Mathijsen's Guide to European Union Law

Mathijsen's Guide to European Union Law

P.S.R.F. Mathijsen

Advocaat
Professor of Law, University of Brussels
Former Director-General with the Commission of the European Union

P Dyrberg

Advokat
Visiting Professor at the University of Reykjavik
Former Head of Legal Service in the EFTA Surveillance Authority

SWEET & MAXWELL

 THOMSON REUTERS

Eleventh Edition   2013   by Mathijsen and Dyrberg

Published in 2013 by Sweet & Maxwell, 100 Avenue Road, London NW3 3PF part of
Thomson Reuters (Professional) UK Limited (Registered in England & Wales, Company No
1679046.
Registered Office and address for service: Aldgate House, 33 Aldgate High Street, London
EC3N 1DL)

For further information on our products and services, visit *www.sweetandmaxwell.co.uk*

Typeset by Letterpart Limited, Caterham on the Hill, Surrey CR3 5XL

Printed and bound in Great Britain by CPI Group (UK) Ltd, Croydon, CR0 4YY.

No natural forests were destroyed to make this product; only farmed timber was used and
re-planted.

A CIP catalogue record of this book is available for the British Library.

ISBN: 978-0-414-027701

To Beverly

Acknowledgments

This 11th Edition of the Guide is quite different from the preceding ones which were written practically entirely by me. However, this book endeavors to cover all major aspects of Union Law, and although each subject cannot be covered exhaustively, the volume, complexity and novelties have, frankly, become too much for one writer.

I was, therefore, most fortunate to have shared offices, here in Brussels, with Peter Dyrberg, Resident Partner in Brussels of the Norweigan law firm Schjødt, and who agreed to work with me on this 11th edition. Peter also took over the organization of the work, since we decided to involve a group of seasoned scholars and practitioners in Union law to take care of various chapters.

The following authors have revised various chapters of this 11th edition:

Auke Baas, European Parliament: the chapters on the European Parliament and on Financing Union Activities.

Ernesto Vallejo Lobete, Madrid: the chapters on Transport, Agriculture and the Common Fisheries Policy.

Jan Magne Juuhl-Langseth, law firm Schjødt, Oslo and Brussels: the chapter on Competition Policy.

Jose Ramon Bengoetxea, University of the Basque Country: the chapters on Energy and the General Provisions concerning the Union's External Action, and with the assistance of Xabier Ezeizabarrena, University of the Basque Country: the chapter on Environment.

Morten Broberg, University of Copenhagen: the chapter on Development Co-operation.

Niels Fenger, University of Copenhagen: the chapter on the Court of Justice.

Peter reviewed: the chapters of Part III of the book: the Internal Market, and the chapters on the Council, the Commission, the ECB, Taxation, Approximation of Laws, Economy and Monetary Union, Common Commercial Policy and Enlargement.

The remaining chapters were reviewed by me.

We were greatly helped by Maria Feckova, Hulda Magnúsdóttir, Paula Wojtysiak and Raluca Radu; all currently or formerly with the law firm Schjødt.

I am also particularly grateful to the publisher Sweet & Maxwell, London, and Nicola Thurlow, publishing editor, for having thought it useful to publish this new edition (they published the first one in 1972 just before the accession of the United Kingdom, Ireland and Denmark); and to Marie Clare, senior content editor.

ACKNOWLEDGMENTS

I have freely made use of information published by the Union Institutions on the Internet and elsewhere and endeavored to always make reference to the places where I found it.

P. Mathijsen
August 2013

viii

Note on the Practical methodology for how to find and work with EU legislation and case-law

This Note will provide the reader with a short guidance for searching relevant EU legislation and case-law applicable to a specific topic, in the complex world of the Internet by illustrating how to navigate through the official websites of the European Union, the Commission, the Parliament and the Courts of Justice in order to find relevant resources.

1. Identifying the main legal aspects applicable to a given case with the help of the official general website of the European Union (*www.europa.eu*).
    The general website of the European Union, available in the official languages of the European Union, acts like an umbrella database that explains (i) how the EU works (e.g. what are the European Institution, what their role is and how citizens can become involved in their work), (ii) what are the policies and activities of the EU (e.g. environment, climate action, employment and social affairs, environment), (iii) how to access EU funding, (iv) basic answers to some of the frequently asked questions by the citizens regarding certain top interest topics (e.g. work and retirement, healthcare, travel, consumer rights). It also provides a link to the official databases containing most of the publications and documents of the EU (e.g. preparatory acts, laws, statistics, opinion polls).
    One of the features of the website is that it provides approximately 3,000 legislation summaries of European legislation, divided into 32 areas corresponding to the activities of the EU (e.g. agriculture, audiovisual and media, economic affairs, external trade, budget, education, training, youth and sports, budget, energy, environment, employment and social policy) which can represent a starting point for identifying what laws and case-law might be applicable to a given case.

2. The official European legislation database: EUR-Lex (*www.eur-lex.europa. eu*)
    The EUR-Lexis an effective search engine that provides a handful of criteria which one can use to search for EU law (both primary and secondary) and case-law: e.g. by word, author, document number, date, Official Journal reference, CELEX numbers (which is the unique identifier of each document in EUR-Lex, regardless of language, based on the document sector—e.g., treaties, international agreements, secondary legislation, EFTA documents).

It also represents the access gate to the Official Journal of the EU.[1]

When the user does not know the identification algorithms of a piece of legislation or case-law, the recommended research method is the one by key words in the title or the title and text of the documents in EUR-Lex. However, as this search may end up retrieving a lot of results, the user can alternatively use the resources in the official website of the EU described above or the websites of the EU Institutions (e.g., the Commission or the Parliament).

When the relevant document is finally displayed, there are several other features of the EUR-Lex data base that the user can use.

Let us take the example of a directive: the Solvency II Directive 2009/138/EC.

After the user had looked for it based on the above-mentioned research algorithms, the displayed result indicates: (i) the CELEX number of the document (e.g., *32009L0138*), (ii) the complete official title of the directive (e.g., Directive 2009/138/EC of the European Parliament and of the Council of November 25, 2009 on the taking-up and pursuit of the business of Insurance and Reinsurance (Solvency II)), (iii) the number of the Official Journal where it was published (e.g., O.J. L335, December 17, 2009, p. 1–155) and (iv) the bibliographic notices.

The bibliographic notices are a very useful tool for navigating through the lifespan of the legal act, providing the following:

(i)   The adoption date of the document (e.g. November 25, 2009), the entry into force based on the subsequent modifications as well (e.g. January 6, 2010 and January 1, 2014) and the end of validity or the transposition deadline (e.g. June 30, 2013);

(ii)   The various classifications (e.g., EUROVOC: life assurance, insurance company, financial solvency; directory code: right of establishment and freedom to provide services);

(iii)   The adoption procedure (e.g. co-decision) with the procedure number and legislative history;

(iv)   The relationship of the act with the various other documents: the Treaty legal basis (e.g. adoption based on Title III of the Treaty Establishing the European Community—Free movement of persons, services and capital); all the other acts that were subsequently adopted based on it, those that were amended or repealed by it and also the acts that amend it.

If there are acts that amend the act the user was looking for, there is also a possibility to display a consolidated version of it. In case of Solvency II Directive, there is a consolidated version containing the changes brought by Directive 2011/89/EU (the amended provisions are marked with the "M1" code). However, keep note that the consolidated versions are only meant to be working tools, see below.

This section also reveals the amendment or repeal proposals concerning the act, the national implementation measures adopted by the Member States for its transposition (when this is relevant), the documents that refer or

---

[1] As from August 1, 2013 the O.J. in the online version will be the authentic version, see Regulation 206/2013.

mention it, and the case-law of the European courts in connection with it (usually categorized considering the referred articles of the act).

3. Preparatory acts: Pre-Lex (*http://ec.europa.eu/prelex/*) and Oeil (*www. europarl.europa.eu/oeil*).

    The main websites for searching for preparatory acts are the Pre-Lex and the Oeil.

    The Pre-Lex is the database of the European Commission on inter-institutional procedures and follows the major stages of the decision-making process between the Commission and the other institutions.

    The Oeil is the legislative observatory of the European Parliament for monitoring the EU decision-making process, with a particular focus on the activities of the Parliament. According to their website, the database contains records for all procedures still ongoing, irrespective of when they began and all procedures that have completed their passage through Parliament since July 1994.

4. Case-law searches

    There are two databases which provide access to the case-law of the EU courts (the European Court of Justice, the General Court and the Civil Service Tribunal): the Curia website (*http://curia.europa.eu/*) or the EUR-Lex. They offer search mechanisms such as: name of the parties, number or other identifications of the cases, subject area or key words. When using EUR-lex it is advisable to use the option called "bibliographic notice and text" when one has found the ruling or the AG conclusions searched for. EUR-Lex contains also, ahead of each document, a list of articles from legal literature which deal specifically with the judgment, so-called case notes. Cases of the Court of Justice bear after 1989 a "C-" before the case number. Cases before the General Court bear a "T-" before the case number (T for "Tribunal", the name of the Court in French). Cases before the Civil Service Tribunal bear a "F-" before their number (F for "function publique"—civil service in French).[2] There is also a heading called "documents mentioning this document". By clicking that one gets a list of all the documents that mention, for instance, a judgment. If the hits list is too long, EUR-Lex offers several options to narrow down the search, for instance limiting the list by "author" or by "time span". If one knows the case number of a case, the easiest option to find it is probably to search on the Internet for it.

5. How to work with the EU Treaties

    The EU treaties can be found in EUR-Lex. As they have been amended multiple times and their articles renumbered, it might be difficult to find the corresponding treaty article to a certain legal document or law institution. For example, the Treaty of Lisbon amended the EU and EC treaties, without replacing them and renumbered their articles. Therefore, when reading a source (e.g. law, book, journal) from before the Lisbon Treaty, it might not be easy to follow the mentioned treaty articles against the new Lisbon Treaty ones. For an easy reference, the user can use the

---

[2] The OJ and Eur-Lex also contains references to the cases of the EFTA Court, set up in the context of the Agreement on the European Economic Area. Cases before the EFTA Court bear an "E-" before their number.

correspondence tables between the new and the old article numbers provided at the end of the Lisbon Treaty.

On the general EU website there are also online versions and summaries concerning other important treaties like the Convention for the Protection of Human Rights and Fundamental Freedoms, the Schengen Agreement, as well as all the other previous treaties that formed the legal basis of the European Union and the European Community.

6. The linguistic equality of the versions of an EU piece of legislation

Most of the acts of secondary law exist in all the official languages of the European Union having an equal legal value and force (they are equally binding). This reflects the general principle of linguistic equality between the EU Member States. Therefore, when performing a research, it is advisable to check more than one language version of an official document.

7. Consolidated and codified versions

Some acts of secondary law are subject to frequent amendments. As in other legal orders, it is a nuisance for the user of the act to have to check all subsequent amending acts to the act to see whether the provisions of interest are still unaltered. In the EU legal order, the problem has been solved much in line with what one finds in some national legal orders, i.e. periodically the Union institutions provide a version of the original act, incorporating all subsequent amendments. One distinguishes between consolidated versions and codified versions. Consolidated versions are produced by administrative services; they have no legal force but for all practical purposes they can be trusted; they can be found on EUR-Lex. For instance, if one searches Regulation 1408/71, EUR-Lex will list all amending acts. Thereafter, there is a heading where the consolidated versions of the act are listed. A codified version is established by the same institution that produced the original act, typically the Union legislator. The codified version of the act will typically be a new act in its own right that repeals the original act and it is typically established at the occasion of amending the original act. For instance, Regulation 40/94 on the Community trademark was amended a number of times. When amending it in 2009, the legislator brought all the previous amendments into the amending act, which then became the codified act, repealing the original act, namely Regulation 207/2009.

TABLE OF CONTENTS

CONTENTS

CONTENTS

CONTENTS

CONTENTS

CONTENTS

CONTENTS

CONTENTS

Part 4
OTHER UNION POLICIES

22. Competition Policy

CONTENTS

CONTENTS

CONTENTS

CONTENTS

TABLE OF CASES

TABLE OF CASES

TABLE OF CASES

TABLE OF CASES

TABLE OF CASES

TABLE OF CASES

TABLE OF CASES

TABLE OF CASES

TABLE OF CASES

1

TABLE OF CASES

lii

TABLE OF CASES

TABLE OF CASES

Court of First Instance [General Court (GC)] of the European Communities (Chronological)

TABLE OF CASES

TABLE OF CASES

TABLE OF CASES

TABLE OF CASES (ALPHABETICAL)

TABLE OF CASES (ALPHABETICAL)

TABLE OF CASES (ALPHABETICAL)

TABLE OF CASES (ALPHABETICAL)

COMMISSION DECISIONS

DECISIONS OF THE EFTA COURT

NATIONAL COURTS

Belgium

France

Germany

United Kingdom

TABLE OF TREATIES AND CONVENTIONS

TABLE OF TREATIES AND CONVENTIONS

TABLE OF TREATIES AND CONVENTIONS

TABLE OF SECONDARY LEGISLATION OF THE EUROPEAN UNION

TABLE OF NATIONAL LEGISLATION

Basic Statistics of the 28 Member States

(in alphabetical order according to national spelling)

Country	Area in KM2	Pop. in Millions[1]	GDP per inh.[2]
Belgium	30.510	11.1	37.883
Bulgaria	110.912	7.3	14.312
Czech Rep.	78.886	10.5	27.191
Denmark	43.100	5.6	37.657
Germany	356.900	81.8	39.028
Estonia	45.227	1.3	21.713
Greece	132.000	11.3	24.505
Spain	504.800	46.2	30.557
France	547.030	65.3	35.548
Croatia	56.542	4.4	17.810
Italy	301.300	59.4	30.136
Ireland	70.300	4.6	41.921
Cyprus	9.250	0.9	27.086
Latvia	64.600	2	18.255
Lithuania	65.301	3	21.615
Luxembourg	2.600	0.5	79.785
Hungary	93.000	9.9	19.638
Malta	316	0.4	27.022
Netherlands	41.526	16.7	42.194
Austria	83.900	8.4	42.409
Poland	312.685	38.5	20.592
Portugal	92.400	10.5	23.385
Romania	237.500	21.4	12.808
Slovenia	20.273	2.1	28.195
Slovakia	48.845	5.4	24.249
Finland	337.100	5.4	36.395
Sweden	450.000	9.5	41.191
UK	244.820	63.3	36.941
TOTAL		506.7	

---

[1] Eurostat 2012.
[2] International Monetary Fund 2012.

Principal Abbreviations

ACP	African, Caribbean, and Pacific countries party to the Lomé Convention.
Bull.	Bulletin of the European Communities edited by the Secretariat of the Commission; there are 11 issues per year (July-August are published together).
CAP	Common agricultural policy.
CCT	Common Customs Tariff.
CFSP	Common Foreign and Security Policy.
C.M.L.R.	Common Market Law Reports.
CMO	Common Market Organisation.
CST	Civil Service Tribunal.
Competition Report	Report on the Competition Policy, published yearly, also on the Internet.
EAGF	European Agricultural Guidance and Guarantee Fund.
EAFRD	European Agricultural Fund for Rural Development.
EASA	European Aviation Safety Agency.
E.C.R.	Official reports in English of most[1] cases decided by the Community Courts (Courts of Justice numbered I-... and General Court II-...) and the Civil Servant Tribunal. The numbering of the pages is the same now in all languages. They can be found on the Internet. A further distinction was established in 1994: Community personnel cases were published in a separate volume "Reports of European Community Staff Cases" E.C.R.S.C. Judgements in staff cases are no longer translated in other official languages.
EC	European Community.
ECB	European Central Bank.
ECSC	The Euopean Coal and Steel Community.
EEC	European Economic Community.
EDF	European Development Fund.
EEA	European Economic Area.
EFTA	European Free Trade Association.
EFSF	European Financial Stability Facility.

EFSM	European Financial Stability Mechanism.
EIB	European Investment Bank.
E.L.Rev.	European Law Review.
EMI	European Monetary Institute.
EMU	European Monetary Union.
ERDF	European Regional Development Fund.
ESCB	European System of Central Banks.
ESF	European Social Fund.
ESM	The European Stability Mechanism.
EUR-ATOM	European Community of Atomic Energy.
FIFG	Financial Instrument for Fisheries Guidance.
GATT	General Agreement on Tariffs and Trade (UN).
GC	General Court.
GDP	Gross Domestic Procuct.
GMOs	Genetically Modified Organisms.
GSP	Generalised System of Preferences.
IGC	Intergovernmental conference.
JHA	Justice and Home Affairs; although this denomination of the so-called "third pillar" was replaced by "Provisions on Police and Judicial Co-operation in criminal matters", the logo JHA is still used.
J.O.	Journal Officiel: French edition of the Official Journal of the European Communities.
MEPs	Members of the European Parliament.
MPS	Market Price Support.

O.J.	Official Journal of the European Union. Remarks 1. This Journal was published under the name *Journal Officiel de la Communauté Européenne du Charbon et de l'Acier* from 1952 to April 19, 1958; on April 20, 1958, the first issue of the *Journal Officiel des Communauté Européennes* appeared, without modifying the structure of the Journal itself; this lasted until December 31, 1967. References to publications in the *Journal Officiel* for the period 1952 to July 1, 1967, are made by mentioning the page and the year or vice versa such as J.O. 849/65. Between July 1 and December 31, 1967, each issue is paged separately. 2. After January 1, 1968 (see O.J. 1968, L.30), the Journal was divided into two separate editions designated by the letters "L" (legislation) and "C." (communications). Legislative texts are published in the edition marked "L" and are again subdivided in: I. Acts adopted under the EC Treaty/Euratom Treaty whose publication is obligatory; II. Acts whose publication is not obligatory; III. Acts adopted under the EU Treaty. All other texts are published in the edition marked "C" except "Notices and public contracts" which are published in O.J. Supplement. References to publication in the *Journal Officiel* after January 1, 1968, are made by mentioning the letter "L" or "C", the year, the No. of the issue and the page, e.g. J.O. 1970, 31/1. 3. The Journal is also published in all the official languages in the union. 4. In accordance with Article 155 of the Act of Accession, provision was made in Council Regulation 857/72 of April 24, 1972, for Special Editions of the *Official Journal* for the publication *inter alia* of the English text of acts of the institutions of the Communities adopted and published before accession. Consequently an authentic English translation now exists of the most important Community acts. This special edition was published in December 1972 and a subsequent edition was published in 1974 (see O.J. 1972, L.101/1). All references to an O.J. publication prior to January 1, 1973 are necessarily in the Special Edition. 5. The numbering of pages is the same in all the languages of the Community.
OECD	Organisation for Economic Co-operation and Development.
OEEC	Organisation of European Economic Co-operation.
R&TD	Research and Technological Development.
Rules	Rules of Procedure of the Court of Justice (O.J. 1975, L.102/1).
SCE	European Co-operative Society.
SEA	Single European Act.
SIS	Schengen Information System.
SPS	Single Payment Scheme.
SSM	Single Supervisory Mechanism.
TAC	Total Allowable Catch.
TACIS	Programme for Technical Assistance to the Commonwealth of the Independent States.

TENs	Trans-European Networks.
UN	United Nations.
UAA	Utilised Agricultural Area.
WEU	Western European Union.
WTO	World Trade Organisation.
TFEU	The Treaty on the functioning of the European Union.

PART 1

THE EUROPEAN UNION—THE TREATIES, THE HISTORY, THE ACTS AND THE LAW

CHAPTER 1

The European Treaties

INTRODUCTION

The reader who approaches the "European" subject for the first time will be easily forgiven if she or he feels confused by the terminology commonly used. The more so since the expressions "European Union", "European Community", "European Communities", "Common market", "Single market" and "Internal market" are often used indiscriminately to designate the same concept. The debate about the European Constitution has not been very helpful in this respect either. As this book hopes to make clear, these expressions do not cover the same realities; therefore some clarification is certainly called for at the outset. The more so since reference is also made, in this context, to the "Treaty on European Union" or "Maastricht Treaty", the "Amsterdam Treaty", the "Treaty of Nice", the "Treaty of Lisbon", the "Treaty on the Functioning of the European Union" (TFEU), the "Economic and Monetary Union" (EMU), the "European Council" and the "Council" and the "Euro", which is not even accepted in all the Member States.

1–01

An examination of the subject "Europe" should logically start with the European Coal and Steel Community (ECSC), created in 1952 by six States: Belgium, France, Germany, Italy, Luxemburg and The Netherlands (this Treaty no longer exists). To this "European Community" were added, in 1958, the European Economic Community (EEC) and the European Community for Atomic Energy (Euratom). It was only in 1992 that the European Union (EU) was established among the, at that time, 12 Member States by the Maastricht Treaty.[1] Those Member States were, according to the Preamble to that Treaty, "resolved to mark a new stage in the process of European integration undertaken with the establishment of the European Communities". It also shows, among other things, the resolve of these Member States to "continue the process of creating an ever closer union among the peoples of Europe".[2]

The Maastricht or EU Treaty added new dimensions, new fields of activity to the ones provided for by the Treaties which established the three original European Communities; the EU Treaty modified the existing Treaties. The Union replaced and succeeded the European Community.[3]

---

[1] It was signed at Maastricht, the Netherlands, on February 7, 1992 and entered into force on November 1, 1993 [1993] O.J. L293/61, after having been ratified by the parliaments of the Member States, in certain cases after it was approved by referendum. It was modified by the Amsterdam, Nice and Lisbon Treaties. Consolidated version now: [2008] O.J. C115/1.
[2] Art. A.2 Maastricht Treaty.
[3] EU Treaty Art. 1,3.

3

The EU Treaty has specific features of its own and its own objectives. In addition to those features, it was founded on three elements: (1) the three European Communities; (2) a Common Foreign and Security Policy (CFSP)[4]; and (3) provisions on co-operation in the fields of justice and home affairs.[5] These three elements constituted the so-called three pillars of the European construction. They no longer exist as separate sets of provisions.

1–02   The Treaties, which established the European Atomic Energy Community (Euratom) and the European Economic Community (EEC), are also referred to as the "Treaties of Rome"; it was in that city that these two Treaties were signed in March 1957. However, when reference is made in this book to the "Treaties", it is the EU Treaty and the Treaty on the Functioning of the European Union (TFEU), which are generally meant. Euratom no longer plays a very important independent role: for all practical purposes most of its activities have been absorbed into the TFEU.

The "common market", now "internal market", often confused with the Union as such, of which it is the main feature, means the so-called basic freedoms (free movement of goods, free movement of persons, freedom of establishment, freedom to provide services and free movement of capital and of payments). The internal market does not include, for instance, external relations, except for the common commercial policy.

The "internal market" is defined in the TFEU as "an area without frontiers in which the free movement of goods, persons, services and capital is ensured".[6] The completion of the internal market, at the end of 1992, was the object of the Single European Act (SEA),[7] signed in February 1986.

This book, as already indicated, is mainly about the EU and the TFEU; their nature will be discussed in this chapter. The "internal market" will be examined in detail further on, but it seems necessary to start with a brief overview of the European Union.

1.   THE TREATY ON EUROPEAN UNION (EU)

1–03   A "Union" among the Member States constitutes the ultimate objective of European integration, the precise scope of which is, as yet, not determined in detail. But, all the nationals of the Member States are now "citizens" of that Union, which grants them certain rights,[8] and the various elements of the Union are held together by:

---

[4] Maastricht Treaty Title V.

[5] EU Title VI. This third element used to be designated "Co-operation in the field of Justice and Home Affairs" (CJH).

[6] Art.26(2) TFEU. It is curious, to say the least, that the freedom of establishment is not mentioned here.

[7] This Act is called "single" because it is the combination of two different instruments, which were, for practical purposes, put together into a single one. The first instrument contains modifications to the three European Treaties, while the second constitutes, in fact, an agreement among the Member States concerning co-operation in the field of external relations.

[8] Contrary to the European Communities, the Union had, at first, no legal personality, but it now has one: Art.47 EU. For the rights granted to the citizens, see "Non-Discrimination and Citizenship of the Union" Arts 20—25 TFEU. It provides, among other things, for the right of citizens to move and reside in the territory of all the Member States, under certain conditions (Arts 20(2)(a) and 21(1)

"[A]n institutional framework, which aims to promote its values, advances its objectives, serves its interests, those of its citizens and those of the Member States and ensure the consistency, effectiveness and the continuity of its policies and actions."[9]

This institutional framework now consists of seven institutions: the European Parliament (hereinafter "Parliament"), the European Council, the Council (of ministers), the Commission, the Court of Justice, the European Central Bank and the Court of Auditors.

The objectives of the Union can be summarised as follows,[10] the Union is to:

- promote peace, its values and the wellbeing of its people;
- offer its citizens an area of freedom, security and justice: free movement of persons, but with external border controls, asylum and immigration measures, and combating of crime;
- establish an internal market;
- develop Europe based on balanced economic growth and price stability;
- establish a competitive social market economy, aiming at full employment and social progress;
- ensure a high level of protection and improvement of the quality of the environment;
- promote scientific and technological advance;
- combat social exclusion and discrimination, and promote social justice and protection;
- promote equality between women and men, solidarity between generations and protection of the rights of the child;
- promote economic, social and territorial cohesion and solidarity among Member States;
- respect the rich cultural and linguistic diversity and ensure that Europe's cultural heritage is safeguarded and enhanced;
- establish an economic and monetary union whose currency is the Euro;
- and, in relation to the wider world:
  - uphold and promote its values and interests and contribute to the protection of its citizens;

TFEU), the right to vote and to stand as a candidate in elections to the European Parliament and in municipal elections in the Member State of residence, under the same conditions as nationals of that State: Arts 20(2)(b) and 22 TFEU. See Directive 1994/80, laying down detailed arrangements for the exercise of the right to vote and to stand as a candidate in municipal elections by citizens of the Union residing in a Member State of which they are not nationals: [1994] O.J. L368/38; see *Commission v Belgium* (C-323/97) [1998] E.C.R. I-4291. In third countries where their own State is not represented, citizens are entitled to diplomatic and consular protection from any other Member State: Arts 20(2)(c) and 23 TFEU; see Decision regarding protection for the citizens of the EU by diplomatic and consular representatives [1995] O.J. L314/73. The citizen also has the right to petition Parliament (Art.24,2 TFEU) and to apply to the Ombudsman (Art.24,3 TFEU). It should be noted that the Council may propose to the Member States to extend those rights (Art.25,2 TFEU).
[9] Art.13(1) EU. *Acquis Communautaire* means everything that was decided and agreed upon since the establishment of the three European Communities, whatever the form in which this was done, whether legally binding or not. It refers to the body of rules which govern the Union in whatever field of activity. In other words it encompasses everything that was "acquired" by the previous Communities and the Union.
[10] Art.3 EU.

–   contribute to peace, security, the sustainable development of the Earth;
–   promote solidarity and mutual respect among peoples, free and fair trade, eradication of poverty;
–   ensure the protection of human rights, in particular the rights of the child; and
–   ensure strict observance and development of international law, including respect for the principles of the United Nations Charter.

The "Common Foreign and Security Policy" (CFSP) shall be examined in the last part of this book; but let it be noted here that this policy could lead to a "common defence", which would need to be approved by all the Member States in accordance with their constitutional requirements.[11]

As for the "Police" and "Judicial Co-operation in Criminal Matters", it will be discussed in the chapter on Free Movement of Persons.

2.   ENHANCED CO-OPERATION[12]

1–04   Enhanced Co-operation is provided for in Title IV of the EU Treaty and Title III of the TFEU—it was previously called "Closer Co-operation".[13]

There are various areas of Union activity in which certain Member States are prepared to go further and faster than other Member States. This is possible under the following conditions.

Once the Council has established[14] that the objectives of such co-operation cannot be attained within a reasonable period by the Union as a whole,[15] the Member States wishing to establish enhanced co-operation between themselves in one of the areas covered by the Treaties, with the exception of the Union's exclusive competences[16] and the common foreign and security policy,[17] may "make use of the institutions and exercise those competences by applying the relevant provisions of the Treaties".[18] Provided, however, that this co-operation:

- is aimed at furthering the objectives of the Union, at protecting its interests and at reinforcing its integration process[19];
- complies with the Treaties and Union law[20];
- does not undermine the internal market or economic, social and territorial cohesion;

---

[11] Art.7(1) EU.
[12] Art.20 EU and Arts 226–334 TFEU.
[13] Art.1(10) EU.
[14] Art.330 TFEU: "unanimity" shall be constituted by the votes of the representatives of the participating Member States only and a "qualified majority" shall be defined in accordance with the voting procedures laid down for the Council: Art.238 TFEU.
[15] Art.20(2) EU.
[16] See Art.3 TFEU.
[17] Arts 23–46 EU.
[18] Art.43 EU.
[19] Art.20(1) EU.
[20] Art.326,1 TFEU.

- does not constitute a barrier to or discrimination in trade between Member States, nor distorts competition;
- involves at least nine Member States[21];
- respects the competences, rights and obligations of the non-participating Member States, the latter may not impede the implementation of the enhanced co-operation; and
- is open to all Member States; the Commission and the participating Member States must promote participation by as many Member States as possible.[22] Any Member State wishing to participate in enhanced co-operation in progress must notify its intention to the Council and the Commission, which must ascertain that the conditions for participation have been met and, if not, indicate the arrangements to be adopted. The Member State concerned may refer the matter to the Council.[23]

Authorisation to proceed with enhanced co-operation shall be granted by the Council acting unanimously, on a proposal from the Commission, and after obtaining the consent of Parliament.[24] A request for enhanced co-operation within the framework of the CFSP shall be addressed to the Council; it shall be forwarded to the High Representative of the Union for Foreign Affairs and Security Policy, for an opinion on consistency with that policy and to the Commission for an opinion on consistency with other Union policies. It shall be forwarded to Parliament for information.[25]

Expenditure resulting from implementation of enhanced co-operation, other than administrative costs, shall be borne by the participating Member States.[26]

3. THE TREATY ON THE FUNCTIONING OF THE EUROPEAN UNION (TFEU)

In 1951, the drafters of the Treaty establishing the European Coal and Steel   1–05
Community (ECSC) coined the word "supranational" to describe the particular character of the functions fulfilled by the members of the High Authority, which later on became the European Commission.[27] The term was from the start also used to designate the specific nature of the Union itself, and of the law it embodied. It was understood to mean that the Union was more than a grouping of member nations, and that its law was more than their national laws and, although the ECSC was set up by an international treaty concluded among sovereign States, the signatories were conscious of having created something very different indeed from other entities set up under the Law of Nations.

---

[21] Art.20(2) EU.

[22] Art.328(1),2 TFEU.

[23] Art.331(1) TFEU.

[24] Art.329(1), 2 TFEU.

[25] Art.329(2) TFEU.

[26] Art.332 TFEU.

[27] Art.9 (5 and 6) ECSC "They shall abstain from any act incompatible with the supranational character of their function", and "Each Member State undertakes to respect this supranational character." The concept did not refer to the Union itself. Since the ECSC Treaty (1952) was concluded for 50 years, it is no longer in force.

As the Court of Justice so clearly put it, back in 1962: the Contracting States were not merely accepting mutual obligations,[28] they were limiting their own sovereign rights, transferring some of them to institutions over which they had no direct control, and endowing the ECSC with powers they did not always possess themselves. Furthermore, the Treaty did not only create new rights and obligations for the Member States, it also granted rights to, and directly included, their citizens, who thereby became subjects, now "citizens", of the Union[29] with the right to defend these rights in the national courts.

By contrast with ordinary international treaties, the European Treaties thus created their own legal system to which the term "international" does not apply, since it is not international law; the term "supranational" expressed the difference.

1–06
Furthermore, it follows from the terms and the spirit of the European Treaties that the Member States, as a corollary, may not give precedence to their national law over a legal system accepted by all of them on the basis of reciprocity. Indeed, the executive force of Union law cannot vary from one State to another in deference to domestic law, without jeopardising the attainment of the objectives of the Treaties.[30] The law of the European Union cannot, therefore, be regarded as national law either. It is different, independent, it is separate, it is not national law; since it is common to 2 nations, it is truly supranational. The term "supranational" has now fallen into disrepute and was even eliminated from the ECSC Treaty.[31] This, however, does not change the specific nature of the Union and of the law it created. More importantly, the concept is now universally accepted and expressed by the words "Union Law".

Union law[32] is to be found mainly in the European Treaties (also referred to as "primary" Union law) and in the implementing legislation or the "secondary" Union law, not to be confused with the *acquis communautaire,* about which later.

Primary Union law now consists of the Treaty establishing the European Atomic Energy Community (Euratom), the Treaty establishing the European Union (EU) and the Treaty on the Functioning of the European Union (TFEU), as amended over the years.[33] The first can be considered as a sectoral treaty, while

---

[28] *Van Gend & Loos v Nederlandse Administratie der Belastingen* (26/62) [1963] E.C.R. 1 at 12; [1963] C.M.L.R. 105.

[29] Forty years later, the EU Treaty formally confirmed this by providing for a "citizenship" of the European Union. See now: Arts 17–22 EU.

[30] *Costa v ENEL* (6/64) [1964] E.C.R. 585 at 594.

[31] The Merger Treaty repealed Art.9 of the ECSC Treaty and replaced it with a text which is identical in the three European Treaties, and, since the term "supranational" did not appear in the two Treaties of Rome, it was entirely left out.

[32] See the chapter on the Legal Acts of the Union.

[33] Chronologically, amendments were introduced by: the Convention on certain institutions common to the three Communities (March 25, 1957); the Treaty establishing a Single Council and a Single Commission of the European Communities (April 8, 1965); the Decision creating the Communities' own resources (April 21, 1970); the Treaty amending certain budgetary provisions (April 22, 1970); the Treaty on the accession of Denmark, Ireland and the United Kingdom (January 22, 1972); the Treaty amending certain financial provisions (July 22, 1975); the Act concerning the direct election of the European Parliament (September 20, 1976); the Treaty on the secession of Greenland (September 20, 1976); the Treaty on the accession of Greece (May 28, 1979); the Treaty concerning the accession of Portugal and Spain (March 9/30, 1985); the Single European Act (February 17/28, 1986); the Maastricht Treaty or Treaty on European Union (February 7, 1992); the Treaty concerning the accession of Austria, Finland, (Norway) and Sweden (June 24, 1994); the Treaty of Amsterdam

the TFEU covers the economic and social fields in general. (Hereinafter, as already indicated, "Treaties" refers mainly to the EU Treaty and the TFEU.)

By "secondary legislation" is meant the legislative texts issued by the institutions, which implement and, in certain cases, complement the original Treaties.

Union law has gradually evolved over the past half-century, from the 100 Articles of the ECSC Treaty, into an impressive body of law comprising thousands of regulations, directives, decisions, agreements and other acts and measures, and, above all, the case law of the Court of Justice.

1–07

It is impressive, not only because of its sheer volume, but because of its specific character and its growth potential. It is worthwhile considering this particular aspect of Union law: except for the original three Treaties just mentioned, none of the Union Acts finds their origin with the national institutions, bodies and organs with which lawyers and citizens were familiar and over which they exercise, through democratic elections, some sort of control. Union regulations, directives, decisions, etc. are issued outside most citizens' own countries, according to complex and remote procedures the citizens cannot easily grasp and over which they have practically no say.[34] They are nevertheless directly involved. Indeed, if those measures may impose upon them obligations, they also grant them rights, which, as already mentioned, they can ask the national courts to uphold, against fellow citizens, undertakings and even against the government of any Member State. Those rights arise not only where they are expressly granted by Union law, but also as a corollary to the obligations, which this law, in a clearly defined way, imposes upon the Member States and the institutions of the Union.[35] Those citizens can also challenge the legality of Union measures in the Union courts, under certain conditions (see TFEU Arts 263,4): they are definitely part of the system!

The apparent aloofness of the European authorities, combined with this direct involvement might be bewildering for the citizens. However, the direct election of the Members of Parliament and the increasing number of cases involving Union law, introduced by private parties, both in the European and in the national courts, seems to indicate a familiarity with at least some aspects of this new system of law. But, if democratic control by the citizens of the Union is to become a reality, some knowledge of the basic rules and procedures is required. This applies not only to the law student, but also to the practitioner, the politician and the general public. Unless one realises what the Union's objectives are, and what means and -procedures have been provided for attaining them, no participation is possible, no criticism is justified, no suggestion can be pertinent.

(October 2, 1997); the Treaty of Nice (February 26, 2001); the Accession Treaty of the Czech Republic, Estonia, Cyprus, Latvia, Lithuania, Hungary, Malta, Poland, Slovenia and Slovakia (April 16, 2003); the Accession Treaty of Bulgaria and Romania (April 25, 2005), (these dates correspond to those of the signature); and, finally, the Treaty of Lisbon (2007).

[34] In order to remedy this situation, Art.1, 2 of the EU Treaty provides that that Treaty marks a new stage in the process of creating an ever closer union among the peoples of Europe, "in which decisions are taken as openly as possible and as closely as possible to the citizens". It should be noted, however, that the situation of aloofness and ignorance referred to above, also prevails within the Member States themselves, with regard to their own legislative processes.

[35] See *Van Gend & Loos* (quoted above, fn.28).

1–08   The objectives of the Union were set out in detail above, and the means to attain them are analysed in detail in the chapters of this book corresponding to the various areas of Union activity.

The Treaties provide precise rules and timetables for the establishment of the internal market and of the economic and monetary union, while the other policies are, as shall be seen, described in rather general terms, leaving it to the institutions, and, in the first place, to the Commission, which must make proposals for the Union's legislative action, to take the initiative. However, notwithstanding this absence of a timetable, Union activities have penetrated more and more social, economic and related fields, some of which were not even, until recently,[36] explicitly provided for in the Treaties. Union law, it seems, is in the process of integrating most of the economies and social policies of the Member States.

The dynamic development of the Union is not the only proof of its vitality; notwithstanding economic recession and political turmoil, the Union not only held together, but expanded its field of activity geographically, economically and politically. This seems to indicate that it fulfils a basic need and responds to a profound aspiration of the peoples of Europe.

4.   MODIFICATION OF THE TREATIES

1–09   The EU Treaty provides for three different procedures to amend the Treaties:

- the "ordinary" revision procedure,[37] which may, inter alia, serve either to increase or reduce the competences of the Union, on a proposal from a government, Parliament or the Commission to the Council, which submits it to the European Council and notifies the national parliaments. After consulting Parliament and the Commission, the European Council decides, by a simple majority, in favour of examining the proposed amendments.
  The President of the European Council then convenes a Convention composed of representatives of the national parliaments, of the Heads of State or governments, of Parliament and of the Commission. The Convention adopts, by consensus, a recommendation to a conference of representatives of the governments of the Member States. In case the convening of the Convention is not justified by the extent of the proposed modifications, the European Council defines the terms of reference for a Conference. The latter determines, by common accord, the amendments to be made to the Treaties, which shall enter into force after being ratified by all the Member States.

---

[36] Education, culture, public health and industry, which were added by the EU Treaty, are examples of fields wherein the Union was active, although they were not mentioned as such. The same applies to Regional Policy, the European Monetary System, Economic and Monetary Union and Political Co-operation, that were introduced into the Treaty by the Single European Act (SEA). Activities in those fields were made possible, in the meantime, through unanimous ad hoc decisions of the Council based upon Art.352 TFEU.

[37] Art.48(2)–(5) EU.

If two years after the signature of the treaty amending the Treaties, four-fifths of the Member States have ratified it, and one or more Member States have encountered difficulties with ratification, the matter shall be referred to the European Council;

- the "simplified" revision procedure[38]: this revision procedure concerns only provisions of Part III[39] of the TFEU relating to the internal policies and action of the Union. The European Council, after consulting Parliament and the Commission, adopts an amending decision, which must be approved by the Member States. The decision may not extend the competences of the Union; for an example see the Decision amending Art.136 TFEU[40] and Court's decision confirming the validity of that amendment.[41] In 2013, the European Council published a decision on the examination by a conference of the governments of the Member States of the amendment to the Treaties proposed by the Irish Government in the form of a Protocol on the concerns of the Irish people on the Treaty of Lisbon, to be annexed to the Treaty on European Union and to the Treaty on the Functioning of the European Union, and not to convene a Convention.[42]
- the so-called "bridging" amendment[43]: where the TFEU or Title V of the EU Treaty provides for a unanimous decision of the Council, the European Council may authorise the Council to act by qualified majority, except in the area of defence. Similarly, where adoption by the Council is provided via a special legislative procedure,[44] the European Council may authorise adoption via the ordinary legislative procedure.[45] These initiatives must be notified to the national parliaments, which have six months to oppose the revision. The European Council must act by unanimity, after obtaining the consent of Parliament, given by a majority of its component members.

5.   TREATY ESTABLISHING THE EUROPEAN STABILITY MECHANISM (ESM)[46]

This Treaty was signed in July 2011 by the 17 ministers of the euro area. It follows a European Council Decision of March 25, 2011 and builds on an amendment of Art.136 TFEU; it entered into force on July 1, 2013. The ESM assumed on that date the tasks of the European Financial Stability Facility (EFSF)[47] and of European Financial Stabilisation Mechanism (EFSM). Although the treaty was signed by the 17 euro-area countries, the ESM is also open to non-European countries for ad hoc participation in financial assistance

1–10

---

[38] Art.48(6) EU.
[39] Part III "Union Policies and Internal Action" includes practically all the activities of the Union, except any external action.
[40] [2011] O.J. L91/1.
[41] *Pringle* (C-370/12) judgment of November 27, 2012, not yet reported.
[42] [2013] O.J. L60/129. For the Protocol, see idem page 131.
[43] Art.48(7) EU.
[44] Art.289(2) TFEU.
[45] Art.294 TFEU.
[46] This part is largely based upon *http://ec.europa.eu/economy_finance/articles/financial_operations/pdf/2012-12-21-blending-funds_en.pdf* [accessed August 23, 2013].
[47] For the EFSF and the EFSM see the chapter on Economic and Monetary Union.

operations. The Treaty had to be ratified by the euro-area member States before December 31, 2012 to enter into force following approval of signatories representing no less than 95 per cent of the total subscriptions.

The Court of Justice decided that provisions of the EU Treaty and of the TFEU do not preclude the conclusion and ratification of the ESM Treaty.[48]

Based in Luxemburg, the ESM will provide financial assistance to euro-area Member States following mutual agreement and under strict conditions.

For further information on the ESM see hereunder the chapter on Economic and Monetary Union (Policy).

6. COUNTRIES TO WHICH THE EUROPEAN TREATIES APPLY[49] AND TERRITORIAL SCOPE OF THESE TREATIES

1–11 Broadly speaking, the Treaties apply to the 28 Member States. However, a distinction must be made between the territories (1) to which what is referred to as "the Treaties" apply, (2) those to which only the Customs Union applies, and (3) those referred to as the "Fiscal Territory".

As for the territory to which the Treaties apply, it is defined[50] as follows: it covers, in the *first place,* all the Member States; *secondly*—with special conditions to be laid down by the Council after consultation of Parliament—the French overseas departments, the Azores, Madeira and the Canary Islands; *thirdly*, Part IV of the Treaty "Association of the Overseas Countries and Territories" applies to those listed in Annex II to the TFEU; and *fourthly*, it "shall apply to the European territories for whose external relations a Member State is responsible". This last provision was included to cover the Saarland, that part of Germany that, after the Second World War, was occupied by France: according to certain writers, it now applies only to Gibraltar.[51] This application is, however, restricted by Art.28 of the British Accession Act of 1972.

The territory of the "Customs Union" corresponds to that to which the Treaties apply with the exception of Gibraltar, Ceuta, Melilla, the communes of Livigno and Campione d'Italia, Heligoland, Greenland, Faeroe Islands and that part of Cyprus[52] over which Cyprus does not exercise effective control. As for Andorra, Monaco, San Marino and the Vatican, although they are independent States, they are included in the Customs Union. In this context it is perhaps interesting to note that Monaco, San Marino[53] and also the Vatican, issued their own Euro coins when they were introduced in 2002.

The "Fiscal or VAT Territory" is identical to the territory to which the Treaties apply, excepting the Äland Islands (Finland), Heligoland Island, Büssingen Territory (Germany), Guadeloupe, Martinique, French Guyana and Réunion

---

[48] *Pringle* (C-370/12) judgment of November 27, 2012, not yet reported.
[49] Art.52(1) EU.
[50] Art.349 TFEU.
[51] Gibraltar falls outside the Customs Union, the Fiscal Territory and even the Common Agricultural Policy. See Regulation 1298/07; [2007] O.J. L289/3.
[52] Art.355(5)(a) and (b) TFEU.
[53] In 2002, the EC and the Republic of San Marino concluded an Agreement on Co-operation and Customs Union, [2002] O.J. L84/43.

(France),[54] Mount Athos (Greece), Ceuta, Melilla and the Canary Islands (Spain), Livigno, Campione d'Italia and Lake Lugano (Italy), and Gibraltar and the Channel Islands (UK).[55]

The Treaties do not apply to:

- the Faeroe Islands[56]; and
- the United Kingdom Sovereign Base Areas of Akrotiri and Dhekelia in Cyprus.

FURTHER READING

Koen Leanarts and Marlies Desomer, "Bricks for a Constitutional Treaty of the European Union: values, objectives and means" (2002) E.L.Rev. 377.

    1–12

    Alan Dashwood, Michael Dougan, Christophe Hillion, Angus Johnston and Eleanor Spaventa, "Draft Constitutional Treaty of the European Union and related documents" (2003) E.L.Rev. 3.

    Fiona Muray, *EU and Member State Territories, the Special Relationship under Community Law* (Sweet & Maxwell, 2004).

---

[54] Art.349 TFEU.
[55] See Directive 77/388: [1977] O.J. L145/1.
[56] See Decision 1997/126 concerning the conclusion of an Agreement between the EC and the Government of Denmark and the Home Government of the Faeroe Islands [1997] O.J. L53/1 amended [2008] O.J. L212/3.

CHAPTER 2

History

Every institution is the product of a series of historical events, and, at the same time, it reflects the convictions, hopes and concerns of those who were instrumental in establishing it. The European Communities, now European Union, are no exception to this rule. For a full understanding and a correct interpretation of the European Treaties, some knowledge of the historical background seems, therefore, necessary.

2–01

Although the expression "United States of Europe" was already used by Victor Hugo in 1849,[1] there seems to be no need to go that far back. The end of the Second World War provides a fair starting point.

1. CHURCHILL'S SPEECH

The agreement made at Yalta in 1945, by the United Kingdom, the United States and the U.S.S.R., left Europe more divided than ever, and the growing antagonism among the victorious Allies created only more tensions and catastrophes. It was on September 19, 1946, barely a year after the end of the Second World War, in a speech at Zurich University, that Winston Churchill, the British Prime Minister, proposed a "sovereign remedy", for Europe's problems, i.e. to "recreate the European family, or as much of it as we can, and provide it with a structure under which it can dwell in peace, in safety and in freedom. We must build a kind of United States of Europe". He went on to "say something that will astonish you. The first step in the recreation of the European family must be a partnership between France and Germany".

2–02

At that time it needed a lot of courage, and foresight, to make such a suggestion about these former arch-enemies. [As will be seen, it was this (British) idea that also inspired the French Government, in 1950, to propose the establishment of the European Coal and Steel Community.] Towards the end of his Zurich speech, Churchill also proposed to start by setting up a regional structure, and to form a Council of Europe.[2]

---

[1] See Henri Brugmans, *L'Idée* Européenne, 1920–1970 (Bruges, 1970).
[2] The Treaty establishing the Council of Europe was signed in London on May 5, 1949.

2. MARSHALL PLAN—OEEC

2–03   If Churchill's words were well received, the European States, in those days, lacked the necessary stamina to proceed with such far-reaching plans, since they were preoccupied with their daily fight for economic survival. Once again, the United States came to the rescue. In another famous university speech, at Harvard this time, George Marshall, United States Secretary of State, announced on June 5, 1947, that the United States would do "whatever it is able to do, to assist in the return of normal economic health in the world". This offer was accepted by 16 European countries on July 15, 1947, and so the Marshall Plan was born; but more important for the future of European integration, was the setting up of the Organisation of European Economic Co-operation (OEEC)[3] in 1948; this was in response to the American request for an agreement among Europeans about the distribution of the American aid. Within that forum, the European States re-learned to work together.

3. ROBERT SCHUMAN: MAY 9, 1950

2–04   In the meantime, Churchill's words about a partnership between France and Germany had not been forgotten, and on May 9, 1950, Robert Schuman, French Foreign Minister, declared that a united Europe was essential for world peace, and that a gathering of the European nations required the elimination of the century-old opposition between France and Germany. As a first practical step towards this end, he proposed "to place the whole Franco-German coal and steel production under one joint High Authority, in an organisation open to the participation of the other countries of Europe". He described this pooling of production as the "first stage of the European Federation". Germany, the Netherlands, Belgium, Luxembourg and Italy accepted in principle, and negotiations started at once.

4. THE EUROPEAN COAL AND STEEL COMMUNITY (ECSC)

2–05   The negotiations progressed rapidly, and were simplified by the fact that all the future partners had accepted the proposed principles; the work consisted of mainly giving them legal form. A sense of urgency was probably added to the existing goodwill by the communist invasion in South Korea. The Treaty establishing the European Coal and Steel Community (ECSC) was signed in Paris on April 18, 1951. Ratification by the national parliaments met with little opposition and on July 23, 1952, the Treaty entered into force for a period of 50 years. The ECSC therefore ceased to exist on July 23, 2002.[4] From that moment

---

[3] In 1961, it became the Organisation for Economic Co-operation and Development (OECD), with the participation of the USA and Canada.

[4] See the Decision of the Representatives of the Governments of the Member States, meeting in Council, of February 27, 2002 on the financial consequences of the expiry of the ECSC Treaty, and on the research fund for coal and steel [2002] O.J. L79/42.

on, acts of the European institutions could no longer be based upon the provisions of that Treaty.[5] However, infringements against ECSC provisions, committed before that expiration date, are to be sanctioned by the European Commission, even after that date; as the Court put it: "it would be contrary to the objectives of the treaties and irreconcilable with the continuity of the legal order of the European Union, if the Commission did not have jurisdiction to ensure the uniform application of the rules from the ECSC Treaty, which continue to produce effects, even after the expiry of that treaty."[6]

The rights and obligations arising under the international agreements concluded by the ECSC were taken over by the European Community, now European Union.[7]

5. THE EUROPEAN DEFENCE COMMUNITY AND THE EUROPEAN POLITICAL COMMUNITY

The following two years were difficult. It has been said that the easing of the international political situation—Stalin died on March 5, 1953, and July 27, 1953 marked the end of the Korean war—diminished the necessity for "closing the ranks". In any case, two additional proposals for close co-operation among the "Six"—in the form of the European Defence Community and a European Political Community—failed miserably.

2–06

6. THE EUROPEAN ECONOMIC COMMUNITY (EEC) AND THE EUROPEAN ATOMIC ENERGY COMMUNITY (EURATOM)

Undaunted by those setbacks, the Benelux (BElgium, the NEtherlands and LUXemburg) countries proposed in 1955, to their partners in the Coal and Steel Community, to take another step towards economic integration, by setting up a "common market" and jointly developing transportation, classical energy and atomic energy. This led to the conference of Messina, in the same year, at which Mr Spaak, Belgian Foreign Minister, was asked to report on the feasibility of those plans. At that time an invitation was issued also to the British Government to join the negotiations of the Six; alas, to no avail.[8]

The Spaak Report was ready in 1956, and was discussed in Venice, where the decision was taken to start negotiations for drafting treaties that would establish a common market and an Atomic Energy Community. With incredible speed (June 1956–February 1957), these two complex Treaties were prepared for signature in

2–07

---

[5] *SP v Commission* (Joined Cases T-27/03, etc.) [2007] E.C.R. II-4331.
[6] *ArcelorMittal Luxemburg v Commission* (Joined Cases C-201/09 and C-216/09) [2011] E.C.R. I-2239, § 66.
[7] [2002] O.J. L194/35 and 36.
[8] See Hans Joachim Heiser, British Policy with regard to the unification efforts on the European Continent (Leyden, 1959), p.96.

Rome on March 25, 1957,[9] ratified by the six parliaments, and on January 1, 1958, the European Economic Community[10] (EEC) and the European Atomic Energy Community (Euratom), became a reality.

In 1961, the British Government decided to apply for negotiations to determine whether satisfactory arrangements could be made to meet the needs of the United Kingdom, of the Commonwealth and of EFTA.[11] The Government were, "baulked in their objective, so that it was not possible to determine whether satisfactory conditions of entry could be obtained".[12]

7. THE TREATY ESTABLISHING A SINGLE COUNCIL AND A SINGLE COMMISSION

2–08   On April 8, 1965, the institutional set-up of the Communities, which had been "streamlined" a first time by the Convention on certain institutions common to the European Communities,[13] was simplified, once again, by the so-called Merger Treaty, the Treaty establishing a Single Council and a Single Commission of the European Communities. It entered into force on July 1, 1967. Until that date, there had been three Councils and three Commissions (one for each Community), while, in accordance with the above-mentioned "Convention" there was only a single Court of Justice, and a single Assembly for the three Communities. The Convention and the Merger Treaty were taken over by the EU Treaty (1992).

8. THE CUSTOMS UNION

2–09   The Customs Union, provided for by the EEC Treaty, became fully operational on July 1, 1968. It meant that tariffs and quotas between the Member States had, by then, been completely abolished, and that the replacement of the national external tariffs by the common (external) customs tariff (CCT) had been completed. The Community was 18 months ahead of the schedule laid down in the Treaty.[14] This, however, still left differences in taxation and charges and measures with equivalent effect to tariffs and quotas, as obstacles to free trade between Member States.

---

[9] The story goes, however, that, since there was no time to print the full text in the four languages, the documents that were signed, only contained printed first and last pages, all the others being blanks!
[10] The Treaty was modified many times, for the last times in 2005 in view of the accession of Bulgaria and Romania; the next time was the Treaty of Lisbon.
[11] The European Free Trade Association (EFTA) was set up, at the instigation of the UK, with, among others, the Scandinavian countries, to "counter" the European Communities; it never amounted to very much, compared with the Communities. It still exists, however, with only Iceland, Norway, Switzerland and Liechtenstein as members.
[12] The UK and the European Communities, 1971 (Cmnd. 4715), para.6.
[13] Signed in Rome on March 25, 1957, together with the two European Treaties.
[14] Twelve years, see Art. 8 EEC (abolished) and Acceleration Decisions: [1960] J.O. 1217 and [1962] J.O. 1284.

9. THE COMMUNITY'S (NOW UNION'S) OWN RESOURCES

The replacement of the Financial Contributions from Member States by the Union's own Resources,[15] inaugurated a new era in the history of the Union. It became, in a certain way, financially independent, and the Treaty amending Certain Budgetary Provisions of the ECSC, EEC and Euratom Treaties and of the Merger Treaty, conferred specific budgetary powers upon, what had become the European Parliament (hereafter "Parliament"). The Union's own resources are provided by the agricultural levies, the customs duties, a percentage of the VAT collected by the Member States and, since February 1988, a rate applied to an additional base, representing the sum of the GNP at market prices.[16]

10. THE BRITISH, DANISH AND IRISH MEMBERSHIP

After a debate in both Houses of Parliament, at the end of which the **2–10** Government's decision was approved in the Commons by a majority of 426, the British Government applied to the Council for membership of the Communities on May 10, 1967. By December of the same year it was clear, however, that the Six could not reach the unanimity necessary under the Treaties to return a reply to Britain's application. Thus ended the second endeavour of the United Kingdom to enter "Europe". The British Government, however, decided to maintain its application for membership and it was discussed at many meetings of the Council, in the following two years.

At the meeting of Heads of State or Government on December 1 and 2, 1969 at The Hague, it was finally agreed to open negotiations with Denmark, Ireland, Norway and the United Kingdom, who had applied for membership. Other important decisions, taken at this "Summit", concerned the Economic and Monetary Community, and the above mentioned "own resources". The Treaty of Brussels, relating to the accession of the United Kingdom, Ireland, Norway and Denmark, was signed on January 22, 1972; this Treaty entered into force on January 1, 1973, except for Norway which, as a result of a referendum on the subject, did not ratify the Treaty. Consequently, several provisions of this Treaty, and of the Act concerning the conditions of accession, and the adjustments to the Treaties attached thereto, were modified by the Council in the Decision of January 1, 1973, adjusting the documents concerning accession of the new Member States (hereinafter referred to as the "Adaptation Decision").

---

[15] Decision 70/243 of April 21, 1970: [1970] J.O. L94/19; [1970(I)] O.J. 224. It became effective on January 1, 1971, after ratification by the six national Parliaments.
[16] For more details see the chapter on Financing Union Activities;

11. THE ENLARGEMENT TO GREECE, PORTUGAL AND SPAIN

2–11 On June 12, 1975, Greece applied for membership of the Union—the Treaty of Accession, together with an Act concerning the conditions of accession, and the adjustments to the Treaties, was signed at Athens on May 28, 1979[17]; it was ratified by the Greek Parliament on June 28, 1979. Greece became a member on January 1, 1981. On March 28, 1977, Portugal and on July 28, 1977, Spain applied for membership. Formal negotiations with Portugal started on October 16, 1978, and with Spain on February 5, 1979. They were successfully concluded at the European Council of March 29 and 30, 1985, and the third enlargement became effective on January 1, 1986, bringing the total of Member States to 12.

12. THE DIRECT ELECTION OF PARLIAMENT AND THE DECLARATION ON DEMOCRACY AND FUNDAMENTAL RIGHTS

2–12 On September 20, 1976, the Representatives of the Member States in Council agreed on the conditions for direct election of the members of Parliament, and signed the Act concerning the Election of the Representatives of [what was then] the "Assembly" by Direct Universal Suffrage,[18] which was subsequently ratified by the, at that time, nine national parliaments. The first elections were held in June 1979,[19] giving "Europe" its democratic legitimacy.

On April 5, 1977 Parliament, the Council and the Commission issued a "Joint Declaration on Fundamental Rights",[20] with which the Heads of State and Government associated themselves in their "Declaration on Democracy". In this Declaration they confirmed their will to ensure that the values of their legal, political and moral order are respected, and to safeguard the principles of representative democracy, of the rule of law, of social justice, and of respect for human rights. They stated that the application of these principles implies a political system of pluralist democracy.

On June 19, 1983, the, by that time, 10 Heads of State and Government signed the "Solemn Declaration on European Community" expressing, among others, their determination "to achieve a comprehensive and coherent common political approach" and their will to transform the whole complex of relations between their States into a "European Community".

13. THE SECESSION OF GREENLAND

2–13 On February 1, 1985, Greenland ceased to be part of the [Union] to which it had belonged since January 1, 1973, as part of the Kingdom of Denmark. Greenland has enjoyed a special status within the Kingdom since the Home Rule Act of

---

[17] [1979] O.J. L291/1.
[18] [1976] O.J. L278/1.
[19] See below, the chapter on the European Parliament.
[20] [1977] O.J. C103/1.

1979, and the Greenland Government has exclusive competence, among others, for fishing, agriculture and stock farming.

Greenland's special features, i.e. remoteness, climatic conditions and the cultural particulars of its non-European population, pleaded in favour of new arrangements after the people of the island had decided in 1982, by referendum, to withdraw from the Union and to seek a new type of relationship. The EC Treaty provisions applicable to overseas countries and territories provided an appropriate framework for these relations, although additional specific provisions were needed.[21]

In 2003, the Council decided to broaden and strengthen future relations with Greenland after 2006, and took a decision in 2006 to that effect, and a Joint Declaration was adopted by the Union, on the one hand, and the Home Rule Government of Greenland and the Government of Denmark, on the other, on partnership between the Union and Greenland.[22]

14. THE COMPLETION OF THE INTERNAL MARKET BY 1992

In June 1985, the Commission sent a White Paper to the European Council [to be distinguished from the "Council"] entitled "Completing the Internal Market".[23] This was the beginning of "Operation 1992". It lays down a comprehensive programme and timetable for the abolition of barriers of all kinds in inter-State trade, the harmonisation of rules, the approximation of legislation and of the tax structures, and the strengthening of monetary co-operation. To complete the internal market, the White Paper provided for removal of physical, technical and fiscal barriers. It was, among other things, to make the implementation of this comprehensive programme possible, that the Member States decided to amend the existing Treaties through the "Single European Act".

2–14

15. THE SINGLE EUROPEAN ACT (SEA)

It was signed in Luxembourg on February 17, and at The Hague on February 28, 1986; it entered into force on July 1, 1987. The SEA's[24] objective is the completion of the "internal market"' defined as "an area without internal frontiers in which the free movement of goods, persons, services and capital is ensured".[25] It provides, among other things, for the strengthening of the decision-making process by extending the number of decisions to be taken by qualified majority,

2–15

---

[21] See Commission opinion on the status of Greenland ([1983] E.C. Bull. 1–13) and text of amending Treaty with various Council regulations [1985] O.J. L29/1.

[22] [2006] O.J. L208/28.

[23] White Paper from the Commission to the European Council (Milan, June 28–29, 1985), COM(85) 310 final.

[24] As already indicated, the Act was designated as "Single" because, in fact, it combines two different instruments: the first one provides for modifications to the three European Treaties, and the second constitutes an agreement between the Member States to jointly formulate and implement, among others, a European foreign policy.

[25] Art.26(2) TFEU.

the inclusion in the Treaty of chapters on Economic and Social Cohesion (Regional Development), Research and Technological Development, and Environment. It also provides for closer involvement of Parliament in the legislative procedures. The SEA makes reference to a Treaty on an "Economic and Monetary Community" and to co-operation in the sphere of Foreign Policy.

16.   THE TREATY ON EUROPEAN UNION OR MAASTRICHT TREATY (EU TREATY)

2–16   The Treaty was signed in Maastricht, the Netherlands, on February 7, 1992 and came into force on November 1, 1993. It contains seven parts. Title I provides for a European Union, sets out its objectives, among others: the establishment of an economic and monetary union, ultimately including a single currency; a common foreign and security policy, including the eventual framing of a common defence policy; the introduction of a citizenship of the Union for the nationals of the Member States; co-operation on justice and home affairs; the mainte-nance of the *acquis communautaire*; and the respect of the principle of subsidiarity.

It also "officialises"[26] the European Council, which must provide the necessary impetus and define the general political guidelines for Union action, and it indicates that to be a Member of the Union, a State's government must be founded on the principles of democracy, while the fundamental rights are considered to be general principles of Union law.

Titles II, III and IV contain amendments to the three European Treaties.

17.   THE EUROPEAN ECONOMIC AREA (EEA) AND THE EUROPEAN FREE TRADE ASSOCIATION (EFTA)

2–17   The European Economic Area (EEA) now unites the 28 Member States and three of the four EFTA States (Iceland, Liechtenstein and Norway; Switzerland having voted to stay out) into an internal market governed by the same basic rules as the Union's internal market.[27]

The Agreement establishing the EEA was signed in Oporto on May 2, 1992 between the, at that time, seven[28] EFTA countries and the "European Community", and their Member States. It entered into force in 1994. Following a referendum in Switzerland, this country dropped out of the EEA, but remained in EFTA. The signature of the EEA Agreement was held up by an Opinion delivered by the Court on the conformity of the draft agreement with the Treaty.[29] Following that Opinion, the Agreement, instead of setting up an EEA Court, now provides for an EEA Joint Committee to settle disputes between the two sides, and to ensure the uniform interpretation of the Agreement, by keeping under permanent review the decisions of the Court and of the newly created EFTA

---

[26] The European Council became an "institution" of the Union under the Lisbon Treaty of 2009.
[27] See below the chapter on the Free Movement of Goods.
[28] Austria, Finland, Iceland, Liechtenstein, Norway, Sweden and Switzerland. See [1994] O.J. L1/1.
[29] Opinion 1/91 of December 14 [1991] E.C.R. I-6079 and Opinion 1/92 of April 10 [1992] E.C.R. I-2825.

Court.[30] The first case was introduced before that court on April 27, 1994. The latter's jurisdiction is confined to the EFTA countries. Decisions of the Committee will have no impact on the case law of the Union courts. The autonomy of the Union legal system is thus preserved. In case parties cannot agree on a uniform interpretation, they may agree to apply to the Court of Justice for an interpretation of the rules at issue.[31]

The EEA Agreement, which entered into force on January 1, 1994, establishes an integrated structure based on common rules and equal conditions of competition, together with the necessary means to implement it. The free movement of goods and persons, the right of establishment and the right to provide services, and the free movement of capital and payments are achieved on the basis of existing Union legislation, as it has evolved over the years (*acquis communautaire*). Subject to a limited number of exceptions and transitional provisions, it is now applicable in the three EEA EFTA countries. In addition to the basic freedoms, the EEA Agreement provides for co-operation in areas that are directly relevant to the economic activity, such as research and development, social policy, social security, consumer protection, the environment, statistics, and company law. It also provides for a permanent information and consultation process covering all stages of the "preparation" of Union instruments. It includes surveillance and enforcement rules.

The Agreement provides for an EEA Council, comparable to the European Council, an EEA Joint Committee, comparable to the European Commission,[32] and an EEA Parliamentary Committee. The EEA has its own decision-making procedure.[33]

2–18

The EEA Agreement was extended to include the 10 new Member States on November 11, 2003, and entered into force retroactively on October 14, 2003 (date of the signature of the enlargement Treaty). The new Members enjoy the same transitional periods as those provided for in the enlargement Treaty. In order to apply on May 1, 2004, the extension was ratified by 28 States (at that time 25 Members of the EU and the three EEA EFTA members). A new extension took place on January 1, 2007 with the accession of Bulgaria and Romania to the Union.

The European Free Trade Association (EFTA) was established, as indicated above, in 1960. Most of the original EFTA members are now Union Member States; the present EFTA members are Iceland, Liechtenstein, Norway and Switzerland. EFTA is served by three institutions: the EFTA Secretariat, the EFTA Surveillance Authority and the EFTA Court.

---

[30] [1994] O.J. L344/1.
[31] Twenty-Sixth General Report (1992), p.421.
[32] See Rules of Procedure of the EFTA Surveillance Authority [1994] O.J. L113/19.
[33] See, e.g. Decisions of the EEC-EFTA Joint Committee. [1994] O.J. L12/32 and of the EFTA Surveillance Authority: [1994] O.J. C158/5 and [1994] O.J. L138/39.

18. THE ACCESSION OF AUSTRIA, FINLAND AND SWEDEN

2–19 At the December 1992 Edinburgh European Council meeting, it was agreed that negotiations with Austria, Finland and Sweden could start in early 1993, to be followed by similar talks with Norway, once the Commission had delivered its opinion on that country's application. It will be remembered that the Treaty provides that:

> "[A]ny European State which respects the values referred to in Art. 2,[34] and is committed to promoting them, may apply to become a member of the Union. It shall address its application to the Council, which shall act unanimously, after consulting the Commission, and after receiving the consent of Parliament, which shall act by a majority of its component members".[35]

The Maastricht European Council of December 1991 added a proviso to that effect, by noting "that any European State whose system of government was founded on the principle of democracy, could apply to become a member of the [Union]".[36]

It is interesting to note that the Commission drew up a set of criteria, with which applicant States should comply. First they must fulfil the three basic conditions of European identity, democratic status and respect for human rights. Secondly, they must accept the *acquis communautaire* in its entirety, but must also, subject to transitional and temporary arrangements, be able to implement it. Thirdly, this presupposes that the country in question possesses a functioning and competitive market economy and an adequate legal and administrative framework.

On the basis of the Commission's report, the Lisbon European Council of June 1992 invited the institutions to speed up preparatory work on negotiations with EFTA countries, stating that official negotiations could begin as soon as the EU Treaty had been ratified,[37] and the second package of financial[38] and structural[39] measures had been agreed upon. Consequently, the Commission adopted opinions on Sweden's application in July 1992 and on Finland's in November. Norway formally applied in November 1992, but withdrew following a negative referendum. The Commission's opinion on Austria's accession was delivered in July 1991. The three countries became Member States on January 1, 1995. They thereby accepted all the provisions of the European Treaties and the *acquis communautaire* in its entirety. This enlargement, which marks a significant step forward in the history of European integration, brought the number of Member States to 15 and the number of European citizens to 368 million.

---

[34] Art.2 EU provides that the, "Union is founded on the values of respect for human dignity, freedom, democracy, equality, the rule of law and respect for human rights, including the rights of persons belonging to minorities. These values are common to the Member States in a society in which pluralism, non-discrimination, tolerance, justice, solidarity and equality between women and men prevails."

[35] Art.49,1 EU.

[36] Twenty-Third General Report (1992), p.249.

[37] November 1, 1993.

[38] See below the chapter on Financing Union Activities.

[39] See below the chapter on Economic, Social and Territorial Cohesion/Regional Policy.

19. THE TREATY OF AMSTERDAM

The intergovernmental conference (IGC), which was provided for in the EU   2–20
Treaty, opened in Turin on March 29, 1996, after the agenda was adopted by the
European Council. The main titles were: (1) a [Union] closer to its citizens; (2)
the institutions in a more democratic and efficient [Union]; and (3) a strengthened
capacity for external action by the Union. On all three accounts the conference
failed miserably. The new Treaty was supposed to prepare the Union for further
expansion by the inclusion of the countries of Central and Eastern Europe. This
required, in the first place, a profound reform, as suggested in the "Agenda 2000"
of the Common Agricultural Policy and of the structural funds, besides the long
overdue reform of the institutions. Where the latter is concerned, the only
progress that was achieved concerns the Parliament, which saw its direct
participation in the legislative field enlarged.[40] None of the other subjects were
even touched upon at Amsterdam, as if the lack of reforms were to be kept as an
excuse for postponing enlargement! The difficulties encountered with the
ratification of the EU Treaty had clearly shown that the citizens had to be
associated with the activities of the Union institutions. One of the ways to achieve
this is by more openness. And although the EU Treaty now provides that
decisions must be taken, "as openly as possible and as closely as possible to the
citizen", nothing much has changed. As will be seen, it is theoretically possible,
but still difficult, to accede to the archives of the institutions, but *im*possible to
get hold of preparatory documents for Union legislation, except at an early stage,
in the Green papers. By refusing to communicate drafts, under the pretext that
they might be amended or have not yet been approved by the hierarchy, the
institutions ignore the obligations the Treaties impose upon them. What has
become of the much-heralded transparency, democracy and openness?

The Treaty also provides that one year before the EU membership exceeds 20
States a conference of representatives of the governments of the Member States
shall carry out a comprehensive review of the composition and functioning of the
institutions. Nothing has come of this either.

The Treaty of Amsterdam entered into force on May 1, 1999.

20. THE TREATY OF NICE[41]

This Treaty was signed at Nice on February 26, 2001 and amends the EU Treaty,   2–21
the Treaties establishing the European Communities and certain related acts.

According to one of the Recitals, the idea was to "complete the process started
by the Treaty of Amsterdam of preparing the institutions of the European
Community to function in an enlarged Community". Whether they succeeded is
more than questionable, and furthermore the drafters "messed up" once again the

---

[40] See, however, the Protocol on institutions with the prospect of enlargement of the European
Community, annexed to the four Treaties which provides that, on accession, the Commission shall
comprise one national of each of the Member States, and that Member States which have two
nationals will give up one, on the condition that the weighting of the votes in the Council has been
modified in a manner acceptable to all Member States.
[41] See [2001] O.J. C80/1.

texts of the Treaties (which had been "cleaned up" by the Treaty of Amsterdam) by inserting all kinds of new provisions, so that one had, once more, articles a, b, c, etc.

21.   ACCESSION OF 10 NEW MEMBER STATES

2–22   The process leading to the accession of Cyprus, Hungary, Poland, Estonia, the Czech Republic, Slovenia, Latvia, Lithuania, Malta and Slovakia was set in motion by the Luxembourg European Council in 1997; it was decided that the process would comprise a single framework, an enhanced pre-accession partnership between each candidate country and the Union, and aid for each applicant country. Although it was decided at first to proceed in two stages, this approach was later abandoned and negotiations took place with all the candidates in parallel. Association Agreements, also known as European Agreements were signed with each candidate country. The Treaty of Accession was signed in Athens on April 16, 2003. It was provided that the 10 new Member States would join the Union on May 1, 2004.

22.   THE EUROPEAN CONVENTION ON THE FUTURE OF THE EUROPEAN UNION AND THE DRAFT CONSTITUTION[42]

2–23   At its meeting in Laeken (Belgium) in December 2001, the European Council convened a Convention on the future of the European [Union] (the Laeken Declaration). The task of the Convention was to pave the way for the next intergovernmental conference as broadly and openly as possible. It was to consider the key issues arising for the Union's future development, for example: what do European citizens expect from the Union? How is the division of competence between the Union and the Member States to be organised? Within the Union, how is the division of competence between the institutions to be organised? How can the efficiency and coherence of the Union's external action be ensured? and How can the Union's democratic legitimacy be ensured?

The Convention opened its proceedings with a period of listening in order to find out what people wanted and expected from the Union. The second phase was a period of analysis for comparing the pros and cons of the proposals put forward for organising the Union. The third phase sought to draw together the different proposals and draft recommendations.

2–24   The Convention terminated its work on July 1, 2003 and a draft Constitution[43] was presented to the European Council of Rome by its President, Valérie Giscard d'Estaing, on July 18, 2003. An intergovernmental conference was convened in

---

[42] *http://european-convention.eu.int/EN/bienvenue/bienvenue2352.html?lang=EN* [accessed August 23, 2013]. See also the Decision of the Representatives of the Member States meeting within the Council of February 21, 2002 setting up a Fund for the financing of the Convention [2002] O.J. L349.
[43] Doc. No. CONV 850/03; http//www.european-convention.eu.int/docs/treaty/cv00850.en03.pdf [accessed August 23, 2013].

October 2003, under the Italian Presidency, to adopt a Constitution, but without success. It was finally signed in Rome in November 2004 and published in the Official Journal.[44]

Several ill-advised Member States decided to submit the ratification of the Constitution to a referendum, with the consequence, among others, that the French and Dutch voters, for reasons that more often than not had nothing to do with the content of the draft, rejected it, although Parliament (with a large majority) and 18 Member States, out of 25 at that time, had ratified the draft. The Member States decided at the European Council of June 17, 2005 that they needed a "period of reflection" to enable a broad debate in each country.[45] In July 2005 it was decided to temporarily suspend the ratification procedure, also because the European Council of June 2005 did not succeed in adopting the pluri-annual budget for 2007–2013.

23. THE ACCESSION OF BULGARIA AND ROMANIA

Following the statement of the Commission of September 26, 2006 that Bulgaria and Romania "can join the EU in 2007", these two candidates became the 26th and 27th Member States on January 1, 2007. However, the final monitoring report of the Commission indicated tough conditions for their entry. Both countries were to be closely monitored on the remaining areas of concern, such as the justice system, the fight against corruption, organised crime and agriculture. If the conditions were not met, the Commission could invoke safeguards. Under the Accession Treaty there are three types of such measures: economic, internal market and JHA (Justice and Home Affairs) that can be invoked up to three years after accession. These could affect food export bans and cuts to EU funds,[46] such as agricultural and structural funds. In addition there are transitional arrangements, such as the restriction of free movement of workers from the new Member States. Also the Commission can take remedial measures to ensure the functioning of EU policies; this concerns the areas of food and air safety, agricultural funds, the judiciary and the fight against corruption. **2–25**

24. THE TREATY OF LISBON

The rejection of the Draft Constitution by the French and Dutch voters seemingly caused nearly a two-year period of quasi-immobility in the European Union (maybe also an excuse to do nothing!), but behind the scenes work was carried on, through diplomatic channels, to draft a new text; these efforts resulted in the adoption at the European Council of June 20 and 21, 2007 of a draft "Reform Treaty". It contained very precise indications concerning the modifications to be introduced in the existing three European Treaties (contrary to the draft **2–26**

---

[44] [2004] O.J. C310/1.
[45] Declaration by the Heads of State or Government of the Member States of the Community on the ratification of the Treaty establishing a constitution for Europe (European Council, June 16 and 17, 2005), SN 117/05.
[46] This actually happened for Bulgaria in 2008.

Constitution that provided for one single Treaty), by a so-called intergovernmental conference. The latter was, in fact, a meeting of lawyers, with the task to draft the decisions that had been taken by the European Council in June 2007.

Noteworthy are some passages of the Presidency Conclusions of that European Council: (1) "Europe is united in its resolve that only by working together can we represent our interests and goals in the World of tomorrow"; and (2) ". . . secure our future as an active player in a rapidly changing World." This reference to the world, rather than to Europe, is remarkable since it shows an evolution from a Union centred on itself ("determined to lay the foundation of an ever closer Community among the peoples of Europe"[47]), to a player on the world scene. It constitutes an important further step in the Union's development.

2–27 Compared to the existing Treaties, as last modified by "Nice", (rather than the draft Constitution), the major changes are the following:

- Where the institutions are concerned:
    - the six-month rotating presidency of the European Council is replaced by a, once-renewable, period of two-and-a-half years—it does not affect the rotating presidency of the Council;
    - a Vice-President of the Commission becomes the High Representative of the Union for Foreign Affairs and Security Policy;
    - the number of members of the Commission shall be equal to two-thirds of the number of Member States (in 2009 this means 18), instead of one member per Member State (presently 28), as it was before; however, this was modified to placate the Irish, and to allow them to vote "yes" in a second referendum [they had rejected the new Treaty in a first referendum, see hereunder], after they seemingly wanted to keep an Irish "commissioner"[48];
    - the voting procedure in the Council, the so-called "co-decision procedure", becomes "ordinary legislative procedure", i.e. Parliament and Council acting jointly; Council decisions are now, except when otherwise provided, taken by qualified majority, the latter remaining unchanged until 2014, it is then slightly modified until 2017, after which a decision must be approved by 55 per cent of the Council members, representing 15 Member States and 65 per cent of the Union population: a blocking minority must include at least four Member States, the so-called double majority;
- other modifications concern mainly:
    - the specific nature of the Foreign and Security Policy;
    - the enhanced role of the national parliaments with regard to draft Union acts;
    - the Charter of Fundamental Rights of the European Union[49] has the same legal value as the Treaties; however, for the Court to have jurisdiction, a connection with European law is necessary.[50] For its

---

[47] Former EC Treaty, Preamble, para.1.
[48] See Conclusions of the European Council of June 19, 2009.
[49] For an interpretation of Arts 16 and 17 see *SKY Österreich* (C-283/11) judgment of January 22, 2013, not yet reported.
[50] *Claude Chartry* (C-457/09) [2011] E.C.R. I-819.

field of application: Art.51, see *Aklagaren v Åkerberg Fransson* (C-617/10) judgment of February 26, 2013, not yet reported.
- "increased co-operation" is extended from the EMU (Euro) and Schengen to Judicial co-operation in the area of Police and Criminal Matters;
- the competences of the Union are now clearly divided into "exclusive competences" and "competences shared with the Member States", the latter being allowed to exercise their own competences, and Union competences "to support, coordinate or supplement the actions of the Member States"[51];
- under "environment", reference is now made to "climate change";
- the control of "subsidiarity" by the national parliaments is reinforced;
- more questionable modifications are:
  - after having been widely used for more than 50 years, the terms "European Community", "Community" and "common market" simply disappear and are replaced by "Union", "European Union" and "internal market";
  - the "EC Treaty" becomes the "Treaty on the Functioning of the European Union"(TFEU);
  - the "Court of First Instance" becomes the "General Court", and the "Judicial Panels" become "Specialised Courts";
  - voluntary withdrawal from the Union is now possible;
  - the numbering of all the articles is modified;
  - there are too many "opt-outs"!

25.   IRELAND AND THE TREATY OF LISBON

In order to make it possible for the Irish people to vote in favour of the Treaty of Lisbon, during a second referendum on October 2, 2009, after having rejected it by a first referendum in 2008, the following legal guarantees were agreed upon.   **2–28**

At the European Council meeting of June 18 and 19, 2009, it was mentioned that, at its meeting of December 11 and 12, 2008, it was agreed (in order to meet the concerns of the Irish people) that a decision would be taken, in accordance with the necessary legal procedures, to the effect that the Commission shall continue to include one national of each Member State. At the June meeting it was also agreed that other concerns of the Irish people relating to taxation policy, the right of life, education, the family and Ireland's traditional policy of military neutrality, would be addressed to the mutual satisfaction of all the Member States, by way of the necessary legal guarantees. It was also agreed that the high importance attached to a number of social issues, including workers' rights, would be confirmed.

Consequently, a decision was taken by the Heads of State or Government, meeting within the European Council, on the concerns of the Irish people on the Treaty of Lisbon, and a Solemn Declaration on Workers' Rights, Social Policy and other issues.

---

[51] Art.6 TFEU.

The Decision is legally binding and took effect on the date of entry into force of the Treaty of Lisbon. At the time of the conclusion of the next accession treaty, the provisions of the Decision will be set out in a Protocol to be attached to the EU Treaty and the TFEU.

The outcome of the second Irish referendum was positive.

26.   THE CZECH REPUBLIC AND THE TREATY OF LISBON

2–29   Arrangements similar to the Irish ones were made for the Czech Republic, concerning the application of the Charter of Human Rights: the Czech President claimed that the Charter would allow descendants of the Germans, who were expulsed from the country after the Second World War, to reclaim their former lands. An exemption was granted.

Another obstacle to the final ratification was an appeal by 17 senators to the Constitutional Court on whether or not the Treaty of Lisbon conflicts with the Czech Constitution. The Court ruled on November 3, 2009 that there was no conflict, and the President, on the same day, signed the Treaty, which thereby was ratified by the 27 Member States, in accordance with their respective constitutional requirements.

The Treaty on European Union and the Treaty on the Functioning of the European Union entered into force on December 1, 2009.

27.   ACCESSION OF CROATIA

2–30   Croatia applied for membership in 2003 and on December 9, 2011 leaders from the EU and Croatia signed the accession treaty. Throughout the interim period until accession, Croatia as an acceding country had active observer status in the European Institutions, allowing it to become familiar with the EU working methods and to be involved in the decision-making process.

Croatia became the 28th Member State on July 1, 2013.

FURTHER READING

2–31   Lenaerts and Van Nuffel, *Constitutional Law of the European Community*, 2nd edn (Sweet & Maxwell, 2004).

Finn Laursen, *The Treaty of Nice* (Martinus Nijhoff, 2006)

CHAPTER 3

The Legal Acts of the Union[1]

The main lines of the Union decision-making process, i.e. the procedures for the adoption of Union legal acts by the institutions will be outlined in the following chapters, when analysing the role played therein by, respectively, the Parliament, the Council and the Commission.

    For those who are subject to Union law, the main question with regard to the acts is to be able to determine whether or not they are binding on them, i.e. confers on them certain rights and/or imposes on them certain obligations, and, if this is the case, whether the institution issuing the acts is indeed competent to do so. According to the Court, an act is binding when it "brings about a distinctive change in the legal position of a party".[2] Regarding the competence of the issuing institution, it is extremely important to note that "the limits of Union competences are governed by the principle of *conferral*".[3] This is further emphasised in the TFEU as follows:

> "Under the principle of conferral, the Union shall act only within the limits of the competences conferred upon it, by the Member States, in the Treaties to attain the objectives set out therein. Competences, not conferred upon the Union in the Treaties, remain with the Member States."[4]

    As will be seen in the following chapters of this book, among the competences conferred upon the Union, there is, in the first place, the creation of the "internal market", characterised by the fundamental freedoms: free movement of goods, free movement of persons, freedom of establishment, freedom to provide services and free movement of capital and of payments. Those freedoms are further sustained and developed by various policies concerning the rights and obligations of Member States and natural and legal persons, living and operating within this internal market. They concern, for instance, competition, agriculture, fisheries, transport, social policy, industrial policy, territorial cohesion, research and information society and foreign policy. All these policies, and several others (such as the area of freedom, security and justice and the Economic and monetary union whose currency is the euro) are to be implemented by the Union and by the Member States, each acting in its own sphere of competence.

    Indeed, one of the fundamental distinctions to be made when reference is made to "competences" of the Union is the distinction between the "exclusive"

3–01

---

[1] Arts 288–292 TFEU.
[2] *IBM* (60/81) [1981] E.C.R. 21639.
[3] Art.5(1) EU.
[4] Art.5(2) EU.

competences of the Union, the competences the Union "shares" with the Member States, and the competence to carry out actions to "support, coordinate or supplement" the actions of the Member States.

3–02
The "exclusive" competences of the Union[5] concern: the customs union; the establishing of the competition rules; the monetary policy of the Member States whose currency is the euro; the conservation of marine biological resources under the common fisheries policy; and the common commercial policy.

The competence "shared"[6] with the Member States apply, *grosso modo*, in the following areas: internal market; social policy; economic, social and territorial cohesion; agriculture and fisheries (excluding conservation of marine biological resources); environment; consumer protection; transport; trans-European networks; energy; the area of freedom, security and justice; public health; and development co-operation and humanitarian aid.

Thirdly, there are the competences of the Union to carry out actions to support, co-ordinate or supplement the actions of the Member States[7]; they are: protection and improvement of human health; industry; culture; tourism; education, vocational training, youth and sport; civil protection; and administrative co-operation.

It must be noted that the "principle of subsidiarity" and the "principle of proportionality" also apply to the exercise by the institutions of the powers conferred upon them by the Treaties.[8]

Under the principle of subsidiarity, in areas which do not fall within its exclusive competence,[9] the Union shall act only if and in so far as the objectives of the proposed action cannot be sufficiently achieved by the Member States, either at central level or at regional and local level, or, by reason of the scale or effects of the proposed action, can be better achieved at Union level. This principle must be applied as laid down in the Protocol on the application of the principles of subsidiarity and proportionality.[10]

3–03
Under the principle of proportionality, the content and form of Union action may not exceed what is necessary to achieve the objectives of the Treaties. This principle must be applied by the institutions, as laid down in the above-mentioned Protocol.

Under that Protocol, the Commission must, before proposing legislative acts, "consult widely" taking into account the local and regional dimension of the act.[11] This obligation also applies to initiatives from a group of Member States, to initiatives from Parliament, to requests from the Court, to recommendations from the European Central Bank (ECB) and to requests from the European Investment Bank (EIB), for the adoption of legislative acts. For more details, see below Ch.8: The Commission.

---

[5] Art.3 TFEU.
[6] Art.4 TFEU.
[7] Art.6 TFEU.
[8] Art.5(3) and (4) EU.
[9] See Art.3(1) TFEU: customs union, competition, monetary policy (Euro), conservation of marine biological resources, common commercial policy and the conclusion of certain international agreements.
[10] Protocol No.2 attached to the TFEU.
[11] Protocol No.2, Art.2.

As for the various forms which the Union acts can take, it should be pointed out from the onset that the actual practice does sometimes differ from what the Treaty provides. As shall be seen below, the TFEU provides only for regulations, directives, decisions and agreements as binding acts.[12] However, the tendency, it seems, has been to multiply the forms of the Union acts, the procedures leading up to them,[13] and the bodies issuing them. Indeed, besides those acts already mentioned, there are: joint actions,[14] common positions,[15] Communiqués, Declarations and Conclusions of the European Council. Furthermore one finds: Programmes, Resolutions, Recommendations,[16] and, especially, Communications.[17]

Some acts are issued, for instance, not only by the Council, but also by the Representatives of the Governments of the Member States within the Council, or by the Council and the Representatives of the Governments. Then there are also the Notices of the Commission, by which it publishes Guidelines[18] or gives definitions[19] in the competition field. Since, generally speaking, these acts are not binding, i.e. do not create rights and obligations for those who are subject to Union law, not all of the above-mentioned measures constitute Union "acts" whose legality the Court can review. Neither are they always issued, as provided for in the Treaty, on the basis of a Commission proposal, although often there will be one. Nor is Parliament or the Social and Economic Committee or the Committee of the Regions necessarily consulted. Nonetheless, these acts shape essential Union policies, and consequently the development of the Union itself. They are part of the *acquis communautaire*. It sometimes appears that the more important the decision, politically speaking, the less formal the procedures that lead to them and the forms of the acts.

Nevertheless, the acts expressly provided for by the Treaties (regulations, directives, decisions, agreements) play, by far, the most important role. The conditions laid down for the decision-making process and for the contents of those acts must be seen as so many guarantees for lawfulness and judicial control, and for the protection of the rights of the citizens.

3–04

---

[12] Art.288 TFEU.

[13] As was seen, normally the Council acts on a proposal from the Commission, there are also cases where the Council acts on a "recommendation" of the Commission: for instance Art.207(3)1 TFEU.

[14] Art.14(1) EU.

[15] Art.15 EU.

[16] Art.126(7) TFEU .

[17] One look at the Commission's General Reports shows that, in all sectors of activity, matters are dealt with mainly in the form of "communications", referred to as "COM(year) No."; see, for instance, the General Reports.

[18] Some of these Guidelines are extremely important, and although they do not bind anybody except the Commission itself, no undertaking can afford to ignore them: they interpret, explain and somehow expand the provisions of binding regulations. See for instance Guidelines on the application of Art.101 of the TFEU to horizontal co-operation agreements [2001] O.J. C 3/2. See *P, JCB Service v Commission* (C-167/04) [2006] E.C.R. C-9028, where the Court held that "in adopting such rules of conduct and announcing them that they will henceforth apply to the cases to which they relate, the Commission imposes a limit on the exercise of its discretion and cannot depart from those rules under pain of being found, where appropriate, to be in breach of the general principles of law, such as equal treatment or the protection of legitimate expectations."

[19] See for instance the Commission Notice on the definition of relevant market for the purposes of Union competition law [1997] O.J. C 372/5. See comment fn.18.

The Treaties invest in the Council, the Parliament and the Commission, the responsibility for implementing the objectives of the Union. To carry out this task, they have empowered them to adopt regulations, directives, decisions, recommendations and opinions[20]; to those must be added, although not mentioned in the same Treaty provision, "international agreements".

Furthermore, each one of those acts fulfils a specific function in the development of Union law, and the Treaties therefore explicitly provide, in many cases, what kind of act must be adopted, by which institution and in which circumstances. Different rules apply to each category of acts and, more important, the extent of the legal protection afforded legal and natural persons varies widely from one category to another.[21]

1. BINDING ACTS PROVIDED FOR IN THE TREATIES: LEGAL ACTS/LEGISLATIVE ACTS[22]

3–05   Not all "legal acts of the Union" (regulations, directives and decisions) are "legislative acts": the latter are only those acts adopted by "legislative procedure",

- whether "ordinary", i.e. joint adoption by Parliament and Council on a proposal from the Commission, or
- whether "specific", i.e. adoption by Parliament with the participation of the Council, or by the latter with the participation of Parliament, or adopted on the initiative of a group of Member States or of Parliament, or on a recommendation of the ECB or at the request of the Court of Justice.

The other legal acts are "non-legislative acts". However, both legislative and non-legislative acts constitute Union "legislation" i.e. are binding.[23] See Art.289 TFEU.

A *regulation* has general application; it is binding in its entirety and is directly applicable in all the Member States.[24] Regulations may be adopted by the Council, or by the Council jointly with Parliament, under the *ordinary legislative procedure*,[25] by the Council with the participation of Parliament, or by Parliament with the participation of the Council, under a *special legislative procedure*,[26] by

---

[20] Art.288(1) TFEU.

[21] It should be noted that it is not the name given to an act that places it in one of the above-mentioned categories, but rather the contents and objectives of its provisions. See *Chevalley v Commission* (15/70) [1970] E.C.R. 975 at 980(10). The Court has also admitted that the same act can contain provisions pertaining to different categories. See *Producteurs de fruits v Council* (Joined Cases 16/62 and 17/62) [1962] E.C.R. 471 at 479; [1963] C.M.L.R. 160.

[22] Art.289(3) TFEU.

[23] The consequence is that, when those acts are published in the *Official Journal,* as required, one can be confronted with the seemingly contradictory classification "Legislation", followed by "non-legislative acts": mostly Commission regulations! The reason why the Treaty of Lisbon adopted these new classifications was to indicate that, contrary to what was previously provided in the Treaty, the Commission no longer has "its own power of decision" (former Art.211).

[24] Art.288,2 TFEU.

[25] Arts 289(1) and 294 TFEU.

[26] Art.189(2) TFEU.

the Commission and by the European Central Bank.[27] The criterion for the distinction between a regulation and other acts, especially decisions, must be sought in its "general application". Being essentially of a "legislative nature, a regulation is applicable, not to a limited number of persons, defined or identifiable,[28] but to categories of persons viewed abstractly and in their entirety".[29]

Secondly, a regulation is, as was mentioned, "binding in its entirety". This distinguishes it from a directive, which only imposes on the Member States, to which it is addressed, the obligation to achieve specific results. The Court has considered that, since a regulation is binding in its entirety, it cannot be accepted that a Member State should apply provisions of a [Union] regulation in an incomplete and selective manner so as to "render abortive certain aspects of [Union] legislation".[30]

Finally, a regulation is "directly applicable" in all the Member States. This means that it does not require a national measure, such as ratification, to become binding upon institutions, States, undertakings and natural persons all over the Union. There are, however, cases where regulations provide for national administrative implementing measures.[31] Directly applicable also means that the national authorities and national legal or administrative measures, even those posterior to the Union act, cannot prevent its application.[32] By this is meant the *precedence* of Union law over national law.[33]

3–06

Direct applicability must not be confused with "direct effect". Union measures have direct effect when they create, for those who are subject to Union law, rights that the national judge is bound to uphold. This is the case every time Union rules impose, in a clear and unconditional way, an obligation (affecting a third party) upon a Member State, an institution or a natural or legal person.[34] The beneficiaries of those obligations can invoke them in the national courts and tribunals, to protect the rights, which result from these obligations, and those

---

[27] Protocol on the Statute of the ESCB and of the ECB, Art.34(1).

[28] *Calpak v Commission* (Joined Cases 789/79 and 790/79) [1980] E.C.R. 1949 at 1961(9); [1981] 1 C.M.L.R. 146.

[29] *Producteurs de fruits* (Joined Cases 16/62 and 17/62), quoted above, fn.21.

[30] *Commission v UK* (128/78) [1979] E.C.R. 419 at 428(9); [1979] 2 C.M.L.R. 45.

[31] See also *Zuckerfabrik Süderdithmarschen and Zuckerfabrik Soest* (Joined Cases C-143/88 and C-92/89) [1991] E.C.R. I-415 at 540(16); [1993] 3 C.M.L.R. 1: "In cases where national authorities are responsible for the administrative implementation of [Union] regulations, the legal protection guaranteed by [Union] law includes the right of individuals to challenge, as a preliminary issue, the legality of such regulation, before national courts, and to induce those courts to refer questions to the Court of Justice for a preliminary ruling." But, in the absence of required implementing national measures, the regulation cannot be relied on before a national court: *Monte Arcosu* (C-403/98) [2001] E.C.R. I-103.

[32] See *Eridania v Ministry of Agriculture* (230/78) [1979] E.C.R. 2749 at 2772(35). Certain provisions contained in a regulation might need national implementing measures to become applicable, but the regulation itself does not have to be transposed into national law by a national measure.

[33] The French Conseil d'Etat only recognised this basic principle in 1989, 37 years after the first Community was established!

[34] For a more extensive analysis of direct effect, see Ch.4: Union Law (Section 2. Direct effect).

courts and tribunals are under Treaty obligation to uphold them.[35] This applies, as mentioned, even when these obligations conflict with national provisions or measures, whether anterior or posterior.

Not all Union provisions have direct effect, but the Court considers that a regulation, by reason of its very nature and its function in the system of sources of Union law, has direct effect, i.e. it is capable of creating individual rights which national courts must protect.[36]

Directives are issued by the Council, by the Council jointly with Parliament, or by the Commission. They constitute the appropriate measure when existing national legislation must be modified, or national provisions must be enacted, in most cases, for the sake of harmonisation. Directives are binding upon the Member States to which they are addressed, as to the results to be achieved. Although this means that Member States are obliged to take the national measures necessary to achieve the results set out in the directive, they are free to decide how they "transpose" this piece of Union legislation into national law. It is, for instance, indifferent whether the national measures are administrative, as opposed to legislative, in nature as long as they are binding and as long as they fully meet the requirements of legal certainty.[37] On the other hand, when transposing a directive into national law, Member States must take care to rely on an interpretation of the directive that allows a fair balance to be struck between the various fundamental rights protected by the Union's legal order. Furthermore, when implementing the measures transposing the directive, the authorities and courts of the Member States must not only interpret their national law in a manner consistent with the directive, but also make sure that they do not rely on an interpretation which would be in conflict with those fundamental rights or with the other general principles of Union law, such as the principle of proportionality.[38]

3–07   Although directives are not directly applicable, since they must first be transposed into national law, certain of their provisions can nevertheless have direct effect.[39] This must be ascertained on a case by case basis, taking into account their nature, background and wording.[40] According to the Court, provisions of a directive are capable of producing direct effect, in the legal

---

[35] Art. 4(3),2 EU: "Member States shall take all appropriate measures, whether general or particular, to ensure fulfilment of the obligations arising out of the Treaties or resulting from the acts of the institutions of the Union." In the Treaties "Member States" means all the authorities of the State: executive, legislative and judiciary.

[36] It is for the national legal system to determine which court or tribunal has jurisdiction to give this protection and, for this purpose, to decide how the individual position thus protected is to be classified. *Politi v Italy* (43/71) [1971] E.C.R. 1039 at 1048(9); [1973] C.M.L.R. 60. See also *Leonesio v Italian Ministry of Agriculture and Forestry* (93/71) [1972] E.C.R. 287 at 295, (22–23); [1973] C.M.L.R. 343.

[37] *Commission v Belgium* (239/85) [1986] E.C.R. 3645; [1988] 1 C.M.L.R. 248.

[38] *Promusicae* (C-275/06) [2008] E.C.R. I-271.

[39] See, for instance, *Farrell* (C-356/05) [2007] E.C.R. I-3067, where the Court found that art 1 of Directive 90/232 fulfilled all the conditions to produce direct effect and *Arcor E.A.* (Joined Cases C-152/07, C-153/07 and C-154/07) [2008] E.C.R. I-5959.

[40] See, for instance, *Wells* (C-201/02) [2004] E.C.R. I-723, where the Court stated that, "In circumstances such as those in the main proceedings, an individual may, where appropriate, rely on Art.2(1) of Directive 85/337, read in conjunction with Arts 1(2) and 4(2) thereof." See also *Arcor* (Joined Cases C-152/07, C-153/07 and C-154/07) (quoted above, fn.39), and *Antoine Boxus et Alia* (128/09) E.C.R. 18.10.11 regarding scope and concept of "specific act of national legislation".

relationship between the addressee of the act and others, i.e. the Member State and third parties, for instance their citizens.[41] Furthermore, in the absence of full transposition, a public authority may not rely on that directive "against" an individual; this has been established in order to prevent a Member State from taking advantage of its own failure to comply with Union law.[42] As for the national judge, he may not refuse to apply a national provision contrary to a not-yet-transposed directive,[43] but where rules of national law fall within the scope of that directive, the national courts are bound to interpret that law as far as possible in light of the wording and purpose of the directive, so as to achieve the results it has in view.

On the other hand, an individual can, under certain circumstances, invoke the not-yet-transposed or partly-transposed directive against the Member State to which it is addressed. Indeed, although a directive imposes obligations upon a Member State, but cannot and does not impose obligations upon private parties,[44] it can confer rights upon an individual. As the Court re-stated recently:

> "It is clear from settled case law that, whenever the provisions of a directive appear, so far as their subject matter is concerned, to be unconditional and -sufficiently precise, they may be relied upon, before the national courts, by individuals against the Member State where it has failed to implement the directive correctly."[45]

Once a directive has been properly transposed into national law, Member States are entitled to impose criminal penalties for breach of national legislation implementing that directive, even if this is not provided for by the directive.[46] However, as already mentioned, a directive cannot be relied upon as such against accused persons by a Member State within the context of criminal proceedings, in view of the fact that a directive cannot, of itself and independently of national legislation, have the effect of determining or increasing the criminal liability of the accused persons.[47]

3–08

This relationship between Member State and natural/legal persons is what is referred to as "vertical direct effect of a directive", as opposed to "horizontal direct effect". The latter would occur if private parties could claim rights under a directive in their bilateral relationship. As already mentioned, since a directive may not, of itself, impose obligations on an individual (it may only impose them on a Member State), it may not be relied upon by an individual against another private party.[48] In another instance, however, where a question concerning the interpretation of a directive was raised in a case involving two persons, the Court

---

[41] *Grad v Finanzamt Traunstein* (9/70) [1970] E.C.R. 825 at 839(5); [1971] C.M.L.R. 1. The Court used as an argument the fact that Art. 267 TFEU empowers the national courts to refer to the Court all questions regarding the validity and interpretation of all acts of the institutions, without distinction. This implies that individuals may invoke such acts before the national courts. See also *Mazzalai v Ferrovia* (111/75) [1976] E.C.R. 657 at 666; [1977] 1 C.M.L.R. 105 and *Nederlandse Ondernemingen v Inspecteur der Invoerrechten en Accijnzen* (51/76) [1977] E.C.R. 113 at 127(23). This last decision is referred to in many subsequent judgments.

[42] *FacciniDori v Recreb* (C-91/92), [1994] E.C.R. I-3325; [1994] 1 C.M.L.R. 665.

[43] *FacciniDori v Recreb* (quoted above, fn.42)

[44] *Arcaro* (C-168/95) [1996] E.C.R. I-4705; [1997] 1 C.M.L.R. 179.

[45] *Arcor E.A.* (Joined Cases C-152/07, C-153/07 and 154/07) (quoted above, fn.39).

[46] *Gallotti* (Joined Cases C-58 etc./95) [1996] E.C.R. I-4345; [1997] 1 C.M.L.R. 32.

[47] *Mulliez E.A.* (Joined Cases C-23 etc./03) [2006] E.C.R. I-3923.

[48] *Marshall* (152/84) [1986] E.C.R. 723 (15, 16); [1986] 1 C.M.L.R. 688.

did not hesitate to give an answer to the preliminary question. By doing so, the Court seems to be admitting that the directive can be relied upon, at least indirectly, in the relationship between two third parties.[49]

The obligation imposed upon Member States to transpose directives into national legislation[50] makes these Member States responsible for the consequences of their failure to do so.[51] In other words, the State is liable for loss and damage caused to individuals as a result of a breach of Union law for which the State can be held responsible.[52] This obligation applies, provided that three -conditions are fulfilled. First, the purpose of the directive must be to grant rights to individuals.[53] Second, it must be possible to identify the content of those rights on the basis of the provisions of the directive and, finally, there must be a causal link between the breach of the State's obligation and the damage suffered.[54] Recently the Court added that, "the liability of the Member State concerned is contingent on a finding of manifest and grave disregard by the State for the limits set on its discretion".[55] See Ch.4: Union Law (4. Member States' Liability for Breach of Union Law).

3–09 It should be noted that as long as a Member State has not transposed a directive into national law, it must, from the moment of entry into force of the directive, abstain from adopting measures liable seriously to compromise attainment of the objectives of the directive.[56] Also, from that date, the national courts are bound to ensure that the application of rules of national law is consistent with the principle of non-discrimination, as recognised by the Union's legal order.[57]

Furthermore, in case a directive was not timely transposed into national rules, national jurisdictions must nevertheless, from the moment the time limit for the transposition expired, interpret, as much as possible, national law in the light of the text and finality of the directive in order to achieve the results envisaged by

---

[49] *Beets-Proper v Van Lanschot Bankiers* (262/84) [1986] E.C.R. 773; [1987] 2 C.M.L.R. 616.

[50] This obligation follows from Art.4(3) EU and Art.288,3 TFEU. It imposes upon the Member States, according to the Court, an obligation not to take any measure liable seriously to compromise the result prescribed in the directive, during the period after the adoption of the directive, but preceding the expiration of the time limit, provided therein, for its transposition by the Member States into national law: *Inter-Environnement Wallonie v Région Wallonne* (C-129/96) [1997] E.C.R. I-7411.

[51] *Francovich* (Joined Cases C-6/90 and C-9/90) [1991] E.C.R. I-5357; [1993] 2 C.M.L.R. 66.

[52] See *Francovich* (Joined Cases C-6/90 and C-9/90) (quoted above, fn.51) and *Brasserie du Pecheur and Factortame* (Joined Cases C-46/93 and C-48/93) [1996] E.C.R. I-1029(31); [1996] 1 C.M.L.R. 889.

[53] This is another expression of the so-called Schutznorm theory which one also finds in the Court's case law concerning reparation of damage caused by the Union's non-contractual liability. The Court explains its restrictive approach to State liability for breach of Union law, by referring to the reasons already given by the Court to justify the strict approach to non-contractual liability of Union institutions: see *HNL v Council and Commission* (Joined Cases 83 etc./76) [1978] E.C.R. 1209; [1978] 3 C.M.L.R. 566.

[54] *El Corte Ingles v Blazquez Rivero* (C-192/94) [1996] E.C.R. I-1283; [1996] 2 C.M.L.R. 507.

[55] *Robins E.A.* (C-278/05) [2007] E.C.R. I-1053.

[56] *Adeneler E.A.* (C-212/04) [2006] E.C.R. I-6057.

[57] *Navarro* (C-246/06) [2008] E.C.R. I-105.

the directive, by privileging the interpretation of the national rule most in conformity with that finality, in order to find a solution compatible with the provisions of said directive.[58]

As for a *decision*, it is binding in its entirety upon those to whom it is addressed; in other words, it is not binding on any other person.[59] The addressee can be a Member State or a legal or natural person. A decision can be taken by the Council, by the Council jointly with Parliament, by Parliament with the participation of the Council or by the Council with the participation of Parliament, under the *ordinary* or *special legislative procedure*,[60] by the Commission and by the ECB.

Decisions are normally of an administrative nature, implementing other Union rules, e.g. granting of an exemption or authorisation, or imposing fines.[61]

There are no requirements as to the form of a decision, so that it may, in certain cases, be doubtful whether a given act constitutes a binding decision or not. Obviously, the institutions must ensure that a decision is recognisable as a binding act by its very form.[62] Being binding in its entirety, a decision can have direct effect.[63]

3–10

The TFEU also provides for *recommendations* and *opinions*, which, however, have no binding force. Nonetheless, according to recent case law, recommendations should not be dismissed as having no legal effect at all. They do not, it is true, create rights which can be invoked in the courts, but the national judges must take recommendations into consideration when solving cases submitted to them. This is especially so if the recommendations can help with the interpretation of other national or Union legal measures.[64]

There are cases where the Court annulled a recommendation, pointing out that an action for annulment is available in the cases of all measures adopted by the institutions, whatever their nature or form, which are intended to have legal effects. This applies also to a Commission Communication which sets out to specify the manner of application of a provision of a directive.[65]

Generally speaking, recommendations aim at obtaining a given action or behaviour from the addressee. They play an important role in many sectors, such as Approximation of Laws,[66] Economic and Monetary Policy[67] and Education, Vocational Training and Youth.[68]

An *opinion*, on the other hand, expresses a point of view, often at the request of a third party. Having no binding effect, the legality of recommendations and opinions cannot, in theory, be reviewed by the Court. Neither can they be

3–11

---

[58] *Vassilakis E.A.* (C-364-07) [2008] E.C.R. 1–90* (only summary published, but on the Internet in the original language).

[59] *Mensch und Natur v Freistaat Bayern* (C-327/09) [2011] E.C.R. I-2897.

[60] Art.289(1) and (2) TFEU.

[61] See *Commission v Greece* (226/87) [1988] E.C.R. 3611; [1989] 3 C.M.L.R. 569, where the Court rejected the Greek Government's contention that the Commission decision adopted pursuant to the now Art.106(3) TFEU should merely be considered a non-binding opinion.

[62] *Hoogovens v High Authority* (28/63) [1963] E.C.R. 231 at 235; [1964] C.M.L.R. 125.

[63] *Grad v Finanzamt Traustein* (9/70) [1970] E.C.R. 825 at 837 [1971] C.M.L.R. 1.

[64] *Fonds des maladies professionnelles* (322/88) [1989] E.C.R. 4407; [1991] 2 C.M.L.R. 265.

[65] *France v Commission* (C-325/91) [1993] E.C.R. I-3283.

[66] Art.117 TFEU.

[67] Arts 121 and 219(2) TFEU.

[68] Art.166(4) TFEU.

submitted to the Court for a preliminary ruling concerning their validity or interpretation. The Court has nevertheless agreed to examine whether recommendations had legal effect when a Member State failed to take the recommended action.[69]

The sequence in which the acts are mentioned in the Treaty does not indicate a hierarchy, it was therefore decided at Maastricht that the intergovernmental conference to be convened in 1996, would examine to what extent it might be possible to review the classification of Union acts with a view to establishing an appropriate hierarchy between the different categories of acts. This is one of the many tasks entrusted to that intergovernmental conference which were not carried out.

A major problem exists as a result of the profusion of regulations, directives and decisions, often amending existing ones. Without even mentioning the sometimes doubtful quality and transparency of Union legislation, the citizen is confronted by an ever increasing array of measures, which it becomes impossible to understand, in the absence of systematic codification. The Union institutions are aware of this and have concluded an Inter-institutional Agreement on the accelerated working method for official codification of legislative texts,[70] and one on "better law-making".[71] Unfortunately, not much has been achieved so far and it seems that the method that was chosen creates, in fact, more confusion.[72] The same problem exists with the Treaties themselves: there are too many of them and too many amendments—the Amsterdam Intergovernmental Conference, therefore, adopted a Declaration on the Consolidation of the Treaties, according to which the aim is to draft a consolidation of all the relevant Treaties, including the Treaty on European Union. However, this will be done for "illustrative purposes" only and "shall have no legal value".[73]

2. REGULATIONS, DIRECTIVES AND DECISIONS MUST BE REASONED

3–12   Regulations, directives and decisions must indicate for which reasons they are taken and must refer to the proposals and opinions which the issuing institutions were required by the Treaties to be obtained.[74]

Reasons must be understood as referring both to the Treaty provision which entitle the institution to take the measure in question, and what motivated the

---

[69] *France v Commission* (C-325/91) (quoted above, fn.65).

[70] [1996] O.J. C102/2.

[71] [2003] O.J. C321/1.

[72] For instance, when an act was modified several times, the simple solution would have been to include all the amendments in the text and re-issue it without further ado; unfortunately, the Council has decided that the act including all the amendments (it had previously agreed upon) has to be re-submitted, and needs a new decision on the part of the institutions, at which occasion more often than not, new amendments are proposed, discussed and introduced! It so becomes a never-ending process. See, however, the Declaration on the Quality of the Drafting of Union Legislation, adopted by the Amsterdam Intergovernmental Conference, which provides for guidelines for improving the quality of the drafting of Union legislation; and for the institutions to make best efforts to accelerate the codification of legislative texts [1997] O.J. C340/139.

[73] [1997] O.J. C340/140.

[74] Art.296(2) TFEU.

institution to act. The mention of the Treaty provisions on which they are based is particularly important since, as was mentioned, the Union institutions may only exercise those powers which are explicitly conferred upon them by the Member States in the Treaties.

Problems may arise when an act can be based simultaneously on several treaty provisions and a choice must be made by the legislator between them. According to the Court, it may not depend simply on an institution's conviction as to the objective pursued, but must be based on objective factors which are amenable to judicial review. Those factors include, in particular, the aim and content of the measure.[75]

As for the motives which prompted the institution to act, they must be mentioned in order to make it possible for the interested parties, and for the Court, to reconstruct the essential elements of the institution's reasoning,[76] thereby permitting the parties to defend their rights, the Court to exercise its control, and the Member States (and in the same way all the interested citizens) to know the conditions under which the institution has applied the Treaty.[77]

To attain those objectives, it is sufficient for the act to set out, in a concise but clear and relevant manner, the principal issues of law and fact upon which it is based and which are necessary in order that the reasoning, which has led the institution to its decision, may be understood.[78] The extent of this requirement depends on the nature of the measure in question. The condition can also be considered as fulfilled when reference[79] is made to the reasons developed in an earlier act.[80]

3–13

Furthermore, the question whether a statement of reasons satisfies the requirements must be assessed with reference not only to the wording of the measure but also to its context and to the whole body of legal rules governing the matter in question. If the contested measure clearly discloses the essential objective pursued by the institution, it would be excessive to require a specific statement of reasons for each of the technical choices made by the institution.[81]

If an act is not sufficiently reasoned, this constitutes an "infringement of an essential procedural requirement"[82] that can be invoked in an action for review by the Court of the legality of the act concerned.[83] The Court can, and must of its

---

[75] *Commission v Council* (C-300/89) [1991] E.C.R. I-2867; [1993] 3 C.M.L.R. 359: in this case the Council could base the act on two different Treaty provisions one of them involved the co-operation procedure with Parliament. The use of both provisions jointly would have excluded this procedure and therefore the involvement of the Parliament. In this case recourse to a dual legal basis is excluded. The Court decided that the act must be based on Art.110 TFEU.

[76] *Hoogovens v High Authority* (14/61) [1962] E.C.R. 253 at 275; [1963] C.M.L.R. 73. *Fedesa* (C-331/88) [1990] E.C.R. I-4023 at 4066 (30); [1991] 1 C.M.L.R. 507: an effect of Council legislation must be mentioned in the latter's reasoning as one of its objectives, only if it was the genuine or main ground for the act. If it is merely a side-effect, it does not have to be mentioned.

[77] *Germany v Commission* (24/62) [1963] E.C.R. 63 at 69; [1963] C.M.L.R. 347.

[78] *Germany v Commission* (24/62) (quoted above, fn.77). See also *Geitling v High Authority* (Joined Cases 36/59, 37/59, 38/59 and 40/59) [1960] E.C.R. 423 at 439.

[79] *Mollet v Commission* (75/77) [1978] E.C.R. 897 at 906(12).

[80] *Italy v Commission* (1/69) [1969] E.C.R. 277 at 285(9); [1970] C.M.L.R. 17. See, however, *Papiers peints v Commission* (73/74) [1975] E.C.R. 1491 at 1514 (31); [1976] 1 C.M.L.R. 589.

[81] *Arnold André* (C-434/02) [2004] E.C.R. I-11825.

[82] Art.263,2 TFEU.

[83] See, for instance, *Elf Aquitaine v Commission* (C-521/09 P) [2011] E.C.R.I. 8947; where the Court annulled a Commission Decision for lack of sufficient motivation.

own motion, take exception to any deficiencies in the reasons which would make such review more difficult.[84] The Court has repeated, over and over again, that an institution is obliged "to state the reasons on which a decision is based".[85]

As for the reference to the required proposals and opinions, a simple mention is considered sufficient; the institutions are not required to indicate whether or not the opinion was favourable,[86] still less must they refute dissenting opinions expressed by the consultative bodies.[87]

3. PUBLICATION, LANGUAGES AND ENTRY INTO FORCE[88]

3–14   Since regulations are of a legislative nature, and therefore concern an unidentifiable group to whom they apply, they must be published in the *Official Journal of the European Union (Official Journal)*,[89] which appears on the internet[90] in the 23 official languages[91] of the Union. The same applies to directives and decisions, since they are binding acts and may concern persons other than the one(s) to whom the act is addressed. Even if it is not published in the official language of a given Member State, a national regulatory authority may refer to Commission "Guidelines" in a decision by which it imposes certain regulatory obligations on a national operator.[92] But acts neither translated in the *Official Journal* nor in national publications may not be applied to individuals of the State in question *AS Pimix v Maksu-ja Tolliameti Louna maksu-ja tollikeskus* (C-146/11) judgment of July 12, 2012, not yet reported.

With regard to competition decisions, the Commission has decided to no longer publish the full texts in the *Official Journal*.

---

[84] Art.263 TFEU; *Nold v High Authority* (18/57) [1959] E.C.R. 41 at 52 and *Rewe v Hauptzollamt Kiel* (158/80) [1981] E.C.R. 1805 at 1834 (27); [1982] 1 C.M.L.R. 449, where Regulation 3023/77 was declared void for not containing a statement of the reasons on which it is based. *Silo e Mangini Martini* (C-228/99) [2001] E.C.R. I-8401(12).

[85] See, for instance, *Stichting Al-Aqsa* (joined cases C-539/10 P and 550/10 P) judgment of November 15, 2012, not yet reported.

[86] This, however, is no secret, since both the Commission's proposals and the Parliament's opinions are published in the *Official Journal*.

[87] *I.S.A. v High Authority* (4/54) [1954–56] E.C.R. 91 at 100(6).

[88] Art.297 TFEU.

[89] Before May 1, 2003, date of the entry into force of the Treaty of Nice, it used to be called *Official Journal of the European Communities*; Art.2,38 Treaty of Nice.

[90] See Council Regulation 216/213 of 7 March 2013, on the electronic publication of the *Official Journal*: the only publication considered authentic and having legal effect.

[91] Regulation 1/58 [1958] O.J. B 017/385, determining the languages to be used by the Union, amended several times. The official languages of the institutions of the Union were Danish, Finnish, German, English, French, Greek, Italian, Dutch, Spanish, Swedish and Portuguese; to which are now added Estonian, Slovakian, Slovene, Hungarian, Czech, Latvian, Polish, Maltese and Lithuanian; and, since January 1, 2007, Bulgarian, Irish and Romanian. In the case of discrepancies among the languages, the requirement of a uniform interpretation across the Union excludes the consideration of one such text in isolation, obliging it to be interpreted in the light of the other versions in the other official languages: *Koschniske* (9/79) [1979] E.C.R. 2717(16); [1989] 1 C.M.L.R. 87. See Regulation 930/2004 [2004] O.J. L196/1 on temporary derogation for the Maltese language and Regulation 920/05 [2005] O.J. L156/3, introducing temporary derogation measures, which were extended by Regulation 1257/10 [2010] O.J. L343/5.

[92] *Polska Telefonia* (C-410/09) [2011] E.C.R. I-3853.

Publication must, as indicated, necessarily take place in all the official languages of the Union; the absence of publication precludes the obligations contained in Union legislation from being imposed on individuals, even though those persons could have learned of that legislation by other means.[93]

Acts enter into force on the day specified therein or, in the absence thereof, on the twentieth day following their publication.[94] This rule raises the question of possible retroactive effect. In this regard, the Court ruled that:

3–15

> "Although in general the principle of legal certainty precludes a [Union] measure from taking effect from a point in time before its publication, it may exceptionally be otherwise, where the purpose to be achieved so demands, and the legitimate expectations of those concerned are duly respected."[95]

Directives and decisions concern only a limited number of persons (Member States or natural or legal persons) and must therefore be notified directly to those to whom they are addressed. However, since the Court may review the legality of decisions at the request of parties which are not addressees of such acts, when the latter are of "direct and individual concern"[96] to them, it is important that they be informed of the contents of all such decisions. The same applies to directives; as was seen, citizens may invoke them in the national courts, and request the latter to ask the Court for a preliminary ruling on their validity or interpretation. Consequently, as just mentioned, directives are always published in the *Official Journal*, as are decisions which may affect the rights of third parties.[97]

4. ENFORCEMENT OF PECUNIARY OBLIGATIONS[98]

Decisions, whether of the Council, the Parliament and the Council, the Commission or the ECB, which impose a pecuniary obligation[99] on persons other than Member States and, similarly, judgments of the Courts imposing such obligations,[100] are enforceable. Enforcement of Union acts is governed by the rules of civil procedure, in force within the Member State where it is to be carried out. The following steps must be taken. The institution which wants to enforce a decision presents it for verification of authenticity to the national authority that

3–16

---

[93] *Skoma-Lux* (C-161/06) [2007] E.C.R. I-10841 and *Heinrich* (C-345/06) E.C.R. I-1659.

[94] A typical example was Regulation 17 giving effect to the principles of competition (replaced by Regulation 1/2003 [2003] O.J. L1/1): the Regulation was adopted by the Council on February 6, 1962, published in the *Official Journal* on February 21, 1962 and, since it did not mention the date of entry into force, it became effective on March 13, 1962. See also *Racke v Hauptzollamt Mainz* (98/78) [1979] E.C.R. 69 at 84 (15) and *Decker v Hauptzollamt Landau* (99/78) [1979] E.C.R. 101 at 109(3).

[95] *SAFA* (337/88) [1990] E.C.R. I-1 at 1885(12); [1991] 1 C.M.L.R. 507. See also *Fedesa* (331/88) [1990] E.C.R. I-4023 at 4069(45), [1991] 1 C.M.L.R. 872 and *Diversinte* (Joined Cases C-260/91 and C-261/91) [1993] E.C.R. I-188.

[96] Art.263 TFEU.

[97] See in this respect *Handelsvereniging Rotterdam v Minister van Landbouw* (Joined Cases 73/63 and 74/63) [1964] E.C.R. 1 at 14; [1964] C.M.L.R. 198 and *Salumificio di cornuda v Amministrazione delle Finanze* (130/78) [1979] E.C.R. 867; [1979] 3 C.M.L.R. 561.

[98] Art.299 TFEU.

[99] For instance, decisions of the Commission imposing fines pursuant to Regulation 1/2003 [2003] O.J. 1/1 for violation of the competition rules.

[100] Art.280 TFEU.

the government of each Member State has designated for this purpose[101] and made known to the Commission and the Court. That authority appends to the decision an order for its enforcement.[102] The institution can then proceed to enforcement, in accordance with national law, by bringing the matter directly before the competent national authorities. From that moment on, the national rules of civil procedure apply, with the exception that suspension of the enforcement may only be decided by the Court.

An action brought before the Court against a decision which is being enforced has no suspensory effect.[103] However, the interested party, in case it has introduced an action against the decision, can always ask for interim measures consisting of a suspension of the enforcement.[104]

5. BINDING ACTS NOT PROVIDED FOR UNDER TFEU ARTICLE 288

3–17   As indicated at the beginning of this chapter, Union acts are not limited to regulations, directives and decisions. Judgments of the courts are also binding upon the parties and can be enforced (see previous section). As for international agreements concluded by the Union with third countries or international organisations, they are binding upon the institutions of the Union and on the

---

[101] Austria: Bundesministerium für Auswertige Angelegenheiten, Abteilung IV/3 "Legalisierungsbüro". The Netherlands: Law of February 24, 1955, Stb 73, modified by Law of January 13, 1960, Stb 15: Minister of Justice is addressee of request, Griffier of Hoge Raad implements. Belgium: Law of August 6, 1967: Greffier en Chef of the Court of Appeal at Brussels. Finland: Ministry of Justice, 1994 Act No.1554/94 concerning the European Union. France: Décret No. 57/321 of March 13, 1957, *Journal Officiel*, March 19, 1957, 2885, designates (1) persons who have received delegation from the Prime Minister and (2) Secrétariat Géneral du Comité Interministériel. Germany: Bundesgesetzblatt, February 3, 1961, II, 50, Minister of Justice. Italy: Decree of December 2, 1960, *Gazzetta Officiale*, February 21, 1961, No. 46, 738, Minister of Foreign Affairs. Luxembourg: Regulation of October 17, 1962, Memorial of October 31, 1962, No. 58, 1028, verification by Minister of Foreign Affairs, and order for enforcement appended by Minister of Justice. United Kingdom: European Communities (Enforcement of Union Judgments) Order 1972 (SI 1972/1590) which provides for the registration in the High Court of England and Northern Ireland and the Court of Session in Scotland of Union judgments and orders to which the Secretary of State has duly appended an order for enforcement. Ireland: (SI 1972/331); enforcement order appended by the Master of High Court. Denmark: by the Minister of Justice, Greece: the head of the Tribunal of First Instance at Athens. Spain: B.O.E. No.160, July 5, 1986, 17843, Minister of Justice. Portugal: Diano da Republica, Law No.104/88 of August 31, 1988, verification of authenticity, Minister of Foreign Affairs; apposition of formula through Minister of Justice, competent tribunal. Sweden: Domstolverket (National Courts Administration), Ordonance SFS 1995: 105.

[102] In the UK "order for enforcement" means an order by or under the authority of the Secretary of State that the Union judgment to which it is appended is to be registered for enforcement in the UK (SI 1972/1590).

[103] When the Commission takes a decision imposing fines on a person, it usually does not seek enforcement in case an appeal has been lodged against the decision. The Court has approved this practice, but only on condition that interest is paid in respect of the period of suspension, and that a bank guarantee is lodged covering the amount of the fine; see *Hasselblad v Commission* (86/82 R) [1982] E.C.R. 1555; [1984] 1 C.M.L.R. 559.

[104] See Ch.9: The Court of Justice of the European Union.

Member States[105] and may be invoked by persons in court.[106] The same applies to acts of bodies created by international agreements when such acts are published in the *Official Journal*[107] and to agreements concluded by the Member States among themselves regarding matters connected with the Treaty.

Somewhat different is the position of international agreements concluded by the Member States with third countries: in so far as, under the Treaty, the Union has assumed the powers previously exercised by Member States in the area governed by such international agreement, the provisions of that agreement have the effect of binding the Union.[108] These agreements can be submitted to the control of legality exercised by the Court, when the Union is a party to them[109] and they constitute rules of law relating to the application of the Treaty[110]; the result being that regulations, directives and decisions can be annulled in case of infringement of these rules. These agreements can also have direct effect, which means that natural and legal persons can ask the national judge to uphold the rights that derive for them from these agreements even against their own national authorities.[111]

Besides the acts already mentioned, there are the decisions of the Representatives of the Governments of the Member States meeting within the Council; these cannot be submitted to the Court, since they do not emanate from the Council, the Parliament or the Commission, but they can be binding within the whole Union.[112] However, it will have to be established on a case by case basis as to whether those decisions are binding only for the Member States or also for the institutions of the Union and even for natural or legal persons. Although those decisions constitute a flexible instrument to solve a number of questions within the scope of the Treaties, they are not without danger for the institutional equilibrium. Besides immunity from the Court's control, these acts neither require a Commission proposal nor an opinion of Parliament. Of course, nothing can prevent the latter from trying to exercise its political control over these acts anyway.

---

[105] Art.300(7) TFEU. See *International Fruit Company v Produktschap voor Groenten en Fruit* (Joined Cases 21/72, 22/72, 23/72 and 24/72) [1972] E.C.R. 1219; [1975] 1 C.M.L.R. 1 and *Singer and Geigy v Amministrazione delle Finanze* (Joined Cases 290/81 and 291/81) [1983] E.C.R. 847 concerning direct effect of GATT rules.

[106] See for instance, *Cordis v Commission* (T-18/99) [2001] E.C.R. II-913; see Ch.4: Union Law.

[107] See for instance [2008] O.J. L72/1.

[108] *International Fruit Company* (Joined Cases 21/72, 22/72, 23/72 and 24/72) (quoted above, fn.103); [1975] 2 C.M.L.R. 1.

[109] See for instance *Commission v Council* (22/70) [1971] E.C.R. 263; [1971] C.M.L.R. 335.

[110] Art.263 TFEU.

[111] See for instance *Syndicat professionnel coordination des pêcheurs de l'étang de Berre et de la Région v EDF* (C-213/03) [2004] E.C.R. I-7357.

[112] See for instance the "acceleration" decisions by which the Member States agreed to establish the Customs Union within a shorter time limit than provided for under the EEC Treaty ([1960] J.O. 1217 and [1962] J.O. 1284). These decisions are not to be confused with decisions of the Member States, such as the appointment of the Members of the Commission (Art.17 EU) or of the Judges of the European courts (Art.253 TFEU).

6.   OTHER FORMS OF UNION "ACTS"

3–18   A form often used is the Resolution, either of the Council[113] or of the "Council and of the Representatives of the Governments of the Member States meeting within the Council".[114] This latter kind of resolution was used to establish the European Passport: "a passport of which the uniform format and scope" was described in an annex to the Resolution![115] These Resolutions are not to be confused with the decision of the Representatives of the Governments of the Member States in Council or a Resolution of Ministers within the Council.[116] In the first place the decisions of the Representatives of the Member States are legally binding upon the latter, while resolutions sometimes only constitute a political commitment; secondly, the fact that the Member States act within the institutional framework is intended to indicate that the matter directly concerns the implementation of the Treaty. On the other hand, resolutions, generally speaking, concern matters directly connected with the Union, but not explicitly provided for under Union law.

There are, furthermore, Programmes,[117] General Action Programmes,[118] Framework Programmes[119] and Programmes of Action,[120] which intend to lay down general principles for future action, both by the Member States and by the institutions of the Union. Such Programmes are generally adopted by the Council, either by a Decision,[121] a Declaration[122] or a Resolution.[123]

Other matters are decided upon by decisions which are not formal binding acts[124]; they are used to settle questions related to Union affairs but do not impose rights or obligations upon the institutions of the Union nor upon natural or legal persons.[125]

The General Court considered "binding" a unilateral declaration by the Commission, annexed to the minutes of a Coreper meeting![126]

---

[113] See for instance Council Resolution of February 6, 1979 concerning the guidelines for Union Regional Policy ([1979] O.J. C36/10), and the Conclusions of the Council of December 4, 1984, concerning measures necessary to guarantee the implementation of the conclusions of the European Council concerning budgetary discipline [1984] E.C. Bull. 12–24. In one case, the Court was asked to interpret a Council Resolution in a request for a preliminary ruling: *Schlüter v Hauptzollamt Lörrach* (9/73) [1973] E.C.R. 1135 at 1162—the Court interpreted the Resolution by stating that it did not impose a prohibition on the Member States.

[114] See [1991] O.J. C178/1. Another form used is the "Conclusions", [1991] O.J. C188/4.

[115] [1981] O.J. C241/1.

[116] See [1991] O.J. L188/2.

[117] For instance: Medium term economic policy programme [1982] O.J. L236/10.

[118] Art.192(3) TFEU.

[119] Art.182 TFEU.

[120] For instance: Programme of action of the EC on the environment [1973] O.J.C112/1.

[121] [1982] O.J. L236/10.

[122] [1973] O.J. C112/1.

[123] [1977] O.J. C139/1.

[124] Other languages such as Dutch and German use a word (Besluit; Beschluss) which clearly distinguishes this act from an Art.288 TFEU decision (Beschikking; Entscheidung).

[125] See for instance [1973] O.J. L207/46.

[126] *Germany v Commission* (T-236/07) [2010] E.C.R. II-5253.

FURTHER READING

Thomas A.J.A. Vandamme, *The invalid Directive. The legal authority of a Union*   **3–19**
Act requiring domestic law making (Groningen, Europa Law Publishing, 2005);
book review: (2006) E.L.Rev. Feb. 140.

   Paul Craig, "The legal effect of Directive: policy, rules and exceptions" (2009)
E.L.Rev. June 349.

CHAPTER 4

Union Law

Union law is laid down in the European Treaties (primary Union law)[1] and in the acts of the institutions and other Union bodies (secondary Union law); the first was examined in the previous chapters; the second is mainly the object of the present one.

Although, as will be seen, other institutions and bodies of the Union are also empowered to issue binding acts, it is mainly the Council acting jointly with Parliament which exercises legislative and budgetary functions. They carry out policy-making and co-ordinating functions.[2]

The exercise of those competences is "governed by the principle of conferral"[3] and by the principles of subsidiarity and proportionality. Indeed, one of the most important provisions concerning the exercise of power by the institutions of the Union is to be found at the very beginning of the EU Treaty: "The Union shall act only within the limits of the competences conferred upon it by the Member States in the Treaties".[4] In other words, the Union institutions are not endowed with a general regulatory competence; they can only act when this is specifically provided for in a Treaty provision, and this is the reason why that provision must always be mentioned in every Union act.[5]

There may, however, be cases where action by the Union:

> "should prove necessary, within the framework of the policies defined by the Treaties, to attain one of the objectives set out in the Treaties, and the Treaties have not provided the necessary powers".[6]

In such a case, the Council acting unanimously on a proposal from the Commission, and after obtaining the consent of Parliament, shall adopt the appropriate measures. However, several stringent conditions have to be fulfilled, and this possibility may not, therefore, be considered as an unlimited opportunity for the institutions to increase their powers of decision. Indeed, the appropriate measures may only be taken when action is necessary "to attain one of the objectives set out in the Treaties", which indicates that the powers exercised in such cases are exclusively destined to implement Treaty objectives. Also, the

4–01

4–02

---

[1] See Ch.3: The Legal Acts of the Union.
[2] Art.16(1) EU.
[3] Art.5(1) EU.
[4] Art.5(2) EU.
[5] Art.296,2 TFEU.
[6] Art.352(1) TFEU; at the 1972 Paris Summit, it was agreed that for the purpose of carrying out the tasks laid down in the different programmes of action, "it was desirable to make the widest possible use of all the dispositions of the Treaty, including Art.352"!

required unanimity within the Council should provide the necessary guarantees; indeed, the extension of the Union's powers will, almost inevitably, reduce the powers of the Member States in the same proportion. Unanimity therefore constitutes a brake on a possible extension of the powers of the Union. Furthermore, the Commission's proposal and the consent of Parliament should ensure that the Union's interests are sufficiently taken into consideration—and there is always the judicial control of the Court.[7]

The Treaty of Lisbon added other limitations: for measures taken under this procedure, the Commission must, under the subsidiarity principle, draw national parliament's attention to such proposals; furthermore, they may not entail harmonisation of Member States' laws or regulations where such harmonisation is excluded by the Treaties,[8] and, finally, it cannot be used as a basis for attaining objectives pertaining to the foreign and security policy.[9]

This procedure does, nevertheless, constitute a way of "supplementing" the Treaty provisions without going through one of the rather cumbersome procedures provided for amending them.[10]

4–03   As was pointed out at the beginning of this book, the Treaties establishing what were, at the time, the "European Communities", and now the "Union", are more than classical international agreements creating mutual obligations between the High Contracting Parties. Indeed, by ratifying those Treaties, the Member States intended to do much more than that, though they most probably did not, at the time, foresee all the consequences which, for instance, the Court has, over the years, drawn from the specific nature of those Treaties. Hence the question: what is it that distinguishes these Treaties from other international agreements?

In the first place, they have, as the Court pointed out, created quasi-governmental bodies (the institutions), independent from the national public authorities, and endowed with legislative, administrative and judicial sovereign rights, which were transferred to them by the Member States.[11] Furthermore, the Treaties lay down basic principles that are either worked out in the Treaties themselves, or defined and implemented by acts of the institutions. The Treaties and the acts constitute a set of rules which directly, i.e. without interference or intervention of national authorities, impose obligations upon, and consequently create rights for, the Member States and the natural and legal persons within the Union. The Treaties therefore present many analogies with national constitutions. It can also be said that, although they started out as international treaties, these texts have become, in fact if not in law, the "Constitution" of the Union.

As was shown, the rules embodied in the Treaties are constantly being expanded and implemented by new treaties, while being made more specific, interpreted and applied by the various acts and measures of the institutions, especially the courts. The European Treaties have, therefore, as was ascertained by the Court, established a specific legal order. Indeed:

---

[7] See *Hauptzollamt Bremerhaven v Massey-Fergusson* (8/73) [1973] E.C.R. 897.
[8] See, for instance, Art.149 TFEU.
[9] Art.352 (3) and (4) TFEU.
[10] See Art.48 EU.
[11] See for instance *Van Gend & Loos v Nederlandse Administratie der Belastingen* (26/62) [1963] E.C.R. 1 at 12 and *Costa v ENEL* (6/64) [1964] E.C.R. 585 at 594.

"[B]y creating a [Union] of unlimited duration, having its own institutions, its own personality, its own legal capacity and capacity of representation on the international plane and, more particularly, real powers stemming from a limitation of sovereignty or a transfer of powers from the States to the [Union], the Member States have limited their sovereign rights, albeit within limited fields, and have created a body of law which binds both their nationals and themselves".[12]

It took years before all national courts and tribunals came to share the view **4-04** that the European Treaties create a separate legal order but, at the time, several of them were quick to agree, as was the German Supreme Administrative Court. It stated that Union law constitutes, "a separate legal order, whose provisions belong neither to international law nor to the municipal law of the Member States".[13]

It must be clearly understood that Union law only applies in cases involving cross-border situations; in other words, purely internal occurrences do not come within the ambit of Union Law.[14]

Union law is, generally speaking, characterised by its direct applicability within the Member States, its direct effect and its primacy over national law. These concepts are briefly examined below.

1. DIRECT APPLICABILITY

Union law, being distinct from national law, is also independent from it. This **4-05** means that rights can be conferred and obligations imposed both on the Member States and on natural and legal persons directly by Union provisions, i.e. without interference from or intervention by national authorities. There is indeed no need for Member States to intervene in order to ensure that Union decisions, regulations and, in certain cases, directives have binding effect throughout the Union.[15] Referring to regulations, the Treaty uses the words, "shall be directly applicable in all Member States".[16] The latter should not be taken too literally. The territory of the Union is defined in the Treaty[17] and thereby the geographical application of Union law. However, as the Court has indicated, this does not

---

[12] *Costa v ENEL* (6/64) [1964] (quoted above, fn.11). It should be pointed out that the "unlimited duration" only applied to the EC and Euratom Treaties; the ECSC Treaty had a duration of 50 years (Art.97 ECSC) and is no longer in force.

[13] (1967) *Common Market Law Revue* (C.M.L.Rev.) 483.

[14] Some authors have suggested that, on account of the growing trend towards regional devolution and to ensure the *effet utile* of Union law, the requirement of a cross-border link should be abolished: see, for instance, (2009) E.L.Rev.433.

[15] This is what is meant by s.2(1) of the (British) European Communities Act of 1972: these provisions "are without further enactment to be given legal effect or use in the United Kingdom." In other words "reception" of Union law into the sphere of national law is not and cannot be required. Anyway, reception is only required by those who adhere to the dualist theory, and furthermore "if one accepts, as is logical and in one view inevitable, that Union law is sui generis then, in strictness the monist/dualist argument is excluded, since it is an argument properly limited to international law strictly so called", which is not the case with Union law. John Mitchell, "British law and British membership", Europarecht, April–June 1971, 109.

[16] Art.288,2 TFEU.

[17] Art.52 EU and Art.355 TFEU.

preclude Union rules from applying outside the territory of the Union, when the activity in question retains sufficient links with the Union.[18]

In addition, Member States are committed not to interfere with the application of Union law, on the contrary, they are under Treaty obligation to make sure that Union law is indeed applied and, in case of conflict with their national law, to set the latter aside. This also follows from the Treaties, which provide that Member States "shall refrain from any measure which could jeopardise the attainment of the Union's objectives"[19] and that they are under obligation to actively support the implementation of that law by taking "any appropriate measure, general or particular, to ensure fulfilment of the obligations arising out of the Treaties or resulting from the acts of the institutions of the Union".[20]

More important than the acceptance of the legal autonomy of the Union legal order in regard to national law is the understanding of its raison d'être. The European Treaties, it will be remembered, aim at establishing within the territories of the Member States an "internal market" characterised by the basic freedoms (goods, persons, establishment, services, capital and payments), and constituting a geographical area wherein Union rules apply with the same force and with the same meaning and effect for all who operate therein.[21] Therefore, the very nature of the law created by the European Treaties implies uniform interpretation and application. Without those characteristics there can be no Union. Union law is either uniform in all the Member States or it simply cannot exist. This does not mean that Union rules should not take into account the specificities of the various Member States or of their regions[22]; as long as the fundamental principles are safeguarded, the way of implementing them must be adapted to local circumstances. Indeed, applying the same rule to different situations constitutes discrimination just as much as applying different rules to comparable situations.[23]

2. DIRECT EFFECT

4–06   If the consequence of direct applicability means, for the Member States, non-interference with the implementation of Union law and, where required, implementation and application of its rules, for the citizens it means, in most cases, the possibility of invoking those Union rules in their national courts and tribunals to defend the rights which flow for them from these rules; this is what is

---

[18] See *Boukhalfa v Germany* (C-214/94) [1996] E.C.R. I-2253; [1996] 3 C.M.L.R. 22: it concerned a Belgian citizen, a local resident employed in the German embassy in Algiers, who claimed the same employment conditions as the German employees.

[19] Art.4(3)2 EU.

[20] Art.4(3)2 EU.

[21] *Costa v ENEL* (6/64) (quoted above, fn.11) at 594, and *Rheinmhlen v Einfuhr-und Vorratstelle Getreide* (166/73) [1974] E.C.R. 33 at 38(2); [1974] 1 C.M.L.R. 523.

[22] See in this regard Art.27 TFEU, which provides that when drawing up proposals for establishing and ensuring the functioning of the internal market, "the Commission shall take into account the extent of the effort that certain economies showing differences in development will have to sustain for the establishment of the internal market, and may propose appropriate provisions." These provisions may take the form of derogations.

[23] *Procureur du Roi v Debauve* (52/79) [1980] E.C.R. 833 at 858(21); [1981] 2 C.M.L.R. 362 and *Webb* (279/80) [1981] E.C.R. 3305 at 3324(16); [1982] 1 C.M.L.R. 719.

meant by "direct effect". This allows all those who are subject to Union law to require the national judge to uphold these rights.[24]

Applicability of Union law must indeed be understood in two ways: on the one hand, the obligations and prohibitions (i.e. obligations to abstain) imposed upon national authorities, institutions and persons, and, on the other hand, the obligation to sustain the rights granted to those in favour of whom those obligations/prohibitions were imposed. Indeed, in law, every obligation imposed upon someone creates, as its corollary, a right for someone else, although this right is not always clearly specified. It is the same in Union law: obligations imposed upon Member States have, generally speaking, as their corollary, corresponding rights for the natural and legal person of the Union. For instance, by prohibiting the Member States from hindering the free movement of goods, the Treaty grants these persons within the Union the right to move goods unhindered from one Member State to another. The same applies to the other freedoms.

It is this kind of right that the national authorities–legislative, administrative and judiciary–must, by virtue of the direct effect of most Union provisions, uphold in pursuance of the Treaty.[25]

Where the judiciary is concerned, the question has been raised as to whether **4–07** the national judge must, of his own volition, apply Union rules that have direct effect. The Court accepted the domestic law principle of "judicial passivity" in civil cases, and the concomitant rule that, in civil suits, it is for the parties to take the initiative.[26] On the other hand, a Member State may not prevent a national judge from raising the question of the compatibility of national law with Union rules.[27] It is thus not only the directly applicable[28] regulations that are, as such, suited to "grant to the citizens rights which the national tribunals are under obligation to protect",[29] but all binding Union acts whatever their nature or form.[30] Consequently, the question: "which provisions of Union law have direct effect?" should rather be put the other way: "which Union provisions that impose a clear and unconditional obligation upon a Member State, an institution or a person, do not have direct effect?"[31] The answer is: only those which leave to the

---

[24] This was clearly stated by the Court in *Defrenne v Sabena* (43/75) [1976] E.C.R. 455, para.24; [1976] 2 C.M.L.R. 98; the same was already apparent in *Reyners v Belgium* (2/74) [1974] E.C.R. 631, para.25; [1974] 2 C.M.L.R. 305, although less clearly stated.

[25] Art.4(3) EU. This provision refers to "Member States", which must be understood as covering all national authorities whether legislative, administrative or judicial. See *Rewe v Landwirtschaftskammer Saarland* (33/76) [1976] E.C.R. 1989, para.5; [1977] 1 C.M.L.R. 533.

[26] *Van Schijndel* (Joined Cases C-430/93 and C-431/93) [1995] E.C.R. I-4705.

[27] *Peterbroeck* (C-312/93) [1995] E.C.R. I-4599.

[28] Art.288 TFEU. See Ch.3: The Legal Acts of the Union.

[29] *Leonesio v Italian Ministry for Agriculture and Forestry* (93/71) [1972] E.C.R. 287 at 293(5); [1973] C.M.L.R. 343.

[30] For instance provisions of directives, decisions or agreements; for directives, see *Delkvist v Anklagemyndigheden* (21/78) [1978] E.C.R. 2327 at 2340(21); [1979] 1 C.M.L.R. 372; for decisions see *Rewe* (33/76) (quoted above, fn.25) and for agreements see *International Fruit Company v Produktschap voor Groenten en Fruit* (Joined Cases 21/72, 22/72, 23/72 and 24/72) [1972] E.C.R. 1219 at 1227; [1975] 2 C.M.L.R. 1. Also *Kziber* (18/90) [1991] E.C.R. I-221.

[31] Originally, the question was put the other way round: see *Molkerei Zentrale Westfalen v Hauptzollamt Paderborn* (28/67) [1968] E.C.R. 143 at 153; [1968] C.M.L.R. 187. See, however, *Defrenne* (43/75) (quoted above, fn.24) at 471. If the acts are not clear and unconditional, the exact obligation cannot be established, neither can it, therefore, be upheld (that seems to go without saying).

addressee of the obligation discretionary latitude. For instance, with regard to public undertakings, the Court stated that:

"Its application involves an appraisal of the requirements, on the one hand, of the particular task entrusted to the undertaking concerned and, on the other hand, the protection of the interests of the [Union]. This appraisal depends on the objectives of general economic policy pursued by the States under the supervision of the Commission. Consequently... Art.106 (2) cannot at the present stage create individual rights which the national courts must protect."[32]

In other words, this Treaty obligation is subject to a Commission appreciation and cannot therefore have direct effect.

However, the Court made it clear that in cases where the latitude is limited in time, the expiration of the time limit suffices to give direct effect to Union rules. This applies notwithstanding the absence of implementing regulations that were to be adopted by the institutions or by the national authorities. The Court found also that, even in the areas in which they have no direct effect, the Union provisions cannot be interpreted as reserving to the national legislature exclusive powers to implement those rules. Indeed, such implementation may be relieved by a combination of Union and national measures.[33]

4–08   The fact that the European Treaties have created a new legal order, directly applicable and conferring upon the natural and legal persons of the Union rights, which the national courts must uphold, was not only ascertained by the Court, but also recognised from the beginning by most national jurisdictions. Indeed, the judiciaries of all the Member States have implicitly recognised this fact for many years by making extensive use of the possibility, offered them by the Treaty, to ask the Court for a "preliminary ruling" on questions concerning Union law raised before them.[34] By referring those questions to the Court, they accepted that Union rules do apply within the territory of their jurisdiction and may confer rights which they, as national courts, must uphold.

Under the principle of co-operation laid down in the EU Treaty,[35] it is for Member States to ensure judicial protection of an individual's rights under Union law. In the absence of Union rules governing the matter, it is for the domestic legal system of each Member State to designate the courts and tribunals having jurisdiction, and to lay down the detailed procedural rules governing actions for safeguarding rights which individuals derive from Union law. Those rules must be no less favourable than those governing similar domestic actions (principle of equivalence), and must not render practically impossible or excessively difficult the exercise of rights conferred by Union law. Moreover it is for the national courts to interpret the procedural rules governing actions brought before them in such a manner as to contribute to ensuring effective judicial protection of an individual's rights under Union law.[36]

The fact that Union law constitutes a new legal order was recognised explicitly, years ago, by the highest national courts and tribunals. This was the

---

[32] *Ministre Public Luxembourgeois v Muller* (10/71) [1971] E.C.R. 723 at 730 (14–16); at the time Art.90 EEC.
[33] *Defrenne* (43/75) (quoted above, fn.24) at 480(68).
[34] Art.267 TFEU.
[35] Art.4(3) EU.
[36] *Unibet* (C-432/05) [2007] E.C.R. I-2271.

case, among others, for the Italian *Corte Costituzionale*, the German *Bundesverfassungsgericht* and the Belgian *Cour de Cassation*. Although of historical value only at this stage of the development of Union law, these decisions were extremely important at the time, when the novelty of those issues often resulted in provoking adverse reactions from national judges. All the implications of the autonomy of the Union legal order did not always become immediately clear either. In many cases it was a lengthy process of adaptation and learning in which the Court played a decisive role.[37]

3. PRECEDENCE OR PRIMACY OF UNION LAW

In retrospect it might seem evident that the autonomy of the Union legal order   4–09
and the necessity for its uniform interpretation and application in all the Member States, automatically imply that Union provisions have precedence over national legislation in case of conflict. Since national authorities (especially national courts and tribunals) are under obligation, as was just seen, to apply Union rules alongside the provisions of national law, it is not unlikely that conflicts will result from this simultaneous application. The European Treaties contain no explicit provisions regarding the solution to be applied in such cases.[38] Attempts were therefore made to solve such conflicts in accordance with provisions of national law. However, few national legal systems provide for conflict rules of this nature.

In the United Kingdom, for instance, the European Communities Act 1972 provides for the necessary precedence by accepting the "legal effect" of Union provisions in the United Kingdom.[39] The same applies to the decisions of the Court regarding the meaning or effect of any of the Treaties, or the validity, meaning or effect of any Union instrument.[40] In relation to statute law, this means that the directly applicable Union provisions shall prevail even over future Acts of Parliament, if the latter are inconsistent with those instruments. It also means that by ratifying the European Treaties, the United Kingdom, like any other Member State, has assented to refrain from enacting legislation inconsistent with Union law.[41]

---

[37] First General Report (1967), p.563.
[38] One could, however, argue that Art.4(3) EU constitutes a legal ground on which to base this precedence.
[39] European Communities Act 1972 s.2(1). See *Factortame* (C-213/89) [1990] E.C.R. I-2433; [1990] 3 C.M.L.R. 1, where the Court held that, "a court [in a dispute governed by Union law] which would grant interim relief, if it were not for a rule of national law, is obliged to set aside that rule", at E.C.R. I-2474(21). See also [2005] EWCA Civ 1191; *Oakley*, before the English Court of Appeal: sui generis nature of s.2.
[40] European Communities Act 1972 s.3(1).
[41] European Communities Act 1972 s.2(4) provides therefore that present and future enactments shall be construed and have effect subject to s.2. See *Hansard*, February 15, 1972, Vol. 831. This basic principle derives not only from the obligations explicitly accepted by the Member States when they became members of the Union, but, as was explained, from the very nature of the Union and Union law. Indeed, as mentioned, the existence of the Union depends upon the simultaneous and uniform application, throughout the Union, of all the provisions of the Treaties and of the acts of the institutions. This was clearly stated over and over again by the Court. See, for instance, *Pigs Marketing Board v Redmond* (83/78) [1978] E.C.R. 2347 at 2371(56); [1979] 1 C.M.L.R. 177 and *Commission v UK* (128/78) [1979] E.C.R. 419 at 428(9); [1979] 2 C.M.L.R. 45.

In the Netherlands, the Basic Law (Constitution) not only provides that the provisions of international treaties have precedence over existing national laws and regulations, it also specifies that the same applies to measures enacted by the institutions set up under those treaties and adds that this precedence applies in case of conflict between an existing Union rule and subsequent national law.[42]

The French Constitution provides, in general terms, that treaties or agreements, duly ratified or approved, shall, upon their publication, have authority superior to that of laws, subject, however, for each agreement or treaty, to its application by the other party.[43]

4–10   The German Constitution provides that the Federal Republic may, by legislation, transfer sovereign powers to intergovernmental institutions[44] and refers to the precedence of the general rules of international law.[45] It is only with difficulty that one can equate Union measures with the latter.

The Italian Constitution is even less precise. It only provides that "Italy's legal system conforms with the general principles recognised by international law".[46]

These German and Italian texts, and even the French Constitution, form a rather meagre legal basis for the obligation that national courts should give precedence to Union law over national law in case of conflict between the two; and what of those Member States whose Constitution contains no provisions in this respect? Furthermore, in certain cases the above-mentioned constitutional provisions were not considered by national judges as obliging them to accept the precedence of Union provisions over national rules.[47]

---

[42] Arts 66 and 67 of the Dutch Constitution; these provisions were incorporated in the Constitution in 1953.

[43] Art.55 of the French Constitution of 1958. In a judgment of 1962, the French Cour de Cassation held that a contested action had been carried out under an EEC decision and regulation which were, "acts regularly published and having acquired force of international treaties" (*Gazette du Palais*, December 9 to 11 (1970) 6–7). See also *Administration des Douanes v Jacques Vabre* [1975] C.M.L.R. 336, where the French Supreme Court clearly stated that the Treaty has an authority greater than that of national acts and is binding on the national courts. See, however, the decision of the Conseil d'Etat: *Syndicat Général des Fabricants de Semoules v Direction des Industries Agricoles* [1970] C.M.L.R. 395. It was only in October 1989 (31 years after the EEC Treaty came into force) that this French highest administrative jurisdiction finally recognised the precedence of Union law over national law!

[44] Art.24(1) of the German Constitution. See, however, the German Constitutional Court on the Treaty of Maastricht, October 12, 1993, 89 BVerfGE 155, at 185. As a former German Judge of the Court of Justice wrote: "[i]n the past, after some hesitations, the German Constitutional court assented to the developing supranational power of the European Union, though with provisions for extreme situations. The judgment on the EU Treaty reversed this situation fundamentally. The [German] Court returned to a nationalistic view of democracy and opened up ways of leaving the European Union regardless of juridical bonds and declared German authorities competent to ignore Union law. It is uncertain whether this tendency to re-nationalisation will continue or whether it will be overcome by another change in the case law of the Constitutional Court." Manfred Zuleeg, "European Constitution under Constitutional Constraints: The German Scenario", (1997) 22 E.L.Rev. Feb.

[45] Art.25 of the German Constitution.

[46] Art.10(1) of the Italian Constitution.

[47] By a ruling of March 1, 1968 ((1968) *Recueil Dalloz-Sirey Jurisprudence* 286) the French Conseil d'Etat ruled that a French Court is bound to ensure the application of the national *lex posterior* to an existing Union rule, whatever the meaning and scope of Union law (Second General Report (1968), 453). The Commission considered this ruling incompatible with the legal obligations deriving from the Treaty. See also Cour de Cassation, October 22, 1970, *Contributions Indirectes v Ramel* [1971] C.M.L.R. 315.

Even in the case of the Dutch Constitution, that is so explicit about precedence, doubts might subsist as to the precise consequences. Furthermore, if the sole legal basis for primacy of Union law over national law were national law itself, this supremacy would be at the mercy of the next constitutional amendment.

Another ground had therefore to be found which would be accepted by all national jurisdictions without reference to their particular national legal orders. This ground was obviously to be found in the Union legal order itself. It is indeed accepted by all the Member States which "have adhered to the Treaty on the same conditions, definitively and without any reservations other than those set out in the supplementary protocols".[48] The Court has always considered that the wording and the spirit of the Treaty make it impossible for Member States to accord precedence to a unilateral and subsequent measure over a legal system accepted by them on the basis of reciprocity. The Court also added that:

4–11

> "[T]he executive force of [Union] law cannot vary from one State to another in deference to subsequent domestic laws, without jeopardising the attainment of the objectives of the Treaty set out in Art.4(3) and giving rise to the discrimination referred to by Art.12."[49]

Therefore:

> "[T]he law stemming from the Treaty, an independent source of law, could not, because of its special and original nature, be overridden by domestic legal provisions, however framed, without being deprived of its character as [Union] law and without the legal basis of the [Union] itself being called into question."[50]

This also applies with regard to national constitutional provisions. The Court states that the effect of a Union measure cannot be affected by allegations that it runs counter to fundamental rights as formulated by the Constitution of a State.[51]

To put it simply once more: either Union law stands by itself, is uniformly applied and has precedence over all domestic law, or it does not exist. This view is now generally accepted in all the Member States.[52]

Attached to the Treaty of Lisbon is a Declaration concerning primacy, which reads as follows:

---

[48] *San Michele v High Authority* (Joined Cases 9/65 and 58/65) [1967] E.C.R. 1 at 30.

[49] *Costa v ENEL* (6/64) [1964] E.C.R. 585 at 594; [1964] C.M.L.R. 425. This was once again emphasised by the Court in *Commission v UK ("Tachographs")* (128/78) [1979] E.C.R. 419 at 429; [1979] 2 C.M.L.R. 45.

[50] *Costa v ENEL* (6/64) (quoted above, fn.49). See also *Internationale Handelsgesellschaft v Einfuhr-und Vorratsstelle Getreide* (11/70) [1970] E.C.R. 1125 at 1134(3); [1972] C.M.L.R. 255.

[51] *Costa v ENEL* (6/64), (quoted above, fn.49) and *Nold v Commission* (4/73) [1974] E.C.R. 491; [1974] 2 C.M.L.R. 338.

[52] It might be of interest to mention some of the earliest and most important rulings of national courts, since they constitute essential steps towards recognition of the Union legal order and its implications. In Belgium, reference must be made to a decision of 1971 of the Cour de Cassation in the case *Belgian State v Fromagerie Franco-Suisse* [1972] C.M.L.R. 373: the primacy of the Treaty results from the very nature of international treaty law. In France, Cour de Cassation, 1975, *Administration des Douanes v Jacques Vabre et al.* ([1972] C.M.L.R. 336) and finally also the French Conseil d'Etat: *Maurice Boisdet*, September 24, 1990: [1991] 1 C.M.L.R. 3.

"The Conference recalls that, in accordance with well settled case law of the Court of Justice of the European Union, the Treaties and the law adopted by the Union on the basis of the Treaties have primacy over the law of Member States, under the conditions laid down by the said case law."[53]

4–12   The general principle of Union law's precedence over national law having been established, it is necessary to examine some of its more concrete consequences. As far as any national court or tribunal is concerned, the Court has described their obligations as follows. Directly applicable rules of Union law are a direct source of rights and duties for all those affected thereby. The latter also include any national court whose task it is, as an organ of a Member State, to protect, in cases within its jurisdiction, the rights conferred upon individuals by Union law. In accordance with the principle of precedence, Treaty provisions and directly applicable Union measures, by their coming into force, automatically render any conflicting provisions of current national law inapplicable.

It follows that every national court, in cases within its jurisdiction, must apply Union law in its entirety and protects the rights the latter confers upon natural or legal persons. As mentioned before, it must set aside any conflicting provision of national law, whether prior or subsequent to the Union provision. It is not necessary for the national court to request or await the prior setting aside of such national provisions by legislative or other means.[54]

As far as legislative bodies are concerned, the Court indicated that the principle of precedence precludes the valid adoption of new national legislative measures to the extent that they would be incompatible with Union provisions.[55]

Where other national authorities are concerned, it is clear that respect for the precedence of Union law and the obligations resulting for Member States from the Treaties,[56] not only prevents them from enacting measures, which are incompatible with existing Union provisions, but also imposes upon them the obligation to abolish all *existing* contrary measures, whatever their nature. Even where these measures are no longer applied, their maintenance gives rise to an ambiguous situation: "by maintaining, as regards those subject to the law who are concerned, a state of uncertainty as to the possibilities, which are available to them of relying on [Union] law".[57]

4–13   The question was raised as to whether or not national authorities were obliged to modify a decision based on incorrect interpretation of Union law after this was established by a Court judgment clarifying Union law. The Court here made a distinction between decisions of national courts not subject to appeal or other remedies and decisions of an administrative body. In the first case, the Court ruled that the, "principle of cooperation under Art.4 EU does not require a national court to disapply its internal rules of procedure in order to review and set

---

[53] Declaration 17 [2008] O.J. C 115/344.
[54] *Amministrazione delle Finanze dello Stato v Simmenthal* (106/77) [1978] E.C.R. 629 at 643–644 (14–18 and 21, 22, 24); [1978] 3 C.M.L.R. 263.
[55] *Simmenthal* (106/77), (quoted above, fn.54) at 17. See also *Eridania v Minister of Agriculture and Forestry* (230/78) [1979] E.C.R. 2749.
[56] Art.4(3) EU.
[57] *Commission v France* (167/73) [1974] E.C.R. 359 at 372(41); [1974] 2 C.M.L.R. 216. See also *Commission v Italy* (159/78) [1979] E.C.R. 3247; [1980] 3 C.M.L.R. 446 and *Commission v Ireland* (61/77) [1978] E.C.R. 417 at 442; [1978] 2 C.M.L.R. 466.

aside a final judicial decision if that decision should be contrary to Union law".[58] In the case of an administrative body, Art.4(3) EU imposes an obligation to review a final administrative decision, where an application for such review is made to it, in order to take account of the interpretation of the relevant provision given in the meantime by the Court. This, however, only applies where, under national law, the body has the power to reopen its decision; in the case under review, the administrative decision became final only as a result of a national court judgment against whose decision there is no judicial remedy; that judgment was incorrect, in the light of a subsequent judgment of the Court, and without a preliminary question being asked as provided for under the Treaty; finally, the person concerned complained to the administrative body immediately after becoming aware of the preliminary decision.[59]

It follows from the preceding remarks that autonomy of the Union legal order, direct effect and precedence of Union rules over national measures all result from the particular nature of Union law.

A final aspect, which needs to be mentioned in this respect, is the reference by the Court to the usefulness[60] or effectiveness[61] of Union acts to justify the right of individuals to rely on obligations imposed by directives. Those acts are not directly applicable, since the choice is left to the national authorities as to the form and method of implementing the obligations imposed upon them by those acts. In other words, the implementation is left, within limits, to their discretion. Consequently, according to the present case law, directives have no direct effect and persons cannot invoke them in national courts. However, the Court admits, as was seen before,[62] that provisions of directives can have direct effect, especially after the time limit set for their transposition into national law has elapsed. Similarly, interested parties have the right to ask national courts to determine whether the competent national authorities, in exercising the choice which is left to them in transposing the directive, have kept within the limits of their discretionary powers.[63] However, whether national authorities have, or have not, exercised their discretionary power, for instance, to make derogation, is a matter for the discretion of the legislative or administrative authorities of the Member State. It cannot, therefore, be subject to legal review on the basis of the provisions of the directive. "It is the duty of the national court before which the directive is invoked to determine whether the disputed national measure falls outside the margin of the discretion of the Member State."[64]

But it is also the duty of the national court when it applies domestic law, and in   **4–14**
particular legislative provisions specifically adopted for the purpose of implementing the requirements of a directive, to interpret national law, so far as possible, in the light of the wording and the purpose of the directive concerned in order to achieve the results sought by the directive and consequently comply with

---

[58] *Kapferer v Schlank & Schick GmBH* (C-234/04) [2006] E.C.R. I-2585.

[59] *Khne & Heitz* (C-453/00) [2004] E.C.R. I-837.

[60] Nederlandse Ondernemingen v Inspecteur der Invoerrechten en Accijnzen (51/76) [1977] E.C.R. 113 at 127(29); [1977] 1 C.M.L.R. 413.

[61] *ENKA v Inspecteur der Invoerrechten en Accijnzen* (38/77) [1977] E.C.R. 2203 at 2211(9); [1978] 2 C.M.L.R. 212.

[62] See Ch.3: The Legal Acts of the Union.

[63] *ENKA* (38/77) (quoted above, fn.61) at 2212(10).

[64] *Nederlandse Ondernemingen* (51/76) (quoted above, fn.60) at 127(29).

the obligation provided for in the Treaty and according to which "a directive shall be binding as to the results to be achieved".[65] It might be useful to repeat once more that this duty of the national court follows from the obligation imposed by the Treaty on the Member States to take all appropriate measures to ensure the fulfilment of the obligations arising out of the Treaty or resulting from action taken by the institutions (here the directive) and that that obligation is binding on all the authorities of the Member States, including, for matters within their jurisdiction, the courts.[66]

In this respect it should be noted that, as will be discussed below, Member States that breach Union law, are, under given conditions, liable for the harm caused to individuals by this breach.

4. MEMBER STATES' LIABILITY FOR BREACH OF UNION LAW

4–15 Failure of a Member State to properly transpose a directive (which constitutes an infringement of Union law) makes that State liable for loss and damages caused to natural and legal persons by that breach, the so-called Francovich[67] liability. More generally, as is explained below in Ch.8: The Commission, Member States are not only responsible to the Union for their infringements of Union law; they are also liable for possible damage caused by their infringement to legal or natural persons. This liability of a Member State applies for acts or failures to act not only of the executive, but also of the legislature and even, in certain circumstances, of the judicature.[68]

According to the Court,[69] this liability is "inherent in the system of the Treaty," and a "further basis is to be found in Art.4(3) of the EU Treaty". The Court added that although the liability of the Member State to make good loss and damage caused to individuals by breaches of Union law, for which it can be held responsible, is required by Union law, the conditions under which there is a right to reparation depend on the nature of the breach, and whether the breached provision did confer rights upon individuals.[70]

Like the principles of "direct effect" and "supremacy of Union law over national law", the principle of state liability for breaches of Union law, finds its origin in Union law itself, as interpreted by the Court. No other justifications are necessary, the Court being, by agreement among the Member States, the "supreme arbiter". The moment one starts discussing what might have influenced the Court in reaching its conclusions, one risks bringing not only the conclusions, but even the basic principles into question. The consequence might be that

---

[65] Art.288,3 TFEU.
[66] *Pfeiffer and Others* (Joined Cases C-397/01, C-398/01, C-399/01, C-400/01, C-401/01, C-402/01 and C-403/01), [2004] E.C.R. I-8835.
[67] *Francovich and Others* (C-6/90 and C-9/90), [1991] E.C.R. I-5357.
[68] See, for instance, *Kbler* (C-224/01) [2003] E.C.R. I-10239 and *Traghetti v Italy* (C-173/03) [2006] E.C.R. I-5177, where the Court found Italy had infringed the Treaty by limiting the responsibility of the courts to cases of intentional fault and serious misconduct, excluding liability in connection with the interpretation of provisions of law.
[69] *Kbler* (C-224/01), (quoted above, fn.68).
[70] See *Paul* (C-222/02) [2004] E.C.R. I-9425.

national courts, like the German Supreme Court, would decide, for instance, that their constitutions prevail over Union law. This approach risks creating tension, and unsettles the Union legal order itself. These speculations might find their place in political science but not in an analysis of a legal system whose acceptance by the Member States and in particular by the national judges is not always evident, although they are bound, by the obligations assumed by the States, to accept and apply the law as it is handed down by the European courts. This does not mean uncritical agreement (which is different from acceptance) with all Court decisions. Although a critical approach might lead the Court itself to modify its case law, as it did in the *Keck and Mithouard* judgment,[71] it has no place in a book that endeavours to describe the law as it stands.

5. INFRINGEMENT OF UNION LAW BY NATURAL OR LEGAL PERSONS

It follows from the Treaty provisions concerning the jurisdiction of the Court[72]   **4–16**
that regulations adopted jointly by Parliament and the Council, or by the Council, may provide for penalties to be imposed upon individuals or undertakings, in case of infringement by them of provisions of said regulations.[73]

As for infringement of Union law by natural and legal person when the Union legislation does not specifically provide any penalty, the Treaty requires, according to the Court, the Member States to take all measures necessary to guarantee the application and effectiveness of Union law.[74] While the choice of penalties remains within their discretion, they must ensure that the infringements are penalised under conditions, both procedural and substantive, which are analogous to those applicable to infringements of national law of a similar nature and importance, and which in any event, make the penalty effective, proportionate and dissuasive.[75]

In order to ensure the efficacy of the rules adopted by the institutions, non-compliance with which may have serious consequences, Member States may be required to apply criminal penalties to certain forms of conduct. However, the determination of the type and level of the criminal penalties to be applied does not fall within the Union's sphere of competence.

---

[71] *Keck and Mithouard* (Joined Cases C-267/91 and C-268/91) [1993] E.C.R. I-6097.
[72] Art.261 TFEU.
[73] Examples are Regulation 1/2003 [2003] O.J. L1/1, implementing the rules on competition, Arts 23 and 24; Regulation 1017/68 [1968] O.J. L175/3, applying rules of competition to transport, Art.22 (amended by Regulation 1/2003, above); and Regulation 726/2004 [2004] O.J. L136/1 laying down Union procedures for the authorisation and supervision of medicinal products, Art.84(3). See also Directive 91/308 [1991] O.J. L166/77 on the prevention of the use of the financial system for the purpose of money laundering, as amended, accompanying statement committing the Member States to enact criminal legislation for infringement of the Directive.
[74] This obligation follows from Art.4(3) EU.
[75] *Hansen* (326/88) [1990] E.C.R. I-2911.

6. SOURCES OF UNION LAW

4–17   As was previously indicated, the Union legal order has its own sources, which consist not only of the European Treaties and the acts of the institutions issued in pursuance of the powers conferred upon them (regulations, directives, decisions, agreements, etc.),[76] but also of the rules relating to the application of this primary and secondary Union law. These rules comprise international law, in so far as applicable[77] and the general principles of law such as equal treatment (non-discrimination), proportionality, legal certainty, etc.[78] including the fundamental rights. The latter play an important role, as the Court pointed out: "respect for fundamental rights forms an integral part of the general principles of law protected by the Court of Justice", and added that "the protection of such rights, whilst inspired by the constitutional traditions common to Member States, must be ensured within the framework . . . and objectives of the [Union]".[79] A reference to those fundamental rights is to be found in the Treaty on European Union, which provides amongst others, that the:

> "Union recognises the rights, freedoms and principles set out in the Charter of Fundamental Rights of the European Union of 7 December 2000, as adopted at Strasburg on 12 December 2007, which shall have the same legal value as the Treaties."[80]

The Treaty adds that:

---

[76] See Ch.3: The Legal Acts of the Union.

[77] Agreements concluded by the Union with third States or international organisations under Art.218 TFEU, are governed by the rules of international law. But, according to the Court (see, e.g. *Greece v Commission* (30/88) [1989] E.C.R. 3711; [1991] 2 C.M.L.R. 169), "the provisions of an agreement concluded by the Council under [Arts 218 and 217 TFEU], form, as from the entry into force of the agreement, an integral part of the [Union] legal system". On the other hand, as the Court pointed out, when exercising their rights to lay down Union rules, the institutions are not bound by provisions of international law, unless the Union itself has assumed the rights and obligations resulting, for the Member States, from international agreements to which they are parties, and unless the provisions of those agreements have direct effect within the Union: *International Fruit Company v Productschap voor Groenten en Fruit* (Joined Cases 21/72, 22/72, 23/72, 24/72) [1972] E.C.R. 1219 at 1226(8); [1975] 2 C.M.L.R. 1. See also [1972] E.C.R. 1219 at 1227(18), and *hlstrm v Commission* (Joined Cases "wood pulp" 89 etc./85) [1988] E.C.R. 5233; [1988] 4 C.M.L.R. 901, "the conduct of the Commission is covered by the territoriality principle, as universally recognised by public international law". As for Treaty precedence over agreements concluded between Member States before its entrance into force, see *Commission v Italy* (10/61) [1962] E.C.R. 1 at 10; [1962] C.M.L.R. 187. The precedence of Union law over all other applicable provisions, including international law, is recognised by the European Communities Act 1972 ss.2(1) and (4).

[78] See *Verli-Wallace v Commission* (159/82) [1983] E.C.R. 2711 at 2718 (8) and Ch.9: The Court of Justice of the European Union.

[79] *Internationale Handelsgesellschaft v Einfuhr-und Vorratstelle Getreide* (11/70) [1970] E.C.R. 1125 at 1134 (4); [1972] C.M.L.R. 255. See also *Einfuhr-und Vorratstelle v Kster* (25/70) [1970] E.C.R. 1161 at 1176 (36); [1972] C.M.L.R. 255, where the Court found that a system of licences for import and export, involving a deposit, did not violate any right of a fundamental nature and *Hauer v Land Rheinland-Pfalz* (44/79) [1979] E.C.R. 3727; [1980] 3 C.M.L.R. 42, where the Court examined whether a Union regulation violated the right of property and the free exercise of professional activity. Also the inviolability of the domicile in *Hoechst v Commission* (46/87 R) [1987] E.C.R. 1549; [1991] 4 C.M.L.R. 410.

[80] Art.6(1) EU.

"Fundamental rights, as guaranteed by the European Convention for the Protection of Human Rights and Fundamental Freedoms and as they result from the constitutional traditions common to the Member States, shall constitute general principles of the [Union]'s law".[81]

The EU Treaty also provides that the Union shall accede to this European Convention.[82]

A Charter of fundamental rights of the European Union was "solemnly proclaimed" (whatever legal meaning that has) by the Parliament, the Council and the Commission at the end of the year 2000.[83] It refers to the above-mentioned source of Union law, in addition to the Social Charters adopted by the Union and the Council of Europe, and the case law of the Court of Justice and of the European Court of Human Rights. According to the EU Treaty this Charter now has "the same legal value as the Treaties."[84]

7. SOME BASIC PRINCIPLES OF THE UNION

The EU Treaty establishes that the Union is founded, inter alia, on the values of respect for human dignity, freedom and respect for human rights, including the rights of persons belonging to minorities, and that those values are common to the Member States in a society in which pluralism, non-discrimination, tolerance, justice, solidarity [also between Member States] and equality between women and men,[85] and that the Union shall combat exclusion and discrimination, and shall promote, inter alia, social justice and protection.[86]

4–18

The TFEU prohibits "any discrimination on grounds of nationality",[87] and adds that Parliament and the Council may, in accordance with the ordinary legislative procedure,[88] "adopt rules designed to prohibit such discrimination". The TFEU also provides that the Council, after obtaining the consent of Parliament may take appropriate action to combat discrimination, including on the ground of disability.[89] The Council adopted a Resolution on a European Disability Framework,[90] a Resolution on the situation of persons with disabilities in the European Union,[91] and Conclusions on the support of the implementation of the European Disability Strategy 2010-2020.[92]

---

[81] Art.6(3) EU.
[82] Art.6(2) EU.
[83] [2000] O.J. C364/8.
[84] Art.6(1) EU.
[85] Art.2 EU.
[86] Art.3 EU.
[87] Art.18(1) TFEU.
[88] Art.289(1) TFEU.
[89] Art.10 and Art.19 TFEU.
[90] Doc.101/73/10.
[91] [2008] O.J. C75/1.
[92] [2011] O.J. C300/1.

The same prohibition of discrimination is to be found, among others, in the provisions concerning the free movement of goods,[93] and of persons,[94] the freedom of establishment,[95] and provisions of services[96] and the free movement of capital and of payments.[97]

The number of times the expression "non-discrimination", or, preferably (because it is positive), "equal treatment", is used in the Treaties, clearly indicates that this is indeed a basic principle of Union law.

8. APPLICATION OF NATIONAL AND INTERNATIONAL LAW BY THE EUROPEAN COURT

4–19   The question of the applicability of the national law of the Member States by the Union institutions was raised on several occasions before the Court. The latter, however, decided that it lacked the competence to apply the internal law of the Member States.[98] Consequently, the Court cannot accept a claim that, by taking a decision, an institution has violated national law. Neither can the Court decide on the interpretation of a national provision.[99] However, application of national law by the Court takes place where the Treaty refers explicitly to national concepts.[100] This is the case, for instance, where reference is made to companies and firms formed in accordance with the law of a Member State.[101] Also when the Treaty provides that, in the case of non-contractual liability, the Union shall make good any damage caused by its institutions or by its servants "in accordance with the general principles common to the laws of the Member States".[102] Similarly, when the Court is called upon to solve a question for which there are no Treaty provisions, it must solve the problem, "by reference to the rules acknowledged by the legislation, the learned writings and the case law of the member countries".[103]

In numerous cases the Court was called upon to interpret[104] and apply international law. According to the General Court (GC), it is only in case the

---

[93] See for instance *Marimex* (Case 29/72) [1972] E.C.R.1309.

[94] See for instance *Watson and Belmann* (Case 118/75) [1976] E.C.R. 1185.

[95] Art.49,2 TFEU.

[96] Art.57,3 TFEU.

[97] Art.65(3) TFEU.

[98] See, e.g. *Stork v High Authority* (1/58) [1959] E.C.R. 17; *Geitling v High Authority* (Joined Cases 36/59, 37/59, 38/59, 39/59 and 40/59) [1960] E.C.R. 423. See, however, *Klckner v High Authority* (Joined Cases 17/61 and 20/61) [1962] E.C.R. 325 and *Commission v Italy* (159/78) [1979] E.C.R. 3247.

[99] *Deutsche Grammophon v Metro* (78/70) [1971] E.C.R. 487 at 498 (3); [1971] C.M.L.R. 631.

[100] See *Wnsche v Einfuhr- und Vorratstelle Getreide* (50/71) [1972] E.C.R. 53 at 64(6); [1973] C.M.L.R. 35.

[101] Art.54 TFEU. See, e.g. *Nold v High Authority* (18/57) [1959] E.C.R. 41 at 48.

[102] Art.340 TFEU.

[103] *Algera v Common Assembly* (Joined Cases 7/56, 3/57, 4/57, 5/57, 6/57 and 7/57) [1957–1958] E.C.R. 39 at 55. Another example is the definition of "misuse of power" (Art.263 TFEU) based on a comparative study by the Advocate-General of this concept in the municipal law of the Member States: *ASSIDER v High Authority* (3/54) [1954–1955] E.C.R. 63 at 74.

[104] See *Dior E.A.* (Joined Cases C-300/98 and C-392/98) [2000] E.C.R. I-11307, where the Court stated that when the judicial authorities of the Member States are called upon to protect rights falling within the Agreement establishing the WTO, approved on behalf of the Union, and a case is brought before the Court in accordance with Art.267 TFEU, the Court has jurisdiction to interpret Art.50 of the TRIPS Agreement set out in an annex to the WTO Agreement.

Union intended to implement a specific obligation assumed in the framework of an international agreement, or when a Union act refers explicitly to a specific provision of an international agreement, that the Union courts are called upon to control the legality of the Union act in regard to that agreement.[105] The Court held that the validity of the Directive on ship-source pollution,[106] could not be assessed either in the light of the International Convention for the prevention of pollution from ships, nor in the light of the United Nations Convention on the Law of the Sea (Montego Bay).[107]

With regard to World Trade Organisation (WTO) agreements, the Court stated   **4–20**
that they are "not in principle among the rules in the light of which the Court is to review the legality, of Union measures".[108] However, the Court also stated that the WTO agreement has been signed by the Community and subsequently approved by decision; therefore the provisions of that convention form an integral part of the Community legal order. Within the framework of that legal order the Court has jurisdiction to give preliminary rulings concerning the interpretation of that agreement.[109] The same applies, for instance, to the 1999 Montreal Convention for the unification of certain rules for international carriage by air; the Court found that it was an integral part of Union law and had primacy over secondary Union legislation.[110]

Neither can the WTO rules constitute a basis for reparation of damages caused by a violation by the Union of WTO rules, despite the existence of actual and certain damage, and a direct causal link between the damage suffered and the conduct of the defendant institutions.[111]

Where bilateral agreements concluded before accession are concerned, the Treaty provides[112] that the rights and obligations arising from them are not affected by the Treaty and these provisions of international law must therefore be applied by the Court. However, the Treaty adds that Member States must take all appropriate steps to eliminate the incompatibilities with the Treaties.[113] The Court also decided that, even when a Union act had been declared incompatible with WTO rules by the dispute settlement body, an economic operator could not invoke this incompatibility in a national court.[114]

---

[105] *Cordis v Commission* (T-18/99) [2001] E.C.R. II-913 (45–46).
[106] Directive 2005/35 [2005] O.J. L255/1.
[107] *Intertanko and Others* (C-308/06) [2008] E.C.R. I-4057.
[108] *Portugal v Council* (C-149/96) [1999] E.C.R. I-8395.
[109] *Merck Genericos* (C-431/05) [2007] E.C.R. I-7001.
[110] *Wallentin-Hermann* (C-549/07) [2008] E.C.R. I-11061.
[111] *Fiamm and Others v European Communities* (T-69/00) [2005] E.C.R. II-5393.
[112] See Art.351 TFEU.
[113] See *Budejovicky Budvar* (C-216/01) [2003] E.C.R. I-13617 and *Commission v Sweden* (C-249/06) [2009] E.C.R. I-1335; where the Court found that Sweden had breached Art.351,2 TFEU.
[114] *Van Parys NV* (C-377/02) [2005] E.C.R. I-1465.

9. APPLICATION OF UNION LAW BY THE NATIONAL AUTHORITIES: ADMINISTRATION, LEGISLATURE AND JUDICIARY

4–21   The obligation of all national authorities to apply Union law is laid down, as indicated above, in one of the initial provisions of the EU Treaty: "The Member States shall take any appropriate measure, general or particular, to ensure fulfilment of the obligations arising out of the treaties or resulting from the acts of the institutions of the Union"[115] As indicated elsewhere, the expression "Member State" covers all the territorial parts of a State and all its authorities: legislative, administrative and judiciary. Consequently, a Member State is responsible for damages caused to a third party by a failure of any of those authorities of that State to abide by Union law.[116]

On the other hand, since these national authorities must apply Union law, they enjoy "procedural autonomy" i.e. they apply Union law according to their national procedures; this autonomy is, in turn, tempered, as was seen in the previous chapter, by the principle of equivalence and the principle of effectiveness. As was seen, direct effect of Union rules means that:

> "[I]t is the national courts, which are entrusted with ensuring the legal protection, which citizens derive from the direct effect of the provisions of [Union] law. Accordingly, in the absence of [Union] rules on the subject, it is for the domestic legal system of each Member State to designate the courts having jurisdiction and to determine the procedural conditions governing actions at law intended to ensure the protection of the rights which the citizens have from the direct effect of [Union] law, it being understood that such conditions cannot be less favourable than those relating to similar actions of a domestic nature".[117]

As was briefly pointed out above, Union law does not require national courts to raise of their own motion an issue concerning a possible breach of provisions of Union law, where examination of that issue would oblige them to abandon the passive role assigned to them, by going beyond the ambit of the dispute defined by the parties.[118] However, where, by virtue of domestic law, courts must raise of their own motion points of law based on binding domestic rules which have not been raised by the parties, such an obligation also exists where binding Union rules are concerned.[119] The situation is the same if domestic law confers on courts a discretion to apply of their own volition binding rules of law.

---

[115]   Art.4(3)2 EU.

[116]   See above para.4 of this chapter.

[117]   *Rewe v Landwirtschaftskammer Saarland* (33/76) [1976] E.C.R. 1989.

[118]   *Van Schijndel* (Joined Cases C-430/93 and C-431/93) [1995] E.C.R. I-4705; see also *Peterbroeck* (C-312/93) [1995] E.C.R. I-4599, where the Court held that Union law precluded the application of a national procedural rule that prevented the courts from raising of their own motion a question concerning the compatibility of a national rule with Union law, when the parties were prevented from doing so after a given period. In *Océano Grupo Editorial and Salvat Editores* (Joined Cases C-240/98, C-241/98, C-242/98, C-243/98 and C-244/98) [2000] E.C.R. I-4941, the Court went much farther and stated that "the requirement for an interpretation in conformity with the Directive requires the national court, in particular, to favour the interpretation that would allow it to decline of its own motion the jurisdiction conferred upon it by virtue of an unfair term."

[119]   *Rewe* (33/76) [1976] E.C.R. 1989; [1997] 2 C.M.L.R. 1.

Indeed, pursuant to the principle of co-operation laid down in the Treaty,[120] it is for the national courts to ensure the legal protection which persons derive from the direct effect of provisions of Union law.[121] The basic rule remains, indeed, that it is the national judge who is, in the first place, responsible for the implementation, application, and interpretation of Union law when the parties refer to it in disputes brought before him.

In a 2003 judgment the Court confirmed once more that in the case of a breach of a directive by legislative provisions or by provisions of collective agreements introducing discrimination contrary to that directive:

> "[T]he national courts are required to set aside that discrimination, using all the means at their disposal, and in particular by applying those provisions for the benefit of the class placed at a disadvantage, and are not required to request or await the setting aside of the provision by the legislature, by collective negotiation or otherwise".[122]

In 1993, the Commission published a Notice on the co-operation between the Commission and the national judges, according to which the national judge can, among other things; call upon the Commission for any help he might need in cases before him involving Union law.[123]

10. CONCLUSIONS

As shown by the foregoing considerations, the Union legal order grew and developed mainly at the hands of the Union judges.[124] Over the years, the Court has played an essential role in consolidating the autonomy of Union law, vis–vis municipal and international law, by emphasising its originality and by imposing its precedence. It goes without saying that this task would have been impossible without the co-operation, understanding and adaptability of the national judges; for example, by asking for preliminary rulings, they gave the Court the opportunity to fulfil its task. Nonetheless, the Union Court was, and still is, the driving force.

It should be clear also that the task of the Court is not limited to applying, developing and interpreting Union law *stricto sensu*. According to the Treaty,[125] the Court shall ensure that "the law" is observed. The term "law" in this provision, and as it is understood by the Court, refers to the concept of what is right, much more so than to anything that is described and analysed in this book. Seen in this light, the European Union appears—beyond all the limitations, ambiguities, hesitations and conflicts—as a legal, political, social and economic

4–22

4–23

---

[120] Art.4(3) EU.
[121] *Factortame* (C-213/89) [1990] E.C.R. I/243; [1990] 3 C.M.L.R. 375.
[122] *Kutz-Bauer* (C-187/00) [2003] E.C.R. I-2741.
[123] [1993] O.J. C39/6. See also *Tremblay* (C-91/95 P) [1996] E.C.R. I-5547; [1997] 4 C.M.L.R. 211.
[124] Of course, the Member States and the institutions did also contribute to the consolidation and development of Union law; see, e.g. the Convention on the Law applicable to Contractual Obligations ([1980] O.J. L266/1).
[125] Art.19 EU.

system that, thanks to its balanced institutional structure and inherent potential, constitutes the only possible solution for Europe's problems and the only hope for its development.

FURTHER READING

4–24   René Barents, *The Autonomy of Community Law* (Kluwer Law International, 2004).

Marten Breuer, "State liability for judicial wrongs and Community law: the case *Gerbhard Kbler v Austria*" (2004) E.L.Rev. 243.

Mario Mendez, "The Impact of WTO rulings in the Community legal order", (2004) E.L.Rev. 517.

Liv Jaeckel, "The duty to protect fundamental rights in the European Community", (2003) E.L.Rev. 508.

Margot Horspool and Matthieu Humphreys, *European Union Law*, 5th edn (2008, Oxford University Press).

PART 2

The Institutions and Bodies of the Union and the Financing of its Activities

INTRODUCTION

Among the various bodies established by, or in pursuance of, the Treaties, seven are referred to as being part of the "institutional framework" of the Union: the European Parliament ("Parliament"), the European Council, the Council ("Council"), the European Commission ("Commission"), the Court of Justice ("Court"), the European Central Bank ("ECB") and the Court of Auditors. The aim of this framework is to promote the values of the Union, advance its objectives, serve its interests (those of its citizens and those of the Member States) and ensure the consistency, effectiveness and continuity of its policies and actions.[1]

II–01

What distinguishes an institution from other Union bodies is the fact that an Institution, generally speaking, can "act", i.e. take binding decisions[2] and that its members are either elected nationally (Council and Parliament) or appointed by the governments of the Member States or by the Council. The other organs operate in specific fields and either have a purely advisory task, or take decisions which are not generally binding.

Only the Union,[3] the EIB, the Supply Agency of Euratom, the ECB and a few other bodies and agencies have legal personality and capacity.[4] When the Union acquires or disposes of property or is party to legal proceedings (outside the

---

[1] Art.13(1) EU. Other bodies set up by the Treaties are, for instance, the Economic and Social Committee (Arts 300 and 301 to 304 TFEU) , the Committee of the Regions (Arts 300 and 305 to 307 TFEU), a European System of Central Banks and a European Central Bank (Art.8 EC), the European Investment Bank (EIB) (Arts 308 and 309 TFEU and Protocol on the Statute of the EIB), the Monetary Committee (Art.134 TFEU) and the Committee of Permanent Representatives (Art.240(3) TFEU). For bodies/agencies set up by the institutions in pursuance of powers conferred upon them by the Treaties, see, for instance, the European Environmental Agency (Regulation 1210/90 [1990] O.J. L 120/1 and below, the chapter on Decentralised Bodies of the Union).

[2] This follows from the wording of Art.13(2) TFEU: "each institution shall act within the limits of the powers conferred on in the Treaties".

[3] Art.47 TFEU.

[4] Art.335 TFEU; see *Lachmüller v Commission* (Joined Cases 43 etc. /59) [1960] E.C.R. 463 at 472: "that personality is one of public law." See also *Commission v Council* (22/70) [1971] E.C.R. 263 at 274(4); C.M.L.R. 335, where the Court decided that having this legal personality, "means that in its external relations, the Union enjoys the capacity to establish contractual links with third countries, over the whole field of objectives defined in Part I of the Treaty." For the EIB see Art.129 TFEU, and for the Supply Agency, Euratom, Art.54; see also Court Ruling 1/78, [1978] E.C.R. 2151. Other organs with legal personality are, among others, the European Centre for the Development of

Court), it is represented by the Commission. However, the Union is represented by each of the institutions, by virtue of their administrative autonomy, in matters relating to their respective operation.[5] With the exception of the Common Foreign and Security Policy and other cases provided in the Treaties,[6] agreements with one or more States or international organisations are negotiated by the Commission and concluded by the Council for the Union.[7]

II–02 The first European institutions, i.e. the High Authority, the Common Assembly, the Special Council of Ministers and the Court of Justice were set up by the Treaty of Paris of 1951 establishing the European Coal and Steel Community (ECSC).[8] Similar institutions: an Assembly, a Council, a Commission and a Court of Justice, were set up by the Treaties of Rome establishing the European Economic Community (EEC), and the European Community for Atomic Energy (Euratom). In theory this meant 12 institutions: three of each kind. However, the Convention on certain institutions common to the European Communities[9] provided for a single Assembly and a single Court of Justice for the three Communities.

Nonetheless this left three Councils and the High Authority plus two Commissions, beside the one Assembly and the one Court; a total of eight institutions. A further rationalisation was introduced by the so-called Merger Treaty,[10] which established the "Council of the European Communities" to replace the three Councils and the "Commission of the European Communities" to replace the High Authority and the EEC and Euratom Commissions. These four institutions exercised, from then on, the powers and jurisdiction conferred by the three Treaties on the various institutions they replaced, in accordance with the provisions of the relevant Treaties.[11] A fifth institution was added by the EU Treaty that "upgraded" the Court of Auditors. As indicated above, the Treaty of Lisbon included the European Council and the ECB among the institutions.

It might be interesting to note that, according to the Preamble of the Merger Treaty, the merger of the institutions is seen as a step in the direction of the "unification of the three Communities". This "exercise" was carried out in the draft Treaty on a Constitution for Europe that amalgamated all the existing Treaty texts, as amended, into a single one. This draft Treaty was not ratified and the Treaty of Lisbon maintains the three Treaties.

Vocational Training, the European Foundation for the Improvement of Living and Working Conditions and the European Environment Agency; these are described below in the chapter on Decentralised Bodies of the Union.

[5] Art.335 TFEU.

[6] Art.27(1) EU; for the representation in other matters, see Art.335 TFEU.

[7] Art.218 TFEU).

[8] Art.7 ECSC (no longer exists).

[9] This Convention was annexed to the EEC and Euratom Treaties, and signed, together with these Treaties, at Rome on April 25, 1957. It was repealed by then Art.9(1) EU which, however, retained its essential elements.

[10] Treaty establishing a single Council and a single Commission of the European Communities, signed at Brussels on April 8, 1965. This Treaty was also repealed by then Art.9(1) EU. Its essential provisions were, however, retained, and according to its then Art.11(2) there will be no change in the legal effects of the Acts in force adopted on the basis of the Treaties.

[11] Arts 1 and 3 Convention; Arts 1 and 9 Merger Treaty.

CHAPTER 5

The European Parliament[1]
("Parliament")

The European Treaties originally referred to this institution as the "Assembly". In 1962, the Assembly decided to call itself the "European Parliament[2] and since then the other institutions adopted that denomination, also in legislative acts[3]. The name was only formally changed in the Treaties as from the Single European Act (SEA) but only in the articles modified by it. The general replacement of the name "assembly" intervened only as a result of the Treaty of Maastricht.

    Under the original Treaties, Parliament's competences were limited to a consultative role. This situation was considered unsatisfactory. Under the Treaties powers were transferred to the Communities but democratic control at this level was insufficient. However, the decision making process, until the Treaty reforms from the end of the 20th century mainly invested in the Council only, was not subject anymore to control by national parliaments.

    This situation, generally called *the democratic deficit*, gave a boost to Parliament's competences in budgetary and budgetary control matters (1970 and 1975 Reform Treaties), and in legislative and other fields in the Treaties of Maastricht, Amsterdam, Nice and Lisbon.

    In most of the areas of Union competence the democratic deficit has been substantially reduced or eliminated. However, the role of Parliament is still not comparable to the role of national parliament. The budgetary powers comprise expenditure, but there are no corollary powers in terms of revenues. And though Art.225 TFEU caters for a right of Parliament to request the Commission to take legislative initiatives, a right of legislative initiative does not exist. The emergence of the European Council and the increase of its role reinforces the democratic deficit.

    Some critics contend that Parliament is not a parliament in the generally accepted sense of the word, or, as the German Constitutional Court recently wrote: the European Parliament "is not a body of representation of a sovereign European people"[4]. Comparisons with national Parliaments are thus difficult to make. Parliament is the representative body of the Union citizens within the Union context and exercises a parliamentary role of democratic control here. The

5–01

5–02

---

[1] Art.14 EU and Arts 223–234 TFEU.
[2] Resolution of March 30, [1962] J.O.1045. On March 20, 1958 the Assembly had decided to call itself the "European Parliamentary Assembly".
[3] See, e.g. Regulation 214/79 concerning the European Regional Development Fund [1979] O.J. L35/1.
[4] BVerfG, 2vE 2/08vm 30.6.2009, *Absatz-Nr* (1–421).

Union is no State, and the role of Parliament has to be seen in the constitutional structure of the Union, based on conferral, checks and balances between the Institutions, and between the Union and its member States. Within this context, and despite the persistence of a democratic deficit in some areas, Parliament operates as a genuine parliamentary body.

1. THE MEMBERS OF PARLIAMENT, THEIR MANDATE AND LEGAL POSITION

(1) Composition

5–03 Parliament consists of "representatives of the Union's citizens".[5] The TEU establishes the maximum number of Members at 750 plus the President (see below for this formula) and provides for basic parameters as to the number of members per State: representation of citizens shall be degressively proportional, with a minimum threshold of six members per State, and a maximum of 96. The exact composition is to be decided by the Council, on the initiative of Parliament and with its consent.[6]

Due to accessions, the maximum number of seats has been gradually increased throughout the years. Upon each accession, during a transitional period until the following legislative period, the seats for new Member States were allocated on top of the maximum, followed by a slight revision of the maximum number of seats as from the new legislative period which means that all the Member States see their membership numbers reduced after that later date.

Likewise, the Nice Treaty provided that the number "shall not exceed 732".[7] From January 1, 2007, until the end of the 2004–2009 legislative period, there were 785 members,[8] and as from the beginning of the 2009–2014 legislative period the maximum was initially set at 736 members in the latest Accession act signed in 2005.[9]

Before the Treaty of Lisbon, the Treaties consistently provided, apart from the maximum number, the breakdown of seats per Member State. The main criterion for the allocation of seats was (and is) the population of the States concerned and degressive proportionality was de facto applied: the smallest member State, Malta, currently has 5 seats for 300,000 inhabitants, Germany currently 99 seats for 82 million inhabitants.

5–04 Until the Treaty of Lisbon comprehensive criteria were never explicitly laid down and politico-historical developments influenced the number of seats rather than the real size of the population in some cases[10].

The draft Constitutional Treaty already laid down the system of—what was to become—Art.14 of the TEU, be it with a maximum of 750 seats. When the

---

[5] Art.14(2) EU, which also provides that the number shall not exceed 750, plus the President.
[6] Art.14 EU.
[7] Art.2,17 Treaty of Nice modifying the then Art.189(2) of the EC Treaty, [2001] O.J. C80/20.
[8] Art.24 Act of Accession Bulgaria and Romania [2005] O.J. L157/203.
[9] Act of Accession Bulgaria and Romania [2005] O.J. L 157/203, Art.9.
[10] Since the 1950s parity always existed between the 4 largest member States, only Germany received more seats upon the German reunification. In 1986, Spain obtained a second commissioner but paid this politically through les seats in parliament. Population growth was not taken into account.

Lisbon mandate (June 2007) confirmed the line taken, Parliament and European Council reached a political agreement on the breakdown which was based on degressive proportionality more realistically—within the limits of the Treaty, i.e. the minimum a maximum number of seats—based on population in October 2007[11].

A short historical and mathematical survey is required to understand the current composition. Seventeen new seats were expected to be allocated during the 2009 elections: to the increase in seats (750 compared to 736), 3 seats were to be added due to the lower number of German seats (96 instead of 99). Italy, seeing the historical equal footing with France and the UK lost, obtained *in fine* an extra seat during the IGC, which explains the formula of 750 plus the president. Upon the signing of the Treaty of Lisbon, the package was reflected in Declarations 4 and 5.

However the Treaty of Lisbon only entered into force after the 2009 elections. A specific protocol was needed in order to accommodate the extra seats[12], entering in force on December 1, 2011. As it would be inappropriate to reduce the number of German MEPs during the legislature, the 18 new seats added up to the 736 seats. The accession of Croatia in July 2013 brought about a temporary top-up of 12 seats above the 754 thus established, bringing the total to 766.[13]

As of the legislative period starting in 2014, the total number will be 751. On the basis of the 2007 parameters, but taking into account the accession of Croatia, the European Parliament made a revised proposal in spring 2013 and the European Council adopted the final Decision on Parliament's composition in June 2013.[14]

(2) Election of the Members

Until the first direct elections in 1979, the members of Parliament were designated by the respective national parliaments from among their members,[15] which meant dual membership. Although the ECSC Treaty[16] already provided for election by direct universal suffrage, it was not until September 20, 1976 that the Act concerning direct election was finally adopted by the Representatives of the Member States in Council: according to this Act, elections by direct universal suffrage should be held "in accordance with a uniform procedure in all Member

5–05

---

[11] See Resolution EP P6_TA(2007)0429 of October 11, 2007, based on Report A6-0351/2007 ("Lamssoure-Severin report") of the Committee on constitutional affairs, for the reasoning.

[12] Protocol amending the Protocol on Transitional Provisions annexed to the Treaty on European Union, to the Treaty on the Functioning of the European Union and to the Treaty establishing the European Atomic Energy Community, 23-06-2010: Brussels, O.J. 2010, C263/1.

[13] Breakdown per Member State on *http://www.europarl.europa.eu* [accessed August 23, 2013].

[14] European Council Decision of June 28, 2013 on the composition of the European Parliament, O.J. 2013, L181/57.

[15] This was done according to a procedure laid down by each Member State. See former Art.138 EC which lapsed on July 17, 1978, in accordance with Art.14 of the Act concerning direct election. MEPs receive a uniform salary of €5,677 (Council Decision of April 27, 1999). However, this is not the case presently (2012).

[16] Art.21(3) ECSC (no longer valid).

States".[17] The Rules of Procedure of Parliament[18] provide in rule 1 that: "[T]he European Parliament is the assembly elected pursuant to the Treaties, the Act of September 20, 1976, concerning the election of the members of the European Parliament by direct universal suffrage, and national legislation deriving from the Treaties".[19]

Parliament was to draw up proposals and the Council, after obtaining the assent of Parliament, was to lay down the appropriate provisions, which it shall recommend to Member States for adoption in accordance with their respective constitutional requirements. For the Member States, nothing binding, in other words. Since it was not possible to agree on such procedures, the 1979, 1984, 1989, 1994, 1999 and 2004 elections were held in accordance with the method of voting decided nationally.[20] In 2002, the Act concerning direct election was amended by a Council Decision to enable members to be elected by direct universal suffrage in accordance with principles common to all Member States, while leaving Member States free to apply their national provisions in respect of aspects not governed by the Act.[21] The latter now provides that the members of Parliament, "shall be elected on the basis of proportional representation, using the list system or the single transferable vote", but added that, "Member States may authorise voting based on a preferential list system in accordance with the procedure they adopt."

The necessary measures are now to be laid down by the Council, "acting in accordance with a special legislative procedure, upon proposal and with the consent of Parliament. The national ratification procedures still apply."[22] Parliament's constitutional affairs committee aims to achieve, at least partially, a genuine European list system[23] but politically this effort seems to be a bridge too far in this stage.

Citizens of the Union residing in a Member State of which they are not a national have the right to vote and to stand in elections for Parliament.[24] A Council directive lays down detailed arrangements.[25]

---

[17] Act concerning direct election of representatives of the European Parliament by direct universal suffrage annexed to Council Decision 76/787 of September 20, 1976, [1976] O.J. L278/1, amended: Decision 2002/772 (see below).

[18] Parliament's Rules of Procedure are regularly modified. They are published in a booklet version (last edition "7th parliamentary term - December 2012" and on Parliament's website *http://www.europarl.europa.eu* [accessed August 23, 2013].

[19] See Arts 223–234 TFEU and Art.14 EU.

[20] Act concerning direct election, Art.7(2): "pending the entry into force of the uniform electoral procedure, and subject to other provisions of the Act, the electoral procedure shall be governed in each Member State by its national provisions". All the Member States apply, with some variations, a proportional representation system, via party lists.

[21] Decision 2002/772, [2002] O.J. L283/1; corrigendum: [2009] O.J. L.126/23.

[22] Art.223(1)2 TFEU.

[23] Report A7-0027/2012, 2.2.2012, not yet adopted in Plenary.

[24] Art.22(2) TFEU. See *Spain v UK* (C-145/04) [2006] E.C.R. I-7917, where the Court stated that the right to vote is not limited to citizens!

[25] See Directive 93/109 laying down detailed arrangements for the exercise of the right to vote, and to stand as a candidate in elections to the EP, for citizens of the Union, residing in a Member State of which they are not a national [1993] O.J. L329/34.

(3) The Member's Mandate and legal position

(a) Electoral Act

Members of the European Parliament (MEPs) are elected for a term of five years, by direct universal suffrage in a free and secret ballot.[26] Anyone can stand for Parliament,[27] it being understood that, upon election, the rules concerning incompatibility[28] apply.

    5–06

Before 1979, MEPs had to be members of a national parliament; as from the 2004 and for some Member States the 2009 elections the Act concerning direct election fully prohibits combined mandates. [29] Already before 2004 incompatibilities existed at national level and many political parties have done the same in their internal rules. This situation has not ended the debate on combined mandates. The reason for their abolition is that fulfilling two mandates is an extremely demanding task and that conflicts of interests should be avoided. However, those in support of combined mandates contend that the disjunction between the two has somehow estranged the European Parliament from the national ones, thereby not only eliminating a chance for political integration, but also decreasing the political clout of the MEPs.

Substantive provisions on the Members' mandate are laid down in Art.6 of the 1976 electoral Act (individual and personal vote, no instructions or binding mandate). The provisions on the mandate and the term of office are also worked out in the Rules of Procedure. Further, the Members' Statute (see below) also contains provisions on the nature of the mandate. They are partially overlapping with the two above instruments, but add a reference to the Members being "free and independent", and a provision that agreements on resignation are null and void.

(b) Members' Statute

The Statute for members of Parliament was adopted in September 2005[30] after a lengthy procedure; it covers the rules and general conditions applicable to the exercise of their mandate, as well as provisions on remuneration and reimbursement of expenses. Parliament already paid the expenses of Members, but the remuneration was prior to the Statute paid by the Member state of election, according to provisions applicable to national MPs.

    5–07

---

[26] Art.14(3) EU.

[27] Including, e.g. in the UK, peers and ministers of religion, who are excluded from election to Westminster.

[28] Act concerning direct election, Art.6(1) and (2).

[29] Act concerning direct election, Art.7. The last derogations for Ireland and the UK lapsed as from the 2009–2014 legislative period.

[30] [2005] O.J. L262/1. Legal basis is Art.223(2) TFEU: "Regulations and general conditions governing the performance of the duties of the members are laid down by Parliament, acting by means of regulations, on its own initiative, in accordance with a special legislative procedure, after seeking the opinion of the Commission, and the approval of the Council. All rules or conditions relating to the taxation of members and former members require unanimity within the Council".

The Statute is applicable as from the 7th legislative period (July 2009). Implementing provisions are adopted by the Bureau of Parliament[31] and regularly updated.

(c) Privileges and Immunities

5–08   Under the Protocol on the privileges and immunities of the European Union, Members' privileges and immunities consist of three elements:

1.   freedom from administrative restrictions and, in terms of customs control, assimilation to national diplomats;
2.   freedom from inquiry, detention or legal proceedings in respect of opinions expressed or votes cast in the performance of their duties;
3.   during the sessions of Parliament, as to privileges and immunities, assimilation to members of national parliaments when in their own countries, and immunity from detention and legal proceedings when on the territory of another Member State.[32]

Under Art.9 of the Protocol, immunity can be waived by Parliament, but Parliament can decide to uphold immunity. The internal procedure is described in the Rules of Procedure.

Cases on administrative restrictions and detention are rare; most issues concern legal proceedings.

Formally, in an action before a national court for damages brought against a member, in respect of opinions he has expressed, the national court, which has not received information from that member regarding his request to Parliament seeking defence of his immunity,[33] is not obliged to request Parliament to give a decision on whether the conditions of that immunity are met. When the national court is informed that the member has made a request to Parliament for defence of its immunity, the national court must stay procedure, and request Parliament to issue its opinion as soon as possible.

5–09   Where the national court considers that the member enjoys the immunity provided in the Protocol, it must dismiss the action brought against the member.[34] Immunity can only be waived by Parliament.[35]

In substance, as to legal proceedings not duty-related (civil, administrative, ordinary criminal matters) Parliament tends to waive immunity. The more difficult item is the question whether a proceeding has a link with the

---

[31] See Decision of the Bureau concerning implementing measures for the Statute of the members of the E.P. [2009] O.J. C159/1.

[32] Protocol no.7 on the Privileges and Immunities of the European Union , Arts 7 to 9. See, e.g. *Wybot v Faure* (149/85) [1986] E.C.R. 2403; [1987] 1 C.M.L.R. 819 from which it follows that Parliament is always "in session", and *Rothley* (T-17/00) [2000] E.C.R. II-2085, concerning the right of the Union Antifraud Office to inspect the offices of MEPs. This right was provided for by an amendment of Parliament's Rules, following an inter-institutional agreement ([1999] O.J. L136/20); the amendment was contested by a number of MEPs, first in the CFI, and later in the Court of Justice (*Rothley and Others v Parliament* (C-167/02) [2004] E.C.R. I-3149); in both instances the request for annulment was rejected.

[33] Protocol on Privileges and Immunities, Art.8 and Rules, Art.6(3).

[34] *Marra* (Joined Cases C-200/07 and C-201/07) [2008] E.C.R. I-7929.

[35] Protocol on Privileges and Immunities, Ch.III, Art.18, last indent.

performance of the duty—in that case immunity cannot be waived. Parliament's position is subject to judicial control. The Court may decide on the question of immunity and is not bound by the outcome of Parliament's internal consideration.

In 2012, the Court, interpreting Art.8 of the Protocol, decided that a statement made by a member beyond the precincts of Parliament and giving rise to prosecution in his Member State of origin for the offence of insulting behaviour does not constitute an opinion expressed in the performance of his parliamentary duties unless that statement amounts to a subjective appraisal having a direct, obvious connection with the performance of those duties.[36]

2. PARLIAMENT'S INTERNAL ORGANISATION

Like any national Parliament, the internal organisation of Parliament is laid down in Rules of Procedure. Parliament's Rules are a living instrument: they were initially established in 1958 but are regularly revised, not only due to Treaty changes but also as a result of internal reconsideration. Traditionally, fundamental revisions take place before each new legislative period (like in 2004 and 2009).   **5–10**

Parliament's Rules define the role and tasks of its bodies of which the main, apart from the Plenary, are:

- the President;
- the Bureau (consisting of the President and the Vice-Presidents), responsible for internal organisation and internal financial matters. A body linked to the Bureau are the Questers, responsible for financial and administrative entitlements of Members;
- the Conference of Presidents, consisting of the President of the Political groups, responsible for political guidance and setting the agenda.

They also regulate *in extenso* the work of the Committees, the legislative and other procedures, and the work of the Plenary. In a Parliament of over 750 Members, much comes down to a tight internal organisation and the Committees have important preparatory tasks, together with the political groups. The successive amendments to Parliament's Rules have invested important decision-making and preparatory powers in the Conference of Presidents and the Committees, notably in inter-institutional negotiations. This contributes to efficiency but is often considered to entail a weakening of the Plenary, less attractive debates, and a reduction of Parliament's visibility.

The Rules of Procedure play an important part in the development of Parliament's position within the Union. Like the system of inter-institutional agreements (see below) providing Parliament with influence where this is sometimes not expressly provided in the Treaties, Parliament has used the Rules of Procedure as an instrument to increase its powers, often with success.[37]   **5–11**

---

[36] Patriciello (C-496/10) order of January 19, 2012, not yet reported.

[37] Good examples are the hearings of candidates for senior offices (Commission, Court of Auditors) and the right to put questions to (and obtain answers from) the Council. Except for the Foreign Affairs and Security policy, it is still not provided for by the Treaty (see Art.230,3 TFEU), but the Council does answer the questions put to it by Parliament.

However, as shall be seen in respect of the approval of the designated members of the Commission, it seems that Parliament has attributed to itself more powers than provided for under the Treaties, and, since the Rules do not bind the other institutions, it remains to be seen whether they will comply with what are, after all, only Parliament's wishes.[38]

For the sake of providing a comprehensive guide, Parliament annexes sometimes Regulations and inter-institutional agreements to its Rules—though they are not adopted according to the same procedure.

Mention must be made here of the right of access to documents of Parliament, of the Council and of the Commission, granted to any citizen of the Union, and to any natural or legal person residing or having its registered office in a Member State.[39] See, in this respect, a Bureau Decision of Latest version of the Rules: 7th parliamentary term—March 2011.[40]

Parliament's bodies

(a) The Political Groups and the Conference of Presidents

5–12   Political groups are not to be confused with national political parties; since the 2004 elections, some 157 national political parties were represented in Parliament and, for instance, in the PPE-DE Group, 50 members ware representatives of 50 different national political parties. Indeed, representatives sit in *multinational* political groups,[41] each having its own statute and enjoying a degree of financial and organisational autonomy.

The representatives are free to choose the Group to which they want to belong, and unless they are a member of a national political party that is a member of that group, they must ask to belong and be accepted.

The groups play a central role in coordinating the political line to be taken as to committee proposals and votes, though the "intra group discipline" is finally a political process, the Act concerning direct election provides that representatives shall vote on an individual basis, and that they shall not be bound by any instruction, nor receive a binding mandate.[42] Many groups consist of members of various political families. As the members not belonging to a group, the so-called "non-attached", enjoy fewer facilities in terms of resources than groups, there is a dynamic to create groups. Thus especially outside the mainstream political families, a number of groups consist of component entities that have few points of their agenda in common. Rules lay down only a limited number of conditions, and require only a minimum of political affiliation—purely technical groups are not accepted.[43]

---

[38] Rules of Procedure, r.106 "Election of the Commission"! Art.17 TFEU: "the President and the other Members of the Commission shall be subject as a body to a vote of approval by the European Parliament."

[39] Regulation1049/2001 [2001] O.J. L145/43.

[40] [2011] O.J. L116/1.

[41] For recent figures on composition per Member State and per Group see *http://www.europarl. europa.eu* [accessed August 23, 2013].

[42] Act concerning direct elections, Art.4(1); ([1976] O.J. L278/1).

[43] See *Front National* (C-486/01 P) [2004] E.C.R. I-6289.

According to the Rules of Procedure, a political group must comprise **5–13** members "elected in, at least, one-quarter of the Member States. The minimum number of members required to form a political group shall be 25".[44] Clearly, this rule was made to encourage the formation of transnational groups, which is one of the characteristics of the European Parliament.

The Chairs of the political groups are reunited in the Conference of Presidents. The Conference of Presidents takes the important decisions on the organisation of Parliament's work and matters of legislative planning, sets the competences of the committees, sets the agenda for the plenary, and is responsible for the relations with other institutions.

Political groups should neither be confounded with political parties at European level, referred to in the Treaty on European Union. They have a role as contributing to forming European political awareness and expressing the will of the citizens of the Union.[45] Parliament and Council must lay down, acting in accordance with the ordinary legislative procedure,[46] the regulations governing them and, in particular, the rules regarding their funding.[47] These parties[48] have legal personality in the Member State, in which their seat is located. These conditions were laid down in 2003, by Parliament and Council; they also lay down rules regarding the funding of the parties.[49]

Though there is certainly a philosophy behind that, these European political parties may at some moment replace national parties for European elections—in 2012 the Commission proposed a reform in the direction of a genuine European statute—there is no absolute convergence between European parties and groups.

(b) Parliamentary Committees and the Conference of Committee Chairs

The Rules of Procedure provide that Parliament can set up standing or temporary **5–14** committees,[50] which in turn, may appoint one or more subcommittees. The chairmen of all the Committees form the "Conference of Committee Chairmen". These Chairmen may make recommendations to the Conference of Presidents[51] about the work of the Committees and also discuss horizontal issues. The Conference of Committee Chairmen can be instructed to carry out specific tasks.[52]

The members of the Committees are elected by Parliament after nominations have been submitted by the political groups. It is within the Committees that the

---

[44] Rules of Procedure, r.30,2. See *Front national and Martinez v Parliament* (Joined Cases C-486/01 and C-488/01 P-R) [2002] E.C.R. I-1843.

[45] Art.10(4) EU.

[46] Art.294 TFEU.

[47] Art.224 TFEU.

[48] Rules of Procedure, rr.208–210.

[49] Regulation 2004/2003 on the regulations governing political parties at European level, and the rules regarding their funding [2003] O.J. L297/1, see Decision of the Bureau laying down the procedure for implementing Regulation 2004/2003 [2011] O.J. C112/1; see also Decision of the Bureau of Parliament, laying down the procedures for implementing said Regulation [2004] O.J. C155/1.

[50] Rules of Procedure, rr.183–192. See, for instance, Temporary Committee on policy challenges and budgetary means of the enlarged Union 2007–2013.

[51] Rules of Procedure, r.25.

[52] Rules of Procedure, r.27.

real parliamentary work is carried out. When, for instance, a proposal is sent to Parliament by the Commission, it is assigned to a given Committee (which becomes the leading Committee) to examine the proposal and report on it. Other Committees act as advisory committees. In horizontal issue, this advisory procedure is reinforced whilst sometimes two or more committees are jointly competent. Conflicts occurring are settled by the Conference of Presidents. In the leading Committee, each Political Group has a co-ordinator, who owns a number of points, depending on the strength of his Group in Parliament; these points count when it comes to designate the rapporteur, who plays an extremely important role, since he drafts the resolution that will be sent to the plenary for approval. Only he can put a draft resolution on the agenda of the Committee, when he thinks he has a majority in favour of it. The other Groups designate their own rapporteur—"shadow-rapporteur"—so there are, in fact, 1+7 rapporteurs! The leading Committee adopts a draft resolution to be submitted to Parliament in plenary session. At that point, amendments may be proposed, either in writing or orally, by a Group or 32 MEPs. Parliament expresses its final position in the form of a legislative act.[53]

There are presently 20 committees,[54] 2 subcommittees[55] and 2 special committees.[56]

(c)   The Bureau and the Quaestors

5–15   Parliament elects its President[57] and 14 Vice-Presidents,[58] which together form the Bureau, i.e. the executive body. The Bureau is responsible for the internal financial and logistic organisation of the Parliament, its Secretariat, and drafts the estimates of Parliament's section of the general budget.[59]

The Rules of Procedure also provide for a Conference of Presidents,[60] mentioned above, consisting of the President of Parliament and the Presidents of the political groups. The Bureau constitutes the ultimate centre of decision-making for all internal matters of Parliament. The Rules of Procedure also provide for the election of Quaestors; they are responsible for administrative and financial matters directly concerning Members, pursuant to guidelines laid down by the Bureau[61]—they are members of the Bureau with advisory capacity.

---

[53] Rules of Procedure, r.180.
[54] Foreign Affairs, Development, International Trade, Budgets, Budgetary Control, Economic and Monetary Affairs, Employment and Social Affairs, Environment, Public Health and Food Safety, Industry, Research and Energy, Internal Market and Consumer Protection, Transport and Tourism, Regional Development, Agriculture, Fisheries, Culture and Education, Legal Affairs, Civil Liberties, Justice and Home Affairs, Constitutional Affairs, Women's Rights and Gender Equality and Petitions.
[55] Security and Defence and Human Rights.
[56] One on the financial crisis and the other on the financial perspective.
[57] Art.14(1) EU.
[58] Rules of Procedure, r.15.
[59] Rules of Procedure, r.75b.
[60] Rules of Procedure, r.24.
[61] Rules of Procedure, r.16.

(d)   Parliament's Secretariat

Parliament has its own staff totalling, in 2012, around 6,000 posts, grouped in a   **5–16**
Secretariat headed by a Secretary-General. It is divided over 11 Directorates-
General located in Luxembourg and Brussels.[62] Staff is subject to the Staff
regulations. In 2009 the Staff Regulations were amended in order to
accommodate personal assistants of Members.

(e)   Sessions and Meeting Place(s)

Parliament holds annual sessions, i.e. legally lasting 12 months, but actually sits   **5–17**
only during 12 part-time sessions, which last four days.[63] Parliament meets,
without requiring to be convened, on the second Tuesday in March. Parliament
may also meet in extraordinary[64] session, and has instituted so-called additional
sessions.
   At the Edinburgh European Council in December 1992, it was decided that
the:

> "European Parliament shall have its seat in Strasburg, where 12 periods of monthly
> plenary sessions, including the budget session shall be held. The periods of
> additional plenary sessions shall be held in Brussels. The Committees of the
> European Parliament shall meet in Brussels. The Secretariat of the European
> Parliament, and its departments shall remain in Luxemburg".[65]

Historically, the choice of Strasbourg had both a symbolic (French–German
reconciliation) and a practical political function (Strasbourg is the seat of the
Council of Europe's Parliamentary Assembly, which already existed when the
Communities were founded). However, the obligation to hold 12 sessions in
Strasbourg while Parliament's main political activities now take place in Brussels
are considered outdated, inefficient and too resource-consuming by many.
However, the Treaties have never been changed and attempts of Parliament to
modify its modus operandi have proven unsuccessful in Court.[66]

---

[62] I. Presidence, II. Committees and delegations, III. Information/public relations, IV. Studies, V. Personnel, VI. Administration, VII. Translation/General services and VIII. Finances and Financial control.

[63] Parliament is understood to be in session even when not actually sitting, and is so until the session is declared closed; see *Wagner v Fohrman* (101/63) [1964] E.C.R. 195 and *Wybot v Faure* (149/85) [1986] E.C.R. 2391.

[64] Art.229,2 TFEU.

[65] Conclusions of the Presidency: Decision taken by common agreement between the Representatives of the Governments of the Member States, on the location of the seats of the institutions and of certain bodies and departments of the European Communities, Art.1(a): [1992] Bull.12–24. This Decision was incorporated in the Protocol on the location of the institutions and of certain bodies and departments of the EC and of Europol, attached to the TFEU: [1997] O.J. C340/112; [2010] O.J. C83/265.

[66] Parliament's decisions to hold its sessions wherever it decides was successfully attacked by Luxembourg: *Luxembourg v Parliament* (230/81) [1983] E.C.R. 255; [1983] 2 C.M.L.R. 726, *Luxembourg v Parliament* (108/83) [1984] E.C.R. 1945; [1986] 2 C.M.L.R. 507: Parliament has no right to decide on the location of its departments, and *France v European Parliament* (358/85) [1986] E.C.R. 2149; [1988] 3 C.M.L.R. 786, *France v European Parliament* (C-345/95) [1997] E.C.R. I-5215 and *France v European Parliament* (Joined cases C-237/11 and C-238/11) judgment of December 1, 2012, not yet reported.

Members of the Commission may (and do) attend all the meetings of Parliament and, on invitation, those of the Committees; the Council is represented at all the plenary sessions. The minutes of the meetings are published in the *Official Journal of the European Union* and the full debates in an annex thereto.

Except for the adoption of a motion of censure, and certain decisions within the co-operation, co-decision and budgetary procedures, Parliament acts by a majority of the votes cast.[67] There is a quorum when the majority of the representatives are present; however, as long as there is no request to do so, the number of members present is not ascertained.[68]

3.   TASKS AND POWERS OF PARLIAMENT

5–18   As set out above the competences of the Union are based on the principle of conferral. Like all the Union institutions, Parliament, "shall act within the limits of the powers conferred on it by the Treaties".[69] These are the only powers the institutions may exercise.

Parliament exercises, jointly with the Council, legislative and budgetary functions. It also exercises functions of political control and consultation; as laid down in the Treaties. Furthermore Parliament exercises competences in matters of key appointments of which the TEU mentions the election of the President of the Commission[70]. Previously, Parliament only had "advisory and supervisory" powers, but this changed with the SEA and even more so, with the Maastricht, Amsterdam, Nice and Lisbon Treaties. The Amsterdam Treaty, as shall be seen, provided for the so-called "co-decision power" which is now called the ordinary legislative procedure.

It should be noted, however, that since 1970, Parliament exercises certain deciding powers in the budgetary field.[71] Nonetheless, as was just mentioned, Parliament does not yet fully exercise all the attributes of an elected representative body, i.e. legislation and the raising of taxes. The TFEU provides for jurisdictional control of the Court over "acts of the European Parliament intended to produce legal effects vis–vis third parties."[72] There are no further indications in the Treaties concerning the precise meaning of those acts. The same provision existed in the EC Treaty, and one example could be a "legislative resolution".[73]

The tasks and powers of Parliament, in the order in which they appear in Art.14 TEU shall be examined hereunder.

---

[67] Art.231 TFEU .

[68] Act concerning direct election, Art.6(1) and (2) (quoted above).

[69] Art.13(2) EU.

[70] Art.14(1) EU.

[71] Arts 313–316 TFEU .

[72] Art.263 TFEU.

[73] [2009] O.J. L21/7: legislative resolution with a view to adopting a Council Decision adjusting the basic salaries and allowances applicable to Europol.

(1) Exercise, Jointly with the Council, Legislative Functions

As mentioned already, it is in this area that the SEA, and more so the EU,   **5–19**
Amsterdam, Nice and Lisbon Treaties, introduced the most far-reaching changes.
The SEA increased the cases wherein Parliament must be consulted by the
Council before the latter adopts an act, and introduced the "co-operation
procedure". The EU Treaty provided for the so-called "co-decision" procedure,
which was extended by the Amsterdam and Nice Treaties. Presently there are,
besides the simple consultation of Parliament by the Council, two different
legislative procedures[74]: the "ordinary" one and the "special" one. The Treaties
also provide for "consultationé" of Parliament by the Council and the "consent"
of Parliament for a limited number of acts to be adopted by the Council.

(a) Types of procedures

(i) Consultation

At the beginning, this used to be the general rule and practically all Treaty   **5–20**
provisions dealing with acts of the Council would read: "the Council shall, on a
proposal from the Commission and after consulting the European Parliament . . .".[75]

The successive Treaty revisions enhanced Parliament's role in legislation by
introducing and enhancing co-decision (the former name of what is now the
ordinary legislative procedure) and assent procedures. Presently there are only a
few instances, where Parliament is merely "consulted".[76]

When the Council enacts regulations, directives or decisions, the consultation
of Parliament is initiated by the Council on the basis of a proposal submitted to it
by the Commission. This proposal may be altered by the Commission as long as
the Council has not acted on it at any time during the procedure leading to the
adoption of the Act.[77] This, for example, allows the Commission, when
Parliament has expressed an opinion on the proposal, to take it into account by
submitting a modified proposal. In February 1990, the Commission proposed a
Code of Conduct that would ensure more effective co-operation in the
decision-making process, with a bigger role for Parliament in the field of external
relations.[78]

---

[74] Art.289(1) and (2) TFEU.
[75] See, e.g. former Art.37(2) EC, last sub-paragraph.
[76] Art.48(2) and (6) EU, modification of the Treaties; Art.19 TFEU: combat discrimination;
Art.148(2) TFEU: guidelines on employment; Art.150 TFEU: establishment of an Employment
Committee.
[77] Art.293(2) TFEU.
[78] [1990] EC Bull.4–81: the Code stipulates that the Commission will take care to remind the
Council, not to come to a "political agreement", before Parliament has given its opinion, keep the
House informed of the guidelines set out by the Council, and ensure that, in accordance with the
principles laid down by the Court, Parliament is re-consulted should the Council substantially amend
a Commission proposal. The Commission also undertakes to set up its contact with Parliament and the
Council, concerning the choice of the legal base to be adopted for its proposals, and to take individual
decisions on any amendment adopted, at second reading, by Parliament, which the Commission does
not wish to incorporate in its proposal. Parliament, for its part, undertakes to adopt any appropriate
operational and statutory measures, to make the inter-institutional process more effective, and ensure,

5–21   Parliament's opinions have no binding force; however, mention must be made, in the relevant acts, of the fact that Parliament was indeed consulted.[79] However, the Treaty does not require the Council to mention whether the opinion was favourable or not, nor to refute, in the latter case, the arguments brought forward by Parliament against the proposal.[80]

It should also be noted that where the Council acts, on a proposal from the Commission, unanimity,[81] except in certain cases,[82] is required for the adoption by the Council of an act constituting an amendment to that proposal.[83] This seems to indicate that the power of the Council to adopt an act which differs from the Commission's proposal is limited to amending the latter, while respecting the essential content of the proposal. In the case where the Council introduces a modification, the question arises whether Parliament must be consulted again, this time on the amended text. According to the Court, this is only necessary when the amended text is substantially different from the one on which Parliament gave its opinion.[84]

It should be pointed out that Parliament may, acting by a majority of its component Members, "request the Commission to submit any appropriate proposal on matters on which it considers that a Union act is required, for the purpose of implementing the Treaties". If the Commission does not submit a proposal it must inform Parliament of the reasons for its refusal.[85] The question has been raised as to whether this right to request proposals infringes upon the "exclusive" right of initiative of the Commission. This seems unlikely since it is only a "request" and, on the other hand, the Council has had the same right from the beginning,[86] and this was never considered as limiting the Commission's freedom to decide on the opportunity of making proposals. It seems that the matter rests there, unless the Commission is obliged, under the Treaty, to act; in that case, Parliament may bring an action against the Commission before the Court for failure to act.[87]

---

in particular, that opinions on the proposals linked with the creation of a frontier-free area before the end of 1992, are adopted swiftly. (Report of proceedings: [1990] O.J. Annex 3–389.)

[79] Art.296,2 TFEU.

[80] See *Government of the Kingdom of the Netherlands v High Authority* (6/54) [1954–56] E.C.R. 103 at 111. The Commission undertook, starting with the July 1973 session of Parliament, to inform it systematically of actions taken on its opinions.

[81] However, this rule does not apply during the conciliation procedure: Art.294(10) and (13) TFEU, for the establishment of the budget (Arts 310 and 314 TFEU), for the adoption of the multi-annual financial framework, and for authorising expenditure in excess of one-twelfth, in case the budget has not been adopted at the beginning of the year (Art.315,2 TFEU).

[82] Art.293(1) TFEU. The exceptions are Art.294 TFEU paras 10 (Conciliation Committee) and 13 (period after approval in the Conciliation Committee), Art.310 (budget), Art.312 (multi-annual financial framework), Art.314 (establishment of the budget), and Art.315,2 (propose expenditure in excess of one-twelfth).

[83] Art.293(1) TFEU;

[84] See *ACF Chemiefarma v Commission* (41/69) [1970] E.C.R. 661 at 689(69), *Buyl v Commission* (817/69) [1982] E.C.R. 245 and *Parliament v Council* (C-65/91) [1992] E.C.R. I-4593. Similar text in *Parliament v Council* (C-65/93) [1995] E.C.R. I-643; [1996] 1 C.M.L.R. 4.

[85] Art.225 TFEU. See r.42, Rules of Procedure.

[86] Art.241 TFEU.

[87] Art.265 TFEU.

In certain cases the Treaties confer on Parliament a right of initiative.[88] The latest version of Parliament's Rules of Procedure refers to "Rights of initiative conferred on parliament by the Treaties".[89] The Commission itself has pointed out that it is the Treaty which confers upon it the power to initiate legislation in the areas covered by the Treaty, and that it is therefore legally and politically responsible for its proposals, regardless of the fact that they are drawn up at the request of another institution or of economic operators.[90]

5–22

Finally, mention must be made of the fact that, when provided for in the Treaty, consultation of Parliament, constitutes an "essential procedural requirement", and failure of the Council to comply with it constitutes a ground for annulment of the relevant act by the Court.[91]

Besides the opinions given following the consultation procedure, Parliament has always formulated resolutions whenever it considered it necessary.[92] According to the Rules of Procedure, such resolutions must, however, concern matters falling within the activities of the European Union.

With a view to furthering the inclusion of Parliament in the decision-making process, a Code of Conduct has laid down, since 1990, a number of reciprocal commitments of Parliament and Commission.[93] In 2005, for instance, Parliament was consulted 113 times.

(ii)   The Ordinary Legislative Procedure[94]

The introduction of this co-decision procedure by the EU Treaty, and the extension of its scope, and of the role of Parliament in it by the Treaties of Amsterdam, Nice and Lisbon, represents a real breakthrough for Parliament. Where, before those Treaties, its function was purely consultative, the Parliament from then on shared with the Council real legislative power. Consequently, most acts were no longer designated as "Council" regulations, directives or decisions,

5–23

---

[88] In the December 2009 Rules of Procedure, Art.41 provides that "in cases where the Treaties confer a right of initiative on Parliament, the committee responsible may decide to draw up an own-initiative report. The report shall comprise: (a)...; (b) where appropriate, a draft proposal; ...Where the adoption of an act of Parliament requires the approval or the consent of the Council, and the opinion or the consent of the Commission, Parliament may, following the vote on the proposal ... decide to postpone the vote ... until the Council or the Commission have stated their position."

[89] Rules of Procedure, r.41. General Report 2005/20, reference is made to "Own initiative procedures".

[90] See answer to written question No.3471/92: [1993] O.J. C292/22.

[91] See *Roquette Freres v Council* (138/79) and *Maizena v Council* (139/79) [1980] E.C.R. I-3149, where the Court annulled a regulation because the Council, although it had transmitted the Commission's proposal to Parliament for its opinion, adopted the regulation without having received it. However, see also *Parliament v Council* (C-65/93) [1995] E.C.R. I-643: Parliament was duly consulted, but, according to the Court, failed to meet the obligation of genuine co-operation, by adjourning the last plenary session during which the draft could have been adopted. No reproach to the Council, which adopted the measure, without having received the opinion of Parliament, because of urgency.

[92] Rules of Procedure, r.113(1).

[93] The Code provides, e.g. for individual Commission Decisions on any amendment adopted at second reading. See [1990] EC Bull.5–80.

[94] Art.294 TFEU.

but as regulations, directives or decisions "of the European Parliament and the Council".[95] The procedure creates an interplay between Parliament and Council in successive stages.

The rather lengthy and complex ordinary legislative procedure can best be described on the more familiar basis of the three classical phases in Union legislation: the Commission's proposal, the role of Parliament and the role of the Council.

5–24   *First Reading*

1.   The Commission submits a proposal to Parliament and to the Council[96];
2.   Parliament adopts its position in first reading, and communicates it to the Council;
3.   If the Council approves Parliament's position, the act shall be adopted in the wording corresponding to Parliament's position;
4.   If the Council does not approve Parliament's position, it shall adopt its own position, at first reading, and communicate it to Parliament;
5.   The Council informs Parliament fully of the reasons that led it to adopt its own position. The Commission also informs Parliament of its position.

Second Reading

5–25   If, within three months of such communication, Parliament:

●   approves Council's position at first reading, or has not taken a decision, the act concerned shall be deemed to have been adopted, in the wording, which corresponds to the position of the Council;
●   rejects, by a majority of its component members, Council's position at first reading, the proposal shall be deemed not to have been adopted;
●   proposes, by a majority of its component members, amendments to the Council's position at first reading, the text thus amended shall be forwarded to the Council and the Commission, which shall deliver an opinion on those amendments.

If within three months of receiving Parliament's amendments, the Council, acting by a qualified majority[97]:

●   approves all those amendments, the act shall be deemed to have been adopted (however, unanimity is required for the amendments on which the Commission has delivered a negative opinion)[98];

---

[95] In 2005, 122 acts were adopted via this procedure.

[96] In the other procedures, the proposal is sent to the Council, which then consults Parliament on it.

[97] For a definition of qualified majority, see Ch.7: The Council. As will be seen, there are a number of cases, wherein the Council must decide unanimously throughout the whole co-decision procedure: for instance, Art.21(3) TFEU—provisions to facilitate the exercise by the citizens of the Union of the right to move and reside freely within the territory of the Union.

[98] Art.294(9) TFEU. This is logical, because, where the Council acts on a proposal from the Commission, (and this 'negative opinion' is equivalent to a 'proposal'), it may only amend it unanimously: Art.293(1) TFEU.

- does not adopt all the amendments, the President of the Council, in agreement with the President of Parliament, shall within six weeks convene a meeting of the Conciliation Committee.

Conciliation

The Conciliation Committee, which shall be composed of the members of the Council or their representatives and an equal number of members representing Parliament, shall have the task of reaching agreement on a joint text by a qualified majority of the members of the Council or their representatives, and by a majority of the members representing Parliament, within six weeks of being convened, on the basis of the positions of Parliament and the Council at second reading.   **5–26**

The Commission shall take part in the Conciliation Committee's proceedings and shall take all necessary initiatives, with a view of reconciling the positions of Parliament and of the Council.

If, within six weeks of it being convened, the Conciliation Committee does not approve the joint text, the proposed act shall be deemed not to have been adopted.

Third Reading

If, within that period, the Conciliation Committee approves a joint text, Parliament, acting by a majority of the votes cast, and the Council, acting by a qualified majority, shall each have a period of six weeks from that approval in which to adopt the act in question in accordance with the joint text. If they fail to do so, the proposed act shall be deemed not to have been adopted.   **5–27**

The periods of three months and six weeks mentioned above, shall be extended by a maximum of one month and two weeks respectively, at the initiative of Parliament or of the Council.

Special Provisions

Where, in the cases provided for in the Treaties, a legislative act is submitted to the ordinary legislative procedure on the initiative of a group of Member States, or on a recommendation by the European Central Bank, or at the request of the Court of Justice, a proposal of the Commission is not provided for,[99] neither shall the Commission inform Parliament of its position,[100] nor can the Council act on a Commission's negative opinion.[101] However, Parliament and Council must, in such case, communicate the proposed act to the Commission, with their position at first and second reading. They may request the opinion of the Commission.   **5–28**

---

[99] Art.294(2) TFEU.
[100] Art.294(6) TFEU second phrase.
[101] Art.294(9) TFEU.

Type of Act to be Adopted

5–29   Normally the Treaties indicated what type of act can, or must, be adopted. When this is not the case, Parliament, the Council and the Commission must select it on a case by case basis in compliance with the applicable procedures, and with the principle of proportionality.[102]

The ordinary legislative procedure, described above, has now become the most common way for Parliament to participate in the legislative process of the Union. A problem might arise when the power to legislate can be based on two different Treaty provisions. The Court has held that in such cases, the act must be adopted on the basis of the two relevant provisions.[103] In case this would result in divesting the procedure of its essential element, i.e. Parliament's intervention in the legislative process, that rule is now not applicable. For instance, if one of the provisions requires the ordinary legislative procedure, and the other requires the Council to act unanimously, after merely consulting Parliament, the essential element of the ordinary legislative procedure would be undermined. Consequently, the dual legal basis is excluded. Which one should be used depends on the content of the act to be adopted.[104]

Implementing Measures

5–30   Some acts adopted under the ordinary legislative procedure need implementing measures, which are normally adopted by the Commission. It is clear, however, that such implementing measures can be extremely important, since they often determine the actual content of the act. The Council therefore provided that such implementing regulations could only be adopted by the Commission in co-operation with a specific committee, as provided for in the basic act.[105] This "comitology" procedure is described in Ch.8: The Commission, paras 8–16 to 8–18. Furthermore, a *modus vivendi*[106] was adopted by the three institutions in 1995 containing guidelines to overcome difficulties which had arisen, for reasons connected with the question of committee procedure, in order to allow a direct involvement of Parliament in the implementing procedure. It provides that drafts submitted by the Commission to the committee provided for in the basic act, shall be sent, at the same time and under the same conditions, to the appropriate committee of Parliament, which then delivers an opinion. Parliament shall be informed by the Commission when the implementing measure is not in accordance with that opinion or when the Commission must submit a proposal to the Council. The latter informs Parliament and will take due account of any unfavourable opinion. The same applies to the Commission.

---

[102] Art.296,1 TFEU.

[103] *Commission v Council* (165/87) [1988] E.C.R. 5545; [1990] 1 C.M.L.R. 457.

[104] *Commission v Council* (C-100/89) [1991] E.C.R. I-2867 at 2897; [1991] 1 C.M.L.R. 2867.

[105] Art.290 TFEU. Decision 1999/468 laying down the procedure for the exercise of implementing powers conferred on the Commission [1999] O.J. L184/23.

[106] Regulation concerning the implementation measures, for acts adopted in accordance with the procedure laid down in Art. [251] of the EC Treaty [1996] O.J. C102/1, now Art.290 TFEU.

(iii) The Special Legislative Procedure[107]

In specific cases provided for by the Treaties, the adoption of a regulation, directive or decision, which must be done:

- by Parliament with the participation of the Council, or
- by the Council with the participation of Parliament,

constitutes a special legislative procedure.

The procedure to be adopted shall, in each case, be determined in agreement by the two institutions.

(iv) Consent Procedure

The consent procedure was introduced by the SEA,[108] and extended by the EU Treaty.[109] It constitutes, in fact, a veto right of Parliament,[110] rather than a right of co-decision, where Council and Parliament decide "together", as under the ordinary legislative procedure.[111] When consent is required, the Council may only act after it has obtained the agreement of Parliament.

(b) Inter-institutional relations and agreements in legislation

A section on legislative powers would be incomplete without taking into account the political reality of inter-institutional arrangements and agreements. The procedures described, such as the ordinary legislative procedures and assent procedures, are static. Throughout the process negotiations take place.

Article 4 TEU (formerly Art.10 EC) provides for a principle of genuine and mutual "loyal" cooperation between Member States and the Union. In the ECJ on March 30, 1995, *European Parliament v Council of the European Union* C-65/93 ECR 1995 Page I-00643 the Court held that the dialogue between institutions, on which the consultation procedure in particular is based, is subject to the same mutual duties of genuine cooperation as those which govern relations between Member States and the Community institutions.

Throughout the years a number of agreements between institutions (inter-institutional agreements or IIA's) have seen the light. They are a necessary complement to the provisions of the Treaty. They are adopted under different names as "common declaration", "modus vivendi" or even plainly "inter-institutional agreement". They were mainly seen as deriving from the duty of loyal co-operation.

5–31

5–32

5–33

---

[107] Art.289(2) TFEU.

[108] Arts 8 and 9 SEA respectively action on application for membership of the Union, and international agreements; these are the only two cases introduced by the SEA.

[109] It was reduced by the Treaty of Amsterdam, and now applies in the following cases: Art.7(1) EU—serious and persistent breach by a Member State; Art.14(2)2 EU—composition of Parliament; Art.18(7)3 EU—nomination of President and members of the Commission, and of the High Representative; Art.49 EU—accession of new members; Art.223(1)2 TFEU —procedure for election of MEPs; Art.218(6)(a) TFEU —certain international agreements.

[110] Indeed Parliament can only refuse its assent, and cannot discuss the case with the Council.

[111] See above: ordinary legislative procedure.

Article 295 TFEU now provides for a legal basis. IIA's may be binding according to this provision[112]. It mainly confirms practice and case law—whether an IIA is binding depends on the substance, not on the name. Presently a binding character is affirmed if institutions have a clear intention to be bound and if IIA serves to clarify/implement Treaty procedures. Many IIA's are policy arrangements.

In the field of legislation we note a substantive number of agreements. They relate to:

(i)   information and coordination procedures in the (pre) legislative stage, like the Framework Agreement between Parliament and Commission.

5–34   This agreement is traditionally renewed each 5 years after the "new" Parliament and Commission have taken up their duties. The most recent version was adopted October 20, 2010.[113] Arrangements exist on, for example, transmission of documents, negotiation of international agreements, exchange of confidential information, dialogues but also on, for example, institutional relations between EP and Commission.

NB: the Council issued a Declaration stating that some elements of this Declaration are ultra vires (e.g. the individual responsibility of the Commissioner).

(ii)   the legislative procedure; and mainly increase the role of the EP beyond the treaty provisions.

5–35   See, for example, the framework agreement EP/Commission and also the enhanced consultation procedure for legislation with important financial implications; see Joint Declaration of March 4, 1975, O.J.1975 C89/1. It introduced a "conciliation" procedure after the EP opinion was given. As many procedures have been shifted to OLP or consent, they became obsolete or their importance has been reduced.

(iii)   Other agreements cover the legislative process itself.

5–36   Some are purely technical like the technical arrangements for the composition of conciliation committees, 25.10.1995, Bull.1993, nr.10, p.126.

The practical arrangements for the co-decision procedure (May 22, 2007, O.J.2007 C145/5.) have departed from a rather technical agreement into an agreement facilitating political compromises in order to achieve OLP's without conciliation (see under IV).

(iv)   Others govern the content of legislation.

5–37   The budgetary IIAs (see IIA between the EP, the Council and the Commission on budgetary discipline and sound financial management, concluded May 17, 2006,

---

[112] For more details see Bart Driessen, *Inter-institutional Conventions in EU Law* (Cameron, May 2008).
[113] O.J. 2010, L304/48.

O.J.2006 C331/1) concern mainly items related to the budgetary procedure and the multiannual financial framework[114]; they also provide for arrangements on the interaction of budget and legislation, e.g. financial provisions in legislation and the co-ordination between budgetary and legislative authority in a specific file.

Another set of agreements deals with legislative quality. Quality of legislative texts/drafting is governed in the IIA of December 22, 1998 (O.J.1998 C73/1), which was completed by the Institutions implemented jointly a "joint practical guide").

(v) The complete legislative environment, from the pre-legislative phase (notably impact assessments) to the post-legislative (implementation) is now governed in the "better law making" IIA of December 16, 2003 (O.J.2003 C321/1).

The main features of this agreement are in fact not new, but consist of a codification of a practice already existing. Some elements of this agreement were preceded by the White Paper on European Governance of 2001, notably those on broad consultation.   **5–38**

There are provisions on, for example, enhanced planning and legislative programming (including processes of exchange of information in all stages). Others concern explanations by the Commission of choice of legislative instrument and legal basis. The more interesting elements are—as an implementation of the subsidiarity principle—provisions on co-regulation and self-regulation. There is also attention for pre-legal consultation (white papers), impact assessments (by the Commission as to the proposal and by the Council and EP as to their amendments) and attention is given to the implementation by Member States. The latter issue has gained notoriety in 2010/2011, after the new Framework agreement EP-Commission. Parliament stresses upon the submission, by Member States, of "correlation tables" showing implementation of Directives.

(c) The role of national parliaments

The necessity of closer links between the Union and the national Parliaments is now generally recognised.   **5–39**

To that effect a Protocol on the role of national parliaments in the European Union was annexed to the Treaties already in 1997.[115] In its current wording this Protocol provides that Commission consultation documents (Green and White Papers and Communications) and other key documents are to be sent to national parliaments. The same applies to proposals—"draft legislative acts"—regardless of their authors.

National parliaments may send to the President of the European Parliament, to the Council or to the Commission a reasoned opinion,[116] on whether the draft

---

[114] See for the MFF now Art.312 TFEU—conversion into a Regulation required.
[115] [1997] O.J. C340/113.
[116] Protocol No.1 to the TFEU, Arts 1–2.

legislative act complies with the principle of subsidiarity.[117] An eight-week period must elapse between the draft legislative act being made available, in the official languages of the Union, and the date when it is placed on a provisional agenda of the Council for adoption; exceptions are possible in case of urgency.

The Protocol provides also for inter-parliamentary co-operation, recognising the need for more cooperation between the national parliaments among themselves and the European parliament and the national parliaments.

5–40   It provides for a structure—a Conference of Parliamentary Committees for Union Affairs—that may submit any contribution it deems appropriate for the attention of Parliament, the Council and the Commission; it must also promote the exchange of information and best practice between national parliaments and Parliament, including their special committees.[118]

Such a structure already exists, namely COSAC (Conference of Parliamentary Committees for Union Affairs of Parliaments of the European Union) which was set up in Paris in 1989, and which has an organisational structure of its own.[119]

In addition to the protocol on the role of national parliaments, the Treaty of Lisbon introduced a second Protocol on the application of the principles of subsidiarity and proportionality. Quintessence of this protocol is a review procedure based on a reasoned opinion that a proposal does not comply with the principle of subsidiarity, to be issued by a substantive number of national parliaments, and possibly leading to a review or even a withdrawal of the proposal.

(2)   Functions of political control and consultation

(a)   Setting up of a Temporary Committee of Inquiry

5–41   Parliament may, at the request of a quarter of its component members, set up a Temporary Committee of Inquiry to investigate, without prejudice to the powers conferred by the Treaties on other institutions or bodies, alleged contraventions or maladministration in the implementation of Union law.[120]

There are, however, a certain number of limitations. In the first place, as the name indicates, such a committee is only temporary, which means that it shall cease to exist on the submission of its report.[121] Secondly, the investigation does not supersede actions undertaken by other institutions or bodies on the basis of the powers conferred on them by the Treaties. When, for example, the Court of Auditors submits a special report,[122] it cannot be contradicted by the report of the Committee of Inquiry, and to avoid this, Parliament must consult this institution before setting up the Committee.

---

[117] See Protocol No.2 to the TFEU on the application of the principles of subsidiarity and proportionality.

[118] Protocol No. 1 to the TFEU, Arts 9–10.

[119] For information see *http://www.cosac.eu* [accessed August 23, 2013]

[120] Art.226,1 TFEU. See, for example, Decision of Parliament of July 17, 1996 setting up a temporary committee of inquiry to investigate alleged contraventions or maladministration in the implementation of Union law in relation to BSE [1996] O.J. C239/1.

[121] Art.226,2 TFEU.

[122] Art.287(4) TFEU.

The same applies, and this is the third limitation, where facts are being examined before a court and while the case is still subject to legal proceedings.[123] Detailed provisions governing the right of inquiry must be determined by Parliament, acting by means of regulations, on its own initiative, in accordance with a special legislative procedure, after obtaining the consent of the Council and the Commission.[124] In May 2012, Parliament adopted an initiative proposal for a new Regulation, increasing its powers. This proposal is blocked for the moment.[125]

(b)   Right of Petition and Appointment of an Ombudsman

The right of petition[126] is granted not only to citizens of the Union, but also to "any natural or legal person residing, or having its registered office, in a Member State", individually or in association with other citizens or persons. Petitions may be sent concerning a matter which comes within the Union's field of activity by persons directly affected by them. A right of petition has been in existence for quite some time,[127] and is widely used. In 2008, Parliament received over 1,000 petitions.

5–42

An *Ombudsman*, appointed by Parliament,[128] after each election of Parliament for the duration of its term of office (eligible for reappointment), is empowered to receive (from the same category of persons as those referred to above) complaints concerning instances of maladministration in the activities of the institutions,[129] or of bodies of the Union.[130] See Parliament's publication on "How to complain to the European Ombudsman".[131] If the Ombudsman finds such a case, he shall refer the matter to the institution concerned, which shall inform him of its views within three months. He then sends a report to Parliament and to the institution with, if needed, suggestions for remedies. It should be noted that expenses incurred by applicants for lodging a complaint are not considered "caused" by the institutions![132]

Parliament, acting by means of regulations, on its own initiative, in accordance with a special legislative procedure,[133] must, after seeking an opinion from the Commission, and with the approval of the Council, lay down the regulations and general conditions governing the performance of the Ombudsman's duties.[134]

---

[123] Art.226,1 TFEU.
[124] Art.226,3 TFEU. See Decision of Parliament, the Council and the Commission, on the detailed provisions governing the exercise of the Parliament's power of inquiry [1995] O.J. L78/1.
[125] P7_TA(2012)0219, May 23, 2012, *http://www.europarl.europa.eu* [accessed August 23, 2013].
[126] Art.227 TFEU.
[127] See Rules of Procedure, r.191, 2007 version.
[128] Art.228 TFEU. See Decision 94/262 on the Regulation and General Conditions governing the performance of the Ombudsman's duties [1994] O.J. L113/15, amended [2008] O.J. L189/25. Council Decision approving those acts [1994] O.J. L54/25, and Parliament's Resolution on the role of the Ombudsman [1995] O.J. C249/226. See also Parliament's Decision appointing an Ombudsman [2010] O.J. L37/41.
[129] [1996] O.J. C157/1.
[130] In 2008 an agreement was signed between the Ombudsman and the EIB: [2008] O.J. C244/1.
[131] *http://www.ombudsman.europa.eu* [accessed August 23, 2013].
[132] *Internationalen-Hillfonds* (C-331/05) [2007] E.C.R. I-5475.
[133] Art.289(2) TFEU.
[134] Art.228(4) TFEU.

(c)   Questions to the Council, the Commission and the ECB[135]

5–43   The Treaty provides that the Commission shall reply orally or in writing to questions put to it by Parliament, i.e. by a committee, a political group or at least 37 members.[136]

Parliament's right to obtain answers to its questions constitutes an important aspect of its supervisory powers. It has been widely used.[137] This right, and the use of it, was considerably extended over the years, both as to form and as to addressees. The most important extension was probably the right to obtain answers from the Council,[138] especially when one takes into account that it was introduced in 1958 unilaterally by Parliament and accepted by the Council. It was again extended by the EU Treaty to include questions to the Councils of the Common Foreign and Security Policy[139] and of the Police and Judicial Co-operation in Criminal Matters.[140] Presently, the Treaties provide that Parliament may ask questions of the Council, and make recommendations to it under the chapter concerning the Common Foreign and Security Policy, and that twice a year it shall hold a debate on progress in this field, including the Common Security and Defence Policy.[141] In this field also, Parliament must be consulted by the High Representative of the Union for Foreign Affairs and Security Policy ("High Representative") on the main aspects and the basic choices and be informed of how these policies evolve; the High Representative must ensure that the views of Parliament are duly taken into consideration.[142]

In other fields, the European Council and the Council "shall be heard" by Parliament, in accordance with the conditions laid down in their respective rules of procedure.[143]

5–44   To the questions for written and oral answers provided for in the Treaty, Parliament added in 1962 the Oral Questions followed by a Debate.[144] This was accepted by the Commission; as for the Council, it was accepted, with the proviso that the debate may not be concluded by a vote on a resolution concerning the debate in question.[145] This is presently the only form of questioning. In 1973, Parliament introduced the Question Time,[146] in which the Council and the Commission agreed to participate. In this case, only the answers from the Commission can give rise to a debate. Finally, there are the questions for written answers that are published in the *Official Journal of the European Union*.[147]

---

[135] Rules of Procedure, r.115–118.

[136] Art.230,2 TFEU and Rules of Procedure, r.115.

[137] For instance, during 2008 Parliament addressed, out of a total of 7,322 questions, 6,570 written questions, 659 oral questions with debate and 93 during question time to the Commission: 1,037 were addressed to the Council—547 written, 413 oral with debate and 50 during question time. See, for instance, the publication in the O.J. of written questions with answers: [2010] O.J. C189/1.

[138] Rules of Procedure, r.115,1, 2007 version. See Art.197(4) EC.

[139] Art.36,2 EU. For the Common Foreign and Security Policy see Ch.36: External action byt he Union, the Common Foreign and Security Policy and Enlargement.

[140] Repealed Art.39(3) EU.

[141] Art.36,2 EU.

[142] Art.36,1 EU.

[143] Art.210,3 TFEU.

[144] Rules of Procedure, r.115.

[145] Rules of Procedure, r.115.

[146] Rules of Procedure, r.116.

[147] Rules of Procedure, r.117.

It is clear from the above that Parliament has succeeded in including the Council in its work, far beyond what was provided for in the Treaties. Indeed, not only the Council, as such, accepted to participate, but also the Presidency of the Common Foreign and Security Policy.[148] As indicated, there are differences in the ways the above-mentioned procedures are applied to the Council and to the Commission. This distinction reflects the particular character of the relationships existing between Parliament, on the one hand, and the other two institutions, on the other. Indeed, as far as the Commission is concerned, the relationship is one of political supervision and co-operation. The latter sometimes becomes a conspiracy against the Council, which, after all, in certain cases, still wields the ultimate legislative power within the Union.

Where the Council is concerned, the relationship should rather be seen as political co-operation and partnership, especially after the modifications introduced by the EU Treaty. This relationship tends to find expression in what can be considered a kind of dialogue between the two institutions. Besides the formal contacts already mentioned, each incoming President of the Council, presents, at the beginning of his mandate, a "Programme of the Presidency", and a survey of significant developments, at the end of his six-month term. Similarly, a representative of the Council presents an oral report to Parliament twice a year, on the activities of the Council.[149]

(d) The General Report

According to the TFEU, Parliament must "discuss in open session the General Report" on the activities of the Union,[150] which the Commission publishes annually.[151] It is submitted to Parliament before the opening of its session, i.e. the second Tuesday in March.[152] In the old days, the discussion of the General Report, gave rise to a general debate on all the facets of Union life, since the Report covers the activities of all the institutions and bodies of the Union. It should be noted that the work of the other institutions and of the EIB is described, in detail, in their own reports.

The General Report is supplemented by an Annual Report on the Agricultural Situation of the Union,[153] a Report on the Development of the Social Situation in the Union,[154] and a Report on Competition Policy.[155] Furthermore, on the basis of the Treaties or on the basis of sectoral legislation, or on request of Parliament, the Commission produces a large number of annual or periodical reports on different sectoral topics.

All those reports constitute an invaluable source of information on the activities of the Union, although the General Report no longer contains detailed information as it used to do. This report is less important, however, for the supervisory task of Parliament, since the latter is kept well-informed through the

5–45

---

[148] Art.36,2 EU. Rules of Procedure, r.115.
[149] Art.15(6)(d) EU.
[150] Art.233 TFEU.
[151] Art.18 Merger Treaty. No longer "published", but on the Internet.
[152] Art.229 TFEU. The Commission has always scrupulously respected this obligation.
[153] This practice was started in 1975 at the request of Parliament.
[154] Art.161 TFEU.
[155] Undertaking given by the Commission to Parliament on June 7, 1971.

permanent contacts it maintains, mainly with the Commission, through the work of the Parliamentary Committees, in which the Commission always participates, and especially through the budgetary discharge procedure.

The discussion of the General Report is no longer a standalone debate, but takes place within the framework of the debate on the annual work programme of the Commission under the aforementioned Framework Agreement between parliament and Commission. The 2007 version of the Rules of Procedure provides, among other things, that Parliament shall work together with the Commission and the Council to determine the legislative planning of the European Union, and that Parliament and the Commission shall co-operate in preparing the Commission's legislative and work programme in accordance with the timetable and arrangements agreed between the two institutions, and annexed to the Rules of Procedure.[156]

(e) The Motion of Censure

5-46   Parliament has the power to dismiss the members of the Commission, as a body, by adopting a "motion of censure", in case it disagrees with activities of the Commission.[157] This is, by far, the most impressive power of control vested in Parliament; but, although motions have been tabled in the past, never yet has one been carried.[158] The procedural requirements are the following. First, the Treaty prescribes a "reflexion time": Parliament shall not vote on the motion until at least three days after it was tabled, and shall decide by open vote. Secondly, the Treaty requires a two-thirds majority of the votes cast, representing a majority of the component Members of Parliament.

It must be underlined that the censure only affects the Commission. The Council, which is the co-legislator within the Union, and therefore co-responsible for most of the activities of the Commission, remains outside Parliament's reach. In case of a regularly adopted motion, the Commission shall resign as a body. However, the Commissioners shall remain in office until they are replaced,[159] and continue to exercise their functions normally.[160] It would be difficult for the governments, it seems, to re-nominate the same persons since the President and the members of the Commission, after having been nominated by the governments, must be approved as a body by Parliament before they can be appointed.

Until now, as mentioned, no motion of censure has ever been carried. It is interesting though to note that, in 1999, the fear for such a motion brought about the resignation of all the members of the "Santer" Commission six months before the expiration of their mandate. This most unusual and controversial act, not specifically provided for in the Treaty, was triggered by criticism as to an individual Commissioner whose alleged behaviour brought discredit to the Commission as an institution. This event reopened the political debate on the

---

[156] Rules of Procedure, r.35 and 11907 and Annex XIV.

[157] Art.234,1 TFEU. Rules of Procedure, r.107.

[158] The first motion was tabled in November 1972; it was later withdrawn. In order to avoid the motion of censure, the Commissioners can resign, as they did on March 16, 1999.

[159] Arts 234 and 246 TFEU.

[160] Art.246 TFEU: "they shall remain in office and continue to deal with current business". Rules of Procedure, r.98(1).

responsibility of individual commissioners. It is true that the Treaty already provided for compulsory retirement in cases of qualified misconduct (Arts 245 and 247 TFEU) according to a specific procedure. What is not governed is individual political responsibility and the possibility for Parliament to force a specific commissioner to resign. As the Treaty provides that a Commissioner shall resign if the President so requests (Art.17 TEU), Parliament and the Commission adopted provisions in the 2010 Framework Agreement to ensure a procedure in case of parliamentary criticism.

(f)   Control over implementation of the budget—discharge

Parliament's role in the budgetary field does not end with the adoption of the budget: it also exercises control over its implementation. In this task, Parliament and the Council are assisted by the Court of Auditors.[161] The Treaty [Art.319 TFEU] provides that Parliament shall give discharge to the Commission in respect of the implementation of the budget.

5–47

As shall be seen, when discussing the financing of the Union's activities, the Commission is entrusted with the implementation of the budget, on its own responsibility, and in accordance with the so-called "financial" regulations.[162]

The Commission submits annually the accounts of the preceding year, together with a financial statement of the assets and liabilities of the Union, to the Council and to Parliament.[163] The latter receives from the Court of Auditors a "statement of assurance" as to the reliability of the accounts, and an Annual Report.[164] Though the Treaty wording could give rise to the presumption that this is a mere accounting exercise—basic documents are the accounts and the report of the Court of Auditors on the financial year under consideration [Arts 318 and 287 TFEU] the discharge procedure involves a wider appreciation of the financial and general management by the European Commission, involving a procedure of hearings and questionnaires—the Treaty provides explicitly for a duty to co-operate before and after the discharge decision has been taken [see Art.319, paras 2 and 3 TFEU]. Parliament's Rules of Procedure, notably Annex VI, the Framework Agreement between Parliament and Commission and the main rules for the implementation of the budget, the Financial Regulation [Regulation 966/2012/EU, Euratom, O.J.2012 L298, legal basis Art.322 TFEU] provide further rules. Parliament gives discharge but may also postpone, or refuse it; as Parliament is the sole discharge authority—the Council gives a recommendation—this power is not to be underestimated. Within the procedure, Parliament often obtains important concessions. It should not be forgotten that (see above) the collective resignation of the Commission in 1999 found its origin in a refusal of discharge in 1998.

---

[161] See below for an analysis of this institution.
[162] Art.317 TFEU which refers to Art.322 TFEU.
[163] Art.318 TFEU.
[164] Art.287 TFEU.

(3) Key nominations

5-48 Parliament has also powers as to the nomination of key office holders. The most important one is the approval of the President and Members of the Commission "Taking into account the elections to the European Parliament, and after having held the appropriated consultations",[165] the European Council, acting by a qualified majority, proposes to Parliament a candidate for President of the Commission. He shall be elected by Parliament, by a majority of its component members, in practice, after this person has made a statement to Parliament, followed by a debate.[166] In case the candidate is not elected, the European Council must propose a new candidate within one month.

The Council, by common accord with the President-elect, adopts the list of the other persons it proposes for appointment as Members of the Commission. The President, the High Representative and the other members of the Commission, are then subject, as a body, to a vote of consent by Parliament.[167] In conformity with Parliament's wish, those members appear "before the appropriate committee, according to their prospective field of responsibility".[168] There is criticism that this is not provided for by the Treaty—in this view portfolios are only officially attributed by the Commission itself, after it takes office. If this were to be decided beforehand, this would mean that the Council, i.e. the Member States, decide, in fact, on this attribution. Some held this to violate the institutional balance, i.e. the principle of the independence of the Commission and its members, so clearly provided for in the Treaty.[169] On the other hand the treaty provides that the Commission is to be approved by Parliament as a body and is, as a body, responsible to the European parliament. This relation of confidence can be held to imply that Parliament is to be involved in the question of "the right person for the right job". Where Parliament did criticise proposed commissioners, it was correct to do so because it was not convinced on the match between the Commissioner designate and his portfolio.

Other key nominations include the nomination of the Ombudsman as already discussed.

Parliament also gives opinions on the nomination of the members of the Court of Auditors, this equally after a hearing in the competent committee based on its Rules of Procedure.

(4) Participation in the Budgetary Procedure

5-49 The budgetary procedure, and the role of Parliament in it, can best be described as follows.[170]

The annual budget of the Union is established by Parliament and the Council, acting in accordance with a special legislative procedure.[171]

---

[165] Art.17(7) EU.
[166] Rules of Procedure, r.105.
[167] Art.17 EU.
[168] Rules of Procedure, r.106 and Annex XVII.
[169] Art.245,1 TFEU.
[170] Arts 314–316 TFEU.
[171] Art.289(2) TFEU.

1. The Commission consolidates, in a "draft budget", the estimates of expenditure for the following year, drawn up by the various institutions, with the exception of the European Central Bank, before July 1. The draft budget, which may contain different estimates, also contains an estimate of the revenues.

2. The Commission submits a proposal containing the draft budget to Parliament and to the Council not later than September 1, preceding the budget year. The Commission may amend the draft budget during the procedure, until such time as the Conciliation Committee is convened.

3. The Council defines its position on the draft, forwards it to Parliament not later than October 1, and informs Parliament in full of the reasons which led it to adopt its position.

4. If, within 42 days of such communication, Parliament:
   (a) approves the position of the Council, the budget shall be adopted;
   (b) has not taken a decision, the draft budget shall be deemed to have been adopted;
   (c) adopts amendments by a majority of its component members, the amended draft is forwarded to the Council and to the Commission— the President of Parliament, in agreement with the President of the Council, shall immediately convene a meeting of the Conciliation Committee.

   However, if within 10 days of the amended draft being forwarded to the Council, the latter informs Parliament that it has adopted all its amendments, the Committee shall not meet.

5. The Conciliation Committee, composed of the members of the Council or their representatives and an equal number of members representing Parliament, shall have the task of reaching agreement on a joint text, by a qualified majority of the members of the Council or their representatives and by a majority of the representatives of Parliament, within 21 days of its being convened, on the basis of the positions of Parliament and the Council. The Commission takes part in the Conciliation Committee's proceedings, and must take all the necessary initiatives with a view to reconciling the positions of Parliament and the Council.

6. If, within the 21 days mentioned above, the Conciliation Committee agrees on a joint text, Parliament and the Council shall each have a period of 14 days from the date of the agreement to approve the joint text.

7. If, within that period of 14 days:
   (a) Parliament and Council both approve the joint text or fail to take a decision, or if one of these institutions approves the joint text while the other one fails to take a decision, the budget shall be deemed to be definitively adopted in accordance with the joint text;
   (b) Parliament, acting by a majority of its component members, and the Council both reject the joint text, or if one of these institutions rejects the joint text while the other one fails to take a decision, a new draft budget shall be submitted by the Commission; or
   (c) Parliament, acting by a majority of its component members, rejects the joint text while the Council approves it, a new draft budget shall be submitted by the Commission; or

(d) Parliament approves the joint text while the Council rejects it, Parliament may, within 14 days from the date of the rejection by the Council and acting by a majority of its component members and three-fifths of the votes cast, decide to confirm all or some of the amendments referred under (c) above—where a Parliament amendment is not confirmed, the position agreed in the Conciliation Committee on the budget heading which is the subject of the amendment shall be retained, the budget shall be deemed to be adopted on this basis.

8. If, within the 21 days referred to in para.5 above, the Conciliation Committee does not agree on a joint text, a new draft budget shall be submitted by the Commission.

9. When the procedure provided for in the treaty, has been completed, the President of Parliament shall declare that the budget has been definitively adopted.[172]

10. Each institution must exercise the powers conferred upon it in compliance with the Treaty and the acts adopted thereunder, with particular regard to the Union's own resources and the balance between revenue and expenditure.

The Treaty thus establishes a procedure which shows similarities with the ordinary legislative procedure, be it that—for reason of deadlines—there is only one written "reading" followed immediately—in case of non-agreement in the written phase between parliament and Council (which is traditionally the case)—by a conciliation process. The conciliation has to lead ultimately to a joint text, to be approved by both institutions.

5–50 It follows, however, from the procedural requirements in this special legislative procedure that Parliament declares the budget to be finally adopted; the budget of the Union is signed by Parliament's president only.[173] A case in which the Council claims the right to co-sign the budget is currently under consideration in the Court [C-77/11, *Council v Parliament*]. On May 28, 2013, the Adovate-General delivered an opinion favourable to Parliament's position.

Before the entry into force of the Treaty of Lisbon, the budgetary procedure was not aligned on a full agreement between Parliament and Council on the entire budget, but on a system of compulsory and non-compulsory expenditure, where Council respectively Parliament had some autonomous margin to decide. Council had the last word on compulsory expenditure, and Parliament had the last word on non-compulsory expenditure, be it within a certain ceiling. Numerous conflicts arose on the application of this system. From the end of the 1980s—when, for reasons of economic convergence and an increased tension for structural policies—the difficulties of a year-by-year setting of priorities in a legal environment of an annual budget were considered to jeopardize long-term policies of the Union, calling for some multiannual financial planning.

---

[172] Art.114(9) TFEU.
[173] It could happen, of course, that the budget is not voted in time for the beginning of the financial year, or is rejected by Parliament; in that case a sum equivalent to no more than one-twelfth of the budget appropriations for the preceding year, may be spent each month: Art.315 TFEU.

In order to avoid the repetition of the numerous conflicts which arose between the Council and Parliament regarding the adoption of the Union budget, the institutions involved concluded as from 1988 inter-institutional agreements[174] covering budgetary discipline, and improvements of the budgetary procedure. In 1988 its main feature was a medium-term (five years) Financial Perspective,[175] but especially the versions of 1999 and 2006 provide for comprehensive and detailed procedures on the annual budgetary procedure, implementation of the budget, negotiation processes, and a detailed Multiannual Financial Framework—since 2006 the new name of the Financial Perspective, in anticipation of what was to become the Lisbon Treaty. It also provides for the possible mobilisation of a "Flexibility Instrument" that allows the use of certain funds for unforeseen structural operations.[176] It is true that this system, in fact, reduces powers of parliament as to the annual budget procedure, and in return a degree of stability and consensus is provided.

The Treaty of Lisbon has codified the system that, on the while, has catered for stable multiannual financial planning. The TFEU [Art.312 TFEU] now provides for the Multiannual Financial Framework (MFF) to be adopted as a regulation, according to a special legislative procedure, with the assent of Parliament. The annual budget has to be in compliance with the MFF. Negotiations on the regulation and a "residual" inter-institutional agreement are pending between the Institutions.

(5) Procedures before the Court of Justice

Until recently, Parliament could only play a rather secondary role in the proceedings before the Union Courts. It could "intervene" in cases before the Courts,[177] institute third-party proceedings to contest a judgment and bring an action against the Council and/or the Commission for failure to act and thereby infringing the Treaty.[178] However, its *locus standi* was considerably enhanced by the Treaty of Nice.[179] Presently, the Member States, Parliament, the Council and the Commission have a general right to request the Court to review the legality of Union acts.[180] The Court may also review the legality of acts when actions are brought by the Court of Auditors and by the ECB, "for the purpose of protecting their prerogatives".[181] The same applies to the right to "obtain the opinion of the Court of Justice as to whether an agreement envisaged, is compatible with the provisions of the Treaty"; this possibility is now also open to Parliament.[182]

5–51

---

[174] See currently the Inter-institutional Agreement between the European Parliament, the Council and the Commission on budgetary discipline and sound financial management, O.J. 2006, C139/1 succeeding that of May 6, 1999 [1999] O.J. C172/1.

[175] [1988] O.J. L185.

[176] See, for instance, Decision 2002/158, [2002] O.J. L53/28.

[177] See, e.g. Resolution of December 14, 1979 ([1980] O.J. C4/52) to intervene in cases *Roquette Frères v Council* (138/79) [1980] E.C.R. 3333 and *Maizena v Council* (139/79) [1980] E.C.R. 3393.

[178] Art.265 TFEU. See, e.g. *Parliament v Council* (13/83) [1985] E.C.R. 1556; [1986] 1 C.M.L.R. 138.

[179] Art.2(34) Treaty of Nice.

[180] Art.263 TFEU. See *Parliament v Council* (302/87) [1988] E.C.R. 5637.

[181] Art.263 TFEU.

[182] Art.218(11) TFEU.

(6) Consultative function

5–52   Apart from legislative consultation and ex post involvement (e.g. in the case of the discussion on annual reports) Parliament also has its voice heard through participation in other Union Activities.

Several agreements of association between the Union and third States provide for a joint Parliamentary Committee. This is the case with the EEC Turkey Association,[183] the EEA, and also with the so-called European Agreements with the candidate countries from Central and Eastern Europe.[184] These Parliamentary Committees are composed of Members of Parliament and Members of the national parliaments of the associated States. These Committees constitute discussion forums, rather than decision-making bodies. Similarly, the ACP-EEC Convention provides for a Joint Assembly.[185] Parliament actively supports inter-parliamentary co-operation through inter-parliamentary bodies set up in their own right, such as Euromed (together with the Mediterranean countries) and Euronest (together with the non-mediteranean neighbouring countries).

4. CONCLUSION

5–53   The European Parliament has, over the years, thanks to its determination, and strongly supported by the popular claim for more democracy within the Union, succeeded in increasing its powers. It is rapidly becoming an institution with a status equal to that of the Council, and the Commission.[186] In fact, Parliament wields more power than would appear from the Treaty provisions. It needs to be noted that there is one overall tendency in the constitutional reforms of the last 20 years: together with the increase of Parliament's competences and powers, the competences and powers of the National Parliaments and the European Council are also substantially increased; defining its position towards these actors on the scene is Parliament's constitutional challenge for the next years.

FURTHER READING

5–54   R. Corbett, F. Jacobs and M. Schackelton, *The European Parliament*, 8th edn (John Harper Publishing, 2011).

Peter Gjerloeff Bonnor, "The European Ombudsman: a novel source of soft law in the European Union", (2003) E.L.Rev.39.

Magdalena Elisabeth de Leeuw, "The Regulation on public access to European Parliament, Council and Commission documents in the European Union: are citizens better off?", (2003) E.L.Rev. 324.

Lenaerts-Van Nuffel, *Constitutional Law of the European Union*, 3rd edn (Sweet & Maxwell, 2011).

---

[183] See Art.27 of the Agreement ([1964] O.J. 3687).
[184] The first agreements were signed on December 16, 1991.
[185] The Cotonou Agreement was signed on June 23, 2000; for meetings of the Joint Assembly, see, for instance, General Report (1998).
[186] See Framework Agreement on relations between the European Parliament and the Commission: [2010] O.J. L304/47.

Panos Koutrakos, "New links in the Union's institutional chain", (2010) E.L.R. 1.

CHAPTER 6

The European Council

1. INTRODUCTION

To avoid confusion, it must be made clear at the outset that among the seven   **6–01**
institutions of the Union[1] there are—besides Parliament, the Commission, the
Court of Justice, the European Central Bank and the Court of Auditors—two
Councils: a "European Council" composed of Heads of State or of Government
and a "Council" composed of government ministers. These two institutions shall
be examined separately.

2. THE EUROPEAN COUNCIL

(1) History

There came a time when Council decisions were no longer taken by majority   **6–02**
voting, although this was provided for in the Treaties, but by consensus/
unanimity. Furthermore, the subjects to be decided upon became more and more
political because, with the evolution towards economic and monetary union, they
were of vital importance for the general economic development of the Member
States themselves. Consequently, the decision-making process within the Union
virtually came to a halt. It became obvious that new impetus had to be given and
new methods of decision-making had to be found. Since the Council is already a
gathering of high-level politicians (government ministers), the solution was
sought more and more in the so-called "Conferences of Heads of State or of
Government".[2] At the 1974 "Summit", as those Conferences were also called, the
participants:

> "[R]ecognised the need for an overall approach to the internal problems involved in
> achieving European unity, and the external problems facing Europe—consider it
> essential to ensure progress and overall consistency in the activities of the
> Communities, and the work on political co-operation—and [have] therefore decided

---

[1] Art.13(1) EU.
[2] The original idea was to organise gatherings of heads of government and the denomination "Heads
of State or Government" was made necessary by the fact that in France the function of head of
government is assumed by the Head of State. The first such conference was held in Paris on February
10/11, 1961; see Communiqué in [1961] EC Bull.3–13, and the second in Bonn on July 19, 1961,
where it was decided to hold such meetings at regular intervals; see Communiqué in [1961] EC Bull.
7–40.

to meet, accompanied by the Ministers of Foreign Affairs, three times a year and, whenever necessary, in the Council of the Communities and in the context of Political Co-operation".[3]

Consequently, since 1975, the Heads of State or of Government meet as the "European Council", at the onset three times a year, later on twice a year, and presently (2012), twice every six months, with the possibility for the President of the European Council to convene a special meeting when the situation so requires.[4] A record of conclusions is issued on the authority of the Presidency after each meeting.[5]

(2) Composition

6–03
The European Council is composed of the Heads of State, or of Government, of the Member States, its President, and the President of the Commission. The High Representative of the Union for Foreign Affairs and Security Policy ("High Representative") takes part in its work.

In case the agenda of the meeting requires it, the members may decide, each to be assisted by a minister and, in the case of the President of the Commission, by a member of the Commission.

(3) The President of the European Council

6–04
The President is elected by the European Council, by a qualified majority, for two-and-a-half years, renewable once. It used to be presided over by the Member State, which holds the presidency of the Council, on the basis of equal rotation every six months. Presently, the conditions of that rotation for Council meetings, except those concerning Foreign Affairs,[6] are established by the European Council.[7] Those conditions establish also the way these two Presidents work together.

In the event of an impediment or serious misconduct of its President, the European Council can end the President's term of office, in accordance with the same procedure.[8]

The President of the European Council chairs the meetings, and drives forward its work, he ensures the preparation and continuity of the work in co-operation with the President of the Commission and on the basis of the decisions of the "General Affairs Council", he must endeavour to facilitate cohesion and consensus and he presents a report to Parliament after each meeting.[9] The President ensures, at his level and in that capacity, the external representation of

---

[3] General Report 1974, p.297.
[4] Art.15(3) EU.
[5] Those conclusions are published on the Internet: *http://www.europa.eu/european-council/index_eu.htm* [accessed August 23, 2013]
[6] Art.16(9) EU.
[7] Art.236(b) TFEU.
[8] Art.15(5) EU.
[9] Art.15(6) EU.

the Union on issues concerning its Common Foreign and Security Policy, without prejudice to the powers of the High Representative. The President may not hold a national office.[10]

(4) Voting

Decisions are taken by consensus, unless the Treaties provide otherwise.[11] The latter is the case, among others, when the European Council adopts a decision establishing the list of Council configurations, other than those of the General Affairs Council and of the Foreign Affairs Council,[12] and a decision on the presidency of the Council configurations other than that of Foreign Affairs[13]; in those cases, the European Council acts by a qualified majority, the latter being defined in accordance with the relevant Treaty provisions.[14] The European Council shall act by simple majority for procedural questions, including the adoption of the Rules of Procedure.

6–05

Where a vote is taken, any member of the European Council may also act on behalf of not more than one other member. Abstention by members present in person, or represented, shall not prevent the adoption by the European Council of acts which require unanimity. Where the European Council decides by vote, its President and the President of the Commission shall not take part in the vote.[15]

(5) Tasks

The task of the European Council is defined as follows: it "shall provide the Union with the necessary impetus for its development, and shall define the general political directions and priorities thereof. It shall not exercise legislative functions".[16] The European Council has, so far, mostly limited itself to issuing general guidelines, which have been acted upon by the Council and the Commission. One of the tasks attributed to the European Council is to define the principles of, and general guidelines for, the Common Foreign and Security Policy (CFSP), which was provided for by the EU Treaty and modified by the Amsterdam Treaty.[17] The CFSP is the object of a later chapter in part six of the book.

6–06

(6) Existence of a "serious and persistent breach" by a Member State of the Union's Values

The European Council may, on a proposal by one-third of the Member States, or by the Commission, and after obtaining the consent of Parliament, and inviting the Member State in question to submit its observations, determine the existence of a serious and persistent breach (as opposed to a "clear risk of a serious breach"

6–07

---

[10] Art.15(6)2 and 3 EU.
[11] Art.15(4) EU.
[12] Art.16(6) EU.
[13] Art.16(9) EU.
[14] Art.16(4) EU and Art.238(2) TFEU. See Ch.7: The Council.
[15] Art.235 TFEU.
[16] Art.15(1) EU.
[17] Art.26 (13) EU.

which is determined by the Council[18]), by a Member State,[19] of the values referred to in the Union Treaty. These values are: respect for human dignity, freedom, democracy, equality, the rule of law and human rights, including the rights of persons belonging to minorities.[20] The Treaty provides that, to make this determination, the European Council must be "acting by unanimity",[21] but the TFEU provides that the member representing the Member State in question shall not take part in the vote.[22]

Where such a determination is made by the European Council, the Council, acting by a qualified majority, may decide to suspend certain rights deriving from the application of the Treaty, including the voting rights of the representative of the government of that Member State in the Council.[23] In doing so, the Council must take into account the possible consequences of such suspension on the rights and obligations of natural and legal persons. The Council, acting by a qualified majority, may subsequently decide to vary or revoke these measures in response to changes in the situation which led to their being imposed. Before imposing such sanctions, the European Council must obtain the assent of Parliament. The latter shall decide by a two-third majority of the votes cast, representing a majority of its members.[24]

(7) Organisation

6–08   The Rules of procedure are laid down in a Decision from 2009.[25] The main points are the following:

- the President, in close co-operation with the General Affairs Council and the Commission, prepares the meetings of the European Council and draws up the agenda;
- in principle the meetings of the European Council last for maximum two full days;
- in principle, the meetings take place in Brussels;
- each delegation has two seats in the meeting room, while the total size of each delegation is limited to 20 persons per Member State, and the Commission.

FURTHER READING

6–09   Jan Werts, *The European Council* (London, John Harper, 2008).

---

[18] Art.7(1) EU, where the determination is made by the Council on a reasoned proposal by one-third of the Member States, by Parliament or by the Commission.

[19] Art.7(2) EU.

[20] Art.2 EU.

[21] Art.7(2) EU.

[22] Art.354,1 TFEU; the Treaty adds that the Member State in question shall be counted in the calculation of the one-third or four-fifths of Member States referred in paras 1 and 2 of that article.

[23] Art.7(3) EU.

[24] Art.354 TFEU.

[25] Decision 2009/882 [2009] O.J. 315 L315/51.

CHAPTER 7

The Council

INTRODUCTION—THE OBJECTIVES OF THE TREATIES AND THE MEANS TO ACHIEVE THEM: THE ROLE OF THE COUNCIL

Although the distinction between the objectives of the Treaties and the means to attain them is not as clear as it was under the EC Treaty,[1] the present Treaties provide for several means to attain the "objectives" assigned to the Union.[2] The objectives are in particular: firstly, that the Union must offer its citizens an Area of Freedom, Security and Justice in which the free movement of persons is ensured[3]; secondly, the Union must establish an internal market[4]; thirdly, it must establish an Economic and Monetary Union whose currency is the Euro[5]— furthermore, the Union must define and implement a Common Foreign and Security Policy, including the progressive framing of a Common Defence Policy[6]; and, finally, it must develop a special relationship with neighbouring countries.[7]

7–01

Detailed means are provided for in the TFEU for the exercise of the Union's competences in order to implement the above-mentioned objectives. This is to be done either exclusively by the Union, or by implementing competences shared between the Union and the Member States, or by the Union carrying out actions to support, co-ordinate or supplement the actions of the Member States.[8]

"Exclusive" Union competence exists in the following areas: the Customs Union, competition rules, monetary policy for the Euro area, conservation of marine biological resources, the common commercial policy and the conclusion of certain international agreements.[9]

---

[1] See former Art.2 EC, which defined the means as "by establishing a common market and monetary union and by implementing common policies or activities (the Community shall have as its task . . .)".
[2] Art.3 EU: "promote peace, its values and the well-being of its peoples", "combat social exclusion and discrimination, etc.", "promote economic, social and territorial cohesion and solidarity among Member States", "ensure that Europe's cultural heritage is safeguarded and enhanced", "in its relations with the wider world uphold and promote its values and contribute to the protection of its citizens, etc.".
[3] Art.3(2) EU.
[4] Art.3(3) EU.
[5] Art.3(4) EU.
[6] Art.2(4) TFEU.
[7] Art.8 EU.
[8] Arts 3 to 6 TFEU.
[9] Art.3 TFEU.

7–02   "Shared" competences between the Union and the Member States concern, among others: the internal market; social policy; economic, social and territorial cohesion (regional policy); agriculture and fisheries; environment; consumer protection; transport; trans-European networks; energy; area of freedom; security and justice; public health; research; technological development; and space.[10] Also in development of co-operation and humanitarian aid, in which area the Union may also conduct a common policy.[11]

Then there are the areas[12] where the Union has competence to carry out activities, in particular to define and implement programmes, while the Member States are not prevented from exercising their own activities: protection and improvement of human health; industry; culture; tourism; education; vocational training; youth and sports; civil protection; and administrative co-operation.[13] These competences of the Union are commonly referred to as "supporting competences."

In areas which do not fall within the exclusive competence of the Union, it shall take action in accordance with the principle of subsidiarity, i.e.:

> "[O]nly if and in so far as the objectives of the proposed action cannot be sufficiently achieved by the Member States, either at central level or at regional and local level, but can rather, by reason of the scale or effects of the proposed action, be better achieved at Union level".[14]

7–03   All those activities shall be examined in detail in Parts Three, Four and Five of this book, but it is important at this juncture to notice the distinction the Treaty makes between the "exclusive tasks of the Union" and the "activities of the Member States and the Union, either sharing competences or each exercising its own", both being destined to implement the Treaty objectives. This distinction indicates that certain tasks can only be accomplished by the Union institutions and the Member States acting together, each in its own sphere. It calls for closer integration of the policies of the Member States with those of the Union proper.

This is particularly relevant for the Council. Indeed, it is within this institution, that the two spheres come together: the Council is an institution of the Union, but it is composed of representatives of the Member States. In other words, it is at the same time intergovernmental and supranational. This dichotomy does often create friction between the general interest of the Union and the national interests of the individual Member States, which can only be resolved by what the Treaties refer to as "solidarity among the Member States".[15] If the powers provided for in the Treaties for the establishment of the Customs Union typically come within the ambit of the Union institutions, the situation is different with regard to the activities in the economic and social policy fields. Those must necessarily be based "on the close co-ordination of Member States' economic policies",[16] and this co-ordination necessarily takes place within the Council. Indeed, according

---

[10] Art.4(1),(2) TFEU.
[11] Art.4(3) TFEU.
[12] Art.4(3) TFEU.
[13] Art.4(4) TFEU.
[14] Art.5(3) EU. The principle of subsidiarity must also be seen in connection with Art.1 EU which provides that "decisions are taken as closely as possible to the citizen".
[15] Art.3(3)3 TFEU.
[16] Art.119(1) TFEU.

to the EU Treaty, the Council is to "carry out policy-making and coordinating functions".[17] On the other hand, the Council is also, together with Parliament, the Union's lawmaker, which is expressed in the Treaty by the words: it shall, jointly with Parliament, "exercise legislative and budgetary functions".[18]

1.   MEMBERS OF THE COUNCIL

The Council consists of a representative of each Member State at ministerial level,[19] who may commit the government of the Member State in question and cast its vote".[20] These last words were added by the EU Treaty to allow members of State governments in federal Member States to represent the central government, but ensures that whoever represents a government within the Council, for example a regional minister, she or he can indeed commit said central government. It is left to each government to decide which one of its members shall represent it at a given Council meeting and, although the Treaty refers to "a" representative, it sometimes happens that two or more ministers of the same Member State are present at the same Council meeting.[21]

7–04

A member of the Council who is prevented from attending a meeting may arrange to be represented.[22] Neither the Treaty nor the Rules of Procedure of the Council specify who can represent a Council member. It is clear, however, that unless the representative is "at ministerial level", he or she shall not be able to cast a vote.[23]

Being representatives of the Member States, the members of the Council act on instruction from their government. They do not, however, constitute an intergovernmental conference of ministers, nor are they in a position similar to that of their colleagues within international organisations, where decisions are practically always taken unanimously and only bind those States which afterwards ratify them.

As mentioned, the members of the Council do represent the interests of their respective States, but they must, at the same time, act as an institution of the Union and in the interest of the latter. It is not evident that this is always clearly perceived by all the members of the Council.

---

[17] Art16(1) EU.

[18] Art.16(1) EU.

[19] The Rules of Procedure of the Council, Annex I, last sub-paragraph, refer to "the minister or State secretary of its choice" [2004] O.J. L106/22.

[20] Art.16(2) EU; this means 28 members as from the accession of Croatia to the Union in summer 2013.

[21] This is specifically provided for in Art.15(3) EU.

[22] Rules of Procedure, Art.4.

[23] The wording of the Treaty allows the Member State to be represented by a person who would not be considered a minister in the State concerned.

2. TASKS AND POWERS OF THE COUNCIL

(1) Decision-making

(a) Principles

7–05 The Council exercises, jointly with Parliament, legislative and budgetary functions. It carries out policy-making and co-ordinating functions.[24]. Those competences are like all Union competences "governed by the principle of conferral".[25] Indeed, as indicated, the most important provision concerning the exercise of power by the institutions of the Union is to be found at the very beginning of the EU Treaty: "The Union shall act only within the limits of the competences conferred upon it by the Member States in the Treaties".[26] In other words, the Union is not endowed with a general regulatory competence; it can only act when this is specifically provided for in a Treaty provision, the reason why the latter is almost always mentioned in Union acts.[27]

There may be cases, however, where action by the Union:

> "[S]hould prove necessary, within the framework of the policies defined by the Treaties, to attain one of the objectives set out in the Treaties, and the Treaties have not provided the necessary powers".

In such a case, the Council, acting unanimously on a proposal from the Commission and after obtaining the consent of Parliament, shall adopt the appropriate measures.[28]

However, several stringent conditions have to be fulfilled, and this possibility may not, therefore, be considered as an unlimited opportunity for the institutions to increase their powers of decision. Indeed, the appropriate measures may only be taken when action is necessary "to attain one of the objectives set out in the Treaties", which indicates that the powers exercised in such cases are purely implementing Treaty objectives. Also, the required unanimity within the Council should provide the necessary guarantees; indeed, the extension of the Union's powers will, almost inevitably, reduce the powers of the Member States in the same proportion. Unanimity therefore constitutes a brake on a possible extension of the powers of the Union. Furthermore, the Commission's proposal and the consent of Parliament should ensure that the Union's interests are sufficiently

---

[24] Art.16(1) EU.

[25] Art.5(1) EU.

[26] Art.5(2) EU.

[27] Art.296(2) TFEU: "Legal acts shall state the reasons on which they are based". See Ch.3: The Legal Acts of the Union.

[28] Art.352(1) TFEU; at the 1972 Paris Summit it was agreed that for the purpose of carrying out the tasks laid down in the different programs of action, "it was desirable to make the widest possible use of all the dispositions of the Treaty, including Art.[352]". Earlier, the use of Art.352 was more common than nowadays. The frequent Treaty changes over the last 25 years, adding detailed provisions on the Union's competences to the Treaty, have made it less necessary in practice to have recourse to Art.352.

taken into consideration—and there is always the judicial control of the Court.[29] The Treaty of Lisbon added other limitations: measures taken under this procedure may not entail harmonisation of Member States' laws or regulations where such harmonisation is excluded by the Treaties[30] and it cannot be used as a basis for attaining objectives pertaining to the foreign and security policy.[31] This procedure does, nevertheless, constitute a way of "supplementing" the Treaty provisions without going through one of the rather cumbersome procedures provided for amending it.[32]

Beside the fact that the Council (together with Parliament) may only act when this is expressly provided for in the Treaty, there is another limitation which results from the balance of powers among the Union institutions. Indeed, in practically all cases, the Council can only use its decision-making power on the basis of a proposal from the Commission. Although there are many cases where the Commission must, in pursuance of the Treaties,[33] make a proposal to the Council[34] (and to Parliament), and, although the Council (and Parliament) may "request the Commission to submit any appropriate proposal",[35] such a proposal for which only the Commission is responsible, remains a prerequisite for the Council's (and Parliament's) action. If Commission refuses to submit a proposal, it must inform the Council and/or the Parliament of its reasons.

7–06

It is not only the impossibility to act, in most cases,[36] without a proposal from the Commission that constitutes a limitation of the Council's decision-making power. The limitation resides also, and probably more so, in the content of the Commission's proposal. Indeed, although the Council is empowered, acting unanimously, to amend the Commission's proposal, the Council is still bound by its general content.[37] It could only adopt a content different from the original proposal if the Commission agrees to modify it.[38]

The "conferred powers" principle is not an obstacle to the use of the "implied powers" theory as a basis for action by the institutions. The "implied powers" theory means in short: When the Union has a competence to act internally, it must

---

[29] See *Hauptzollamt Bremerhaven v Massey-Fergusson* (8/73) [1973] E.C.R. 897 and *Commission v Council* (242/87) [1989] E.C.R. 1449, where the Court accepted the use of what is now Art.308 TFEU [1991] 1 C.M.L.R. 478.

[30] See, for instance, Art.149(2) TFEU.

[31] Art.352(3) and (4) TFEU.

[32] See Art.48 EU.

[33] In case the Commission were to fail to make a proposal when required to by the Treaty, the Court could be called upon to establish that this failure constitutes an infringement under Art.265 TFEU, thereby obliging the Commission to "take the necessary measures to comply with the judgment of the Court" (Art.266 TFEU).

[34] This is the case each time the Treaty provides that the Council, acting on a proposal from the Commission, "shall . . .", e.g. Art.31 TFEU, as opposed to the Council "may", on a proposal from the Commission, e.g. Art.18,2 TFEU.

[35] Arts 225 and 241 TFEU.

[36] As shall be seen, there are cases where the Treaties provide that other institutions and bodies and Member States may make proposals for legislative acts, such as the High Representative Art.238(2) TFEU.

[37] Art.293(1) TFEU. If the Council were to modify the proposal substantially, it would no longer be an amendment. One must apply here, by analogy, the Court's view on the requirement of renewed consultation of Parliament in case the Council modifies the proposal on which Parliament was consulted, in such a way as to affect its substance. *ACF Chemiefarma v Commission* (41/69) [1970] E.C.R. 661 at 662(3).

[38] Art.293(2) TFEU.

also have the competence to act externally, for instance by entering into international commitments with third countries or international or jurisdictions in the area where it has internal competences.[39]

The principle of conferred powers does not imply that provisions conferring power on the Union must necessarily be interpreted narrowly. On the contrary, case law shows that the provisions are often interpreted extensively.[40] One of the arguments to which the Court has referred to in order to arrive at an extension interpretation (or of narrow interpretation of exceptions to Treaty provisions, is the *effet utile;* that is that otherwise the provisions would not be effective or reach their full effect.[41]

(b) Scope

7–07
Being the Union (co)legislator, the Council's decision-making power covers the whole spectrum of the Union's activities. The Council may bestow on the Commission in the acts which it adopts, powers to adopt the necessary non-legislative acts of general application to supplement or amend certain non-essential elements of the legislative act.[42] Such powers are referred to delegated powers. If the legislative act requires the adoption of implementing provisions, it will normally be for the Commission to adopt these; the powers of the Commission are in that case referred to as implementing powers.[43]

As was seen, most of the Council's legislative powers are now shared with Parliament. This was, from the introduction of the "own resources", already the case with the budgetary powers[44]; it now applies to most legislative acts.[45] Both were examined in some detail in the previous chapter concerning Parliament.[46]

(c) Voting Procedure

7–08
The voting procedure provided for under the European Treaties is one of the more interesting aspects of the Union, since it provides for the possibility of taking, by a majority vote, decisions which are nonetheless binding on all the Member States. Under the majority voting system, even under the qualified majority voting, no single Member State has a veto right.[47] It is this system that has allowed the Union to move steadily towards the implementation of its objectives.

---

[39] *Fédération Charbonnire de Belgique v High Authority* (8/55) [1954–1956] E.C.R. 245 at 299 and *Commission v Council* (22/70) [1971] E.C.R. 263 at 280(72); C.M.L.R. 335.

[40] See for instance *Blaizot v University of Liege* (24/86) [1988] E.C.R. 379 where the Court held the notion of "vocational training" in Art.128 of the EEC Treaty to include university studies; and *Continental Can* (6-72) [1973] E.C.R. 215, where the Court held that the strengthening of a dominant position in itself could constitute an "abuse of dominant position" under Art.102 TFEU.

[41] See for instance *Reyners* (2/74) [1974] E.C.R. 631, and *Van Binsbergen* (33/74) [1974] E.C.R. 1299.

[42] Art.290 TFEU. See consolidated version of Council "Comitology" Decision 1999/462, now repealed through Regulation 182/2011 [2011] O.J. L55/13. For more details see Ch.8: The Commission, paras 8–16 to 8–18.

[43] Art.291(2) TFEU.

[44] See former Art.272 EC.

[45] Art.294 TFEU.

[46] See Ch.5: The European Parliament.

[47] Obviously this only exists when unanimity is required; there still are a few such cases, see below.

This system is unique, and it differentiates the Union from other bodies established under international law, since the latter, generally speaking, only operate on the basis of consensus or unanimous decisions.

However, according to the Rules of Procedure,[48] a vote is only taken within the Council if a majority of the members of the Council so decide, or on the initiative of its President, or on the initiative of a member of the Council, or of the Commission.

The basic rule with regard to voting in the Council is that it acts "by a qualified majority, except where the Treaties provide otherwise".[49] The same applies to the European Council which only acts by simple majority for procedural questions.[50] The presence of a majority of the members of the Council who are entitled to vote is required in order to enable the Council to vote (= quorum).[51] Any member of the European Council,[52] and of the Council, may also act on behalf of not more than one other member.[53] On the other hand, there are cases in which, according to the Treaties, one or more members of the Council may not participate in the vote[54]; in such a case "due account will be taken, in accordance with Annex III [of the Rules of Procedure] of such cases".[55]

The voting procedures are: simple majority; qualified majority; and unanimity.

(i) Simple majority[56]

This majority exists in a limited number of cases.[57] When required, the Council shall act by a majority of its component members, i.e. presently 15 out of 28.

    The simple majority does not apply unless the Treaties specifically provide for it,[58] since the general rule is, as mentioned, that the Council acts by qualified majority.[59]

                                      7–09

(ii) Qualified majority

Three different calendar periods must be borne in mind when calculating the qualified majority, in the European Council and in the Council, for the adoption of acts requiring qualified majority:[60]

                                        7–10

---

[48] Rules of Procedure, Art.7.1.

[49] Art.16(3) EU.

[50] Art.235(3) TFEU.

[51] Rules of Procedure, Art.11(4).

[52] Art.235(1) TFEU.

[53] Art.239 TFEU.

[54] See, for instance, Art.20(3) EU (provisions on enhanced co-operation).

[55] Rules of Procedure, Art.16. According to a Council agreement, this does not cover the situation provided by Art.7 EU: serious and persistent breach by a Member State; see 1 under Art.16.

[56] Art.238(1) TFEU.

[57] See, for instance, Art.240(2) and (3) TFEU: organization of the General Secretariat, adoption of the Rules of Procedure; Art.241 TFEU: Request the Commission to undertake studies or to submit proposals; Art.242 TFEU: rules governing the committees.

[58] See, for instance, Art.243 TFEU.

[59] Art.16(3) EU.

[60] Provisions concerning these periods and the applicable rules are to be found in the EU Treaty, the TFEU and Protocol No.36, which makes the understanding of the system rather complicated!

- *Until October 31, 2014.*[61] Until October 31, 2014, "transitional provisions" are applicable[62]—member's votes, both in the European Council and in the Council, shall be weighted as follows:

Belgium	12	Luxembourg	4
Bulgaria	10	Hungary	12
Czech Republic	12	Malta	3
Denmark	7	Netherlands	13
Germany	29	Austria	10
Estonia	4	Poland	27
Ireland	7	Portugal	12
Greece	12	Romania	14
Spain	27	France	29
Slovenia	4	Lithuania	7
Croatia	7	Slovakia	7
Italy	29	Finland	7
Cyprus	4	Sweden	10
Latvia	4	United Kingdom	29

Acts shall be adopted if there are at least 260 votes in favour, representing a majority of the members (14), where, under the Treaties, they must be adopted on a proposal from the Commission. In other cases, decisions are adopted if there are at least 260 votes in favour, representing at least two-thirds of the members (19).

When a decision is to be adopted by a qualified majority, a member of the European Council or of the Council (as the case may be) may request that a check is made to ensure that the Member States comprising the qualified majority represent at least 62 per cent of the total population of the Union[63] (+/– 500 million); if that proves not to be the case, the act shall not be adopted.

When not all the members of the Council participate in the voting, namely in the cases where reference is made to the qualified majority, as defined in the TFEU,[64] the qualified majority shall be defined as the same proportion of the weighted votes and the same proportion of the number of Council members and, if appropriate, the same percentage of the population of the Member States concerned as laid down by Protocol No.36 on Transitional Provisions.[65]

---

[61] Protocol No.36 attached to the TFEU "On Transitional Provisions", Art.3(1), [2008] O.J. C115/322.

[62] Art.16(5) EU.

[63] For the population figures see Rules of Procedure, new Annex III [2006] O.J. L285/65. The population figures are recalculated and published at the end (or beginning of each year). See also Basic Statistics at the beginning of this book.

[64] Art.238(3) TFEU.

[65] Protocol No.36, Art.3(4).

- *Between November 1, 2014 and March 31, 2017.*[66] During that period "transitional provisions" will also be applied[67]—as from November 1, 2014, a qualified majority shall be defined as at least 55 per cent of the members of the Council (15), comprising at least 15 of them and representing Member States comprising at least 65 per cent of the population of the Union (+/− 500 million).

  A blocking minority must include at least four Council members, failing which the qualified majority shall be deemed to be attained.[68]

  When a decision is to be adopted by a qualified majority, a member of the European Council or of the Council (as the case may be) may request that the act be adopted in accordance with the rules applying before November 1, 2014.[69]

  When, under the Treaties, not all the members of the Council participate in the voting, namely in the cases where reference is made to the qualified majority as defined in the TFEU,[70] the qualified majority shall be defined as at least 55 per cent of the members of the Council representing the participating Member States, comprising at least 65 per cent of the population of these States.[71]

  A blocking minority must include at least the minimum number of Council members representing more than 35 per cent of the population of the participating Member States, plus one member, failing which, the qualified majority shall be deemed attained.[72]

  When the Council does not act on a proposal from the Commission or from the High Representative, the qualified majority shall be defined as at least 72 per cent of the members of the Council (19), representing the participating Member States comprising at least 65 per cent of the population of these States.[73]

- *After March 31, 2017.* The provisions provided for the period between November 1, 2014 and March 31, 2017 shall apply.[74] However, a member of the European Council or of the Council may no longer request that the act be adopted in accordance with the rules applying before November 1, 2014.

(iii)   Unanimity

Initially, the EEC Treaty provided for unanimity in many cases until the end of the transitional period[75] and majority thereafter. Unanimity, for instance, is still required when the Council, acting on a proposal from the Commission, wants to

7–11

---

[66] Art.16(4)1 EU.

[67] Art.16 (4) and (5) EU, Art.238(2) TFEU and Protocol No.36, Art.3(2).

[68] Art.16(4)2 EU.

[69] Protocol No.36, Art.3,2.

[70] Art.238(3) TFEU.

[71] Protocol No.36, Art.3(4).

[72] Art.16(4)2 TFEU.

[73] Art.238(2) TFEU.

[74] This follows from a concurrent reading of Art.16(4) and (5) EU and Art.238(2) and (3) TFEU and Protocol No.36 Art.3(1) and (2).

[75] The transitional period ended on December 31, 1965.

adopt an act which constitutes an amendment to that proposal.[76] As indicated, unanimity had, in the beginning, become common practice.[77] Presently it is only required in a limited number of cases by the Treaties.[78] Abstentions by members present in person or represented do not prevent the adoption by the Council of acts which require unanimity.[79]

A final observation concerning the voting procedure of the Council is that, in case of urgency, acts may be adopted by "written procedure"; agreement of the Commission is required where the written vote is on a matter the Commission has brought before the Council.[80]

(2)   Co-ordination of Economic Policies: Broad Guidelines of the Economic Policies of the Member States and the Union

7–12   Member States must conduct their economic policies with a view to contributing to the achievement of the objectives of the Union, as defined in the Treaty on European Union, and in the context of the broad guidelines set out by the Council. The Member States and the Union must act in accordance with the principle of an open market with free competition, favouring an efficient allocation of resources,[81] based on an economic policy founded on the close co-ordination of the Member States' economic policies, on the internal market and on the definition of common objectives.[82]

Besides having the power to take decisions in all the cases provided for by the Treaty, the Council has the task to "adopt broad guidelines of the economic policies of the Member States and the Union".[83] To this end, the Council, on a

---

[76] Art.293(1) TFEU this rule does not apply in the case of Art.294(10) and (13) TFEU; conciliation committee, Art.310 TFEU; financial provisions, Art.312 TFEU; multiannual financial framework, Art.314 TFEU; budget and Art.315 TFEU—in case the budget is not approved at the beginning of the financial year.

[77] This practice finds its origin in the Arrangement regarding majority voting, adopted by the Council at its meeting of January 28 and 29, 1966, at Luxembourg. This arrangement is sometimes improperly referred to as the "Luxembourg Compromise" or "Luxembourg Accord": it is no such thing. It is only an internal arrangement of the Council, which ended the most serious crisis the Union had known and which was started by the over-nationalist government of Général De Gaulle. The arrangement provided, among others: "1. Where, in the case of decisions which may be taken by majority vote on a Commission proposal, and very important interests of one or more partners are at stake, the members of the Council will endeavor, within a reasonable time, to reach solutions, which can be adopted by all the members of the Council while respecting their mutual interests and those of the Union, in accordance with Art.2 of the EEC Treaty." For the French, the discussion must be continued until unanimous agreement is reached; this was not accepted by the other five members, and the question always remained: what happens in the event of failure to reach complete agreement? This is the reason why the Luxembourg arrangement was, in fact, an agreement to disagree. Anyway, after the SEA, EU, Amsterdam and Nice Treaties, one should be able to assume that the Luxembourg arrangement is dead. It should be remembered, however, that the arrangement only concerned cases where qualified majority voting is provided for. This means that, where unanimity is required, each Member State has indeed a veto right.

[78] Art.92 TFEU transport; Art.108(2)3 TFEU State aids to be considered compatible by the Council; Art.203 TFEU association with ACP countries; and Art.346(2) TFEU protection of security interests.

[79] Art.238(4) TFEU.

[80] Art.12 Rules of Procedure.

[81] Art.120 TFEU.

[82] Art.119 TFEU.

[83] Art.121(2) TFEU.

recommendation from the Commission, formulates a draft for the broad guidelines and reports it to the European Council. The latter formulates a conclusion on the basis of which the Council adopts a recommendation setting out the broad guidelines.[84] These guidelines must be consistent with the guidelines for employment policies of the Member States.[85] Together they form the "Integrated Guidelines for growth and jobs".

As was pointed out at the beginning of this section, the Union and the Member States are also to establish an "Economic and Monetary Union", whose currency is the Euro and implement the common policies and activities referred to in the Treaty.[86] Mention should be made here of the fact that the "close coordination of Member States' economic policies" constitutes a necessary complement to the establishment of the internal market. As will be seen, the latter consists of the basic freedoms[87] and a number of Union policies. The list of the various policies entrusted to the Union and the Member States has grown with the SEA, the EU, Nice and Lisbon Treaties.

As was pointed out, most of the above-mentioned activities of the Union require co-operation between the Union and the Member States, and it is the task of the Council to organise this co-operation. However, it is extremely difficult to describe with great precision how this task is to be carried out. Indeed, while the activities of the Union with regard to the establishment of the internal market are described in the TFEU with some precision (the Treaty indicates, for instance, whether the Council must act through regulations, directives, decisions or agreements) and contains an indication as to the timetable for their implementation (such as the EMU phases),[88] the situation is rather different when it comes to the co-ordination of the economic activities of the Member States.

Although regulations, directives and decisions are by no means excluded, the Treaty refers, as far as the Council is concerned, to "broad guidelines",[89] "multilateral surveillance",[90] "coordinated strategy",[91] "appropriate measures",[92] "general orientations",[93] "adoption of measures to contribute to the objectives referred to",[94] besides the "resolutions", "declarations", "work programmes", "multi-annual framework programmes"[95] and "general action programmes" provided for in various Treaty provisions.

7–13

---

[84] See for instance, Council Recommendation on the broad guidelines for the economic policies of the Member States and the Union (2010–2014) [2010] O.J. L191/28.

[85] Art.146(1) TFEU and 148(2).

[86] Art.3 EU.

[87] Freedom to move goods, to accept work, to establish oneself, to provide services, to transfer capital and payments in any of the Member States.

[88] Art.139 TFEU.

[89] Art.121(2–3) TFEU. See, for instance, Council Recommendation of February 12, 2001, "with a view of ending the inconsistency with the broad guidelines, of the economic policies in Ireland", [2001] L69/22 and the Decision of the same day "making public" said Recommendation, [2001] O.J. L69/24. See also the Council Opinions on the updated stability programmes for various Member States, [2002] O.J. C51/1.

[90] Art.121(3)2 TFEU.

[91] Art.145 TFEU.

[92] Art.117(1) TFEU.

[93] Art.219(2) EC.

[94] Art.166(4) TFEU.

[95] Art.182(1) TFEU.

Clearly, the Council's task with regard to co-ordination of economic policies is ill-defined as regards its means. Nevertheless, this loose system has, so far, worked in a rather satisfactory way: to be effective, co-ordination needs to be flexible.

As for the obligations imposed upon the Member States in the above--mentioned fields, they are often just as vague. The Treaty mentions, for example that the Member States "shall regard their economic policies as a matter of common concern and shall coordinate them with the Council".[96] Not a very precise obligation. The question can therefore be asked whether the procedures provided in the Treaty for implementing the co-ordination of the economic policies by the Council correspond to the requirements of a democratic exercise of powers.

(3) Guidelines on Employment Policy

7–14 Under the EU Treaty,[97] the Union must "work for the sustainable development of Europe based on balanced economic growth and price stability, a highly competitive social market economy, aiming at full employment".[98]

Each year, the European Council must consider the employment situation in the Union and adopt conclusions thereon, on the basis of a joint annual report from the Council and the Commission. On the basis of these conclusions, the Council, on a proposal from the Commission and after consulting Parliament, the Economic and Social Committee, the Committee of the Regions and the Employment Committee,[99] shall draw up guidelines for the Member States.[100] These guidelines must be consistent with the Guidelines on Economic Policy mentioned above. Parliament and the Council, acting in accordance with the ordinary legislative procedure,[101] may adopt incentive measures designed to encourage co-operation between Member States, and to support their action in the field of employment.[102] The Treaty also provides for the establishment of an Employment Committee with advisory status to promote co-ordination between Member States on employment and labour market policies.[103] For further details see Ch.29: Social Policy.

---

[96] Art.121(1) TFEU.
[97] Art.3(2) EU.
[98] Art.3(3) EU.
[99] Art.150 TFEU.
[100] See 2010 Guidelines [2010] O.J. L308 /46.
[101] Art.294 TFEU.
[102] Art.149 TFEU.
[103] Art.150 TFEU.

3. ORGANISATIONAL ASPECTS OF THE COUNCIL

(1) Configurations of the Council

The Council meets in different configurations according to the subject matter to   **7–15**
be dealt with. The list of these configurations is, according to the EU Treaty,[104]
fixed by the European Council acting by qualified majority.[105]

The various configurations of the Council are presently[106] the following:

1. General Affairs;
2. Foreign Affairs;
3. Economic and Financial Affairs, including budget (generally referred to as "Ecofin");
4. Justice and Home Affairs, including Civil Protection;
5. Employment, Social Policy, Health and Consumer Affairs;
6. Competitiveness (Internal Market, Industry, Research and Space) including Tourism;
7. Transport, Telecommunications and Energy;
8. Agriculture and Fisheries;
9. Environment;
10. Education, Youth, Culture and Sport, including Audiovisual Affairs.

Consequently, it is not unusual to have various Council meetings in session at the same time in Brussels where, according to the Rules of Procedure, the Council shall have its seat, or in Luxembourg.[107]

The office of President of the Council is held, for periods of six months, in turn by each Member State, in the order decided by the European Council.[108] The same rotation applies to all the subordinate bodies of the Council, such as the Committee of Permanent Representatives (COREPER)[109] (see below), the working groups and other meetings of ministers.

However, the presidency of the Foreign Affairs Council is assumed by the High Representative.[110]

The meetings of the Council are always attended by the Commission, represented by its President and/or the Commission member who is more particularly responsible for the subject under discussion. Commission officials also attend the meetings, and participate in the work of COREPER (see hereunder) and other Council bodies.

---

[104] Art.2(1) Rules of Procedure.
[105] Art.236 TFEU.
[106] Modified [2010] O.J. L263/12.
[107] Art.1(3), Rules of Procedure; see also [1997] O.J. C340/112 on the location of the seats of the institutions.
[108] Art.16(9) EU, which provides that the presidency shall be held by member States' representatives on the basis of equal rotation and Art.236(b) TFEU: see Decision of the European Council of December 1, 2009 on the exercise of the Presidency of the Council [2009] O.J. L315/50, and implementing Decision [2009] O.J. L322/28, corrigendum [2009] O.J. L349/56.
[109] See hereunder.
[110] Art.18(3) EU. See below, Ch.37: The Common Foreign and Security Policy.

(2) COREPER[111] (COmité des REprésentants PERmanents—Committee of Permanent Representatives)

7–16   The creation of this Committee stems from the fact that the Council meets no more than a few days a month and that, with the increase of Union activities, a more permanent presence of the Member States in Brussels was required. The Permanent Representatives—high-level civil servants with the rank of Ambassador—closely follow the various Union activities on a day-to-day basis. They are not deputies of the Council members, they only have very limited administrative decision-making power, since they may adopt "procedural decisions" in cases provided for in the Council's Rules of Procedure[112]; they constitute an organ within the Council structure.

Their task is to prepare the work of the Council and to carry out the tasks assigned to them by the Council.[113] They meet several days each week and, although COREPER has, as was stated, no decision-making power, once it has reached agreement, for instance, on a proposal from the Commission, it can safely be assumed that the Council will decide accordingly. This is expressed by the fact that, in such cases, the matter is put on the agenda of the Council as an "A" point.[114] The practice is that the Council accepts the A points, without further ado at the beginning of its meeting, thereby transforming them into legislative (binding) acts. It must, however, be emphasised that the Council is in no way bound to accept the A points, and any Council member is free to ask for a discussion on the subject, in which case it is placed on the agenda of the next Council meeting, but this time as a "B" point or sent back to COREPER. It may also happen that a member maintains a "reserve", due, for example, to the need for a national parliamentary scrutiny. This reserve can, however, be lifted in time for the next Council meeting, allowing the latter to adopt the act as an "A" point. When no agreement can be reached at COREPER level, but it is thought that a solution can be found at the ministers (political) level or there is a deadline, the matter is placed on the Council's agenda as a "B" point, i.e. a subject on which discussion is needed.

7–17   COREPER is assisted in its work by a whole series of "working groups", some permanent, some temporary, which prepare the work of COREPER. These working groups are composed of civil servants from the Member States and convene whenever necessary. When a Commission proposal is sent to the Council, it first comes before COREPER, which can examine it and agree on it directly, but normally sends it to one of the working groups. The latter examines it and reports to COREPER. All the meetings of COREPER and of the working groups are attended by officials of the Commission; it would be more correct to say that these Commission officials participate in their work. Indeed, real negotiations often take place inside those working groups (and at COREPER level) in order to arrive at a text which is acceptable to all Member States, or at least to enough of them to reach a qualified majority when this is provided for.

---

[111] It is sub-divided into COREPER I, composed of the deputy permanent representatives, which handle, among others the agricultural policy; and COREPER II, formed by the Ambassadors.
[112] Council's Rules of Procedure [2004] O.J. L106/22, amended [2010] O.J. L338/47.
[113] Art.240(1) TFEU.
[114] Art.2(6), Rules of Procedure.

This might result in the Commission modifying its proposal.[115] The meetings of the working groups are presided over by a national from the country which holds the office of President at the Council.

One great advantage of these working groups composed of national civil servants, is that the national view is clearly expressed in Brussels, while the national administrations are, in turn, directly confronted with the views of the Commission, and those of the other Member States.

In the same way, it can be said that the Permanent Representatives fulfil a double function: they defend the national interests within the Union, and at the same time, represent the Union's point of view at home. They thus constitute an indispensable link between the national administrations and the European institutions.

(3) The Rules of Procedure

The Rules of Procedure are adopted by the Council, by a simple majority vote.[116] **7–18**
They provide, among others, for the following:

- The adoption of a multi-annual strategic programme for the three years to come, on the basis of a joint proposal from the presidency and the Commission, and an annual operating programme. The latter shall have regard to relevant points resulting from the "dialogue on the political priorities" for the year, conducted at the Commission's initiative.
- Measures relating to co-operation between presidencies of successive six-month periods, and the chairing of certain working parties by a member of the General Secretariat of the Council.
- The Council meets in public when it deliberates and votes on draft legislative acts. To this end each meeting is divided into two parts dealing, respectively, with Union legislative acts and non-legislative activities.[117]
- The conduct of the meetings: the presidency is responsible for taking any measure required to achieve the best possible use of the time available, including: limiting contributors' speaking time, determining the order in which they speak, etc.

The present Rules of Procedure were adopted in 2006 and amended several times[118] Mention should be made here of public access to Council documents,[119] as provided for by the Treaty: "[a]ny citizen of the Union and any natural or legal person residing or having its registered office in a Member State, shall have the

---

[115] Art.293(2) TFEU.
[116] Art.240(3) TFEU.
[117] Art.16(8) EU and Art.15(2) TFEU.
[118] [2009] O.J. L325/351, amended [2011] O.J. L346/17.
[119] See Art.240(3) TFEU. Decision 93/731 on public access to Council documents [1993] O.J. L340/43, Art.22, Rules of Procedure amended [1993] O.J. L304/1 and Code of Conduct concerning public access to Council and Commission documents [1993] O.J. L340/41; see also *The Carvel and Guardian Newspapers* (T-194/94), [1995] E.C.R. II-2765; [1995] 3 C.M.L.R. 359; *Netherlands v Council* (C-58/94), [1996] E.C.R. I-2169; [1996] 2 C.M.L.R. 996; *Svenska Journalist Forderbundet* (T-174/95), [1998] E.C.R. II-2289 and *Kuijer v Council* (T-188/98), [2000] E.C.R. II-1959, where the Court found a breach of Decision 93/731.

right of access to European Parliament, Council and Commission documents".[120] See also the Council Decision on the improvement of information on the Council's legislative activities and the public register of Council documents.[121] It provides that the General Secretariat shall make accessible to the public, via the Internet, the provisional agendas of meetings of the Council and its preparatory bodies.

In 2001 the Council adopted its "security regulations" concerning classified information regarding the Security and Defence Policy[122] and, in 2011, a decision was taken on the security rules for protecting EU classified information.[123]

(4) The Secretariat of the Council

7–19 According to the Treaty, the Council is assisted by a General Secretariat, under the responsibility of a Secretary General,[124] who is appointed by the Council which also decides on the organisation of the Secretariat. It is, like the Commission's departments, divided in Directorates General, whose competences correspond to the main activities of the Union.

FURTHER READING

7–20 Hayes-Renshaw & Wallace, *The Council of Ministers* (Palgrave Macmillan, 2006).

Jan Werts, *The European Council* (London, John Harper, 2008).

Jeffrey Lewis, *Council of Ministers and European Council* in The Oxford Handbook of the European Union (Oxford University Press, 2012).

Naurin & Wallace, *Unveiling the Council of the European Union* (Palgrave Macmillan, 2010).

Westlake & Galloway, *The Council of the European Union* (London, John Harper, 2006).

---

[120] Art.15(3) TFEU. See Regulation 1049/2001 of Parliament and the Council regarding public access to Parliament, Council and Commission documents, [2001] O.J. L145/43 and the Joint Declaration relating to Regulation [2001] O.J. L173/5. The rules on public access gives rise to much litigation, see for instance *Sweden and Turco v Council* (Joined Cases C-39/05 P and C-52/05 P), where the Court annulled a decision of the General Court (CFI) misinterpreting Art.4(2): [2008] E.C.R. I-4753, *Access Info Europe* (T-233/09) [2011] O.J. C139 exception relating to the protection of the decision-making process.

[121] [2000] O.J. L9/22.

[122] [2001] O.J. L101/1.

[123] [2011] O.J. L141/17.

[124] Art.240(2) TFEU.

CHAPTER 8

The Commission

According to the EU Treaty,[1] the Commission's task is to:

- promote the general interest of the Union and take appropriate initiatives to that end;
- ensure the application of the Treaties and of measures adopted by the institutions pursuant to them;
- oversee the application of Union law under the control of the Court of Justice of the European Union;
- execute the budget and manage programmes;
- exercise co-ordinating, executive and management functions as laid down in the Treaties;
- ensure the Union's external representation with the exception of the common foreign and security policy, and other cases provided for in the Treaties; and
- initiate the Union's annual and multi-annual programming with a view to achieving inter-institutional agreements.The former EC Treaty provided that the Commission shall "have its own power of decision"; this has disappeared and the TFEU contains a general provision concerning the powers of all the institutions to adopt acts. This, plus the fact that, as shall be seen, the Commission no longer has the exclusive monopoly of legislative proposal, indicates a certain reduction in the Commission's special position among the institutions.

Nevertheless, the Commission is the moving power of the Union's activities, and its uninterrupted presence at Brussels, the main seat of the Union institutions,[2] its competent staff and its world-wide relations create the necessary conditions for it to play a major role within the institutional system of the Union. The Commission embodies and represents the common or Union interest and seeks to ensure that this interest prevails when Union decisions are taken. The various tasks of the Commission will be examined in more detail, after a short analysis of some organisational aspects.

---

[1] Art. 17(1) EU.
[2] See Protocol on the location of the seats of the institutions and certain bodies and departments of the European Union and of Europol annexed to the Treaty on European Union and the Treaties establishing the European Union and the European Atomic Energy Union [1997] O.J. C340/112.

1. THE MEMBERS OF THE EUROPEAN COMMISSION

(1) The Number of Commissioners

8–02   While the EC Treaty provided that the Commission "shall include one national of each of the Member States"[3] (this means 28 members) and that that number may be altered by the Council,[4] the EU Treaty now provides that:

> "[B]etween the entry into force of the Treaty of Lisbon and 31 October 2014, the Commission shall consist of one national of each Member State, including the President and the High Representative of the Union for Foreign Affairs and Security Policy ('High Representative'), who shall be one of its Vice-Presidents"[5]

and that:

> "[A]s from 1 November 2014, the Commission shall consist of a number of members, including the president and the High Representative, corresponding to two thirds of the number of Member States, unless the European Council, acting unanimously, decides to alter this number. The members shall be chosen from among the nationals of the Member States on the basis of a system of strictly equal rotation among the Member States, reflecting the demographic and geographical range of all the Member States. This system shall be established unanimously by the European Council.[6]"[7]

After the rejection of the Treaty of Lisbon in an Irish referendum, specific legal guarantees for Ireland were agreed upon by the European Council in order to make it possible for the Irish people to vote in favour of the Treaty in a second referendum.[8] Among these guarantees is the number of Commission members: one from each Member State.[9] Thus, there are, after the accession of Croatia in the summer 2013, 28 commissioners. The members are appointed for a period of five years.[10]

(2) The Choice of the Members of the Commission

8–03   They are to be chosen on the ground of their competence and European commitment from persons whose independence is beyond doubt.[11]

The required independence applies not only to the qualities of the candidate-commissioner; the Treaty also specifies that the members of the Commission shall, in the general interest of the Union, be completely

---

[3] Art.213(3)4 EC.
[4] Art.213(1) EC.
[5] Art.17(4) EU.
[6] The system of rotation must be established on the basis of the following principles: (a) Member States shall be treated on a strictly equal footing, as regards determination of the sequence of, and the time spent, by their nationals as members of the Commission, and (2) each successive Commission shall reflect satisfactorily the demographic and geographic range of all the Member States.
[7] Art.17(5) EU.
[8] Decision 2013/278 [2013] O.J. L165/98.
[9] See Ch.2: History.
[10] Art.17(3) EU.
[11] Art.17(3)2 EU.

independent "in the performance of their duties".[12] Since the most obvious problem with regard to this independence is the relationship between the Commissioner and the government that nominated him, the Treaty explicitly imposes upon the Member State the obligation "to respect this principle, and not to seek to influence the members of the Commission in the performance of their duties".[13]

As for the members of the Commission themselves, they are bound by certain obligations, both during and after their term of office.[14] In order to underline the importance of the independence and the other obligations, the Treaty provides that the members of the Commission shall, when entering upon their duties, give a solemn undertaking to respect the obligations arising from their office.[15]

A last remark concerning this all-important aspect of the duties of the members of the Commission: in the event of a breach of the above-mentioned obligations, the Court of Justice may, on application by the Council or the Commission, rule that the member concerned be, according to the circumstances, either compulsorily retired or deprived of his rights to a pension or other benefits in its stead.[16] The Commissioner is also under obligation to resign if the President requests him to do so.

(3) The Nomination Procedure of the Members of the Commission

As concerns the President of the Commission, the European Council, acting by qualified majority, shall propose a candidate to the Parliament. The European Council shall do so, taking into account the elections to the Parliament and after holding appropriate consultations.[17] This candidate is elected by a majority of the component members of Parliament. In case the candidate does not obtain said majority, a new candidate must be proposed within one month.

8–04

The High Representative of the Union for Foreign Affairs and Security Policy ("High Representative") is appointed by the European Council acting by a qualified majority.[18] He shall be one of the Vice-Presidents of the Commission.[19]

---

[12] Art.245 TFEU.

[13] Art.245 TFEU.

[14] Art.245 TFEU.

[15] Art.245,2 TFEU; the solemn undertaking is given before the Court of Justice during a special session. Each member undertakes to perform his duties as specified in the Treaty: complete independence in the general interest of the Union, no instructions, no action incompatible with the office, integrity and discretion; they also formally take note of the fact that the governments of the Member States have undertaken to respect their independence. One can only hope that the Commissioners strictly adhere to those obligations.

[16] Art.245(2) TFEU. So far there has only been two cases in which this procedure was initiated; in one case it ended with a settlement. See Council Decision of July 9, 1999 on the referral of the case of Mr Bangemann to the Court of Justice [1999] O.J. L192/53 and *Council v Bangemann* (C-290/99) removed from the register ([1999] O.J. C314/8) and *Bangemann v Council* (T-208/99) also removed from the register, and Council Decision of December 17, 1999 on the settlement of the *Bangemann* case: [2000] O.J. L16/73; and case C-432/04 *Commission v Edith Cresson* [2006] E.C.R. I-06387.

[17] A new Commission takes up its functions in November and the elections to Parliament are held the preceding summer.

[18] Art.18(1) EU.

[19] Art.18(4) EU.

The *other members* of the Commission: the Council, by common accord with the President-elect, shall adopt the list of the other persons it proposes for appointment; they are selected on the basis of suggestions made by the Member States.[20]

The President, the High Representative and the other members are then subject, as a body, to a vote of consent by Parliament. On the basis of this consent, the Commission shall be appointed by the European Council, acting by a qualified majority.[21]

8–05 Once the members have been nominated, they form a college: they do not have an individual role under the Treaty, although each one of them is put in charge of a given Commission service. They are jointly responsible to Parliament for the activities of the Commission; consequently they must resign, as a body, when Parliament votes a motion of censure of the Commission,[22] except the High Representative who then resigns but only from his duties in the Commission.[23]

The President of the Commission shall lay down guidelines within which the Commission is to work, decide on the internal organisation, ensuring that it acts consistently, efficiently and as a collegiate body and appoint Vice-Presidents other than the High Representative.[24] Since the President decides on the "internal organisation", he assigns the members to the different Directorates-General which composes the Commission. The President may reshuffle the allocation of those responsibilities during the Commission's term of office.[25] This allocation of responsibilities is a particular delicate task since each Member State desires the member of its nationality to be responsible for the most important services and strongly "lobbies" for it.[26]

2. THE COMMISSION'S TASKS AND POWERS

8–06 The Commission's tasks and powers have been enumerated at the beginning of this chapter and shall be examined in detail hereunder.

---

[20] Art.17(7)2 EU.

[21] Art.17(7)3 EU.

[22] Art.234 TFEU. See Ch.5: The European Parliament.

[23] Art.17(8) EU.

[24] Art.17(6) EU.

[25] Art.248 TFEU.

[26] Enormous pressure is put on the President right from the beginning of the selection process and it is, obviously, difficult for the President to ignore the wishes of the Member States. Furthermore, Parliament, before giving its consent, subjects the candidate members to questioning on the basis of their assumed future tasks which are not supposed to be known until the Commissioners have been nominated by the European Council!

(1) "Ensure the application of the Treaties, and of measures adopted by the institutions pursuant to them" and "oversee the application of Union law under the control of the Court of Justice of the European Union"[27]

The Commission is therefore often referred to as the "guardian of the Treaties", 8–07
which, indeed it is; but one should not conclude from this that it is the only body
responsible for the correct application of the Union law provisions. This task
belongs, as shall be seen, also to the national authorities and especially to the
national judge.

The measures adopted by the institutions are referred to as "secondary law",
the Treaties constituting the "primary law". Both impose obligations upon the
Member States, the institutions and natural and legal persons. It is the
Commission's task to ensure that they all abide by the law. For this purpose the
Commission is endowed with powers consisting mainly of the right to obtain
information and to institute proceedings against trespassers.

The right to *obtain information* is provided for, in a general way, by the
Treaty,[28] and by various Union acts.[29] Furthermore, the general obligation
imposed upon the Member States to "facilitate the achievement of the Union's
tasks"[30] should provide the necessary legal ground for the Commission to obtain
all the required data. Based upon the information obtained,[31] the Commission can
then, if necessary, start the following actions.

(a) With Regard to Member States[32]

When the Commission considers that a Member State has failed to fulfil an 8–08
obligation under Union law:

---

[27] Art.17(1) EU.

[28] Art.337 TFEU: "The Commission may, within the limits and under the conditions laid down by the
Council and collect any information and carry any checks required for the performance of the tasks
entrusted to it." See for instance Art.108(3) TFEU (plans to grant or alter aids).

[29] As for acts see, for instance, Regulation 2186/93 obliging Member States to draw up harmonised
business registers and *Germany v Council* (C-426/93) [1995] E.C.R. I-3723; according to the Court,
that Regulation is a measure necessary to allow the Commission to carry out its task: therefore the
Regulation does not infringe the Treaty and Regulation 1/2003, Arts 4 and 5 (Regulation
implementing Art.101 TFEU and 102, [2003] O.J. L1/1).

[30] Art.4(3) EU. See *R v Ministry of Agriculture* (C-5/94 R) [1996] E.C.R. I-2553; [1996] 2 C.M.L.R.
391: Member States are obliged to take all measures necessary to guarantee the application and
effectiveness of Union law.

[31] The Commission can also obtain information in the course of an investigation following a
complaint from a Member State or from natural or legal persons; see for instance Regulation 1/2003,
Art.3 ([2003] O.J. L1/1.) See *Smanor* (T-182/97) [1998] E.C.R. II-271, Order of the CFI: refusal of
the Commission to start proceedings against Member States for failure to fulfil an obligation; natural
or legal persons are not admissible, when challenging a refusal of the Commission to start an Art.258
procedure and *Sateba* (T-83/97) [1997] E.C.R. II-1523; [1998] 4 C.M.L.R. 528: the procedural
position of a party complaining to the Commission on the basis of Regulation 17 (now 1/2003) for
violation of Regulation 99/63, [1963] O.J. 127, 2269, is fundamentally different from the one of a
complainant requesting action for failure by a Member State: Art.258.

[32] Art.258 TFEU. It is settled case law that the Commission cannot be sued for its failure to act
against a Member State's possible incompliance with Union law

- it shall[33] remind the government in question of its obligations, and invite it to take the necessary measures or submit its observations, all within a time limit set by the Commission, usually two months; this "reminder" is commonly referred to as the "letter of formal notice";
- if no action is taken by the Member State, or no observations are received, or if those that were submitted do not convince the Commission, it shall deliver a "reasoned opinion" on the matter, and lay down a time limit with which the Member State must comply;
- if the Member State does not comply, the Commission may[34] bring the matter before the Court;
- if the Court finds that the Member State has indeed failed to fulfil its obligation, it rules accordingly and "the State shall be required to take the necessary steps to comply with the judgment".[35]

What happens when the Member State fails to implement the Court's judgment? Until the entering into force of the Union Treaty, there was nothing the Union institutions could do, except start the procedure over, in order to have the Court ascertain that the Member State concerned did not comply with the judgment.[36]

8–09   The Treaty now provides that, in case the Commission considers that the Member State has not taken the necessary measures to comply with the judgment, it shall, after having given the Member State the opportunity to submit its observations, issue a reasoned opinion specifying the points on which the Member State has not complied and fixing a time limit to do so. In case of non-compliance, the Commission may bring the matter before the Court and "specify the amount of the lump sum or penalty payment to be paid" which it considers appropriate in the circumstances.[37]

If the Court finds that the Member State has, indeed, not complied with its judgment, it may impose a lump sum[38] or penalty payment. So now[39] there exists

---

[33] The terms used here indicate that, once the Commission has determined that a Member State has indeed failed to fulfil an obligation under the Treaty (and in this determination the Commission enjoys discretionary power: it must, among other things, weigh the political implications), there is an obligation for the Commission to act. The existence of this obligation is essential within a system, where the plea of *non adimpletus contractus* is inadmissible; see *Commission v Luxembourg and Belgium* (Joined Cases 90/63 and 91/63) [1964] E.C.R. 625 at 631; [1965] C.M.L.R. 58.

[34] At this point the Commission's powers are entirely discretionary.

[35] It is interesting to note that Art.258 TFEU refers to the judgment of the Court, rather than to the Treaty obligation, which was the point of departure of the whole proceedings. The Court cannot impose upon the Member States obligations, which differ from what the Treaty prescribes; anyway, in its judgments based upon Art.258, the Court only ascertains that the Member State "has failed to fulfil its obligation under the Treaty"; see, e.g. *Commission v Belgium* (Joined Cases 227/85, 228/85, 229/85 and 230/85) [1988] E.C.R. 12; [1989] 2 C.M.L.R. 797.

[36] See, e.g. *Commission v Belgium* (Joined Cases 227/85, 228/85, 229/85 and 230/85) quoted above, fn.37.

[37] Art.258(2)1 TFEU. See *Commission v France* (C-304/02) [2005] E.C.R. I-6263, where the Court decided that by not controlling the fishery activities, in conformity with Union law, and by not insuring that violations of the fishery's provisions be prosecuted, France had not taken the measures necessary to implement the judgment of June 11, 1991 (*Commission v France* (C-64/88) [1991] E.C.R. I-2727). It therefore condemned France to pay the Commission a penalty of 57,761,250 Euros, for each period of six months during which said judgment would not have been implemented.

[38] See, for instance, *Commission v France* (C-121/07) [2008] E.C.R. I-9159, where the Court imposed on France the payment of €10 million.

a coercive measure against Member States that flout Union law. A further slight improvement was introduced by the Treaty of Lisbon: when a case is brought against a Member State for failing to fulfil its obligation to notify measures transposing a directive, the Commission may already specify the amount of the lump sum or penalty payment to be paid by the Member State concerned.[40] This amount may not be exceeded by the Court. The payment obligation shall take effect on the date set in the judgment.[41]

The Commission enjoys a large discretionary power when deciding whether or not to pursue a Member State before the Court.[42] It should also be noted that, in most cases, problems with the implementation of Union law by the Member States are settled out of court.

Responsibility of Member States towards private and legal persons for infringement of Union law.   Member States are not only responsible towards the Union for their own infringements of Union law; there is also their responsibility for possible damages caused, by the infringement, to natural or legal persons. The responsibility of the administration (government) for damage caused by failure to correctly apply Union law was amply confirmed by the Court.[43] Less evident, maybe, is the responsibility of the Member State for infringement by the legislature or the judicature. The Court decided that where a breach of Union law by a Member State is attributable to the national legislature acting in a field in which it has a wide discretion to make legislative choices, individuals suffering loss or injury thereby, are entitled to reparation. This rule only applies, however, where the breached rule of Union law is intended to confer rights upon the said individual, the breach is sufficiently serious and there is a direct causal link between the breach and the damage sustained by the individual.[44]

8–10

Where the judiciary is concerned, the Court held that this could only be incurred in the exceptional case where the national court against whose decisions there is no judicial remedy, manifestly infringed the applicable law, and the European courts' case law in the matter. In the case in question, the Court

---

[39] The ECSC Treaty also provided for some kind of coercive measures (see Art.88 ECSC), but they were never applied.
[40] Art.260(3)1 TFEU.
[41] Art.260(3)2 TFEU. The Commission publishes annually a report on Monitoring the Application of European Union Law, for instance COM (2012) 714 final. The Report contains figures on the cases that the Commission has processed in the course of the preceding year.
[42] The Commission's exercise of that power cannot be challenged in Court, see for instance *Star Fruit* (C-247/87) [1989] E.C.R. 00291.
[43] See the following cases referred to by the Court in *Köbler* (C-224/01) [2003] E.C.R. I-10239; *Francovich* (Joined Cases C-6/90 and C-9/90) [1991] E.C.R. I-5357(35); *British Telecommunications* (C-392/93) [1996] E.C.R. I-1631(38); *Hedley Lomas* (C-5/94) [1996] E.C.R. I-2553(24); *Dillenkofer* (Joined Cases C-178/94 etc.) [1996] F.C.R. I-4845(20); *Norbrook Laboratories* (C-127/95) [1998] E.C.R. I-1531(106) and *Haim* (C-424/97) [2000] E.C.R. I-5123(43). See also *Traghetti v Italy* (C-173/03) [2006] E.C.R. I-5177.
[44] *Brasserie du Pêcheur and Factortame* (Joined Cases C-46/93 and C-48/93) [1996] E.C.R. I-1029; [1996] 1 C.M.L.R. 889. Idem. in case *Heddley Lomas* (C-5/94) [1996] E.C.R. I-2553 and *Sutton* (C-66/95) [1997] E.C.R. I-2163; [1997] 2 C.M.L.R. 382.

considered that the national court did not commit a manifest, and thus sufficiently serious breach of Union law and that, consequently, the State in question did not incur liability for it.[45]

(b) With Regard to Acts of Institutions and Other Bodies

8–11 The institutions concerned here are the Council, Parliament, the EIB[46] and the ECB.[47] The Commission can initiate a court action against those authorities when it is of the opinion that they infringe a Union provision[48] or when a failure of those authorities to act is considered by the Commission to be an infringement of the Treaty.[49] These actions will be examined in more detail in Ch.9: The Court of Justice of the European Union.

(c) With Regard to Legal or Natural Persons

8–12 The administration of the bulk of Union law towards citizens and undertakings does not lie with the Commission, but with national authorities. It is only within very limited areas that the Commission is also charged with the direct administration of Union rules, most notably in the field of competition. Within this field the Commission is endowed with important powers as regards undertakings both public[50] and private and natural persons. The Commission may impose fines and penalties[51] in case of violation, or order enterprises to disinvest themselves when investigating mergers and acquisitions.[52] The Commission may also start proceedings against companies before national courts in Member States or third countries.[53]

(2) "Adopt regulations, directives, decisions, recommendations and opinions"

8–13 The TFEU refers, as indicated, to the "institutions" adopting regulations, directives, decisions, recommendations and opinions.[54] This is not without importance since, as pointed out, the legislative institutions within the Union are,

---

[45] Case *Köbler v Austria* (C-224/01) [2003] E.C.R. I-10243.

[46] Art.271(a) TFEU; see, for instance, *SGEEM v EIB* (C-370/89) [1992] E.C.R. I-6211.

[47] Art.263,1 TFEU. On the other hand the ECB itself can initiate an action in the Court against a national central bank in case it is of the opinion that the latter has failed to fulfil an obligation under the Treaty.

[48] Art.263 TFEU. Those cases are brought either by governments, Union institutions or by individuals.

[49] Art.265 TFEU.

[50] Art.106 TFEU.

[51] See Regulation 1/2003 (implementing Arts 101 and 102 TFEU), Art.15 ([2003] O.J. L1/1); Regulation 11/60 (implementing Art.75(3))[1960] O.J. 52/1121; Regulation 1017/68 (applying the rules of competition to transport by rail, road and inland waterways) [1969], Art.22, O.J. L175/1 and Regulation 139/2004 (the Merger Regulation) [2004] O.J. L24/1; see, e.g. the *Nestlé/Perrier* Decision [1992] O.J. L356/1.

[52] Regulation 139/2004, Art.8(4), quoted above, fn.53.

[53] See *Philip Morris v Commission* (Joined Cases T-377/00, T-379/00, T-380/00, T-260/01 and T-272/01) [2003] E.C.R. II-1 and Court (in appeal), Case C-131/03 P, [2006] E.C.R. I-7795: both jurisdictions confirmed the right of the Commission to start proceedings in a court in a third State.

[54] Art.288,1 TFEU.

in principle, Parliament and Council, acting jointly, or the Council acting alone. The fact that the Commission also exercises a decision-making power might create the impression that the legislative power is shared by several institutions. Although all those institutions may indeed issue acts which are binding for the subjects of Union law, a distinction must be made between "legislative" powers, which are the prerogative of Parliament and Council, and "executive" and/or "implementing" powers, which befall the Commission. Although both the Legislator and the Executive may adopt binding acts, Parliament, the Council and the Commission do not operate on quite the same level, although it must be recognised that no clear-cut distinction exists between them.[55]

It should be remembered that in both cases the powers are "conferred" powers, i.e. the institutions are not endowed with a "general" decision-making power; the Treaties now refer to "conferral" of powers.[56] The institutions only enjoy those powers which have been conferred upon them by the Treaties.[57]

As for non-binding acts, it is mostly the Commission which adopts recommendations and opinions: the many Notices and Communications of the Commission[58] fall under this category. It should be remembered that recommendations and opinions have no binding force,[59] so that in fulfilling this task the Commission acts in a purely informative or advisory capacity. The most that can be said is that the Commission binds itself politically.[60] The Treaty provides for several cases where an opinion of the Commission is required,[61] and others where it is referred to as a possibility.[62]

It is in the areas where the Union exercises exclusive powers that the Commission's role comes to the fore, both in the development of the legislative procedure, and in the implementation of the adopted rules. They concern the Customs Union,[63] competition,[64] the conservation of marine biological resources,[65] the common commercial policy[66] and the execution of the Union budget.[67] When exercising its right to act, the Commission has, in certain cases, a

8–14

---

[55] See, e.g. Commission Directive 80/723 on the transparency of financial relations between Member States and public enterprises [1980] O.J. L195/35 and *France, Italy and United Kingdom v Commission* (Joined Cases 188/80, 189/80, 190/80) [1982] E.C.R. 2545; [1982] 3 C.M.L.R. 144, where the Court ruled that the Commission Directive in question was in conformity with the Treaty; and Commission Directive 88/301on competition in the markets in telecommunications terminal equipment, challenged before and partially annulled by the Court, *France v Commission* (C-202/88) [1991] E.C.R. I-1223.

[56] Art.5(1) EU.

[57] See Ch.7: The Council (2.(1) Decision-making).

[58] See, e.g. Communication of the Commission following the famous *Cassis de Dijon* judgment [1980] O.J. C256/2.

[59] Art.288,5 TFEU. See, however the Ch.3: The Legal Acts of the Union.

[60] However, these can have a certain self-binding effect in that the Commission cannot depart from rules that it has imposed on itself, see for instance case *Hüls AG v Commission* (T-9/89) [1992] E.C.R. II-00499.

[61] See, e.g. Art.156 TFEU (opinion on problems arising at national level in the social field).

[62] Art.97 TFEU: reduction of charges and dues in respect of crossing of frontiers.

[63] Art.3(1)(a) EU.

[64] Art.101(3) TFEU, 105(2), 106(3) and 108(2).

[65] Art.17(1) EU.

[66] Art.17(1) EU.

[67] The Commission is responsible for implementing the budget and administering the various Union funds: social fund, regional fund, cohesion fund, etc.

choice as to the form of the measure,[68] in other instances no form is prescribed,[69] and sometimes a given act is required.[70] Decisions of the Commission are adopted, in case a vote is taken at any Commission's Member's request, "if a majority of the number of Members specified in the Treaty vote in favour,"[71] and when at least "a majority of the number of Members specified in the Treaty" are present.[72]

Such decisions must be authenticated to guarantee legal certainty[73]; failure to do so constitutes an infringement of an essential procedural requirement.[74] The Commission may, provided the principle of collective responsibility is fully respected, empower one or more of its members to take management or administrative measures on its behalf and subject to such restrictions and conditions as it shall impose. Powers, conferred in this way, may be sub-delegated to the Directors-General or Heads of Service, unless this is expressly prohibited in the empowering decision.[75] The Commission may not delegate its powers to autonomous bodies, i.e. bodies outside its control.[76]

It is of interest to note that the Commission is obliged to "reconsider" a decision, which has become definitive, when a request thereto is based on substantial new facts.[77]

The Rules of Procedure of the Commission are published in the *Official Journal*, see further below.

(3) Adoption of non-legislative acts of general application[78] and Implementation of legally binding Union acts[79]

(a) Adoption of non-legislative acts

8–15 A legislative act[80] may delegate to the Commission the power to adopt non-legislative acts of general application to supplement or amend non-essential elements of a legislative act.

This delegation of powers must necessarily be limited: the objectives, content, scope and duration of the delegation must be explicitly defined in the legislative act. The delegation cannot encompass essential elements of the rule laid down by

---

[68] See, e.g. Art.160(3) TFEU: the Commission shall address "appropriate directives or decisions"; of course, the form depends on the content of the act.

[69] See, e.g. Art.44 TFEU: the Commission shall fix the amount of the charges.

[70] See, e.g. Art.105(2) TFEU.

[71] Art.250 TFEU. Art.7 Rules of procedure, [2000] O.J. L308/26.

[72] Art.8 Rules of Procedure.

[73] Art.11,2 Rules of Procedure.

[74] *Commission v ICI* (C-286/95 P) [2000] E.C.R. I-2341.

[75] Art.213 Rules of Procedure. See, for instance, Decision 183/68 authorising certain management measures to be taken within the framework of the common organisation of the agricultural markets [1968] O.J. L89/13. See *Cementhandelaren v Commission* (8/72) [1972] E.C.R. 977; [1973] C.M.L.R. 7 concerning the legality of a document signed by a Director-General rather than by a Commissioner.

[76] See *Meroni v High Authority* (9/56) [1957 and 1958] E.C.R. 133.

[77] *INPESCA v Commission* (T-186/98) [2001] E.C.R. II-557.

[78] Art.290 TFEU.

[79] Art.291(2) TFEU.

[80] Art.289(3) TFEU "Legal acts adopted by legislative procedure shall constitute legislative acts"; there are two "legislative procedures": the "ordinary" one (Art.289(1) TFEU and the "special one" (Art.289(2) TFEU).

the legislative act. This delegation is subject to conditions: Parliament or the Council may decide to revoke the delegation, and the delegation may enter into force only if no objection has been expressed by Parliament or the Council, within a period set by the legislative act. Parliament shall act by a majority of its members and the Council by a qualified majority.

(b) Implementing powers of the Commission

While Member States must adopt all measures of national law necessary to implement legally binding Union acts, where uniform conditions for implementing such acts are needed, those acts must confer implementing powers on the Commission or, in duly specified cases,[81] on the Council.

8–16

The provisions implementing the "legally binding Union acts" may be adopted by the Commission (or the Council) according to a different procedure.[82] Furthermore, the Member States, via the committees that are part of the Commission's decision procedure, play an important, sometimes even a decisive, role in the procedure leading up to the adoption of an implementing act. As was explained above, the Council only meets a few days a month and has neither the opportunity nor the means to work out the detailed rules for implementing the Union legislation it enacts. This is, therefore, normally entrusted to the Commission.

The procedures to be followed by the Commission in exercising implementing powers are laid down in the new Comitology Decision of the Council.[83] There are two comitology procedures: the "advisory" one and the "examination" one.

A legally binding act (basic act) may provide for the application of the advisory procedure or the examination procedure, taking into account the nature, or the impact of the implementing act required.

The *examination procedure* applies, in particular, for the adoption of:

8–17

(a) implementing acts of a general scope;
(b) other implementing acts relating to programmes with substantial implications, the common agricultural and the common fisheries policies, the environment, security and safety, or protection of the health or safety of humans, animals or plants; the common commercial policy, taxation.

The *advisory procedure* applies, as a general rule, for other acts, but may also apply, in duly justified cases to the above mentioned acts.

In both cases the Commission shall be assisted by a committee, composed of representatives of the Member States, and chaired by the Commission; the latter does not take part in the vote.

In the advisory procedure, the committee shall deliver its opinion, if necessary by taking a vote; in that case, the committee decides by a simple majority of its composing members. The Commission shall decide on the draft implementing act

---

[81] This applies also in the cases provided by Arts 24 and 25 EU Treaty, concerning the common foreign and security policy.
[82] *Koster* (25/70) [1970] E.C.R. 1161(6).
[83] Regulation 182/11, laying down the rules and general principles concerning mechanisms for control, by Member States, of the Commission's exercise of implementing powers.

to be adopted, taking the utmost account of the conclusions drawn from the discussions within the committee and of the opinion delivered.

Under the examination procedure, the committee delivers its opinion by majority vote, as defined in EU Art.16(4) and (5).[84] Where the committee delivers a positive opinion the Commission shall adopt the draft implementing act.[85]

8–18
In case the committee delivers no opinion, the Commission may adopt the draft, except in certain cases, provided for in the Regulation.[86]

If the committee delivers a negative opinion, the Commission shall not adopt the draft implementing act. Where an implementing act is deemed to be necessary, the chair may either submit an amended version to the same committee within two months, or submit the draft implementing act within one month to the "appeal committee".[87] The latter shall deliver its opinion, by the same majority as described above. Until an opinion is delivered, any member of the appeal committee may suggest amendments to the draft implementing act, and the chair may decide whether or not to modify it. The chair must endeavour to find solutions which command the widest possible support within the appeal committee.

Where the appeal committee delivers a positive opinion or no opinion, the Commission shall adopt the implementing act. In case of a negative opinion, the Commission may not adopt the implementing act.

The Regulation contains rules concerning, among others, the adoption of implementing acts in exceptional cases,[88] the immediately applicable implementing acts on the rules of procedure[89] and on the right of scrutiny for Parliament and the Council: this applies when the basic act was adopted under the ordinary legislative procedure; Parliament or the Council may, at any time, indicate to the Commission that, in its view, a draft implementing act exceeds the implementing powers provided in the basic act. In that case, the Commission shall review the draft, taking into account the position expressed, and inform Parliament and the Council whether it intends to maintain, amend or withdraw the draft.

---

[84] This means: the same as for the Council, i.e. as from November 1, 2014, a qualified majority shall be defined as at least 55 per cent of the members of the Council (15), comprising at least 15 of them, and representing Member States comprising at least 65 per cent of the population of the Union; for the period until October 31, 2014 and after November 1, 2014, see Protocol No.9 on transitional provisions attached to the Treaties; according to the latter, the Council must hold a preliminary deliberation in case any draft would amend or abrogate any provision of that Protocol; reference is also made to Art.238(3) TFEU, which provides for cases where, under the Treaty, not all the members of the Council participate in voting.

[85] Regulation 182/11 [2011] O.J. L55/13. However, in a Statement attached to the Regulation, the Commission indicated that this does not preclude the Commission to decide not to adopt a draft implementing act, in very exceptional cases, taking into consideration new circumstances, that have arisen after the committee's vote.

[86] See Regulation 182/2011 (quoted above, fn.87), Art.5(4).

[87] The appeal committee must adopt its own rules of procedure by a simple majority of its component members, on a proposal from the Commission, Regulation 182/2011 (quoted above, fn.87), Art.3(7)2.

[88] Regulation 182/2011 (quoted above, fn.87), Art.7, i.e. where the act needs to be adopted without delay in order to avoid creating a significant disruption of the markets in the area of agriculture, or a risk for the financial interests of the Union, within the meaning of Art.325 TFEU (combating fraud).

[89] Ibidem Art.9.

(4) Participation in the Legislative Process

As was pointed out in the chapters on the Parliament and on the Council, the two can, in most cases, only legislate on the basis of a proposal submitted by the Commission. The Commission no longer enjoys a complete monopoly in this respect since the Treaties now provide for initiatives from a group of Member States, initiatives from Parliament, requests from the Court of Justice, recommendations from the ECB and requests from the EIB.[90] However, the main rule remains that the Commission has the legislative initiative.

8–19

By submitting proposals for regulations, directives and decisions, the Commission does indeed participate directly in the shaping of measures taken by the Council and Parliament. Whenever the Commission makes such a proposal in pursuance of the Treaties, it exercises its right of initiative in the law-making process of the Union. There are cases where the Commission is required to make a proposal within a given time limit,[91] but in most cases the Commission must use its own judgement as to the suitability of making a proposal.[92] Although the Commission enjoys the near-exclusive right of initiative, the Treaty provides that both the Council[93] and Parliament[94] may "request" the Commission to submit to it any appropriate proposals. Of course, it is only a request, but it will be difficult in many cases for the Commission to ignore it; nonetheless, neither Council nor Parliament can generally take legislative initiatives. When the Commission makes a proposal at the request of another institution, it remains politically and legally[95] responsible for the proposal. The submission by the Commission of a proposal for legislation constitutes the start of the decision-making process in which the three institutions—Commission, Parliament and Council—each play an essential role. The roles of Parliament and of the Council have been described above in the chapters concerning those institutions, and it is therefore necessary to briefly describe here the role of the Commission.

This role doesn't start with the submission of the proposal, nor does it end with it. Before drafting its proposal for a legislative act, the Commission must "consult widely".[96] Consequently, it holds informal consultations with, among others, national experts. This allows the Commission to judge the possible reactions of each of the Member States, which is essential, especially in cases of majority voting in the Council. In most cases the Commission will issue preparatory documents, such as Green Papers, which contain a description of a given problem and the possible legislative solutions envisaged by the Commission. Those papers are widely distributed or sent to selected groups in

8–20

---

[90] Protocol No.2, Art.3.

[91] See, e.g. Arts 25 and 249 TFEU.

[92] See, e.g. Art.109 TFEU.

[93] Art.241 TFEU.

[94] Art.225 TFEU: the Treaty requires that such request be voted by a majority of the members of Parliament, and when it considers that a Union act is required for the purpose of implementing the Treaties. Although one could argue that the latter goes without saying, Parliament shall have to show, in each case, that an act is indeed required; such an obligation is not imposed on the Council.

[95] *Werhahn v Council* (Joined Cases 63/72, 64/72, 65/72, 66/72, 67/72, 68/72, and 69/72) [1973] E.C.R. 1229 at 1247(8).

[96] Protocol No.2, Art.2.

order to obtain reactions and proposals.[97] The Green Paper is usually followed by a White Paper; available for anyone, it contains the broad lines of the legislation the Commission is planning to propose. Here, again, the Commission is looking for reactions from interested parties. The purpose of those consultations is, in general, to fulfil an obligation provided for in the EU Treaty, namely that decisions should be "taken as closely as possible to the citizen",[98] but also, and for practical purpose, to allow the Commission's staff to gather the necessary information they need to draft their proposals. In certain cases the Commission will organise consultations of certain groups[99] and/or organise hearings. Although those consultations are quite time-consuming, they constitute, for the Commission, an invaluable source of information, in view of the drafting of the definitive proposal or its modification, in case it was already submitted. It might be of interest to note that in 2012, for instance, the Commission submitted 168 proposals for legislative acts.[100]

Once a draft proposal has been approved by the Commission, it is, generally speaking, published in the *Official Journal*,[101] For the application of the principles of subsidiarity and proportionality, the Commission must also, before proposing legislative acts, forward the drafts or the amended drafts to national parliaments at the same time as to the Union legislator. Any such draft must contain a detailed statement making it possible to appreciate compliance with the above-mentioned principles. The reasons invoked must be substantiated by qualitative and, where possible, by quantitative indicators. The statement must also contain some assessment of the proposal's financial impact and, in case of a directive, of its implications for the rules to be put in place by the Member States. Any burden imposed by the envisaged act upon the Union, national governments, regional or local authorities, economic operators or citizens, must be minimised.[102]

8–21 National Parliaments have eight weeks to send a reasoned opinion to the Presidents of Parliament, the Council and the Commission stating why they consider that the draft does not comply with the principle of subsidiarity. In case the initiative originated with another body, the latter will be informed by the President of the Council. The drafters of the proposal shall "take account of the reasoned opinion". Each national parliament has two votes, and if the reasoned opinion represents one-third of all the votes allocated, the draft must be reviewed. This threshold is reduced to one-quarter, when it concerns the area of freedom, security and justice.

After such review, the drafter(s) may decide to maintain, amend or withdraw the draft. However, under the ordinary legislative procedure,[103] the Commission must review its proposal when the non-compliance reasoned opinion represents a

---

[97] They are available under the reference COM, followed by the year in brackets and a number. They are normally available on the Internet.

[98] Art.1 EU.

[99] See, e.g. [1994] O.J. C199/10.

[100] General Report 2012, p.201.

[101] Proposals are published in the "C" series of the O.J. also available on the Internet, or available from the Commission and known as COM documents; the latter are also to be found in the *Official Journal*.

[102] Art.5 of Protocol No.2. The Protocol applies to any "draft legislative act" and thus also to those that do not originate from the Commission.

[103] See Art.294 TFEU.

simple majority of the allocated votes. In case the Commission then decides to maintain its proposal anyway, it must justify its position in a reasoned opinion. The two opinions are then submitted to the legislator. If 55 per cent of the members of the Council, or a majority of the votes cast by Parliament, is of the opinion that the proposal is not compatible with the principle of subsidiarity, it shall be given further consideration.[104]

The Court has jurisdiction in actions on grounds of infringement of the principle of subsidiarity, in accordance with the procedure for the review of legality of acts of the institutions.[105]

All this to indicate that there is much more to the drafting of a proposal for Union legislation, than the terms of the Treaty suggest: the Council, or the Parliament and the Council, shall decide "on a proposal from the Commission".

The Commission will closely follow the work of Parliament and more particularly that of the parliamentary committees that examine the draft. Representatives of the Commission are always present when those committees meet to discuss its proposals. This allows the Commission both to explain its position in drafting the proposal and to better understand Parliament's reactions to it. The Commission is therefore fully prepared to eventually modify its proposal, which it may do as long as the Council has not acted, at any time during the procedures leading up to the adoption of a Union act.[106]

8–22

In parallel with the discussions within Parliament, the Commission is present when the proposal is discussed within the Council, either by COREPER or by the working groups set up by the latter. In many cases those groups are composed of the same national civil servants which were consulted informally by the Commission before the proposal was drafted; undoubtedly this allows for a smoother basis for the final decision of the Council.

If the latter wishes to amend the proposal without the argument of the Commission, unanimity is required,[107] except in the conciliation procedure,[108] the budgetary procedure,[109] the establishment of the multi-annual financial framework[110] and the establishment of the Union's annual budget.[111] As pointed out before, the right of the Council to modify the proposal is certainly not unlimited: the modification may not, as the Court indicated, alter substantially the proposal,[112] unless the Commission accepts the proposed modification. This would be the case when, during the discussion in the Council on the proposal, the

---

[104] Art.7(3) of Protocol No.2.

[105] Art.263 TFEU. This very complex and time-consuming procedure risks to prolong the already lengthy legislative procedures, were it not that, according to some, very few national parliaments are able to react, within the allocated eight weeks! This pessimistic view is belied by the facts: in 2008, for instance, the Commission sent 420 proposals and received 200 opinions; for more details see General Report 2008, p.235.

[106] Art.293(2) TFEU. See, for instance, the amended proposal for a Council Directive amending Directive 91/440 on the development of the Union railways [1998] O.J. C321/6.

[107] Art.293(1) TFEU.

[108] Art.294(10) and (13) TFEU.

[109] Art.310 TFEU.

[110] Art.312 TFEU.

[111] Art.314 TFEU.

[112] See, e.g. *Parliament v Council* (C-65/91) [1992] E.C.R. I-4593.

presidency makes a compromise proposal to break a deadlock; it is not unusual for the Commission itself to suggest such a compromise to the presidency.[113]

Finally, it must be noted that the Commission might be called upon to justify its proposal before the Court, since the latter has recognised the right of applicants, in an action concerning the extra-contractual liability of the Union to bring proceedings not only against the Council for having adopted the act, but also against the Commission for having proposed it.[114]

(5)   External Relations

8–23   The external relations of the Union will be analysed in detail in Part Six of this book, it may therefore suffice here to point out two aspects which concern the Commission in particular.

Where the Treaty provides for the conclusion of international agreements, mainly within the framework of the Union's commercial policy, the Commission makes recommendations to the Council. The latter may then authorise the Commission to open the necessary negotiations, and formulate directives for such negotiations. The Commission negotiates the international agreements in consultation with special committees appointed by the Council to assist it in this task.[115] Parliament, the Council, the Commission or a Member State may obtain the opinion of the Court as to whether an envisaged agreement is compatible with the provisions of the Treaties. Where the opinion is adverse, the agreement may not enter into force unless it is amended or the (European) Treaties are revised.[116] As to the word "agreement", the Court held that it covers "any undertaking entered into by a subject of international law, which has binding force".[117] Besides negotiating international agreements, the Commission:

> "[S]hall be instructed, together with the High Representative, to establish all appropriate forms of cooperation with the organs of the United Nations, and its specialised agencies, the Council of Europe, the Organisation for Security and Cooperation in Europe, the Organisation for Economic Co-operation and Development (OECD) and other international organisations".[118]

(6)   Implementation of the Union Budget

8–24   The budgetary procedure, and the role of the Commission in it, was examined in Ch.5: The European Parliament. The role of the Commission is formally limited to drafting its own budget and consolidating the estimates of the other institutions, except the ECB, in a draft budget to be submitted to Parliament and

---

[113] *Parliament v Council* (C-65/91), quoted above, fn.114.
[114] *Werhahn v Council* (Joined Cases 6372 to 69/72, etc) [1973] E.C.R. 1229, para.8.
[115] Art.218(4) TFEU.
[116] Art.118(11) TFEU. See, e.g. Court Opinion 1/91 on the compatibility of the Agreement establishing an European Economic Area (EEA) [1991] E.C.R. I-6079.
[117] Opinion 2/92 concerning the competence to participate in the Third Revised Decision of the OECD on National Treatment [1995] E.C.R. I-521. The Court also decided that the fact that certain questions could be dealt with by means of other remedies, for instance Art.190 TFEU does not preclude the Court from being asked an opinion under Art.218(11) TFEU .
[118] Art.220(1) TFEU.

the Council.[119] Once the budget is adopted, it falls to the Commission to implement it in accordance with the regulations laid down by the Council.[120] Detailed rules are provided in these regulations for each institution concerning its part in effecting its own expenditure.[121] Afterwards, the Commission must seek discharge in respect of the implementation of its part of the budget. To this end, it must submit annually to the Council and to Parliament the accounts for the preceding financial year relating to the implementation of the budget, together with a financial statement of the assets and liabilities of the Union.[122] In exercising their powers of control over the Commission's implementation of the budget, the Council and Parliament are assisted by the Court of Auditors, which forwards to them an annual report after the close of each financial year.[123] The Council and Parliament examine the accounts, the financial statement and the report. Discharge is given to the Commission by Parliament, on a recommendation from the Council, acting by a qualified majority.[124]

As part of the implementation of the budget, the Commission administers the European Agricultural Guarantee Fund, the European Agricultural Fund for Rural Development, the European Fisheries Fund, the European Social Fund, the European Regional Development Fund and the Cohesion Fund. The Commission is also responsible for administering the European Development Fund for the African, Caribbean and Pacific States, financed by direct contributions from the Member States.[125]

The Commission is also empowered to borrow on the world financial markets **8–25** and loan money for the financing of atomic energy projects,[126] and to finance infrastructure and industrial projects.[127] The borrowing is done by the Commission, but the administration of the resources is delegated to the European Investment Bank.

The Commission must carry out external administrative investigations for the purpose of strengthening the fight against fraud, corruption and any other illegal activity adversely affecting the Union's financial interests. To exercise those powers the Commission established the European Anti-Fraud Office (OLAF).[128]

(7) Publication of the Annual General Report

Each year, one month before the opening of the session of Parliament, the **8–26** Commission must publish a General Report on the activities of the European Union.[129] This report covers the activities of all the institutions and organs of the

---

[119] Art.314 TFEU.
[120] Art.322(1) TFEU. Financial Regulation 1605/2002 applicable to the general budget of the EC [2002] O.J. L248/1.
[121] Art.317 TFEU.
[122] Art.318 TFEU.
[123] Art.287 TFEU. See also Ch.10: The Court of Auditors.
[124] Art.319 TFEU. In 1984, Parliament refused to give discharge for the 1983 budget implementation; [1994] EC Bull. 12–67. In 1987 it deferred the discharge in respect of the implementation of the 1985 budget; Twenty-Second General Report (1988), 75.
[125] See General Report 2003, the chapter on ACP countries.
[126] Art.172(4) Euratom and [1977] O.J. L88/9.
[127] See [1978] O.J. L298/9.
[128] For more details see hereunder the chapter on Financing Union Activities, and [1999] O.J. L136/1.
[129] Art.249(2) TFEU. Since 2010, only found on the Internet.

Union, and as such is an invaluable source of information. Several areas, however, are covered very summarily because they are the object of separate reports either from the Commission or from other institutions or bodies.[130]

3. RULES OF PROCEDURE AND THE COMMISSION'S STAFF

8–27 The Commission must adopt its rules of procedure so as to ensure that both it and its departments operate in accordance with the provisions of the Treaty.[131] The departments consist of Directorates-General and Services whose responsibilities correspond more or less to the various tasks assigned to the Union by the Treaty.[132] With regard to the Union staff, two texts should be mentioned: the Protocol on the Privileges and Immunities of the European Communities[133] and the Staff Regulations of Officials of the European Communities and the Conditions of Employment of other Servants of the European Communities.[134] It might be worth mentioning at this point that the Union civil servants don't pay taxes to the Member State whose citizens they are on their Union salaries, but that they pay income tax to the Union itself and cannot, like other citizens in their own countries, deduct anything, like costs or interest payments, from their taxable income. Officials are recruited by the various institutions from the pool of candidates selected by the European Personnel Selection Office (EPSO)[135]; in other words, they are mostly not seconded by the national administrations[136] this should guarantee their independence and objectivity. Lately, however, the institutions, unable because of budgetary restraints, to recruit more personnel, have engaged, on a temporary basis, officials from the Member States; some fear

---

[130] For those reports see Ch.5: The European Parliament (3.(2)(d) The General Report).

[131] Art.249(1) TFEU. See [2000] O.J. L308/26; amended [2002] O.J. L21/23 and [2004] O.J. L251/9, adding an Annex containing provisions on electronic and digitised documents; amended [2005] O.J. L347/83 replacing Arts 1-28; amended [2006] O.J. L19/20, setting-up the ARGUS general rapid alert system. The Rules were amended in 2008, as regard detailed rules for the application of Regulation 1367/06 on the application of the provisions of the Aarhus Convention on Access to Information, Public Participation in Decision-making and Access to Justice in Environmental Matters to Community Institutions and Bodies [2008] O.J. L140/22. Arts 12 and 23 were amended in 2011 with regard to the co-ordination and surveillance of the economic and budgetary policies of the Member States [2011] O.J. L296/58.

[132] Arts 3, 4, 5 and 6 TFEU. See also the Declaration adopted by the Conference of the Representatives of the Governments of the Member States convened in Turin on March 29, 1996 to adopt the amendments to be made to the Treaties, concerning the organisation and functioning of the Commission; the Conference noted the intention to undertake, in parallel with the reorganisation of the tasks within the college, a corresponding reorganisation of its departments [1997] O.J. C340/137. Presently there are, besides the Secretariat General and the Legal Service, 32 Directorates General and 10 services.

[133] Protocol No.7 on the privileges and immunities of the European Union.

[134] Regulation 723/2004 [2004] O.J. L124/1.

[135] EPSO was set up by Decision 2002/60 of the institutions, the Committees and the Ombudsman, [2002] O.J. L197/53 and Decision 2002/621 of the same on the organisation and operation of EPSO [2002] O.J. L197/56.

[136] It goes without saying that when recruiting officials, the Union institutions must take the nationality of the candidates into account, and although "no post may be reserved for a given nationality" (Staff Regulation Art.27), a "geographical distribution" must exist, based upon the size of the population of the respective Member States.

that this may create a problem with regard to their independence and the influence the Member States can exercise.

4. ACCESS TO DOCUMENTS

Access by the public to Commission documents is, as for the other institutions,   **8–28**
provided for[137] and a refusal to grant access must state reasons for refusal.[138] Access to documents is, however, to be distinguished from access to information.[139]

FURTHER READING

Dionyssis Dimitrakopoulos, *The Changing European Commission* (Manchester   **8–29**
University Press, 2004)

Walter Van Gerven, *The European Union. A Polity of States and Peoples* (Hart Publishing, 2005)

Anna Michalski, *Governing Europe: the future role of the European Commission* (Clingendael, Netherlands Institute of International Relations, 2002)

Neill Nugent, *At the Heart of the Union: Studies of the European Commission* (St. Martin's Press and Palgrave, 2000)

Neill Nugent, *The European Commission* (Palgrave, 2001)

Jeremy Richardson, *European Union, Power and Policy-Making* (Routledge, 2006)

Andy Smith, *Politics and the European Commission: Actors, Independence, Legitimacy* (Routledge, 2004)

David Spence, *The European Commission* (John Harper Publishing, 2006).

---

[137] Regulation 1049/2001 regarding public access to European Parliament, Council and Commission documents [2001] O.J. L145/43. See among the many cases concerning public access, *Sweden v ASBL* (Joined Cases C-514/07 P, 528/07 P and 532/07 P) [2010] E.C.R. I-8533.

[138] [1994] O.J. L46/58 and *Interporc* (T-124/96) [1998] E.C.R. II-231. See also Notice on the internal rules of procedure for processing requests for access to files: [1997] O.J. C23/3.

[139] Case *Meyer v Commission* (T-106/99) [1999] E.C.R. II-3273.

CHAPTER 9

The Court of Justice of the European Union

The task of the Court of Justice of the European Union is to ensure that "in the interpretation and the application of the Treaties the law is observed".[1] Indeed, as the Court has underlined, the Union is:

> "based on the rule of law, inasmuch as neither it's Member States nor its institutions can avoid a review of whether measures adopted by them are in conformity with the basic constitutional charter, the [Treaties]. The [Treaties] established the Court as the judicial body responsible for ensuring that both the Member States and the [Union] institutions comply with the law".[2]

9–01

With this statement the Court highlights several essential points: First, that the Union is "based on the rule of law". Second that the Treaties constitute the basic legal text from which other rules derive. This is expressed, among others, by Art.13 TEU according to which "each institution shall act within the limits of the powers conferred upon it by the Treaties and in conformity with the procedures, conditions and objectives set out in them". Finally, there is the reminder that the last word, with regard to the legality and interpretation of Union acts, lies with the Court of Justice.

In the following, we will first look at the organisation of the Court of Justice and its various bodies, see section 1 below. Thereupon follows, in section 2, an account of the different types of actions that may be brought before the Court. Finally, in section 3, the most important aspects of the procedure before the Court will be described.

I. THE COURT OF JUSTICE

---

[1] Art.19 TEU.
[2] *Les Verts v Parliament* (294/83) [1986] E.C.R. 1357. See also Art.6(1) TEU according to which the Union is founded on the rule of law.

1. OVERVIEW

9–02   According to Art.19 EU, the Court of Justice of the European Union shall include the Court of Justice, the General Court and specialised courts.

Of those courts, the Court of Justice (hereafter the Court), is placed on top of the hierarchy and is thus the ultimate arbiter of Union law. Hereunder follows the General Court. The General Court was established in 1989 in order to alleviate the case load of the Court and was originally called the Court of First Instance. Finally, the Treaties allow the European Parliament and the Council to establish specialised courts attached to the General Court to hear and determine at first instance certain classes of action or proceedings brought in specific areas.[3] On this basis, the European Union Civil Service Tribunal was set up in 2004 and started functioning in 2005.[4]

2. THE COURT

9–03   The main types of cases that fall within the jurisdiction of the Court are:

1)   Preliminary reference cases;[5]
2)   Cases brought by the Commission or a Member State concerning the failures of Member States to respect their obligations under Union law;[6]
3)   Some cases concerning the legality of Union acts where the plaintiff is a Member State or a Union institution;[7] and
4)   Cases whereby decisions of the General Court are appealed.[8]

The Court consists of one Judge per Member State, i.e. with the accession of Croatia, 28 Judges[9] and eight Advocates General. As from October 2015 the number of Advocates General will be increased to 11.

The Judges and the Advocates General shall be chosen from persons whose independence is beyond doubt and who possess the qualifications required for appointment to the highest judicial offices in their respective countries or who are jurisconsults of recognised competence. They are appointed for a term of six years by common accord of the Governments of the Member States.[10] The appointment takes place after consultation of a panel, set up in order to give an

---

[3] Art.19 TEU and Art.257 TFEU.
[4] Decision establishing the European Union Civil Servants Tribunal [2004] O.J. L 333/7 and [2005] O.J. L 325/2.
[5] Art.267 TFEU and see point II.5 below.
[6] Arts 258 and 259 TFEU and see point II.2 below.
[7] Art.51 of the Court's Statute and Arts 263 and 265 TFEU.
[8] Art.256 TFEU. Only decisions taken by the General Court as a first instance court may be appealed to the Court. However, decisions of the General Court on appeals against decisions of the European Union Civil Service Tribunal may, in exceptional circumstances, be reviewed by the Court as provided in the Protocol on the Statute of the Court of Justice of the European Union.
[9] Art.19 TEU.
[10] Art.253 TFEU.

opinion on the candidates' suitability.[11] The President and the Vice-President of the Court are elected by the Judges, from among their number, for a term of three years; they may be re-elected.[12]

The Court sits in chambers, or in a Grand Chamber, in accordance with the rules laid down in the Statute of the Court, which also provides for a full Court.

The Grand Chamber is currently composed of 15 Judges.[13] The Chambers are **9–04** composed of five or three Judges.[14] The Court shall assign to the Chambers of five and of three Judges any case brought before it in so far as the difficulty or importance of the case or particular circumstances are not such as to require that it should be assigned to the Grand Chamber. It shall also assign the case to the Grand Chamber if a Member State or an institution of the European Union participating in the proceedings has so requested.[15]

The Court sits in full court where the European Parliament requests the dismissal of the Ombudsman.[16] The same applies where the Council or the Commission apply for the retirement of a member of the Commission[17]; and where the Court of Auditors requests the Court to find that one of its members no longer fulfils the requisite conditions.[18] Finally, when it considers that a case before it is of exceptional importance, the Court may decide to refer the case to the full Court.[19]

In 2012, the Grand Chamber dealt with roughly 9 per cent of the cases, chambers of five Judges with 54 per cent, and chambers of three Judges with approximately 34 per cent of the cases brought to a close by judgments or by orders.

The Advocate General is a member of the Court. He has the same status as the Judges, particularly in so far as concerns immunity and the grounds on which he may be deprived of his office. The Advocate General participates publicly and personally in the process leading up to the Court's decision, but does not participate in the deliberations of the Court. Instead, at the end of the oral proceedings, the Advocate General presents his suggestions for how to solve the case before the Court in a so-called Opinion that will be part of the deliberations between the Judges when deciding the case at hand.

Consequently, the submissions presented by the Advocate General do not **9–05** necessarily reflect the Court's views. Rather they constitute the individual reasoned opinion of a member of the Court.[20] However, when the Court follows the views of its Advocate General, those views often constitute a precious source of information concerning the reasoning which led to the Court's decision. Occasionally, the Court simply refers, for certain questions, to the reasons set out

---

[11] Art.255 TFEU. The panel comprises seven persons chosen from among former members of those courts, members of national supreme courts and lawyers of recognised competence, one of which shall be proposed by Parliament. The members of the panel are appointed by the Council.

Art.253 TFEU and Art.8 of the Court's Rules of Procedure.

[12] Art.9a of the Court's Statute.

[13] Art.27 of the Court's Rules of Procedure.

[14] Art.28 of the Court's Rules of Procedure.

[15] Art.60 of the Court's Rules of Procedure

[16] Art.228 TFEU.

[17] Arts 245 and 247 TFEU.

[18] Art.286 TFEU.

[19] Art.16 of the Court's Statute.

[20] *Emesa Sugar* (17/98) [2000] E.C.R. I–665.

by the Advocate General in his Opinion, and which the Court adopts. Moreover, it regularly happens that the Advocate General advises on matters which the Court of Justice does not itself touch upon in its ruling. Generally speaking, the parties are not admitted to submit observations in response to the Opinion of the Advocate-General.[21]

An Advocate General's Opinion does not have binding effect. One cannot, therefore, consider a question of interpretation or validity as having been settled solely on the basis of such an Opinion. The Opinion should, however, not be underestimated. It is presumably most correct to characterise the Advocate General's Opinion as being a source of law which can and should be taken account of when clarifying the state of the law, much in the same way as writings of leading legal theorists.

The Court may decide that a case shall be determined without a submission from the Advocate General, where it considers that the case raises no new points of law.[22] In 2012, 53 per cent of the Court's judgments were delivered without an Opinion of an Advocate General.

In 2012, the Court completed 527 cases and had 632 new cases brought before it. In the case of references for a preliminary ruling, the average duration amounted to 15.7 months. The average time taken to deal with direct actions and appeals was 19.7 months and 15.3 months respectively.

3.   THE GENERAL COURT

9–06   The General Court basically deals with five types of cases:

1)   cases whereby actions are made against the validity of Union acts,[23]
2)   cases whereby it is argued that a Union body illegally has failed to act,[24]
3)   actions seeking compensation for damage caused by the institutions of the European Union or their staff,[25]
4)   appeals, limited to points of law, against the decisions of the Civil Service Tribunal,[26] and finally
5)   actions based on contracts made by the European Union which give jurisdiction to the General Court.[27]

---

[21] *Makedoniko Metro* (C-57/01) [2003] E.C.R. I-1091, and *Radlberger* (C-309/02) [2004] E.C.R. I-11763.

[22] Art.20 of the Court's Statute.

[23] Arts 256 and 263 TFEU. This includes actions brought by the Member States against the Commission and actions brought by the Member States against the Council relating to acts adopted in the field of State aid, dumping and acts by which it exercises implementing powers. Other actions made by Member States against the Union Institutions are brought directly before the Court, cf. Art.51 of the Court's Statute. A substantial number of cases before the General Court concerns trademark cases in the form of proceedings brought against the Office for Harmonisation in the Internal Market, Trade Marks and Designs (OHIM). Amongst the General Court's competence is also actions brought against decisions of the Community Plant Variety Office or of the European Chemicals Agency.

[24] Arts 256 and 265 TFEU. Under the same conditions as those set out in the previous footnote, some of these cases must be brought directly before the Court, cf. Art.51 of the Court's Statute.

[25] Arts 256, 268 and 340 TFEU.

[26] Art.256 TFEU.

[27] Arts 256 and 272 TFEU.

The General Court is made up of at least one Judge from each Member State. With the accession of Croatia to the Union, there are now 28.[28] The judges are chosen from persons whose independence is beyond doubt, and who possess the ability required for appointment to high judicial office. They are appointed by common accord of the governments of the Member States after consultation of the same panel as that which is responsible for giving an opinion on the suitability of candidates for judgeships at the Court.[29] As is the case for the Court, the term of appointment is six years with retiring members being eligible for reappointment.[30] The judges in the General Court elect their President, for a period of three years.

Unlike the Court, the General Court does not have permanent Advocates General. However, that task may, in exceptional circumstances, be carried out by a Judge.[31]

The General Court sits in Chambers of five or three Judges or, in some cases, as a single Judge. It may also sit as a Grand Chamber (13 Judges) or, exceptionally, as a full court when this is justified by the legal complexity or importance of the case.[32] More than 80 per cent of the cases brought before the General Court are heard by a Chamber of three Judges.

The General Court has its own Registry, but uses the services of the Court for its other administrative and linguistic requirements.

In 2012, the General Court completed 688 cases while it received 617 new cases the same year. The duration of cases averaged 24.8 months. The same year 1,237 cases were pending before the General Court.

4.   THE CIVIL SERVICE TRIBUNAL

As its name indicates, the Civil Service Tribunal has jurisdiction to hear and determine at first instance disputes between the European Union and its servants.[33] The Civil Service Tribunal also has jurisdiction in disputes between all bodies or agencies and their staff in respect of which jurisdiction is conferred on the Court of Justice, such as disputes between Europol, OHIM or the European Investment Bank and their staff. In contrast, the Civil Service Tribunal may not hear and determine cases between national administrations and their employees.

The Civil Service Tribunal is composed of seven Judges appointed by the Council for a period of six years, following a call for applications and after taking the opinion of the same panel which advises on the appointment of members of the Court and of the General Court. When appointing the Judges, the Council seeks to ensure a balanced composition of the Civil Service Tribunal on as broad a geographical basis as possible from among nationals of the Member States and with respect to the national legal systems represented. The Judges may be renewed. They elect their President from among their number for a term of three years. He may be renewed.

9–07

---

[28] Art.19 TEU and Art.48 of the Court's Statute.
[29] See, in this respect, point I.2 above.
[30] Art.254 TFEU.
[31] Art.49 of the Court's Statute.
[32] Art.11 of the General Court's Rules of Procedure.
[33] Arts 257 and 270 TFEU and annex I to the Court's Statute.

The Civil Service Tribunal normally sits in Chambers of three Judges. However, whenever the difficulty or importance of the questions of law raised justifies it, a case may be referred to the full court. Furthermore, in cases determined by its Rules of Procedure, it may sit in a Chamber of five Judges or as a single Judge. The Civil Service Tribunal has its own Registry, but makes use of the services of the Court for its other administrative and linguistic needs.

In 2012 the number of cases brought before the Civil Service Tribunal was 178, and the number of cases brought to a close 121, with 235 cases pending by the end of that year.

II. THE TYPES OF CASES THAT MAY BE BROUGHT BEFORE THE COURT OF JUSTICE

1. OVERVIEW

9–08 The jurisdiction of the Court of Justice basically falls into six main groups:

1) It hears cases concerning the issue as to whether a Member State has failed to fulfil an obligation under the Treaties;[34]
2) It reviews the legality of Union acts and the failure of the institutions to act.[35] In this respect the Court may be given unlimited jurisdiction with regard to penalties imposed by an institution, as provided for in certain regulations;[36]
3) It may order damages in case of non-contractual liability of a Union body;[37]
4) It gives preliminary rulings on the basis of questions from the national courts;[38]
5) It gives so-called Opinions as to whether an envisaged international agreement is compatible with the provisions of the Treaties and as to whether the European Union or any institution of the European Union has the power to enter into that agreement;[39]
6) It gives judgement pursuant to arbitration clauses in contracts concluded by or on behalf of the Union just as it may decide in disputes between Member States, submitted under special agreements between the parties.[40]

In the following we examine the most important aspects of this multiple jurisdiction.

---

[34] Arts 258 and 259 TFEU.
[35] Arts 263 and 265 TFEU.
[36] Art.261 TFEU.
[37] Arts 268 and 340 TFEU.
[38] Art.267 TFEU.
[39] Art.218 TFEU.
[40] Arts 272 and 274 TFEU.

2. FINDING THAT A MEMBER STATE HAS FAILED TO FULFIL AN OBLIGATION UNDER THE TREATIES

The Commission may bring before the Court a complaint that a Member State has failed to fulfil an obligation under the Treaties. Such a complaint could, for example, be that the Member State concerned has not transposed a directive correctly and in time, or that a given piece of national law conflicts with Union law. This type of cases is brought directly before the Court of Justice and not before the General Court.

9–09

For the Commission, the possibility to initiate an infringement action constitutes its main instrument for fulfilling the task of "guardian of the Treaty".[41] In 2012, 73 such cases where brought. The procedure is laid down in Art.258 TFEU. This provision specifies that if the Commission considers that a Member State has failed to fulfil an obligation under the Treaties, it shall deliver a reasoned opinion on the matter after giving the State concerned the opportunity to submit its observations; something which takes place in the form of a so-called "letter of formal notice". Only if the State concerned does not comply with the Commission's reasoned opinion within the period laid down by the Commission, may the latter bring the matter before the Court.

Also a Member State may bring another Member State before the Court for failure to fulfil its obligations under the treaties. With regard to such cases, Art.259 TFEU prescribes that a Member State which considers that another Member State has failed to fulfil an obligation under the Treaty, must first bring the matter before the Commission. The Commission then gives each State the opportunity to submit its own case, and its observations on the other party's case, both orally and in writing. The Commission must, after that, deliver a reasoned opinion within three months after the date the matter was brought before it. The absence of such an opinion cannot prevent the matter from being brought before the Court by the complaining Member State. Very few cases of this type have been formally submitted to the Commission, and of those only three ended with a judgment.[42]

With regard to cases brought by a Member State against another Member State, attention must be drawn to the obligation, undertaken by the Member States, not to submit a dispute concerning the interpretation or application of the Treaty to any method of settlement other than those provided for therein.[43] The principal method provided for in the Treaty is recourse to the Court. The obligation not to seek other means of legal settlement seeks to guarantee uniformity in the interpretation and application of Union law. The Court also has jurisdiction in disputes between Member States that relate to the subject matter of the Treaty, when such a dispute is submitted to it, under a special agreement.[44]

---

[41] If the alleged infringement concerns the fulfilment by Member States of obligations under the Statute of the European Investment Bank, the Board of Directors of the Bank shall enjoy the powers normally conferred upon the Commission by virtue of Art.258 TFEU, cf. Art.271 TFEU.

[42] *France v United Kingdom* (141/78) [1979] E.C.R. 2923; *Belgium v Spain* (C-388/95) [2000] E.C.R. I–3123; and *Hungary v Slovakia* (C-364/10) judgment of 16.10.2012, not yet reported.

[43] Art.344 TFEU. In *Commission v Ireland* (C-459/03) [2006] E.C.R. I-4635, the Court held that Ireland had infringed the Treaty by starting an arbitration procedure against the UK in the framework of the UN.

[44] Art.273 TFEU.

9–10   In cases against Member States under Arts 258 and 259 TFEU, the Court can only "find" that the State has failed to fulfil an obligation.[45] It cannot annul the national legislation that has been held to conflict with Union law, nor can the Court order the Member State to take any specific measures in order to remedy the breach of Union Law.

If the State does not take the necessary measures to comply with the judgment of the Court, the Commission can bring the case before the Court again, after having given the State the opportunity to submit its observations. In that case the Commission must specify the amount of the lump sum or penalty payment to be paid by the Member State, which it considers appropriate in the circumstances.[46] The Court has jurisdiction to impose a financial penalty not suggested by the Commission.[47] Whereas the Commission launches this procedure each year close to 100 times, only very few cases are referred to the Court, as the Member States usually take the necessary measures to end the infringement before then.

The Treaty of Lisbon added the possibility for the Commission, when it brings an action against a Member State for failing to fulfil its obligation to notify measures transposing a directive adopted under a legislative procedure,[48] to specify right away, in its action to the Court, the amount of the lump sum or penalty payment to be paid by the Member State concerned. In this situation as well the Court remains free to impose the amounts it considers adequate.[49]

In certain types of cases, the Treaties limit the Court's power to review the fulfilment by the Member States of their obligations under Union law. For example, in the area of freedom, security and justice, the Court of Justice has no jurisdiction to review the validity or proportionality of operations carried out by the police or other law enforcement services of a Member State.[50] The same applies to the exercise of the powers of Member States with regard to the maintenance of law and order and the safeguarding of internal security. However, the fact that the Court does not have jurisdiction for such types of conflict does not mean that there can be no judicial review of the legality of such operations. It merely means that such review must be carried out by the national courts of the Member States, which must apply the fundamental principles of EU law when conducting such reviews.

---

[45] Art.260 TFEU.

[46] Art.260 TFEU. In *Commission v Spain* (C-610/10), judgment of December 11, 2012, Spain had not recovered illegal and incompatible aid pursuant to a judgment from 2002. The Court ordered Spain to pay a lump sum of EUR 20 million and a penalty payment of EUR 50,000 for each day of delay in adopting the measures necessary to comply with the judgment.

[47] *France v Commission* (C-304/02) [2005] E.C.R. I-6263.

[48] Art.289 TFEU.

[49] For further information see Communication from the Commission on the implementation of Art.260(3) of the Treaty (TFEU), [2011] O.J. C 12/1.

[50] Art.276 TFEU.

3. REVIEW OF THE LEGALITY OF AN ACT AND OF THE FAILURE OF AN INSTITUTION TO ACT

Articles 263 and 265 TFEU

(a) Annulment actions

The second type of cases that can be brought before the Court is cases concerning   9–11
the legality of acts taken be the EU Institutions and other Union bodies.[51] As
already indicated, such cases must, in general, be brought before the General
Court with right of appeal to the Court of Justice.[52]

In reviewing the legality of Union acts, the Court ensures that the activities of
the Union bodies remain within the boundaries laid down by the Treaties and that
institutions respect the balance of powers within the Union. It also provides legal
protection for those submitted to Union law, although most cases brought by
individuals against Union legislation cannot be brought directly before the Court
of Justice (the General Court), but must be brought before national courts and
directed against national measures implementing the relevant piece of Union
legislation. Indeed, when assessing the judicial protection afforded by Union law,
one should keep in mind that the Court of Justice is not the only judicial body
capable of giving legal protection of Union law rights. It is via the combination of
actions before the Court of Justice and the procedure for preliminary rulings that:

> "...the Treaty has established a complete system of legal remedies and procedures
> designed to ensure review of the legality of acts of the institutions, and has entrusted
> such review to the Community Courts. Under that system, where natural or legal
> persons cannot, by reason of the conditions for admissibility laid down in [Art.263
> on the annulment procedure], directly challenge Community measures of general
> application, they are able, depending on the case, either indirectly to plead the
> invalidity of such acts before the Community Courts under [Art.277 concerning
> objections of Illegality] or to do so before the national courts and ask them, since
> they have no jurisdiction themselves to declare those measures invalid, to make a
> reference to the Court of Justice for a preliminary ruling on validity."[53]

(i) Acts Submitted to the Control of Legality

According to Art.263 TFEU, the following acts may be subject to control under   9–12
the annulment procedure: Legislative acts; acts adopted by Parliament jointly
with the Council, acts issued by the Council, acts issued by the Commission and
by the ECB, other than recommendations and opinions; and acts of Parliament
and of the European Council, intended to produce legal effects vis-à-vis third

---

[51] Art.263 TFEU. In contrast, the Court does not have competence to assess the legality of national
measures, be that legislation, administrative acts or court decisions, outside the ambit of the
above-discussed Arts 258 and 259 TFEU.

[52] Art.256 TFEU and see point I.2 above. If the case concerns a dispute between EU officials and
their institution the action should be brought before the Civil Service Tribunal with right of appeal to
the General Court, cf. Art.257 TFEU and point I.3 above.

[53] *Commission v Jégo-Quéré & Cie SA* (C-263/02 P) [2002] E.C.R. I-3425.

parties. The list also includes acts adopted by bodies, offices and agencies of the Union intended to produce legal effects vis-à-vis third parties, and when this is provided for in the founding act.

Examples of acts that can be challenged under this procedure are regulations, directives, and decisions. That being said, the form in which such acts are cast is, in principle, immaterial as regards the question as to whether they are open to challenge in court or not. It is the content that counts.[54] Thus, the General Court has accepted as admissible an action for annulment brought against an oral statement.

Acts of a procedural nature which are taken in order to issue a final act (so-called preparatory acts) may not be attacked separately under an annulment procedure. For example, a decision of the Commission not to gather more evidence or not to hear a party before the Commission issues a decision concerning fines for breach of the Union's competition rules does not constitute a challengeable act. This does not, however, mean that such preparatory decisions cannot be subject to judicial control. It merely entails that this control must take place in relation to an attack on the Commission's final decision during which the lack of evidence or the violation of the right to a hearing may be adduced as an argument for why the final decision should be quashed.[55]

9–13   In some types of cases, the Court's general competence to review Union measures have been limited. This is most notably the case with regard to the area of the Common Foreign and Security Policy. The clear starting point remains that the Court does not have jurisdiction in this area.[56] The Court does, however, have powers to control that provisions on the Common Foreign and Security Policy are not applied in such a way as to involve an unjustified restriction of the EU's other policies. This means that the Court will be able to review the content of a legal act adopted pursuant to Common Foreign and Security Policy provisions, with a view to determining whether the legal act ought to have been adopted pursuant to the authority of a provision which does fall within the Court's jurisdiction. Moreover, the Court has jurisdiction to monitor compliance with the procedures and the extent of the powers of the institutions, laid down by the Treaties, by reviewing the legality of decisions providing for restrictive measures against natural or legal persons, adopted by the Council applying specific provisions concerning the Common Foreign and Security Policy.

In principle, the Court has jurisdiction to decide on the legality of acts adopted by the Council or the European Council concerning a serious breach by a Member State of the values on which the Union is founded.[57] In such cases, the Court's powers are, however, limited to control the procedural stipulations

---

[54] *Commission v Council* (22/70) [1971] E.C.R. 263. See similarly *Le Pen v Parliament* (C-208/03 P) [2005] E.C.R. I-6051, and *Luxembourg v Parliament* (108/83) [1984] E.C.R. 1945, where the Court annulled a Resolution of the Parliament, and *France v Commission* (C-325/91) [1993] E.C.R. I–3283, where the Court annulled a Commission Notice.

[55] *IBM v Commission* (60/81) [1981] E.C.R. 2639.

[56] See Art.24 TEU and Art.275 TFEU. This applies both to direct proceedings and to preliminary rulings under Art.267 TFEU.

[57] Arts 2 and 7 TEU and Art.269 TFEU.

contained in the EU Treaty.[58] It is, in other words, not up to the Court, but only to the Council and the European Council, to determine as to whether such a serious breach does indeed exist.

(ii)   Who may Lodge an Appeal for Annulment?

A claim for annulment is only admissible if the applicant has a legal interest in seeing the contested measure annulled. In this respect, Union law distinguishes between so-called privileged and semi-privileged plaintiffs who do not need to show any specific interest in having a legal act declared void, and other plaintiffs who will only be entitled to bring proceedings if they have a sufficiently strong interest in the outcome of a specific case.

9–14

Under Art.263 TFEU, the Member States, the Council, the Commission and the European Parliament always have standing, in other words they are privileged plaintiffs. Moreover, the Court of Auditors, the European Central Bank and the Committee of the Regions always have standing for the purpose of protecting their prerogatives under the Treaties; hence the fall in the group of semi-privileged plaintiffs. In contrast, the Economic and Social Committee, the European Ombudsman and the European Data Protection Supervisor, for example, are neither privileged nor semi-privileged plaintiffs and will therefore only be able to bring action on the same terms as private persons and businesses.

As for such non-privileged plaintiffs, Art.263 TFEU lays down the general requirement that the legal act in dispute must be addressed to the plaintiff or be "of direct and individual concern to them". The same persons may also bring proceedings for annulment of a "regulatory act which is of direct concern to them and does not entail implementing measures". As for such regulatory acts, it is thus not a condition for the plaintiff to be individually affected, but only that he is directly affected. The concept of a "regulatory act" covers all acts of general application apart from so-called legislative acts.[59] Hence, e.g. directives and regulations that are not adopted by the legislative procedure fulfil this requirement. In contrast, a legislative act may form the subject-matter of an action for annulment brought by natural or legal persons only if it is of both direct and individual concern to them.

An act is of *direct* concern when it affects the applicant's legal position and when there is a causal relationship between the act and the modified legal position of the applicant. In other words, the act must affect directly the legal situation of the applicant and leave no discretion to its addressees, who are entrusted with the task of implementing it, such implementation being purely automatic and resulting from Union rules without the application of other intermediate rules.[60]

9–15

That being said, actions for annulment brought by individuals against European Union acts have been admitted where the effects of those acts on the respective applicants are not legal, but merely factual, because they are directly

---

[58] Art.269 TFEU.
[59] *Microban International* (T-262/10), judgment of October 25, 2011. As for the condition that the act does not entail implementing measures, reference is made to *Iberdrola v Commission* (T-221/10), judgment of March 8, 2012, and *Eurofer v Commission* (T-381/11), order of June 4, 2012.
[60] *Commission v Infront WM* (C-125/06 P) [2008] E.C.R. I-1451, and *Bavaria and Bavaria Italia* (C-343/07) [2009] E.C.R. I-5491.

affected in their capacity as market participants in competition with other market participants. For example, the Court has confirmed the standing of competitors to institute proceedings against Commission decisions to authorise State aid even if the actual aid does not follow from the Commission's decision but from separate acts of the Member States. Moreover, in some cases direct concern to a person has been recognised even in the existence of a certain margin of discretion for the authorities responsible for implementing an EU act, provided it could be predicted with sufficient probability that that discretion would be exercised in a certain way.

As for the second condition, *individual* concern means that the act affects the individuals by reason of certain attributes, which are particular to them, or by reason of circumstances, which are peculiar to them, or by reason of circumstances in which they are differentiated from all other persons, and by virtue of these factors, distinguishes them individually, just as in the case of the person addressed.[61]

9–16 With regard to acts of general application, not having the character of a "regulatory act", this condition means that such acts can only seldom be challenged directly before the Court of Justice by individuals or undertakings. In practice, this will only be the case if they can show that these acts contain provisions, which in reality have an individual rather than a general application.[62] In comparison, where a decision affects a group of persons who are identified or identifiable when that measure was adopted by reason of criteria specific to members of the group, those members might be individually concerned by that measure inasmuch as they form part of a limited class of traders. That can sometimes be the case when the decision alters rights acquired by the individual prior to its adoption.[63]

As for associations of undertakings, they are admissible in at least three kinds of circumstances:

- When the legal provision grants procedural powers to the association in question;
- When the association represents the interests of undertakings, which would, themselves, be entitled to bring proceedings; and
- when the association is distinguished individually because its own interests, as an association, are affected, in particular because its negotiating position has been affected by the measure whose annulment is being sought.[64]

In some special cases private enforcement is precluded, as the Treaties prescribe that only some may bring proceedings for specific types of claim. This is, for example, so with regard to cases on the legality of acts adopted by the European Council, or by the Council, concerning a serious breach, by a Member

---

[61] *Plaumann v Commission* (25/62) [1963] E.C.R. 95. This is not the case when the applicant is affected by the act because he belongs to a category designated abstractly and as a whole.

[62] In those situations, the avenue is instead either the objection of illegality (see point iv below) or a case before a national court that may make a preliminary reference concerning the validity of the EU act concerned (see point 5 below).

[63] *Commission v Infront WM* (C-125/06 P) [2008] E.C.R. I–1451.

[64] *Union de Pequenos Agricultores v Council* (T-173/98) [1999] E.C.R. II–3357.

State, of the values on which the Union is founded.[65] Such actions may only be brought at the request of the Member State concerned.

(iii) Grounds for Annulment

There are four grounds for annulment which may be invoked by the applicant. Some of these grounds may also be invoked by the Union judge, acting on his own motion (*ex officio*).[66] That being said, the Court may not rule *ultra petita*. In other words, the scope of the annulment, which the Court pronounces, may not go further than that sought by the applicant.[67]

9–17

Lack of competence. This ground embodies the basic principle of conferral, under which the institutions of the Union may only exercise those powers which have been granted to them, by the Member States, in the Treaties.[68] Hence, the Court will annul legislation or individual acts issued by an institution without the necessary conferred powers. This includes the situation where the Commission adopts an act without having the necessary implementing powers and situations where the Treaties actually confer the powers that is needed to issue that act, but where the institution used a wrong legal basis in the Treaties.[69] For those reasons, the choice of the provision for the legal basis of an act is of essential importance. According to Art.296 TFEU, every Union act must indicate on which Union provision it is based.

9–18

Infringement of an essential procedural requirement. This heading brings together violations of the various types of procedural rules for the coming into being of the legal act in question. If, for instance, the Council were to take a decision without a proposal from the Commission, or without including the European Parliament, when this is required by the Treaties, the Council would have infringed an essential procedural requirement and the decision will be annulled. The same would apply if the Commission, for instance, were to make a proposal without asking for the opinion of the Economic and Social Committee, when this is required by the Treaties.

9–19

Failure to state sufficient reasons for a Union act also constitutes a ground for annulment, and the same is the case for violations of unwritten principles of administrative procedure. As examples, one can mention the right to be heard and rights of the defence; principles that have previously been unwritten, but now find their basis in Art.41 of the Charter on Fundamental Rights.[70]

---

[65] Arts 2 and 7 TEU and Art.269 TFEU.

[66] In *Commission v Ireland* (C-89/08 P) [2009] E.C.R. I-11245, the Court found that an absence of or inadequate statement of reasons constituted an infringement of procedural requirements for the purpose of Art.263 TFEU and a plea involving a matter of public policy that could be raised by the Union judicature of its own motion.

[67] *Commission v Assidoman Kraft Products* (C-310/97 P) [1999] E.C.R. I-5363.

[68] Art.5 TEU.

[69] *Parliament v Commission* (C-403/05) [2007] E.C.R. I-9045.

[70] According to *Lisrestal* (C-32/95 P) [1996] E.C.R. I-5373, the right to be heard applies in all proceedings initiated against a person, and which are liable to culminate in a measure adversely affecting that person. It constitutes a fundamental principle of EU law, even in the absence of any specific rules.

9–20   **Infringement of the Treaties or of any rule of law pertaining to their application.**   This heading relates to situations where an act is in conflict with a higher norm of law. It covers not only the Treaties, but also an act of secondary legislation having a higher legal status than the challenged act, for instance the accordance of an implementing regulation of the Commission with the underlying basic regulation of the Council and the Parliament.

    As for the expression "any rules relating to its application", it refers mainly to the general principles of law, to international law, and to fundamental rights. It includes the Charter of Fundamental Rights, which has the same legal value as the Treaties.[71] As unwritten principles, which an EU act shall respect in order to be valid, one may mention the protection of legitimate expectations;[72] legal certainty;[73] equal treatment (non-discrimination);[74] and proportionality.[75]

9–21   **Misuse of power.**[76]   There is misuse of power when a public authority uses its lawful powers to attain an objective for which the powers were not intended. Although this ground has been invoked many times, the Court seldom accepts this as a ground for the annulment of an act.[77]

(iv)   Consequences of the Annulment of an Act by the Court

9–22   Unless the Court has been given unlimited jurisdiction by a special provision (which is the case for penalties), it may only, when it finds the action for annulment well founded, declare the act void.[78] In other words, the Court cannot order the Union institution concerned to take any specific measures in order to remedy the illegality, nor may the Court change the content of the attacked act in order to make it compatible with Union law.

    The institution whose act has been declared void is required to take the necessary measures to comply with the judgment of the Court.[79] Such measures involve the removal of the effects of the illegalities found in the judgment

---

[71] Art.6 TEU.

[72] According to *Tea-Cegos E.A.* (T-376/05 and T-383/05) [2006] E.C.R. II–205, the right to claim protection of legitimate expectations encompasses any party that finds itself in a situation from which it follows that the Union administration by furnishing precise assurances, whatever the form in which they were communicated, created for it grounded hopes.

[73] *Aventis Pasteur* (C-358/08) [2009] E.C.R. I-11305; and *Altun* (C-337/07) [2008] E.C.R. I-10323.

[74] *Lianakis* (C-532/06) [2008] E.C.R. I-251; *Lindorfer v Council* (C-227/04) [2007] E.C.R. I-6767. The principle of equality has now been codified in Art.21 of the Charter.

[75] The principle of proportionality consists of three interlinked requirements. First, the act in question must be suitable to achieve its goals, cf. *Bonnier Audio* (C-461/10) judgment of April 19, 2012, not yet reported and *Corporación Dermoestéti* (C-500/06) [2008] E.C.R. I-.5785. Second, it should not be more intrusive than necessary for that purpose, cf. *Afton Chemical* (C-343/09) [2010] E.C.R. I-10427, and *Faust* (C-24/90) [1991] E.C.R. I-4905. Finally, the effects of the act should be proportionate in the absolute sense, something which includes a balancing exercise between the aims of the act in question and its effects, cf. *Ze Fu Fleischhandel* (C-201/10 og C-202/10) [2011] E.C.R. I-3545, and *Urbán* (C-210/10) judgment of February 9, 2012, not yet reported.

[76] Maybe better known by its French equivalent: *détournement de pouvoir.*

[77] One rare example is *Simmenthal v Commission* (92/78) [1979] E.C.R. 777. See also *Antonio Giannini v Commission* (T-282/97 and T-57/98) RecFP I–A-33 and II–151 and *Commission v Gianni* (C-153/99 P) [2000] E.C.R. I–2891.

[78] Art.264 TFEU.

[79] Art.266 TFEU.

annulling the act. The institution may thus be required to take adequate steps to restore the applicant to its original situation or to avoid the adoption of an identical measure.[80]

Unless otherwise specified, the Court's declaration has effect *ex tunc* so that the judgment has retroactive effect from the moment the act was adopted. Since, theoretically, annulment means that the act is to be considered as never having existed, the institution must endeavour to recreate the situation which would have existed had the act not been issued. However, the Court may, if it considers this necessary, state which of the effects of the act which it has declared void shall be considered as definitive.[81] It may also declare that the act or the implementing measures remains valid until replaced.[82] Moreover, in certain cases, where an annulment *ex tunc* would have unacceptable financial consequences, the Court has decided that the annulment should not have retroactive effect. This is referred to as limitation of the temporal effect of judgments.[83]

The annulment does not affect the validity of identical or similar acts, the legality of which has not been contested, within the time limits provided for by the Treaty.

(v)   The Objection of Illegality

Proceedings for annulment must be instituted within two months[84] of the publication of the measure in the Official Journal of the European Union,[85] or of its notification[86] to the claimant, or, in the absence thereof, of the day on which it came to the knowledge of the latter.[87] If an application for annulment is filed after the expiry of that deadline, the case will be dismissed as inadmissible. However, notwithstanding the expiry of the period for when a case for annulment may be brought before the Court, any party may, in proceedings in which an act of general application adopted by a Union body is at issue, plead the grounds specified in Art.263 (2) TFEU, in order to invoke before the Court of Justice the inapplicability of that act.[88]

9–23

This so-called "objection of illegality" constitutes an expression of:

> "… a general principle conferring upon any party to proceedings the right to challenge, for the purpose of obtaining the annulment of a decision of direct and

---

[80] *Antillean Rice Mills* (T-480 and T-483/93) [1995] E.C.R. II–2310.

[81] Art.264 TFEU.

[82] See, e.g. *Commission v Council* (275/87) [1988] E.C.R. 259, where the act was annulled only because the legal basis chosen by the Council was not considered to be the right one. In *Parliament v Council* (C-22/96) [1998] E.C.R. I–3231, the Court annulled Decision 95/468 since it could not be adopted on the basis of what is now Art.352 TFEU. That judgment, however, maintained the effects of the implementing measures already adopted by the Commission on the basis of that decision.

[83] See in more detail point II.5(viii) below.

[84] Art.263 TFEU For the calculation of this time limit see Arts 49–53 of the Court's Rules of Procedure. It follows from Art.51 of those rules that the procedural time-limits shall be extended on account of distance by a single period of 10 days.

[85] Art.297 TFEU.

[86] Notification necessarily involves the communication of a detailed account of the contents of the measure notified and of the reasons on which it is based, cf. *Socurte* (C-143/95 P) [1997] E.C.R. I–1, and *Parliament v Commission* (C-403/05) [2007] E.C.R. I-9045.

[87] Art.263 TFEU.

[88] Art.277 TFEU.

individual concern to that party, the validity of previous acts of the institutions, which form the legal basis of the decision, which is being attacked, if that party was not entitled, under Article [263 TFEU], to bring a direct action, challenging those acts, by which it was thus affected, without having been in a position to ask that they be declared void".[89]

Hence, together with the below-discussed preliminary ruling procedure and the claim for compensation for damage, the objection of illegality constitutes a third way for natural and legal persons to challenge a measure, whose legality they cannot directly ask the Court to review.

A declaration of inapplicability is only possible in proceedings brought before the Court itself, under some provision of the Treaty, other than the one for annulment. Moreover, the plea may only be used against a measure, which is the basis for the act in dispute. In other words, the objection of illegality does not constitute an independent action, and may only be sought incidentally.[90]

(b)   Actions against Failure of an Institution to Act

9–24   If the European Parliament, the European Council, the Council, the Commission or the European Central Bank, in infringement of the Treaties, fails to act, the Member States and the other institutions of the Union may bring an action before the Court to have the infringement established. The same goes for other bodies, offices and agencies of the Union which fail to act.[91]

Also any natural or legal person may complain to the Court that an institution, body, office or agency of the Union has failed to address to that person any act other than a recommendation or an opinion.

The action shall be admissible only if the Union body concerned has first been called upon to act. If, within two months of being so called upon, the Union body has not defined its position, the action may be brought within a further period of two months. In case the body, within the said deadline, defines its position by refusing to act, this position does not become an act which can be challenged under the annulment procedure, since the failure has not ceased. In such a case, the right approach is still to bring an action for failure to act.[92] On the other hand, where the body concerned does adopt an act, then the procedure for failure to act may not be used to impose a given result; if the person concerned is unhappy with the content of the act so issued, then the right means of redress will be an annulment action under Art.263 TFEU.

Where the failure to act is held to be unlawful, it is for the Union body concerned to put an end to the failure by adopting appropriate measures.

Jurisdiction to hear actions for failure to act is shared between the Court of Justice and the General Court according to the same criteria as for actions for annulment.

---

[89] *Hauts Fournaux de Chasse v High Authority* (15/57) [1957–1958] E.C.R. 211, and *Meroni v High Authority* (9/56) [1957–1958] E.C.R. 133.
[90] *CSF and CSME v Commission* (T-154/94) [1996] E.C.R. II–1377.
[91] Art.265 TFEU.
[92] *Parliament v Council* (302/87) [1988] E.C.R. 5615.

4. COMPENSATION FOR DAMAGES CAUSED BY INSTITUTIONS

The Court of Justice has jurisdiction in disputes relating to compensation for damages resulting from the non-contractual liability of the Union.[93]   **9–25**

Actions for annulment and claims for damages are different proceedings. In providing for an action for damages, the Treaty has introduced an autonomous form of action, subject to conditions on its use dictated by its specific nature. Indeed, the end of an action for damages is not the abolition of a particular measure, but the compensation for the damages inflicted by the measure or action of the administration.[94] That being said, if successful, an action for damages can nevertheless constitute a declaration on the part of the Court that the act is illegal. On the other hand, the unlawful nature of an act does not automatically make the Union responsible for compensation in case of damage.

According to settled case law, the European Union may incur non-contractual liability only if three conditions are fulfilled, namely 1) the unlawfulness of the conduct of which the Union institution is accused, 2) the occurrence of actual damage, and 3) the existence of a causal link between that conduct and the harm alleged.[95]

In so far as the three conditions giving rise to liability must be satisfied cumulatively, the fact that one of them has not been satisfied is a sufficient basis on which to dismiss an action for damages.

As for the requirement of causation, there is no obligation on the Union to make good every harmful consequence, even a remote one, of conduct of its institutions. Case law requires a sufficiently direct causal nexus between the conduct of the institutions and the damage.[96] Hence, it is necessary that such damage was actually caused by the conduct alleged against the institution. Even in the case of a possible contribution by the institution concerned to the damage for which compensation is sought, that contribution might be too remote because of some responsibility resting on others, including the one seeking damages.[97] Moreover, damages will be refused if the causal link is interrupted by elements attributable to causes other than the unlawful action taken by the institution concerned, such as unilateral decisions taken by the applicant.[98]

As for the requirement of a fault on behalf of the institution concerned,   **9–26**
"negligence" entails an act or omission by which the party responsible breaches the duty of care which it should have discharged, and could have discharged, in view of its attributes, knowledge and abilities. It is therefore possible for the

---

[93] Arts 268 and 340 TFEU.

[94] *Zuckerfabrik Schöppenstedt v Council* (5/71) [1971] E.C.R. 975.

[95] *Lucaccioni v Commission* (C-257/98 P) [1999] E.C.R. I-5251, *Bouma and Beusmans v Council and Commission* (C-62/01 P and C-163/01 P) [2004] E.C.R. I-4509, and *Sviluppo Italia Basilicata* (C-414/08 P) [2010] E.C.R. I-2559.

[96] *Finsider* (C-363/88 and C-364/88) [1992] ECR I-359, and *É.R.* (T-138/03) [2006] ECR II- 4923, as confirmed on appeal in C-100/07 P [2007] ECR I-136.

[97] *Trubowest Handel* (C 419/08 P) [2010] E.C.R. I-2259.

[98] *Schneider Electric* (C-440/07 P) [2009] E.C.R. I-6413.

Union administration to be non-contractually liable for wrongful conduct where it fails to act with all necessary care and, as a result, causes harm.[99]

Where the unlawfulness of a legal measure is at issue, the existence of a sufficiently serious breach of a rule of law intended to confer rights on individuals is a necessary condition for liability to arise. The decisive criterion for establishing that a breach of Union law is sufficiently serious is whether the Union institution concerned manifestly and gravely disregarded the limits on its discretion. Where that institution has either no or only considerably reduced discretion, the mere infringement of Union law may be sufficient to establish the existence of a sufficiently serious breach. The determining factor in deciding whether there has been such an infringement is not the general or individual nature of the act in question.[100] Rather, the system of rules which the Court of Justice has worked out in relation to the Union's non-contractual liability takes into account, inter alia, the complexity of the situations to be regulated, the difficulties in the application or interpretation of the legislation, and the margin of discretion available to the author of the act in question.[101]

As for the damage for which compensation is sought, it must be actual and certain and have been assessed or, at least, be assessable. The Court has, however, accepted the admissibility of an action, in which it was asked to declare the Union liable for imminent damage, foreseeable with sufficient certainty, even if the damage could not yet be precisely assessed.[102]

9–27   Sometimes the existence of discretion on the part of the sued institution entails that it can be difficult to determine the exact amount of the loss compared to what would have happened had the institution not violated its obligations. However, such considerations authorise the Court only to find that there is uncertainty with regard to the extent of the damage claimed, but not to find that the very existence of the damage is uncertain and thus not recoverable. To claim the contrary would be to deprive actions for compensation of all useful effect in those areas, such as the common organisation of markets where the EU institutions enjoy, in the exercise of their regulatory or decision-making powers, wide discretion having regard, inter alia, to the economic imperatives and choices inherent in these matters.[103]

The Court also admits that the damage can be fixed by agreement between the parties.[104] Non-economic moral prejudice may be covered.[105]

The Union courts have exclusive jurisdiction to hear cases concerning compensation based on the non-contractual liability of the Union.[106]

---

[99] *Intertanko* (C-308/06) [2008] E.C.R. I-4057; and *Internationaler Hilfsfonds v Commission* (C-331/05 P) [2007] E.C.R. I-5475.

[100] *Bergaderm and Goupil v Commission* (C-352/98 P) [2000] E.C.R. I-5291; and *Commission v Fresh Marine* (C-472/00) [2003] E.C.R. I-7541.

[101] *Holcim v Commission* (C-282/05 P) [2007] E.C.R. I-2941.

[102] *Agraz E.A. v Commission* (C-243/05 P) [2006] E.C.R. I-10833.

[103] *Agraz v Commission* (C-243/05 P) [2006] E.C.R. I-10833.

[104] *Pauls Agriculture v Council and Commission* (256/81) [1983] E.C.R. 1707, and *Biovilac v EEC* (59/83) [1984] E.C.R. 4057. See also *Adams v Commission* (145/83) [1985] E.C.R. I–3539.

[105] *Dreyfus* (T-485/93) [1996] E.C.R. II–1101; and *Hautem v EIB* (T-11/00) [2000] E.C.R. II–4036.

[106] *Asteris v Greece* (106/87, 107/87, 108/87, 109/87, 110/87, 111/87, 112/87, 113/87, 114/87, 115/87, 116/87, 117/87, 118/87, 119/87 and 120/87) [1988] E.C.R. 5531. A question relating to the application of Art.340 TFEU cannot be determined in proceedings for a preliminary ruling, cf. *Granaria v Hoofd produktschap voor Akkerbouwprodukten* (101/78) [1979] E.C.R. 623.

Actions for compensation for damage are subject to a five-year period of limitation which begins to run once the requirements governing the obligation to provide compensation for damage are satisfied and, in particular, once the damage to be made good has materialised.[107] In the case of disputes arising from individual measures, the limitation period begins to run as soon as the decision has produced its effects vis-à-vis the persons concerned by it.[108]

5. PRELIMINARY RULINGS

(i) Overview

According to Art.267 TFEU, the Court has jurisdiction to give so-called "preliminary rulings". A reference for a preliminary ruling is a request from a national court of a Member State to the Court to give an authoritative interpretation of Union law or a decision on the validity of an EU act.

9–28

When answering such preliminary questions the Court does not function as a court of appeal which rules on the outcome of the main proceedings before the referring court: it makes judgment neither on the facts in the main proceedings nor on the interpretation and application of national law. Moreover, in principle, it does not pronounce itself on the concrete application of EU law in the main proceedings before the referring court. Finally, while a preliminary ruling is normally given in the form of a judgment, the ruling is addressed only to the referring court, but not to the parties to the main proceedings. Only the referring court's subsequent decision can be enforced against those parties. As a matter of principle, the preliminary reference procedure is therefore an expression of an interplay and allocation of tasks between national courts and the Court. The preliminary references make the bulk of the Court's case law, and in 2012 the Court received 404 references out of a total of 632 new cases.

(ii) Which bodies may refer a preliminary question?

It is not every national body which has a right to refer a preliminary question to the Court for a preliminary ruling. According to Art.267 TFEU this right is only given to "a court or tribunal of a Member State".

9–29

The decision as to whether a given body constitutes a "court or tribunal" entitled to make a reference must be made on the basis of a uniform and independent definition under EU law. In other words, the definition does not refer to national law. This means that although private bodies and administrative authorities normally will not be able to make preliminary references,[109] some independent appeal boards may satisfy the conditions for being considered a "court or tribunal" for the purposes of Art.267, even if they are considered

---

[107] Art.46 of the Statute of the Court and see *Evropaïki Dynamiki* (C-469/11 P), judgment of November 12, 2012. The period of limitation shall be interrupted if proceedings are instituted before the Court of Justice or if prior to such proceedings an application is made by the aggrieved party to the relevant institution of the Union.

[108] *Inalca* (C 460/09 P), judgment of February 28, 2013.

[109] *Município de Barcelos* (C-408/09), order of February 12, 2010.

administrative bodies under national law. For instance, on several occasions the Court of Justice has given preliminary rulings on questions referred by Member States' public procurement appeal boards.[110]

The Court works on the assumption that a referring body will be a "court or tribunal" as long as it is part of a Member State's ordinary court system, and the reference is made as part of judicial proceedings which are intended to lead to the settlement of a dispute. Where the Court cannot rely on this assumption, it will normally make a more detailed assessment taking into account, in particular, whether the reference is made as part of judicial proceedings which are to lead to the settlement of a dispute. If this is not the case, it can be expected that the Court will refuse to accept the reference. If the reference is made as part of judicial proceedings which are to lead to the settlement of a dispute, but the referring body is not part of a Member State's ordinary court system, it will be particularly important whether the body is independent, and whether it has compulsory jurisdiction.[111] It is to be expected that the Court of Justice will reject references from bodies that are only set up with a view to resolve a particular individual dispute, or which are not established by law.

As the purpose of the preliminary reference procedure is that the Court should assist national courts with the interpretation of EU law in connection with the referring bodies' decisions on disputes, the Court will decline jurisdiction if the case in question does not concern the settlement of a dispute. This applies regardless of whether, according to its organisational characteristics, the body is classified as a "court or tribunal" according to the above criteria.[112]

What types of question may be referred?

9–30   Not every question from a body that fulfils the conditions for being categorised as a court or tribunal of a Member State in accordance with Art.267 TFEU can be accepted for a preliminary ruling. The categories of questions that can be referred for a preliminary ruling are listed in Art.267(1)(a)–(b).

According to these provisions, the Court has, with a few exceptions primarily linked to the Common and Foreign Security Policy, jurisdiction to give preliminary rulings on the interpretation of the Treaties, and on the validity and interpretation of acts of the institutions, bodies, offices or agencies of the Union. In this respect, it is not a condition that the Union act in question has direct effect. Moreover, a number of international agreements entered into by the EU have

---

[110] *Unitron Scandinavia* (C-275/98) [1999] E.C.R. I-8291 (the Danish Procurement Review Board); *Dorsch Consult* (C-54/96) [1997] E.C.R. I-4961 (the German Federal Public Procurement Awards Supervisory Board); *HI* (C-92/00) [2002] E.C.R. I-5553 (the Public Procurement Review Chamber of the Vienna Region); *Köllensperger and Atzwanger* (C-103/97) [1999] E.C.R. I-551 (the Public Procurement Office of the Land of Tyrol); and *Felix Swoboda* C-411/00 [2002] E.C.R. I-10567 (the Austrian Federal Public Procurement Office).

[111] *Pilato* (C-109/07) [2008] E.C.R. I-3503; *RTL Belgium* (C-517/09) [2010] E.C.R. E.C.R. I-14093, and *Nidera Handelscompagnie* (C-385/09) [2010] E.C.R. I-10385.

[112] *Job Centre* (C-111/94) [1995] E.C.R. I-3361; and *Standesamt Stadt Niebüll* (C-96/04) [2006] E.C.R. I-3561.

been deemed to constitute acts of the institutions of the European Union with the effect that they fall within the jurisdiction of the Court to interpret or rule on their validity.[113]

In contrast, the Court does not have jurisdiction to rule on the interpretation or validity of international law or national laws. Likewise, in principle, the Court is prevented from giving a binding ruling on the facts before a national court. That being said, this doctrine does not preclude the Court showing in the preliminary ruling how the EU rule will apply to a situation such as the one in the main proceedings. Where a preliminary ruling contains such guidance, it *de facto* amounts to the Court of Justice applying EU law to the facts and national law aspects in the main proceedings. Hence, to a fair extent, the distinction between interpretation and application, where the former falls within the Court's competence whereas the latter is a matter solely for the referring court, is more a question of form than a substantive delimitation of the Court's competence.[114]

Hypothetical questions

As it is not the task of the Court to rule on hypothetical questions, a preliminary question will only be admissible if the answer of the Court of Justice to the question referred will be relevant to the decision in the main proceedings before the referring court.

9–31

In this respect, it is, in the first place, for the national court to decide whether it is necessary to make a reference for a preliminary ruling in order to give judgment. This competence is naturally linked to the fact that it is the national court which is seized of the substance of the dispute and which must bear the final responsibility for the decision to be taken. The Court, however, regularly checks whether a preliminary question is hypothetical, and the Court refuses to treat the question as admissible if it is quite obvious that the interpretation of EU law or the examination of the validity of a rule of EU law sought by that court bears no relation to the actual nature of the case or the subject-matter of the main action.[115] For example, a question concerning the proportionality of criminal sanctions will not be found admissible if it is made in connection with a civil action between two private parties.[116] Similarly, the Court tries to restrict its interpretation of EU law to the factual situation before the national court, without venturing into other issues the resolving of which is not necessary for the resolution of the case before the national court. Thus, for instance, in a case concerning the validity of a national law which prohibits advertisements, a ruling will only be given in relation to the form of advertisement or type of product which is in fact involved in the case.[117]

---

[113] *Walz* (C-63/09) [2010] E.C.R. I-4239, *Lesoochranárske zoskupenie VLK* (C-240/09) [2011] E.C.R. I-1255, and *The Air Transport Association of America* (C-366/10), judgment of December 21, 2011.

[114] See point II.5.(viii) below.

[115] *Caja de Ahorros y Monte de Piedad de Madrid* (C-484/08) [2010] E.C.R. I-4785.

[116] *IP* (C-2/97) [1998] E.C.R. I-8597.

[117] *Leclerc-Siplec* (C-412/93) [1995] E.C.R. I-179.

When is there a duty to refer?

9–32 Assuming that the above-mentioned condition of relevance is fulfilled, the main rule is that a national court is free to decide whether or not to make a preliminary reference. In this respect, the national court may take into account, e.g., the difficulty of the legal question at stake, the delay and cost connected to a preliminary reference, the wishes of the parties, and the need not to overload the Court.

There are, however, two exceptions to that main rule on the national court's discretion. First, where a national court considers that an argument for invalidity of an EU act is well founded, it must stay proceedings and make a reference to the Court of Justice for a preliminary ruling on the act's validity, as it cannot itself set aside an EU act.[118] Second, Art.267(3) TFEU provides that where a question of the validity or interpretation of EU law is raised in a case pending before a national court against whose decisions there is no judicial remedy under national law, that court or tribunal shall bring the matter before the Court of Justice.

According to its wording, Art.267 TFEU requires national courts of last instance to refer questions for preliminary rulings in all situations where a case gives rise to a question of the interpretation or validity of EU law. However, the obligation to make such a reference must be understood in the light of the purpose behind the provision, which is to ensure the uniform and correct application of EU law by the national courts. This has considerable importance, not least today where EU law covers so many areas that there would inevitably be an excessively large number of cases referred if every court of last instance were to make a reference every time it was faced with a case that contained elements of EU law.

9–33 For those reasons, the Court has stated that there is no obligation to refer a preliminary question in the so-called acte éclairé situations, meaning situations where in other cases the Court has already made a decision on the question.[119] The same applies in cases of acte clair, i.e. situations where the question for interpretation has not previously been put before the Court, but where there is no real doubt about the proper interpretation of EU law. However, in the latter case the Court has laid down strict conditions for when a national court is justified in refraining from making a preliminary reference and instead taking upon itself the responsibility for resolving the question. In particular, not only must the national court itself be convinced as to the correct interpretation of EU law, it must also "be convinced that the matter is equally obvious to the courts of the other Member States and to the Court of Justice."[120]

This condition, that the national court invoking acte clair must be convinced about how other judges will view the interpretative issue at stake, is virtually impossible to fulfil and is a much stricter requirement than the need for the judge himself to feel certain about the correct interpretation of the rule in question. The very fact that the Court of Justice has a tendency to develop its case-law in a

---

[118] *Foto-Frost* (314/85) [1987] E.C.R. 4199. In comparison, unless the national court is a court of last instance (or there is acte clair), it may refute an argument of invalidity of an EU act without seeking prior advice from the Court.

[119] In this situation, under Art.99 of the Court's Rules of Procedure, the Court may limit itself to answering the question by a reasoned order.

[120] *CILFIT* (283/81) [1982] E.C.R. 3415.

dynamic fashion and that it retains the right to overrule previous case-law often makes it difficult to be absolutely certain about the correct interpretation of EU law. However, the bar is set even higher when the national court must also be convinced not only that other national courts will arrive at the same result, but also that they will consider the outcome to be "obvious". Ultimately, the national court can only rely on its own judgement. In contrast, it cannot realistically engage in imagining the workings of the minds of other judges whom it has never met and actually convince itself about the minds of these other persons.

The Court has ruled that there can be an infringement of EU law entailing Member State liability if a national court does not make a reference for a preliminary ruling in a situation where it has a duty to do so, and on this basis renders a judgment which is not in accordance with EU law.[121]

The form and content of the reference

An order for preliminary reference should be formulated in such a way as to be in accordance with Art.267 TFEU. The questions may therefore not (directly) concern the actual application of EU law to the case in question, nor may they invite the Court to perform an evaluation of the facts in the main proceedings, nor may they relate to the interpretation or validity of national law.   **9–34**

In order to ensure that the Court of Justice receives the necessary information to render an adequate ruling, Art.94 of its Rules of Procedure lays down that a request for a preliminary ruling shall contain:

(a)   a summary of the subject-matter of the dispute and the relevant findings of fact as determined by the referring court or tribunal, or, at least, an account of the facts on which the questions are based;

(b)   the tenor of any national provisions applicable in the case and, where appropriate, the relevant national case-law;

(c)   a statement of the reasons which prompted the referring court or tribunal to inquire about the interpretation or validity of certain provisions of European Union law, and the relationship between those provisions and the national legislation applicable to the main proceedings.

A reference for a preliminary ruling which raises one or more questions in the areas covered by Title V of Part Three of the TFEU may, at the request of the referring court or, exceptionally, of the Court of Justice's own motion, be dealt with under an urgent procedure derogating from the provisions of these Rules. In such cases the referring court should explicitly state its request for an application of the urgent procedure and advance reasons therefore.

---

[121] *Köbler* (C-224/01) [2003] E.C.R. I-10239, and *Traghetti del Mediterraneo* (C-173/03) [2006] E.C.R. I-5177.

Proceedings before the referring court after a reference has been made

9–35   Normally, the national court stays the proceedings when it refers a preliminary question to the Court. However, to make a preliminary reference does not imply that the case as such is transferred to the Court. On the contrary, the main proceedings remain pending before the referring court and that court thus retains jurisdiction to take any procedural measures which it is empowered to take under national law. For example, it may order protective measures to safeguard the interests of the parties pending the preliminary ruling. Furthermore, EU law does not prevent the referring court from withdrawing a preliminary question, and there is no duty to give reasons for such a withdrawal.

The preliminary ruling

9–36   The preliminary ruling—that may take the form of a judgment or an order—answers the preliminary question referred by the national court. That being said, the Court of Justice often reformulates preliminary questions and gives its answer based on such reformulations. This is not only so where the questions exceed the Court's powers under Art.267 TFEU. In order to be able to give a useful answer to the questions asked, the Court can provide the referring court with all the elements of interpretation of EU law that are relevant for deciding the dispute in the main proceedings. This frequently means that the Court refers to EU rules which the national court have not mentioned in the order for reference and appears not to have taken into account. The Court is more reticent in cases where an assessment of other EU rules will raise problems other than those which the national court has chosen to lay before the Court.

   As explained above under point (iii), it is, in principle, the task of the Court only to interpret EU law, but not to apply it in the actual case. On this basis, preliminary rulings were originally given in abstract and general terms. What lay behind this practice was presumably a view that the distinction between abstract interpretation and its application to the facts required the Court to leave a certain scope for the national court concerning the application of the preliminary ruling.

   The distinction between interpretation and application is far from unambiguous, however. Furthermore, an abstract and general answer will often be of limited value to the referring court, just as there sometimes will be a risk that different national courts will apply the interpreted EU provision in divergent ways, contrary to the purpose behind Art.267. On this basis, the Court of Justice has long been moving towards a more concrete style of interpretation, where the preliminary ruling is formulated in a manner that takes into account relevant aspects of the facts in the main proceedings and of the national law. Thereby, depending on the circumstances, an interpretation will be given which is still formulated in abstract terms but which in reality is tantamount to application. This is regularly expressed in the rulings themselves in the formulation whereby a given factual and legal situation, such as the one before the referring court, is or is not in accordance with EU law.[122]

---

[122] For recent examples see *Ze Fu Fleischhandel* (C-201/10 and C-202/10) [2011] E.C.R. I-3545; and *Q Beef* (C-89/10 and C-96/10) judgment of September 2011.

The response that the Court gives to a preliminary question binds the referring   9–37
court in its application of EU law. Hence, if the referring court fails to comply
with a preliminary ruling it not only risks its decision being reversed on appeal; it
also constitutes a breach of EU law so that the Commission may commence an
infringement action under Art.258 TFEU against the State concerned. Moreover,
failure to comply with a preliminary ruling can constitute such a serious
infringement of EU law that it will trigger State liability.

Not only the referring court, but also any appeal court which decides on the
case in the main proceedings is bound by a preliminary ruling on the case in
question. The same applies to any other national court dealing with the case at a
later stage of the proceedings.

The interpretation which the Court gives to a rule of EU law clarifies and
defines the meaning and scope of that rule as it must be or ought to have been
understood and applied from the time of its coming into force. In other words, the
interpretation has effect *ex tunc*, not *ex nunc*. This also applies to judgments on
the validity of an EU act. Hence, a preliminary ruling declaring an EU act invalid
has retroactive effect, similar to a judgment annulling an act under Art.263 TFEU.

However, in application of the general principle of legal certainty inherent in
the EU legal order, the Court may in exceptional circumstances limit the temporal
effect of a preliminary ruling. For this to happen, several conditions must be
fulfilled for the temporal effects of a preliminary ruling to be limited. First, the
affected individuals or national authorities must have been prompted to adopt
practices which did not comply with EU law by reason of objective, significant
uncertainty regarding the implications of the relevant EU provisions.[123] Second,
without a limitation on the temporal effect the preliminary ruling must be liable
to cause serious financial consequences because a considerable number of
measures have been taken on the basis of the now overturned legal provision.[124]
Third, an exemption from a possible temporal limitation must be made for those
who have initiated legal proceedings prior to the handing down of the preliminary
ruling.

6.   OPINIONS

Upon a request made by a Member State, by the European Parliament, by the   9–38
Council or by the European Commission, the Court may give a so-called Opinion
as to whether an envisaged agreement is compatible with the Treaties and as to
whether the European Union or any institution of the European Union has the
power to enter into that agreement.[125]

The purpose of this procedure is to forestall complications which would result
from legal disputes concerning the compatibility with the Treaties of international
agreements binding upon the European Union.[126] Indeed, a decision of the Court,
after the conclusion of an international agreement binding upon the European

---

[123] *Mednis* (C-525/11) judgment of October 18, 2012; *Sürül* (C-262/96) [1999] E.C.R. I-2685; and
Bosman (C-415/93) [1995] E.C.R. I-4921.
[124] *Skov Æg* (C-402/03) [2006] E.C.R. I-199; and *Test Claimants in the FII Group Litigation*
(C-446/04) [2006] E.C.R. I-11753.
[125] Art.218 TFEU.
[126] Opinion 2/94 [1996] E.C.R I-1759, and Opinion 1/08 [2009] E.C.R. I-1129.

Union, to the effect that such an agreement is, by reason either of its content, or of the procedure adopted for its conclusion, incompatible with the provisions of the Treaties could provoke, not only in the internal European Union context, but also in that of international relations, serious difficulties and might give rise to adverse consequences for all interested parties, including third countries.[127]

For the Court to rule on the compatibility of the provisions of an envisaged agreement with the rules of the Treaty, it must have sufficient information on the actual content of that agreement. This entails, inter alia, that the decision-making process in relation to the draft agreement must have reached a sufficiently advanced stage so as to enable the Court to rule on the compatibility of that draft with the Treaties. Otherwise, the request for an Opinion might be held inadmissible.

On the other hand, a request for an Opinion can be submitted to the Court before the commencement of international negotiations, where the subject-matter of the envisaged agreement is known, even though there are a number of alternatives still open and differences of opinion on the drafting of the texts concerned, if the documents submitted to the Court make it possible for the Court to form a sufficiently certain judgment on the question raised by the request for an Opinion.[128] Therefore, the admissibility of a request for an Opinion cannot be challenged solely on the ground that the relevant institutions have not yet adopted the decision to open the international negotiations. Nor is it a prerequisite condition of being able to submit a request for an Opinion pursuant to Art.218 TFEU that the institutions concerned have reached final agreement. The right accorded to the Council, the Parliament, the Commission and the Member States to ask the Court for its Opinion can be exercised individually, without any co-ordinated action and without waiting for the final outcome of any related legislative procedure.[129]

7. ATTRIBUTION OF COMPETENCE

9–39 Competence may be attributed to the Court pursuant to an arbitration clause contained in a contract concluded by or on behalf of the Union.[130] The same applies to disputes between Member States that relate to the subject matter of the Treaty, if the dispute is submitted to the Court under a special agreement.[131]

In the case of a contract, the arbitration clause is necessary, since Art.274 TFEU provides that disputes to which the Union is a party shall not, on that ground, be excluded from the jurisdiction of the courts of the Member States. In other words, if no arbitration clause provides that disputes under the contract shall be decided by the Court of Justice, the national courts are the only competent forum for the resolution of such disputes. As the Court has held, any other solution would entail that the Court would be exercising jurisdiction beyond

---

[127] Opinion 3/94 [1995] E.C.R. I-4577.
[128] Opinion 1/78 [1979] E.C.R. 2871.
[129] Opinon 1/09 of March 8, 2011.
[130] Art.272 TFEU. See *Evropaïki Dynamiki* (C-200/10 P) [2011] E.C.R. I-67.
[131] Art.273 TFEU.

the limits placed by Art.274 TFEU.[132] It is not so that a plaintiff can freely choose whether he wants to avail himself of the Court of Justice or of the national court system.[133] Finally, only the parties to a contract containing an arbitration clause may be parties to an action brought on the basis of Art.272 TFEU, whereas the same option is not available to third parties which find that the contract has affected their legal position in an illegal manner.[134]

III.   PROCEDURE

1.   OVERVIEW

The rules concerning the procedure before the Court are laid down in the Protocol on the Statute of the Court of Justice of the European Union, and in the Rules of Procedure of the Court of Justice and the parallel rules of the General Court and the Civil Service Tribunal.[135] These rules are complemented by so-called "Practice Directions to Parties" relating to direct actions and appeals and by the Court's "Recommendations to national courts and tribunals in relation to the initiation of the preliminary ruling proceedings". All the said documents can be found in continuously updated form on the Court's homepage.

9–40

2.   THE WRITTEN PROCEDURE

The procedure before the Court consists of two parts: a written and an oral. In direct cases, the written procedure starts with the submission to the Court of a written application from the Applicant. It shall be addressed to the Registry, and it may now be transmitted by electronic means. The Registrar publishes a notice of the action in the Official Journal, setting out the applicant's claims and arguments. At the same time, the application is served on the defendant, who has two months within which to lodge a defence.[136] The plaintiff's application and the defence may (but need not) be supplemented by a Reply from the applicant and a Rejoinder from the defendant.[137]

9–41

In addition to the information provided by the parties on their own initiative, the Court may prescribe the measures of inquiry and other preparatory measures that it considers appropriate such as: personal appearance of the parties; a request

---

[132] *Mutal Aid Administration Services v. Commission* (T-186/89 R) [1997] II-1633, and *Hanssens-Ensch* (C-377/09) [2010] E.C.R. I-7751.
[133] *Flemmer* (C-80/99, C-81/99 & C-82/99) [2001] E.C.R. I-7211.
[134] *Marinova* (C-29/09 P) [2009] E.C.R. I-115.
[135] Unless the Statute of the Court provides otherwise, the Treaty provisions relating to the Court apply to the General Court, cf. Art.254 TFEU. In the following all the references to the Rules of Procedure are those pertaining to the Court and not those found in the General Court's Rules of Procedure.
[136] Arts 120 and 124 of the Court's Rules of Procedure.
[137] Art.126 of the Court's Rules of Procedure.

for information and production of documents; oral testimony; the commissioning of experts, and/or an inspection of the place or thing in question.[138] The Court may also, either on its own motion, or on application by a party, order that certain facts be proven by witnesses.[139] Finally, it may request the parties to submit all such information, relating to the facts, and all such documents and other particulars, as they may consider relevant.[140]

3.   THE ORAL PROCEDURE

9–42   Once the written procedure is closed, the parties may state, within three weeks, whether and why they wish a hearing to be held. The Court decides then whether any preparatory inquiries are needed, what type of formation the case should be assigned to, and whether a hearing should be held for oral argument. In order words, the parties do not have an unconditional right to have an oral hearing. However, in preliminary cases an interested party who could have presented written observations, but chose not to do so, has a right to insist on an oral hearing.[141]

When it has been decided that an oral hearing will be held, the case is argued at a public hearing, before the bench and the Advocate General. It often happens that the Judges or the Advocate General put to the parties questions in order to better understand the facts or the arguments of the parties. A month or two after the oral hearing, the Advocate General delivers his or her Opinion.[142]

4.   LANGUAGE

9–43   The language of the proceedings must be one of the 24 official languages of the Union. It is in general determined by the applicant. However, when the defendant is a Member State or a natural or legal person having the nationality of a Member State, the language of the case shall be the official language of that State. Moreover, at the joint request of the parties, the use of another of the 24 languages may be authorised, for all or part of the proceedings. Finally, at the request of one of the parties, and after the opposite party have been heard, another language may be authorised, for all or part of the proceedings.[143]

In the case of a preliminary ruling, the language shall be that of the national court or tribunal, which has referred the question. However, representatives from Member States presenting observations may use the language of their respective states.

---

[138] Art.64 of the Court's Rules of Procedure.
[139] Art.66 of the Court's Rules of Procedure.
[140] Art.62 of the Court's Rules of Procedure.
[141] Art.76 of the Court's Statute.
[142] See point I.2 above.
[143] Art.37 of the Court's Rules of Procedure.

5. REPRESENTATION

The Member States and the institutions of the Union shall be represented before the Court of Justice by an agent appointed for each case. The same applies to States, other than the Member States, which are parties to the EEA Agreement and to the EFTA Surveillance Authority. Other parties must be represented by a lawyer who is authorised to practise before a court of a Member State or of another State which is a party to the EEA Agreement.[144]

9–44

6. INTERVENTION

Member States and institutions of the Union may intervene in cases before the Court of Justice. The same right is open to the bodies, offices and agencies of the Union, to the EFTA Surveillance Authority and to members of the EEA Agreement, not being members of the EU. As for others, there is a right to intervene if the person concerned can establish an interest in the result of a case submitted to the Court. However, such other natural or legal persons may not intervene in cases between Member States, between institutions of the Union or between Member States and institutions of the Union.[145]

9–45

The submissions of an intervener must be limited to supporting the form of order sought by one of the parties.[146] An intervener cannot, therefore, argue that a case should be declared inadmissible if the defendant has not himself put forward a claim to that effect, but only argued that the case should be dismissed on its merits.[147] However, an intervener is not precluded from advancing arguments which are new or which differ from those of the party he supports, as long as those arguments do not attempt to modify the frame of the dispute by presenting new grounds.[148]

In preliminary references cases there is no right to intervene properly speaking. Instead, the Court's Rules of Procedure lay down, exhaustively, that the following are authorised to submit observations to the Court:

(a)   the parties to the main proceedings,
(b)   the Member States,
(c)   the European Commission,
(d)   the institution which adopted the act of which the validity or interpretation is in dispute,
(e)   the States, other than the Member States, which are parties to the EEA Agreement, and also the EFTA Surveillance Authority, where a question concerning one of the fields of application of that Agreement is referred to the Court for a preliminary ruling,

---

[144] Art.19 of the Court's Statute.
[145] Art.40 of the Court's Statute.
[146] Art.129 of the Court's Rules of Procedure.
[147] *Commission v. Ireland* (C-13/00) [2002] E.C.R. I-2943; and *DLD Trading* (T-146/01) [2003] II-6005.
[148] *Regione autonoma della Sardegna* (T-171/02) [2005] E.C.R. II-2123; and *Boehringer Ingelheim Vetmedica* (T-125/96 & T-152/96) [1999] E.C.R. II-3427.

(f)   non-Member States which are parties to an agreement relating to a specific subject-matter, concluded with the Council, where the agreement so provides and where a court or tribunal of a Member State refers to the Court for a preliminary ruling a question falling within the scope of that agreement.[149]

7. ORDER OF CASES AND EXPEDITED PROCEDURES

9–46   In principle, the Court of Justice deals with the cases in the order in which they are received. However, whilst all cases should of course be decided as rapidly as possible, some cases present particular characteristics that entail a special need for a speedy resolution. The Court disposes of several ways of allowing it to accelerate the procedure.

First, the Court may, in some situations, decide the case by a reasoned order.[150] In this way it dispenses both with the oral arguments of those entitled to submit observations and with the written Opinion of the Advocate General.

Second, if the Court believes that there should be an oral hearing whilst at the same time the proceedings should be expedited, the Court may decide the case by a judgment whilst dispensing with the Advocate General's written Opinion.[151]

Third, on proposal by the referring court or by one or more of the persons or bodies entitled to submit observations, the President may, in special circumstances, order that a case be given priority over others.[152] Such prioritisation does not affect the time limits for providing observations in the case or other time limits applying to the "external" participants in the case. It merely means that the Court will give priority to the resolution of the case in its internal planning, translation and case distribution.

Fourth, the Court may apply a so-called expedited procedure if the nature of the case requires that it be dealt with within a short time.[153] The expedited procedure enables the Court to give its rulings quickly by reducing the time-limits as far as possible and giving such cases absolute priority. Under this procedure, in direct cases, reply and rejoinder may only be filed, if the Court so decides.[154] In preliminary cases, written observations shall be delivered within a shorter time-frame than normally, Moreover, the President may request those interested persons to restrict the matters addressed in their observations to the essential points of law raised by the request for a preliminary ruling.[155]

Finally, a special urgent procedure has been introduced for cases referred for a preliminary ruling in the areas covered by Title V of Part Three of TFEU.[156]

---

[149] Art.96 of the Court's Rules of Procedure.
[150] Arts 53, 99 and 181-182 of the Court's Rules of Procedure
[151] Art.20 of the Court's statute.
[152] Arts 53 and 133 of the Court's Rules of Procedure.
[153] Art.53 of the Court's Rules of Procedure.
[154] Art.114 of the Court's Rules of Procedure.
[155] Art.105 of the Court's Rules of Procedure.
[156] Arts 109-114 of the Court's Rules of Procedure.

8. SUSPENSION OF OPERATION OR ENFORCEMENT AND OTHER INTERIM MEASURES

Applications for annulment have no suspensory effect. However, the Court may, if it considers that circumstances so require, order the application of the contested act to be suspended just as it may order interim measures against the contest act.[157]

9–47

Interim measures are granted only if the following three conditions are all met:

1) The action in the main proceedings must appear, at first sight, not to be without merits;[158] this also entails that main action must not be manifestly inadmissible, e.g. because it has been brought too late or because the plaintiff obviously lacks standing;[159]
2) The applicant must show that the requested interim measures are urgent and that it would suffer serious and irreparable harm without them;[160]
3) The interim measures must take account of the balance of the parties' interests and of public interest.[161]

The order is provisional in nature and in no way pre-judges the decision in the main proceedings. Where the decision is taken by the General Court, an appeal against it may be brought before the Court of Justice. Similarly, when the decision is taken by the Civil Service Tribunal, an appeal can be made to the General Court.

The interim measures, prescribed by the Court, have been varied. The Court has, for instance, ordered the parties to start negotiations to agree upon an alternative solution,[162] authorised a Member State to take temporary measures, but with the consent of the Commission, and suspended the application of a measure on condition that a party continues to provide security.

The Court of Justice has no jurisdiction to entertain an application for interim relief in a preliminary reference case. It is therefore exclusively for the referring court to grant interim relief in order to ensure the legal protection which persons derive from EU law.[163]

9–48

In this connection, the Court has held that a national court seized of a dispute governed by EU law must be in a position to grant interim relief against a national law or administrative order that is claimed to be incompatible with EU law in order to ensure the full effectiveness of the judgment to be given on the existence of rights claimed under EU law.[164]

---

[157] Arts 278 and 279 TFEU. See, for instance *Oakley v OHIM* (T-116/06 R) [2006] E.C.R. II-2627
[158] *Commission v Malta* (C-76/08 R) [2008] E.C.R. I-64.
[159] *Bactria* (C-380/04 P R) unpublished order of December 13, 2004.
[160] In principle, purely pecuniary damage cannot be regarded as irreparable as it can be the subject of future pecuniary compensation. That being said, there may be situations where such damage cannot subsequently be compensated, for instance because it will not be possible to prove the extent of the damage or because the party that will be required to compensate the loss will not be able to do so, cf. *Melli Bank* (T-246/08 R) [2008] E.C.R. I-146; and *United Phosphorus* (T-95/09 R) [2009] E.C.R. II-47.
[161] *UK v Commission* (C-180/96 R) [1996] E.C.R. I-3903.
[162] *Commission v Ireland* (61/77 R) [1977] E.C.R. 937.
[163] *Alexander Dory* (C-186/01 R) [2001] E.C.R. I-7823.
[164] *Factortame* (C-213/89) [1990] E.C.R. I-2433; and *Unibet* (C-432/05) [2007] E.C.R. I-2271.

National courts may also suspend the enforcement of a national measure based on an EU act where the legality of the latter is contested. However, in such cases, the substantive conditions for ordering the suspension are regulated by EU law and are thus the same for all Member States. Moreover, these uniform conditions are largely identical to those regulating the same matter in cases brought before the Court and the General Court in accordance with Arts 278-279 TFEU. Finally, it is a condition that at the same time as ordering the suspension, the national court makes a preliminary reference to the Court for a ruling on the validity of the disputed EU act, should the validity question not already have been brought before the Court in another case.[165] Indeed, this requirement follows logically from the Court's case law according to which it has exclusive competence to declare an EU act invalid.[166]

The competence of national courts to provide for positive interim relief does not go so far as to allow for such measures in cases where the existence and extent of the applicant's EU rights are yet to be established in a future legal act that has still to be adopted by the EU legislator.[167]

9.   THE JUDGMENT

9-49   The Judges deliberate on the basis of a draft judgment drawn up by the Judge-Rapporteur. Each Judge of the formation concerned may propose changes. Decisions of the Court of Justice are taken by majority and no record is made public of any dissenting opinions.

According to the Rules, a judgment contains 12 items, among which are the operative part, including the decision as to costs and the grounds for the decision.[168] The latter are not only important because they explain how the Court arrived to the operative part, but also because the grounds for the decision constitute its essential basis, in so far as they are necessary to determine the exact meaning of what is stated in the operative part.[169] The judgment (i.e. the "operative part") is read in open court. Moreover, judgments and the Opinions of the Advocates General are available on the CURIA Internet site on the day they are delivered. They are, in most cases, subsequently published in the European Court Reports.

Judgments of the Court are designated with the letter "C", before the number of the case, and published in part I of the E.C.R. The judgments of the General Court are preceded by the letter "T" (for Tribunal) and published in part II of the E.C.R. In case of appeal from a General Court judgment to the Court, the number of the case is followed by the letter "P" (Pourvoi). Summary procedures are indicated by the letter "R" (Référé).

---

[165] *Zuckerfabrik Süderditmarschen* (C-143/88 and C-92/89) [1991] E.C.R. I-415, and *Krüger* (C-334/95) [1997] E.C.R. I-4517.
[166] See point II.5.v above.
[167] *Port* (C-68/95) [1996] E.C.R. I-6067.
[168] Art.87 of the Court's Rules of Procedure.
[169] *Spain v Commission* (C-415/96) [1998] E.C.R. I-6993.

10. COSTS

The unsuccessful party shall be ordered to pay the costs if they have been applied   **9–50** for in the successful party's pleadings. Where each party succeeds on some and fails on other heads, the parties shall bear their own costs. However, if it appears justified in the circumstances of the case, the Court may order that one party, in addition to bearing its own costs, pay a proportion of the costs of the other party. Moreover, the Court may order a party, even if successful, to pay costs if the Court considers that party to have unreasonably or vexatiously caused the opposite party to incur unreasonable or vexatious costs.[170]

As for interveners the rule is that the Member States, the other EEA States and institutions which have intervened in the proceedings shall bear their own costs. As for other interveners, the Court may order them to bear their own costs.[171]

In general, the following are to be regarded as recoverable costs: 1) sums payable to witnesses and experts, and 2) expenses necessarily incurred by the parties for the purpose of the proceedings, in particular the travel and subsistence expenses and the remuneration of agents, advisers or lawyers.[172] Proceedings before the Court are normally free of charge.[173]

There is no taxation of the lawyers' costs in the judgment. If a dispute arises between the parties about the costs, the dispute may be brought before the Court that will then decide by way of an order.[174] As Union law does not lay down any provisions for the scales of costs, the Court must freely assess the circumstances of the case. In this respect, it does not have to take account of a national scale of costs fixing lawyers' fees.

A party to the main proceedings who is wholly or in part unable to meet the costs of the proceedings before the Court may at any time apply for legal aid.[175]

In preliminary reference cases, it is for the referring court to decide as to the costs of the preliminary ruling proceeding.[176]

11. APPEALS

Appeal against decisions of the General Court may be brought before the Court   **9–51** within two months of the notification of the contested decision.[177] The appeal may concern a final decision, a decision disposing of the substantial part of the substantive issues only, or a decision disposing of procedural issues concerning a plea of lack of competence or inadmissibility.

An appeal to the Court shall be limited to points of law. Indeed:

---

[170] Arts 138-139 of the Court's Rules of Procedure. In *Svenska Journalistforbundet v Council* (T-174/95) [1998] E.C.R. II-2293, the Court ordered the successful party to bear part of its own costs in view of the abuse of procedure committed by the applicant who had published an edited version of the defence on the Internet with an invitation to the public to send their comments to the Agents of the Council.
[171] Art.140 of the Court's Rules of Procedure.
[172] Art.144 of the Court's Rules of Procedure.
[173] Art.143 of the Court's Rules of Procedure.
[174] Art.145 of the Court's Rules of Procedure.
[175] Art.115 of the Court's Rules of Procedure.
[176] Art.102 of the Court's Rules of Procedure.
[177] Art.56 of the Court's Statute.

"The [General Court] has exclusive jurisdiction, first to establish the facts except where the substantive inaccuracy of its findings is apparent from the documents submitted to it and, second, to assess those facts. When the [General Court] has established or assessed the facts, the Court of Justice has jurisdiction to review the legal characterisation of those facts and the legal conclusions it has drawn from them".[178]

An appeal may be brought by any party which has been unsuccessful, in whole or in part, in its submissions. However, interveners other than the Member States and the institutions of the Union may bring such an appeal only where the decision of the General Court directly affects them. With the exception of cases relating to disputes between the Union and its servants, an appeal may also be brought by Member States and institutions of the Union which did not intervene in the proceedings before the General Court. If the appeal is well founded, the Court sets aside the judgment of the General Court. Where the state of the proceedings so permits, the Court may itself decide the case. Otherwise, it refers the case back to the General Court, which is bound by the decision given by the Court on the appeal.[179]

FURTHER READING

9–52   Anthony Arnull, *The European Union and its Court of Justice*, 2nd edn (Oxford University Press, 2006).
Herwig Hoffmann, Gerard Rowe and Alexander Türk, *Administrative Law and Policy of the European Union*, (Oxford University Press, 2011).
Koen Lenaerts, Dirk Arts, Ignace Macelis, *Procedural law of the European Union*, 2nd edn (Sweet & Maxwell, 2006).
Koen Lenaerts & Courthaut, "Judicial Review as a Contribution to the Development of European Constitutionalism", in Tridimas & Nebbia (eds.), *European Union Law for the Twenty-first Century*, (Oxford: Hart Publishing, 2004).
Morten Broberg and Niels Fenger, *Preliminary References to the European Court of Justice* (Oxford University Press, 2010).
Rene Barents, "The Court of Justice after the Treaty of Lisbon", C.M.L.Rev. 2010, p.709.

---

[178] *New Holland Ford v Commission* (C-8/95) [1998] E.C.R. I–3175.
[179] Art.61 of the Court's Statute.

CHAPTER 10

The Court of Auditors

The Court of Auditors[1] was set up by the Treaty amending Certain Financial **10–01**
Provisions of the European Treaties and the Merger Treaty.[2] Previously a simple
organ of the Union, it was "upgraded" to an "institution" by the EU Treaty.[3] Its
task is to "carry out the Union's audit."[4] Since it is an institution, albeit without
the power to issue binding acts, which could be challenged in the courts, it has,
nonetheless, the power to go to court, like the ECB and the Committee of the
Regions, for the purpose of protecting its prerogatives.[5]

1. MEMBERS OF THE COURT OF AUDITORS

The Court of Auditors consists of one national for each Member State,[6] presently **10–02**
28, appointed for a term of six years; this term is renewable. The Council, after
consultation of Parliament, adopts the list of Members drawn up in accordance
with the proposals made by each Member State.[7] They are chosen from among
persons who belong or have belonged, in their respective countries, to external
audit bodies or who are especially qualified for this office. They elect their
President from among their number, for a term of three years; he may be
re-elected.[8]

Their independence, like that of the members of the Commission and the
Judges, must be beyond doubt. Similarly, they must be completely independent in
the performance of their duties, not take any instructions, engage in no other
occupation, give a solemn undertaking on beginning their duties and behave with
integrity and discretion during and also after their term of office.[9]

Members may be compulsorily retired by a ruling of the Court if the latter
finds, at the request of the Court of Auditors, that they no longer fulfil the
requisite conditions or meet the obligations arising from their office.[10]

---

[1] Art.285 TFEU.
[2] This Treaty was signed at Brussels on July 22, 1975, but entered into force only on June 1, 1977
([1977] O.J. L359/10), see Art.15.
[3] Art.286(7) TFEU.
[4] Art.285,1 TFEU.
[5] Arts 263,3 and 265,1 TFEU.
[6] Art.285,2 TFEU.
[7] Art.286 (2) TFEU.
[8] Art.286(2)2 TFEU.
[9] Art.286(4) TFEU.
[10] Art.286(6) TFEU.

2. TASKS OF THE COURT OF AUDITORS[11]

10–03   The Court of Auditors examines the accounts of all revenue and expenditure of the Union and of all bodies, offices and agencies set up by the Union,[12] in so far as their relevant constituent instrument does not preclude such examination.[13] As the Court of auditors writes, its purpose "is to ensure that EU taxpayers get maximum value for their money. It has the right to check ('audit') any person or organisation handling EU funds."[14]

It must present Parliament and the Council with a:

> "[S]tatement of assurance as to the reliability of the accounts and the legality and regularity of the underlying transactions which shall be published in the *Official Journal*. This statement may be supplemented by specific assessments for each major area of Union activity".[15]

It shall examine the legality and regularity of all income and expenditure and whether the financial management was sound. In doing so it must report in writing to the Commission and the EU national governments, in particular on any cases of irregularity.[16]

The auditors have the right to examine all records and visit all the premises of the other institutions and of any body, office or agency which manages revenue or expenditure on behalf of the Union; with regard to the Member States, the audit must be carried out in liaison with the national audit bodies. The other institutions, any body, office or agency managing revenue or expenditure on behalf of the Union, any natural or legal person in receipt of payments from the budget and the Member States, must forward to the Court of Auditors any document and information necessary to carry out its task. In respect to the EIB managing Union expenditure and revenue, the Court of Auditors' right of access to information shall be governed by an agreement between the Court, the Bank and the Commission.[17]

10–04   The Court of Auditors has no legal powers of its own. In case its auditors discover fraud or irregularities, they inform OLAF, the European Anti-Fraud Office.

The Court of Auditors also has to give its opinion on EU financial legislation and how to help the EU to combat fraud.

The Court of Auditors draws up an annual report which is published, with the observations of the various institutions, in the *Official Journal*.[18] Although this is not provided for in the Treaty, the Court of Auditors also publishes its own replies to those observations, which leaves the institutions at a disadvantage, since they have no possibility of making their views on those answers known. The Court of

---

[11] Art.287 TFEU.

[12] See, for instance, Reports on the financial statements and management of 10 bodies set up by the Union [2003] O.J. C319/1. While in this book I refer, in Ch.13, to "Decentralised Bodies", the Court of Auditors refers to "Union satellite bodies"; it does not, however, refer to Europol.

[13] Art.287 TFEU.

[14] *http://europa.eu/about-eu/institutions-bodies/court-auditors/* [accessed August 23, 2013].

[15] Art.287(1)2 TFEU.

[16] Art.287(2) TFEU.

[17] Art.287(3)3 TFEU.

[18] See for instance [2011] O.J. C134/1.

Auditors may also submit special reports on specific questions and deliver opinions at the request of another institution. It adopts its reports by a majority of its component members; it may establish internal chambers.

In a declaration adopted by the Conference which adopted the Nice Treaty, the Court of Auditors and the national audit institutions were invited to improve the framework and conditions for co-operation between them, while maintaining the autonomy of each. To that end, the President of the Court of Auditors may set up a contact committee with the chairmen of the national audit institutions.[19]

The Court of Auditors only published its Rules of Procedure in 2002; new rules were published in 2005[20] and in 2010.[21] Its role can best be summarised, in the words of the Treaty, as "assisting the European Parliament and the Council in exercising their powers of control over the implementation of the budget".[22]

The Court of Auditors is situated in Luxembourg. It has a staff of some 800 persons, including translators and administrators.

---

[19] Art.287(2) TFEU. For a Special Report see, for instance; [1994] O.J. C13/1 concerning business and innovation centres.
[20] [2001] O.J. C 80/80.
[21] [2010] O.J. L103/1.
[22] [2002] O.J. L 210/1.

CHAPTER 11

The European Central Bank

1. THE EUROPEAN SYSTEM OF CENTRAL BANKS AND THE EUROPEAN CENTRAL BANK

The European System of Central Banks (ESCB) (composed of the European   **11–01**
Central Bank and the 28 national central banks) and the European Central Bank
(ECB) were established by the EC Treaty.[1] They exercise their powers and carry
out their tasks to implement the Economic and Monetary Policy of the Union that
shall be examined hereafter within that framework (see below, Ch.28: The
Economic and Monetary Union (Policy) The Euro). The institutional aspects shall
be briefly described here.

2. INSTITUTIONAL PROVISIONS CONCERNING THE ESCB AND THE ECB

The ESCB was established, together with the ECB, at the start of the third stage   **11–02**
of achieving the Monetary and Economic Union;[2] its primary objective is "to
maintain price stability".[3] It must support the general economic policies in the
Union with a view to contributing to the achievement of the objectives of the
Union.[4] It must act in accordance with the principles of an open market economy
with free competition, favouring an efficient allocation of resources, and in
compliance with the principles of the Union's economic policy.[5]

The basic tasks of ESCB are:

- to define and implement the monetary policy of the Union;
- to conduct foreign exchange operations;
- to hold and manage the foreign exchange reserves of the Member States;
- to promote the smooth operation of payment systems.

---

[1] Art.13(1) EU, last indent and Art.282 TFEU and Statute of the ESCB and of the ECB annexed to
the TFEU. The Eurosystem comprises the ECB and the national central banks of the Member States
that have adopted the euro.
[2] For details on the stages, see below Ch.28: The Economic and Monetary Union (Policy) The Euro.
[3] Art.127(1) TFEU.
[4] Art.3 EU.
[5] Art.119 TFEU.

The ESCB must also contribute to the smooth conduct of policies pursued by the competent authorities relating to the prudential supervision of credit institutions and the stability of the financial system.[6]

It is governed by the decision-making bodies of the ECB.[7] Its statute is laid down in a Protocol attached to the TFEU.

The ECB replaced the European Monetary Institute (EMI). As was decided by the European Council on October 29, 1993, the seat of the EMI, and consequently of the ECB, is in Frankfurt.

The ECB, which has legal personality,[8] is headed by a Governing Council and an Executive Board.[9]

11–03   The *Governing Council* consists of the members of the Executive Board and the governors of the national central banks. One of the most impressive tasks of the Governing Council is to set, for the Euro area,[10] the interest rates at which commercial banks can obtain money from their central bank. This rate practically determines the interest to be paid by anyone borrowing or investing money. However, one of the problems encountered in the financial crisis is the lack of transmission of the monetary policy to markets in some Member States, i.e. interest rate cuts are not transmitted to the rates banks offer their customers.

The *Executive Board* comprises the President, the Vice-President and four other members of the Governing Council. They are appointed for eight years from among "persons of recognised standings and professional experience in monetary and banking matters", by common accord of the governments of the Member States. The appointments are decided by the latter at the level of the European Council, on a recommendation of the Council. The latter must first consult Parliament and the Governing Council. The meetings of the Governing Council may be attended, without voting right, by the President of the Council and a member of the Commission.[11] The President of the ECB shall be invited to attend meetings of the Council when the latter discusses matters relating to the objectives and tasks of the European System of Central Banks (ESCB). Clearly everything has been provided to establish close links both with the highest national monetary institutions and with the highest political decision-making authorities within the Union.

The *capital* of the ECB was €5,000 million.[12] It was increased to €5,760,652,402.58 as a consequence of Member States acceding to the Union and their national central banks joining the European System of Central Banks.[13] Presently, after a new increase, the ECB's capital is €10,760,652,402.58.[14] The national central banks are the sole subscribers to and holders of that capital,

---

[6] Art.127(5) TFEU.

[7] Art.129(3) TFEU.

[8] Art.129(2) TFEU.

[9] Art.283(1) TFEU. Rules of Procedure [1998] O.J. L338/28.

[10] The Euro area presently includes 16 Member States.

[11] Art.294(1) TFEU.

[12] Statute of the ESCB, first sentence of Art.28(1).

[13] See Preamble (1) of Decision of the European Central Bank of December 13, 2010 [2011] O.J. L11/53.

[14] same, Art.1.

which is subscribed according to a key established by the bank on the basis of statistical data provided by the Commission.[15]

3. TASKS OF THE ECB

The ECB has the exclusive right to authorise the issue of Euro banknotes within the Union. The ECB and the national central banks may issue such notes.

11–04

The ECB must ensure that the tasks conferred upon the ESCB under the TFEU[16] are implemented either by its own activities pursuant to the Statute or through the national central banks.[17] Its prime objective is to maintain price stability by defining the monetary policy of the Euro area so as to preserve the value of the Euro.

The ECB addresses an annual report to Parliament, the European Council, the Council and the Commission. This report is presented by the President to the Council and to Parliament, which may hold a general debate on that basis. The ECB may make regulations[18] to the extent necessary to implement a limited number of tasks[19] and to take decisions necessary for carrying out the tasks entrusted to the ESCB. Those acts are open to review and interpretation by the Court. It may also make recommendations and deliver opinions.

The ECB may institute proceedings under the conditions laid down in the TFEU.[20] Within the limits and under the conditions adopted by the Council,[21] the ECB may impose fines or periodic penalty payments on undertakings for failure to comply with obligations under its regulations and decisions.[22]

The ECB adopts its own rules of procedure[23] and it hires its own staff.[24] A Monetary Committee with advisory status was set up to promote co-ordination of the policies of Member States to the full extent needed for the functioning of the

11–05

---

[15] See Regulation 1009/2000 concerning capital increases of the ECB [2000] O.J. L115/1 and Regulation 1010/2000 concerning further calls of foreign reserve assets by the ECB [2000] O.J. L115/2.

[16] Art.105(2) Statute ESCB and ECB: the basic tasks to be carried out through the ESCB are: "to define and implement the monetary policy of the Union"; to conduct foreign exchange operations; to hold and manage the official foreign reserves of the Member States (the latter may hold and manage foreign exchange working balances (Art.127(3) TFEU); to "promote the smooth operation of payment systems"; and Art.127(5) TFEU: "The ESCB shall contribute to the smooth conduct of policies pursued by the competent authorities relating to the prudential *supervision* of credit institutions and the stability of the financial system."

[17] Arts 12(1) and (3) and 14 Statute ESCB and ECB.

[18] Art.132(1) TFEU first indent. See for instance Regulation 1921/2000 [2000] O.J. L229/34.

[19] Art.34(1) Statute ESCB and ECB.

[20] Art.35 Statute ESCB and ECB.

[21] Art.34.3 Statute ESCB and ECB: in accordance with the procedure laid down in Art.41 of the Statute.

[22] Art.34(3) Statute ESCB and ECB. See Regulation 2532/98 [1998] O.J. L318/4 and ECB Regulation 2157/99 (also referred to as ECB/1999/4) [1999] O.J. L264/21, amended [2001] O.J. L137/24.

[23] [1999] O.J. L125/34; see Rules of Procedure of the Executive Board [1999] O.J. L314/34 and of the General Council of the ECB [1999] O.J. L75/36.

[24] See conditions of employment [1999] O.J. L125/32 and Decision concerning public access to documentation and the archives [1999] O.J. L110/30.

internal market.[25] At the start of the third stage the Monetary Committee was replaced by an *Economic and Financial Committee* with similar tasks.[26] Its tasks are:

- to deliver opinions at the request of the Council or of the Commission, or on its own initiative for submission to those two institutions;
- to keep under review the monetary and financial situation of the Member States and to report regularly thereon, especially on financial relations with third countries and international institutions;
- to contribute to the work of the Council regarding movement of capital, the guidelines for the economic policies of the Member States, guidelines on monetary policy instruments and procedures of the Eurosystem,[27] access to financial institutions, commitments of public authorities, government deficits and the transitional provisions of the economic and Monetary Union (EMU)[28];
- to examine, at least once a year, the situation regarding the movement of capital and the freedom of payments; the Committee must report on the outcome of this examination to the Commission and to the Council.

The composition of the Committee is decided by the Council on a proposal from the Commission and after consulting the ECB and the Committee.

4. THE FINANCIAL CRISIS AND THE EURO CRISIS[29]

11–06   The above mentioned crisis required quite a number of decisions on the part of the ECB, the Member States and the Union.

Too numerous to be all mentioned here, a certain number of recent ones concern the effective enforcement on budgetary surveillance in the euro area,[30] the enforcement measures to correct excessive imbalances in the euro area,[31] the strengthening of the surveillance of budgetary positions and the surveillance and co-ordination of economic policies,[32] the prevention and correction of microeconomic unbalances,[33] on speeding up and clarifying the implementation of excessive deficit procedure[34] and on requirements for budgetary frameworks of the Member States.[35]

See, for instance, Guidelines on monetary policy instruments and procedures of the Eurosystem.[36]

---

[25] Art.134(1) TFEU.
[26] Art.134(2) TFEU.
[27] See, for instance, [2002] O.J. L185/1.
[28] See the EIB's Annual Report.
[29] See also Ch.18: Freedom to Provide Services/Financial Services.
[30] Regulation 1173/11, O.J.L306/1.
[31] Regulation 1174/2011, O.J.L306/8.
[32] Regulation 1175/2011, O.J.L306/12.
[33] Regulation 1176/2011, O.J.L306/25.
[34] Regulation 1177/2011, O.J.L306/33.
[35] Directive 2011/85, O.J. L306/41.
[36] [2011] O.J. L331/1.

The financial crisis led to the setting up of European System of Financial Services at the core of which one finds a European Systemic Risk Board.[37] The Board has its seat in Frankfurt and the ECB is heavily represented on the Board, chaired by the President of the ECB.

The Euro crisis made it clear that the link between weak banks and (weak) Member States had to be severed. Banks that are "too large to fall" have also become too large for one single Member State to bail out; the debt in which Ireland incurred in order to save its largest banks is an example. The obligations assumed by the Irish State brought it to its knees and eventually it needed a rescue package from the IMF and the Union.

11–07

The way to sever that link is establishment of a banking union. A banking union includes several components, in particular a common framework for resolution of banks and a single resolution authority, a common deposit guarantee scheme and a common and a single supervisory mechanism (SSM). The work as concerns resolution of banks is still outstanding, and as concerns the common deposit guarantee scheme its materialisation is probably not within a near future. However, the SSM has in principle been agreed and it entails that the ECB assumes the role as supervisor. All banks in the Euro case will come under the SSM—there are around 6,000. However, the ECB will only supervise itself the banks of systemic relevance—of which the estimated number is 150. The supervision of the remainder will be done by national authorities on the basis of common rules, and with the ECB having the power to step in if need be.

FURTHER READING

De Haan et al., *Financial Markets and Institutions: A European Perspective* (Cambridge University Press, 2009).

11–08

Fabian Amtenbrink, *The Democratic Accountability of Central Banks* (Hart, 1999).

Fritz Breuss & Eduard Hochreither (eds.), *Challenges for Central Banks in an Enlarged EMU* (Springer, 2005).

Jakob De Haan, *The European Central Bank: Credibility, Transparency and Centralization* (MIT Press, 2005).

Karl Kaltenthaler, *Policymaking in the European Central Bank: The Masters of Europe's Money* (Rowman & Littlefield Publishers Inc., 2006).

Mads Andenas, Gormley, Hadjiemmanuil and Harden, *European Economic and Monetary Union: The Institutional Framework* (Kluwer, 1997).

Marek Jarocinski et al., *Approaches to Monetary Policy Revisited: Lessons from the Crisis* (European Central Bank, 2011).

Otmar Issing, *Monetary Policy in the Euro Area: Strategy and Decision-Making at the European Central Bank*, (Cambridge University Press, 2001).

Paul De Grauwe, *Economics of Monetary Union* (Oxford University Press, 2005).

---

[37] Regulation 1092/2010, O.J. L/331/1. Regulation 1096/2010, O.J. L331/162, sets out the tasks of the ECB in relation to the Board.

CHAPTER 12

Other Bodies of the Union[1]

1. THE ECONOMIC AND SOCIAL COMMITTEE (ESC)

The Economic and Social Committee[2] is one of the "Union's advisory bodies", **12–01** which assist Parliament, the Council and the Commission.[3] It plays a consultative role, mainly within the decision-making process of the Union: it must be consulted by Parliament, the Council or by the Commission where the Treaty so provides.[4] If Parliament, the Council or the Commission were to fail to consult it when it is provided for by the Treaties, the final act could be annulled by the courts for infringement of an essential procedural requirement.[5] The fact that consultation has taken place must be mentioned in the relevant Union act.[6]

The ESC may also be consulted, by Parliament, the Council or the Commission, in all cases where they consider it appropriate. At the 1972 Paris Summit meeting, the Heads of State or Government decided to invite "the [Union] institutions to recognise the right of the Economic and Social Committee in future to advise on its own initiative on all questions affecting the [Union]".[7]

The number of ESC members is 353 and as many alternate members. The Committee's composition is decided unanimously by the Council on a proposal from the Commission.[8] The members are appointed for five years by the Council acting by a qualified majority, in accordance with the proposals made by each Member State and after consulting the Commission; the Council may also obtain the opinion of the various social and economic sectors and of civil society to which the Union's activities are of concern. The term of office is renewable.[9]

The members are representatives of organisations of employers, of the employed, and of other parties representative of civil society, notably the

---

[1] These are bodies provided for in the Treaties, as opposed to agencies set up by the institutions (see next chapter).

[2] Art.301 TFEU.

[3] Art.300 TFEU.

[4] See, for instance, Art.46 TFEU: Parliament and the Council must issue a Directive or Regulation to ensure freedom of movement for workers, and Art.50,1 TFEU: Directives to attain freedom of establishment.

[5] See Ch.9: The Court of Justice of the European Union (3.(a)(iii) Grounds for annulment).

[6] See Ch.3: The Legal Acts of the Union (2. Regulations, Directives and Decisions must be Reasoned).

[7] Examples of own-initiative opinions in [1988] O.J. C95/12 and C134/10.

[8] Art.301,1 TFEU.

[9] Art.302 TFEU: each Member State makes proposals to the Council. The number of members for each country are laid down in Protocol No.36 on Transitional Provisions: the four large countries each have 24 members; Spain and Poland 21; Romania 15; Netherlands, Bulgaria, the Czech Republic, Belgium, Greece, Hungary, Portugal, Austria and Sweden 12; Slovakia, Denmark, Lithuania, Ireland,

socio-economic, civic, professional and cultural areas.[10] However, they shall not be bound by any mandatory instructions. They shall be completely independent in the performance of their duties.[11]

A summary of the ESC's proceedings is published in the *Official Journal*. The ESC adopts its own Rules of Procedure[12]; it has its seat in Brussels. A Decision provides for public access to ESC documents.[13]

See Protocol on co-operation between the Commission and the ESC.[14]

2. THE COMMITTEE OF THE REGIONS[15]

12–02 This Committee was established by the EU Treaty and is composed of representatives of regional and local bodies who either hold a regional or local authority electoral mandate or are politically accountable to an elected assembly. The Committee has an advisory status.[16]

Like the Economic and Social Committee, the number of its members is now 353, but it also has an equal number of alternate members, appointed for five years by the Council in accordance with the proposals made by each Member State. The number of seats for each country is the same as for the SEC (see above). The term of office is renewable.

The members may not be bound by any mandatory instructions, they must be completely independent in the performance of their duties, in the general interest of the Union. They may not at the same time be Members of Parliament.[17]

12–03 There are several cases where consultation of the Committee of the Regions by Parliament, the Council or the Commission is provided for by the Treaties.[18] It is also consulted in all cases, in particular those that concern cross-border co-operation, in which one of those institutions considers it appropriate.[19]

The Committee of the Regions must be informed of requests for opinions from the Economic and Social Committee pursuant to the Treaty; when the Committee of the Regions is of the opinion that specific regional interests are involved it may issue an opinion on the matter.[20]

Croatia and Finland 9; Latvia, Slovenia and Estonia 7; Luxembourg and Cyprus 6; and Malta 5. See *CIDA v Council* (297/86) [1988] E.C.R. 3549; [1989] 3 C.M.L.R. 851, asking for annulment of the Council's Decision nominating the members.

[10] Art.300(2) TFEU.
[11] Art.300(4) TFEU.
[12] [2002] O.J. L 268/1, amended [2004] O.J. L310/77, codified version: [2007] O.J. L93/1.
[13] [1997] O.J. L339/18.
[14] [2012] O.J. C102/1.
[15] Art.300 and following TFEU.
[16] Arts 300 and 305 TFEU.
[17] Arts 300 and 305 TFEU.
[18] See for instance, Art.175 TFEU: actions necessary outside the Regional Fund and Art.192 TFEU: measure in the field of environment protection.
[19] Implementation of the transport policy: Art.91(1) TFEU; the social provisions: Art.153(3) TFEU; education, vocational training and youth: Art.166(4) TFEU; public health: Art.168(4) TFEU; Trans-European Networks: Art.172,1 TFEU; actions outside the structural funds: Art.175,3 TFEU; definition of tasks, priority objectives and organisation of the structural funds: Art.177,1 TFEU; implementing decisions concerning the ERDF: Art.178,1 TFEU and the environment: Art.192(1) TFEU.
[20] Art.307,3 TFEU.

Its opinions and a record of the proceedings are forwarded to the Council and the Commission. A summary of the proceedings is published in the *Official Journal*. See Rules of Procedure, which have to be approved by the Council, and a Decision concerning public access to documents of the Committee of the Regions.[21]

See Protocol on co-operation between the Commission and the Committee.[22]

3. THE SCIENTIFIC AND TECHNICAL COMMITTEE OF EURATOM

This Committee, set up by the Euratom Treaty,[23] is attached to the Commission; it consists of 33 members appointed for five years, in their personal capacity, by the Council after consultation with the Commission. It has an advisory status. The Commission must consult this Committee, among others, before setting up the Joint Nuclear Research Centre and before working out the basic standards for the protection of the health of workers and the general public against dangers arising from ionising radiations.[24]

12–04

4. EURATOM'S SUPPLY AGENCY

Provided for in the Euratom Treaty, the Supply Agency has a right of option on ores, source materials and special fissile materials produced in the territories of the Member States and an exclusive right to conclude contracts relating to the supply of those materials coming from inside or outside the Union.[25] In 2006, the Commission exempted from this obligation the transfer of small quantities of ores, source materials and special fissile materials.[26]

12–05

However, the Agency is entitled to refuse to purchase material on grounds of origin of the fuel[27] and is not obliged to guarantee disposal of uranium output accumulated by Union producers.[28]

New Statutes of the Supply Agency, replacing the 1958 ones, were adopted in 2008.[29] The Agency has legal personality and is situated in Brussels.

See also Ch.35: Energy Policy.

---

[21] [2007] O.J. L23/10. For the Rules of Procedure see [2010] O.J. L6/14.
[22] [2012] O.J. C102/6.
[23] Art.134 Euratom.
[24] See, e.g. Directive 84/467/Euratom [1984] O.J. L265.
[25] Art.52(2)(b) Euratom. See also Arts 53 to 56.
[26] Regulation (Euratom) 66/2006 [2006] O.J. L11/6.
[27] *Lippe-EMS* (Joined Cases T-149/94 and T-181/94) [1997] E.C.R. II–161; [1997] 3 C.M.L.R. 136 and *Kernkraftwerke Lippe-Ems v Commission* (C-161/97 P) [1999] E.C.R. I–2057.
[28] *ENU* (C-357/95 P) [1997] E.C.R. I–1329; [1997] 3 C.M.L.R. 95.
[29] [2008] O.J. L41/15.

5. THE GROUP OF THE EUROPEAN INVESTMENT BANK (EIB)

12–06 The "Group" is made up of the EIB[30] and the European Investment Fund (see below). Detailed provisions concerning the functioning of the EIB are laid down in the Statute of the Bank, which is the object of Protocol No.5 attached to the TFEU.

(1) Task

12–07 The task of the EIB[31] is to contribute to the balanced and steady development of the internal market in the interest of the Union. It does so by having recourse to the capital market and utilising its own resources on a non-profit-making basis.[32] Notwithstanding this obligation, it follows from the decision of the Board of Governors that there was, for 1996 alone, for instance, a so-called operating surplus of one billion ECU.[33]

The subscribed capital of the Bank is, according to Protocol No.5, attached to the TFEU €164,808,169,000[34]; it is subscribed by the Member States, which are liable only up to the amount of their share of the capital subscribed and not paid up.[35] They decided on a capital increase to €232 billion in April 2009. The subscribed capital is paid up by the Member States[36] to the extent of slightly more than 9 per cent.[37] However, instead of "paying up", the Board of Governors decided, in June 1997, that the remaining contributions would be financed using part of the proceeds of the operating surplus for 1996. The legality of this measure can be questioned.[38]

The same "solution" was applied when the capital was increased from €62 to €100 billion in 1992.

In 1998, the Board of Governors took a number of decisions laying down a Strategic Framework for the Bank.[39] This followed the invitation of the Amsterdam European Council to the Bank to step up its activities, with special reference to a number of sectors, in order to promote the creation of employment. Accordingly, the Bank introduced its Amsterdam Special Action Programme (ASAP), involving the creation of a special small and medium-size enterprise (SME) window, the development and reinforcement of EIB activities in the sectors of education, health, urban environment and environmental protection, and a new impetus to the financing of trans-European networks and other large infrastructure networks.

12–08 It is against this background that the Board of Directors has discussed the strategic framework, the main pillars of which are the following:

---

[30] Art.308 TFEU.
[31] Art.258 TFEU and Protocol EIB annexed to the Treaty.
[32] Art.309 TFEU.
[33] [1997] O.J. C211/6.
[34] See now: Annual Report 2012 , Activity and Corporate Responsibility Report, 2.
[35] Art.4 Statute EIB.
[36] Art.4 Protocol No.5.
[37] Art.5(1) Statute EIB.
[38] [1997] O.J. C211/16.
[39] [1998] O.J. C269/9. See also [1999] O.J. C247/6.

- concentration on "peripheral economic areas";
- continuing support to key EU policy areas such as development of Trans-European Networks (TENs), international competitiveness, SMEs, energy and the environment.

This must be viewed in the light of recent developments, i.e. recognition that the disciplines of the EMU must be accompanied by a concerted policy to reduce unemployment and the Council's decision on enlargement.[40]

The EIB grants loans and gives guarantees that facilitate the financing of:

- projects for developing less-developed regions[41];
- projects for modernising and converting undertakings under certain conditions; and
- projects of common interest to several Member States which cannot be financed by individual States.

In carrying out its task the Bank must facilitate the financing of investment programmes in conjunction with assistance from the structural fund[42] and other Union financial instruments.[43]

The EIB grants loans to its members (the Member States), and private and public undertakings for investment projects to be carried out, unless authorised otherwise by the Board of Governors, in the European territories of the Member States.[44] As far as possible, loans are granted only on condition that other sources of finance are also used.[45] When granting a loan to a body other than a Member State, it is conditional on an adequate guarantee, for example, from the Member State where the project is to be carried out.[46] The necessary funds are borrowed on the international capital markets or those of the Member States.[47]

(2) Procedure for Granting Loans or Guarantees

Requests for loans are sent either directly or through the Commission or the Member State concerned. Decisions regarding applications for loans or guarantees[48] are taken by the Board of Directors on a proposal from the Management Committee. Before deciding on the financing of a project the Bank

12–09

---

[40] For further details on this important document, see [1998] O.J. C269/89.

[41] The Commission finances similar projects with the European Regional Development Fund (ERDF) and other Funds, hence the need for close co-operation between the Commission and the EIB. The Director-General of "Regional Policy" is always an alternate member of the Bank's board.

[42] The ERDF, the Social Fund and the Guidance Section of the European Agricultural Guarantee and Guidance Fund (EAGGF).

[43] For example the Cohesion Fund.

[44] Art.18(1) Statute EIB.

[45] Art.18(2) Statute EIB.

[46] Art.18(3) Statute EIB. See Council Decision of December 22, 1999 granting a Union guarantee to the EIB against losses under loans for projects outside the Union: Central and Eastern European countries, Mediterranean countries, Latin American and Asian countries and South Africa [2000] O.J. L9/24.

[47] In 2009, the EIB approved loans for a total of €79.1 billion. In 2013 it intends to borrow a total of €70 billion. Outstanding loans amount to €350,289 billion and borrowings to €266,989.

[48] The Bank may also guarantee loans contracted by public or private undertakings or other bodies; Art.18(4) Statute EIB. Guaranties provided in 2008: €262 million.

must secure the opinion of the interested Member State and of the Commission. If the latter delivers an unfavourable opinion, the Board of Directors may not grant the loan (or guarantee) unless its decision is unanimous, the Director nominated by the Commission abstaining.

Originally the Bank was mainly intended to provide financial resources for the economic development of Southern Italy, the Mezzogiorno. This is still the case today, but other regions have been added, first by the successive enlargements of the Union and secondly by the economic crisis of the 1970s and 1980s. About 80 per cent of the Bank's loans go to the development regions of the Union[49] as a means of increasing economic and social cohesion.

In 2001, the governors approved the setting up of the Bank's Structured Finance Facility (SFF) that allows the EIB to finance projects with a higher degree of risk, especially in the areas of research and innovation projects and the Trans-European Networks (TENs) to be financed from the Bank's surplus. It focuses on quality projects and objectives shared by the EIB and the Commission and endorsed by the European Council. Lending for the Innovation 2010 in support of the EU's Lisbon strategy increased to almost €11 billion.

In 1994 the Council established a Guarantee Fund for external operations; its main function is to shield the general budget of the Union against shocks due to defaults on loans or guaranteed loans.[50] See Decision of Parliament and Council granting an EU guarantee to the EIB against losses under loans and loan guarantees for projects outside the Union.[51]

(3) Internal Structure of the EIB

12–10 The Bank is directed and managed by a Board of Governors, a Board of Directors and a Management Committee.

The Board of Governors consists of Ministers (of Finance) of the Member States. It lays down general directives for the credit policy of the Bank; it also decides on possible increases in the subscribed capital,[52] on grants of special interest-bearing loans to the Bank to finance specific projects by Member States and on the granting of loans for investment projects to be carried out entirely or partially outside the European territory of the Member States. Decisions are taken by a majority of the members: either simple majority representing at least 50 per cent of the subscribed capital; or qualified majority (e.g. for financing outside the Union) requiring a favourable vote of members representing 68 per cent of the subscribed capital.[53]

The Board of Directors consists of 29 directors and 19 alternate[54] nominated by each Member State and the Commission and appointed by the Board of Governors for five years. Each Director has one vote. Decisions are normally taken by at least one-third of the members representing at least 50 per cent of the

---

[49] In 2005, out of €42.3 billion lent in the Union, €28 billion went in loans for regional development.
[50] [1994] O.J. 1.293/3, amended [2007] O.J. 10223/3.
[51] Decision 1080/2011 [2011] O.J. L280/1.
[52] €100 billion.
[53] Art.8 Protocol No.5.
[54] Art.9(2) Protocol No.5. The Council acting unanimously, at the request of the EIB and after consultation of Parliament and the Commission, may amend those figures.

subscribed capital. A qualified majority shall require 18 votes in favour and 68 per cent of the subscribed capital. The quorum is laid down in the Rules of Procedure of the Bank.[55]

The Management Committee consists of a President and eight Vice-Presidents appointed for six years by the Board of Governors. The Management Committee is responsible for the current business of the Bank under the authority of the President and the supervision of the Board of Directors. The officials and other employees of the Bank are not servants of the Union, but under contract to the Bank.

An Audit Committee of six members verifies annually that the operations of the Bank have been conducted properly and its books kept in a proper manner. The Bank has legal personality and its members are the Member States. The EIB is submitted to the jurisdiction of the Court.[56] The Management Committee has adopted Rules on public access to document[57] and on historical archives.[58]

6. THE EUROPEAN INVESTMENT FUND

The Fund is part of the EIB group. The Statutes of the Fund were adopted by the Board of Governors of the EIB on May 25, 1994,[59] and amended in 2009.[60] The Fund has legal personality and financial autonomy. The task of the Fund is to support the development of Trans-European Networks (TENs), in the areas of transport, telecommunications and energy infrastructure[61] (see Ch.32: Regional Policy/Economic, Social and Territorial Cohesion – The Europe 2020 Strategy), and the development of small and medium-size enterprises (SMEs): close to one million SMEs received support from the EIB Group in 2008.[62] The Fund accomplishes its task by providing its guarantee for loans and by acquiring, holding or managing equity participations in any enterprise. In addition the Fund may carry out any other ancillary operations connected with its tasks. **12–11**

The capital of the Fund—two billion—is provided by the EIB (since the year 2000, more than 50 per cent), the Union[63] and commercial banks. The EIB operates as manager of the Fund. By the end of 2008 the Fund had a portfolio of €15.867 billion, of which €4.754 billion was in venture capital operations and €13.017 billion in guarantees.[64]

---

[55] Art.10 Protocol No.5.The Rules of Procedure, amended several times, were last published in [2011] O.J. L266/3.
[56] See, e.g. *Commission* v EIB, [1988] E.C.R. 1281 and *SGEEM v EIB* (C-370/89) [1992] E.C.R. I–6211.
[57] [2002] O.J. C292/10.
[58] [2005] O.J. C289/12.
[59] [1994] O.J. L173/1.
[60] [2009] O.J. C216/6.
[61] See Ch.31: Enterprise and Industrial Policy/Information Society.
[62] EIB Annual Report 18. New credit lines with financial intermediaries increased to €8.1 billion.
[63] See Council Decision 94/375 of June 6, 1994 on Union membership of the Fund [1994] O.J. L173/12 and Decision 2007/247 on the Union participation in the capital increase of the EIF: [2007] O.J. L107/5.
[64] EIB 2008 Report, 2.

7.   THE ECONOMIC AND FINANCIAL COMMITTEE

12–12   This Committee is provided for in the TFEU in order to promote co-ordination of the policies of the Member States to the full extent needed for the functioning of the internal market.[65] It has the following tasks:

- to deliver opinions at the request of the Council or Commission or on its own initiative;
- to keep under review the economic and financial situation of the Member States and of the Union and to report regularly thereon to the Council and the Commission, in particular on financial relations with third countries and international institutions;
- without prejudice to the work of COREPER, to contribute to the preparation of the work of the Council concerning:
  - safeguarding measures with regard to movement of capital from and to third countries[66];
  - administrative measures with regard to capital movement[67];
  - guidelines of the economic policies of the Member States[68];
  - Union's financial assistance to Member States in difficulties[69];
  - definitions concerning overdraft facilities and privileged access to financial institutions[70];
  - measures concerning excessive government deficit[71];
  - conferral to ECB of tasks relating to prudential supervision of credit institutions[72];
  - harmonising denominations of Euro coins[73];
  - adoption of provisions concerning ESCB and ECB[74];
  - establishing common positions within international financial institutions[75];
  - assistance to Member States in difficulties as regards balance of payments[76];
  - abolishment by Member States of protective measures[77];
  - abrogation of derogation from Euro[78];
  - agreement on exchange rate systems for the Euro with third States.[79]

---

[65]   Art.134 TFEU.
[66]   Art.66 TFEU.
[67]   Art.75 TFEU.
[68]   Art.121 TFEU.
[69]   Art.143 (1)2 TFEU.
[70]   Arts 123–124 and 125 TFEU.
[71]   Art.126 TFEU.
[72]   Art.127(6) TFEU.
[73]   Art.128(2) TFEU.
[74]   Art.129(4) TFEU.
[75]   Art.138 TFEU.
[76]   Art.143 TFEU.
[77]   Art.144 TFEU.
[78]   Art.140 TFEU.
[79]   Art.219 TFEU.

Detailed provisions concerning the composition of the Committee are laid down by the Council after consulting the ECB and the Commission. The Statutes of this Committee were revised in 2012.[80]

The Committee must keep under review the monetary and financial situation and the general payment system of the Member States with a derogation.

8.   THE EUROPEAN DATA PROTECTION SUPERVISOR

The TFEU provides for rules relating to the protection of individuals with regard   **12–13** to the processing of personal data by the Union institutions and bodies, offices and agencies, and by the Member States when carrying out activities which fall within the scope of Union law, and the rules relating to the free movement of such data.[81] In 2001, Parliament and Council adopted a regulation[82] setting up an independent supervisory authority referred to as the Data Protection Supervisor. His task is to monitor the application of the regulation to all processing operations carried by Union institutions or bodies.[83] The Supervisor is located in Brussels.

FURTHER READING

Michael Keating, *Regions and regionalism in Europe* (Edward Elgar Publishing,   **12–14** 2004).

---

[80] Council Decision [2012] O.J. L121L22.
[81] Art.16 TFEU.
[82] Regulation 45/2001: [2001] O.J. L8/1.
[83] See the Annual Reports published by the Publication Office of the Communities.

CHAPTER 13

Decentralised Agencies and Bodies of the Union

GENERAL REMARKS

It is interesting to note what the Commission wrote at the beginning of 2008: "There are two types of agency—regulatory and executive—each with different characteristics and raising different issues." "Regulatory" or "traditional" agencies have a variety of specific roles set out in their own legal basis, case by case. They are independent bodies often with their own legal personality. Most are funded by the EU budget as well as, in some cases, by the direct receipt of fees or payments. The agencies were, at the beginning, set up in successive waves in order to meet specific needs on a case by case basis. They are typified by their diversity. They were, later on, established in accordance with a Council Regulation adopted in 2002, published in 2003.[1] They operate under full responsibility of the Commission. The latter believes that these agencies can bring real added value to the Union's governance structure. Their work is particularly relevant in fields of shared competences where the implementation of new policies, at Union level, needs to be accompanied by close co-operation between the Member States and the EU.

It is important to note that the Court decided that the acts of the Agencies, not being provided for in the Treaty provisions on annulment of Union acts,[2] cannot be the subject of the Court's review of legality.[3] On the other hand, all these bodies are held accountable to Parliament (execution of budgets), the Court of Auditors and are also subject to controls by the European Anti-Fraud Office (OLAF).[4]

They have an important role in implementing EU policies, especially tasks of a technical, scientific, operational and/or regulatory nature.

13–01

---

[1] Regulation 58/03 [2003] O.J. L11/1.
[2] Art.263 TFEU.
[3] *Spain v Eurojust* (C-160/03) [2005] E.C.R. I-2077.
[4] See Ch.14: Financing Union Activities.

THE 2012 OVERHAUL

13–02   "Because the agencies where set up on a case-by-case basis over the years, to respond to emerging individual policy needs, they have been operating under quite diverse conditions. In 2012, the EU rectified this by adopting a comprehensive set of guiding principles—a "common approach—to make the agencies more coherent, effective and accountable."[5]

See also the "Joint Statement" of the European Parliament, the Council of the EU and the European Commission on decentralised agencies.[6] It points out that the decentralised agencies have become an established part of the way the EU operates. In 2011, 31 such agencies performed a wide range of implementing tasks, using a significant amount of resources. They contribute to the implementation of important Union policies, thus helping all the institutions, in particular the Commission, to concentrate on core policy-making tasks. Agencies also have a role in supporting the decision-making process by pooling the technical and specialist expertise available at European and national level, and thereby help enhance the co-operation between the Member States and the EU in important policy areas.

It is interesting to read the last sentence of this introduction: "the spread of agencies beyond Brussels and Luxemburg adds to the visibility of the Union in the different Member States."

13–03   It should be noted that this "Common Approach" is of a legally non-binding character and does not apply to agencies operating in the field of Foreign and Security Policy, nor to "executive agencies" (see hereunder).

For more details reference is made to the documents mentioned in the foot notes, but it is of interest to note that the Common Approach provides for a Management Board in each agency composed of one representative from each Member State, two representatives from the Commission, and, where appropriate, one member designated by Parliament and a fairly limited number of stakeholders' representatives. Besides the management Board, which gives general orientations for the agency's activities, there should be a small sized Executive Board, with the presence of a Commission representative, more closely involved in the monitoring of the agency's activities.

A last important remark: there is no official "classification" of the decentralised bodies[7]; therefore the titles under which they are mentioned in this chapter do not determine their nature (as always: *titulus non lex*" !).

I.   DECENTRALISED UNION AGENCIES[8]

---

[5] *http://europa.eu/about-eu/agencies/index_en.htm* [accessed August 23, 2013].

[6] *http://europa.eu/agencies/documents/joint_statement_and_common_approach_2012_en.pdf* [accessed August 23, 2013].

[7] *http://europa.eu/agencies/documents/fiche_1_sent_to_ep_cons_2010-12-15_en.pdf*   [accessed August 23, 2013].

[8] The Agencies are mentioned in the chronological order of their establishment.

1. THE EUROPEAN CENTRE FOR THE DEVELOPMENT OF VOCATIONAL TRAINING (CEDEFOP)

The Centre was set up in 1975.[9] It is a scientific and technical body entrusted **13–04** with promoting, at Union level, the exchange of information and experience, the distribution of documentation and the launching of research and experimental projects to facilitate the attainment of vocational training objectives set by the Treaty.[10]

The Centre is endowed with legal personality to ensure its independence. The Management Board consists of representatives of the Member States, workers' organisations, employers' organisations and the Commission. The Centre has its own budget.[11] Its seat is at Thessalonica with a staff of some 35 permanent positions and 53 temporary ones.

2. THE EUROPEAN FOUNDATION FOR THE IMPROVEMENT OF LIVING AND WORKING CONDITIONS (EUROFOUND)

It was set up in 1975 with seat in Dublin.[12] The Foundation deals specifically **13–05** with the following issues: men at work; organisation at work and particularly job design; problems peculiar to certain categories of workers; long-term aspects of the improvement of the environment and special distribution of human activities and their distribution in time.

It provides authoritative guidance and advice to social policy makers, assesses and analyses living and working conditions, reports on developments and trends, especially those driving change, and contributes to improving the quality of life.

The structure is similar to that of Cedefop and it has a staff of about 91 officials.[13]

3. THE EUROPEAN ENVIRONMENT AGENCY (EEA)

The objective of the Agency and of the Information and Observation network, set **13–06** up in 1990[14] and operational since 1994, is to provide the Union and the Member States with objective and reliable information at the European level in order to allow them to take the necessary measures to protect the environment, to evaluate

---

[9] Regulation 337/75 [1975] O.J. L39/1; modified many times; see *http://www.cedefop.europa.eu* [accessed August 23, 2013]

[10] Art.156,1 TFEU third indent.

[11] See, for instance, statement of revenue and expenditure for 1994 ([1994] O.J. L35/1), which constitutes an annex to the Union budget.

[12] Regulation 1365/75 [1975] O.J. L139/1, amended several times; *http://www.eurofound.europa.eu* [accessed August 23, 2013].

[13] See Statement of revenue and expenditure, quoted above. See also *Ryan-Sheridan, Staff Cases* (T-589/93) [1996] E.C.R. II–77.

[14] Regulation 1210/90 [1990] O.J. L120/1, amended many times; *http://www.eea.europa.eu* [accessed August 23, 2013]. Codified version: Regulation 401/09: [2009] O.J. L126/13.

their implementation and to ensure that correct information reaches the public on the state of the environment. A number of non-member countries participate in the work of the Agency.[15]

Its main tasks are:

- establish an Information and Observation Network;
- provide the information necessary to formulate and implement efficient environmental policies;
- register, check and evaluate environmental data;
- ensure the comparability of the data at European level;
- integrate the European information into international programmes;
- disseminate the information[16];
- precipitate the development of methods for calculating the damage caused to the environment, etc.

The agency has a Management Board, an Executive Director and a Scientific Committee. It is situated at Copenhagen, with a staff of around 115.

4. THE EUROPEAN TRAINING FOUNDATION (ETF)

13–07 The purpose of this foundation[17] is to contribute, in the context of EU external relations policy, to improving human capital development, in the following countries:

- countries eligible for support from the Instrument for Pre-accession Assistance (IPA)[18] and subsequent legal acts;
- countries eligible for support from the European Neighbourhood and Partnership Instrument[19];
- certain countries designated by decision of the Governing Board (these countries are designated as "Partner Countries").

The Foundation may provide assistance in: facilitating adaptation to industrial changes, in particular through vocational training and retraining; improving initial and continuing vocational training in order to facilitate vocational integration and reintegration into the labour market; facilitating access to vocational training; stimulating co-operation between educational establishments and firms; developing exchange of information; increasing the adaptability of workers and designing, introducing and implementing reforms in education and training systems.

13–08 The Foundation shall have the following functions:

---

[15] See, for instance, the agreement with the Swiss Confederation: [2006] O.J. L90/36.

[16] The EEA publishes four distinct reports, with Environmental Signals Reports being the Agency's main brand.

[17] Regulation 1360/90 [1990] O.J. L131/1, amended several times and recast by Regulation 1339/2008 [2008] O.J. L354/82.

[18] [2006] O.J. L210/82.

[19] [2006] O.J. L310/1.

- provide information, policy analyses and advice on human capital development;
- promote knowledge and analysis of skills;
- support relevant stakeholders in building capacity in human capital development;
- facilitate the exchange of information and experience among donors;
- support the delivery of Government assistance;
- disseminate information and encourage networking and the exchange of experience and good practice;
- contribute to the analysis of the overall effectiveness of training assistance; and
- undertake such other tasks as may be agreed between the Governing Board and the Commission.

It is managed by a Governing Board, a Consultative Committee and a Director. With regard to non-contractual liability, it is submitted to the jurisdiction of the Court. See the Decision of the Governing Board on public access to ETF documents.[20] The Foundation has legal personality and its seat is at Turin with a staff of about 100 officials.

5. THE EUROPEAN MONITORING CENTRE FOR DRUGS AND DRUG ADDICTION (EMCDDA)[21]

The Centre's objective is to provide the Union and its Member States with objective, reliable and comparable information at European level concerning drugs and drug addiction and their consequences. Its tasks are:

13–09

- collection and analysis of existing data;
- improvement of data-comparison methods;
- dissemination of data[22]; and
- co-operation with European and international bodies and organisations and with non-Union countries. In 2008 an Agreement was concluded with Turkey for the participation of the latter in the work of the Centre.[23]

The centre works closely together with, among others, the World Health Organisation, Interpol and Europol. It has legal personality, has a Management Board, a Director and a Scientific Committee and is submitted to the jurisdiction of the Court. It became operational in December 1993, i.e. after the Member States agreed on its location: Lisbon.

---

[20] [1997] O.J. C369/10.
[21] Regulation 302/93 [1993] O.J. L36/1, modified [1994] O.J. L341/7. Recast [2006] O.J. L3767/3.
[22] *http://www.emcdda.europa.eu* [accessed August 23, 2013].
[23] Decision 2008/375 [2008] O.J. L128/48.

6.   THE EUROPEAN MEDICINES AGENCY (EMA)

13–10   Parliament and Council replaced the 1993 Regulation laying down Union procedures for the authorisation and supervision of medicinal products for human and veterinary use and establishing a European Agency for the Evaluation of Medicinal Product,[24] with a Regulation of March 2004[25] that also modified the name of the Agency. Since 1995, the Union has had a twin-track approach to drug licensing. Companies are able to submit a conventional medicine either to the EMEA (the "centralised" route) or to one of the 28 national regulatory agencies (the "decentralised" route). The rule applicable in both cases is that no medicine may be put on the market without prior authorisation. The centralised route is compulsory in a certain number of cases.[26]

The new regulation corrects some of the operating procedures and makes adaptations to take account of the probable development of science and technology and the enlargement of the European Union. The general principles previously established that govern the centralised procedure are maintained. Directives were adopted on the Union code relating to medicinal products for human use[27] and on the Union code relating to veterinary medicinal products.[28]

At the Agency's request, the Commission may impose financial penalties to holders of marketing authorisations if they fail to observe certain obligations laid down in connection with the authorisation.[29]

A centralised authorisation procedure was also set up for the placing on the market of high-technology medicinal products, particularly those resulting from biotechnical processes.[30] The same need for centralisation exists for Orphan Medicinal Products; this task is assumed by the Committee on Orphan Medicinal Products.[31] As regards Herbal Medicinal Products the responsibility is vested in the Committee on Herbal Medicinal Products.[32]

The Agency has legal personality and is situated in London with a staff of about 315 persons. Its organs are: a Director, a Council of 34 members (representatives from the Member States, from Parliament and from the

---

[24] Regulation 2309/93 [1993] O.J. L214/1. See, for instance, Summary of Union decisions on marketing authorisations in respect of medicinal products, taken pursuant to Art.12 or 34 of Regulation 2309/93.

[25] Regulation 726/2004 [2004] O.J. L136/1, amended [2012] O.J. L316//38.

[26] See Annex to Regulation 726/2004, quoted above fn.25.

[27] Directive 2001/83 [2004] O.J. L311/67, amended [2012] O.J. L299/1 . See *Merck Sharp and Others v Commission* (T-273/03) [2006] E.C.R. II-141: the Commission is not competent to modify the summary of the characteristics of a product and *Synthon* (C-452/06) [2008] E.C.R. I-7681: Art.28 precludes a Member State to which an application is made for mutual recognition of a marketing authorisation granted by another Member State under the abridged procedure, from refusing that application on the ground of lack of similarity with the reference product. See also *Commission v Spain* (C-88/07) marketing of herbal medicines [2009] E.C.R. I-1353: herbal medicinal products produced and sold in another Member State and Decision 3052/95 on mutual recognition, repealed by Regulation 764/08 [2008] O.J. L218/21. Interpretation of Art.77 of Directive 2001/83; *Caronna* (C-7/11) judgment of June 28, 2012, not yet reported.

[28] Directive 2001/82: [2004] O.J. L311/1.

[29] Art.83 TFEU.

[30] See Directive 87/22 [1987] O.J. L 15/38, repealed [1993] O.J. L 214/40.

[31] [2000] O.J. L18/1.

[32] Directive 2001/83 [2001] L311/67.

Commission) and a Committee of Pharmaceutical Specialities. See also Committee for Proprietary Medicinal Products.[33]

The fees payable to the Agency are set by the Council[34]; special fees and assistance are provided for micro, small and medium-sized enterprises.[35]

7. THE OFFICE FOR HARMONISATION IN THE INTERNAL MARKET (TRADE MARKS, DESIGNS AND MODELS) (OHIM)

The Office was established on December 22, 1993.[36] It grants a uniform Union-wide protection which allows its owner to prohibit the use of the mark, design or model for similar goods and services.[37]

13–11

Before granting the protection, the Office examines whether any absolute motive prevents the grant from being made; the latter can also be withdrawn, for instance, if the owner does not make use of it for five years, or if someone else proves prior claim. The protection is granted for a renewable period of 10 years to anyone having his domicile in one of the Member States or in one of the countries party to the Paris Convention on the Protection of Industrial Property Rights. There is a right of appeal at every stage of the procedure, before the Boards of Appeal.[38] It is possible to appeal the decisions of the Boards of Appeal in the Union courts. This gave rise to abundant case law, both in the GC[39] and on appeal in the Court.[40] In some cases national courts are competent to hear the appeals.

The Union protection does not replace the existing national protections, and the economic operators have the choice between the two. The systems have been conceived to ensure that formalities and management are kept simple:

13–12

- a single application in one of the languages of the Union;
- a single file at a single administrative centre;
- defence against opposition, cancellation and invalidity actions, in the language of application, or in German, English, French, Spanish or Italian;
- links with national registrations and the Madrid Protocol System for the International Registration of Trade Marks OAMI-ONLINE, the website of

---

[33] Directive 93/39, 93/40 and 93/41 [1993] O.J. L214/22, 31 and 40.
[34] Regulation 1905/2005 [2005] O.J. L304/1. Regulation 297/95 lays down the categories and levels of the fees; amended [2013] O.J. L70 /1.
[35] Regulation 2049/2005 [2005] O.J. L329/4.
[36] Regulation 40/94 on the Union Trade Mark [1994] O.J. L11/1; modified [2009] O.J. L109/3. See *Nokia* (C-316/05) [2006] E.C.R. I-12083, where the Court stated that a Union trade mark court which has issued an order prohibiting the defendant from proceeding with infringement of a Union trade mark, is required to take from among the measures provided for under national law, such as are aimed at ensuring that the prohibition is complied with, even if those measures could not be taken under national law in the case of a corresponding national infringement.
[37] *Yamanouchi* (C-110/95) [1997] E.C.R. I–3251; [1997] 3 C.M.L.R. 749.
[38] See Order of the President of the GC [CFI] of June 19, 1997, *Chaves Fonsica Ferrao v OHIM* (T-159/97 R) [1997] E.C.R. II–1049, concerning the independence of the members of the boards of appeal. See also Rules of Procedure of the Board of Appeal: Regulation 216/96 [1996] O.J. L28/11, amended [2004] O.J. L360/8.
[39] See, for instance, *Vedial v OHMI—France distribution Hubert* (T-110/01) [2002] E.C.R. II–5275.
[40] See, for instance, *DKV v OHMI* (C-104/00) [2002] E.C.R. I–7561.

the Office offers the possibility of online filing of applications for both trademarks and designs. See also CTM-ONLINE database of trademarks and decisions of the Office. The office publishes its own monthly *Official Journal*, a weekly Union Trade Marks Bulletin and a fortnightly Union Design Bulletin.

The Office charges fees.[41] It is situated in Alicante (Spain), and started operating on April 1, 1996.

8.   TRANSLATION CENTRE FOR BODIES OF THE EUROPEAN UNION (CDT)

13–13   The Centre was set up in 1994[42] and its task was enlarged in 1995[43]; it is a legal person in its own right and self-financed. It was set up to meet the translation needs of other decentralised Union Agencies; it also serves the institutions and their bodies that have their own translation services, on the basis of voluntary co-operation agreements.

It participates in the Inter-institutional Committee for Translation that works to promote co-operation between the services on the basis of the principle of subsidiarity and to achieve economies of scale in the translation field. It has a Management Board and a Director; it has over 160 staff members and is established at Luxembourg.

9.   THE UNION PLANT VARIETY OFFICE (CPVO)

13–14   This Office was set up by the Regulation on Plant Variety Rights,[44] and the rules for the proceedings before the Office were published in 1995.[45] Parliament and the Council created a supplementary protection certificate for plant protection products[46] indicating that the competitiveness of the plant protection sector, by the very nature of the industry, requires a level of protection for innovation,[47]

---

[41] Regulation 2869/95 on the fees payable to the OHIM [1995] O.J. L303/1, amended [2009] O.J. L109/3.

[42] Regulation 2965/94 [1994] O.J. L 314/1, amended [2003] O.J. L245/13.

[43] Regulation 2610/95 [1995] O.J. L268/1.

[44] Regulation 40/94 on the Union Trade Mark [1994] O.J. L11/1, implemented by Regulation 2868/95 [1995] O.J. L303/1, amended [2005] O.J. L172/4 and [2009] O.J. L109/3. Article 30 of Regulation 2100/94 on Union Plant Variety Rights [1994] O.J. L227/1, amended [2004] O.J. L162/38.

[45] Regulation 1239/95 [1995] O.J. L121/37, amended [1996] O.J. L62/3; see for recourse *Federacion v OCVV* (T-95/06) [2008] E.C.R. II-38. See also Directive 91/414 concerning the placing of plant protection products on the market [1991] O.J. L230/1,amended [2011] O.J. L58/41,45 and 49, [2011] O.J. L59 /26,29,32 and 37, and [2011] O.J. L102/24; *Suède v Commission* (T-229/04) [2007] E.C.R. II-2437, where the GC annulled a Commission directive for non-application of procedural provisions; Directive 97/57 establishing Annex VI of Directive 91/414 [1997] O.J. L265/87 and Regulation 1238/95 establishing implementing rules for the application of Regulation 2100/94 as regards the fees payable to the Union Plant Variety Office [2005] O.J. L189/26.

[46] Regulation 1610/96 [1996] O.J. L198/30.

[47] See *Schulin* (C-305/00) [2003] E.C.R. I–3525, on the interpretation of Regulation 2100/94 and Regulation 1768/95. See also *Federacion de cooperativas de la Communidad Valenciana* (T-95/06) [2008] E.C.R. II-31.

which is equivalent to that granted by the Council when creating a supplementary protection certificate for medicinal products.[48] The Office grants rights ensuring industrial property protection for eligible new varieties; these rights are valid for a duration of either 25 or 30 years. A regulation provides for the grant of compulsory licences and the rules on public inspection and access to documents held by the Union Plant Variety Office.[49] A regulation establishes the level of the annual fee and the fees relating to technical examination payable to the Office and the manner of payment.[50]

In 2005, the European Union acceded to the International Convention for the Protection of New Varieties of Plants.[51]

Every two months the Office publishes an official gazette including extracts from the registers. It also publishes an Annual Report listing valid Union plant variety rights, the names of their holders and the dates on which they were granted and will expire. The Office is situated at Angers (France) with a staff of around 37 persons. An Application fee is payable to the Office.[52]

10. THE EUROPEAN AGENCY FOR SAFETY AND HEALTH AT WORK (OSHA)

The Agency[53] started work in 1996 and is based in Bilbao, Spain. The objective   **13–15**
of the Agency is to encourage improvements in the working environment. It shall provide the Union bodies, the Member States and those involved in health and safety at work with the technical, scientific and economic information of use in the field of occupational safety and health. The Agency is managed by a Director and has a Board, which is made up of representatives of the governments, employers and workers from the Member States and representatives of the Commission. Its staff counts about 38 people.

11. THE EUROPEAN FOOD SAFETY AUTHORITY (EFSA)

Set up by Parliament and the Council[54] in 2002, with legal personality and   **13–16**
privileges. The Regulation lays down the general principles and requirements of food law and procedures in matters of food safety. It also provides the basis for the assurance of a high level of protection of human health and consumer interest in relation to food. Its purpose is to approximate the concepts, principles and procedures of the Member States so as to form a common basis for measures governing food and feed taken in the Member States and at Union level.

---

[48] See above the section titled "6. The European Medicines Agency (EMA)".
[49] Regulation 2100/94 [1994] O.J. L227/1 and Regulation 1239/95 establishing implementing rules, modified [2005] O.J. L170/7.
[50] Regulation 1238/95, amended [2008] O.J. L161/7.
[51] [2005] O.J. L192/63.
[52] Regulation 1238/95, amended [2012] O.J. L156/38.
[53] Regulation 2062/94 [1994] O.J. L216/1; modified [2005] O.J. L184/5.
[54] Regulation 178/02 [2002] O.J. L31/1. See also Regulation 2230/04 laying down detailed rules for the implementation of Regulation 178/02.

The Authority must provide scientific advice and scientific and technical support for the Union legislation and policies in all fields which have a direct or indirect impact on food and feed safety; it must also provide scientific opinions on other matters relating to animal health and welfare and plant health, and on products other than food and feed relating to genetically modified organisms.[55] The Authority comprises a Management Board, an Executive Director and Staff (about 140), an Advisory Forum and a Scientific Committee and Scientific Panels. It is situated at Parma.

For more information see also "call for expression of interest for scientific experts to be considered for membership of the Scientific Panels and the Scientific Committee.[56]

12. THE EUROPEAN MARITIME SAFETY AGENCY (EMSA)

13–17 This Agency was set up by Parliament and the Council[57] in 2002, following several catastrophic maritime accidents. Its task is to assist the Commission in the preparatory works for updating and developing and, afterwards, implementing Union legislation in the field of maritime safety and prevention of pollution by ships. It shall work with the Member States and facilitate co-operation between the Member States and the Commission. For more details see the chapter on Transport.[58] The Agency is located in Lisbon.

13. THE EUROPEAN AVIATION SAFETY AGENCY (EASA)

13–18 Established in 2002 by regulation,[59] the Agency started operating in September 2003; its mission is to assist the Union in:

- establishing and maintaining a high, uniform level of civil aviation safety and environmental protection;
- facilitating the free movement of goods, persons and services;
- promoting cost efficiency in the regulatory and certification processes;
- assisting Member States in fulfilling International Civil Aviation Organisation (ICAO) obligations on a common basis; and

---

[55] See Directive 2001/18 [2001] O.J. L106/1 and *Commune de Sausheim* (C-552/07) [2009] E.C.R. I-987 on the scope of the Directive. Interpretation of Art. 23 *Monsanto SAS and Others* (Joined Cases C-58/10 to C-68/10) judgment of 8 September 2011, not yet reported.

[56] [2011] O.J. C99/33.

[57] Regulation 1406/02 [2002] O.J. L208/1. Modified [2013] O.J. L39/30. The institutions' powers to issue this regulation are based upon Art. 100(2) TFEU.

[58] See Ch.27: Transport.

[59] Regulation 1592/02 [2002] J.O. L240/1, amended [2003] O.J. L240/1; repealed by Regulation 216/2008 [2008] O.J. L79/1 on common rules in the field of civil aviation and establishing a European Aviation Safety Agency, the latter was amended [2009] O.J. L199/6, modified: [2013] O.J. L4/34. (See also Regulation 1178/11 [2011] O.J. L311/1 laying down technical requirements and administrative procedures related to civil aviation aircrew and modifying Regulation 216/2008 (see above). See also Regulation 965/12 laying down technical requirements and administrative procedure related to air operations pursuant to regulation; Regulation 1178/11 modified [2012] O.J. L100/1

- promoting worldwide Union views regarding civil aviation safety standards.

The first steps concern the certification of aeronautical products and the organisations and personnel involved in the design, production and maintenance. The EASA must also assist the Commission in the monitoring of the application of the regulation; the Commission is empowerd to impose fines or periodic penalty payments on holders of certificates for the intentional or negligent breach of any of the obligations laid down in Regulation 216/08 or its implementing rules;[60] a regulation lays down the working methods of the Agency for conducting standardisation inspection.[61]

The Agency was entrusted with the management of the Safety Assessment of Foreign Aircrafts (SAFA).[62] For more information see Ch.27: Transport.

The revenues of the Agency consist of contributions from any European third country which has entered into an agreement under the regulation, the fees[63] paid by applicants for certificates and approvals issued, maintained or amended by the Agency, and charges for publications, handling of appeals, training and other services provided by the Agency.

The Regulation permits the association of as many European partners as possible. Parliament and Council issued a regulation establishing common rules in the field of civil aviation security.[64] It provides, amongst other things, for the Commission to adopt measures for the implementation of common basic standards for aviation security throughout the European Union.[65] It is interesting to note that the annex to said regulation "should be secret and should not be published", "in order to prevent unlawful acts",[66] consequently the annex is non-binding in so far as it seeks to impose obligations on individuals.[67]

The Agency has a Management Board and a Director and is situated in Cologne with a staff of about 100 persons.

---

[60] Regulation 646/12 [2012] O.J. L187/29.

[61] Regulation 736/06 [2006] O.J. L129/10, amended [2012] O.J L31/1.

[62] See Directive 2004/36 on the safety of third-country aircraft using Union airports [2004] O.J. L143/76, as amended, complemented by Regulation 768/06 [2006] O.J. L134/16, as regards the collection and exchange of information on the safety of aircrafts using Union airports and the management of the information system entrusted to the Agency. Directive 2004/36 was repealed [2013] O.J. L4/34.

[63] Regulation 593/07 on the fees and charges levied by the EASA [2007] O.J. L140/3, amended [2012] O.J. L.151/22.

[64] Regulation 2320/02 establishing common rules in the field of civil aviation security: [2002] O.J. L355/1, repealed and replaced by Regulation 300/08 [2008] O.J. L97/72; annex supplemented by Regulation 272/09 [2009] O.J. L91/7, amended [2011] O.J. L293/22. See now Regulation 483/09 [2009] O.J. L 145/23 laying down measures for the implementation of the common basic standards on aviation security.

[65] Regulation 622/03 [2003] O.J. L89/9, amended [2004] O.J L10/14, [2005] O.J. L143/9 [2007] O.J. L200/3 [2008] O.J. L9/12 and L111/5.

[66] See Regulation 781/05 amending Regulation 622/2003 [2005] O.J. L131/24.

[67] *Heinrich* (C-345/06) [2009] E.C.R. I-1659.

14. THE EUROPEAN NETWORK AND INFORMATION SECURITY AGENCY (ENISA)

13–19   The Agency was established in 2004 for five years,[68] which were extended by three years in 2008.[69] It was again extended until 2013 in 2011.[70] Its mission is to assist the Commission and the Member States in developing a culture of network and information security for the benefit of the citizens, consumers, enterprises and public sector organisations. ENISA will ultimately serve as a centre of expertise for Member States, the business community and the EU institutions to seek advice on matters related with network and information security. Its task is focused on:

- collecting and analysing data on security incidents and emerging risks;
- co-operating with different players notably through the establishment of public/private partnership with industry operating at EU and global level;
- raising awareness and promoting risk assessment methods and best practices for interoperable risk management solutions; and
- tracking the development of standards for products and services on Network and Information Society.[71]

The Agency is located at Heraklion in Crete, Greece.

15. THE EUROPEAN CENTRE FOR DISEASE PREVENTION AND CONTROL (ECDC)

13–20   The communicable disease outbreaks pose a significant threat to the health and wellbeing of the European citizens. Since 1999, the Commission has managed a Communicable Disease Network based on ad hoc co-operation between Member States. Substantial reinforcement was needed for the Union to be in a position to control communicable diseases effectively. In 2004[72] the Centre was set up to provide a structured and systematic approach to this control and that of other serious health threats; it will also reinforce the synergies between the national centres for disease control.

The Centre is situated in Stockholm.

---

[68] Joint Action 2004/551 [2004] O/J/ L245/17, amended [2008] O.J. L102/34 and L293/1; Regulation 460/04 [2004] O.J. L77/1, based on Art.114 TFEU. The validity of this legal basis for the Regulation was contested by the UK: *UK v Parliament and Council* (C-217/04) [2006] E.C.R. I-3771, to no avail.
[69] Regulation 1007/08 [2008] O.J. L293/1.
[70] Regulation 580/11 [2011] O.J. L165/3.
[71] *http://www.enisa.europa.eu* [accessed August 23, 2013].
[72] Regulation 851/2004 [2004] O.J. L142/1.

16. THE EUROPEAN RAILWAY AGENCY (ERA)

The Agency was set up in 2004.[73] Its objective is to contribute, on technical   **13–21**
matters, to the implementation of the Union's legislation aimed at improving the
competitive position of the railway sector by enhancing the level of interoperability of railway systems and at developing a common approach to safety on the
European railway system, in order to contribute to creating a European railway
area without frontiers guaranteeing a high level of safety. In pursuing these
objectives, the Agency shall take full account of the process of enlargement of the
EU and of the specific constraints relating to rail links with third countries.

The Agency is a body of the Union and it has legal personality; it has an
Administrative Board and an Executive Director; it is located at Lille/
Valencienne (France) with a staff of about 30.

17. THE EUROPEAN GNSS (GLOBAL NAVIGATION
SATELLITE SYSTEM) SUPERVISORY AUTHORITY

This Authority was set up in 2004[74] given the strategic nature of the European   **13–22**
satellite positioning and navigation programmes and the need to ensure that
essential public interests in this field are adequately defended and represented.
The Authority was entrusted with, among others, the following tasks:

- managing the European satellite navigation programmes such as Galileo
  and AGNOS and controlling the use of the funds allocated to them;
- being the licensing authority vis-à-vis the private concession holder
  responsible for implementing and managing the Galileo deployment and
  operating phases;
- all matters related to the right to use the frequencies necessary to the
  operation of the system;
- being the owner of the tangible and intangible assets created and developed
  under the Galileo and AGNOS programmes; and
- assisting the Commission in matters involving satellite radio-navigation.

It is a Union agency and is located at Prague.

---

[73] Regulation 881/2004 [2004] O.J. L161/1, amended [2008] O.J. L354/51.
[74] Regulation 1321/2004 [2004] O.J. L246/1.

18. THE EUROPEAN AGENCY FOR THE MANAGEMENT OF OPERATIONAL CO-OPERATION AT THE EXTERNAL BORDERS OF THE MEMBER STATES OF THE EUROPEAN UNION (FRONTEX)

13–23 This agency was set up in 2004[75] to improve integrated management of the Union's external borders. Although responsibility for the control and surveillance of external borders lies with the Member States, the Agency will facilitate co-ordination of existing and future Union measures relating to the management of these borders. "External borders" means land and sea borders and airports and seaports to which the provisions of Union law on the crossing of external borders by persons apply.

An agreement was concluded with Iceland and Norway on the modalities of their participation in the Agency.[76]

The main tasks of the Agency are to:

- co-ordinate operational co-operation between Member States;
- develop a common integrated risk assessment model;
- help Member States to train their national border guards;
- follow up on the development of research relevant to the control and surveillance of external borders;
- assist Member States in circumstances requiring increased technical and operational assistance—a Rapid Border Intervention Team was set up in 2007[77];
- provide Member States with the necessary support in organising joint return operations.

The Agency is a Union body with legal personality and is represented by an Executive Director. It has a Management Board composed of representatives of the Member States and two of the Commission; it is situated at Warsaw.

19. THE UNION FISHERIES CONTROL AGENCY (CFCA)

13–24 The CFCA was set up in 2005[78] as a key part of the drive to improve compliance with the rules under the 2002 reform of the Common Fisheries Policy (CFP); see Ch.24: The Common Fisheries Policy (CFP) and Marine Policy. It should strengthen the uniformity and effectiveness of enforcement of control by pooling EU and national means of fisheries control and co-ordinating enforcement activities. It should also improve the flow of information between and among the

---

[75] Regulation 2007/2004 [2004] O.J. L349/1, amended [2011] O.J. L304 /1 . The validity of this Regulation was contested by the UK, but to no avail: *UK v Council* (C-77/05) [2007] E.C.R. I-11459.
[76] [2007] O.J. L188/15.
[77] Regulation 863/07 establishing a mechanism for the creation of a Rapid Border Intervention Team [2007] O.J. L199/30.
[78] Regulation 768/2005 [2005] O.J. L128/1, amended [2009] O.J. L341/1, amending Regulation 2847/93 establishing a control system applicable to the common fisheries policy [1993] O.J. L261/1, repealed [2009] O.J. L343/1.

Member States and the Commission. It should also lead to better relations between the EU and its international partners by centralising contact points and promoting more uniform control and inspection methods. To help the Agency, an EU Fisheries Monitoring Centre using satellite technology to provide information regarding the location and movements of EU vessels was established.

The Agency has an Administrative Board composed of representatives of the Commission and the Member States, an Executive Director and an Advisory Board made up of representatives of the regional Fisheries Councils. It is located at Vigo, Spain.[79]

20. THE EUROPEAN INSTITUTE FOR GENDER EQUALITY

Set up in 2006[80]. It became operational on January 19, 2008. The main aims of the Institute are to help:

13–25

- promote and strengthen gender equality;
- include gender mainstreaming in all Community policies and resulting national policies;
- fight discrimination based on sex; and
- raise EU citizens' awareness.

Mission and tasks are:

- collection, analysis and dissemination of information;
- promotion of dialogue at European level;
- raising of public awareness; and
- transparency.

The Institute will also raise the profile of such issues among Union citizens.

Operation: The Institute will perform its tasks within the framework of Community powers and in accordance with the EU's priorities in the field of gender equality.

The Institute will be organised in such a way as to operate independently from national authorities, civil society and the Community institutions, thereby ensuring transparency of action.

13–26

The Institute has legal personality and comprise a Management Board, a Director and his staff, and an Advisory Forum. Its seat is in Vilnius (Lithuania).

In order to avoid duplication, the Institute co-operates as closely as possible with all the Community programmes and agencies, notably the European Foundation for the Improvement of Living and Working Conditions, the European Agency for Safety and Health at Work, the European Centre for the Development of Vocational Training and any future agency for fundamental rights.

The Institute may enter into contractual relations, in particular subcontracting arrangements, with other organisations.

---

[79] According to [2008] O.J. L278/78 it is situated at Brussels.
[80] Regulation 1922/06 [2006] O.J. L403/9.

21. THE EUROPEAN CHEMICALS AGENCY

13–27   This agency was set up together with the adoption of the regulation on the Registration, Evaluation, Authorisation and Restriction of Chemicals (REACH).[81] It is a body of the Union and has legal personality. It is composed of a Management Board, an Executive Director, a Committee for Risk Assessment, a Committee for Socio-economic Analysis, a Member State Committee, a Forum for Exchange of Information on Enforcement, a Secretariat and Board of Appeal. The regulation provides that the Agency's work may not affect the activities of the European Agency for Health and Safety at work nor those of the European Medicines Agency, or the Food Safety Authority.

The Board of Appeal hears cases against individual decisions of the Agency concerning registration of chemical substances. Detailed rules concerning the qualifications required for the members of the Board were laid down by the Commission.[82] The Court has jurisdiction in any dispute relating to compensation of damages caused by the non-contractual responsibility of the Agency.

The Agency shall provide the Member States and the institutions of the Union with the best possible scientific and technical advice on questions relating to chemicals which fall within its remit and which are referred to it in accordance with the provisions of the regulation.

See Regulation concerning the export and import of dangerous chemicals.[83]

22. THE EUROPEAN UNION AGENCY FOR FUNDAMENTAL RIGHTS

13–28   It replaced the European Monitoring Centre on Racism and Xenophobia (EUMC).[84]

The Centre was set up in 1997; it is situated in Vienna with a staff of around 34 persons—its task is to provide the Union and the Member States with objective, reliable and comparable data at European level on the phenomena of racism, xenophobia and anti-Semitism. It must study the extent, development, causes and effect of the said phenomena in the following fields:

- free movement of persons;
- information, TV and the media;
- education, vocational training and youth;
- social policy, including employment;
- free movement of goods; and
- culture.

---

[81] Regulation 1907/06 [2006] O.J.L396/1, amended [2012 O.J. L37/1 , as regards Annex XVII and [2009] O.J. L220/1; amended [2012] O.J. L41/1 as regards annex xiv; [2010] O.J. L86/7 as regards annex xvi; amended again [2010] O.J. L133/1, and in 2011 [2011] O.J. L44/2, [2011] O.J. L58/27, annex XVII amended [2013] O.J. L43/24 annex XIV amended [2013] O.J. L108/1; [2012] O.J. L193/1.

[82] Regulation 1907/06 [2006] O.J. L396/1, amended [2012] O.J. L252/1 and Regulation 1238/07.

[83] Regulation 689/08 [2008] O.J. L204/1, amended [2010] L60/5 and L253/1 and 5.

[84] Replaced as from March 1, 2007 by the European Union Agency for Fundamental Rights [2007] O.J. L53/3.

The very core of its activities is the European Information Network on Racism and Xenophobia (RAXEN) whose objective it is to collect, co-ordinate and disseminate data at national and EU level.

The Centre was replaced by the European Union Agency for Fundamental Rights in 2007 (see hereunder).

The Agency was established[85] upon the premise that greater knowledge of, and broader awareness of, fundamental rights issues in the Union are conducive to ensuring full respect of fundamental rights. For a description of the latter, the Regulation refers to the Charter of Fundamental Rights of the European Union,[86] the constitutional traditions and international obligations of the Member States, the European Treaties, the European Convention for the protection of Human Rights and Fundamental Freedoms, the Social Charter adopted by the Union and by the Council of Europe, the case law of the Union courts and of the European Court of Human Rights.[87] The task of the Agency is to provide information and data on fundamental rights matters. Moreover, it is considered that developing effective institutions for the protection and promotion of human rights is a common value of the international and European societies.[88]

13–29

The Agency is built upon the European Monitoring Centre on Racism and Xenophobia described above, situated in Vienna, which it succeeds.

The Agency comprises a Management Board, an Executive Board, a Scientific Committee and a Director. The Court of Justice has jurisdiction among others in disputes relating to compensation for damages caused by the Agency and its servants.

A multi-annual framework for the Agency (2007–2012) was adopted in 2008.[89] An agreement was signed between the Union and the Council of Europe on co-operation between the Agency and the Council of Europe.[90]

23. EUROPEAN INSTITUTE FOR INNOVATION AND TECHNOLOGY (EIT)

The European Institute for Innovation and Technology is to be a key driver of sustainable European growth and competitiveness through the stimulation of world-leading innovations with a positive impact on economy and society.

13–30

The mission of the EIT is to grow and capitalise on the innovation capacity and capability of actors from higher education, research, business and entrepreneurship from the EU and beyond through the creation of highly integrated Knowledge and Innovation Communities (KICs).

It is managed by a Governing Board and is situated in Budapest.

---

[85] Regulation 168/07 [2007] O.J. L 55/1.
[86] [2000] O.J. C364/1.
[87] This reference is particularly interesting since this Court has no legal links with the Union; the Agency is to work closely with the Council of Europe.
[88] Reference is made to Recommendation R (97)14 of the Committee of Ministers of the Council of Europe of 30.09.97.
[89] [2008] O.J. L63/14.
[90] [2008] O.J. L186/7.

24.   THE EUROPEAN ASYLUM SUPPORT OFFICE

13–31   Established in 2010,[91] the Support Office is to help to improve the implementation of the Common European Asylum System (CEAS), to strengthen practical co-operation between Member States on asylum and to provide and/or coordinate the provision of operational support to Member States subject to particular pressure on the asylum and reception systems. It shall provide scientific and technical assistance in regard to the policy and legislation of the Union in all areas having a direct or indirect impact on asylum.

The Regulation provides, among others, for an Asylum Intervention Pool and a Support Office with interpreters.

The administrative and management structure comprises a management Board, an Executive Director and the staff of the Support office. The Support Office's budget must be balanced in terms of revenue and of expenditure. The Support Office is a body of the Union with legal personality. The regulation provides for co-operation with third and associated countries.

25.   THE EUROPEAN GNSS[92] AGENCY

13–32   The European Satellite radio-navigation policy used to be implemented through the EGNOS and Galileo programmes.[93] In 2004 was established a European agency called the European GNSS Supervisory Authority. A new framework for the public governance and financing of the programmes was defined in 2008.[94] It set out the principles for the strict division of responsibilities between the Commission, the Authority and the European Space Agency (ESA).

The European GNSS Agency was set up in 2010 by regulation;[95] it has an Administrative Board, a Security Accreditation Board and an Executive Director. It is a body of the Union and has legal personality. It is located in Prague.[96]

26.   THE EUROPEAN AGENCY FOR THE OPERATIONAL MANAGEMENT OF LARGE-SCALE IT SYSTEMS IN THE AREA OF FREEDOM, SECURITY AND JUSTICE

13–33   Established by Regulation[97] in 2011 to ensure the operational management of SIS II, VIS and Eurodac and of certain aspects of the communication infrastructure.

---

[91] [2010] O.J. L132/11.
[92] Global Navigation Satellite System.
[93] Regulation 912/10, Preamble (1) [2010] O.J. L276/11.
[94] Regulation 683/08 [2008] O.J. L196/1.
[95] Regulation 912/10 [2010] O.J. L276/11. which repealed Regulation 1321/04 and amended Regulation 683/08 (above).
[96] Decision of the Representatives of the Governments of the M.S. [2010] O.J. L342/15.
[97] [2011] O.J. L286/1. See also Ch.16: The Free Movement of Persons: *Schengen*.

27. THE EUROPEAN ANTI-FRAUD OFFICE (OLAF)

Established by Commission Decision[98] in 1999 to carry out external administra-   **13–34**
tive investigations for the purpose of strengthening the fight against fraud,
corruption and any other illegal activity adversely affecting the Union's financial
interests, as well as any other act or activity by operators in breach of Union
provisions. It exercises the Commission powers as they are defined by the
Treaties. The office may be entrusted with investigations in other areas by the
Commission or by the other institutions or bodies. It shall be in direct contact
with the police and judicial authorities. It shall exercise the powers of
investigation in complete independence. The Director of the Office shall neither
seek nor take instructions from the Commission, any government or any other
institution or body. A Surveillance Committee is responsible for the regular
monitoring of the investigative function.

28. EUROPEAN INSURANCE AND OCCUPATIONAL PENSIONS AUTHORITY (EIOPA)

Established by regulation[99] in 2010. Before and during the financial crisis of   **13–35**
2007 and 2008, Parliament called for a move towards more integrated European
supervision to reflect the increasing integration of financial markets in the Union.
It is part of a European System of Financial Supervisors that comprises three
European Supervisory Authorities: besides EIOPA, an authority for the securities
sector and the European Systemic Risk Board. Its main goals are: better
protecting consumers, rebuilding trust in the financial system; ensuring a high,
effective and consistent level of regulation and supervision; greater harmonisation and coherent application of rules for financial institutions and markets;
strengthening oversight of cross-border groups, and promote co-ordinated EU
supervisory response.[100]
   It is based in Frankfurt am Main, Germany.

29. THE EUROPEAN POLICE COLLEGE (CEPOL)

Established in 2000 by Council Decision pursuant to Title VI of the EU Treaty; it   **13–36**
was replaced by an organ with the same name and to be regarded as its successor
by a Council decision in 2005! It started as a network bringing together the
national training institutes for senior police officers in the Member States,
applicant countries and Iceland and Norway but it does not preclude the
establishment of a permanent institution at a later stage. The EU has been active
in this field with a common programme for the exchange and training of, and
co-operation between, law enforcement authorities (OISIN). It also promotes a

---

[98] [1999] O.J. L136/20. The decision took effect on the entry into force of Parliament and Council
Regulation 1073/1999 concerning investigations conducted by OLAF [1999] O.J. L136/1.
[99] Regulation 1094/10 [2010] O.J. L331/48.
[100] *http://eiopa.europa.eu* [accessed August 23, 2013].

programme for exchange, training and co-operation for persons responsible for action to combat crime (Falcone). For further details see the Council Decision.

The College is situated at Bramshill (UK).

30. THE EUROPEAN POLICE OFFICE (EUROPOL)

13–37 It was established in 1995 by a Council act consisting of a Convention concluded by the Member States and based on Title VI of the EU Treaty, the "Europol Convention".[101] The office is therefore financed by the Member States. (In 2008 it was decided to transform the Office into a European Agency on January 1, 2010.) It became operational on July 1, 1999, after ratification by the, at that time, 25 Member States. Some of its tasks are now provided for in the TFEU, such as:

- the collection, storage, processing, analysis and exchange of relevant information, in particular that forwarded by the authorities of the Member States or third countries or bodies;
- the co-ordination, organisation and implementation of investigative and operational action carried out jointly with the Member States' competent authorities or in the context of joint investigative teams, where appropriate in liaison with Eurojust.[102]

In 1998, a Council act laid down rules governing Europol's external relations with third States and non-European related bodies[103] and an act laying down rules governing the receipt of information from third parties.[104] Another Council act was adopted in 1999 concerning rules governing the transmission of personal data by Europol to third States and third bodies.[105] Its mandate was extended in 1999 to deal with forgery of money and means of payment.[106] A protocol on the interpretation, by way of preliminary ruling[107] by the Court of Justice of the Europol Convention was accepted by all the Member States, except the UK.

Any operational action of Europol must be carried out in liaison and in agreement with the authorities of the Member State or States whose territory is concerned. The application of coercive measures is the exclusive responsibility of the competent national authorities.

---

[101] [1995] O.J. C316/2; see Rules implementing Art.6a of the Convention—automatic processing of personal data: [2007] O.J. L155/78.
[102] Art.88 TFEU.
[103] [1999] O.J. C26/19. See Decision of March 27, 2000 authorising the Director of Europol to enter into negotiations on agreements with third States and non-European bodies [2000] O.J. C106/1, amended O.J. L56/14.
[104] [1999] O.J. C26/17.
[105] [1999] O.J. C88/1.
[106] [1999] O.J. C149/16.
[107] See Ch.9: The Court of Justice of the European Union.

Europol is headed by a Supervisory Board and a Director and has its own staff.[108] It is situated at The Hague (the Netherlands), like Eurojust.

31. THE EUROPEAN SECURITIES AND MARKETS AUTHORITY (ESMA)

Established by regulation[109] in 2010. ESMA is to contribute to the establishment of regulatory and supervisory standards and practices, monitoring and assessing the market in the area of its competence and fostering the protection of investors. It has a leading role in developing draft regulatory and implementing technical standards, issuing guidelines and recommendations, and providing a centrally accessible database of financial institutions. The ESMA also carries out activities relating to consumer protection. ESMA is situated in Paris.

13–38

32. EUROJUST (THE EUROPEAN BODY FOR THE ENHANCEMENT OF JUDICIAL CO-OPERATION)

Eurojust was set up in 2002 by the Council as "a body of the Union"[110]; it has legal personality. It is composed of one national member seconded by each Member State in accordance with its legal system; being a prosecutor, judge or police officer of equivalent competence. Its objectives are: (in the context of investigations and prosecutions concerning two or more Member States, of criminal behaviour in relation to serious crime, particularly when it is organised) to stimulate and improve co-ordination between the competent authorities, to improve co-operation and to support otherwise the competent authorities.

13–39

Eurojust may also assist investigations and prosecutions concerning only one Member State and a non-Member State where a co-operation agreement has been concluded with said State.

The general competences of Eurojust cover:

- the types of crime and offences in respect of which Europol (see above) is at all times competent to act;
- the following types of crime:
  - computer crime;
  - fraud and corruption and any criminal offence affecting the EC's financial interests;
  - the laundering of the proceeds of crime;
  - participation in a criminal organisation;

---

[108] See [2001] O.J. C65/1 laying down the rules on Europol personnel files and Staff Regulations applicable to Europol employees: [1999] O.J. C26/23 as amended by act of March 15, 2001 [2001] O.J. C112/1. See act of the Management Board: [2006] O.J. C68/1. The rules of procedure were adopted in 2010.

[109] Regulation 1095/10 [2010] O.J. L331/84

[110] Decision 2002/187 [2002] O.J. L63/1, setting up Eurojust with a view to reinforcing the fight against serious crime, modified by Decision 2009/426 on the strengthening of Eurojust [2009] O.J. L138/14.

- other offences committed together with the types of crime and offences referred to above.

Eurojust can act either through its national members or as a College; the latter consists of all the national members, each one having one vote. The Commission is also associated with the work.

An Independent joint supervisory body was set up to monitor collectively the activities concerning the processing of personal data.

Eurojust is assisted by a Secretariat headed by an Administrative Director; it has its own staff of about 80 persons, subject to the rules and regulations applicable to the officials of the Union. It is situated at The Hague (Netherlands).

33. THE AGENCY FOR CO-OPERATION OF ENERGY REGULATORS (ACER)

13–40 Established in 2009,[111] it constitutes a key measure for completing the internal markets in electricity and natural gas. It replaces the European Regulators Group for Electricity and Gas (ERGEG) established by the Commission.[112] This group is composed of representatives of the national regulatory authorities established pursuant to Directive 2003/54 concerning common rules for the internal market in electricity[113] and Directive 2003/55 concerning common rules for the internal market in natural gas.[114]

It assists the regulatory authorities in exercising, at Union level, the regulatory tasks performed in the Member States and, where necessary, co-ordinate their action.

It is situated in Ljubljana, Slovenia. It has legal personality. It comprises an Administrative Board, a Board of Regulators, a Director (who represents the Agency) and a Board of Appeal.

34. THE EUROPEAN INSTITUTE OF INNOVATION AND TECHNOLOGY (EIT)

13–41 Set up by regulation[115] in 2008 with reference to the task entrusted by the TFEU to the Union and the Member States to, "ensure that the conditions necessary for the competitiveness of the Union's industry exist."[116]

The EIT's objective is to contribute to sustainable European economic growth and competitiveness by reinforcing the innovation capacity of the Member States and the Union. It must do this by promoting and integrating higher education, research and innovation of the highest standards. The EIT operates through

---

[111] Regulation 713/09 [2009] O.J. L211/1.
[112] [2003] O.J. L296/34.
[113] [2003] O.J. L176/37.See bilateral agreement on the protection of investments concluded prior to accession *Commission v Slovak Republic* (C-264/09) judgment of September 15, 2011, not yet reported.
[114] [2003] O.J. L176/57.
[115] Regulation 294/08: [2008] O.J. L97/1.
[116] Art.173(1) TFEU.

autonomous partnerships of higher education institutes, research organisations, companies and other stakeholders; they are designated as Knowledge and Innovation Communities (KICs).

There is a Governing Body, an Executive Committee and a Director. For more details see the above-mentioned regulation. It is situated in Budapest, Hungary.

II. UNION AGENCIES UNDER COMMON SECURITY AND DEFENCE POLICY

1. THE EUROPEAN DEFENCE AGENCY (EDA)

The Agency was set up by a Council Joint Action pursuant to the Treaty on European Union. It is now provided for in the EU Treaty.[117] It is subject to the authority of the Council and open to participation by all Member States. Its task is to:

13–42

- contribute to identifying the Member States' military capability objectives and evaluating observance of their capability commitments;
- promote harmonisation of operational needs and adoption of effective, compatible procurement methods;
- propose multilateral projects to fulfil the objectives in terms of military capabilities;
- support defence technology research; and
- contribute to identifying and, if necessary, implementing any useful measure for strengthening the industrial and technological base for the defence sector and for improving the effectiveness of military expenditure.

The statute, seat and operational rules of the Agency are defined by the Council, acting by a qualified majority. It shall carry out its task in liaison with the Commission where necessary.

The Agency should contribute to the implementation of the Common Foreign and Security Policy (CFSP), in particular the European Security and Defence Policy (ESDP).

It has legal personality and has its headquarters in Brussels.[118] The Council fixed its financial rules, rules on procurement and rules on financial contributions

---

[117] Arts 42(3)2 and 45 EU.
[118] See Council Decision of September 24, 2004 concerning the Staff Regulation of the Agency [2004] O.J. L310/9 and Decision concerning the Rules applicable to national experts and military staff on secondment to the Agency [2004] O.J. L310/64.

from the operating budget of the Agency.[119] See also Ch.37: The Common Foreign and Security Policy (CFSP) and the establishment of a European Security and Defence College.[120]

The statute, seat and operational rules of the Agency were laid down by Decision in 2011.[121]

2.   THE EUROPEAN UNION SATELLITE CENTRE (EUSC)

13–43   Established on the basis of Art.14 of the EU Treaty in July 2001, operational since January 1, 2002, the Centre has the legal personality "necessary to perform its functions and attain its objectives".[122] The Centre supports the decision-making of the Union in the context of the Common Foreign and Security Policy (CFSP), in particular of the European Security and Defence Policy (ESDP), by providing material resulting from the analysis of satellite imagery and collateral data, including aerial imagery as appropriate.

The initial staff of the EUSC was recruited from among the staff of the West European Union (WEU) Satellite Centre, which it replaces.

It is situated at Torrejón de Ardoz, Spain.

3.   THE EUROPEAN UNION INSTITUTE FOR SECURITY STUDIES (ISS)

13–44   Established on the basis of Art.14 EU in July 2000[123] by a Council Joint Action and operational since January 1, 2002, the Institute contributes to the development of the Union Foreign and Security Policy (EFSP), including the European Security and Defence Policy (ESDP), by conducting academic research and analysis in relevant fields. The Institute has the legal personality "necessary to perform its functions and attain its objectives". The initial staff was recruited from among the staff of the West European Union (WEU) Institute for Security Studies, of which it incorporates the relevant features. It is situated in Paris. The staff regulations were published in 2005.[124]

III.   EUROPEAN EXECUTIVE AGENCIES

---

[119] [2007] O.J. L269/1.
[120] Council Joint Action 2008/550 [2008] O.J. L176/20 replacing Joint Action 2005/575 [2005] O.J. L194/15.
[121] Council Decision 2011/411/CFSP, repealing Joint Action 2004/551/CFSP [2011] O.J. L183/16.
[122] [2001] O.J. L200/5, Art.6, amended [2006] O.J. L405/60, amended [2009] O.J. L297/18.
[123] [2001] O.J. L200/3, amended [2006] O.J. L409/181.
[124] [2005] O.J. L235/1.

1. EUROPEAN RESEARCH COUNCIL EXECUTIVE AGENCY (ERC)

It is part of the Union's Seventh Research Framework Programme. Set up by the **13–45** Commission to support investigator-driven frontier research, with a total budget for 2007–2013 of €7.5 billion. Its main aim is to stimulate excellence in Europe by supporting and encouraging creative scientists, scholars and engineers who are invited to submit their individual proposals in any field of research.

It consists of an independent Scientific Council which defines the strategy and methodology and an Executive Agency acting on behalf of the European Commission and which applies them.

The Executive Agency manages the following tasks:

- executing the annual work programme;
- implementing calls for proposals;
- providing information and supporting the applicants;
- organising peer review evaluation;
- establishing and managing grant agreements; and
- providing assistance to the Scientific Council.

It has about 380 staff members; it is situated in Brussels.

2. TRANS-EUROPEAN TRANSPORT NETWORK EXECUTIVE AGENCY

This Agency was established in 2007[125] and the target date for it to be fully **13–46** operational was the end of 2007. It manages the Union funds available for the promotion for the Trans-European Transport Network in close co-operation with the Commission's Directorate-General for Energy and Transport. Its main tasks are to ensure the technical and financial management of projects co-financed under the Trans-European Transport Network's budget,[126] to collect, analyse and transmit to the Commission all information required for the implementation of said networks and to assist in programming and checking the conformity of projects financed by the Union with the transport policy rules and principles. Its tasks and period of operation were modified in 2008,[127] it also became responsible for projects receiving financial aid.[128]

The Agency is located in Brussels and is managed by a Steering Committee and a Director appointed by the Commission.

---

[125] Decision 2007/60 [2007] O.J. L32/88.
[126] The Agency receives a subsidy entered in the general budget of the Union and taken from financial allocations for Union action in the field of Trans-European Transport Network and, where appropriate, other Union programmes or actions whose implementation is entrusted to the Agency.
[127] Decision 2008/593 [2008] O.J. L190/35.
[128] Regulation 680/07 [2007] O.J. L162/1, amended [2012] O.J.204/1.

3. THE EDUCATION, AUDIO-VISUAL AND CULTURE EXECUTIVE AGENCY (EACEA)[129]

13–47 It was set up in 2005 by Commission Decision[130] with a seat in Brussels; its mission is to implement and manage a number of parts of more than 15 Union-funded programmes and action in the fields of education and training, active citizenship, youth, audio-visual and culture.[131]

It operates under the supervision of its three parent Directorates-General of the Commission: Education and Culture; Information Society and Media; and the Europe Aid and Co-operation Office—it is managed by a Steering Committee and a Director appointed by the Commission.

4. THE EXECUTIVE AGENCY FOR COMPETITIVENESS AND INNOVATION (EACI)[132]

13–48 This is, in fact, the new name given in 2007 to the Intelligent Energy Executive Agency[133] (which started operating in Brussels in 2004), following the integration of the Intelligent Energy programme into the Competitiveness and Innovation Framework Programme (2007–2013). The Agency is responsible for implementing the tasks concerning Union aid under the programme and it disseminates the resulting know-how and best practices. Its official lifetime is until 2015. It is located in Brussels.

From 2008 on, it started managing the European Commission's SME support network and eco-innovation initiatives, which form part of the Framework Programme and the Marco Polo Programme. It reports to three Directorates-General of the Commission: Energy and Transport; Enterprise and Industry; and Environment, which remain responsible for programming and evaluation.

5. THE RESEARCH EXECUTIVE AGENCY (REA)

13–49 The Research Executive Agency, located in Brussels, was created in December 2007. Managing over €6.5 billion, it started its work in 2008, and became fully independent in 2009. The REA reports to the Directorates-General for Research; Enterprise; Information Society and Media; and Energy and Transport.

The evaluation of proposals and the management of projects are at the heart of research support. The Research Executive Agency will carry out these evaluation and management processes for a large part of the current Research Framework Programme. With increasing research budgets, dedicating facilities and services

---

[129] Decision 2005/56, [2007] O.J. L49/21, amended [2008] O.J. L205/47.
[130] Decision 2005/56, [2007] O.J. L49/21, amended [2008] O.J. L205/47.
[131] See *http://www.eacea.ec.europa.eu*.
[132] See *http://ec.europa.eu/eaci/* [accessed August 23, 2013].
[133] Set up by Decision 2004/20 under the Union programme "Intelligent Energy-Europe" created by Decision 1230/03.

to these tasks is at the core of the Framework Programme. These dedicated facilities and services will enable the Union to improve the delivery of support to the research community.

The REA will manage the following tasks:

- the Marie-Curie fellowships and related awards;
- specific research grant agreements for the benefit of small and medium-sized enterprises;
- multi-partner projects in the field of space research;
- multi-partner projects in the field of security research;
- operate the proposal reception and evaluation facility in the Covent Garden building in central Brussels;
- operate a one-stop shop helpdesk for enquiries about FP7; and
- operate the unique registration facility for project partners to reduce the amount of paperwork involved in project management.

6.   THE EXECUTIVE AGENCY FOR HEALTH AND CONSUMERS (FORMERLY THE PUBLIC HEALTH EXECUTIVE AGENCY)

This Agency was established in December 2004 for a period beginning on January 1, 2005 and ending on December 31, 2010 and is situated in Luxembourg, with about 30 staff members. It is entrusted with implementing tasks concerning Union aid under the Union programme in the field of public health established by a 2002 Framework Decision.[134]

13–50

It is entrusted with the following tasks:

- managing all the phases in the lifetime of specific projects and in the work plan provided for;
- adopting the instruments of budget execution for revenue and expenditure and carrying out, where the Commission has empowered it to do so, all the operations necessary for the management of the programme, in particular those linked to the award of contracts and grants; and
- providing logistical, scientific and technical support.

The Agency is managed by a Steering Committee and a Director appointed by the Commission.

It receives a grant entered in the general budget of the Union and taken from the funds allocated to the programme on public health.

Although it does not come under any of the categories examined above, mention should be made here of the European Personnel Selection Office (EPSO) responsible for selecting staff for the European institutions.[135]

---

[134] Decision 1786/2002 [2002] O.J. L271/1, amended [2004] O.J. L138/7.
[135] Decision 2002/621 [2002] O.J. L197/53, amended [2010] O.J. L26/24.

7. THE EDUCATION, AUDIO-VISUAL AND CULTURE EXECUTIVE AGENCY (EACEA)

13–51 Set up in 2012,[136] for the management of Community action in the fields of education and training, citizenship, youth, audiovisual and culture.

IV. JOINT UNDERTAKINGS[137] AND OTHER STRUCTURES[138]

13–52 Joint Undertakings—the following were set up: Artemis Joint Undertaking (embedded computer systems); Clear Sky Joint Undertaking (air transport); ENIAC Joint Undertaking (nanoelectronics); FCH Joint Undertaking (fuel cells and hydrogen); IMI Joint Undertaking (innovative medicines); SESAR Joint Undertaking (air traffic management).

Other structures: The European Research Infrastructure Consortium (ERIC).[139]

Those joint undertakings were set up within the Seventh Framework Programme of the Union for research, technological development and demonstration activities (2007–2013),[140] which provides for a long-term public private partnership in the form of Joint Technology Initiatives, to be implemented through joint enterprises as provided for in the Treaty.[141]

For more details see Ch.33: Research and Technological Development and Space.

V. INTER-INSTITUTIONAL OFFICE: THE PUBLICATIONS OFFICE[142]

13–53 The Publications Office of the European Union has competence for:

- publishing the Official Journal of the European Union;
- publishing other mandatory publications;
- publishing non-mandatory publications under the prerogative of each institution;
- publishing publications on its own initiative, the Office may procure translations by means of a service contract;
- developing, maintaining and updating electronic publishing for the public;
- all legislation and other official texts (making them available to the public);

---

[136] Regulation 58/2003 [2003] O.J. L11/1.

[137] See General Report 2008, 261.

[138] Art.187 TFEU: The Union may set up joint undertakings or any other structure necessary for the efficient execution of Union research, technological development and demonstration programmes.

[139] [2009] O.J. L206/1.

[140] [2006] O.J. L.412/1.

[141] Art.187 TFEU.

[142] Decision 2009/496 of Parliament, Council, Commission, Court of Justice, Court of Auditors, ECSC and Committee of the Regions [2009] O.J. L168/41. Amended [2012] O.J. L179/15.

- preserving all publications;
- allocating international standard numbers;
- managing reproduction and translation rights in respect of the institutions publications;
- proposing and selling the publications.

A Management Committee was established in which all the signatory institutions are represented.

FURTHER READING

Stefan Griller and Andreas Orator, "Everything under control? The 'way forward' **13–54** for European agencies in the footsteps of the *Meroni* doctrine", (2010) E.L.Rev. 3.

Timothy Millett, "Community plant variety rights—Extent of the information that a holder may claim from a farmer about his use of the 'agricultural exception'", (2004) E.L.Rev. 124.

CHAPTER 14

Financing Union Activities

The financing of the Union's activities has over the last years become a key topic   14–01
for debate, not in the last place as a result of the economic crisis. The Treaty
provides rules on the revenue side (Own resources) and on the expenditure
side—the main basic acts are here the Multiannual Financial Framework
(MFF)—to be adopted as a regulation, according to a special legislative
procedure, with the assent of Parliament [Art.312 TFEU] and the annual budget
[Art.314 TFEU] which has to be in compliance with the MFF. Negotiations on
the regulation and a "residual" inter-institutional agreement are pending between
the Institutions. The MFF and the annual budget are more specifically discussed
in Ch.5: The European Parliament.

1.   FINANCIAL CONTRIBUTIONS OF THE MEMBER
STATES AND THE UNION'S OWN RESOURCES

The Decision to replace the Financial Contributions from the Member States   14–02
(which was the original way of financing Union activities) with the Union's
"Own Resources"[1] inaugurated a new era in the history of the Union. On the one
hand, it made it, in a certain way, financially independent, with all the economic
and political consequences this entails. On the other hand, the Treaty of April 22,
1970 Amending Certain Budgetary Provisions of the ECSC, EEC and Euratom
Treaties and of the Merger Treaty, conferred at the same time certain budgetary
powers upon Parliament, as a necessary complement to the transfer of national
resources to the Union.[2]

   In 1975 the budgetary provisions were again modified and complemented by
the creation of the Court of Auditors.[3]

(1)   The Decision on the Union's own Resources

The Decision on the Own Resources is adopted according to a special legislative   14–03
procedure (unanimity in Council with Parliament's opinion only). On top of this,
it is one of the acts of secondary legislation which is to be ratified by the Member
States. This situation has not changed under the Lisbon Treaty, showing the grip

---

[1] Decision 70/243 of April 21, 1970 [1970] J.O. L94/19.
[2] This Treaty became effective on January 1, 1971. The budgetary powers of Parliament are analysed
in Ch.5: The European Parliament (3. (4) Participation in the Budgetary Procedure).
[3] Treaty amending Certain Financial Provisions of the Treaties establishing the European
Communities and the Merger Treaty of July 22, 1975 [1977] O.J. L359/1.

of the Member States on the revenue side as well as—since the Treaty of Lisbon—part of the expenditure side (unanimity for the MFF). It is renewed regularly, and follows normally the duration of the MFF thus ensuring cohesion between revenue and expenditure in a given period. Thus, the current own resources decision was adopted in 2007 [Decision 2007/436/EC, Euratom, [2007] O.J. L 163/17], and negotiations are pending on the draft Decision for the period 2014–2020.

The main features of this Decision in its historical context can be summarised as follows:

- both the agricultural levies and the Common Customs Tariff (CCT) duties constitute own resources to be entered in the budget of the Union. These are the traditional own resources;
- since the revenue accruing from the duties and levies did not suffice to cover the expenditures of the Union, revenue from the Value Added Tax (VAT) was also allocated.[4] It will be remembered that the revenue and expenditure shown in the Union budget must be in balance.[5] As from January 1, 1980, the Union's expenditures were entirely financed by the revenue accruing from the agricultural levies, the customs duties[6] and a percentage of the VAT collected in the Member States. However, the traditional own resources gradually diminished as a result of CAP reforms and developments within the WTO-GATT. The VAT based own resource came under pressure as the Member States with a GNP below Union average—thus spending relatively more money on VAT objected consumption—considered further development of this resource as unfair.

14–04   The Decision on the system of the Union's own resources, adopted in June 1988,[7] introduced the changes adopted by the European Council at Brussels, in February 1988. This 1988 decision set the tone for the decisions to come:

- the overall ceiling on own resources was set at 1.20 per cent of total Union GNP for payments (1.30 per cent for commitments), it was 1.27 per cent in 1999 but 1.24 per cent in the 2007 decision. Note that for the MFF 2007–2013 (27 Member States) the ceiling is actually 1.045 per cent, which is thus lower than the Own resources ceiling;
- the third source (VAT) was collected in 1988 at a rate of 1.4 per cent applied to a VAT base limited to 55 per cent of GNP to take account of the

---

[4] Directive 77/388 [1977] O.J. L145/1. The revenue results from the application of a rate not exceeding 1.4 per cent of the basis used for assessing VAT, determined in a uniform manner for the Member States. The decision to increase the rate from 1 per cent to 1.4 per cent from January 1, 1986 and to 1.6 per cent on January 1, 1988 was taken by the European Council at Fontainebleau in June 1984; see [1984] Bull. 6–11. The Decision of April 21, 1970 was implemented by Regulation 2892/77 [1977] O.J. L336; see the Commission's report on the implementation of this Regulation: COM(88) 99 final.

[5] Decision 88/376 [1988] O.J. L185 and [1988] Bull. 3–105. See Regulation 3464/93 implementing Decision 88/376 [1993] O.J. L317, and Commission proposal for replacing Decision 88/376: General Report 1993 377.

[6] In case a Member State fails to collect customs duties, it is nonetheless financially responsible for their transfer to the Community: *Commission v Denmark* (C-19/05) [2007] E.C.R. I–8597.

[7] Art.210(1)3 TFEU.

situation of Member States where consumption accounts for a high proportion of GNP—currently the rate is 0,3 per cent with even a lower percentage for Austria, Germany, The Netherlands and Sweden, and the VAT base is 50 per cent of GNP, showing the decreased importance of the VAT based resource.

- a fourth resource, based on a GNP scale, was introduced.[8] It was meant to replace VAT as the resource for balancing the budget; it is obtained by applying a rate fixed each year under the budget procedure to a base representing the sum of the gross national products at market prices. It is calculated by reference to the difference between expenditure and the yield of the other resources. Under the current 2007 Own Resources decision, this now "third" resource (next to the traditional resources and VAT) is the most important own resource. It is in substance close to a contribution.

The Brussels European Council (1998) and the 1988 Own Resources Decision resolved a long-standing feud about the Union's own resources which had become insufficient to cover the expenditures. This "liberated" the Union and allowed it to go ahead with the completion of the internal market by the end of 1992.[9] However, it also consolidated developments which were to become major touchstones for the years to come: **14–05**

- The "budget correcting mechanism" introduced in 1976 to enable payments to be made to Member States which, due to special economic conditions, are considered to bear a disproportionate burden in financing the budget,[10] remained applicable. The compensation to the United Kingdom[11] was continued and financed on the basis of a GNP scale (it gives the UK a rebate equivalent to 0.66 per cent of its net balance and is shared by the other Member States according to their share of GNP, except Germany, whose share is reduced by a third), and for Spain and Portugal abatement arrangements were applied in accordance with their Act of Accession.[12] Furthermore, an adjustment was made to offset the effect of the introduction of the fourth resource and the costs of collecting the own resources was deducted from the Member States' payments (10 per cent). These were piecemeal operations in order to provide de facto compensations and reductions to several member States—triggering at their turn "corrections on corrections". Such arrangements have been formalised and individually fine-tuned ever since. The system has lost much of its clarity and transparency, despite efforts to come to a more comprehensive mechanism. Like in the case of the MFF, some underline the need to come

---

[8] For details see, for example, [1988] Bull.2, 13, and following. This resource became the most important Community resource.

[9] See the Introduction to Part III of this book: The Internal Market.

[10] This means the UK: General Report 1980, 59; [1980] Bull. 5–7 and Regulation 2744/80 [1980] O.J. L284/4.

[11] In 1980 agreement was reached on the United Kingdom's contribution to the budget: the financial correcting mechanism was modified to allow a reduction for the UK and supplementary Union expenditures were provided for to help reduce certain regional disparities in the UK. The correction for 1990 was 2,430 million ECUs.

[12] Arts 187 and 374 Act of Accession.

to a political achievement under difficult circumstances, whilst others deplore the horse-trading and lack of transparency.

- the system is mainly based on GNP contributions, thus departing the Unions financing from identifiable sources. Efforts have been taken (Co2 tax based resources) and are taken (financial transaction tax based resources) to cater again for a real "own" resource, but are politically extremely sensitive.

2. THE UNION BUDGET, REVENUE AND EXPENDITURE

14–06   As the Commission remarked about the budgetary procedure of 1988: "Thanks to the new instruments governing [Union] finances the problems which have beset the budgetary procedure in the past were very largely avoided."[13] The Commission was referring to the Inter-institutional Agreement on budgetary discipline and improvement of the budgetary procedure,[14] and the Regulation amending the implementing regulation of the Decision of April 21, 1970 creating the Union's own resources.

The budgetary procedure has been discussed in Ch.5: The European Parliament. It is noted that the budget must be in compliance with the MFF.

As to the substance, all items of revenue and expenditure of the Union are to be included in estimates to be drawn up for each financial year and be shown in the budget.[15] The revenue and expenditure shown in the budget must be in balance.[16] The financial year runs from January 1 to December 31.[17] The structure of the general budget and the form in which it is to be presented are determined by Financial Regulations.[18] The budget consists of separate sections dealing with the revenue and expenditure of each institution. The section dealing with the Commission provides for expenditure in 40 different titles corresponding more or less to the activities described in the rest of this book.[19] After giving some general indications, a few examples are given below.

14–07   The general budget for 2012 provides for the following:

- Expenditures:

---

[13] General Report 1988, p.66.
[14] This agreement came into force on July 1, 1988 [1988] O.J. C142. A novelty is the Financial Perspective 1988–92; another important aspect of the agreement is the mutual obligation to comply with the financing objectives set by the European Council for certain priority policy areas (structural funds, integrated Mediterranean programmes, framework research programme). See [1988] Bull. 6–112. A new Agreement was signed on October 29, 1993 [1993] O.J. C331 and a new financial framework laid down for 1993–1999 at the Edinburgh European Council; see General Report 1993, 375. For the latest version of the Agreement see section 3 of this chapter titled "Financial Framework and Inter-institutional Agreement".
[15] One important item not covered by the Union budget is the European Development Fund (resources destined to finance aid to developing countries), because the funds for this activity are provided directly by the Member States; the activities of the European Investment Bank do not appear on the budget either.
[16] Art.310(1)3 TFEU.
[17] Art.313 TFEU.
[18] See Regulation 966/2012 [2012] O.J. L298. Also Regulation 1268/2012 [2012] O.J. L362.
[19] See [2009] O.J. L69/II/1.

- Commitments: €147 232 172 662 compared to 2011: 3.54 per cent more.
- Payments: €129 088 042 928 compared to 2011: 1.86 per cent more.
- Revenue: €129 088 042 988[20] composed of the following resources:
  - VAT: 0.3278 per cent, representing 16.90 per cent of the revenue,
  - GNI: 0.5847 per cent, representing 65.39 per cent of the revenue,
  - own resources: 16.54 per cent of revenue and other revenue: €1,359,720,000.
- Common agricultural policy and rural development and accompanying measures (markets, set-aside, income aids): €53,301,727,905.
- Fisheries and maritime affairs: €953,145,213.
- Regional policy (cohesion fund and solidarity fund): €984,534,647.
- External relations (European Development Fund, food aid, co-operation with third countries, Common Foreign and Security Policy, etc.): €3,919, 361,607.
- ACP: €1,317,126,477.
- Enlargement: €1,093,326,691.
- Administrative expenditure of the institutions (salaries, pensions, etc.): €968,732,046.
- Reserves: €1,824,993,050.

The 2013 general budget, adopted in times of constraints, does not depart fundamentally from these figures.

(1) Commitment and Payment Appropriations

The Union budget contains "non-differentiated" and "differentiated" appropriations. Under the former, commitments can be made during the financial year and the corresponding payments can be made practically at the same time, i.e. during that financial year and the next. The differentiated appropriations consist of both commitments, i.e. the maximum that may be committed during that financial year, and the corresponding payments which may be disbursed either during that same year or at any time thereafter. This system is particularly suited for medium and long-term operations such as research projects and infrastructure investments. The advantage of this method is that the total amount of the Union's financial participation can be committed at the start of the project but the payments only have to be made as the work progresses over the years.[21] The problem is that the commitment appropriations are set at a higher level than the payment appropriations, both in the Own Resource decisions, the MFF and the budget. A certain degree of under-spending is calculated, and the Council tends to save on payments. This leads to the consequence that, especially at the end of the MFF duration, when the projects committed over the years need to be paid, the payment appropriations are insufficient and amending budgets need to be adopted. This gives rise to tough negotiations as the Member States reunited in the Council see this as a budget increase, rather than paying the bills they themselves signed up for.

14–08

---

[20] [2012] O.J. L561/1.
[21] The commitment and payment appropriations are now used for all expenditures.

(2) Compulsory and Non-compulsory Expenditure

14–09   The Treaty of July 22, 1975 amending Certain Financial Provisions of the existing Treaties introduced the concept of "expenditure necessarily resulting from this Treaty or from acts adopted in accordance therewith" otherwise referred to as "compulsory" expenditures. This differentiation no longer exists for procedural purposes under the budgetary procedure (see above).[22] However, the Treaty still provides that legal commitments and obligations have to be reflected in the budget and financial means are to be made available, thus sustaining a substantive concept of compulsory expenditure.[23]

3.   FINANCIAL FRAMEWORK AND INTER-INSTITUTIONAL AGREEMENT

14–10   As discussed in Ch.5: The European Parliament, the quintessence of the Inter-institutional Agreements and especially the MFF over the years is to enable multi-annual planning of expenditure. Its advantage is obvious: it gives the Union a solid base for its future planning and it eliminates the inter-institutional haggling from which the Community suffered for many years.

In the political process, the MFF, be it as an inter-institutional agreement (1988, 1993, 1999 and 2006) or as, under the Treaty of Lisbon, a Regulation, is concluded by Parliament and Council, but always with strong political guidance of the European Council.

The Edinburgh European Council of December 1992 agreed on the resources for the financing of the Union in the period 1993–99. This allowed the Union to finance its internal and external policies.

On May 6, 1999, Parliament, the Council and the Commission concluded a new Inter-institutional Agreement on budgetary discipline and improvement of the budgetary procedure. This Agreement entered into force on January 1, 2000 and replaced agreements concluded previously. It was intended to ensure, besides what is indicated in the title itself, that, in the medium term, Union expenditure develops within the limits of the own resources. It covers all expenditure.

An Agreement on budgetary discipline and sound financial management as regards the multi-annual financial framework for the 2007–2013 period was agreed by the Council, Parliament and Commission in May 2006.[24] It provides for EU spending of up to 864 billion that represents an increase of 4 billion over the preceding agreement allowing for an increase in expenditure for, for instance: life-long learning (Erasmus and Leonardo programmes), TENs, competitiveness and innovation, future actions (Life and Natura), culture, health and consumer protection. It also allows for flexibility in allocation of spending: *flexibility*

---

[22] Art.313 TFEU.
[23] Art.323 TFEU.
[24] [2006] O.J. C139/1, amended [2008] O.J. L51/7and [2009] O.J. L132/8; amended again [2012] O.J. L4/12.

instrument,[25] Solidarity Fund, Globalisation Fund and Emergency Aid Reserve. It provides—and this is a recent development—for a review in 2008/2009.

The 2007–2013 multiannual financial framework (replacing, as to the terminology, the Financial Perspectives) was adopted, after very difficult and protracted discussions between Parliament and Council—and also among the 25 Member States—in April 2006 after orientations of the European Council in December 2005. The figures for commitments look roughly as follows:

14–11

Year	2007	2008	2009	2010	2011	2012	2013
Total	120,601	121,307	122,362	122,752	123,641	125,055	126,646

with a grand total of 862,363 billion for seven years (in the meantime these figures have been adapted to inflation).

Negotiations on the MFF for 2014–2020 are currently pending. Also here, political guidance if not detailed instructions were provided by the European Council on February 8, 2013, this to the discomfort of Parliament expressed in a resolution of March 13, 2013.

The European Council has formally no role in the process apart from a possible decision to apply qualified majority instead of unanimity in Council to adopt the MFF—a decision unrealistic in this stage. Parliament considers the ever more detailed involvement as an unwarranted attempt to reduce the negotiation margin. However, without a position of the European Council negotiations would not have been given the final impetus. It is a main controversy in the budget procedures.

4.   PROTECTION OF THE UNION'S FINANCIAL INTERESTS

The Treaty provides that the Union and the Member States shall "counter fraud and any other illegal activity affecting the financial interests of the Union".[26]

14–12

Several acts of secondary legislation were already adopted in 1995 and 1996 in order to establish a mechanism of detection and addressing fraud and irregularities to the detriment of the EU budget in the Member States—where 80 per cent of the budget is spent—and to enhance co-operation between the Member States and the Commission.

After the fall of the Santer commission due to a refusal of discharge, having its origin in a number of alleged irregularities and the way they were addressed, Parliament and Commission considered that effective protection of the Union's financial interests required the establishment of a European Anti-Fraud Office (OLAF).[27] This office replaced the Task Force for Co-ordination of Fraud Prevention (the "UCLAF") and implements the Commission's powers to carry out external administrative investigations. Besides combating fraud, its task is,

---

[25] Necessary in order to face unforeseen events which cannot be predicted when the financial framework is adopted. See Decision of December 15, 2010 on the mobilisation of said Instrument [2011] O.J. L14/20.

[26] Art.325(4) TFEU.

[27] See Decision of 28.04.99 [1999] O.J. L136/20.

therefore, to investigate serious facts linked to the performance of professional activities by officials and servants of the institutions and other bodies of the Union. The Office is responsible for providing the Commission's support in co-operating with the Member States. It shall be in direct contact with the police and judicial authorities.

The independence of the Office is ensured by the obligation imposed upon its Director to neither seek nor take instructions from the Commission, any government or any institution or body.[28] The establishment of a Surveillance Committee is also provided for.[29] The Office became operational together with the Parliament and Council Regulation concerning investigations conducted by the Office,[30] on-the-spot checks[31] and an Inter-institutional Agreement of Parliament, Council and Commission concerning internal investigations by the Office.[32]

14–13   The investigations conducted by the OLAF are the subject of two Regulations.[33] The Court has held that OLAF can also investigate the European Investment Bank, the European Central Bank and Parliament.[34]

In summer 2013, Parliament and Council agreed on an overhaul of the OLAF Regulation.[35]

The role and investigative powers of OLAF are currently also regarded under the angle of protection of fundamental rights and its position in the institutional framework: OLAF remains an administrative, and not a judiciary body that has to apply strict procedural safeguards for individuals under investigation.

With a view to strengthen the legal framework, and on the basis of the new provision of the Treaty enabling the establishment of a European Public Prosecutor's Office from Eurojust[36], the Commission has submitted legislative proposals on the establishment of the European Public Prosecutor in summer 2013.[37]

The Member States have important responsibilities as to both the collecting of own resources and the spending of EU funds: around 80 per cent of the EU budget is allocated to final recipients by Member States on the basis of sectoral legislation.

Obligations of Member States to combat fraud to the detriment of the EU budget have to be commensurate with their responsibilities. Apart from the Regulation 2186/96 (see footnote 32), a Convention was signed between the Member States containing obligations can now be imposed by secondary EU law.

---

[28] Decision of 28.04.99 [1999] O.J. L136/20, Art.3.

[29] Rules of Procedure of the Committee [2000] O.J. L41/12.

[30] Regulation 1073/99: [1999] O.J. L136/1 and Regulation 1074 [1999] O.J. L136.

[31] Regulation 2185/96 [1996] O.J. 292/1.

[32] Inter-institutional Agreement between Parliament, Council and Commission concerning internal investigations by the European Anti-Fraud Office [1999] O.J. L136/15, with attached to it the model of an internal decision for all the institutions and bodies of the Community.

[33] Regulation 1073/1999 of Parliament and Council, and Regulation 1074/1999 (Euratom) of the Council (1999) O.J. L136/1 and 8.

[34] See, for instance, *Commission v ECB* (C-11/00) [2003] E.C.R. I-7147.

[35] See Parliament legislative resolution A7-0225/2013 of July 3, 2013 (not yet published in the *Official Journal*).

[36] Art.86 TFEU.

[37] COM (2013) 534 final, 17.7.2013. See also the related proposals COM (2013) 535 final (reform of Eurojust) and two communications on the proposals and the reform of OLAF, COM (2013) 532 and 533 final, 17.7.2013.

A proposal for a directive on the protection of the financial interests of the Union by criminal law, aiming to replace the Convention, was adopted by the Commission in 2012.[38]

---

[38] Convention drawn up on the basis of Article K.3 of the Treaty on European Union, on the protection of the European Communities' financial interests, O.J. C316, 27.11.1995, p.49.

PART 3

THE INTERNAL MARKET

INTRODUCTION

(1) The term

When someone uses the term "internal market", what is usually envisaged is that persons, goods, services and capital can flow freely across the national borders of the Member States that form part of the Union. However, sometimes the speaker may use the term with a wider meaning. The central idea remains, though, that the whole Union constitutes one single economic area, similar to a national market, wherein trade can develop without obstacles, making allowance, however, for differences in development of certain economies.[1] *Art 27(1) TFEU* [handwritten annotation: *Definition of Internal market: General idea.*]

III–01

The absence of obstacles is extremely significant since it is generally admitted that free trade contributes to the creation of wealth, i.e. employment and rising living standards that are objectives of the Union. Any producer within the Union now has a potential market of some 500 million customers, which should allow him, among others, to fully use the advantages of the economies of scale. Every consumer, on the other hand, is free to "shop" wherever he can obtain the best conditions. The original Rome Treaty did not know the term "internal market". It used the term "common market" without defining it. That term encompassed not only the usual meaning of "internal market" but also various common policies such as the establishment of a customs union and the common agricultural policy. The term was eliminated by the Treaty of Lisbon.[2]

The Single European Act introduced the term "internal market". The background was political in the sense that by the mid-1980s, it was clear that the establishment of the originally envisaged "common market" had not been accomplished. The re-launch of the original idea of a common market required a new term, and two appeared: "the single market" and the "internal market". Of these two the latter found its way into the Treaty. The core of the internal market provision introduced by the SEA remains still in the TFEU: "The internal market shall comprise an area without internal frontiers in which the free movement of goods, persons, services and capital is ensured in accordance with the provisions

---

[1] Art.27(1) TFEU; "When drawing up proposals with the aim [of establishing or ensuring the functioning of the internal market], the Commission must take into account the extent of the effort that certain economies showing differences in development will have to sustain for the establishment of the internal market and propose appropriate provisions."

[2] For a discussion of the different terms, see *Moortelmans*, "The Common Market, the Internal Market and the Single Market. What's in a Market?" C.M.L.R. (1998) p.101.

of the Treaties."[3] In conjunction with that definition it is provided that the Union shall undertake the necessary action for "establishing or ensuring the functioning of the internal market." It is of limited value, practically and for the present purposes, to search for the exact legal boundaries of the definition.[4] At the core of the internal market are the TFEU rules pertaining to five disciplines, namely the free movement of goods, the free movement of workers, the freedom of establishment, the free movement of services, and the free movement of capital and payments.[5] These are rules of primary law. They seek to do away with national measures that discriminate on grounds of nationality, directly or indirectly, or other unwarranted obstacles to the freedoms mentioned; or with a term that encompasses all these kind of obstacles: "restrictions". Each set of rules are presented in the following chapters.

III–02   In addition to primary law the Union has adopted secondary law to facilitate free movement within the internal market. Such rules may range from regulating bottle sizes, denominations of crystal glass, the recognition of foreign diplomas, to capital requirements for financial undertakings, just to give a few examples. The myriad acts of secondary law cannot be presented here. However, central rules of secondary law will be included in the presentation in order to give a more comprehensive view of the area of law. Most of these rules seek to harmonize national legislations. There are different types of harmonisation; they are presented in Ch.26: Approximation of Laws.

Moreover, subjects such as the transport policy and the common agricultural policy, which have a claim to be part of the internal market, are dealt with in separate chapters as they are to a great extent governed by particular rules. To some the rules relating to competition have an equal claim to pertain to the internal market; however, those rules are also better presented on their own, namely in Ch.22: Competition Policy.

(2)   Restrictions and justification

III–03   The provisions of primary law on free movement of goods, persons, services and capital seek to do away with national restrictions on free movement. The overall trust of the provisions is that Member States shall not hinder cross-border economic activity unless it is necessary to do so.

Each set of rules has its own particularities. However, the main features are common and so is the analytical roadmap for analysing whether a national measure is compatible with the provisions. It is useful to present the common features.

---

[3] Art.26(2) TFEU. The term "Single Market" has not fallen into disuse. It is, for instance, used in various communications of the European Commission; see for instance COM 2012/259 "Better Governance for the Single Market".

[4] That is not the same thing as saying that it will never have a value. Proposals of the Commission with a view to achieving the internal market must for instance take into account "the effort that certain economies showing differences in development will have to sustain for the establishment of the internal market"—thus a limitation, although very broad, on the Commission's powers, cf. Art.27(1) TFEU.

[5] The freedoms are commonly referred to as the "four freedoms", namely for goods, persons, services and capital, although legally there are not just four. They may also be referred to as the six freedoms, in which case one counts the freedom to provide payments as a separate freedom. The four freedoms are also referred to as the Internal Market freedoms.

The bans on restrictions apply only to cross-border situations. The rules of primary law, banning restrictions, are concerned with free movement across national borders. Therefore, they do not find application in situations that are entirely confined to one Member State; they do not apply in purely internal situations.[6]

Next, the restriction must, as a rule, result from a measure adopted by a public authority. However, to some extent, the bans also apply to private action. A measure of a public authority can be rules that are on the Statute book of a Member State. It can also be administrative rules, an administrative practice or case law established by the courts of the Member State at issue.[7] Because of the wide variety of rules and practices that can be caught under the bans, one uses commonly the term "measures" instead of, for instance, the narrower term "rules".[8] As to the private action which may fall under the bans, it is well-established case law that the bans on restrictions in free movement of workers, free movement of services and freedom of establishment apply to rules of private origin that regulate in a collective manner employment, self-employment and the provision of services.[9] Industrial action may also be susceptible to come within those bans.[10]

III–04

Not all national measures are caught by the bans; only measures that are discriminatory or restrictive, i.e. restrictions. The notion of restrictions is construed widely. This is to ensure the effectiveness of the internal market. Without a wide notion of restrictions, there is a risk that many national measures that in fact obstruct the free movement would legally fall outside the scope of European law. However, measures whose restrictive effects are too indirect or too uncertain do not fall within the bans.[11]

---

[6] See for instance *Guimont* (C-448/98) [2000] E.C.R. I-10663, para.21. It is important to note that the provisions do not apply by virtue of *Union law.* That does not hinder that they may apply indirectly by virtue of *national law.* For instance, the law of some Member States requires that nationals may not be treated worse than foreigners. Such a type of prohibition is commonly referred to as a prohibition of reverse discrimination. Thus, in such Member States a restriction that cannot be opposed against a national from another Member State cannot be opposed against its own nationals, even if the latter situation is not governed by Union law; see for instance *Guimont*, para.23. It is also important to stress that most acts of secondary law apply independently whether or not the situation is a cross-border situation or not. For instance a trader has to comply with the Union norms on food safety, regardless as to whether the foodstuffs are sold cross border or internally.

[7] See for instance *Commission v France (Postal Franking Machines)* (21/84) [1985] E.C.R. 1355, para.13.

[8] To come within the scope of the bans, it is not necessary that the national measure applies on the entire territory of the Member State at issue; regional and municipal measures are also caught by the bans, see for instance *Aragonesa de Publicidad* (Joined Cases C-1/90 and C-176/90) [1991] E.C.R. I-4151.

[9] See for instance *Wouters* (C-309/99) [2002] E.C.R. I-1577, *Angonese* (C-281/98) [2000] E.C.R. I-4139, *Bosman* (C-415/93) [1995] E.C.R. I-4921, *Dona* (13/76) [1976] E.C.R. 1333, and *Walrave and Koch* (36/74) [1976] E.C.R. 1405.

[10] *Viking Line* (C-438/05) [2007] E.C.R. I-10779. In free movement of goods, some actions that in the national legal order would be considered to be of private law may come within the ban or restrictions, see Ch.15: The Free Movement of Goods.

[11] See for instance *Peralta* (C-379/92) [1994] E.C.R. I-3453, and *BASF* (C-44/98) [1999] E.C.R. I-6269. "Too indirect or too uncertain effect" must be distinguished from "minor effect". If it is established that a national measure has a discriminatory or restrictive effect, it is caught by the bans regardless as to whether the effect is only limited or present in only few instances, see for instance *Commission v France (Taxation of Insurance Companies)* (270/83) [1986] E.C.R. 273.

The legal point of departure is that restrictions are banned. The term "restrictions" may be used in the wide sense as above. Then it covers direct discrimination, indirect discrimination and restrictions in the narrow sense, i.e. non-discriminatory obstacles to free movements. Direct discrimination occurs when a national measure distinguishes on the basis of nationality; for instance the national measure provides that television stations may be owned only by nationals. Indirect discrimination occurs when the national measure, on the basis of criteria other than nationality, leads to similar results as a directly discriminatory measure.[12] Residence requirements are the classical example of indirect discrimination; if a national measure provides that television stations may be run only by persons resident in the State, it will, all things being equal, be easier for nationals of that State to fulfil the requirement, most nationals already having residence in the State. Restrictions in the narrow sense are present when the national measure prohibits, impedes or otherwise renders less attractive the exercise of one of the four freedoms.[13]

III–05 However, there are exceptions to the bans. In the terminology usually employed in Union law, one speaks about "justifying" restrictions. Thus, after having established that a national measure qualifies as a restriction, one must ask oneself whether it can be justified. The justification implies that the restriction must pursue a legitimate objective, i.e. there must be a valid justification ground, and the measure must be in compliance with the proportionality principle.

The justification grounds follow from the Treaty and case law. Those established by the Treaty are in particular public policy, public security and public health. Those established by case law are for instance consumer protection, the protection of workers, the protection of the environment, the protection of creditors, safeguarding the sound administration of justice, just to name a few. The list of legitimate objectives established in case law is open-ended, i.e. the Court may recognise in the future new and different objectives as legitimate, adding thus to the current number of objectives.[14] There are, however, two kinds of objectives that the Court refuses in principle to accept, that is financial and economical ones and reasons of administrative convenience.[15]

---

[12] See for instance *Sotgiu* (152/73) [1974] E.C.R. 153 and *O'Flynn* (C-237/94) [1996] E.C.R. I-2617.

[13] See for instance *FA Premier League* (Joined Cases C-403/08 and C-429/08), judgment of April 22, 2011, not yet reported, para.85 and *Anton Las* (C-202/11), judgment of April 16, 2013, not yet reported, para.20. The notion of restriction largely converges in the four freedoms. However, in free movement of goods a special rule called the *Keck* (Joined Cases C-267/91 and C-268/91) [1993] E.C.R. I-6097) rule applies, which entails that certain non-discriminatory measures, for instance concerning advertising, fall outside the notion of restrictions, see Ch.15: The Free Movement of Goods. Moreover, in some particular fields the bans are largely just bans on discrimination, see for instance below concerning tourists in Ch.18: Freedom to Provide Services/Financial Services and Ch.25: Taxation.

[14] The justification grounds made by the judge are referred to in the case law as, for instance, "mandatory requirements in the public interest" or "overriding requirements relating to the public interest". In legal literature one sees also the term "rule of reason" which originates in US anti-trust law. The essence of a "rule of reason" is in short that the judge goes against or beyond the wording of the legal provision; in this case: although the Treaty only provides for few justification grounds, the Court has recognised more.

[15] See for instance *Gration* (C-398/95) [1997] E.C.R. I-3091, para.22. However, the Court has recognised the risk of undermining the financial balance of social security system as a legitimate ground for justifying restrictions, see for instance *Müller-Fauré* (C-385/99) [2003] E.C.R. I-4509,

The Court holds that discriminatory measures can only be justified on the grounds established by the Treaty.[16] This case law of the Court leaves one with the question as to whether it applies both to directly and indirectly discriminatory measures. The answer is in short that it is only directly discriminatory measures that can only be justified on the grounds established by the Treaty. Indirectly discriminatory measures may be justified on both the grounds established in the Treaty and those that follow from case law.[17]

The justification grounds must be construed narrowly.[18] As concerns the health and life of humans, the Court has consistently held that it ranks foremost amongst the assets and interests protected by the Treaty.[19] In relation to health and the environment, the Court allows the so-called precautionary principle to apply; that is that in case of scientific uncertainty about the detrimental effects of a product the Member State is allowed to take measures against the product without having to wait for science to demonstrate fully those detrimental effects.[20]   III–06

It must be noted that the justification grounds are notions of Union law. Most often this will not matter in a practical case; for instance, if a Member State limits the sales outlets for prescription medicine for reasons of public health to pharmacies, Union law accepts that the reasons underlying the restriction are qualified as public health. However, in some instances this may matter.[21]

The justification that a Member State puts forward for defending a restriction must be in conformity with fundamental rights and general principles of law. Union law integrates those rights and principles and therefore cannot accept national restrictions on free movement which violate those rights and principles.[22]

Once a valid justification ground has been established, it must be examined whether the restriction is in compliance with the proportionality principle. The principle implies that the restriction must be both suitable and necessary to attain   III–07

---

para.73. Moreover, the Court does not accept that reasons of administrative convenience can justify restrictions, for instance arguments from a State to the effect that the field of law is easier to administer with a restriction, see for instance *Persche* (C-318/07) [2009] E.C.R. I-359, para.55.

[16] See for instance *Svensson and Gustavsson* (C-484/93) [1995] E.C.R. I-3955, para.15. In practice the Court seems however willing to accept that the protection of the environment—which is a ground developed in case law—can also be a valid justification ground for discriminatory measures, see *Commission v Belgium (Walloon Waste Case)* (C-2/90) [1992] E.C.R. I-4466 and *Preussen Elektra* (C-379/98) [2001] E.C.R. I-2099.

[17] See for instance *Clean Car* (C-350/96) [1998] E.C.R. I-2521. In cases concerning indirect discrimination the Court will often express itself to the effect that it must first be examined whether the indirectly discriminatory measure is based on objective considerations independent of nationality and is in accordance with the principle of proportionality, see for instance *Clean Car*, para.31. If the result of that examination is negative, then the only defence left for the Member State is that the measure is justified on the grounds in the Treaty.

[18] See for instance, as concerns public policy, *Omega* (C-36/02) [2004] E.C.R. I-9609; as concerns public security, *Campus Oil* (72/83) [1984] E.C.R 2727 and *Scientology* (C-54/99) [2000] E.C.R. I-1335.

[19] See for instance *Ker-Optika* (C-108/09) [2010] E.C.R. I-12213, para.58.

[20] See for instance *Commission v Denmark (Fortified foodstuffs)* (C-192/01) [2003] E.C.R. I-9693 which also sets out the different stages of the application of the principle.

[21] See for instance *Commission v Luxembourg (Posted Workers)* (C-319/06) [2008] E.C.R. I-4323, para.30: "...the public policy exception is derogation from the fundamental principle of freedom to provide services...the scope of which cannot be determined unilaterally by the Member States."

[22] See for instance *ERT* (C-260/89) [1991] E.C.R. I-2925.

the objective.[23] The suitability test is failed if the national measure is not conducive to the objective sought. The necessity test is failed if the objective may be attained by less restrictive measures. When national measures fail the justification test, it is most often because they fail the necessity test. The proportionality principle entails that restrictions of a Member State that just duplicate requirements to which the goods or the persons in their Member State of origin are submitted are unnecessary.

It must be stressed that the proportionality principle does not concern the level of protection of a given interest that a Member State seeks to attain. A Member State is free to set the level of protection and the level of protection may differ from that set by another Member State. For instance: If a Member State limits the sales of food and beverages of no or low nutritional value because it seeks to achieve a high level of public health, that objective cannot be put into question simply for the reason that in other Member States there are no restrictions on the sales of such food. The proportionality principle concerns the means that the Member State deploys to attain the objective.

The proportionality principle appears simple in theory; however, its application in practice is often fraught with difficulties. The difficulties can for instance be related to establishing what the exact objective is, what exactly the less alternative measures are and what the context is. With an example: if a Member State bans alcohol advertising, the overall objective is to enhance public health: the measure is, all things being equal, suitable, i.e. it is not implausible that alcohol consumption may be reduced by a ban; but is the ban necessary? Is it relevant that the Member State has one of the highest alcohol taxes in the world or no alcohol tax at all? Is it relevant that the Member State claims that it seeks to change attitudes to alcohol in the long term, not just to reduce consumption in the short term?

III–08   The review of the compliance with the proportionality principle may in practice differ from one type of case to another. It may be lax. It may be intense. When restrictions are based on grounds of public morality, for instance, it will

---

[23] The proportionality test thus falls in two stages: suitability and necessity. This is the way the Court of Justice normally describes the test. However, many in legal literature consider that it is more appropriate to describe what the Court actually does by a three-stage test; namely, suitability, necessity and proportionality in the narrow sense. The third stage of the test relates to the question as to whether the national measure, although necessary to attain its aim, should, however, be set aside because it entails an excessive encroachment of the fundamental freedom. Moreover, it must be noted that occasionally one sees in the case law that the proportionality review also encompasses a consistency test, see for instance *Gambelli* (C-243/01) [2003] E.C.R. I-13031, para.67, and *Hartlauer* (C-169/07) [2009] E.C.R. I-1721, para.55. The consistency test may probably best be described as a wider suitability test. The difference between the suitability test and the consistency test may be illustrated with this example: A Member only knows two types of alcoholic drinks: beers and strong spirits. The State bans sales of beer but not the sales of strong spirits, for reasons of public health. It is assumed that there are no particular circumstances pertaining to the situation in that Member State such as the population having a particular liking for beer and a disliking for strong spirits. In general one must then hold that the measure, viewed in isolation, is suitable, i.e. beer drinkers that do not like strong spirits will stop consuming alcohol, i.e. an enhancement of public health. On the other hand, the ban seems inconsistent, as strong spirits normally represent a greater danger to public health than beer; drinkers of strong spirits who also consumed beer will, all things being equal, consume more strong spirits; beer drinkers that also consumed strong spirits will make the same move.

typically be lax.[24] The Court of Justice is in no good position to be a judge of the moral values prevailing in the different Member States. For instance: if a Member State bans prostitution for reasons of public morality, the Court will accept that without going into any detailed scrutiny as to the suitability or necessity of such a ban.[25]

Many of the cases that come before the Court of Justice do so by way of a reference for preliminary ruling from national judges. In such cases the Court may make the proportionality assessment itself or leave it to the national court.

It is for the party that invokes a ban on restrictions to prove the restriction. On the other hand, it is the State that bears the burden of proof for the justification.[26]

(3) Positive integration and negative integration

These two terms are not to be found in any legal text. However, they are often used in order to describe in a short way how the rules of primary law and secondary law mainly function. By negative integration one understands that the rules of primary law described do away with unjustified restrictions. When a national measure is contrary to those rules, it must be set aside by virtue of the supremacy of Union law. However, Union law does not provide a norm to replace it. Hence, the integration is "negative".

III–09

Secondary law, on the other hand, mostly seeks to replace divergent national rules by common Union rules. In replacement of the national rule, a Union rule is provided. Hence, the integration is "positive".

---

[24] See for instance *Henn and Darby* (34/79) [1979] E.C.R. 3795. In its case law concerning gambling services the Court has often also performed extremely lax proportionality review, see for instance *Santa Casa* (C-42/07) [2009] E.C.R. I-7633. This case law is subject to much criticism in legal literature.

[25] On the other hand, if the Member State bans prostitution and then tolerates it by not prosecuting any national offenders, but expulses foreign prostitutes, hereunder those from other Member States, the Court of Justice will react to that, not on the basis of principle of proportionality, but on the basis of the ban on discrimination on grounds of nationality, see *Adoui and Cornuaille* (Joined Cases 115 and 116/81) [1982] E.C.R. 1655.

[26] See for instance *Humanplasma* (C-421/09) [2010] E.C.R. I-12869, para.38.

CHAPTER 15

The Free Movement of Goods

The first of the Internal Market freedoms—the free movement of goods—means   **15–01**
that goods can circulate unimpeded across the whole Union.[1] By "goods" must be
understood "products which can be valued in money and which are capable, as
such, of forming the subject of commercial transactions".[2] Goods are both
industrial and agricultural.[3]

Under the heading "free movement of goods" the Treaty deals with tariff
barriers to trade (customs and equivalent charges) and with some non-tariff
barriers to trade (quantitative restrictions and measures with equivalent effect;
discriminatory internal taxation), as well as with State monopolies of a
commercial character.

The elimination of the tariff barriers will be briefly examined in the next
section on the Customs Union, and then follows a section on the elimination of
quantitative restrictions and measures having equivalent effect. Thereafter
follows a section on State monopolies. The ban on discrimination in the internal
taxation of goods is dealt with in Ch.25: Taxation. At the end is a section on an
instrument of secondary law that is of particular importance to the free
movement, concerning notification to the Commission of national measures that
can hinder trade.

1.   THE CUSTOMS UNION

The Treaty provides that the: **15–02**

> "Union shall comprise a customs union which shall cover all trade in goods and
> which shall involve the prohibition between Member States of customs duties on

---

[1] For the territorial scope of the Union see Art.50 EU and Art.355 TFEU.
[2] *Commission v Italy* (7/68) [1968] E.C.R. 423 at 428. See also the definition in *Commission v
Belgium (Walloon Waste)* (C-2/90) [1992] E.C.R. I–4466(26) which concerned waste: "all objects,
which are being shipped across a frontier for the purpose of commercial transactions, are subject to
Art.[34] whatever the nature of those transactions". Electricity is considered a good, see *Commission
v Netherlands* (C-157/94) [1997] E.C.R. I-5699. A lottery ticket is just the physical carrier of a right;
lotteries therefore fall under the Treaty rules on free movement of services, see *Schindler* (C-275/92)
[1994] E.C.R. I-1039. Coins that are not legal tender—for instance historical coins, gold coins—are
also considered as goods, see *Thompson* (7/78) [1978] E.C.R. 2247.
[3] The agricultural products to which the Treaty applies are listed in Annex I to the Treaty.

imports and exports and of all charges having equivalent effect, and the adoption of a common customs tariff in their relations with third countries".[4]"

Thus, the free movement of goods requires in the first place the creation of a Customs union involving:

- the prohibition, among the Member States, of all customs duties and of all charges having equivalent effect; and
- the adoption of a common customs tariff (CCT) in relations with third countries. Without this CCT, products from third countries would enter the Union through the country with the lowest external tariffs, since once inside, those products can circulate freely throughout the whole Union. This would "deflect" trade from the other Member States.[5]

Where goods imported from outside the Union are concerned, as soon as the import formalities have been complied with and all customs duties and charges have been paid, those imports are "in free circulation" just like Union goods. This means that such goods can benefit from the provisions on free movement.[6]

(1) Prohibition of Customs Duties and Charges having Equivalent Effect[7]

15–03 "Charges having equivalent effect" have been defined by the Court:

"[A]ll charges demanded on the occasion or by reason of importation which, imposed specifically on imported products and not on similar domestic products, alter their cost price, and thus produces the same restrictive effect on the free movement of goods as a customs duty".[8]

Such a charge will fall under this prohibition no matter its amount.[9] A charge will not escape this prohibition because it is levied for the benefit of someone other than the State.[10] Such a charge can only be accepted if it is a consideration

---

[4] Art.28 TFEU. The Customs Union among the original six Member States was established over a period of 10.5 years, shorter thus than the 12 years provided for in the original EEC Treaty.

[5] If third country products were not covered by the Union rules, it would be difficult to eliminate fully customs check points in the trade between Member States, as there would be a need to verify whether a given imported product is a third country product, not benefitting from free movement, or a product originating in the Union, benefitting from free movement. A customs union is thus different from a "free trade area" (FTA) where only products originating within the participating States are included. FTAs therefore have (normally complex) rules on the origin of products; see for instance Protocol 4 to the EEA Agreement.

[6] See for instance *Donckerwolcke* (41/76) [1976] E.C.R. 1921 (in relation to Art.34 TFEU) and *Co-Frutta* (193/85) [1987] E.C.R 2085, at para.28 (in relation to Art.110 TFEU). However, see case *Tabouillot* (C-284/96) [1997] E.C.R I-7471, at para.21.

[7] Art.30 TFEU.

[8] *Marimex v Amministrazione Finanziaria Italiana* (29/72) [1972] E.C.R. 1309 at 1318(6); [1973] C.M.L.R. 486. Charges of equivalent effect must be distinguished from charges that form part of an internal taxation system which are covered by Art.110 TFEU, for instance: a charge on the registration of a car will form part of the latter and will thus not be a charge equivalent to customs duties, see below Ch.25: Taxation.

[9] See for instance *Commission v Italy* (24/68) [1969] E.C.R. 193.

[10] See for instance *Diamantarbeiders* (Joined Cases 2 and 3/69) [1969] E.C.R. 211.

for a benefit provided for the importer or exporter.[11] The concept "charge having an equivalent effect" gave rise to abundant case law in the 1960s and, in one of its first judgments, the Court stated that the Treaty provisions on this point create individual rights which the national courts must uphold.[12] In other words, those provisions have direct effect.[13]

(2) The Common Customs Tariff (CCT)

The CCT constitutes, in the first place, a measure of commercial policy towards third countries. It is interesting to note that actions undertaken by the Union for its internal functioning have repercussions worldwide. The CCT had to coincide with the elimination of customs duties and charges among the Member States. This was necessary in order to avoid, as was mentioned already, deflection of trade, since all imports would obviously take place through the borders of the Member State with the lowest external customs duties. Consequently, it also constitutes an integral part of the Customs Union which could not have been established without it. The CCT was adopted by a Council regulation[14] and gradually introduced in parallel with the elimination of the customs duties. Since that time, Member States no longer have jurisdiction over the duties they levy on the goods entering their territory from third countries. They may not modify them, nor keep the proceeds,[15] which now belong to the Union as "own resources".[16] Modification or suspension of CCT duties is an exclusive Union matter[17] and is decided by the Council.[18] Important reductions were introduced following multilateral trade negotiations within the framework of the General Agreement on Tariffs and Trade (GATT, now World Trade Organisation WTO), such as the Kennedy Round (1964–1967), the Tokyo Round (1973–1979), the Uruguay Round (1988–1993) and the present Doha Round (2001–present).

15–04

Mention should also be made of the possible exception to the CCT where tariff quotas at a reduced rate or at zero-rate and generalised preferences are provided for.[19]

It should be noted, however, that from a commercial point of view a reduction of customs tariffs is less important than the elimination of non-tariff trade barriers, which are much more difficult to detect. This applies also to trade within the Union itself. See below on measures with equivalent effects to quantitative restrictions.

In terms of trade, the creation of the Customs Union resulted in shifts in the trade patterns, since industrial goods are sometimes less expensive for Union

---

[11] This is not the case, for instance, when the service is rendered in the general interest such as health inspections or charges covering the costs of customs activities: *Dubois* (C-16/94) [1995] E.C.R. I–2421; [1995] 2 C.M.L.R. 771.

[12] *Van Gend & Loos v Nederlandse Administratie der Belastingen* (26/62) [1963] E.C.R. 1 at 12; [1978] 3 C.M.L.R. 630.

[13] See Ch.4: Union Law.

[14] Regulation 950/68 O.J. L172/1; it is regularly updated.

[15] Except for 25 per cent, which they may keep to cover administrative costs; see Ch.14: Financing Union Activities.

[16] For "own resources" see Ch.14: Financing Union Activities.

[17] *Cadi Surgelés* (C-126/94) [1996] E.C.R. I–5647; [1997] 1 C.M.L.R. 795.

[18] Art.31 TFEU.

[19] See Ch.38: Common Commercial Policy and Relations with Third Countries.

users and consumers when imported from other Member States than from third countries. Also trade among the Member States has grown much faster than trade between the Union and third countries. In relation to the latter, the Union also uses the CCT as an instrument to guarantee the effectiveness of its commercial and external policy.[20]

15–05   Setting identical tariff levels for Union's borders is only one step in establishing the CCT. Indeed, the latter also calls for uniform interpretation, continuing administration, harmonisation of customs rules, simplification of checks and formalities and, generally speaking, the reinforcement of the structure of the Customs Union.[21]

Goods that are imported must be classified in order for the right duty to be levied; for instance, shall "lightweight knitted garments, intended to cover the upper body, loose fitting, boat-necked, short-sleeved or sleeveless, extending down to the knee or thigh" be classified as "women's nightdresses" with a corresponding custom duty or as "dresses of synthetic textile fabrics", with another level of duty?[22] The classification system of goods is currently laid down in a Regulation from 1987.[23] The classification system must be common. If not, imports from third countries could in one Member State be classified differently than as done by another Member State, with resulting application of different tariffs. It follows that there is also a need to ensure the uniform application of the CCT, and numerous references to the ECJ by national judges have concerned the question under which tariff position a good shall be rightly classified.

In 1992, the Council, wishing to assemble in a Code the provisions of custom legislation that were contained in a large number of Union regulations and directives, and which would contain the general rules and procedures which ensure the implementation of the tariffs and other measures in connection with trade in goods between the Union and third countries, adopted the Union Customs Code.[24]

An electronic-customs system was established and a Modernised Customs Code was adopted in 2008.[25]

The decision[26] establishing electronic customs systems in Europe provides for a series of measures and deadlines with a view to replacing all customs procedures with interconnected national computerised procedures and creating a common electronic portal. The Modernised Union Customs Code[27] replaces the

---

[20] See Ch.38: Common Commercial Policy and Relations with Third Countries (1. Commercial Policy Instruments and Import and Export Arrangements).

[21] See the Convention on the use of information technology for customs purposes and Agreement on provisional application between certain Member States [1995] O.J. C316/33.

[22] *Wiener S.I. GmbH* (338/95) [1997] E.C.R. I-6495.

[23] Regulation 2256/87 on the tariff and statistical nomenclature and on the Common Customs Tariff, with later amendments. The classification system builds on the Harmonised Commodity Description and Coding System, established within the framework of the World Customs Organisation and widely used in the world (there are more than 140 States using it).

[24] Regulation 2913/92 establishing the Union's Custom Code [1992] O.J. L302/1 and Regulation 2454/93 laying down provisions for the implementation of Regulation 2913/92 [1993] O.J. L253/1, both constantly amended.

[25] Regulation 450/08 [2008] O.J. L145/1.

[26] Decision 70/08 [2008] O.J. L23/21, on a paperless environment for customs and trade.

[27] Regulation 450/08 [2008] O.J. L145/1.

Customs Code of 1992, in order to adapt to developments in international trade; the aim is to simplify the legislation and to introduce computerised customs procedures.

2. PROHIBITION OF QUANTITATIVE RESTRICTIONS ON IMPORTS AND EXPORTS[28]

The elimination of customs duties and charges having equivalent effect is not sufficient to guarantee the free circulation of goods within the Union. There are indeed many other ways of hindering imports and exports; quantitative restrictions are one such way and they are in principle banned under the Treaty (see below for the possibility of justifying quantitative restrictions).

15–06

The Court has defined quantitative restrictions as "measures which amount to a total or partial restraint of, according to the circumstances, imports, exports or goods in transit".[29]

Thus, for instance quotas amount to quantitative restrictions. Moreover, the Court has in line with the definition above held that total bans on import qualify as quantitative restrictions; a ban on import of pornographic articles thus amounted to a quantitative restriction.[30]

(1) Measures with equivalent effect to Quantitative Restrictions on Imports

The ban on quantitative restrictions has nowadays limited relevance in practice. The contrary is the case with the ban on measures with equivalent effect to quantitative restrictions on imports. (MEQR). Such measures are in principle prohibited by the Treaty [31]—see below for the possibility of justifying such measures. The prohibition has sparked off extensive case law which is not always easily comprehended.

15–07

For a measure to fall under the prohibition, the measure must be attributable to the public authorities of a Member State.[32] Measures are normally rules but can also be for instance an established administrative practice in the State.[33] This applies both in relation to imports and to exports. Acts of private persons fall in principle outside the prohibition.[34]

---

[28] Arts 34 and 35 TFEU.

[29] *Geddo v Risi* (2-73) [1973] E.C.R. 865.

[30] *Henn and Darby* (34/79) [1979] E.C.R. 3795.

[31] Art.34 TFEU.

[32] The measure can thus be adopted by whatever public authority in the State, for instance municipalities or bodies that are independent under national law.

[33] *Commission v France (Postal Franking Machines)* (21/84) [1985] E.C.R. 1355, paras 13-14.

[34] The ECJ has construed public measures widely and has found that measures adopted by entities, which under national law were subjects of private law, come within the notion see for instance *Commission v Ireland (Buy Irish)* (249/81) [1982] E.C.R. 4005, and *Commission v Germany (Markenqualität)* (C-325/00) [2002] E.C.R. I-9977. The State's failure to take measures against private activities may also, under certain circumstances, be considered as a MEQR, see *Commission v France (Strawberries)* [1997] E.C.R. I-6959.

The Court of Justice has construed the notion of MEQR in relation to imports widely.[35] However, measures caught by other provisions of primary law do not come within the notion, such as for instance charges with equivalent effect to customs. MEQR are often referred to as "invisible trade barriers", since they are, generally speaking, difficult to detect and only discovered by their effects on trade.

15–08   The Court's definition of MEQR in relation to imports was given in 1974 in the *Dassonville* Case; [36] it is therefore often referred to as the *Dassonville* formula. Although the Court revisited the definition subsequently, the definition is still relevant. The definition implies that the notion of MEQR covers all measures[37] enacted by Member States[38] "which are capable of hindering, directly or indirectly, actually or potentially, intra-[Union] trade". This means that the prohibition applies not only when trade is actually prevented, but already when it is simply made unnecessarily difficult. Secondly, it means that the hindrance does not have to be actual. It suffices that it can be shown that the possibility exists that interstate trade may be hampered. In other words, one does not have to wait until the measure has produced its ill effects. It is not necessary, either, that those trading rules have an appreciable effect on intra-Union trade.[39] Thirdly, the word "indirect" means that there is an infringement of the principle of the free movement of goods even when the hindrance is only indirectly attributable to the contested measure. The *Dassonville* formula is thus very wide and a host of national measures has been considered to fall under it. However, in a few cases the Court has held that the effects of the measure on trade were too uncertain and indirect to make it qualify as a MEQR.[40]

In 1993, the Court limited the *Dassonville* formula in the Case *Keck*.[41] The Court did so by holding that "selling arrangements" do not qualify as MEQR provided that they apply to all traders without any discrimination in fact or in law. "Selling arrangements" are for instance national rules concerning advertising;[42]

---

[35] The understanding of MEQR has been a matter of controversy in legal literature, throughout the life of the Union. To put matters simply, there are two contrasting views. One is that the notion and thus the prohibition of MEQR should in principle only cover discriminatory/protectionist measures. The other view is that the notion should cover all national measures that have restrictive effects on trade, independently of whether the measures are discriminatory or not.

[36] *Procureur du Roi v Dassonville* (8/74) [1974] E.C.R. 837.

[37] Instead of "measures" the Court has in some instances also referred to "trading rules", included in *Dassonville*. Case law shows that it is not just national trading rules, but all national measures that may have restrictive effects on trade that are covered by the notion of MEQR, see for instance Case *Schmidberger v Austria* (112/00) [2003] E.C.R. I-5659 where the Court found a permit to hold a demonstration on a motorway to qualify as a MEQR. National rules restricting the use of a given product may also qualify as a MEQR; see *Commission v Portugal (Tinted films)* (265/06) [2008] E.C.R. I-2245 (prohibition on the use of tinted films on windows in cars), and *Commission v Italy (Trailers)* (110/05) [2009] E.C.R. I-519 (prohibition of trailers being towed by mopeds, motorcycles and tricycles). MEQR also includes rules of a temporary nature: *Openbaar Ministerie v Van Tiggele* (82/77) [1978] E.C.R. 25, para.20.

[38] The prohibition also applies to measures adopted by the Union institutions: *Kieffer and Thill* (C-114/96) [1997] E.C.R. I-3629.

[39] *Prantl* (16/83) [1984] E.C.R. 1299.

[40] For instance *BASF* (C-44/98) [1996] E.C.R. I-626, para.21, and *Guarnieri* (C-291/09), not yet reported, para.17.

[41] *Keck and Mithouard*, joined cases (267/91) and (268/91) [1993] E.C.R. I-6097.

[42] See for instance Case *Leclerc-Siplec* (412/93) [1995] E.C.R. I-179. Note that one and the same national rule on advertising may in one relation qualify as a selling arrangement and not in another.

rules on opening hours;[43] rules limiting the sales to certain type of outlets (for instance sales of medicine in pharmacies).[44] These rules do not qualify as MEQR provided that they are applied to all traders equally in fact and in law. Thus, if a national measure fulfils the *Keck* test, it is not a MEQR and there is no need to justify it. In other words, the national rules fall outside the scope of the ban on quantitative restrictions and MEQRs. There is no authoritative definition of what a "selling arrangement" is. In order to determine whether a given measure is a selling arrangement it is useful to ask two questions: in the first place, does the national measure in some way regulate trade? If the answer is no, the national measure may still fall under the *Dassonville* formula and it must be assessed whether the measure qualifies under that formula. If the answer is yes, the next question to ask is whether the application of the national measure would require an alteration of the product, product being here understood in the wide sense as including packaging, labelling, language used. If the answer is no, then the national measure qualifies as a selling arrangement and it must be examined whether it fulfils the *Keck* test, i.e. whether it applies to all traders without any discrimination in law or in fact; on the contrary, if the answer is yes, then the national measure implies a requirement to the product and it must be examined whether it falls within the *Dassonville* formula, which it most certainly will. If the product must be altered to gain access to the importing State, the hindrance that the national measure implies seems clearly direct and actual.[45]

The *Keck* ruling has been subject to much controversy in legal literature; many authors consider that the ruling leaves the regulatory autonomy of the Member States too unrestrained, in the sense that the ruling allows Member States to enact rules on selling arrangements, no matter how restrictive they are, as long as the rules comply with the principle of non-discrimination. A particular question that has attracted much attention is whether it is right that bans, in particular comprehensive bans, on advertising should be considered selling arrangements.[46] However, the *Keck* ruling is still valid law.[47]

For instance, a ban on advertising for soft drinks will normally be a selling arrangement. However, if the ban implies that a magazine, produced abroad and carrying such publicity, cannot gain access to the State, then the rule is not a selling arrangement in relation to the magazine. The magazine must be altered, i.e. taking out the publicity, in order to gain access. That implies an actual and direct hindrance to trade under the *Dassonville* formula. See Case *Familiapress* (368/95) [1997] E.C.R. I-3689.

[43] *Tankstation 't Heukske* (Joined Cases 401/92 and 402/92) [1994] E.C.R. I-2199. Even before establishing the *Keck* formula, the ECJ had found that national rules banning trading on Sundays fell outside the scope of the prohibition on MEQR, see *Stoke-on-Trent* (C-169/91) [1992] E.C.R. I-6635. This ruling overruled some previous and seemingly inconsistent rulings on the matter; see for instance *Conforama* (312/89) [1991] E.C.R. I-997 and case *Torfaen Borough* (145/88) [1989] E.C.R. I-3851.

[44] *Commission v Greece (Infant Milk)* (C-391/92) [1995] E.C.R. I-1621.

[45] For applying the *Keck* test the distinction between product requirements and selling arrangements is useful. However, that distinction must not lead the user to believe that Art.30 only covers product requirements and selling arrangements. As mentioned above, Art.30 also includes such national measures as the permit to hold a demonstration on a motorway.

[46] See in particular the Opinion of Jacobs AG in *Leclerc-Siplec* (412/93) [1995] E.C.R. I-179.

[47] For the application of the *Keck* test to total bans on advertising, see in particular *Gourmet International* (C-405/98) [2001] E.C.R. I-1795. See also the ruling of the EFTA Court in *Phillip Morris* (E-16/10), judgment of September 12, 2011, not yet reported. The practical importance of the question has to some extent vanished with the adoption of Directive 2005/29 on unfair commercial practices in business-to-consumer relations. The overall trust of the Directive is that as a rule, national

15–09   In 2009 the Court gave a ruling in a case normally referred to as *Trailers* that sought to bring together the different strands as to what qualifies as a MEQR into one overall definition.[48] According to *Trailers* the notion of MEQRs cover:

- Discriminatory rules.
- Rules on product requirements.
- All other measures that hinder access to the market.

There has been much legal writing on the question as to which extent this ruling may imply an alteration of the previous case law.[49] The better view is probably that, if there is any alteration, it is very limited: Discriminatory rules would hitherto have been caught by the *Dassonville* formula (if national rules favour national production, then there will most likely be a hindrance to trade, no matter whether it would be only indirect or potential); and discriminatory rules on selling arrangements would not be able to fulfil the *Keck* test. Next, rules on product requirements will certainly qualify under the *Dassonville* formula. So far, the new definition seems definitely to be in line with what was the law previously. As concerns the last group of measures mentioned in *Trailers*, the open question is whether it must be understood fully in line with the *Dassonville* formula or rather as a limitation to the *Dassonville* formula in the sense that now, the hindrance must be more clear and material, i.e. some indirect hindrances now qualifying under the *Dassonville* formula may not qualify under the *Trailers* formula. This remains to be seen.

Finally, it must be recalled that the fact that a national measure amounts to a MEQR does not automatically entail that the measure is incompatible with Union law. Restrictions may be justified, i.e. if they pursue a legitimate objective and do so without restricting cross-border trade unnecessarily, cf. below.

(2) Measures with equivalent effect to Quantitative Restrictions on Exports

15–10   The Treaty contains, in parallel to the ban on quantitative restrictions on import and MEQR, a ban on such restrictions on exports and MEQR.[50] The Treaty provision has sparked off much less case law and much less interest in legal literature. The obvious reason is that while States may seek to limit imports to protect national markets and production, it is much rarer that they have an interest in limiting exports, i.e. imposing restrictive measures on exports.

---

rules banning in general commercial practices on grounds of consumer protection, hereunder advertising, are banned unless allowed under the Directive.

[48] Case *Commission v Italy (Trailers)* (110/05) [2009] E.C.R. I-00519 and Case *Mickelson and Roos (Jetski)* (142/05) [2009] E.C.R. I-4273.

[49] See for instance Niels Fenger, *Article 28 EC and restrictions on the use of a legally marketed product, in European Law Reporter* 2009, p.326 and Peter Pecho, *Good-Bye Keck?, A Comment on the Remarkable Judgment in Commission vs Italy, in Legal Issues of Economic Integrations* 2009, p.257.

[50] Art.35 TFEU.

The Court holds that the notion of MEQR in relation to exports covers just discriminatory measures.[51] Thus, the *Dassonville, Keck* and *Trailers* formulas stated above do not apply. The relevant question to ask, to know whether a national measure comes within the notion of MEQRs on exports, is whether the measure is discriminatory. If the answer is no, then the measure falls outside the ban on MEQRs on exports. If the answer is yes, the measure must be justified, cf. below.

One may wonder why there is this difference in the notion of MEQR, depending on whether it applies to exports or imports.[52] The better view is probably that there are good reasons for limiting the notion of MEQRs on exports to discriminatory measures. If not, the notion would become much too wide and would apply, for instance, to a host of national requirements related to the production process; it would also be difficult for the Court to handle.

(3) Justification

Every rule has its exceptions. They can be found either in the legal provisions laying down the rule, or in the interpretation of the rule by the courts. The same applies to the basic rules concerning the free movement of goods in the Union. The Treaty provides for several exceptions to the bans on quantitative restrictions and MEQRs (in short: restrictions). The normal term for referring to this is that the restriction is justified. The terminology signals that the restriction does not as such fall outside the bans. On the contrary, the restriction is at the outset within the bans; however, it may be accepted provided it is justified.

15–11

Before entering into the details of justification, it must be recalled that the question as to whether a restriction can be justified is normally not relevant at all to ask if the national measure is the result of a Union measure. For instance, if a directive lays down that contact lenses may only be sold to consumers when they are accompanied by detailed instructions, and the national measure does nothing more than to transpose that requirement, the national measure does not need to be justified. The measure is in accordance with the directive.[53] If for instance the national measure lays down that the instructions must also be accompanied by a health warning, while the directive does not foresee such a health warning, the question arises as to whether the health warning requirement is excluded by the directive or not. So-called total harmonisation directives exclude States from laying down any requirements that go further than the harmonisation established by the directive. In this example, total harmonisation will imply that the national health warning requirement will be held contrary to Union law by the mere fact that the directive does not allow national regulators to establish requirements beyond those of the directive. There will thus be no issue of justifying the national measure. On the other hand, if the directive is a so-called minimum directive, it will allow States to adopt requirements that go beyond the minimum requirements laid down by the directive, provided that they are in accordance

---

[51] *Groenveld* (15/79) [1979] E.C.R. 3409, *Oebel* (155/80) [1981] E.C.R. 01993. The notion of discrimination is construed widely, see *Gysbrechts* (205/07) [2008] E.C.R. I-9947.

[52] See for instance Trstentak AG in *Gysbrechts* (205/07) [2008] E.C.R. I-9947.

[53] If a private party still holds that the requirement is unlawful, it will have to argue that the directive is contrary to primary law, for instance by lacking sufficient legal basis in the Treaty, see Ch.26: Approximation of Laws.

with Union law, in particular the free movement of goods provisions of the Treaty. Here the question of justification will thus arise, namely in relation to the health warning that is not foreseen by the directive.

15–12   The justifications grounds are to be found either in the Treaty[54] or have been (are) developed in case law. The only relevant difference attached to the question as to whether a justification ground follows from the Treaty or from the case law is whether discriminatory measures may be justified also under justification grounds developed in the case law. The traditional stance of the Court of Justice has been that discriminatory measures can only be justified under the grounds stated in the Treaty.[55] However, the stance is in movement.[56]

The Treaty provides for a very limited set of justification grounds. Restrictions on imports, exports and transit of goods may be justified on grounds of public morality,[57] public policy or public security,[58] the protection of health and life of humans, animals and plants,[59] the protection of national treasures possessing artistic, historic or archaeological value[60] or the protection of industrial and commercial property.[61]

The TFEU provides that, in case difficulties arise in a Member State, the Council may decide upon "measures appropriate to the economic situation",[62] in particular if they arise in the supply of certain products. Such measures could have effects equivalent to quantitative restrictions. Although this text was

---

[54] Art.36 TFEU.

[55] *Commission v Belgium (Wallon waste)* [1992] E.C.R. I-4431. Indirect discrimination may be justified on the grounds given in the Treaty or on the grounds developed in case law.

[56] See for instance *PreussenElektra AG v Schleswag AG* (379/98) [2001] E.C.R. I-2099 where the Court accepts environmental protection—a ground developed in case law—as a justification ground for discriminatory measures.

[57] See *Henn and Darby* (34/79) [1979] E.C.R. 3795; [1980] 1 C.M.L.R. 246; prohibition of imports of pornographic articles.

[58] See *Thompson* (7/78) [1978] E.C.R. 2247; [1979] 1 C.M.L.R. 47: export ban on silver alloy coins.

[59] The Court considers that "health and the life of humans' ranks first among the interests protected by Art.36": *De Peijper* (104/75) [1975] E.C.R. 613 at 635(15); [1976] 2 C.M.L.R. 271. This ground for exception has given rise to numerous Court rulings: see, for instance, *Brandsma* (C-293/94) [1996] E.C.R. I–3159, prohibition of import of biocidal products containing dangerous substances which have not yet been the subject of Union legislation is justified even if they have already been authorised in another Member State. In *Bellon* (C-42/90) [1990] E.C.R. I–4863, the Court added that a Member State may prohibit the marketing of foodstuffs containing certain preservatives, provided that the principle of proportionality underlying the last sentence of Art.36 TFEU is observed and authorisation can be obtained under a procedure which is readily accessible and which can be completed within a reasonable period, where the additive meets a genuine need and represents no danger to public health.

[60] See *Commission v Italy* (7/68) [1968] E.C.R. 423. See also Directive 93/7 on the return of cultural objects unlawfully removed from the territory of a Member State [1993] O.J. L74/74 and Regulation 3911/92 on the harmonisation of controls on the export of cultural goods [1993] O.J. L395/1, codified version [2009] O.J. L39/1.

[61] See *Keurkoop v Nancy Keen Gifts* (144/81) [1982] E.C.R. 2853; [1983] 2 C.M.L.R. 47 and *Bristol-Myers Squibb v Paranova* (Joined Cases C-427/93, C-429/93 and C-436/93) [1996] E.C.R. I–3457; [1997] 1 C.M.L.R. 1151. As concerns the justification ground referring to industrial and commercial property, see also Ch.20: Intellectual Property Rights.

[62] Art.122(1) TFEU.

introduced by the EU Treaty and has not yet been tested in court, there seems to be no doubt that it would apply in situations similar to those created by the oil crises of the 1980s.[63]

Finally, mention must be made in this context of the possibility for Member States to take such measures as they consider necessary for the protection of the essential interests of their security which are connected with the production or trade in arms, munitions and war material. A list of the products benefitting from these exceptions was drawn up by the Commission on April 15, 1958 and has never been published.[64] Similarly, Member States may be called upon to take certain measures[65] in the event of serious internal disturbances affecting the maintenance of law and order,[66] in the event of war, serious international tension constituting a threat of war, or in order to carry out obligations they have accepted for the purpose of maintaining peace and international security.[67] In both cases, the measures taken by the Member States may limit the free movement of goods. **15–13**

In the latter case the Treaty simply provides that the Member States shall consult each other with a view to taking steps together to prevent the functioning of the common market being affected. If, in both cases, the measures affect competition in the common market, the Commission shall, together with the Member State concerned, examine how those measures can be adjusted. In case the Commission or a Member State considers that another Member State is making improper use of the powers provided in the above-mentioned circumstances, they may bring the matter directly before the Court, which shall give its ruling in camera.[68]

It is a plausible assumption that the narrow set of justification grounds in the Treaty reflected the view that the notion of MEQRs was correspondingly narrow. For instance, when the Treaty was negotiated, environmental protection did not exist as a policy area; consumer protection was also hardly a policy area.

The *Dassonville* ruling had the potential to include a vast number of national measures from almost any field of law under the notion of MEQRs. This could be problematic if measures could only be justified on grounds stated in the Treaty and when the set of grounds stated in the Treaty is very limited. **15–14**

The answer to this problem came with the ruling of the Court in *Cassis de Dijon* from 1979. In the ruling the Court made clear that States can also rely on other justification grounds than those stated in Treaty. The justification grounds developed in the case law are normally referred to as "mandatory requirements" or "imperative requirements in the public interest". They are for instance consumer protection, environmental protection, the protection of workers, the protection of cultural and linguistic diversity, just to give a few examples.

Once it is established that a measure pursues a valid justification ground, the measure must also be in accordance with the proportionality principle. The principle implies that the measure must be suitable and necessary to attain its

---

[63] See, for instance, *Campus Oil Ltd v Minister for Industry and Energy* (72/83) [1984] E.C.R. 2727; [1984] 3 C.M.L.R. 544.

[64] Art.346 TFEU.

[65] Art.347 TFEU.

[66] One could think of the situation that prevailed in Northern Ireland.

[67] Think about the intervention in former Yugoslavia.

[68] Art.348 TFEU.

objective. For instance, a ban on a product given for reasons of consumer protection will not be necessary if the objective, consumer protection, can be attained with a less restrictive measure such as an obligation to give information about the product on the label.

(4) Mutual recognition

15–15   One will often see the term "principle of mutual recognition" in texts concerning the free movement of goods.[69] The origins of the principle can be found in the Treaty[70] but it was not until the judgment in *Cassis de Dijon* and the use the Commission made of that judgment that the principle became prominent.[71] The Court held that when a product is legally produced and marketed in a Member State, it should be able to move freely into another Member State, unless this latter State has a valid justification to oppose it. The principle is thus a short-hand term for saying what was explained above, namely that a Member State cannot impose restrictions on the free movement of goods, unless it has a valid justification for doing so. The principle, though, has a narrower scope than the Treaty provision banning restrictions on imports. The Treaty provision also applies to products from third countries that are in free circulation, while the principle refers to goods produced in another Member State. Moreover, the application of the principle is linked to what above has been called product requirements; the Treaty provision has a wider scope in that it also covers other measures that can have restrictive effects on imports.

The principle is also often referred to in the context of harmonisation of Member States' legislation. The principle serves here normally to express that the harmonising measure will not lay down all the requirements that a product has to satisfy, but only the essential requirements. Member States are then free to lay down more detailed rules on how those requirements are satisfied; however, a Member State must accept a product produced in another Member State in accordance with the directive, hence, the expression "mutual recognition".

The principle of mutual recognition has had considerable influence in the Union's development of the internal market, politically and on the legislative level.[72] It is a short way to express the view that there should be free flow of goods and services in the Union because one Member State must trust that the legislation of other Members States has sufficiently regulated the goods and services at issue.

---

[69] The principle is also referred to in the ambit of freedom of establishment and free movement of services.

[70] See for instance Art.53 TFEU.

[71] See for instance Commission communication concerning the consequences of the judgment given by the Court of Justice on February 20, 1979 in case 120/78 *Cassis de Dijon* O.J. 1980 C256/2.

[72] Before the judgment in *Cassis de Dijon* the efforts to harmonise national legislations had mainly been to the effect of harmonising all requirements to a product, even in great detail. The judgment contributed to the re-orientation of the harmonisation efforts to be limited to essential requirements on which it was easier to reach agreement amongst Member States—the so-called new approach, see Council Resolution of May 7, 1985 on a new approach to technical harmonisation and standards, O.J. 1985 C136/1.

3. STATE MONOPOLIES OF COMMERCIAL CHARACTER

Member States are required by Art.37 TFEU to "adjust" their monopolies of a commercial[73] character, so as to ensure that by the end of the transitional period[74] no discrimination regarding the conditions under which goods are procured and marketed exists between nationals of the Member States.[75] However, the:

15–16

> "[A]rticle does not apply to national provisions which do not concern the exercise by a public monopoly of its exclusive right, but apply in a general manner to the production and marketing of goods, whether or not they are covered by the monopoly in question".[76]

The delimitation between Art.37 TFEU and the general provision on free movement of goods, i.e. Art.34 TFEU gives rise to some problems in practice. It is often important to establish under which provision a national measure has to be assessed. The reason is simple: the former provision only contains a ban on discrimination while the latter provision contains a broader ban, i.e. on discrimination and restrictions. The Court has established that the criterion for establishing the delimitation between the provisions is whether the national rule forms part of the inherent operation of the monopoly; in that case it must be assessed under Art.37 TFEU.[77]

4. TECHNICAL STANDARDS

Another important element with regard to the free movement of goods is technical standards; it is up to the Commission to make sure that the Member States:

15–17

> "[R]ecognise the technical specifications, standards and rules applicable in other Member States and the validity of tests carried out by approved laboratories in other Member States offering adequate guarantees of reliability and efficacy" ("mutual recognition").[78]

The Commission monitors the compliance by Member States with the principle of free movement of goods, mainly through the procedure under which the Member States have to notify to the Commission of the technical standards

---

[73] The term "commercial" indicates that production monopolies are not affected by the Treaty. Indeed, in an internal market, production monopolies do not constitute an obstacle to free trade between Member States, this freedom being the test for the existence of competition. Neither are the common agricultural organisations affected by Art.43 TFEU, since, under Art.38(2), the rules laid down for the establishment and functioning of the internal market apply, "save as otherwise provided in Arts 39 to 44". See *Pigs Marketing Board v Redmond* (83/78) [1978] E.C.R. 2347; [1979] 2 C.M.L.R. 573.

[74] For the original six Member States this was the December 31, 1969; other dates were, of course, provided by the different Accession Treaties.

[75] Art.37(1) TFEU.

[76] *Banchero* (C-387/93) [1995] E.C.R. I–4663; [1996] 1 C.M.L.R. 829.

[77] See for instance *Franzén* (C-189/95) [1997] E.C.R. I-5909 and *Rosengren* (C-170/04) [2007] E.C.R. I-4071.

[78] General Report 1992, 48.

and regulations which they intend to introduce. The procedures are laid down in a directive and are fairly detailed.[79] In case a Member State fails to comply with the procedures, the national rule adopted may not be invoked against an individual.[80] When the Commission is of the opinion that proposed standards or regulations will infringe the principle of free movement, it issues a "detailed opinion". The Member State may adopt its intended rule in spite of such an opinion; but it goes without saying that it exposes itself to private operators contesting it. The Commission operates a database with all national notifications made, called TRIS, which is available on-line. The Commission periodically issues reports on the operation of the Directive, the latest being COM (2011) 853 final.

5. THEORY AND REALITY OF THE FREE MOVEMENT OF GOODS

15–18 What explains that 20 years after the completion of the internal market on December 31, 1992, people and undertakings still experience difficulties when moving goods within the Union? The answer, of course, is not a simple one. A fair shot at an answer is that establishing an internal market is a more difficult task than most people realise. Relevant factors in this context are for instance that national authorities, and national politicians, will in all likelihood always be under pressure to adopt measures that protect local production. Those who are involved in local production, commonly are possible voters; they can vote but the foreign trader cannot. Sheer ignorance of the Union rules is probably also a factor. The Union is still a fairly recent phenomenon and its rules are very pervasive; many national authorities, be it at central level or at local level, may still have very limited knowledge of the limits that Union law puts to their activities. Another factor is probably the very development of markets; national regulators are closest to those developments and they may be the first ones to adopt regulations concerning the new developments. Those rules may then turn out to imply a restriction to free movement. In short, it is a reasonable assumption that the establishment of the internal market will never be a goal that is achieved once and for all. On the contrary, the establishment of the internal market is a continuous enterprise.

As concerns violations of the free movement rules that may be attributable to insufficient knowledge of national authorities, it must be noticed: the Commission created the Internal Market Problem Solving Network (SOLVIT).[81] It is an online network which helps find out-of-court solutions to complaints by consumers and enterprises regarding the misappropriation of internal market laws by public authorities. Each Member State and the EFTA EEA countries have a SOLVIT centre which networks with the other centres forming part of the public administration in which it is located. Each centre is connected to a central database, which boasts a high level of transparency and makes it possible to

---

[79] Directive 83/189 [1983] replaced by Directive 98/34 [1998] O.J. L204/37 amended [1998] O.J. L217/18. The range of measures that Member States have to notify under the Direction is very wide, see for instance *Schwibbert* (C-20/05) [2007] E.C.R. I-9447.

[80] See *CIA* (C-194/94) [1996] E.C.R. I-2201 and *Schwibbert* (C-20/05) [2007] E.C.R. I-9447.

[81] [2001] O.J. L331/79.

monitor performance and the progress made. It has been operational since November 2003. It is free of charge and attempts to find solutions within a short 10-week deadline; if a centre regards the complaint received from a customer or enterprise as justified, it forwards it to the SOLVIT centre in the country where the problem has arisen for it to be solved within 10 weeks. The solutions proposed are not binding; if the customer does not consider the proposed solution acceptable, it may recommend that the dispute be resolved through the courts. The Member State concerned is responsible for settling the dispute, but if it does not take action, the Commission reserves the right to initiate proceedings.

FURTHER READING

Christian Joerges & Renaud Dehousse, *Good Governance in Europe's Integrated Market* (Oxford University Press, 2002).   **15–19**

Daniel Wilsher, "Does *Keck* discrimination make any sense? An assessment of the non-discrimination principle within the European Single Market" (2008) E.L.Rev.3.

Laurence Gormley, *EU Law of Free Movement of Goods and Customs Union* (Oxford University Press, 2009).

Lorna Woods, *Free Movement of Goods and Services within the European Union* (Aldershot, Ashgate, 2004).

Nic N. Schuibne, *Regulating the Internal Market* (Edward Elgar Publishing, 2006).

Peter Oliver, assisted by Malcolm Jarvis, *Free movement of goods in the European Union*, 5th edn (Hart Publishing, 2010).

CHAPTER 16

The Free Movement of Persons

INTRODUCTION

There is no chapter in the Treaties entitled "free movement of persons". Title IV **16–01** of Part III of the TFEU is entitled "Free movement of persons, services and capital" and it contains the chapters on free movement of workers, services and capital and the freedom of establishment. Free movement of workers is one of the Internal Market freedoms, in line with the others mentioned and the free movement of goods, and thus entails a ban on discrimination and other restrictions to which the worker could be exposed.

The Maastricht Treaty of 1992 introduced the "Citizenship of the Union". Citizens of the Union are the nationals of the Member States.[1] The provisions governing citizenship are to be found in Part II of the TFEU. The citizenship entails some disperse rights, amongst which in particular the right to free movement, namely "the right to move and reside freely within the territory of the Member States", in accordance with the "conditions and limits defined by the Treaties and by the measures adopted thereunder".[2] The right to enter and reside in another Member State is regulated more in detail by an instrument of secondary law, namely a Directive from 2004.

Since the Maastricht Treaty co-operation in Justice and Home affairs has been an area for Union activity. The background to the introduction of these rules in the Treaty was inter alia the abolition of internal border controls of persons. The abolition of internal border controls of persons was put in motion by an intergovernmental agreement called the Schengen Agreement. The abolition led to need of co-operating between police forces and the judiciary in the Member States; the same abolition led to a need to define common rules for the entry of third country nationals to this borderless area and for their movement within the area. The collapse of the communist regimes in Central and East Europe also played a role in the process; when the communist regimes strictly controlled their borders to the Member States, the Union and its Member States had less reason to worry about their external borders. The fall of the regimes created a need for a control of the external borders. International terrorism also put co-operation amongst security forces high on the agenda. The current Treaty rules are to be found in a Protocol to the TFEU—the Schengen Protocol—and Title V of Part III

---

[1] Art.20(1) TFEU. The citizenship of the Union is additional to and does not replace citizenship of a Member State. Switzerland knows of a similar construction: To become a citizen of Switzerland, one must first become citizen of a canton.
[2] Art.20(2) TFEU.

of the TFEU, entitled "Area of Freedom, Security and Justice". The provisions in that Title are characterised by mainly just providing the legal basis for the Union to adopt measures.

This chapter deals with this cluster of subjects. First the citizenship and the rules to enter and reside in a Member State will be presented. Thereafter follows the free movement of workers. At the end follows a presentation of Schengen and the co-operation under Title IV Area of Freedom, Security and Justice.

I. CITIZENSHIP OF THE UNION AND FREE MOVEMENT OF UNION CITIZENS

1. THE RIGHTS CONFERRED BY THE CITIZENSHIP

16–02 The TFEU establishes the citizenship of the Union by providing that every person holding the nationality of a Member State shall be a "citizen of the Union" and adds that this citizenship complements and does not replace national citizenship.[3] Consequently, the loss of national citizenship entails the loss of EU citizenship.[4]

The citizenship entails the right to move to and reside in another Member State in accordance with the Treaty, hereunder the principle of non-discrimination on grounds of nationality.[5] The Court has held that when a child born in a Member State from third country parents has acquired the nationality of that Member State, by virtue of the law of said State, the parents cannot be denied the right of residence nor the right to work there if this would deprive that child of the genuine enjoyment of the substance of the rights attaching to the status of Union citizen.[6]

Besides the right to move and reside freely within the territory of the Member States, citizens have the right to vote and stand as candidate in municipal elections in the Member State of residence of which they are not a national, under the same conditions as nationals of that State.[7] Detailed arrangements were adopted by the Council acting unanimously in accordance with a special legislative procedure[8] and after consulting Parliament.[9] According to the Treaty, these arrangements may provide for derogations where warranted by problems specific to a Member State.

---

[3] Art.20(2) TFEU.

[4] *Janko Rottman* (C-135/08) [2010] E.C.R. I-1449. Because the decision to strip a person of his nationality of a Member State entails loss of the Union citizenship, the Court of Justice held that the decision can be reviewed on the basis of Union law.

[5] Art.20 TFEU. On the importance of Art.20 TFEU as a basis for rights, see for instance *Martinez Sala* (C-85/96) [1998] E.C.R. I-2691, *Trojani* (C-456/02) [2004] E.C.R. I-7573, *Commission v Netherlands* (C-50/06) [2006] E.C.R. I-4383, and *Grunkin* (C-353/06) [2007] E.C.R. I-7639.

[6] *Luiz Zambrano* (C-34/09) [2011] E.C.R. I-1177.

[7] Arts 20(2)(b) and 22(1) TFEU.

[8] Art.289(2) TFEU.

[9] Directive 94/80 [1994] O.J. L368/38, with later amendments.

Citizens also have the right, when residing in a Member State of which they are not a national, to vote and to stand as candidate in elections to the European Parliament[10]; detailed arrangements are adopted by the Council under the above conditions.[11]

Furthermore, citizens have the right to enjoy, in the territory of a third country in which the Member State of which they are a national is not represented, the protection of the diplomatic and consular authorities of any Member State on the same conditions as the nationals of that State.[12] Member States must adopt the necessary provisions and start the international negotiations to secure this protection.[13] The Council, acting in accordance with a special legislative procedure and after consulting Parliament may adopt directives establishing the co-ordination and co-operation measures necessary to facilitate such protection.[14]

16–03

Citizens also have the right to petition Parliament,[15] to apply to the European Ombudsman[16] (these two rights are not limited to Union citizens, but are open to any person (natural or legal) legally residing in the Union) and to address the institutions and advisory bodies of the Union in any of the Treaty languages and to obtain a reply in the same language.[17]

The Lisbon Treaty introduced the mechanism of citizens' initiative, which exists in some Member States. Not less than one million citizens, who are nationals of a significant number of Member States, may take the initiative of inviting the Commission, within the framework of its powers, to submit any appropriate proposal on matters where citizens consider that a legal act of the Union is required for the purpose of implementing the Treaties.[18] Provisions for the procedure and conditions required for such initiative—including the minimum number of Member States from which the citizens must come—shall be adopted by Parliament and the Council by regulation in accordance with the ordinary legislative procedure.[19]

Every three years the Commission reports on this citizenship, assesses the application of Union rules on citizens' rights and proposes concrete measures to further their complete and effective implementation. The Council, acting unanimously, in accordance with a special legislative procedure,[20] may, following a three-yearly report by the Commission, adopt provisions to strengthen or to add

---

[10] Arts 20(2)(b) and 22(1) TFEU.

[11] Directive 93/109 [1993] O.J. L329/34.

[12] Art.20(2)(c) TFEU.

[13] See European Union guidelines on the implementation of the consular lead State concept [2008] O.J. C317/6.

[14] Art.23 TFEU. See Decision regarding protection [1995] O.J. L314/73.

[15] Art.227 TFEU.

[16] Art.228 TFEU.

[17] Art.20(2)(d) TFEU.

[18] Art.11(4) EU.

[19] Art.24,1 TFEU See Regulation 211/2011 on the citizen's initiative [2011] O.J. L65/1; with later amendments. See Commission implementing Regulation laying down technical specifications for online collection systems pursuant to the regulation on the citizens' initiative, Regulation 1179/11 [2011] O.J. L301/3.

[20] Art.289(2) TFEU.

to the above rights; these provisions shall enter into force after their approval by the Member States in accordance with their respective constitutional requirements.[21]

2. FREE MOVEMENT OF UNION CITIZENS

16–04   The Treaty furthermore provides, as already mentioned, that every citizen of the Union "shall have the right to move and reside freely within the territory of the Member States", but that those rights "shall be exercised in accordance with the conditions and limits defined by the Treaties and by the measures adopted there under".[22]

The measures referred to may be adopted by Parliament and the Council in accordance with the ordinary legislative procedure[23] with a view to facilitating the exercise of these rights. It must be noted that before the Union citizenship, nationals of a Member State also had a right to enter and reside in another Member State; the right followed mainly from their quality as worker, provider of services, etc. under the respective Internal Market freedoms. The details were laid down by various instruments of secondary law. An overhaul of the field in 2004 brought the provisions into one single Directive which also builds on the relevant case law that had developed on those instruments and the underlying Treaty provisions.[24]

Under the Directive Union citizens have the right of residence in the territory of another Member State:

- for a period of up to three months without any condition or formalities other than holding a valid passport or valid identity card;
- for a period of longer than three months, if they:
  - are workers or self-employed persons (see below), or
  - have sufficient resources for themselves and their family members and sickness insurance cover not to become an unreasonable burden on the social assistance system of the host State, or
  - are enrolled in an establishment accredited and financed by the host State to follow a course of study, including vocational training and

---

[21] Art.25(2) TFEU.

[22] Art.20(2)2 TFEU. The Court determined that this provision precludes legislation under which a Member State refuses to pay certain benefits granted to surviving spouses of victims of war solely because they are domiciled in certain specific Member States: *Weyhermiller* (C-221/07) [2008] E.C.R. I-9029.

[23] Art.289(1) TFEU.

[24] Directive 2004/38 on the right of citizens of the Union and their family members to move and reside freely within the territory of the Member States, amending Regulation 1612/68 and repealing Directives 64/221, 68/360, 72/194, 73/148, 74/35, 90/364, 90/365 and 93/96 [2004] O.J. L158/77. There are numerous cases on the Directive and the previous instruments of secondary law and the underlying Treaty provisions, see amongst others: *Jipa* (C-33/07) [2008] E.C.R. I-5157: Member State may restrict travel to another Member State on account of "illegal residence" there, provided the personal conduct constitutes a genuine, present and sufficiently serious threat. See *Lassal* (C-162/09) [2010] E.C.R. I-9217. Article 16: period of five years. *Panagiotis Tsakouridis* (C-145/09) E.C.R. [2011] I-11453: interpretation of "serious grounds of public policy or public security". *Ziolkowski and Szja* (C-424 and 425/10) (2010) E.C.R. I-13459: interpretation of Art.16, legal residence, etc.

have comprehensive sickness insurance cover and sufficient resources for themselves and their family not to become a burden on the social assistance system of the host State, or

– are family members (even when not a national of a Member State[25]) accompanying or joining a Union citizen who satisfies the above conditions;[26]

- for permanent residence: citizens who have resided in the host Member State, in compliance with the conditions laid down in the Directive, during a continuous period of five years without becoming subject to an expulsion measure.[27]

Union citizens must be able to prove that they are indeed citizens of one of the Member States; this proof normally consists of a valid identity card or a passport, but the identity and nationality may also, according to the Court, be brought, without ambiguity, by other means.[28]   **16–05**

Member States may require persons to report their presence to the national authorities; the time limit for reporting and the penalties for failing to do so have to be reasonable (if not, the principle of proportionality would be infringed).[29]

Expulsion or refusal of entry can only be justified on grounds of public policy, public security and public health.[30]

Finally it must be recalled that the provisions presuppose a cross border movement. The Court has held that the provisions referred to above are "not applicable to a Union citizen who has never exercised his right of free movement, who has always resided in a Member State of which he is a national, and who is also a national of another Member State", adding, however, that a Member State may not apply measures restricting for that person the enjoyment of the fundamental rights of a citizen of the Union.[31]

Free movement of citizens was also facilitated, in some way, by the issue of a "European Passport",[32] i.e. a passport of uniform pattern (format and colour) in

---

[25] See *Metock and others* (C-127/08) [2008] E.C.R. I-6241 where the Court held that a Member State may not require that the spouse of a citizen residing in a Member State of which the latter is not a national, has resided legally in another Member State before entering the host State and independently of the location and date of their marriage and the way in which the citizen entered the host Member State.

[26] It must be recalled that the right to enter and stay applies in a cross border situation. The national of a Member State that has resided all the time in that Member State cannot therefore rely on the Directive to require that Member State to give a right of residence to a member of this family who is a third country national, see *Dereci and others* (C-256/11), judgment of November 15, 2011, not yet reported.

[27] Directive 2004/38 [2004] O.J. L158/77, Preamble (17). See *Taous Lassal* (C-162/09) [2010] E.C.R. I-9217. For the interpretation of Art.16(1) of this Directive, see *Secretary of State v Maria Dias* (C-325/09), judgment of July 21, 2011, not yet reported.

[28] *Oulane* (C-215/03) [2005] E.C.R. I-1215.

[29] Art.5(5) of Directive 2004/38. See also *Watson and Belmann* (118/75) [1976] E.C.R. 1185; [1976] 2 C.M.L.R. 552. In the ruling the Court also held that the time limit for reporting and the penalties for failing to do so had to be reasonable (if not, the principle of proportionality would be infringed).

[30] Art.27 of Directive 2004/38. These justification grounds must be construed narrowly. The Directive contains a particular definition of public health, applicable within the scope of the Directive, Art.29.

[31] *McCarthy* (C-434/09) [2011] E.C.R. I-3375.

[32] Several Resolutions were adopted by the Representatives of the Governments of the Member States meeting within the Council; [1981] O.J. C241/1, amended by [1995] O.J. C 200/1; [1982] O.J.

which national passports are issued. Presently the passports of all citizens of the Union are "same-looking EU passports".

II. THE FREE MOVEMENT OF WORKERS[33]

16–06   The principle of freedom of movement of workers forms, according to the Court, one of the foundations of the Union and consequently has to be given a broad interpretation.[34] The ban on restrictions on the free movement of workers has direct effect.[35] It does not apply in purely internal situations.[36] The beneficiaries are nationals of the Member States.

Access to employment in another Member State is a fundamental aspect of the free movement of persons within the EU. A wide area of labour mobility represents a large number of opportunities for workers to find work and for the employer to find people with adequate skills, thereby enhancing employment and economic growth. The purpose is to open European labour markets to all EU workers, which is one of the tangible aspects of European integration. The right of access to national labour markets includes a right to equal treatment with respect to working conditions, as well as the right to social, economic and cultural integration of the migrant worker and her or his family in the host State.[37]

Workers are not defined in the Treaty. The definition of worker gave rise to some case law of the Court, which has always maintained that the term "has a [Union] meaning and, inasmuch as it defines the scope of one of the fundamental freedoms of the [Union], must be interpreted broadly".[38] The Court furthermore indicates that the concept must be defined in accordance with objective criteria which distinguish the employment relationship by reference to the rights and duties of the persons concerned and that "the essential feature of an employment relationship is that for a certain period of time, a person performs services for, and under the direction of, another person, in return for which he receives

---

C179/1; [1986] O.J. C185/1. See Resolution of the Representatives of the Governments of the Member States, meeting within the Council of June 8, 2004 supplementary to the resolution of June 23, 1981, June 30, 1982, July 14, 1986 and July 10, 1995 concerning the introduction of a passport of uniform pattern [2004] O.J. C245/1.

[33] See also above the Introduction to the Internal Market, the section concerning restrictions and justification.

[34] *Commission v Belgium* (C-344/95) [1997] E.C.R. I–1035, para.14, and *Levin v Staatssecretaris van Justitie* (53/81) [1982] E.C.R. 1035, para.13.

[35] *Dona* (13/76) [1976] E.C.R. 1333.

[36] See *Moser v Land Baden-Württemberg* (180/83) [1984] E.C.R. 2539; [1984] 3 C.M.L.R. 720, which concerned a national who had never resided or worked in another Member State.

[37] *Royer* (48/75) [1976] E.C.R. 497; [1976] 2 C.M.L.R. 619.

[38] *Bettray v Staatssecretaris van Justitie* (344/87) [1989] E.C.R. 1621 at 1644(11); [1991] 1 C.M.L.R. 459. It must be added that the notion of worker under Union law may vary from one context to another, see for instance *Martinez Sala*, quoted above, para.31: "...there is no single definition of worker in Community law: it varies according to the area in which the definition is to be applied. For instance, the definition of worker used in the context of Art.48 of the EC Treaty [Art.45 TFEU] and Regulation No 1612/68 does not necessarily coincide with the definition applied in relation to Art.51 of the EC Treaty [Art.48 TFEU] and Regulation No 1408/71."

remuneration".[39] Thus, a bank teller or a university professor are workers within the meaning of the Treaty; so are employed professional football players.[40]

Free movement of workers, as the other Internal Market freedoms, applies only to persons pursuing or wishing to pursue an economic[41] activity and consequently, it only covers the pursuit of an effective and genuine activity.[42] The latter is defined by the Court as excluding "activities on such a small scale as to be regarded as purely marginal and ancillary".[43] The Court also added that neither productivity nor the origin of the 'funds used for the remuneration can have any consequence with regard to the question as to whether or not the person is to be regarded as a worker. The same applies to the nature of the legal relationship between the employee and the employer.[44] Furthermore, the employment must not necessarily be full-time employment: free movement of workers also applies to persons who pursue an activity on a part-time basis, even if, by virtue of that fact, that person obtains remuneration lower than the minimum guaranteed wage in a given sector.[45] There is neither any requirement to the duration of the employment relation for considering a person as a worker.[46] The Court also determined that the motives which may have prompted a worker to seek employment are of no account and must not be taken into consideration.[47]

As with the other freedoms, the free movement of workers protects against discrimination and other restrictions.[48] The main obstacles to the free movement of workers within the Union are:

- discriminatory conditions of work and employment for non-nationals;
- law, regulations and administrative action, which impose on workers from other Member States obligations which are different from those governing nationals; and
- lack of co-ordination among the social security systems with harmful consequences for the migrant worker.

As shall be seen hereunder, the Treaty addresses each one of those obstacles. The Treaty grants rights to any person who desires to exercise an economic

16–07

---

[39] *Bettray* (344/87) at 1645(12), (quoted above, fn.38).

[40] *Bosman* (C-415/93) [1995] E.C.R. I-4921.

[41] See *Walrave and Koch v Association Union Cycliste Internationale* (36/74) [1974] E.C.R. at 1405(5); [1975] 1 C.M.L.R. 320, concerning the nationality of the motorcycle pacemakers and the cyclists. See also *Deliège* (Joined Cases C-51/96 and C-191/97) [2000] E.C.R. I-2549 concerning a judoka and the free movement of services; and *Lehtonen* (C-176/96) [2000] E.C.R. I-2681 concerning professional basketball players and free movement of workers.

[42] The employment can be effective and genuine although the remuneration is in kind and limited, see *Steymann* (196/87) [1988] E.C.R. 6159.

[43] *Levin* (53/81) (quoted above, fn.34), at 1050(17).

[44] *Sotgiu v Deutsche Bundespost* (152/73) [1974] E.C.R. 153.

[45] See also *Jenkins v Kingsgate* (96/80) [1981] E.C.R. at 911(11); [1981] 2 C.M.L.R. 24.

[46] *Ninni-Orasche* (C-413/01) [2003] E.C.R. I-13187.

[47] *Levin* (53/81) (quoted above, fn.34), at 1052(22).

[48] Discriminatory measures taken by a private employer also come within the scope of the provisions, see *Angonese* (C-281/98) [2000] E.C.R. I-4139. Although the Treaty provisions are drafted such as to protect "workers", they may also be relied upon by employers, see *Clean Car* (C-350/96) [1998] E.C.R. I-2521.

activity as an employed person and is a national of one of the Member States. Those rights have been further implemented by the Union legislator.[49]

16–08   The TFEU provides that the worker enjoys the following rights:

1.   the right "to accept offers of employment actually made".[50] This, however, does not mean that the worker, in order to benefit from the freedom to move to another Member State, must have in his possession a duly executed employment contract. Freedom of movement also extends to persons who "seriously wish to pursue activities as an employed person"[51];

2.   the right "to move freely within the territory of Member States".[52] This means the right to move to any Member State for the purpose of employment;

Taking into account the fact that the right to enter and reside can also be claimed by a person looking for a job, the question was raised as to how long this person could go on looking. The answer given by the Court is a reasonable time. The Court also held that a national rule limiting the period to six months was not unreasonable unless the person in question provides evidence that she or he is continuing to seek employment and that there is a genuine chance of being engaged[53];

3.   the right "to stay in the Member State for the purpose of employment".[54] This right follows from the Treaty and thus not from the national authorities issuing a residence permit, this latter just being a proof;[55]

4.   the right "to employment in accordance with the provisions governing employment of nationals".[56] This is by far the most important right of the migrant worker; it is the embodiment of the prohibition of discrimination on grounds of nationality, be it direct or indirect. The principle applies, according to the Treaty, to "employment, remuneration and other conditions of work and employment".[57] It means, among other things, that the worker must have access to all economic activities within the territory of the host State under the same conditions as the nationals. Save exceptions, no economic activity may be reserved for nationals. Individual and collective employment agreements are subject to all the above rules.[58] Important are the words "and other conditions of work and employment": they include conditions as regards dismissal, re-instatement or re-employment, social and tax advantages, access to training in vocational schools and re-training centres, membership of trade unions and the exercise of the rights attached thereto, including the right to vote, eligibility

---

[49] See in particular Regulation 1612/68, codified [2011] O.J. L141/1.

[50] Art.45(3)(a) TFEU.

[51] *Levin* (53/81) (quoted above, fn.34), para.21. See also *Collins* (C-138/02) [2004] E.C.R. I-2703.

[52] Art.45(3)(b) TFEU.

[53] *Queen v Immigration Appeal Tribunal* (C-292/89) [1991] E.C.R. 1745 at 1780(18); [1991] 2 C.M.L.R. 373, where the Court found that an obligation to automatically leave after three months infringes Union law.

[54] Art.45(3)(c) TFEU.

[55] *Royer* (48/75) (quoted above, fn.37).

[56] Art.45(3)(c) TFEU.

[57] Art.45(2) TFEU.

[58] Regulation 1612/68 [1968] O.J. L 257/2, on freedom of movement of workers within the Union; codified by Regulation 492/2011 [2011] O.J. L141/1; see Art.7(4).

for workers' representative bodies in the undertaking. The migrant worker shall also enjoy all the rights and benefits accorded to national workers in matters of housing, including ownership;

5. the right to be joined by his family; although this right is not expressly provided for in the Treaty chapter on workers, it is obvious that preventing the family from joining the migrant worker would constitute an obstacle to his freedom of movement. It should be noted that the freedom to be joined by the family applies irrespective of the nationality of the members of this family.[59] In case the worker returns to his Member State of which he is a national, the accompanying family member who is a national of a third country has the right to accompany the worker in that Member State even if the worker does not there exercise a real and effective activity.[60]

By "family member", in this context, is meant the worker's spouse, registered partner, and their descendants who are under the age of 21 years or are dependents,[61] and dependent relatives in the ascending line of the worker, registered partner or his spouse.[62] Furthermore, the spouse and the children under the age of 21 years or dependent on him shall have the right to take up any activity as an employed person throughout the territory of the same State, even if they are not nationals of any Member State.[63] Important here is the term "dependent"; it means the family member needs the material support of the worker or his or her spouse in order to meet their essential needs in their State of origin or in the State from which they come at the time they apply to join the worker. Proof of the need for material support may be adduced by any appropriate means, but a mere undertaking from the worker or his or her spouse to support the family member concerned need not be regarded as establishing the existence of real dependence.[64]

The worker's children shall be admitted to the host State's general educational,[65] apprenticeship and vocational training[66] courses under the

---

[59] See for instance *Baumbast* (C-413/99) [2002] E.C.R. I-7091 where the Court had to consider whether a person continued to enjoy the protection of Union law after she ceased to qualify as a member of the family of the migrant worker; she had custody of the children. Since the children had the right of residence, the mother had to have it also on the basis of her right to respect for family life provided for in Art.8 of the European Convention for the Protection of Human rights; *Metock and others* (C-127/08) [2008] E.C.R. I-6241 where the Court held that a Member State may not require that the spouse of a citizen residing in a Member State of which he is not a national, has resided legally in another Member State before entering the host State and independently of the location and date of their marriage and the way in which the citizen entered the host Member State. See also *JIA* (C-1/05) [2007] E.C.R.I-1 and the right to family reunification: a necessary way of making family life possible; a directive determines the conditions for the exercise of the right to family reunification by third country nationals residing lawfully in the territory of the Member States: Directive 2003/86 [2003] O.J. 251/12.

[60] *Minister voor vreemdelingen Zaken v Eind* (C-291/05) [2007] E.C.R. I-10719.

[61] *Confédération Générale du Travail E.A.* (C-1/05) [2007] E.C.R. I-1 where the Court held that "the proof of the need for material support may be adduced by any appropriate means". The English Court of Appeal decided that the time and place of dependency is not relevant *Pedro v Secretary of State* [2009] EWCA Civ 1358.

[62] Art.2 of Directive 2004/38.

[63] Art.23 of Directive 2004/38.

[64] *JIA* (C-1/05) [2007] E.C.R. I-1.

[65] Directive 77/486 on the education of the children of migrant workers [1977] O.J. L199/32 and Council Conclusions concerning the implementation of Directive 77/486 [1985] O.J. C165/1.

same conditions as the nationals of that State, if such children are residing in its territory.[67] They must also have access to special employment programmes.[68] Generally speaking, the rights constituting the free movement of workers, especially the right of entry, movement and residence also apply to the worker's family, even if the latter are not nationals of a Member State[69];

6. the right "to remain in the territory of a Member State after having been employed in that State",[70] subject to the conditions embodied in "regulations to be drawn up by the Commission.".[71] For a person reaching pensionable age, the general rule is the following: the worker, at the time of termination of his activity as an employed person, must have reached the age laid down by the law of the host Member State for entitlement to an old-age pension; the worker must also have been employed in that State for at least the last 12 months and resided there continuously for more than three years.[72] If the worker has acquired the right to remain in the territory of a Member State, the members of his family shall be entitled to remain there permanently even after his death[73];

7. aggregation of all rights acquired anywhere in the Union under a social security system.[74] The rights mentioned above would be useless if the migrant worker, when moving from one Member State to another, would lose even partially the benefits acquired under social security regulations of the first Member State. The Treaty therefore provides that all the rights acquired or periods acquired under the laws of the several countries where the worker exercised his activity shall be aggregated "for the purpose of acquiring and retaining the right to benefit and of calculating the amount of benefit of all periods taken into account under the laws of the several countries".[75] Those benefits will be paid to the worker by one social security institution, normally the one in the Member State of residence or

---

[66] Vocational training: "Any form of education which prepares for a qualification for a particular profession, trade or employment or which provides the necessary training and skills for such a profession, trade or employment": *Gravier v City of Liege* (293/83) [1985] E.C.R. 593; [1985] 3 C.M.L.R. 1. See also Art.166 TFEU.

[67] Art.1 of Regulation 492/2011 concerning education and training facilities and the rights of children of a deceased worker. 1 C.M.L.R. 357. A national of a Member State who was employed in another Member State, in which its child is in education, can claim, in the capacity of primary carer for that child, a right of residence in the host Member State on the sole basis of Art.12 of Regulation 1612/68: *Teixeira* (C-480/08) [2010] E.C.R. I-1107.

[68] *Commission v Belgium* (C-278/94) [1996] E.C.R. I-4307; [1997] 1 C.M.L.R. 1040: tide-over allowances to young people seeking their first employment may not be subject to them having completed their secondary education in an establishment subsidised or approved by that Member State.

[69] *Christini v SNCF* (32/75) [1975] E.C.R. at 1085(19). This applies also to the member of the family from a third country when the worker returns to his country of origin after being gainfully employed in another Member State: *Eind* (C-291/05) [2007] E.C.R. I-10719.

[70] Art.45(3)(d) TFEU.

[71] Regulation 1251/70 on the right of workers to remain in the territory of a Member State after having been employed in the State, repealed by Regulation 635/2006 [2006] O.J.L112/9. The relevant provisions can now be found in Directive 2004/38.

[72] Art.17(1) of Directive 2004/38.

[73] Art.17(4) of Directive 2004/38.

[74] Art.48 TFEU.

[75] Art.48(a) TFEU.

the Member State of his work.[76] The purpose of the Treaty therefore is not to harmonise the existing social security systems of the different Member States into a single Union social security system, but to co-ordinate them. As the Court pointed out, the Treaty allows for separate systems to exist "creating separate claims against separate institutions against which the beneficiary has direct rights", either under national law alone or under national law supplemented by the Treaty. The Council must take such measures as are necessary to provide freedom of movement to workers and it "shall make arrangements to secure for the migrant workers and their dependents" the aggregation and payments just mentioned.[77] Those measures gave rise to an abundance of case law, which is not surprising considering the complexity and the scope of the matter. The following branches of social security are covered by Council's Regulations:

(a)   sickness benefits;
(b)   maternity and equivalent paternity benefits;
(c)   invalidity benefits;
(d)   old-age benefits;
(e)   survivors' benefits;
(f)   benefits in respect of accidents at work and occupational diseases;
(g)   death grants;
(h)   unemployment benefits;
(i)   pre-retirement benefits;
(j)   family benefits.

Social and medical "assistance" is not included. The distinction between social assistance and social security covered can be difficult to draw in practice.[78]   **16–09**

An Administrative Commission and an Advisory Committee on Social Security for Migrant Workers[79] were set up to help the Member States and the Commission with the implementation of the measures adopted in favour of migrant workers.

Restrictions to the free movement of workers may be justified.[80] The Treaty mentions first the following justification grounds: public policy, public security or public health[81]; next it excludes "employment in the public service" from the

---

[76] Art.48(b) TFEU.

[77] Regulation 1408/71 on the application of social security schemes to employed persons and their families moving within the Union [1971] O.J. L149/71; replaced by Regulation 883/2004; Regulation 574/72 fixing the procedure for implementing Regulation 1408/71, replaced by Regulation 987/2009 laying down the procedure for implementing Regulation 883/2004.

[78] See *Beerens v Rijksdienst voor Arbeidsvoorziening* (35/77) [1977] E.C.R. 2249; [1978] 2 C.M.L.R. 320 where the Court found that social and medical assistance are excluded in the Netherlands from social security, while in Belgium they are included.

[79] Arts 80–83 Regulation 1408/71 [1971] O.J. L149/2, as modified (quoted above, fn.77). Internal Rules in [1995] O.J. C163/3.

[80] See also the Introduction to Part III of this book: The Internal Market, 2. Restrictions and justification.

[81] Art.45(3) TFEU.

application of the Treaty rules.[82] The meaning of the concepts "public policy", "public security" and "public health" have been elucidated in extensive case law of the Court.[83]

As concerns public policy, it must be mentioned that the expulsion or the refusal of entry of a migrant worker on the ground of public policy requires that his presence or conduct constitutes a genuine and sufficiently serious threat to fundamental values of society. A Member State's decision, whether it concerns refusal of entry[84] or expulsion[85] must be based on the individual circumstances of any person under the protection of Union law, and not on general considerations.[86] Furthermore, and this is essential, in each Member State, nationals of other Member States should have appropriate legal remedies available to them in respect of such decisions of the administration.[87]

Concerning the non-applicability of the free movement of workers to employment in the public service, the exception has been construed narrowly to the effect that it concerns posts that are closely associated with the exercise of official authority.[88] For instance: the fact that school teachers in one Member State are public servants cannot serve to exclude national from other Member States from becoming a school teacher in that State. Moreover, once a national of another Member State has been admitted into such a post, the exception cannot be invoked to justify discrimination on grounds of nationality.[89]

1. FREEDOM OF MOVEMENT OF WORKERS—TEMPORARY MEASURES AFTER THE LATEST ENLARGEMENTS (2004, 2007 AND 2013)

16–10   The 2004 Accession Treaty[90] sets out the conditions for freedom of movement of workers to and from the then 10 new Member States after enlargement. The above-mentioned Treaty provides for transitional arrangements that allow the EU 15 Member States to restrict for a period of seven years the free movement of workers coming from the new ones. There was an initial period of two years during which national law or bilateral agreements had to be applied. After that, the EU 15 Member States had to give formal notice to the Commission of their intention to either apply in full Union law as explained above or maintain restrictive measures for a maximum of three more years; during a further two-year period a Member State could apply restrictions provided that it could show that its labour market would otherwise be seriously affected.

---

[82] Art.45(4) TFEU.

[83] See for instance *Rutili v Minister for the Interior* (36/75) [1975] E.C.R. 1219; [1976] 1 C.M.L.R. 140.

[84] *Van Duyn v Home Office* (41/74) [1974] E.C.R. 1337; [1975] 1 C.M.L.R. 1.

[85] *Pecastaing v Belgian State* (98/79) [1980] E.C.R. 691; [1980] 3 C.M.L.R. 685, a person against whom an expulsion order has been issued may exercise all the remedies available to nationals in respect of acts of the administration.

[86] Art.27(2) of Directive 2004/38. The provision builds on case law.

[87] Arts 30 and 31 of Directive 2004/38. The provision builds on case law, see for instance *Singhgara and Radiom* (Joined Cases C-65/95 and C-111/95) [1997] E.C.R. I–3343; [1997] 3 C.M.L.R. 703.

[88] *Sotgiu* (152/73) [1974] E.C.R. 153; [1975] 1 C.M.L.R. 91.

[89] *Commission v Greece* (C-290/96) [1996] E.C.R. I–3285.

[90] [2003] O.J. 326/1.

The Accession Treaty also provides for a "safeguard clause"[91] and a "standstill clause".[92]

Three Member States: the United Kingdom, Sweden and Finland did not apply restrictions. It is interesting to note that a study carried out by the Commission indicates that the number of persons with the firm intention of taking advantage of mobility after May 1, 2004 accounted for just 1 per cent of the population of working age of the new Member States; so the fear of massive arrival of workers from the new Member States seemed unfounded.

Similar conditions applied to Bulgaria and Romania, (accession 2007). Similar conditions also apply to Croatia (accession 2013).

2. WORKERS FROM THIRD COUNTRIES

As indicated, the Treaty rules, generally speaking, apply only to citizens of the Union; this is the case concerning "workers". Indeed, the Treaty refers to "workers of the Member States".[93] Nonetheless, where workers from third countries are employed by an undertaking in a given Member State for more than six months on the basis of an employment contract of unlimited duration, another Member State may not make their entry and employment on its territory, by the undertaking employing them in the other Member State, more difficult than for citizens; this follows from the freedom to provide services, i.e. the freedom of the undertaking from one Member State to move its work force to another Member State when the undertaking is delivering services there.[94]

16–11

Conditions of entry and residence of third country-nationals for the purpose of highly qualified employment were laid down in 2009.[95] See a Directive on a single application procedure for third country nationals to reside and work in the Union.[96]

III. AN AREA OF FREEDOM, SECURITY AND JUSTICE—INTERNAL BORDERS AND FREE MOVEMENT OF THIRD COUNTRY NATIONALS

---

[91] The clause makes it possible for a Member State that has decided to no longer apply the restrictions to ask the Commission for authorisation to re-introduce restrictions if its labour market is threatened by, or experiences, serious difficulties.

[92] The EU 15 Member States could not make access to their labour market more restrictive for workers who are nationals of the new Member States than it was on the date the Accession Treaty was signed (April 16, 2003).

[93] Art.45(2) TFEU.

[94] *Commission v Luxembourg* (C-445/03) [2004] E.C.R. I-10191. Directive 96/71 regulates the terms and conditions of employment that the host Member State may require the service provider to comply with.

[95] Directive 2009/50 [2009] O.J. L155/17.

[96] Directive 2011/98 [2011] O.J. L343/1.

1. SCHENGEN

16–12 First mention must be made of the Schengen arrangements. The term refers to the Schengen Agreement of 1985[97] on the gradual abolition of controls at the common (inner) frontiers of the signatories and of the 1990 Convention Implementing the Schengen Agreement (CISA).[98] The Schengen Agreement was an agreement outside the framework of the Treaty, and only Belgium, France, Germany, Luxembourg and the Netherlands were parties to it; it sought to do away with internal border controls. Later other Member States joined the Agreement, and so did a few third countries. In 2005 followed the Schengen III Agreement concerning the deepening of cross-border co-operation in the fields of the fight against terrorism, cross-border criminal activities and illegal migration. It enables the signatories to exchange all data regarding DNA fingerprints; the contracting parties having made a commitment to create and maintain national DNA analysis databases for the purpose of prosecuting criminal offences.

The Treaty now integrates the "Schengen *acquis*".[99] The Schengen *acquis* comprises the Agreement of 1985, the CISA, the Accession Protocols for Italy, Spain, Portugal, Greece, Austria, Denmark, Finland and Sweden, Ireland and the UK (the latter adhering to parts of Schengen), Iceland and Norway,[100] Switzerland,[101] where the full application took place in 2008[102], Liechtenstein, where full application took place in 2011[103] and the 10 new Member States which adhered from the moment of their accession[104] and also the Decisions and Declarations of the Executive Committee and those of the Central Group.[105]

16–13 In order to protect against terrorism and other crimes, the Schengen Information System (SIS) was set up; it allows the exchange of data on people's identities and description of objects stolen or lost. Later on, new functions were attributed to the SIS,[106] which became SIS II.[107] The Commission laid down the network requirements for the SIS II[108] and adopted the SIRENE manual[109] and

---

[97] Agreement of June 14, 1985, published for instance in Moniteur Belge of April 29, 1986 (the text can also be obtained from the Benelux Secretariat in Brussels, fax 02/513.42.06).

[98] [2000] O.J. L239/19. See *Kretzinger* (C-288/05) [2007] E.C.R. I-6441 concerning the "*ne bis in idem*" principle. See also *Bourquain* (C-297/07) [2008] E.C.R. I-9425, where the Court held that the *ne bis in idem* principle also applies when a first sentence could never have been directly enforced.

[99] Protocol 19 TFEU on the Schengen *acquis* integrated into the framework of the Union. The Schengen *acquis* thus does not formally form part of the Title of the Treaty "Area of Freedom, Security and Justice".

[100] [1999] O.J. L176/31.

[101] [2004] O.J. L370/78; see agreement between the European Union and the Swiss Confederation of the latter's association with the implementation, application and development of the of the Schengen *acquis* [2008] O.J. L53/1.

[102] [2008] O.J. L127/15.

[103] [2008] O.J. L83/5; [2011] L334/27.

[104] However, a decision of the EU Council is needed before controls at their borders are lifted.

[105] Romania and Bulgaria do not yet—spring 2013—participate.

[106] [2005] O.J. L68/44 with later amendments.

[107] Regulation 2424/2001 on the development of the second generation SIS [2001] O.J. L328/4, amended by Regulation 1988/2006 and Decision 2007/533 on the establishment, operation and use of the second generation Schengen Information System [2007] O.J. L205/63.

[108] [2007] O.J. L79/29.

[109] See Regulation 378/04 on procedures for amending the Sirene Manual [2004] O.J. L64/5 and Implementing Decision amending the Sirene Manual [2011] O.J. L186/1.

other implementing measures for the second generation SIS.[110] See Regulation on migration from SIS I to SIS II.[111] See also the *Schengen Borders Code*,[112] a Union Code on the rules governing the movement of persons across borders, the *Visa Information System* (VIS)[113] and the *Schengen consultation network*.[114] A European Agency for the operational management of large-scale IT systems in the area of freedom, security and justice was established in 2011 in order to ensure the operational management of SIS II, VIS and Eurodac and of certain aspects of the communication infrastructure after the transitional period, and potentially that of other large-scale information technology (IT) systems.[115]

One of the consequences of this integration of the Schengen *acquis* into the Treaty is that the Court of Justice can be called upon to interpret the Schengen Agreement via a preliminary question. This allowed the Court to determine, for instance, that when a citizen travels within the Union, his spouse who is a national of a third country is covered to a large extent by the freedom of movement, but may be refused entry on grounds of public policy or public security. However, where such a person for whom alerts are entered into the Schengen Information System (SIS) for the purpose of refusing entry, a Member State must verify whether the presence of such person constitutes a genuine, present and sufficiently serious threat affecting one of the fundamental interests of society before refusing it entry into the Schengen area. The Court clearly stated that the Schengen Protocol confirms that the Schengen *acquis* is applicable only and in so far as it is compatible with European Union Law.[116] In the same ruling the Court also held that the concept of public policy within the meaning of the 2004 Directive presented above[117] does not correspond to that of the CISA.

2. AREA OF FREEDOM, SECURITY AND JUSTICE

The TFEU provides that the Union shall constitute an area of freedom, security **16–14** and justice.[118] A programme adopted in 2010—the "Stockholm Programme—an open and secure Europe serving and protecting citizens"—seeks to detail the implications.[119] The main elements of this programme are: 1. Towards a citizens' Europe in the area of freedom, security and justice; 2. Promoting citizens' rights: a Europe of rights; 3. Making peoples' lives easier: a Europe of law and justice; 4. A Europe that protects; 5. Access to Europe in a globalised world; 6. A Europe of

---

[110] [2008] O.J. L123/1. See [2008] O.J. L149/78 on declassifying Annex IV.

[111] [2008] O.J. L299/1, amended [2010] O.J. L155/19.

[112] This Code was supplemented, as regards the surveillance of the sea external borders: Decision 10/252 [2010] O.J. L111/20.

[113] Regulation 562/06 [2006] O.J. L105/1, with later amendments; see List of residence permits referred to in Art.2(15) [2006] O.J. C247/1. See Notification of the Swiss Confederation concerning penalties for unauthorised crossing [2009] O.J. C3/11.

[114] [2008] O.J. L328/38, amended [2009] O.J. L353/49, and [2011] O.J. L126/22.

[115] [2011] O.J. L286/1.

[116] *Commission v Spain* (C-503/03) [2006] E.C.R. I-3969.

[117] Directive 2004/38 [2004] O.J. L158/77.

[118] Art.67(1) TFEU.

[119] [2010] O.J. C115/1.

responsibility, solidarity and partnership in migration and asylum matters and 7. Europe in a globalised world—the external dimension of Freedom, Security and Justice.

Concretely speaking this Area means: the absence of internal border controls for persons; the framing of a common policy on asylum, immigration and external border control; a high level of security through measures to prevent and combat crime, racism and xenophobia[120]; measures for co-ordination and co-operation between police and judicial authorities; the mutual recognition of judgments in criminal matters[121] (if necessary, through the approximation of criminal law); and facilitating access to justice, in particular through the mutual recognition of judicial and extra-judicial decisions in civil matters.[122] Quite a programme!

"Strategic guidelines for legislative and operational planning" in the above-mentioned areas shall be defined by the European Council,[123] which indicates the great importance of the activities provided for in this field. The Council, on the other hand, may adopt measures laying down the arrangements whereby Member States, in collaboration with the Commission, conduct objective and impartial evaluation of the implementation of the Union's policies referred to above, by Member State's authorities.[124] To this end a standing Committee will be set up within the Council,[125] which must adopt measures to ensure administrative co-operation between the relevant departments of the Member States, as well as between those departments and the Commission.[126]

3. POLICIES ON BORDER CHECKS, ASYLUM AND IMMIGRATION

16–15 The objectives of the "Policies on border checks, asylum and immigration"[127] are multiple:

- ensuring the absence of any controls on persons, whatever their nationality, when crossing internal borders;
- carrying out checks and efficient monitoring of the crossing of external borders; and
- the gradual introduction of an integrated management system for external borders.

---

[120] Art.75 TFEU complements this with a reference to "terrorism and related activities" and providing that Parliament and Council must define a framework for administrative measures with regard to capital movements and payments, such as freezing of funds, etc. Measures to implement the framework are to be taken by the Council on a proposal from the Commission.

[121] In these domains the TFEU assigns a role to the national Parliaments: ensure that the measures comply with the principle of subsidiarity: Art.69 TFEU. Measures in those fields shall be adopted by the Council on a proposal from the Commission or on the initiative of a quarter of the Member States: Art.76 TFEU, which constitutes a departure from the Commission's right to propose legislation.

[122] Art.67 (2–4) TFEU.

[123] Art.68 TFEU.

[124] Art.70 TFEU.

[125] Art.71 TFEU.

[126] Art.74 TFEU.

[127] Arts 77–80 TFEU.

In order to achieve these objectives, Parliament and the Council, acting in accordance with the ordinary legislative procedure,[128] must adopt measures concerning, among others: a common policy on visas and other short-stay residence permits,[129] the checks at the external borders (*External Borders Fund*[130]) and the conditions under which nationals of third countries shall have the freedom to travel within the Union for a short period.[131]

Where *asylum*[132] is concerned, the Union will develop a common policy in accordance with the Geneva Convention of July 28, 1951 and the Protocol of January 31, 1967 relating to the status of refugees and other relevant treaties. It is for Parliament and the Council, acting in accordance with the ordinary legislative procedure,[133] to adopt the necessary measures for a *Common European Asylum System (CEAS)*; the first phase comprises four instruments: the "Dublin Regulation",[134] the "Reception Condition Directive",[135] the "Qualification Directive"[136] and the "Asylum procedure Directive".[137] The main components of the system are:

- a uniform status of asylum for nationals of third countries;
- a uniform status of protection for other nationals of third countries in need of international protection;
- a common system of temporary protection for displaced persons in the event of a massive inflow;
- a common procedure for the granting and the withdrawal of the above;
- criteria and mechanisms for determining which Member State is responsible for considering corresponding applications established by the Dublin Convention[138]; EURODAC was established creating a system for comparing fingerprints of asylum seekers and illegal immigrants for the effective application of the Dublin Convention[139];
- standards concerning the conditions for the reception of applicants;
- partnership and co-operation with third countries for the purpose of managing inflow of asylum seekers. In case a sudden inflow creates an emergency situation in a Member State, the Council may adopt provisional measures.

---

[128] Art.294 TFEU.

[129] See Regulation 767/08 [2008] O.J. L218/60 concerning the visa information system (VIS) and the exchange of data between the Member States (VIS Regulation) amended [2009] O.J L243/15 and Decision 2009/377 [2009] O.J. L117/3, adopting implementing measures.

[130] The External Borders Fund for the period 2007 to 2013 with €1.820 million was established as part of the General Programme "Solidarity and Management of Migration Flows": Decision 574/07 [2007] O.J. L144/22, amended [2013] O.J. L82/6; see Decision 2008/456 laying down rules for the implementation of Decision 574/07, amended [2011] O.J. L61/28.

[131] Art.77(2) TFEU.

[132] Art.78 TFEU.

[133] Art.294 TFEU.

[134] Regulation 343/2003 [2003] O.J. L50/1 amended [2008] L304/80.

[135] Directive 2003/9 [2003] O.J. L31/18.

[136] Directive 2004/83 [2004] O.J. L304/12.

[137] Directive 2005/85 [2005] O.J. L326/13.

[138] [1997] O.J. C254/1. Regulation 343/03 [2003] O.J. L50/1 amended [2008] O.J. L304/80 and Regulation 1560/03 [2003] O.J. L222/3 laying down detailed rules for its application; see *Petrosian* (C-19/08) [2000] E.C.R. I-495.

[139] Regulation 2725/00 [2000] O.J. L316/1 concerning the establishment of EURODAC.

16–16   The second phase consisted in the establishment of a *European Asylum Support Office* in 2010 in order to increase co-ordination of operational co-ordination between the Member States so that the common rules are implemented effectively.[140]

A *European Refugee Fund*[141] for the period 2008–2013 was established as part of the General Programme "Solidarity and Management of Migration Flows" (see below).

A directive was adopted on minimum standards for procedures in Member States for granting and withdrawing refugee status.[142] See also the Directive on minimum standards for the qualification and status of third-country nationals as stateless persons; as refugees or as persons who otherwise need international protection and the content of the protection granted.[143]

As for *immigration*,[144] the TFEU provides for the development of a "common immigration policy aimed at ensuring, at all stages, the efficient management of migration flows, fair treatment of third-country nationals residing legally in Member States, and the prevention of, and enhanced measures to combat, illegal immigration and trafficking in human beings". Measures are to be adopted by Parliament and Council, acting in accordance with the ordinary legislative procedure,[145] in the following areas:

- conditions of entry and residence and standards on the issue of long-term visas and residence permits; Member States remain free to determine volumes of admission of third-country nationals[146];
- the definition of the rights of third-country nationals residing legally in the Member States and their integration[147] therein;
- illegal immigration and unauthorised residence, including removal and repatriation[148]; for the latter, the Union may conclude agreements with third countries[149]; a directive provides for minimum standards on sanctions and measures against employers of illegally staying third-country nationals[150];
- combating trafficking in persons, especially women and children.[151]

---

[140] Regulation 439/10 [2010] O.J. L132/11.

[141] Decision 573/07 [2007] O.J. L144/1, endowed with €628 million for the period 2007–2013; amended [2010] O.J. L129/1 removing funding for certain actions, etc.

[142] Directive 2005/85 [2005] O.J. L326/13.

[143] Directive 2004/83 [2004] O.J. L304/12. See *Elgafaji* (C-465/07) [2009] E.C.R. I-921 and *Aydin Salahadin and others* (Joined Cases C-175/08, etc.) [2010] E.C.R. I-1493 minimum standards for determining who qualifies for refugee status.

[144] Art.79 TFEU.

[145] Art.294 TFEU.

[146] Art.79(5) TFEU.

[147] For this purpose an Integration Fund endowed with €825 million for the period 2007–2013 was established as part of the general programme "Solidarity and Management of Migration Flows" [2007] O.J. L168/18 amended [2013] O.J. L82/1.

[148] See also the *External Borders Fund* [2007] O.J. L144/22 amended [2013] O.J. L82/6.

[149] Art.79(3) TFEU.

[150] Directive 2009/52 [2009] O.J. L168/24.

[151] See Decision of December 8, 2000 on the signing, on behalf of the Union, of the UN Convention against trans-national organised crime and its Protocol on combating trafficking in persons, especially women and children, and the smuggling of migrants by land, air and sea [2000] O.J. L30/44.

The above policies must be governed by the principle of solidarity and fair sharing of responsibilities, including its financial implications,[152] between Member States.

A General Programme "Solidarity and Management of Migration Flows" was, as already indicated, set up for this purpose.[153] It provides for a fair share of responsibility between Member States as concerns the financial burden arising from the introduction of an integrated management of the external borders of Member States and the implementation of common policies on asylum and immigration.

16–17

In 2008 the Council established a European Migration Network (EMN)[154]; the objective is to meet the information needs of Community institutions and the Member States on migration and asylum by providing up-to-date, objective reliable and comparable information with a view to supporting policymaking in the Union and in 2011 an immigration liaison officers' network.[155]

A European Fund for the Integration of third-country nationals for the period 2007–2013 was established in 2007, as part of the of the General Programme "Solidarity and Management of Migration Flows", mentioned above.[156]

A *European Return Fund* was established for the period 2008–2013 as part of the general programme "Solidarity and Management of Migration Flows": endowed with €676 million[157]. A Directive provides for common standards and procedures in Member States for returning illegally staying third-country nationals.[158]

4. JUDICIAL CO-OPERATION IN CIVIL AND COMMERCIAL MATTERS[159]

Of great lasting importance are the measures provided for in the TFEU on judicial co-operation in civil matters having cross-border implications. These measures include:

16–18

- a regulation on the mutual recognition and enforcement between Member States of judgments in civil and commercial matters.[160] The regulation replaces the Brussels Convention of 1968 and is known as Brussels 1;

---

[152] See the establishment of a European Refugee Fund [2007] O.J. L144/1 with later amendments.

[153] COM(2005) 123 final (not published in the O.J.).

[154] Decision 2008/381 [2008] O.J. L131/7.

[155] Regulation 493/11 [2011] O.J. L141/13.

[156] Decision 435/07 and Decision 2008/457 laying down rules for the implementation of Decision 435/07, amended [2009] O.J. L179/64.

[157] Decision 575/07 [2007] O.J. L144/45; see Decision 2008/458, amended [2011] O.J. L77/32, laying down rules for the implementation of Decision 575/07.

[158] [2008] O.J. L348/98. When told to leave and the foreign individual stays on illegally, that person should not, according to the Court, be put in prison *Hassen El Dridi* (C-61/11 PPU) [2011] E.C.R. I-3015.

[159] Art.81 TFEU.

[160] Regulation 44/2001 [2001] O.J. L12/1, modified [2012] O.J. L50/3. The main rule as concerns jurisdiction is found in Art.2 which provides that the courts of the Member States, on whose territory the defendant resides, are competent. The Regulation does not apply to Denmark that stands outside the co-operation in Title V TFEU; cf. the Protocol on the position of Denmark. Here, as in other

- the cross-border service of judicial and extra-judicial documents[161]; a manual of receiving agencies and a glossary of documents that may be served was adopted[162];
- the compatibility of the rules applicable in the Member States concerning conflict of laws and of jurisdiction;
- co-operation in the taking of evidence[163]; see Council Framework Decision on the execution in the European Union of orders freezing property or evidence[164];
- effective access to justice (this includes legal aid): see Council Directive,[165] which aims at improving access to justice in cross-border disputes by establishing common rules relating to legal aid for such disputes; the Commission established a standard form for legal aid applications;
- establishment of a *European Judicial Network* in civil and commercial matters[166];

---

matters, Denmark, however, participates through concluding an international agreement with the Union; see Decision 2009/430 concerning the conclusion of the Convention on jurisdiction and the recognition and enforcement of judgments in civil and commercial matters [2009] O.J. L147/1. Iceland, Norway and Switzerland participate also through an international agreement. The Regulation and the previous Brussels Convention have on numerous occasions been interpreted by the Court of Justice, see for instance *Color Drack* (C-386/05) [2007] E.C.R. I-3699 for an interpretation of Art.5(3)(b) when there are several places of delivery of a good within a single Member State: the principal place of delivery, *FBTO* (C-463/06) [2007] E.C.R. I-11321: Art.9 an injured party may bring an action directly against the insurer before the court in the Member State where the party is domiciled provided the insurer is domiciled in a Member State; and *Freeport* (C-98/06) [2007] E.C.R. I-8219: Art.6, point 1 can be applied although the claims introduced against several defendants have different legal bases. See also *ASML* (C-283/05) [2007] E.C.R.I-12041, concerning the possibility of a defendant to proceed against a default judgment, Art.34(2). See *Hasset and Doherty* (C-372/07) [2008] E.C.R. I-7403, interpretation of Art.22, point 2, of the Regulation *Allianz* (C-185/07) [2009] E.C.R. I-663: it is incompatible with the Regulation for a court of a Member State to make an order to restrain a person from proceeding before the court of another Member State on the ground that it would be contrary to an arbitration agreement. In *Falco* (C-533/07) [2009] E.C.R. I-3327, the Court found that a contract whereby the exploitation of an IPR is conceded against payment is not a service contract and in order to determine the competent jurisdiction, refers to the case law concerning Art.5(1) of the Convention of September 27, 1968. With regard to Art.43(1) see *Draka NK Cables* (C-167/08) [2009] E.C.R. I-3477. For interpretation of Art.5(1)(b) first indent see *Electrosteel Europe SA* (C-87/10) Court of the place of performance of the contractual obligation, sale of goods, place of delivery, contract containing the clause "Delivery EX Works": place where the purchaser has obtained actual power of disposal. Enforcement/grounds for refusing enforcement: *Prism Investment BV* (C-139/10), judgment of October 13, 2011, not yet reported.

[161] Regulation 1348/2000 [2000] O.J. L160/37, replaced by Regulation 1393/07 on the service in the Member State of judicial and extrajudicial documents in civil and commercial matters [2007] O.J. L324/79 amended [2009] O.J. L292/48; Commission Decision 2001/781 adopting a manual of receiving agencies and a glossary of documents that may be served in the Member State [2008] O.J. L173/17; see *Leffler* (C-443/03) [2005] E.C.R. I–9611 on the consequences of the absence of a translation and *Weiss and Partner* (C-14/07) [2008] E.C.R. I-3367, concerning the language of the notification.

[162] Decision 2007/500 [2007] O.J. L185/24.

[163] Regulation 1206/2001 [2001] O.J. L 174/1 amended [2008] O.J. L304/8 and [2009] O.J. L351/6.

[164] Framework Decision 2003/577 [2003] O.J. L196/45.

[165] Directive 2003/8 [2003] O.J. L26/41.

[166] Decision 2001/470 [2001] O.J. L174/25, amended [2009] O.J. L168/35. Its purpose is to improve, simplify and expedite effective judicial co-operation between the Member State (with the exception of Denmark), through the establishment of contact points, etc.

- eliminating obstacles to the good functioning of civil proceedings, if necessary by promoting the compatibility of the rules on civil procedure applicable in the Member States;
- the development of alternative methods of dispute settlement;
- support for the training of judiciary and judicial staff;
- mediation in civil and commercial matters[167];
- jurisdiction, applicable law, recognition and enforcement of decisions and co-operation in matters relating to maintenance obligations[168]; the regulation applies to maintenance obligations arising from a family relationship, parentage, marriage or affinity.

Before the Treaty of Lisbon became applicable several measures had already been taken by the Union institution concerning judicial co-operation in civil matters; they concern, among others: **16–19**

- jurisdiction and the recognition and enforcement of judgments in matrimonial matters and in matters of parental responsibility.[169] See below, in this respect, the 1996 Hague Convention on parental responsibility and protection of children[170];
- a European Enforcement Order for uncontested claim[171];
- Convention on the law applicable to contractual obligations, Rome Convention, (Rome I); a regulation of 2008[172] replaced the Rome Convention in the Member States, it concerns mainly which law is applicable to the contract;

---

[167] Directive 2008/52 [2008] O.J. L136/3.

[168] Regulation 4/2009 [2009] O.J. L7/1 with later amendments.

[169] Regulation 1347/2000 [2000] O.J. L160/19 replaced by Regulation 2201/2003 [2003] O.J. L338/1 with later amendments. The Regulation is commonly referred to as "Brussels 2". The Regulation has on numerous occasions been interpreted by the Court of Justice, see for instance *Sundelind Lopez* (C-68/07) [2007] E.C.R. I-10403, jurisdiction of Member State; (C-435/06) [2007] E.C.R. I-10106, interpretation of Art.1(1) on the meaning of "civil matters"; *PPU, Inga Rinau* (C-195/08) [2008] E.C.R. I-5271, opposition to recognition of judgment; *Sundelind Lopez* (C-68/07) [2007] E.C.R. I-10403, competence in divorce matters; *C* (C-435/06) [2007] E.C.R. I-10141, a single decision ordering a child to be taken into care is covered by the term "civil matters"; in this case the regulation in question applies *ratione temporis*; *A.*(C-523/07) [2009] E.C.R. I-2805: interpreting "civil matter", "habitual residence", conditions for deciding a "protective measure" (taking into care of children) and obligation for the national court to inform the court of another Member State having jurisdiction. Also *Purrucker* (C-256/09) [2010] E.C.R. I-7452. Arts 21 et seq. do not apply to provisional measures relating to rights of custody, falling within the scope of Arts 21 and following of Regulation 2201/2003. *J.McB. v L.E.* (C-400/10 PPU) [2010] E.C.R. I-10381: children whose parents are not married, father's right of custody, interpretation of "right of custody", general principles of law and Charter of Fundamental Rights; concept of "habitual residence" of an infant and concept of "right of custody" *Mercredi* (C-497/10) [2010] E.C.R. I-14309; power of the requested court to refuse enforcement *Zarraga* (C-491/10) [2010] E.C.R. I-14247.

[170] Decision 2003/93 [2003] O.J. L48/1.The principle concerning the rights of children was laid down by Art.24 of the European Charter of fundamental rights. See approval of the Hague Convention of 23.11.07 on the International Recovery of Child Support and other Forms of Family Maintenance [2011] O.J. L192/39.

[171] Regulation 805/2004 [2004] O.J. L143/15, modified [2005] O.J. L300/6, [2007] O.J. L174/22 and [2008] O.J. L304/80, based on Art.81 TFEU. The same enforcement can be obtained under Regulation 44/2001 concerning jurisdiction and enforcement of judgments in civil and commercial matters [2001] O.J. L12/1, amended [2012] O.J. L50/3.

[172] Regulation 593/08 [2008] O.J. L177/6 amended [2009] O.J. L309/87.

- European contract law[173];
- insolvency proceeding[174];
- creation of a European order for payment procedure[175];
- establishment of a European Small Claims Procedure[176]; and
- law applicable to non-contractual obligations (Rome II).[177]

16–20   The implementation of the rules and measures described above also have their exceptions. They concern, for instance, the responsibility incumbent upon Member States with regard to maintenance of law and order and the safeguarding of internal security.[178]

See also, with regard to civil matters, the Hague Programme 2005–2010[179] that lists 10 key areas for priority action:

- development of policies enhancing citizenship, monitoring and promoting respect for fundamental rights;
- fight against terrorism: prevention, preparedness and response;
- migration management: developing a common EU immigration policy and countering illegal migration;
- internal and external borders, visas: integrated management of external borders and a common visa policy;
- a common asylum policy;
- maximising the positive impact of migration on society and economy;
- privacy and security in sharing information;
- fight against organised crime[180] effective access to justice for all and enforcement of judgments; and
- reviewing the effectiveness of policies and financial instruments in meeting the objectives of freedom, security and justice.

---

[173] Communication from the Commission [2001] O.J. C255/1. See also Decision on the accession of the Union to the Hague Conference on Private International Law [2006] O.J. L297/3.

[174] Regulation 1346/2000 [2000] O.J. L160/1, see O.J. L121/1, amending lists of insolvency proceedings, winding-up proceedings and liquidators of annexes A, B and C, amended [2011] O.J. L160/52 Regulation 681/07 [2007] O.J. L159/1. See *Eurofood* (C-341/04) [2006] E.C.R. I-3813: interpreting Arts 3 and 16. *Seagon* (C-339/07) [2009] E.C.R. I-767: According to Art.3(1) the court of a Member State within which insolvency proceedings have been opened has jurisdiction to decide an action to set a transaction aside brought against a person registered in another Member State.

[175] Regulation 1896/2006 [2006] O.J. L399/1 amended [2012] O.J. L283/1.

[176] Regulation 861/07 [2007] O.J. L199/1.

[177] Regulation 864/07 [2007] O.J. L199/40.

[178] Art.72 TFEU.

[179] [2005] O.J. L198/1.

[180] See Framework Decision 2008/841 on the fight against organised crime [2008] O.J. L300/42.

A 2002 regulation establishes a general framework for Union activities to facilitate the implementation of judicial co-operation in civil matters.[181] The plans to develop electronically Justice (*e-Justice*) would greatly facilitate the access to justice.[182]

In 2010, a Council Decision authorised enhanced co-operation in the area of the law applicable to divorce and legal separation[183], it was later implemented.[184]

5. JUDICIAL CO-OPERATION IN CRIMINAL MATTERS[185]

Judicial co-operation is based on the principle of mutual recognition of judgments and judicial decisions and includes the approximation of the laws and regulations of the Member States in the relevant areas. Parliament and the Council, acting in accordance with the ordinary legislative procedure[186] are to adopt measures to:

16–21

- lay down rules and procedures for ensuring recognition throughout the Union of all forms of judgments and judicial decisions[187]; see the Framework Decision on the application of the principle of mutual recognition to judgments in criminal matters imposing custodial sentences or measures involving deprivation of liberty for the purpose of their enforcement in the European Union and a Framework Decision of 2008 on taking account of convictions in the Member States in the course of new criminal proceedings[188]; recognition of decisions rendered in the absence of the person concerned at the trial[189];
- prevent and settle conflicts of jurisdiction between Member States;
- support the training of judiciary and judicial staff; and
- facilitate co-operation between judicial or equivalent authorities of the Member States in relation to proceedings in criminal matters and the enforcement of decisions.

Parliament and Council may also, in the same way, adopt directives establishing minimum rules concerning: mutual admissibility of evidence; the

---

[181] [2002] O.J. L115/1. See date of entry into force of the Convention on jurisdiction and recognition and enforcement of judgments in civil and commercial matters, signed in Lugano on October 30, 2007 [2011] O.J. L138/1.

[182] Multi-annual European E-Justice action plan 2009–2013 [2009] O.J. C75/1. See also "E-Justice in Europe": l'Observateur de Bruxelles July 2008, p.12; *http://www.dbfbruxelles.eu* [accessed August 23, 2013].

[183] [2010] O.J. L189/12.

[184] [2010] O.J. L343/10.

[185] Arts 82–86 TFEU. See *Advocaten voor de Wereld* (C-303/05) [2007] E.C.R. I-3633, concerning, among others, the European arrest warrant and Framework Decision 2002/584.

[186] Art.294 TFEU.

[187] See Framework Decision 2008/67 on taking account of convictions in the Member States of the European Union in the course of new criminal proceedings [2008] O.J. L220/32 and Framework Decision 2008/909 [2008] O.J. L327/27 amended [2009] O.J. L81/24. See also Directive 2010/64 on the right to interpretation and translation in criminal proceedings and proceedings for the execution of the European arrest warrant: [2010] O.J. L280/1.

[188] Framework Decision 2008/675 [2008] O.J. L220/32. Member States must take the necessary implementing measures before August 15, 2010.

[189] Framework Decision 2009/299 [2009] O.J. L81/24.

rights of individuals in criminal procedure; the rights of victims of crime[190]; and any other specific aspects of criminal procedure. In case of disagreement within the Council concerning these rules, they shall be referred to the European Council.[191]

16–22   Furthermore, Parliament and the Council can, in the same way, adopt directives concerning the definition of criminal offences and sanctions in the areas of particularly serious crimes with a cross-border dimension resulting from the nature and the impact of such offences. Those areas of crimes are the following: terrorism; trafficking in human beings and sexual exploitation of woman and children[192]; illicit drug trafficking[193]; and illicit arms trafficking; money laundering; corruption; counterfeiting of means of payment; computer crime; and organised crime.

In case of disagreement within the Council, reference is to be made to the European Council.[194] Parliament and the Council may establish measures to promote and support the action of Member States in the field of crime prevention.[195]

The *Daphne III Programme* to combat violence against children, young people and women and to protect victims and groups at risk was established for the period 2007–2013 with a total budget of €30 million.[196] The funds are used to support activities submitted to and selected by the Commission.[197]

The *European Protection Order*: the Stockholm Programme[198] provided for special protection measures of crime victims, which should be effective within the Union. Consequently, rules were established allowing judicial or equivalent authorities in a Member State, in which a protection measure has been adopted with a view to protect a person against a criminal act by another person, to issue a European Protection Order, enabling an authority in another Member State to continue the protection.[199]

16–23   *Eurojust* (European Body for the Enhancement of Judicial Co-operation)[200] was set up by the Council in 2002 to improve co-operation between competent authorities.

---

[190] See Directive 2012/29 establishing minimum standards on the rights, support and protection of victims of crime and *Katz* (C-404/07) [2008] E.C.R. I-7607, Arts 2 and 3 do not oblige the national judge to allow the victim to be heard as witness but must be authorised to make a deposition.

[191] Art.82(3) TFEU.

[192] See Decision 779/07 establishing for the period 2007–2013 a specific programme to prevent and combat violence against children, young people and women and to protect victims and groups at risk (Daphne III programme) as part of the general programme "Fundamental Rights and Justice" [2007] O.J. L173/19.

[193] See European Union action plan for the fight against drugs and *http://www.consilium.europa.eu/uedocs/cms_Data/docs/pressdata/en/jha/125709.pdf* [accessed August 23, 2013]. In 2012, the European Council endorsed the EU Drug Strategy (2013-2020); see EU Drugs Action Plan (2009–2012) [2008] O.J. C326/7. See also Council Framework Decision 2004/757 laying down minimum provisions on the constituent elements of criminal acts and penalties in the field of drug trafficking [2004] O.J. L335/8.

[194] Art.83(3) TFEU.

[195] Art.84 TFEU.

[196] Decision 779/07 [2007] O.J. L173/19.

[197] Art.67 TFEU.

[198] [2010] O.J. C115/1.

[199] [2011] O.J. L338/2.

[200] See Ch.13: Decentralised Agencies and Bodies of the Union.

Its mission is to support and strengthen co-operation and co-ordination between national investigating and prosecuting authorities in relation to serious crime affecting two or more Member States or requiring a prosecution on common bases, on the basis of operations conducted and information supplied by Member States' authorities and by Eurojust. It is for Parliament and Council to determine, in accordance with the ordinary legislative procedure,[201] Eurojust's structure, operation, field of action and tasks. The latter include: the initiation of criminal investigations, particularly those relating to offences against the financial interests of the Union; the co-ordination of investigations and prosecutions; and the strengthening of judicial co-operation, including by resolution of conflicts of jurisdiction and by close co-operation with the European Judicial Network.[202]

A *European Public Prosecutor's Office* from Eurojust may be established in order to combat crimes affecting the financial interests of the Union.[203] It shall be established by regulation from the Council acting unanimously after obtaining the consent of Parliament. It shall be responsible for investigating, prosecuting and bringing to judgment, where appropriate in liaison with Europol,[204] the perpetrators of, and accomplices in, offences against the Union's financial interests. This task may be extended to include serious crime having a cross-border dimension.[205]

It might be interesting to note that "provisions on police [below] and judicial co-operation in criminal matters" constituted Title VI of the Treaty on European Union and that the Court agreed with the GC in that no action for damages are possible under that Title.[206]

6. THE EUROPEAN CASE LAW IDENTIFIER (ECLI)

Member States were invited to introduce, on a voluntary basis at the national level, the European Case Law Identifier and a minimum set of uniform metadata for case law. It would apply to all decisions rendered by all the national courts and tribunals and provide all such decisions published on public websites with a minimum set of metadata, as provided in the Council's Conclusions.[207]

16–24

7. POLICE CO-OPERATION

The Union is to establish police co-operation involving all the Member States' competent authorities, including police, customs and other specialised law enforcement services in relation to the prevention, detection and investigation of criminal offences.[208] Parliament and the Council, acting in accordance with the

16–25

---

[201] Art.294 TFEU.

[202] European Judicial Network in civil and commercial matters [2008] O.J. L348/130.

[203] Art.86 TFEU. The Commission made a proposal in July 2013.

[204] See Ch.13: Decentralised Agencies and Bodies of the Union.

[205] Art.86(4) TFEU.

[206] *Gestores Pro Amnistia E.A. v Council* (C-354/04 P) [2007] E.C.R. I-1579.

[207] [2011] O.J. C127/1.

[208] Art.87 TFEU.

ordinary legislative procedure,[209] may establish measures concerning the collection, storage, processing, analysis and exchange of relevant information, support for the training of staff and co-operation on the exchange of staff, on equipment and on research into crime-detection, and common investigative techniques in relation to the detection of serious forms of organised crime. The Council, acting in accordance with a special legislative procedure,[210] may establish measures concerning operational co-operation between national authorities.[211]

The following were set up:

- a framework for the exchange of liaison magistrates[212];
- a network of contact points in respect of people responsible for genocide and crimes against humanity[213];
- the *European arrest warrant* that, de facto, replaces the lengthy and difficult extradition procedure[214];
- surrender of procedures between Member State[215];
- mutual recognition of financial penalties[216];
- convention on driving disqualification[217];
- combating cross-border vehicle crime.[218]

In 2002, the Council established a framework programme on police and judicial co-operation in criminal matters (AGIS).[219]

---

[209] Art.294 TFEU.

[210] Art.289(2) TFEU.

[211] Art.87(3) TFEU.

[212] Joint Action 96/277/JHA [1996] O.J. L105/1.

[213] Decision 2002/494/JHA [2002] O.J. L167/1. See also: the investigation and prosecution of genocide, crimes against humanity and war crimes, Decision 2003/535/JHA [2003] O.J. L118/12; and network of contact points in respect of persons responsible for genocide and crimes against humanity, Decision 2002/494/JHA [2002] O.J. L167/1.

[214] Framework Decision 2002/584/JHA on the European arrest warrant and the surrender procedure between Member States [2002] O.J. L190/1 amended [2009] O.J. L81/24, thereby enhancing the procedural rights of persons subject to criminal proceedings and fostering the application of the principle of mutual recognition to decisions rendered in the absence of the person concerned at the trial, amended Decision 2009/299 [2009] O.J. L81/24. See (urgent procedure!) *Santesteban* (C-296/08 PPU) [2008] E.C.R. I-6307: the decision is only applicable for facts committed after the date indicated by the relevant Member State in a declaration provided for in Art.32 of the Decision, see, for example, Italy's declaration [2009] O.J. L97/26. For the interpretation of the notion "staying" in a given Member State see *Kozlowski* (C-66/08) [2008] E.C.R. I-6041; for a definition of "same acts" see *Mantello* (C-261/09) [2010] E.C.R. I-11477. See report from the Commission on the implementation since 2007 of Decision 2002/494, published on 11 April 2011.

[215] Framework Decision 2002/584/JHA (quoted above). For an interpretation of Art.4,6, European arrest warrant, see *Kozlowski* (C-66/08) [2008] E.C.R. I-6041. For non-execution of arrest warrant see *Wolfzenburg* (C-123/08) E.C.R. I-9621 and for the possibility for the executing judicial authority to refuse to execute a European arrest warrant and a definition of "same acts": *Mantello* (C-261/09) [2010] E.C.R. I-11477.

[216] Framework Decision 2005/214/JHA of February 24, 2005 amended Decision 2009/299 [2009] O.J. L 2009/81.

[217] Convention [1998] O.J. C216/1.

[218] Decision 2004/919 [2004] O.J. L389/28.

[219] [2002] O.J. L203/5.

All Member States signed the 1959 European Convention on Mutual **16–26** Assistance in Criminal Matters.[220] The Convention regulates mutual assistance in criminal matters in a fast and efficient manner compatible with the basic principles of national laws, and in compliance with the individual rights and principles of the European Convention, signed in Rome in 1950. A network of judicial contact points was set up[221] under the name "European Judicial Network"[222]; those contact points must be active intermediaries with the task of facilitating judicial co-operation between Member States. See also a 2008 decision on the European evidence warrant for the purpose of obtaining objects, documents and data for use in proceeding in criminal matters.[223]

The fight against *terrorism* also became an important preoccupation for the Union, and the Council, in consultation with Parliament, adopted a Framework Decision on combating terrorism,[224] a common position on the application of specific measures to combat terrorism,[225] a decision on specific restrictive measures directed against certain persons and entities with a view of combating terrorism,[226] a decision establishing a mechanism for evaluating national legal provisions relating to the fight. See also specific restrictive measures directed against certain persons and entities with a view of combating terrorism.[227]

The provisions on Police and Judicial Co-operation in Criminal Matters (TFEU Title V) fall under the jurisdiction of the Court of Justice.

FURTHER READING

Anja Wiesbrock, *Legal Migration to the European Union* (Martinus Nijhoff **16–27** Publishers, 2010).

Anne Pieter Van der Mei, *Free Movement of Persons within the European Community: Cross-border access to public benefits* (Hart Publishing, 2003).

Carlier & Guild, *The Future of Free Movement of Persons in the EU* (Bruylant, 2006).

Joanna Apap, *Freedom of movement of persons* (Kluwer International 2002).

Peter J. van Krieken, *The Consolidated Asylum and Migration Acquis. The EU Directives in an Expanded Europe* (T.M.C. Asser Press by Cambridge University Press, 2004).

Robin White, *Workers, Establishment and Services in the European Union* (Oxford University Press, 2004).

---

[220] Council Act adopted in accordance with Art.34 EU (now repealed) [2000] O.J. C197/3. See Protocol providing additional measures for the purpose of the fight against crime, including organised crime, money laundering and financial crime; it concerns information on bank accounts held by persons subject to criminal investigation, on banking transactions, fiscal offences, etc. [2001] O.J. C326/1.

[221] Joint Action 98/428 [1998] O.J. L191/4.

[222] Decision 2008/976 [2008] O.J. L348/130.

[223] Decision 2008/978 [2008] O.J. L350/72.

[224] [2002] O.J. L164/3 amended [2008] O.J. L330/21.

[225] Common Position 2007/448 updating Common Position 2001/931 on the application of specific measures to combat terrorism [2007] O.J. L169/69.

[226] [2005] O.J. L144/59.

[227] [2011] O.J. L343/10.

Rogers & Scannell, *Free Movement of Persons in the Enlarged European Union* (Sweet & Maxwell, 2012).

Steve Peers, "EU Criminal Law and the Treaty of Lisbon", (2008) E.L.R. 507.

Steve Peers, *EU immigration and asylum law: text and commentary* (Leiden, 2012).

CHAPTER 17

Freedom of Establishment/Company Law

1. INTRODUCTION

This chapter first presents the Treaty rules on freedom of establishment. As is the case with the other freedoms, the freedom of establishment entails a ban on discrimination and other restrictions and the scope of the ban in the Treaty has been determined by case law. As with the other freedoms, the ban is directly applicable.[1] It does not apply in purely internal situations. The case law concerning the freedom of establishment has to a large extent been codified by the general Services Directive.[2] The Directive does not only deal with free movement of services, but also with freedom of establishment. The Directive will also be presented below—after the presentation of the Treaty provisions, as otherwise the Directive makes difficult reading. In addition, the Directive excludes from its scope of application various sectors of the economy and obstacles to the freedom of establishment in those sectors will continue to have to be assessed on the basis of the provisions of the Treaty.

Obstacles to the freedom of establishment may result from national rules concerning the qualifications needed to exercise a profession. For the realisation of the freedom of establishment it is important to harmonise such rules or to provide for mutual recognition of professional qualifications. The matter is now mainly governed by one directive, generally referred to as the General Directive on Recognition of Professional Qualifications.[3] The main elements of the Directive are presented below.

This chapter also gives an overview of the harmonisation of company law. Most economic activity is carried out through companies and the Union has considered it important that there is a level playing field, i.e. that the same rules apply as concerns matters such as capital and annual accounts. The harmonised rules facilitate the cross-border movement of companies. The last section concerns European forms of legal persons.

17–01

---

[1] *Reyners* (2/74) [1974] E.C.R. 631.
[2] Directive 2006/123 [2006] O.J. L376.
[3] Directive 2005/36 [2005] O.J. L255.

2.   FREEDOM OF ESTABLISHMENT

17–02   The Treaty provides that restrictions on the freedom of establishment of nationals in the territory of another Member State are prohibited; the prohibition also applies to restrictions on the setting-up of agencies, branches or subsidiaries by nationals of a Member State established in the territory of another Member State. The freedom includes the right to take up and pursue activities as self-employed persons and to set up and manage undertakings on the same conditions that apply to nationals of the Member State of establishment.[4] Within the meaning of the Treaty "establishment" is a broad notion, allowing a national of a Member State to participate, on a stable and continuous basis, in the economic life of another Member State and to profit therefrom, thus contributing to economic and social interpretation within the Union in the sphere of activities as self-employed persons.[5]

The crucial term to delimit the freedom of establishment from the free movement of workers is "self-employed". Free movement of workers applies to employees while freedom of establishment applies to self-employed persons.[6] The crucial terms to delimit freedom of establishment from free movement of services are "stable and continuous"; if a person, be it legal or natural (as a self-employed), wants to exercise its activity in another Member State only on a temporary basis, the rules concerning free movement of services apply. The temporary nature of the activities has to be determined in the light of the duration of the provision of the services, the regularity, periodicity or continuity.[7] The temporary nature thus can vary in function of the individual circumstances of a case; for instance, in the construction sector, a building firm may be present for years in another Member State—for instance for the construction of a large stadium—and still fall within the scope of the provisions on free movement of services.[8] As concerns the free movement of capital, there is also a delimitation to be made. The Treaty rules on free movement of capital cover cross-border purchases of shares in a company. If the share purchase confers a definite influence over the company's decisions and thus allows the shareholder to determine its activities, the cross-border purchase falls within the scope of freedom of establishment.[9] As the said freedoms largely converge, it will for the

---

[4] Art.49 TFEU. The right of establishment includes freedom to set up and maintain, subject to observance of the professional rules of conduct, more than one place of work within the Union. *Ordre des Avocats du Barreau de Paris v Klopp* (107/83) [1984] E.C.R. 2971 para. 10; [1985] 1 C.M.L.R. 99.

[5] *Gebhard* (C-55/94) [1995] E.C.R. I-4165, para.25.

[6] That free movement of workers applies to workers does not hinder that a company, as employer, may invoke the freedom; for instance, if a national rule provides that the director of a company must be resident in the State, the company may invoke that the rule is a restriction to free movement of workers, see *Clean-car* (C-350/96) [1998] E.C.R. I-2521.

[7] *Gebhard* (quoted above, fn.5) para.27.

[8] *Schnitzer* (C-215/01) [2003] E.C.R. I-14847, para.30. The permanent presence in a Member State does not require a legal person from another Member State to set up a branch in the first Member State. A permanent presence may follow from simply having "an office managed by the undertaking's own staff" or a "person who is independent but authorized to act on a permanent basis for the undertaking", see *Commission v Germany (Insurance)* (205/84) [1986] E.C.R. 3755, para.21.

[9] *Baars* (C-251/98) [2000] E.C.R. I-2787, para.21-22.

assessment of an individual case often not matter whether one or another freedom applies; however, it may matter in some instances, as will appear from below.

Those that benefit from freedom of establishment are both physical and legal persons. The physical persons are nationals of a Member State.[10] Who is a national of a Member State is determined by that State, and other Member States have to accept that; other States cannot question the citizenship that a Member State has conferred upon a person.[11] As concerns legal persons, the Treaty provides that companies or firms formed in accordance with the law of a Member State and having their registered office, central administration or principal place of business within the Union shall be treated in the same way as natural persons who are nationals of Member State.[12] Once these two conditions are fulfilled, the undertaking establishing itself in another Member State enjoys in that State all the rights normally exercised by undertakings, such as the possibility to appear in court[13] and to acquire land and buildings.[14] The Treaty adds that "companies or firms" means companies or firms constituted under civil or commercial law, including co-operative societies, and other legal persons governed by public or private law, save for those which are non-profit making.[15]

The measures that can be caught by the ban on restrictions to the freedom to establishment are "all measures which prohibit, impede or render less attractive the exercise of that freedom".[16] The grounds on which Member States can justify restrictions are those enumerated in the Treaty, namely exercise of public authority, public policy, public security and public health, and the imperative requirements in the general interest that the Court recognises in its case law, such as for instance the protection of consumers or the environment. **17–03**

In its case law the Court has dealt with a wide variety of national measures, for instance: tax rules,[17] industrial action,[18] rules prohibiting that on sight bank accounts carry interests,[19] rules reserving the offering of gambling services to a State monopoly,[20] and rules reserving the right to carry out certain examinations to ophthalmologists.[21] Restrictions must comply with the proportionality principle to be lawful. If the Court, in a preliminary case, disposes of all the

---

[10] The national of a Member State does not necessarily mean a national from another Member State. A national of one Member State may invoke freedom of establishment against his own Member State, for instance when the State puts obstacles to its nationals leaving the State.

[11] *Micheletti* (C-369/90) [1992] E.C.R. I-4239. See also *Zhu and Chen* (C-200/02) [2004] E.C.R. I-9925, para.37. The Union rules on citizenship set some wide limits on Member States' withdrawal of citizenship, as loss of a Member State nationality also entails loss of Union citizenship, see *Rottman* (C-135/08) [2010] E.C.R. I-1449.

[12] Art.54(1) TFEU.

[13] *Überseering* (C-208/00) [2002] E.C.R. I–9919.

[14] Art.50(2)(e) TFEU.

[15] Art.54(2) TFEU.

[16] *Payroll and Others* (C-79/01) [2002] E.C.R. I-8923, para.26.

[17] *Cadbury Schweppes* (C-196/04) [2006] E.C.R. I-7995.

[18] *Viking Line* (C-438/05) [2007] E.C.R. I-10779.

[19] *Caixa Bank* (C-442/02) [2004] E.C.R. I-8960.

[20] *Zeturf* (C-212/08), judgment of June 30, 2011, not yet reported.

[21] *Mac Quen* (C-108/96) [2001] E.C.R. I-837.

elements to carry out the proportionality assessment, it will often do so[22]; if not, the Court will leave the proportionality assessment to be undertaken by the national referring court.[23]

The detailed rules on the right to enter and to remain in a Member State are laid down in Directive 2004/38 which is examined in Ch.16: The Free Movement of Persons.[24]

3.   THE SERVICES DIRECTIVE

17–04   The Services Directive was adopted in 2006. It seeks to lay down general rules to facilitate the exercise of the freedom of establishment and the free movement of services.[25] Although the Directive is general, many economic activities are excluded from its scope of application.[26] The activities excluded are governed by specific acts of secondary law and/or primary law.[27] Chapter II of the Directive is entitled "Administrative Simplification" and enacts notably an obligation for Member States to establish "points of single contact" where all procedures and formalities for providing a service can be completed,[28] and Members States shall ensure that this can be done by electronic means at a distance, i.e. over the Internet.[29] The provisions of Chapter II apply both to freedom of establishment and free movement of services.

Chapter III of the Services Directive concerns in particular freedom of establishment. The provisions concerning freedom of establishment involve two major deviations from what follows from the Treaty provisions and the case law developed in relation to those provisions. In the first place, in the area of freedom of establishment the Directive does not, contrary to the Treaty, require a cross-border link for its provisions to be applicable. In the second place, the Directive contains a list of national restrictions, in the terminology of the Directive, requirements, that are banned in all circumstances, i.e. those restrictions cannot at all be justified.[30]

17–05   The Chapter on freedom of establishment also contains provisions on authorisation requirements which are based on the case law that the Court has

---

[22] See for instance *Cadbury Schweppes* and *Caixa Bank* (quoted above, at fn.17 and fn.19 respectively).

[23] See for instance *Viking Line, Mac Quen* and *Zeturf* (quoted above, at fn.18, fn.21 and fn.20 respectively).

[24] It shall be noted that the entry of the staff of a company exercising its right to freedom of establishment is not limited to nationals of a Member State; this is particularly important for undertakings from third countries established in the Union, cf. Art.50(2)(f) TFEU.

[25] Art.1 of the Services Directive.

[26] Art.2 of the Services Directive.

[27] If the Services Directive conflicts with an act of secondary act, that act shall prevail, see Art.3 of the Services Directive.

[28] Art.6 of the Services Directive.

[29] Art.8 of the Services Directive.

[30] Art.14 of the Services Directive. The outlawed requirements are restrictions that generally have failed the proportionality test in the Court's case law. Requirements banned by Art.14 are for instance nationality requirements for the provider, his staff, persons holding the share capital or members of the provider's management or supervisory bodies. Art.14 surely fulfils the conditions for having direct effect.

developed on the basis of the Treaty.[31] The overall conditions that must be fulfilled for allowing a Member State to enact an authorisation scheme are:

a) The authorisation scheme does not discriminate against the provider in question.

b) The need for an authorisation scheme is justified by an "overriding reason relating to the public interest".[32]

c) The objective pursued cannot be attained by means of a less restrictive measure, in particular because an *a posteriori* inspection would take place too late to be genuinely effective.[33]

If an authorisation scheme meets those conditions and thus its existence as such is warranted, the individual procedures must still meet detailed conditions spelled out in the subsequent provisions of the Directive. Those conditions are in particular that the criteria in the authorisation procedure must be: non-discriminatory; justified by an overriding reason relating to the public interest; proportionate to that public interest objective; clear and unambiguous; objective; made public in advance; transparent and accessible; and the conditions for granting an authorisation must not duplicate requirements to which the person is already subject in his home Member State.[34]

If the authorities fail to reply to a request for authorisation within a reasonable period, the authorisation shall be deemed granted.[35]

4. PROFESSIONAL QUALIFICATIONS FOR NATURAL PERSONS

In each Member State there are regulated or unregulated professions. In one Member State the profession as real estate agent may for instance be unregulated, so that no particular professional qualifications are required for setting up a real estate agency or for working as a real estate agent. In another Member State the profession may be regulated, for instance by providing that only persons having fulfilled a certain education may exercise the profession. The reasons why a Member State may choose to regulate a profession vary greatly; mostly, however, it is to ensure a certain quality of the services to the benefit of those purchasing those services, be this consumers or businesses; for instance, hair-dressing may be a regulated profession because the national authorities have considered that anybody that goes to a hair-dresser should be able to trust that the person who will cut their hair has a minimum of professional qualifications. It also varies considerably from one Member State to another which professions are regulated,   **17–06**

---

[31] See for instance *Canal Satelite* (C-390/99) [2002] E.C.R. I-607 and *Hartlauer* (C-169/07) [2009] E.C.R. I-1721.

[32] The term is defined in Art.4(8) of the Services Directive and it refers both to the justification grounds, enumerated in the Treaty, and those developed in case law. Restrictions on freedom of establishment may be justified on all those grounds, while restrictions on free movement of services may be based only on a limited number of grounds, cf. Art.16 of the Services Directive.

[33] Art.9 of the Services Directive.

[34] Art.10 of the Services Directive.

[35] Detailed rules on this "deemed consent" are given in Art.13 of the Services Directive.

although there are commonalities, for instance the profession of a doctor is regulated in all Member States. The number of regulated professions also differs significantly between Member States; some States have few, some have many. In total it is estimated that there are around 800 regulated professions in the Union.

It does not require much imagination to see that national regulation of professions may cause an obstacle to free movement, not just to freedom of establishment, and it is a kind of obstacle that it may be difficult to deal with for the Court of Justice directly on the basis of the Treaty provisions; for instance, is two or three years of experience needed in order to exercise the profession of hair-dresser?

Before entering into how the Union has sought to address the problem that regulated professions poses, a few words on unregulated professions are warranted. If a Member State has not regulated a profession, it means that the access to the profession is free. It may be that in the Member State concerned there are educations that lead to the profession. However, as long as the access to the profession is free, there is no issue concerning access to the profession to be addressed by Union Law: nationals of other Member States can also access the profession at issue. As concerns regulated professions, the drafters of the original Rome Treaty were aware of the problem that they entail. The relevant Treaty provision in its current version provides that the Union legislator shall issue directives for the mutual recognition of diplomas, certificates and other evidence of formal qualifications and for the co-ordination of national provisions concerning the taking-up and pursuit of activities as self-employed persons.[36] The Treaty adds that as concerns medical and allied and pharmaceutical professions, the progressive abolition of restrictions shall be dependent upon co-ordination of the conditions for their exercise in the various Member States.[37]

17–07   During the 1960s and 70s a number of directives were adopted. The directives fall largely into two groups. Within the first group one finds a wide range of professions within commerce, industry, craft and retail.[38] The directives were of a limited scope in the sense that they would do away with flagrant and specific restrictions in the Member States or would for instance provide the minimum period during which a given profession had to have been exercised in order for the professional to exercise the profession in another Member State. The directives in this group were in 1999 brought together in one directive which established a general system for recognition of professional qualifications in the professions concerned.[39]

In the second group there were a few directives concerning particular professions such as nurses, doctors and veterinarians. The directives in this group sought to regulate in detail the requirements to be fulfilled for the regulated

---

[36] Art.53(1) TFEU.
[37] Art.53(2) TFEU.
[38] See for instance Council Directive 68/367 [1968] O.J. L260/16 concerning the attainment of freedom of establishment and freedom to provide services in respect of self-employed persons in the personal services sector; 1. restaurants, cafés, taverns and other drinking and eating places; 2. hotels, rooming houses, campus and other lodging places.
[39] Directive 1999/42 [1999] O.J. L201/77 establishing a mechanism for the recognition of qualifications in respect of the professional activities covered by the Directives on liberalisation and transitional measures and supplementary the general system for the recognition of qualifications.

profession.[40] By the late 1980s it was clear that this later harmonisation method was too cumbersome. Taking inspiration from the principle of mutual recognition, a general directive was adopted in 1989.[41] Instead of regulating in detail individual professions, the 1989 Directive laid down general rules for Member States' recognition of professional qualifications from other Member States. This 1989 Directive was later supplemented in 1992 concerning professions not covered by the 1989 Directive.[42] These two Directives were repealed in 2005 and their provisions incorporated into Directive 2005/36, into which the provisions of the harmonisation directives on individual professions, mentioned above, were also incorporated, along with the provisions of the above mentioned Directive of 1999 concerning professions in trade, industry, craft and retail.[43] Directive 2005/36 is currently being revised; however, the main components will remain relatively unaltered and they will be presented below.

A condition sine qua non for the applicability of the Directive is that the profession at issue is regulated in the Member State to which the person wants to move (the host State).[44] The Directive gives a detailed definition of "regulated profession". The core is: "a professional activity or group of professional activities, access to which, the pursuit of which, or one of the modes of pursuit of which is subject, directly or indirectly, by virtue of legislative, regulatory or administrative provisions to the possession of specific professional qualifications; in particular, the use of a professional title limited by legislative, regulatory or administrative provisions to holders of a given professional qualification shall constitute a mode of pursuit." "Professional qualifications" is in turn defined as qualifications attested by evidence of formal qualifications, an attestation of competence and/or professional experience. "Professional experience" is defined as "the actual and lawful pursuit of the profession concerned in a Member State." The Directive thus concerns access to regulated professions.[45]

17–08

The Directive applies not just in case of establishment, i.e. when a national of a Member State wants permanently to establish and exercise a regulated profession in a Member State other than the one in which the professional

---

[40] See for instance Council Directive 77/452 [1977] O.J. L176 concerning the mutual recognition of diplomas, certificates and other evidence of the formal qualifications of nurses responsible for general care, including measures to facilitate the effective exercise of the right of establishment and freedom to provide services and Council Directive 77/453 [1977] O.J. L176 concerning the coordination of provisions laid down by law, regulation or administrative action in respect of the activities of nurses responsible for general care.

[41] Directive 89/48 [1989] O.J. L19/16 on a general system for the recognition of higher-education diplomas awarded on completion of professional education and training of at least three years' duration.

[42] Directive 92/51 [1992] O.J. L209/25 on a second general system for the recognition of professional education and training to supplement Directive 89/48.

[43] Directive 2005/36 thus covers almost all professions. Free movement of services and freedom of establishment of practicing laws are though still governed by two separate directives, Directive 77/249 [1977] O.J. L78/17 to facilitate the effective exercise by lawyers of freedom to provide services, and Directive 98/5 [1998] O.J. L77/36 to facilitate practise of the profession of lawyer on a permanent basis in a Member State than that in which the qualification was obtained.

[44] Art.1 of the Directive.

[45] This must be distinguished from access to an economic activity. The distinction is not always easy to draw. In many Member States the access to the civil service is conditioned by successfully passing a competition for entering the civil service. Such a competition in itself does not make the profession a regulated profession within the meaning of the Directive, see *Rubino* (C-586/08) [2009] E.C.R. I-12013. See also *Penarroja* (Joined cases C-372/09 and C-373/09) [2011] E.C.R. 1785.

qualifications were obtained. The Directive also applies to workers that want permanently to move to another Member State to exercise a regulated profession; as well as to workers and self-employed persons who want temporarily or occasionally to exercise regulated professions in another Member State.[46] The Directive states that the temporary and occasional nature of an activity "shall be assessed case by case, in particular in relation to its duration, its frequency, its regularity and its continuity."[47] This must be understood as referring to the corresponding delimitation that the Court has made between freedom of establishment and free movement of services.

The Directive operates a major distinction between free movement of services[48] and freedom of establishment.[49] The terminology of the Directive thus differs from the habitual one, as free movement of services also covers the situation of the employee working temporarily or occasionally in another Member State[50]; and freedom of establishment covers also the situation of workers permanently exercising the regulated profession in another Member State.

17–09   The regime concerning free movement of services is relatively simple. The core provision establishes that a Member State shall not restrict, for any reason relating to professional qualifications, the free provision of services in another Member State:

- if the service provider is legally established in a Member State for the purpose of pursuing the same profession there (hereinafter referred to as the Member State of establishment),
- and where the service provider moves, if he has pursued that profession in the Member State of establishment for at least two years during the 10 years preceding the provision of services when the profession is not regulated in that Member State. The condition requiring two years' pursuit shall not apply when either the profession or the education and training leading to the profession is regulated.

The host Member State may require the service provider to make a declaration prior to providing any services including the details of any insurance cover or other means of personal or collective protection with regard to professional liability. The host Member State may also require that the first application be accompanied by certain documents listed in an annexe to the Directive. In case the host State requires pro forma registration with the competent professional association, this must occur automatically.

---

[46] Note that the Directive also applies in the following situation: a national from Member State A acquires his professional qualifications in Member state B after which he returns to Member State A, to exercise a regulated profession. The Directive applies to Member State A's recognition of the professional qualification obtained. See also from the time before the Directive, *Knoors* (115/78) [1979] E.C.R. 399.

[47] Art.5(2).

[48] Regulated in Title II of the Directive, Arts 5–9.

[49] Regulated in Title III of the Directive, Arts 10–52.

[50] Posted workers are thus also covered, i.e workers that are posted to another Member State within the provision of services, for instance workers of a construction firm in Member State A that are sent to Member State B to work there on a building that the firm is constructing, exercising its right to freedom to provide services.

The regime concerning freedom of establishment is more complex. It falls in to three parts, which in want of better names are commonly referred to as the "sectoral professions", "professions in trade, industry or business" and the "general system". The "sectoral professions" regroup the individual professions that were previously regulated by detailed harmonisation directives. The professions in question are: Doctors, nurses responsible for general care, dental practitioners, veterinary surgeons, pharmacists, midwifes and architects. For these professions the rule is that if the person holds the relevant qualifications enumerated in Annex V to the Directive, other Member States must automatically recognise them. If the person does not meet those requirements, he must seek recognition of his qualifications under the general system.

The professions in trade, industry and business are enumerated in Annex IV to **17–10** the Directive. They are for instance professions in hair-dressing, laundry services, hotels and restaurants. The rule for the Annex IV professions is that recognition is made on the basis of professional experience. The Directive operates a distinction according to in which kind of position the experience has been acquired, so that for instance recognition follows from three years' professional experience in a self-employed or managerial position, while more years of professional experience are required if the experience has been obtained as an employee. If the person has the experience required, recognition is also automatic. If the person does not have the experience, he must seek recognition under the general system.

The general system entails that the host Member State must evaluate the qualifications to see whether they meet the national requirements. If the host Member State finds the qualifications insufficient, it must suggest "compensation measures". A compensation measure is either that the person completes an adaptation period of up to three years or takes an aptitude test.[51]

The 2005 Directive provides for "common platforms" defined as a set of criteria of professional qualifications that are suitable for compensating substantial differences as mentioned above.[52] These platforms may be submitted to the Commission by Member States or by professional associations or organisations that are representative at national or European level. If these platforms are adopted, the host State shall waive the application of compensatory measures.[53]

5. LAWYERS IN PRIVATE PRACTISE

The legal profession, and particularly the right to practise as a lawyer, is regulated **17–11** in detail in the individual Member States of the Union and these regulations can hinder the free movement of lawyers in private practice.

The very first "opening" occurred with the *Reyners* judgment:[54] Mr. Reyners, of Dutch nationality, got his law degree in Belgium and applied to become a member of the Brussels bar. He was refused because of his nationality and Art.(now)51 TFEU: freedom of establishment "shall not apply, so far as any

---

[51] Art.14 contains the detailed rules on compensation measures.
[52] For more details see *http://ec.europa.eu/internal_market/qualifications/docs/future/platforms_en.pdf* [accessed August 23, 2013].
[53] Art.15 of Directive 2005/36.
[54] *Reyners v Etat Belge* (C-2/74) E.C.R. 1974, p.631.

given Member State is concerned, to activities which in that State are connected, even occasionally, with the exercise of official authority." However, according to the Court, this requires a direct and specific connection with that exercise, and it is not possible to recognise such a connection for the profession of a lawyer. Until the year 2000, lawyers having obtained their qualification in their home country and wishing to practise on a permanent basis in another Member State had to rely on the Directive to facilitate the effective exercise by lawyers of freedom to provide services.[55] The second lawyers' directive[56] became applicable on March 14, 2000. It allows a lawyer to become established in a Member State and to practise the host country's law immediately after simply proving that he is already registered as a lawyer in another Member State, without the need for either a test or an adaptation period. Moreover, after effectively and regularly pursuing, for a period of three years, an activity involving the law of the Member State in question, including Union law, a lawyer will be entitled to gain admission to the profession in the host Member State and so acquire the professional title of that Member State. For example, under the Directive, a Danish advokat could settle in Germany, practice German law immediately as an advokat and, after three years, obtain the German title of Rechtsanwalt. He must, however, fulfil certain obligations, like becoming a member of a body such as a Bar Association.[57]

6.   RECOGNITION ON THE BASIS OF THE TREATY

17–12   In case secondary law does not regulate access to a profession, the issue must be dealt with on the basis of primary law, i.e. the Treaty. The requirements in the host State will, all things being equal, qualify as a restriction which then must be justified. As there will in general be a valid justification ground for those requirements, the compatibility of the requirements with Union law will therefore turn on the question as to whether they comply with the principle of proportionality. Referring to that principle the Court has held that the national authorities must in general proceed in a manner similar to the one of the general

---

[55] Directive 77/249 [1977] O.J. L78/17.

[56] Directive 98/5 [1998] O.J. L77/36 to facilitate practise of the profession of lawyer on a permanent basis in a Member State other than that in which the qualification was obtained. See also Directive 77/249 [1977] O.J. L78/17 to facilitate the effective exercise by lawyers of the freedom to provide services on a temporary basis. See *Wilson* (C-506/04) [2006] E.C.R. I-8613, the Directive precludes an appeal procedure in which the decision refusing registration must be challenged at first instance before a body composed of lawyers practising under the professional title of the host country and on appeal before a body composed for the most part of such lawyers; registration cannot be made subject to a prior examination of proficiency in the language of the host Member State and Arts 3 and 4 preclude national legislation imposing penalties. See *van Leuken* (C-197/06) [2008] E.C.R. I-2627. This Directive precludes legislation by a Member State which makes the performance on its territory by a service provider established in another Member State subject to obtaining an authorisation the grant of which is conditional upon success in an aptitude test in law.

[57] *Donat Ebert* (C-359/09) [2011] E.C.R. I-269. It might be of interest to note that the reimbursement of a lawyer, established outside a given judicial district, is limited to the amount corresponding to that claimed by a lawyer established in the judicial district of the court having jurisdiction at first instance, see *Gebhard Stark* (C-293/10) [2011] E.C.R. I-4711. Also, the limitations put, by national authorities, on the remuneration of a lawyer, do not impede the access of lawyers from other Member States, see *Commission v Italy* (C-565/08) [2011] E.C.R. I-2101.

system under the 2005 Directive. That is the authorities must compare the qualifications of the person with the national requirements and determine the extent to which the requirements are met.[58]

In 2004, Parliament and Council established a "single Union framework for the transparency of qualifications and competences" (EUROPASS). This consists of a personal, co-ordinated portfolio of documents that citizens can use on a voluntary basis to better communicate and present their qualifications and competences throughout Europe. Its purpose is to facilitate the mobility within the Union.

7. COMPANY LAW

The free movement of companies and firms is obviously facilitated if the safeguards for the protection of the interests of the members and the public that are required by Member States are equivalent throughout the Union. The Treaty therefore entrusts the Union to take the necessary action which shall take the form of directives.[59] Below an overview of the directives harmonising company law will be given.

17–13

Before entering into secondary law it is appropriate to recall that the free movement of companies and firms has been greatly facilitated by the case law that the Court has developed on the basis of the Treaty's ban on restrictions to freedom of establishment. In this context, it must first be recalled that companies and firms, i.e. legal persons, are "creations" of national law.[60] That means that in the absence of harmonising secondary law, it is for the Member States to set the conditions for recognising an entity as a company or a firm within its legal order. The connecting factor between a company or a firm and a Member State is normally that the entity has its registration, central administration or principal place of business within the State. If the entity moves out that connecting factor of the Member State of its location and into another Member State, but still wants to maintain its status in the first Member State, is the first Member State obliged to accept that transfer by virtue of the Treaty ban on restrictions to freedom of establishment? The answer is in principle no.[61] On the other hand, the Member State of origin may not seek to prevent the company from converting itself into a company governed by the law of another Member State, unless such attempts can be justified.[62]

As concerns the situation where a company or firm wants to move into another Member State, for instance through a secondary establishment in the form of a branch, the Court has held that this Member State must in principle allow that, unless it can justify any restrictions in that regard.[63] If a company moves for

---

[58] See for instance *Vlassopoulos* (C-340/89) [1991] E.C.R. I-2357 and *Penarroja* (joined cases C-372/09 and C-373/09) [2011] E.C.R. I-1785.

[59] Art.50(1) and (2) TFEU.

[60] Expression used by the Court in *R v Treasury and Commissioners of Inland Revenue Ex p. Daily Mail and General Trust PLC* (81/87) [1988] E.C.R. 5483 at 5510(16).

[61] See *Daily Mail* (quoted above, fn.60) and *Cartesio* (C-210/06) [2008] E.C.R. I-9641.

[62] *Cartesio* (quoted above, fn.61) paras 111-113.

[63] *Centros* (C-212/97) [1999] E.C.R. I-1459. The case concerned a Danish couple that set up a company in the UK, primarily to avoid complying with Danish rules on minimum capital, and with a

instance its central administration from one Member State to another Member State complex situations can arise, for instance when the first Member State still considers it to be a company because according to the laws of that Member State the connecting factor is incorporation in the State and not having its central administration in the State; while the second State considers that the place of the central administration is the connecting factor and because the company has not complied with formalities in that State, denies to recognise it as a company. In such a situation the Court has held that the Member State to which the company has moved its central administration must recognise the company, as it is still validly a company under the laws of the first Member State, under which it was created.[64] The attention can now turn to secondary law.

17–14   The company law directives are:

The *first* directive concerns the co-ordination of safeguards in the case of companies with limited liability. It provides for the protection of the interests of third parties by disclosure of information concerning such companies, the particulars of persons authorised to bind the company, restriction of the grounds on which obligations are not valid and limitation of the cases in which nullity can arise.[65]

The *second* directive deals with the formation of public liability companies and the maintenance and alteration of their capital; it restricts the right of a company to acquire its own shares.[66] This restriction was extended to the acquisition of shares by companies over which the first can exercise a dominant influence.[67]

The *third* directive concerns mergers of public limited liability companies and requires publication to the shareholders of the merger plan, accounts and reports.[68]

The *fourth* directive provides for similar legal requirements concerning the financial information that must be made public, such as annual accounts; in this respect attention must be drawn to the International Accounting Standards (IAS),

---

view to doing business mainly in Denmark. The Danish authorities refused to register a branch of the company in Denmark. The Court held that the refusal was a restriction on free establishment and rejected most of the Danish authorities' attempts to justify it. See also *Inspire Art* (C-167/01) [2003] E.C.R. I-10155 which concerned Dutch rules which sought to keep the directors of a company personally liable for the company's engagements in case it was just "formally a foreign company". The Court held that to be an unjustified restriction. The gist of this case law is that nationals of the Union are free to set up companies in the Union where it best suits their interests.

[64] *Überseering* (208/00) [2002] E.C.R. I-9919.

[65] Directive 68/151 regarding disclosing requirements in respect of certain types of companies [1968] O.J. L65/8, amended [2003] O.J. L221/13, codified by Directive 2009/101 [2009] O.J. L258/11. See *Daihatsu-Händler v Daihatsu Deutschland* (C-97/96) [1997] E.C.R. I–6843: national legislation may not restrict to certain persons the right to apply for imposition of penalties in the event of failure of a company to disclose the annual accounts. See also *Berlusconi* (Joined Cases C-387/02, C-391/02 and C-403/02) [2005] E.C.R. I–3565, concerning false accounting.

[66] Directive 77/91 [1977] O.J. L26/3, modified [2006] O.J. L264/32, amended [2009] O.J. L259/14 as regards reporting and documentation requirements in the case of mergers and divisions; further amended by Directive 2012/30 [2012] O.J. L315/74. See *Pafitis v TKE* (C-44/93) [1996] E.C.R. I–1347: increase of bank capital by administrative measure not allowed; *Siemens* (C-42/95) [1996] E.C.R. I–6017: Art.29 of the Directive does not prohibit the grant of a preferential right to shareholders in case of capital increase; and *Kefalas* (C-367/96) [1998] E.C.R. I–284: the right of a shareholder to invoke Art.25(1) of the Directive cannot be exercised abusively.

[67] Directive 92/101 [1992] O.J. L347/64.

[68] Directive 78/855 [1978] O.J. L295/36. Codified by Directive 2011/35 [2011] O.J. L110/1.

the International Financial Reporting Standards (IFRS) and the International Financial Reporting Interpretation Committee (IFRIC).[69] Extended to banks and other financial institutions[70] and to branches in the Union of credit or financial institutions with head offices in third countries.[71] The switch-over to the new IFRS was not an easy operation; it is now applied by the 27 Member States, Australia and South Africa and, in the coming years, by Japan, South Korea and Canada and will necessarily have to be adopted, at some point, also by the United States in view of their many subsidiaries within the Union.

The *fifth* directive never passed the stage of Commission proposal.[72] It concerned the structure of public limited liability companies and the powers and obligations of their organs.

The *sixth* directive is about the division of public liability companies either by acquisition or by the formation of new companies, or both.[73] It complements the previous one on mergers.

The *seventh* directive concerns consolidated accounts,[74] and was extended to banks and other financial institutions.[75] A complementary directive concerns the annual accounts and consolidated accounts of insurance undertakings.[76]

The *eighth* directive deals with approval of persons responsible for carrying out statutory audits of accounting documents.[77]

There is no *ninth* directive, and the *tenth* never got beyond the draft stage: it was supposed to concern cross-frontier mergers of public liability companies.[78]

---

[69] Fourth Directive 78/660 [1978] O.J. L222/11, amended [1990] O.J. L317/60 and [2009] O.J. L164/42; Regulation 1126/08, amended [2009] O.J. L80/5. See *Springer* (Joined Cases C-435/02 and C-103/03) [2004] E.C.R. I-8663; see also *BIAO v Finanzamt fur Grossunternehmen* (C-306/99) [2003] E.C.R. I-1; see below, seventh Directive 83/349 [1983] O.J. L193/1, amended [2009] O.J. L164/42 and Directive 86/635 extending the seventh Directive to financial institutions [1986] O.J. L372/1 and Directive 91/674 on the annual accounts and consolidated accounts of insurance undertakings [1991]. Important is Regulation 1606/02 on the application of International Accounting Standards (IAS)/[2002] O.J. L 243/1 (for the implementing powers conferred on the Commission, see Regulation 297/09 [2009] O.J. L97/62), and Regulation 1126/08 adopting certain international accounting standards in accordance with Regulation 1606/02 [2008] O.J. L320//32, amended [2009] O.J. L21/10 and corrigendum [2009] O.J. L68/33, amended again [2009] O.J. L139/6 as regards the IFRIC and [2009] O.J. L149/6, amended [2011] O.J. L305/16. See also Regulation 70/09 as regards improvements to international Financial Reporting Standards (IFRSs) [2009] O.J. L21/16, amended [2009] O.J. L244/6.

[70] Directive 86/635 on the annual accounts and the consolidated accounts of banks and other financial institutions [1986] O.J. L372/1. See Regulation 1606/2002 (quoted above, fn.69).

[71] Directive 89/117 [1989] O.J. L44/40. See also Directive 89/299 on the own funds of credit institutions [1989] O.J. L124/16.

[72] [1983] O.J. C240/2.

[73] Directive 82/891 [1982] O.J. L378/47, amended [2009] O.J. L259/14.

[74] Directive 83/349 [1983]; see also Regulation 1606/2002 on the application of international accounting standards [2002] O.J. L243/1, amended [2005] O.J. L299/45 and [2008] O.J. L320/1, modified [2008] O.J. L338/10, amended [2009] O.J. L191/5 and [2010] O.J. L166/6, and Regulation 2086/04 [2004] O.J. L363/1.

[75] Directive 86/635 [1986] O.J. L372/1, amended several times; see also Regulation 2423/2001 concerning the consolidated balance sheet of the monetary financial institutions [2001] O.J. L333/8 and Regulation 63/2002 concerning statistics on interest rates applied by monetary financial institutions top deposits and loans vis-à-vis households and non-financial corporations ([2002] O.J. L10/24); the latter were modified by Regulation 2181/2004 [2004] O.J. L371/42.

[76] Directive 91/674 [1991] O.J. L374/7.

[77] Directive 84/253 [1984] O.J. L126/20.

[78] [1985] O.J. C203/211.

The *eleventh* directive concerns disclosure requirements with respect to branches opened in a Member State by certain types of companies governed by the law of another State.[79]

The *twelfth* directive deals with single-member private limited liability companies.[80]

17–15 Application of the International Accounting Standards (IASs); published by the International Accounting Standards Board (IASB), interpreted by the Standing Interpretation Committee (SIC), and the International Financial Reporting Interpretations Committee (IFRICs).[81] According to the Preamble of the relevant Regulation, the reporting requirements set out in the existing Directives[82] cannot ensure the high level of transparency and comparability which is a necessary condition for building an integrated capital market. It was considered important for the competitiveness of Union capital markets to achieve convergence of the standards used in Europe for preparing financial statements with international accounting standards that can be used globally, for cross-border transactions or listing anywhere in the world.

Mention must also be made of three directives on the admission of shares to official stock exchange listing,[83] the requirements for the drawing up, scrutiny and distribution of particulars to be published for that admission,[84] and information to be published on a regular basis by companies whose shares were admitted.[85]

In order to protect the interests of holders of the securities of companies that are the subject of takeover bids or of changes of control and whose securities or at least some of them are admitted to trading on a regulated market in a Member State, a directive on takeover bids was issued in 2004.[86] By "takeover bid" is meant, "a public offer (other than by the offered company itself) made to the holders of the securities of a company to acquire all or some of those securities, which has as its objective the acquisition of control of the offered company". The

---

[79] Directive 89/666 [1989] O.J. L395/36.

[80] Directive 89/667 [1989] O.J. L395/40, codified [2009] O.J. L258/20.

[81] Regulation 1606/2002 [2002] O.J. L243/1 IFRS, see above, Regulation 1725/2003 on the application of international accounting standards [2003] O.J. L261/1, amended [2005] O.J. L337/16 and Regulation 1606/02; Regulation 2236/04, 2237/04 and 2238/04 respectively O.J. L392/1, 393/1 and 394/1. See Regulation 211/2005 amending Regulation 1725/2003 adopting certain international accounting standards [2005] O.J. L41/1, see also Regulation 1751/05 amending Regulation 1725/03 [2005] O.J. L282/3. See also Regulation 1126/08 on IFRIC, amended [2009] O.J. L314/15 and Regulation 1171/09 [2009] O.J. L314/43.

[82] Directive 78/660 [1978] O.J. L22/11 on the annual accounts of certain types of companies, modified [2009] O.J. L164/42; Directive 83/349 on consolidated accounts [1983] O.J. L193/1, modified [2009] O.J. L164/42; Directive 86/635 on the annual accounts and consolidated accounts of banks and other financial institutions [1986] O.J. L372/1 and Directive 91/674 on the annual accounts and consolidated accounts of insurance companies [1991] O.J. L374/7.

[83] Directive 79/279 [1979] O.J. L66/21, see also Directive 2001/34 on the admission of securities to official stock exchange listing and on information to be published on those securities [2001] O.J. L184/1 amended by Directive 2004/109 on the harmonisation of transparency requirements in relation to information about issuers whose securities are admitted to trading on a regulated market [2004] O.J. L390/38, amended [2010] O.J. L327/1, and Directive 2007/14 [2007] O.J. L69/14, laying down detailed rules for the implementation of Directive 204/109. With regard to "listing particulars" (Art.21 Directive 2001/34), see *Ntion et Pikoulas* (C-430/05) [2007] E.C.R. I-5835.

[84] Directive 80/390 [1980] O.J. L100/1.

[85] Directive 82/121 [1982] O.J. L48/26.

[86] Directive 2004/25 [2004] O.J. L142/12.

latter meaning, "a company, the securities of which are the subject of a bid". The Directive lays down, among other things, "general principles", defines the "supervisory authority and the applicable law", the "protection of minority shareholders, the mandatory bid and the equitable price", "information concerning bids", "time allowed for acceptance", "information for and consultation of employee's representatives", etc.

A 2003 directive[87] concerns the *prospectus* to be published when securities are offered to the public or admitted to trading, harmonises requirements for the drawing up, approval and distribution of the prospectus to be published. It provides that no Member State shall allow any offer of securities to be made to the public without prior publication of a prospectus, but with some exceptions. The prospectus must contain all information, which, according to the particular nature of the issuer and of the securities offered or admitting to trading, is necessary to enable the investor to make an informed assessment of the assets, liabilities, financial position, profit and losses, prospects of the issuer and rights attached. Responsibility for the information given in a prospectus shall attach, at least, to the issuer or its administrative, management or supervisory bodies, the offer or the person asking for admission to trading or the guarantor, as the case may be. The Commission shall define the minimum information to be included. A prospectus is valid for 12 months after its publication. **17–16**

Furthermore, there are directives concerning taxation in the case of mergers, divisions, transfer of assets and exchanges of shares concerning companies of different Member States[88] and in the case of parent companies and subsidiaries of different Member States.[89]

In 2005, a directive on cross-border mergers of limited liability companies[90] was adopted in order to reduce costs, while guaranteeing the requisite legal certainty and enabling as many companies as possible to benefit. **17–17**

The Market Abuse Directive[91] requires Member States to amend their national legislation so that in relation to financial instruments traded on EEA regulated markets, insider dealing and market manipulation are prohibited, issuers are required to announce inside information to the public as soon as possible, issuers

---

[87] Directive 2003/71 [2003] O.J L345/68, amended [2008] O.J. L76/37, also amending Directive 2001/34 [2001] O.J. L184/1 on the admission of securities to official stock exchange listing and on information to be published. Directive 2003/71 was amended again by Directive 2010/73 [2010] O.J. L327/1. See *Ntionik and Picoulas* (C-430/05) [2007] E.C.R. I-5835 establishing all the parties responsible in case of incorrect information. Directive 2010/73 also amended Directive 2004/109 on the harmonisation of transparency requirements in relation to information about issuers whose securities are admitted to trading on a regular market [2004] O.J. L145/1. Directive 2003/71 was amended again in 2012 [2012] O.J. L103/11; it was implemented by Regulation 809/2004 which was amended by Commission Delegated Regulation 311/12 [2012] O.J. L103/13.

[88] Directive 90/434 [1990] O.J. L225/1, repealed by Directive 2009/133.

[89] Directive 90/435 [1990] O.J. L225/6, repealed by Directive 2011/96. See *Crédit Mutuel* (C-27/07) [2008] E.C.R. I-2767, regarding taxable income of parent company, nature of "tax credit"; in *Cobelfret* (C-138/07) [2009] E.C.R. 12.02.09 where the Court stated that Directive 90/435, first indent of Art.4(1) "is unconditional and sufficiently precise to be capable of being relied on before national courts".

[90] Directive 2005/56 [2005] O.J. L310/1. amended by Directive 2009/109/EC [2009] O.J. L259/14 as regards reporting and documentation requirements in the case of mergers and divisions.

[91] Directive 2003/6 [2003] O.J. L96/16. The description of the Directives is borrowed from Herbert Smith, corporate briefing, July 2004. See *Spector v Commission* (C-45/08) E.C.R. 23.12.09 concept of "use".

insure that they and those acting for them draw up "insider lists", those with managerial responsibilities for the issuer, and persons closely associated with them, are under an obligation to notify their dealings in the issuer's shares or any financial instrument linked to them, there is appropriate regulation of investment research to ensure presentation and disclosure of interest, and market professionals are required to notify the relevant competent authority of suspicious transactions. There are four sets of more detailed provisions, known as the level 2 implementing measures, which expand on the following provisions in the Directive: definition of inside information and market manipulation[92]; fair presentation of investment recommendations and disclosure of conflict of interest[93]; the exemptions from market abuse for buy-back programmes and stabilisation[94]; and accepted market practices, definition of insider information in relation to derivatives on commodities, insider lists and notification of managers' transactions and suspicious transactions.[95] A 2008 Directive further amended the implementing powers conferred on the Commission with regard to insider dealing and market manipulation.[96]

8.   EUROPEAN FORMS OF LEGAL PERSONS

(1)   The European Company: Societas Europaea (SE)

17–18 Back in 1970, the Commission made a proposal for a European Company Statute that would allow the setting up of a company according to Union law and to be recognised in all the Member States. The main difficulty was the workers' representation in such a company; this is still unacceptable for certain Member States, although rules were laid down in 1994 on the establishment of a European Work Council or a procedure for informing and consulting employees.[97] The Statute for a European Company was finally adopted by regulation in 2001.[98]

According to the recitals, the Council considered the following:

- the structures of production must be adapted to the Union dimension—companies should be able to carry out the re-organisation of their business on a Union scale;
- the necessity of cross-border mergers with their legal, psychological and fiscal problems;
- the legal framework is still largely based on national law, which forms a considerable obstacle to the creation of groups of companies from different Member States;

---

[92] Directive 2003/124 [2003] O.J. L339/70.
[93] Directive 2003/125 [2003] O.J. L339/73.
[94] Regulation 2273/2003 [2003] O.J. L336/33.
[95] Directive 2004/72 [2004] O.J. L162/70.
[96] Directive 2008/26/EC [2008] O.J. L81/42.
[97] Directive 94/45 [1994] O.J. L254/64, replaced by Directive 2009/38 [2009] O.J. L122/28. See *Betriebsrat der Firma ADS v ADS Anker* (C-349/01) [2004] E.C.R. I–6803.
[98] Regulation 2157/2001 on the Statute for a European company (SE) [2001] O.J. L294/1, modified [2004] O.J. L168/1.

- next to the different national laws, it should be possible to form companies and carry on business under the new Statute that is directly applicable in all the Member States.

When harmonisation is impossible, reference may be made to the law governing public limited liability companies in the Member State where it has its registered office. The SE itself must take the form of a company with share capital, that being the form most suited, in terms of both financing and management, to the needs of a company carrying on business on a European scale. A minimum capital is required (€120,000). Since there are presently two different systems for the administration of public limited liability companies, an SE should be free to choose between the two, as long as the respective responsibilities of those responsible for management and those responsible for supervision are clearly defined. The rules and general principles of private international law do apply both where the SE exercises control and where it is the controlled company.

17–19

The rules with regard to the involvement of employees in the SE are laid down in a second act, a directive[99] whose provisions form an indissociable part of the first act, the Regulation, and must be applied concomitantly. It provides that concrete procedures of employee trans-national information and consultation, as well as, if applicable, participation, should be defined primarily by means of an agreement between parties concerned, or, in the absence thereof, through the application of a set of subsidiary rules. It is a fundamental principle to secure employees' acquired rights as regards involvement in company decisions. Employee rights in force before the establishment of SEs should provide the basis for employee rights of involvement in the SE (the "before and after" principle). Member States must lay down "standard rules" satisfying the provisions set out in the Annex to the Directive. Transposition had to take place no later than October 8, 2004.

(2) The European Co-operative Society

Similarly, the Council adopted, in 2003, a regulation on the statute for a European Co-operative Society (SCE).[100] Those societies can acquire a single legal personality and exercise their trans-national activities with a single statute and structure. Minimum capital is set at €30,000 and the responsibility is limited. It can be set up by natural or legal persons. The Regulation entered into force on August 18, 2006. The Council also adopted a directive concerning the involvement of workers in the co-operative society in order to preserve their rights such as information, consultation and participation.[101]

17–20

---

[99] Directive 2001/86 [2001] O.J. L294/22 supplementing the Statute for a European company with regard to the involvement of employees. See also Directive 2002/14 establishing a general framework for informing and consulting employees in the European Union [2002] O.J. L80/29; see *Confédération Internationale du Travail E.A.* (C-385/05) [2007] E.C.R. I-611 Art.3(1) precludes national legislation which excludes a specific category of workers from the calculation of staff members and *Ingeniorforeningen* (C-405/08) [2010] E.C.R. I-985: Art.7 of Directive 2002/14 does not require more extensive protection against dismissal for employees' representatives.

[100] Regulation 1435/03 [2003] O.J. L207/1, corrected [2007] O.J. L49/35.

[101] Directive 2003/72 [2003] O.J. L207/25.

In 2008 the Commission made a proposal for societas private europea—a European private company—which is intended for the small and medium-sized enterprises (SMEs).[102] It has not yet been enacted.

(3) The European Economic Interest Grouping

17–21 A kind of forerunner to the SE, albeit on a much more modest scale, is the European Economic Interest Grouping (EEIG),[103] which constitutes a very simple form of association between economic entities, based on Union law. When registered in one Member State, it is recognised as a legal entity in all the others. The only requirement is the drafting and registration of the bylaws; it enjoys legal personality if the Member State of registration so provides. It suffers, however, from an important drawback constituted by the fact that all the members of an EEIG are individually responsible for its debts. A problem might arise with the denomination of an EEIG, since this is done on the basis of national law.[104]

FURTHER READING

17–22 Andrew Johnston and Phil Syrpis, "Regulatory competition in European company law after *Cartesio*", (2009) E.L Rev. June 378.

Dashwood, Wyatt et al, *Wyatt and Dashwood's European Union Law* (Hart Publishing, 2011).

Edith Loozen, "Professional ethics and restraints of competition", (2006) E.L.Rev. Feb.

Frank Dornseifer, *Corporate Business Forms in Europe* (Sweet & Maxwell, 2006).

Jukka Snell, *Goods and Services in EC Law: A Study of the Relationship between the Freedoms* (Oxford University Press, 2002).

Rachel Crauford Smith, *Old Wine in New Bottles? From the 'Country of Origin Principle' to 'Freedom to Provide Services' in the European Community Directive on Services in the Internal Market* (Europa Institute—Mitchell Working Paper Series, University of Edinburgh, 2007).

Robin White, *Workers, Establishment and Services in the European Union* (Oxford University Press, 2004).

Roger Blanpain, Involvement of Employees in the European Union (Kluwer, 2002).

---

[102] General Report 2008, 55.

[103] Regulation 2137/85 [1985] O.J. L199/1; incorporated [1994] O.J. L1/517.

[104] *European Information Technology Observatory (EITO)* (C-402/96) [1997] E.C.R. I–7515.

CHAPTER 18

Freedom to Provide Services/Financial Services

1. INTRODUCTION

This chapter first presents the Treaty provisions on free movement of services. Thereafter follows a presentation of the Services Directive. As mentioned in Ch.17: Freedom of Establishment/Company Law, the Directive codifies to a large extent case law of the Court on the Treaty provisions. However, the Directive also contains deviations from case law and moreover, many sectors are exempted from the Directive. Therefore, it is useful to present the Treaty provisions and the Directive separately. The last section of the chapter gives an overview of the harmonisation undertaken in the financial sector, given the importance of the sector. The measures have been adopted by the Union institutions to ensure both freedom of establishment and freedom to provide services.

18–01

2. FREEDOM TO PROVIDE SERVICES[1]

Restrictions on freedom to provide services within the Union are prohibited in respect of nationals of Member States who are established in a State of the Union, other than that of the person for whom the services are intended.[2] As the other bans within the four freedoms, the ban has direct effect.[3] And the ban does not apply to purely internal situations.[4] The beneficiaries are nationals of the Member States and the companies benefitting from freedom of establishment, i.e. companies set up under the laws of a Member State and having their registered office, central administration or principal place of business within the Union.[5] The freedom entails that the provider of the service may move temporarily to the State of the recipient of his services. A surgeon who moves to another Member State to perform an operation does not "establish" himself in that other State: he remains "established" in the Member State where he resides and normally carries out his activities. For the performance of the operation in another Member State,

18–02

---

[1] See the Introduction to Part III of this book: The Internal Market.

[2] Art.56 TFEU.

[3] *Van Binsbergen v Bedrijfsvereniging voor de Metaalnijverheid* (33/74) [1974] E.C.R. 1299; [1975] 1 C.M.L.R. 298.

[4] See for instance *Gervais* (C-17/94) [1995] E.C.R. I-4353, paras 24-26.

[5] See, however, Art.56(2) TFEU: the Council may extend the right to provide services to nationals of third countries established within the Union; this was done, among others, for architects.

he therefore comes under the provisions concerning the freedom to provide services, and not those providing for the right of establishment. The recipient of services can also move freely to another Member State to receive services. This is not explicitly provided for in the Treaty but the Court determined that the right to provide services also entails the freedom to receive services and, in order to be able to do so, the recipient is just as free to move to any other Member State to receive a service, as the provider is to provide services; and the recipient may invoke the freedom against the Member State where he resides.[6] There are indeed numerous cases where it is the receiver of the service who necessarily moves to another Member State. Examples are the patients who go to consult a doctor or the businessman on business trips. The provisions on free movement of services may also apply in a situation where both the service provider and the service recipient are located in the same Member State. For instance, the executor of a testament in the UK, where also the heirs are present, may rely on the freedom to provide services when the estate includes a property in Germany and German measures put an obstacle to the exercise of his tasks, for instance by requiring foreign nationals to provide security for costs in judicial proceedings.[7] Tourists are recipients of services and they may therefore also invoke the provisions on free movement of services, but in the Member State of their tourist destination probably just to the extent that the national provisions are discriminatory, be it directly or indirectly: in 1989 the Court had to deal, within a reference for preliminary ruling, with the situation of a British tourist in France, Cowan.[8] He suffered an act of aggression while he was visiting Paris. He could not claim victims' compensation under the applicable French rules as they were discriminatory. As Cowan was a tourist and thus a recipient of services, the Court found in the first place that the situation came within the scope of the Treaty. Next, the Court found the French rules to be in violation of the general ban on discrimination on grounds of nationality, enshrined in Art.18 TFEU. Thus the Court, at that time, held that the discrimination did not come within the scope of the free movement of services.[9] It is recalled that the general ban on discrimination only comes into play if the national measure cannot be assessed under one of the more specific provisions of the Treaty, such as the provisions on free movement of services.[10] The Court has later been confronted with national provisions concerning entrance fees to museums; the rules implied that residents, be it nationals or foreigners, would not pay fees charged to tourists.[11] The Court held the rules to be discriminatory. The Court based that finding on the provisions on free movement of services *and* the general ban on discrimination.

---

[6] *Luisi and Carbone* (Joined Cases 286/82 and 26/83) [1984] E.C.R. 377.

[7] See *Hubbard* (C-20/92) [1993] E.C.R. I-3777. See also *Skatteministeriet v Bent Vestergaard* (C-55/98) [1999] E.C.R. I-7641.

[8] *Cowan* (186/87) [1989] E.C.R. 195.

[9] The Council later adopted a directive relating to compensation to crime victims, Directive 2004/80 [2004] O.J. L261/15. In *Dell'Orto* (C-467/05) [2007] E.C.R. T-5557 the Court gave a definition of "victim" within the Directive.

[10] See for instance *Mutsch* (137/84) [1985] E.C.R. 2681.

[11] *Commission v Spain (Museum admission)* (C-45/93) [1994] E.C.R. I-911, and *Commission v Italy (Museum admission)* (C-388/01) [2003] E.C.R. I-721.

Services may also be delivered cross-border without any physical movement **18–03** of the persons involved, for instance when a patent agent in one Member State delivers patent renewal services electronically or by mail to a client in another Member State.[12]

For the delimitation between the free movement of services and the freedom of establishment, the reader is referred to Ch.17: Freedom of Establishment/ Company Law. As concerns the delimitation from free movement of goods, it is recalled that cross-border movement of lottery tickets is dealt with under free movement of services, the ticket just being the physical bear of a right.[13] National regulations on advertising may be analysed both under the angle of free movement of goods and free movement of services; a national ban on advertising for a given product for instance affects the free movement of goods as, all things being equal, it makes market penetration more difficult; at the same time the ban hinders that, for instance, marketing firms from other Member States can deliver advertising services to economic operators in the State of the ban.[14] If a national measure relates to more freedoms, the Court of Justice will examine the national measure only under the provisions concerning one freedom provided that the other(s) are entirely secondary to the first one. However, in the field of telecommunications, it may in some instances be difficult to determine whether free movement of goods or free movement of services should take priority; in such a case the Court will examine the national measures under both freedoms.[15]

Services are "services" within the meaning of the Treaty "where they are normally provided for remuneration, in so far as they are not governed by the provisions on free movement of goods, capital and persons."[16] In its case law the Court has held that the remuneration does not necessarily have to be provided by the recipient of the service; it may be provided in another manner. An example is the case of a Belgian judoka who contended that her federation impeded her from participating in international tournaments. Although the spectators at such tournaments would not pay remuneration to her, she could invoke free movement of services as the remunerations would stem from, for instance, sponsoring.[17] Broadcasting is also a service within the meaning of the Treaty: For instance, a Belgian municipality imposed a tax on satellite dishes which was opposed by a resident in the municipality. The Court held that transmission of television signals

---

[12] *Säger* (C-76/90) [1991] E.C.R. I-4221.
[13] *Schindler* (C275/92) [1994] E.C.R. I-1039. After this ruling there have been numerous cases concerning gambling services, which have been decided on the basis of free movement of services or freedom of establishment.
[14] *Gourmet* (C-405/98) [2001] E.C.R. I-1795 and *De Agostini and Tv Shop* (Joined Cases C-34/95, C-35/95 and C-36/95) [1997] E.C.R. I-3843.
[15] See *Canal Satelite* (C-390/99) [2002] E.C.R. I-607.
[16] Art.57(1) TFEU. The Court has clarified that the provision does not imply an order of priority between free movement of services and other freedoms. The meaning is that the notion of "services" covers services not governed by other freedoms "in order to ensure that all economic activity falls within the scope of the fundamental freedoms", see Fidium Finanz (C-452/04) [2006] E.C.R. I-9521.
[17] See also *Smits and Peerbooms* (C-157/99) [2001] E.C.R. I-5473 which concerned claims against sickness insurance schemes, brought by insured persons who had received hospital treatment abroad. The Court held that the fact that hospitals were paid by the schemes did not hinder qualifying the hospital service as a service in relation to the patient. See also *Humbel* (263/86) [1988] E.C.R. 5365(17); [1989] 1 C.M.L.R. 393, where the Court held that the State's provision of general education to its population did not constitute services within the meaning of the provisions concerning free movement of services.

came within the provisions on free movement of services and that the tax made the provision of services between Member States more difficult than the provision of services purely within one Member State.[18]

18–04   Transport services are regulated separately in the Treaty and are dealt with in Ch.27: Transport.

It must be noted that the Treaty provides that "the person providing a service may, in order to do so, temporarily pursue his activity in the State where the service is provided, under the same conditions as are imposed by that State on its own nationals".[19] This provision could give the impression that a Member State can submit the service provider from another Member State, exercising his right to free movement of services, to all the requirements to which it submits the person seeking establishment in the State; such requirements can concern for instance qualifications, the organisation of the profession or professional ethics. The Court has held that such a reading is out of place as it would imply that the provisions "securing freedom to provide services would be deprived of all practical effect."[20]

The ban on restrictions to the free movement of services is broad and applies, as in the other freedoms, to discriminatory measures, directly or indirectly,[21] and to restrictive measures, i.e. measures "liable to prohibit or otherwise impede the activities of a service provider established in another Member State where he lawfully provides similar services."[22] The broadness of the ban may be seen from the examples given above. Restrictions to the freedom of services may also result from national authorities' actions in relation to public contracts, see below Ch.21: Public Procurement.

A Member State can submit the service providers only to restrictions that are justified, hereunder proportionate.[23] Only such measures are compatible with Union law.[24]

18–05   If the service provider in the Member State of his establishment is submitted to equivalent requirements, the Member State where he provides his services temporarily or occasionally must take account of that.[25] One refers often to this as a ban on duplication of requirements; i.e. for the restriction to be justified, it cannot simply duplicate requirements to which the service provider is already submitted. The duplication ban can be seen as a logical consequence of the

---

[18] *De Coster* (C-17/00) [2001] E.C.R. I-9445. See also *ERT* (C-260/89) [1991] E.C.R. I-2925, and *Sacchi* (155/73) [1974] E.C.R. 409. The reader must not be led to believe that cross-border broadcasting is just regulated by primary law. On the contrary, a directive intensively regulates the matter, Directive 2010/13 [2010] O.J. L95 on audiovisual services. To the extent a matter is not regulated by the Directive, it may of course still be governed by primary law.

[19] Art.57(3) TFEU.

[20] *Commission v France (Tourist Guides)* (C-154/89) [1991] E.C.R. I-659, para.12.

[21] See for instance *Seco v Evi* (Joined Cases 62/81 and 63/81) [1982] E.C.R. 223(8).

[22] See for instance *Säger* (C-76/90) [1991] E.C.R. I-4221, para.12.

[23] *Commission v France (Co-insurance)* (220/83) [1986] E.C.R. 3663, para.20.

[24] "To be compatible with Union law" is a cumbersome way to express that the measure is lawful under Union law. The expression reflects the fact that it is in principle for the national legal order to draw the consequences as concerns legality or not of a measure's incompatibility with Union law. The Union legal order cannot declare a measure from another legal order illegal.

[25] See for instance *Van Wesemael* (Joined Cases 110 and 111/78) [1979] E.C.R. 35 and *Webb* (279/80) [1981] E.C.R. 3305.

principle of proportionality; a restriction that in essence just duplicates a requirement to which the service provider is already submitted cannot be necessary.

As concerns the service provider's right to enter and stay in another Member State, the reader is referred to Ch.16: The Free Movement of Persons, where Directive 2004/38 is presented.

Finally, a particular judge-made rule concerning the circumvention of national establishment rules through the freedom to provide services must be mentioned. The "rule" is sometimes also referred to as the *Van Binsbergen* principle—so named after the first Court case where it was enounced. The kind of situation that the "rule" seeks to address is for instance the following: Member State A prohibits non-lawyers from providing some legal services, although the services are of a simple nature. A person sets up a business in Member State B which allows the provisions of such services, and then targets exclusively or mainly clients in Member State A, for instance by establishing advertising material in the language of Member State A, different from the language of Member State B. When Member State A seeks to hinder the provision of services, the person invokes the freedom to provide services. In such a situation the Court has held that Member State A "cannot be denied the right to take measures to prevent the exercise by a person whose activity is entirely or principally directed towards its territory of the freedoms guaranteed by the Treaty for the purpose of avoiding the professional rules of conduct which would be applicable to him if he were established within that State."[26]

3. THE SERVICES DIRECTIVE

The Services Directive[27] has been introduced in Ch.17: Freedom of Establishment/Company Law. The regulation of the Directive in relation to free movement of services entails three major departures from the case law concerning the Treaty provisions. In the first place, the Directive limits the justification grounds that a Member State may invoke to justify a restriction, caught by the Directive, to just four, namely: public policy, public security, public health and the protection of the environment. Thus, if a Member State imposes for instance a restriction for reasons of consumer protection, that restriction cannot at all be opposed against the service provider from another Member State; the justification ground is not valid and thus no proportionality assessment is called for. In the second place, the Directive provides that all restrictions must be non-discriminatory. Under the case law concerning the Treaty provisions, discriminatory measures can in principle be justified, but just on the grounds provided by the Treaty.[28] The Directive thus alters that within its scope of application; discriminatory measures are ruled out per se. In the third place, the Directive contains a "black list" of national measures that are outlawed when the

18–06

---

[26] *Veriniging Veronika* (C-148/91) [1993] E.C.R. I-487, para.12. The pertinence and the scope of this case law have been much discussed in legal literature. The case law does not detract from the objective contents of the notion of restriction, i.e. a national measure coming within the notion of restriction will continue to do so, no matter any circumvention intent of the person concerned.

[27] Directive 2006/123 on services in the internal market [2006] O.J. L376/36.

[28] See the Introduction to Part III of this book: The Internal Market.

service provider does not have to move to the other Member State to provide his service, e.g. when the service can be provided electronically.[29] It should also be noted that the terminology of the Directive in relation to the justification test differs from the habitual one. When the Directive talks about "the necessity" of a restriction it does not refer to the necessity test as part of the proportionality review; it refers to whether there is a valid justification ground for the restriction.

4. FINANCIAL SERVICES AND SUPERVISION

18–07   Of particular importance within the single market is the financial services sector, i.e. banking, insurance and securities. A well-functioning financial services sector ensures the transmission of capital from investors and depositors to undertakings and persons in the real economy. When the financial sector works well, the costs in raising capital for undertakings and firms is reduced, and the savings and funds of investors and depositors are allocated more efficiently. The free circulation of financial services is also made constantly easier by the development of modern technology in the communications field.

According to the Treaty,[30] banking and insurance services were to be liberalised in step with the liberalisation of movement of capital, in so far as those services are connected with such movement. The liberalisation of capital movements did not take off until in 1988 when the Council adopted the Second Capital Movements Directive.[31] In 1992, the Maastricht Treaty introduced new provisions on free movement of capital into the Treaty, in conjunction with the introduction of the provisions on Economic and Monetary Union, which ensured the liberalisation.[32] Liberalisation of capital movements, however, does not detract from the necessity of adopting harmonising measures governing the financial services sector. National regulations of the sector are based on important considerations of public interest, notably to protect customers, investors and depositors as well as financial stability. The divergence of national rules on issues such as licensing, financial supervision, solvency ratio and own funds, was a hindrance to cross-border activity in the sector.

The Union legislation is complex and rich in details. The legislation was so even before the onset of the financial crisis in 2008 and the ensuing Euro debt crisis. The legislation has come in waves: in the 1970s timid steps at

---

[29] Art.16(2) of the Services Directive.

[30] Art.58(2) TFEU.

[31] Directive 88/361 [1988] O.J. L178/88. Previously, i.e. before the liberalisation it was common to distinguish between capital movements and "payments", i.e. the money movements necessary for the purchase of goods and services. The distinction was appropriate since free movement of payments was liberalised and the Treaty provision thereupon had direct applicability while the provision on capital movements was not, see *Casati* (C-203/80) [1981] E.C.R. 2595 and *Luisi and Carbone* (Joined cases 286/82 and 26/83) [1984] E.C.R. 377. After the liberalisation of capital movements the distinction is made less often. However, in the wake of the financial crisis of 2008 some States have had to adopt restrictions on capital movements, for instance Cyprus in 2013 and the EEA EFTA State Iceland in 2008; in that context the distinction becomes relevant in the sense that the restrictions apply to capital movements but not to payments.

[32] The Second Capital Movements Directive thereafter became superfluous. However, the annex to the Directive contains a listing of different types of capital movements—referred to as the nomenclature—to which the Court still often refers.

harmonisation were taken; in the push for the establishment of the Internal Market, after the Single European Act, numerous acts were adopted; a new wave came after the Commission adopted, in 1999, a Financial Services Action Plan (FSAP) and later in 2005 a programme for a Financial Services Policy (FSP).[33] Then came the financial crisis. The crisis showed shortcomings in existing regulations, for instance as concerns banks, a need for regulating matters hitherto unregulated (i.e. regulatory gaps), for instance as concerns credit rating agencies and certain financial instruments, and it entailed a fragmentation of the internal market in the financial services sector, i.e. financial institutions withdrawing from cross-border activities. The crisis showed also that there was a need for rules at macro level, or with another term, rules concerning financial stability at the systemic level. The crisis triggered off a true avalanche of regulatory activity, for instance with a view to bolstering the capitalisation of banks or to enhancing the supervision of the sector, notably by providing a European level of supervision, supervision having been so far a national matter. Many of the measures proposed originate in work done in international fora such as the OECD, the Financial Stability Board, the G20 group or the Basel Committee on Banking Supervision. Some of the measures proposed have been passed but a good number are still pending before the legislative instances. It is impossible here to make a meaningful enumeration of the many acts of secondary law in the sector, existing or currently in the legislative process. Below a few remarks of general nature are made on the harmonisation in the sector. Then mayor acts in the different areas of the financial sector will be presented; at the end is a section on the emerging European level of supervision and governance of the financial services sector and the banking union.

The harmonisation in the sector has generally taken the character of minimum **18–08** harmonisation, coupled with an obligation of mutual recognition.[34] Thus, a Member State has at least to lay down the requirements prescribed by the acts of secondary law, and it has to allow financial entities from other Member States that comply with those minimum requirements to operate in its territory. This is often referred to as the "principle of home State control" or "the single passport" system, i.e. once a financial entity has been authorised by the State of its establishment, i.e. its home State, it can unhindered provide services in other Member States, i.e. it has a "passport to cross borders." Thus, for instance a bank licensed as such in Germany can provide services in France, for instance through a branch, without having to show to the French authorities that it complies with all the requirements needed for being licensed as a bank; the French authorities have to recognise the German license, just as German authorities will have to recognise a French license—principle of mutual recognition.[35] There are though limits to the principle of home State control. The host State can for instance normally require the financial entity to comply with its rules that concern the conduct of business (COB). COB rules are for instance rules on when and how the financial services can be offered.

---

[33] COM(2005) 629 final.
[34] For minimum harmonisation, see Ch.26: Approximation of Laws; for mutual recognition, see Ch.15: The Free Movement of Goods.
[35] If the bank wishes to set up a subsidiary in the other Member State, for instance a new bank, it must comply with the latter's requirements, hereunder the national rules that implement the relevant directives.

Within the context of the harmonisation in the financial services sector it is often stated that the harmonisation process is conducted in accordance with the *Lamfalussy* principle/report/process. The name is of a Belgian economist who headed a committee to see how one could improve the mechanisms for regulating financial services in the Union. The committee suggested that regulation should be made in accordance with a multiple-level structure, notably: at the first level, there should be regulation enacted by the Union legislator, laying down the main rules; at level two there should be implementing regulation established by the Commission; at level three one should ensure consistent transposition and implementation of Union rules at the national level. The *Lamfalussy* principle is laudable; most persons will agree to the fact that overriding norms and principles should be decided at the top level of the regulatory machinery and details should be left for levels below. However, it must be added that the principle has its limitations in practice. As all lawyers know, "the devil is in the detail", and thus in practice the *Lamfalussy* principle has also entailed that on the top level, one leaves the detailed matters on which agreement cannot be reached to the level below, on which (surprisingly) agreement cannot either be reached, thus with the end result that not much is gained by moving detailed matters from a higher level to a lower level of decision-making.

5. BANKING

18–09 The first directive adopted in this sector concerned the abolition of restrictions on freedom of establishment and freedom to provide services in respect of self-employed activities of banks and other financial institutions.[36] In 1977 followed a directive on the taking up and pursuit of the business of credit institutions which had a very limited scope.[37] Later, in 1989 and in 2000, followed directives co-ordinating the laws, regulations and administrative provisions relating to the taking up and pursuit of the business of credit institutions.[38] These directives laid down the principle of the single banking authorisation and supervision and control by the home Member State. They also enabled banks to set up branches and provide financial services freely throughout the Union. Currently the key acts are two directives from 2006.[39] The two directives cover issues such as the own funds of credit institutions, the solvency ratio for credit institutions, the supervision of credit institutions on a consolidated basis and the monitoring and control of large exposures of credit institutions.

Currently the directives are being recast in particular to meet the capital-ratio requirements that follow from the so-called Basel III agreement. The Union is in favour of complying with Basel III but has been awaiting actions in the United

---

[36] Directive 73/183 [1973] O.J. L194/1, now repealed.

[37] Directive 77/780 [1977] O.J. L322/30, now repealed. The Directive is commonly referred to as the first banking directive. It had a limited scope as it did not ensure mutual recognition, see for instance *Parodi v Banque H. Albert de Bary* (C-222/95) [1997] E.C.R. I–3899.

[38] Directive 89/646 [1989] O.J. L386/1 (commonly referred to as the second banking directive) and directive 2000/12 [2000] O.J. L126/1, both repealed.

[39] Directive 2006/48 relating to the taking up and pursuit of the business of credit institutions and Directive 2006/49 on the capital adequacy of investment firms and credit institutions, both [2006] O.J. L177, with later amendments.

States which, although having formally agreed to Basel III, are hesitating to pass the internal legislation needed to comply with Basel III. Basel III sets stricter capital ratio requirements to banks than hitherto.

A directive from 2001 concerns the re-organisation and winding up of credit institutions.[40] The Directive lays down rules concerning the winding-up when the credit institution has branches in other Member States. The background to this is that in practice the State of the branch may seek to ring-fence the activities of the branch in order to satisfy claims of domestic creditors. The Directive seeks to prevent that by ensuring that the winding up proceedings in the home State also include the branches and creditors in other Member States. Within the context of the discussions for a banking union—see below—the need for a single resolution (i.e. re-organisation or winding-up) mechanism (SRM) is generally acknowledged. SRM goes far beyond the matter regulated by the Directive and is addressed further below.[41]

In 1994, a directive on deposit guarantee schemes was adopted.[42] The scope of the harmonisation is limited. The Directive obliges Member States to ensure that credit institutions are members of a deposit guarantee scheme.[43] Member States are free to decide on how to fund the schemes, as long as they are not funded through State aid.[44] There are two funding models: ex-ante funding or ex-post funding; in practice there may be combinations of the two. In both models the schemes are funded through contributions from the entities that are affiliated to the scheme. In some Member States there are more schemes and the schemes are private; in others the schemes are public. The guaranteed sum was originally set at €20,000 per depositor, with the possibility that Member States could provide for higher coverage. After the onset of the financial crisis the sum was raised so that currently it is €100,000, without a possibility to deviate from that sum. A proposal for further harmonisation has been made by the Commission.[45] There is in general agreement amongst economists to the effect that a banking union—see below—eventually entails a deposit guarantee scheme at European level. However, there is also a general sentiment that the time is not yet ripe for that; thus the proposal mentioned is made with a view to further harmonising Member States' legislation in the matter.

18–10

---

[40] Directive 2001 /24 [2001] O.J. L125/15. A similar directive was adopted in relation to insurance undertakings, Directive 2001 /17 [2001] O.J. L110/28 repealed by Directive 2009/138 [2009] O.J. L 335/2009.

[41] The Insolvency Directive—that applies cross-sectors—does not address the daunting challenges that the collapse of financial groups may entail, Directive 1346/2000 [2000] O.J. L160/1, with later amendments.

[42] Directive 94/19 [1994] O.J. L135/5, latest amended by Directive 2009/14 [2009] O.J. L68/3. A similar directive was adopted in 1997 concerning investor-compensation schemes, Directive 97/9 [1997] O.J. L84/22.

[43] The scope and nature of the obligation imposed upon Member States has been the subject of litigation, see *Peter Paul* (C-222/02) [2004] E.C.R. I-9425. See also the ruling of the EFTA Court: *EFTA Surveillance Authority v Iceland* (E-16/1) judgment of January 28, 2013, not yet reported.

[44] Another matter is that the State may exceptionally have to come to the rescue of a scheme—in that case the State aid rules must be complied with, see for instance Commission Decision in State aid Case N-17/2009 (the decision is available on-line and can easily be searched for, using the Case number).

[45] COM/2010/368 final. It appears from the proposal that the Commission expects the schemes to be able to resist a medium-sized bank failure.

Mention must also be made of a directive on the taking up, pursuit and prudential supervision of the business of electronic money institutions.[46] Rules concerning capital and own funds requirements, limitations of investments, verifications by the authorities, etc. are provided for in the Directive. Electronic money institutions cannot take deposits and their possibilities for granting credit are very limited. A directive from 2007 concerns payment services.[47] Credit institutions and electronic money institutions are, by being such, permitted to carry out payment transactions. In addition payment institutions, authorised in accordance with the Payment Services Directive, can carry out such transactions. Payment institutions are not allowed to take deposits and their possibilities for granting credit are very limited.[48]

The financial crisis showed that a large number of entities active in the financial sector performed "bank-like" activities such as accepting funding similar to deposits, without being regulated like banks, i.e. as credit institutions. Such entities are for instance money market funds. The common term for referring to this phenomenon is "shadow banking". The sector is huge as it is estimated to represent 25-30 per cent of the financial system on a global level. Given that fact and that the entities are not submitted to banking regulations and thus not to the supervision and the requirements adopted in the public interest to which banks are submitted, it is in general considered that the sector poses a risk to financial stability and must be regulated. In 2012 the Commission presented a first paper on the issue.[49]

Finally, it is worth noting that Union legislation in the field of consumer protection applies in general also to financial services.[50]

6. FINANCIAL MARKETS AND INVESTMENTS

18–11   The Union has liberalised access to stock exchange membership and financial markets in other Member States for investment firms authorised to provide the services concerned in their home Member State. An initial directive on investment services was adopted in 1993 and applied, generally speaking, to all investment firms.[51] It sought to establish the conditions under which authorised investment firms could provide specified services or establish branches in other

---

[46] Directive 2000/46 [2000] O.J. L275/39, repealed by Directive 2009/110 [2009] O.J. L 267/7.

[47] Directive 2007/64 [2007] O.J. L319/1, amended by Directive 2009/111 [2009] O.J. L302/97.

[48] As concerns payments, mention must be made of the Single Euro Payments Area (SEPA) initiative that aims to overcome technical, legal and market barriers between countries in order to create a single market for retail payments in euros. Two SEPA instruments were introduced in 2008 (SEPA credit transfer) and 2009 (SEPA direct debit). Regulation 260/2012 O.J. L94/22 establishes the technical and business requirements for credit transfers and direct debits in euros. The Regulation is also referred to as the "SEPA end-date Regulation" and defines the deadlines for the migration to the new SEPA instruments. The deadline for the euro area is February 1, 2014.

[49] COM(2012) 102 final: Green Paper on Shadow Banking.

[50] See for instance *BHW v Dietzinger* (C-45/96) [1998] E.C.R. I–1199, concerning Directive 85/577 to protect consumers in respect of contracts negotiated away from business premises, and *Mohamed Aziz* (C-415/11), judgment of March 14, 2013, not yet reported, concerning Directive 93/13 on unfair terms in consumer contracts. A directive from 2002 lays down rules concerning distance marketing of consumer financial services, Directive 2002/65 [2002] O.J. L271/16.

[51] Directive 93/22 [1993] O.J. L197/58, now repealed.

Member States, based on the principle of home country authorisation and supervision. It also aimed to harmonise the initial authorisation and operating requirements for investment firms and provided for the harmonisation of some conditions governing the operation of regulated markets. Thus, the Directive entailed the necessary harmonisation for mutual recognition, the home Member State being responsible for the prudential supervision and the host Member State responsible for ensuring compliance with conduct of business rules.

In 2004, a new directive was adopted for the regulation of the markets in financial instruments and investment firms.[52] It aimed to establish a comprehensive regulatory regime regarding the execution of transactions in financial instruments irrespective of the used trading methods. Therefore, it applies to the investment firms and, under certain conditions to credit institutions, with the exclusion of central banks and other bodies performing similar functions, as well as public bodies responsible for public debt.

A directive on undertakings for collective investments in transferable securities (UCITS) was adopted as early as in 1985.[53] The Directive sought to ensure uniform protection of unit-holders and thereby to enhance the undertakings' possibility of marketing its units in other Member States. The Directive was replaced by a new directive in 2009.[54]

After the FSAP and the FSP a number of acts were adopted which should be mentioned, although they do not all relate strictly to investments and some of them are dealt with in Ch.17: Freedom of Establishment/Company Law.

18–12

- Directive on the taxation of the savings income in the form of interest[55];
- Directive on insider dealing and market manipulation (Market Abuse Directive)[56];
- Directive on the prospectus to be published when securities are offered to the public or admitted to trading (Prospectus Directive)[57];
- Directive on takeover bids[58];
- Directive on the harmonisation of transparency requirements in relation to information about issuers whose securities are admitted to trading on a regulated market (Transparency Directive)[59];

A directive adopted in 2011 address the issue of alternative investment fund managers (AIFM), including hedge funds.[60] It seeks to lay down harmonised regulatory standards and to enhance transparency towards investors.

---

[52] Directive 2004/39 [2004] O.J. L145/1, with later amendments. The Directive is commonly referred to as the MIFID Directive. The Directive is currently being revised.
[53] Directive 85/611 [1985] O.J. L375/3, now repealed.
[54] Directive 2009/65 [2009] O.J. L302/32.
[55] Directive 2003/48 [2003] O.J. L157/38, amended [2006], O.J. L363/129.
[56] Directive 2003/6 [2003] O.J. L96/16, amended [2010] O.J. L331/120. The Directive has been interpreted in *Spector and Van Raemdonck* (C-45/08) E.C.R. I-12073, and *Markus Geltl v Daimler AG* (C-19/11), judgment of June 28, 2012, not yet reported.
[57] Directive 2003/71 [2003] O.J. L345/64, amended [2010] O.J. L327/1 and Regulation 809/04 [2004] O.J. L149/1.
[58] Directive 2004/25 [2004] O.J. L147/12, amended 2010, O.J. L 87/109.
[59] Directive 2004/109 [2004] O.J. L390/38, amended [2010] O.J. L327 /1, and Directive 2007/14 laying down the detailed rules for its implementation [2007] O.J. L69/27.
[60] Directive 2011/61 [2011] O.J. L174/1.

The financial crisis showed that the credit ratings established by credit rating agencies were trusted by markets to an extent that was not warranted. A regulation from 2009 seeks to protect investors against the risk of malpractice in credit rating agencies.[61]

The crisis also showed that the over-the-counter sales of derivatives could entail significant risk to financial stability. Derivatives create a complex web of interdependence in the financial system and therefore also a risk of contagion. As such sales were made privately, with information thereabout normally just available to the private parties concerned, the allocation of risk became opaque. A directive from 2012 now regulates the matter.[62]

7. INSURANCE

18–13 The establishment of the internal market in this sector was completed years ago, according to the Commission,[63] with the third Insurance directives of 1992[64] that introduced a single system for the authorisation and financial supervision of insurance undertakings by the Member State in which they have their head office (the home Member State). Such authorisation enables an insurance undertaking to carry out its insurance business anywhere in the Union, by opening agencies or branches in other Member States or providing services cross-border from its home State. When carrying out business in another Member State, the insurance undertaking must comply with the conditions under which, for reasons of the general good, such business must be conducted in the host Member State.

National laws have also been harmonised with regard to insurance against civil liability in respect of the use of motor vehicles,[65] the activities of insurance agents and brokers,[66] co-insurance,[67] legal expenses insurance,[68] reorganisation

---

[61] Regulation 1060/2009 [2009] O.J. L302/1.

[62] Regulation 648/2012 [2012] O.J. L201/1.

[63] See Commission Interpretative Communication "Freedom to provide services and the general good in the insurance sector" [2000] O.J. C43/5.

[64] Directive 92/49 on the co-ordination of laws, regulations and administrative provisions relating to direct insurance other than life insurance (third non-life insurance directive) [1992] O.J. L228/1, and Directive 92/96 on the co-ordination of laws, regulations and administrative provisions relating to direct life assurance (third life insurance directive) [1992] O.J. L360/1, both repealed by Directive 2009/138 [2009] O.J. L335/1, amended [2011] L326/113.

[65] Directive 72/166, on the approximation of the laws of the Member States relating to insurance against civil liability in respect of the use of motor vehicles, and to the enforcement of the obligation to insure against such liability [1972] O.J. L103. This was the first motor insurance directive which was followed by three more directives. Both it and the subsequent directives are now repealed by a codifying directive, Directive 2009/103 [2009] O.J. L263/11. The harmonisation concerns insurance cover and not the national rules on civil liability. The distinction may be difficult to draw in practice, see for instance *Carvalho Ferreira Santos* (C-484/09) [2011] E.C.R. I-1821. In *Farrel* (C-356/05) [2007] E.C.R. I-3067 the Court held that Art.1 of the third motor insurance directive, Directive 90/619, had direct effect.

[66] Directive 77/92 [1977] O.J. L26/14 on measures to facilitate the effective exercise of freedom of establishment and freedom to provide services in respect of the activities of insurance agents and brokers repealed by Directive 2002/92 on insurance mediation [2002] O.J. L9/3. As there are amongst others still many inconsistencies between Member States as to the level of consumer protection, the Commission has presented a proposal for recast of the Directive, see COM(2012) 360/2.

[67] Directive 78/473 [1978] O.J. L151/25, repealed by Directive 2009/138 [2009] O.J. L335/1, amended [2011] O.J. L326/113.

and winding-up of insurance undertakings[69] and on the annual accounts and consolidated accounts of insurance undertakings.[70]

A major overhaul of the legislation in the insurance sector was made in 2009 through the adopting of the Solvency II Framework Directive.[71] The Directive seeks to strengthen the supervision of insurance undertakings, hereunder the risk management. The Directive is an example of the *Lamfalussy* process. The Directive will be supplemented by implementing measures adopted by the Commission, more precisely, delegated acts. Those measures will be supplemented by technical standards set by the European Insurance and Occupational Pensions Authority (EIOPA). Next, EIOPA will provide guidance to national authorities so as to ensure consistent application and co-operation amongst said authorities. Detailed regulation of the powers of EIOPA in this respect will be laid down by an envisaged directive, commonly referred to as the Omnibus II Directive, which is currently pending before the Council and the Parliament.[72] The application in practice of Solvency II has been delayed; however, it is expected that the Directive will be applicable as from January 2014.

8. CROSS SECTOR AND MISCELLANEOUS ISSUES

In 1991, the Council adopted a directive on prevention of the use of the financial system for the purpose of money laundering.[73] The notion of money laundering has gradually expanded and now the applicable rules also apply to terrorist financing. The Directive does not apply only to undertakings in the financial sector; notaries and independent legal professionals for instance also come within the scope of the Directive.

18–14

In the financial sector there are many groups of undertakings, or with another term, "financial entities in a financial conglomerate". Conglomerates can for instance consist of banks, insurance firms and investment firms and they pose additional risks, for instance as concerns contagion from one part of the conglomerate to other parts. In 2002, a directive was adopted to ensure supplementary supervision of such conglomerates and in 2011 it was substantially amended.[74]

---

[68] Directive 87/344 [1987] O.J. L185/77 repealed by Directive 2009/138 [2009] O.J. L 335/1, amended [2011] L 326/113; see *Stark* (C-293/10) [2011] E.C.R. I-4711: freedom of the insured person to choose his lawyer, limitation of the reimbursement allowed.

[69] Directive 2001/17 [2001] O.J. L110/28 repealed by Directive 2009/138 [2009] O.J. L 335/1, amended [2011] L326/113.

[70] Directive 91/674 [1991] O.J. L374/7 amended [2006], O.J. L 224/1. See Regulation 1606/02 on the application of international accounting standards [2002] O.J. L243/1 amended [2008] O.J. L 97/62 and Regulation 2086/04 [2004] O.J. L363/1. For more information concerning the international accounting standards, see Ch.17: Freedom of Establishment/Company Law.

[71] Directive 2009/138 [2009], O.J. L 335/1, amended [2011] L 326/113.

[72] COM(2011) 8 final.

[73] Directive 91/308 [1991] O.J. L166/77 repealed by Directive 2005/60 [2005] O.J. L306/15, with later amendments. See *Ordre des barreaux Francophones et Germanophones* (C-305/05) [2007] E.C.R. I-5305 concerning the obligation of lawyers to divulge to the competent authorities all facts that could indicate money laundering.

[74] Respectively Directive 2002/87 [2002] O.J. L35/1 and Directive 2011/89 [2011] O.J. L326/113.

The financial crisis showed that remuneration structures in the financial sector could induce excessive risk-taking. Even before the financial crisis and after the Enron scandal in the beginning of the 2000s there had been voices to the effect that shareholders should have a more effective say in the policy of remuneration of CEOs and other top employees in firms. Two Commission recommendations in the matter[75] were followed by the adoption in 2010 of some rather general provisions applicable in the banking sector.[76] Late spring 2013, Parliament and Council came to an agreement on provisions that will put a ceiling on the variable remuneration, namely two times the annual fixed remuneration, unless the assembly general of the company decides otherwise.

The financial crisis entailed that massive sums from the public purse went to rescuing undertakings in the financial sector, i.e. sums that ultimately have to be provided by the taxpayers. Politically the idea that the financial sector also should contribute more generally to the public purse gained ground and thus, the idea of a tax on financial transactions.[77] Many Member States, in particular the UK which fears for London's position as a financial centre, opposed the idea. In January 2013, the Council authorised 11 Member States to make use of the mechanism of enhanced co-operation with a view to adopting such a tax.

9. SUPERVISION AND GOVERNANCE

18–15   The Union realised that the financial crisis exposed important shortcomings in financial supervision, both in particular cases and in relation to the financial system as a whole.

Three agencies were created. As a group they are commonly referred to as the European Supervisory Authorities (ESA) and each is active within a specific part of the financial sector:

The European Banking Authority (EBA) has broad competences, including preventing regulatory arbitrage, guaranteeing a level playing field, strengthening international supervisory co-ordination, promoting supervisory convergence and providing advice to the EU institutions.[78]

The European Insurance and Occupational Pensions Authority (EIOPA) have powers in relation to the areas of activities of insurance/reinsurance undertakings, institutions for occupational retirement provisions and insurance intermediaries.[79]

The European Securities and Markets Authority (ESMA) oversee financial and securities markets, including matters of corporate governance, auditing, financial reporting, take-over bids, clearing and settlement and derivatives issues.[80]

---

[75] Recommendation 2004/913 fostering an appropriate regime for remuneration of the CEO of listed companies [2004] O.J. L385/55 and Recommendation on remuneration policies in the financial services sector [2009] O.J. L120/22.

[76] Directive 2010/76 amending Directives 2006/48 and 2006/49 [2010] O.J. L329/3.

[77] The Commission made a proposal for a directive in 2011, COM(2011) 594 final. It was based on the Treaty provisions allowing for measures to be adopted to ensure the proper functioning of the internal market and to avoid distortion of competition.

[78] Regulation 1093/2010 [2010] O.J. L331/12.

[79] Regulation 1094/2010 [2010] O.J. L331/48.

[80] Regulation 1095/2010 [2010] O.J. L331/84.The powers of the three ESA's are also regulated by Directive 2010/78 [2010] O.J. L331/120.

Moreover, a new system for the supervision of the financial system within the   **18–16**
Union was established with the creation of the European System of Financial
Supervision (ESFS).[81] The ESFS aims at bringing together the actors of financial
supervision at national level and at the level of the Union. The ESFS is composed
of the following authorities:

- The European Systemic Risk Board (ESRB).[82] It has its seat in Frankfurt
  am Main. It is chaired by the President of the ECB. The ECB is also
  represented on the organs of the ESRB, such as the Steering Committee and
  the General Board. The national central banks are also represented on the
  General Board. ESRB must co-operate with international players such as
  the IMF. The ESRB is in charge of the macro-prudential oversight of the
  financial system within the Union in order to contribute to the prevention or
  mitigation of systemic risks to financial stability.
- the European Banking Authority (EBA);
- the European Insurance and Occupational Pensions Authority (EIOPA);
- the European Securities and Markets Authority (ESMA);
- the Joint Committee of the European Supervisory Authorities[83];
- the competent authorities in the Member States.[84]

The Euro crisis also leads to changes. In June 2012, the European Council
decided that steps should be taken to establish a banking union. The decision was
taken against the background of the deepening of the Euro crisis and to
overcome, at least for the future, the link between weak banks and States that
financially are not, or only with difficulty, in the position to bail out banks. There
is no exact definition of the term "banking union" but there is general agreement
amongst economists that four components are needed, namely common rules
governing the banking sector, a single supervisory mechanism (SSM), a single
resolution mechanism (SRM), and a common deposit guarantee system. As
concerns the first component, it is overall in place within the Union, as the
previous pages show. The three other components are politically and technically
very difficult. The Commission presented in autumn 2012 its first proposal for
SSM. By the end of 2012, Member States reached political agreement concerning
the main elements of the SSM. In principle the ECB will be in charge of the
SSM; however, ECB will only supervise itself financial institutions that are
systemically important, while national authorities will carry out the supervision
of the others—which are numerous, but not systemically important. Currently—
spring 2013—the agreement has not materialised in regulations. SRM is with all
probability the next issue on the political agenda; the issue is technically very
difficult, for instance co-ordinated reorganisation and winding-up of financial
conglomerates operating in more Member States and globally. A common deposit
guarantee scheme is not on the political agenda within a foreseeable future.

---

[81] Regulation 1092/2010 [2010] O.J. L331/1.
[82] Set up by Regulation 1092/2010. The tasks of the ECB in relation to the ESRB are set out in
Regulation 1096/2010 [2010] O.J. L331/162.
[83] The Committee is set up under the Regulations setting up the ESA's.
[84] They are referred to in the Regulations setting up the ESA's.

FURTHER READING

18–17   Lorna Woods, *Free Movement of Goods and Services within the European Community* (Aldershot, Ashgate, 2004).

Ulla Neergaard, Ruth Nielsen and Lynn M. Roseberry, *The Services Directive-Consequences for the Welfare State and the European Social Model* (DJOF Publishing 2008).

CHAPTER 19

Free Movement of Capital and Payments[1]

Capital movements are for instance: 19-01

1. direct investments;
2. investments in real estate;
3. operations in securities normally dealt in on the capital market;
4. operations in units of collective investment undertakings;
5. operations in securities and other instruments normally dealt in on the money market;
6. operations in current and deposit accounts with financial institutions;
7. credits related to commercial transactions or to the provision of services in which a resident is participating;
8. financial loans and credits;
9. sureties, other guaranties and rights of pledge;
10. transfers in performance of insurance contracts;
11. personal capital movements;
12. physical import and export of financial assets; and
13. other capital movements.

Capital movements are in general related to investments. They can be distinguished from payments. A payment is consideration for instance for a good or a service. This distinction is now in general not relevant legally.[2] Both capital movements and payments are liberalised.[3] Previously the distinction was relevant for the simple reason that payments were liberalised, while capital movements were not. The liberalisation of payments went hand in hand with the other freedoms; nobody would profit from those freedoms if the economic results of the activities carried out under them could not be "brought home" to wherever in the Union the operator had his business; there would for instance not be much value for a seller to sell his goods cross border if he cannot receive the purchase sum.[4]

---

[1] Arts 63–66 TFEU. See also the Introduction to Part III of this book: The Internal Market.
[2] It may be in other contexts statistically or economically.
[3] Art.63(1) and (2) TFEU.
[4] It must be noted that although the distinction between capital movements and payments are generally of no legal relevance, it is not always so. The financial crisis has shown that exceptionally a Member State may need to control and restrict capital movements. In this context the distinction becomes relevant. Payments will namely still be allowed, the State limiting itself to verify that the payment is indeed such and not a disguised capital movement.

19–02   Contrary to what is the case with the other Internal Market freedoms, the Treaty provisions on free movement of capital have been substantially altered in the course of the life of the Union, namely with the Maastricht Treaty and the establishment of the Economic and Monetary Union. The provisions are now in line with those governing the other freedoms. That is all restrictions on capital movements are banned unless they can be justified.[5] The ban has direct effect.[6] It does not apply in purely internal situations.[7]

It must be noted that the ban also applies to extra-Union movements, i.e. movements of capital with third countries. The distinction between movements intra-Union and extra-Union has importance because of the different possibilities to restrict them.[8] As concerns movements with third countries, national restrictions existing on December 31, 1993 are grandfathered into the Treaty.[9] Moreover, these movements may be regulated in more detail by the Union legislator, in accordance with the ordinary legislative procedure;[10] and a "step backwards" in the liberalisation may be decided under the special legislative procedure. If such movements cause serious difficulties for the Economic and Monetary Union, the Council may impose safeguard measures, i.e. restrictions for a limited time.[11]

As is the case with the other Internal Market freedoms, the notion of restrictions is wide. It covers for instance national measures concerning the currency in which a mortgage can be registered, under which the currencies of other Member States were excluded;[12] national measures concerning the valuation of assets for the purpose of inheritance taxes, which implied that assets in other Member States were evaluated differently;[13] national measures requiring the acquirer of an agricultural property to take up his residence of the property;[14] national measures submitting the acquisition of certain shareholdings to the consent of national authorities;[15] national discriminatory rules concerning the taxation of dividends.[16] The Court has also held that the ban applies to national

---

[5] The liberalisation started before the Maastricht Treaty, namely with Directive 88/361. The Directive is commonly referred to as the Second Capital Movements Directive. After the Maastricht Treaty the Directive has lost its importance, i.e. the liberalisation is provided for by the Treaty provisions. However, the Directive contains in its Annex I a non-exhaustive list of capital movements, often referred to as the nomenclature. The Court of Justice still refers to that list in its case law, see for instance *Scheunemann* (C- 31/11), judgment of July 19, 2012, not yet reported. The list at the beginning of this chapter is from that Annex.

[6] *Sanz de Lera* (Joined Cases C-163/94, C-165/94 and C-250/94) [1995] E.C.R. I-4821.

[7] *Reischl* (Joined Cases C-515/99, C-519 to 524/99 and C-526 to 540/99) [2002] E.C.R. I-2157, para.24.

[8] The EEA EFTA States are not third countries in this relation, see *Ospelt* (C-452/01) [2003] E.C.R. I-9743, the reason being in short that they participate in the Internal Market: for the EEA see Ch.38: Common Commercial Policy and Relations with Third Countries. The overseas countries and territories, listed in Annex II TFEU are considered as third-countries in this context, see *Prunus and Polonium* (C-384/09) [2011] E.C.R. I-3319.

[9] Art.64(1) TFEU. A "grandfather clause" is a clause that allows previous rules, which would be in contradiction with the future rules, to subsist.

[10] Art.64(2) TFEU.

[11] Art.66 TFEU.

[12] *Trummer and Mayer* (C-222/97) [1999] E.C.R. I-1661.

[13] *Jäger* (C-256/06) [2008] E.C.R. I-123.

[14] *Festersen* (C-370/05) [2007] E.C.R. I-1129.

[15] *Commission v Greece* (C-244/11), judgment of November 8, 2012, not yet reported.

[16] *Verkooijen* (C-35/98) [2000] E.C.R. I-4071.

measures under which national authorities seek to obtain or preserve special rights in companies, those rights going beyond what the size of the authorities' shareholding in the companies entitles them to.[17] Such measures may for instance be the right to veto certain strategic decisions of the company or to appoint extra members of a company's board.

As for the justification the Treaty provides in the first place that the principle of free movement of capital shall not prevent Member States from applying their tax laws that "distinguish between taxpayers who are not in the same situation with regard their place of residence or with regard to the place where such capital is invested".[18] National tax laws draw in many aspects such a distinction which is prima facie at odds with the fact that residence requirements constitute prima facie indirect discrimination. The case law on the impact of the four freedoms on national tax rules is presented in Ch.25: Taxation.

19–03

In the second place the Treaty provides that Member States may "take all requisite measures to prevent infringements of national tax law regulations, in particular in the field of taxation and the prudential supervision of financial institutions, or to lay down procedures for the declaration of capital movements for purposes of administrative and statistical information,[19] or to take measures which are justified on grounds of public policy or public security."[20] The Treaty adds that all measures may not constitute arbitrary discrimination of a disguised restriction of free movement of capital.

Case law has added more justification grounds, such as for instance the objective of preserving viable farming communities[21] and town and country planning.[22]

Restrictions must, as in the other freedoms, be in compliance with the proportionality principle.

---

[17] See for instance *Commission v Netherlands (Golden shares)* (Joined Cases C-282/04 and C-283/04) [2006] E.C.R. I-9141 and *Commission v Germany (Volkswagen)* (C-112/05) [2007] E.C.R. I-8995.

[18] Art.65(1) letter a) TFEU.

[19] See for instance from the time when Directive 88/361 was applicable, *Bordessa* (Joined Cases C-358/93 and C-416/93) [1995] E.C.R. I-36.

[20] Art.65(1) letter b) TFEU. If a Member State imposes an authorisation system of certain movements on grounds of public policy or public security it must be able to articulate its rules in such a way that the persons concerned can ascertain under which conditions the authorisation will be granted or not, see *Scientology* (C-54/99) [2000] E.C.R. I-1335.

[21] See *Ospelt* (quoted above, fn.8).

[22] See for instance *Konle* (C-302/97) [1999] E.C.R. I-3099.

CHAPTER 20

Intellectual Property Rights

1. INTRODUCTION

The first reference in the Treaty to those rights is in connection with the free movement of goods: prohibition or restrictions on imports, exports or transit of goods may be justified by the protection of industrial and commercial property (hereinafter: IP rights).[1] National IP rights confer on the holder an exclusive right within a given territory, and there is an inherent tension with the objective of free flow of goods across borders; to the extent that the holder of the IP rights enjoys protection, similar or identical goods to the product protected cannot flow freely into the Member State concerned. The way in which the Union has dealt with this problem, in case the goods originate from the IP rights holder, is set out below under "Exhaustion".

20–01

There is also an inherent tension between IP rights and competition. To the extent of his IP right the holder is protected against competition. However, it is generally recognised that in a more general perspective, competition benefits from IP rights as they create incentives to innovation. Occasionally, however, competition rules may interfere with the exercise of IP rights. This is briefly addressed in section 3.

The Union has been very active in seeking harmonisation of national laws concerning IP rights. Moreover, the Union has created a number of IP rights. Section 4 gives an overview of the main measures adopted.

Before setting out Union law it should be recalled that IP rights are thoroughly regulated through international agreements and conventions to which the Union and/or the Member States are parties. The most important ones are: the Paris Convention on the Protection of Industrial Property of 1883, with later revisions, the Berne Convention for the Protection of Literary and Artistic Works of 1886, with later revisions (both falling now within the ambit of WIPO), the Universal Copyright Convention of 1952, the WIPO Performance and Phonograms Treaty, and the TRIPS agreement, concluded in the context of WTO.

2. EXHAUSTION

IP rights may be used to partition markets. That can for instance occur in the following way: in France there is a company A that owns the trademark "XYZ". The company establishes a subsidiary B in Germany which produces the same

20–02

---

[1] Art.36 TFEU.

goods as the parent company. In Germany the subsidiary registers the trademark "XYZ" for the goods. A trader, independent of A and B buys goods produced by B and marked "XYZ" in Germany and imports them into France. Here, however, company A opposes the marketing of the goods, alleging that the marketing will infringe its trademark right, registered in France. How shall that conflict between the independent trader and the trademark owner be solved? The answer follows from the Court's case law and it is that the trademark owner cannot invoke his trademark right because the trade-marked goods at issue have been put on the market in the Union by him or with his consent, in this case by the subsidiary B. One says that in relation to these goods the trade mark rights are exhausted; hence the name of "exhaustion doctrine" or "exhaustion principle".[2] The Court reached this result by establishing a distinction between the "existence" of IP rights and the "exercise" of IP rights; Union law does not interfere with the existence of national IP rights but with the exercise.[3] The Court later nuanced this to the effect that Union law does not interfere with the specific subject matter of the IP right;[4] in the example above, the specific subject matter of a trade mark is in particular to provide an indication of commercial origin. That function of the trade mark is not interfered with by letting the trade-marked goods from Germany move into France. The principle of exhaustion applies when the goods have been put on the market in an EEA State by the IP owner or with his consent. It does not occur when the marketing has occurred without consent, for instance in case of compulsory licensing.[5] In case the IP owner sells his right to a third party, there is no consent to the subsequent marketing and thus no exhaustion. In the example above, if company B) sells its trademark right in Germany to an unrelated trader, the company A) will be able to oppose the marketing by that trader of the trade-marked goods in France—where A) has maintained its trade mark right—because there is a likelihood of confusion. Denying the company A) that right would be tantamount to putting the specific subject matter of a trade mark right in jeopardy; the two marks are identical but the commercial origin is not the

---

[2] Exhaustion occurs when the goods have been put on the market in the Union by the IP owner or with his consent, Union-wide exhaustion. However, as the exhaustion doctrine also applies when the first marketing has been made in one of the three EFTA States that participate in the EEA (European Economic Area), one refers often to "EEA exhaustion".

[3] *Consten and Grundig* (Joined Cases 56/64 and 58/64) [1966] E.C.R. 299.

[4] See for instance See *Centrafarm v Sterling Drug* (15/74) and *Centrafarm v Winthrop* (16/74) both [1974] E.C.R. 1147 and 1183; [1974] 2 C.M.L.R. 480, where the Court defined what is the subject matter of a patent: the guarantee that the patentee, to reward the creative effort of the inventor, has the exclusive right to use an invention with a view to manufacturing industrial products and putting them into circulation for the first time, either directly or by the grant of licences to third parties, as well as the right to oppose infringements (*Centrafarm v Sterling drug* (15/74) (quoted above, para.9) and of a trade mark (*Centrafarm v Winthrop* (16/74) (quoted above, para.8); from *Parke, Davis* (24/67) [1968] E.C.R. 55 it follows that one can legally oppose the import and distribution of an unpatented product, otherwise one's own patent becomes useless. The same applies where the holder of a specific right prevents the import of a product from another Member State where there is no longer a protection: *EMI Electrola v Patricia In -und Export* (341/87) [1989] E.C.R. 92; [1989] 2 C.M.L.R. 413.

[5] *Pharmon v Hoechst* (19/84) [1985] E.C.R. 2281. In a case commonly known as *HAG I—Van Zuylen v HAG* (192/73) [1974] E.C,R. 731 the Court held that in case of compulsory division of a trade mark, the principle of exhaustion applied. *HAG I* is no longer valid law as it was later overruled by *HAG II—CNL-Sucal v HAG* (C-10/89) [1990] E.C.R. I-3711.

same.[6] The owner of the IP right may only oppose exhaustion when he has legitimate reasons for doing so, for instance when the actions of the independent trader impair the IP right.[7] The principle of EEA exhaustion can be summarised in the following main points:

1. The Treaty does not affect the existence of IP rights recognised by the law of the Member States.
2. The exercise of those rights may, nevertheless, depending on the circumstances, be restricted by the prohibitions of the Treaties.
3. The principle of exhaustion may not jeopardise the rights which constitute the specific subject matter of the IP right. Therefore the principle of exhaustion does for instance not apply to the right to rent out a work, protected by copyright, as the specific subject matter is to ensure the owner the right to control public use of the work.[8]
4. The principle of exhaustion applies to all IP rights.
5. The principle does not apply when the IP owner has legitimate reasons to oppose it, for instance when the independent trader's actions alter or impair the IP right.

Above it has been stressed that exhaustion occurs when the good protected by the IP right is put on the market in the EEA by the owner or with his consent. Now, what happens if the goods at issue are put on the market outside the EEA by the owner or with his consent, and an independent trader thereafter imports them into the EEA? The answer is that in that case, there is no exhaustion: the IP owner may invoke his IP right in the EEA to oppose the import into the EEA. A principle of international exhaustion thus does not apply in the Union legal order.[9]

---

[6] *IHT Internationale Heiz-technik v Ideal Standard* (C-9/93) [1994] E.C.R. I-2789. Whether the assignment in the example could imply market partitioning, illegal under the competition rules is another issue.

[7] Within the field of trademarks there is much case law on this, in particular as concerns pharmaceutical products. The reason is that in some instances the independent trader, in order to get access to the market in another Member State must re-package the trade-marked good or affix labelling to it, in order to comply with mandatory rules in the importing Member State; for instance a pharmaceutical product may only be sold if the text on the package is in the language of the consumer; the independent trader in order to comply with that requirement may need to re-package the product; the trade mark owner then objects arguing that the re-packaging has entailed an impairment of his trademark right. The case law on re-packaging is rather complex, but the main guiding principle for resolving such a dispute is that the independent trader may only re-package the product if it is necessary to access the market in the importing Member State, and not just done to obtain commercial gain, see for instance *Boehringer Ingelheim* (C-143/00) [2002] E.C.R. I-3759.

[8] *Warner Brothers v Christiansen* (158/86) [1988] E.C.R. 2605.

[9] The leading ruling on the matter is *Silhouette* (C-355/96) [1998] E.C.R. I–4799, which concerned the first Trade Mark Directive. The reasons that led the Court to the result are complex but the essence may be summarised to the effect that the Union legislator had reserved the question of international exhaustion or not for itself and the Directive did not provide for international exhaustion. As the regulation of the Directive pre-empted national regulations of the question—see Ch.26: Approximation of Laws—an individual Member could not either provide for international exhaustion in its internal legal order. The absence of international exhaustion in the Union legal order has been extensively discussed and also criticised in legal literature. It is by now also established that the three EEA EFTA States do not apply the principle of international exhaustion, see *L'Oreal* (Joined Cases E-9/07 and E-10/07) [2008] EFTA Court Report 210.

3.   IP RIGHTS AND "ABUSE OF DOMINANT POSITION"

20–03   As mentioned above, the owner of an IP right can occupy a dominant position and the question therefore arises as to whether a refusal to grant a licence can constitute an "abuse of a dominant position" under the competition rules of the Union. According to the Court, an obligation imposed upon the proprietor of an IP right to grant to third parties, even in return for a reasonable royalty, a licence for the supply of products making use of the IP right would lead to the proprietor thereof being deprived of the substance of his exclusive right and the refusal to grant such a licence cannot in itself constitute an abuse of a dominant position.[10] The Court has also held that the mere fact that the owner of an intellectual property right has granted to a sole licensee an exclusive right in the territory of a Member State, while prohibiting the grant of sub-licences, is not sufficient to justify a finding that such a contract infringes competition rules.[11] This is the clear principle of departure for assessing the relationship between IP rights and the Treaty's ban on abuse of dominant position. However, the refusal to supply spare parts by an undertaking holding a dominant position to independent traders may constitute an abuse prohibited by the Treaty.[12] The refusal to grant a licence on a copyright constitutes, according to the Court, an abuse of a dominant position where the following conditions are fulfilled: the undertaking that requests the licence intends to offer new products or services not offered by the copyright owner and for which there is a potential consumer demand, the refusal is not justified by objective considerations and the refusal is such as to reserve to the copyright owner the supply of a service by eliminating all competition on the relevant market.[13] Such a situation was the object of a Commission decision forcing television companies to supply a third party (Magill) with their individual advance weekly programmes listing and permitting reproduction of those listings that were covered by copyright. This decision was confirmed by the General Court and, on appeal, by the Court of Justice.[14]

4.   UNION LEGISLATION

20–04   The Union has enacted harmonisation measures for a host of IP rights. Moreover, the Union has created a few Union wide IP rights.[15] Below is an overview of the most important developments.

---

[10]   *Volvo v Veng* (238/87) [1988] E.C.R. 6211.

[11]   *Tiercé Ladbroke v Commission* (T-504/93) [1997] E.C.R. II–923.

[12]   See the Commission's decision in *Hugin* [1978] O.J. L22/23. The decision was annulled by the Court but on the ground that the Commission had not established that there was an effect on trade between Member States; a condition sine qua non for the prohibition on abuse of dominant position to apply; *Hugin* (22/78) [1979] E.C. R. 1869.

[13]   *IMS Health v NDC Health* (C-418/01), [2004] E.C.R. I–5039. See also *Microsoft* (T-201/04) [2007] E.C.R. II-3601.

[14]   See *RTE and ITP v Commission* (Joined Cases C-241/91 P and C-242/91 P) [1995] E.C.R. I–743.

[15]   The Lisbon Treaty introduced a specific provision as legal basis for the Union's creation of IP rights, Art.118 TFEU.

The different IP rights

(a) Patents

The Convention on the Grant of a European Patent[16] of 1973, revised in 2000, **20–05**
known as the European Patent Convention, is a multilateral treaty setting up the
European Patent Organisation (EPO), and provides an autonomous legal system
according to which a European (not a Union) patent is granted. The Convention is
not a legal instrument of the Union. A European patent is not a unitary right, but
a group of essentially independent, nationally enforceable and revocable patents.
Those patents are granted via a single harmonised procedure before the European
Patent Office at Munich, at its branches at The Hague and Berlin, or at a national
patent office of one of the Contracting Parties. National patents continue to exist.
For decades, the Union sought to create a Union patent but the efforts failed, inter
alia because of disagreement among Member States concerning the judicial
system and the language regime that should apply. In 2012 a breakthrough came
in the negotiations, by way of using the mechanism for enhanced cooperation.[17]
The system that will be put in place builds upon the existing European patent
system. A system of patent courts will also be set up, based in London, Paris and
Munich.

Attention must also be drawn to the Directive on the legal protection of the
topographies of semi-conductor products,[18] and the Directive on the legal
protection of biotechnical inventions.[19]

(b) Copyrights and Related Rights

In 2001, Parliament and the Council adopted a directive on the harmonisation of **20–06**
certain aspects of copyright and related rights in the information society.[20]
According to the Commission it complements the existing framework on
copyright and related rights to respond to the new challenge[21] of technology and
the information society. There exists presently a directive on the legal protection
of computer programs[22]; on rental right and lending right and on certain rights
related to copyright in the field of intellectual property[23]; on the co-ordination of
certain rules concerning copyright and rights related to copyright applicable to

---

[16] See *http://www.epo.org/law-practice/legal-texts/epc.html* [accessed August 23, 2013].
[17] All Member States, except Spain and Italy, participate.
[18] [1987] O.J. L24/36.
[19] [1998] O.J. L213/13.
[20] [2001] O.J. L167/10.
[21] Directive 2006/115 [2006] O.J. L376/28.
[22] [1991] O.J. L111/16. It includes neighbouring rights that are protected by specific legislation. See,
for instance, Council Directive 92/100 on film rental rights and lending rights and on certain rights
related to copyright in the field of intellectual property [1992] O.J. L346/61, amended O.J. L167/10.
Art.5(1) precludes a system of remuneration calculated exclusively according to the number of
borrowers *VEWA* (C-271/10) E.C.R.10.03.11; Art.8, para.2 was interpreted in *SENA* (C-245/00)
[2003] E.C.R. I–12151 and Art.2(1) in *Commission v Portugal* (C-61/05) [2006] E.C.R. I-6779
extending those rights to videogram producers constitutes a breach of that article. See also Council
Resolution on increased protection for copyright and neighbouring rights [1992] O.J. C138/1.
[23] [2006] O.J. L376/28.

satellite broadcasting and cable re-transmission[24]; on harmonising the term of protection of copyright and certain related rights[25]; and on the legal protection of databases.[26]

The 2001 Directive defines the scope of the acts covered by the reproduction rights with regard to the different beneficiaries. The right covers any transmission and air re-transmission of a work to the public by wire or wireless means, including broadcasting. For authors it applies to their work; for performers: to their performance; for phonogram producers: to their phonograms; for producers of the first fixation of films: to the original and copies of their films; and, for broadcasting organisations: to fixations of their broadcastings, whether transmitted by wire or over the air, including by cable or satellite. The Directive provides for exceptions and limitations, for sanctions and remedies, etc.

(c) Trade Marks

20–07   The trade mark laws of the Member States have legally been harmonised through the first Council Directive to approximate the laws of the Member States relating to trade marks.[27] The Directive has been subject of numerous Court rulings, inter alia on the core concept of "likelihood of confusion", which according to the Court includes the notion of association between two marks.[28]

A Union-wide trade mark right was created through the Regulation on the Union Trade Mark that provides uniform trade mark protection for the entire territory of the European Union.[29]

The Regulation provides that each Member State must designate, in their territory, as limited a number as possible of national courts and tribunals of first and second instance, referred to as "Community trade mark courts", to perform the tasks assigned to them by the Regulation to the extent permitted under national law. They have exclusive jurisdiction (1) for all infringement actions, and of threatened infringement relating to Union trademarks, (2) for actions for declaration of non-infringement, (3) for all action brought as a results of acts referred to in Art.9(3) and (4) for counter claims for revocation or for a declaration of invalidity of the Union trademark.[30]

20–08   This Regulation was amended in 2003 to give effect to the accession of the European Union to the Protocol relating to the Madrid Agreement concerning the international registration of marks.[31]

The Union trade mark is obtained by filing one single application with the Office for Harmonisation in the Internal Market (Trade Marks, Designs and Models) (OHIM). The protection lasts 10 years and can be renewed. There is an

---

[24] [1993] O.J. L248/15.

[25] [2006] O J. L372/12.

[26] [1996] O.J. L77/20.

[27] Directive 89/104 [1989] O.J. L40/1, codified by Directive 2008/95 [2008] O.J. L299/25. The Directive is currently being revised.

[28] See, for instance *Canon v Cannon* (C-37/97) [1998] E.C.R. I–5507 and *Lloyd v Klijsen* (C-342/97) [1999] E.C.R. I–3819.

[29] Regulation 40/94 [1994] O.J. L349/93; codified version [2009] O.J. L78/1.

[30] The Decisions of these Community trademark courts have affect in the territory of Member States other than the Member State of the court seized, see *DHL Express France v Chronopost* (C-235/09) [2011] E.C.R. I-2801.

[31] [2003] O.J. L296/1.

implementing regulation,[32] a regulation on the fees payable to the Office, a regulation on the fees payable in respect of the registration of Union design[33] and a regulation laying down the rules of procedure of the Board of Appeal of the Office.[34]

(d) Designs

A directive of the Parliament and the Council aims at approximating national legislations on the protection of designs.[35]   **20–09**

The Union has also created a Union design. Its creation was decided at the end of 2001. It sets up a system for obtaining a Union design to which uniform protection is given, with uniform effect throughout the entire territory of the Union.[36] It lays down a simple and inexpensive procedure for registering designs with the Office for Harmonisation in the Internal Market.

The Office registers Union designs as from April 1, 2003. The aim is to remove legal uncertainty facing industry as a result of the differences in national legislation. It also aims at encouraging creativity and innovation. The Union system co-exists with the national protection systems. To qualify for protection, designs must be new and have an individual character. The regulation provides for two types of protection: without any formality—an "unregistered Union design"—protection for three years from the moment the design is made available to the public against systematic copying; and the "registered Union design", five years against both copying and development of similar design.

Only national courts are competent for dealing with infringements.   **20–10**

A registered design may be declared invalid by the Office; such a decision may be appealed before the Board of Appeal whose decisions are open to appeal before the General Court.

The Regulation was implemented by a Commission regulation[37] supplementing the legal framework for the registration and setting the fees to be paid to the Office for registration; this regulation had to be amended following the accession of the Union to the Geneva Act of The Hague Agreement concerning the international registration of industrial designs.[38] The Union acceded to the Geneva Act of The Hague Agreement concerning the international registration of industrial design[39]; a regulation was adopted to give effect to this accession.[40]

---

[32] Regulation 2868/95 [1995] O.J. L303/1.
[33] Regulation 2246/02 [2002] O.J. L341/54.
[34] Regulation 216/96 [1996] O.J. L28/11.
[35] Directive 98/71 [1998] O.J. L289/71.
[36] [2002] O.J. L3/1.
[37] Regulation 2245/2002 [2002] O.J. L 341/28, amended by Regulation 876/07 [2007] O.J. L193/13 and Regulation 2246/02 [2002] O.J. L341/54 amended by Regulation 877/07 [2007] O.J. L193/16.
[38] Regulation 876/07 [2007] O.J. L193/13.
[39] Decision of December 18, 2006 [2006] O.J. L386/28.
[40] Regulation 1891/06 [2006] O.J. L386/14.

(e)   Counterfeit Goods and Piracy

20–11   A Parliament and Council directive[41] provides for measures and procedures to be applied by the Member States to ensure the enforcement of the intellectual property rights and apply appropriate measures against those responsible for counterfeiting and piracy.

See also a directive on the legal protection of services based on, or consisting of, conditional access.[42]

(f)   Protection of IP rights

20–12   In 2004 the Parliament and the Council adopted a directive on the enforcement of intellectual property rights.[43] While other harmonisation measures have intended to harmonise the substantive rules applying to IP rights, this Directive obliges the Member States to set up the necessary measures and procedures to safeguard those rights.

(g)   Protected Geographical Indications and Designations of Origin

20–13   This regime applies to agricultural products. It seeks to protect the names of agricultural products which are produced in accordance with the traditions of a particular region and whose characteristics are determined thereby, for instance "feta" is reserved for cheese produced in Greece. There are two types of food quality names based on their geographical origin: the protected geographical indication (PGI); and the protected designation of origin (PDO). Once these names are registered, they are protected against the sale of any other competing imitation product seeking to use the reputation of the name of origin.[44]

FURTHER READING

20–14   David T. Keeling, *Intellectual Property Rights in EU law—Free Movement and Competition Law, Volume 1* (Oxford, 2003).

Panos Koutrakos, "In search of a common vocabulary in free movement of goods: the example of repackaging pharmaceuticals" (2003) E.L.Rev. 53.

Morag McDonald and Dr Uma Suthersanen, *Copyright: World Law and Practice* (Sweet & Maxwell, 2006).

Prof. Spyros Maniatis, *Trade marks in Europe: A Practical Jurisprudence* (Sweet & Maxwell, 2006).

---

[41] Directive 2004/48 [2004] OJ.J L195/16. See *Promusicae* (C-275/06) [2008] E.C.R. I-271: Directive neither compelling nor precluding obligation to disclose personal data in civil proceedings.
[42] Directive 98/84 [1998] O.J. L320/54. See European Convention on the legal protection of services based on, or consisting of, conditional access [2011] O.J. L336/1.
[43] [2004] O.J. L 195/16.
[44] See Regulation 2081/92 [1992] O.J. L208/1, now replaced by Regulation 510/2006 [2006] O.J. L93/12. The Regulation lays down a rather complex procedure for the protection of those rights, involving both national authorities and the Commission.

CHAPTER 21

Public Procurement

1. INTRODUCTION

The volume of public procurement contracts represents about 18 per cent of the GDP of the Union or €1,500 billion, which shows its economic importance. It is in the interest of the internal market that companies from all Member States can compete for such contracts. Competition for such contracts also serves to ensure that public authorities and thus in the last instance the taxpayers do not pay too high a price for the services and goods they buy. Competition also serves to lower the risk of fraud and corruption in the award of such contracts.   **21–01**

The bulk of the Union's rules on public procurement are found in secondary law, namely in two directives adopted in 2004. The two Directives are presently being reviewed. One applies only to the procurement procedures of entities operating in the water, energy, transport and postal sectors.[1] The other one concerns award of public work contracts (for instance the construction of a government building), public supply contracts (for instance an authority's purchase of furniture for public schools) and public service contracts (for instance purchase of IT-services).[2] The fact that this field of law is extensively regulated by acts of secondary law must not lead one to forget about primary law. Questions not regulated by the Directives and public contracts outside the scope of the Directives are governed by primary law, such as the provisions of primary law banning restrictions on intra-Union trade. The fundament of the law governing public contracts is the principles of equal treatment, of transparency and of non-discrimination on grounds of nationality.[3] The rules of the Union must conform to the rules adopted within the framework of the WTO, i.e. the Agreement on Government Procurement (GPA).

---

[1] Directive 2004/17 with later amendments [2004] O.J. L134/1.

[2] Directive 2004/18 with later amendments [2004] O.J. L134/114.The Directive is often referred to as the "Classical" Directive while Directive 2004/17 is often referred to as the "Utilities" Directive. The first directive in this field concerned public works and was adopted in 1971.

[3] The principle of equal treatment implies that one company may not be advantaged over another one and the principle thus has a wider scope than the principle of non-discrimination on grounds of nationality.

2. PUBLIC WORKS, PUBLIC SUPPLY AND PUBLIC SERVICE CONTRACTS

21–02   The Directive applies to public contracts which are defined as "contracts for pecuniary interest concluded in writing between one or more economic operators and one or more contracting authorities and having as their object the execution of works, the supply of products or the provision of services". Contracting authorities means the State, regional or local authorities, bodies governed by public law, associations formed by one or several of such authorities or one or several of such bodies governed by public law.[4] The Directive only applies to such contracts when the value of the contract (exclusive of VAT) is above a certain threshold. There are different thresholds for different kinds of contracts, and the thresholds are periodically revised.[5] The current thresholds can be shown as in the following table[6]:

Central contracting authorities	
Works contracts, works concessions contracts, subsidised works contracts	5,000,000 EUR
All contracts concerning so-called Annex II B Services, inter alia legal and health services, certain telecommunications services and R&D services; all design contests concerning these services and all subsidised services	200,000 EUR
All contracts and design contests concerning services listed in Annex II A **except** contracts and design contests concerning certain telecommunications services and R&D services	130,000 EUR
All supplies contracts awarded by contracting authorities not operating in the field of defence	130,000 EUR
Supplies contracts awarded by contracting authorities in the field of defence concerning products listed in Annex V[7]	130,000 EUR
Supplies contracts awarded by contracting authorities operating in the field of defence concerning other products	200,000 EUR
Non-central contracting authorities	

---

[4] Body governed by public law is also defined in the Directive. The definition has given rise to some case law, see for instance *Mannesman* (C-44/96) [1998] E.C.R. I-73 and *Cambridge University* (C-380/98) [2000] E.C.R. I-8035.

[5] The differences in thresholds are also linked to commitments under the GPA.

[6] Source: the Commission.

[7] The classical Directive and the Utilities Directive only apply to defense procurement to the extent that it is not governed by the specific "Defense Directive", Directive 2009/81 [2009] O.J. L216/76.

Works contracts, works concessions contracts, subsidised works contracts	5,000,000 EUR
All service contracts, all design contests, subsidised services contracts, all supplies contracts.	200,000 EUR

A certain number of contracts are excluded from the scope of the Directive,[8] and contracts concerning some services are only submitted to the rules of the Directive to a limited extent (so called Annex II B services).[9] The application of the Directive entails in the first place that the award of a contract must result from a tendering procedure, and that an invitation to the tender must be published in the Official Journal, thus enabling competition from across the Union.[10] The main procedures for awarding a public contract are the open procedure and the restricted procedure. The open procedure means a procedure whereby any interested economic operator may submit a tender for the contract. The restricted procedure means a procedure in which any economic operator may request to participate and whereby only those economic operators invited by the contracting authorities may submit a tender.[11] That the Directive gives priority to these two procedures follows from the overall purpose of opening up the market to all possibly interested economic operators. During any procedure the contracting authority must adhere strictly to the principles of equal treatment, transparency and non-discrimination on grounds of nationality. For instance, if the contracting authority refers to a national standard to be complied with, it must include the terms or "equivalent" so as not to discourage economic operators from other Member States from tendering.[12] The contracting authority may award the contract on the basis of one of the following two criteria; the lowest offer or the economically most advantageous offer. This last criterion permits the contracting authority to take into account other elements than price such as quality and security of supply. The contracting authority may for instance also take into account environmental concerns as long as they are related to the subject matter of the contract.[13] In order to enhance the effectiveness of the rules on public contracts the Union has established an electronic information system for European Public Procurement, "Simap", which can be found within the Union's general europa.eu website. The system encompasses TED, (for Tenders Electronic Daily) which provides electronic access to the Supplement of the Official Journal (OJ S) where all notices under the Directives must be published.

---

[8] See Section 3 of the Directive.

[9] Art.21 of the Directive.

[10] A notice on the award of the contract must also be published.

[11] Another procedure foreseen by the Directive, only to be used under very specific circumstances, is the negotiate procedure, where the contracting authority picks directly the economic operator to whom it intends awarding the contract. As the procedure thus is not open to all interested economic operators and therefore not to competition, its scope of application is very narrow. Other specific procedures, foreseen by Directive 2004/18 are competitive dialogues, design contests, framework agreements and electronic auctions.

[12] Art.23. See also *Mousten Vestergaard* (C-59/00) [2001] E.C.R. I-9505.

[13] Art.53. See also *Concordia Bus Finland* (C-513/99) [2002] E.C.R. I-7213.

21–03   A directive provides for the use of standard forms in the publication of public contract notices.[14] The use of these standard forms harmonises the way notices shall be published, with an aim at enhancing openness, efficiency and transparency, thus making easier the dissemination of electronic procurement. In addition, potential suppliers may use electronic search engines which make it easier for them to seek procurement notices they may be interested in. Furthermore, the standard forms cut the burden and costs contracting authorities normally bear for complying with the Directives on public procurements.

With a view to harmonising the public contracts vocabulary, the Union legislator adopted a regulation on the Common Procurement Vocabulary (CPV).[15] This Regulation should be considered as a tool that sets a single classification system applicable to public procurement. The Annexes to the regulation consist of correlation tables which permit to gather and compare a number of existing nomenclatures used in diverse countries, such as: the Statistical Classification of Products by Activity in the EEC (CPA); the Provisional Central Product Classification (CPC Prov.) of the United Nations; the General Industrial Classification of Economic Activities within the European Communities (NACE Rev.1); and the Combined Nomenclature (CN). A group of independent experts assists the Commission by providing it with legal, economic, technical and/or practical expertise with a view to shaping the public procurement policy.[16]

3.   THE WATER, ENERGY, TRANSPORT AND POSTAL SERVICES SECTORS

21–04   These sectors have always been considered as forming a separate sector requiring specific regulation, hence their exclusion from the Classical Directive examined above. The activities covered by the Utilities Directive are: gas, heat and electricity, water, transport services, postal services and exploration for, or extraction of, oil, gas, coal or other solid fuels, as well as ports and airports. Various kinds of contracts are excluded from the Directive.[17]

For supply and service, the Directive applies to contracts which have a value, excluding VAT, of no less than €400,000 and for works contracts the threshold value is €5,000,000.[18] Generally speaking, the rules are similar to the ones in the Classical Directive though in some aspects less strict.

The Utilities Directive does not apply to markets where the participants pursue an activity which is directly exposed to competition and the access to which is not limited within the relevant Member State.[19]

---

[14] Directive 2001/78 [2001] O.J. L285/1.
[15] Regulation 2195/2002 [2002] O.J. L 340/1.
[16] Commission Decision [2011] O.J. C291.
[17] Art.26 and following of Directive 2004/17.
[18] Art.16 of Directive 2004/17.
[19] Art.30 of Directive 2004/17. Thus, if a sector in a Member State is sufficiently exposed to competition the Commission may exempt the sector from the Directive, see for instance Commission Implementing Decision 2013/154 exempting services in the postal sector in Hungary from the application of Directive 2004/17 [2013] O.J. L86/22.

4. CONTRACTS BELOW THE THRESHOLDS OF THE DIRECTIVES AND PUBLIC CONCESSIONS

Public concessions mean a public contract where the consideration to the contractor consists solely or partly in the right to exploit the works or the services object of the contract. For instance, the constructor, who constructs a motorway for a public authority may be entitled to claim toll for the use of the motorway for 30 years. Public concessions are not governed by the Directives, except for public work concessions.[20] Contracts below the thresholds of the Directives and concessions are, however, still submitted to the general rules of the Treaty including the principles of equal treatment, transparency and non-discrimination on grounds of nationality. This entails that for contracts that could potentially be of interest to economic operators from other Member States, a sufficient degree of advertising must be ensured; the impartiality of the procedures must equally be ensured.[21] Whether a contract can potentially interest economic operators from other Member States must be evaluated on the basis of the individual circumstances of each case, such as the subject matter of the contract, its estimated value, the specifics of the sector concerned and the geographic place (for instance smaller contracts may in border regions be of interest to economic operators from the bordering Member States). A Commission communication sets out in more details the requirements that must be observed.[22]

21–05

5. "IN-HOUSE"

Union law applies where the contracting authority awards the contracts to an entity distinct from the public authority. Union law concerning public contracts does not bar the contracting authority from supplying the service itself; a municipality may decide that it wants waste collection within the municipality to be carried out by its own services.[23] Such a provision of services by the contracting authority itself is often referred to as "in-house" provision. The question that now shall be examined is to what extent, one may consider the award of a public contract to be "in-house" even though the contractor legally is a distinct subject from the contracting authority. The practical background against which this question arises is that contracting authorities may be organised in myriad ways; for instance, one municipality may have decided to organise waste collection as a department within the municipality, while another municipality may have chosen to establish a public limited company to handle waste collection: should the latter municipality, because of that organisational difference, be banned from entrusting the waste collection directly to its company? The question as to the scope of permitted "in-house" awards is of great practical importance. In many Member States local authorities are landed with

21–06

---

[20] Art.18 of Directive 2004/18 and Art.18 of Directive 2004/17.
[21] See *Telaustria* (C-324/98) [2000] E.C.R. I-10745 and *Coname* (C-231/03) [2005] E.C.R. I-7287.
[22] Communication on the Community law applicable to contract awards not or not fully subject to the provisions of the Public Procurement Directives [2006] O.J. C179/2.
[23] Another question is whether the *Altmark* case law applies; see Ch.22: Competition Policy, concerning competition and the State aid rules.

tasks that the authority cannot perform on its own or only at a very high cost. Local authorities may therefore decide to co-operate to perform the task; for instance by setting up jointly a company to handle waste collection.

There is by now well-established case law on the question as to when a contracting authority may award a contract directly to an outside entity without complying with the Union law on public contracts that would normally be applicable.[24] Two criteria have to be complied with in order to consider such a direct award as "in-house"; a "control criterion" and an "activity criterion". The control criterion implies that the contracting authority exercises over the contractor "a control similar to that which it exercises over its own departments". The activity criterion implies that the contractor "carries out the essential part of its activities with the controlling authority". The criteria are cumulative. When both are fulfilled, the contracting authority can lawfully make a direct award to a contractor that is legally distinct from the contracting authority; the award is considered to be "in-house". The control criterion serves to ensure that private interests cannot take control of the contractor.[25] The activity criterion entails that the contractor cannot extend its activities to other markets. When several contracting authorities together set up the external contractor, it suffices to meet the control criterion that they exercise joint control over it.[26]

6. THE REMEDIES DIRECTIVES[27]

21–07 The Directives ensure effective implementation of the above-mentioned directives at national level and guarantees access to justice to aggrieved contractors and interested parties against illegal or wrongful award decisions. The procedures to be set up by Member States are defined,[28] and the Court has considered that it is up to the Member States to secure a judicial system able to deal with any complaint.[29] In this respect, Member States are to ensure the existence of procedures for taking interim measures with a view to correcting an alleged infringement or preventing further damage, setting aside decisions taken unlawfully, and awarding damages to persons harmed by an infringement.[30] As far as the scope of the Remedies Directives is concerned, they apply to decisions taken by contracting authorities within the scope of the Classical Directive and the Utilities Directive.[31]

As far as the possibility for any person to make use of those Directives is concerned, it is provided that "(. . .) review procedures [must be] available at

---

[24] See in particular *Teckal* (C-107/98) [1999] E.C.R. I-8121, *Parking Brixen* (C-458/03) [2005] E.C.R. I-8585, *Coditel Brabant* (C-324/07) [2008] E.C.R. I-8457, and *Econord* (joined cases C-182/11 and C-183/11) judgment of November 29, 2012, not yet reported.

[25] See in this context *Coname* (quoted above, fn.21).

[26] See *Econord* (quoted above, fn.24).

[27] Directive 89/665 [1989] O.J. L395/33 which applies to the "classical" sectors and Directive 92/13 [1992] O.J. L76/14 which applies to the utilities sectors.

[28] See *Alcatel Austria* (C-81/98) [1999] E.C.R. I-7671.

[29] *Dorsch Consult Ingenieursgesellschaft v Bundesbaugesellschaft Berlin* (C-54/96) [1997] E.C.R. I-4961; in *Gebietskrankenkasse* [1998] E.C.R. I-5357, and *HI* (C-258/97) [1999] E.C.R. I-1405.

[30] See Art.2(1)(a), (b) and (c) of Directive 89/665 (quoted above, fn.27).

[31] See for instance Art.1(1) of Directive 89/665. It is every decision, i.e. every act producing legal effects, that falls within the scope of the Remedies Directives, see *HI* (C-92/00) [2002] E.C.R. I-5553,

least to any person having or having had an interest in obtaining a public contract who has been or risks being harmed by an alleged infringement".[32]

Outside the scope of the Remedies Directives, the Treaty rules apply. That entails that the contracting authority must give reasons for its decision to the economic operator concerned and that the decision must be subject to judicial review.[33] The principles of equivalence and effectiveness apply, that is that the procedures set up must be at least equivalent to similar national procedures and they must not render the exercise of the interested party's rights impossible or excessively difficult.

7. REFORM

As in many other fields of Union law, there are on-going discussions on how to improve the rules. A concern often raised, in particular on behalf of public authorities with limited resources or know-how, is that compliance with the Directives causes high costs and delays. Currently—spring 2013—a proposal for amending the Directives is pending before the Union legislator, the Council and Parliament; a major contentious issue is whether the contracting authority, in its award decisions, may take account of social considerations. Moreover, a proposal for regulating public concessions is pending.

21–08

FURTHER READING

Albert Graells Sánchez, *Public procurement and the EU competition rules* (Hart, 2011).

Christopher Bovis, *EU public procurement law* (Edward Elgar, 2012).

Lee Digings and Prof. John Bennett *EU Public Procurement: Law and Practice* (Sweet & Maxwell, 2012).

Robert Caranta & Dacian Dragos, *Outside the EU procurement directives—inside the Treaty?* (DJØF Publishing, 2012).

Steen Treumer & Francois Lichère, *Enforcement of the EU public procurement rules* (DJØF Publishing, 2011).

21–09

---

para.37, and *Makedoniko Metro and Mikhaniki* (C-57/01) [2003] E.C.R. I–1091, para.68. This applies regardless of the decision being part of the formal award procedure, see *Stadt Halle and RPL Lochau* (C-26/03) [2005] E.C.R. I–1, para.34.

[32] *Stadt Halle and RPL Lochau* (C-26/03), (quoted above, fn.31) para.40.

[33] See for instance *Heylens* (222/86) [1987] E.C.R. 4097.

PART 4

OTHER UNION POLICIES

CHAPTER 22

Competition Policy

INTRODUCTION

Competition policy is considered as one of the key driving forces behind the single market by the Commission:

    22–01

> "[T]he single market is Europe's best asset for generating sustainable growth. An effective internal market requires the deployment of two instruments: first, regulation to create one integrated market without national borders and, second, competition policy including State aid control to ensure that the functioning of that internal market is not distorted by anticompetitive behaviour of companies or by Member States favouring some actors to the detriment of others. Competition is a major driver of growth; it incentivises enterprises, including new ones, to enter markets and innovate, improving productivity and competitiveness in a global context".[1]

The campaign against restrictive cartels and abuse of dominance remains at the forefront of the Commission's competition agenda.[2] Regulation 1/2003 has fostered a more effective and efficient enforcement of these types of anti-competitive behaviour and has as such played an important role in the competition policy of the European Union.[3] Due to the financial crisis an increased emphasis has been placed on the state aid rules since 2008. The sovereign debt crisis has put a pressure on the banking system in Europe as well as posing a threat to financial stability of many of the Member States. This has called for both effective enforcement and review of the state aid legal framework.[4] At the same time there has been a sharp decline in the number of merger notifications.[5]

---

[1] COM(2012) 209 final, EU State Aid Modernisation (SAM), para.2.
[2] COM(2012) 253 final, Report on Competition Policy 2011, p.11.
[3] COM(2009) 206 final, Report on the functioning of Regulation 1/2003, para 41.
[4] See resolution of the European Parliament of January 17, 2013 on state aid modernisation ((2012/2920(RSP)) and COM(2012) 725 final, *Proposal for a council regulation amending Regulation EC No 659/199 laying down detailed rules for the application of Art.93 of the EC Treaty*.
[5] Statistical information on merger control can be found on the homepage of DG Competition at *http://ec.europa.eu/competition/mergers/statistics.pdf* [accessed August 23, 2013].

I. COMPETITION RULES APPLYING TO UNDERTAKINGS[6]

22–02   The competition rules applicable to undertakings are contained mainly in three sets of provisions: the first concern which is generally referred to as "cartels", the second "abuse of dominant positions" and the third "concentrations". The term cartel designates all forms of anti-competitive co-operation and collusion among undertakings; the second expression refers to anti-competitive behaviour of an undertaking(s) in a dominant position; while concentrations covers limitation of competition through the creation or strengthening of a dominant position via joint ventures, mergers, take-overs or the establishment of permanent control by other means. Whether or not a cartel is prohibited or whether or not there is abuse of a dominant position is decided by the national competition authorities, national judges or by the Commission; all of which can determine the legality of an act or a measure under Arts 101 and 102 TFEU. As for concentrations that have a so-called Community dimension in so far as the turnover of the undertakings involved are above the thresholds set out in Regulation 139/2004, these must be notified to the Commission for assessment prior to being implemented.[7] Concentrations that do not have Community dimension shall nevertheless, if specific criteria are fulfilled, be examined by the Commission if the concentration is capable of being reviewed by the national competition law of at least three Member States[8] or when a Member State refers the concentration to the Commission for examination as it affects trade between Member States and poses a significant threat to competition within that Member State.[9] However, a Member State can ask for the whole or part of the concentration to be assigned to it when it considers that it would affect competition on a market within that State, which "presents all the characteristics of a distinct market".[10]

According to the TFEU, "the establishing of the competition rules necessary for the functioning of the internal market"[11] falls within the exclusive competence of the Union. However, both the Commission and the competition authorities of the Member States are also entrusted, as already indicated above, in close co-operation with each other,[12] with the application of these rules. Both can require that an infringement be brought to an end,[13] both can order interim measures,[14] accept commitments and impose fines and periodic payments;[15] national competition authorities may also impose other penalties provided for in their national law.[16] It can also be briefly mentioned that private parties with

---

[6] Arts 101–105 TFEU and Merger Regulation, see below.

[7] Art.2 Regulation 139/2004 on the control of concentrations between undertakings, the so-called Merger Regulation [2004] O.J. L24/1.

[8] Art.4(5) Merger Regulation.

[9] Art.22 Merger Regulation.

[10] Art.4(4) Merger Regulation.

[11] Art.3(1) TFEU.

[12] See, for instance, Commission "Notice on co-operation between national competition authorities and the Commission in handling cases falling within the scope of Art.101 and 102 TFEU" [1997] O.J. C313/3.

[13] Arts 5 and 7 Regulation No 1/2003 on the implementation of the rules on competition laid down in Arts 81 and 82 of the Treaty [2003] O.J. L1/1.

[14] Arts 5 and 8 Regulation 1/2003.

[15] Arts 5, 9 and 23 of Regulation 1/2003.

[16] Art.5 Regulation 1/2003.

locus standi before the national courts may bring proceedings claiming damages, termination of alleged infringements and interim measures.[17]

1. THE CONCEPT OF A MARKET

Market definition is a tool to identify and define the boundaries of competition between firms. It serves to establish the framework within which competition policy is applied by the Commission. The main purpose of market definition is to identify in a systematic way the competitive constraints that the undertakings involved face. The objective of defining the market is to identify the actual competitors in a defined relevant product market and a relevant geographic market.[18]

22–03

The relevant market definition forms the basis of all competition law analysis as it defines the market wherein two or more goods compete and identifies and define the boundaries of competition between undertakings. The relevant market is determined by assessing successively the "relevant product market" and the "relevant geographic market". The relevant product market also comprises services. Indeed, it is only after having defined the relevant product market that the Commission and the courts will be able to determine whether and to what extent competition occurs. From there the question: when does competition exist between products or services? Basically, the answer is very simple. There is competition when the end consumer has a choice between different products/ services, which, because of their characteristics, their price and their intended usage, are "interchangeable". The Court defined this as follows:

> "[T]he concept of relevant market, in fact, implies that there can be effective competition between the products, which form part of it and this presupposes that there is a sufficient degree of inter-changeability between all the products forming part of the same market in so far as the specific use of the product is concerned".[19]

Probably the best example of a non-interchangeable product is the banana. The Court was called upon to determine whether bananas constitute a relevant market on their own or whether it was part of the larger market of fresh fruits. In one of its most cited and early competition cases the Court found that:

> "[T]he banana has certain characteristics, appearance, taste, softness, seedlessness, easy handling, a constant level of production, which enables it to satisfy the constant needs of an important section of the population consisting of the very young, the old and the sick".[20]

The Court concluded that "consequently, the banana market is a market which is sufficiently distinct from the other fresh fruit markets".

22–04

---

[17] White paper on damages actions for breach of the EC antitrust rules (COM) 2008 165.

[18] See also below the section on Control of Concentrations for the definition of the geographic market.

[19] *L'Oréal v De Nieuwe AMCK* (31/80) [1980] E.C.R. 3775; [1981] 2 C.M.L.R. 235.

[20] *United Brands v Commission* (27/76) [1978] E.C.R. 207 at 273(31); [1973] C.M.L.R. 612. Another example is to be found in *Hoffmann-La Roche* (85/76) [1979] E.C.R. 461 at 547(111).

It follows that the Commission, when examining whether or not an infringement of the competition rules has taken place, must, in the first place determine the limits of the product/service market. With regard to services, an example of the difficulty this might present is to be found in the definition of the banking sector. The Commission ascertained that a significant number of non-financial companies have subsidiaries involved in financial services, such as financing subsidiaries of car manufacturers, payment cards or retail banking subsidiaries of big retailers.

In order to answer the question of the substitutability between products, which in turn determines whether they are part of the same product market, a key criterion is price sensitivity of demand. This can be demonstrated by considering whether a small, permanent increase in price of 5 to 10 per cent of a product would be sufficient to render any such price increase unprofitable.[21] Consider two competing soft drinks. The question is whether consumers of a soft drink A would switch to another soft drink when confronted with a permanent price increase of 5 to 10 per cent. If a sufficient number of consumers would switch to soft drink B to such an extent that the price increase would not be profitable, then the market would be comprised of at least soft drink A and B.

Besides defining the relevant product market, the Commission must also determine the geographic market. This is considered as the area within which the conditions of competition are sufficiently homogeneous and which can be distinguished from neighbouring areas of demand. The limits of this market depend on the structure of the product market, especially as far as production, supply and demand are concerned.[22] The Court did underline "how necessary it is to define the market concerned in order that the relative strength for the undertakings in such a market might be considered".[23] The limits of the geographic market do not necessarily coincide with the territories of the Member States, nor of the Union, although they normally do, for the simple reason that statistics are generally available for those areas only. The Treaty refers to the "internal market or a substantial part of it".[24] However, the geographic market can be very small indeed.[25] In order to clarify and detail its methodology when defining a relevant market, the Commission published a "Notice on the definition of the relevant market for the purpose of the [Union] competition law".[26]

---

[21] This is known as a Small but Significant Non-Transitory Increase in Price, or *SSNIP*.
[22] See *Alsatel v Novasam* (247/86) [1988] E.C.R. 5987, where the Court did not accept the existence neither of a relevant product market, nor of a national geographic market, but only of a regional one.
[23] *Hoffmann-La Roche* (85/76) (quoted above, fn.20).
[24] Art.102,1 TFEU.
[25] See, e.g. Decision of December 13, 1995, *Eurotunnel* [1988] O.J. L311/36.
[26] [1997] O.J. C372/5.

2. CARTELS (AGREEMENTS, DECISIONS OF ASSOCIATIONS OF UNDERTAKINGS AND CONCERTED PRACTICES)[27]

The TFEU[28] refers not only to "agreements between undertakings", but also to "decisions by associations of undertakings" and "concerted practices". These are prohibited when they may affect trade between Member States and have as their object or effect the prevention, restriction or distortion of competition. When caught by the prohibition, such agreements are automatically void and unenforceable, unless they satisfy the conditions for an exemption from the prohibition.[29] Each one of these expressions needs to be clarified and interpreted.

22–05

> "The notions of agreements, decisions and concerted practices are autonomous concepts of [Union] competition law covering the coordination of behaviour of undertakings on the market as interpreted by the [Union] Courts".[30]

Hereinafter the concepts "agreements, decisions of associations of undertakings and concerted practices" shall globally be referred to by the word "agreements", unless indicated otherwise. The following will now be successively examined: (1) the prohibition, (2) the nullity and (3) the exemptions from the prohibition.

(1) The Prohibition

Obviously, only certain agreements between undertakings are prohibited; indeed, the whole economy thrives on such agreements and could not function without them, and the Commission has done a lot to encourage undertakings to co-operate, especially across borders, in order to further European economic integration. However, agreements between undertakings are prohibited when they may affect trade between Member States, and the agreement's object or effect is to restrict competition or cause it to be restricted in the internal market. This basic rule seems simple enough, but what exactly is meant by "undertaking", "agreement", "decision by associations of undertakings", "concerted practices", "have as their object or effect", "may affect trade between Member States", and "distortion of competition"? Those terms will be successively examined hereafter.

22–06

(a) Undertakings

According to the Court:

22–07

---

[27] Art.101 TFEU.
[28] See Art.101 TFEU.
[29] Art.1(2) Regulation 1/2003 (quoted above).
[30] Eighth recital Regulation 1/2003.

"[T]he concept of an undertaking encompasses every entity engaged in an economic activity, regardless of the legal status of the entity and the way in which it is financed".[31]

Economic activity was in subsequent case law defined as any activity offering goods or services on a given market.[32] The fact that the offer of goods or services is made without profit motive does not prevent the entity that carries out those operations on the market from being considered an undertaking, since that offer exists in competition with that of other operators which seek to make a profit.[33]

The term "undertaking" also covers natural persons,[34] public enterprises and even public authorities[35] when the latter carry out commercial and economic activities.[36] Consequently, only those entities engaged in purely social,[37] religious, artistic or scientific activities provided in a non-market context on the basis of solidarity[38] are not caught by the competition rules.

22–08 An undertaking must be an "economic" entity, in other words it must have economic independence.[39] This is not the case, under certain conditions, with undertakings belonging to the same group and having the status of a subsidiary in relation to a parent company. Whether or not a subsidiary is subject to control of the parent undertaking must be determined on a case-by-case basis taking into consideration factors such as shareholding of the parent undertaking in the subsidiary, composition of the board of directors in the subsidiary and the ability of the parent undertaking to influence decision making in the subsidiary.[40] When the subsidiary is not free to determine its market behaviour independently of the parent company,[41] and the agreements concluded between them merely constitute internal allocations of tasks, such undertakings together form a single economic unit. Therefore, the agreement concluded between them is not an "agreement between undertakings". The same applies to agreements concluded between

---

[31] *Höfner and Elser v Macrotron GmbH* (C-41/90) [1991] E.C.R I-1979, para.21; See also e.g. *CNOP and CCG v Commission* (T-23/09) [2010] E.C.R. II-5291.

[32] Case (C-180/98) *Pavlov* [2000] E.C.R I-6451, para.75.

[33] *MOTOE* (C-49/07) [2008] E.C.R. I-4863 and *OTOC* (C-1/12), judgment of February 28, 2013, not yet reported.

[34] See e.g. *Reuter/BASF* Decision [1976] O.J. L254/40; *Wolfgang Heiser* (C-172/03) [2005] E.C.R I-1627 and *FMBV v Commission* (C-101/07 P and C-110/07) [2008] E.C.R I-10193.

[35] See *Pig Marketing Board v Redmonds* (83/78) [1978] E.C.R. 2347; [1979] 1 C.M.L.R. 177; *Banchero* (C-387/93) [1995] E.C.R. I-4663 and as *Italy v Commision* (41/83) [1985] E.C.R. 873.

[36] See *Commission v Italy* (C-35/96) [1998] E.C.R. I–3851(36): "Constitute an economic activity, any activity which consists in offering products or services on a given market".

[37] See for instance *Cisal di Batistello* (C-218/00) [2002] E.C.R. I–691, where the Court held that an entity participating in the management of one of the traditional branches of social security, fulfils an exclusively social function and does not therefore constitute an undertaking within the meaning of Art.101 TFEU.

[38] See definition in Case C-70/95 *Sodemare v. Regione Lombardia* [1997] ECR I-3395.

[39] See *Christiani and Nielsen* Decision [1969] O.J. L165/72 and confirmed in *Asia Motor France* (T-387/94) [1996] E.C.R. II–961; [1996] 5 C.M.L.R. 537.

[40] *AEG Telefunken* (107/82) [1983] E.C.R. II-3151.

[41] The question is whether or not the parent company controls the subsidiary; see, e.g. *Welded Steel Mesh Cartel* Decision [1989] O.J. L260/1: a 25 per cent interest held by one company in a competitor does not give rise to a parent-subsidiary relationship. See also *Viho* (C-73/95) [1996] E.C.R. I-5457.

subsidiaries.[42] This means that agreements between companies, or undertakings, within the same group of companies are not as such caught by Art.101 TFEU.

On the other hand, when the market behaviour of the subsidiary is determined by the parent company and the subsidiary violates the competition rules, it is the parent company which may be held responsible.[43] Whether the parent company in such a case is situated within the Union or not is irrelevant since the violation has its effects within the internal market and is therefore caught by the Union rules.[44] This is commonly referred to as the effects doctrine: whether the behaviour is inside or outside the Union is irrelevant and Union Competition rules will apply as long as the agreements have effect inside it, or has as its object to create such an effect.

(b) Agreements and Concerted Practices

Agreement within the meaning of Art.101 TFEU are defined as "[centred] around the existence of a concurrence of wills between at least two parties, the form in which it is manifested being unimportant so long as it constitutes the faithful expression of the parties' intention".[45] A contract which is legally binding, and thus an enforceable commitment, would naturally fall within the concept.[46] However, not only legally binding acts are covered by the term but also 'gentleman's agreements',[47] 'understandings' and even a simple 'genuine concurrence of wills'.[48] In other words, it is not the form of the agreement that is the important factor but rather whether there has been a concurrence of wills between at least two undertakings. Conversely, unilateral conduct does not fall under the scope of Art.101 of the TFEU.[49]

The expression *concerted practice*, on the other hand, refers to an anti-competitive parallel market behaviour of several undertakings that is caught

22–09

---

[42] See *Kodak* Decision [1970] O.J. L147/24 and *DaimlerChrysler v Commission* (T-325/01) [2005] E.C.R. II-3319.

[43] See *KNP BT v Commission* (T-309/94) [1998] E.C.R. II–1007, *General Quimica e.a* (C90/09 P) [2011] E.C.R. I-1, attribution of liability to the parent company at the head of the group and *Elf Aquitaine v Commmission* (C-521/09 P), judgment of September 29, 2011, not yet published.

[44] See, for instance, *ICI v Commission* (48/69) [1972] E.C.R. 619 at 662; [1972] C.M.L.R. 557; *Europemballage and Continental Can v Commission* (6/72) [1973] E.C.R. 215; [1973] C.M.L.R. 199; *Instituto Chemioterapico Italiano* and *Commercial Solvents v Commission* (Joined Cases 6/73 and 7/73) [1974] E.C.R. 223; [1974] 1 C.M.L.R. 309; *United Brands v Commission* (27/76) [1978] E.C.R. 207; [1978] 1 C.M.L.R. 429 and *Hoffmann-La Roche v Commission* (85/76) [1979] E.C.R. 461; [1979] 3 C.M.L.R. 211.

[45] Case (T-41/06) [2000] E.C.R. II-3383 para.96 cf. Case (C-2/01 P and C-3/01) *Bundesverband der Arzneimittel-Importeure eV v Bayer AG er* [2004] E.C.R. I-23, para.97.

[46] Such a commitment is not limited to certain forms; see *Van Landewijck v Commission* (Joined Cases 209/78–265/78 and 218/78) [1980] E.C.R. 3125; [1981] 3 C.M.L.R. 134. Also *Sandoz v Commission* (C-277/87) [1990] E.C.R. I–45: the systematic dispatching by a supplier to his customers of invoices bearing the words "exports prohibited", constitutes a prohibited agreement. Idem: Commission Decision of January 10, 1996, Adalat (Bayer): [1996] O.J. L201/1, implicit acceptance by wholesaler through continued dealing, so agreement reached.

[47] Case 41/69 *ACF Chemiefarma NV v Commission* [1970] ECR 661 and Case (T-53/03) *BPB plc v Commission* [2008] E.C.R II-1333, para.82.

[48] *HOV SVZ/MCN* [1994] OJ L 104/34, para.46.

[49] Case (C-2/01 P and C-3/01) *Bundesverband der Arzneimittel-Importeure eV v Bayer AG er* [2004] E.C.R. I-23.

by the prohibition when this behaviour is the result of a "concentration" or "concurrence of wills" among said undertakings.[50] According to the Court, a concerted practice:

> "[R]efers to a form of coordination between undertakings which, without having been taken to a stage where an agreement properly so called has been concluded, knowingly substitutes for the risk of competition, practical co-operation between them."[51]

22–10   In subsequent case law the Court further elaborated on the concept of concerted practices and stated that Art.101 TFEU prohibited:

> "any direct or indirect contact between such operators, the object or effect whereof is either to influence the conduct on the market of an actual or potential competitor or to disclose to such a competitor the course of conduct which they themselves have decided to adopt or contemplate adopting on the market.[52]"

In essence this means that it is for each undertaking to determine its commercial policy independently and conditions offered to its customers.[53]

The difference between an agreement and a concerted practice is important with regard to the conditions for the existence of a prohibition and the proof of an infringement. Indeed, in the case of an agreement, it suffices for a violation of the competition rules to occur, that the clauses of the agreement show that the *object* is to distort competition. Whether or not competition was actually distorted is irrelevant.[54] If the object is to restrict competition, this is commonly referred to as a "hard core restriction" that amounts to an infringement almost per se.[55] In the case of a concerted practice, the fact that undertakings consult each other is not, in itself, prohibited; it is the market behaviour, the practice, that eventually follows the consultation or even looser contacts, that is caught by the prohibition.[56] As for the proof of the existence of a concerted practice, this could be, for instance, the existence of a gentleman's agreement or information exchanges that relate to, in particular, future business conduct.[57] However, it may not always be easy to establish that the object of a given practice is to distort

---

[50] For an example of a concerted practice see *Musique Diffusion Française v Commission* (Joined Cases 100/80, 101/80, 102/80 and 103/80) [1983] E.C.R. 1825; [1983] 3 C.M.L.R. 221 and (C-8/08) *T-Mobile Netherlands BV* [2009] E.C.R. I-4529.

[51] This concept was originally defined by the Court of Justice in case (48/69) *ICI v Commission* [1972] E.C.R.619. See also *Commission v Anic* (C-49/92 P) [1999] E.C.R. I-4125 (112–138).

[52] Case (40/73) *Suiker Unie v Commission* [1975] E.C.R. 1663.

[53] Guidelines on the applicability of Art.101 of the Treaty on the Functioning of the European Union to horizontal co-operation agreements [2011] OJ C11/1, para.60.

[54] See *Société Technique Minière v Machienenbau Ulm* (56/65) [1966] E.C.R. 235 at 249; [1966] C.M.L.R. 357.

[55] Art.4 of Commission Regulation (EU) No 330/2010 [2010] O.J. L102/1.

[56] Case (C-199/92) *Hüls AG v Commission* [1999] E.C.R I-4287.

[57] Gentlemen's agreements and other arrangements, binding in honour only, are not, in this writer's view, prohibited by the Treaty whatever their content; it is only the resulting "practice", which can be prohibited. See *ACF Chemiefarma* Decision [1969] O.J. L192/5, where the Commission considered a gentlemen's agreement to be a binding agreement in the sense of Art.101 TFEU because it was concluded together with a binding agreement which referred to the former. This view was accepted by the Court: *ACF Chemiefarma v Commission* (41/69) [1970] E.C.R. 661 at 693 (113,114). See also Opinion of the Advocate-General, *ACF Chemiefarma* (41/69) at 714.

competition. This is illustrated by the fact that parallel price increases by several undertakings are not, in themselves, prohibited; they could indeed be purely coincidental or the result of a particular market situation known as oligopoly with price leadership.[58] On the other hand, such parallel price increases are prohibited when they are the result of prior consultation. Proof of such consultation will often have to be based on circumstantial evidence[59] such as the participation in meetings with an anti-competitive object.[60] According to the Court, the participation in one single such meeting is sufficient proof of concerted practices in violation of Art.101 TFEU.[61]

(c) Decisions by Associations of Undertakings

Decisions must be understood to include the constitutive act of a trade association **22–11** and its internal rules,[62] decisions made in accordance with those rules and which are binding upon the members of the association,[63] and also recommendations such as the fixing of target prices by an association.[64] Whether an agreement must be regarded as one "between undertakings" or one "between associations of undertakings" is irrelevant. The same applies to the framework within which decisions of associations are taken and the classification given to that framework by the national authorities.[65] As for the term "association",[66] it is not limited to any particular form of association. It also includes associations of associations[67] with or without legal personality as well as non-profit-making associations. According to the General Court an association representing a significant number of manufacturers in a relevant sector can be directly and individually concerned by a decision addressed to another association and is therefore admissible to challenge that Commission decision in court.[68]

(d) Which may affect Trade between Member States

This criterion confines the scope of Art.101 TFEU to agreements that have a **22–12** minimum level of cross-border effects. The concept of trade is not limited to

---

[58] In *Hoffmann-La Roche v Commission* (85/76) [1979] E.C.R. 461 at 520(39); [1979] 3 C.M.L.R. 211, the Court refers to "parallel courses of conduct which are peculiar to oligopolies".

[59] See, for example, *ICI v Commission* (48/69) [1972] E.C.R. 619; [1972] C.M.L.R. 557 and *Suiker Unie v Commission* (Joined Cases 40, etc./73) [1975] E.C.R. 1663; [1976] C.M.L.R. 295: in both cases the Court admitted the existence of a concerted practice. Not admitted in *Cram and Rheinzink v Commission* (Joined Cases 29/83 and 30/83) [1984] E.C.R. 1679 at 1702(19); [1985] 1 C.M.L.R. 688.

[60] *SCA Holdings v Commission* (T-327/94) [1998] E.C.R. II–1374.

[61] *T-Mobile A.O.* (C-8/08) (quoted above, fn.51).

[62] *ASPA* Decision [1970] O.J. L148/1.

[63] *Bomee-Stichting* Decision [1975] O.J. L329/30.

[64] *Cementhandelaren v Commission* (8/72) [1972] E.C.R. 977 at 991(19); [1973] C.M.L.R. 7. See also *Van Landewyck* (Joined Cases 209, etc./78) [1980] E.C.R. 3125 at 3254(102); [1981] 3 C.M.L.R. 134.

[65] *BNIC v Clair* (123/83) [1985] E.C.R. 391 at 423 (17–20); [1985] 2 C.M.L.R. 430.

[66] See *Metropol Television* (Joined Cases T-528/93 etc.) [1996] E.C.R. II–649; [1996] 5 C.M.L.R. 386.

[67] A *de facto* association of associations was considered by the Commission to be an association of undertakings. See *Cecimo* Decision [1969] O.J. L69/13 and *van Landewyck* (Joined Cases 209, etc./78) (quoted above, fn.55).

[68] *AIUFFASS* (T-380/94) [1996] E.C.R. II–2169; [1997] 3 C.M.L.R. 542.

traditional exchange of goods and services but also where competition is affected by agreements.[69] The notion of "may affect" has been defined in several judgments of the Court:

> "[I]n order that an agreement between undertakings may affect trade between Member States it must be possible to foresee with a sufficient degree of probability on the basis of a set of objective factors of law and fact that it may have an influence, direct or indirect, actual or potential, on the pattern of trade between Member States such as might prejudice the realisation of the aim of a single market in all the Member States."[70]

When an agreement, for instance, prevents undertakings from importing certain goods from another Member State or prohibits them from re-exporting those goods to other Member States, those agreements indisputably affect trade between Member States. Other examples are agreements which grant an exclusive right; the Court stated that they do not necessarily, of their very nature, contain elements incompatible with the internal market. But, in such a case special attention must be given to the question as to whether or not the agreements are capable of partitioning the market in certain products between the Member States.[71]

It is also clear from the wording of the Treaty and the judgments of the Court that the effect on trade does not have to be actual; it suffices that the agreement is "capable of constituting a threat" to freedom of trade between Member States.[72] In other words, the effect on trade has to be appreciable, which in turn is dependent on factors such as the nature of the agreement and/or practices, the underlying market and position of the undertakings concerned on the relevant market.[73] Only in rare instances has the Court deemed an agreement not to have effect on trade.[74]

(e) "Which have as their Object or Effect"

22–13   When the object of an agreement is to restrict competition, the question as to whether competition was indeed distorted becomes irrelevant.[75] Whether or not an agreement has as its objective to restrict competition is based on assessment of

---

[69] Commission Notice: Guidelines on the effect on trade concept contained in Arts 81 and 82 of the Treaty (2004/C 101/07) para.19–20.

[70] *Remia v Commission* (42/84) [1985] E.C.R. 2545 at 2572(22); [1987] 1 C.M.L.R. 1. See also *Consten and Grundig v Commission* (Joined Cases 56/64, 57/64 and 58/64) [1966] E.C.R. 299 at 341; [1966] C.M.L.R. 418, where the Court added that the fact that an agreement encourages an increase, even a large one, in the volume of trade between Member States is not sufficient to exclude the possibility that an agreement "may affect" trade in the above-mentioned manner. In *Bilger v Jehle* (43/69) [1970] E.C.R. 127 at 135(5); [1974] 1 C.M.L.R. 382, the Court stated that trade may be affected even though the agreement does not concern imports or exports; *Comenteries CBR* (25/95) [2000] E.C.R. II-491.

[71] *Société Technique Minière* (56/65) (quoted above, fn.55).

[72] *Consten and Grundig* (Joined Cases 56/64, 57/64 and 58/64) (quoted above, fn.71) and *Compagnie Maritime Belge Transport* (T24/93) [1996] E.C.R. II-1201.

[73] Commission Notice: Guidelines on the effect on trade concept contained in Arts 81 and 82 of the Treaty (2004/C 101/07). Section 2.4, paras 44-57.

[74] See, for example, *Emanuela* Sbariga (C-383/08) [2010] E.C.R. I-06337.

[75] *T-Mobile A.O.* (C-8/08) (quoted above, fn.51), para.31.

the "content of its provisions, the objectives it seeks to attain and the economic and legal context of which it forms a part [...]."[76] The intention to distort competition may result from all or some of the clauses of the agreement; only those clauses which indicate that the object of the agreement is to interfere with competition will be caught by the prohibition and are therefore automatically void, and not necessarily the whole agreement.[77] When the terms of the agreement do not disclose the intention of the parties to distort competition, the consequences of implementing the agreement must be considered. For an agreement to have anti-competitive effect, whether actual or potential, it must have an adverse impact on at least one of the factors of competition, e.g. price, output, quality.[78] In order to be able to prove violation of the competition rules, factors must be found by the Commission or the national competition authorities, that show that competition was in fact distorted, or, at least that a danger of distortion existed.[79] This can notably be shown by assessing what the situations would be in the absence of the agreement, the so-called "counterfactual" assessment.[80]

(f) "Prevention, Restriction or Distortion of Competition"

Competition exists when economic operators in the common market act independently from one another and have freedom of choice.[81] Or, as the Court put it, "undistorted competition ... can be guaranteed only if equality of opportunity is secured as between the various economic operators."[82]   **22–14**

The Court has developed and specified the meaning of "distortion of competition" by indicating that, in order to be prohibited, an agreement must distort competition "to an appreciable extent". For instance, an "exclusive dealing agreement, even with absolute territorial protection, may, having regard to the weak position of the persons concerned in the market and the products in question, escape the prohibition" of the Treaty.[83] Another point emphasised by the Court is that the anticipated effect on competition may not be purely theoretical, but that "the competition in question must be understood within the actual context in which it would occur in the absence of the agreement in dispute". It is therefore appropriate:

---

[76] *GlaxoSmithKline* (C-501/06 P) [2009] E.C.R. I-9291, para.58.

[77] See *Consten and Grundig* (Joined Cases 56/64, 57/64 and 58/64) (quoted above, fn.71) where the Court annulled the Commission's decision because it considered the whole agreement as void. See also *Sociéteé de Vente de Ciments et Betons v Kerpen & Kerpen* (319/82) [1983] E.C.R. 4173 at 4184(12), where the Court reiterated that the consequences of the nullity of certain provisions for other parts of the agreement are not a matter for Union law, but must be determined by the national court on the basis of its own national law.

[78] Guidelines on the applicability of Art.101 of the Treaty on the Functioning of the European Union to horizontal co-operation agreements [2011] O.J. C11/1, para.27.

[79] *Brasserie de Haecht* (23/67) [1967] E.C.R. 407; *Braug AG* (C-234/89) [1991] E.C.R. I-935.

[80] *O2 GmbH* (T-328/03) [2006] E.C.R. II-1231.

[81] *Suiker Unie* (Joined Cases 40, etc./73) [1975] E.C.R. 1663, at 1942(173).

[82] *France v Commission* (C-202/88) [1991] E.C.R. I–1223(51).

[83] Case 5/69 *Völk v Vervaecke* [1969] E.C.R. 295, para.7; Case 1/71 *Cadillon* [1971] E.C.R. 351, para.8; Case C-226/11 *Expedia v Autorité de la concurrence* Judgment of December 13, 2013, not yet reported.

"[T]o take into account the nature and quantity, limited or otherwise, of the products covered by the agreement, the position and importance of the [parties] on the market for the products concerned, the isolated nature of the disputed agreement or, alternatively, its position in a series of agreements, the severity of the clause intended to [limit trade] or alternatively the opportunities allowed for other commercial competitors in the same product by way of parallel re-exportation or importation."[84]

Listed in Art.101(1) TFEU are types of agreement which contain provisions that are likely to have adverse effect on competition:

- price fixing;
- trading conditions;
- limitation of production;
- applying dissimilar conditions to equivalent transactions;
- making the conclusion of contracts subject to acceptance of supplementary conditions.

This applies both to horizontal and vertical agreements. The Commission published guidelines on both the applicability of Art.101 TFEU to vertical restraints and horizontal co-operation agreements, which will be explained in more detail below.[85]

(g)   "Within the Internal Market"

22–15   According to the TFEU the distortion of competition must take place within the internal market. The Court has stated:

"It should be observed that an infringement of Art.101, such as the conclusion of an agreement which has had the effect of restricting competition within the common market, consists of conduct made up of two elements, the formation of the agreement, decision or concerted practice and the implementation thereof. If the applicability of prohibitions laid down under competition law were made to depend on the place where the agreement, decision or concerted practice was formed, the result would obviously be to give undertakings an easy means of evading those prohibitions. The decisive factor is therefore the place where it is implemented."[86]

This doctrine established by the Court has often been referred to as the implementation doctrine or the effects doctrine as it only takes into account the implementation of the agreement and not where it was formed. Thus if an agreement is formed within the EU by undertakings established there but implemented in a third country where it has anti-competitive effects it falls outside the scope of Art.101 TFEU.[87] If, however, an agreement that is formed

---

[84] Case 56/65 *Société Technique Minière* [1966] E.C.R. 337
[85] Guidelines on the applicability of Art.101 of the Treaty on the Functioning of the European Union to horizontal co-operation agreements [2011] O.J. C11/1 and Guidelines on Vertical Restraints SEC(2010) 411 final.
[86] *Älström v Commission* (Joined Cases C-89, etc./85) [1988] E.C.R. 5193 [1988] 4 C.M.L.R. 901, concerning a concerted practice between undertakings situated in non-member countries affecting selling prices to purchasers established in the Union.
[87] *Distillers Company* (30/78) [1980] E.C.R. I-2229.

outside the EU but has anti-competitive effects within the internal market it is caught by Art.101 TFEU. For example, a distribution agreement for export from a Member State to a third country that prohibits re-importation into the EU is considered to have an anti-competitive effect on the internal market.[88]

Finally, it should be noted that the expression "between the Member States" does not mean that agreements must concern all the Member States or even some of them. An agreement limiting competition in one of the Member States can have distorting consequences in other Member States and affect trade within the Union. This will practically always be the case when the agreement in question covers the whole territory of one Member State, since it creates what the Court calls a "threshold effect" with regard to imports.[89]

(2) The Nullity Sanction

Prohibited cartels are automatically void.[90] Consequently, no declaration to this effect is needed.[91] For agreements caught by the prohibition, the nullity applies without a prior decision being required.[92] This nullity applied to agreements concluded after March 13, 1962[93] and not notified to the Commission[94]; different dates applied for the new Member States.[95] Since the entry into force of "Regulation to give effect to the principles of TFEU Art.101 and 102",[96] agreements can only be implemented at the parties' own risks.[97] They must determine whether or not the agreement is prohibited[98] and, if so, whether an exemption applies. If an agreement is implemented anyhow, it could, later on, be found void ab initio and the parties could then be fined; furthermore, third parties that have been damaged by the agreement could also seek for redress.[99]

22–16

---

[88] *Javico Interational v YSL* (C-306/96) [1998] E.C.R. I-1938.
[89] See, for example, *Cementhandelaren* (8/72) (quoted above, fn.65).
[90] Art.101(2) TFEU.
[91] See Art.1(1) Regulation 1/2003 where the same is provided for the prohibition [2003] O.J. L1/1.
[92] This follows from the wording of Art.101(2) TFEU.
[93] Entry into force of Regulation 17, replaced by Regulation 1/2003 [2003] O.J. L1/1.
[94] As indicated below, this notification obligation no longer exists.
[95] For the new Member States: the date of accession was substituted for the original date, January 1, 1973 for Denmark, Ireland and the UK; January 1, 1981 for Greece; January 1, 1986 for Portugal and Spain; and January 1, 1995 for Austria, Finland and Sweden; and with regard to the Czech Republic, Estonia, Cyprus, Latvia, Lithuania, Hungary, Malta, Poland, Slovenia and Slovakia, the prohibition shall not apply to cartels which were in existence at the date of accession of Austria, Finland and Sweden or at the date of accession of the 10 new Member States and which, by reason of accession, fall within the scope of Art.81(1), if within six months from the date of accession, they are so amended that they comply with the conditions laid down in the various regulations.
[96] Regulation 1/2003 (quoted above).
[97] This means that they must seek the necessary advice.
[98] According to the Preamble of the new Regulation, existing practice and case law provide sufficient information for such determination.
[99] There is currently no effective legal framework for antitrust damages actions on European level. Although listed in the Commission Work Program in 2012 there was no legislative proposal for action for damages for breaches of antirust law made public in that year. The Commission has recently focused on collective reddress by publishing a staff working paper for hearing SEC(2011) 173 final *Towards a coherent European Appraoch to Collective Redress* and quantifying harm by publishing a Draft Guidance Paper Quantifying Harm in Actions for Damages Based on Breaches of Arts 101 or 102 of the TFEU.

(3) Block exemption

22–17 Agreements caught by the prohibition but that satisfy the conditions of Art.101(3) TFEU are not prohibited.[100] Before May 1, 2004, an exemption could only be granted by the Commission, either in individual cases notified to it, or within the framework of a so-called block exemption that applies the exemption automatically to certain categories of agreements. However, today undertakings are required to make their own assessment as to whether the conditions set out in Art.101(3) TFEU and/or under the block exemption framework are met. By doing so the Commission has been able to free up considerable resources to focus on other enforcement priorities. In turn undertakings are tasked with conducting a self-assessment of the compatibility of their behaviour. The Commission has published extensive guidance which, when read in conjunction with the relevant Block Exemption Regulations, facilitates the task of self-assessment for undertakings.

(a) Individual Exemptions

22–18 According to the Commission: 40 years of Court case law and Commission decisional practice have established a homogeneous body of clear rules on the circumstances under which antitrust exemption is available. The Commission is, however, ready to provide guidance for novel questions that arise in individual cases by issuing an informal "guidance letter".[101] In practice, this rarely happens.[102]

An exemption automatically applies when, although the agreement affects trade between Member States and restricts competition, the fulfilment of the following four conditions outweighs those limitations:

- the agreement must contribute to improving the production or distribution of goods or to promoting technical or economic progress; however, the restriction of competition must be "indispensable" to the "improvement", which must in particular show appreciable objective advantages of such a character as to compensate for the disadvantages caused in the competition field[103]; this condition is referred to by the Commission as "efficiency gains";
- consumers must get a fair share of the resulting benefit;
- the agreement may not impose on the undertakings concerned restrictions which are not indispensable to the attainment of the above objectives; and
- the agreement may not afford such undertakings the possibility of eliminating competition in respect of a substantial part of the products or services in question.

---

[100] Art.101(3) TFEU and Art.1(2) Regulation 1/2003 [2003] O.J. L1/1.

[101] See Commission Guidelines on the application of Art.101(3) TFEU [Art.81(3) EC] [2004] O.J. C101/97 and Notice on informal guidance to novel questions concerning Arts 101 and 102 TFEU that arise in individual cases [2004] O.J. C101/78.

[102] Notice on informal guidance to novel questions concerning Arts 101 and 102 TFEU that arise in individual cases [2004] O.J. C101/78.

[103] *Consten and Grundig v Commission* (Joined Cases 56/64 and 58/64) (this is the official name of the cases in the ECR, but they are always referred to as *Grundig/Consten*) [1966] E.C.R. 299.

In fact, the four conditions overlap and constitute only different viewpoints to be considered in an evaluation of the benefits and detriments of an agreement.

(b) De Minimis

As mentioned above, the Court has indicated that in order to fall under the **22–19** prohibition of the competition rules, the agreements must affect intra-Union trade and restrict competition to an "appreciable" extent. In a Notice on agreements of minor importance which do not appreciably restrict competition,[104] the Commission quantifies, with the help of market share thresholds what is not an appreciable restriction of competition. The notice aforementioned does not quantify what does not constitute an appreciable effect on trade.

However, the Commission holds the view that agreements that affect trade between Member States do not appreciably affect competition:

- where the parties are potential or actual competitors: if the aggregate market share held by the parties does not exceed 10 per cent on any of the relevant product and geographic markets;
- where the parties are not competitors: if the market share held by each of the parties does not exceed 15 per cent on any of the relevant product and geographic markets;
- (in case of doubt whether the parties are competitors or not, the 10 per cent threshold applies);
- where competition is restricted by cumulative foreclosure effect of parallel networks of agreements having similar effects on the market, the above-mentioned thresholds are reduced to 5 per cent;
- where individual suppliers or distributors with a market share not exceeding 5 per cent are in general not considered to contribute significantly to a cumulative foreclosure effect, neither is there a cumulative foreclosure effect if less than 30 per cent of the relevant market is covered by parallel agreements having similar effects (these thresholds may be exceeded by two percentage points during two consecutive years).

The above provisions do not apply to hardcore restrictions. Hardcore **22–20** restrictions are those that have as their object: the fixing of prices, the limitation of output or sales or the allocation of markets or consumers. As for agreements between non-competitors the de minimis rule does not apply when they have as their object:

- the restriction of the buyer's ability to determine its sale price (does not apply to a maximum sales price or a recommended price);
- the restriction of the territory into which the buyer may sell the contract goods or services (does not apply to restriction of active sales into other territories, restriction of sales to end-users by a wholesaler, nor to restriction of the buyer's ability to sell components for the purpose of incorporation in the same type of goods as those of the supplier);

---

[104] [2001] O.J. C368/13.

- the restriction of active or passive sales to end-users by members of a selective distribution system;
- the restriction of cross-supplies within a selective distribution system; and
- the limitation of the supplier's ability to sell components as spare parts to end-users or to repairers.

The Notice contains various definitions and references to Court cases and other Commission publications.

(c) Exemptions for Categories of Agreements

22–21   The Commission's experience has shown that certain agreements are almost always anti-competitive whilst others usually are not. This experience forms that basis for the so-called block exemption regulations which exempt certain categories of agreements from competition rules altogether provided that certain circumstances are met.[105] Such exemptions are reserved for agreements for which it can be assumed with sufficient certainty that they satisfy the conditions set by the Treaty for exemptions from the prohibition. The exemptions for categories are provided by a regulation of the Commission, acting in pursuance of a Council regulation. The Council establishes the principle of the exemption and delegates to the Commission the task of working out the details. This technique has been used for several categories which will be further seen below.

All the regulations granting block exemptions follow, generally speaking, the same pattern. They provide in detail which restriction may be imposed upon the parties, which other restrictions do not infringe the prohibition and which restrictions are excluded from the exemption (the so-called black list). It should be noted that agreements which are not exempted under the block exemption may nonetheless be considered exempted by the parties, as indicated above.

(i)   Horizontal Co-operation Agreements

22–22   Agreements are of a horizontal nature if entered into between actual or potential competitors. The likelihood that such agreements could have a negative impact on competition is greater than for vertical agreements. This is because they can prevent competing undertakings from independently determining their competitive strategy. These agreements can lead to substantial economic benefits, but also to competition problems; this is, for instance, the case if the parties agree to fix prices or output or to share markets, or, if the co-operation enables the parties to maintain, gain or increase market power and thereby is likely to give rise to negative market effects with respect to prices, output, product quality, product variety or innovation.

In 2011 the Commission published "Guidelines on the application of Art.101 TFEU to horizontal cooperation agreements".[106] The purpose of the Guidelines is to provide an analytical framework for the most common types of permissible horizontal co-operation agreements; they deal with research and development agreements, production agreements including sub-contracting and specialisation

---

[105] See also below: 4. Competition Rules Applying to Various Branches of the Economy.
[106] [2011] O.J. C11/1.

agreements, standardisation agreements including standard contracts, and information exchange. The Guidelines apply to the most common of horizontal co-operation agreements irrespective of the level of integration they entail, with the exception of operations constituting a concentration within the meaning of the Merger Regulation.

(ii)   Vertical agreement and concerted Practices[107]

Vertical agreements cover those agreements entered into between undertakings that, for the purpose of the agreement, are present at different levels of the production or distribution chain. This is for instance the case for an agreement between a supplier and distributor. Vertical agreements are amongst the most common in business relations and usually have a neutral or positive impact on competition.[108] For instance, certain types of vertical agreements can improve economic efficiency by facilitating better co-ordination between the participating undertakings, leading to a reduction in costs and optimisation of sales and investment level.

22–23

Vertical agreements which determine elementary aspects of commerce, such as price and quantity in a purchase and sales contract, do not normally restrict competition. Yet a restriction of competition may occur if the vertical agreement contains restraints on the supplier or buyer, such as an obligation not to purchase competing products.

Vertical restraints can be both pro and anti-competitive. On the one hand, they can offer protection against "free riders" that profit from the sales and marketing efforts of another distributor (for example, through regulated distribution networks). On the other hand, vertical restrictions can also lead to input foreclosure. It is therefore important to balance the overall impact of the agreement on competition as certain restraints can be balanced by overriding imperatives that prevail on the market in question. Accordingly, the market structure is of primary importance. In order to facilitate self-assessment amongst undertakings, the Commission has adopted a block exemption regulation which provides a "free harbour" for agreements that meet certain requirements. The block exemption regulation is thus the first port of call when undertaking an assessment of a vertical agreement's compatibility with competition law.[109]

The vertical block exemption regulation (VBER) applies as from June 1, 2010 and expires on May 31, 2022. It replaces the Regulation on the application of Art. EC 81(3) to categories of vertical agreements and concerted practices.[110] The benefit of the block exemption is limited to vertical agreements for which it can be assumed with sufficient certainty that they satisfy the conditions of Art.101(3) TFEU. The Court has held that it is not necessary to give a broad interpretation of

22–24

---

[107] As indicated "agreements" covers also "concerted practices". Commission Regulation (EU) No 330/2010 [2010] O.J. L102/1.

[108] Guidelines on vertical restraints [2010] O.J.C130/1, para.98, 106-107.

[109] Vertical Guidelines para.24.

[110] Regulation 2790/99 [1999] O.J. L336/21] which, in turn, replaced the Regulation on bilateral exclusive distribution (supply) agreements Regulation 1983/83 [1983] O.J. L173/1; the literature refers to those agreements as "exclusive supply agreements", the Regulation on bilateral exclusive purchasing agreements Regulation 1984/83 [1983] O.J. L173/5 and the Regulation concerning franchising agreements Regulation 4073/88 [1988] O.J. L359/46.

the provisions of the VBER as parties can always argue that the restrictions are individually exempt under Art.101(3) TFEU.[111]

The safe harbour provided by the block exemption regulation is contingent upon cumulative conditions, relating to the market share of the parties to the agreement and the absence of certain pre-defined restraints.

The first condition relates to the market share held by the parties to the agreement. Article 3 of the VBER provides that in order for the exemption to apply, the market share held by the supplier on the relevant market where it sells the contract products to the buyer, and the market share of the buyer on the relevant market where it purchases the contract products, must each be 30 per cent or less.[112] It is important to note that if one, or both, of the parties' market shares exceed 30 per cent this does not necessarily imply that the agreement will fall foul of competition rules.[113] Rather, it means that an individual analysis must be undertaken.

22–25   The second condition relates to the existence of certain restraints which can be further divided into two distinct categories, the hard-core restraints and the excluded restraints. Hard-core restraints are so called because experience has shown that they almost always cause harm to consumers.[114] The presence of a hard-core restriction means that the whole agreement falls outside the scope of the VBER, regardless of the parties' market share. It is also considered unlikely, although not impossible, that agreements containing hard-core restrictions can be justified under an individual analysis.[115] Hard-core restrictions are defined in Art.4 of the Block Exemption Regulation:

- The first hard-core restriction concerns resale price maintenance. This term relates to situations where an undertaking operating upstream in the distribution chasing imposes a minimum price at which distributors can resell their products. However, it is permissible for a supplier to impose a "maximum" sales price or a "recommended", on the condition that this is not, in fact, a disguised minimum price.[116]
- The second hard-core restriction concerns the territory into which, or the customers to whom, the buyer may sell. Both of these are instances of market partitioning, with the only difference being whether this is done in terms of customers or territory. In principle, distributors must remain free to decide where and to whom they sell. However, there are certain exceptions to this rule:
  - Active sales by a buyer into a territory reserved to another distributor. The term active sale denotes active commercialisation and solicitation where the distributor actively pursues customers in the territory.
  - Restrictions of sales to end-users by buyers operating at the wholesale level of trade, thereby allowing a supplier to keep the

---

[111] *Pierre Fabre Dermo-Cosmétique* (C-439/09) judgment of October 13, 2011, not yet published, para.57.

[112] *Pierre Fabre Dermo-Cosmétique* (C-439/09). Art.3.1. See further in the Vertical Guidelines para.87-95.

[113] *Activision Blizzard v Commission* (C-260/09P) [2011] E.C.R. I-00419.

[114] See Vertical Guidelines para.47-59.

[115] Vertical Guidelines, para.60-64.

[116] Vertical Guidelines, para.48. See also *JCB Service v Commission* (T-67/01) [2004] E.C.R. II-49.

wholesale and retail levels of trade separate so as to, for instance, for specialisation at each level of trade.[117]

–   Restriction of sales of members of a selective distribution system to unauthorised distributors within the territory reserved by the supplier to operate the system.

–   Restriction of the buyer's ability to sell components, supplied for the purposes of incorporation, to customers who would use them to manufacture the same type of goods as those produced by the supplier.

- The third and fourth hard-core restrictions concern selective distribution. Firstly, selected distributors, while being prohibited to sell to unauthorised distributors, cannot be restricted in the end-users to whom they may sell. Secondly, the appointed distributors must remain free to sell or purchase the contract goods to or from other appointed distributors within the distribution network.

- The fifth hard-core restriction concerns the supply of spare parts. An agreement between a manufacturer of spare parts and a buyer which incorporates these parts into its own products may not prevent or restrict sales by the manufacturer of these spare parts to end users, independent repairers or service providers.

Furthermore, the VBER does not apply to so-called "excluded" restrictions. These vertical restraints are excluded from the exemption by the VBER. However, the VBER continues to apply to the remaining part of the vertical agreement if that part is severable (i.e. can operate independently) from the non-exempted vertical restraints.[118] The excluded restrictions include: **22–26**

- any direct or indirect non-competing obligation the duration of which is indefinite or exceeds five years;

- obligations preventing the buyer from manufacturing, purchasing, selling or reselling unless it:
  –   relates to competing goods or services;
  –   is limited to the land or premises from which the buyer has operated during the contract period;
  –   is indispensable to protect know-how;

- obligations preventing members of selective distribution systems to sell brands of particular competing suppliers.

The exemption applies to vertical agreements entered into between an association and its members or between such an association and its suppliers, but only if all its members are retailers of goods, and no member, together with its connected undertakings, has a total turnover of more than €50 million.[119] The exemption applies also to the assignment to the buyer or use by the buyer of intellectual property rights, when those do not constitute the primary object of the agreement and are directly related to the use, sale or resale of goods and services

---

[117] Vertical Guidelines, para.137; see *Metro v Commission* (26/76) [1977] E.C.R. 1875.
[118] On the notion of severability see Vertical Guidelines, para.70-71.
[119] Regulation 330/10 Art.2,2; for the calculation of the turnover see Art.8.

by the buyer or its customer.[120] The exemption applies on condition that the provisions do not contain restrictions of competition.

22–27   The exemption does not apply to vertical agreements entered into between competing undertakings, except where these enter into a non-reciprocal vertical agreement and (a) the supplier is a manufacturer and distributor of goods, while the buyer is a distributor but not a competing manufacturer and (b) the supplier is provider of services at several levels of trade, while the buyer provides its goods or services at the retail level and is not competing with the level of trade where it purchases the contract services.[121]

Furthermore, the exemption does not apply to vertical agreements which fall within the scope of any other block exemption regulation.

Finally, when parallel networks of similar vertical restraints cover more than 50 per cent of the relevant market, the Commission may declare the regulation not applicable.

The Commission published rather extensive *Guidelines on Vertical Restraints* setting out, among other things, which vertical agreements fall outside the Treaty's prohibition, an analysis of the Regulation and of specific vertical restraints.[122]

(iii)   Certain Categories of Vertical Agreements and Concerted Practices in the Motor Vehicle Sector

22–28   The motor vehicle sector has been subject to a special block exemption scheme since 1985, where the latest regulation was adopted in 2010.[123] The main change introduced in the new regulation is that as of June 1, 2013 the general block exemption regulation will also be applied to the motor vehicle sector.[124] The new Regulation makes a clear distinction between agreements relating to the purchase, sale or resale of vehicles, and agreements relating to the aftermarket.

The exemption is granted for vertical agreements where they relate to the conditions under which the parties may purchase, sell or resell new motor vehicles, spare parts for motor vehicles or repair and offer maintenance services for motor vehicles and which contain vertical restraints.

In relation to the purchase, sale or resale of new cars, the main conditions for exemption are as follows:

- manufacturers must choose between a selective and an exclusive distribution system;
- exemption is not granted to any restriction of passive sales, etc. in order to strengthen intra-brand competition;
- the link between selling and after-sales services is no longer exempted;
- the prohibition of multi-branding within the same showroom is no longer exempted;
- limiting a distributor's right to sell motor vehicles with different specifications from those covered by the agreement are not exempted;

---

[120] Regulation 330/10 Art.2.3.
[121] Regulation 330/10 Art. 2.4.
[122] [2010] O.J. C130/1 replacing [2000] O.J. C29/1.
[123] [2010] O.J. L129 /52.
[124] [2010] O.J. L102/1.

- intermediaries acting on behalf of consumers are no longer subject to conditions;
- the independence of vehicle distributors from their suppliers is increased by enabling them to freely represent more than one brand.

Where vertical agreements relating to the motor vehicle aftermarket are concerned, the Regulation introduces a 30 per cent market share threshold above which agreements between car manufacturers and authorised repairers will no longer be block exempted. It provides that the prohibition of Art.101 TFEU shall not apply to vertical agreements relating to the conditions under which the parties may purchase, sell or resell spare parts for motor vehicles or provide repair and maintenance services for motor vehicles, which fulfil the requirements for an exemption under VBER and do not contain any of the hard-core clauses listed in Art.4 VBER.

22–29

Other conditions concern the notice given by the supplier: a minimum time period of five years or, in case of an agreement for unlimited period, that the notice has to be at least two years for both parties, and, finally, the exemption shall apply on condition that the agreement provides for each of the parties the right to refer disputes to an independent expert or arbitrator.

The Regulation provides for "hard-core restrictions" concerning the sale of new motor vehicles, repair, maintenance or spare parts, or concerning some of these activities, and "specific conditions", which exclude the application of the derogation, such as restriction of the sale of spare parts to independent repairers.[125]

(iv)   Specialisation agreements[126]

The Regulation exempting specialisation agreements from the prohibition is based on the second Council Regulation.[127] It was adopted on December 14, 2010, and shall expire on December 31, 2022. Specialisation agreements can take many forms but essentially encompass agreements whereby two parties each focus their abilities on a distinct facet of a final product, thereby "specialising" themselves from one part of production. Specialisation agreements may be pro-competitive in particular because such agreements enable smaller market players to "join forces" and compete in markets where they may not have been able to enter effectively unless specialisation occurred.

22–30

Unilateral specialisation agreements cover agreements between two parties active on the same product market by virtue of which one party agrees to fully or partly cease production of certain products or to refrain from producing those products and to purchase them from the other party, who agrees to produce and supply those products. Reciprocal specialisation agreements are those between two or more parties active on the same product market, by virtue of which two or more parties on a reciprocal basis agree to fully or partly cease or refrain from producing certain but different products and to purchase these products from the other parties, who agree to produce and supply them.

---

[125]   See Art.5 of Regulation 461/10,quoted above.
[126]   Regulation 1218/10 [2010] O.J. L335/43, replacing [2000] O.J. L304/3.
[127]   Regulation 2821/71 [1971] J.O. L258/46.

The Specialisation Block Exemption Regulation further applies to agreements which relate to the assignment or licensing of intellectual property rights to one or more of the parties, provided that those provisions do not constitute the primary object of the agreement, but are directly related to and necessary for their implementation, and whereby the parties accept an exclusive purchase and or an exclusive supply obligation, or the parties do not independently sell the specialisation products, but jointly distribute them.

22–31   In order to benefit from the exemption, specialisation agreements must satisfy a market share threshold and be free of hard-core restraints. The exemption thus only applies if the combined market share of the participating undertakings does not exceed 20 per cent of the relevant market. This market share is calculated on the basis of (a) the market sales value and (b) the data relating to the preceding calendar year; special rules apply for connected undertakings. If the market share rises above 25 per cent, the exemption continues to apply for one year. With respect to hard-core restrictions the exemption does not apply, whether directly or indirectly, in isolation or in combination with other factors under the control of the parties:

- fixes prices of the product to third parties (except those charged to immediate customers in the context of joint distribution),
- limits output or sales (except provisions on the agreed amount of products in the context of reciprocal or unilateral specialisation agreements or in the context of joint production agreements), the setting of sales targets, and;
- allocates markets or customers.

(v)   Research and development agreements[128]

22–32   The exempting Regulation is based on the second Council Regulation.[129] It exempts research and development agreements entered into by two or more undertakings containing provisions which relate to the assignment or licensing of intellectual property rights to one or more of the parties or to an entity the parties establish to carry out the joint research and development, paid-for research and development or joint exploitation, provided that these provisions do not constitute the primary object of such agreements, but are directly related to and necessary for their implementation. There are, however, conditions: all the parties must have access to the results of the joint research and development including any resulting intellectual property rights and know-how for the purpose of further research and development and exploitation, as soon as they become available. Access may be limited in accordance with the Regulation; an example of this is where access is restricted by an obligation to pay royalties.

Research institutes, academic bodies or undertakings which supply R&D as a commercial service without being active in the exploitation of results, may agree to limit the use to future research, but the compensation may not be so high as to effectively impede such access.

Where the research and development agreement provides only for joint research and development or paid-for research and development, the agreement

---

[128] Regulation 1217/10 [2010] O.J. L335/36 replacing [2000] O.J. L304/7.
[129] Regulation 2821/71 [1971] J.O. L258/46.

must stipulate that each party must be granted access to any pre-existing know-how of the other parties, if it is indispensable for the exploitation of the results. Compensation may be provided for parties charged with the manufacture of the contract product by way of specialisation must be required to fulfil orders from the other parties, except where the agreement provides for joint distribution or where the agreement provides that only one party shall manufacture the contract product.

The exemption is valid for a limited number of years which is contingent upon   **22–33**
the competitive relationship between the parties to the agreement. Where the parties to the agreement are not competing undertakings, the exemption applies for the duration of the R&D. Where the results are jointly exploited, the exemption shall continue to apply for seven years from the time the contract products are first put on the market within the internal market.

Where two or more parties are competitors, the exemption shall apply for the periods mentioned above only if, at the time the agreement is entered into, the combined market share of the participating undertakings does not exceed 25 per cent of the relevant market for the products capable of being improved or replaced by the contract products.

At the end of said periods, the exemption continues to apply as long as the combined market share of the parties does not exceed 25 per cent of the relevant market for the contract products.

The exemption does not apply to R&D agreements which have as their object: **22–34**

- to restrict the freedom of the parties to carry out R&D independently or in co-operation with third parties in unconnected fields or, after completion of the R&D in connected fields, or, after the completion of the joint R&D, or of the paid-for research, in the field to which it relates or in a connected field;
- the limitation of output or sales, with some exceptions;
- the fixing of prices for contract products when sold to third parties;
- the restriction of territory or customers;
- the prohibition to make passive sales of the contract products;
- the prohibition to put contract products on the market or to pursue active sales policies in territories reserved for other parties, after the end of seven years from the time the products were first put on the market;
- the requirement not to grant licenses to third parties;
- the requirement to refuse to meet demand from resellers in their respective territories who would market in other territories;
- the requirement to make it difficult for users or resellers to obtain the contract products from other resellers.

Restrictions excluded from the exemption:

- the obligation not to challenge, after completion of the R&D, the validity of intellectual property rights;
- the obligation not to grant licences to third parties to manufacture the contract production to supply contract technology, unless the agreement provides for the exploitation of the results by at least one of the parties.

The regulation expires on December 31, 2022. The publication of the Regulation on specialisation agreements and the R&D block exemption was followed by a Commission Notice containing "Guidelines on the applicability of Art.81 of the EC Treaty [now Art.101 TFEU] to horizontal co-operation agreements"[130] setting out the principles for assessment of horizontal co-operation agreements. This Notice replaces two previous Notices on co-operation agreement[131] and on co-operative joint ventures.[132]

(vi)   Technology transfer agreements

22–35   Intellectual property secures exclusive rights to holders of patents, copyrights, registered trademarks and other protected rights. A holder of intellectual property rights is thereby enabled to prevent any unauthorised use of its intellectual property and to exploit such property, in particular by licensing it to third parties. Technology transfer agreements concern the licensing of technology.

The Commission Regulation (TTBE)[133] granting a block exemption in this field is based upon the first Council Regulation.[134] It combines the former Regulation on patent licensing agreements[135] and the Regulation on know-how licensing agreements.[136] The Commission decided that those two block exemptions ought to be combined into a single regulation covering the vast majority of technology transfer agreements.

Such agreements will usually be pro-competitive as they can reduce duplication of research and development, strengthen incentives for initial research and development, spur incremental innovation, facilitate diffusion and generate product market competition. However, licensing agreements may also be used for anti-competitive purposes. This may be the case where two competitors use a licensing agreement to divide markets between them or where an important licence holder excludes competing technologies from the market. Striking a balance between these often conflicting interests of protecting innovation and safeguarding competition was at the core of the TTBE.

22–36   The TTBE applies to the Member States' patents, Union patents[137] and European patents[138] ("pure" patent licensing agreements). It also applies to agreements for the licensing of non-patented technical information such as descriptions of manufacturing processes, recipes, formulae, designs or drawings, commonly termed as "know-how" (known as "pure" know-how licensing agreements) and, to combined patent and know-how licensing agreements ("mixed agreements"), which play an increasingly important role in the transfer of technology. Agreements containing ancillary provisions relating to intellectual property rights other than patents are also covered by the exemption.

---

[130] [2001] O.J. C3/2.
[131] [1968] O.J. C75/3.
[132] [1993] O.J. C43/2.
[133] Regulation 240/96 [1996] O.J. L31/2. Replaced [2004] O.J. L123/11; see Guidelines [2004] O.J. C101/2.
[134] Regulation 19/65 [1965] O.J. L533/65, modified by Regulation 1/2003 [2003] O.J. L1/1.
[135] Regulation 2349/84 [1984] O.J. L219/15.
[136] Regulation 556/89 [1989] O.J. L61/1.
[137] Convention for the European patent for the common market (Union Patent Convention) of December 15, 1975 [1975] O.J. L17/1.
[138] Convention on the grant of European patents (European Patent Convention) of October 5, 1973.

In order to benefit from the exemption the parties must satisfy a market share test that is contingent upon the parties' competitive relationship.[139] Where the parties are competing undertakings the combined market share of the parties must not exceed 20 per cent of the affected relevant technology and product market. Where the parties are not competing undertakings the combined market share of the parties must not exceed 30 per cent on the affected relevant technology and product market. If the market share is initially not more than 20 per cent or 30 per cent but subsequently rises above that level, the exemption continues to apply for a period of two consecutive calendar years following the year in which the 20 per cent or 30 per cent threshold was first exceeded.[140] Further to satisfying the market share thresholds, the agreement must not contain any hard-core or excluded restrictions. With respect to hard-core restrictions, these are different depending on whether the parties are competitors or not.

An agreement containing a hard-core restriction is automatically void and unenforceable. Hard-core restrictions are not severable, and bring the entire agreement outside the scope of the TTBE.[141] Moreover, it is very unlikely that a license containing a hard-core restriction will qualify for individual exemption. The list of hard-core restrictions differs depending on whether the agreement is concluded between competitors or non-competitors.

With respect to agreements between competitors, the following restrictions are **22–37** to be considered as hard-core: price fixing, reciprocal output restrictions, market and customer allocations (although important exceptions apply), and the restriction of the licensee's ability to exploit its own technology or to carry out R&D.

With respect to agreements between non-competitors, the following restrictions are considered as hard-core: resale price maintenance, passive sales restrictions on licensees (although important exceptions apply), and the restriction of active or passive sales to end users by a licensee which is a member of a selective distribution and which operates at the retail level.

As regards excluded restrictions these are slightly less numerous with the following restrictions considered as excluded: exclusive grant backs by the licensee; no challenge clauses; restrictions on exploiting technology.[142]

The application of Union law to patents and know-how was further examined **22–38** in Ch.20: Intellectual Property Rights; however, mention must be made here of the effect the competition rules have on the use that can be made of intellectual property rights. Normally such rights are used by their owner to prevent third parties from producing products covered by such rights, and/or by reserving the use of such rights to particular (national) territories. Although the owner acts in accordance with national law, by preventing imports and exports among the Member States, he prevents the free movement of goods within the internal market. It is in connection therewith that several cases concerning the use of intellectual property rights were submitted to the appreciation of the Court, which declared that such use is contrary to the Union competition rules.[143]

---

[139] See Technology Transfer Guidelines para.26–33.
[140] See Technology Transfer Guidelines para.19–23.
[141] See Technology Transfer Regulation Art.4(1).
[142] Technology Transfer Guidelines, para.107–117.
[143] *Transacctiones Maritimas* (C-12/95 P(R)) [1995] E.C.R. I-467; [1996] 2 C.M.L.R. 580.

The position of the Court with regard to the use of intellectual property rights can be summarised as follows: the Treaty provisions do not affect the existence of the exclusive rights attached to patents, know-how, trademarks, copyrights, registered designs, plant breeder's rights and other similar rights. They do, however, limit their use in so far as that use restricts trade between Member States. Nonetheless, the Court upholds the use of those rights when this is "justified by the purpose of safeguarding rights which constitute the specific subject matter of such property".[144] As was seen in Ch.20: Intellectual Property Rights, the Court introduced another restriction in the form of the principle of exhaustion of intellectual and industrial property rights, when the product is put on the market in another Member State by the owner himself or with his consent.

3. ABUSE OF A DOMINANT POSITION[145]

22–39 Competition and inter-State trade can be adversely affected by agreements between undertakings, decisions of associations of undertakings and concerted practices. However, they can also be restricted by an undertaking or undertakings in a quasi-monopoly situation, known as "dominant position", that behave in a manner amounting to an "abuse". Such abuse is prohibited by the Treaty in so far as it affects trade between Member States.

Both the rules of competition concerning cartels and those applying to abuses have as their object to ensure that "competition in the internal market is not distorted"[146] and thereby ensuring free movement of goods within the internal market.

The TFEU refers to the expressions: "dominant position"; "abuse"; and "may affect trade between Member States". The latter was examined in relation to prohibited cartels; the other two concepts will be briefly analysed hereafter.

(1) Dominant Position/Joint Dominant Position

22–40 A dominant position exists, according to the Court, when the economic strength of an undertaking on a given market is such that it:

> "[E]nables it to hinder the maintenance of effective competition on the relevant market by allowing it to behave to an appreciable extent independently of its competitors and customers and ultimately of its consumers."[147]

It follows that an undertaking is not in a dominant position merely because of the size of its market share.[148] Rather the notion of dominance is contingent upon the undertaking being able to act independently from other market factors, effectively according it the ability to unilaterally dictate market parameters. Generally speaking an undertaking will be presumed to be dominant where it holds a market share above 50 per cent, also known as the *Akzo* presumption of

---

[144] *Pharmon v Hoechst* (19/84) [1985] E.C.R. 2281.
[145] Art.102 TFEU.
[146] *SFEI* (C-39/94) [1996] E.C.R. I–3549; [1996] 3 C.M.L.R. 369.
[147] *United Brands Continental BV v Commission* (C-27/76) [1978] E.C.R. 207.
[148] Communication from the Commission [2009] OJ C 45/7, replacing [2002] OJ C 152/5.

dominance.[149] Although market shares are a good indication of dominance, this can also derive from a combination of several factors which, taken separately, would not necessarily be determinative. They are, for instance, the relationship between the market share of the undertaking in question and the shares of the next largest undertaking(s), the technological lead of the undertaking in question, the existence of a highly developed sales network and the absence of potential competition.[150] An undertaking vested with a legal monopoly may be regarded as occupying a dominant position.[151] It should here also be noted that it is not illegal for a company to merely hold a dominant position per se. Rather, it is the abuse thereof which is sanctionable and which will be further examined below.

Since the TFEU refers to one or more undertakings, a dominant position can also be held by several undertakings together, the so-called joint or collective dominance.[152] This requires, however, the existence of "links which are sufficiently strong for there to be a collective dominant position" between the undertakings in question.[153] The Court was also referred to "economic links or factors which give rise to a connection between the undertakings concerned".[154] The Court added that:

22–41

> "[T]he existence of a collective dominant position may therefore flow from the nature and terms of an agreement, from the way in which it is implemented and, consequently, from the links or factors which give rise to a connection between undertakings which result from it."[155]

This applies to both horizontal and vertical relationships.[156] The concept of joint dominance was further developed by the Commission within the framework of the Merger Regulation, which will be examined below. As for the General Court, it determined[157] that a collective dominant position may arise as the result of a concentration where in view of the characteristics of the relevant market and

---

[149] *Akzo v Commission* (C-62/86) [1991] ECR I-3359.

[150] Those criteria and others have been analysed in P. Mathijsen in "Oligopolistic Dominance under the Merger Regulation", Festschrift fur Dr Jurgen Gundich, Carl Heymans, Verlag1 KG, (1999) p.161, see also *AstraZeneca v Commission* (T-321/05) [2010] ECR II-2805.

[151] *Höfner and Elser* (C-41/90) [1991] E.C.R. I-1979.

[152] See *Compagnie Maritime Belge Transports and Others* (Joined Cases T-24/93, T-25/93 and T-26/93) [1996] E.C.R. II–1201(65–66); [1977] 4 C.M.L.R. 273 and Decision of May 14, 1997, in *Irish Sugar Plc* (IV/34.621) [1997] O.J. L258/1 (11–112). See also *RTE v Commission* (T-69/89) [1991] E.C.R. II–485 and *(Flat Glass) SIV v Commission* (Joined Cases T-68/89 etc.) [1992] E.C.R. II–1403; [1992] 5 C.M.L.R. 302. In Decision IV/M.1524 [2000] O.J. L93/1, the Commission indicated that "it is not a necessary condition of collective dominance for the oligopolists always to behave as if there were one or more explicit agreements between them. It is sufficient for the oligopolists, in adapting themselves to market conditions, to act, individually, in ways which will substantially reduce competition between them".

[153] *Almelo* (C-393/92) [1994] E.C.R. I–1520(43).

[154] *Compagnie Maritime Belge Transport and others* (Joined Cases C-395/96 P and C-396/96 P) [2000] E.C.R. I–1365(41).

[155] *Compagnie Maritime Belge Transport and others* (Joined Cases C-395/96 P and C-396/96 P), above, (45).

[156] See *Irish Sugar v Commission* (T-228/97) [1999] E.C.R. II–2969.

[157] *Airtours v Commission* (T-342/99) [2002] E.C.R. II–2585, where the GC annulled the Commission's Decision prohibiting the merger. For the existence of a joint dominant position see *Compagnie Maritime Belge and others* (Joined Cases T-24/93, T-26/93 and T-28/93) [1996] E.C.R. II-1201.

of the alterations in its structure that the transaction would entail the latter would make each member of the dominant oligopoly adopt a common policy on the market on a lasting basis. Consequently, three conditions are necessary for the creation of a collective dominant position significantly impeding effective competition:

1. there must be sufficient market transparency for all members of the dominant oligopoly to be aware, sufficiently, precisely and quickly, of the way in which the other members' market conduct is evolving;
2. there must be adequate deterrents to ensure that there is a long-term incentive in not departing from the common policy; and
3. it must be established that the foreseeable reaction of current and future competitors, as well as of consumers, would not jeopardise the results expected from the common policy.

(2) Abuse

22–42   A more burdonsome task is the definition of "abuse". It will be remembered that cartels are prohibited when two conditions are fulfilled: trade between Member States must be affected and competition must be restricted. According to the Court, the concept of abuse is an objective concept relating to the behaviour of an undertaking enjoying a dominant position in a given market.[158] This behaviour constitutes an abuse when it is such as to influence the structure of the relevant market. Such behaviour must have the effect, through recourse to methods different from those which condition normal competition, of hindering the maintenance or growth of existing competition.[159] It has been said that the categories of abuse are open, and include practices such as "trying" the purchase of one product to another, predatory pricing and loyalty rebates.

Any behaviour of an undertaking in a dominant position, which interferes with one of the basic freedoms or with the free choice of the purchaser or consumer, or with freedom of access to the market or to an essential facility,[160] constitutes an abuse.[161] The most obvious criterion is the freedom of choice left to the other participants in the market. Such a choice only exists when there is a sufficient offer to supply; this offer is practically non-existent in the case of an undertaking which owns an essential facility and either refuses to grant access in the absence of objective justification or only against excessive prices. An essential facility can be defined as a "facility or infrastructure, without access to which competitors cannot provide services to customers".[162] It is determined by the technical, legal or economic obstacles preventing a would-be user of the facility from competing

---

[158] For instance, an undertaking abuses its dominant position where it charges, for its services, fees which are unfair or disproportionate to the economic value of the services provided, see *TNT Traco* (C-340/99) [2001] E.C.R. I–4109.

[159] *Hoffmann-La Roche* (85/76) (quoted above, fn.59) (91).

[160] See, for example, Decision of January 18, 1994, Case IV/34.689, *Sea Containers v Stena Seelink* [1994] O.J. L15/8.

[161] See, for example, Decision of June 28, 1995, *Landing fees at Zaventem* [1995] O.J. L216/8 and *Job Centre* (C-55/96) [1998] E.C.R. I–7119: abuse of dominant position "unavoidable", caught by Arts 101–102 TFEU [8182].

[162] Commission Decision *Sea Containers v Stena Sealink* [1994] O.J. L15/08.

on the relevant (downstream) market.[163] The Court, however, never uses the expression "essential facilities", but rather refers to "refusal to deal".

It should be noted that abuse can also take place on a market different from the **22–43** dominated one and without effects on the latter, but the markets must be closely linked.[164] In other words, the prohibition also concerns abuses on, and affecting, associated non-dominated markets in special circumstances.

Although the Treaty refers to abuse "of" a dominant position, this does not mean that a link of causality must exist between the dominant position and the abuse. Indeed, the strengthening of the position of an undertaking may constitute an abuse and be prohibited regardless of the means and procedures by which it is achieved. However, such situations are to a certain extent regulated by the control of concentrations.

As for abuse by undertakings in a joint dominant position, the abuse does not necessarily have to be the action of all the undertakings in question. Such undertakings may engage in joint or individual abusive conduct; it suffices that that conduct relates to the exploitation of a joint dominant position which the undertakings hold on the market.[165]

4. COMPETITION RULES APPLYING TO VARIOUS BRANCHES OF THE ECONOMY

The Treaty also entrusts the Council, acting by a qualified majority on a proposal **22–44** from the Commission and after consulting Parliament, to lay down appropriate regulations or directives to define, if need be, in the various branches of the economy, the scope of the competition provisions.[166]

(1) Telecommunications

Telecommunications, information industries and innovation constitute one of the **22–45** most important industrial sectors for the economic development of the European Union. They will be further examined in the chapter on Enterprise and Industrial Policy/Information Society. Full competition in the telecommunications market was only introduced in 1998, after the abolition of national monopolies for equipment[167] and value-added services.[168] But, given the fact that the infrastructure remained governed by monopoly rights, the Council introduced the

---

[163] *Bronner v Mediaprint* (C-7/97) [1998] E.C.R. I–7791.
[164] *Tetra Pak* (T-83/91) [1994] E.C.R. II-755 and *Tetra Pak* (C-333/94) [1996] E.C.R. I–5951.
[165] See *Irish Sugar v Commission* (T-228/97) [1999] E.C.R. II–2969.
[166] Art.103(2)c TFEU.
[167] Directive 88/301 [1988] O.J. L131/73, incorporated [1994] O.J. L1/446, modified [1994] O.J. L268/15 and repealed by [2008] O.J. L462/20.
[168] Directive 2002/77 on competition in the markets for electronic communications network and services [2002] O.J. L249/21, which replaces Directive 90/388. For interpretation of Art.4 of Directive 2002/77 (Competition Directive) together with Art.7(3) of Directive 2002/20 (Authorisation Directive) and Art.9(1) of Directive 2002/21 (Framework Directive), see *Centro Europa 7* (C-38/05) [2008] E.C.R. I-349: they preclude, in television broadcasting matters, national legislation which makes it impossible for an operator holding rights to broadcast.

Open Network Provision Directive,[169] requiring the telecommunication organisations to lease lines to new market entrants on reasonable terms and to provide open and fair access to their networks. From 1992 onwards, the satellite[170] and mobile[171] services and the cable television networks[172] were progressively opened to competition.

In 1996, the Commission adopted its so-called Full Competition Directive[173] amending and extending its earlier Services Directive. The Directive's aim is at the introduction of full competition in the Union telecommunications market. It requires the Member States to abolish the last remaining areas of monopoly rights in that market.

22–46   In 2002, the liberalisation of the European telecom markets was pushed forward by the adoption of a new regulatory framework, the so-called telecom package. With regard to electronic communications networks and services, Parliament and the Council issued a series of directives on a common regulatory framework, among others on roaming charges for calls on mobile telephones within the Union,[174] on access and interconnection,[175] on authorisation[176] and on universal services and users' rights.[177] According to this framework, the national regulatory authorities have to define the relevant markets. The Commission has published guidelines in which the principles for the analysis of markets and

---

[169] Directive 90/387 on the establishment of the internal market for telecommunications services through the implementation of open network provision [1990] O.J. L192/1, repealed by [2002] O.J. L108/33 modified [2007] O.J. L171/32, [2009] O.J. L167/12, [2009] O.J. L337/37.

[170] Directive 94/46 amending Directive 88/301 and Directive 2002/77 (quoted above) in particular with regard to satellite communications [1994] O.J. L268/15.

[171] Directive 92/2 amending Directive 90/388 with regard to mobile and personal communications [1996] O.J. L20/59.

[172] Directive 95/51 amending Directive 90/388 with regard to the abolition of the restrictions on the use of cable television networks for the provision of already liberalised telecommunications services [1995] O.J. L256/49.

[173] Directive 96/19 amending Directive 90/388 regarding the implementation of full competition in telecommunications markets [1996] O.J. L74/13.

[174] Directive 2002/21 (Framework Directive) [2002] O.J. L108/33, amended by Regulation 717/07 on roaming on public mobile telephone networks within the Union [2007] O.J. L171/32; Regulation 544/2009 [2009] O.J. L667/12 and Directive 2009/140/EC [2009] O.J. L337/37. See *Deutsche Telekom* (C-262/06) [2007] E.C.R. I-10057, provisional maintenance of obligations to obtain authorisation regarding tariffs and *Vodafone Espana* (T-109/06) [2007] E.C.R. II-5151, Commission letter under Art.6(5) not binding. For interpretation of Art.9(1), Art.5(2) and Art.7(3) of Directive 2002/20 and Art.4 of Directive 2002/77 on competition in the markets for electronic communication, see *Centro Europa 7* (C-380/05) [2008] E.C.R. I-349, precludes national legislation that makes it impossible for an operator holding rights to broadcast in the absence of broadcasting radio frequencies granted on the basis of objective criteria. *Kabel* (C-336/07) [2008] E.C.R. I-10889, telemedia services fall within the scope of Art.31(1) and *Commission v Germany* (C-424/07) [2009] E.C.R. I-11431: failure to fulfil obligations. Also *Commission v Belgium* (C-222/08) [2010] E.C.R. I-9017: concerning Arts 12 and 13.

[175] Directive 2002/19 (Access Directive) [2002] O.J. L108/7, modified [2009] O.J. L337/37. See *Commission v Germany* (C-424/07), quoted above, fn.176.

[176] Directive 2002/20 (Authorisation Directive) [2002] O.J. L108/21. See above, *Deutsche Telekom* (C-262/06) and *Centro Europa 7* (C-380/05).

[177] Directive 2002/22 (Universal Service Directive) [2002] O.J. L108/51, modified [2009] O.J. L337/14. See *Commission v Germany* (C-424/07) quoted above, fn.176; interpretation of Art.25(2) *Deutsche Telekom AGv Deutschland* (C-194/05): precludes national legislation under which undertakings assigning telephone numbers to end-users must make available data in their possession.

effective competition under the new regulatory framework are laid down.[178] The Directive also introduced the basic principles for licensing new entrants to both voice telephony and telecommunications infrastructure markets. It furthermore requires interconnection to the voice telephony service and public switched telecommunications networks to be granted on non-discriminatory, proportional and transparent terms, based on objective criteria.

In 2002, the Commission also adopted a Directive on "Competition in the markets for electronic communication networks and services"; amending and consolidating a similar directive from 1990[179] and in 2008 the Commission adopted a Directive on competition in the markets in telecommunications terminal equipment.[180]

(2) Transport

Although, as indicated above, the Council must, if need be, define the scope of the competition rules in the various branches of the economy, there is no obligation to do so with regard to transport. In the past, the Council excluded transport services from the application of the first regulation implementing the competition rules,[181] but this exemption was repealed by the Regulation that replaced the latter in 2003.[182] This left in place rules[183] of competition for transport by rail, road and inland waterway,[184] maritime transport and air transport. These shall be briefly examined below, but more extensively in Ch.27: Transport.

22–47

Another regulation concerns the limitation periods in proceedings and the enforcement of sanctions under the Union competition rules relating to transport.[185]

(a) Maritime Transport

Reference must be made here to the Regulation laying down detailed rules for the application of the Union competition rules to maritime transport and to the block exemption for Liner Conferences.[186] The regulation provided for the possibility

22–48

---

[178] Commission guidelines on market analysis and the assessment of significant market power under the Union regulatory framework for electronic communications networks and services [2002] O.J. C165/6.

[179] Directive 2002/77 [2002] O.J. L249/21. See *Centro Europa 7* (C-380/05) [2008] E.C.R. I-349.

[180] Directive 2008/63 [2008] O.J. L162/20 (codified version).

[181] Regulation 141/62 exempting transport from the application of Council Regulation No.17 [1962] O.J. 124/2750.

[182] Regulation 1/2003 [2003] O.J. L1/1.

[183] Regulation 17/62 [1962] O.J. 13/204, repealed by Regulation 1/2003 [2003] O.J. L1/1.

[184] Regulation 1017/68 [1968] O.J. L175/1, amended by Regulation 1/2003 (quoted above, fn.184), replaced by codified version Regulation 169/2009 [2009] O.J. L61/1. For the scope of Regulation 1017/68 see *UIC (Union Internationale des Chemins de Fer)* (C-264/95 P) [1997] E.C.R. I–1287; [1997] 5 C.M.L.R. 49. Art.26 of Regulation 1017/68 on hearings was implemented by Regulation 1630/69 [1969] O.J. L209/11; this Regulation was repealed by Regulation 773/2004 [2004] O.J. L123/18, modified [2008] O.J. L171/3.

[185] Regulation 2988/74 [1974] O.J. L319/1, amended by Regulation 1/2003 (quoted above, fn.184).

[186] Regulation 4056/86 [1986] O.J. L378/4, amended by Regulation 1/2003 (quoted above, fn.184). See *Compagnie Maritime Belge Transports and others v Commission* (Joined Cases T-24/93, etc.) [1996] E.C.R. II–1201.

to exempt certain technical cartels and also for block exemptions of Liner Conferences under well-defined conditions and with specific obligations. However, this regulation was repealed and maritime transport is now governed by the general competition enforcement regime. In order to assist companies in carrying out self-assessment of their practices, the Commission has published a set of extensive guidelines on the application of Art.101 TFEU to maritime transport services.[187]

The Council also adopted a regulation on the application of the competition rules to certain categories of cartels between liner shipping companies, described in shipping circles as "consortia".[188] The Regulation remains in force and authorises the Commission to declare that the competition rules shall not apply to certain categories of agreements. It concerns agreements that have as their object to promote or establish co-operation in the joint operation of maritime transport services between liner shipping companies, for the purpose of rationalising their operations by means of technical, operational and/or commercial arrangements, with the exception of price-fixing consortia.

In order to benefit from the exemption the consortia must not have a market share above 30 per cent, omit hard-core restrictions and give members the opportunity to withdraw without financial or other penalty.

(b)   Air Transport

22–49   The Treaty provides that the Title on transport shall only apply to transport by rail, road and inland waterway and that the Council may decide, "whether, to what extent and by what procedure appropriate provision may be laid down for sea and air transport".[189] Having recognised that the rules on competition form part of the Treaty's general provisions which also apply to air transport,[190] the Council adopted a regulation laying down the procedure for the application of the competition rules to undertakings in the air transport sector.[191]

In that regulation the Council considered that air transport is characterised by features which are specific to this sector and that, furthermore, international air transport is regulated by a network of bilateral agreements between States. Those agreements define the conditions under which air carriers designated by the parties to the agreement may operate routes between their territories.[192] On the

---

[187] Martime Transport Guidelines [2008] O.J. C245/02.

[188] Regulation 479/92 [1992] O.J. L55/3, amended by Regulation 1/2003 (quoted above, fn.184), codified version [2009] O.J. L79/1. See block exemption Regulation 870/95 [1995] O.J. L89/7, which was replaced by Regulation 823/2000 on the application of Art.101(3) [81(3)] of the Treaty to certain agreements between liner shipping companies (consortia) [2000] O.J. L100/24, extended and amended 2009 IP/09/1367, arguing that consortia generally bring about improvements of productivity and service quality; it was renewed until April 25, 2010 [2005] O.J. L101/10, repealed by [2009] O.J. L256/31 and renewed until April 25, 2015.

[189] Art.100(2) TFEU.

[190] This recognition only occurred after the Court had so decided, see *Ministère Public v Asjes* (Joined Cases 209/84, 210/84, 211/84, 212/84 and 213/84) [1986] E.C.R. 1425; [1986] 3 C.M.L.R. 173.

[191] Regulation 411/2004 [2004] O.J. L68/1, partially repealed by [2009] O.J. L148/1.

[192] Regulation 1617/93 only applies to air transport between Member States; with regard to air transport between Member States and third countries see, among others, the *Open Sky* cases (see below); this Regulation was renewed by Regulation 1105/02 [2002] O.J. L167/6.

other hand, it is clear that practices which affect competition relating to air transport between Member States may have substantial effect on trade between Member States. It was therefore necessary to authorise the Commission to take the requisite measures for the application of the competition rules to air transport.

Consequently, the Council adopted a regulation allowing the Commission to exclude from the prohibition provided by the Treaty, certain categories of agreements in the air sector.[193] The regulation provides in particular for block exemptions in relation to agreements concerning: (i) joint planning and co-ordination of airlines schedules; (ii) consultation on tariffs for the carriage of passengers, baggage and freight on scheduled air services; (iii) joint operation on new less busy scheduled air services; (iv) slots allocation at airports and airport scheduling; and (v) common purchase, development and operation of computer reservation system relating to timetabling, reservations and ticketing by air transport undertakings. Altogether, the main preoccupation of the Union remains the opening of the markets, i.e. the right of access for Union air carriers to intra-Union air routes.[194]

(c) International Aviation[195]

The Commission has no effective and efficient enforcement tools to ensure that **22–50** competition is preserved and promoted in the field of international air transport, i.e. between Member States and third countries.[196] The Commission sought, without success to extend the scope of certain regulations to encompass this.[197] A Court judgment in the *Open Sky* cases,[198] where the Court found that the bilateral agreements concluded by several Member States were contrary to Union rules,[199] resulted in the Commission obtaining a mandate from the Council to start negotiations with the US (see Ch.27: Transport). These negotiations resulted in the adoption on April 30, 2007 of an Air Transport Agreement between the EU and the Member States on one hand, and the US on the other, authorising EU and US airlines to fly between any cities in the EU and any cities in the US.

---

[193] Regulation 487/09 [2009] O.J. L148/1 on the application of Art.101(3) to certain categories of agreements and concerted practices in the air transport sector.

[194] See Regulation 2408/92 [1992] O.J. L240/8 repealed by [2008] O.J. L293/3 and *Air Inter* (T-260/94) [1997] E.C.R. II–997.

[195] XXXIInd Report on Competition Policy, 108.

[196] Interesting also is Decision 98/710 on the Italian traffic distribution rules for the airport system of Milan [1998] O.J. L337/42. See also *Aéroports de Paris v Commission* (T-128/98) [2000] E.C.R. II–3929.

[197] Regulation 411/2004 on procedure for application of the rules of competition to undertakings in the air transport sector [1987] O.J. L374/1 and Regulation 3976/87 allowing the Commission to adopt block exemptions in that sector [1987] O.J. L374/9, amended [2004] O.J. L68/1 and repealed by [2009] O.J. L148/1.

[198] *Open Sky* cases (Joined Cases C-466/98, C-467/98, C-468/98, C-471/98, C-472/98, C-475/98 and C-476/98) against the UK, Denmark, Sweden, Finland, Belgium, Luxembourg, Austria and Germany [2002] E.C.R. I–9427.

[199] Art.49 TFEU [43].

(d) Rail Transport

22–51   Historically, the rail transport sector has been characterised by the existence of State monopolies, with the result that national markets were absolutely closed to operators from other Member States. Subsequent privatisations which have taken place have not necessarily changed this. Consequently, the Union has tried to pry open the national markets to operators from other Member States by providing for a "right of access".[200] Under the present Directive this right is granted only to "international groupings" and to "railway undertakings operating international combined transport goods services".[201] Where the former are concerned they have the right of access in the Member States of establishment of their constituent railway undertakings and the right of transit in other Member States for international services between the Member States of establishment. As for the combined goods services, they have access to the infrastructure of all the Member States.

Various regulations were adopted over the years concerning the application of competition rules to rail operators; see for instance the rules concerning aid in the form of compensation for discharging public service obligation.[202]

Further provisions concerning transport will be examined in Ch.27: Transport.

(3) Postal Service[203]

22–52   Although the Court stated,[204] back in 1993, that competition rules of the Treaty (cartels, abuses of dominant positions, and also State aid provision[205]), apply to the postal sector, the latter enjoyed a privileged position until the end of the 1990s. The application of the competition rules was carried out very progressively. This is surprising when one realises that the revenue of the postal sector represents 0.62 per cent of the Union's GDP (2012) and that it provides more than five million direct and indirect jobs. The national postal services constitute "undertakings entrusted with the operation of services of general economic interest" specifically referred to in the TFEU.[206] The Commission published a Notice[207] setting out the:

---

[200] Directive 91/440 [1991] O.J. L237/25 on the development of the Union's railways, amended [2001] O.J. L75/1 and [2007] O.J. L315/44. See the landmark Decision *Ferrovie dello Stato (FS)/Georg Verkehrsorganisation (GVG)*. Press release IP/03/1183, according to which FS was required to allow new train operators to provide cross-border passenger services into Italy. See also Directive 2001/14 on the allocation of railway infrastructure capacity and the levying of charges for the use of railway infrastructure and safety certification [2001] O.J. L75/291, amended [2002] O.J. L289/30 and [2007] O.J. L315/44.

[201] Art.10 Directive 91/440.

[202] Regulation 1370/07 [2007] O.J. L315/1 and Regulation 169/2009 [2009] O.J. L61/1.

[203] Some of the data in this section is borrowed from "La libéralisation des services postaux dans l'UE" by Stéphane Rodrigues, L'Observateur de Bruxelles, No. 63, p.II.

[204] *Netherlands and Others v Commission* (Joined Cases C-48/90 and C-66/90) [1992] E.C.R. I–565; [1993] 5 C.M.L.R. 316 and *Corbeau* (C-320/91) [1993] I–2533; [1995] 4 C.M.L.R. 621.

[205] *Banco Exterior de España* (C-387/92) [1994] E.C.R. I–877; [1994] 3 C.M.L.R. 473.

[206] Arts 14 and 106(2) TFEU. The latter provides that these undertakings "shall be subject to the rules contained in this Treaty, in particular to the rules on competition, in so far as the application of such rules does not obstruct the performance, in law or in fact, of the particular tasks assigned to them."

[207] [1998] O.J. C39/2.

"[G]uiding principles according to which the Commission intends to apply the competition rules to the postal sector in individual cases, while maintaining the necessary safeguards for the provision of a universal service. It also gives the enterprises and the Member States clear guidelines so as to avoid infringements of the Treaty."

The Commission also ascertains that "the traditional structures of some services of general interest,[208] which are organised on the basis of national monopolies, constitute a challenge for European economic integration".

The Notice sets out rules concerning the duties of dominant postal operators, cross-subsidisation, public undertakings and special or exclusive rights, freedom to provide services, measures adopted by Member States, postal operators and aid, services of general economic interest and the conditions for the application of the exception provided for undertakings entrusted with the operation of such services.[209]

In 1997, Parliament and Council adopted a Directive on common rules for the development of the internal market of Union postal services and the improvement of quality of service; this Directive was modified in 2002.[210] It is based upon five elements:

22–53

- a progressive and controlled liberalisation of the postal services: different steps were taken in 2003 and 2006. Notably this results in a liberalisation. 43 per cent of the French postal service (outgoing trans-frontier mail and mail of more than 50g whose price is two-and-a-half times the basic rate);
- the maintenance, in each Member State, of a universal postal service, i.e. an offer of quality service on a permanent basis at every point of the territory and at affordable prices. Concretely, this means at least one delivery and one clearance every weekday at the home or premises of every natural and legal person. Furthermore, it should include the following minimum facilities: the clearance, sorting, transport and distribution of postal items up to 2kg and of postal packages up to 10kg and services for registered and insured items;
- besides the obligation of affordable prices, the Directive requires transparency of accounts; see in this respect also the obligation of transparency imposed on the relation between the State and public enterprise[211];
- the quality of the postal services: besides the quality of the internal postal service that comes under the national competences, the quality of the trans-border services is established in an Annex to the Directive and is based on the duration of the forwarding[212];
- the Directive requires the Member States to establish one or more National Regulatory Authorities (NRA) that are legally distinct and functionally independent of the postal operators.

---

[208] Communication from the Commission, Services of general interest in Europe [2001] O.J. C17/4.
[209] Art.106(2) TFEU.
[210] Directive 97/67 [1998] O.J. L15/14, amended [2002] O.J. L176/21, with regard to the further opening of Union postal services. Scope of Art.19: *DHL* (C-148/10) judgment of October 13, 2011.
[211] Directive 80/723 [1980] O.J. L195/35, modified: [2005] O.J. L312/47, repealed by [2006] O.J. L318717.
[212] J+3 for 85 per cent of the deliveries and J+5 for 97 per cent of them.

A European Regulators Group for Postal Services was established in 2010 to ensure a consistent application of the relevant rules in all the Member States.[213] A third postal directive[214] was published in 2008 providing for abolishing legal monopolies of postal services by December 31, 2010. It provides for the accomplishment of the internal market of Union postal services via abolition of the reserved areas in all Member States, the confirmation of the scope and standard of universal service, the reinforcement of consumers' rights and upgrading of the role of national regulatory authorities and the offering of a list of measures Member States may take to safeguard and finance, if necessary, the universal service. The Directive requires Member States to continue to ensure a universal service for all customers including collection and delivery of mail at least five days per week at affordable prices throughout the territory.[215]

(4) Insurance[216]—Financial Sector

22–54 In May 1991, the Council adopted a Regulation concerning the exemption from the competition rules of certain categories of agreements in the field of insurance. It authorises the Commission to issue a regulation exempting this category from the prohibition of certain agreements.[217] On that basis the Commission issued, in December 1992, a Regulation[218] exempting four types of agreements—out of the six provided for in the Council regulation—that seek co-operation with respect to:

- the establishment of common risk-premium tariffs based on collectively ascertained statistics or on the number of claims;
- the establishment of standard policy conditions;
- the common coverage of certain types of risks; and
- the establishment of common rules on the testing and acceptance of security devices.

The Regulation was replaced, with effect from April 1, 2003.[219] The new 2003 Regulation provided for two types of agreements not previously included: the settlement of claims; and registers of, and information on, aggravated risks, but also moves away from the previous approach of listing exempted clauses; it placed greater emphasis on defining categories of agreements which are exempted up to a certain level of market power[220] and on specifying the

---

[213] [2010] O.J. C217/7.

[214] Directive 2008/6 [2008] O.J. L52/3 modifying Directive 97/67 (quoted above).

[215] For more info. See *http://www.ec.europa.eu//internal_market/post/index_en.htm* [accessed August 23, 2013].

[216] See also above, Ch.18: Freedom to Provide Services/Financial Services.

[217] Regulation 1534/91 [1991] O.J. L143/1, ameded [2003] O.J. L1/1.

[218] Regulation 3932/92 [1992] O.J. L398/7.

[219] Regulation 358/03 [2003] O.J. L53/8, amended [2004] O.J. L168/14.

[220] In the case of co-insurance groups, the insurance products underwritten within the grouping arrangement by the participating undertakings or on their behalf, should not be more than 20 per cent of the relevant market (which may rise to 22 per cent) and in the case of co-reinsurance groups, not more than 25 per cent (which may rise to 27 per cent).

restrictions or clauses which are not to be contained in such agreements.[221] This Regulation expired on March 31, 2010 and was replaced by a new Regulation[222] as from April 1, 2010. The 2010 Regulation is narrower in scope than its predecessor in that it removes the benefit of the block exemption from agreements on standard policy conditions and security devices.

The Commission closely supervises the application of the Union competition rules to banks[223] and other financial institutions.

(5) Intellectual Property Rights

As already mentioned, such rights are used by their owner to prevent others from producing and commercialising the product covered by the right or to limit the use of this right to particular national territories. Consequently, the owner divides the Union once more into separate markets, and, although he acts in conformity with national law, he thereby prevents trade between Member States. This, of course, constitutes an infringement of the basic principle of free movement of goods and it was in relation to this principle that the Court defined the implementation of the competition rules in this important sector. This subject is discussed below in Ch.31: Enterprise and Industrial Policy/Information Society.

22–55

(6) Agriculture

The Treaty provides that "rules on competition shall apply to production of, and trade in, agricultural products only to the extent determined by the Council".[224] In other words, the Council could, in theory, have decided that those rules do not apply to agriculture[225]; however, the Council opted for a limited application.[226]

22–56

The point of departure is that the rules of competition do apply to agriculture, but only in so far as their application does not impede the functioning of national organisations of agricultural markets—those were later replaced by the common organisations of agricultural markets—or jeopardise the attainment of the objectives of the common agricultural policy. In order to clarify the scope of the application of competition rules to the agricultural sector, a Council Regulation of July 24, 2006 sets out categories of agricultural agreements that are exempt from the competition rules.[227] The agreements so excluded are:

- farmers' cartels;
- farmers' associations;

---

[221] This has been the new approach of the Commission with the group exemption regulations since a few years.

[222] Regulation 267/10 [2010] O.J. C83/1.

[223] The Commission imposed fines totalling €124,260 million on eight Austrian banks.

[224] Art.42 TFEU.

[225] See first recital of Regulation 26/62 [1962] O.J. 30/993: "where as one of the matters to be decided under the common agricultural policy is whether the rules on competition . . . are to apply to production of and trade in agricultural products". The regulation has been replaced by [2006] O.J. L 214/7 , amended by [2007] O.J. L299/1, [2008] O.J. L121/1 and [2009] O.J. L154/1.

[226] Regulation 1184/2006 (quoted above). See *Dijkstra* (Joined Cases C-319/94, C-40/94 and C-224/94) [1995] E.C.R. I–4471; [1996] 5 C.M.L.R. 178, on the interpretation of Art.2 of Regulation 26/62 which is identical in wording to Art.2 in Regulation 1184/206.

[227] Council Regulation (EC) No 1184/2006 of July 24, 2006.

- associations of such associations belonging to a single Member State, and which concern the sale of agricultural products or the use of joint facilities for the storage, treatment or processing of agricultural products and under which there is no obligation to charge identical prices.

The Commission has sole power to determine which cartels fulfil those conditions; its decisions must be published.

(7) Energy

22–57 The main objective of the application of the competition rules to the energy sector is to ensure the effective liberalisation of the electricity and gas sectors. For more details, see Ch.35: Energy Policy.

(8) Coal and Steel

22–58 Until the expiry of the ECSC Treaty on July 23, 2002, these two sectors were subject to the specific competition rules of that Treaty.[228] Although "the Commission had over the years aligned the application of the ECSC and the EC Treaties", it thought it useful "to provide guidance for companies…" and consequently adopted a Communication concerning certain aspects of the treatment of competition cases resulting from the expiry of the ECSC Treaty.[229] An interesting point is that restrictive agreements which were exempted under the ECSC Treaty will not lose this exemption because of the expiry of that Treaty. Even after the expiry of the ECSC Treaty, the Commission can, according to the Court,[230] impose fines on the basis of the ECSC Treaty.

5. IMPLEMENTATION OF THE RULES ON COMPETITION[231]

22–59 Regulation 1/2003 replaced Regulation 17,[232] which was in force for just over 40 years (from March 1962 to April 30, 2004). According to the Council, it allowed a Union competition policy to develop that has helped to disseminate a competition culture within the Union. In the light of experience it had to be replaced by legislation designed to meet the challenges of an integrated market and of the enlargement of the Union.[233]

Furthermore, according to the TFEU,[234] legislation in this field must take into account the need to ensure effective supervision on the one hand, and to simplify

---

[228] Art.65 ECSC for agreements, Art.66 for concentrations and Art.67 for interference with conditions of competition by Member States. No longer in force.

[229] [2002] O.J. C152/5.

[230] *ArcelorMittal Luxembourg v Commission* and *Commission v ArcelorMittal Luxembourg* (C-201/09 and C-216/09 P) E.C.R. 29.03.11.

[231] [2003] O.J. L1/1, modified [2004] O.J. L68/12 (air transport) and [2006] O.J. L269/1 (maritime transport).

[232] [1962] O.J. p.204/62.

[233] Regulation 1/2003 first recital [2003] O.J. L1/1.

[234] Art.103(2)(b) TFEU.

administration to the greatest possible extent on the other. This balance could no longer be secured under Regulation 17. Historically, Regulation 17 provided for a system where all agreements that violated the provision corresponding to Art.101 TFEU then in force and that were not covered by the de minimis notice or one of the block exemptions had to be notified to the Commission. If not, the agreements were deemed void according to Art.101(2) TFEU and its "pre-decessor" Art.81(2). The workload on the Commission was tremendous and in practice seldom issued so-called negative clearances or individual exemptions, but rather issued so-called non-binding "comfort letters". For all practical purposes the system had become obsolete and very bureaucratic.

The Commission also, at the time, realised that in order to ensure effective application of the Union competition rules, the competition authorities of the Member States had to be more closely associated with their application.[235]

(1) Role of the Member States and the European Competition Network

The role of the national competition authorities is complemented by the national courts and it was decided that national courts should be allowed to apply the competition provisions in full, including the application of exemptions from the prohibition, for certain agreements. The latter constitutes the most far-reaching change, since until then this was the sole prerogative of the Commission under the notification system.

22–60

The Commission and the competition authorities of the Member States also put in place a European Competition Network (ECN).[236] It allows for greater co-operation and provides for an allocation of cases according to the principle of the best placed authority. The Commission remains at the centre of the ECN. It will, as the guardian of the Treaty, ensure that decisions taken by national authorities are consistent and that the antitrust rules are applied in a uniform manner. In this context it may be mentioned that the Commission has not taken an active role interfering formally with national competition authorities, for instance under Art.11(6) of Regulation 1/2003, which provides that "[t]he initiation by the Commission of proceedings for the adoption of a decision [. . .] shall relieve the competition authorities of the Member States of their competence to apply Arts 101 and 102 of the Treaty. If a competition authority of a Member State is already acting on a case, the Commission shall only initiate proceedings after consulting with that national competition authority." Several other mechanisms of co-operation with the national authorities designated by the Member States[237] are provided for.[238]

1. when national competition authorities apply national competition law to agreements within the meaning of Art.101(1) TFEU which may affect interstate trade, they must also apply Art.101(3) TFEU; the same applies for abuses of a dominant position. This application may not lead to the

---

[235] Regulation 1/2003, recital 6 (quoted above).
[236] Notice on co-operation within the Network of Competition Authorities [2004] O.J. C101/43.
[237] Art.35(1) Regulation 1/2003.
[238] Art.11 Regulation 1/2003.

prohibition of agreements which do not restrict competition in the common market, or which fulfil the conditions for an exemption or which are covered by a block exemption regulation. The latter does not apply to *unilateral* conduct engaged in by undertakings; nor does it apply to mergers[239];

2. national competition authorities may not take decisions which would run counter to decisions already adopted by the Commission[240];

3. the Commission must transmit to the competition authorities of the Member States copies of the most important documents it has collected with a view of finding and ordering an infringement to be terminated, ordering interim measures, accepting binding commitments, deciding the competition rules do not apply or withdraw the benefit of a block exemption;

4. the national competition authorities must inform the Commission in writing before (or without delay after) commencing the first formal investigative measure;

5. the national competition authorities must, not later than 30 days before the adoption of a decision concerning infringements, undertakings or withdrawal of the benefit of a block exemption, inform the Commission;

6. the national competition authorities may consult the Commission on any case involving the application of Union law;

7. the initiation by the Commission of proceedings shall automatically relieve the national authorities of their competence to apply the Union competition Rules;

8. the Commission and national competition authorities may exchange and use in evidence any matter of fact or of law, including confidential information[241];

9. the Commission may reject a complaint on the ground that a national authority is dealing with the case[242];

10. as for the national courts, it is explicitly provided that they "have the power to apply Arts 101 and 102 TFEU of the Treaty."[243] For this purpose, they may ask the Commission to transmit information in its possession and its opinion on questions concerning the application of Union competition rules. A copy of any written judgment deciding on the application of Arts 101 and 102 TFEU, must be forwarded to the Commission. The latter may, where the coherent application of the Union rules so require, submit written observations to the national courts; with their permission it may also submit oral observations.[244]

---

[239] The concept of unilateral behaviour and Art.7(2) of Regulation 1/2003 is an area where unceatainty persits due to different rules and regulations among member states, typically in Germany and France.

[240] Art.16(2) Regulation 1/2003.

[241] Art.12 Regulation 1/2003.

[242] Art.13 Regulation 1/2003. See also the Notice on co-operation between the Commission and the courts [2004] O.J. C101/54.

[243] Art.6 Regulation 1/2003.

[244] Art.15 Regulation 1/2003.

National courts may not adopt decisions running counter to decisions adopted **22–61** by the Commission; they must also avoid adopting decisions which would conflict with a decision "contemplated" by the Commission. When the enforcement is entrusted to administrative and judicial authorities, Member States may allocate different powers and functions to those different national authorities, whether administrative or judicial. In case courts are designated to make decisions requiring that an infringement be brought to an end, ordering interim measures, accepting commitments or imposing fines, they shall be relieved of their competence the moment the Commission initiates proceedings for the adoption of decisions under the Regulation.[245] This, however, applies only to the prosecuting authority, when for the adoption of the above-mentioned decisions; an authority brings an action before a judicial authority that is separate and different from the prosecuting authority. That prosecuting authority shall, when the Commission opens proceedings, withdraw its claim before the judicial authority.[246]

(2) Role of the Commission

Generally speaking, the Regulation provides for procedures to be followed by the **22–62** Commission when it takes one of the following decisions[247]:

1. When acting on a complaint from a Member State or a natural or legal person who can show a legitimate interest[248] or on its own initiative, the Commission finds that there is an infringement and requires undertakings or associations of undertakings to end such an infringement.[249] In this connection attention should be drawn to the limitation period of five years for enforcement procedures.[250] The time of the limitation period shall begin to run upon the day on which the infringement is committed. In the case of continuing or repeated infringements, time shall begin to run on the day on which the infringement cases.

---

[245] Art.35(3) Regulation 1/2003.

[246] Art.35(4) Regulation 1/2003.

[247] Lists of decisions taken by the Commission can be found in the Annual Reports on Competition policy published in conjunction with the annual General Reports.

[248] Art.7(1) Regulation 1/2003. See Regulation 27, first Regulation implementing Council regulation 17, fixing form, content and other details concerning applications [1962] J.O. 35/1118. No longer in force. See *Koelman* (T-575/93) [1996] E.C.R. II–1; [1994] 4 C.M.L.R. 636, where in the GC ruled that the now repealed Regulation 27 fixing form, content and other details concerning complaints does not confer upon a person who lodges a complaint (application), the right to obtain from the Commission a decision within the meaning of Art.288 TFEU. See Notice on the handling of complaints by the Commission under Arts 101 and 102 TFEU [2004] O.J. C101/65.

[249] See *Camera Care v Commission* (792/79 R) [1980] E.C.R. 119 at 131(18); [1980] 1 C.M.L.R. 334: the powers which the Commission holds under Art.3 (now Art.7 Regulation 1/2003) include the power to take interim measures which are indispensable for the effective exercise of its function. See also *Ford Werke v Commission* (Joined Cases 228/82 R and 229/82 R) [1982] E.C.R. 3091, where interim measures were suspended.

[250] Regulation 2988/74 concerning limitation periods in proceedings and the enforcement of sanctions under the rules of the EEC relating to transport and competition [1974] O.J. L319/1, Arts 4–6 as amended by Regulation 1/2003.

2. Order interim measures in case of urgency due to the risk of serious and irreparable damage to competition, on the basis of, prima facie, finding of infringement.[251]

3. Make commitments offered by undertakings binding.[252] This was a novelty since it allows the Commission to end a procedure without having to decide whether or not the Union competition rules were infringed; for the relevant undertaking(s) it created legal certainty by avoiding statements of objections and possible fines since the commitments must meet the concerns expressed by the Commission in its "preliminary assessment" of a matter.

4. Find that the prohibition is not applicable in case the Union public interest relating to the application of the prohibitions so requires.[253] This possibility had not yet been used at the time of publishing this book.

5. To interview any natural or legal person who consents to be interviewed for the purpose of collecting information relating to the subject matter of an investigation.[254]

6. To obtain all necessary information from governments and national authorities and from undertakings, either by simple request or by decision. In both cases the Commission must state the legal basis and specify what information is required, fix a time limit for providing them.[255] In case of incorrect information or absence of information within the set time limit, the Commission may impose fines.[256] The power to ask questions is widely used by the Commission during its investigations and constitutes an indispensable means for gathering the required data. Both the Court and the GC recognised that:

> [A]n undertaking in receipt of a request for information can be recognised as having a right to silence only to the extent that it would be compelled to provide answers, which might involve an admission on its part of the existence of an infringement, which it is incumbent upon the Commission to prove.[257]

Self-infringement is thus not an obligation upon the undertakings under EU law, and practice in this area is rather extensive.[258] The core is that objective facts must be handed over to the Commission, but not "subjective assessments" of documents and facts that may be deemed self-incriminating.

7. To undertake inspections of undertakings.[259] To this end officials authorised by the Commission to conduct an inspection (written authorisation) are empowered to:

---

[251] Art.8 Regulation 1/2003.

[252] Art.9 Regulation 1/2003.

[253] Art.10 Regulation 1/2003.

[254] Art.19 Regulation 1/2003.

[255] Art.18(2) and (3) Regulation 1/2003.

[256] Regulation 1/2003. See, for instance, Decision 2001/271 imposing fines on Deutsche Post/trans-o-flex [2001] O.J. L97/1.

[257] *Orkem v Commission* (374/87) [1989] E.C.R. 3350(35) and *Mannesmannroehren-Werke v Commission* (T-112/98) [2001] E.C.R. II–729(67).

[258] *Commission v SGL Carbon AG* (C-301/04 P) [2006] E.C.R. I-5915.

[259] Art.20 Regulation 1/2003.

(a)   enter any premises, land or means of transport[260];
(b)   to examine books and business records irrespective of the medium in which they are stored[261];
(c)   to take copies of or extracts from the books and business records;
(d)   to seal any business premises and books or records to the extent necessary for the inspection;
(e)   to ask for oral explanations on the spot.

Legal privilege. The confidentiality of written communications between lawyer and client is protected when: (i) such communications are made for the purpose and in the interest of the client's defence and (ii) they emanate from independent lawyers, i.e. lawyers who are not bound to the client by a relationship of employment ("in-house" lawyers).[262] If the Commission were to read documents covered by the legal privilege it could not use them nor show them to third parties. For several years undertakings' and lawyers' organisations continued to plead for inclusion of their in-house lawyers within the legal privilege but this has been rejected by the Court.[263]

Undertakings must submit to inspections ordered by a Commission Decision, which shall specify the subject matter and purpose, the date on which it is to begin, the penalties provided in case of refusal and the right to have the decision reviewed by the Court. At the request of the national authorities concerned or the Commission, the Commission inspectors may be assisted by national officials. Where it is found that an undertaking opposes an inspection, the Member State concerned shall afford the necessary assistance of the police or of an equivalent enforcement authority so as to enable the inspection to proceed.[264]

If such assistance requires authorisation from a judicial authority it shall be applied for. The national authority shall control that the Commission decision is authentic and that the coercive measures envisaged are neither arbitrary nor excessive. In the control of the proportionality the national authority may ask the Commission for detailed explanation in particular on the grounds the Commission has for suspecting infringement of the Union competition rules, the seriousness of the infringement and the nature of the involvement of the undertaking concerned. However, the national authority may not call into question the necessity for the inspection nor demand that it

---

[260] Art.20(a)b Regulation 1/2003. This right to enter premises was contested, but to no avail, by several undertakings: *Hoechst v Commission* (46/87 R) [1987] E.C.R. 1549 and *Dow Chemical Nederland BV v Commission* (85/87) [1987] E.C.R. 4367. See also Explanatory Notes on authorisation to investigate: Thirteenth Report on Competition policy, 1993, 270–271.

[261] Art.20(2)(b) Regulation 1/2003.

[262] *AM&S* (155/79) [1982] E.C.R. 1575. This was confirmed by the Court: *Akzo Nobel v Commission* (C-550/07) [2010] E.C.R. I-8301.

[263] *Akzo Nobel and Akcros Chemicals v Commission* (Joined Cases T-125/03 and T-253/03) Order of the President [2003] II-4771 and *Commission v Akzo and Ackros* (C-07/04) [2004] E.C.R. I-8739 and *Akzo Nobel Chemicals Ltd v Commission of the European Communities* [2007] E.C.R.II-3523, C-550/07 *Akzo Nobel v Commission* [2010] E.C.R. I-8301.

[264] Art.20(6) Regulation 1/2003.

be provided with the Commission file. The lawfulness of the Commission decision is, of course, submitted to the review of the Court[265];

(f) inspection of other premises,[266] including the homes of directors, managers and other members of staff. Such decision must be taken after consultation of the competent authorities of the relevant Member State. It also needs the prior authorisation of the national judicial authorities. The same conditions as set out above apply in this case;

(g) request the relevant national authorities to undertake inspections.[267]

8. To impose fines and penalties.[268]

Fines can range up to 10 per cent of the firm's total sales in the preceding business year[269]; for credit and other financial institutions, sales may be replaced by assets.[270] For the calculation of fines see "Guidelines on the Method of Setting Fines"[271]: the combination of the value of the sales to which the infringement relates and of the duration of the infringement is regarded by the Commission as an appropriate proxy to reflect the economic importance of the infringement as well as the relative weight of each undertaking involved. This information is used to set a "basic amount".[272] There are also aggravating and mitigating circumstances which may increase or decrease the basic amount.

It might be interesting to note that the amount of fines collected by the Commission in competition cases amounted to over €3.3 billion in 2007 in eight final decisions in which it fined 41undertakings[273]. The level of fines in 2008 were €2.2 billion in 2008, €1.5 billion in 2009, €2.8 billion in 2010, €614 million in 2011 and €1.8 billion in 2012.

Settlement Procedure. The Regulation relating to the conduct of proceedings by the Commission pursuant to the cartel and dominant position rules[274] lays down rules concerning the participation of the parties concerned in such proceedings. These parties may be prepared to acknowledge their participation in a cartel violating the competition rules

---

[265] See *France Télécom v Commission* (T-339/04) [2007] E.C.R. II-521, where the GC examined the role of the national judge and of the national competition authorities.

[266] Art.21 Regulation 1/2003.

[267] Art.22 Regulation 1/2003.

[268] Art.23 Regulation 1/2003. The undertakings must be told, in the statement of objections, that the Commission intends to impose fines. Fines have been imposed for submitting incomplete information ([1971] EC Bull.11–55) and periodic fines were imposed for each day an undertaking failed to fulfil an obligation imposed by the Commission: Decision MA-Statuut [1980] O.J. L318/1.

[269] Art.23 Regulation 1/2003. The expression "total sales" refers to total "world" sales: see *Lafarge* (T-54/03) [2008] E.C.R. II-120*.

[270] By analogy to Art.5(3) of the Merger Regulation.

[271] [2006] O.J. C210/2. In *Cheil Jedang v Commission* (T-220/00) [2003] E.C.R II–2481, the GC decided that the fact of an enterprise having been fined in the US does not give rise to a *no bis in idem.*

[272] In case of a company heading a group and owning 100 per cent of the capital of the daughter companies, that head company may be held responsible for the total: see *Akzo Nobel and Others v Commission* (T-112/05) [2007] E.C.R. II-5049; see appeal C-97/08 cf. *Elf Aquitiane v Commmission* (C-521/09P), not yet published.

[273] XXXVII Report (2008), 1.1.2.

[274] Regulation 773/04 [2004] O.J. L123/18, amended [2006] O.J. L362/1 and [2008] O.J. L171/3.

and their liability, if they can reasonably anticipate the Commission's findings and the fines they are likely to incur. In that case those parties might submit settlements submissions. The Commission therefore established a Settlement Procedure.[275] At the time of publication, the latest and sixth cartel settlement took place on June 27, 2012. The Commission then fined producers of water management products €13 million in a cartel settlement.[276] The settlement procedure allows the Commission to apply a simplified procedure to suitable cases and thereby reduce the length of the investigation. This is, according to the Commission, good for consumers and for taxpayers as it reduces costs; good for antitrust enforcement as it frees up resources to tackle other suspected cases; and good for the companies themselves that benefit from quicker decisions and a 10 per cent reduction in fines.[277]

After the initiation of proceedings, the Commission may set a time limit within which the parties may indicate that they are prepared to engage in settlement discussions with a view to introducing settlement submissions. The Commission, on its part, may indicate the range of potential fines. A time limit for introducing the submissions may be set by the Commission. In order to be able to deal more quickly with cartel cases the Commission introduced a "fast-track" settlement system under which undertakings will be able to receive a 10 per cent reduction of their fines.[278] The co-operation covered by this Notice is different from the voluntary production of evidence to trigger or advance the Commission's investigation, which is covered by the Notice on Immunity from fines or reduction of fines in cartel cases, the "Leniency Notice", discussed below. Provided that the co-operation offered by an undertaking qualifies under both Notices, it can be cumulatively rewarded accordingly.

Like all other decisions, the one to impose fines constitutes a decision "imposing a pecuniary obligation"[279] and is subject to the control of legality by the Union courts which can, as already indicated, lower or increase[280] a fine imposed by the Commission. In case a reduction is decided by the Court, the Commission must not only reimburse the amount of the fine exceeding the one set by the Court, but also default interests on that sum. When an appeal is filed against a decision imposing a fine, the latter does not, as the main rule[281], have to be paid as long as a bank guarantee is provided for the full amount; if the decision imposing the fine is annulled, the Commission must repay not only the full amount of the fine

---

[275] Regulation 622/08 [2008] O.J. L171/3 and Commission Notice on the conduct of settlement procedures [2008] O.J.C167/1.

[276] *http://europa.eu/rapid/press-release_IP-12-704_en.htm* [accessed August 23, 2013].

[277] See IP/08/1056 and MEMO/08/458).

[278] Commission Notice on the conduct of settlement procedures in view of the adoption of Decisions pursuant to Arts 7 and 23 of Regulation 1/2003 in cartel cases.

[279] Art.299 TFEU. See *Commission v Ferriere Nord* (C-516/06) [2007] E.C.R. I-10685.

[280] A very rare case where a fine was increased: *BASF* and *UCB v Commission* (Joined Cases T-101/07 and T-111/07) [2007] E.C.R. II-4949; in the same judgment the fine imposed upon UCB was reduced by 90 per cent. See also *Tokay Carbon E.A.* (Joined Cases T-236/01, etc.) [2004] E.C.R. II-1181.

[281] See Art.90 Commission Regulation No 1268/2012 [2012] OJ L362/1.

(in case it was paid) but also the default interests; however this obligation does not extend to the guarantee cost in case the latter was provided.

The Court stated that when the General Court, for instance, establishes the amount of the fine to be paid, it is not bound by a mathematical calculation method based solely on the turnover of the defendant.[282]

Notice on immunity from fines and reduction of fines in cartel cases: a first Notice was published in 1996,[283] a second one in 2002,[284] which was replaced in 2006.[285] This so-called Revised Leniency Notice provides as follows.

(a)   **Immunity.**[286] Under this Notice, the Commission will grant total immunity from any fines to the first company to disclose its participation in an alleged cartel and submit contemporaneous, incriminating information and evidence on a cartel which, in the Commission's view, will enable it to carry out a targeted inspection in connection with an alleged cartel affecting the Union or to find an infringement of Union competition rules in connection with the alleged cartel. To obtain full immunity, a company must provide the Commission with the following: a detailed description of the alleged cartel—including name and address of the legal entities involved, name, position, office location and home address of all individuals involved; information on other competition authorities inside or outside the Union which have been approached or are intended to be approached; and all other evidence in the possession of the applicant. The information must be contained in a corporate statement.

Immunity shall not be granted in case the Commission was already in possession of sufficient information to adopt a decision to carry out an inspection. Neither shall the undertaking be eligible that took steps to coerce other undertakings to join the cartel or to remain in it.

To qualify for immunity the following conditions must be fulfilled:

(i)   the undertaking must co-operate genuinely, fully, on a continuous basis and expeditiously throughout the administrative procedure by providing the Commission with all relevant information and evidence in its possession or available to it, by remaining at the Commission's disposal to answer promptly to any request, by making current and former employees and directors available for interviews, by not destroying, falsifying or concealing relevant information or evidence and by not disclosing anything before the Commission has issued a statement of objections;

---

[282] *Evonik Degussa v Commission* (C-266/06) [2008] E.C.R.I-81*.

[283] [1996] O.J. C207/4. See *Hoechst v Commission* (T-410/03) on the application of the Notice [2008] E.C.R. II-881.

[284] [2002] O.J. C45/3. However, the question of confidentiality does not seem to have been satisfactorily solved. See *SCA Holding v Commission* (T-327/94) [1998] E.C.R. II–1373, where mitigation was refused. There is one case where a fine paid was refunded. *Assidoman Kraft* (T-227/95) [1997] E.C.R. II–1189; [1997] 5 C.M.L.R. 364.

[285] [2006] O.J. C298/17.

[286] In 2007, the Commission received 20 applications for immunity.

      (ii)   the undertaking must have ended its involvement in the alleged cartel immediately following its application, except for what would, in the Commission's view, be reasonably necessary to preserve the integrity of the inspections.

(b)   **Reduction of fines.**[287] Reduction of fines is provided for companies that do not qualify for immunity but provide evidence that represents "significant added value" to the information in the Commission's possession and terminate their involvement in the cartel. "Added value" refers to the extent to which the evidence provided strengthens by its very nature and/or its level of detail, the Commission's ability to prove the alleged cartel. This is commonly referred to as a "Leniency".

The first company fulfilling those conditions could receive a reduction of 30 to 50 per cent of the possible fine, the second successful applicant, 20 to 30 per cent and subsequent successful applicants a reduction of up to 20 per cent.[288]

Immunity can, of course, not be granted in case the infringement is covered by the five-year limitation period.[289]

It should finally be noted that an Undertaking is under no obligation to reveal its infringements to the Commission and the principle of non-self-incrimination applies. Indeed, the leniency and immunity procedures merely serve as incentives to undertakings for undertaking to co-operate with the Commission in exchange for a reduction of fines. However, in so co-operating with the Commission and, as it where, confessing to the participation in an illegal cartel, an undertaking will open itself up to potential claims for damages by the "victims" of the cartel. Such "private" enforcement is high on the Commission's policy agenda, it is therefore necessary to balance the risk and cost of third party damages claims against the benefits of applying for leniency/immunity.

(3) Limitation Periods

For imposing penalties, the following limitation periods apply: three years in the case of infringements concerning information or inspections and five years for all other infringements. Enforcement of penalties is subject to a limitation period of five years.[290] Continued infringements are subject to limitation only if they have been "inactive" for at least five years, meaning that no investigative measures have been taken by the Commission.

22–63

---

[287] Under the 2006 Notice until the end of 2007, the Commission received 11 applications.
[288] For an example of reduction, see Cases COMP/C–3/35.587, COMP/C–3/35.706 and COMP/C–3/36.321.
[289] Art.25(1)(b) Regulation 1/2003.
[290] Arts 25 and 26 Regulation 1/2003.

(4) Hearings

22–64   Before deciding on an obligation to put an end to an infringement, on interim measures, to accept binding commitments or decide that the Union competition rules do not apply, the Commission must give the undertakings which are the subject of the proceedings the opportunity to be heard.[291] The Commission decision may only be based on objections on which the parties concerned have been able to comment. Complainants must also be associated closely with the proceedings.[292] The Commission normally informs the undertakings concerned about the points to which the Commission objects by sending a "Statement of objections" (SOs), to which the undertaking can respond.

The hearings are chaired by the *Hearing Officer* whose terms of reference were laid down by a Commission decision[293] and were complemented by a Decision of the President of the Commission in 2011 on the function and the terms of reference of the hearing officer in certain competition proceedings.[294] This was done in order to ensure the effective exercise of the procedural rights of the parties concerned, other involved parties,[295] complainants,[296] other persons,[297] and third persons.[298]

This officer is totally independent from the competition administration: he reports exclusively to the Commissioner responsible for competition. The rights of defence must be fully respected; the parties must have access to the Commission's files, subject to the legitimate interests of undertakings in the protection of their business secrets. The right of access does not extend, among others, to confidential information and internal documents of the Commission or national authorities.

22–65   Decisions are published in the *Official Journal*[299]; they must state the name of the parties and the main content of the decision, including any penalty imposed.

As mentioned, the Commission can act on its own initiative or on the basis of a complaint filed by a natural or legal person.[300] The Union courts accept that the Commission could reject a complaint where it finds that the case does not display sufficient "Union interest" to justify further investigation of it.[301] According to the Court, it is consistent with the Commission's obligations under Union law for it to apply different degrees of priority to the cases submitted to it. In order to do this, the Commission is entitled to refer to the Union interest, i.e. significance of

---

[291]   Art.27 Regulation 1/2003.
[292]   Art.27(1) Regulation 1/2003.
[293]   Decision 2001/462 on the terms of reference of hearing officers in competition procedures [2001] O.J. L162/21.
[294]   Decision 2011/695/EU [2011] O.J. L275/29.
[295]   Within the meaning of Art.11(b) of Regulation 802/04.
[296]   Within the meaning of Art.7(2) of Regulation 1/2003.
[297]   Other than those referred to in Art.54 and 11 of Regulation 773/2004.
[298]   Within the meaning of Art.11 of Regulation 802/04.
[299]   See *Lisrestal* (T-450/93) [1994] ECR II-01177, upheld on appeal in Case C-32/95 P.
[300]   See *Hoffmann-La Roche v Commission* (85/76) [1979] E.C.R. 461; [1979] 3 C.M.L.R. 211.
[301]   *BEMIM (Bureau Européen des Médias de l'Industries Musicales) v Commission* (T-114/92) [1995] E.C.R. II–147.

the alleged infringement as regards the functioning of the internal market, the probability of establishing the existence of the infringement[302] and the scope of the investigation required.[303]

6. CONTROL OF CONCENTRATIONS[304]—THE MERGER REGULATION[305]

Concentrations may lead to permanent structural changes that may seriously impede competition in one or more relevant product and geographic markets. Those concentrations must therefore be controlled. This control applies to all types of industries provided that the turnover thresholds in the Merger Regulation are fulfilled.

22–66

The EU merger control regime was originally established by Council Regulation 4064/89 and was later replaced with Regulation 139/2004 ("Merger Regulation"). The recast Merger Regulation introduced a number of substantive and procedural changes. A review had found that, notwithstanding the introduction of the new turnover thresholds under Art.1(3), there was still further scope for improved case allocation between the Commission and the national competition authorities ("NCAs"). Therefore, a set of voluntary pre-notification referral mechanisms was introduced in order to "further improve the efficiency of the system for the control of concentrations within the Community".[306] The principles guiding the system were those that decisions taken with regard to the referral of cases should take due account "in particular which is the authority more appropriate for carrying out the investigation, the benefits inherent in a 'one-stop-shop' system, and the importance of legal certainty with regard to jurisdiction".[307]

Another reform is currently under way, but the coming reform is "minor" and the backbone of the Merger Regulation will remain the same.[308] In February 2013, the Commission proposed a series of amendments to the existing merger

---

[302] Art.32 Regulation 1/2003.

[303] *Automec* (T-24/90) [1992] E.C.R. II–2223. See, however, *Asia Motor France and Others v Commission* (T-387/94) [1996] E.C.R. II–961; [1996] 4 C.M.L.R. 305, where the Court concluded that the Commission had made an error of assessment.

[304] For the concept "Concentration", see Commission Consolidated Jurisdictional Notice adopted by the Commission on 10.07.07.

[305] [2004] O.J. L24/1.

[306] Recital 16 of the EC Merger Regulation. Other instruments are: the Commission Notice on Case Referral in respect of concentrations (Commission Notice on Case Referral in respect of concentrations—OJ C 56, 5.3.2005, p. 2), which sets out the guiding principles of the referral system. On July 10, 2007, the Commission adopted the Consolidated Jurisdictional Notice under Council Regulation (EC) No 139/2004 on the control of concentrations between undertakings. [2008] O.J. C95/1. The Consolidated Jurisdictional Notice replaces the previous four jurisdictional Notices, all adopted by the Commission in 1998 under the previous EC Merger Regulation. The Consolidated Jurisdictional Notice covers all issues of jurisdiction relevant for establishing the Commission's competence under the EC Merger Regulation, including in particular, the concept of a concentration, the notion of control, the concept of full-function joint ventures and the calculation of turnover.

[307] Commission Notice on Case Referral in respect of concentrations (OJ C 56, 5.3.2005, p.2-23, para.8).

[308] Cf. Public consultation on the Draft Revision of simplified procedure and merger implementing regulation of April 2013.

control framework in order to further simplify it. The onus is on extending the scope of the simplified merger control procedure (see below) and updating and reducing the information requirements for notifying a merger or making a request to refer a merger case to the Commission or to a Member State.

22–67   The term "Merger Regulation" is somewhat confusing since what is at stake is the control of "concentrations" and that includes not only mergers, but also acquisitions and joint ventures as further defined in the Merger Regulation. However, the Merger Regulation covers mainly two operations: mergers and acquisitions, on the one hand, and joint ventures on the other. Mergers are operations whereby two legally and economically independent companies form a single undertaking (total absorption), while acquisitions are operations whereby one undertaking acquires sole control of the whole or part of another. Joint ventures are transactions whereby two or more firms (parent companies), which remain independent, acquire joint control[309] of another firm, existing or to be created. Control is constituted by rights, contracts or any other means which confer the possibility of exercising decisive influence on an undertaking and which is determined by both legal and factual considerations.[310] Decisive influence can be achieved not only by ownership but also through "any other means" which confer the possibility of exercising decisive influence on an undertaking on a lasting basis, for example by means of veto rights on strategic decisions such as approval of the annual budget or designating general managers.[311] Full-function joint ventures that have a Union dimension.

A joint venture is deemed to be full-function when it can be deemed to perform, "on a lasting basis all the functions of an autonomous economic entity", and constitutes a concentration.[312] The key criterion here is independence from the "parents", since, without that, it is not autonomous. Mergers which would significantly impede effective competition on the internal market or in a substantial part of it, in particular as a result of the creation or strengthening of a dominant position, shall be prohibited by a Commission decision.[313] "Restriction of competition" therefore becomes the key words of the prohibition. The definition of "dominance" under the Merger Regulation is the same as under Art.102 TFEU analysed above. Summarily said, an undertaking occupies a dominant position when it can operate on the market independently of its competitors, its customers and the end consumers, for example as an unavoidable trading partner for other market players. There are, however, important differences; indeed, the dominant position in the case of Art.102 TFEU refers to an existing situation, while under the Merger Regulation it concerns in particular the potential future dominant position resulting from structural changes due to the transaction. As was seen, Art.102 TFEU prohibits a certain behaviour, while the Merger Regulation prohibits a modification of the market structure which might impede competition. The latter, therefore, is prospective, while the former concerns conduct the past. The analytical standpoint is thus different. On the one

---

[309] For the concept "joint control" see below the Commission Consolidated Jurisdictional Notice.
[310] Art.3 Merger Regulation.
[311] Art.3(2) Merger Regulation.
[312] Art.3(4) Merger Regulation.
[313] Art.2(3) Merger Regulation.

hand, in Art.102 cases the Commission must establish a position of dominance ex-post facto. On the other hand in merger cases the Commission must identify potential issues ex-ante.

As the Court pointed out "a proper definition of the relevant market is a necessary precondition for any assessment of the effect of a concentration on competition."[314] The Court refers to both the geographic and the product/service markets. With regard to the former, the Court gave the following definition:

22–68

> "the relevant geographical market is a defined geographical area in which the product concerned is marketed and where the conditions of competition are sufficiently homogeneous for all economic operators, so that the effect on competition of the concentration notified can be evaluated rationally."

The Consolidated Jurisdictional Notice is the most useful guidance for a comprehensive overview of the Commission's interpretation of market definitions and many other terms used in the Merger Regulation.

The main features of the Merger Regulation are the following.

22–69

1. The Regulation applies to concentrations with a "Union dimension", i.e:
    (a) where three conditions are fulfilled:
        (i) the aggregate worldwide turnover of all the undertakings concerned is more than €5 billion;
        (ii) the aggregate Union-wide turnover of at least two of them is more than €250 million; and
        (iii) each undertaking realises at least one-third of its Union turnover in another Member State;
    (b) a concentration that does not meet the above-mentioned thresholds nonetheless has a Union dimension when:
        (i) the combined aggregate worldwide turnover of all undertakings concerned is more than €2.5 billion;
        (ii) in each of at least three Member States the combined aggregate turnover of all undertakings concerned is more than €100 million;
        (iii) in each of those three Member States the aggregate turnover of at least two of the undertakings concerned is more than €25 million;
        (iv) the aggregate Union-wide turnover of at least two of the undertakings concerned is more than €100 million;
        (v) unless each of the undertakings concerned achieves more than two-thirds of its aggregate turnover within one and the same Member State.[315]

    In other words, a concentration between two or more undertakings situated in the same Member State has no Union dimension when all of them achieve more than two-thirds of their turnover in that same Member State. Indeed, in that case it is an internal affair of that Member State. However, if the concentration also triggers merger notification obligations in other

---

[314] *France v Commission* (Joined Case C-68/94 and C-30/95) [1998] E.C.R. I–1375.
[315] Art.1 Merger Regulation.

Member States, these will also have to be addressed to the appropriate national authorities. Where the Commission finds that a notified concentration falls within the scope of the Regulation, it must publish the fact of the notification, at the same time indicating the names of the parties, the nature of the concentration and the economic sector involved.[316]

2.   A "concentration" is deemed to arise where two or more previously independent undertakings merge, or where one or more persons or undertakings already controlling one or more undertakings acquire direct or indirect control of the whole or parts of one or more other undertakings; the main criterion therefore is "control".[317]

3.   The above-mentioned concentrations must be notified[318] to the Commission prior to their implementation. Failure to notify a concentration falling within the scope of the Merger Regulation can be sanctioned by fines. Notification may also be made before a binding agreement is signed, where the undertakings involved demonstrate a good faith intention to conclude an agreement and have publicly announced an intention to make a bid.[319] It should be noted—this is very important—that the Commission encourages pre-notification contacts of the notifying parties with the Commission. The business community has found those pre-notification contacts very beneficial.

In 2012, the Commission received 283 notifications. The amount of notifications received by the Commission is a reflection of the general economic climate in the Union. For example in 2007 the Commission received 402 notifications and in 2009 it received 259 notifications, mirroring the decrease in merger and acquisitions generally in the wake of the 2008–2009 financial crises. The number of notifications have not picked up to their prior levels with 309 in 2011 further down to 283 in 2012.

4.   The Commission assesses the concentration by taking into account the need to maintain and develop competition within the internal market in view of, among other things, the structure of all the markets concerned and the actual and potential competition from undertakings located within or outside the Union. The Commission will also consider the market position of the undertakings concerned[320] and their economic and financial power, the alternatives available to suppliers and users, their access to supplies and markets, any legal or other barrier to entry, supply and demand trends for the relevant goods and services, the interests of the intermediate and ultimate consumers and the development of technical and economic

---

[316] Art.4(3) Merger Regulation.

[317] Art.3 Merger Regulation.

[318] Art.4 Merger Regulation. Notification must be made by using Form CO issued by the Commission. See Annex to Regulation 447/98 [1998] O.J. L61/1. In their notification the parties must define the relevant product market and the relevant geographic market and also any "affected market", i.e. a relevant market where two or more of the parties are engaged in business activities in the same product or individual group product market and would acquire a combined market share of more than 10 per cent; this threshold applies to both horizontal and vertical relationships.

[319] Art.4(1) Merger Regulation. The Commission imposed a fine of 33,000 ECU on Samsung (South Korea) for late notification and for having put the merger into effect prematurely.

[320] See below: Commission Consolidated Jurisdictional Notice 7.

progress.[321] In order to undertake this, the Commission will conduct market tests and request information from competitors on the market as to how they perceive the impact of a particular concentration.

Finally, the Commission will take into account restrictions directly related and necessary to a concentration: "ancillary restraints".[322] This concerns agreements which do not form an integral part of the concentration, but which limit the parties' freedom of action in the market. Such agreements are covered by the decision declaring the concentration compatible with the common market.

It should be noted that the Commission in its assessment of a merger is not bound by decisions taken by national authorities in allegedly identical situations, having regard to the clear division of powers on which the Merger Regulation is based.[323]

5.   Straightforward cases will be cleared within 25 working days from the date of notification, increased to 35 working days where the internal receives a request from a Member State to refer[324] the case to it or where the undertakings concerned offer commitments to render the concentration compatible (Phase I).[325] When the Commission has "serious doubts", it opens an in-depth procedure which may last no more than 90 working days (Phase II).[326] Such a procedure is opened by a decision, after which the parties will receive a "statement of objections" setting out the Commission's concerns raised by the concentration. The undertakings may contest the Commission's objections in writing and, if they requested, during hearings. Outright prohibitions are rare and in the period 1990 to 2012, the Commission has only prohibited 24 concentrations out of 5,140 notified concentrations.

In order to allow for a more expedite assessment of objectively unproblematic concentrations, in March 2005, the Commission introduced a Notice allowing for a simplified procedure for treatment of certain concentrations.[327] This procedure applies to three categories of concentrations:

(a)   two or more undertakings acquire joint control of a joint venture the turnover of which and/or the turnover of the contributed activities, is less than €100 million within the EEA and the total value of assets transferred to the joint venture is less than €100 million in the territory;

(b)   two or more undertakings merge, or one or more undertakings acquire sole or joint control of another undertaking, provided that none of the parties to the concentration are engaged in business activities in the same product and geographical market, or in a

---

[321] Art.2(1) Merger Regulation.

[322] [2001] O.J. C188/3.

[323] See *Cementbouw* (C-202/06 P) [2007] E.C.R. I-12129.

[324] See Notice on referrals [2005] O.J. C56/2.

[325] In 2007, the Commission cleared 368 merger cases without conditions, out of 402 during Phase I; another 18 transactions were cleared with conditions.

[326] In 2007, 10 decisions were adopted, five without conditions; one (*Ryanair Aer Lingus*) was prohibited.

[327] Notice of 05.03.05 [2005] O.J. C56/32.

product market which is upstream or downstream of a product market in which any other party to the concentration is engaged;

(c)   two or more undertakings merge, or one or more undertakings acquire sole or joint control of another undertaking and although two or more parties have a horizontal or a vertical relationship, their combined market share is not 15 per cent or more for horizontal and 25 per cent or more for vertical relationships.

(d)   a party is to acquire sole control of an undertaking over which it already has joint control.

In February 2013, the Commission submitted a revision of the current simplified procedure to public consultation. Under the current proposals, the market share thresholds set out in point (c) above would be revised and the simplified procedure would be available for mergers with limited horizontal overlaps of up to 20 per cent or vertical relationships of up to 30 per cent.

Prior to a notification, it is recommended although not technically necessary to undertake an informal "pre-notification" consultation with the Commission where the parties set out the concentration and give the Commission officials a chance to put together a "case-team" prior to submitting the official notification.[328]

After the notification, parties may present, during the first or second phase, modifications (known as *remedies*) to their proposed merger or acquisition in order to make it acceptable to the Commission.[329] In order to facilitate and clarify the proposal of remedies, the Commission published a Notice on acceptable remedies.[330] The rights of the defence must be fully respected and the parties directly involved will have access to the file, subject to the protection of business secrets.

After having consulted the Advisory Committee,[331] the concentration must be declared either compatible or incompatible[332] with the internal market. This decision must be published in the *Official Journal*. If no decision is taken within the prescribed time limit, the merger is deemed compatible. The Commission may impose conditions and/or accept modifications to the merger agreement proposed by the parties[333] to allow it to clear the merger.

6.   The Commission may order suspension of the merger until it reaches a final decision, but within given time limits.[334]

7.   The Commission has powers to investigate and to impose fines or periodic penalty payments.[335]

---

[328] See DG Comp "Best Practices on the Conduct of EC merger control procedures", January 20, 2004.

[329] Art.6(2) Merger Regulation, which refers to "modifications by the undertakings concerned".

[330] Commission Notice on remedies acceptable under Council Regulation (EC) No 139/2004 and under Commission Regulation (EC) No 802/2004 [2008] O.J. C267/1. The Notice sets out the applicable general principles, the main types of commitments, such as divestiture, which have been accepted in the past, the specific requirements which proposals of commitments need to fulfil in both phases of the procedure and the main requirements for their implementation.

[331] Art.19 Merger Regulation.

[332] Art.2(1)1 Merger Regulation.

[333] Art.6(2) Merger Regulation.

[334] Arts 7 and 10 Merger Regulation.

[335] Arts 13, 14 and 15 Merger Regulation.

8.   The Commission has exclusive jurisdiction over mergers with a Union dimension; however, at a Member State's request, the Commission may and, under certain circumstances, must[336] refer the case, in whole or in part, to the competition authorities of that State.

A Commission Regulation[337] implementing the basic Regulation[338] and modifying an earlier regulation[339] was issued in 2008. It lays down rules for notifications, time limits and hearings provided for in the Merger Regulation.[340] It updates the notification form in particular the Form RS, relating to reasoned submissions, which deals with information requirements for pre-notification referrals; these forms are used for concentrations which require certain information based on a list of all Member States. In order to ensure that the Commission is in a position to carry out a proper assessment of commitments offered by the notifying parties,[341] with a view to rendering a concentration compatible with the internal market, the notifying parties are required to submit detailed information concerning the commitments offered and, in particular, to submit specific information if the commitments offered consist in the divestiture of a business. These commitments may include details on the appropriate mechanism proposed by the parties, including the appointment of an "independent trustee", at the own expenses of the undertakings, to assist the Commission in overseeing compliance.[342] The Trustee may be appointed by the parties after the Commission has approved its identity, or by the Commission.[343] **22–70**

The Commission was published several Notices to provide maximum transparency and legal certainty for all interested parties. These "Notices" are not legally binding; they reflect the Commission's decisional practice and views on key aspects concerning the meaning, implementation, practice and case law with regard to the Merger Regulation. For instance, they concern, besides the Notices mentioned above, Guidelines on the assessment of *horizontal mergers* under the Merger Regulation.[344] See also the Guidelines on the assessment of *non-horizontal mergers*, i.e. concentrations where the undertakings concerned are active on different relevant markets; two broad types can be distinguished: vertical mergers and conglomerate mergers.[345]

In 2008, the Commission published a "Consolidated Jurisdictional Notice under the Merger Regulation"[346]; it defines, among other things, the concept of concentration; the concept of control—acquisition of control, sole control, joint **22–71**

---

[336] Those conditions are that within three weeks after having received copy of the notification, the Member State communicates to the Commission, who informs the parties, that a concentration affects a distinct market within its territory, which is not a substantial part of the internal market and that the Commission considers that such a market is indeed affected; see Art.9(3)(b), last sub-paragraph.

[337] Regulation 1033/08 [2008] O.J. L279/3.

[338] Regulation 139/04 on the control of concentrations between undertakings [2004] O.J. L24/1.

[339] Regulation 802/04 [2004] O.J. L133/1.

[340] Regulation 447/98 on the notifications, time limits and hearings provided for in the Merger Regulation [1998] O.J. L61/1, repealed by Regulation [2004] O.J. L133/1.

[341] Notification of commitments pursuant to Art.6(2) or 8(2) of Regulation 139/04.

[342] New Art.20a.

[343] See also Commission Notice on remedies acceptable under the above-mentioned Regulations. [2008] O.J. C267/1.

[344] [2004] O.J. C31/5.

[345] [2008] O.J. C265/6.

[346] [2008] O.J. C95/1.

control,[347] joint venture; Union Dimension—undertaking concerned, jurisdiction and turnover, financial institutions and insurance. This Notice replaces four previous Notices concerning "concentration",[348] "full function joint venture",[349] "undertakings concerned"[350] and the "calculation of turnover".[351] All these aspects will be covered by the decision, if any, declaring the concentration compatible or not with the internal market.[352]

The decisions of the Commission taken under the Merger Regulation are subject to review by the Union courts.[353] Several decisions declaring a merger incompatible had in fact been annulled.[354] A delicate problem, as with cartels, is the confidentiality of information provided to the Commission by the parties to a concentration as business secrets. It should be remembered, in the first place, that the Treaty itself requires the members of the Commission, the officials and other servants of the Union "not to disclose information of the kind covered by the obligation of professional secrecy".[355] Furthermore, the Regulation provides that information acquired shall be used only for the purpose of the relevant request, investigation or hearing. It also specifies that neither the Commission nor the competent authorities of the Member States shall disclose information they have acquired through the application of the Regulation.[356] The protection of business secrets is further guaranteed both in the Merger Regulation and in the implementing Regulation. See below: (3) Access to the Files.

With the adoption of the Merger Regulation, the arsenal of Union instruments at the disposal of the Union institutions and national authorities to ensure that competition is not distorted in the internal market by undertakings, can now be considered complete.

7. OTHER COMMISSION NOTICES

22–72   In order to clarify its competition policy, the Commission has issued several notices. These notices seek to issue guidance to undertakings when they vet their agreements for compliance with competition but, contrary to block exemptions, they have no binding effect. They simply provide guidance and information concerning the Commission's views on the implementation of the competition rules.

---

[347] See *Dow Chemical v Commission* (T-77/08), judgment of February 2, 2012, not yet reported: on the imputability of unlawful conduct in a joint venture.
[348] [1998] O.J. C66/5.
[349] [1998] O.J. C66/1.
[350] [1998] O.J. C66/14.
[351] [1998] O.J. C66/25.
[352] Arts 6(1)(b) and 8(2) Merger Regulation.
[353] Art.21(1) Merger Regulation.
[354] See, for instance, *Schneider Electric v Commission* (T-310/01) [2002] E.C.R. I-4071 and *Tetra Laval v Commission* (T-5/02) [2002] E.C.R. II-4381.
[355] Art.339 TFEU, which refers "in particular [to] information about undertakings, their business relations or their cost components".
[356] Art.17 Merger Regulation. See detailed examination by the CFI in *Gencor v Commission* (T-106/96) [1997] E.C.R. II-879, concerning requests for confidential treatment. See also Opening to the Public of Documents and Files from the Historical Archives of the Commission, which are covered by the Obligation of professional or Business Secrecy [1997] O.J. C218/3.

(1) Agency agreements

Contracts concluded with commercial agents, in which those agents undertake for   22–73
a specified part of the territory of the internal market to negotiate transactions on
behalf of an enterprise, or conclude transactions in the name or on behalf of an
enterprise will not fall foul of the prohibition set out in Art.101 TFEU. This
entails that in agency agreements, the principal can impose restrictions upon the
agent that would otherwise be caught by the Art.101 TFEU prohibition, such as
restrictions on prices and customers.

The Vertical Guidelines have replaced the earlier Notice on Exclusive Dealing
Contracts with Commercial Agents.[357] With regard to relations between
commercial agents and their principal, see the 1986 Directive on the
co-ordination of laws of the Member States relating to self-employed commercial
agents.[358] Commercial agents need not be registered in the Member State where
they operate.[359] See also a directive on the co-ordination of the laws of the
Member States relating to self-employed commercial agents[360] and another on
temporary agency work.[361] Accordingly, the Vertical Guidelines must be read in
conjunction with the 1986 Directive.

(2) Subcontracting Agreements[362]

Such agreements are is considered by the Commission as a form of resource   22–74
allocation, which in particular concerns SMEs[363] and whereby technology is
made available by one party to the other with restrictions as to its use.
Restrictions which are not prohibited are the following:

1. Technology and equipment provided by the contractor may only be used for
    the purposes of the agreement, and may not be made available to third
    parties, and the goods and services resulting from the use of such
    technology may be supplied only to the contractor or used on his behalf,
    provided that the technology and equipment are necessary to enable the
    subcontractor to carry out his obligations.
2. The above proviso is satisfied where performance of the subcontracting
    agreement makes necessary the use of industrial property rights of the
    contractor, of know-how of the contractor, of studies, plans or documents
    which have been prepared by the contractor or patterns or tools and
    accessory equipment which belong to the contractor and, which permit the
    manufacture of goods which differ in form, function or composition from
    other goods manufactured or supplied on the market.
3. The following restrictions are also authorised: an undertaking by either
    party not to reveal manufacturing processes or other know-how, an

---

[357] [1962] O.J. 292/1.

[358] [1986] O.J. L382/17.

[359] *Centrosteel* (C-456/98) [2000] E.C.R. I–6007.

[360] Directive 86/653 [1986] O.J. L382/17. For more details see Ch.17: Freedom of Establishment/
Company Law (1. Introduction).

[361] Directive 2008/104 [2008] O.J. L327/9.

[362] [1979] O.J. C1/2.

[363] See Commission Recommendation concerning the definition of SMEs (quoted above).

undertaking by the subcontractor not to make use, even after expiration of the agreement, of the above, and an undertaking by the subcontractor to pass to the contractor on a non-exclusive basis any technical improvement which he has made during the execution of the subcontracting agreement.

4.   The contractor may forbid the use by the subcontractor of trademark, trade names and get-up in the case of goods, which are not to be supplied to the contractor.

(3)   Access to the Files

22–75   The right of access to the files is laid down in a Notice on the internal rules of procedure for processing of requests for access to the file of cases pursuant to Arts 101 and 102 TFEU[364] and Regulation 139/2004.[365] Among other things, this Notice defines "non-communicable" and "communicable" documents; the former are "internal documents" and "business secrets and other confidential information". These definitions are clarified in the revised Notice.[366]

The Notice was updated in 2005 in order to increase the transparency of competition procedures and underline the Commission's commitment to due process and parties rights of defence. The access is granted only to addressees of a Statement of Objection; limited access to specific documents is provided for complainants in antitrust cases and other involved parties in merger cases.

(4)   Guidance on Commission's enforcement priorities in applying Article [102 of the TFEU] to abusive exclusionary conduct by dominant undertakings[367]

22–76   Besides setting out the enforcement priorities the Communication was intended provide greater clarity and predictability as regards the general framework of analysis which the Commission employs in determining whether or not it should pursue cases concerning various forms of exclusionary conduct.

It only applies to undertakings holding a single dominant position (as opposed to collective dominance).

In it, the Communication examines successively, among others the general approach to exclusionary conduct, foreclosure leading to consumer harm "anti-competitive foreclosure", price-based exclusionary conduct and objective necessity and efficiencies; specific forms of abuse: exclusive dealings, tying and bundling, predation and, finally, refusal to supply and margin squeeze.[368]

---

[364] [1997] O.J. C23/3.

[365] [2004] O.J. L24/1.

[366] IP/05/1581.

[367] [2009] O.J. C45/7.

[368] See Anne C. Witt, "The Commission's Guidance Paper on Abusive Exclusionary Conduct—More radical than it appears?" European Law Review, Volume 35 No. April 2, 2010, 214.

(5) Notice on best practices for the conduct of proceedings

On October 17, 2011, the Commission adopted a series of measures aimed to 22–77
increase interaction with parties in antitrust proceedings and strengthening
procedural rights.[369] The Notice on best practices sets out the general framework
for the Commission's investigative process and the rights of defence. This
includes informing parties under investigation of the initiation of proceedings
sufficiently in advance to enable them to prepare their own communications
strategy before the Commission makes the investigation public. It also sets out
the framework for undertakings to discuss an ongoing case with the Commission
by means of "State of Play" meetings. The Notice further deals with the issue of
self-incrimination, legal professional privilege, confidentiality and business
secrets, as well as the submission of economic evidence.

(6) Co-operation between Member States competition authorities and the Commission

The Regulation 1/2003 imposes obligations on NCAs and the Commission to 22 78
ensure that they co-operate closely with each other. To this end the Commission
has published guidance on the manner in which the Commission will
communicate with the National Competition Authorities of the EU Member
States in cases falling within the Regulation, as well as how the National
Competition Authorities communicate amongst each other.[370] Essentially, the
notice sets out the framework within which each authority must report cases
falling within the scope of the Modernisation Regulation and the timeframe
within which this should occur as well as procedures for identifying the Authority
best suited to handle a matter that spans several jurisdictions.

(7) Implementing Provisions

The Commission was authorised to take measures to apply the Regulation on the 22–79
implementation of the rules on competition.[371] The following regulation, notices
and communication were adopted:

1. A Regulation relating to the conduct of proceedings by the Commission
    pursuant to the cartel and abuse provisions.[372] It concerns the initiation of
    proceedings, investigations by the Commission, the handling of complaints
    (including: the participation of complainants in proceedings, the rejection
    of complaints), statement of objections, the right to be heard, and access to
    the file. This Regulation repealed three previous regulations.[373]

---

[369] Commission Notice on the best practices for the conduct of proceedings concerning Arts 101 and
102 TFEU [2011] O.J. C308/6.
[370] Notice on Co-operation within the Network of Competition Authorities [2004] O.J. C101/43.
[371] Art.33(1) Regulation 1/2003 (quoted above).
[372] Regulation 773/2004 relating to the conduct of proceedings by the Commission pursuant to TFEU
Art.101 and 102 [2004] O.J. L123/18, modified [2008] O.J. L171/3.
[373] Were repealed: Regulation 2842/98 on hearings, Regulation 2843/98 concerning complaints,
applications and hearings in the air transport sector and Regulation 3385/94 on the form, content and
other details of applications and notifications provided for in Regulation 17.

2. A Notice on co-operation within the network of Competition Authorities.[374] Although, as the Notice mentions, "consultations and exchanges within the network are matters between public enforcers and do not alter any rights or obligations arising from Union or national law for companies", it might be of interest for the latter to understand how cases are allocated between the enforcers. Under the system of parallel competences (introduced by the new cartel Regulation), cases will be dealt with either by a single authority, possibly with the assistance of other Member States, or by several authorities acting in parallel, or by the Commission. In general the authority that receives the complaint or starts an ex-officio procedure will remain in charge of the case. Reference is also made to the position of applicants claiming the benefit of a leniency programme.

3. A Notice on the co-operation between the Commission and the national courts.[375] The term "courts" refers to those courts and tribunals of the Member States that have jurisdiction to apply Union competition rules and are authorised to ask a preliminary question. The national courts can apply Union competition rules without it being necessary to apply national competition rules. However, and this could be important for undertakings, when a national court applies national competition rules to agreements or abuses that may affect trade between Member States, they must, as indicated above, also apply Union competition rules. Consequently, cartels that do not infringe the Union prohibition or that fulfil the condition for an exemption may not be prohibited under national competition law. Similarly, prohibited cartels that do not fulfil these conditions cannot be upheld on the basis of national competition rules.

Generally speaking, national courts may not apply national law which contravenes a Union rule. They are bound by the case law of the Union courts and by the general principles of Union law. Where there is an infringement of Union law, national law must provide for sanctions that are effective and dissuasive; and where the infringement of Union law causes harm to an individual, the latter should, under given conditions, be able to ask the national court for damages.[376]

Finally, the rules on procedure and sanctions that national courts apply to enforce Union law must not make such enforcement excessively difficult or practically impossible (the principle of effectiveness) and may not be less favourable than the rules applicable to the enforcement of equivalent national law (principle of equivalence).

4. A Notice on the handling of complaints by the Commission under the cartel and abuse provisions.[377] As was seen above, some rules concerning complaints are to be found in the regulation concerning the conduct of proceedings by the Commission.[378] Since complaints play an essential role in the application of the Union competition rules, this Notice is a must for undertakings and lawyers. The Commission emphasises that national courts have an essential role to play and encourage undertakings to bring their

---

[374] Notice on co-operation with authorities [2004] O.J. C101/43.

[375] Notice on co-operation with courts [2004] O.J. L101/54.

[376] See, for instance, *Dillenkofer* (Joined Cases C-178/94, etc.) [1996] E.C.R. I-44845.

[377] Notice on complaints [2004] O.J. C101/65.

[378] Arts 5–9 Regulation 773/2004, as modified [2008] O.J. L171/3 (quoted above).

complaints rather in the form of actions before the national courts. Indeed, the latter may award damages for loss suffered as a result of the infringement, something neither the Commission, nor the national competition authorities can do. Also, national courts may rule on claims for payment; it is indeed for the national court to apply the civil sanction of nullity in contractual relationships between individuals. Furthermore, national courts are better placed to adopt interim measures and before national courts it is possible to combine claims under national law with claims under Union law; finally, national courts normally have the power to award legal costs to the successful applicant.

The Notice contains detailed rules concerning the making of a complaint that must be made in conformity with Form C that is annexed to the Notice and also to the above-mentioned Regulation. It should be noted that filling in the Form is no simple matter; in fact the questions asked are not very different from the information that was required in the past under Form A/B for notifications.[379]

Only natural and legal persons who can show a "legitimate interest"[380] can be formal complainants; the Notice provides some guidance in this matter. The Commission is entitled to give differing degrees of priority to complaints based on the "Union interest" they present; if the latter is not sufficient, the Commission may reject the complaint on that ground, although it is not obliged to do so.[381]

Of great interest are the "Procedural rights of the complainant": he is entitled to receive a copy of a statement of objections, if any, he is invited to comment on them in writing and eventually orally. He may submit documents that contain business secrets, he may submit observations in case the Commission decides not to further examine the complaint, etc.

A rejection of a complaint is done in the form of a decision that can be challenged in court.

5.   Notice on informal guidance relating to novel questions concerning the cartel and abuse rules that arise in individual cases.[382] Under the previous system, undertakings would, in case of doubt about the legality of their agreements or the applicability of the exemptions, simply notify their agreements to the Commission. They would ask the Commission, for example, for a confirmation of the applicability of the exemptions. Since the new Regulation came into force, this is no longer possible. Undertakings are now on their own: it is up to them to decide whether or not their agreements are prohibited and, if so, whether or not the exemptions apply. As the Commission points out in its Notice:

---

[379] See in this respect the comments in the Notice on the "Assessment under Arts 101 and 102", points 46–52.
[380] Art.5(1) in the Notice on the "Assessment under Arts 101 and 102".
[381] Notice on complaints (quoted above) point 45.
[382] Guidance letter [2004] O.J. C101/78.

"Undertakings are generally well placed to assess the legality of their actions . . . They have at their disposal the framework of block exemption regulations, case law and case practice as well as extensive guidance in Commission guidelines and notices."[383]

It could have added "and the advice of knowledgeable lawyers and advisers"! Where despite these elements cases give rise to genuine uncertainty because they present a novel or unresolved question for the application of the Union competition rules, individual undertakings may wish to seek informal guidance from the Commission.[384] The Notice contains information, among other things, on the, "framework for assessing whether to issue a guidance letter", "information on how to request guidance" and, most important, "the effects of guidance letters".

6. Guidelines on the "effect on trade" concept.[385] The criteria "may affect trade between Member States" is an essential element for ascertaining the prohibition of cartels and abuses of dominant positions. The courts have clarified that concept by distinguishing three elements: "trade"; "may affect"; and "appreciable". The Guidelines examine these concepts on the basis of the existing case law and decisional practice of the Commission. They then apply these principles to common types of agreements and abuses. These Guidelines constitute an[386] indispensable tool for natural and legal persons and their advisers.

7. Guidelines on the application of the exemptions to the cartel prohibition.[387] This lengthy and impressive study of academic quality unfortunately contains few practical elements able to "guide" natural and legal persons in the application of the exemption. After analysing the prohibition itself, the document examines in detail the four conditions which must be fulfilled for the exemption to be applicable. This information might be useful to help undertakings and their advisers decide whether or not a prohibited agreement can claim an exemption.

8. Commission Notice on best practices for the conduct of proceedings concerning Arts 101 and 102 TFEU.[388] The principal purpose is to provide practical guidance on the conduct of proceedings before the Commission. The Notice seeks to increase understanding of the Commission's investigation process and thereby enhance the efficiency of investigations and ensure a high degree of transparency and predictability of the process. Proceedings are in particular regulated, as was seen above, by Regulation 1/2003 and the implementing Regulation,[389] by the Notices on access to file[390] and handling of complaints.[391]

---

[383] Guidance letter point 3.
[384] Guidance letter, point 5.
[385] Guidelines on trade [2004] O.J. C101/81.
[386] Regulation 773/04 [2004] O.J. L123/18 amended [2008] O.J. L171/3.
[387] Guidelines on 81(3) [2004] OJ. C101/97.
[388] [2011] O.J. C308/6.
[389] Regulation 773/04 [2004] O.J. L123/18 amended [2008] O.J. L171/3.
[390] Regulation 139/04 [2005] O.J C325/7.
[391] [2004] O.J. C101/65.

(8) International Co-operation

In 1995, an agreement was concluded between the Commission and the United   **22–80**
States Government regarding the implementation of their competition laws.[392]
This agreement contains provisions on exchange of information, consultation,
notification and other procedural aspects. It also provides for co-operation in
cases where the parties to the agreement apply their competition rules to identical
or related situations. They agree to take into account the important interests of the
other party, referred to as "comity".

This co-operation has allowed the competition authorities of both parties to
harmonise, for instance, the content and timing of their final decisions in identical
cases,[393] thereby avoiding discrepancies, which might create embarrassing
situations when the object of the investigations concerns cases with worldwide
ramifications, as is more and more the case in this period of globalisation.[394] This
first agreement was complemented by another agreement between the European
Union and the Government of the United States of America[395] on the application
of positive comity principles in the enforcement of their competition laws.

In 2002, the European and US competition authorities issued a set of best
practices on co-operation in reviewing mergers that require approval of both sides
of the Atlantic with a view to enhancing the good relationship developed over the
last decade.[396] The document defines objectives and provides indications
concerning co-ordination on timing, collection and evaluation of evidence,
communication between the two reviewing agencies and remedies and
settlement.

An agreement similar to the first EU-US agreement was signed with Canada in
1999[397]. It provides for:

1. the reciprocal notification of cases under investigation where they affect the
    important interests of the other party;
2. the co-ordination of the enforcement activities and the rendering of
    reciprocal assistance;
3. the possibility to request the other party to take enforcement action
    (positive comity)[398] and for a party to take into account the interests of the
    other in the enforcement procedure; and
4. the exchange of information.

---

[392] Exchange of letters [1995] O.J. L95/45.
[393] See, for example, *Boeing v McDonnell Douglas* (IV/M 877) [1997] O.J. L 336/16 and *Price Waterhouse v Coopers & Lybrand* [1999] O.J. L50/27.
[394] This was the case with *General Electric/Honeywell* (Case M.2220, Decision of July 3, 2001) and *Microsoft*.
[395] [1998] O.J. L173/28.
[396] Case M.2220, Decision of July 3, 2001.
[397] [1999] O.J. L175/5.
[398] [2001] O.J. C363/10.

22–81   An agreement was signed in 2004 between the EU and China on a structured dialogue on competition.[399] The primary objective is to establish a permanent forum of consultation, transparency and co-operation.[400]

On a broader front mention must be made of a Communication from the Commission to the Council: "Towards an international framework of competition rules"[401] and a Recommendation of the Council concerning "co-operation between Member Countries on Anti-Competitive Practices Affecting International Trade".[402]

22–82   In 2009, a Memorandum of understanding and co-operation was entered into between the Commission and the Brazilian Competition Authorities (CADE, SDE and SEAE) setting the groundwork for the exchange of non-confidential information, alerting each other on possible competition law infringements in the other's jurisdiction and providing for greater co-operation and meetings in the future.

In 2012, a Memorandum of Understanding was entered into between the Commission and the competition authorities of the people Republic of China (NDRC and SAIC) setting out a framework for future talks and collaboration as well as the exchange of non-confidential information.

The Commission further has in place agreements or memorandums of understanding with the competition authorities in Japan (2003), Republic of Korea (2009) and the Russian Federation (2011).

II.   COMPETITION RULES APPLYING TO MEMBER STATES

1.   PUBLIC UNDERTAKINGS

22–83   A public undertaking is any undertaking, whatever its public or private status, whose economic behaviour the State can control. This control can be based, for instance, on the State's direct or indirect financial participation or on legal provisions governing the establishment of the undertaking in question.[403]

The logical consequence of the subordinate position of the public undertaking in relation to the public authority which controls it, is that the latter is responsible for the market behaviour of said undertaking. The object of the Treaty provisions examined here is to prevent that a Member State could exercise, through a public undertaking, an activity which it is prohibited from exercising itself. This would constitute a circumvention of the Treaty rules by that public authority to which these rules apply in the first place. Indeed, very few Treaty rules apply directly to

---

[399] IP/04/595.
[400] IP/04/1325.
[401] COM(96) 284 final, [1996] EC Bull. 6–125.
[402] COM(95) 130 final.
[403] See Directive 2006/111 on the transparency of financial relations between Member States and public undertakings as well as on financial transparency within certain undertakings [2006] O.J. L 318/17 and *Commission v Italy* (118/85) [1987] E.C.R. 2599 at 2621(8).

undertakings, the most important ones being the competition rules. On the other hand, when a public undertaking infringes rules applying to undertakings, it can be held directly responsible by the Commission notwithstanding the fact that it might have been induced to do so by a public authority. Legislation that has inducing effects does not excuse the public undertaking from its obligation to comply with the Union competition rules. However, if national law requires the undertaking to engage in anti-competitive behaviour or eliminates all possibility for the undertaking to compete on a given market, the undertaking may be excused for the simple reason that it is not accountable.[404]

However, these competition rules only apply when the public undertaking is in competition with undertakings not controlled by the State.[405] They do not apply when the public undertaking acts for the State in the exercise of an activity which is connected by its nature, its aim and the rules to which it is subject, with the exercise of powers relating, for instance, to the protection of the environment, which, typically, constitute powers of a public authority.[406] However, in the case of infringement by a public undertaking of these competition rules, the State and its legislation can also be challenged by the Commission.[407] The Commission is empowered to determine that a given State measure is incompatible with the Union competition rules. Such powers are essential to allow the Commission to discharge the duty imposed upon it to ensure the application of the rules on competition and to contribute to the institution of a system of undistorted competition in the internal market. It would be impossible for the Commission to discharge its duty completely if it could take action only in respect of anti-competitive conduct of undertakings and could not take action directly against Member States enacting or maintaining in force measures having the same anti-competitive effect.[408]

2. SERVICES OF GENERAL ECONOMIC INTEREST

Undertakings entrusted with the operation of "services of general economic interest" are subject to the Treaty rules on competition and state aid in so far as it does not obstruct the performance of the task which they are entrusted with in law or fact.[409] There is no uniform definition of what constitutes a service of general economic interest as it is dependent on the social and political preferences in each of the Member States.[410] Generally speaking service of general economic interest is a type of service in relation to which the State considers that there is a market

22–84

---

[404] *Commission and France v Ladbroke Racing* (C–359/95 P and C–379/95 P) [1997] ECR I–6265; *CIF* (Case C–198/01) [2003] E.C.R. I-8055; *Glaxosmithkleine Services v Commission* (T-168/01) [2006] E.C.R. II-2369.

[405] *Luxembourg* (10/71) [1971] E.C.R. 723.

[406] *Cali & Figli v SEPG* (C-343/95) [1997] E.C.R. I–1547.

[407] This challenge would be based on Art.4 EU and Arts 101 and 106(3) TFEU.

[408] Art.106(3) TFEU. *The Netherlands v Commission* (Joined Cases C-48/90 and C-66/90) [1992] E.C.R. I–565; *Portugal v Commission* (C-163/99) [2001] E.C.R. I–2613.

[409] Art.106(2) TFEU.

[410] See further Communication from the Commission on the application of the European Union State aid rules to compensation granted for the provison of services of general economic interest [2012] OJ C-8/4, para.45.

failure, i.e. the services are not provided to the extent or at the price deemed satisfactory, for instance as social and health services.

A problem that has drawn much attention in practice and theory is whether the State pays too much compensation to an undertaking that has been entrusted with a service of general economic interest. An excessive compensation entails that the undertaking receives State aid and in that case, the State aid rules must be observed, see below.

3.   AIDS GRANTED BY STATES[411]

22–85   Aid granted by public authorities to an undertaking distorts competition. If an undertaking A receives aid while its competitor B does not receive any, B is disfavoured. Moreover, States have historically granted aid to domestic undertakings to the detriment of the undertaking's competitors from abroad. When a domestic industry is suffering decline the national authorities will be under pressure to take supporting measures, for multiple reasons such as preserving domestic employment or ensuring the survival of national "champions", for instance a domestic airline.

The Treaty bans aid. This is the legal point of departure. However, there are many exceptions to the ban, and the amounts of State aid granted in the Union in 2011 total around €64 billion.[412] That amount just represents so-called non-crisis aid, i.e. aid that is not related to the financial crisis of 2008. The amount of State aid in response to the financial crisis stands at €682 billion.[413]

Below the notion of State aid will first be set out, i.e. the criteria that must be fulfilled to consider a public measure to be State aid within the meaning of the Treaty. The procedural rules governing State aid are crucial for an understanding of this field of law and they are therefore presented in the next section. Thereafter follows a presentation of the rules under which State aid may be compatible "with the internal market".

(1)   The Notion of Aid

22–86   Any aid granted by a Member State or through State resources in any form whatsoever which distorts competition by favouring certain undertakings or the production of certain goods is, in so far as it affects trade between Member States, incompatible with the internal market.[414]

In other words, for a measure to be regarded as an aid that is subject to the principle of incompatibility with the common market, it must satisfy four conditions, which are cumulative. The measure must: "advantage" an undertaking; the aid must be granted by a "Member State or through State resources"; it must favour "certain" undertakings or the production of "certain" goods; and it

---

[411] Arts 107–109 TFEU.

[412] For figures on State aid for 2011, see SEC (2012) 443 final.

[413] SEC (2012) 443 final. It is not clear from the document whether the figure includes State guarantees. State Guarantees constitute State aid but there are instances where State guarantees will never materialise. For statistical purposes it may be said that the aid is not given and therefore can be kept out of the figures on State aid.

[414] Art.107(1) TFEU.

must "distort competition" and "affect trade between Member States". By "State" one means not just aid granted by State, but aid granted by any public authority or through public resources. Aid granted for instance by a municipality or a region is thus also covered.[415]

(a)   "advantage an undertaking"

According to the Court[416], a measure constitutes aid when it confers upon an undertaking an economic or financial advantage, which it would not have enjoyed in the normal course of events and which reduces the charges it would otherwise have borne.[417] The notion of advantage must be taken in the broadest possible sense.[418] It embraces not only positive benefits, such as subsidies, but also measures which, in various forms, mitigate the charges which are normally included in the budget of an enterprise and therefore have the same effect.[419] Cross-subsidisation, for instance, between a public company operating in a non-competitive market and one of its subsidiaries operating in a market where there is free competition, may constitute aid granted through State resources.[420] On the other hand, compensation for the costs connected, for instance, with public service obligations does not constitute State aid.[421]

22–87

Likewise, when the State sells for example land and buildings, there is no aid if the price is set at market price. If the price is set below market price, however, the sales will entail aid to the buying undertaking. To ensure that there is no element of aid, it is therefore advisable to make such sale through an open bidding procedure; in that case the Commission will assume that no aid is involved.[422] As regards privatisations, the Commission applies similarly the principle that there is no aid when the shares are sold to the highest bidder following an open and unconditional bidding procedure.

---

[415] *Germany v Commission* (C-248/84) [1987] ECR 4013, para.17. The aid must also be attributable to the "State". For instance, the mere fact that the State controls a public undertaking does not mean that all action taken by the undertaking can be attributed to the State, see for instance *Stardust Marine* (C-482/99) [2002] E.C.R. I-4397.

[416] See, for example, *Amministrazione delle Finanze dello Stato v Denkavit Italiana* (61/79) [1994] E.C.R. 709; [1981] 3 C.M.L.R. 694.

[417] See, for instance, *Banco Exterior de Espana* (C-387/92) [1994] E.C.R. I–877 (12, 13); [1994] 3 C.M.L.R. 473.

[418] See, for instance, *Italy v Commission* (C-305/89) [1991] E.C.R. I–1603 and *Belgium v Commission* (234/84) [1986] E.C.R. 2263; [1988] 2 C.M.L.R. 331.

[419] *Ecotrade v AFS* (C-200/97) [1998] E.C.R. I–7907(34). Advantages that a State's legislation confers on a certain undertakings but which are not financed through State resources, do not constitute State aid, see *PreussenElektra v Schhleswag* (C-379/98) [2001] E.C.R. I-02099 and joined cases *Sloman Neptun* (C-72/91,C-73/91) [1993] E.C.R. I-00887.

[420] See Commission Decision in *Société Française de Messageries Chronopost and Securitpost* I.P. (96) 126. See also *SFEI* (C-39/94) [1996] E.C.R. I–3547; [1996] 3 C.M.L.R. 369.

[421] Commission Decision Financing of Portuguese radio and television of 07.11.96 and *SIC v Commission* (T-46/97) [2000] E.C.R. II–2125.

[422] Commission Communication on State aid elements in sales of land and buildings by public authorities, [1997] O.J. C209/3.

(b)   "granted by a Member State or through State resources"

22–88   Normally it is not difficult to verify whether this criterion is fulfilled. As for State participation in undertakings, the "private investor" principle applies; the principle is also commonly referred to as the "market economy investor" principle. It allows to determine whether the transfer of public funds to public or private undertakings constitutes an aid. This is the case if a private investor, operating under normal market conditions, would provide the funds on less favourable conditions or would not provide them at all.[423]

State aid can also be granted through the tax system, for instance through tax credits or special depreciation rules that apply only to a particular section of the economy, so-called fiscal aid.[424] Several court cases have clarified the concept of fiscal aid.[425]

(c)   "selectivity"[426]

22–89   This is the case when the measure concerns a well-defined category of undertakings, such as "road haulers operating for hire or reward".[427] Selectivity stands in contrast to generality. Selectivity does not exist in the case of general economic, fiscal or social measures which apply to all firms in the Member State implementing them. If a State lowers its company tax from 30 per cent to 25 per cent, the measure is general and there is no aid.

From the moment a measure only benefits undertakings in a given economic sector or a given region, there can be little doubt about it constituting an aid; the measure does not apply to the economy as a whole; it only applies to the given sector or region.[428] A good example is national legislation intended to reduce the tax burden on road haulers operating for hire or reward.[429] As for distortions resulting, in the internal market, from advantages granted by general measures to

---

[423] *Commission v Électricité de France (EDF)* (C-124/10 P), judgment of June 5, 2012, not yet reported.

[424] Commission Notice on the application of state aid rules to measures relating to direct business taxation [1998] O.J. C384/3; Council Conclusions concerning the establishment of the Code of Conduct Group for business taxation [1998] O.J. C99/1. See also Council Conclusions of the ECOFIN meeting of 01.12.97 [1998] O.J. C2/1.

[425] See, for instance, (all five cases) *Diputacion Foral de Alava v Commission* (Joined Cases T-129/99, T-129/99 and T-148/99 and Joined Cases T-92/00 and T-103/99) [2002] E.C.R. II-1275 and II-1423.

[426] Favour "certain" Undertakings or the Production of "certain" Goods.

[427] *Italy v Commission* (C-6/97) [1999] E.C.R. I-2981(17).

[428] If a region has fiscal autonomy in a Member State, e.g. under the constitutional law of that State it has the power to raise its own taxes, a regime adopted by that region, more favourable to the general regime of the State may, however, not qualify as selective under the State aid rules: for the detailed conditions to be fulfilled in that respect, see *Commission v Portugal (Azores)* (C-88/03) [2006] E.C.R. I-7115.

[429] See *Italy v Commission* (C-6/97) [1999] E.C.R. I-2981. If the selectivity of a tax measure is justified by the nature or general scheme of the tax system, the measure is, however, not aid. It is often difficult to apply this test in practice. See for instance *British Aggregates Association v Commission* (T-210/02 RENV.), not yet reported.

the undertakings of one Member State, as compared to the undertakings of other Member States, they can only be eliminated through approximation of legislation.[430]

Another element for assessing selectivity is the discretion enjoyed by the subsidising authority in choosing the beneficiaries; with an example: if a State provides that all undertakings must pay social security contributions due within 18 months, that rule does not constitute State aid. The rule may be generous in comparison to rules in other Member States that set the time limit to for instance three months; still the rule is general. However, if the Member State may waive that time limit in relation to some undertakings, that possibility is selective.[431] Therefore, according to the Court, for a measure to be described as "general", it is necessary, in particular, that the State should have no discretionary power enabling it to vary the application of the measure according to such considerations as the choice of recipient, the amount, or the conditions of the intervention.[432]

(d) "distort competition and affect trade between Member States"

Generally it takes little to show that the aid may affect trade between Member States. Even if the beneficiary company offers goods or services only within one Member State, it may have competition from other Member States wanting to enter the market or domestic competition may be owned by foreign interests from other Member States. It also takes little to show that aid distorts competition.[433] However, incompatibility of aid with the internal market is "neither absolute, nor unconditional".[434] The distortions must therefore not be merely hypothetical.

22–90

Aids which fulfil the four above-mentioned criteria are incompatible with the internal market, unless they belong to the categories of compatible aids established by the Treaty or are declared compatible by the Commission. The notion of State aid does not leave any margin of appreciation to the Commission or national courts. However, the assessment of the compatibility of the aid with the internal market often entails complex economic, social, regional or sectorial assessments in which broad discretion is conferred upon the Commission.[435]

---

[430] See Ch.26: Approximation of Laws and Arts 114, 115 116 TFEU.

[431] See for instance *Demenagements-Matutention Transport (DMT)* (C-256/97) [1999] E.C.R. I-3913, para.27.

[432] *France v Commission* (C-241/94) [1996] E.C.R. I–4551; [1997] 1 C.M.L.R. 983. For a measure declared general although favouring only certain undertakings, but justified by the nature or the general economy of the system, see *Netherlands v Commission* (T-233/04) [2008] E.C.R. II-591.

[433] In *Philip Morris v Commission* (730/79) [1980] E.C.R. 2671; [1981] 2 C.M.L.R. 321, the Court rejected the applicant's argument that in order to show that an aid falls within the terms of Arts 107(1) 87(1) TFEU, the Commission must apply the tests which determine the existence of restriction of competition under Arts 101 and 102 TFEU (relevant markets, market structure, etc.). The Court held that simpler grounds (a more favourable treatment of certain undertakings affects inter-State trade) are adequate. See, however, *Intermills v Commission* (323/82) [1984] E.C.R. 3809; [1986] 1 C.M.L.R. 614 the granting of aid cannot be regarded as automatically contrary to the Treaty; *Spain v Commission* (joined Cases C-278/92 to C-280/92) [1994] ECR I-4103 and finally see *Maribel* (C-5/97) [1999] ECR I-3671.

[434] *Iannelli v Meroni* (74/76) [1977] E.C.R. 557(11); [1977] 2 C.M.L.R. 688.

[435] *France v Ladbroke Racing and Commission* (C-83/98 P) [2000] E.C.R. I–3271.

(e)   Particularities concerning public service compensation

22–91   When undertakings perform public service obligations, there is a risk that the compensation is too high and thus includes an element of State aid.

It is difficult to establish in practice what should be the right compensation. The Court has developed formal criteria, normally referred to as the Altmark-criteria, to delimit the situations where State aid could possibly be involved.[436] If the following four conditions are cumulatively met the general service obligation does not constitute State aid:

i.   the recipient undertaking has a public service obligation and the obligation is clearly defined;

ii.   the parameters for calculating the compensation are objective, transparent and established in advance;

iii.   the compensation does not exceed what is necessary to cover all or part of the costs incurred in the discharge of the public service obligations, taking into account a reasonable profit;

iv.   where the undertaking which is to discharge public service obligations is not chosen pursuant to a public procurement procedure which would allow for the selection of the tenderer capable of providing those services at the least cost to the community, the level of compensation needed must be determined on the basis of an analysis of the costs of a typical well-run company.

22–92   If these four conditions are not met and, in addition, the State aid criteria examined above are met, State aid is involved. The aid may nevertheless be compatible with the internal market subject to approval of the Commission.

In December 2011, the Commission adopted a new set of rules on State Aid for services of general economic interest. The new rules consist of four instruments:

- Communication on application of the European Union State aid rules to compensation granted for the provision of services of general economic interest.[437]
- De Minimis Regulation establishing a threshold below which compensation is deemed not to constitute state aid.[438]
- Commission Decision declaring certain types of service of economic interest compatible with the internal market with the Treaty pursuant to Art.106(2) TFEU although constituting state aid.[439]

---

[436] *Altmark* (C-280/00) [2003] E.C.R. I–7747.

[437] Communication from the Commission on the application of the European Union State aid rules to compensation granted for the provision of services of general economic interest [2012] O.J. C8/4.

[438] Commission Regulation on the application of Arts 107 and 108 of the Treaty on the Functioning of the European Union to de minimis aid granted to undertakings providing services of general economic interest [2012] O.J. L114/8.

[439] Commission Decision on the application of Art.106(2) of the Treaty on the Functioning of the European Union to State aid in the form of public service compensation granted to certain undertakings entrusted with the operation of services of general economic interest [2012] O.J. L7/3.

- Framework declaring when state aid falling outside the scope of the Commission Decision nevertheless to be compatible with the Treaty also under Art.6(2) of the TFEU.[440]

The objective of the new rules is to clarify when State aid rules apply to services of general economic interest and when it is compatible with the Treaty.

(f) De Minimis Aid[441]

Minor aids are presumed not to pose a problem to the Union. The current general threshold below which aid is not considered to be so within the meaning of the Treaty and therefore does not have to be notified to the Commission, see below, is €200 000 over a period of three years.[442] For undertakings providing services of general economic interest the limit is €500 000 over a period of three years.[443]

22–93

(2) Procedural Rules

The Treaty contains only a few rules for the administration of the State aid rules but they are crucial. It was not until 1999 that the Council adopted a regulation setting out more in detail specific procedural rules for State aid. The regulation is to a large extent a codification of the case law of the Court and is often referred to as the Procedural Regulation.[444] The Procedural Regulation is supplemented by an implementing Regulation of the Commission, normally referred to as the Implementing Regulation.[445]

22–94

The TFEU makes a fundamental distinction between existing aid and new aid. Existing aid is aid that was in existence when the Treaty came into force, i.e. in 1958, or as concerns Member States that have later joined the Union, on the day of the accession. The Procedural Regulation contains additions to this, in particular that aid approved by the Commission is existing aid. All aid that is not existing aid, is new aid, in particular aid that is put into effect after the Treaty or in the case of new Member States, after the accession.[446]

The importance of the distinction between existing aid and new aid is crucial. Existing aid is subject to review of the Commission, which shall propose to the Member State concerned appropriate measures if it finds that the aid is not compatible with the internal market.[447] If the Member State does not accept the

---

[440] Communication from the Commission, European Union framework for State aid in the form of public service compensation [2012] O.J. C-8/15.

[441] The expression "de minimis" stems from a principle of Roman law—"de minimis non curat praetor", i.e. the judge does not deal with inferior details.

[442] Commission Regulation 1998/2006 [2006] O.J. L379/5. The other conditions in the Regulation must also be fulfilled for the de minimis rule to apply. The Regulation is currently—spring 2013—being reviewed.

[443] Commission Regulation (EU) No 360/2012 [2012] O.J. L114/8.

[444] Regulation 659/99, OJ 1999 L 83/1. With regards to codification of the case law see for instance *Austria v Commission* (C-99/98) [2001] ECR I-1101.

[445] Regulation 794/2004, OJ 2004 L140/1.

[446] Existing aid and new aid are defined in Art.1 of the Procedural Regulation. See also *Namur-Les Assurances* (C-44/93) [1994] E.C.R. I-3829, and *Gibraltar v Commission* (Joined Cases T-195/01 and T-207/01) [2002] E.C.R. II-2309.

[447] Arts 17 and 18 of the Procedural Regulation.

proposal for appropriate measures, the Commission may eventually adopt a binding decision to the effect that the aid is not compatible with the internal market.[448] This means that existing aid *can lawfully be disbursed* by the Member State until such a decision is adopted. On the contrary new aid cannot be put into effect until the Commission has examined and approved it. To ensure that only aid that is compatible with the TFEU is implemented, Member States are obliged to notify new aid to the Commission (notification obligation) for examination and not to put the aid into effect pending the Commission's examination (stand-still obligation).[449] The stand-still obligation has direct effect.[450] Thus, a private party may bring an action before a national court, invoking the obligation, and the national court may thus order the disbursement of the un-notified aid to be stopped.[451] The direct effect provides Member States with a strong incentive to comply with the notification and stand-still obligations. So does the fact that disbursed aid which the Commission does not approve of, must be recovered from the beneficiary undertaking.[452]

22–95   If aid has not been notified by a Member State, interested parties may file a complaint to the Commission regarding illegal aid.[453] If an interested third party files a complaint with the Commission concerning a non-notified aid, the institution is obliged to examine such complaint.[454]

The Commission has exclusive competence to find that an aid is illegal. The examination of new aid falls in two parts: the preliminary examination and the formal investigation procedure. The preliminary examination may lead to the following outcomes[455]:

a)   the aid is not aid;
b)   the aid is compatible with the internal market;
c)   there are doubts as to whether the aid is compatible with internal market.[456] In that case the Commission must open the formal investigation procedure.[457]

The Commission has two months, often referred to as the *Lorenz* time limit, to examine aid under the preliminary examination procedure.[458] The *Lorenz* time limit only applies to notified new aid. Once the *Lorenz* time limit expires the aid shall be deemed authorised by the Commission unless it acts within 15 working

---

[448] Art.19 of the Procedural Regulation.

[449] Arts 2 and 3 of the Procedural Regulation.

[450] *Steinicke* (78/76) [1977] E.C.R. 595.

[451] The Commission has adopted a notice on enforcement of state aid law by national courts that explains this procedure in detail. See Commission Notice on the Enforcement of State Aid law by National Courts [2009] OJ C85/1.

[452] Art.14 of the Procedural Regulation.

[453] Art.20(2) of the Procedural Regulation.

[454] *Commission v Sytraval and Brink's France* (C-367/95 P) [1998] E.C.R. I–1719: in its examination the Commission is not constrained to limit itself to the element raised by the complainant; it may even have the obligation to go beyond.

[455] Art.4 Procedural Regulation and *Gestevision v Commission* (T-95/96) [1998] E.C.R. II–3407.

[456] *SIC v Commission* (T-46/97) [2000] E.C.R. I–2125(71). The notion of doubts is objective, i. e. it must be assessed objectively whether there are doubts or not, see *Bouygues and Bouygues Télécom v Commission* (C-431/07) [2009] ECR I-2665(63).

[457] Art.6 Procedural Regulation.

[458] It was originally laid down by the Court, namely in case (120/73) [1973] E.C.R. 1471.

days on the notice sent by the Member State on its intention of implementing the aid.[459] It should be noted that the *Lorenz* time limit begins running from the moment the Commission considers the notification complete.[460] In practice it is common that the Commission considers the notification incomplete and thus the average length of a preliminary examination is normally longer than two months. To reduce the *Lorenz* time limit in straightforward cases the Commission adopted a simplified procedure for State aid that is fully in line with its communications and framework.[461] The simplified procedure can be applied to three categories of aids: (i) aid measure falling under the standard assessment under existing guidelines and frameworks, (ii) aid measures corresponding to well-established Commission decision-making practice and (iii) prolongation and extensions of existing schemes.

If at the end of the preliminary investigation the Commission has doubts as to whether the aid is compatible with the internal investigation it must open a formal investigation. Such "serious doubt" is presumed, by the Court, to exist when, for instance, the Commission has requested supplementary information several times and has taken much time to reach a decision.[462] **22–96**

Under the formal investigation procedure the Commission is able to gather information from third parties for its assessment and not only the Member State notifying the aid like in the preliminary procedure. When a formal investigation is opened a notification is published in the *Official Journal* where the relevant law and facts are summarised along with possible preliminary views of the Commission. The formal investigation procedure is meant to allow for in-depth investigation of the aid and there is no binding time limit applicable to it. Although the Commission shall endeavour to adopt a decision within 18 months under the Procedural Regulation that time limit is often not respected in practice.

With regards to the possibility of challenging a decision declaring aid compatible with the internal market (positive decision), it is easier for a third party to fulfil the requirement of being individually and directly affected by the decision following a preliminary investigation rather than a formal investigation procedure. This comes from the fact that under a preliminary procedure the third party, e.g. complainant, has not been given the opportunity to exercise its procedural right by lodging comments like under the formal investigation procedure.[463] A third party wishing to challenge a positive decision following a formal investigation procedure must, however, show that he is directly and individually affected by the aid. It is not sufficient for the third party to be one of many competitors of the aid beneficiary.

---

[459] Art.4(6) Procedural Regulation.

[460] Art.4(5) Procedural Regulation.

[461] Notice from the Commission on a simplified procedure for treatment of certain types of State aid. [2009] OJ C136/9.

[462] *Prayon-Rupel v Commission* (T-73/98) [2001] E.C.R. II–867. Much time in taking a decision is in itself not proof of serious doubts. It may together with other elements be indicative of such doubts.

[463] See *Cook v Commission* (C-198/91) [1993] E.C.R. I-2487; *Matra v Commission* (C-225/91) [1993] E.C.R. I-3203 and *Aktionsgemeinschaft Recht und Eigentum (ARE) v Commission* (C-78/03 P) [2005] E.C.R. I-10737.

22–97   The Commission may withdraw, because of the illegality affecting it, a decision declaring an aid compatible, as long as it is done within a reasonable delay and the legitimate expectation and the principle of legal security are both respected.[464]

The reader may have gathered from above that the procedural set-up for administering the State aid rules is rather cumbersome: the only instance competent to declare State aid compatible with the Treaty is the Commission which has limited resources. On the other hand, the notion of State aid is wide and covers myriad measures that may be taken by national authorities; the State aid notion covers, for instance, the sale of a minor municipal plot of land in a far-away region of the Union, or a municipality's decision to support the building of a stadium for the local professional football club although the club has no national or international ranking of importance. Given the time and resources involved in a notification procedure national authorities have an inclination to seek to avoid it. On the other hand, if the measure adopted does turn out to involve aid, the consequences of a failure to notify may be wide-ranging: national courts may enforce the stand-still obligation; and if the Commission should later find that the measure does involve incompatible State aid, it will order the recovery of the aid, see below. The national authorities will therefore, all things being equal, notify. Given the limited effects of certain aids to competition in the Internal Market and the Commission's limited resources, there is a need in the first place for standardised rules for the assessment of the compatibility of aid with the Internal Market, by providing that certain aids do not constitute State aid within the meaning of the Treaty or that they do not need to be notified to the Commission. In the second place, aids which may have appreciable effects on the Internal Market need closer and more detailed analysis by the Commission.

Finally it should be noted that the Procedural Regulation is currently being re-cast. The objective of the re-cast is to make state aid control more transparent, efficient and predictable. The main theme of the proposed amendments is thus to ensure that the Commission obtains all the necessary information for its assessment as soon as possible by clarifying the requirements for lodging a complaint and to enable the Commission to request information directly from market participants.[465]

(3) Aids Compatible with the Internal Market

22–98   Although State aid is in principle prohibited by the Treaty, there are certain categories of aid, which either must or may be considered by the Commission[466]—or in exceptional cases by the Council[467]—as being compatible with the internal market.

---

[464] *Région Nord-pas-de-Calais v Commission* (T-267/08) [2011] E.C.R. II-1999; Appeal C-389/11.

[465] COM (2012) 735 final. Proposal for a Council Regulation amending Regulation (EC) No 659/1999.

[466] This category of aids can be extended by the Council pursuant to Art.107(3)(e) TFEU.

[467] Art.108(2) TFEU. On application by a Member State, the Council may, acting unanimously, decide that an aid which that State is granting or intends to grant shall be considered to be compatible. This application suspends the Commission procedure. See for instance Council Decision of May 3, 2002 on the granting of national aids by the Netherlands in favour of road transport undertakings

(a)   Treaty provisions

According to the Treaty the following aids must be held compatible with the   **22–99**
internal market:[468] (i) those having a social character, granted to individual
consumers, provided it is granted without discrimination related to the origin of
the products concerned; (ii) aids to make good the damage caused by natural
disasters or exceptional occurrences; and (iii) aids granted to certain areas of
Germany and required to compensate for the economic disadvantages caused by
the previous division of that country.[469]

Moreover the TFEU provides for five categories of aid which may be
compatible with the internal market: (i) aids to promote the economic
development of less-developed areas; (ii) aids for important projects of common
European interest or to remedy a serious disturbance in the economy of a
Member State; (iii) aids to certain economic activities or economic areas; (iv)
aids to promote culture and heritage conservation, where such aid does not affect
trading conditions and competition in the Union to an extent contrary to the
common interest; (v) and other categories of aids specified by the Council on a
proposal from the Commission.[470]

The Treaty provisions are supplemented by a vast body of secondary law.
Many of the acts of secondary law take the form of communications from the
Commission, e.g. Guidelines on regional aid for 2007–2013.[471] This means that a
large part of the law in this area is formally seen as non-binding. The background
to this is in short that the Treaty entrusts the Commission with the administration
of the State aid rules. It is a prerogative of the Commission which the
Commission has guarded well. The Treaty provides that the Council may enact,
on a proposal from the Commission, regulations in the field of State aid.
Historically, the Commission was reluctant to make proposals as this implied the
risk that the Member States in Council would seek to relax the State aid regime.
The Commission thus did not make proposals to the Council, effectively barring
the Council from exercising its regulatory power. In place of regulations, the
Commission had recourse to its own non-binding communications as to how it
would administer the Treaty rules, be it a particular type of aid, for instance
regional aid, or within a given sector of the economy, for instance shipbuilding,
or as concerns a particular kind of aid instrument, for instance State guarantees.

In its practice the Commission has consistently been reluctant to accept aid the   **22–100**
purpose of which is simply to keep an unprofitable undertaking running.
Commonly one refers to this by saying that operative aid is not allowed, while
investment aid may be allowed. There are exceptions to this general rule, for
instance in the guidelines for rescuing and restructuring firms in difficulty under

---

[2002] O.J. L131/12. The Council cannot make use of this power when the Commission has declared
the aid incompatible with the internal market, see *Commission v Council* (C-110/02) [2004] E.C.R.
I-6333.

[468] Art.107(2) TFEU.

[469] The last point may be repealed by the Council, acting on a proposal from the Commission, five
years after the entry into force of the Treaty of Lisbon.

[470] Art.107(3) TFEU.

[471] O.J. 2006 C-54/13.

which operative aid may be given for a limited period while a restructuring plan for the undertaking is being drawn up.[472]

It is not possible here to make a meaningful review of the many instruments of secondary law; a list of the instruments can be found on the web page of the Commission's directorate general, responsible for State aid, DG COMP. Below follows a short presentation of a few major instruments.

Before doing so, a few words concerning the relation between the rules on compatibility of State aid with the Internal Market and other provisions of the Treaty are called for. State aid is distortive of competition. It is normally also discriminatory in the sense that it only benefits national undertakings; it also implies a restriction to cross-border trade; to the extent that a State supports for instance domestic production of shoes, the volume of imported shoes from other Member States will fall. Therefore it is relevant to address the question as to the relation of the State aid rules with other provisions of the Treaty. The Court's answer to that question is in short that violations of other Treaty provisions are only acceptable to the extent that they follow from the very notion of State aid. With an example: a Member State provides for State aid to its automobile industry. The measure fulfils the conditions for being considered compatible with the Internal Market. However, the Member State also wants to impose a condition under which the domestic automobile industry may only source its supplies from domestic companies. Such a condition implies a violation of the principle of free movement of goods and it is not inherent to the notion of State aid. Therefore, such a condition cannot stand and it bars the notified aid from being approved by the Commission.[473]

(b) General Block Exemption Regulation

22–101 The Commission adopted a simple and user-friendly General Block Exemption Regulation (GBER) declaring aid which is likely to promote economic development without distorting competition compatible with the internal market.[474] The categories of aid covered by the GBER are aid for:

- Regional aid.
- SME investment and employment aid.
- Aid for the protection of small enterprises by women.
- Aid for the protection of the environment.
- Aid in favour of SMEs.
- Risk capital aid.
- Aid for research, development and innovation.
- Training aid.
- Aid for disadvantaged or disabled workers.[475]

---

[472] [2004] O.J. C244/2. The validity of the guidelines, originally limited until 2009, has been extended, latest by [2012] O.J. C296/3.

[473] For the particularities concerning parafiscal charges that may be caught by the ban on customs duties or equivalent charges or the ban on discriminatory taxation in internal taxation, while at the same time implying State aid, see Ch.25: Taxation.

[474] Commission Regulation No 800/2008 [2008] OJ L214/3.

[475] Art.1 GBER.

Aid that fulfils all of the conditions set out in Chapter I (general conditions) and Chapter II (specific conditions depending on the type of aid) of the GBER is deemed to be compatible with the internal market and exempted from the notification obligation.[476] Chapter I of the GBER entails general conditions which aid must fulfil such as aid thresholds,[477] transparency of the aid and incentive effect. The GBER only applies to transparent aid[478] which includes the following types of aid: (i) grant and interest rate subsidies; (ii) loans where it is possible to calculate the gross grant equivalent[479]; (iii) guarantee schemes; (iv) fiscal measures; and (v) repayable advance only if the total amount does not exceed the applicable threshold.[480] A particular emphasis is placed on whether the aid has an incentive effect requirement, meaning that without the aid the project would not have been undertaken.[481]

To understand how the GBER works it is helpful to examine for example how **22–102** State aid aimed at environmental protection is assessed under the regulation. Under the GBER the following types of aid for environmental purposes may be granted:

- Investment aid enabling undertakings to go beyond Community standards for environmental protection or increase the level of environmental protection in the absence of Community standards.
- Aid for the acquisition of new transport vehicles which go beyond Community standards or which increase the level of environmental protection in the absence of Community standards.
- Aid for early adaptation to future Community standards for SMEs.
- Environmental investment aid for energy saving measures.
- Environmental investment aid for high-efficiency cogeneration.
- Environmental investment aid for the promotion of energy from renewable energy sources.
- Aid for environmental studies.
- Aid in the form of reductions in environmental taxes.

Accordingly the GBER provides for the ability for authorities to grant undertakings aid to achieve energy savings. For the environmental aid to be exempted under the GBER it must fulfil the general conditions in Chapter I such as being transparent and not exceeding the threshold of €7.5 million per undertaking per investment project.[482] Further, the specific conditions for environmental investment aid for energy saving measures are set out in Chapter II of the GBER.[483] According to the special conditions the aid intensity for

---

[476] Art.3 GBER.
[477] Art.6 GBER.
[478] Transparent aid means aid in respect of which it is possible to calculate precisely the gross grant equivalent *ex ante* without need to undertake a risk assessment.
[479] The amount of State aid is calculated gross, without any deductions for tax, etc. The value of the aid is obvious when the aid is paid out as a (cash) grant. When the aid takes other forms, for instance guarantees, or aids to be paid over a period of for instance 10 years, the amount of aid must be assessed on the basis of the aid's gross grant equivalent.
[480] Art.5 GBER.
[481] Art.8 GBER.
[482] Art.6(1)(b) GBER.
[483] Art.21 GBER.

environmental aid shall not exceed 20 per cent or 60 per cent of the eligible cost, which is the extra investment cost necessary to achieve energy savings beyond the level required by Community standards. Eligible costs shall be established by an external auditor and should be equal to the precise environmental protection-related costs or by comparing the investment with a counterfactual situation in the absence of state aid where it cannot be identified.[484]

The GBER is currently subject to review by the Commission with the view of simplifying it in accordance with the objectives of the State Aid Modernisation Plan.

(c) Regional aid

22–103 The TFEU provides for two kinds of regional development aids, which may be considered by the Commission to be compatible with the common market.[485] They are, firstly, the aids to promote the economic development of areas where the standard of living is abnormally low or where there is serious underemployment and of regions where development is severely restrained in view of their structural, economic and social situation.[486] Secondly, the aids to promote the development of certain economic areas, where such aid does not adversely affect trading conditions to an extent contrary to the common interest. The first concern areas in general, while the second ones concern "economic" areas, which are areas economically developed, but subject to acute and temporary difficulties.

As the Commission indicated in its 1998 Guidelines,[487] regional aid is designed to develop the less-favoured regions by supporting investment and job creation in a sustainable context. It promotes the expansion, modernisation and diversification of the activities of establishments located in those regions and encourages new firms to settle there. The granting of such aid must be conditional on the maintenance of the investment and the jobs created during a minimum period. In exceptional cases those aids might have to be supplemented by operating aids. The current Guidelines are applicable until the end of 2013. Those guidelines provide for the selection of the most disadvantaged regions and the maximum aid intensities that Member States can allow, the definition of eligible costs, the incentive effect, the rules on large investment projects, operating aid, accumulation and transparency.[488] The distortions of competition resulting from the granting of regional aids must be accepted if the equilibrium between those distortions and the advantages of the aid in terms of development of the less-favoured regions can be guaranteed. Furthermore, it must be neutral towards the allocation of resources between the various economic sectors and activities. The Guidelines on regional State aid for 2014–2020 are currently under consultation.[489]

---

[484] Art.18(6) GBER.
[485] Art.107(3)(a) and (c) TFEU.
[486] Art.107(3)(a) TFEU refers to Art.349 TFEU which mentions: Guadeloupe, French Guiana, Martinique, Réunion, Saint Barthélemy, Saint Martin, the Azores, Madaira and the Canary Islands.
[487] [1998] O.J. C74/9, amended [2000] O.J. C258/5. See also the new multi-sectoral framework on regional aid to large investment projects [1998] O.J. C107/7.
[488] IP/06/851.
[489] Further informaton can be found on the homepage of the Commission at *http://ec.europa.eu/ competition/consultations/2013_regional_aid_guidelines/index_en.html* [accessed August 23, 2013].

(d)   Compatibility assessment—balancing test

Aid that does not meet standardised criteria or is above the thresholds under **22–104** which standardised criteria apply, requires an individual assessment by the Commission as concerns the aid's compatibility with the Internal Market. In its analysis of such measures the Commission seeks increasingly to use a "refined economic approach". The approach implies a balancing test to ensure that the positive effects of State aid outweigh any negative effect on competition or trade. The balancing test was explained in detail in a Staff Working Paper on Common Principles for an Economic Assessment of the Compatibility of State Aid under Art.107(3) TFEU and consists of the following questions:[490]

1.   Is the aid measure aimed at a well-defined objective of common interest?[491]
2.   Is the aid well-designed to deliver the objective of common interest, i.e. does the proposed aid address the market failure or other objectives?
    i.   Is the aid an appropriate policy instrument to address the policy objective concerned?
    ii.   Is there an incentive effect, i.e. does the aid change the behaviour of the aid recipient?
    iii.   Is the aid measure proportionate to the problem tackled, i.e. could the same change in behaviour not be obtained with less aid?
3.   Are the distortions of competition and effect on trade limited, so that the overall balance is positive?

This test for balancing the positive and negative effects on State aid has been adopted by the Commission in subsequent guidelines concerning particular types of aids.

4.   RECOVERY OF AID

Non-compatible aids must be recovered. The Commission can even seek the **22–105** payment of interests on the sums recovered[492] and has published a Communication on the interest rates to be applied when aid granted unlawfully is recovered.[493]

In the event that the beneficiary or the public authority which granted the aid obtains an interim order from the Court to suspend the repayment, a suspension will be conditional upon the provision of a bank guarantee; the judge is entitled to take into account the overall financial resources of the applicant and the Union interest in securing effectiveness of the judgment to be given.[494]

The Commission may also authorise an aid that a Member State is planning to give to an undertaking, but prohibit payment thereof until the undertaking has

---

[490] The Staff Working Paper is accessible on DG COMP's web page.
[491] The objectives can either be efficiency or equity, i.e. correction of market failures or equal distribution of wealth.
[492] *Siemens* (T-459/93) [1995] E.C.R. II–1675.
[493] [2010] O.J. C166/6.
[494] *Transacciones Maritimas* (C-12/95 P(R)) [1995] E.C.R. I–468; [1996] 2 C.M.L.R. 580.

repaid previously received aid which has been found to be unlawful by a decision of the Commission, which has become final.[495]

22–106   In case of unforeseen and unforeseeable difficulties encountered by the Member State in the recuperation of the aid, the Commission and the Member State must work together in good faith with a view to overcoming the difficulties whilst fully observing the Treaty provisions and especially those on aid.[496] Many cases have dealt with the question as to whether recovery can be opposed on the grounds of legitimate expectations. It is by now settled case law that the national authorities cannot oppose recovery on that ground.[497] As concerns the aid beneficiary the possiblity is not completely ruled out; however, it must be noted that the beneficiary's ignorance about the State aid rules cannot qualify as good faith; a diligent economic operator should be able to determine whether the State aid procedures have been complied with, i.e. whether the aid has been notified to and approved by the Commission.[498] In case the Commission has attached conditions to the authorisation to grant an aid and the beneficiary was not informed of those conditions:

> "[I]t is not contrary to Union law to apply the principle of legal certainty so as to preclude repayment by that beneficiary of the amounts wrongly paid, provided that it is possible to establish the beneficiary's good faith."[499]

The right of the Commission to claim repayment of illegally granted aid expires after 10 years.[500]

In 2007, the Commission published a Notice "towards an effective implementation of Commission decisions ordering Member States to recover unlawful and incompatible State aid".[501] The Commission indicated that it is prepared to take strong action against unlawful aid ever since the entry into force of the Procedural Regulation.[502]

5.   MODERNISATION OF STATE AID RULES

22–107   In 2005, the Commission launched the State Aid Action Plan[503] outlining the guiding principles for a comprehensive reform of State aid rules and procedures over the following five years.[504] The reform is still on-going. The Commission hoped to encourage Member States to focus aid on improving the competitiveness of Union industry and creating sustainable jobs (aid for R&D, innovation and risk capital for small firms), ensuring social and regional cohesion and

---

[495] *TWD v Commission* (Joined Cases T-244/93 and T-486/93) [1995] E.C.R. II–2265; [1996] 1 C.M.L.R. 332.

[496] *Commission v Italy* (C-349/93) [1995] E.C.R. I–343.

[497] *Spain v Commission* (169/95) [1997] E.C.R. I-135.

[498] *Alcan Deutschland* (C-24/95) [1997] E.C.R. I-1591.

[499] *Stichting ROM-Projecten* (158/06) [2007] E.C.R. 21.06.07.

[500] Art.8 Regulation 659/99 [1999] O.J. L83/1; see *Scott v Commission* (C-276/03 P) [2005] E.C.R. I–8437 concerning interruption of the time limit.

[501] [2007] O.J. C272/4.

[502] Regulation laying down detailed rules for the application of Art.113 TFEU [1999] O.J. L83/3.

[503] 2005 Report on competition policy, 119.

[504] *http://ec.europa.eu/competition/state_aid/reform/archive.html* [accessed August 23, 2013].

improving public services. The Commission also aimed at rationalising and streamlining procedures, so that the rules are clearer and less aid has to be notified, and to accelerate decision-making.

The Action Plan was based on the following elements:

- Less and better targeted state aid.
- A more refined economic-based approach so that less distorting aid, particularly where money is less readily available, can be approved more easily and quickly.
- More streamlined and efficient procedures: the Commission intends to exempt more planned subsidies from the obligation to notify.
- A shared responsibility between the Member States and the Commission who cannot improve State aid rules and practice without their co-operation.

The State Aid Action Plan introduced an important change into state aid control, namely the economic approach to the compatibility assessment of the aid. However due to the financial crisis the Commission deemed it necessary to introduce a reform in state aid control in 2013 with the aim of modernising it.[505] The modernisation of the state aid control is an important component in Europe's growth strategy for this decade, i.e. the Europe 2020.[506] The objective of the modernisation is: (i) to foster growth in a strengthened, dynamic and competitive internal market; (ii) to foster enforcement on cases with the biggest impact on the internal market; and (iii) to streamline rules and faster decisions. The European Parliament adopted a Resolution on State aid Modernisation in 2013 supporting the initiative of the Commission.[507]

FURTHER READING

Alison Jones & Brenda Sufrin, *EU Competition Law*, 4th edn (Oxford University **22–108** Press, 2010).

Alister Lindsay & Alison Berridge, *The EU Merger Regulation: Substantive Issues*, 4th edn (Sweet & Maxwell, 2012).

Andrea Biondi, Piet Eeckhout and James Flynn, *The Law of State Aid in the European Union* (Oxford University Press, 2004).

Ariel Ezrachi, *EU Competition Law: An Analytical Guide to the Leading Cases*, 3rd edn (Hart Publishing, 2012).

Christopher Kerse and Nicholas Khan, *EU Antitrust Procedure*, 6th (revised) edn (Sweet & Maxwell, 2012).

Christopher Jones and Marc van der Woude, *EU Competition Law Handbook*, published annually (Sweet & Maxwell, 2012).

Damian Chalmers, Gareth Davies, Giorgio Monti, *European Union Law: Cases and Materials*, 2nd edn (Cambridge University Press, 2010).

---

[505] COM(2012) 209 final. EU State Aid Modernisation (SAM).
[506] Information on the growth strategy can be found here: *http://ec.europa.eu/europe2020/index_en.htm* [accessed August 23, 2013].
[507] European Parliament resolution of January 17, 2013 on state aid modernisation (2012/2920(RSP)).

F. Wijckmans, F. Tuytschaever, *Vertical Agreements in EU Competition Law*, 2nd edn (Oxford University Press, 2011).

Frauke Henning-Bodewig, Unfair Competition law, *European Union and Member States* (Kluwer Law International, 2006).

Gerhard Dannecker & Oswald Jansen, "Competition Law Sanctioning in the European Union", European Monographs 46, 2004.

Joanna Goyder, *EU Distribution Law*, 5th edn (Hart Publishing, 2011).

John Cook, Christopher Kerse and Riccardo Celli, *EC merger Control*, 5th (revised) edn (Sweet & Maxwell, 2009).

Leigh Hancher, Tom Ottervanger and Piet Jan Slot, *EU State Aids*, 4th edn (Sweet & Maxwell, 2012).

Lennart Ritter, W. David Braun, *E.C. Competition Law. A Practitioner's Guide*, 3rd edn (Kluwer, 2004).

Luis Ortiz Blanco, *EC Competition procedure*, 2nd edn (Oxford Unversity Press, 2006).

Michael Sachez Rydelski, *The EC State Aid Regime—Distortive effects of state aid on competition and trade* (Cameron May Ltd, 2006).

Nihoul P. & Rodford P., *EU Electronic Communications Law. Competition and Regulation in the European Telecommunications Market*, 2nd edn (Oxford University Press, 2011).

Richard Whish and David Bailey, *Competition Law*, 7th edn (Oxford University Press 2012).

Robert O'Donoghue and Jorge Padilla, *The Law and Economics of Article 82 EC* (Hart Publishing, 2006).

Thomas Hays, *Parallel Importation under European Union Law* (Sweet & Maxwell, 2004).

Van Bael & Bellis, *Competition Law of the EC*, 5th edn (Kluwer Law International, 2009).

CHAPTER 23

Agriculture and Fisheries[1]

According to the Commission, the Common Agricultural Policy (CAP) is:

"[F]undamental to the strength and competitiveness of EU farming and the agro-food sector as a whole, with its 19 million jobs. The policy ensures that farming and preservation of the environment go hand in hand. It helps develop the economic and social fabric of rural communities. It plays a vital role in confronting new challenges such as climate change, bioenergy and biodiversity."[2]

As will be briefly shown below:

"EU agricultural policy is constantly evolving. In the earliest days, 50 years ago, the emphasis was on providing enough food for a Europe emerging from a decade of war-induced shortages. Subsidising production on a large scale and buying up surpluses in the interest of food security are now largely a thing of the past. The focus of EU policy is to get food producers—of all forms of food from crops and livestock to fruit and vegetables, or wine—to be able to stand on their own feet on EU and world markets."[3]

"Agriculture" in the Union is no longer centred on agricultural markets, i.e. production and marketing of agricultural products, but now rests on two so-called pillars: the CAP, on the one hand, and Rural Development, on the other. Until the beginning of the 1990s, the main content of the CAP, which on its own devoured nearly 70 per cent of the Union budget, was agriculture per se. However, as the Commission indicated, new challenges appeared in the form of globalisation of world trade (especially trade in agricultural products), consumer-led quality requirements and Union enlargement. These changes affected not only the agricultural markets (see hereunder), but also local economies in rural areas. The Commission underlined that the future of agriculture itself is closely linked to a balanced development of rural areas that account—few European citizens realise this—for 80 per cent of the European territory (before accession of the 10 new Member States). Consequently, not only "agriculture", but also "rural policy" has an important role to play in the cohesion of the Union's territorial, economic and social policies. This double approach is also reflected in the Union budgets and in

---

[1] The term "Fisheries" was added in the denomination of Title III of Part Three of the TFEU by the Treaty of Lisbon; the fisheries policy will be examine in the next chapter of this book, but it should be noted that the TFEU provides that "Reference to the common agricultural policy or to agriculture and the use of the term 'agricultural', shall be understood as also referring to fisheries, having regard to the special characteristics of that sector." (Art.33(1)2 TFEU).

[2] EUROPA. Activities of the European Union. Agriculture.

[3] EUROPA. Overviews of European Union activities Agriculture.

the Financial Perspectives,[4] where the amounts for agriculture are divided between the Common Agricultural Policy (CAP) and Rural Development and accompanying measures. The amounts for these two Union activities still represent today around 46 per cent of Union expenditures.

23–02 The TFEU[5] now provides that the "internal market shall extend to agriculture,[6] fisheries and trade in agricultural products",[7] and that "save as otherwise provided in Arts 39 to 44, the rules laid down for the establishment and functioning of the internal market shall apply to agricultural products"[8]. The latter are defined as the products of the soil, of stock farming and of fisheries and products of first-stage processing directly related to those products.[9]

The Treaty also provides that the "operation and development of the internal market for agricultural products must be accompanied by the establishment of a common agricultural policy".[10] In other words, an unqualified application, for instance, of the Union competition rules to agricultural products was, from the start, deemed impossible. Special complementary rules, known as agricultural policy, were needed. The more so since agriculture has always represented, due to its particular nature,[11] difficult problems in all the Member States. Elaborate and costly national measures to aid agriculture existed (and still exist) practically everywhere. Consequently, the inclusion of agriculture in, what was then called the common market, was agreed upon, but on special terms, i.e. via "the establishment of a common agricultural policy"[12] and the "need to effect the appropriate adjustments by degree".[13]

Consequently, the provisions relating to the CAP have precedence, in case of conflict, over the rules relating to the establishment of the internal market, such as those on the free movement of goods.[14] On the other hand, it means that, in the absence of specific provisions, the general rules of the Treaties fully apply to the agricultural sector since the end of the transitional period.[15] As for the national measures existing at the time of the establishment of the CAP, they were replaced

---

[4] See above Ch.14: Financing Union Activities.

[5] Art.38(1) TFEU.

[6] One could, in theory, have established an internal market without agricultural products (today, agriculture only represents 1.3 per cent of Union GDP), but in the 1950s agriculture constituted, in all the Member States, a sector closely linked with the economy as a whole (see Art.39(2)(c) TFEU), and could therefore not be left out of the internal market. The food industry, which processes more than three-quarters of the agricultural products of the Union, also constitutes its most important industrial sector in terms of turnover and employment.

[7] Art.38(1)2 TFEU.

[8] Art.38(2) TFEU.

[9] They are listed in Annex II to the Treaty. In pursuance of old Art.32(3) EC a number of products were added to this list in 1960. See Regulation 7a [1961] J.O. 71/61 and [1959–1962]68.

[10] Art.38(4) TFEU.

[11] Art.39(2)(a) TFEU refers to the "particular nature of agricultural activity which results from the social structure of agriculture and from structural and natural disparities between the various agricultural regions".

[12] Art.38(4) TFEU.

[13] Art.39(2)(b) TFEU.

[14] *Pig Marketing Board v Redmond* (83/78) [1978] E.C.R. 2347; [1979] 1 C.M.L.R. 177.

[15] *Charmasson v Minister for Economic Affairs and Finance* (48/74) [1974] E.C.R. 1383; [1975] 2 C.M.L.R. 208.

by a "common organization of agricultural markets"[16] that took the form of various European Market Organisation[s][17], now replaced by a single Common Market Organisation (see below).

1. THE COMMON AGRICULTURAL POLICY (CAP)

It is important to mention the objectives assigned by the TFEU to the CAP, since, **23–03** as the Court stated, taken separately, they appear to conflict with one another and it is up to the Union Institutions to allow, where necessary, temporary priority to one of them.[18] The objectives of the common agricultural policy still are, after all those years the following:

"(a)   to increase agricultural productivity by promoting technical progress and by ensuring the rational development of agricultural production and the optimum utilisation of the factors of production, in particular labour;

(b)   thus to ensure a fair standard of living for the agricultural community, in particular by increasing the individual earnings of persons engaged in agriculture;

(c)   to stabilise markets;

(d)   to assure the availability of supplies;

(e)   to ensure that supplies reach consumers at reasonable prices."[19]

Looking back over the past 50 years or so, it is easy to ascertain that only some of those objectives were actually attained. There is no doubt that agricultural productivity and production increased dramatically; it could be said, out of all proportion to the internal and external needs. However, one should not forget that the CAP was established by people who had lived through World War II and that the memories about the scarcity of food during that period and about those who died of hunger, were still very vivid at the time. What was more natural than the strong desire "to assure the availability of supplies",[20] preferably home-grown to avoid dependency upon outside suppliers? One has to add to that the claim of the farmers' organisations, which have long enjoyed and exercised an excessive influence[21] on political decisions concerning agriculture. They pretended that the "increase of individual earnings of persons engaged in agriculture"[22] was guaranteed to them by the Treaty, ignoring the other objectives. The result was the impossibility to "stabilise the markets"[23] and "to ensure that supplies reach consumers at reasonable prices".[24]

These above-mentioned Treaty objectives were complemented under "Agenda   **23–04** 2000" by a reform whose purpose was:

---

[16]   Art.40(1) TFEU.

[17]   Art.40(1)(c) TFEU.

[18]   *Balkan-Import-Export v Hauptzollamt Berlin-Packhof* (5/73) [1973] E.C.R. 1091.

[19]   Art.39(1) TFEU.

[20]   Art.30(1)(d) TFEU.

[21]   This influence, fortunately, has waned with the years, together with the decline in the number of farmers (which before enlargement represented less than 2 per cent of the working population), and the economic importance of farm products in the GNP of the Member States.

[22]   Art.39(1)(b) TFEU.

[23]   Art.39(1)(c) TFEU.

[24]   Art.39(1)(e) TFEU.

"[T]o preserve the European model of agriculture by insuring that farming throughout the Union, even in the regions with special problems, is sustainable and competitive, capable of maintaining the landscape, conserving nature, contributing to the vitality of the countryside and responding to the concerns and demands of consumers in terms of food quality and safety, environmental protection and animal welfare."[25]

The basic principles which determined the orientation of the CAP were adopted by the Council in 1960 and still apply today:

1. free movement of agricultural products within the Union;
2. a common price level for all agricultural products;
3. fair earnings for those employed in agriculture (i.e. price support);
4. a uniform system of levies imposed on all imported products and export restitutions;
5. co-ordination of national measures for structural reform.

(1) A Bit of History: Mixed Results of the Successive Reforms of the CAP

23–05 After several decades of operation, with outstanding positive results, the problems created by appalling overproduction in some sectors and the resulting unbearable costs to the Union, among others, for storing them, made a revision of the CAP mandatory.[26] A first reform of the CAP took place in 1984.[27] Although it was considered by the Commission as "a milestone in the development of the [agricultural] policy"[28] the Union faced a major crisis a few years later due to a combination of accumulated surplus stocks and acute budgetary difficulties. A turning point came at the meeting of the European Council in Brussels, in February 1988. The Council approved a Commission Communication entitled "The Single European Act: a new Frontier for Europe". At that meeting the Union endowed itself with the political and financial resources it needed to finally complete the internal market.

Notwithstanding all those efforts, the CAP continued to suffer from a fundamental deficiency: agricultural production was guided by price-setting rather than by demand. Farmers continued to produce huge quantities of products for which the Union offered the highest guaranteed prices, irrespective of the need for those products. So, once again the Council approved, in May 1992, a number of measures redirecting agriculture in the Union. This so-called Mac Sharry re-orientation was prolonged by the above-mentioned Agenda 2000 and was restructured in the course of 2003 (see below).

---

[25] General Report 1999, 494.
[26] See the Communiqué of the European Council of June 1983 [1983] Bull.6 at 19.
[27] [1983] EC Suppl. Bull. 4 at 19. The following adaptations were proposed:
  1. co-responsibility principle, guaranteed thresholds and delivery quotas for milk;
  2. a prudent and, in certain cases, restrictive price policy, and for cereals a reduction of the gap between Union and World prices;
  3. existing aids and premiums to be discontinued;
  4. promotion of agricultural exports; and
  5. dismantling of the monetary compensatory amounts. See General Report 1983, 172.
[28] General Report 1984, 64.

On June 26, 2003, EU farm ministers adopted a new fundamental reform of the CAP: it completely changed the way the EU supports its farm sector. The new CAP is geared towards consumers and taxpayers, while giving EU farmers the freedom to produce what the market wants. One can only deeply regret that after all those years of subsidised wild overproduction geared at support rather than demand, that sentence doesn't read as follows "while forcing farmers to produce only what the market demands". [That would finally have introduced some economic common sense into the CAP.] However, since then, the vast majority of subsidies have been paid independently from the volume of production; this makes farmers more competitive and market-orientated, while providing the necessary income stability. Exceptions are possible. These new "single farm payments"[29] or "single payment scheme (SPS)" are also linked to the respect of environmental, food safety and animal welfare standards.

The two pillars of the 2003 reform are the decoupling of direct aid to producers (cutting the link between support and production) and introduction of the single payment scheme. Direct aid no longer depends on the type of production.   **23–06**

Cross-compliance: farmers may receive direct payments provided that they maintain their land in good agricultural condition and comply with the standards of public health, the environment and animal welfare.

Degressivity, modulation and financial discipline: between 2005 and 2012, direct payments (other than in the outermost regions[30] and the Aegean Islands[31]) are to be reduced each year (3 per cent in 2005, 4 per cent in 2006 and afterwards 5 per cent each year).

They entered into force in 2005 for those Member States that decided to start on January 1, 2005: Austria, Belgium, Denmark, Germany, Ireland, Italy, Luxembourg, Portugal, Sweden and the United Kingdom. The five other old Member States applied the SPS in 2006, while two new Member States, Malta and Slovenia, started in 2007. The other new Member States will apply the new system in 2009 at the latest. The reform also provides for a revision of the tobacco, olive oil, cotton and sugar sectors.

The key elements of the reformed CAP can therefore be summarised as follows[32]:   **23–07**

- Single Payment Scheme for EU farmers, independent from production;

---

[29] Regulation 1782/03 establishing common rules for direct support schemes and establishing certain support schemes for farmers [2003] O.J. L270, amended [2010] O.J. L106/16; see *Arnold and Johan Harms* [2010] E.C.R. 20.05.10. concerning the single payment scheme.

[30] For details, see below in Ch.32: Regional Policy/Economic, Social and Territorial Cohesion—the Europe 2020 Strategy.

[31] See Regulation 615/08 [2008] O.J. L168/1 providing for two support schemes.

[32] See IP/04/1540 23.12.04. Direct support for Farmers Regulation 73/09 [2009] O.J. L30/16, amended [2012] O.J. L204 /11or stateless persons as beneficiaries of international protection, Annexes IV and VIII modified [2012] O.J.L103/17; detailed rules for its application, in Regulation 1121/09, amended [2011] O.J. L341/33. Annex I of Reg.73/09.amended: [2012] O.J. L160/13. See Implementing Regulation 776/12 on advances to be paid from October 16, 2012 of the direct payments listed in Annex I of Regulation 73/09 [2012] O.J. L231/8.

- payment is linked to the respect of environmental, food safety, animal and plant health and animal welfare standards, as well as the requirement to keep all farmland in good agricultural and environmental condition (cross-compliance);
- a strengthened rural development policy with more EU money, new measures to promote the environment, quality and animal welfare and to help farmers to meet Union production standards starting in 2005;
- a reduction in direct payments ("modulation") to bigger farms to finance the new rural development policy;
- a "financial discipline" mechanism to prevent spending exceeding the ceiling agreed upon, until 2013.

Hopefully these changes will give consumers what they want, offer taxpayers more transparency and contribute towards more market-orientated world trade. It is important to note that farmers are no longer paid just to produce food. Today's CAP is, according to the Commission,[33] demand driven.

(2) The Single Common Market Organisation (CMO)[34]

23–08   As was indicated, the Treaty provides for the establishment of "common organisations of agricultural markets" in order to attain the objectives of the CAP.[35] Some kind of organisation exists for the following products classified in: on the one hand, "plant products", also referred to as "crop products"[36]—arable crops, wine, olive oil, fruit and vegetables, sugar, tobacco, cotton and hops; and, on the other hand, "animal products", also referred to as "livestock products"— milk and milk products, beef and veal, sheep-meat and goat-meat, pig-meat, poultry-meat, eggs and honey. These markets will be briefly examined hereunder. In addition, the Council adopted three regulations with specific rules for ethyl alcohol of agricultural origin,[37] on measures improving general conditions for the production and marketing of agricultural products[38] and special measures to encourage silkworm rearing.[39]

The 21 existing common market organisations were replaced in 2008 by the Single Common Market Organisation (Single CMO).[40] According to the Commission it constitutes the most significant technical simplification of the CAP yet undertaken; it allows the repeal of almost 50 Council acts and replaces more than 650 legal articles in the Regulations.[41] However, all the existing policies remain unchanged and, consequently, it has no financial impact. It does not include those parts of CMOs which are subject to policy reforms; this was the

---

[33] See under http://www.ec.europa.eu/agriculture [accessed August 23, 2013].
[34] Some of the following text has been borrowed from http://ec.europa.eu/agriculture/markets/index_en.htm [accessed August 23, 2013].
[35] Art.39 TFEU.
[36] This is the expression used in the General Report 2004, 116.
[37] [2003] O.J. L97/6.
[38] [2004] O.J. L125/1.
[39] [2006] O.J. L286/1.
[40] Regulation 1234/2007 "Single CMO Regulation", establishing a common organisation of agricultural markets and on specific provisions for certain agricultural products [2007] O.J. L299/1, amended [2008] O.J. L121/1, [2009] O.J. L154/1 and [2009] O.J. L312/4.
[41] European Commission "Agriculture and Rural Development" simplifying the CAP.

case with regard to most parts of the fruit and vegetables, processed fruit and vegetables and the wine sector; the substantive provisions of the relevant Regulations will be incorporated in the CMO once the respective reforms have been enacted.

It is important to note the possibility under the TFEU[42] to change existing price levels with regard to all sectors covered by the Regulation.

(a) Plant Products

(i) Cereals[43]

They cover a wide range of annual crops of primary importance, such as wheat, barley, maize, rye, colza, sunflower, peas, etc. They cover 40 per cent of the EU's utilised agricultural area, and are found in all the Member States. Since 1992, they have been eligible for a hectare-based aid scheme, which also includes set-aside measures. In the cereals sector, Union prices are, on average, still higher than world prices; to allow for exports, "refunds" are granted covering the difference between those two prices. The subsidised exports are limited each year in terms of volume and value, as part of the Union's international commitments to the WTO. A solution is to be found in aligning the Union prices with those of the world market.

23–09

As for oil seeds, the alignment of payments per hectare on those of cereal, should eliminate their specific character.

(ii) Wine[44]

The Union occupies a leading position in the world wine market, accounting for 45 per cent of wine-growing areas, 65 per cent of production, 57 per cent of global consumption (although this is now declining) and 70 per cent of exports in global terms. The Union wine market went through several transformations including a serious structural surplus, a ban on planting, the obligation to distil the surplus, incentives to giving up vineyards, etc. Following the GATT agreements, demand being in constant decline, the necessity to develop towards a qualitative level that the vineyard could not always guarantee, the introduction of a new CMO became necessary.[45] It simplified the legislation in this field, recognised the role of producers and inter-branch organisations, provided for restructuring of the vineyards and was supposed to put an end to intervention, except in special circumstances. See financial transfer of the common

23–10

---

[42] Art.43(2) TFEU.

[43] See CMO, Annex I, Part I, which applied to cereals on July 1, 2008 [2007] O.J. L299/1.

[44] Regulation 1493/99 [2008] O.J. L148/1, amended [2008] O.J. L335/32, and Regulation 1227/00 detailed rules for the application of Regulation 1493/99 now CMO, Annex I, Part XII; applicable since August 1, 2008. See *Schneider* (C-285/06) [2008] E.C.R. I-1501 interpreting Art.47 of Regulation 1493/99.

[45] Regulation 1493/1999 [1999] O.J. L179/1. No longer applicable. See CMO Regulation 134/2007 [2007] O.J. L299/1.

organisation of the market in wine to rural development.[46] Now replaced by the Single Common Market Organisation. The common organisation for the market in wine was reformed in 2008.[47]

(iii) Olive oil and table olives

23–11   The Union is the leading world producer, accounting for 80 per cent and consuming 70 per cent of the world's olive oil. World demand is steadily increasing to the benefit of many Union regions in whose economies it plays an important role. The Union encourages production of a high quality product for the benefit of growers, processors, traders and consumers. It is based on a single payment system. 40 per cent of the funding is an area aid for the upkeep of olive groves of environmental and social value. Since July 1, 2008 it is part of the single CMO.[48]

(iv) Fresh fruit and vegetables

23–12   There are three categories: fresh fruit and vegetables,[49] processed fruit and vegetables[50] and certain citrus fruits.[51] The CMO was modified in 2000 including the special arrangements for certain types of fruits and vegetables, like tomatoes, peach, pear and citrus fruit processing. The changes aim at boosting support for the sector in a resolutely market-orientated way; simplification of aid schemes increased their transparency. Of interest here is the fact that aid is paid directly to producer organisations, which make the scheme more flexible and increase producers' responsibility. Since January 1, 2008 replaced by the Single CMO.[52]

(v) Processed fruit and vegetables

23–13   The provisions governing this market organisation are now, without modification, included in the single Market Organisation, which became applicable for these agricultural products, on January 1, 2008.[53]

(vi) Raw tobacco

23–14   The CMO was set up in 1992[54] and amended in 1998 and 2002.[55] It comprises a premium system, a system of production orientation and limitation and measures

---

[46] Regulation 479/08 [2008] O.J. L335/32.
[47] Regulation 479/08 [2008] O.J. L148/1.
[48] Regulation 1234/07 [2007] O.J. L299/1.
[49] Regulation 2200/96 [1996] O.J. L297/1, modified [2004] O.J. L106/10, implemented by Regulation 1580/07 [2007] O.J. L350/1, amended [2008] O.J. L336/1. Since January 1, 2008 Single CMO, Regulation 1234/07 [2007] O.J. L299/1.
[50] Regulation 2201/96 [1996] O.J. L297/29, modified [2004] O.J. L64/25. Since January 1, 2008 Single CMO, Regulation 1234/07 (quoted above, fn.48).
[51] Regulation 2202/96 [1996] O.J. L297/49, modified [2001] O.J. L262/6. Now Single CMO Regulation 1234/07 (quoted above, fn.48).
[52] Since January 1, 2008 Regulation 1234/07 (quoted above, fn.48).
[53] Regulation 1234/07 (quoted above, fn.48).
[54] Regulation 2075/92 [1992] O.J. L215/70, amended [2003] O.J. L345/17 and [2005] O.J. L271/1. Since July 1, 2008 Single CMO, Regulation 1234/07 (quoted above, fn.48).

to convert production (including the Union Tobacco Fund[56] and a quota buy-back programme). Detailed rules were laid down for the implementation of the system[57] and with regard to the Fund.[58]

(vii) Sugar[59]

The CMO for sugar was set up in 1968 to ensure fair income for producers and self supply for the Union. Import levies provided protection against external competition and export refunds allowed for sales to third countries. A major reform became effective on July 1, 2006; the key to the reform is a 36 per cent cut in the guaranteed minimum price, generous compensation for farmers and a Restructuring Fund as an incentive to uncompetitive sugar producers to leave the industry.

23–15

(viii) Rice

The common organisation was based on a 1995 regulation.[60] It provides for intervention on the internal market, including the fixing of an intervention price and certain support measures for European products when they are traded on international markets. In addition it is heavily influenced by certain international agreements under the WTO. It is part of the Single CMO since September 1, 2008.

23–16

(ix) Cotton

This agricultural sector suffers from overproduction and severe competition from third countries. The CMO has undergone several changes; since the 2000/2001 marketing year, the price reduction mechanism has been significantly strengthened above certain production thresholds in order to respect budgetary discipline, the main concern, and to avoid the environmental problems caused by extreme intensification and the spread of cotton growing. There is a special aid scheme for small producers.[61] A 2008 regulation[62] established national restructuring programmes for the cotton ginning industry and to enhance the quality and marketing of the cotton produced.

23–17

(x) Hops[63]

The CMO covers three products: cones, powder and extracts. Aid is granted to producers at 480 per hectare. From January 1, 2005, the sector was integrated into

23–18

---

[55] Regulation Fixing the premiums and guarantee thresholds for leaf tobacco by variety group and Member State [2002] O.J. L84/4. Now Single CMO.
[56] See Regulation 470/08 [2008] O.J. L140/1.
[57] Regulation 2848/98 [1998] O.J. L358/17. Now Single CMO [2007] O.J. L.299/1.
[58] Regulation 2182/02 [2002] O.J. L 331/16. Now Single CMO (quoted above).
[59] See single CMO, Regulation 1234/07 (quoted above, fn.48).
[60] Regulation 370/95.
[61] Regulation 1152/90 [1990] O.J. L116/1. Now Single CMO (quoted above).
[62] Regulation 637/08 [2008] O.J. L178/1.
[63] Since July 1, 2008 Single CMO (quoted above).

the single farm payments system (see above). With enlargement, the Union areas under hops increased by almost 50 per cent. The trend is, however, towards area reduction as a consequence of increased yields of the bitter constituent of hops that gives beer its bitter taste. There are practically no unsold stocks within the Union, which is traditionally a net exporter.

(xi) Bananas

23–19   This CMO was based on a 1993 regulation and should allow the Union market to receive satisfactory supplies of quality bananas at fair prices for producers and consumers and ensure a balance between the various sources of supply. It was based on a tariff-only system. It was reformed in 2006 and is absorbed in the Single CMO[64] since January 1, 2008.

(b)   Animal Products

(i)   Milk and milk products

23–20   The CMO is based on a 1999 regulation.[65] It refers to the additional levy which was introduced in 1992 for the purpose of reducing the imbalance between supply and demand. In order to stimulate consumption within the Union and improve competitiveness on the international markets, the level of market support was reduced through a gradual reduction of the target prices and the intervention prices starting on July 1, 2005. Milk production was increased by 2 per cent from April 2008.[66]

Besides the intervention in respect of butter and fresh cream, the regulation provides for:

1.   buying-in of skimmed milk powder with a minimum protein content;
2.   defraying part of the costs for supplying milk to pupils in schools;
3.   the introduction of individual income support;
4.   import duties and export refunds based on the undertakings accepted under the Uruguay Round; and
5.   application of the Treaty provisions concerning the granting of State aid to this sector. Several other measures are provided for in case of difficulty in implementing the above-mentioned regulation.

(ii)   Beef and veal

23–21   The CMO is based on a 1999 regulation.[67] To re-balance supply and demand, market support was gradually reduced by 20 per cent, farmers being compensated by direct payments set up under Agenda 2000. One of them is to encourage

---

[64] Regulation 1234/07 [2007] O.J. L299/1.
[65] Regulation 1255/99 [1999] O.J. L160/48, amended several times. Since July 1, 2008 Single CMO [2007] O.J. L299/1.
[66] Regulation 248/08 [2008] O.J. L76/6.
[67] Regulation 1254/99 [2000] O.J. L263/34, amended several times. Since July 1, 2008 Single CMO [2007] O.J. L199/1.

producers to adopt extensive grazing methods ("extensification payment"); these were not very successful and the Commission proposed measures to curb the tendency towards intensive production.

(iii) Sheep-meat and goat-meat[68]

This CMO was based on a 2001 regulation brought into effect on January 1, 2002. A fixed premium for producers has replaced a price-dependent variable compensatory payment. The main components of the regulation are: rules on direct payments, rules on trade with third countries and market monitoring.

23–22

(iv) Pig-meat[69]

Measures were provided to ensure that supply is in-line with market demand. It provides for (1) a basic price and the possibility of intervention (not used in the last 20 years), (2) rules concerning trade with third countries: possibly import and export licences, additional import duties in case of risk to destabilise the Union market, export refunds; prohibition of taxes equivalent to customs duties and quotas and application of Treaty rules on State aids. Many other regulations were adopted concerning, for instance, export licences.[70]

23–23

(v) Poultry-meat[71]

This CMO was established by a 1975 regulation still in force but amended many times. It covers: cocks, hens, ducks, geese, turkeys and guinea-fowl. Marketing standards related to grading by category, quality and weight and to labelling are mandatory. The Regulation contains rules on trade with third countries: import and export licences, customs tariffs, additional import duties, tariff quotas, export refunds, safeguard measures, trade barriers, animal diseases and State aid.

23–24

(vi) Eggs

This market was based on a 1975 regulation[72] amended several times. It covers eggs of domestic fowl, eggs not in shell and egg yolks however preserved. Union measures in support of trade or joint trade initiatives may be taken. Marketing standards related to grading by category and weight and to labelling are mandatory. Rules on trade with third countries refer to import and export licences, the common customs tariff, quotas, safeguard measures, animal diseases and State aids.

23–25

---

[68] Since July 1, 2008 Single CMO Regulation 1234/07 [2007] O.J. L299/1.
[69] Since July 1, 2008 Single CMO (quoted above).
[70] Regulation 1518/03 [2003] O.J. L320/07 now Single CMO (quoted above, fn.57).
[71] Since July 1, 2008 Single CMO (quoted above).
[72] Regulation 2771/75 [1075] O.J. L282/49. Since July 1, 2008 Single CMO Regulation 1234/2007 [2007] O.J. L199/1.

(vii)   Honey

23–26   The legal basis for this CMO was a 1997 regulation.[73] This Regulation gives Member States the chance to lay down national annual programmes, in close co-operation with trade organisations and co-operatives. The following may be included in those programmes: technical assistance, control of varroasis, rationalisation of transhumance, support for laboratories carrying out analyses of honey and applied research to improve the quality of honey. Details for these programmes were laid down in a Commission regulation.[74] See also a directive relating to honey, which establishes a definition of honey and rules concerning labelling in order to inform the consumer of the country of origin of the honey and possible mixtures.[75]

A very important point is that all decisions to be taken in the various fields briefly described above are proposed by the Commission and need the agreement of the Management Committee set up for each variety.

The market organisations for floriculture (since January 1, 2007), dried fodder (since April 1), seeds (since July 1), flax and hemp[76] (since July 1), were all replaced at various dates in 2008 by the Single CMO.

There also is an organisation for "spirit drinks": their definition, description, presentation, labelling and protection of geographical indication.[77]

(3)   The Structural Measures

23–27   They concern, among others, the protection of the environment and forestry. The former provides for agricultural production methods compatible with the requirements of the protection of the environment and the maintenance of the countryside. Its object is to reduce the harmful effects and pollution caused by agriculture, while ensuring recognition of the fundamental function performed by farmers in terms of management of the countryside and protection of natural resources. The latter introduces a Union aid scheme for forestry, measures in agriculture, intended to enable farmers to adjust to the changes arising from the adjustments to the market organisations, particularly by providing economically viable alternatives to the agricultural use of land. In the context of the protection of forests against atmospheric pollution and fire, the Council adopted measures to ensure the extension, improvement and reinforcement of the mechanisms set up previously.

See also the specific measures for agriculture in the outermost regions of the Union.[78]

---

[73] Regulation 1221/97 [1997] O.J. L 173/1. Now Single CMO (quoted above).
[74] Regulation 2300/97 [1997] O.J. L319/4. Now Single CMO (quoted above).
[75] Directive 2001/110 [2001] O.J. L10/47. Now Single CMO (quoted above).
[76] Regulation 246/08 [2008] O.J. L76/1.
[77] Regulation 110/08 [2008] O.J. L39/16.
[78] Regulation 247/06 [2006] L42/1, modified [2010] O.J. L194/23.

(a)   Organic Farming[79]

"Organic farming" implies that the farmers use only organically produced seed. It   **23–28**
differs from other farming systems in a number of ways. It favours renewable
resources and recycling, returning to the soil nutrients found in waste products.
Where livestock is concerned, meat and poultry production is regulated with
particular concern for animal welfare and by using natural foodstuffs. Organic
farming respects the environment's own systems for controlling pests and
diseases in raising crops and livestock and avoids the use of synthetic pesticides,
herbicides, chemical fertilisers, growth hormones, antibiotics and gene manipulation. Instead organic farmers use a range of techniques that help sustain
ecosystems and reduce pollution.

Increased consumer awareness of food safety issues and environmental
concerns have contributed to the growth of organic farming developing into one
of the most dynamic agricultural sectors. It has to be understood as part of a
sustainable farming system and a viable alternative to the more traditional
approaches in agriculture. Union rules came into force in 1992.[80] For organic
farming to enjoy the confidence of consumers, stringent regulations covering
production and quality were necessary, as well as measures to prevent fraudulent
claims to organic status. Present regulations have evolved into a comprehensive
framework for the organic production of crops and livestock and for the labelling,
processing and marketing of organic products.[81]

(b)   Genetically Modified Food and Feed[82]

Modern biotechnology has many applications in the pharmaceutical and   **23–29**
agri-food industries. One example is the use of genetically modified organisms
(GMOs) in the food production chain. GMOs are organisms such as plants,
animals and micro-organisms (bacteria, viruses, etc.) the genetic characteristics
of which have been modified artificially in order to give them a new property (a
plant's resistance to a disease or insect, improvement of food's quality or
nutritional value, increased crop productivity, a plant's tolerance of a herbicide,
etc.). In order to ensure that this development of modern biotechnology, and more
specifically of GMOs, takes place in complete safety, the EU has established a
legal framework comprising various acts. In this field, the Union issued a

---

[79] See General Report 2004, 111 and *http://ec.europa.eu/agriculture/organic/home_en* [accessed
August 23, 2013].
[80] Regulation 2092/91 on organic production of agricultural products and indications referring thereto
on agricultural products and foodstuffs [1991] O.J. L198/1, supplemented by Regulation 1804/1999
[1999] O.J. L219/1; corrigendum [2000] O.J. L83/35. See also Regulation 1452/2003 [2003] O.J.
L206/17, maintaining the derogations provided in Regulation 2092/91 with regard to certain species
of seed and vegetative propagating material and laying down procedural rules and criteria relating to
that derogation.
[81] See, for instance, Regulation 834/07 [2007] O.J. L189/1 on organic production and labelling of
organic products with regard to organic production; labelling and control and implementing detailed
rules: Regulation 889/08 [2008] O.J. L250/1, modified [2008] O.J. L337/80 and [2012] O.J. L41/5 as
regards documentary evidence and amending Regulation 1235/2008, as regards the arrangements for
imports of organic products from the United States.
[82] *http://www.ec.europa.eu./food/food/biotechnology/index_en.htm* [accessed August 23, 2013].

Directive on the contained use of genetically modified micro-organisms,[83] a Directive on the deliberate release into the environment of genetically modified organisms,[84] a Regulation on genetically modified food and feed, a Regulation on trans-boundary movements of genetically modified organisms[85] and a Regulation concerning the traceability and labelling of genetically modified organisms and traceability of food and feed products produced from genetically modified organisms.[86]

See, for instance, Commission decisions authorising the placing on the market of products containing, consisting of, or produced from genetically modified maize.[87]

(c)   Food Safety

23–30   According to the Commission,[88] the food safety policy is based on a series of principles established or updated at the beginning of 2000. These principles, applied in line with the integrated approach "From the Farm to the Fork", specifically include transparency, risk analysis and prevention, the protection of consumer interests and free circulation of safe and high quality products. A certain number of bodies, in particular the European Food Safety Authority[89] are responsible for helping to guarantee food safety. See Ch.30: Culture and Education, Public Health, Consumer Protection for more details.

2.   RURAL DEVELOPMENT

23–31   As indicated at the beginning of this chapter, rural development has become the second pillar of the Union's agricultural policy. In 1999, the Council adopted a "Framework for [Union] support for sustainable rural development"[90] to accompany and complement other instruments of the CAP. The new rural development policy aims at providing for the improvement of agricultural holdings, to guarantee safety and quality of foodstuffs, to ensure fair and stable incomes for farmers, to ensure that environmental issues are taken into account, to develop complementary and alternative activities, to improve living and working conditions, etc. Rural development is based on the following principles:

- the multi-functionality of agriculture over and above the production of foodstuffs; it recognises and encourages the range of services provided by farmers;

---

[83] Directive 90/219 [1990] O.J. L117/1.

[84] Directive 2001/18 [2001] O.J. L106/1, modified [2003] O.J. L268/24; see *Commune de Sausheim* (C-552/07) [2009] E.C.R. 17.02.09 on scope of Directive.

[85] Regulation 1946/03 [2003] O.J. L287/1 *Monsanto* (C-58/10 and C-68/10) E.C.R. 08.09.11 interpretation of Arts12 and 23.

[86] Regulation 1830/03 [2003] O.J. L268/24.

[87] Decisions of October 30, 2009 [2009] O.J. L289/ 21, 25 and 29.

[88] *http://ec.europa.eu/food/food/intro/white_paper_en.htm* [accessed August 23, 2013].

[89] See above Ch.13: Decentralised Agencies and Bodies of the Union.

[90] Regulation 1257/99: [1999] O.J. L160/80, amended [2004] O.J. L91/11.*Hehenberger* (C-188/11) financial support for agri-environmental methods E.C.R. 24.05.12.

- a multi-sectoral and integrated approach to the rural economy in order to diversify activities, create new sources of income and employment and protect the rural heritage;
- flexible aids for rural development based on subsidiarity and promoting decentralisation, consultation at regional, local and partnership level;
- simplified and more accessible legislation.

The main features are:

- strengthening the agricultural and forestry sector;
- improving the competitiveness of rural areas; and
- preserving the environment and rural heritage.

The Union set up a new Union initiative for rural development: LEADER. It was designed to help rural actors consider the long-term potential of their rural region. A total of €5,046.5 million was available for the period 2000–2006.

3. FINANCING THE CAP AND RURAL DEVELOPMENT

As was also mentioned at the beginning of this chapter, one of the basic principles adopted at the onset for the CAP was the financial responsibility of the Union for all the expenses, or "financial solidarity". The European Agricultural Guarantee and Guidance Fund (EAGGF), maybe better known by its French abbreviation, FEOGA, was a Union household name since the very beginning. It was set up in 1962,[91] but it no longer exists as such. It consisted of a guarantee section (expenditures for the price system) and a guidance section (for financing the socio-structural measures). The EAGGF was replaced in 2005 by two Funds: the European Agricultural Guarantee Fund (EAGF) and the European Agricultural Fund for Rural Development (EAFRD).[92] It will be remembered that the European Council approved a European Economic Recovery Plan (EERP) which envisages the initiation of priority action to enable Member States' economies to adjust rapidly to the current challenges and based on a figure amounting to around €200 billion. Of this amount, €1.020 billion is made available to all the Member States via the EAFRD, with a view to developing broadband Internet in rural areas and to strengthen the operations related to priorities laid down in the regulation on support for rural development.[93]

A little history seems called for here to be able to understand references made left and right to the way the CAP was financed. Long acclaimed as the first and

23–32

---

[91] [1962] O. J. 991. Spec. Ed. O.J. 1959–1962, 126.
[92] Regulation 1698/05 on support for rural development by the EAFRD, amended [2009] O.J. L30/100 and L144/3, and Regulation 1974/06 lying down detailed rules for the application of Regulation 1698/05 [2006] O.J. L368/15, amended [2013] O.J. L105/1; see implementing Regulation 147/2012 [2012] O.J. L48/7, as regards the implementation of control procedures as well as cross-compliance in respect of rural development support measures; also Decision 2007/383 fixing the annual breakdown by Member State of the amount for Union support to rural development for the period from January 1, 2007 to December 31, 2013 [2007] O.J. L147/21, amended [2009] O.J.L181/49 and Decision 2009/434 amending Decision 2006/493 [2009] O.J. L144/25 on the minimum amount to be concentrated in the regions eligible under the Convergence Objective.
[93] Regulation 473/09: [2009] O.J. L144/3.

only totally integrated economic sector of the Union, the EAGGF grew over the years to absorb nearly 70 per cent of the total Union budget. It not only became a financial burden but a danger for the Union itself. Some Member States were no longer prepared to contribute to the open-ended system that benefitted only some Member States, mainly France. The ever-increasing agricultural expenditures were one of the reasons, if not the main one, for the various reforms referred to above and especially the 1992 one. However, outside pressures also played a role. As mentioned, the multilateral trade negotiations within the GATT, the Uruguay Round, forced the Union to strengthen its negotiation position by making some of the required adaptations to its policy with the ensuing reductions in agricultural expenditure.

It resulted, as was explained above, in a shift from market price support to direct payments to farmers. It has ensured transparency and somewhat allowed restoring of market balance.

23–33   This however applied only to the Guarantee Section. As described above, the guaranteed price system has been severely curtailed by the latest reform and expenditures were from then on fixed in advance in order to avoid over-spending; this was one of the main results of Agenda 2000, adopted in Berlin, and that put a ceiling on the Communities expenditures for a period of seven years. A new reform became inevitable when the Union decided to enlarge to the countries of Central and Eastern Europe. The latter are still overwhelmingly agricultural and the application of the present CAP to those countries would, as the Commission expresses it mildly, "create difficulties".

A re-orientation of the CAP with less focus on price support and more on direct income support, as well as on rural development and environment policy helped to reduce the price gap and provided support for the structural adjustment process of acceding countries. Finally, adequate implementation and enforcement of the Union acquis in the candidate countries was essential for the protection of plant, animal and public health in an enlarged Union as a whole. It must be accomplished before the movement of agricultural products without border control can be established.

The Fund is administered by the Commission and the Member States, co-operating within the EAGF Committee, which consists of representatives of the Member States and the Commission.[94] The EAGF finances, among others, refunds for export, intervention measures to regulate agricultural markets, direct payments to farmers and contribution to information and promotion for agricultural products. The EAFRD finances contributions to rural development programmes.

23–34   Payments are made by paying agencies accredited by the Member States since only they offer reasonable assurance that the necessary controls have been carried out before granting Union aid to beneficiaries. Maximum expenditure for the EAGF and the EAFRD for each year is laid down by the budgetary authorities by reference to the amounts fixed by the Inter-institutional Agreement and the Financial Perspective set out in Annex 1 to that Agreement.[95] The annual

---

[94] See Decision 1999/468 [1999] O.J. L184/23, modified several times; see above Ch.8: The Commission, laying down procedures for the exercise of powers conferred by the Council.
[95] [2003] O.J. L147/25. See Regulation 1290/05 on the financing of the common agricultural policy [2005] O.J. L2009/1.

breakdown by Member State of the amount for Union support to rural development for the period 2007–2013, and the minimum amount to be concentrated in regions eligible under the Convergence Objective, was fixed by Council decision.[96]

An implementing Decision of 2012 excludes from European Union financing certain expenditures incurred by the Member States under the EAGGE, EAGF and EAFRD.[97]

It can only be hoped that the latest reform will allow an improvement of the market equilibrium and of the internal and international competitiveness of Union agriculture, as well as ensuring a greater stability in farm incomes and a more equitable distribution of the Union's resources. The reform also aimed at helping to secure quality production which is more respectful of the environment and at lower prices for the consumer. It should also mark a new approach to the developing countries, especially in Africa. Agriculture on that continent has suffered over the years a very important reduction in agricultural production because of the competition from subsidised agricultural products from the Union, both within it and in the world. Here more than anywhere else the Union should head the African request of "no aid, but trade": the African countries could produce at much lower cost and equal quality, if given a chance to compete on equal ground with Union producers.

FURTHER READING

B. Sheridan, *EU Biotechnology Law and Practice. Regulating Genetically Modified and Novel Food Products* (Palladian Law Publishing, 2001).   **23–35**

J. A. Usher, E. C., *Agricultural Law*, 2nd edn (Oxford University Press, 2002).

Melaku Geboye Desta, *The law of international trade in agricultural products* (Kluwer, 2002).

Naomi Salmon, "A European perspective on the precautionary principle. Food safety and the free trade imperative of the WTO" (2003) E.L.Rev. 138.

Raymond O'Rourke, *European Food Law* (Palladian Law Publishing, 2002).

Yearly Report of the European Commission, *The Agricultural Situation in the European Union* (Office for Official Publications of the European Communities, Luxembourg).

---

[96] Decision 2006/636 [2006] O.J. L261/32, amended [2010] O.J. L106/13.
[97] [2012] O.J. L244/11.

CHAPTER 24

The Common Fisheries Policy (CFP)[1] and Marine Policy

As the Commission indicated:

24–01

"[F]ishing and aquaculture are two of the most important uses of the sea. As well as providing a healthy and enjoyable source of food, they create much-needed jobs in coastal areas and promote the social and economic well-being of the European Union's fishing regions."[2]

The Commission sees it as its task, among others in this field, to ensure sustainable, i.e. responsible, fishing and aquaculture and secure the future of the fishing industry through the Common Fisheries Policy. Fishing and aquaculture activities are regulated also through international co-operation in order to allow for the continuous renewal of stocks and the protection of the marine ecosystem. The competence of the Union in regard to fisheries is based on the same Treaty provisions as those for agriculture[3] of which they are a part: there are no specific provisions regarding fisheries and/or maritime policies—the TFEU specifies that:

"[R]eference to the common agricultural policy or to agriculture and the use of the term agricultural shall be understood as also referring to fisheries having regard to the specific characteristics of this sector".[4]

Nevertheless, fisheries acquired a momentum of their own and developed into an autonomous policy, which is examined below.

24–02

Since the Second World War, fishery products have become an important food resource, and although this sector only provides a few hundred thousand jobs, compared with millions in agriculture, the industry is also of crucial economic importance to many otherwise disadvantaged coastal areas. It was not until 1970 that the first decisions concerning fisheries were taken by the Union, which used its powers in the following fields. The CFP is based on the principle of common access to all fishing grounds in the Union, monitoring fishing activities, the

---

[1] Arts 38–44 TFEU.

[2] *http://ec.europa.eu/dgs/maritimeaffairs_fisheries/about_us/mission_statement/index_en.htm* [accessed August 23, 2013]; some of the data in this chapter has been borrowed from this website.

[3] See *France v United Kingdom* (141/78) [1979] E.C.R. 2923; [1990] 1 C.M.L.R. 6. The shared powers of the Union and the Member States in fishing matters are provided for in Art.4(1)(d) TFEU and Art.38(3) and Annex I to the Treaty, which includes fisheries within the sphere of the common agricultural policy.

[4] Art.38(1)2 TFEU.

common organisation of the market,[5] agreements with third countries and structural measures. It came into being in 1983 and takes account of the biological, social and economic dimension of fishing. Its main aspects will be briefly examined hereunder, they are: conservation of fish stocks; the common market organisation; agreements with third countries; and structural measures. The Union has a new CFP since 2003 (date of the reform of the PAC); indeed, a new policy was needed to ensure conservation of resources, protection of the marine environment, economic viability of the fishing fleets and good quality food to consumers. As the Commission put it: too many fish had been taken from the sea by fishing, leaving too few adult fish to reproduce and rebuild the stocks. Today, several important fish stocks, such as cod, are on the verge of collapse. Beyond the damage done to fish stocks, such a situation has a significant negative effect on fisherman's income, the balance of the marine ecosystem and the supply of fish to the market.

1. ACCESS TO FISHING GROUNDS

24–03 Access to coastal waters, i.e. coastal bands 6 to 12 miles deep, is reserved for fishermen from local ports to protect their fishing rights and help ensure that fishing remains an essential part of the local economy. However, the restriction was not absolute: small fishing boats from a given Member State, which have traditionally operated in the coastal waters of another continued to do so.

Outside the 12-mile band, the general principle of free access to fishing grounds still applies, except for predetermined protected areas where the right to fish is restricted or completely withdrawn. Corresponding decisions are based on biological advice and implemented to protect rich breeding grounds of fish for human consumption.

In 1995, a new system of fishing licences—a kind of identity paper—was introduced for Union fishing boats operating in and outside Union waters. Moreover, a system of fishing permits provides a management mechanism to limit the fishing effort of individual vessels having access to certain fisheries.

2. CONSERVATION OF FISH STOCKS

24–04 Fish stocks need to renew themselves as fish die through natural causes and fishing: to have enough mature fish to renew stocks, small fish must be left to grow and reproduce. It is most surprising, however, that this evidence is not understood and often not accepted by those most closely connected with these products of the sea, i.e. the fishermen. Indeed, in many cases they oppose, by all possible means, the limitations necessarily imposed on their catches to allow renewal of stocks.

---

[5] Regulation 3759/92 on the common organisation of the market in fishery and aquaculture products [1992] O.J. L388/1. The establishment of a common market organisation is based on producer organisations, a price support mechanism and protection for the Union market, a structural policy, conservation and administration of resources, and relations with third countries.

To limit the capture of small fish, a number of technical rules have been adopted by the Union: minimum mesh sizes, certain areas are closed, some fishing gears are banned, selective techniques are imposed, minimum fish sizes are imposed and catches and landings have to be recorded in special log books. Conservation was ensured by the annual fixing of Total Allowable Catches (TACs)[6] for all species threatened because of overfishing,[7] taking into account the international agreements and arrangements made with interested third countries. This was complemented by the setting of long-term objectives for attaining and/or maintaining safe levels of adult fish.[8]

Various regulations were adopted in specific sectors and places, such as: measures to reduce incidental catches of cetaceans in fisheries,[9] transposition of the new technical recommendations of the International Commission for the Conservation of Atlantic Tunas,[10] establishment of a definitive plan for the recovery of cod stocks[11] and for Northern hake stock.[12] The importance of Mediterranean fisheries was recognised by an ambitious Action Plan and conservation measures relating to waters around Malta.[13]

The TACs are divided among the Member States, in the form of quotas, in pursuance of the principle of relative stability that allows for a global equilibrium among the fishing fleets. Concretely speaking, each Member State concerned keeps a fixed percentage for each stock as originally established.[14]   **24–05**

The accession of new Member States required, of course, an adaptation of the existing quotas especially in so far as they concerned also non-Union waters.[15] After accession, Spain and Portugal, for instance, contested the principle of relative stability before the Court, which however, rejected most of their complaints.[16] Another problem resulted from the so-called quota hopping. This was the transfer of fishing boats from one Member State to the flag of another in order to use the quota allocated to the latter. Certain Member States therefore restricted access to their quotas. The Court has admitted that conditions be imposed in the sense that the boat in question should have some economic ties with that country; it did not admit, however, restrictions based on the nationality

---

[6] *Commission v Council* (C-25/94) [1996] E.C.R. I–1469: exclusive competence of the Union in matters relating to conservation of the biological resources of the sea.

[7] For 2009 see Regulation 43/09 fixing for 2009 the fishing opportunities and associated conditions for certain fish stocks and groups of fish stocks, applicable in Community waters and, for Community vessels, in waters where catch limitations are required [2009] O.J. L22/1, corrigendum [2009] O.J. L124/75; for 2010, Regulation 23/2010 [2010] O.J. L21/1.

[8] See Regulation 2371/2002 on the conservation and sustainable exploitation of fisheries resources under the CFP [2002] O.J. L358/59, modified [2012] O.J. L343/30.

[9] Regulation 812/04 O.J. L150/12.

[10] Regulation 831/04 O.J. L127/33.

[11] Regulation 423/04 O.J. L70/8, modified [2009] O.J. L343/1.

[12] Regulation 811/04 O.J. L185/1.

[13] Regulation 813/04 O.J. L150/32.

[14] Regulation 894/87 relating to technical measures for the conservation of fisheries resources [1997] O.J. L132/1, modified [1998] O.J. L171/17.

[15] Regulation 170/83 is no longer in force. See Regulation 1796/94 [1994] O.J. L187/1.

[16] *Portugal and Spain v Council* (Joined Cases C-63/90 and C-67/90) [1992] E.C.R. I–5073.

or residence of the crew, limitations to the right to land the captures in other Member States or restrict normal fishing activities.[17]

At the end of 2002, the Council adopted various regulations on conservation measures.[18] On that basis, the Council established financial measures for the implementation of the common fisheries policy and in the area of the Law of the Sea.[19]

In 2008, the Council adopted a dozen regulations fixing, for instance, fishing opportunities for certain fish stocks, cod fishing quotas in the Baltic sea, in the Black sea, for certain deep-sea fish, etc.[20]

3. MONITORING FISHING ACTIVITIES

24–06   The Member States are in charge of implementing the preservation measures taken on their territory and in their waters and, for the vessels flying their flag, outside their territorial waters. The task of the Commission was to monitor their correct application until the end of 2005, when the Union inspection system became operative.[21] The Commission also monitors compliance with TACs (Total Acceptable Catches) and quotas in Union and in certain international waters; the same applies to fishery agreements with third countries and international agreements. The Commission also contributes to the financing of programmes presented by Member States for the acquisition and improvement of means of monitoring and inspection.[22] Satellite technology to check vessel movements is used for all 15 metres vessels.

In 2008, a regulation was adopted establishing a Union system to prevent, deter and eliminate illegal, unreported and unregulated fishing.[23] This Regulation aims to ensure the viability of the fish stocks and improve the situation of Union fishermen facing unfair competition from illegal products. Another regulation updates the system of authorisation for fishing activities of Union fishing vessels outside Union waters and of third-country vessels in Union waters.[24] It is intended to better align Union authorisation procedures with international obligations. A new Union framework for the collection, management and use of

---

[17] *Agegate* (C-3/87) [1989] E.C.R. 4459; [1990] 1 C.M.L.R. 366 and *Jaderow* (216/87) [1989] E.C.R. 4509; [1991] 2 C.M.L.R. 556; *Commission v United Kingdom* (C-246/89) [1991] E.C.R. I–4585; *R v Secretary of State for Transport Ex p., Factortame* (C-221/89) [1991] E.C.R. I–3905.

[18] Regulation 2371/02 on the conservation and sustainable exploitation of fish stocks under the common fisheries policy [2002] O.J. L358/59 and Regulation 742/2006 adapting certain fish quotas pursuant to Regulation 847/96 introducing additional conditions for year-to-year management for TACs and quotas [2006] O.J. L130/7, modified [2009] O.J. L343/1. Regulation 2347/02 on specific access requirements and associated conditions for deep-sea stocks [2002] O.J. L351/28 and Regulation 254/02, measures to be applicable in 2002 for the recovery of the stock of cod in the Irish sea [2002] O.J. L41/1.

[19] Regulation 871/2006 [2006] O.J. L160/1.

[20] See General Report 2008, 118.

[21] Regulation 2241/87 establishing certain control measures for fishing activities [1987] O.J. L207/1. See Regulation 1224/09 establishing a Union control system for ensuring compliance with the rules of the Common Fisheries Policy and Commission implementing Regulation [2011] O.J. L112/1.

[22] Council Decision 89/631 [1989] O.J. L364/64 modified [1992] O.J. L213/35 extending the programme to include the Mediterranean. It was extended by Decision 2001/431 [2001] O.J. L154/22.

[23] Regulation 1005/08 [2008] O.J. L286. Borrowed from General Report 2008, 117.

[24] Regulation 1006/08 [2008] O.J. L286.

data in the fisheries sector and support for scientific advice was also issued[25]; it covers the whole process from the collection of data at ports or at sea to their use by the end-users. Another regulation provides a temporary specific action aiming to promote the restructuring of the fishing fleets affected by the economic crisis.[26]

See also the Regulation establishing a list of vessels engaged in illegal, unreported and unregulated fishing.[27]

4. AQUACULTURE

Aquaculture means the rearing or culture of aquatic organisms using techniques designed to increase the production of the organisms in question beyond the natural capacity of the environment; the organisms remain the property of a natural or legal person throughout the rearing or culture stage, up to and including harvesting.[28] The principal aquaculture products of the EU are fish (trout, salmon, sea bass, sea bream) and molluscs (mussels, oysters and clams). Aquaculture constitutes 17 per cent of the volume and 27 per cent of the value of the total fishery production of the EU. It is essentially made up of three sub-sectors: freshwater fish farming—unfortunately there is limited demand for freshwater fish; marine mollusc farming—locally extremely important in economic terms and for job creation; marine fish farming—the most recent development and the most complex, it suffers from over-production and environmental problems since fish are fed with industrial feed.

Aquaculture is spread widely over the EU and often in rural areas which depend on fishing. The EU has a vast legal armour[29] on aquaculture; it has to cope with problems in the context of health protection, environment and market instability.

24-07

5. THE COMMON ORGANISATION OF THE MARKET

The common organisation of the market in fishery and aquaculture products was set up in 1970 with the following objectives:

24-08

- applying common marketing standards;
- establishing producers' organisations;

---

[25] Regulation 199/08 [2008] O.J. L60.

[26] Regulation 744/08: [2008] O.J. L202.

[27] Regulation 468/10 [2010] O.J. L131/22.

[28] Regulation 1263/99 [1999] O.J. L161/54 and Regulation 2792/99 laying down the detailed rules and arrangements regarding Union structural assistance in the fishery sector [1999] O.J. L337/10 were replaced by Regulation 1198/06 (the basic Regulation) which was implemented by Regulation 498/07 [2007] O.J. L120/1 laying down detailed rules for the implementation of Regulation 1198/06 on the European Fisheries Fund.

[29] See, for instance, Directive 1999/29 on the undesirable substances and products in animal nutrition [1999] O.J. L6/45, modified [2001] O.J. L115/32; Regulation 466/2001 setting maximum levels for certain contaminants in foodstuffs [2001] O.J. L77/1, amended [2001] O.J. L321/1; Directive 91/67 on measures governing the placing on the market of aquaculture animals and products [1991] O.J. L46/1, amended [2003] O.J. L122/1; and Directive 93/53 on measures for the control of certain fish diseases [1993] O.J. L175/28, amended [2001] O.J. L99/11.

- instituting a price support system based on intervention mechanisms or compensation mechanisms; and
- establishing a regime for trade with non-member countries.

It was, as was the rest of agriculture, reformed in 1992. In 1993, a new regulation[30] strengthened the controls and extended monitoring beyond the catching of fish, to other aspects of the CFP, such as structures, fish marketing and aquaculture. In addition, all links in the fishery chain from producer to consumer, whether catches themselves, landings, transport or actual sales, are now monitored and documented. This provides for much more detailed checks of the data recorded in the fishermen's logbooks. Penalties are decided by national courts. They may range from heavy fines, confiscation of fishing nets, of fish caught and even of the boat itself, to temporary suspension or permanent withdrawal of fishing licences.

Various regulations were adopted to tighten the control on fishing activities: for instance, electronic transmission of information on fishing activities and for remote sensing,[31] implementing rules on the Union fleet policy,[32] detailed provisions regarding a satellite-based vessel monitoring system.[33]

24–09   The Union also encourages research with various programmes such as the Fisheries and Aquaculture Research (FAR) and AIR, an integrated programme in agriculture and agro-industry.

A new Common Organisation for the Markets in fishery and aquaculture products was adopted in 2000 and entered into force in 2001. It aims to:

- encourage fisherman to fish only what can be sold;
- strengthen industry organisations, particularly Producers' Organisations, and make them more competitive;
- enable consumers to know what they are buying;
- ensure a better match between supply and demand; and
- protect employment in the catching sector as well as in the processing industry.

To achieve these aims, new measures were introduced:

- obligation for the Producers' Organisations to set up fishing programmes to adapt supply to demand;
- support for the development of inter-professional organisations;
- updating the intervention mechanism[34];
- the obligation for retailers to provide better information to consumers; and
- improving supply conditions for the processing industry.

---

[30] Regulation 2847/93 establishing a control system applicable to the common fisheries policy, adapted for bluefin tuna by Regulation 446/08 [2008] O.J. L134/11. See *Commission v Italy* (C-249/08) [2009] E.C.R. I-173.
[31] Regulation 1461/03 [2003] O.J. L208/14.
[32] Regulation 1438/03 [2003] O.J. L204/21.
[33] Regulation 2244/03 [2003] O.J. L333/17 implementing Regulation 2371/02 on the conservation and sustainable exploitation of fisheries resources under the CFP [2004] O.J. L240/17.
[34] Regulation 2792/1999 (quoted above).

6. AGREEMENTS WITH THIRD COUNTRIES AND INTERNATIONAL CONVENTIONS

Since 1976, the Union has been exclusively competent to handle international **24–10** fishing negotiations. Fishing agreements were signed with a number of third countries[35] in order to safeguard traditional fishing rights of Union vessels or to seek new opportunities.

Indeed, without those agreements the general extension of fishing zones to 200 miles and the resulting substantial reduction in fishing opportunities would have had serious repercussions for Union fishermen. Furthermore, in the present circumstances of surplus capacity in Union waters, these agreements represent a means of reducing fishing efforts in those waters. Multilateral agreements have also been concluded with a view to the Union's participation in the international agreements covering the North-West,[36] North-East, East, Central and South-East Atlantic: the North-Atlantic Salmon Conservation Organisation (NASCO), the North-East Atlantic Fisheries[37] Commission (NEAFC), The Southern Indian Ocean Fisheries Agreement,[38] the International Commission for the South East Atlantic Fisheries (ICSEAF), the Fishery Committee for the Eastern-Central Atlantic (CECAF), the International Whaling Commission, etc.[39]

To date, the Union has concluded several dozen agreements with countries from Africa[40] and the Indian Ocean and from the North Atlantic area. In the latter area problems developed mainly with Canada, which forced the Council to regulate access and catches for the North-West Atlantic Fisheries Organisation (NAFO) Convention area.[41]

Different categories of fisheries agreements exist, which are distinguished according to the type of concession offered: reciprocal arrangements; access to surplus stock; access to stocks in return for market access; access to stocks in return for financial compensation; and access to stocks in return for payment and market access. For more details see the annual General Reports published by the Commission in February of each year.[42]

---

[35] See various General Reports.
[36] See Regulation 1386/07 laying down conservation and enforcement measures applicable in the Regulatory Area of North-West Atlantic Fisheries Organization [2007] O.J. L318/1, modified [2008] O.J. L157/1, amended [2008] O.J. L157/1.
[37] See, for instance, Regulation 770/04 [2004] O.J. L123/4. Also [2012] O.J. L136/41 Schemes of control and enforcement.
[38] [2006] O.J. L196/14.
[39] See General Report 1989, 270. See, for instance the Convention on the Conservation and management of High Seas Fishery Resources in the South Pacific Ocean [2012] O.J. L67/1.
[40] See, for instance, fishery partnership agreements with Côte d'Ivoire: Regulation 242/08 [2008] O.J. L75/51; and Guinea-Bissau: Regulation 241/08 [2008] O.J. L75/49.
[41] Regulation 3927/92 laying down certain conservation and management measures for fishery resources in the Regulatory Area as defined in the Convention on Future Multilateral Co-operation in the North-West Atlantic Fisheries [1992] O.J. L397/67 and Regulation 3928/92 establishing a NAFO pilot observer scheme applicable to Union fishing vessels operating on the Regulatory Area of the North-West Atlantic Fisheries Organisation (NAFO) [1992] O.J. L397/78.
[42] General Report 2002, 442 and 443. See for instance Council Regulation 1765/03 on the conclusion of an agreement with the government of the republic of Guinea setting out the fishing opportunities and financial contribution [2003] O.J. L256/1.See, for instance, the Convention on the Conservation and Management of High Seas Fishery Resources in the South Pacific Ocean, signed by the Union [2011] O.J. L81/1.

7. STRUCTURAL MEASURES—THE EUROPEAN FISHERIES FUND[43]

24–11   These measures help the fishing sector to adapt to present needs. Funding is available for projects in all branches and for market and development research, for modernisation of fishing fleets as well as getting rid of excess fishing capacity. The first rules laying down a common structural policy for the fishing industry were enacted in 1970.[44] Following enlargement, a new regulation was adopted in 1976.[45] Those provisions enabled the Union to support financially, through the agricultural fund, fish processing and marketing development projects, building of inshore fishing vessels, refitting of vessels and extension of fish farming schemes. In 1977, common measures were adopted to improve the conditions under which agricultural and fishery products are processed and marketed[46] and in 1983 the Council adopted common measures for restructuring, modernising and developing the fishing industry and for developing aquaculture[47] and measures to encourage exploratory fishing.[48] Once again new structural aspects of the fisheries policy were adopted, this time in 1986,[49] to finance the construction of fishing vessels, aquaculture and structural work in coastal waters, modernisation of fishing vessels and exploratory fishing voyages, while at the same time financing programmes to reduce the capacity of the Member States' fishing fleets to bring them into line with the available fish stocks.[50]

The actions relating to the transformation and the commercialisation of products of fishery and aquaculture have as their objective the modernisation and the rationalisation of the factories, mainly sanitary conditions. Following the reform of the Structural Funds, the Union established, within that framework, a Financial Instrument for Fisheries Guidance (FIFG).[51] This permitted a doubling of the available resources. The Union adopted a regulation in 2002 lying down the detailed rules and arrangements regarding Union structural assistance in the fisheries sector.[52]

The Union fisheries suffer from overcapacity of fleets in comparison to diminishing resources; it is essential to re-establish equilibrium. This can only be achieved through several activities: the Union must increase the effectiveness of the TACs—reinforce the monitoring, reduce the fishing capacity; compensate the

---

[43] Regulation 1198/06 [2006] O.J. L223/1 on the European Fishery Fund.

[44] Regulation 2141/70 [1970] O.J. L236/1.

[45] Regulation 101/76 [1976] O.J. L20/19.

[46] Regulation 355/77 [1977] O.J. L51/1.

[47] Regulation 2908/83 [1983] O.J. L290/1 and Regulation 3166/83 L316/1.

[48] Regulation 2909/83 [1983] O.J. L290/9.

[49] Regulation 4028/86 [1986] O.J. L376/7.

[50] General Report 1988, 297 and Directive 83/515 [1983] O.J. L290/15).

[51] Regulation 2080/93 laying down provisions for implementing Regulation 2052/88 as regards the financial instrument of fisheries guidance [1993] O.J. L193/1 and Regulation 4253/88:*Chambre de Commerce et d'Industrie de l'Indre* (C- 465/10) E.C.R. 21.12.11: concept of "irregularity" and "continuous irregularity". See *Vereniging Nationaal Overlegorgaan Sociale Werkvoorziening A.O.* (Joined Cases C-383/06, C-384/06, C-385/06 and C-386/06) [2008] E.C.R. I–1597, concerning obligations of Member States to recover any amount lost as a result of irregularity or negligence.

[52] Regulation 2369/02 [2002] O.J. L 358/49. See also Regulation 498/2007 laying down detailed rules for the implementation of the European Fisheries Fund [2007] O.J. L120/1.

socio-economic consequence with accompanying measures; and, at the same time, guarantee a constant supply at reasonable prices. Important changes are required while the Union, on the other hand, needs to import huge quantities to satisfy the internal demand.

Union financial measures were established for the implementation of the common fisheries policy and in the area of the law of the sea.[53]   **24–12**

Mention must also be made of the adoption of the PESCA Union initiative[54] that seeks to generate clearly focused projects to help the fishing sector to adapt and coastal areas to diversify their economic activities[55] and of the Multi-annual Programme to restructure the Union fishing industry providing for cuts in fleet tonnage and engine power. Member States finally accepted the need for a common set of vessel measurements and agreed on the creation of a Union register of vessels to make the information on fishing capacity more open and easy to check. This had been lacking due to Member States' reluctance to accept the inevitable. However, cuts are now expressed in "fishing efforts" calculated by multiplying the capacity of a fishing vessel expressed in tonnage and engine power by the number of days spent at sea. Furthermore, to protect depleted stock from over-fishing, the totality of fish stocks was divided into three groups and Union vessels were also split into groups or "segments", according to the main fisheries. These measures were designed to match stocks and vessels.

On the basis of a scientific study (the Gulland Report), the Commission made recommendations for cuts and the Council agreed to reduce fishing efforts for fish living at the bottom of the sea (demersal) by 20 per cent (the Commission had recommended 30 per cent) and flat fish (benthic) by 15 per cent (the Commission had recommended 20 per cent). Fishing efforts can also be reduced, of course, by scrapping vessels or keeping them in port for set periods of time. The choice was left to the Member States; all chose to eliminate excess capacity and, as a result, overall fleet was cut by 7 per cent.[56]

The Multi-annual Guidance Programme (MAGP) IV (1997–2001) further   **24–13** reduced fishing efforts. The validity of this MAGP was prolonged by the Council.[57] Actions for the fisheries sector outside Objective 1 region[58] will be supported, according to the decisions taken by the Berlin European Council of March 24–25, 1999, by the Financial Instrument for Fisheries Guidance (FIFG) with an amount of €1.1 billion over the period 2000–2006. A new European Fisheries Fund (EFF) was established in 2006[59] establishing a framework for Union support for a sustainable development of the fisheries sector, fisheries areas and inland fishing.

---

[53] Regulation 861/06.

[54] See Ch.32: Regional Policy/Economic, Social and Territorial Cohesion—The Europe 2020 Strategy.

[55] In 1997, this initiative was endowed with 21,456 million ECUs. See also Decision 97/292 on a specific measure to encourage Italian fishermen to diversify out of certain fishing activities [1997] O.J. L121/20.

[56] See General Report 2002, 435.

[57] See Ch.32: Regional Policy/Economic, Social and Territorial Cohesion—The Europe 2020 Strategy.

[58] Regulation 1198/2006 [2006] O.J. L223/1.

[59] Regulation 639/2004 on the management of fishing fleets registered in the Union outermost regions [2004] O.J. L102/9 and Regulation 2104/04 laying down detailed implementation rules [2004] O.J. L365/19, corrected [2005] O.J. L252/6, amended [2008] O.J. L327/1.

With regard to State aids to the fisheries sector, see the de minimis Regulation.[60]

In 2004, the Council introduced special arrangements for the management of the fishing fleets of the outermost regions in order to take account of their structural, social and economic situation.

The European Fisheries Fund (EFF) was set up in 2002 and renewed in 2006[61]; it forms part of the Structural Funds; for more information see Ch.32: Regional Policy/Economic, Social and Territorial Cohesion—The Europe 2020 Strategy.

8.   MARINE ENVIRONMENTAL POLICY[62]

24–14   In line with the Decision of Parliament and the Council of 2002 laying down the Sixth Community Environment Action Programme,[63] a thematic strategy for the protection and conservation of the marine environment was developed with the overall aim of promoting sustainable use of the seas and conserving marine ecosystems.

The establishment of marine protected areas, including areas already designated or to be designated under the Directive on the conservation of natural habitats and of wild fauna and flora (Habitats Directive),[64] and under the Directive on the conservation of wild birds (Birds Directive)[65] and also under international and regional agreements to which the Union[66] or Member States concerned are Parties, constitute an important contribution to the achievement of good environmental status under the 2008 Directive establishing a framework for Union action in the fields of marine environmental policy (Marine Strategy Framework Directive).[67]

The Directive only applies to Member States with coastal waters.

The Commission is empowered[68] to lay down criteria and methodological standards to be used by the Member States and to adopt specifications and standardised methods for monitoring and assessment.

---

[60] Regulation 875/07 [2007] O.J. L193/6.

[61] Regulation 1198/06 [2006] O.J. L223/1.

[62] Regulation 744/08 [2008] O.J. L202/1.

[63] [2002] O.J. L242/1.

[64] [1992] O.J. L206/7, amended by Directive 2006/105 [2006] O.J. L363/368.

[65] [1979] O.J. L103/1, amended by Directive 2006/105 (quoted above).

[66] Convention on the Protection of the Marine Environment in the Baltic Sea Area [1994] O.J.L73/19; Convention on the Protection of the Marine Environment of the North-East Atlantic [1998] O.J. L104/1, Convention on the Protection of the Marine Environment and the Coastal Region of the Mediterranean [1977] O.J. L240/1, [1999] O.J. L322/32, [1983] O.J. L67/1; and [1999] O.J. L322/18.

[67] [2008] O.J. L164/19. The above passage is quoted from that Directive.

[68] Since those measures are of general scope and are designed to amend non-essential elements, the measures must be adopted in accordance with the regulatory procedure with scrutiny (Decision 1999/468, Art.5a).

9.   INTEGRATED MARITIME POLICY

A programme to support the further development of an Integrated Maritime   **24–15**
Policy was established in 2011.[69]

---

[69] Regulation 1255/11 [2011] O.J. L321/1.

PART 5

POLICIES OF THE UNION AND THE MEMBER STATES

CHAPTER 25

Taxation

1. INTRODUCTION

Taxation is an issue that generally interests taxable undertakings and persons   **25–01**
highly; and seeking to reduce one's tax burden lawfully is a legitimate purpose.
Taxation is also of high importance to public authorities as without the
appropriate tax incomes, they are not able to provide the services and goods that
citizens demand from them. A modern welfare State cannot provide social
security, efficient infrastructure, proper education, just to give a few examples,
without disposing of a proper tax base. Moreover, citizens collectively and the
public authorities are normally in agreement that tax evasion must be hindered;
tax evasion makes public authorities lose tax revenue and makes tax complying
citizens pay more tax, to compensate for the loss.

Taxation is obviously at the very core of the sovereign powers of a State; it is
one of the prerogatives for which national parliaments historically have fought
heavily. There is therefore a reticence on behalf of the Member States to cede
powers in taxation matters to the Union. This reticence is reflected in the Treaty
in the sense that there are hardly provisions of primary law that explicitly concern
taxation, and adoption of harmonisation measures in the field of taxation requires
unanimity in the Council, i.e. adoption of measures of secondary law is difficult.[1]
However, there is a growing recognition, not just in the Member States and in the
Union, but also elsewhere, for instance in the OECD, that globalisation and
liberalisation of capital movements requires enhanced co-operation in tax
matters. Capital will, all things being equal, seek to the places where it is taxed
less, and States may seek to attract capital by lowering in particular corporate
taxes.[2] Resourceful multinational companies may be able to set up tax
arrangements so that ultimately they may pay extremely limited tax, in some
cases even just a few per cent on incomes of billions. Although such
arrangements do not imply tax evasion, such a situation is politically not
sustainable and the issue is in spring 2013 becoming a top priority of the political
agenda in the Union. On the other hand, lack of co-ordination or harmonisation of
national tax systems may hit hard at persons and undertakings—for instance
SMEs—with insufficient know-how as to reduce their tax burden; they may have
to pay tax on the same income in more jurisdictions.

---

[1] See Ch.26: Approximation of Laws.
[2] Over the last decades corporate tax rates have declined considerably in OECD countries. There is
no similar trend as concerns personal taxation. There may thus be a "race to the bottom" as concerns
corporate tax; an expression generally used to express that States, holding that they are in competition
amongst others to attract business, lower taxes or regulatory standards.

25–02   The Treaty contains a provision that deals explicitly with taxation, on a substantive level, i.e. it is a substantive norm that is not just limited to providing competence for the Union to enact secondary law.[3] The provision prohibits discrimination in taxation of goods and it is mirrored on a similar provision that is found in the WTO context.[4] The provision just represents the bare minimum for dealing with tax issues in cross-border contexts, namely that national provisions may not discriminate domestic goods and imported goods. The provision has direct effect and it is presented below.[5]

Next, it will be recalled from the Introduction to Part III of this book: The Internal Market, that the Treaty provisions on the four freedoms contain a prohibition on discrimination and other restrictions. For many years it was not clear that these provisions could have an impact on national tax rules. However, as from the late 1980s and the beginning of the 1990s it became clear from the Court's case law that national tax rules were within the scope of the provisions.[6] This case law has grown considerably in importance since then. An introduction to that case law is given below. National tax measures that imply State aid are dealt with in Ch.22: Competition Policy.

After the presentation of the provisions of primary law follows an overview of the main measures of secondary law that the Union has enacted in this field.

2.   THE PROHIBITION OF DISCRIMINATION IN INTERNAL TAXATION OF GOODS

25–03   Article 110(1) TFEU prohibits the direct or indirect imposition of tax on products from other Member States[7] or of "any internal taxation of any kind in excess" of that imposed on similar domestic products. Article 110(2) TFEU prohibits internal taxation "of such a nature as to afford indirect protection to other products". Despite its apparent simplicity, this Treaty provision has given rise to an abundance of case law.

In the first place, it is useful to delimit the term "taxation". The fact that the Treaty refers to "any kind", indicates that it must be interpreted widely. This was confirmed by the Court.[8] Even an import surcharge, which, at first sight, might be viewed as a charge having an equivalent effect to a customs duty, must be, according to the Court, assessed in the light of the tax provisions, where the surcharge is added to a general duty that forms part of a general system of

---

[3] Art.110 TFEU.

[4] Art.III of the General Agreement on Tariffs and Trade (GATT) 1994 which mirrors a provision in the original GATT.

[5] See for instance *Finck-Frucht v Hauptzollamt München-Landsbergerstrasse* (27/67) [1968] E.C.R. 223; [1968] C.M.L.R. 187.

[6] See for instance *Commission v France (Tax credits)* (270/83) [1986] E.C.R. 273 and *Schumacker* (C-279/93) [1995] E.C.R. I-225.

[7] The expression "other Member States" includes products from third countries in free circulation; see *Co-Frutta* (193/85) [1987] E.C.R. 2085.

[8] *Schottle v Finanzamt Freudenstadt* (20/76) [1977] E.C.R. 247; [1977] 2 C.M.L.R. 98: taxation imposed indirectly on products must be interpreted as including a charge imposed on international transport of goods by road according to the distance covered on the national territory and the weight of the goods.

internal dues.[9] Obviously, stamp duties[10] and fees for a mark on precious metal[11] constitute internal taxation. A distinction between the latter and customs duties and charges having equivalent effect should be possible on the simple basis that the latter are levied at the occasion of a product crossing a border between Member States. Internal taxes, on the other hand, are levied as part of a general system that is applicable to both imported and national products.[12] The distinction, however, is not always easy to draw in practice.

When thinking of discrimination in taxation, what first comes to mind are differences in rates. The wording of Art.110(1) also leads the thought in that direction, given the terms "in excess of". However, it must be noted that the discrimination ban applies not just to rates but to the taxation system as such. Thus, rules for determining the taxable basis and for levying the tax also come within the scope of Art.110.[13] Moreover, even if the taxation system as such does not discriminate between imported and national products, it may be caught by the ban if the proceeds of the tax are ear-marked for the national production. Taxes that are levied on a certain sector of the economy and the proceeds of which are ear-marked for the same sector of the economy are commonly referred to as "parafiscal charges". With an example: a State considers that the production of oak trees should be promoted; however, the State finds that the industry itself should bear the costs. So the State imposes a levy on imports and domestic production of oak trees and sets up a body to select national firms who shall benefit from the income that the levy brings in. In this situation, the national product and the imported product are treated equally as concerns imposition; both have to pay the same levy. However, the Court has held that the fact that the proceeds are channelled back to national producers, albeit not all, makes the tax objectionable under Union law. According to the Court, if the proceeds are fully channelled back to the national industry, the parafiscal charge implies a charge with equivalent effect to an import duty; if the proceeds are only partially channelled back to the national industry, the parafiscal charge comes within Art.110.[14]

---

[9] *Haahr Petroleum v Abenra Havn* (C-90/94) [1997] E.C.R. I-4085; [1998] 1 C.M.L.R. 771.

[10] *Commission v Belgium* (77/69) [1970] E.C.R. 237; [1974] 1 C.M.L.R. 203: the rate was the same, but the basis on which it was applied resulted in heavier taxes for the imported products.

[11] *Statens Kontrol v Larsen* (142/77) [1978] E.C.R. 1543; [1979] 2 C.M.L.R. 680.

[12] Taxes on registration of cars are an example. The fact that triggers the taxation is *not* that a car is imported; it is the regisration of the car that triggers the taxation and that applies equally to national and imported cars. Many Member States do not have a national car industry. That does not alter that car registration taxes form part of an internal, general system, see for instance *FinckFrucht* (quoted above, fn.5). See also *Commission v Denmark (Car Registration Duties)* (C-47/88) [1990] E.C.R. I-4509 where it was not contested that the Danish system for car registration duties fell under Art.110 even though there is no production of cars in Denmark. If there is no relevant comparable national products to the imported product, there cannot be discrimination under Art.110.

[13] See for instance *Iannelli & Volpi* (74/76) [1977] E.C.R. 557.

[14] *Celulose Beira Industrial* (C-266/91) [1993] E.C.R. I-4337. The channelling of the proceeds to national industry also constitutes State aid. As mentioned in Ch.22: Competition Policy, State aid must be notified to the Commission. In its examination the Commission will detect the problems that the State aid represents under Arts 30 or 110 TFEU—and which bars the Commission from approving of the aid—and thus such issues will in practice be sorted out before any approval of the aid. Thus, in practice, issues concerning parafiscal charges typically arise when the State has not complied with its notification obligation.

25–04   The ban of Art.110 does not only apply to the taxation system and the destination of the proceeds. It may also apply to the criminal sanctions that the national legal order establishes for offences against its rules in tax matters. An example is the case of a German citizen by the name of Drexl who imported a car into Italy for his private use, without settling VAT. He was prosecuted for that offence and the national court submitted a reference for preliminary ruling to the Court. Under the case it appeared that in Italy, VAT offences, be it in internal situations or in cross-border situations, attracted criminal sanctions; however, the sanctions in cross-border situations were, by far, much more severe than those applying in internal situations. The Italian authorities sought to justify this by referring to the fact that the possibility of discovering an offence in the cross border situation was much more limited and therefore the sanctions, to be dissuasive, had to be more severe. The Court accepted that some differentiation was allowed, given the differences between the two situations; however, it held that the Italian rules were disproportionate and therefore caught by the ban in Art.110.[15]

The term "similar" in Art.110(1) refers, according to the Court, to products having the same characteristics and meeting the same needs from the point of view of the consumer.[16] It is therefore necessary to determine the scope of the prohibition on the basis, not of the criterion of the strictly identical "nature" of the products, but on that of their similar and comparable "use". As concerns Art.110(2) TFEU the provision covers all forms of indirect taxation that protects products which, without being similar, are nevertheless in competition, even partial, indirect or potential, with imported products. The test as to whether two products are in competition turns on whether the products are substitutable; that means whether, in view of the consumer, they satisfy the same need, i.e. largely whether they have the same use. The similarity test under Art.110(1) and the competition test under Art.110(2) thus to a large extent ask the same question, albeit in different terms; the answer will depend on the individual circumstances of each case.[17] The fact that the two paragraphs of Art.110 largely overlap is not of much material importance in the sense that the legal consequence of either paragraph is the same: the discrimination that the tax entails is banned. As an

---

[15] *Drexl* (299/86) [1988] E.C.R. 1213.

[16] *Commision v France* (168/78) [1979] E.C.R. 855.

[17] It must be noted that the competition test under Art.110(2) appears identical, but is not, to the substitutability test used in competition law to delimit the relevant market—see Ch.22: Competition Policy for market definition; in *Commission v Italy (Bananas)* (184/85) [1987] E.C:R. 2013 the Court held, under Art.110(2), that bananas were at least partially in competition with other fresh fruit, such as pears; in *United Brands* (27/76) [1978] E.C.R. 207 the Court held, under the competition rules, that bananas constituted a separate market, distinct from other fresh fruit. The difference in the two tests translates the different concerns underlying the provisions. An example may help to convey understanding of that: In a Spanish speaking country, one would hardly find that books in Spanish are on the same market, within the meaning of the competition rules, as books in German; a book in Spanish cannot be substituted by a book in German for the majority of the population that does not read German. Whether an undertaking engages in anti-competitive conduct in the country must, all things being equal, be assessed in relation to separate markets for books in Spanish and German (or other languages). Now imagine that the government of that country imposes a tax on books, of 10 per cent in general, but of 50 per cent for books in German. Most people will subscribe to the view that such a tax is deeply unfair to readers of books in German. Such discrimination can be caught by Art.110 through finding that at least in some cases, namely for those who read both Spanish and German, the two types of books are similar or in competition.

example of the tests one may mention wine and beer; are they similar products; are they competing products? The Court has held that beer and wine, at least the lightest and cheapest varieties, are in competition under Art.110(2).[18] The Court held so in 1983 in relation to the UK market and perhaps because the finding would fail to convince many, the Court stated in its reasoning that a national taxation system must not "crystallise" consumer habits so as to consolidate an advantage acquired by national industry. In other words: if the UK taxed wine higher than beer, a largely domestically produced product, the likelihood is that it would never occur to the beer-consuming UK customer that wine could actually be an alternative to beer; that is that the two products are at least potentially in competition.

The tests under Art.110 seek to establish whether the imported product and the **25–05** national product are in a comparable situation, i.e. that there are no objective reasons to differentiate between them.[19] When it is established that the domestic product and the imported product are in a comparable situation, then *any* discrimination is banned, no matter how minor it is or that it only applies to a few imported products. Two examples can illustrate this. A Member State decides to levy a tax on energy produced nationally according to how "green" it is, the idea being that the most-green energy attracts the lowest tax rate, while the less-green energy attracts the highest rate. The State establishes a scale with five rates accordingly. The question that arises now for the State is: how shall it deal with imported energy? The State has two problems in dealing with that question. In the first place, the State does not know how green the imported energy is; it comes through the grid from abroad, but nobody knows how it has been produced. In the second place, the State cannot politically leave imported energy untaxed while national energy is taxed. The State solves this dilemma by taxing imported energy at the middle rate, i.e. at the rate three of the five available rates. In that way it considers that on average it may be dealing fairly with imported energy; some of it, if one knew the details, would perhaps attract the highest rate; some of it would perhaps attract the lowest rate. Such a solution would not be acceptable under Art.110, the reason being: if imported energy has in fact been produced in a way such that if it were nationally produced, it would only attract the lowest rate, then by paying the middle rate it is suffering discrimination.[20] The next example concerns the import of second-hand cars which is a complex issue and which has given rise to quite some case law. The reason is that taxation of new cars differs enormously from one Member State to another. Thus, a new car in State A may be subject to taxation of a level around 150 per cent while the same car in State B may be subject to taxation at the level of around 20 per cent. A new car whose price ex-factory is €100 will thus cost €250 in State A while it would cost €120 in State B. The value of a car depreciates over time, for instance in average by 50 per cent over five years. So after five years the State A car will be at €125 while the State B car will be at €60. It goes without saying that there is an economic interest for a resident in State A to buy a second-hand car in State B and seek to import it into State A. On the other hand the State A authorities will subject that

---

[18] *Commission v UK (Tax arrangements applying to wine)* (170/78) [1983] E.C.R. 2265.
[19] It is recalled that a ban on discrimination also implies that objectively different situations must not be treated equally. Thus, a Member State that considers that a difference in treatment between the two situations can be justified, must seek to argue that the two situations are objectively different.
[20] *Outokumpu Oy* (C-213/86) [1998] E.C.R. I-1777.

imported State B car to taxation. That they will do so is not a problem. The question is how will they establish the value of the State B car, i.e. the taxable basis on which they levy the tax? As there are numerous second-hand cars being imported, they cannot proceed to an individual, detailed evaluation of each car. They fall back on general depreciation guidelines such as for instance that a 5-year-old car has lost 50 per cent of its original value. Now imagine that the State B car at issue has had a particularly rough owner, has done excessive mileage and is in a thoroughly bad state so that its value is actually just 10 per cent of its original ex-factory value, i.e. €10. The evaluation method of the authorities in State A in that case leads to paying an excessive tax. The general deprecation guidelines will set the ex-factory value of the car at €50 instead of the €10 that is actually worth. The imported car, after tax, will thus become much more expensive than the equivalent national second-hand car that also has had a rough owner, done excessive mileage and is in a thoroughly bad state. Is this permitted under Art.110? The Court has accepted that national authorities may make use of general rules for evaluating the value of imported second-hand cars. However, the Court has submitted that acceptance to the condition that it must be possible for the importer to contest the evaluation and obtain an individual evaluation. Thus, for the system to exclude *any* discrimination, it must give the importer the possibility for an individual evaluation.[21]

3.   REIMBURSEMENT OF TAX IN CASE OF EXPORTS

25–06   For the sake of completeness, mention must be made of the prohibition imposed on the Member States to repay internal taxation exceeding that taxation imposed directly or indirectly, where products are exported to any Member State.[22] The same prohibition applies to remissions or repayments, in respect of exports to other Member States, of charges other than turnover taxes, excise duties and other forms of indirect taxation, unless the measures contemplated have been previously approved for a limited period by the Council.[23] The same prohibition applies to the imposition of countervailing charges in respect of imports from Member States.

4.   NATIONAL TAX RULES AND THE INTERNAL MARKET FREEDOMS

25–07   Direct taxes, such as taxes on income or wealth, remain within the competence of the Member States. However, the Court has consistently held that, in the absence of harmonisation, the taxation by Member States must respect primary law. The four freedoms thus apply also to national rules of taxation, in the first place for the simple reason that no national rule falls outside the scope of the four freedoms because of the qualification that the national legal order gives to its rules; for instance, national rules no matter what they are called in their national legal

---

[21] See for instance *Gomes Valente* (C-393/98) [2001] E.C.R. I-1327.
[22] Art.111 TFEU.
[23] Art.112 TFEU.

system, cannot discriminate on grounds of nationality if the rules apply within the material scope of the Treaty.[24] Next, national tax rules very often treat residents in another State than the taxing State differently. When the person at issue is residing in another Member State of the Union, the national tax rules are obviously at the risk of being considered indirectly discriminatory, cf above in the Introduction to Part III: The Internal Market. Thus, if the national rule shall be compatible with Union law, it must be shown to be justified, or that the difference of treatment it entails follows from the fact that the situations treated are not identical but different. The Union law notion of indirect discrimination is thus potentially at odds with national tax rules as the national tax rules distinguish between resident taxpayers (submitted to tax as concerns their global income, with possibilities of tax allowances and credits) and non-resident taxpayers (submitted to tax only as concerns income that originates from the State, normally with limited possibilities of tax allowances and credits).[25] Thus, at the outset, a difference in tax treatment that derives from this basic distinction between resident and non-resident taxpayers must be justified. Now, the reasons underlying national tax rules may very often be reduced to one that is very simple: ensure that most tax revenues accrue to the State. That reason is a financial or economic ground and, as was mentioned in the Introduction to Part III of this book: The Internal Market, such grounds are not valid justification grounds. The scene is thus clearly set for an uneasy relationship between the four freedoms and national tax rules.[26]

Over the years, Member States have developed and the Court has accepted justification grounds that are specific to taxes. In the first place, the need to avoid tax evasion is a valid justification ground[27] although often the Court finds that national rules fail the proportionality test. The reason is that national tax rules, in order to ensure revenue and avoid evasion, are generally very broad; the Court on the contrary expects the rules to be exactly to the point, to pass the proportionality test.[28]

Next, the Court has held that the need to ensure the cohesion of the national **25–08** tax system may be a valid justification ground.[29] This ground has had over the years an ever more limited application in the case law. It is useful to dwell shortly at it as an illustration of the relation between the four freedoms and national tax rules as well as the development of the Court's case law. First, when the Court

---

[24] See for instance *Hubbard* (C-20/92) [1993] E.C.R. I-3777, and *Bickel and Franz* (C-274/96) [1998] E.C.R. I-7637. The reader is invited to note that when Member States do not reach agreement on harmonisation of national laws, the issues that call for regulation do not go away; it falls upon the Court of Justice to confront them, in the context of references for preliminary rulings from national judges, and on the basis of primary law.

[25] The Treaty recognises the relevance of the distinction when Art.65 TFEU provides that the principle of free movement of capital shall not restrain the Member States' right to "apply the relevant provisions of their tax law which distinguish between taxpayers who are not in the same situation with regard to their place of residence or with regard to the place where their capital is invested."

[26] The assessment in an individual case turns on the question as to whether the cross-border situation is objectively different from the internal situation or on what for all practical purposes is the same, namely whether the difference in treatment can be justified. The assessment is fraught with difficulties. For a very instructive and critical analysis of the case law, see Ruth Mason, "A theory of Tax Discrimination" (NYU Jean Monnet Working Paper 09/06), available online.

[27] *Cassis de Dijon* (C-120/78) [1979] E.C.R. 649.

[28] *De Lasteyrie du Saillant* (C-9/02) [2004] E.C.R. I-2409.

[29] *Bachman* (C-204/90) [1992] E.C.R. I-249.

refers to the cohesion of the tax system, what is meant is that the disadvantage imposed by a given tax system must be levelled out by an advantage, the both being clearly and directly related. For instance; Belgium exempts from tax contributions to an old-age pension scheme. The counterpart in Belgium is that when the pension is paid out, it is taxable. As the scheme is based in Belgium, the Belgian authorities know that they will be able to enforce their tax claim. However, when the contributions are paid to, for instance, a German insurance scheme, Belgium levies tax, the reason being that when the German scheme—many years afterwards—pays out the pension, the Belgian authorities cannot be sure that they will be able to levy tax: the scheme is in Germany and the person may in the meantime have left Belgium. Belgium will therefore submit contributions to Belgian and foreign schemes to different rules. The Court was originally understanding of this on the basis of the ground of ensuring cohesion of the national tax system. In the Court's view it was fair that Belgium would tax contributions to a foreign scheme now while not doing it when the scheme was national. However, the Court has later reckoned that the true problem relates to the question as to whether the person benefitting from the pension remains in the country when the pension is paid, i.e. in the case of the Belgian resident, the true problem is whether the person has left Belgium when the pension is paid.[30] If the person has not left Belgium, the Belgian authorities can still tax. If the person in the meantime has left Belgium, the authorities can seek to tax him at his departure—commonly referred to as "exit tax". An "exit tax" would thus be a less restrictive measure to obtain the legitimate objective of the Belgian authorities. However, it should be noted that "exit taxes" are by their very nature also discriminatory, and they can also be very hard to bear for the person at the moment of departing the Member State. In the example given, the person leaving Belgium will be submitted to tax in relation to a pension that will not be paid out until 20 years later when the person becomes pensionable. Such a tax burden may make the person desist from moving to another Member State. The Court has therefore in general held that "exit taxes" are only acceptable when they defer the payment of the tax to the moment when the person actually disposes of the sums that trigger the taxation.[31]

The Court has also accepted that Member States have a right to exercise their tax jurisdiction in relation to the activities carried out in their territory so as to ensure a balanced allocation between Member States of the power to impose taxes.[32] It was not until after many years of litigation that the Court was in a position to formulate this justification ground, and reading of the case law leaves the impression that it was not much helped by the submissions made by Member States. The ground is very broadly formulated. When the Court develops such a broad justification ground, the question that one must ask oneself is whether the Court will also enlarge the scope of the notion of restrictions in this field; as the reader will have noticed, the notion of restriction is in practice hitherto largely limited to discrimination. The answer is still open.

Moreover, an instrument of secondary law often plays an important role in cases concerning national tax rules and the four freedoms, namely a directive

---

[30] See *Commission v Denmark* [2007] E.C.R. I-1163.
[31] See for instance *N* (C–470/04) [2006] E.C.R. I–7409.
[32] *Cadbury Schweppes* (C-196/04) [2006] E.C.R. I-1163.

from 1977 concerning co-operation between tax authorities.[33] In order to defend national tax rules that treat internal situations differently from cross-border situations, national authorities often put forward that they do not have the means to be sufficiently informed about cross-border movements. The reply of the Court has in general been that the authorities can rely on the Directive to obtain the necessary information or that they can request the information directly from the taxable person. Thus, to the extent the facilitation of information under the Directive is sufficient for accommodating a Member State's concerns, stricter national rules will not be accepted.[34] This follows from the principle of proportionality.

5. SECONDARY LAW: INDIRECT TAXATION

(1) Value Added Tax (VAT)

VAT is a general turnover tax on the consumption of goods and services and any exclusion of it requires a specific provision. The main legal instrument for this cumulative multi-stage turnover tax was adopted in 1977 by the Sixth VAT Directive which was replaced in 2006 by a new directive.[35] The Directive bans Member States from adopting taxes, duties or levies that can be characterised as turnover taxes.[36] It is therefore important to know what characterises a turnover tax. According to the Court, the characteristics of a turnover tax are: VAT applies generally to transactions relating to goods and services; it is proportional to the price of those goods and services; it is charged at each stage of the production and distribution process; and it is imposed on the added value of goods and services, as the tax payable on the transaction is calculated after deducting the tax paid on the previous transaction.[37]

25–09

The Directive establishes a uniform VAT coverage. Currently the main rule is that the standard rate must not be less than 15 per cent; in addition Member States may apply one or two reduced rates of not less than 5 per cent (only for supplies of goods and services referred to in an exhaustive list). However, there are still a great number of derogations to this Directive, especially for new Member States or special services. The VAT regime covers also electronically delivered services.[38]

---

[33] Directive 77/388/EEC of May 17, 1977, replaced by Directive 2010/88/EU of December 7, 2010.

[34] The relevance of the Directive is highlighted by the ruling in *Rimbaud* (C-72/09) [2010] E.C.R. I-10659.

[35] The Sixth Council Directive 77/388 on the harmonisation of the laws of the Member States relating to turnover taxes—Common system of value added tax: uniform basis of assessment [1977] O.J. L145/1 was repealed by Directive 2006/112 on a common system of VAT [2006] O.J. L347/1, with later amendments.

[36] Art.401 of Directive 2006/112. The provision has direct effect.

[37] See for instance *KÖGÁZ* (C-283/06 and C-312/06) [2007] E.C.R. I-8463 and *Dansk Denkavit* (C-200/90) [1992] E.C.R. I-2217.

[38] For instance services covered by the E-commerce Directive, Directive 2002/38 [2002] O.J. L128/41, with later amendments.

The persons that have to VAT register are so-called taxable persons, i.e. persons and undertakings that carry out economic activities independently.[39] Thus, employees do not VAT register.

25–10   The taxable transactions are the supply of goods or services. "Technically" they are divided into four categories, namely: supply of goods, intra-EU acquisition of goods (i.e. buying goods from a seller in another Member State), supplies of services, and imports. The "place of supply" and thus the place of the chargeable event differs from one category to the other. For instance for an intra-EU acquisition of goods the place of supply is deemed where the transport of the goods to the person acquiring them ends.

Products or services sold on markets outside the Internal Market are not subject to VAT. In order to combat VAT evasion and avoidance, a framework for co-operation between the national tax authorities of the Member States was set up; it provides in particular for closer co-operation and mutual assistance. In addition, in 1993 a VAT information exchange system (VIES) was established.[40] The co-operation has since been simplified, decentralised and reinforced.

Finally, the importance of VAT for the Union derives, inter alia, from the fact that since 1970 a percentage of VAT collected by Member States belongs to the Union as "own resource".[41]

(2) Excise Duties

25–11   Excise duties are indirect taxes on the consumption or the use of certain products. The point of departure is that Member States are free to decide on which products that they submit to excise duties, and the rates on them. There are a few products that normally attract the attention of Member States as object of excise duties. They are in short: tobacco, alcohol and energy products such as petrol. Harmonisation measures have been adopted concerning those products.

A basic directive was adopted in 1992, laying down the general framework for excise duties and applicable to the said products.[42] It is based on the principles that the imposition of excise duties should be identical in all Member States; that products subject to excise duties that are bought and transported by private people for their own use are to be taxed in the Member State of origin[43] and that, for commercial traffic, the excise duty on goods is imposed by the Member State of destination. The range of rates for the said products is laid down in individual directives applicable to each of the products.[44]

---

[39] Art.9 of Directive 2006/112.

[40] Now under a single legal framework, Regulation 1798/2003 on administrative co-operation in the field of value added tax [2003] O.J. L264/1.

[41] See above Ch.14: Financing Union Activities.

[42] Directive 92/12 on the general arrangements for products subject to excise duty [1992] O.J. L76/1, repealed by Directive 2008/118 [2009] O.J. L9/12.

[43] See *Joustra* (C-5/05) [2005] E.C.R. I-11075.

[44] See for instance Directive 92/84 on the approximation of the rates of excise duty on alcohol and alcoholic beverages [1992] O.J. L316/29; Directive 95/59 on taxes other than turnover taxes which affect the consumption of manufactured tobacco [1995] O.J. L291/40; replaced by Directive 2011/40 [2011] O.J. L176/24; Directives 92/81 and 92/82 concerning mineral oils, replaced by Directive 2003/96 restructuring the Community framework for the taxation of energy products and electricity [2003] O.J. L283/51.

The directives relating to excise duties deal with three main groups of questions:

- the structure of the tax to be applied to a particular group of products;
- the rates; and
- the movement and storage of goods subject to excise duties.

Within the framework of this chapter on Taxation, a word must be said about so-called "duty free". This system of turnover tax and excise duty exemption was set up in 1969 in order to allow travellers crossing a border between two Member States to be exempted from reclaiming taxes already paid when leaving one Member State, and paying new taxes on arrival in the other Member State. The traveller was therefore allowed to purchase goods to be transported in his personal luggage at a price which does not include VAT, nor excise duty; the amounts of goods which the traveller could thus purchase were strictly limited. To put this system into practice, vendors at airports and on board ships and planes were allowed to purchase those goods at "duty free" prices in order to sell them at those same prices to the traveller. The system was not successful in the sense that the vendors kept for themselves most of the profit which the Council had intended for the traveller. The vendors made huge profits that, in addition, distorted competition. Furthermore, the system discriminated between categories of travellers.

Notwithstanding the entry into force of the internal market at the end of 1992, and the elimination of the fiscal frontiers, which were the origin of the whole system, the Council, in 1992, extended the duty free exemption to June 30, 1999. This system has now disappeared for intra-Union travellers but still applies to travellers leaving or entering the EU.

25–12

(3) Other indirect taxes

In 1969, a directive was adopted. concerning indirect taxes on the raising of capital[45] that gives the Member State the right, but not the obligation to impose such taxes, secondly, to impose capital tax at a minimum level of 1 per cent on the creation of a company in that Member State. A directive from 2008 seeks to phase out the tax.[46]

A directive from 1999 concerns the charging of heavy goods vehicles for the use of certain infrastructures.[47] It harmonises vehicle taxes and tolls and charges for using roads.

25–13

---

[45] Directive 69/335 [1969] O.J. L245/25.
[46] Directive 2008/7 [2008] O.J.L124/1.
[47] Directive 1999/62 [1999] O.J. L53/5.

6. SECONDARY LAW: DIRECT TAXES

25–14   The Council and the Representatives of the Governments of the Member States adopted in 1998 a resolution on a Code of Conduct for Business Taxation and Taxation of Saving.[48] The aim was to tackle tax obstacles to cross-border activities within the internal market, prevent significant losses of tax revenue and to help tax structure to develop in a more employment-friendly way. In order to combat harmful tax competition, the Council adopted in 1997 a Code of Conduct that requires the Member States to refrain from introducing any new harmful tax measures and to phase out existing harmful tax measures.[49]

In order to avoid harmful tax competition between the Member States, to avoid double taxation and to safeguard the Treaty freedoms, the Commission proposed, in 2001, a "Tax Package" consisting of:

- a code of conduct to eliminate harmful business tax regimes;
- a measure to ensure an efficient minimum level of taxation of savings income; and
- a measure to eliminate source taxes on cross-border payments on interests and royalties between associated companies.[50]

As for taxes on personal income the Council adopted a directive on the taxations of saving income in the form of interest payments.[51] Although the Commission had wanted to also eliminate obstacles to the taxation of pensions,[52] the Council did not come to an agreement. As concerning dividend income of individuals, the Commission established a communication where it concludes that the Court's case law obliges Member States to treat in-bound dividends as domestic dividends.[53]

25–15   Concerning company tax, several rules were adopted:

---

[48] [1998] O.J. C99/1 and C2/6. At the same time the Commission adopted a notice on State aid guidelines relating to direct business taxation [1998] O.J. C384/3.

[49] [1998] O.J. C2/1. As concerns relations with third countries, the Commission issued, in 2012, a recommendation regarding measures intended to encourage third countries to apply minimum standards of good governance in tax matters [2012] O.J. C338/37.

[50] See for more details Communication on "Tax policy in the European Union-Priorities for the years ahead", COM(2001) 260.

[51] Directive 2003/48 [2003] O.J. L157/38. It is applicable since January 1, 2005; it established an exchange system of information reporting. It was supported by all Member States except for Belgium, Luxembourg and Austria because of their banking secrecy as well as their fear of losing bank clients to other countries with a banking secrecy such as Switzerland, the Principality of Andorra, Liechtenstein and Monaco and the Republic of San Marino. For this reason, the Union has negotiated special agreements in order to ensure that those countries adopt measures equivalent to those provided for in Directive 2003/48 (see [2004] O.J. L385/28; L385/50; L359/32; L379/83; L381/32 and [2005] O.J. L19/53). The financial crisis has led to the three said Member States being under considerable pressure for lessening their bank secrecy rules. In spring 2013, Austria is reportedly the only State that holds on to its bank secrecy rules.

[52] COM(2001) 214 final.

[53] COM(2003) 810 final. Dividend taxation of individuals in the Internal Market.

In 1990, a directive on cross-border mergers[54] was adopted and so was a directive on a common system of taxation in the case of parent companies and subsidiaries in different Member States.[55]

In 1993, followed a directive on a common system of taxation applicable to interest and royalty payments made between associated companies of different Member States (I + R Directive).[56] This Directive abolishes the withholding tax on royalty payments and interest payments made in a Member State, provided that the beneficial owner of the payments is a company established in another Member State.

Multinational companies can allocate their profits by transfer pricing; the Council has therefore adopted a Code of Conduct on that subject.[57] However, it only reflects a political commitment without limiting the competences of the Member States.

In 2001, the Commission established a strategy for providing companies with a consolidated corporate tax base for their Union-wide activities in order to reduce the compliance costs, administrative burdens and the lack of cross-border loss-relief.[58] As from the end of 2004 a working group dealt with this subject and in 2006 the Commission issued a Communication on the progress to date and next steps towards a Common Consolidated Corporate Tax Base (CCCTB).[59] The Commission made a proposal for directive in 2011.[60] It proposes a mechanism for Member States' sharing of the tax revenue generated by the corporations coming within the scope of the proposed act. Currently—spring 2013—it appears that the matter is stalled.

A system for the exchange of information between the competent authorities of the Member States in the field of direct taxation was set up by the Mutual Assistance Directive, mentioned above.[61]

---

[54] Directive 90/434 [1990] O.J. L225/1, replaced by Directive 2009/133 [2009] O.J. L310/34.

[55] Directive 90/435 [1990] L225/6, replaced by Directive 2011/96 [2011] O.J. L345/8 (commonly referred to as the Parent-Subsidiary Directive). The Directive concerns distributed profits, not undistributed profits, see also *Cadbury Schweppes* (C-196/04) [2006] E.C.R. I-7995.In *Cobelfret* (C-138/07) [2009] E.C.R. I-731 the Court found that Art.4(1) of Directive 90/435 had direct effect. The Directive is likely to be reviewed within the context of the efforts to combat artificial tax arrangements.

[56] Directive 2003/49 [2003] O.J. L157/49, with later amendments.

[57] [2006] O.J. C176/1.

[58] COM(2001) 582.

[59] COM(2006) 157.

[60] COM(2011) 121 final.

[61] Directive 77/799 [1977] O.J. L336/15, replaced by Directive 2011/16 [2011] O.J. L64/1. In 1998, Parliament and the Council established a programme of Union action to ameliorate the internal taxation systems on the internal market; the FISCALIS programme [1998] O.J. L126/1. Originally established for four years it was extended to 2007 and subsequently to 2013. The programme is intended to improve the operation of the taxation systems in the internal market. It is designed to: improve tax officials' knowledge of Union law; secure wide-ranging and effective co-operation among the Member States as well as between them and the Union; combat tax evasion; and reduce compliance burdens on administrations and taxpayers.

FURTHER READING

25–16 Ben Terra and Peter Waddell, *European Tax Law*, 3rd edn (Kluwer, 2001).
Pascal Pistone, *The Impact of Community Law on Tax Treaties* (Kluwer, 2002).
Pinto Carlo, *Tax competition and EU law* (Kluwer, 2003).
Servaas van Thiel, "Removal of income tax barriers to market integration in the EU litigation by the Community citizens instead of harmonisation by the Community legislation?", EC Tax Review 2003, Vol.12, No.1, pp.4–19.

CHAPTER 26

Approximation of Laws[1]

1. THE GENERAL LEGAL BASIS FOR HARMONISATION

The term "approximation of laws" is the term used by the Treaty to refer to   **26–01**
harmonisation of the provisions laid down by law, regulation and administrative
action in the Member States. It is clear that the many differences existing between
the laws, etc. of the Member States impede the development and functioning of
the internal market on which the Union is based. Harmonisation is a means to
overcome such obstacles to the establishment of the internal market.

Harmonisation consists of replacing existing national provisions by rules
whose content is common to all the Member States. That does not necessarily
mean that the rules must be completely identical. The instrument most commonly
used to achieve the objective of approximation is the directive, and the latter, as
was seen in the chapter on Union acts, is only binding as to the results to be
achieved. It leaves to the national authorities the choice of form and methods.[2]
There are many provisions in the Treaty that provide the legal basis for the
harmonisation of national laws.[3] The Treaty, however, also contains a chapter
entitled "approximation of laws" that contains the general provisions for
harmonising the laws of the Member States.[4]

The Treaty makes a distinction between national provisions that "directly
affect the establishment or functioning of the internal market",[5] and rules which
have as their "object" the establishment and functioning of the internal market.[6]
As regards national rules that "directly affect" the establishment or functioning of

---

[1] Arts 114–118 TFEU.

[2] Art.288 TFEU. However, mention must be made of the fact that many directives are very detailed
and do not leave the Member States with much choice. Moreover, the case law of the Court has also
a bearing on Member State's implementation of directives; overall it can be said that the
implementation of the directive must be such as to ensure its effective application in the Member State
concerned. That means that private persons must be able to ascertain, when the directive entails rights
for individuals that the implementing measure confers upon them these rights. Therefore, mere
administrative practices in the Member State will normally not suffice to comply with the
implementation obligation of the Member State, see for instance *Commission v Germany (Right of
residence)* (C-96/95) [1997] E.C.R. I-1653.

[3] For instance Arts 48, 50, 53 and 75 TFEU. If the provision establishes different legislative
procedures for the adoption of an act, the choice of legal basis becomes a matter of much importance.
It is well-established case law that the choice of legal basis, i.e. the right Treaty article(s), must be
determined objectively, according to the content and main object of the act to be adopted, see for
instance *Commission v Council* (Case C-155/91) [1993] E. C. R. I-939.

[4] Arts 114-118 TFEU, of which the main ones are Arts 114 and 115.

[5] Art.115 TFEU.

[6] Art.114(1) TFEU.

475

the internal market, the Treaties provided and still now provides for directives issued by the Council, acting unanimously in accordance with the special legislative procedure,[7] on a proposal from the Commission and after consulting Parliament and the ESC. The requirement of unanimity makes the use of this provision as legal basis extremely time-consuming, if not practically impossible. It became clear that another solution had to be found to expedite the establishment and functioning of the "internal market" before the end of 1992.[8] The simplification of the harmonisation procedure consisted of replacing the required unanimity by qualified majority. To this end the EU Treaty introduced a new provision for "the achievement of the objectives set out in Art.14" (the latter defined the internal market). The TFEU now provides that Parliament and the Council, "acting in accordance with the ordinary legislative procedure,[9] after consulting the ESC, shall adopt the measures for the approximation of the provisions laid down by law, regulation or administrative action in Member States which have as their object the establishment and functioning of the internal market",[10] as distinct from national measures which "directly affect" the establishment and functioning of the internal market.[11] This provision, Art.114 TFEU, must by now be considered the main and general provision for harmonising national rules. To delimit its scope from Art.115 is not obvious. However, a negative delimitation follows from Art.114(2) which excludes from its scope "fiscal provisions, those relating to the free movement of persons" and "those relating to the rights and interests of employed persons". Harmonisation measures concerning such provisions must thus, unless another legal basis may be found in the Treaty, be based on Art.115, which requires unanimity in the Council.[12] In contrast to many other provisions, Art.114 does not prescribe the use of any particular type of act. By this, according to the Court, the authors of the Treaty intended to confer on the Union legislature discretion, depending on the general context and the specific circumstances of the matter to be harmonised, as regards the harmonisation technique most appropriate for achieving the desired results, in particular in fields that are characterised by complex technical features.[13] The harmonisation measures adopted under Art.114 may also encompass the establishment of a Union body.[14] For Art.114 to be used as legal basis for a harmonisation measure, the measure must envisage to overcome obstacles to trade or distortions of competition that are not just "remote and indirect".[15]

---

[7] See Art.189(2) TFEU.

[8] Former Art.14 EC.

[9] Art.294 TFEU.

[10] Art.114(1) TFEU.

[11] Art.94 TFEU.

[12] As concerns fiscal provisions, let it be noticed that Art.113 TFEU concerns indirect taxes and provides for unanimity in the Council. Harmonisation of fiscal provisions will thus always call for unanimity in the Council, either under Art.113 or 115.

[13] *UK v Parliament and Council (Smoke Flavourings)* (C-66/04) [2005] E.C.R. I-10553.

[14] *UK v Parliament and Council (Network and Information Security Agency)* (C-217/04) [2006] E.C.R. I-3771.

[15] *Germany v Parliament and Council (Tobacco Advertising Directive)* (C376/98) [2000] E.C.R. I-8419. In its ruling the ECJ annulled Directive 98/43 because Art.114, then Art.95 EC, were insufficient as legal basis. Subsequently the Union legislation adopted an altered act, Directive

The Court has held that, in the case of a harmonisation process in stages, two **26–02** conditions have to be fulfilled. First, the basic act must determine the essential elements of the harmonising measure and, second, the mechanism for implementing these elements must be designed in such a way that it leads to a harmonisation within the meaning of the relevant Treaty provision. According to the Court, an act adopted by the Union legislature may be limited to defining the provisions that are essential for the achievement of the objectives in connection with the establishment and functioning of the internal market, while conferring power on the Commission to adopt the harmonisation measures needed for the implementation of the legislative act in question.[16]

However, the Court has held that the harmonisation measures may only be used when the result is the replacement of existing national laws or regulations by Union rules. This is not the case when Union rules are created while the national rules remain unchanged.[17]

Under Art.114, the Commission's proposals concerning health, food safety, environmental protection and consumer protection, must take as a base a high level of protection, "taking account, in particular, of any new development based on scientific facts".[18] The Parliament and the Council are also bound by this objective. As Art.114 allows adoption of harmonisation measures by a qualified majority, some Member States feared when the provision was introduced that they could be forced to lower their standards for protecting for instance public health, the environment or the working environment. Therefore a provision was inserted into Art.114 allowing a Member State to maintain higher standards. The provision has since been split into two, namely paras 4 and 5 of Art.114. A distinction is established between maintenance of national rules, i.e. existing before the harmonisation measure, and the introduction of new rules. The condition for doing the latter are more strict.[19] In both cases the Member State must notify the Commission, which shall normally take a decision within six months. In case the Commission or any Member State considers that another Member State is making improper use of these exceptions, they can bring the matter directly before the Court without going through the normal procedures.[20]

Finally, it should be recalled that certain matters are excluded from the approximation process, namely in areas where the Union only has supporting competences. One example is to be found in the field of employment. The Treaty provides that the Council may adopt "incentive measures designed to encourage co-operation between Member States and to support their action in the field of employment", but adds that those "measures shall not include harmonisation of

---

2003/33 which was upheld by the Court, see *Germany v Parliament and Council (Tobacco Advertising Directive II)* (C-380/03) [2006] E.C.R. I-11573.

[16] *UK v Parliament and Council* (C-66/04) (quoted above, fn.14).

[17] Regulation 1435/2003 lays down a single statute for the European Co-operative Society (SCE) on the basis of Art.352 TFEU; this legal basis was contested by Parliament, which proposed Art.114 TFEU as legal basis. Since the national provisions remained unchanged, the Court ruled that the act did not constitute a harmonisation: *Parliament v Council* (C-436/03) [2006] E.C.R. I-3733.

[18] Art.114(3) TFEU.

[19] In case of introduction of a new rule, it must be based on "new scientific evidence" that can only relate to the environment or the working environment (and thus not to other objectives of protection), and it must concern a problem "specific" to the Member State "arising after the adoption" of the harmonisation measure.

[20] Art.114(9) TFEU.

the laws and regulations of the Member States".[21] Other examples are vocational training policy,[22] culture,[23] public health[24] and education.[25]

2. HARMONISATION TECHNIQUES

26–03   Let it first be noted that harmonisation is not the only way in which the Union may seek to achieve its objectives. Sometimes, but with much less frequency, the Union measure *co-ordinates* national laws. An example is Regulation 883/2004 on the co-ordination of the social security system and its predecessor, Regulation 1408/71. The Regulation seeks to co-ordinate the national social security rules applicable to cross-border situations without seeking to harmonise those rules.[26] To give an example: a worker who has for 20 years been working in Germany while residing in France—where shall he claim benefits if he becomes unemployed, in France or in Germany? The Regulation gives an answer to that question without harmonising the laws on unemployment benefits, e.g. for instance the amount of the benefits and the conditions to obtain them.

Within harmonisation measures one distinguishes between different types of harmonisation. One type of harmonisation is "total harmonisation". As the term implies, the directive will in that case regulate exhaustively the matter. Total harmonisation thus entails there is no room for further legislation of the matter by the national legislator. For instance, if a directive lays down all the information that a product must carry on its label, the national legislator cannot add or subtract from that. Thus, if the national legislator considers that considerations as to consumer protection or public health call for additional information, the directive pre-empts the national legislator from enacting such additional rules.

Minimum harmonisation is the contrary to total harmonisation. In this case, the directive allows the national legislator to go beyond the requirements laid down by the directive. The scope of action of the national legislator is, however, still confined by primary law, i.e. the Treaty. For instance, if the national legislator decides to enact additional labelling requirements to those laid down by a directive for reasons of public health, the requirements must be in accordance with the principle of proportionality; the additional requirements are namely, all things being equal, a restriction which can only be accepted if it is justified, see the Introduction to Part III of this book: The Internal Market. Some minimum harmonisation directives contain, however, a so-called "market access" clause. That means that a Member State that has enacted higher requirement must nevertheless accept imported products that just meet the requirements of the directive.

---

[21] Art.149 TFEU.

[22] Art.166(4) TFEU.

[23] Art.167(5) TFEU first indent.

[24] Art.168(5) TFEU.

[25] Art.165(4) TFEU first indent.

[26] For another example, see Directive 96/71 concerning the posting of workers in the framework of the provision of services, [1996] O.J. L18/1. Although the Directive may appear as a harmonisation measure, it is settled case law that the Directive does not harmonise national rules but only co-ordinates them, see for instance *Commission v Germany* (C-490/04) [2007] E.C.R. I-6095, para.19.

The meaning of the terms "total harmonisation" and "minimum harmonisation" is well-established. As to other type of harmonisation, there is less consistency in the terminology. "Optional harmonisation" is a term often used to convey that a directive obliges the Member State to accept products that meet the requirements of the directive, while leaving the Member State the option of maintaining another set of rules, applicable to the production in the Member State.

To determine the exact nature of a harmonisation measure can be fraught with difficulty, also for experienced lawyers in Union law. Often the directive itself will not state what sort of harmonisation is envisaged. Even if it does so, there may be provisions that do not correspond to the enounced statement.[27]

Finally, one should note the distinction between "old approach" and "new approach". Under the "old approach" the Union laid down detailed requirements for a product. Under the "new approach"—which came into existence after the ruling of the Court in *Cassis de Dijon*, see Ch.15: The Free Movement of Goods—the directive lays down the "essential requirements" for the product and leaves it to European standardisation bodies[28] to establish the detailed technical specifications through which the essential requirements can be met. If a product is produced in accordance with those specifications, this is a presumption that the essential requirements of the directive are met.

---

[27] For cases that have turned on the question as to what sort of harmonisation a directive entails, see for instance *Cidrerie Ruwet* (C-3/99) [2000] E.C.R. I-8749, *Kemikalieinspektionen v Toolex Alpha* (C-473/98) [2000] E.C.R. I-5681, and *Silhouette* (C-355/96) [1998] E.C.R. I-4799.

[28] For instance CEN, the European body for standardisation (CEN is the acronym for its French name: Comité européen de normalization).

CHAPTER 27

Transport

INTRODUCTION

The importance of transport for the Union follows from the fact that the implementation and functioning of the internal market with its fundamental freedoms, provided for in the Treaties, depends on interconnected and interoperable regional and national transport networks, as well as on access to such networks. The TFEU therefore provides that shared competence between the Union and the Member States also applies to transport,[1] and that the objectives of the Treaty are to be pursued within the framework of the Common Transport Policy.[2] It is the task of Parliament and the Council, acting in accordance with the ordinary legislative procedure,[3] and after consulting the ESC and the Committee of the Regions and taking into account the distinctive features of transport,[4] to provide for:

27–01

- common rules applicable to international transport to or from the territory of a Member State or passing across the territory of one or more Member States;
- the conditions under which non-resident carriers may operate transport services within a Member State;
- measures to improve transport safety; and
- any other appropriate provision.[5]

In adopting the Common Transport Policy (or any other policy for that matter), the Union has to take into consideration the obligation to ensure a high level of human health protection,[6] to contribute to the protection of the health,

---

[1] Art.4(2)(G) TFEU.

[2] Arts 90–100 TFEU.

[3] Art.294 TFEU. Account must be taken of cases where their application might seriously affect the standards of living and level of employment in certain regions and the operation of transport facilities: Art.91(2) TFEU.

[4] Regulation 1017/68 applying rules of competition to transport by rail, road and inland waterway [1968] O.J. L175/10, codified version Regulation 169/09 [2009] O.J. L61/1; Regulation 411/2004 laying down the procedure for the application of the rules on competition to undertakings in the air transport sector [2004] O.J. L68/1; and Regulation 4056/86 laying down detailed rules for the application of Arts 101 and 102 TFEU to maritime transport [1986] O.J. L378/4; all three amended by Regulation 1/2003 [2003] O.J. L1/1.

[5] Art.91(1) TFEU.

[6] See Art.168(1) TFEU.

safety and economic interests of consumers[7] and to integrate environmental protection requirements.[8] Until the above-mentioned provisions had been laid down by the Union, the Member States were to observe a standstill with regard to similar national provisions, in the sense that they were not allowed to adopt provisions less favourable, in their direct or indirect effect, on carriers of other Member States as compared with carriers of their own State. This prohibition applies unless the Council has unanimously adopted a measure granting a derogation.[9]

Although mentioned at the very end of Title VI of the TFEU on Transport, the provisions of that Title only apply to transport by rail, road and inland waterways.[10] However, Parliament and the Council acting in accordance with the ordinary legislative procedure,[11] may lay down appropriate provisions for sea and air transport, after consulting the ECS and the Committee of the Regions.[12] That was done and, as will be seen, many Union acts have been adopted concerning those latter means of transport. The *acquis communautaire* supporting the Common Transport Policy has become an impressive law compilation.

1. NEW EUROPEAN TRANSPORT POLICY: ADAPT THE MOBILITY SYSTEM TO NEW CHALLENGES

27–02 At the beginning, the aim of the Common Transport Policy was to open up the transport market and to support the construction of new infrastructure in order to promote the economic competitiveness and economic and cultural exchanges within the Union. Today, this is considered to be insufficient to meet the problems[13] of the increasing demand of mobility as a result of the economic growth, globalisation, the enlarged internal market and the increasing shortage of adequate transport supply due to major bottlenecks in the European infrastructure.

In September 2001, the Commission adopted a White Paper, "European Transport Policy for 2010: time to decide",[14] that sets out steps towards a transport policy which meets the demands of enlargement and sustainable development. The new objectives aim at restoring the balance between modes of transport and developing inter-modality, combating congestion, improving safety and the quality of services, while maintaining the right to mobility. In this new Transport Policy Paper, the Commission proposed an action plan including 60 measures based on the following objectives:

- revitalise the railways by opening up the national and international market both in terms of freight and passengers;

---

[7] Arts 12 and 169(1) TFEU.
[8] Art.11 TFEU and Art. 191.
[9] Art.92 TFEU.
[10] Art.100 TFEU.
[11] Art.294 TFEU.
[12] Art.100(2) TFEU.
[13] For instance: congestion, environmental nuisance, accidents, isolation of outlying regions.
[14] See COM (2001) 370; see as well mid-term review of the European Commission's 2001 Transport White Paper COM (2006) 314.

- improve the quality of road transport by harmonising inspection procedures and penalties as well as ensuring satisfactory working conditions;
- improve road safety and reduce the number of accident victims by half;
- promote short sea and inland waterway transport to combat road congestion and deficiencies in railway infrastructure by building "sea motorways" as part of the Trans-European Network (TEN), and also developing a European maritime traffic management system to improve maritime safety;
- increase air transport while respecting the environment by adopting new regulations to reduce noise and pollution, introducing a "single sky" in order to manage the air traffic better and by 2004, implement Union legislation on air traffic to increase EU co-ordination in air transport;
- increase inter-modality by integrating the modes of transport, harmonise and promote interoperability between systems, and promote alternative solutions to road transport[15];
- develop the Trans-European Networks by removing the bottlenecks in the railway network; completing the routes defined as priorities for absorbing the traffic flows generated by enlargement and improving access to outlying areas;
- adopt a policy on effective charging for transport so that each mode of transport pays for the costs it generates,[16] harmonise fuel taxation for commercial users, particularly in road transport, introduce an infrastructure-charging system and allowing cross-financing by channeling revenues into specific funds;
- recognise the rights and obligations of users by extending measures to improve the quality of service;[17]
- develop quality urban transport by making better use of public transport and the existing infrastructure in order to meet the international commitments to reduce CO2 emissions (Kyoto Protocol); in 2008 a directive was adopted on the inland transport of dangerous goods, which includes provisions for the protection of the environment;[18]
- use research and technology to develop clean and efficient transport;[19]
- manage the effects of globalisation by opening transport markets while continuing to maintain quality and safety in transport by reinforcing the position of the Union in international organisations;[20] and
- develop a European satellite navigation system, "Galileo", a global navigation satellite system (GNSS) and European satellite radionavigation system EGNOS (European Geostationary Navigation Overlay Service).[21] In 2009, Parliament and Council adopted a regulation on the future of these

---

[15] See the Marco Polo programme below.
[16] See also the Commission White Paper, "Fair Payment for Infrastructure Use: A phased approach to a common transport infrastructure charging framework in the EU" COM (1998) 466.
[17] For example transparency of information to passengers, special contract conditions.
[18] Directive 2008/68 [2008] O.J. L260/13.
[19] See the 7th RTD Framework Programme for 2007–2013 and the European Research Area below, in Ch.33: Research and Technological Development and Space.
[20] For instance: the International Civil Aviation Organisation (ICAO), the International Maritime Organisation, the Rhine Navigation Commission, the Danube Commission and Eurocontrol.
[21] See General Report 2007, 81.

European satellite radio navigation programmes.[22] The budgetary resources were set at €3.4 billion for the period 2007–2013. It also provides for improving the governance of these programmes.

2.   SPECIAL FEATURES OF TRANSPORT

27–03   As already mentioned, transport has several characteristics which distinguish it from other services.[23] One is the fact that it extends inevitably beyond the geographic borders of the Union and is thus subject to many international agreements and conventions. It suffices to think about sea and air transport.[24] Furthermore, most kinds of transport infrastructure require high investments, which, due to varying demand, remain temporarily unproductive. In addition, there exists an enormous difference between the infrastructures needed for the various modes of transport. Some, like railways and inland shipping, need heavy and very specific infrastructures, which are only intermittently used by a limited number of carriers. Therefore, the offer exceeds the demand most of the time. On the other hand, the road infrastructure is used by millions of people which do not contribute directly to its cost. Another characteristic is that some means of transport have been until recently (or still are) in the hands of or under the control of the States, either through public undertakings or undertakings to which they grant special or exclusive rights. This is due, among others, to the fact that they are obliged to offer (public) services which are not justified from a purely economic point of view. Finally, all forms of transport, especially public transport, are subject to strict safety requirements.

In order to understand the challenges the Union faces in developing its Common Transport Policy, a few basic facts should be kept in mind.

The first important fact is the constant increase in demand for transport, because of, among other things, the increased standard of living, which allows people to travel more and farther, changing lifestyles and consumer habits. Looking at the development in passenger transport, the continuing growth becomes obvious: the number of cars has tripled in the last 30 years and in the enlarged Union this growth continues.

Secondly, the creation of the internal market has led to substantial changes in the European economy and its system of production: the economic activities are no longer concentrated in urban areas but geographically spread, depending on the production costs (especially labour costs). The same applies to the population in general: suburbia has inevitably increased the demand for transport due to longer distances between home and work.

27–04   Thirdly, the different modes of transport have not grown equally—for reasons of unequal adaptation to the needs of modern economy and society, because of unequal regulations and other factors. Contrary to 20 years ago, inland waterways amount to 3.3 per cent of the EU goods transport market, air 0.1 per cent,

---

[22] Regulation 683/08 [2008] O.J. L196/1; modified [2010] O.J. L276/11. See Commission implementing Decision establishing a list of key decision points to evaluate the implementation of the Galileo programme [2012] O.J.L52/28.

[23] Art.91 TFEU.

[24] Art.100(2) TFEU and, for instance, the Chicago Convention of December 7, 1944 (see *http://www.iasl.mcgill.ca/airlaw* [accessed August 23, 2013]).

railways 9.6 per cent, while maritime transport amounts to 39.3 per cent and road transport to 44.5 per cent (referring to 2005).

Looking at the passenger transport, the predominance of road transport becomes obvious (referring to 2006–7): road transport 77 per cent; railways, including tram and metro, 7 per cent; air transport 8 per cent; sea 1 per cent.[25] Bearing those figures in mind it is clear that, if nothing is done, road transport will continue to grow to the detriment of the other modes of transport, but also, taking into account the problems with regard to the environment and congestion that creates significant external costs, to the detriment of the population and the economy of the Union.

Looking back at the development of the Common Transport Policy, one ascertains that, although the former EC Treaty did from the beginning provide for a "common transport policy", the Council failed for many years to materialise it.[26] It took an action in the Court,[27] lodged by Parliament and supported by the Commission, against the Council for failure to implement the Treaty provisions in this field to get things moving. The Court ruled that "there is not yet a set of rules which may be regarded as a common transport policy" and consequently concluded that:

> "[I]n breach of the Treaty, the Council had failed to ensure freedom to provide services in the sphere of international transport and to lay down the conditions under which non-resident carriers may operate transport services in a Member State".[28]

In the light of this Court judgment, the Council finally adopted a policy approach to transport, rather than the piecemeal one used before. Subsequently, the Treaties reinforced the political, institutional and budgetary foundations for a transport policy. For instance, the unanimity requirement for Council decisions was replaced by qualified majority.[29] Furthermore the Union became responsible for transport safety,[30] which is in line with the new obligations to ensure human health protection[31] and consumer protection.[32]

27–05

Also very important was the introduction of the Trans-European Networks (TENs),[33] among others, in the field of transport and the setting up of a Cohesion Fund to provide financial contributions to projects in the fields of environment and the TENs and in order to build the necessary transport infrastructure in

---

[25] See Statistical Pocketbook 2009, published by Directorate-General for Energy and Transport, European Commission, p.120.

[26] At that time, unanimity was needed for a Council decision related to transport and only a few dispersed provisions had been adopted.

[27] Art.265 TFEU.

[28] *Parliament v Council* (13/83) [1985] E.C.R. 1513; [1986] 1 C.M.L.R. 138.

[29] See Art.91 TFEU.

[30] Art.91(1)(c) TFEU.

[31] Art.168(1) TFEU.

[32] Arts 12 and 169 TFEU.

[33] TFEU Title XVI (Arts 170–172), see Decision 1692/96 on Union guidelines for the development of the trans-European transport network [1996] O.J. L228/1, as amended, and see Ch.31: Enterprise and Industrial Policy/Information Society.

less-developed regions.[34] Community financial aid is provided in the field of the trans-European transport and energy networks.[35]

Another new feature was the necessity to integrate environmental protection requirements into the definition and implementation of other Union policies, and therefore, also into the Common Transport Policy.[36] If one adds to that the necessary international aspects, the conclusion can only be that there was a need for a global Union transport policy. As mentioned, such a policy is based on the free movement of goods, the free movement of persons, the freedom to provide services and the right of establishment, while also taking into account other policies such as social policy.[37] The object remains to provide the carriers with the greatest possible choice while at the same time harmonising technical characteristics.[38]

3. APPLICATION OF COMPETITION RULES TO TRANSPORT

27–06 This subject was examined in some detail in Ch.22: Competition Policy, with special reference to maritime, air and rail transport. It was also pointed out that transport is subject to specific competition rules,[39] but that in 2004 the implementing system was harmonised,[40] which has affected also the transport sector.[41] Furthermore, the specific State aid rules applicable to the transport sector have to be kept in mind. State aid is only considered to be compatible with the common market if it meets the needs of co-ordination of transport or if it represents reimbursement for the discharge of certain obligations inherent in the concept of public service.[42] In 2004, the Commission decided to apply the de

---

[34] Art.177 EFDC and TFEU, see also below Ch.32: Regional Policy/Economic, Social and Territorial Cohesion—The Europe 2020 Strategy.

[35] Regulation 680/07 [2007] O.J. L162/1.

[36] Art.11 TFEU.

[37] See, for instance, Regulation 561/2006 on the harmonisation of certain social legislation relating to road transport [2006] O.J. L102/1 and Regulation 3821/85 on recording equipment in road transport [1985] O.J. L370/8, amended for the ninth time [2009] O.J. L21/3 and [2009] O.J. L29/45. See *Raemdonck* (C-128/04) [2005] E.C.R. I-2445: definition of "material or equipment".

[38] Numerous directives were adopted relating, for instance, to the type-approval of motor vehicles and their trailers, [1970] O.J. L42/1, several times amended [2006] O.J. L65/27.

[39] See Regulation 1017/68 (quoted above), most articles were repealed by Regulation 1/2003 [2003] O.J. L1/1, replaced by Regulation 169/09, codified version [2009] O.J. L61/1. See Regulation 773/2004 relating to the conduct of proceedings by the Commission pursuant to Arts 101–102 TFEU [81 and 82] [2004] O.J. L123/18; Regulation 1419/2006 [2006] O.J. L269/1 (maritime transport); and Regulation 411/2004 [2004] O.J. L68/1 (air transport).

[40] Regulation 1/2003 [2003] O.J. L1/1.

[41] Regulation 1/2003 [2003] O.J. L1/1 on the implementation of the rules on competition laid down in Arts 101–102 TFEU has repealed Regulation 141/62 exempting transport from the application of Regulation 17 [1962] O.J. 124/2751 and amended Regulation 1017/68 [1968] O.J. L175/10 (transport by rail, road and inland waterway), replaced by codified version Regulation 169/09 [2009] O.J. L61/1.

[42] Art.93 TFEU. See Regulation 1191/69 on action by Member States concerning the obligations inherent in the concept of a public service in transport by rail, road and inland waterway [1969] O.J. L56/1, repealed by Regulation 1370/07 on public passenger transport services by rail and by road [2007] O.J. L315/1; Regulation 1107/70 on the granting of aids for transport by rail, road and internal waterway [1970] O.J. L130/1, amended [1997] O.J. L84/6, repealed by Regulation 1370/07 on public passenger transport by rail and road [2007] O.J. L315/1.

minimis rules[43] to the transport sector, i.e. it will no longer examine small amounts, i.e. less than €100.000, of State aid to the transport sector.[44]

As mentioned above, the Treaty entrusts the Union institutions with laying down common rules applicable to international transport, conditions for market access, measures to improve transport safety and any other appropriate provisions.[45] The main provisions will be examined below for the various modes of transport.

4. ROAD TRANSPORT

Road transport can be subdivided into transport of passengers and transport of goods. For the former, a regulation laid down common rules for the international carriage of passengers by coach and bus,[46] a Regulation lays down the rights of passengers in coach and bus transport[47] and another lays down the conditions under which non-resident carriers may operate national road passenger transport services within a Member State.[48] The Union signed the Agreement on the International Carriage of Passengers by Road by means of Occasional Coach and Bus Services (ASOR),[49] and the Agreement on the international occasional carriage of passengers by coach and bus (Interbus Agreement).[50] A Regulation lays down common rules for access to the international market for coach and bus services.[51] The ASOR provides for harmonised liberalisation measures and simplified inspection measures by introducing a single document. The aim of the Interbus Agreement is to harmonise rules and thus to facilitate tourism between the contracting parties. For non-resident carriers conditions have been adopted for the right to operate national road passenger transport services within a Member State (cabotage transport operations).[52] The rights of passengers of bus and coach transport are also provided for.[53]

27–07

Where the carriage of goods is concerned, common rules for international transport of goods by road for hire or reward are provided for.[54] See Customs Convention on the International transport of Goods under Cover of TIR Carnets (TIR Convention, 1975).[55]

---

[43] See Regulation 69/2001 on the application of Arts 106 and 107 TFEU to de minimis aid [2001] O.J. L10/30.

[44] IP/04/290.

[45] Art.91 TFEU.

[46] Regulation 684/92 [1992] O.J. L74/1, amended [1998] O.J. L4/1 and [2006] O.J. L363/1.

[47] Regulation 2006/04 [2004] O.J. L364/1, modified [2011] O.J. L55/1.

[48] Regulation 12/98 [1998] O.J. L4/10.

[49] [1982] O.J. L230/39. See also Regulation 56/83 concerning the implementation of the Agreement [1983] O.J. L10/1 and Regulation 684/92 on common rules for the international carriage of passengers by coach or bus [1992] O.J. L74/1, as amended, and implemented as regards documents by Regulation 2121/98 [1998] O.J. L268/10.

[50] [2002] O.J. L321/11.

[51] Regulation 1073/09 [2009] O.J. L300/88.

[52] Regulation 12/98 [1998] O.J. L4/10.

[53] Regulation 181/11 [2011] O.J. L55/1.

[54] Directive 62/2005 [1962] O.J. 70/2005, as amended. See also Directive 2003/59 on the initial qualification and periodic training of drivers of certain road vehicles for the carriage of goods or passengers [2003] O.J. L226/4, adapted by reason of the accession: [2004] O.J. L168/35; it applied as from September 10, 2008 to drivers of vehicles for the carriage of passengers by road, and as from

The conditions for market access are laid down in a basic regulation,[56] while a regulation concerning the right of non-resident carriers with regard to road haulage services within a Member State, has introduced progressively the free road cabotage for freights.[57] A directive regulates the use of vehicles hired without drivers for the carriage of goods by road[58] and another establishes common rules for certain types of carriage of goods by road.[59] In order to ensure the freedom to provide transport services, the Treaty explicitly provides that:

> "[D]iscrimination which takes the form of charging different rates and imposing different conditions for the carriage of the same goods over the same transport links on grounds of the country of origin or of destination of the goods in question must be abolished".[60]

27–08   It is up to the Council to lay down the necessary rules for implementing this principle.[61] Nevertheless, the Member States remain free to charge tolls on roads, provided they are in line with the Treaty provisions.[62] Charges will become more important in order to meet the "polluter pays" principle and the realisation of a fair principle, some of the objectives are set out in the White Paper.[63] A 2009 directive provides measures to promote clean and energy-efficient road transport vehicles.[64]

For both road haulage and passenger transport, the Council laid down the conditions for admission to the occupation of road transport operator,[65] and the mutual recognition of diplomas in order to facilitate the freedom of establishment. Member States shall issue national driving licences, which shall be

---

September 10, 2009 to drivers of vehicles for the carriage of goods by road; and Directive 2006/1 on the use of vehicles hired without drivers for the carriage of goods by road [2006] O.J. L33/82; see *Bourrasse and Perchicot* (Joined Cases C-228/01 and C-289/01) [2002] E.C.R. I-10213.

[55] Consolidated text published by Decision 2009/477 [2009] O.J. L165/1.

[56] Regulation 881/92 [1992] O.J. L95/1, repealed and replaced by Reg.1072/09 [2009] O.J. L300/72; see correlation table in Annex IV.

[57] Regulation 3118/93 laying down the conditions under which non-resident carriers may operate road haulage services within a Member State [1993] O.J. L279/1, repealed and replaced by Reg.1072/09 (quoted above); see also Regulation 1071/09 establishing common rules concerning the conditions to be complied with to pursue the occupation of road transport operator [2009] O.J. L300/51 and Regulation 792/94 laying down detailed rules for the application of Regulation 3118/93 to road haulage operators on own account [1994] O.J. L92/13.

[58] Directive 2006/1 [2006] O.J. L33/86.

[59] Directive 2006/94 [2006] O.J. L374/5.

[60] Art.95(1) TFEU.

[61] Regulation No.11 concerning the abolition of discrimination in transport rates and conditions [1960] O.J. 52/1121, as amended, and Regulation 4058/89 on the fixing of rates for the carriage of goods by road between Member States [1989] O.J. L390/1. The Court accepted that road haulage tariffs are approved and brought into force by the State: *Autotrasporti Librandi* (C-38/97) [1998] E.C.R. I-5955.

[62] Directive 1999/62 on the charging of heavy goods vehicles for the use of certain infrastructure [1999] O.J. L187/42 contains only a framework and did not harmonise the national systems nor included the environmental costs.

[63] White Paper "European transport policy for 2010: time to decide", COM(2001)370.

[64] Directive 2009/33 [2009] O.J. L120/5.

[65] Regulations 1071/09, 1072/09 and 1073/09, [2009] O.J. L300/51.

mutually recognised, based on a Union model driving licence.[66] In 2008, the Commission issued a decision on equivalence between categories of driving licences.[67]

Other subjects, such as insurance against liability in respect of the use of motor vehicles,[68] the installation and use of speed limitation devices for certain categories of motor vehicles,[69] recording equipment in road transport[70] and elimination of controls performed at the frontiers of Member States,[71] are the subject of several Union rules. See also rules concerning a framework for the approval of motor vehicles and their trailers, and of systems, components and separate technical units intended for such vehicles.[72]

The fact that in 2007 more than 40,000 (in 1990: 70,628) people were killed and more than 1.3 million were injured (in 1990: more than 1.45 million) in road accidents in the Union shows that the implementation of road safety measures is very important.[73] Consequently, legislation concerning roadworthiness tests for motor vehicles and their trailers,[74] the minimum level of training for some road transport drivers,[75] the transport of dangerous goods,[76] the weights and dimension for heavy goods vehicles,[77] and technical conditions were adopted. Where the latter are concerned, Union legislation is very detailed indeed. They concern, for instance, the use of safety belts,[78] safety glazing on motor vehicles and their trailers,[79] the technical roadside inspection of the roadworthiness of commercial

27–09

---

[66] Directive 91/439 on driving licences [1991] O.J. L237/1, amended [2009] O.J. L223/26. See *Wiedemann* (Joined Cases C-329/06 and C-343/06) [2008] E.C.R. I-4635: withdrawal of driver's licence in one Member State and issue of new licence in another Member State: mutual recognition, but possibility of Art.227 EC action. When normal residence condition laid down in Art.7(1)(b) has not been observed in a given Member State, a host Member State may refuse to recognise the driving licence in its territory *Grasser v Bayern* (C-184/10) [2011] E.C.R. I-4057. See also Directive 2006/126 on driving licences [2006] O.J. L403/18, amended [2012] O.J. L321/54.

[67] [2008] O.J. L270/31.

[68] Decision 2003/564 on the application of Directive 72/166 relating to checks on insurance against civil liability in respect of the use of motor vehicles [2003] O.J. L192/23, now Directive 2009/103 [2009] O.J. L263/11; see implementing Decision; *Farrell* (C-356/05) [2007] E.C.R.I-3067 concerning damages to a person without a seat in a car.

[69] Directive 92/6 [1992] O.J. L57/27, as amended; *Elbertsen* (C-449/08) [2009] E.C.R. I-10241.

[70] Regulation 3821/85 [1985] O.J. L370/8, amended [2009] O.J. L2945. Regulation 2135/98: [1998] O.J. L274/1.

[71] Regulation 4060/89 [1989] O.J. L390/18, codified by Regulation 1100/08 [2008] O.J. L304/63.

[72] Framework Directive 2007/46 [2007] O.J. L263/1. Replacement of Annexes I, III, IV, VI, VII, XI and XV [2008] O.J. L292/1. Annexes IV and VI were amended in 2011 [2011] O.J. L53/4. Annex II was replaced and Annexes IV, IX and XI were amended [2011] O.J. L185/30. Amending Annexes IV and XII [2012] O.J. L353/1. Several amendments: [2013] O.J. L55/9.

[73] See also CARE (Community data base on road accidents) Decision 93/704 [1993] O.J. L329/63.

[74] Directive 96/96 [1996] O.J. L46/1, as amended.

[75] Directive 76/914 [1976] O.J. L357/36, repealed [2003] O.J. L226/4, which applied as from September 10, 2008 to drivers of vehicles for the carriage of passengers by road, and as from September 10, 2009 to drivers of vehicles for the carriage of goods by road.

[76] Directive 94/55 [1994] O.J. L319/7, replaced together with Directive 96/49 (see below) by Directive 2008/68 [2008] O.J. L260/13; see also Directive 99/36 on transportable pressure equipment approved for the inland transport of dangerous goods by road and by rail [1999] O.J. L138/20, as amended.

[77] Directive 96/53 laying down for certain road vehicles circulating within the Union the maximum authorised dimensions in national and international traffic and the maximum authorised weights in international traffic [1996] O.J. L235/59, as amended.

[78] Directive 91/671 [1991] O.J. L373/26, as amended.

[79] Directive 92/22 [1991] O.J. L129/11, as amended.

vehicles circulating in the Union,[80] the tread depth of tyres,[81] the external projections forward of the cab's rear panel of motor vehicles of category N,[82] a directive establishing a framework for the approval of motor vehicles and their trailers, and of systems, components and technical units intended for such vehicles (Framework Directive).[83]

And so on. The list seems unending.[84] Then there are the regulations adopted by bodies created by international agreements concerning the approval of vehicles.[85] See also a regulation on type-approval of hydrogen-powered motor vehicles.[86]

The Union also adhered to the European Agreement concerning the work of crews of vehicles engaged in international road transport (AETR),[87] which was the object of a famous judgment establishing the international competence of the Union in a field where no specific powers were granted by the Treaty.[88] Several pieces of legislation were adopted to improve safety and working conditions in the road transport sector.[89] Transport has its competition rules,[90] but certain sectors have their own.[91]

See also the regulation on public passenger transport service by rail and by road applying the concept of "services of general economic interest" to this mode of transport.[92]

---

[80] Directive 2000/30 [2000] O.J. L203/1, as amended.

[81] Directive 89/459 [1989] O.J. L226/4.

[82] Directive 92/114 [1992] O.J. L409/17.

[83] Directive 07/46 [2007] O.J. L263/1,Annexes V, X, XV and XVI replaced [2010] O.J. L110/1.

[84] As mentioned already the complete list of all the Union acts in force can be found in the Directory of Union Legislation, published by the Official Journal, in Luxembourg, or under *http://eur-lex. europa.eu/en/legis/latest/index.htm* [accessed August 23, 2013].

[85] [2010] O.J. L120/1, etc. and [2010] O.J. L130/1, 19 and 50: Regulations of the Economic Commission for Europe of the United Nations (UN/ECE) : uniform provisions concerning the approval of parking lamps, replacement brake lining and protection of occupants in the event of frontal collision. See also [2010] O.J. L177: a number of regulations of the Economic commission for Europe of the United Nations (UN/ECE). See also [2010] O.J. L230.

[86] [2010] O.J. L122/1, etc. [2010] L185/1, etc.

[87] [1978] O.J. L95/1.

[88] *Commission v Council* (22/70) [1971] E.C.R. 263; [1971] C.M.L.R. 335.

[89] Directive 2003/88 on certain aspects of the organisation of working time [2003] O.J. L299/9; see concerning annual sick leave and compensation (Joined Cases C-350/06 and C-520/06): Member State not allowed to make existence of right subject to any precondition E.C.R [2009] 20.01.09; Regulation 3820/85 on the harmonising of certain social legislation regarding road transport [1985] O.J. L370/1, adapted by reason of the accession [2004] O.J. L168/35, amended [2009] O.J. L29/45. See also Regulation 561/2006: [2006] O.J. L102/1. Directive 2002/15 on the organisation of working time of persons performing mobile road transport activities [2006] O.J. L102/1; see *Spain and Finland v Parliament and Council* (Joined Cases C-184/02 and C-223/02) [2004] E.C.R. I-7789, where the Court rejected a request for annulment of said Directive.

[90] Regulation 1017/68 [1988] O.J. L 175/1, amended [2003] O.J. L1.

[91] See below: 6. Air Transport and 8. Maritime Transport.

[92] Regulation 1370/07 [2007] O.J. L315/1.

5.   RAIL TRANSPORT

Rail transport requires extremely heavy expenditure on infrastructure, which in **27–10** addition is only used intermittently, with the consequence that railway companies risk being in deficit[93] and, were in the past all nationalised. While road and air transport, both for passengers and freight, have increased their market share, railway transport has seen its own constantly reduced, not only in relative, but also in absolute terms. This, in turn, deprived it of the sorely needed income to modernise its infrastructure and rolling stock. Nevertheless, rail transport is needed, and it is more environmentally friendly and safer than other means of transport. How to explain this decline? The railways themselves are, of course, partly to blame: inefficiency (except for a few remarkable achievements), corporatism, lack of co-operation with other railway companies[94] and conservatism. The real cause, however, was their monopoly position and the market fragmentation. In other words, there was no competition and therefore closed-off and protected markets. This could only partly be explained by the obligations of public service[95] generally imposed on the railways by the national governments.

More than a decade after liberalising road and air transport in the Union, steps have been taken to develop an internal market for railways. This includes the creation of a high-speed rail network[96] and freight transport "freeways" across the Union. A series of measures aiming to ensure the development of a Union's international railways freight market have been adopted. In 2007, the Commission adopted a communication "Towards a rail network giving priority to

---

[93] Regulation 1192/69 on common rules for the normalisation of the accounts of railways undertakings [1969] O.J. L156/8, as amended.

[94] Council Resolution on co-operation between railway undertakings [1971] O.J. C5/1; for a long time, no "international" trains existed; indeed, when crossing a border, a train, besides changing locomotive, acquired the nationality of the host country and was submitted to all the rules and regulations applying to "national" trains.

[95] Regulation 1191/69 on action by Member States concerning the obligations inherent in the concept of public service in the transport by rail, road and inland waterway [1969] O.J. L156/1, amended several times. See also Art.93 TFEU, which refers to the discharge of certain obligations inherent in the concept of public service.

[96] Directive 96/48 on the interoperability of the trans-European high-speed rail system, [1996] O.J. L235/6, amended [2007] O.J L141/63, repealed by Regulation 1370/07 on public passenger transport by rail and by road [2007] O.J. L315/1 and the Commission Recommendation on the basic parameters of this system [2001] O.J. L100/17; see the Decision concerning a technical specification for interoperability relating to the "infrastructure" sub-system of the trans-European high-speed rail system [2008] O.J. L77/1. See also Decision 2008/386 concerning the technical specification for interoperability relating to the control-command and signalling sub-system of the trans-European conventional and high-speed rail system [2008] O.J. L136/11 and Directive 2008/57 on the interoperability of the rail system within the Union [2008] O.J. L191/1, modified [2011] O.J. L57/21, Annex III amended [2013] O.J. L68/55; see Regulation 454/11 on the technical specifications for interoperability, Annex VII modified [2009] O.J. L273/12 and Decision concerning a technical specification for interoperability relating to the rolling stock subsystem "Locomotives and passenger rolling stock" [2011] O.J. L139/1 and Decision concerning the technical qualifications for interoperability relating to the "operation and traffic management" subsystems of the trans-European conventional rail system [2011] O.J. L144/1. However, see also Commission communication in the framework of the above mentioned Directive 96/48 [2010] O.J. C97/11. Commission Decision amending decision 2012/88 on the technical specifications for interoperability relating to the control-command and signalling systems of the Trans-European rail system [2012] O.J. L310/3.

freight", which aims to make freight transport more competitive, in particular by reducing transit times and improving the reliability of rail and its responsiveness to customers' demands.[97]

The first important piece of legislation required the Member States to manage railway undertakings in a competitive manner, to make railway undertakings independent by giving them a separate budget and system of accounts, to guarantee rights of access for rail transport operators on specific terms in other Member States to international combined transport services, and to have separate accounting for railway infrastructure (track and related equipment) and the operation of transport services as such as from January 1, 1993.[98] Important is as well the "combined" transport, which the Union tries to encourage and regulate.[99]

27–11   The *first railway package* (also called rail infrastructure package) aimed to enable rail companies to provide competitive European services to meet the demands of industry and forwarders. It consists of three Directives on the further development of the Union's railways,[100] on the licensing of railway undertakings[101] and on the allocation of railway infrastructure capacity and the levying of charges for the use of railway infrastructure and safety certification.[102]

The first package also provides for an extension of fair and non-discriminatory access for licensed railway undertakings to the entire network for a transitional period of up to seven years. This includes access to, and supply of, services in major terminals and ports, better organisation of frontier crossings, elimination of the main bottlenecks in the system, independent regulatory bodies qualified to issue safety certificates and allocation of train paths as well as the interoperability of the trans-European conventional rail system.[103] The "Trans European Rail Freight Network" (TERFN) provided for in this package had to be implemented by Member States by March 15, 2003. To the detriment of the liberalisation of the rail freight transport sector, several Member States have failed to implement the first rail infrastructure package within the time limit set.[104] The delays in transposition have had repercussions on the ability of the actors to assert themselves on the European stage due to the resulting uncertainty surrounding the

---

[97] COM(2007) 608.

[98] Directive 91/440 on the development of the Union's railways [1991] O.J. L237/25, amended [2007] O.J. L315/44.

[99] Directive 92/106 on the establishment of common rules for certain types of combined transport of goods between Member States [1992] O.J. L368/38, as amended; and Council Resolution on the development of rail transport and combined transport: [1995] O.J. C169/1.

[100] Directive 2001/12 [2001] O.J. L75/1, amending [1991] O.J. L237/25; see *Commission v Germany* (C-477/03) [2004] E.C.R. 17.11.04, unpublished.

[101] Directive 2001/13 [2001] O.J. L75/28, amending [1995] O.J. L143/70.

[102] Directive 2001/14 [2001] O.J. L75/29, amended [2007] O.J. L315/44.For charges for the use of railway infrastructure: *Commission v Hungary* (C-473/10), judgment of February 28, 2013, not yet reported.

[103] Directive 2001/16 [2001] O.J. L110/1, amended [2007] O.J. L141/63, replaced by Directive 2008/57 on the interoperability of rail systems within the Community [2008] O.J. L191/1.See, however, Commission communication [2010] O.J. C97/18.

[104] Court cases (unpublished, but on the Internet under "Curia"): *Commission v Greece* (C-550/03); *Commission v United Kingdom* (C-483/03) and *Commission v Germany* (C-447/03): non-notification implementation measures for Directives 2001/12, 2001/13 and 2001/14 as well as: *Commission v Luxembourg* (C-481/03): non-notification implementation measures for Directives 2001/12 and 2001/13.

national regulatory situation.[105] In 2008, the Commission launched infringement proceedings against 24 (!) Member States for incorrect transposition of the directives making up the first railway package.[106] As from March 15, 2008, the entire European Rail Network is open to international freight services. The situation for passenger transport, however, remains unchanged.[107]

Safety does, of course, play an important role. In 2012, the Commission published a second set of common safety targets as regards the rail system.[108] A general licensing system for railway undertakings was set up,[109] as mentioned, a Directive on transportable pressure equipment approved for the inland transport of dangerous goods by road and by rail,[110] rules regarding the transport of dangerous goods by rail have been adopted[111] and a European Rail Traffic Management System was backed by the Union to enhance cross-border interoperability and signalling procurement by creating a single European-wide standard for railway signalling. In order to complement the first package and to revitalise the railways by rapidly building an integrated European Railways Area, the Commission published, in 2001, a White Paper[112] concerning a second package.

The *second railways package* was adopted by Parliament and the Council in 2004. It covers the opening of the market for international freight transport to the entire European rail network as of January 1, 2006, the liberalisation of the market for national freight transport (cabotage) as of January 1, 2007, the interoperability of trans-European rail systems,[113] the development of the Union's railways,[114] safety rules[115] and the establishment of an European Railway Agency[116] to steer the technical work on safety and interoperability. With regard to the latter, Parliament and the Council adopted a directive which establishes a legislative framework aimed at reducing barriers to bringing railway vehicles into service. Cross-acceptance between Member States should be improved through the application of the principle of mutual recognition and the harmonisation of national authorisation procedures.[117]

27–12

---

[105] Report from the Commission on the implementation of the first railway package of May 3, 2006; COM (2006) 189 final.

[106] General Report 2008, 83.

[107] But see Commission Decision of August 28, 2003 (COMP/37.685 GVG/FS) which concerned cross-border passenger service.

[108] Decision 2012/226 [2012] O.J. L115/27.

[109] Directive 95/18 [1995] O.J. L143/70, as amended.

[110] Directive 99/36 [1999] O.J. L138/20, as amended.

[111] Directive 96/49 on the approximation of the laws of the Member States with regard to the transport of dangerous goods by rail [1996] O.J. L235/25, replaced, together with Directive 94/55 (see above), by Directive 2008/68 [2008] O.J. L260/13.

[112] White Paper, "European transport policy for 2010: time to decide", COM (2001) 370.

[113] Directive 2004/50 [2004] O.J. L164/114.

[114] Directive 2004/51 [2004] O.J. L164/164.

[115] Directive 2004/49 [2004] O.J. L164/44 (Railway Safety Directive), modified [2008] O.J. L345/62. See Regulation 352/2009 on the adoption of a common safety method on risk evaluation and assessment [2009] O.J. L108/4.

[116] See Ch.13: Decentralised Agencies and Bodies of the Union.

[117] General Report 2008, 83.

In March 2004, the Commission proposed a *third railway package* of measures. The third package of railway measures was adopted by Parliament and the Council in 2007[118]; it consists of one regulation and two directives:

- a Regulation[119] on the rights and obligations of rail passengers, which is intended to enhance and improve these passengers' rights. It covers all journeys and rail services provided throughout the Union by one or more railway undertakings;
- a Directive[120] providing for the opening-up to competition of the international rail passenger transport service market by 2010 and includes the right for international trains to provide cabotage services, i.e. to take up and set down passengers at stations in the same Member State;
- a Directive on the certification of train drivers operating locomotives and trains on the railway system in the Union.[121]

27–13   In 2007, Parliament and the Council adopted the public service obligation regulation on public passengers transport service by rail and by road,[122] similar, in part, to the one adopted in 2004 establishing common rules on compensation and assistance to passengers in the event of denied boarding and of cancellation or long delays of flights,[123] and a Regulation on Public Service Obligations.[124] In 2007, the Commission published a Communication on monitoring development of the rail market providing for: statistical analysis, regular reporting and presenting the regulatory and institutional framework established for the purpose of liberating this market.[125]

See also above Ch.22: Competition Policy for rules applying to transport, e.g. Guidelines for State aid to rail undertakings.[126]

In 2010, Parliament and Council established a Euroepan rail network for competitive freight: [2010] O.J. L276/22.

An Agreement between the Union and the Intergovernmental Organisation for International Carriage by Rail entered into force in 2011.[127]

A *Single European Railway Area* was established in 2012.[128]

An agreement was signed between the Union and the Intergovernmental Organisation for Carriage by Rail on the accession of the Union to the Convention concerning International carriage by Rail (COTIF) in 2011.[129]

---

[118] General Report 2007, 76.

[119] Regulation 1371/07 [2007] O.J. L315/14, became applicable on December 3, 2009.

[120] Directive 2007/58 [2007] O.J. L315/44, amending Directive 91/440 on the development of the Community railways [1991] O.J. L237/25.

[121] Directive 2007/69 on the certification of train drivers operating locomotives and trains on the railway system in the Union [2007] O.J. L315/51.

[122] Regulation 1370/07 [2007] O.J. L315/1 and Regulation 1371/07 on rail passengers' rights and obligations [2007] O.J. L315/14.

[123] [2004] O.J. L46/1.

[124] Regulation 1370/07 [2007] O.J. L315/1.

[125] COM(2007) 609.

[126] [2008] O.J. C 184/13 and Directive 91/440 [1991] 237/25.

[127] [2011] O.J. L183/1.

[128] Directive 2012/34 [2012] O.J. L343/32.

[129] [2013] O.J. L51/1.

6. AIR TRANSPORT

As indicated, air transport was at the beginning not covered by the provisions on   **27–14**
Transport of the EC Treaty, which, according to the Court does not mean that the
general provisions of the Treaty did not apply either.[130] From the beginning, these
two modes of transport were indeed subject to the general rules of the Treaty.[131]

Air transport, although in full expansion, suffered from the same drawback as
rail transport, namely its monopoly position, and was therefore a protected
national market. However, because of reciprocal traffic rights, some competition
from foreign carriers had to be accepted on international routes, but for a long
time, there were no competing national ones. Although the national airlines, the
so-called Flag Carriers, desperately fought to keep foreign airlines from
providing air service within their territory, i.e. from flying passengers from one
city to another within the same country (so-called cabotage), the situation has
changed completely in the last years due to successive liberalisation packages
adopted by the Union.

The *first liberalisation package* was adopted in December 1987. It limited, for
example, the right of governments to object to the introduction of new fares and
enabled airlines of two different states having a bilateral air transport agreement
with each other to share seating capacity. It was in the same year that the Council
laid down the procedure for the application of the competition rules to
undertakings in the air transport sector and for exemptions by category for
agreements and concerted practices.[132] Those measures have been supplemented
in June 1990 by the *second liberalisation package*, which opened up the market
further. It gave the carriers a greater flexibility over the setting of fares and
capacity-sharing and opened up the routes between Member States to all Union
carriers.[133]

The *third liberalisation package* was adopted in July 1992 and has been   **27–15**
applicable since January 1993. It introduced gradually the freedom to provide air
transport services within the Union and led, in April 1997, to the freedom to
provide services within another Member State (cabotage).[134] This package
provides for a Union air carrier's licence,[135] freedom of access to the market[136]

---

[130] Art.100 TFEU.

[131] In *Commission v France* (167/73) [1974] E.C.R. 359, 24–25; [1974] 2 C.M.L.R. 216, where the
Court ruled that the very first words of the Title on Transport: "The objectives of this Treaty shall be
pursued..." refer to the provisions of Arts 2 and 3 EC, and since the fundamental provisions
applicable to the whole complex of economic activities are of prime importance for the attainment of
those objectives, the object of the rules relating to the common transport policy, far from involving a
departure from those fundamental rules, is to implement and complement them by means of common
action; see as well *Nouvelles Frontiéres* (Joined Cases 209/84, 210/84, 211/84, 212/84 and 213/84)
[1986] E.C.R. 1425.

[132] Regulation 3975/87 which was repealed by Regulation 411/2004 [2004] O.J. L68/1 and
Regulation 3976/87 on the application of Art.101(3) of the Treaty to certain categories of agreement
and concerted practices in the air transport sector, replaced by Regulation 487/09 [2009] O.J. L148/1.
See also Regulation 773/2004 [2004] O.J. L123/18, as amended.

[133] Regulation 2408/92 on access for air carriers to scheduled intra-Union air service routes [1992]
O.J. L240/8, as amended.

[134] In 2003, the Commission announced the revision of the third liberalisation package in order to
adapt the current rules to the recent changes.

[135] Regulation 2407/92 [1992] O.J. L240/1.

[136] Regulation 2408/92 [1992] O.J. L240/8, as amended.

and the freedom to set fares and rates for air services.[137] However, this freedom only applies to Union air carriers; where air carriers from third countries operating on intra-Union routes are concerned, the Union has acquired exclusive competence to enter into commitments with non-Member States concerning fares and rates to be charged (external competence of the Union).[138] This was followed by various other regulations: on exemption for agreements and concerted practices concerning consultations on passenger tariffs on scheduled air services and slot allocation at airports,[139] code of conduct for computerised reservation systems,[140] common rules for the allocation of slots at Union airports,[141] access to the ground-handling market at Union airports,[142] and the limitation of noise emission.[143] See also a regulation laying down common requirements for the provisions of air navigation services, as regards working methods and operating procedures,[144] and a regulation on common rules for the operation of air service in the Union—Public service obligations in respect of scheduled air services.[145] The 2013 Regulations lay down a performance scheme for air navigation services and network functions[146] and laying down a common charging scheme for air navigation services.[147]

A common framework regulating the essential feature of *airport charges* and the way they are set, was established.[148]

27–16   In order to strengthen *passengers' rights*, a regulation establishing common rules for a denied-boarding compensation system in scheduled air transport,[149] a

---

[137] Regulation 2409/92 [1992] O.J. L240/15240/15.See Public service obligations in respect of scheduled air services [2011] O.J. C330/8.

[138] See *Commission v Netherlands* (C-523/04) [2007] E.C.R. I-3267.

[139] Regulation 1617/93 [1993] O.J. L155/18, ended June 30, 2005. It was followed by Regulation 1459/2006 [2006] L272/3, whose validity ended October 31, 2006. Presently, Regulation 95/93 [1993] O.J. L14/1 on common rules for the allocation of slots at Union airports applies, modified [2009] O.J. L167/24.

[140] Regulation 2299/89 [1989] O.J. L220/1, amended [2009] O.J. L35/47.

[141] Regulation 95/93 [1995] O.J. L14/1, as amended. See Communication of April 30, 2008 (IP/08/672) clarifying a number of issues in order to ensure a better implementation COM (2008) 227.

[142] Directive 96/67 [1996] O.J. L272/36, as amended. See *Commission v Italy* (C-460/02) [2004] E.C.R. I-7335.

[143] Directive 89/629 [1989] O.J. L363/27. See *Commission v Spain* (C-70/03) [2004] E.C.R. I-7999.

[144] Regulation 2096/05 [2005] O.J. L335/13, amended [2010] O.J. L201/1.

[145] Regulation 1008/08 [2008] O.J. L293/3; See Commission's Notices pursuant to Art.16(4) and Art.17(5) [2011] O.J. C221/5 and 6. Modification of public service obligations [2012] O.J. C-263/7.Modification of public service obligations in respect of scheduled air service [2013] O.J. C65/13.

[146] Regulation 390/13 [2013] O.J. L128/1.

[147] Regulation 391/13 [2013] O.J. L128/31.

[148] Directive 2009/12 [2009] O.J. L70/11.

[149] Regulation 261/2004 [2004] O.J. L46/1. The Court determined that this Regulation only applies for travels within the Union: *Emirate Airlines* (C-173/07) [2008] E.C.R. I-5237. See *IATA and ELFAA* (C-344/04) [2006] E.C.R. I-403, *FINNAIR* (C_22/11 [2012] E.C.R.04.10.12.) denied boarding, cancellation or long delays must be interpreted as relating not only to cases where boarding is denied because of overbooking, but also where boarding is denied on other grounds such as operational reasons. Also interpretation of Arts 2(j) and 4(3). *Cuadrench Moré* (C-139/11), judgment of November 22, 2012, not yet reported; time-limit for bringing actions for compensation is determined in accordance with the rules of each Member state on the limitation of actions. *McDonagh* (C-12/11), judgment of January 31, 2013, not yet reported; the obligation of Art.5(1)(b) and 9 are not affected by "extraordinary circumstances"; also Regulation 2006/2004 on co-operation between national authorities responsible for the enforcement of consumer protection laws [2004] O.J. L364/1 amended

directive on unfair terms in consumer contracts[150] and a directive on package travel, package holidays and package tours[151] have been adopted.

Safety, of course, plays a very important role and several regulations and directives have been adopted,[152] including one on protection of the European sky against unsafe airlines[153] and on a restriction of liquids in carry-on baggage.[154] See also the Regulation laying down detailed measures for the implementation of the common basic standards of aviation security.[155] Common basic standards were laid down on aviation security in respect of explosive detection systems.[156]

Other safety rules have established common rules in the field of civil aviation security,[157] or regulate air carrier liability in the event of accidents.[158] Insurance requirements for air carriers and aircraft operators have been established,[159] while measures for the implementation of the common basic standards on aviation security have also been issued.[160] The principal objective is to establish and maintain a high uniform level of civil aviation safety in Europe.

A European Aviation Safety Agency (EASA), briefly described above in Ch.13: Decentralised Agencies and Bodies of the Union, was established by regulation in 2002.[161] This Regulation applies to the design, production,

27–17

[2011] O.J. L259/1, and Communication pursuant to Art.5(2) of Regulation 2006/2004 [2010] O.J. C244/1, the latter again amended [2011] O.J. L155/1.

[150] Directive 93/13 [1993] O.J. L95/29, amended [2012] O.J. L304/64; see Ch.30: Culture and Education, Public Health Consumer Protection. See *Oceano Grupo Editorial and Salva Editores* (Joined Cases C-240/98 and C-244/98) on the role of the national courts [2000] E.C.R. I-4941 and *Commission v Spain* (C-70/03) [2004] E.C.R. I-7999.

[151] Directive 90/314 [1990] O.J. L158/59.

[152] See, for instance, Regulation 300/08 on common rules in the field of civil aviation security [2008] O.J. L97/72, amended [2010] O.J. L7/3, and repealing Regulation 2320/02; Regulation 185/10 laying down detailed measures for the implementation of the common basic standards on aviation security [2010] O.J. L55/1, amended [2012] O.J. L59 /1; also Regulation 552/2004 on the interoperability of the European Air Traffic Management network [2004] O.J. L96/26, Communication concerning the implementation of Art.4 of Regulation 552/04: [2012] O.J. C332/9; Regulation 3922/91 on the harmonisation of technical requirements and administrative procedures in the field of civil aviation [1991] O.J. L373/4, amended [2008] O.J. L10/1 and [2008] L254/1. In 2007, the Council established a Joint Undertaking to develop the new generation European air traffic management system (SESAR) [2007] O.J. L64/1, amended [2008] O.J. L352/12. See also Regulation 996/2010 on the investigation and prevention of accidents and incidents in civil aviation: [2010] O.J. L295/35.

[153] Regulation 2111/2005 on the establishment of a Union list of air carriers subject to an operating ban ("Airlines black list") within the Union and on informing air transport passengers of the identity of the operating air carrier [2005] O.J. L344/15; Regulation 474/2006 establishing the Union list of air carriers which are subject to an operating ban within the Union referred to in Ch.II of Regulation 2111/2005 [2006] O.J. L84/14, amended [2012] O.J. L333 /7; Directive 2004/36 on the safety of third-country aircraft using Union airports [2004] O.J. L143/76, as amended.

[154] See IP/06/1313.

[155] Regulation 185/10 [2010] O.J. L55/1, amended [2012] O.J. L324/25.

[156] Regulation 1087/2011 [2011] O.J. L281/12.

[157] Regulation 2320/2002 [2002] O.J. L355/1, amended: see Regulation 483/09 [2009] O.J. L145/23.

[158] Regulation 2027/97 [1997] O.J. L285/1, as amended in order to align it with the Montreal Convention of May 28, 1999 [2001] O.J. L194/38. *Bogiatzi* (C-301/08) [2009] E.C.R. I-10185 this Regulation does not prevent the application of Art.29 of the Warsaw Convention. See also damage or delay of baggage.

[159] Regulation 785/2004 [2004] O.J. L138/1.

[160] Regulation 622/2003 [2003] O.J. L89/9, amended [2008] O.J. L9/12 and L111/5; since the Annex was not published in the O.J., for security reasons, it is non-binding on individuals: *Heinrich* (C-345/06) [2009] E.C.R. I-1659.

[161] Regulation 1592/2002 [2002] O.J. L240/1, as amended.

maintenance and operation of aeronautical products, parts and appliances, and to the personnel and organisations involved in the operation of aircraft. Essential requirements for airworthiness are laid down in an annex, and products, parts and appliances must comply with the environmental protection requirements contained in the Chicago Convention of December 7, 1944. Implementing rules for the airworthiness and environmental certification of aircraft and related products, parts and appliances, as well as for the certification of design and production organisations, were laid down in 2012.[162] Several other regulations were adopted.[163]

See also the implementing Regulation concerning the common basic standards on civil aviation security as regards the use of security scanners at EU airports.[164]

In 2012, the Council decided to sign the Agreement providing a general framework for enhanced co-operation between the European Union and the European Organisation for the Safety of Air Navigation.[165]

(1) Single European Sky

27–18 In 2004, a Regulation was adopted laying down the framework for the creation of the single European sky (the Framework Regulation[166]).

In order to achieve the objectives of the Single European Sky Initiative, the Commission is working closely together with the European Organisation for the Safety of Air Navigation (Eurocontrol). The co-operation should avoid duplication of efforts and will also be extended to other areas like Galileo, research and development, support to States and co-ordinated actions in international organisations.[167] The Union will become a member of Eurocontrol[168] and its membership has been implemented on a provisional basis in order to enable it to participate during the ratification process.

In 2009, Parliament and the Council adopted the second *Single European Sky* package in order to improve and reinforce safety, to restructure European airspace as a function of air traffic flow, to create additional capacity and to increase the overall efficiency of the Air Traffic Management system (ATM). It comprises four regulations[169] covering the essential elements for a seamless

---

[162] Regulation748/12 [2012] O.J. L224/1, amended [2013] O.J. L4/36.

[163] See for instance Regulation 1702/03 [2003] O.J. L243/6, amended [2006] O.J. L122/16 and [2007] O.J. L94/3 and Regulation 2042/03 on the continuing airworthiness of aircraft and aeronautical parts O.J. L315/1, amended [2012] O.J. L176/38.See *Techniko Epimelitirio Elladas* (C-271/11), judgment of November 8, 2012, not yet reported; qualifications required of members of staff involved in tasks of inspection.

[164] Regulation 1147/11 [2011] O.J. L294/7.

[165] [2013] O.J. L16/1.

[166] Regulation 549/04 [2004] O.J. L96/1.

[167] Memorandum of Co-operation between the Commission and EUROCONTROL of December 22, 2003, which governs the relationship between the two organisations and points the way for future co-operation.

[168] Council Decision concerning the conclusion by the European Union of the Protocol on the accession of EUROCONTROL, Council Document 5565/1/04.

[169] Regulation 1108/09 laying down the framework for the creation of the single European sky (the Framework Regulation) [2009] O.J. L309/51; Regulation 550/2004 on the provision of air navigation services in the single European sky (the Service Provision Regulation) [2004] O.J. L96/10; Regulation 551/2004 on the organisation and use of the airspace in the single European sky (the Airspace Regulation) [2004] O.J. L96/20 and Notice implementing Art.5 [2009] O.J. C46/26;

ATM. The actions defined in the regulations reinforces as well the integration of the civil and military air traffic control. See regulation laying down detailed rules for the implementation of air traffic management network functions and amending Regulation 691/2010 [2011] O.J. L185/1. The latter was amended [2011] O.J. L271/15 and 23. A Regulation lays down requirements on aircraft identification for suveillance for the Single European Sky[170] and, another, for the performance and the interoperability of surveillance for the Single European Sky.[171]

See also Commisssion Decision setting the European Union-wide perfor-   27–19
mance targets and alert thresholds for the provision of air navigation services for the years 2012 to 2014.[172]

A Directive provides for noice-related operating restrictions at Union airports: noise-level limits that must be observed when flying over built-up areas near an airport.[173] A performance scheme for air navigation services and network functions was laid down in 2011.[174]

A Memorandum of Co-operation was concluded in 2012 with the Internatioi-nal Aviation Organisation providing a framework for enhanced co-operation, and laying down procedural arrangements related thereto.[175]

(2) Safety Assessment of Foreign Aircraft (SAFA)[176]

In 2005, Parliament and Council decided that a Community list would be   27–20
established of air carriers subject to an operating ban within the Community and on informing air transport passengers of the identity of the operating air carriers.[177] The list was established by the Commission in 2006.[178]

Details about this programme can be found above in Ch.13: Decentralised Agencies and Bodies of the Union (I 13. The European Aviation Safety Agency (EASA)).

(3) International Agreements

More than any other mode of transport, air transport extends beyond international   27–21
borders, from there the necessity for agreements with third countries and International Organisations and Conventions stems.[179] Following the so-called "open skies" decisions of the Court, in which agreements of eight Member States

---

Regulation 552/2004 on the interoperability of the European Air Traffic Management network (the Interoperability Regulation) [2004] O.J. L96/26. All modified [2009] O.J. L300/34.

[170] Regulation 1206/11 [2011] O.J. L305/23.

[171] Regulation 1207/11 [2011] O.J. L305/35.

[172] [2011] O.J. L48/16.

[173] Directive 2002/30, [2002] L.85/40. See *European Air Transport* (C-120/10) [2011] E.C.R. I-7865.

[174] Regulation691/10 [2010] O.J. L201L1 amended 2011] O.J. L310/3.

[175] [2012] O.J. L121/16.

[176] See report from the Commission on the European Community SAFA programme [2008] O.J. L42/1.

[177] Regulation 2111/05 [2005] O.J. L344/15.

[178] Regulation 474/06 [2006] O.J. L84/14, amended [2008] O.J. L197/36 and [2009] O.J. L95/16 and [2009] O.J. L182/4, [2011] O.J. L104/10.

[179] See, for instance, Decision on the conclusion by the EC of the Convention for the Unification of Certain Rules for International Carriage by Air (the Montreal Convention) [2001] O.J. L194/38.

with the United States were found to partly infringe Union Law,[180] the Commission requested a negotiation mandate.

It contains first, a mandate for the Commission to open negotiations with the United States on the creation of an Open Aviation Area, consequently an air transport agreement was signed with the United States.[181] As a result all EU airlines can fly direct to the US from any airport in Europe and no longer only from their own country of origin. The agreement does away with all restrictions affecting connections, fares or the number of flights per week. An agreement was also signed on co-operation in the regulation of civil aviation safety.

Second, a mandate for the Commission to negotiate with third countries for the replacement of certain provisions in existing bilateral agreements with a Union agreement, and third, a proposal for a regulation on the negotiation and implementation of air service agreements between Member States and third countries; an agreement was signed with Russia on the utilisation of the trans-Siberian routes, with the Kyrgys Republc,[182] Jordan,[183] the United Arab Emirates,[184] Panama, New Zealand, Armenia, Nepal[185] and Mongolia.[186] Decisions were adopted concerning the conclusion of agreements with Croatia, Macedonia, Georgia, Kyrgyzstan, Lebanon, Malaysia, the Maldives, Moldova, Panama, Paraguay, Singapore, Uruguay,[187] Morocco,[188] Azerbaijan, Australia,[189] India and Pakistan.

27–22   An agreement exists between the Union and the Swiss Confederation[190] and the State of Israel[191] on air transport. An agreement on civil aviation safety was signed with Canada.[192]

Decisions on the signing and provisional application of agreements were also adopted for Australia, Nepal, Pakistan, Israel, India and Armenia.[193]

In order to protect the European air carriers against distortion of competition by non-European carriers, a regulation concerning protection against subsidisation and unfair pricing practices causing injury to Union air carriers in the supply of air services from countries not members of the European Union has been adopted.[194] Mention must also be made of the Agreement between the Union and the USA concerning the application of the "GATT Agreement on Trade in Civil Aircraft" to trade in large civil aircraft.[195] The purpose was to put an end to the

---

[180] See *United Kingdom, Denmark, Sweden, Finland, Belgium. Luxembourg, Austria et Germany v Commission* (C-466/98, C-467/98, C-469/98, C-471/98, C-472/98, C-475/98 and C-776/98) [2002] E.C.R. I-9427.

[181] Decision 2007/339 [2007] O.J. L134/1.

[182] Decision 2007/470 [2007] O.J. L179/38.

[183] [2009] O.J. L173/6.

[184] [2009] O.J. L173/6.

[185] Decision 2009/117 [2009] O.J. L41/3.

[186] General Report 2007, 82.

[187] [2008] O.J. L60/22 and L106/6.

[188] [2008] O.J. L87/9.

[189] [2009] O.J. L173/4.

[190] Agreement of December 16, 2008. See Decision of the Joint Community/Switzerland Air Transport Committee [2009] O.J. L40/38.

[191] [2009] O.J. L90/10.

[192] [2009] O.J. L153/10.

[193] General Report 2008, 86.

[194] [2004] O.J. L162/1.

[195] [1992] O.J. L301/32.

financial support granted on both sides of the Atlantic to the constructors of large aircrafts (Boeing v Airbus). From the complaints recently filed by both parties with the WTO it appears that this endeavour was not successful.

See Memorandum of Co-operation between the European Union and the International Civil Aviation Organisation providing a framework for enhanced co-operation.[196] Decision on their adoption of an Annex on aviation security to the above mentioned memorandum: [2012] O.J. L266/37.

7. INLAND WATERWAY TRANSPORT

Europe is known for its canals and natural waterways used for transport, not only of goods but also of passengers. The Union legislation in this field is particularly extensive, but of interest to only a small group of people. Let it be sufficient to mention a Regulation[197] on a Union-fleet capacity policy to promote inland waterway transport, which aimed to reduce overcapacity in that sector by introducing an "old-for-new" rule and a recent directive laying down technical requirements for inland waterway vessels.[198] No further mention will be made here of the rules applying to this mode of transport. As already mentioned, the *Official Journal Repertory of Union Legislation in force*, contains most of the needed information.[199]

27–23

8. MARITIME TRANSPORT

This mode of transport has, by definition, an international aspect. There is no question, therefore, of treating this field exclusively at Union level. As an example, at the international level the Union has ratified[200] the UN Convention on the Law of the Sea.[201] Within the Union this applies, in the first place, to the rules of competition. Special rules have therefore been adopted: first concerning the application of the competition rules to maritime transport[202] and a Regulation on unfair pricing practices in maritime transport.[203] Since liner shipping companies (consortia) play an important role in shipping, an exemption for certain categories of agreements was also provided for.[204] The same applies to

27–24

---

[196] [2011] O.J. L123/2.

[197] Regulation 718/1999 [1999] O.J. L90/1, as amended, concerning the scope of application, see, e.g. *Josanne E.A. v Commission* (T-82/01) [2003] E.C.R. II-2013 and *Mohr & Sohn v Commission* (T-131/07) [2010] E.C.R. II-190.

[198] Directive 2006/87 [2006] O.J. L389/3, modified [2006] O.J. L399/3, [2008] O.J. L255/5 and [2009] O.J. L32/1 and L109/14, correction [2009] O.J. L150/5; Annexes were amended [2013] O.J. L6/1 and 49.

[199] Office for Official Publications of the European Union, L-2985 Luxembourg.

[200] See *http://www.un.org/depts/los/convention_agreements/texts/unclos/unclos_e.pdf* [accessed August 23, 2013]; The United Nations Convention on the Law of the Sea.

[201] See *http://www.unclos.com* [accessed August 23, 2013].

[202] Regulation 1419/2006 [2006] O.J. L269/1.

[203] Regulation 4057/86 [1986] O.J. L378/14, codified version [2009] O.J. L79/1.

[204] See Regulation 479/92 [1992] O.J. L55/3, as amended, and Regulation 823/2000 on the application of Art.101(3) TFEU to certain categories of agreements, decisions and concerted practices between liner shipping companies (consortia) [2000] O.J. L100/24, amended and prolonged [2005]

Liner Conferences: the Council adopted a Regulation on the ratification by the Member States of the United Nations Convention on a Code of Conduct of Liner Conferences.[205] Market access is crucial, both within the Union and outside of it, for which adequate rules have been adopted granting freedom to provide maritime transport services within Member States (maritime cabotage),[206] or providing for co-ordinated action to safeguard free access to cargoes in ocean trades.[207] In 2008, the Commission published Guidelines on the application of Arts 101 and 102 to maritime transport Services.[208] The latter cover liner shipping services, cabotage and tramp services. The guidelines define their relevant market. With regard to horizontal agreements in the maritime transport sector, certain technical agreements, information exchange between competitors in liner shipping and pool agreements in tramp shipping are acceptable from a competition point of view, under certain conditions set out in the Guidelines.

Understandably, environmental safety and safety at sea was a major preoccupation. In order to ensure the uniform and compulsory application of environmental standards as, for example, provided for in the International Convention for the Prevention of Pollution from Ships (so-called MARPOL)intern,[209] adopted by the International Maritime Organisation and signed by all Member States, a directive has been adopted.[210] The Council recommended the ratification of several international conventions concerning safety at sea,[211] laid down rules for a vessel traffic monitoring and information system with a view to enhancing the safety and efficiency of maritime traffic, improving the response of

---

O.J. L110/10. Regulation 246/09 of the Council on the application of Art.101(3) to certain agreements between liner shipping companies (consortia) [2009] O.J.L79/1 and Commission Regulation 906/09 [2009] O.J. L256/31, applicable until April 25, 2015.

[205] Regulation 954/79 [1979] O.J. L121/1, repealed as from the end of the transition period provided in Regulation 1419/06 [2006] O.J. L269/1. See Commission Decision imposing fines on the Trans-Atlantic Conference Agreement for abuse of a dominant position: press release IP/98/811 of September 16, 1998.

[206] Regulation 3577/92 [1992] O.J. L364/7.See *NavitliakiEtairia e.a.* (Joint Cases C-128 and C-129/09) E.C.R. 17.03.11. Order in ports and public service obligations. Regulation 1419/2006 [2006] O.J. L269/1 extended the scope of Regulation 1/2003 and of Regulation 773/2004 conduct of proceedings by the Commission pursuant to Arts 101 and 102 [81 and 82] [2004] O.J. L123/18) to include cabotage and tramp vessel services.

[207] Regulation 4055/86 applying the principle of freedom to provide services to maritime transport between Member States and between Member States and third countries: [1986] O.J. L378/1, as amended, and Regulation 4058/86 [1986] O.J. L378/21.

[208] [2008] O.J. C245/2.

[209] See *http://www.imo.org/About/Conventions/ListOfConventions/Pages/International-Convention-for-the-Prevention-of-Pollution-from-Ships-(MARPOL).aspx* [accessed August 23, 2013].

[210] Directive 2005/35 on ship-source pollution and on the introduction of penalties for infringement [2005] O.J. L255/1, modified [2009] O.J. L280/52; see also Directive 2000/59 on port reception facilities for ship-generated waste and cargo residues [2000] O.J. L332/81, amended with regard to the former Directive; the Court ascertained that its validity cannot be assessed either in the light of the International Convention for the prevention of pollution from ships or in the light of the UN Convention on the law of the Sea (Montego Bay, December 10, 1982).

[211] Convention on safety in shipping [1978] O.J. L194/17; Convention on standards of training, certification and watch-keeping for sea-farers [1979] O.J. L33/31; Convention for safe containers [1979] O.J. L125/18; and the Convention for the safety of fishing vessels, see Council Resolution [1985] O.J. L72 /110; Convention for the safety of life at sea; Convention for the prevention of pollution from ships [1993] O.J. L194/5; and the Convention on maritime Search and Rescue (SAR) [1983] O.J. L237/34. It will be noticed that all those Council Recommendations were published in the L (Legislation) series of the *Official Journal*, although they do not constitute binding acts.

authorities to incidents, accidents or potentially dangerous situations at sea, including search and rescue operations, and contributing to a better prevention and detection of pollution by ships[212] and ruled on the accelerated phasing-in of double hull or equivalent design requirements for single-hull oil tankers. Since 2008, no oil tanker carrying heavy grades of oil is allowed to enter or leave ports or off-shore terminals or to anchor in areas under the jurisdiction of a Member State, unless it is a double-hull tanker.[213] See Regulation on accelerated phasing-in of double-hull or equivalent design requirements for single-hull oil tankers.[214]

Following several catastrophic accidents with ferries, rules have been adopted on the safety management of roll-on/roll-off passenger ferries[215]; on safety rules and standards for passenger ships[216]; on specific stability requirements for ro-ro passenger ships[217]; requirements and procedures for the safe loading and unloading of bulk carriers[218]; the setting up of a harmonised safety regime for fishing vessels of 24 metres in length or over[219]; on common rules and standards for ship inspection[220]; on the minimum safety and health requirements for improved medical treatment on board vessels[221]; on the minimum level of training of seafarers[222]; concerning enforcement, in respect of shipping using Union ports[223] and sailing in the waters under the jurisdiction of the Member States; of international standards for ship safety, pollution prevention and shipboard living and working conditions (port State control).[224] Furthermore, a European Maritime Safety Agency (EMSA),[225] and a specialised expert body assisting the Commission in its task and facilitating the co-operation within the Union, has been established.[226]

27–25

---

[212] Directive 2002/59 establishing a Union vessel traffic monitoring and information system [2002] O.J. L203/10, amended [2011] O.J. L 49/33 , and by Directive 2002/18 establishing the fundamental principles governing the investigation of accidents in the maritime transport sector [2009] O.J. L131/114, amended [2009] O.J. L314/13.

[213] Regulation 417/2002 [2002] O.J. L64/1, after the Prestige and Erika accidents, amended [2007] O.J. L113/1.

[214] Regulation530/12 [2012] O.J. L172/3.

[215] Regulation 3051/95 [1995] O.J. L320/14, which has been repealed by Regulation 336/2006 on the implementation of the International Safety Management Code within the Union [2006] O.J. L64/1, and Directive 99/35 on a system of mandatory surveys for the safe operation of regular ro-ro ferry and high-speed passenger craft services [1999] O.J. L138/1, amended by Directive 2009/18 establishing the fundamental principles governing the investigation of accidents in the maritime transport sector [2009] O.J. L131/114.

[216] Directive 98/18 [1998] O.J. L144/1, recast by Directive 2009/45 [2009] O.J. L163/1, amended [2010] O.J. L162/1. See also Directive2009/16 as regards expanded inspections of ships [2009] O.J. L131/57, amended [2010] O.J. L125/2.

[217] Directive 2003/25 [2003] O.J. L123/22, as amended.

[218] Directive 2001/96 [2002] O.J. L13/9, as amended.

[219] Directive 97/70 [1998] O.J. L34/1, as amended.

[220] Directive 94/57 [1994] O.J. L319/20, as amended.

[221] Directive 92/29 [1992] O.J. L113/19, as amended.

[222] Directive 2001/25 [2001] O.J. L136/17, as amended.

[223] See Regulation 725/2004 on enhancing ship and port facility security [2004] O.J. L129/6, modified [2009] O.J.L29/53.

[224] Directive 95/21 [1995] O.J. L157/1, as amended. See also Regulation 725/2004 on enhancing ship and port facility security [2004] O.J. L129/6 and Regulation 884/2005 laying down procedures for conducting Commission inspections in the field of maritime security [2005] O.J. L 148/25.

[225] Regulation 1406/2002 [2002] O.J. L208/1, amended [2004] O.J. L129/1.

[226] For more details see Ch.13 Decentralised Agencies and Bodies of the Union.

In 2007, the Commission adopted an action plan for an integrated maritime policy[227] and in 2008 presented a communication on "Guidelines for an integrated approach to maritime policy: Towards best practice in integrated maritime governance and stakeholder consultation".[228]

An agreement on maritime transport was signed with China in 2002 and entered into force in 2008[229]; it was amended in 2009.[230]

A 2010 Regulation establishes the rights of passengers when travelling by sea and inland waterway.[231]

9. INTERMODALITY

27–26   Intermodality plays a major role in the Commission's objectives for the transport policy in order to shift the congestion of road transport to other modes.[232] The concept of intermodal freight transport involves the easy and efficient movement of goods using more than one mode of transport to exploit the advantages of multiple means of transport. The so-called Marco Polo Programme[233] was designed to achieve modal shifts from road transport to transport by sea, rail, and inland waterway. This programme has been replaced in 2006 by the *second* Marco Polo Programme, which started on January 1, 2007.[234] The program has a budget of €400 million for the period 2007–2013; it includes new actions such as motorways of the sea and traffic avoidance measures and has been extended to countries bordering the EU.

A framework for the development of Intelligent Transport Systems in the field of road transport and for interfaces with other modes of transport was the object of a Directive in 2010.[235]

10. TRANS-EUROPEAN TRANSPORT NETWORKS

27–27   A Trans-European Transport Network Executive Agency was set up to manage the Union funds for the promotion of the trans-European transport network.[236] The funds allocated to railway projects under the 2007–2013 programme exceed €1.7 billion. Exploratory talks took place regarding co-operation in the field of transport with neighbouring countries. Discussions with the Western Balkans

---

[227] COM(2007) 575.

[228] COM(2008) 395.

[229] [2008] O.J. L46/25.

[230] [2009] O.J. L144/20.

[231] Regulation 1177/10 [2010] O.J. L334/1.

[232] White Paper "European transport policy for 2010: time to decide", COM(2001) 370.

[233] Regulation 1382/2003 [2003] O.J. L196/1, as amended.

[234] Regulation 1692/2006 establishing the second Marco Polo (Marco Polo II) programme for granting of Union financial assistance to improve the environmental performance of the freight transport system [2006] O.J. L328/1, amended [2009] O.J. L266/1.

[235] Directive 2010/40 [2010] O.J. L207/1.

[236] See Ch.13: Decentralised Agencies and Bodies of the Union, Part III. European Executive Agencies.

have been concluded and the Commission has proposed negotiating directives to establish a transport community in the region.[237]

11. CONCLUSION WITH REGARD TO A "COMMON TRANSPORT POLICY"

As was seen, transport in the Union is the subject of an impressive array of rules and regulations. The question is, however, whether this constitutes a "common policy". As was seen above, important steps were taken to liberalise transport within the Union, cabotage is now possible; another important step was the creation of the Trans-European Networks (TENs) by the EU Treaty, which should help to integrate the national networks into a single system. This aim has been practically achieved with regard to the road system, but is still an on-going process as far as rail transport is concerned. Nevertheless, as is clearly stated in the White Paper, there is now a global approach to the various sectors of transport aiming to tackle the existing imbalance in the different modes of transport and to enhance the environmental problems. The objective remains the establishment and functioning of an Internal Transport Market, which can only be attained through liberalisation, integration and harmonisation. It is to be seen how the Union will manage the challenges of the transport issues in the enlarged internal market. Much has been achieved, much remains to be done.

27–28

FURTHER READING

Liz Heffernan and Conor McAuliffe, "External relations in the air transport sector. The Court of Justice and the open sky agreements", (2003) E.L.Rev. 601.

27–29

---

[237] General Report 2008, 87.

CHAPTER 28

Economic and Monetary Union (Policy)[1]—The Euro

The most tangible aspect of European integration and more particularly of the Economic and Monetary Union (EMU) was, for the European citizens, the introduction of the single currency, called the *Euro*.[2] The introduction of the Euro on January 1, 2002, in replacement[3] of the national currencies of the Member States participating in this aspect of EMU[4] constitutes a major event not only from an economic and monetary point of view, but foremost from the point of view of European integration. Indeed, a corollary of the introduction of the Euro, is the setting up of the European Central Bank (ECB) to which the Member States have surrendered, as shall be seen, the definition of their monetary policies. It was generally held that through this transfer of sovereignty, the process of European integration has reached the point of no return; politically speaking, it was *the* decisive step on the way to European Union. The Euro crisis has shaken this assumption to some extent.

28–01

The introduction of the Euro was the result of a rather short—10 years—but complex procedure with economic, monetary and institutional aspects. Those shall be briefly described in the following sections. The introduction was an unprecedented success thanks to meticulous preparation and to the enthusiastic welcome given to it by a large majority of the public. Title VIII of the TFEU on "Economic and Monetary Policy" is divided into five chapters: "Economic policy"; "Monetary policy"; "Institutional provisions"; "Provisions specific to Member States whose currency is not the euro"; and "Transitional provisions".

It is interesting to note that "Economic and Monetary Policy" is not mentioned among the "Categories and Areas of Union Competence"[5], only "monetary policy for the Member States whose currency is the euro"[6] is; but the Treaty also provides that "the Member States shall co-ordinate their economic policies within

---

[1] Arts 119–144 TFEU.
[2] Regulation 1103/97 [1997] O.J. L162/1. See also Council Regulation 974/98 on the introduction of the Euro [1998] O.J. L139/1.
[3] National currencies ceased to exist on June 30, 2002.
[4] Currently 17 Member States participate: Belgium, Germany, Ireland, Spain, France, Italy, Luxembourg, the Netherlands, Austria, Portugal and Finland, except Denmark, Greece (which joined later on, see Decision 2000/427 [2000] O.J. L167/19), Sweden, which has a derogation, Art.139(1) TFEU and the UK, which decided not to move to the third stage; as indicated, Slovenia joined in 2007, Malta and Cyprus in 2008, Slovakia in 2009 and Estonia in 2011.
[5] Arts 3, 4, 5 and 6 TFEU.
[6] Art.3(1)(c) TFEU.

the Union"[7] and that the Council shall adopt measures, in particular broad guidelines, for these economic policies.[8] See Ch.6: The European Council. This economic policy is based upon "common objectives", which are not further defined.[9] The Treaty, however, makes clear that the economic policy envisaged must be conducted "in accordance with the principle of an open market economy with free competition".[10] At least the basic economic philosophy is here unequivocally affirmed. The TFEU adds that:

> "[T]hese activities shall include a single currency, the euro, and the definition and conduct of a single monetary policy and exchange rate policy the primary objective of both of which shall be to maintain price stability and, without prejudice to this objective, to support the general economic policies in the Union."[11]

28–02   Furthermore, "these activities of the Member States and the Union shall entail compliance with the following principles: stable prices, sound public finances and monetary conditions and a sustainable balance of payments."[12] As for the monetary policy, as shall be seen, the Treaty provides that the primary objective is to maintain price stability and to support the general economic policies in the Union.[13] Here again the principle of an open market economy with free competition is asserted.[14] Those principles correspond more or less to the four criteria[15]that must be fulfilled by the Member States "for the adoption of a single currency".[16]

The above constitutes, in a nutshell, the economic and monetary policy of the Union; its various aspects will, as already mentioned, be examined in some more detail below.

1.   ECONOMIC POLICY[17]

28–03   Although no mention is made of social policy in the context of the economic and monetary policy, the Treaty provides that Member States shall conduct their economic policies with a view to contributing to the achievement of the objectives of the Union, amongst which figures "full employment and social progress".

The chapter on economic policy covers the following subjects:

---

[7] Art.5(1) TFEU.

[8] Art.5(1) TFEU.

[9] Art.121(2) TFEU provides that on the basis of a conclusion of the European Council, the Council shall adopt a recommendation setting out broad guidelines of the economic policies of the Member States and of the Union.

[10] Art.119(1) TFEU.

[11] Art.119(2) TFEU.

[12] Art.119(3) TFEU.

[13] Art.127(1) TFEU.

[14] Art.119 TFEU.

[15] Art.140(1) TFEU.

[16] Art.140(1) TFEU.The criteria are often referred to as the "convergence criteria". They are set out in Protocol 13.

[17] Arts 120–126 TFEU.

- the conduct of economic policies by the Member States in the context of the broad guidelines set out by the Council[18];
- the monitoring of economic developments in each of the Member States by the Council[19];
- Union financial assistance to Member States in difficulties[20]; see below concerning the euro crisis;
- the prohibition of overdraft or any other type of credit facility with the ECB or with central banks of the Member States for public bodies, except public-owned credit institutions[21] and of privileged access to financial institutions[22];
- the Union or a Member State cannot be held liable for the commitments of another Member State, without prejudice to mutual financial guarantees for the joint execution of a specific project[23]; and
- the avoidance of excessive government deficits.[24]

(1)   Co-ordination of the Economic Policies of the Member States[25]

Member States must conduct their economic policies in the context of "broad guidelines". These are drafted by the Council on a recommendation from the Commission and submitted to the European Council. The latter discusses a "conclusion" on the guidelines, after which the Council adopts a "recommendation" setting out these guidelines.[26]

28–04

The implementation of the broad guidelines forms the object of a "multilateral surveillance" by the Council. In order to ensure closer co-ordination of the economic policies and sustained convergence of the economic performances of the Member States, the Council monitors the implementation of the guidelines on the basis of reports submitted by the Commission on the economic developments in each Member State.[27] The latter must forward all relevant information to the Commission.[28] When it is established that the economic policies of a Member State are not consistent with the broad guidelines, the Council may, on recommendation from the Commission, make by qualified majority the necessary recommendations to the Member State concerned.[29] It is worthwhile noting here that none of the binding Union acts provided for in the Treaty, i.e. regulations, directives and decisions, are mentioned here; the terms "report" and "conclusion", in such a context, were novelties in the text of the Treaty. Furthermore, the

---

[18] Art.121(2) TFEU.
[19] Art.121(3) TFEU.
[20] Art.122 TFEU. See Regulation 332/2002 establishing a facility providing medium-term financial assistance to Member States' balance of payments [2002] O.J. L53/1, amended [2008] O.J. L352/11. See for instance assistance to Romania [2011] O.J. L132/15.
[21] Art.123 TFEU.
[22] Art.124 TFEU.
[23] Art.125 TFEU.
[24] Art.126(1) TFEU.
[25] Art.121 TFEU.
[26] See, for instance, Council Recommendation on the broad guidelines 2012–2013 [2012] O.J. C219/95.
[27] Art.121(3), 1 TFEU.
[28] Art.121(3), 2 TFEU.
[29] Art.121(4) TFEU. See for instance Council Recommendation of February 12, 2001.

setting out of "broad guidelines" for the economic policies of the Member States via a non-binding "recommendation" seems to minimise their importance. This is surprising since great weight is attached to the consistency between the economic policies of the Member States and those guidelines and since Parliament and the Council, acting by means of regulations, in accordance with the ordinary legislative procedure,[30] may adopt detailed rules for the multilateral surveillance procedure.[31]

(2) Excessive Government Deficits[32]

28–05   The Treaty introduces the notion of "budgetary discipline" in order to avoid excessive government deficits.[33] Two criteria are provided that allow the Commission to monitor the development of the budgetary situation and the stock of government debt. The ratio of deficit, on the one hand, and of the government debt, on the other, to gross domestic product, may not exceed a reference value specified in the Protocol on the excessive deficit procedure annexed to the Treaty.[34] The application of the Protocol is the object of a regulation.[35]

In case those criteria are not observed by a Member State, the Commission prepares a report which is submitted to the Economic and Financial Committee,[36] that formulates an opinion thereon. If the Commission considers that an excessive deficit exists or may occur, it addresses an opinion to the Member State concerned and informs the Council accordingly.[37] The latter shall, on a proposal from the Commission, after having considered the observations of the Member State concerned, decide, after an overall assessment, whether an excessive deficit does indeed exist.[38] The Council must then adopt, on a recommendation from the Commission, "recommendations" addressed to the Member State in question with a view to bringing the situation to an end within a given period. These recommendations shall not be made public, unless the Council establishes that there has been no effective action in response to its recommendations. If the latter fails to put the recommendations into practice, the Council may decide to give

---

[30] Art.294 TFEU.

[31] Art.121(6) TFEU.

[32] Art.126 TFEU.

[33] Art.126(2) TFEU.

[34] Protocol No. 12. The ratios are respectively 3 and 60 per cent. This Protocol shall be replaced by "appropriate provisions" adopted by the Council, acting unanimously on a proposal from the Commission and after consulting Parliament and the ECB: Art.126(14)2 TFEU.

[35] Regulation 479/09 [2009] O.J. L145/1. The Regulation replaces Regulation 3605/93 and contains detailed rules for the reporting of budgetary data by the Member States. In order to deter excessive general government deficits; the Council adopted Regulation 1467/97 on speeding up and clarifying the implementation of the excessive deficit procedure, [1997] O.J. L209/6.

[36] This Economic and Monetary Committee was set up, under a different name (Economic and Financial Committee), at the start of the third stage; at the time, it replaced the Monetary Committee. Its task is to "promote co-ordination of the policies of the Member States to the full extend needed for the functioning of the internal market." Art.126(4) TFEU.

[37] Art.126(5) TFEU.

[38] Art.126(6) TFEU. See, for instance, Council Decision of June 30, 1997 abrogating the decision on the existence of an excessive deficit in the Netherlands [1997] O.J. L177/23. See Council Decision of November 5, 2002 on the existence of an excessive deficit in Portugal [2002] O.J. L322/30 and decisions concerning the existence of an excessive deficit in France, Greece, Italy and Spain [2009] O.J. L135/19, 21, 23 and 25.

notice to that Member State "to take, within a specified time limit, measures for the deficit reduction".[39] Although failure by the Member State in question to abide by the notice does not constitute a failure "to fulfil an obligation under this Treaty",[40] that can be brought before the Court, the Treaty provides for some measures which can be taken against the recalcitrant Member State.

These measures are the following[41]:

28–06

- require the Member State to publish additional information before issuing bonds and securities;
- invite the EIB to reconsider its lending policy towards said State;
- require a non-interest-bearing deposit of an appropriate size with the Union; and/or
- impose fines of an appropriate size.

The President of the Council informs Parliament.

All decisions are taken by the Council, on a recommendation from the Commission, by qualified majority, weighted as for normal Council decisions.[42]

When the excessive deficit has been corrected, the Council abrogates some or all of its decisions and recommendations.

(3) Prohibition of "overdraft facilities"[43] and "privileged access to financial institutions"[44]

Overdraft facilities with the Central Banks, so called "monetary financing" and privileged access to financial institutions for governments, regional, local or other public authorities have always been a simple means to finance deficits. This is no longer possible. On the other hand, the Treaty provides for mutual assistance, where a Member State is in difficulties or seriously threatened with difficulties as regards its balance of payments, and where those difficulties are liable to jeopardise the functioning of the internal market or the progressive implementation of the common commercial policy.[45] In 2002, the Council established a facility providing medium-term financial assistance for Member States, outside the Euro area. In 2009, the scope and intensity of the international financial crisis required raising the ceiling of outstanding loans from €25 billion to €50 billion.[46]

28–07

---

[39] Art.126(9) TFEU; see, for instance, Council Decision of March 7, 2011 addressed to Greece giving notice to take measures for the deficit reduction [2011] O.J. L110/26.

[40] Art.126(10) TFEU.

[41] Art.126(11) TFEU.

[42] See Ch.7: The Council.

[43] Art.123 TFEU.

[44] Art.124 TFEU.

[45] Arts 122(2) and 143 TFEU.

[46] Regulation 332/02 [2002] O.J. L53/1, modified [2009] O.J. L128/1. See, for instance, Decision 2009/102 providing Community medium-term financial assistance for Hungary [2009] O.J. L57/5.

2. MONETARY POLICY[47]

28–08 Expanding on the task of the European System of Central Banks (ESCB) (described in a previous chapter), it can be noted, once again, that the primary objective of the Union monetary policies is to maintain price stability. In order to make this possible a vast programme for achieving economic and monetary union, of which a part was just described, was devised. It had to be implemented in three stages.[48]

---

[47] Arts 127–133 TFEU.

[48] The *first stage* started on July 1, 1990 and ended on December 31, 1993. It consisted essentially of an attempt at greater convergence of the national economies and the strengthening of the co-operation between the central banks. During that stage, all restrictions on the free movement of capital and payments between Member States, and between Member States and third countries, were abolished and so were the overdraft facilities and the privileged access to financial institutions, mentioned above. Furthermore, the Council was to assess the progress made with regard to economic and monetary convergence, in particular with regard to price stability and sound public finances, and progress made with regard to Union law concerning the internal market. Governments also had to avoid excessive deficits and start the process leading to the independence of their central bank. The *second stage* for achieving economic and monetary union started on January 1, 1994. On that date the European Monetary Institute (EMI) was established (in Frankfurt) and took up its duties. It was replaced five years later by the European Central Bank (ECB), at the start of the *third stage*. The EMI's task was to prepare the third stage; details can be found in the corresponding Treaty provisions. In particular, it should be noted that the EMI had to specify the regulatory, organisational and logistical framework for the European System of Central Banks (ESCB). The latter's task is to define and implement the monetary policy of the Union. The most important decision to be taken during the second stage was which Member States could participate in the single currency system. Since no other date had been set for the beginning of the third stage, it was decided that it would start on January 1, 1999. The Council, meeting in the composition of Heads of State or Government had to confirm, before July 1, 1998, which Member States fulfilled the necessary conditions for the adoption of the single currency and whether a majority of the Member States fulfilled the necessary conditions. Although this is now history, it is of interest to note that this decision was taken on the basis of a report from the Commission and the EMI on, among other things, the achievement of a high degree of sustainable convergence. The latter was judged by reference to the fulfilment by each Member State of four criteria, i.e. inflation, budgetary deficit, exchange rate fluctuations within the European Monetary System and long-term interest rate levels. Those criteria were further developed in a Protocol annexed to the Treaty. The *third stage*. The decision was taken by the Heads of State and Government on May 1, 1998, and all the Member States, except Denmark, Greece, Sweden and the UK, were found to fulfil the necessary conditions for the adoption of a single currency. Greece joined later. Denmak and the UK have "opt-outs", enshrined now in Protocols to the Treaty. Sweden lacked the political will to join. On that date also financial transactions could be carried out in Euros; anyone could open a bank account in that currency. However, the Euro did not become legal tender for current transactions. That had to wait for the issuing of Euro banknotes and coins which started circulating on January 1, 2012. The Treaty confers upon the ECB the "exclusive right to authorise the issue of banknotes within the Union". Both the ECB and the national central banks may issue such notes. Those banknotes are the "only such notes to have the status of legal tender within the Union". With regard to coins, the Treaty provides that they may be issued by the Member States, subject to approval by the ECB of the volume of the issue. Measures were adopted by the Council to harmonise the denominations and technical specifications of all coins intended for circulation to the extent necessary to permit their smooth circulation within the Union. As from January 1, 2002 citizens of the participating Member States carried two different currencies: the Euro and their national currency for a period of six months: until June 30, 2002 at midnight. This date was modified to the last day of February. Until then, both currencies were legal tender at the same time but after that date only the Euro was accepted as current payment. The Treaty also provides that the Council may conclude formal agreements on an exchange-rate system for the euro in relation with non-Union currencies. From the start of the third stage, the value of the Euro was irrevocably fixed, the composition of the Euro basket was not changed from that of the ECU. From that date on also, the Member States

3. PROVISIONS SPECIFIC TO MEMBER STATES WHOSE CURRENCY IS THE EURO[49]—THE EURO GROUP

The Council is to adopt measures specific to the Member States whose currency **28–09** is the Euro in order to strengthen the co-ordination and surveillance of their budgetary discipline and to set out economic policy guidelines for them, while ensuring that they are compatible with those adopted for the whole of the Union and are kept under surveillance.

Interesting and important are the "meetings between finance ministers" of those Member States as laid down by the Protocol on the Euro Group.[50] The latter provides that the Ministers "with responsibility for finance" of those Member States shall "meet informally", when necessary, to discuss questions related to the specific responsibilities they share with regard to the single currency. The Commission takes part and the ECB shall be invited. The president is elected for two-and-a-half years.

This not-very-well-known body plays a role much more important than it appears at first sight.

4. INSTITUTIONAL PROVISIONS

The most interesting institutional provision is the one conferring upon the ECB **28–10** the power to make regulations, take decisions, and make recommendations and deliver opinions.[51] The fact that the ECB has the power to make regulations,[52] which have general application and are binding in their entirety and directly applicable in all Member States, might explain why the Treaty of Lisbon conferred upon the ECB the status of an "institution" of the Union.[53] Like all binding acts of the institutions, the regulations and decisions of the ECB must be reasoned and published in the *Official Journal of the European Union*.[54] They must be made available to the citizens of the Union and when they impose a pecuniary obligation[55] on persons other than States, they shall be enforceable. The binding acts of the ECB are also submitted to the control of legality by the

---

participating in the single currency no longer implemented their own monetary policy. This role was transferred to the European System of Central Banks (ESCB). The ESCB has no legal personality (only the ECB has) and its Statute, together with that of the ECB, is the object of Protocol No. 4 annexed to the TFEU.

[49] Arts 136–138 TFEU.

[50] Protocol No.14.

[51] See for instance, Regulation 2818/98 of the ECB on the application of minimum reserves and Regulation 2819/98 concerning the consolidated balance sheet of the monetary financial institutions sector [1998] O.J. L356/1 and 7.

[52] Art.132(1) TFEU.

[53] Art.13(1) EU.

[54] This is provided for in Art.297 TFEU to which Art.132 TFEU indirectly refers, when it provides that the ECB shall make regulations "in accordance with the provisions of the Treaties".

[55] The ECB may be entitled by the Council to impose fines or periodic penalty payments on undertakings for failure to comply with obligations under its regulations and decisions: Art.132(3) TFEU.

European courts.[56] An Economic and Financial Committee was set up,[57] among others, to keep under review the economic and financial situation of the Member States.[58]

5. TRANSITIONAL PROVISIONS

28–11 Under the heading "transitional provisions" the Treaty contains specific rules for Member States that do not fulfil the conditions for adopting the euro. The Treaty refers to these Member States as "Member States with derogation".

6. STABILITY AND GROWTH PACT

28–12 The Pact consists of a Resolution[59] and two Council Regulations[60] and aims at safeguarding sound government finances as a means to strengthen price stability and strong sustainable growth conducive to employment creation. It is also considered necessary that national budgetary policies support stability oriented monetary policies. According to the Resolution, adherence to the objective of sound budgetary positions close to balance or in surplus will allow all Member States to deal with normal cyclical fluctuations while keeping the government deficit within the *reference value of 3 per cent of GDP*. The Resolution contains firm political guidelines issued to the Member States, the Council and the Commission, in order to implement the Growth and Stability Pact.[61] The first Regulation[62] provides for the strengthening of budgetary surveillance and co-ordination of economic policies (the "preventive arm" of the Pact), while the second Regulation[63] concerns the excessive deficit procedure (the "corrective arm" of the Pact). Unfortunately, the Pact has often not been respected, inter alia by some larger Member States (the same ones that had insisted on the necessity for this Pact!).

The Regulations implement the Treaty provisions concerning mutual surveillance, i.e. the monitoring of "the economic developments in each of the Member States and the Union" by the Council and the obligation for the Member States to "avoid excessive government deficits".[64] They can be briefly described as follows.

---

[56] Art.354 TFEU.

[57] Art.134 TFEU.

[58] Art.134(2) TFEU. See Decision 98/743 on the detailed provisions concerning the composition of the Economic and Financial Committee [1998] O.J. L358/109.

[59] Resolution of the European Council on the Stability and Growth Pact, Amsterdam, June 17, 1997 [1997] O.J. C236/1.

[60] Regulation 1466/97 on the strengthening of the surveillance of budgetary positions and the surveillance and co-ordination of economic policies [1997] O.J. L209/1, and Regulation 1467/97 on speeding up and clarifying the implementation of excessive deficit procedure [1997] O.J. L209/6.

[61] See point (2) of Regulation 1466/97 (quoted above).

[62] Regulation 1466/97 [1997] O.J. L209/1.

[63] Regulation 1467/97 [1997] O.J. L209/6.

[64] Art.126 TFEU.

(1) The Strengthening of Budgetary Surveillance and Co-ordination of Economic Policies

Under this Regulation, Member States are required to submit to the Council and to the Commission a Stability Programme and yearly updated programmes; these programmes are made public. These programmes must present, among others, the "medium-term budgetary objectives" (MTOs). Under changes introduced in 2005,[65] these MTOs are differentiated to take into account the diversity of economic and budgetary positions and their sustainability. They now range from a deficit of 1 per cent of GDP to a balance or surplus for Euro area and ERM II countries.[66] In case they have not yet reached their MTO, these countries will have to pursue an annual improvement of 0.5 per cent of GDP as a benchmark of their cyclically adjusted balance, net of one-off measures. A higher effort must be pursued in good times. Member States having implemented major structural reforms, with a verifiable impact on the long-term sustainability of public finances, will be allowed to temporarily deviate from the MTO or the adjustment path toward it.

28–13

On the basis of an assessment of the Stability Programme by the Commission and the Economic and Financial Committee,[67] the Council examines whether the medium-term budget objective provides for a safety margin to ensure the avoidance of an excessive deficit, whether the economic assumptions are realistic and whether the measures taken or proposed are sufficient to achieve the targeted adjustment path towards the medium-term budgetary objective.[68] The Council delivers an "opinion" and, in case it considers that the objectives and contents should be strengthened, the Council must, in its opinion, invite the Member State to adjust the programme.

Furthermore, the Council must monitor the implementation of the stability programmes, and, in case it identifies significant divergence of the budgetary position from the MTO, it must, with a view to giving early warning in order to prevent the occurrence of an excessive deficit, address a recommendation to the Member State concerned to "take prompt corrective measures and may make its recommendation public".[69] The above described procedure applies to so-called participating Member States, i.e. those that adopt the single currency. A similar procedure applies to the other Member States, referred to in the Regulation as "non-participating Member States".

(2) Speeding-up and Clarifying the Implementation of the Excessive Deficit Procedure

This Regulation provides for the Council to decide that an "excessive deficit" exists in a Member State.[70] The Council must do this on the basis of an assessment by the Commission after consultation of the Economic and Financial

28–14

---

[65] Regulation 1055/2005 [2005] O.J. L174/1.
[66] Member States that do not participate in the euro but who have joined the exchange-rate mechanism.
[67] Art.134 TFEU.
[68] Regulation 1055/2005 [2005] O.J. L174/1.
[69] Art.6(3) Regulation 1466/97.
[70] Art.126(6) TFEU.

Committee. The Council must at the same time make recommendations with a view to bringing that situation to an end within a given period. However, the excessive deficit shall be considered "exceptional and temporary" when resulting, for instance, from a "severe economic downturn",[71] the latter being defined as "an annual fall of real GDP of at least 2 per cent". This definition was modified in 2005 and now refers to a "negative annual GDP volume growth rate" or an "accumulated loss of output during a protracted period of very low annual GDP volume growth relative to its potential".[72]

If a Member State persists in failing to put into practice the recommendations of the Council, the latter may decide to give notice to the Member State to take, within a specified time limit, measures for the deficit reduction. Under the modifications introduced in 2005, the deadlines for taking measures to correct excessive deficits are extended to give more time to take effective and more permanent action; also, the Council shall now request the Member State to achieve a minimum annual improvement of at least 0.5 per cent of GDP and, in case of unexpected adverse economic events with major unfavourable consequences for government finances, the Council may now adopt a "revised notice".[73] In case the Member State fails to comply, the Council may, among other measures, "impose fines of an appropriate size".[74] The regulation also provides for various sanctions.

(3) The Euro Crisis[75]

28–15 In the wake of the financial crisis a Euro crisis emerged. Unsound public finances and/or assumed liabilities for banks triggered off a sovereign debts crisis in many Member States; the State at issue was not able to raise funds on the financial markets or only at rates that in the long term would be unsustainable. The Union with the IMF "bailed out" a number of States, for instance Greece, Ireland and Cyprus, by providing them with funds at affordable terms. To that end the Union first set up a temporary *European Financial Stability Facility (EFSF)*. It was created by the euro area Member States in May 2010 and is based in Luxembourg and financed by euro area Member States. The objective of the EFSF is to preserve financial stability by granting financial assistance to euro area Member States in difficulty. The Union also set up a European Financial Stabilisation Mechanism under which the Commission was authorised to raise funds on the financial markets up to the limit of 60 billion Euro. In 2012, the activities of the two bodies were taken over by a permanent body set up under a Treaty between the euro area Member States, the European Stability Mechanism (ESM).[76] The ESM provides financial assistance to euro area Member States that are, or are threatened to be, in financial difficulties. It has lending capacity up to a limit of 500 billion Euro.

The crisis also showed that there was a need for strengthening the Stability and Growth Pact and the governance of the euro area. Because of a British veto to do

---

[71] Art.2(1) Regulation 1467/97.
[72] Art.1(2) Regulation 1056/2005 [2005] O.J. L174/5.
[73] Art.1(3)1 Regulation 1056/2005 [2005] O.J. L174/5.
[74] Art.126(11) TFEU.
[75] See also Ch.18: Freedom to Provide Services/Financial Services, at the end.
[76] The EFSF will just remain operative for existing engagements.

so through Treaty amendment, it was done through an international treaty, the Treaty on Stability, Co-ordination and Governance in the Economic and Monetary Union, also referred to as the "Fiscal Compact Treaty".[77] It entered into force on January 1, 2013. The Treaty commits the States to ensure that their budgetary position shall be balanced or in surplus and imposes on the States an obligation to make that commitment binding in their internal legal order, preferably by provisions of constitutional ranking.[78] If a State fails on its implementation obligation, another State may bring the matter before the Court of Justice. If the State fails to comply with the judgment of the Court of Justice a new case may be brought before the Court under which a financial sanction of up to 0.1 per cent of the State's GDP may be imposed.

By 2012, works aimed at creating a "banking union" started. The objective is in particular to break the link between weak banks and financially weak Member States. The "banking union" is not an exact legal term; what is envisaged in the first place is in particular the creation of a single supervisory mechanism, where the ECB will carry out supervision of mayor banks, and the creation of a single resolution mechanism, i.e. procedures for winding-up financial institutions. The works on the supervisory mechanism are well advanced.

FURTHER READING

B. Hancké, *Unions, Central Banks and EMU: labour market institutions and monetary integration in Europe* (Oxford University Press, 2013).   **28–16**

C. Zilioli and M. Selmayr, *The Law of the European Central Bank* (Hart Publishing, 2001).

H. James, *Making the European Monetary Union* (Harvard University Press, 2012).

J. de Haan, *Financial Markets and Institutions: a European perspective* (Cambridge University Press, 2012).

P. de Grauwe, *Economics of Monetary Union* (Oxford University Press, 2012).

T. Mayer, *Europe's Unfinished Currency: The Political Economics of the Euro* (Anthem Press, 2012).

---

[77] 25 Member States to the Treaty, i.e. all Member States except the UK and the Czech Republic. Currently it is not known whether Croatia will join once it becomes a Member State in the summer 2013. The non-euro Member States may limit their engagements under the Treaty.
[78] Art.3 of the Fiscal CompactTreaty.

CHAPTER 29

Social Policy[1]

INTRODUCTION

Under this heading will be examined the social provisions of the TFEU,[2] the **29-01** European Social Fund (ESF),[3] education, vocational training, youth and sport,[4] and also, although it is not mentioned under the same heading in the TFEU, employment.[5] The latter was added to the EC Treaty by the Treaty of Amsterdam.

The Union has been accused of giving priority to the economic and monetary developments, forgetting the social aspects, or even at their cost. It suffices, however, to look at the first of the European Treaties establishing the now defunct European Coal and Steel Community, to realise that, from the beginning, the social preoccupations were present; as for the European Economic Community, it not only contained a Title III on Social Policy, with social provisions and a Social Fund, but the free movement of workers was considered as requiring measures in the field of social security. Similarly, the Euratom Treaty contains several provisions on the health and safety of workers.[6] The Court underlined this importance of the "social" by stating that the Union has "not only an economic but also a social purpose".[7] However, only the social provisions of the TFEU shall be examined here.

One of the reasons why the Union is viewed as neglecting the social aspects is because social policy remains largely within the exclusive competence of the Member States. Indeed, the role of the Union is limited: the TFEU provides that social policy, but then only "for the aspects defined in the Treaty",[8] is part of the competences the Union shares with the Member States.[9] This means that both the Member States and the Union are to take implementing measures that take account of the diverse forms of national practices, in particular in the field of contractual relations,[10] and having regard to the conditions and technical rules pertaining to those in each Member State.[11]

---

[1] Arts 151–164 TFEU.
[2] Arts 151–161 TFEU.
[3] Arts 162–164 TFEU.
[4] Arts 165, 166 TFEU.
[5] Arts 145–150 TFEU.
[6] EAEC, Title Two, Ch.3.
[7] *International Transport Workers Association v Viking Line* (C-438/05) [2007] E.C.R. I-10779.
[8] Art.4(2)(b) TFEU.
[9] Arts 4(2) and 153(1) TFEU.
[10] Art.151,2 TFEU.
[11] Art.155(2)(b) TFEU.

29–02   The Treaty also refers to the "need to maintain the competitiveness of the Union economy"[12]; maybe this is a hidden way of reminding the workers and their organisations of the fact that, besides all the rights mentioned in the various charters (see hereunder), workers also have "obligations" with regard, for instance, to productivity and wage-restraint.

In 2012, the Commission wrote that "[t]o do well in the face of competition from new emerging economies, Europe must create the jobs needed by a dynamic knowledge-based society.This requires investment in education, science and employment policies geared to keep up with the pace of change and see the EU through the economic crisis."[13]

1. SOCIAL PROVISIONS

29–03   The social provisions of the TFEU[14] start with a reference to the European Social Charter of 1961 and the 1989 [Union] Charter of the Fundamental Social Rights of Workers (Social Charter). The former was signed at Turin in 1962, within the framework of the Council of Europe. It provides for 19 "rights", such as the rights to work, to just conditions of work, to safe and healthy working conditions, to fair remuneration, to organise, to bargain collectively, to social security, to medical assistance, etc. As for the Social Charter, it was adopted at the Strasbourg European Council, on December 8 and 9, 1989. Although referred to in many Union publications, it was never published officially; only the Agreement on social policy between the Member States, with the exception of the UK, was annexed to the EU Treaty[15]; it no longer is. The purpose of that Agreement was to implement the 1989 Social Charter. This led to the adoption of several directives that were later accepted by the UK, which also adhered to the Charter and the Agreement with the entry into force of the EU Treaty. Most of the rights provided for in the Charter and the Agreement are now to be found in the social provisions of the TFEU.[16]

It is interesting to note that the Union and the Member States included a "credo" in the Treaty (something that is normally done in the recitals), by affirming that they "believe"[17] that the implementation of the objectives outlined above will ensue, among others, "from the functioning of the common market", which will favour the harmonisation of the social systems.[18] The Treaty procedures and the approximation of laws are other means to achieve the objectives set out in this chapter.

29–04   The social provisions refer to four different Union activities:

---

[12] Art.151,2 TFEU.

[13] This statement is based upon Art.151,1 TFEU.

[14] Art.151 TFEU.

[15] Former EC Protocol 14.

[16] Art.151,1 TFEU.

[17] Art.151,3 TFEU.

[18] It will be remembered that with regard to the free movement of workers and self-employed persons, a harmonisation of the social security systems was not envisaged.

1. the Union is to "support and complement"[19] the activities of the Member States in various fields[20];
2. the Commission has the task of promoting the consultation of management and labour[21];
3. the Commission must encourage co-operation between the Member States in given fields[22]; and
4. Member States must ensure the principle of equal pay for male and female workers.[23]

These activities will be briefly examined below.

(1) Union Action Supporting and Complementing Member States' Activities

In the social field also, one of the first tasks of the Union is, as mentioned, to "support and complement" the activities of the Member States in the 11 areas below. This is to be done by adopting measures to encourage co-operation between Member States through various initiatives[24] and by means of directives setting out minimum requirements for gradual implementation, having regard to the conditions and technical rules obtaining in each of the Member States. These requirements relate to:

29–05

- improvement in particular of the working environment to protect workers' health and safety; with regard to the latter, several directives on the protection of workers from certain risks at work[25] were adopted by the Council, and the Agency for Safety and Health at Work was set up[26];

---

[19] This expression is confusing because it is similar to the one used in Art.6 TFEU to describe the third category of Union competences, besides the exclusive and the shared ones: "The Union shall have competence to carry out actions to support, co-ordinate or supplement the actions of the Member States".

[20] Art.153 TFEU.

[21] Art.154 TFEU.

[22] Art.156 TFEU.

[23] Art.157 TFEU.

[24] For more details see Art.153(2)(a) and (b) TFEU.

[25] The basic Directive 80/1107 concerning the protection of workers from the risks related to exposure to chemical, physical and biological agents [1980] O.J. L327/8, see [1998] O.J. L131/11, was implemented through a number of "individual" directives. The basic Directive and some of the implementing Directives were repealed [1998] O.J. L131/11. Still applicable are: Directive 83/477, exposure to asbestos [1983] O.J. L263/25, amended [2003] O.J. L97/48; Directive 80/1107 was replaced by Directive 89/391, on the introduction of measures to encourage improvements in the safety and health of workers at work [1989] O.J. L183/1; see *Lewen v Denda* (C-333/97) [1999] E.C.R. I-7243. This Directive was implemented by a series of individual directives as provided for in its Art.16(1): Directive 89/654 (1st Directive), concerning the minimum safety and health requirements for the workplace [1989] O.J. L393/1; Directive 89/655 (2nd Directive), same for the use of equipment [1989] O.J. L393/13, amended [2001] O.J. L195/46; Directive 89/656 (3rd Directive) same for the use of protective equipment [1989] O.J. L393/18; Directive 90/269 (4th Directive), same for the manual handling of loads where there is a risk of back injury [1990] O.J. L156/9; Directive 90/270 (5th Directive), same for work with display screen equipment [1990] O.J. L156/14; Directive 2004/37 (6th Directive) codified version, risks related to exposure to carcinogens [2004] O.J. L158/50; Directive 2000/54 (7th Directive), same at temporary or mobile construction sites [2000] O.J. L262/21; Directive 2000/54 (8th Directive), risks related to exposure to biological

- working conditions; the European Foundation for the improvement of living and working conditions[27] was created to help achieve this objective;
- social security and social protection of workers; the Nice Treaty provided for the establishment of a Social Protection Committee[28] with advisory status, to promote co-operation on social protection policies between the Member States. The task of this Committee is to monitor the social situation and the development of social protection, promote exchanges of information and prepare reports, formulate opinions or undertake other work within its field of competence. In fulfilling its mandate, the Committee must establish appropriate contacts with management and labour[29];
- protection of workers where their employment contract is terminated; several directives were adopted concerning, among others, collective redundancies,[30] safeguarding employees' rights in the event of transfers of undertakings,[31] the protection of workers in the event of the insolvency of

agents [2000] O.J. L262/21; Directive 92/57 health and safety at temporary and mobile construction sites [1992] O.J. L245; see Communication on practical implementation COM(2008)698; Directive 92/58 (9th Directive), minimum requirements for the provisions of safety and/or health signs [1992] O.J. L245/23; see same Directive 92/85 (10th Directive), pregnant workers or who have recently given birth or are breastfeeding [1992] O.J. L348/1, see *Paquay* (C-460/06) Art.10 prohibits not only the notification of a decision to dismiss, but also the taking of preparatory steps for such a decision before the end of the period of protection, see also *Dita Danosa* (C-232/09) E.C.R. [2010] I-11405 concept of "pregnant worker" and equal treatment of men and women; Directive 92/91 (11th Directive), workers in the mineral-extracting industries through drilling [1992] O.J. L348/9; Directive 92/104 (12th Directive), workers in the surface and underground mineral-extracting industries [1992] O.J. L404/10; Directive 93/103 (13th Directive), work on board fishing vessels [1993] O.J. L307/1; Directive 98/24 (14th Directive), risk related to chemical agents [1998] O.J. L131/11; Directive 99/92 (15th Directive) risks from explosive atmosphere [1999] O.J. L23/57; Directive 2002/44 (16th Directive) risks arising from physical agents (vibration) [2002] O.J. L177/13; Directive 2003/10 (17th Directive) risks arising from physical agents (noise) [2003] O.J. L42/38; Directive 2004/40 (18th Directive) risks from electromagnetic fields [2004] 159/1, transposition post posed, see below, Directive 2008/46; Directive 2006/25 (19th Directive) risks arising from physical agents (artificial optical radiation), [2006] O.J. L114/38. See also Directive 94/33 on protection of young people at work [1997] O.J. L 215/12; Directive 08/46 minimum health and safety requirements regarding the exposure of workers to the risks arising from physical agents (electromagnetic fields) [2008] O.J. L114/88.

[26] Established by Regulation 2062/94 [1994] O.J. L216/1. See Ch:13: Decentralised Agencies and Bodies of the Union.

[27] Regulation 1365/75 [1975] O.J. L139/1, amended [1993] O.J. L181/13. See Ch.13: Decentralised Agencies and Bodies of the Union.

[28] Art.160 TFEU.

[29] Art.160 TFEU.

[30] Directive 75/129 [1975] O.J. L48/29 and Directive 98/59 [1998] O.J. L225/16, modified [2007] O.J. L59/84. See *Rockfon v Specialarbejderforbundet i Danmark* (C-449/93) [1995] E.C.R. I-4291: collective redundancies, definition of "establishment", company forming part of a group. See also for the notion of "redundancy"; *Junk* (C-188/03) [2005] E.C.R. I-885 and *Confédération Internationale du Travail E.A.* (C-385/05) [2007] E.C.R. I-611: Art.1(1)(a) of Directive 98/59 precludes national legislation which excludes a specific category of workers from the calculation of staff members; also *Rodriges Mayor e.a.* ([2009] E.C.R. C-11621:the Court accepts a difference between the loss of job because of collective redundancies and loss because of the death of the employer; equivalence between employer and liquidator: *Claes and Others* (Joint Cases C-235 to 239/10 [2011] E.C.R.I-1113).

[31] Directive 2001/23 on the approximation of the laws of the Member States relating to the safeguarding of employees' rights in the event of transfer of undertakings, business or parts of undertakings or business [2001] O.J. L82/16 (codified version of Directive 77/187, several times

their employer,[32] and the obligation of the employer to notify an employee of the essential aspects of the contract or employment relationship by written declaration not later than two months after the commencement of employment.[33] (A landmark judgment in this field is *Francovich*[34] where the Court held that a Member State is required to make good loss and damage caused to individuals by its failure to transpose a directive.) the Treaty provisions do not apply, however, to pay, the right of association, the right to strike or the right to impose lock-outs[35]

- the information and consultation of workers; the Council adopted a directive on the establishment of a European Works Council or a procedure for informing and consulting employees[36];
- representation and collective defence of the interests of workers and employers, including co-determination;

---

amended and repealed). An "employee" is defined as any person who, in the Member State concerned, is protected as an employee under national employment law (Art.2(1)(d)). See *Henke v Gemeinde Schierke and Verwaltungsgemeinschaft 'Brocken'* (C-298/94) [1996] E.C.R. I-4989; [1997] 1 C.M.L.R. 373, does not apply to the transfer of administrative functions from a municipality to an administrative collectivity. *Rotsart de Hertaing* (C-305/94) [1996] E.C.R. I-5927; [1997] 1 C.M.L.R. 329; the contracts of employment and the employment relationships existing on the date of the transfer of an undertaking, between the transferor and the workers employed in the undertaking transferred, are automatically transferred from the transferor to the transferee by the mere fact of the transfer of the undertaking, despite the contrary intention of the transferor or the transferee. The Directive does not apply in case of termination of a cleaning contract with an independent contractor: *Süzen v Zehnacker Gebäudereinigung* (C-13/95) [1997] E.C.R. 1259; [1997] 1 C.M.L.R. 768; *Francovich v Italian Republic* (C-497/93) [1995] E.C.R. I-3843, gives a definition of insolvency under Directive 80/987: employers who are subject to proceedings, involving their assets, to satisfy collectively the claims of creditors. *Merckx and Neuhuys* (Joined Cases C-171/94 and C-172/94) [1996] E.C.R. I-1253, concept of "transfer": the criterion is whether the entity in question retains its economic identity, as indicated, among others, by the fact that the operation is actually continued or resumed and *Dethier Equipement v Dassy and Sovam* (C-319/94) [1998] E.C.R. I-1061, workers illegally made redundant by the transferor can turn to the transferee on the basis of Art.4.1 of Directive 77/187. *Liikene* (C-172/99) [2001] E.C.R. I-745: Directive 77/187 does not apply in the absence of transfer of tangible assets. *Collino and Chiappero* (C-343/98) [2000] E.C.R. I-6659: the Directive also applies when a body managed by a public entity is transferred in the form of an administrative concession to a private company set up by a public body, which owns all of its capital. As for the date of the transfer, see *Celtec* (C-478/03) [2005] E.C.R. I-4389. In *Klarenberg* (C-466/07) [2009] E.C.R. I-803. The Directive may also apply, under certain conditions, where part of an undertaking is transferred. The Directive does not require the preservation of a commercial lease even if the termination of the lease is likely to entail the termination of contracts of employment transferred to the transferee: *Kirtruna* (C-313/07) [2008] E.C.R. I-7907 meaning of "undertaking" and "transfer": *Ivana Scattolon* (C-108/10) judgment of September 6, 2011, not yet reported.

[32] Directive 80/987 on the approximation of the laws of the Member States relating to the protection of employees in the event of the insolvency of their employer [1980] O.J. L283/23, amended [2002] O.J. L270/10, codified by Directive 08/94 [2008] O.J. L283/36; Art.4 has direct effect. *AGS Assedic* (C-235/95) [1998] E.C.R. I-4531; see *Maria Nunez* (C-498/06) [2008] E.C.R. I-921. Another Directive was adopted in 2008 providing a minimum degree of protection for employees in case of insolvency of their employer: Directive 08/94: [2008] O.J. L283/36.

[33] Directive 91/533 [1991] O.J. L288/32; see *Kampelmann and Others v Landschaftverband Westfalen-Lippe and Others* (Joined Cases C-253/96, C-254/96, C-255/96, C-256/96, C-257/96 and C-258/96) [1997] E.C.R. I-6907: the burden of proving correctness of details notified must be determined by national law.

[34] *Francovich and Others* (Joined Cases C-6/90 and C-9/90) [1991] E.C.R. I-5357.

[35] Art.153(5) TFEU.

[36] Directive 94/45 on establishment of a European Works Council or a procedure in Union-scale undertakings and Union-scale groups of undertakings for the purpose of informing and consulting

- conditions of employment of third-country nationals legally residing in Union territory;
- the integration of people excluded from the labour market; social protection and inclusion[37];
- equality between men and women with regard to the labour market opportunities and treatment at work[38] (not to be confused with equal pay for male and female workers for equal work or work of equal value,[39] which shall be examined below);
- the combating of social exclusion;
- the modernisation of social protection systems; see MISSOC (Mutual Information System on Social Protection in the Member States and the EEA).

29–06   In those areas Parliament and the Council may adopt measures in accordance with the ordinary legislative procedure,[40] after consulting the ESC and the Committee of the Regions.[41] However, in some fields, the Council must act alone and unanimously, in accordance with a special legislative procedure,[42] after consulting Parliament and the said committees: this is the case for social security, social protection of workers where their employment contract is terminated, representation and collective defence of the interests of workers and employers, and conditions of employment for third-country nationals legally residing within

---

employees [1994] O.J. L254/64; extended to the UK by Directive 97/74 [1998] O.J. L10/22; replaced by Directive 2009/38 [2009] O.J. L122/28. See *Bofrost* (C-62/99) [2001] E.C.R. I-2579 and *ADS Anker* (C-349/01) [2004] E.C.R. I-6803.

[37] General Report 2008, 98 and 99.

[38] See, for instance, Directive 76/207 on the implementation of the principle of equal treatment for men and women, as regards access to employment, vocational training and promotion, and working conditions (the "equal treatment directive") [1976] O.J. L39/40. See *Draehmpaehl* (C-180/95) [1997] E.C.R. I-2195; [1997] 3 C.M.L.R. 1107, *Coote* (C-185/97) [1998] E.C.R. I-5199, refusal of employer to provide references, and *Kachelmann* (C-322/98) [2000] E.C.R. I-7505, where the Court held that part-time workers and full-time workers are not comparable when a part-time job must be eliminated for economic reasons. The Directive also applies after the work relationship was terminated. See also *Paquay* (C-460/06) [2007] E.C.R. I-851, dismissal on the ground of pregnancy or childbirth is contrary to Arts 2(1) and 5(1); Council Recommendation on the promotion of positive action for women [1984] O.J. L331/34; Council Directive 86/613 on the application of the principle of equal treatment between men and women engaged in an activity, including agriculture, in a self-employed capacity, and on the protection of self-employed women during pregnancy, repealed by Directive 2010/41 [2010] O.J. L180/1 (see *McKenna* (C-191/03) [2005] E.C.R. I-7631) and motherhood [1986] O.J. L359/56; Resolution on the promotion of equal opportunities for women [1986] O.J. C203/2; Council Recommendation on the balanced participation of women and men in the decision-making process; and Directive 97/80 on the burden of proof in cases of discrimination based on sex [1998] O.J. L14/6, extended to the UK [1998] O.J. L205/66. This Directive applies to any kind of discrimination. Directive 2000/78 establishing a general framework for equal treatment in employment and occupation [2000] O.J. L303/16. See *Wolf* (C-229/08) [2010] E.C.R. I-1, age discrimination; see also *Kucukdevici v Swedex* (C-555/07) precludes national legislation providing that periods of employment completed before the age of 25 are not taken into account. See also below under "equal pay".

[39] Art.157 TFEU.

[40] Art.294 TFEU.

[41] Art.153(2)2 TFEU.

[42] Art.189 TFEU.

the Union[43] (it will be remembered that in those fields the Member States are particularly jealous of their independence).

The Council may also adopt measures designed to encourage co-operation between Member States through initiatives aimed at improving knowledge, developing exchanges of information and best practices, but, here again, excluding any harmonisation of the laws and regulations of the Member States. Furthermore, the Council may, with regard to the nine first activities mentioned above, adopt directives for gradual implementation.

It should also be noted that the above-mentioned directives do not prevent any Member State from maintaining or introducing more stringent protective measures compatible with the Treaty.[44] A similar provision exists in different other fields, where the policy in question is the joint responsibility of the Member States and the Union, for instance "Environment"[45], "Public Health"[46] and "Consumer Protection".[47] Neither do the Treaty provisions affect the right of the Member States to define the fundamental principles of their social security systems and may not significantly affect the financial equilibrium thereof.[48]

(2) Consultation of Management and Labour

With regard to management and labour, the Treaty provides that a Member State may entrust them, at their joint request, with the implementation of the above-mentioned directives.[49] The Commission, on the other hand, has the task of promoting the consultation of management and labour, by doing that before submitting proposals in the social policy field, and following that, consulting them on the content of the envisaged proposals.[50] On that occasion management and labour may inform the Commission that they wish to initiate a dialogue at Union level, which may lead to contractual relations, including agreements. Implementation of such agreements can be done by a Council decision.[51] Of interest in this context is the Commission Communication on the "European social dialogue, a force for innovation and change".[52] It puts forward concrete measures aimed at strengthening the different levels and forms of social dialogue. This approach to social dialogue is based on the social partner's contribution to the Laeken European Council and the reflections of the High Level Group on Industrial relations.

29–07

---

[43] Art.153(2)5 TFEU.
[44] Art.153(4) TFEU second indent.
[45] Art.172 TFEU.
[46] Art.168 TFEU; however, this possibility was provided for in Art.154 TFEU.
[47] Art.169(4) TFEU.
[48] Art.153(4) TFEU.
[49] Art.153(4) TFEU. See, for instance, framework agreement on fixed-term work concluded by ETUC, UNICE and CEEP, Directive 1999/70 [1999] O.J. L175/43. See *Sorge* (C-98/09) E.C.R. [2010] I-5837 concept of "employment contract", *Lorenzo Martinez* (C-556/11) order of February 9, 2012, not yet reported; fixed-term employment contracts in the public sector.
[50] Art.154 TFEU.
[51] Art.155 TFEU.
[52] COM (2002) 341 final.

(3) Encouraging Co-operation Between the Member States and Facilitating Co-ordination of their Action

29–08   This is the task of the Commission and is to take place particularly in matters relating to:

- employment[53]; a Standing Committee on Employment in the European Communities was set up,[54] special measures of Union interest were introduced granting financial assistance[55];
- labour law and working conditions; various measures were taken concerning, for instance, the organisation of working time,[56] safety at work,[57] wages, income and working hours,[58] industrial relations, etc;
- basic and advanced vocational training[59]; it suffices to mention here that the Commission is helped in this task by the European Centre for the Development of Vocational Training[60]; vocational training will be examined below;
- social security[61]; since the task of the Union in this field is limited to encouraging co-operation between Member States, the Commission and the Council only issue Recommendations and Resolutions[62];

---

[53] In December 1993, the Commission forwarded to the European Council, at its request, a White Paper entitled "Growth, Competitiveness, Employment: the Challenge and Ways forward into the 21st Century".

[54] [1970] O.J. L273/25, amended [1975] O.J. L21/17.

[55] [1984] O.J. L177/1.

[56] Directive 93/104: [1993] O.J. L307/18, this Directive was amended to cover sectors and activities that were excluded at first, [2000] O.J. L195/41; see *Michaeler and Subito GmbH* (Joined Cases C-55/07 and C-56/07) [2008] E.C.R. I-3135, on equal treatment of part-time and full-time workers; see also Directive 2003/88 concerning certain aspects of the organisation of the working time [2003] O.J. L299/9. For right to paid annual leave see *Neidel* (C-337/10) judgment of May 3, 2012, not yet reported; and for the right to full annual leave, even when sickness occurred during that leave *ANGED* (C-78/11) judgment of June 21, 2012, not yet reported. For both Directives see cases concerning annual leave, compensation and sick leave *Schultz-Hoff* (Joined Cases C-350/06 and C-520/06) [2009] E.C.R. I-179. Directive 96/71 concerning the "posting" (temporary employ in another Member State) of workers in the framework of the provision of services [1996] O.J. L18/1. See *Rüffert* (C-346/06) [2008] E.C.R. 8-1989: the Directive precludes a legislative measure requiring contracting authorities to designate as contractors for public works only those undertakings which agree in writing to pay their employees at least the remuneration prescribed by collective agreement; see Communication from the Commission (COM(2006)159 final): "Guidance on the posting of workers in the framework of the provision of services" and *Robinson-Steel and Clarke* (Joint Cases C-131/04 and C-257/04) [2006] E.C.R. I-2531. Concerning the requirement of a work permit, see *Vicoplus* Joined Cases C-307/09 and C-309/09 [2011] E.C.R. I-453 .See also Directive 97/81 concerning the framework agreement on part-time work concluded by UNICE, CEEP and ETUC [1998] O.J. L14/9, amended [1998] O.J. L131/10, and *INPS v Bruno and Pettini* (Joined Cases C-395 and 396/08) E.C.R. [2010] I-5119: calculation of period of service, *O'Brien* (C-393/10) judgment of March 1, 2012, not yet reported; distinction between full-time judges and part-time judges not allowed.

[57] Quoted above.

[58] See, for instance, Directive 93/104 concerning certain aspects of the organisation of working time [1993] O.J. L307/18 and Regulation 2744/95 on statistics on the structure and distribution of earnings [1995] O.J. L287/3.

[59] Vocational training was, from the beginning, part of the activities of the Union.

[60] The Centre was set up in 1975, Regulation 337/75 [1975] O.J. L39/1, amended several times [2004] O.J. L355/1; see above, Ch.13: Decentralised Agencies and Bodies of the Union.

[61] It will be remembered that this subject was broached above in Ch.16: The Free Movement of Persons, the Treaty secures for workers, for the purpose of acquiring and retaining the right to social

- prevention of occupational accidents and diseases[63];
- occupational hygiene;
- the right of association and collective bargaining between employers and workers.

As mentioned already, the role of the Union in those fields is rather limited: the Commission, acting in close contact with the Member States, may only act "by making studies, delivering opinions and arranging consultations"[64]; not very much indeed!

(4) The Principle of Equal Opportunity and Equal Treatment of Men and Women[65]

The directive on the implementation of the principle of equal treatment of men and women as regards access to employment, vocational training and promotion, and working conditions[66] was interpreted by the Court as meaning that "absolute priority" to women in case of equivalent qualifications is not provided. The Court ruled that the Directive does not preclude a rule of national case law under which a candidate belonging to the under-represented sex may be granted preference over a competitor of the opposite sex, provided that the candidate possesses equivalent or substantially equivalent merits, where the candidates are subjected to an objective assessment that takes account of the specific personal situations of all the candidates.[67] The Court also ruled that the Directive precludes a refusal to appoint a pregnant woman to a post for an indefinite period on the ground of a national statutory prohibition.[68]

29–09

Equal Pay   The principle of "equal opportunity" also includes the principle of "equal payment" for male and female workers; it only applies, of course, "for equal work or work of equal value". It concerns here an obligation imposed upon

29–10

security benefits, aggregation of all the periods taken into account under the laws of the several Member States and the payment of those benefits in whatever Member State the beneficiary resides. Furthermore, many regulations were adopted on the application of social security schemes to employed persons and their families moving within the Union, see, for instance, Regulation 1408/71 [1971] O.J. L149/2, modified [2008] O.J. L177/1.

[62] Council Recommendation 92/441 on common criteria concerning sufficient resources and social assistance in social protection systems [1992] O.J. L245/46 and Recommendation 92/442 on the convergence of social protection objectives and policies [1992] O.J. L245/49; it will be noticed that those non-binding acts were published in the L series of the O.J. normally reserved for Legislative acts; see also Council Resolution on flexible retirement arrangements [1993] O.J. C188/1.

[63] Commission Recommendation 90/326 concerning the adoption of a European schedule of occupational diseases [1990] O.J. L160/39.

[64] Art.156 TFEU.

[65] Art.157 TFEU. See, for instance, Directive 79/7 on the progressive implementation of the principle of equal treatment of men and women in matters of social security [1979] O.J. L6/24 and *Züchner v Handelskrankenkasse (Erztskasse) Bremen* (C-77/95). [1996] E.C.R. I-5689; [1997] 3 C.M.L.R. 263: not applicable to persons not engaged in an economic activity. Also *Dietz v Stichting Thuiszorg Rotterdam* (C-435/93): right to payment of a retirement pension, Part-time workers [1996] E.C.R. I-5223.

[66] Directive 76/207 [1976] O.J. L39/40. *Kalanke v Bremen* (C-450/93): promotion, equal qualifications, priority to women [1995] E.C.R. I-3051.

[67] *Abrahamsson and Anderson* (C-407/98) [2000] E.C.R. I-5539.

[68] *Mahlburg* (C-207/98) [2000] E.C.R. I-549.

the Member States; Parliament and the Council must, acting in accordance with the ordinary legislative procedure,[69] adopt the necessary measures. Reference to "equal opportunity" was made above, the focus here is on equal "pay". The latter is defined as "ordinary basic or minimum wage or salary and any consideration, whether in cash or in kind, which the worker receives directly or indirectly, in respect of his employment, from his employer".[70] As for "equal pay", it means that "the pay for the same work at piece rates shall be calculated on the basis of the same unit of measurement" and that "pay for work at time rates shall be the same for the same job".[71] It should be noted that this Treaty provision has direct effect. Several directives[72] were adopted by the Council to implement the above-mentioned principles and many Court judgments have clarified the various concepts.[73] Although the Treaty, in the context of its social provisions, refers only to equality between women and men, the Treaty provisions concerning the "Principles" of the Union provide that the Council, acting unanimously, on a proposal from the Commission and after consulting Parliament, may take appropriate action to combat discrimination based on sex, racial or ethnic origin, religion or belief, disability, age or sexual orientation.[74] On that basis, the Council

---

[69] Art.294 TFEU.

[70] Art.157 TFEU.

[71] Protocol No.33 attached to the TFEU provides that "for the purpose of Art.157 of the TFEU, benefits under occupational schemes shall not be considered as remuneration if and in so far as they are attributable to periods of employment prior to May 17, 1990 (date of the Barber judgment, see below), except in the case of workers or those claiming under them who have before that date initiated legal proceedings or introduced an equivalent claim under applicable national law".

[72] See, for instance, Directive 75/117 on the approximation of the laws of the Member States relating to the application of the principle of equal pay for men and women [1975] O.J. L45/19; in *Rummler v Dato-Druck* (237/85) [1986] E.C.R. 2101 the use of the criterion of muscular demand is not prohibited; Directive 76/207 on the implementation of the principle of equal treatment for men and women as regards access to employment, vocational training and promotion and working conditions [1976] O.J. L39/40.

[73] *Barber* (C-262/88) [1990] E.C.R. I-1889; [1990] 2 C.M.L.R. 513 on the notion of "remuneration", on the fact that the benefits paid by an employer to a worker on the latter's redundancy, constitutes a form of pay, also that, unlike the benefits awarded by national statutory social security schemes, retirement pensions paid under private occupational schemes constitute consideration paid by the employer in respect of his employment and consequently fall within the scope of Art.157 TFEU—furthermore, it is unlawful to discriminate between the sexes by providing for their respective pension benefits to be payable at different ages; also *Larsson v Fotex Supermarked* (C-400/95) [1997] E.C.R. I-2757; [1979] 2 C.M.L.R. 915: outside periods of maternity leave, women are not protected against dismissal of ground of absence due to illness attributable to pregnancy. Famous cases are the *Defrenne* cases: *Defrenne v Belgium* (80/70) [1971] E.C.R. 445 and *Defrenne v Sabena* (43/75) [1976] E.C.R. 455. See also *Commission v UK* (61/81) [1982] E.C.R. 2601 and *Commission v UK* (165/82) [1983] E.C.R. 3431; [1984] 1 C.M.L.R. 44. However, the Court admitted that, although a "bridging allowance" falls under the concept of "pay", there are situations where Art.157 TFEU and Directive 75/117, do not preclude the application of a social plan providing for a difference in the treatment of male and female workers in terms of the age at which they are entitled to the bridging allowance, since under national law they are in different situations with regard to the factors relevant to the grant of that allowance: *Hlozek* (C-19/02) [2004] E.C.R. I-11491. The Court also held that when there are important differences between the pay of men and that of women, and they cannot be explained, it is up to the employer to prove that there is no discrimination: *Handelsverband v Danfoss* (109/88) [1989] E.C.R. 3199. *Association Belge des Consommateurs Test-Achat and others* (C-236/09) E.C.R. [2011] I-7730. Art.5(2) of Directive 2004/113 implementing the principle of equal treatment between men and women in the access to and the supply of goods and services is invalid as of December 31, 2013.

[74] Art.19 TFEU.

adopted two directives in 2000,[75] and in 2002 amended the basic Directive ensuring equal treatment between women and men to update its provisions in the light of evolving case law and to ensure consistency with the two Directives just mentioned. A 2004 Directive implements the principle of equal treatment between men and women in the access to and supply of goods and services.[76]

See also "Framework Strategy on gender Equality (2001–2005)".[77] To summarise, directives exist in the following fields:

- equal treatment for men and women as regards access to employment; vocational training and promotion and working conditions[78];
- equal pay[79];
- equal treatment at the workplace;
- equal treatment with regard to statutory social security schemes[80];
- equal treatment with regard to occupational social security systems;
- equal treatment for self-employed[81] and their assisting spouses;
- maternity leave (see *Sass* (C-284/02) [2004] E.C.R. I-11143);
- organisation of working time;
- parental leave;
- burden of proof in sexual discrimination cases[82]; and
- Framework Agreement on part-time work.[83]

In January 2008, the Commission adopted its Annual Report on equality between men and women[84]: it shows that gender gaps remain substantial, especially differences concerning working arrangements, labour market segregation still exists and is on the rise in certain countries, and the pay gap is not diminishing. Numerous challenges still had to be taken up.

---

[75] Directive 2000/43 implementing the principle of equal treatment between persons irrespective of racial or ethnic origin [2000] O.J. L180/22; see *Feryn* (C-54/07) [2008] E.C.R. I-5187, an employer's public statement that it will not recruit employees of a certain ethnic or racial origin constitutes direct discrimination within the meaning of Art.2(2)(a), it is then for the employer to prove that there is no breach of the principle of equal treatment—Art.15 requires that national sanctions be effective, proportionate and dissuasive even when there is no identifiable victim. See also Directive 2000/78 establishing a general framework for equal treatment in employment and occupation [2000] O.J. L303/16. See *Palacios de la Villa* (C-411/05) [2007] E.C.R. I-853, discrimination based on age justified; see also *Maruko* (C-267/06) [2008] E.C.R. I-1757, application to survivor of same sex partners. In *Coleman* (C-303/06) [2008] E.C.R. I-5603 the Court held that the prohibition of direct discrimination and harassment is not limited to people themselves disabled—in this case the child was disabled and was the origin of harassment by the law firm! Prohibition on age discrimination: *Lufthansa* (C-109/09) [2011] E.C.R. I-1309. Directive 200/43 does not preclude national rules which provide that a person's surname and forenames may be entered on the certificates of civil status only in a form which complies with the rules governing the spelling of the official national language *Runevic-Vardyn et Wardyn* (C-391/09) [2011] E.C.R. I-3787.
[76] Directive 2004/113 [2004] O.J. L373/37.
[77] COM (2000) 335.
[78] Directive 2002/73 [2002] O.J. L269/15.
[79] Directive 75/117 [1975] O.J. L45/19.
[80] Directive 79/7 [1979] O.J. L6/24.
[81] Directive 86/613 [1986] O.J. L359/56,repealed by Directive 2010/41 [20101] O.J. L180/1.
[82] Directive 97/80 [1998] O.J. L14/6.
[83] Directive 97/81 [1998] O.J. L128/71. See *Wippel* (C-313/02) [2004] E.C.R. I-9483; part-time workers, sex discrimination, working time.
[84] COM(2008) 10 [2008] O.J. C118/9.

See Guidelines on the application of Directive 04/113 to insurance, in the light of the judgment of the Court of Justice in Case C-236/09 (*Test-Achat*).[85]

2. THE EUROPEAN SOCIAL FUND[86]

29–11   The European Social Fund (ESF)[87] was set up by the EC Treaty in 1958: its objectives were not modified, neither by the Single European Act, nor by the Treaties of Amsterdam, Nice or Lisbon. Those objectives are to:

> "[I]mprove employment opportunities for workers in the internal market and to contribute thereby to the raising of the standards of living; it shall aim to render the employment of workers easier and to increase their geographical and occupational mobility within the Union, and to facilitate their adaptation to industrial changes and to changes in production systems, in particular through vocational training and retraining".[88]

In other words, the ESF is clearly linked to employment (see hereafter), to the free movement of workers (which was examined above in Ch.16: The Free Movement of Persons), and to vocational training (see below).

Of great interest is the addition introduced by the EU Treaty concerning the necessary adaptations of the working force to economic changes; from that it follows that social policy is not only about granting rights to workers and protecting them, but also about helping them to accept the consequences of a changing economic environment, i.e. globalisation. It was pointed out earlier on that the Treaty enjoins the Union and the Member States to implement measures that take account of the "need to maintain competitiveness of the Union economy".[89] Although in a rather indirect way, those two provisions give a clear hint as to the obligations, which rest on the workers and their organisations, to help achieve the objectives of the Union.

29–12   As is explained in Ch.32: Regional Policy/Economic, Social and Territorial Cohesion—The Europe 2020 Strategy, the ESF, together with the European Agricultural Guidance and Guarantee Fund, the Fisheries Fund, the Rural Development Fund and the European Regional Development Fund, are now grouped within the "Structural Funds", which, with the European Investment Bank and the other existing financial instruments, support the achievement of the objective of overall harmonious development.[90] The EFS is examined in that context. Let it, however, be mentioned here that a reform of the ESF was undertaken in order to redefine the framework and political priorities of the Fund for the period 2000–2006 to support the European Employment Strategy as part of the Agenda 2000 reform of the structural funds. It might be of interest to note

---

[85] [2012] O.J. C11/1.
[86] See Regulation 1784/1999 [1999] O.J. L213/5.
[87] Arts 162–164 TFEU.
[88] Art.162 TFEU.
[89] Art.151,2 TFEU.
[90] Arts 174 and 175 TFEU.

that, according to the Court, using ESF assistance in breach of the conditions set out in the relevant Union acts does not constitute a criminal act, but should be penalised by the Member States.[91]

A *European Globalisation Adjustment Fund* was set up to provide additional support for workers who suffer the consequences of major structural changes in world trade patterns.[92]

3. SOCIAL SECURITY

As indicated above, the EU rules on social security do not replace national   **29–13** systems: all Member States remain free to decide who is to be insured under their national legislation, which benefits are granted and under what conditions. The EU provides common rules to protect personal social security rights, when the beneficiary of those rights moves within the 28 Member States and Iceland, Lichtenstein, Norway and Switzerland. Nationals of these countries and their families are protected when they are or were insured in one of these countries. It also applies to stateless persons or refugees, and nationals of non-EU countries, and their families, legally residing in the EU and who have moved between the above mentioned countries.[93]

The four main principles:

1. Persons are covered by one country at a time, and only pay a contribution in that one country.
2. Beneficiaries have the same rights and obligations as the nationals of the country where they reside, known as "equal treatment".
3. When claiming a benefit, the previous periods of insurance, work and residences are taken into account.
4. If entitled to a cash benefit from one country, it may generally be received when living in another country, known as the "principle of exportability".

Since May 1, 2010 new Regulations on the modernised co-ordination of social security systems apply.[94]

4. EMPLOYMENT

Employment is the object of TFEU Title IX,[95] which was introduced by the   **29–14** Treaty of Amsterdam. It is not part of Title X on Social Policy, where it probably belongs; it was inserted into the EC Treaty immediately after the Title on "Economic and Monetary Policy", to function as the social "counterpart", to prevent the Treaty from looking too one-sided in favour of economic preoccupations.

---

[91] *Nunes and de Matos* (C-186/98) [1999] E.C.R. I-4883.
[92] Regulation 1927/06 [2006] O.J. L406/1. For an example, see [2012] O.J. L130.21. For more details see Ch.16: The Free Movement of Persons.
[93] *http://ec.europa.eu/social/main.jsp?langld=en8* [accessed August 23, 2013].
[94] Regulation 883/04 [2004] O.J. L166/1 and 987/2009 [2009] O.J. L284/1.
[95] Arts 145 to 150 TFEU.

The set-up of this Title is similar to the various parts of Social Policy, i.e. shared responsibility of the Union and the Member States for achieving the objectives; the task of the Union is limited to encouraging co-operation between the Member States. This is accomplished through the drawing up by the Council, on the basis of the conclusions of the European Council and after consulting Parliament and the SEC, the Committee of the Regions and the Employment Committee, of Guidelines, which the Member States "shall take into account".[96] The TFEU also provides for the adoption by Parliament and Council of incentive measures, after consulting the above-mentioned Committees. Harmonisation measures are, however, excluded here also.

Furthermore, the Treaty only refers to "co-ordinated strategy", "promotion" of a skilled, trained and adaptable workforce, "employment policy",[97] promoting employment as a "matter of common concern", the "objective of a high level of employment", the European Council, which must "each year consider the employment situation" and adopt "conclusions thereon", the Council and the Commission making a "joint annual report on the employment situation in the Union",[98] "exchange of information and best practice", providing "comparative analysis and advice" and promoting "innovative approaches", "evaluating experiences" and an Employment Committee. One can only hope that all this "soft" action will indeed create jobs.

29–15   Clearly, it is up to the Member States to take the necessary measures and implement their own employment policy, the Union can only encourage co-operation between Member States and support their action in the field of employment. The danger of providing for the kind of Union activity described above is that it might create the illusion that the Union is actively engaged in combating unemployment. This is not its task and it is not equipped to do this; the principle of subsidiarity applies here to the full. The only action the Union can undertake, besides trying to co-ordinate the actions of the Member States, is to help in training and retraining the workforce in order to make it responsive to economic change. Nonetheless the Union publishes "Employment Guidelines",[99] and at the Barcelona European Council it was made clear that the European Employment Strategy had to be reinforced with continuing emphasis on reform of employment and labour-market policies.[100] Incentive measures were adopted

---

[96] Art.148(2) TFEU. The Employment Guidelines for 1998, agreed upon at the Luxembourg Job Summit of November 1997, were built on four main pillars: employability, entrepreneurship, adaptability and equal opportunity. Every year, a set of guidelines is adopted for each of the pillars, which set out a number of specific targets for Member States to achieve in their national employment policies. Those Guidelines are then transposed into concrete and administrative measures by each Member State, through their National Action Plans for Employment (NAPS). See Council Decision on guidelines for Member State, employment policies and Recommendation on the implementation [2012] O.J.119/47.

[97] See Decision on the guidelines for the employment policies of the Member States [2011] O.J. L138/56.

[98] In fact there are two reports: the Joint Employment Report, the objective of which is to present the employment situation in the Member States and to assess the quality of the efforts being undertaken by them to implement their national Action Plans, and the Employment Rates Report on employment performance in the Member States.

[99] See 2010 Decision on Guidelines for the employment policies of the Member States [2010] O.J. L308 /46.

[100] General Report 2003, 150.

to bolster the Union strategy with activities geared to analysis, research and co-operation between Member States.[101]

Unemployment is the most crucial problem facing the Union. The hope is that the Economic and Monetary Union, with its single currency, may play a decisive role in helping to create the necessary jobs, thanks to the greater flexibility it will generate in the exchanges and trade between Member States. Mention must also be made of the European Employment Services (EURES), which is a European labour market network aiming at facilitating the mobility of workers in the European Economic Area. It links more than 450 Euroadvisers—specialists in employment matters—throughout Europe. The Luxembourg European Council in 1997 had initiated the European Employment Strategy (EES), also known as the Luxembourg Process. It is designated as the main tool to give direction to, and ensure co-ordination of, the employment policy priorities to which the Member States should subscribe at Union level. It is the basis for the Employment Guidelines, the National Action Plans, the Joint Employment Report and Council country-specific Recommendations.

A [Union] Programme for Employment and Social Solidarity was established in 2006,[102] and a European Progress Microfinance Facility for employment and social inclusion was created in 2010.[103]

6.   THE SOCIAL AGENDA[104]

Launched by the Commission in 2005, (a renewed Agenda was adopted in 2008)[105] it aims at:

 29–16

> "[M]odernising Europe's social model under the revised Lisbon Strategy for growth and jobs. It focuses on providing jobs and equal opportunities for all and ensuring that the benefits of the Union's growth and job drive reach everyone in society. By modernising labour markets and social protection systems, it will help people seize the opportunities created by international competition, technological advance and changing population patterns while protecting the most vulnerable in society."

The Agenda develops a two-pronged strategy: the first is to strengthen citizens' confidence and, secondly, it presents key measures under two headings: employment and equal opportunity and inclusion. EU funding is assured by mobilising the Structural Funds, the European Globalisation Adjustment Fund and the PROGRESS Programme on employment and social solidarity.

FURTHER READING

Elise Muir, "Enhancing the effects of Ciommunity law on national employment policies: the *Mangold* case", (2006) E.L.Rev. 879.

 29–17

---

[101] Decision 1145/02 [2002] O.J. L170/1.

[102] [2006] O.J. C139/1.

[103] [2010] O.J. L87/1.

[104] COM (2005) 33 final: Communication from the Commission. See also the Internet.

[105] *http://ec.europa.eu/social/main.jsp?catId=547* [accessed August 23, 2013].

SOCIAL POLICY[1]

Henk Overbeek, *The political economy of European employment* (Routledge, 2003).

Marc Bell and Lisa Waddington, "Reflecting on inequalities in European equality law", (2003) E.L.Rev. 349.

Roger Blanpain, *European labour Law*, 10th edn (Kluwer Law International, 2006).

Tamara Herbey and Jeff Kenner, *Economic and Social Rights under the EU Charter of Fundamental Rights* (Hart Publishing, 2003).

Van den Bogaert, Stefaan and Vermeersch, "Sport and the EC Treaty: a tale of uneasy bedfellows", (2006) E.L.Rev. 821.

CHAPTER 30

Culture and Education[1], Public Health, Consumer Protection

Those subjects are treated here together, because they have much in common, **30–01** although they form separate titles in Part Three of the TFEU: "Union policies and Internal actions". In a previous edition, I wrote that "Compared to subjects like the basic freedoms or competition, they constitute 'minor' Union activities". As will be seen hereunder, this is no longer true. Public health is an example, as the Commission puts it: "the 'mad cow' and 'dioxin' crisis and the emergence or re-emergence of certain diseases such as tuberculosis have highlighted the need for a genuine Union-level policy."[2]

However, in accordance with the TFEU provisions, the above-mentioned policies merely tend to "complement", "supplement" or "support" the Member States' actions in those fields. In that respect they are very similar indeed to the policies examined in Ch.29: Social Policy. This means that, for all those activities and policies, the emphasis is on the Member States, not on the Union's activities. The Treaty, furthermore, contains very few provisions (one single long article for each of the subjects examined here), and those are, most of the time, couched in general terms: "the Union shall contribute to", "shall complement national policies", etc. These activities could be called what the Treaty of Amsterdam refers to as "directly related flanking measures".[3] However, the question must be asked as to whether these actions are indeed directly related to other Union activities? For other areas, such as "Trans-European Networks",[4] the Treaty itself indicates that they are to "help achieve the objectives referred to in Articles 26 [internal market] and 174 [regional policy]".[5] Other subjects such as Education and Vocational Training obviously are indispensable for the free movement of workers and the self-employed. Nothing of the sort is provided for the other subjects examined here and, one could indeed wonder why the EU Treaty inserted them into the Treaty. Nevertheless, as is so often the case, even in the absence of specific provisions, the Member States are ready, when a crisis occurs, to endow the Union with the necessary powers to act and help financially. This is especially so when the crisis affects several Member States and its solution

---

[1] One of the reasons for examining together Education and Culture (which previously were in different chapters of this book), is that the Commission has joined these subjects under the Directorate General for Education and Culture, which provides most of the information on the developments of these two subjects and are a source for the information printed in this edition of the book.
[2] See also Commission website on these diseases.
[3] Former Art.61(a) EC.
[4] TFEU Title XVI Art.170–172.
[5] Art.170(1) TFEU.

requires heavy expenditure. However, a question remains concerning the limits of the activities, which genuinely belong to the Union level. It seems that the fact that certain Treaty rules, such as those on competition, apply to various human activities, like sports, means the Union must be endowed with competences in those fields. It is not simply because the Union is no longer referred to as the "Economic" Union, that, therefore, "non-directly related" fields may be legitimately included. What about the principle of subsidiarity[6] and the famous slogan "let's do less, but do it better"? Anyway, the activities are in the Treaty, and they will therefore be examined in this book.

1. CULTURE[7]

30–02 Even before the insertion of the present Title into the Treaty, there were references to activities which can be classified under the heading "culture": to start with, the "protection of national treasures possessing artistic, historic or archaeological value", which justifies prohibitions or restrictions on imports, exports or transit.[8] Other provisions were adopted, for instance, for the return of cultural objects unlawfully removed from the territory of a Member State[9]; the harmonisation of controls on exports of cultural goods[10]; besides more mundane arrangements like the application of the Social Fund to "cultural workers",[11] special conditions of admission of young people to museums and cultural events[12] and the protection of Europe's architectural heritage.[13] Since the entry into force of the EU Treaty, the Union has a task with regard to both the cultures of the Member States, whose national and regional diversities must be respected, and the "common cultural heritage".[14] Access for everyone to the latter was facilitated by the creation of the European digital library EUROPEANA.[15] The heritage will be brought "to the fore", while the Union must "contribute to the flowering"[16] of the former. However, the Union is not to develop its own

---

[6] Art.5 EU.
[7] Art.167 TFEU.
[8] Art.36 TFEU.
[9] Directive 93/7 [1993] O.J. L74/74, amended [1996] O.J. L60/59 and Regulation 3911/92 on the harmonisation of controls on the export of cultural goods [1993] O.J. L 395, codified [2009] O.J. L39/1.1. See also Council Resolution on the implementation of Directive 93/7 [2002] O.J. C 32/3 and list of central authorities nominated by the Member States to deal with the return of cultural objects unlawfully removed [2006] O.J. C123/4.
[10] Regulation 3911/92 [1992] O.J. L395/1, amended [1996] O.J. L335/9; see also Regulation 752/93 laying down provisions for the implementation of Regulation 3911/92 [1993] O.J. L77/24.
[11] Resolution of the Council and of the Ministers responsible for Cultural Affairs meeting within the Council [1985] O.J. L2/2.
[12] Resolution of December 20, 1985 [1985] O.J. C348/2.
[13] Resolution of November 13, 1986 [1986] O.J. C320/1.
[14] Art.167(1) TFEU.
[15] Council Conclusion of November 20, 2008 [2008] O.J. C319/18.
[16] See Art.6(c) TFEU: "The Union shall have competence to carry out actions to support, coordinate or supplement the actions of the Member States. The areas of such actions shall, at European level, be: . . . (c) culture".

independent activity, but simply to encourage co-operation between the Member States and, if necessary, to support and supplement their action in the following areas[17]:

- improvement of the knowledge and dissemination of the culture and history of the European peoples;
- conservation and safeguarding of cultural heritage of European signifi-cance;
- non-commercial cultural exchanges; and
- artistic and literary creation, including the audio-visual sector.

The "supporting and supplementing" will be done by Parliament and the Council[18] in accordance with the ordinary legislative procedure,[19] after consulting the Committee of the Regions. The Council must also adopt recommendations on a proposal from the Commission. All this clearly shows that this field remains solidly in the hands of the Member States, which somehow only consent to receiving (financial) "support" from the Union!

30–03

The TFEU also provides that the Union and the Member States (acting together), shall foster co-operation with third countries and the competent international organisations, in particular the Council of Europe.[20] Interesting is that the cultural aspects must be taken into account by the institutions in all actions under other provisions of the Treaty, in particular in order to respect and to promote the diversity of its cultures.[21] Other activities referred to are audiovisual policy, regional development, employment and training, research and technological development, agriculture, the information society, tourism and business.

---

[17] See, however, Council Resolution on the role of culture in the development of the European Union [2002] O.J. C32/2.

[18] See, for instance, Decision of Parliament and Council establishing a programme to support artistic and cultural activities having a European dimension (Kaleidoscope) [1996] O.J. L99/20 and Decision 792/2004 establishing a Union action programme to promote bodies active at European level in the field of culture [2004] O.J. L138/40; same to support, including translation, in the field of books and reading (ARIANE) [1997] O.J. L291/26; Decision on cross-border fixed book prices in European linguistic areas [1997] O.J. L305/2; idem in the field of cultural heritage (RAPHAËL) [1997] O.J. L305/31; there are also at least two dozen Resolutions and Conclusions (none of them binding) of the Council, or of the Council and the Ministers responsible for Cultural Affairs meeting within the Council, or of those Ministers alone, concerning electronic publishing, a European sculpture competition, the European Foundation, etc. Special mention must be made of the Decision establishing a Union action for the Europe capital of Culture event for the years 2005–2019 [1999] O.J. L166/1.

[19] Art.294 TFEU.

[20] Art.167(3) TFEU. As shall be seen, the Union is to establish all appropriate forms of co-operation with the Council of Europe: Art.220(1) TFEU.

[21] Art.167(4) TFEU.

30–04   **Culture and audio-visual media.**   Following the adoption of the Television without frontiers Directive in 1989, the Commission runs two programmes: the Media Plus programme (2001–2006)[22] and the Multilingual Radio and Television Initiatives.[23]

30–05   **Culture and Regional Development.**   Funds available for regional development make up the lion's share of the European budget for culture. The Commission establishes guidelines on the basis of which the Member States adopt programmes.

30–06   **Culture and Research and Technological Development.**   This co-operation at Union level reflects its cultural choices. Some research programmes of the Seventh Framework Programme (2007–2013) focus their resources on projects relating directly to cultural activities.

30–07   **Culture and agriculture.**   Agriculture is part of European culture. The Treaty provisions promote traditional forms of production, preservation of the cultural heritage and the creation of jobs relating to culture.

30–08   **Culture and the Information Society.**   The emergence of new information technologies brings with it new methods of work in the cultural sphere. The Commission thus encourages the application of these new instruments to culture. See for instance the User-friendly Information Society programme.[24]

30–09   **Culture and the Environment.**   The preservation of natural habitats as cultural heritage is encouraged by the environment financial instruments LIFE III and by European environmental regulations. See the Energy, Environment and Sustainable Development programme.[25]

It should also be noted that the Treaty authorises Member States to provide aid for economic operators in order to promote culture and heritage conservation, provided such aid does not affect trading conditions and competition in the Union, to an extent that is contrary to the common interest.[26] Mention must be made of the Decision of Parliament and Council establishing the Culture 2000 programme supporting artists and cultural projects with a European dimension.[27] The aim of the programme, which combines the Raphaël, Kaleidoscope and Ariane programmes, is to develop a common cultural area by promoting cultural dialogue, knowledge of the history, creation and dissemination of culture, the mobility of artists and their works, European cultural heritage, new forms of cultural expression, the socio-economic role of culture, co-operation between creative artists and the cultural institutions of the Member States. With this programme, the Union is taking a new approach to its cultural action. Besides the

---

[22] [2000] O.J. L336/82. See General Report 2008/74 for the Commission's final assessment report on the implementation and results of the MEDIA Plus and MEDIA Training programmes.

[23] See Council Resolution on the development of the audio-visual sector [2002] O.J. C32/4.

[24] [1999] O.J. L64/20.

[25] [1999] O.J. L64/58.

[26] Art.107(3)(d) TFEU, that defines aid "which may be considered [by the Commission] to be compatible with the common market".

[27] Decision 508/2000 [2000] O.J. L63/1, modified [2004] O.J. L99/3.

aims just mentioned, it promotes the international distribution of European culture and history, development of heritage sites and collections of European importance as well as intercultural dialogue integration.

The financial framework for the implementation of the Culture 2000 programme for the period 2000–2006 was set at €236 million. The programme was open to participation by the countries of the European Economic Area and Romania and Bulgaria.

The *2007–2013 Culture programme* was established at the end of 2008.[28] The   **30–10** Commission is in charge of implementing the programme and addresses a report[29] to the Council, Parliament, the ESC and the Committee of the Regions. It shall be briefly examined here.

It was established to enhance the cultural area shared by Europeans and which is based on a common cultural heritage, through the development of co-operation activities among cultural operators. The Education, Audiovisual and Culture Executive Agency (EACEA) (see Ch.16: The Free Movement of Persons)

The programme proposes funding opportunities to all cultural sections and all categories of cultural operators contributing to the development of cultural co-operation at European level.

The programme mainly promotes trans-national mobility of cultural players,   **30–11** trans-national circulation of artistic and cultural works and products and intercultural dialogue and exchanges.

With a budget of €400 million it allows to co-finance around 300 different cultural actions per year.

The European Commission also designates the European Capitals of Culture and supports the awarding of prizes in cultural heritage, architecture, literature and music.

Finally, cultural activities throughout the Union are facilitated by the implementation of the basic freedoms: free movement of workers and of the self-employed, i.e. the freedom of establishment and the freedom to provide services and the free movement of (cultural) goods. Similarly the protection of copyright and related rights encourages creativity in the cultural field.

In July 2002, the Council adopted a Resolution on a new work plan on   **30–12** European co-operation in the field of culture.[30] This plan was later implemented, among others, by a Resolution concerning "European added value and mobility of persons and circulation of works in the cultural sector".[31]

According to the Commission's website the Union's fields of activity are: architecture, visual arts, cinema and audiovisual media, dance, education and training in fine arts, books, music, cultural heritage and theatre. On the other hand, the Union is active via cultural co-operation, cultural industries, access to culture, the culture professionals, cultural facilities, linguistic diversity, regulatory aspects and international relations. Where the latter are concerned, the Union approved the Unesco Convention on the Protection and Promotion of the Diversity of Cultural Expressions.[32]

---

[28] Decision 1352/08 [2008] O.J. L348/128.
[29] See for the years 2000–2001 COM(2003) 722.
[30] [2002] O.J. C162/5.
[31] [2003] O.J. C13/5.
[32] [2006] O.J. L2001/15.

(1) Education

30–13 Education in this context refers to general education. There are four programmes: Comenius for schools, Erasmus for higher education, Leonardo da Vinci for vocational training, and Grundtvig for adult education, with a budget of around €7 billion (2007–2013).

Education remains the sole responsibility of the Member States, where the content of teaching and the organisation of education systems are concerned— except for the professions.[33] As the Commission indicated: "There is no common education policy". The main task of the Union in this field is therefore to "contribute to the development of quality education".[34] The means at its disposal to fulfil this task are: encouraging co-operation between Member States and, if necessary, supporting and supplementing their action. It is probably to be considered as normal that, even where it is their exclusive responsibility, Member States do not hesitate to ask for the (financial) support of the Union. Indeed, the Treaty provides that the Union may "supplement" the action of the Member States. However, the Treaty adds immediately that, while doing this, the Union must not only respect the responsibility of the Member States just mentioned, but also their cultural and linguistic diversity.

Furthermore, the incentive measures to be adopted by Parliament and the Council acting jointly, may not lead to harmonisation of the laws and regulations of the Member States.[35]

30–14 The Union action shall, according to the Treaty, be aimed at:

- developing the European dimension in education,[36] particularly through the teaching and dissemination of the languages of the Member States. (The reader might wonder about this objective: with 23 official languages, is this a viable proposition? Surely, everyone will want to learn or improve English, since, for all practical purposes, that is the "common" language (lingua franca), but such an idea is, of course, anathema in all the non-English-speaking capitals. Anyway, the Union set up the LINGUA programme[37] to promote the teaching and learning of all the languages[38] of the Union); see also Council's conclusions on multilingualism[39] and the Commission communication on "Multilingualism, an asset for Europe and a shared commitment"[40];
- encouraging mobility of students and teachers; for this purpose the Union Action Programme for the Mobility of University Students (ERASMUS)[41]

---

[33] See Ch.17: Freedom of Establishment/Company Law.

[34] Art.165(1) TFEU.

[35] Art.165(4) TFEU.

[36] See Resolution of the Council and the Ministers of Education meeting within the Council on the European dimension in education [1988] O.J. C177/5; idem for higher education [1992] O.J. C336/4.

[37] Council Decision 89/489 establishing an action programme to promote foreign languages competence in the European Union [1989] O.J. L239/24.

[38] Council Resolution on the early teaching of European Union languages [1998] O.J. C1/2.

[39] [2008] O.J. C140/14.

[40] General Report 2008, 80.

[41] Decision 87/327 [1987] O.J. L166/20. In 2008, the Commission implemented the first phase of the Erasmus Mundus programme (2004–2008) and negotiated the second phase (2009–2013).

and the Trans-European Mobility Scheme for University Students (TEM-PUS)[42] were established; these programmes now also apply to the Mediterranean States; the mobility should be facilitated, among others, by encouraging the academic recognition of diplomas and periods of study.[43]

These programmes, together with the SOCRATES, ORION and EURY-DICE programmes are now grouped in the "Lifelong Learning programme".[44]

The Lifelong Learning Programme (LLP)[45] supports learning opportunities from childhood to old age in every single life situation. It has a budget of €7 billion for the period 2007–2013. It is composed of four sectoral sub-programmes: COMENIUS (action for schools); ERASMUS (higher education); LEONARDO DA VINCI (vocational education and training); and GRUNDTVIG (adult education).See also MINERVA: information and communication technologies (ICT), multimedia and open and distant learning (ODL) in education: improving the understanding of innovation, designing new teaching methods, communicating project results and promoting the exchange of results of experience with regard to ODL and ICT.

The budget for the execution of the programme was set at €7 billion.[46]

There are activities in four themed areas across all sectors: (1) policy co-operation and innovation in education and training; (2) language and language learning; (3) development of ICT-based content and services; and (4) dissemination and exploitation of the results of the programmes.

A regulation on the production and development of statistics on education and lifelong learning was adopted in 2008.[47] The European qualification framework (EQF) for lifelong learning was approved in order to improve mobility by making qualifications obtained in all areas of education across the Union more transparent.[48] A Commission communication on schools intends to support Member States' efforts to improve the quality of their education systems.[49]

There also is a Jean Monnet programme which supports institutions and actions in favour of European integration.[50]

---

[42] Decision 90/233 [1990] O.J. L131/21.

[43] See above, Ch.16 and 17, The Free Movement of Persons and Freedom of Establishment/Company Law. See also [1974] O.J. C98/1, Resolution on mutual recognition of diplomas, certificates and other evidence of formal qualifications.

[44] *http://ec.europa.eu/education/lifelong-learning-programme/doc78_en.htm* [accessed August 23, 2013].

[45] [2006] O.J. L327/45. See the Tempus IV (2007-2013); Tempus supports the modernisation of higher education in the EU's surrounding area: Easter Europe, Central Asia, the Balkans and the Mediterranean region.

[46] *http://ec.europa.eu/education/lifelong-learning-programme/doc78_en.htm* [accessed August 23, 2013].

[47] Regulation 452/08 [2008] O.J. L145/227.

[48] [2008] O.J. C111/1.

[49] COM(2008) 425.

[50] *http://ec.europa.eu/education/lifelong-learning-programme/monnet_en.htm* [accessed August 23, 2013].

- promoting co-operation between educational establishments[51]; this constitutes one of the objectives of the Union action programme SOCRATES,[52] which was endowed with €1.85 billion for the period 2000–2005;
- developing exchanges of information and experience on issues common to the education systems of the Member States; see the EURYDICE network (part of SOCRATES) concerning quality assurance in teachers' education in Europe and the ARION programme[53];
- encouraging the development of youth[54] exchanges and the exchange of socio-educational instructors and encouraging the participation of young people in democratic life in Europe;
- encouraging the development of distance education.[55]

(2) Vocational Training

30–15   The Treaty provides for the Union to implement its own vocational training policy, which, however, must "support and supplement the action of the Member States", the latter remaining responsible for the content and organisation of vocational training.[56] In 2008, a decision was adopted on the comparability of vocational training qualifications between the Member States.[57]

Like in the field of education, measures are to be adopted jointly by Parliament and Council to achieve the objectives referred to in the Treaty, with the exclusion, however, of any harmonisation of the laws and regulations of the Member States. Once again, Member States accept Union support, but are not ready yet for an approximation of their national rules.

Vocational training was provided for by the Treaties from the very beginning; it was referred to as one of the actions of the Member States which could be financed at 50 per cent by the ESF. It has become an activity on its own: see the LEONARDO DE VINCI action programme for the implementation of a Union vocational training policy,[58] which received €1.15 billion for the period 2000–2006 and, as mentioned in Ch.13: Decentralised Agencies and Bodies of the Union, the setting up of the European Centre for the Development of Vocational Training.[59] The latter is a scientific and technical body entrusted with promoting, at Union level, the exchange of information and experience, the distribution of documents and the launching of research and experimental projects to facilitate the attainment of the vocational training objectives. As for

---

[51] Conclusion of the Council and the Ministers of Education meeting within the Council concerning a pilot action for multilateral school partnership in the European Union [1991] O.J. C321/3.
[52] Decision 819/95 was replaced by the programme for education and training.
[53] See EURYDICE: [1992] O.J. C336/7, *http://www.eurydice.org* [accessed August 23, 2013] and ARION programme on study visits for education specialists and administrators; Eur-lex database, Section 16.30.
[54] See the "Youth in Action" programme for the period 2007–2013 [2008] O.J. L348/113.
[55] Conclusions on the development of open and distance learning [1992] O.J. C151/3 and on criteria for actions for open and distant learning [1992] O.J. C336/6.
[56] Art.166 TFEU.
[57] Decision 1065/08 [2008] O.J. L288/4.
[58] Decision 94/819 [1994] O.J. L340/8 and Decision 1999/382 establishing the second phase of the Union vocational training action programme [1999] O.J. L146/33.
[59] Regulation 337/75 [1975] O.J. L39/1, amended several times [2004] O.J. L355/1; see also Decision 96/1025 [1996] O.J. C316/1.

the European Training Foundation, its purpose is to help the countries of Central and Eastern Europe with professional training.[60]

The aims of the Union action in the field of vocational training are the following:

30–16

- facilitate adaptation to industrial changes;
- improve initial and continuing vocational training;
- facilitate access to vocational training and encourage mobility of instructors and trainees and, particularly, young people;
- stimulate co-operation on training between training establishments and firms; and
- develop exchanges of information and experience.

In the field of vocational training also, the Union and the Member States are to foster co-operation with third countries and international organisations.[61] No reference is made here to the Council of Europe.

(3) Youth

The Union's youth policies[62] aim to meet young people's changing expectations, while encouraging them to contribute to society by concrete action in the form of a specific programme for young people called "Youth in Action". In 2005, the European Council established a framework programme, now made up of three main strands:

30–17

- young people's active citizenship with the following instruments: "Youth in Action" programme,[63] "Youth Portal", adopted in 2005, and the "European knowledge centre on youth policy";
- social and occupational integration via the European Youth Pact;
- youth dimension in other Union policies.

See the "Youth in Action" Programme 2007–2013: it aims to inspire a sense of active European citizenship, solidarity and tolerance among young Europeans and to involve them in shaping the Union's future.[64]

See also mobility of young volunteers across the European Union[65] and a renewed framework in the youth field (2010–2018).

---

[60] Regulation 1360/90 establishing the European Training Foundation for Central and Eastern Europe [1990] O.J. L131/1, replaced by Regulation 1339/2008 establishing a European training Foundation (recast) [2008] O.J. L354/82.

[61] Quoted above.

[62] Borrowed from: *http://ec.europa.eu/youth/index_en.htm* [accessed August 23, 2013].

[63] Decision 1719/06 for the period 2007–2013 with a budget of €855 million.

[64] More information is to be found on the web site of the Education, Audiovisual & Culture Executive Agency.

[65] Council Recommendation [2008] O.J. C319/8.

(4) Sports

30–18   The aim here is to develop the European dimension of sport, by promoting fairness and openness in sporting competitions and co-operation between bodies responsible for sports, and by protecting the physical and moral integrity of sportsmen and sportswomen, especially the youngest ones.[66]

The TFEU also provides for the Union and the Member States to foster co-operation with third countries,[67] and the competent international organisations in the field of education and sports, in particular the Council of Europe.[68] Thirty-five new joint projects were launched in 2008 with the United States (16), Canada (5), Australia (4) and New-Zealand (1); these projects are co-financed with the partner countries.[69] A China-EU language exchange programme, sponsored by the Chinese Government, was also launched.

In order to contribute to the achievement of these objectives, Parliament and the Council, acting in accordance with the ordinary legislative procedure,[70] after consulting the ESC and the Committee of the Regions, shall adopt "incentive measures" (not further defined), excluding any harmonisation, and the Council, on a proposal from the Commission, shall adopt recommendations (not very binding!).[71]

2. PUBLIC HEALTH[72]

30–19   In pursuance of the TFEU, the Union must, whenever it defines or implements any of its policies and activities ensure a high level of human health protection;[73] it shall also complement national policies. The field of action is circumscribed as follows: improving public health, preventing human illness and diseases and obviating sources of danger to physical and mental health, that includes the fight against the "major health scourges",[74] by promoting research into their causes, their transmission and their prevention, as well as health information and education.[75] Reference is also made to the reduction of drug-related health damage, including information[76] and prevention[77] and monitoring, early warning of and combating serious cross-border threats to health. Although in this field like

---

[66] Art.165(2) TFEU last indent.

[67] See Agreement between the EU and the US establishing a co-operation programme in higher education and vocational education and training [1995] O.J. L279/13; idem with Canada [1995] O.J. L300/19; also Association in this field with Romania [1997] O.J. L229/5.

[68] Art.165(3) TFEU.

[69] General Report 2008, 80.

[70] Art.294 TFEU.

[71] Art.165 TFEU (4).

[72] Art.168 TFEU.

[73] Art.168(1) TFEU.

[74] See, for instance, Decision 646/96 on action plan to combat cancer [1996] O.J. L95/9 and [2001] O.J. L79/1; Decision 647/96 setting up a Union programme on the prevention of AIDS and certain other communicable diseases [1996] O/J L95/16 and [2001] O.J. L79/1; see also Decision 1295/99 on Union action on rare diseases [1999] O.J. L155/1.

[75] Decision 645/96 programme of Union action on health promotion, information, education and training [1996] O.J. C95/1 and [2001] O.J. L79/1.

[76] Decision 1400/97 on a programme for healthy monitoring [1997] O.J. L193/1 and [2001] O.J. L79/1.

in that of culture, the first task of the Union is to "encourage co-operation between Member States" and, if necessary, lend support to their action, it is also to develop its own activity. The latter came into the limelight when, as pointed out above, the "mad cow" and "dioxine" crises, and the emergence or re-emergence of certain diseases, such as tuberculosis, showed the need for a genuine Union-level health policy. This is to be done by Parliament and the Council, acting in accordance with the ordinary legislative procedure,[78] and after consulting the ESC and the Committee of the Regions, adopting, in order to meet common safety concerns, measures with regard to the quality and safety of organs, and substances of human origin, blood and blood derivatives, the protection of human health in the veterinary and phytosanitary fields, and setting high standards of quality and safety for medicinal products and devices for medical use. Parliament and Council may also, in the same way, adopt incentive measures to protect and improve human health and, in particular, to combat the major cross-border health scourges, which include measures concerning monitoring, early warning of and combating serious cross-border threats to health and measures having as their direct objective the protection of public health regarding tobacco and the abuse of alcohol.[79]

The Treaty makes clear that the Union will not tread on national toes: harmonisation is excluded and the "responsibilities of the Member States for the definition of their health policy and the organisation and the delivery of health services and medical care" must be respected. In particular, adds the Treaty, the above measures "shall not affect national provisions on the donation or medical use of organs and blood".[80]

Obviously, many aspects of health protection overlap with Consumer **30–20** Protection, which is analysed in the next section and in Ch.34: Environment; the object of which is also to protect human health.[81] This applies, for instance, to the classification, packaging and labelling of dangerous substances,[82] restrictions on the marketing and use of certain dangerous substances and preparations,[83] pesticides,[84] asbestos,[85] biotechnology, the quality of drinking[86] and bathing[87] water. Human health is, of course, dependent also on animal health. In this field the Union has been very active, mainly within the framework of the agricultural policy.

Mention must be made of a Parliament and Council Decision setting up a Network for Epidemiological Surveillance and Control of Communicable

---

[77] Decision 102/97 on a programme of Union action on the prevention of drug dependence [1997] O.J. L19/25 and [2001] O.J. L79/1.
[78] Art.294 TFEU.
[79] Art.168(7) TFEU.
[80] Art.168(5) TFEU.
[81] See, for instance, Decision 1296/1999 action programme on pollution related diseases [1999] O.J. C200/1 and [2001] O.J. L79/1.
[82] Directive 67/548 [1967] O.J. 196/1, Repealed by Regulation 1272/08 [2008] O.J. L353/1, amended by Regulation 790/09 [2009] O.J. L235/1, corrigendum [2011] O.J. L16/1.
[83] Directive 76/769 [1976] O.J. L262/201, amended [1997] O.J. L315/13.
[84] Directive 78/631 [1978] O.J. L206/13, amended [1992] O.J. L154/1.
[85] Directive 87/217 [1987] O.J. L85/40.
[86] Directive 75/440 [1975] O.J. L194/26.
[87] Directive 76/160 [1976] O.J. L31/1, amended several times.

Diseases in the Union,[88] and the Decision on the common diseases to be progressively covered by this Union network.[89] It should also be noted that health protection projects may be co-financed in certain regions by the European Regional Development Fund (ERDF) and the European Social Fund (ESF).

On May 16, 2000, the Commission sent a Communication[90] to the Council, Parliament, the ESC and the Committee of the Regions on the Health Strategy of the European Union. This strategy consisted of two main elements: (1) a public health framework, including an action programme in the field of public health (2003–2008)[91] and, (2) the development of an integrated health strategy; it contained specific measures to address the obligation to incorporate health protection into all Union policies.

30–21   An "Executive Agency for the Public health programme" was set up; like other agencies, it is to be entrusted with certain tasks in the management of Union programmes.[92] In addition to the Public Health programme, the framework provided for other legislative measures. These included:

- prevention and monitoring of communicable diseases; an international network of epidemiological surveillance and control of communicable diseases was set up in 1999[93];
- prevention of drug dependence: action plan to combat drugs;
- Union action programme on injury prevention (1999–2003)[94];
- Union action programme on health monitoring (1997–2001)[95];
- DAPHNE, action programme to combat violence against children, young persons and women (2000–2003)[96];
- Union action programme on pollution-related diseases (1999–2001)[97];
- Union action programme on rare diseases (1999–2003).[98] The list of health problems which the Union helps to cure seems endless:
- Cancer: Europe against Cancer action plan (1996–2000); action against smoking; ban on smoking in places open to the public; advertising and sponsorship of tobacco products[99]; health warning on tobacco packages[100]; manufacturing, presentation and sales of tobacco products[101];
- Aids: several actions and programmes: "Europe against Aids" programme[102];
- Bovine spongiform encephalopathy (BSE): identification and labelling of beef and veal;

---

[88] Decision 2119/98 [1998] O.J. L268/1, amended [2012] O.J. L262/1.
[89] [2000] O.J. L28/50.
[90] COM (2000) 285 final.
[91] For 2008–2013, see *http://ec.europa.eu/health/programme/policy/2008-2013/* [accessed August 23, 2013].
[92] Regulation 58/2003 [2003] O.J. L11/1.
[93] [1999] O.J. L268/1.
[94] [1999] O.J. L46/1.
[95] [1997] O.J. L193/1.
[96] [2000] O.J. L34/1.
[97] [1999] O.J. L155/7.
[98] [1999] O.J. L155/1.
[99] Directive 2003/33 [2003] O.J. L152/16.
[100] Decision 2003/641 [2003] O.J. L226/24.
[101] Directive 2001/37 [2001] O.J. L194/26, Annex I amended [2012] O.J. L69/15.
[102] [1995] O.J. L168/1.

- Drugs, see Action Plan to Combat drugs[103];
- Doping: Union support plan to combat doping in sport;
- Alcohol abuse: maximum authorised level of alcohol in the blood of motor-vehicle drivers;
- Food: food law in the EU[104] among others: food information to consumers; genetically modified organisms.

As mentioned before, in September 2002, Parliament and Council adopted a **30–22** programme of Union action in the field of public health (2003–2008).[105] A second programme for Union action in the field of Health (2008–2013) was adopted in 2007,[106] its objectives are to improve citizen's health, to promote health in order to improve prosperity and solidarity and to generate and disseminate health knowledge. The Executive Agency for the Public Health Programme was renamed Executive Agency for Health and Consumers.[107]

The objectives of this second programme are:

1. to improve citizens' health security: developing Union and Member States' capacity to respond to health threats, for example with health emergency planning and preparedness measures and actions related to patient safety;
2. to promote health, including the reduction of health inequalities: action on health determinants, such as nutrition, alcohol, tobacco and drug consumption, as well as social and environmental determinants, measures on the prevention of major diseases and reducing health inequalities across the Union, and increasing healthy life years and promoting healthy ageing;
3. health information and knowledge: action on health indicators and ways of disseminating information to citizens and focus on Union added-value action to exchange knowledge in areas such as gender issues, children's health or rare diseases.

A financing decision for 2011 was adopted, with criteria for financial contributions.[108]

See also the directive on the application of patients' rights in cross-border healthcare.[109]

---

[103] COM (1999) 239 final.
[104] See Directive 2000/13 relating to labelling, presentation and advertising of foodstuffs [2000] O.J. L109/29, repealed [2011] O.J. L30418, replaced by Regulation 1169/2011 [2011] O.J. L304/18 on the provision of food information to consumers and Regulation 178/2002 laying down the general principles and requirements of food law, establishing the European Food Safety Authority (see Ch.13: Decentralised Agencies and Bodies of the Union) and laying down procedures in matters of food safety [2002] O.J. L31/1.
[105] Decision 1786/2002 [2002] O.J. L271/1.
[106] Decision 07/1350 [2007] O.J. L301/3.
[107] Decision 08/544 [2008] O.J. L173/27.
[108] [2011] O.J. C69/1.
[109] [2011] O.J. L88/45.

(1)   Food Safety

30–23   As the Commission writes[110], the EU integrated approach to food safety aims to assure a high level, not only of food safety, but also of animal health, animal welfare and plant health within the Union, through coherent farm-to-fork measures and adequate monitoring, while ensuring the effective functioning of the internal market. This is done in part through the Standing Committee on the Food Chain and Animal Health (SCFCAH).[111]

It is one of the major preoccupations of the European citizens and the year 2000 was not too soon for the Union to develop activities in this field. Indeed, food is a prime example of products which circulate widely across the whole Union and therefore need to be regulated at Union level. The directive issued in 2000 on the approximation of the laws of the Member States relating to the labelling, presentation and advertising of foodstuffs,[112] is a first major step to provide assurance of a high level of protection of human health, and consumers' interest in relation to food. It takes into account in particular the diversity in the supply of food, including traditional products, while ensuring the effective functioning of the internal market. Among others, the following particulars are compulsory on the **labelling**: the name under which the product is sold, the list of ingredients, the quantity of certain ingredients, in the case of pre-packaged foodstuffs the net quantity, the date of minimum durability, any special storage conditions or conditions of use, the name or business name and address of the manufacturer or packager, or of a seller established within the Union.

30–24   The directive was complemented by a regulation[113] with a very broad scope; indeed, it "establishes common principles and responsibilities, the means to provide a strong science base, efficient organisational arrangements and procedures to underpin decision making in matters of food and feed safety". It applies at all stages of production, processing and distribution of food and feed.[114] An essential element is constituted by the traceability of food; all operators in this sector are, since January 1, 2005, obliged to put into place a **traceability** system allowing, for each one of their products, the identification of the provider of the ingredients and to whom they were delivered, to register this data in a given system allowing to keep them for a period longer than the life of the product and, finally, to provide the data quasi-immediately on demand by the competent authorities. Traceability allows the authorities to withdraw from the market products that present a danger to public health. The Union now has a General Food Law providing for risk analysis, precautionary principle, protection of consumers' interests, public consultation, public information, obligations for food trade, food and feed safety requirements, responsibilities, among others, of the food business operators, traceability and liability.

Finally, mention must be made of the **Precautionary Principle**, which allows Member States to take measures when the potentially dangerous effects of a phenomenon, product or process have been identified by a scientific and objective evaluation, which does not, however, allow the risk to be determined

---

[110] *http://ec.europa.eu/food/food/index_en.htm* [accessed August 23, 2013].
[111] Its summary reports are published on the web.
[112] Directive 2000/13, (quoted above), repealed [2011] P O.J. L304/18.
[113] Regulation 178/2002, (quoted above).
[114] Art.1 Regulation 178/2002 (quoted above).

with sufficient certainty. The Treaty contains only one reference to this principle, namely in the Title on the environment,[115] but it is generally accepted that it also covers human, animal and plant health and consumer policy. Since the principle is neither defined in the Treaty nor in secondary Union law, the Council requested the Commission to develop clear and effective guidelines for its application. This was done by a Communication of February 2, 2000,[116] which is examined hereafter in Ch.34: Environment.

(2) Medicinal Products

A major role in the field of health protection is played by medicinal products; the latter to be distinguished from "medicinal devices" and "cosmetics". In those three fields, the European institutions have adopted numerous directives and regulations.[117]

30–25

The basic principle is that no medicinal product may be placed on the market without a prior authorisation either from a Member State[118] or from the Union.[119] For the latter see Ch.13: Decentralised Agencies and Bodies of the Union (The European Medicines Agency (EMA)). See also the Directive on the Union code relating to medicinal products for human use.[120]

Mention should be made also of a Directive setting standards of quality and safety for the collection, testing, processing, storage and distribution of human blood and blood components.[121] A similar Directive concerns human tissues and cells.[122]

In 1976, the Council issued a Directive on the approximation of the laws of the Member States relating to *cosmetic* products,[123] defined as:

30–26

> "[A]ny substance or preparation intended for placing in contact with the various parts of the human body or with the teeth ... with a view to cleaning them, perfuming them or protecting them in order to keep them in good condition, change their appearance or correct body odours."

---

[115] Art.191(2) TFEU.

[116] COM (2000)1 final.

[117] See, for instance: Directive 2000/70 amending Directive 93/42 as regards medical devices incorporating stable derivates of human blood or human plasma and Directive 2003/94 laying down the principles and guidelines of good manufacturing practices in respect of medicinal production for human use and investigational medicinal products for human use [2003] O.J. L262/22.

[118] Directive 65/65 on the approximation of provisions relating to proprietary medicinal products [1965] O.J. p.369, incorporated [1994] O.J. L1/263 and Directive 319/75 [1975] O.J. L147/1, incorporated [1994] O.J. L1/263, amended [2000] O.J. L139/28.

[119] Regulation 2309/93, laying down a Union procedure for the authorisation and supervision of medicinal products for human and veterinary use and establishing a European Medicines Agency [1993] O.J. L214/1. See Ch.13: Decentralised Agencies and Bodies of the Union (The European Medicines Agency). See also below Directive 2001/83 on the Union code relating to medicinal products for human use amended [2009] O.J. L242/3.

[120] Directive 2001/83 [2001] O.J. L311/67 modified [2012] O.J. L299/1; *Gemische Fabrik Kreusler* (C-308/11) judgment of September 6, 2012, not yet reported: meaning of "medicinal product by function" and definition of "pharmacological action" E.C.R. see Ch.13: Decentralised Agencies and Bodies of the Union (6. The European Medicines Agency).

[121] Directive 2002/98 [2003] O.J. L33/30, implemented by Directive 2004/33 [2004] O.J. L91/25.

[122] Directive 2004/23 [2004] O.J. L102/48.

[123] [1976] O.J. L262/169.

The marketing of cosmetics containing certain substances listed in the Directive is prohibited.

In 1993, the Council issued a directive on *medical devices*, defined as:

> "[A]ny instrument, apparatus, appliance, material or other article ... to be used for human beings for the purpose of diagnosis . . . investigation ... or control of conception, and which does not achieve its principal intended action by pharmacological ... means."[124]

3.   CONSUMER PROTECTION[125]

30–27   What the Commission wrote many years ago[126] still applies today for the more than 500 million consumers in the European Union.

> "The Member States and the [Union] have adopted policies designed to protect the specific interests of consumers, who play a key economic and political role in society. Investing them with a certain number of fundamental rights, the Member States have put in place policies designed to reduce inequalities, abolish unfair practices, promote safety and health and improve living standards in general."

The history of consumer protection starts with the Council Resolution of April 14, 1975 concerning a preliminary programme for a protection and information policy of the consumer, followed by an action programme on consumer policy.[127] It referred to a large number of areas, some of which were introduced by the EU Treaty. They are, the protection of the health, safety[128] and economic interests of the consumer, and the right to information—for instance: before a consumer is bound by a contract (other than "distance-" or "off-premises" contract) the trader must provide the consumer with the following information in a clear and comprehensive manner: the main characteristic of the good or service, the identity of the trader, the total price, the arrangements for payment, delivery and performance, guarantee, duration, technical protection measures, if any, and education and to organise in order to safeguard their interests.[129] Other areas not explicitly referred to in the Treaty are, under the heading "protection of the economic interests": misleading advertising,[130] unfair commercial practices,[131] the protection in respect of distance contracts (cross-border) and contracts

---

[124] [1993] O.J. L169/1.

[125] Art.169 TFEU.

[126] See also J.O. C92/2, 25.04.75, p.2.

[127] [1975] O.J. C92/1.

[128] See, for instance, Directive 88/378 on the safety of toys [1988] O.J. L187/1, amended [1993] O.J. L220/1.

[129] Art.169 TFEU. See Directive 98/27 on injunctions for the protection of consumers' interests [1998] O.J. L166/51, amended by the Unfair Commercial Practice Directive, (quoted below) and repealed by Directive 09/22 [2009] O.J. L110/30, protection of the collective interests of consumers. See Commission Communication concerning Art.4(3) [2009] O.J. C 135/1. See Communication concerning Art.4(3) of Directive 98/27 [2011] O.J. C158/1 concerning the entities qualified to bring an action under Art.2.

[130] Directive 84/450 concerning misleading advertisement and comparative publicity [1984] O.J. L250/17, modified by the Unfair Commercial Practice Directive [2005] O.J. L149/23. See *Lidi Belgium* (C-356/04) [2006] E.C.R. I-8501: comparison may be "misleading", where omissions are likely to deceive significant numbers of consumers.

negotiated away from business premises—the customer has, among others, a time limit of at least 14 days to annul the purchase[132]; it applies to any contract concluded between a trader and a consumer, sale of consumer goods and associated guarantees,[133] electronic commerce[134] and, furthermore, advice, help and redress.[135] A regulation was issued in 2004 on co-operation between national authorities responsible for the enforcement of consumer protection laws: the "Regulation on consumer protection co-operation"[136]; a Union Action Programme in the field of consumer policy (2007–2013) was adopted at the end of

---

[131] Directive 2005/29 [2005] O.J. L149/22, based on Art.114 TFEU provides for a complete harmonisation; it increases the legal protection of both the consumer and the undertakings. It provides for a single general prohibition of unfair commercial practices that modify the commercial behaviour of the consumer. It concerns both the misleading and the aggressive practices. Also explicitly prohibited is the lack of necessary information. The Directive contains a blacklist of commercial practices that are always prohibited (Art.5,5); it also contains a list of aggressive practices. See *Plus Warenhousgezellschaft* (C-304/08) [2010] E.C.R. I-217: national law making additional practice unlawful "in principle" precluded. A practical Guide concerning the application of Directive 2005/29 was published by the Commission, in English only: *http://ec.europa.eu/consumers/rights/docs/Guidance_UCP_Directive_en.pdf* [accessed August 23, 2013].

An invitation to purchase exists as soon as the information on the product advertised and its price is sufficient for the consumer to make a transactional decision *Konsumentenombudsmannen v Ving Swerige AB* (C-122/10) [2011] E.C.R. I-3903. See *Peckmans Turhout* (C-559/11) order of October 4, 2012, not yet reported. Directive 32005/29 does not apply to national legislation prohibiting the opening of an establishment seven days a week, because it does not pursue objectives related to consumer protection.

Directive 84/450 approximation of laws concerning misleading advertising [1984] O.J. L250/18, amended, see below. See *VTB and Galatea* (Joined Cases 261/07 and 299/07) [2009] E.C.R. I-2949. The Directive precludes a national regulation prohibiting joined offers.

[132] Directive 97/7 [1997] O.J. L144/19, amended by the Unfair Commercial Practice Directive, (quoted above), corrigendum [2009] O.J. L187/5 repealed [2011] O.J. L304/64;replaced by Directive 2011/83; see, *Gysbrechts et Santurel Inter* (C-205/07) [2008] E.C.R. I-9947: not allowing supplier to request consumer to provide his payment card number constitutes infringement, and modified by Directive 2007/64 on payment services in the internal market [2007] O.J. L319/1. With regard to off-premises and distant contracts see *Hamilton* (C-412/06) [2008] E.C.R. I-2383, concerning the right to cancel provided for in Art.5(1) and *Gysbrecht* (C-205/07) (quoted above), concerning the right of the seller to ask for a down payment in the case of a trans-frontier transaction; with regard to its application to sales of immovable property, see *Schulte* (C-350/03) [2005] E.C.R. I-9215. See *Gonzales Alonzo* (C-166/11) judgment of March 1, 2012, not yet reported; unit-linked insurance contracts not included.

[133] Directive 99/44 [1999] O.J. L171/12. See *Quelle* (C-404/06) [2008] E.C.R. I-2685, Art.3 precludes national legislation under which a seller who has sold consumer goods, which are not in conformity, may require the consumer to pay compensation for the use of those defective goods until their replacement with new goods, since the seller is responsible for having supplied a defective good; however, in case the consumer makes use of the goods in a manner incompatible with the principles of civil law, such as those of good faith and unjust enrichment, he may be required to make compensation for the use of the good, *Messner* (C-489/07) E.C.R. I-7315. In case a defective good is already installed by the customer, the seller is obliged to remove it and install the replacement *Gebr. Weber et Putz* (Joined cases C-65/09 and 67/09) [2011] E.C.R. I-5257.

[134] Directive 2000/31 [2000] O.J. L178/1 on certain legal aspects of information society services, in particular electronic commerce, in the internal market ("Directive on electronic commerce"). See *Promusicae* (C-275/06) [2008] E.C.R. 8-271, the Directive neither compels nor precludes obligation to disclose personal data in civil procedure and *Deutsche Internet Verziecherung* (C-298/07) [2008] E.C.R. I-7841, interpreting Art.5(1)(c), obligation of service provider to supply recipient with information before the conclusion of the contract.

[135] See European Network for Out-of-Court Settlement of Consumer Disputes or European Extra Judicial Network (eej-net) Europa, Consumer Affairs, eej.net, IP/00/445.

[136] [2004] O.J. L 364/1.

2006.[137] See also a Directive promoting the establishment and operation of the internal market in the field of consumer credit and securing a high level of protection for consumers throughout the Union.[138]

Co-operation between national authorities responsible for the enforcement of consumer protection laws was provided.[139]

30–28   **Product liability.**   Of great importance for consumers, distributors and producers are the directives on general product safety,[140] and liability for defective products,[141] under which only the producer can be held responsible, except in certain well-defined cases, where responsibility is shifted to the supplier.[142] The Court determined that, in order for a producer to incur liability for defective products, the victim does not have to prove that the producer was at fault; that, however, in accordance with the principle of fair apportionment of risk between the injured person and the producer,[143] the latter has a defence if he can prove certain facts exonerating him from liability, including that "the state of scientific and technical knowledge at the time when he put the product into circulation, was not such as to enable the existence of the defect to be discovered".[144] The Court determined that national law may establish liability of the supplier without restriction for producer's fault-based liability.[145] The Court also determined that the producer and the distributor may be bound only by obligations imposed on them respectively by directive.[146] There is a time limit of three years. It should also be noted that this liability does not exclude the possibility for the injured party to also claim damage under other liabilities.[147]

---

[137] [2006] O.J. L404/39.

[138] Directive 2008/48 on credit agreements for consumers [2008] O.J. L133/66. See *Pohotovost* (C-76/10) E.C.R. I-11557 power of national court to examine of its own motion whether certain terms are unfair. See *SC Volksbank România* (C-602/10) judgment of July 12, 2012, not yet reported. Obligation to put in place, in national law, adequate and effective out-of-court dispute resolution procedure.

[139] Regulation on consumer protection co-operation [2004] O.J. L364/1. See Commission recommendation guidelines for the implementation of data protection rules [2011] O.J. L57/44.

[140] Directive 2001/95 with a view of ensuring a high level of protection of safety and health of persons as required by Art.168 TFEU; [2001] O.J. L11/04, Commission Communication [2006] O.J. L171/23 and Decision on compliance of certain standards with the general safety requirements [2006] O.J. L200/35. See Rapid Information System [2010] O.J. L22/1.

[141] Directive 85/374 [1985] O.J. L210/29, amended O.J. L141/20 in order to include non-transformed agricultural products; it is also stated that "product" includes electricity. For an interpretation of "put into circulation" see case *Declan O'Byrne* (C-127/04) [2006] E.C.R. I-1313; on what constitutes sufficient prove of damage caused by a product, *Commission v Greece* (C-286 /08) [2009] E.C.R. I-142 (Summ.pub.). See also Directive 98/37 on the approximation of the laws of the Member States relating to machinery [1998] O.J. L207/1 and Commission communication [2009] O.J. C22/1. For substitution of "producer" in case of wholly-owned subsidiary, see *Aventis Pasteur SA v OB* (C-358/08) [2009] E.C.R. C-11305.

[142] Art.3(3) of Directive 87/374.

[143] Preamble of Directive 85/374.

[144] *Commission v UK* (C-300/95) [1997] E.C.R. I-2649.

[145] *SKOV and Bilka* (C-402/03) [2006] E.C.R. I-199.

[146] Directive 2001/95; *Lidl Magyarország* (C-132/08) E.C.R. I-3841.

[147] *Gonzalez Sanchez* (C-183/00) [2002] E.C.R. I-3901.

The protection of the economic interests covers, besides the ones mentioned already, various other areas, such as consumer credit,[148] the indication of the prices on non-food products,[149] unfair terms in consumer contracts,[150] package travel, package holidays and package tours[151] and combating late payments in commercial transactions.[152] The latter is particularly important for undertakings (it does not apply to natural persons); "late" payment means more than 30 days following the date of receipt of the invoice by the debtor (for certain categories of contracts, the Member States may fix the period at 60 days). The interest to be paid in case of late payment is at least €40. In order to facilitate cross-border payments, a *European Order for payment procedure* was set up.[153]

---

[148] Directive 87/102 [1987] O.J. L42/48, modified [1998] O.J. L101/17, repealed by Directive 2008/48 [2008] O.J. L133/66, corrigendum [2009] O.J. L207/14. See *Rampion and Godard* (C-429/05) [2007] E.C.R. I-8017, concerning the interpretation of Arts 11 and 14 and where the Court stated that the Directive allows the national courts to apply of their own motion the provisions transposing Art.11(2) of Directive 87/102 into national law. For the same Article see also *Scarpelli* (C-509/07) [2009] E.C.R. I-3311.

[149] Directive 88/314 [1988] O.J. L142/19 and Directive 98/6 on consumer protection in the indication of the prices of products offered to consumers [1998] O.J. L80/27.

[150] Directive 93/13 [1993] O.J. L95/29; amended [2011] O.J. L304/64 by Directive 2011/83 on consumer right; see *Commission v Spain* (C-70/03) [2004] E.C.R. I-7999: abusive clauses in a contract—rules of interpretation—rules of conflict of laws and *Mostaza Claro* (C-168/05) [2006] E.C.R. I-10421, an arbitration award must be annulled by the national court where the agreement contains an unfair term even if the consumer has not pleaded that invalidity in the course of the arbitration. For an example of an abusive contract term, see *Pannon GSM* (C-243/08) [2009] E.C.R. I-4713. See *Asturcom v Nogueira* (C-40/08) E.C.R. I-06.10.2009: unfair clause not capable of binding consumer. *Caja de Ahorros* (C-484/08) E.C.R. I-9579. Art.4(2) does not preclude national legislation, which authorises judicial review as to the unfairness of contract terms. Also *VB Pénzügji Lizing* (C-137/08) E.C.R. I-10847: examination by the national court of its own motion of the unfairness of a term conferring jurisdiction. For an interpretation of Arts 4(1) and 6(1): consumer credit contract stipulating an usurious interest rate effect on validity of the contract as a whole can continue to exist, unless the Member State provides the contract to be void as a whole where that will ensure better protection of the consumer *Perenicova and Perenic* (C-453/10) judgment of March 15, 2012, not yet reported. *Invitel* (C-472/10) judgment of April 26, 2012, not yet reported; unilateral amendment by seller or supplier.

[151] Directive 90/314 [1990] O.J. L158/59. See *Verein für Konsumenteninformation* (C-364/96) [1998] E.C.R. I-2949, Art.7 protects travellers who have already paid their hotel and who must pay it a second time following the bankruptcy of the travel organisation, and *Leitner* (C-168/00) [2002] E.C.R. I-26321, Art.5 confers on consumers a right in principle to compensation for non-material damage.

[152] Directive 2000/35 on combating late payment in commercial transactions [2000] O.J. L200/35, repealed and replaced by Directive 2011/7 [2011] O.J. L48/1. See *Telecom v Deutsche Telkom* (C-306/06) [2008] E.C.R. I-1923, defining at which date a payment is considered made and *Caffaro* (C-265/07) [2008] E.C.R. I-7095. Directive does not prevent national law providing a time limit of 120 days for forced execution against a public authority. The Directive is repealed with effect from March 16, 2013 and replaced by Directive 2011/7 (recast) [2011] O.J. I48/1, which has to be brought into force by the Member States on that same date. Under the new Directive, public authorities will have to pay for the goods and services that they procure within 30 days or, in very exceptional circumstances, within 60 days; Enterprises will have to pay their invoices within 60 days, unless they expressly agreed otherwise, and if it is not grossly unfair; Enterprises will automatically be entitled to claim interest for late payment and will also be able to obtain a minimum fixed amount of €40 as a compensation for recovery costs; the Statutory interest rate for late payment will be increased to at least 8 percentage points above the European central bank's reference.

[153] Regulation 1896/06 [2006] O.J. L399/1 see *Szyrocka* (C-215/11) judgment of December 13, 2012, not yet reported: exhaustive nature of requirements to be met by the application.

It is worthwhile noting that with regard to consumer protection, the Court decided that the term "consumer" refers exclusively to physical persons.[154]

30–29   Great emphasis was put on foodstuffs following the publication by the Commission of what is sometimes referred to as the "White Paper BIS" on the completion of the internal market for foodstuffs, wherein the Commission points out four areas in which it will continue to propose legislation, leaving the others to mutual recognition. It concerns mainly labelling[155] and nutritional labelling. (See above, "Food Safety".) As with public health, consumer protection requirements must be taken into account in defining and implementing other Union policies and activities.

To help therewith a Consumer Committee was set up.[156] Here also, the Union must take measures to attain the objectives stated above[157] and to support, supplement and monitor the policy pursued by the Member States. The latter measures must be adopted by Parliament and Council in accordance with the ordinary legislative procedure,[158] after consulting the ESC. In 2009, the Commission set up a European Consumer Consultative Group[159] to be consulted on all issues relating to consumer interest at Union level.

Under the Treaty, Union actions must, as pointed out, help protect the health, safety[160] and economic interests of consumers and promote their rights to receive information and education and to join forces in order to protect their interests.[161] A General Framework Decision covered a five-year period (1999–2003) and was allocated an amount of €2.5 million. It was open to the associated countries of Eastern and Central Europe, as well as Cyprus and the countries of the EEA. The activities cover measures (1) taken by the Commission to supplement the policies of the Member States, (2) in support of activities of European consumer organisations and (3) in support of external initiatives to promote consumers' interests. The Decision identifies four areas requiring action at Union level:

---

[154] *Cape and Ideal Service MN RE* (Joined Cases C-541/99 and C-542/99) [2001] E.C.R. I-9049.

[155] Directive 79/112 on the approximation of the laws of the Member States relating to the labelling, presentation and advertising of foodstuffs for the sale to the ultimate consumer [1979] O.J. L33/1, modified [1997] O.J. L4/21; Directive 79/581 on consumer protection in the indication of the prices of foodstuffs [1979] O.J. L158/19; Directive 90/496 on nutritional labelling for foodstuffs [1990] O.J. L276/40; Directive 93/102 relating to the labelling, presentation and advertising of foodstuffs for sale to the ultimate consumer [1993] O.J. L291/14; and Directive 94/54 [1994] O.J. L300/14. See *Diageme* (C-85/94) [1995] E.C.R. I-2955, the requiring of the language of the "Taalgebiet" goes too far and *Goerres* (C-385/96) [1998] E.C.R. I-4431, the language must be on the label in a comprehensible language. Regulation on the protection of geographical indications and designations of origin for agricultural products and foodstuffs [1992] O.J. L208/1, amended [1997] O.J. L156/10 and Regulation 1107/96 [1996] O.J. L148/1, amended [1998] O.J. L87/8 and Regulation 2400/96 [1996] O.J. L327/111; Directive 76/796, approximation of laws relating to the marketing and use of certain dangerous substances and preparations [1976] O.J. L262/201, amended [1997] O.J. L315/13. See also Directive 2000/13 relating to the labelling, presentation and advertising of foodstuffs [2000] O.J. L109/29, amended [2001] O.J. L310/19.

[156] Decision of June 13, 1995 [1995] O.J. L162/37.

[157] See Council Resolution on Union consumer policy 1999 to 2001 [1999] O.J. C206/1.

[158] Art.294 TFEU.

[159] [2009] O.J. L244/21.

[160] See, for instance, Directive 2008/31 modifying Directive 91/477 [1991] O.J. L256/51, on control of the acquisition and possession of weapons [2008] O.J. L179/5.

[161] Art.169(1) TFEU.

- the health and safety as regards products[162] and services;
- protecting the economic and legal interests, including access to dispute resolution;
- educating and informing about protection and rights; and
- promotion and representation of the interests of consumers.

The Commission is responsible for evaluating and monitoring the various measures and must submit an annual report.

30–30

In 2002, the Commission issued the "Consumer policy strategy 2002–2006"[163] with three objectives:

- a high common level of consumer protection;
- effective enforcement of consumer protection rules; and
- proper involvement of consumer organisations in Union policies, and the follow-up actions proposed therein.

This policy strategy was endorsed by the Council.[164]

It is clear that consumer policy has grown from a minor flanking measure to a full-fledged Union policy indicating thereby that the citizens' interests now constitute a major part of the Union's responsibilities and activities.

Mention should also be made here of the Union *Eco-label* award scheme, although the measures concerning this scheme were adopted[165] on the basis of the Treaty provisions concerning "Environment".[166] The scheme is intended to promote the design, production, marketing and use of products which have a reduced environmental impact during their entire life cycle, and to provide consumers with better information on the environmental impact of products. The Regulation does not apply to food, drink and pharmaceuticals. The decision to award the eco-label is taken by competent bodies designated by each Member State.

It might be of interest to note what the Commission refers to as the "Ten Basic Principles of consumer protection"[167]:

30–31

> "1. Buy what you want, where you want
> 2. If it doesn't work, send it back
> 3. High safety standard for food and other consumer goods
> 4. Know what you are eating
> 5. Contracts should be fair to consumers
> 6. Sometimes consumers can change their mind
> 7. Making it easier to compare prices
> 8. Consumers should not be misled
> 9. Protection while you are on holiday
> 10. Effective redress for cross-border disputes."

---

[162] See, for instance, Directive 2009/48 on the safety of toys [2009] O.J. L170/1.

[163] [2002] O.J. C137/2.

[164] [2003] O.J. C11/1.

[165] Regulation 880/1992 [1992] O.J. L99/1, amended by Regulation 1980/2000 on a revised Union eco-label award scheme [2002] L237/1. Now see Regulation 66/2010 [2010] O.J. L27/1.

[166] Art.192(1) TFEU; see Ch.34: Environment.

[167] *http://www.ec.europa.eu./consumers/cons_info/10principles/en.pdf* [accessed August 23, 2013].

The European Consumer Centres Network (ECC-Net) is an EU-wide network to promote consumer confidence.

It should also be noted that consumer health protection allows Member States to adopt measures limiting the free movement of goods, for instance by prohibiting the import of tobacco products.[168]

4. CIVIL PROTECTION

30–32 A Union mechanism to facilitate reinforced co-operation in civil protection assistance intervention was established in 2001.[169] It was implemented in 2004,[170] and replaced by a Union Civil Protection Mechanism.[171] These rules cover the main characteristics of civil protection modules such as their tasks, capacities, components, and deployment time, and define their appropriate degree of self-sufficiency and interoperability.

Protection of personal data.   Although not directly connected with "consumers" as such, a Directive on the protection of individuals with regard to the processing of personal data and on the free movement of such data, should be mentioned here.[172]

FURTHER READING

30–33 Evangelia Psychoglopoulos, *The Integration of Cultural Consideraztions in EU Law and Policies* (Martinus Nijhof, 2008).

Gerazint Howells and Thomas Wilhelmsson, "EC consumer law: has it come of age?" (2003) E.L.Rev. 370.

Nicolas Moussis, *Access to Social Europe* (European Study Service, 2004).

Raymond O'Rourke, *European Food Law*, 3rd edn (Sweet & Maxwell, 2005).

---

[168] *ANETT* (C-456/10) judgment of April 26, 2012, not yet reported.
[169] Decision 2001/792 [2001] L997/7.
[170] Decision 2004/277 [2004] O.J. L 87/20, amended [2010] L236/5.
[171] Decision 2007/779 [2007] O.J. L314/9.
[172] Directive 95/46 [1995] O.J. L281/31. See *Österreichischer Runfunk E.A.* (Joined Cases C-465/00, C-138/01 and C-139/01) [2003] E.C.R. I-4989, where the Court stated that Art.6 (1)(c) and Art.7(c) and (e) had direct effect, i.e. could be invoked by the citizens in their national courts. See also *Parliament v Council and Commission* (Joined Cases C-317/04 and C-318/04) [2006] E.C.R. I-4721, where the Court annulled an agreement with the US for failure to protect personal data. See also *Huber* (C-524/06) E.C.R. I-9705, where the Court determined that this Directive precludes the putting in place, for the purpose of fighting crime, of a system for processing personal data specific to non-nationals and *Rijkeboer* (C-553/07) E.C.R. I-3889: balance between interest in access and obligation to provide access See *Volker and Marcus Schecke* (Joined Cases C-92 and 93/09) E.C.R.I-11063 interpretation of Arts 18 and 20 of Directive 95/46.

CHAPTER 31

Enterprise and Industrial Policy/Information Society

In this chapter, besides general policies, several specific aspects such as the information society, small and medium-sized enterprises and the Trans-European Networks, will also be examined. However, it should be borne in mind that Union legislation in this domain[1] covers another 16 to 20 sectors, which shall not be examined here in detail.[2]

31–01

1. GENERAL REMARKS

In its Communication of 2010 "An Integrated Industrial Policy for the Globalisation Area, Putting Competitiveness and Sustainability at Centre Stage", the Commission wrote: "Now more than ever, Europe needs industry and industry needs Europe. The Single[3] Market with 500 million consumers, 220 million workers and 20 million entrepreneurs, is a key instrument in achieving a competitive industrial Europe. One out of four jobs in the private sector of the European Union is in manufacturing industry, and at least another one out of four, is in associated services that depend on industry as a supplier or as client, 80 per cent of all private sector research and development efforts are undertaken in industry—it is a driver of innovation and a provider of solutions to the challenges our societies are confronted with."[4]

31–02

Of interest for the reader is the reference made in this "Communication", once again, to the Internal Market, which really is, as indicated above, the nucleus of all the other Union policies, and to "Industry" as such, as the necessary framework for development.

It is worthwhile to read the Table of Contents of the 2010 Communication which includes the following subjects: "2. A fresh approach to Industrial policy, 3. Improving framework conditions for industry, 4. Strengthening the (Single)

---

[1] Art.173 TFEU.
[2] Iron and steel industry, shipbuilding, aeronautical industry, textiles, leather, hides, skins and footwear, information technology, telecommunications and data processing, motor vehicles, agricultural and forestry tractors, metrology, electrical material, foodstuffs, proprietary medicinal products, cosmetics, dangerous substances, fertilisers and other industrial sectors.
[3] It is to be regretted that the Commission still uses the term "Single" market, when the Lisbon Treaty (2010) refers to the "Internal" market; this might create confusion.
[4] Sec(2010) 1272 and SEC(2010) 1276.

Internal Market, 5. A new industrial innovation policy, 6. Capitalising on Globalisation, 7. Promoting industrial modernisation and, 8. The sector-specific dimension—a targeted approach."

31–03   On October 10, 2012, this Communication was followed by another Commission Communication: "A Stronger European Industry for Growth and Economic Recovery" Industrial Policy Communication Update,[5] launching a new partnership between the EU, the Member States and industry. It focuses on four pillars:

1.   Investments in innovation, with a focus on six priority areas: advanced manufacturing technologies for clean production; key enabling technologies; bio-based products; sustainable industrial and construction policy and raw materials; clean vehicles and vessels; smart grids.
2.   Better market conditions, both in the internal market, with special reference to goods, entrepreneurship and Intellectual Property Rights protection, and in international markets.
3.   Access to finance and capital, by a better mobilising and targeting of public resources, including from the EIB, and by unlocking private funds.
4.   Human capital and skills, to promote job creation and better anticipation of, and investments in, the skills needed to promote industry competitiveness.

The Communication is accompanied by a "Staff Working Document", which presents progress made in the implementation of the 2010 flagship initiative, and includes evidence of the current situation and performance of EU industry.

However interesting and needed, such "Communications" have no effect by themselves, and it is therefore necessary to find out how the Member States i.e. the European Council and the Council [of ministers] reacted.

2.   INDUSTRIAL POLICY

31–04   "The role of industrial policy is to promote and enhance the growth of industry. Thus, the **Europe 2020 flagship** on integrated industrial policy aims to enhance the competitiveness of EU industry."[6]

31–05   **Europe 2020**   "Europe 2020" is the European Union's 10-year growth strategy. It is about more than just overcoming the crisis, which continues to afflict many economies. It is about addressing the shortcomings of the growth model and creating the conditions for a different type of growth that is smarter, more sustainable and more inclusive.

Five key targets have been set for the EU to achieve by the end of the decade: employment; education; research and innovation; social inclusion and poverty reduction; and climate/energy.[7]

---

[5] SWD(2012) 297, 298 and 299 final. This part of this Chapter is mostly taken from that publication.
[6] *http://ec.europa.eu/enterprise/policies/industrial* [accessed August 23, 2013].
[7] More at above-mentioned place.

As the Commission indicated back in 2009,[8] industrial policy today is vastly different from what it was 30 years ago when some national authorities believed that barriers to shield their companies from competition from abroad was the key to prosperity. Other Member States questioned the need for an industrial policy altogether, arguing that industrial policy had no place in an open market. Unfortunately some traditional governments and industrialists still believe that shielding industry is the solution to their economic and social problems. Consequently, the Commission indicated that: "In this area of intensifying globalisation, the concept of national sectors and industries is obsolete" (one can only wish that Member States and their industrialists would see that, generally speaking, they shun competition in their own backyard, but, don't hesitate to go into other States to compete with the "locals". Once again, the Commission pointed out that: "Only a European Industrial policy targeting competitiveness and sustainability can muster the critical mass of change and co-ordination needed for success." Thus the key question that industrial policy now seeks to address is: what needs to be done to help business and industry to compete in the global marketplace? Inevitably, this is a multi-faced issue and one that cuts across many other policy areas. The response to that question will have implications for education and training, research and development, competition and environment, to name only a few.

This is the task of both the Union and the Member States; indeed, the Treaty, **31–06** (which contains only one article, entitled "Industry", for this so important subject) provides that: "The Union and the Member States shall ensure that the conditions necessary for the competitiveness of the Union's industry exist".[9]

The Treaty, furthermore, provides that the Member States must "consult" each other, in liaison with the Commission, and where necessary, "co-ordinate" their action. Nothing very concrete!

The Commission, on the other hand, may only "take any useful initiative to promote such co-ordination", by establishing "guidelines and indicators", "organise" the exchange of best practice, and prepare the necessary elements for periodic monitoring and evaluation. It is clear from the Communications referred to above, that the Commission does indeed take needed initiatives.

The "Union" and the Member States, in view of the competitiveness of the **31–07** industry, and in accordance with a system of open and competitive markets, shall ensure that the conditions necessary for the competitiveness of the Union's industry exist, by aiming their action at:

- *speeding up the adjustment of industry to structural changes* (this clearly indicates that the drafters of the Treaty were aware of the new market conditions mentioned above);
- *encouraging an environment favourable to initiative and to the development of undertakings throughout the Union, particularly small and medium-sized undertakings* (a clear indication that the action is to consist in flanking measures and not in direct intervention in favour of undertakings); in this context it is noteworthy that the Treaty explicitly indicates that it

---

[8] Parts of this chapter are based on, or have been taken from, *http://ec.europa.eu/enterprise/policies/industrial-competitiveness/index_en.htm* [accessed August 23, 2013].
[9] Art.173(1) TFEU.

does "not provide a basis for the introduction by the Union of any measure which could lead to distortion of competition"[10]; important also are the words "throughout the Union", that can also be found in the introductory provisions of the Treaty,[11] they indicate that the less-developed regions must not be forgotten, but they don't get priority, that being the task of other policies; finally, the reference to the small and medium-sized enterprises (SMEs) should be underlined: it is universally recognised that they are the principal creators of jobs and, as was seen in other places in this book, for instance under competition, they are the object of special measures (see below);

- *encouraging an environment favourable to co-operation between undertakings* (this must be seen in relation with Union competition policy that exempts from the cartel prohibition various forms of co-operation);
- *fostering better exploitation of the industrial potential of policies of innovation, research and technological development* (those policies will be examined below). Although, as was indicated at the beginning of this chapter, the initiative in this area lies, according to the Treaty provisions, with the Member States, the Union is entrusted with the task to "contribute to the achievement of the objectives set out [above] through the policies and activities it pursues under other provisions of the Treaty"[12]; in other words, no specific "industrial" actions. However, the Treaty also provides that the Council may decide on specific measures, but then only "in support of action taken in the Member States," to achieve the objectives set out above.[13]

31–08   **Promotion of intangible investment:**   with the growth in information-based competition, investment training and R&D have become vital. The drafters of the Single European Act were well aware of R&D's importance, when they introduced it in the Treaty. This provision was kept practically unchanged, as already mentioned, by the EU Treaty and the Treaties of Amsterdam and Nice. Since it forms a separate Title in the TFEU[14] it will be examined below. As for the internal market, the removal of the many hidden barriers to trade should continue to boost the competitiveness of Union companies, while the emergence of a continent-wide market should enable them to reduce unit costs, forge links and partnerships across borders and innovate more rapidly and successfully.

Nevertheless, as the Commission recognises,[15] the internal market remains incomplete in a number of areas, including company law, public procurement and fiscal harmonisation. One must, unfortunately, add to that the refusal of many a Member State to implement the rules governing the internal market, especially

---

[10] Art.173(3,2) TFEU.

[11] Art.173(3,2) TFEU, last para.

[12] Art.173(3) TFEU. Under the heading "economic, social and territorial cohesion", the Treaty refers to "overall" harmonious development: Art.174 TFEU.

[13] It seems to be the same old story: Member States want to do it each in their own way, at the most consult each other, but gladly accept the (financial) support of the Union; see what was said about education, vocational training and youth, culture, health protection, consumer protection and trans-European networks.

[14] TFEU, Title XIX, Arts 179–190: "Research and Technological Development and Space"

[15] See above.

with regard to the free movement of goods, services (transport, for instance), the right of establishment and, more generally speaking, the refusal of their administrations to view the territory of the 28 Member States as one single economic entity, where the same rules apply to all. With regard to the free movement of goods, which after all is the cornerstone, so to say, of the European construction, standards, for instance, play an extremely important role (see hereunder). In other areas, it is the telecommunication and information industries (see below), the intellectual and industrial property rights, and public procurement, which greatly influence the competitiveness of the industry (these subjects are examined above in corresponding chapters of this book).

The manufacturing industry still plays a key role in Europe's prosperity, and the Commission has felt the need to put industry back at the heart of policy concerns. It has done this by launching, at the end of 2005, a new, more integrated industrial policy in order to create better framework conditions for manufacturing industries.[16]

The concept of "integrated industrial policy" means that it encompasses a full range of EU policies, such as competition, trade, innovation or energy. In other words, it requires mutually reinforcing policies.   **31–09**

Some industrial sectors have been briefly examined elsewhere in this book, among others, in Ch.22: Competition Policy, to which the reader is referred.

The *Competitiveness and Innovation Framework Programme (2007–2013)*[17] aims to encourage the competitiveness of European enterprises. With small and medium-sized enterprises as its main target, the programme supports innovation activities (including eco-innovation), provides better access to finance and delivers business support services in the regions. It will encourage a better take-up and use of information and communication technology (ICT) and help to develop the "information society". It also promotes the increased use of renewable energies and energy efficiency. It is divided into three operational programmes: "Entrepreneurship and Innovation Programme" (EIP), Information Communication Technologies—Policy Support Programme" (ICT PSP) and "Intelligent Energy Europe" (IEE). It is financed mainly by the European Investment Fund.[18]

3. PROMOTING OPEN STANDARDS/SYSTEMS

The application of open standards by the industry presupposes three related   **31–10**
issues:

- regulations, i.e. mandatory rules adopted and enforced by governments, widely misrepresented as a weapon for imposing uniform European regulations for their own sake! They are in fact the result of the approximation of laws which aim to remove those discrepancies between existing national regulations that hinder trade. The objective is to ensure

---

[16] COM (2010) 614.
[17] Decision 1639/2006 [2006] O.J. L310/15.
[18] See Ch.12: Other Bodies of the Union.

that a product accepted for sale in one Member State has free access to the whole European market[19], with advantages for both the consumer and the competitiveness of the industry;

- standards, i.e. voluntary specifications prepared by autonomous standardisation bodies made up of representatives of industry, consumer groups and administrations, i.e. CEN (for general standards), CENELEC (for electronic standards) and ETSI (for telecommunications standards); equipment and appliances need to be capable of working together in the different Member States without sacrificing quality, safety or environmental principles[20];

- certification, i.e. a means by which manufacturers can declare that their products conform to the appropriate quality and technical requirements. The Commission's role is to reinforce and ensure the mutual equivalence and recognition of the testing, certification and accreditation bodies in Europe.

31–11   In 2008, the Commission adopted a communication "Towards an increased contribution from standardisation to innovation in Europe".[21] Several directives[22] and regulations[23] were adopted to bring various fields into line with the regulatory procedure with scrutiny.

In 2010, EU ministers and the Commission agreed that EU governments should use open standards and interoperable systems to deliver electronic government services

Open specifications and standards offer many benefits, especially the ease with which different Intelligent Transport Systems (ITS) can share and exchange information.[24] Recent developments include the POSSE project; it undertakes a range of activities to facilitate the exchange and sharing of knowledge and experience on how to develop, implement and maintain open specifications and standards for ITS and traffic management. POSSE draws up good practice guidelines covering the processes and considerations required for the specification and implementation of open ITS systems and standards, drawing on lessons learned and tips from two existing open specification frameworks, namely UTMC (Urban Traffic Management and Control) and OCIT/OTS.

---

[19] This would only be the required implementation of the well-known Court judgment *Cassis de Dijon* wherein was laid down the basic rule, concerning the free movement of goods, according to which "all goods legally produced and marketed in one Member State, must be admitted into all the others"; unfortunately, it seems that several Member States and their entrepreneurs still ignore this basic Treaty obligation.

[20] One highly successful example is the GSM (Global System for Mobile communication) standard that allows mobile telephones to work in most of the Union.

[21] COM (2008) 133 [2008] O.J. C202/17.

[22] See [2008] O.J. L76 and L81, General Report 2008, 63.

[23] See [2008] O.J. L97.

[24] See *http://ec.europa.eu/transport/themes/its/* [accessed August 23, 2013].

4. INFORMATION SOCIETY

As the Commission indicated: "Information technologies and especially the   **31-12**
internet and mobile telephony, have enabled the development of the Information
Society. This sector represents nearly 4 per cent of employment in the European
Union (EU). The EU intends to promote the development and dissemination of
new information and communication technologies (ICT), in accordance with Arts
179–180 of the TFEU. The EU completed the liberalisation of the European
Telecommunications market in 1998. This framework has since been reformed
twice: in 2003 and in 2009.

The European Commission's publication in 1987 of the Green Paper on the
development of the Common Market for Telecommunication Services and
Equipment marked the start of the process of liberalisation of the telecommunications sector. The process continued with the gradual introduction of a legal
framework for telecommunications. See hereunder.

In 2009, the Commission revised the "Telecoms Package", by adopting the
"Better Regulation"[25] and "Citizen's Rights"[26] Directives, and setting up the
"Body of European Regulators for Electronic Communications" (BEREK).[27] The
main object of BEREK is to enhance co-operation among national regulatory
authorities (NRAs) and to strengthen the internal market in electronic
communications networks.[28] It advises the Council, Parliament and the
Commission at their request or on its own initiative.

The Office is a Union body within the meaning of the Financial Regulation
applicable to the general budget of the Union.[29] It acts under the guidance of the
Board and comprises a Management Committee, an Administrative Manager and
staff. The seat of the Office is at Riga.[30]

(1) Regulatory framework for electronic communications

The opening-up of the telecommunications market to competition has acted as a   **31-13**
catalyst on a sector previously reserved for oligopolies; this was followed by the
adoption of a new regulatory framework on electronic communications.

1.   The "Framework Directive"[31] on a common regulatory framework for
      electronic communications networks and services. Together with four other
      directives (see hereunder), it constitutes a single regulatory framework for
      the convergence of the telecommunications, media and information
      technology sectors, covering all transmission networks and services.
2.   The Authorisation Directive,[32] on the authorisation of electronic communi-
      cations networks and services.

---

[25] Directive 2009/140 [2009] L337/37. (to be transposed by May 2011).
[26] Directive 2009/136 [2009] L337/11. (same).
[27] Regulation 20091211 [2009].
[28] Regulation 1211/09 O.J. L337.
[29] Regulation 1605/2002, [2002] O.J. L248/1.
[30] [2010] O.J. L156/12.
[31] Directive 2002/21, amended by Directive 2009/140 (see above) and Regulation 544/09.
[32] Directive 2002/20 [2002] O.J. L108/21.

3.   The Access Directive[33] on access to, and interconnection of, electronic communications networks and associated facilities.

4.   The Universal Service Directive[34] on universal service and users' rights relating to electronic communications networks and services.

To these directives were added the so-called "specific Directives":

- Directive 97/66[35] concerning the processing of personal data and the protection of privacy in the telecommunications sector.
- Directive on privacy and electronic communications.[36]

31–14   Notwithstanding all these legislative acts, the Commission felt obliged to write in 2010 that "the common rules for the regulation of electronic communications networks and services are being implemented in the Member States with different degrees of effectiveness. As a result many operators and citizens still perceive Europe as a patchwork of different regulatory regimes."[37]

It was decided that it was necessary to separate the regulation of transmission from the regulation of content. The "framework" does not therefore cover the content of services delivered over electronic communications services, such as broadcasting content, financial services and certain information society services, and is therefore without prejudice to measures taken at Union or national level in respect of such services.[38]

The provisions of those directives are without prejudice to the possibility of each Member State to take the necessary measures to ensure the protection of its essential security interests.

Information and Communication Technologies (ICT) are a key component of the Union's framework programmes for research. In the Seventh Framework Programme (2007–2013). ICT is one of the nine themes of the specific Co-operation Programme. Activities are designed to strengthen Europe's scientific and technology base in ICT, help stimulate innovation through ICT use and ensure that ICT progress is rapidly transformed into benefits for Europe's citizens, businesses, industry and governments.

For the latest developments, see the 2012 General Report.

31–15   **Protection of Personal Data**   New technologies call for specific requirements to ensure that users have a right to privacy. The EU has adopted a legal framework in this respect: a directive ensuring the legal and mutual recognition of electronic signatures,[39] a regulation liberalising intra-Union trade in encryption products and a directive concerning processing of personal data and the protection of privacy in the electronic communications sector.[40] It concerns,

---

[33] Directive 2002/19 [2002] O.J. L 108/7.
[34] Directive 2002/22 [2002] O.J. L 108/51.
[35] Directive 97/66 [1988] O.J. L24.
[36] Directive 2002/58 [2002] O.J. L201.
[37] See paragraph (1) above.
[38] Taken from *http://europa.eu/legislation_summaries/information_society/index_en.htm* [accessed August 23, 2013].
[39] Directive 1999/93 on a Union framework for electronic signature [1999] O.J. L13/12.
[40] Directive 2002/58 [2002] O.J. L201/37, modified [2009] O.J. L337/11.

among others; the preservation of connection data by the Member States for police surveillance purposes, the sending of unsolicited emails and the inclusion of personal data in directories.[41]

Network Security   This concerns measures to tackle cyber-crime and penalise   **31–16**
attacks against information systems. To ensure the highest level of security the EU set up a European Network and Information Security Agency (ENISA) that acts as an advisory and co-ordinating body.[42]

International Dimension   The Commission is involved in the work of several   **31–17**
multilateral organisations such as the International Communication Union (ITU), World Trade Organisation (WTO), General Agreement on Trade in Services (GATS), the World International Property Organisation (WIPO) and the Organisation of Economic Co-operation and Development (OECD). Mention should be made of the Joint Committee established under the Agreement on Mutual Recognition between the European Union and the United States of America. This Committee is empowered to take decisions concerning telecommunications equipment, electromagnetic compatibility, pharmaceutical GMPs and medical devices.[43]

5.   FRAMEWORK PROGRAMMES

As mentioned, the Framework Programmes play an important role with regard to   **31–18**
the information industries. The Fourth Framework Programme for research and development was adopted by Parliament and the Council in 1994 and covers the period 1995–1998. Under this framework, an important role had been attributed to information technologies. They can be divided into three sections: the telematic applications (Telematics programme), the advanced telecommunications technologies (Acts programme), and information technologies (former Esprit programme). One of the four thematic programmes under the Fifth Framework Programme (1998–2002) concerned "users' friendly information society". The Sixth Framework Programme (2003–2006) set out the priorities—including the Information Society Technologies (IST) priority—for the period 2003–2006. In addition to the IST Thematic Priority, Information Society related activities can be funded in the following parts of the Sixth Framework Programme: Research infrastructures—GEANT and GRIDs, research activities involving SMEs (CRAFT), Marie Curie actions—human resources and mobility, co-ordination of research activities (ERA-NET), nanotechnologies and nanosciences, knowledge-based multifunctional materials and new production processes and devices. Most of these activities were continued under the Seventh Framework Programme (2007–2013).[44]

---

[41] All this information is taken from the website address in fn.37.
[42] See above Ch.13: Decentralised Agencies and Bodies of the Union.
[43] [2001] O.J. L43/55.
[44] Decision 1982/2006, [2006] O.J. L412/1 concerning the Seventh Framework Programme of the European Community for research, technological development and demonstration activities. See Ch.33: Research and Technological Development and Space.

Many sectors are directly interested in the further development of information technology, e.g. commerce (among others, electronic commerce); transport; health care; flexible and distant learning; the rural areas; linguistic research; engineering and libraries. A special aspect of this further development consists of computerised communication of data, information and documents, standardisation, dissemination and exploitation of the results of Union and national research programmes and of an information services market.

It should be noted that one of the most important means of conveying information is television broadcasting; the Union has co-ordinated certain provisions laid down by the Member States in this field (Audio-visual Media Services Directive).[45] The Directive is based on the Treaty provisions concerning the taking-up and pursuit of activities as self-employed persons.[46]

6. ENTERPRISE POLICY—(MICRO), SMALL AND MEDIUM-SIZED ENTERPRISES (SMEs)

31–19 Activities in this area include the improvement of the business environment and administrative simplification. To this end the Commission set up an Enterprise Policy Group, consisting of high-level experts from the enterprise community and representatives of the Member States to assist the Commission in the identification and dissemination of good practice.[47]

More specifically with regard to the supply of business services, mention must be made of the Euro-Info-Centres, the Business Co-operation Network and the Business Co-operation Centre and the Business Support Network,[48] which aim to be vehicles for promoting business contacts of a non-confidential nature. As for the small and medium-sized enterprises (SMEs), it is generally recognised that SMEs are the principal creators of jobs, but often lack the knowledge, experience, means and tools for competitive and sustainable investments. However, both at national and Union level innumerable initiatives have been developed to help the SMEs to remedy these shortcomings through publications, seminars, meetings, conferences, etc. For instance, the Union established many programmes such as: experimental training schemes, Euro management, participation in public procurement, the setting up of seed capital, etc. See, for instance, a Council Decision on measures of financial assistance for innovation and job-creating by small and medium-sized enterprises and the Growth and Employment Initiative.[49]

---

[45] Directive 89/552 [1989] O.J. L298/23, amended [2007] O.J. L332/27; codified [2010] O.J. L95/1. See *Infront v Commission* (T-33/01) [2005] E.C.R. II-5897, *stereichischer Rundfunk* (C-195/06) [2007] E.C.R. I-8817, interpretation of Art.1 and *UTECA* (222/07) E.C.R. [2009] I-1407, Directive does not preclude measures which require television operators to earmark 5 per cent of their revenue for the production of works in one of the official languages of that Member State. See also *Eleftheri Tileorasi and Gianikos* (C-52/10) E.C.R. [2011] I-4973 interpretation of Art.1(d): surreptitious advertising. *Mesopotamia Broadcast v Germany* (Joined cases 244 and 245/10) E.C.R. [2011] I-8777 interpretation of Art.22a: does not preclude a Member State from adopting measures against a broadcaster situated in another Member State, on the ground that the activities and objectives of the broadcaster run counter to the prohibition of infringement of the principles of international law.

[46] Art.53 TFEU.

[47] [2000] O.J. L285/24.

[48] COM (2003) 680 of March 5, 2003.

[49] [1998] O.J. L155/43.

Furthermore, and this is important, the SMEs enjoy numerous privileges in the   **31–20**
form of exceptions to many rules that normally condition the economic activities
of large enterprises; this applies, among others, in regard to competition rules,
State aids, financing by Structural Funds, etc. Obviously the qualification of
"small" or "medium-sized" plays an important "access" role for all those
programmes. Consequently, the Commission issued a Recommendation[50]
concerning the definition of small and medium-sized enterprises:

- a "micro" enterprise is:
  - when it employs fewer than 10 persons;
  - has an annual turn-over or an annual balance sheet of less than €2 million.
- a "small" enterprise is when:
  - it has fewer than 50 persons;
  - a turnover or an annual balance sheet total of less than €10 million;
  - it is independent.
- an enterprise is "medium-sized" when:
  - it has fewer than 250 persons;
  - a turnover of less than €50 million, or a balance sheet total of less than €43 million; and
  - it is independent.

See also the Council Resolution of 1996 on the co-ordination of Union
activities in favour of small and medium-sized enterprises and the craft sector.

Also, see the Decision on the Multi-annual programme for enterprises and   **31–21**
entrepreneurship and in particular for small and medium-sized enterprises
2001–2005. It was followed by the Notice of implementation of the EFT start-up
facilities, the SME guarantee facility and the seed capital action under the
multi-annual programme. Those facilities applied also, since the beginning of
2003, to the candidate countries, including Bulgaria and Romania.

In 2008, the Commission launched the "Enterprise Europe Network" the aim
of which is to give SMEs assistance in respect of Union policies, innovation and
technology transfer. The Network provides businesses with integrated support
services and support for innovation thanks to over 550 partners in 44 countries. A
large number of third countries are taking part in the network. The Executive
Agency for Competitiveness and Innovation[51] was entrusted with managing the
network.[52]

To support SMEs that are active in the field of research and development,
Parliament and the Council established the "Eurostar's Joint Programme",[53]
aimed at SMEs for developing technologies, production processes and advanced
services in their fields and those carrying out market-based research.[54]

An important measure, already mentioned, that does apply to all undertakings,   **31–22**
but especially to SMEs, was adopted in 2000 on "combating late payment in
commercial transactions". It provides that, unless a payment date is provided for

---

[50] Recommendation 2003/361 [2003] O.J. L124.
[51] See Ch.13:Decentralised Agencies and Bodies of the Union.
[52] General Report 2008, 61.
[53] Decision 743/08 [2008] O.J. L201/58.
[54] General Report 2008, 62.

in the contract, interest shall become payable automatically without the necessity of a reminder 30 days after the date of receipt by the debtor of the invoice or, in case that date is uncertain, 30 days after the receipt of the goods or services. The level of interest for late payment shall be the sum of the interest rate applied by the ECB, plus at least seven percentage points, unless otherwise specified in the contract.

In Ch.17: Freedom of Establishment/Company Law, mention was made of "company law" that is to say, among others, a series of directives harmonising the legal requirements for Union companies to operate in all the Member States. These Directives form the basis for equal treatment throughout the internal market of companies and firms formed in accordance with the law of one of the Member States and having their registered office, central administration or principal place of business within the Union.[55]

31–23   Enterprise policy was also the subject of various Commission Communications, such as "Challenges for enterprise policy in the knowledge-driven economy" and the "EU Enterprise policy for the New Economy".

See also two 2013 regulations: one on European venture capital Funds (EuVECA) and one on European social entrepreneurship funds. The first one lays down uniform requirements and conditions for managers of collective investments undertakings that wish to use the designation "EuVECA" in relation to the marketing of qualifying venture capital funds in the Union, thereby contributing to the smooth functioning of the internal market.

The second lays down uniform requirements and conditions for managers of collective investment undertakings that wish to use the designation "EuSEF", in relation to the marketing of qualifying social entrepreneurship funds in the Union.

7.   TRANS-EUROPEAN NETWORKS (TENs)

31–24   The TENs are large infrastructure networks of transport, energy and telecommunications, underpinning the development and integration goals of the EU.[56]

The concept of Trans-European Networks (TENs) was introduced by the EU Treaty. It is closely associated with the achievement of the internal market[57] and with Economic, Social and Territorial Cohesion (Regional Policy).[58] It expressly refers to both Union activities where the Treaty provides that the TENs are intended to help achieve the objectives of both those policies. As can be seen in Ch.32: Regional Policy/Economic, Social and Territorial Cohesion—The Europe 2020 Strategy, the European Regional Development Fund may contribute to the financing of the TENs.[59]

---

[55] Art.54 TFEU.
[56] *http://ec.europa.eu/ten/index_en.html* [accessed August 23, 2013]. Much of the present paragraph has been copied from this website.
[57] Art.26 TFEU.
[58] Art.174 TFEU.
[59] Art.1(b) former Regulation 2083/93 first indent [1993] O.J. L193/34.

By "networks" is meant the interconnection and interoperability of national networks, as well as access to such networks in the areas of transport,[60] telecommunications[61] and energy infrastructures.[62] The regional development preoccupation clearly appears when the Treaty provides that account shall be taken in particular of the need to link island and landlocked areas and peripheral regions with the central regions of the Union. Union activity in the TENs field consist of:

- establishing guidelines covering objectives, priorities and broad outlines of envisaged measures;
- implementation of measures that may prove necessary to ensure the interoperability of the networks, in particular in the field of standardisation;
- support for the financial efforts made by Member States for projects of common interest[63]; the Union may also contribute to specific projects in the area of transport infrastructure through the Cohesion Fund.[64]

As for the Member States, they must co-ordinate among themselves the policies used at national level that may have an impact on the achievement of the above-mentioned objectives.[65] The Union may also co-operate with third countries to promote projects of mutual interest.

31–25

Wide powers have been attributed, in the TENs field, to Parliament since the guidelines to be established shall be adopted by the Council together with Parliament and after consultation of the Economic and Social Committee (ESC) and the Committee of the Regions.[66]

In the case of common projects which relate to the territory of a Member State, the latter's approval shall, of course, be required. As was seen, one of the first tasks of the Union was to establish guidelines. Following the modifications introduced by the Treaty of Amsterdam, all the measures concerning the TENs

---

[60] Decision on Union guidelines for the development of trans-European transport networks [1996] O.J. L228/1, amended [2001] O.J. L185/1; Directive 96/48 on the interoperability of trans-European high-speed rail system [1996] O.J. L235/6, amended [2007] O.J. L141/63 and Decision concerning a technical specification for interoperability to the "infrastructure" subsystem of the trans-European high-speed railway system [2008] O.J. L77/1, replaced by Directive 2008/56 on the interoperability of the rail system within the Community [2008] O.J. L191/1; Decision on the basic parameters for the command-and-control and signalling subsystems relating to the trans-European high-speed rail systems [1999 6] O.J. L216/23; Directive on the interoperability of the trans-European conventional rail systems [2001] O.J. L110/1.

[61] Decision 1336/97 on a series of guidelines for trans-European telecommunication networks [1997] O.J. L194/5.

[62] See, for instance, Directive 90/547 on the transit of electricity through transmission grids [1990] O.J. L313/30; Decision 96/39 laying down a series of measures aimed at creating a more favourable context for the development of trans-European networks in the energy sector [1996] O.J. L161/154; Decision 1254/96 of Parliament and the Council laying down a series of guidelines for trans-European energy networks [1996] O.J. L161/147; Decision 2000/761 defining the specifications of projects of common interest identified in the sector of trans-European energy networks by Decision 1254/96 [2000] J.O. L305/22.

[63] Regulation 2236/95 laying down general rules for the granting of Union financial aid in the field of trans-European networks [1995] O.J. L228/1, amended [2005] O.J. L191/16.

[64] See Commission Decisions concerning projects to be co-financed [1993] O.J. L308/1.

[65] Art.171(2) TFEU.

[66] Art.172 TFEU.

are adopted according to the co-decision procedure,[67] and after consultation of the ESC and the Committee of the Regions. The first ones were adopted in 1995, according to the co-operation procedure, and concerned the telecommunications field of Euro-ISDN,[68] they were followed by guidelines for the development of energy,[69] transport[70] and telecommunications[71] networks. On the basis of those guidelines, the Commission determines which projects are of common interest,[72] after having consulted the Member State where the project is to be carried out. However, a first list of 10 priority projects in the energy field and 14 in the transport area was established by the European Council at Essen.[73] To think that it needs Heads of State or Government to select individual projects!

31–26   During the years following the Essen European Council, steady progress was made in implementing some of the selected projects in the transport sector. These are of course large infrastructure projects that take years to construct. The Commission adopted a communication seeking to clarify the application of the competition rules to new rail infrastructure projects.[74] Where telematics and telecommunications are concerned, Parliament and the Council adopted a decision on guidelines for trans-European telecommunication networks.[75]

The EIB decided to provide at least €75 billion for trans-European projects in the period 2004–2013. In 2011, the EIB lent €9.8 billion for transport TENs and major transport axes. In addition the EIB offers a number of special products:

- Public Private Partnerships (PPP). The bank has been entrusted by the Commission and the Member States with establishing the *European PPP Expertise Centre* which aims to facilitate the effective sharing of experience and best practice.
- The Structure finance Facility, which aims to match the types of funding to the requirements of large-scale infrastructure projects.
- The Loan Guarantee Instruments for Trans-European Transport Network Projects.
- The Marguerite Infrastructure Fund: a fund specifically designed to provide direct equity for TEN projects. Copyright © EIN 2013.

Trans-European Energy Networks (TEN-E) cover the electricity and natural gas sectors. They help to create a single energy market and contribute to security of supply.

---

[67] Art.172 TFEU.
[68] Decision 95/489 [1995] O.J. L282/16.
[69] Decision 1229/2003 [2003] O.J. L176/11.
[70] Decision 96/1692 [1996] O.J. L228/1, replaced by Decision 661/10 [2010] O.J. L204/1 on Union Guidelines for the development of the trans-European transport network.
[71] Decision 97/1336 [1997] O.J. L183/12.
[72] See, for instance, for the energy sector, Decision 96/537 [1996] O.J. L230/16 and 97/548 [1997] O.J. L225/25.
[73] See General Report 1994, 112 and 113.
[74] COM (98) 480.
[75] Decision 1336/97 [1997] O.J. L183/12, amended [2002] O.J. L200/1.

FURTHER READING

David Gillies & Roger Marschall, *Telecommunication Law*, 2nd edn. (Butter-   **31–27**
worths).

David Musker, *The Community Design Handbook*, (Sweet & Maxwell, 2005).

Keith Beresford, *Patenting Software under the European Patent Convention*,
2nd edn (Sweet & Maxwell, 2005).

Sebastian Farr and Vanessa Oakley, *EU Communications Law* (Sweet &
Maxwell, 2006).

CHAPTER 32

Regional Policy/Economic, Social and Territorial Cohesion—The Europe 2020 Strategy

I   THE EUROPE 2020 STRATEGY

It was approved by the European Council in June 2010, as the European Union's 10-year growth strategy. It is about more than overcoming the present crisis; it is about addressing the shortcomings of Europe's growth model and creating the conditions for a different type of growth that is smarter, more sustainable and more inclusive. Five key "targets" have been set for the EU to achieve by the end of the decade: employment, education, research and innovation, social inclusion and poverty reduction, and climate/energy. The strategy also includes seven "flagship initiatives" for the EU and national authorities: innovation, the digital economy, employment, youth, industrial policy, poverty and resource efficiency. At the EU level, key decisions are being taken to complete the single market in services, energy and digital products, and to invest in cross-border links. At national level, many obstacles to competition and job creation must be removed.

The delivery of Europe 2020 relies heavily on the new governance structures and the processes that the EU has been putting into place since 2010. At the heart of these, is the *European Semester* a yearly cycle of economic policy co-ordination[1], involving EU-level policy guidance, reform commitments by the Member states and country-specific recommendations prepared by the Commission and endorsed by the European Council.[2]

II.   REGIONAL OR COHESION POLICY

32–01

---

[1] For the first European Semester, see the 2011 General report on the activities of the EU "strengthening economic governance in the EU".

[2] *http://ec.europa.eu/europe2020/index_en.htm* [accessed August 23, 2013].

1.   HISTORY

32–02   As the Commission wrote: "The European Union's regional policy seeks to reduce disparities between EU regions, foster balanced development throughout the EU and promote real equal opportunities for all. Based on the concept of solidarity and economic and social cohesion, it achieves this in practical terms by means of a variety of financing operations, principally through the Structural Funds and the Cohesion Fund."[3]

For the period 2007–2013, the European Union's regional policy is the EU's second largest budget item, after agriculture, with an allocation of €348 billion.

For the period 2014-2020, the Commission published its first ideas in November 2010. The most significant ideas put forward include: linking allocation of funds to the Europe 2020 objectives, inviting Member States to sign partnership contracts, focussing resources on a small number of priorities, making payments dependent on certain conditions, creating a "performance reserve" to reward the best performers, stronger monitoring and evaluation, combining grants with loans, reinforcing the territorial dimension, and strengthening partnerships.

32–03   The objective of economic and social cohesion was introduced in 1986, with the adoption of the Single European Act. The policy was finally incorporated in what was then the EC Treaty[4] in 1992.

It is interesting and useful, at the start of this chapter, to get an idea about the disparities between the levels of development of the various regions.[5] To determine geographic eligibility for funding, the Commission bases its decision on statistical date: common Nomenclature of Territorial Units for Statistics (NUTS). Member States whose Gross National Income (GNI) is lower than 90 per cent of the Union average can benefit from the Cohesion Fund; that is: all the regions from the following States: Bulgaria, Czech Republic, Estonia, Greece, Cyprus, Latvia, Lithuania, Hungary, Malta, Poland, Portugal, Romania, Slovenia and Slovakia.[6] When the Title on Economic and Social Cohesion was added to the EC Treaty, regional policy had already been an important Union activity since 1975.[7] This is acknowledged by the wording of the Treaty which provides that the Union must develop and "pursue its actions leading to the strengthening of its economic, social and territorial cohesion."[8] It was assumed from the moment the internal market was established that it could not function as an economic entity, if the differences in economic development of the composing regions were excessive. That there are and will be differences is inevitable, due, among others, to great differences in geography, climate, tradition and population, but, without some similarity of the levels of economic and social development, the internal market simply cannot function. If, for instance, the purchasing power in one part

---

[3] *http://www.ec.europa.eu/regional_policy/index_en.htm* [accessed August 23, 2013].
[4] Arts 174–178 TFEU.
[5] London as a PPS of 328, while Severozapaden in Bulgaria has a PPS of 26! The average is 100.
[6] *http://ec.europa.eu/regional_policy/index_en.cfm* [accessed August 23, 2013].
[7] The Regulation setting up the European Regional Development Fund (ERDF) was adopted in March 1975: Regulation 724/75 [1975] O.J. L73/1. The Social Fund and the Agricultural Fund have been in existence practically since the very beginning; they were provided for in the EEC Treaty.
[8] Art.174 TFEU. See Decision 2006/702 on Union strategic guidelines on cohesion [2006] O.J. L291/11.

of the Union does not allow its inhabitants to acquire the goods they need, the producers in the richer parts will not be able to sell them their products. Furthermore, since economic integration of the Union is based, in the first place, on inter-State trade, such a situation, not only jeopardises the development of the internal market itself, but makes it practically impossible to pursue the economic and monetary convergence which is required for the smooth functioning of the EMU.[9]

As indicated, economic, social and territorial cohesion is the objective primarily of "regional policy", but other policies such as Social Policy, Agricultural Policy[10] and Fisheries are also involved in the attainment of the objectives of regional policy. Those objectives are clearly set out in the Treaty as "reducing disparities between the levels of development of the various regions and the backwardness of the least favoured regions."[11] According to the TFEU, among the regions concerned, particular attention must be paid "to rural areas, areas affected by industrial transition, and regions which suffer from severe and permanent natural or demographic handicaps, such as the northernmost regions with very low population density and island, cross-border and mountain regions."[12]

32–04

Besides the provisions concerning economic, social and territorial cohesion, there are several other Treaty provisions, which refer to underdeveloped regions[13]; this shows that, from the very beginning and even in the absence of specific provisions, the regional problems were taken into account.[14] However, it appears that the signatories of the Treaty were convinced (or rather, hoped) that the functioning of the internal market, with the resulting development of economic activity throughout the Union would more or less automatically reduce regional disparities. The functioning of the internal market did, indeed, achieve spectacular results in the most depressed areas, as is evidenced by the doubling, even trebling of their per capita income over the years. Nevertheless, this was not enough for achieving the necessary coherence among the regions in a Union where similar developments took place in the well-developed areas. The result was that, although the gap between the richest and poorest regions might not have widened, it was not reduced significantly. It goes without saying that the existing discrepancies are no longer socially and politically acceptable, and they create a major problem for the Union as a whole. Even worse, it becomes very difficult, if not impossible, to achieve the economic convergence that is required for the functioning of the EMU. Indeed, as long as some Member States (and their number increases with each enlargement), have to devote large proportions of their limited resources to the development of their less favoured regions, they will remain subject to inflation, balance of payment problems and excessive budget deficits, as the recent crisis has amply proved.

---

[9] According to Art.3 EU, among the means to achieve the objectives of the Treaty figure the internal market and Economic and Monetary Union.

[10] See Art.175,1 TFEU where reference is made to the Structural Funds, which includes the Agricultural Fund.

[11] Art.174,2 TFEU.

[12] Art.174,3 TFEU. The words "rural areas" were added by the EU Treaty.

[13] The European Investment Bank (EIB), for instance, was set up to facilitate the financing, among other things, of "projects for developing less-developed regions" Art.309(a) TFEU.

[14] See, for instance, Art.137(3)(a) TFEU.

It was at the October 1972 Paris "Conference of Heads of States or of Governments" (as the European Council was then called), that it was agreed to give a high priority to the aim of correcting the structural and regional imbalances that might affect the realisation of the Economic and Monetary Union.[15] The Member States undertook to co-ordinate their regional policies and invited the Union institutions to create a European Regional Development Fund (ERDF).[16] However, it was not until March 1975: that the Council adopted the Regulation setting up the ERDF,[17] and a Decision creating a Regional Policy Committee.[18] It is interesting to note that no reference was made to a Union regional "policy". This had to wait until February 1979, when amendments to the above-mentioned Regulation were made,[19] together with the adoption of a Resolution concerning guidelines for such a policy.[20] Finally, in 1984, a regulation was adopted concerning both a Union Regional Policy and the ERDF.[21]

32–05   Over the past years, the ERDF Regulation was amended several times and one of the novelties was its inclusion into the Structural Funds. This allowed for far-reaching co-ordination of objectives and procedures with other funds: the EIB,[22] the European Agricultural Guidance and Guarantee Fund (EAGGF) Guidance Section,[23] the European Social Fund (ESF),[24] the Financial Instrument of Fisheries Guidance (FIFG)[25] (now the European Fisheries Fund (EFF)),[26] that were also included in the Structural Funds, and, finally, the Cohesion Fund.[27]

The latest revision of the ERDF Regulation was completed, together with the revision of the ESF, EAGGF and Cohesion Fund, in 2006. The provisions concerning the Structural Funds are now embodied in five regulations: a "Framework" regulation laying down general provisions on the ERDF, ESF and

---

[15] Bull. 10 [1972] 9. This was the first "summit" in which Denmark, Ireland and the UK participated.
[16] See the Commission's "Report on Regional Problems in the Enlarged [Union]", 1973 Bull. suppl. 8.
[17] Regulation 724/75 [1975] O.J. L73/1. It was based on what is now Art.352 TFEU (action is necessary but required powers that are not provided for in the Treaties). Initially the ERDF was endowed with the equivalent of €375 million; in 2004, it was, together with the other funds, for the period 2000–2006, more than €195 billion and now, as indicated above, for the period 2007–2013, €348 billion.
[18] [1975] O.J. L73/47.
[19] [1979] O.J. L35/1.
[20] [1979] O.J. C36/10.
[21] [1984] O.J. L169/1.
[22] Art.308 TFEU.
[23] See Ch.23: Agriculture and Fisheries.
[24] See Ch.29: Social Policy.
[25] See Ch.24: The Common Fisheries Policy (CFP) and Marine Policy.
[26] Regulation 1198/06 [2006] O.J. L223/1.
[27] See below in this chapter.

the Cohesion Fund.[28] This Framework Regulation is accompanied by four "sectoral" regulations: regional,[29] social,[30] grouping of territorial co-operation[31] and the Cohesion Fund.[32]

2. BASIC IMPLEMENTATION PRINCIPLES

The Treaty established three basic principles for the implementation of economic, social and territorial cohesion. In the first place, as with many Union activities, the responsibility for attaining the objectives rests both on the Union and on the Member States: indeed, according to the TFEU, it is part of the principal areas of "shared competence".[33] Furthermore, the Member States must conduct their economic policies and co-ordinate them "in such a way as to attain the objectives" set out in the Treaty.[34] Secondly, the Treaty provides that these objectives must be taken into account by the institutions when formulating and implementing other Union policies and actions and the implementation of the internal market, and that those policies and actions must support the achievement of these objectives. A similar obligation is imposed by the Treaties with regard to other policies.[35] In other words, the formulation and implementation of all Union policies must be achieved in a coherent and co-ordinated manner, with special attention given to the so-called horizontal policies.[36] A third point is the indication in the Treaty that the various existing funds, among others the so-called Structural Funds, the Cohesion Fund and the European Investment Bank (EIB), must all be used to attain these objectives.

32–06

If specific actions prove necessary outside the Funds, such actions may be adopted by the Council, acting in accordance with the ordinary legislative procedure,[37] after consulting the ESC and the Committee of the Regions.[38]

As indicated above in Ch.23: Agriculture and Fisheries, Agenda 2000 concerned, besides the Union financing for the next seven years (2000–2006) and the reform of the agricultural policy, the reform of the existing structural funds: ESF, ERDF, the structural part of FEOGA, the Fisheries Fund and the Cohesion Fund. As was mentioned, all those funds were merged so to speak, within the Structural Funds, and the expenditure of the available amounts under those different funds was closely co-ordinated.

---

[28] Regulation 1083/06 [2006] O.J. L 210/25, corrigendum [2008] O.J. L301/40, amended [2008] O.J. L348/19 and [2009] O.J. L25/1, corrigendum [2009] O.J. L33/49, amended [2009] O.J. L94/10 and L250/1, amended as regards simplification of certain requirements and as regards certain provisions relating to financial management [2010] O.J. L158/1. Amended [2012] O.J. L133/1.

[29] Regulation 1080/06 [2006] O.J. L210/1, repealing Regulation 1783/99, amended as regards eligibility of housing intervention in marginalised communities [2010] O.J. L132/1.

[30] Regulation 1081/06 [2006] O.J. L210/12, repealing Regulation 1784/99.

[31] Regulation 1082/06 [2006] O.J. L210/19, repealing Regulation 1085/99.

[32] Regulation 1084/06 [2006] O.J. L210/79, repealing Regulation 1164/94.

[33] Art.4(2)(b) TFEU.

[34] Art.175 TFEU.

[35] For instance, the protection of the environment: Art.4(2)(e) TFEU.

[36] See, for instance, Communication from the Commission to the Member States on the links between regional and competition policy [1998] O.J. C90/3.

[37] See Art.294 TFEU.

[38] Art.175,3 TFEU.

See Council Decision on Union strategic guidelines on cohesion.[39]

Implementing economic, social and territorial cohesion

(a) The Funds

(i)   Structural Operations

32–07   Improving the effectiveness of the structural and cohesion funds in achieving the goal of economic, social and territorial cohesion enshrined in the Treaty, was a central plank of the Agenda 2000 reforms. This goal was maintained even as priorities continued to evolve in a more diverse Union, taking account of the aim of achieving greater concentration of structural assistance, improving the financial management of the structural funds, as well as simplifying their operation and administration. Greater concentration of structural fund assistance in the areas of greatest need was achieved by reducing to three the number of objectives of the funds. In fostering economic, social and territorial cohesion by pursuing these objectives, the Union contributes to the harmonious, balanced and sustainable development of economic activities, the development of employment and human resources, the protection and improvement of the environment, the elimination of inequalities and the promotion of equality between men and women. The Commission and the Member States must ensure that the operations financed by the funds are in conformity with the provisions of the Treaties and the instruments adopted under it, and are consistent with other Union policies and operations. In view of the continued priority accorded to economic, social and territorial cohesion and as a result of more targeted concentration of structural expenditure in line with the Treaties' objectives, it was decided that the overall amounts for the structural and cohesion funds should, in the future, enable the Union to maintain the existing average aid intensity levels, thereby consolidating the overall effort in this field.

(ii)   Objectives of the Structural Funds[40]

32–08   The financial support from the Structural Funds for the period 2007–2013 is provided for three objectives:

- the *"Convergence"* objective: assistance on supporting sustainable inte-grated economic development and the creation of sustainable jobs. Operational programmes are aimed at modernising and diversifying regional economic structures, particularly in the following fields:
  - research and technological development, innovation and entrepre-neurship,
  - information society,
  - environment,
  - risk prevention,
  - tourism,

---

[39] Decision 2006/702 [2006] O.J. L291/11.
[40] Most of the information is borrowed from SCADPlus: European Regional Development Fund.

- investment in culture,
- investment in transport,
- energy,
- investment in education,
- investment in health and social structures,
- direct assistance for investment in SMEs.

60 per cent of the fund goes to the poorest Member States and regions. The other regions come under the second objective;

- the *"Regional Competitiveness and Employment"* objective, intended to support:
  - innovation and the knowledge economy, including the improvement of regional R&TD and innovation capacities (see "implementing the broad-based innovation strategy"[41]), entrepreneurship and creation of new financial instruments for businesses,
  - environment and risk prevention, included restoring contaminated land, encouraging energy efficiency, promoting the use of clean technology in public transport, and formulating plans to anticipate and manage natural and technology-related risks,
  - access to transport and telecommunications services of general economic interest, especially by improving secondary networks and encouraging access to information and communication technologies for SMEs.

16 per cent of the fund is devoted to this objective. A list of regions eligible for funding under this objective was drawn up by the Commission,[42] and thirdly;

- the *"European Territorial Co-operation"* (ETC) objective: provided for a new legal instrument with the aim to facilitate cross-border, transnational and/or inter-regional co-operation between regional and local authorities. It is to support:
  - development of cross-border economic, social and environmental activities, through joint strategies for sustainable territorial development. This involves, for example, encouraging entrepreneurship, protection and management of natural and cultural resources, and the development of collaboration, capacities and the joint use of infrastructures,
  - establishing and developing transnational co-operation, including bilateral co-operation between maritime regions. This co-operation would be invested with legal personality—the "European Grouping for Territorial Cooperation"—for the implementation of territorial co-operation programmes based on a convention agreed between the participating national, regional, local and other public authorities. The priorities are innovation, the environment, better accessibility and sustainable urban development,
  - reinforcing the effectiveness of regional policy by encouraging regional and local authorities to form networks and exchange experience.

---

[41] General Report 2008, 60.
[42] [2006] O.J. L243/49.

Under this objective, the Commission established the ESPON 2013 programme to provide comparable information, evidence, analyses and scenarios on framework conditions for the development of regions, cities and larger territories.

(b) Conditions for Allocation of Financial Support

Convergence Objective

32–09   Eligible are regions corresponding to NUTS[43] level 2, whose gross domestic product (GDP) per capita, measured in purchasing power parity (ppp) and calculated on the basis of Union figures for the period 2000–2002, is less than 75 per cent of the average GDP of the EU-28 for the same reference period. As for Member States, are eligible those whose Gross Domestic Income (GDI) per capita, measured in ppp, and calculated on the basis of Union figures for the period 2001–2003, is less than 90 per cent of the average GNI of the EU-25 and which have a programme for meeting the convergence conditions of the Treaty.[44] Overall resources for the Convergence objective are, for the period 2007–2013, €251,163,134,221.[45] See Commission Decision drawing up the list of the eligible regions[46] and indicative allocation by Member States of the commitment appropriations.[47]

Regional Competitiveness and Employment Objective

32–10   Regions eligible under this objective are those not covered by the Convergence objective. Member States must present the NUTS level 1 and NUTS level 2 regions for which they will present a programme for financing by the ERDF. Overall resources for this objective amount to €49,127,784,318. See Commission Decision allocating by Member State the commitment appropriations.[48]

European Territorial Co-operation Objective

32–11   Eligible for financing NUTS level 3, are regions along all internal and certain external land borders and all NUTS level 3 regions along maritime borders, separated by a maximum of 150km. Overall assistance for this objective is €7,750,081,461.[49]

32–12   For each of these objectives, the Council must establish, at Union level, strategic guidelines on economic, social and territorial cohesion, defining an indicative

---

[43] Common classification of territorial units for statistics within the meaning of Regulation 1059/03 [2003] O.J. L154/1.
[44] Art.126 TFEU.
[45] For a breakdown among the various actions see Art.19 of the Regulation.
[46] Decision 2006/595 [2006] O.J. L343/44. List valid until December 31, 2013 shall be reviewed in 2010.
[47] Decision of August 4, 2006 [2006] O.J. L243/37.
[48] [2006] O.J. L243/32.
[49] For further details see Art.21 of the Regulation.

framework for the intervention of the Funds.[50] See Commission Decision drawing up the list of eligible regions and areas[51] and the decision allocating commitments appropriations per Member State.[52]

Specific Types of Areas

Areas are: 32–13

- urban areas: they are incorporated in operational programmes and aim at resolving economic, environmental and social problems in towns and cities;
- rural areas and areas dependent on the fishing industry: the action concentrates on diversification such as, infrastructure to improve accessibility, telecommunications networks and services in rural areas, development of new economic activities, improving of links between urban and rural areas, and development of tourism and regeneration of rural areas;
- areas with natural handicaps: the ERDF helps finance investment in the improvement of accessibility, economic activities linked to cultural heritage, the sustainable use of resources and tourism development;
- outermost regions: the Azores, Madeira, the four French overseas departments and the Canaries—subsidising freight transport services and the start-up of transport services, operations linked to storage constraints, the maintenance of production tools and lack of human capital in the local market. See Commission Communication "Strategy for the outermost regions: achievements and future prospects".[53]

(iv)   Eligibility

Additionality.   The funds shall provide assistance that complements national   32–14
actions, including actions at the regional and local levels, integrating them into the priorities of the Union. In other words contributions from the Funds may not replace public or equivalent structural expenditure by a Member State; it is the Commission's task to verify the additionality.

Consistency.   The Commission and the Member States must ensure that   32–15
assistance from the Funds is consistent with activities, policies and priorities of the Union and complementary to other financial instruments of the Union.

The assistance, co-financed by the Funds, must target the EU priorities of promoting competitiveness and creating jobs, including meeting the objectives of the Integrated Guidelines for Growth and Jobs (2005–2008) set out by Council Decision[54]; consequently 60 per cent of expenditure for the Convergence objective and 75 per cent of expenditure for the Regional competitiveness and employment objective is set for the above-mentioned priorities.

---

[50] These Guidelines were to be adopted before February 1, 2007 in accordance with Art.177 TFEU.
[51] Decision 2006/769 [2006] O.J. L312/47.
[52] Decision 2006/609 [2006] O.J. L347/26.
[53] [2007] O.J. C138/36. See Communication from the Commission "The outermost regions: an asset for Europe" COM (2008) 642 final of October 17, 2008.
[54] Decision 2005/600 [2005] O.J. L205/21; these guidelines were maintained for 2007, Decision 2007/491: [2007] O.J. L205/21.

32–16   **Co-ordination.**   Co-ordination must be ensured between the assistance from the Funds, the ERDF,[55] the EFF[56] and the intervention of the EIB and other existing financial instruments.

32–17   **Programmes.**   The objectives of the Funds are to be pursued in the framework of a multi-annual programming system organised in several stages comprising the identification of the priorities, the financing and a system of management and control.[57] As part of an operational programme, the ERDF and the Cohesion Fund may also finance major projects. Management and implementation of a part of an operational programme may be entrusted to one or more intermediate bodies.

The Commission approved the national strategic reference frameworks established by the 27 Member States in line with the Community strategic guidelines for 2007. This paved the way for the adoption of the operational programmes financed by the Structural Funds: 302 such programmes were formally adopted at the end of December 2007.[58]

32–18   **Partnership.**   These objectives must be pursued in the framework of close partnership between the Commission and each Member State and, if possible, with competent regional, local and other public authorities, the economic and social partners and any other appropriate body representing civil society, environmental partners, NGOs and bodies responsible for promoting equality between men and women. The partnership shall cover the preparation, implementation, monitoring and evaluation of operational programmes.

Information on "Cohesion" can be found, among others, in the full cohesion report published by the Commission, every three years; in the years in between, progress reports are published.

(c)   Global Financial Resources

32–19   The resources available for commitment from the Funds for the period 2007–2013 are €398 billion at 2004 prices. This amount is indexed at 2 per cent per year. A breakdown is to be found in Annex I to the Regulation.[59]

As already mentioned, the Treaty provides that if specific actions prove necessary outside the Funds, such actions may be adopted by the Council acting in accordance with the ordinary legislative procedure[60] and after consulting the ESC and the Committee of the Regions.[61] The Council, on that basis, established in 2006 the European Globalisation Adjustment Fund which provides specific, one-off support to facilitate the reintegration into employment of workers in areas, sectors, territories, or labour marker regions suffering the shock of serious economic disruption. The Fund is to promote entrepreneurship, for example through micro-credits or for setting up co-operative projects.[62]

---

[55] European Agricultural Fund for Rural Development.
[56] European Fisheries Fund.
[57] See Art.37 of the Regulation.
[58] General Report 2007, 93.
[59] [2006] O.J. L.210/70.
[60] Art.294 TFEU.
[61] Art.175,3 TFEU.
[62] [2006] O.J. L406/1.

Mention must be made of the Joint European Resources for Micro to Medium Enterprises (JEREMIE) an initiative of the Commission and the EIB Group; it uses Union financial know-how to support small businesses in Europe. It provides the framework for a series of coherent financial actions to improve the financial environment for medium, small and micro enterprises at national, regional and local level, increasing small businesses' access to finance and risk capital. The JEREMIE initiative offers new opportunities for Member States and Regions to invest and reinvest. Structural Funds using a range of financial instruments instead of grants, notably guaranties, venture capital, securitisation and loans. JEREMIE operates on market terms to encourage the participation of private as well as public financial institutions, which is of key importance.[63]

In 2006, Parliament and the Council set up the *European Globalisation Adjustment Fund*,[64] with the aim of stimulating economic growth and creating more jobs in the Union; the fund provides support for workers made redundant as a result of major structural changes in world trade patterns due to globalisation, where those redundancies have a significant adverse effect on the regional or local economy.[65]

Reporting.   Member States are to report on the contribution of the operational   **32–20**
programmes co-financed by the Funds; these reports are to be summarised by the Commission in its Annual Progress report to the Spring European Council. The Commission, as provided in the Treaty,[66] must submit a report every three years on the progress made towards achieving economic and social cohesion. In 2007, the Commission adopted its fourth report,[67] which describes the situation in the enlarged Union of 27 Member States and 268 regions. It contains a detailed analysis of the position of the regions in terms of GDP, productivity and employment. It provides a first assessment of the impact of European Cohesion policy in the 2000–2006 programming period. The fifth progress report on economic, social and territorial cohesion was adopted in 2008.[68]

In 2008, the Commission presented the "Regions 2020" report,[69] putting forward a prospective analysis of the probable regional impact of the four key challenges facing Europe: globalisation, demographic change, climate change and the energy challenge.

The Regulation laying down general provisions for the Funds also provides for technical assistance[70] and evaluation linked to the monitoring of operational programmes.[71]

---

[63] See "Jeremie—Regional Funding".
[64] [2005] O.J. L406/1.
[65] The fund was mobilised for a total of €3.8 million for redundancies in the suppliers of Peugeot and Renault: Decision 2007/726 [2007] O.J. L6/9.
[66] Art.175,2 TFEU.
[67] General Report 2007, 92 and COM (2007) 273 [2007] O.J. C191/17.
[68] General Report 2008, 94 and COM (371) [2009] O.J. C10/18: "growing regions, growing Europe".
[69] General Report 2008, 94 and SEC (2008) 2868.
[70] Art.45 of Regulation 1198/06 [2006] O.J. L223/1.
[71] Art.47 of Regulation 1198/06 [2006] O.J. L223/1.

32–21   **Rates of Assistance.**   For details see Title V of the general Regulation.[72] The rates are lower for contributions of the Funds to revenue generating infrastructure investment and investment in firms.[73]

32–22   **Administration and Financial Management of the Structural Funds.**   The administration of the structural funds was substantially simplified by giving practical effect to decentralising decision-making and striking a balance between simplification and flexibility, so as to ensure that funds are disbursed quickly and effectively. To achieve this, responsibilities of Member States, their partners and the Commission were clarified, bureaucracy reduced and monitoring, evaluation and control strengthened, thereby ensuring improved and sound financial management.

(v) The Cohesion Fund

32–23   The basic objective of the Cohesion Fund is to strengthen the economic and social cohesion in the Union in the interest of promoting sustainable development. It is governed by the general Regulation referred to above.[74] Assistance from the Fund is to be given to actions in the following areas, considering an appropriate balance to be agreed in partnership between the Member States and the Commission, and according to the investments and infrastructure needs specific to each Member State receiving assistance:

- trans-European transport networks;
- the environment within the priorities assigned to the Union environmental protection policy, in areas closely related to sustainable development that clearly represent environmental benefits and in the transport sector outside the trans-European networks.

Not eligible for assistance are: interest on debt; the purchase of land for an amount exceeding 10 per cent of the total eligible expenditure; housing; decommissioning of nuclear stations; and recoverable VAT.

32–24   Assistance is conditioned on the following rules: in the case of excessive government deficit[75] the Council may suspend the totality or part of the commitment; it shall be lifted as soon as the Member State in question has taken the necessary corrective action.

Since this Regulation repealed a previous one, the latter's provisions remain applicable under given conditions. As already indicated above, for the period 2007–2013 the following Member States were eligible on January 1, 2007: Czech Republic, Estonia, Greece, Cyprus, Latvia, Lithuania, Hungary, Malta, Poland, Portugal, Slovenia, Slovakia and, on a transitional and specific basis, Spain.[76] In the event of a Member State becoming ineligible, resources for the Cohesion Fund are reduced accordingly.

---

[72] Art.52 of Regulation 1198/06 [2006] O.J. L223/1.
[73] Art.55 of Regulation 1198/06 [2006] O.J. L223/1.
[74] Regulation 1083/06 [2006] O.J. L210/25, modified [2009] O.J. L25/1 and [2009] O.J. L33/49 and L250/1.
[75] Art.126(6) and (7) TFEU.
[76] [2006] O.J. L243/47.

Finally, it must be noted that each Fund has its own characteristic which must be respected; their individual scope can be described as follows:

- the ERDF can finance productive investments, infrastructure, local development and SMEs, pilot projects, investment in education and health, Trans-European Networks and R&D;
- the ESF may give financial assistance for vocational training, start-up aid, innovation measures, training and education schemes and R&D.

The Treaty envisages the possibility of grouping the Funds.[77]

(vi)   The European Union Solidarity Fund

This Fund was established in 2002,[78] for the Union to show its solidarity with the population of the regions concerned, in the event of major disasters, mainly natural disasters. It enables the Union to act swiftly and efficiently, as quickly as possible, in mobilising emergency services to meet peoples' immediate needs and contribute to short-term restoration of damaged key infrastructure so that economic activity can resume.

32–25

"Major disaster" means any disaster within one of the States, resulting in important damage expressed in financial terms or as a percentage of their gross national income (GNI).[79] Assistance may also be granted exceptionally in other cases.

---

[77] Art.177 TFEU.

[78] [2002] O.J. L311/3.

[79] For a Decision on the mobilisation of the Solidarity Fund see [2010] O.J. L318/42.

CHAPTER 33

Research and Technological Development and Space

1. INTRODUCTION

The Union adopted a policy for Research and Technological Development **33–01** (R&TD) with the establishment of the European Atomic Energy Community (Euratom) and the Single European Act, which introduced a new Title in what was then the EC Treaty. In 1984, the European Strategic Programme for Research in Information Technologies (ESPRIT) added a new level of sophistication to the R&TD policy.

R&TD comprises one of the lengthier chapters of the TFEU.[1] The EU Treaty and Treaty of Amsterdam left the policy practically untouched; the latter only modified the unanimity required, among other things, for setting up joint undertakings, in qualified majority and the co-operation procedure or "co-decision", for the other measures. With the level of worldwide competition in the field of research, in addition to security threats faced by the public today, R&TD has become a prominent policy of the Union. It is interesting and worrying to read what the Commission wrote at the beginning of 2000 (with reference to the Union Lisbon Programme[2]):

> "[T]he range of [Union] economic activities exposed to external competition has widened, now including the production of both high-tech and labour intensive goods and services. R&D investment in the EU has become close to stagnation. If current trends continue, R&D investments will be at 2.2 per cent[3] of GDP in 2010, considerably lower than the agreed objective of 3 per cent.[4] Against this background important decisions need to be taken which will determine Europe's economic and social future."

Contrary to other fields examined in the previous chapters, with regard to R&TD, the Union was assigned its own task, mainly through the implementation of the multi-annual framework programmes, while, on the other hand, complementing the activities of the Member States. To avoid wasteful duplication, co-ordination is therefore essential and the Treaty does, indeed, provide for it:

---

[1] Arts 179–190 TFEU, Title XIX.
[2] See COM (2005) 330 final or SEC (2005) 981.
[3] According to another Commission publication, it presently represents only 1.8 per cent of GDP! See the website quoted below.
[4] The 3 per cent figure is the expenditure on RDT in the US and Japan; see website quoted below.

"[T]he Union and the Member States shall co-ordinate their research and technological development activities so as to ensure that the national policies and the Union policy are mutually consistent".[5]

33–02   It is therefore sad to read the following statement of the Commission:

"At the present time, however, it cannot be claimed that there is a European research policy. The research policies of the Member States and that of the Union are conducted in parallel, but do not constitute a coherent whole"

It is interesting to note that the objective of R&TD is not research for its own sake or for scientific purpose, but for:

"[S]trengthening the scientific and technological bases by achieving a 'European research area',[6] in which researchers, scientific knowledge and technology circulate freely and encouraging it to become more competitive, including in its industry, while promoting all the research activities deemed necessary by virtue of other chapters of the Treaty",[7]

one of the main Lisbon Objectives.[8] The whole activity of the Union in this field, is industrially orientated, whether it is carried out in the undertakings themselves, including small and medium-sized ones, or in research centres and at universities. The task of the Union is to encourage such research and to support the efforts of co-operation among all the actors. This is made easier by the establishment of the internal market,[9] the opening of national public contracts,[10] the definition of common standards[11] and the removal of legal[12]and fiscal obstacles to the co-operation. The importance of co-operation between undertakings, research centres and universities is further underlined by the tasks entrusted to the Union.[13]

33–03   The means to achieve the objectives are: firstly, the implementation of the multi-annual programmes[14]; secondly, co-operation with third countries and international organisations[15]; thirdly, the dissemination and optimisation of the

---

[5] Art.181(1) TFEU.

[6] See "The European research area: new perspectives" [2007] O.J. C181/17. So, now the Union has another "area" besides the internal market, which shall comprise an "area without internal frontiers" (Art.26(2)), and the "area of freedom, security and justice" (Title V TFEU): the drafters of these provisions seem to have forgotten that all these areas cover the same geographical "area". Since the free movement of persons is already guaranteed by the internal market, one wonders what this new area can add to it.

[7] Art.179 (1) TFEU.

[8] Bull. 3, 2004, points 1–10.

[9] See Ch.15: The Free Movement of Goods.

[10] See Ch.31: Enterprise and Industrial Policy/Information Society.

[11] See Ch.15: The Free Movement of Goods (5. Theory and Reality of the Free Movement of Goods). See Directive 98/34 laying down a Procedure for the Provision of Information in the Field of Technical Standards and Regulations [1998] O.J. L204/37, amended [1998] O.J. L217/18.See *Belgische Petroleum Unie and others* (C-26/11) E.C.R. 31.01.13.

[12] See Ch.22: Competition Policy.

[13] Art.180 TFEU.

[14] Arts 182 to 186 TFEU.

[15] Art.180(b) TFEU.

results of activities in Union research, technological development and demonstration[16]; and, fourthly, stimulation of the training and mobility of researchers in the Union.[17] It will be noticed, however, that there are, in the R&TD sector, very few binding acts: practically all the activities are regulated by "Communications".

In the "2012 General Report on the Activities of the Union", the Commission's approach is more factual: under the title "Resaerch, Development, Innovation, European Research Area (ERA)" the Commission writes "A reinforced ERA: partnership for excellence and growth, five priority areas were identified: more effective national research systems, optimal transmission co-operation and competition, an open labor market for researchers, gender equality and gender mainstreaming in research and optimal circulation, access to and transfer of scientific knowledge, including via the digital erea."

2. THE SEVENTH FRAMEWORK PROGRAMME (2007–2013) (FP7)[18]

The Seventh Framework Programme for Research, Technological Development and Demonstration Activities is adapted to the EU's needs in terms of growth and employment. It includes the Seventh Framework Programme of Euratom and centres on four specific programmes which correspond to the four main objectives of European research policy:

33–04

1. the "*Co-operation*" *programme*[19]: promoting co-operation between industry and university to achieve greater leadership in key technological areas; this programme[20] aims to stimulate co-operation and improve links between industry and research within a transnational framework. The programme has nine themes that are to be managed autonomously, but will be complementary in terms of implementation:
   (a) health;
   (b) food, agriculture and bio-technology;
   (c) information and communication technologies;
   (d) nano-sciences, nano-technologies, materials and new production technologies;
   (e) energy;
   (f) environment (including climate changes);
   (g) transport (including aeronautics);
   (h) socio-economic sciences and the humanities;
   (i) security and space;
2. the "*Ideas*"[21] *programme*: intended to enhance exploratory research in Europe, i.e. research aimed at discovering new knowledge that fundamentally changes our vision of the world and our way of life. A new European Research Council (ERC) will support the most ambitious and innovative

---

[16] Art.180(c) TFEU.
[17] Art.180(d) TFEU.
[18] Taken from: *http://europa.eu/legislation_summaries/energy/* [accessed August 23, 2013].
[19] [2006] O.J. L400/86.
[20] Decision 2006/974 [2007] O.J. L54/101.
[21] Decision 2006/972 [2007] O.J. L54/81.

research projects. A Commission decision[22] defines its structure, which comprises the Scientific Council, the ERC's Secretary-General and the dedicated implementation structure. The Scientific Council will identify priorities and scientific strategies;

3.   the *"People"*[23] *programme*: mobilises significant funds that can be used to improve the career prospects of researchers in Europe and attract more high-quality researchers. The programme will reinforce the existing Marie Curie actions;

4.   the *"Capacities"*[24] *programme*: intended to give researchers powerful tools that will enable them to enhance the quality and competitiveness of European research.

33–05   Furthermore, the Seventh Framework Programme finances the direct actions of the Joint Research Centre (JRC) and the actions covered by the Euratom Framework Programme in the fields of:

- research into fusion energy;
- nuclear fission and radiation protection.

The duration of the programme was extended from four to seven years; it is placed within the context of the European Research Area. The seventh programme introduces new measures designed to improve the coherence and effectiveness of the Union's research policy; the main innovations are: simplification of the procedures for participation; implementation of the programme and its budget by themes instead of by instruments; creation of the European Research Council; improved co-operation with industry via the Joint Technology Initiatives, which will combine private investment and public funding (see below); the support of a European research infrastructure policy; and the creation of Risk Sharing Finance Facility to facilitate access to EIB loans. This facility is endowed with €1 billion each from the EIB and the Framework Programme.[25] It is an innovation scheme to improve access to debt financing for private companies or public institutions promoting activities in the field of research, technological development, demonstration and innovation investments. It is built on the principle of credit risk sharing between the Union and the EIB and extends thereby the ability of the Bank to provide loans and guarantees with a low and sub-investment grade risk profile.

Rules were laid down for the participation of undertakings, research centres and universities in actions under the programme.[26]

Some actions under the Seventh Framework Programme are to be carried out by the Joint Research Centre.[27]

33–06   **The Eighth EU Framework Programme:**   had not been adopted at the time the manuscript for this chapter was closed, but the Commission did publish some

---

[22] [2006] O.J. L400/243 and Decision 2007/134 [2007] O.J. L57/14.
[23] [2006] O.J. L400/272 and Decision 2006/973 [2007] O.J. L54/91.
[24] [2006] O.J. L400/299 and Decision 2006/974 [2007] O.J. L54/101.
[25] See Decision 1982/2006 O.J. [2006] L412/1.
[26] Regulation 1908/2006 [2006] O.J. L400/1, corrigendum [2007] O.J. L54/4.
[27] [2007] O.J. L54/126, 139 and 149.

information on the Internet allowing some insight into what it might consist of. Horizon 2020 is the financial instrument implementing the Innovation Union, a Europe 2020 flagship initiative aimed at securing Europe's global competitiveness. Running from 2014 to 2020, with a €80 billion budget, the EU's new programme for research and innovation is part of the drive to create new growth and jobs in Europe. Horizon 2020 provides major simplification through a single set of rules; it will combine all research and innovation funding, currently provided through the Framework Programme for Research and Technical Development, the innovation-related activities of the Competitiveness and Innovation Framework Programme (CIP) and the European Institute of Innovation and Technology (EIT). The proposed support for research and innovation under Horizon 2020 will:

- Strengthen the EU's position in science with a dedicated budget of €24.598 million. This will provide a boost to top-level research in Europe, including an increase in funding of 77 per cent for the very successful European Research Council (ERC);
- Strengthen industrial leadership in innovation with a budget of €17.938 million. This includes major investment in key technologies, greater access to capital and support for SMEs;
- Provide €31.748 million to help address major concerns shared by all Europeans such as climate change, developing sustainable transport and mobility, making renewable energy more affordable, ensuring food safety and security, or coping with the challenge of an aging population.

Horizon 2020 will tackle social challenges by helping to bridge the gap between research and the market, by, for example, helping innovative enterprises to develop their technological breakthroughs into viable products with real commercial potential. This market-driven approach will include creating partnerships with the private sector and Member States bringing together the resources needed.

3.   THE JOINT RESEARCH CENTRE

Some of the above-mentioned research is carried out by the Union itself in the Joint Research Centre (JRC) which was set up in pursuance of the Euratom Treaty.[28] The JRC carries out its work in the Centre's four areas of activity: specific research programmes under the framework programme, support for Commission departments, work under contract for outside bodies and exploratory research. It is composed of seven institutes: reference materials and measurement (IRMM: Geel, Belgium), trans-uranium elements (ITU: Karlsruhe, Germany), energy (IE: Petten, Netherlands), protection and the security of the citizen (IPSC: Ispra, Italy), environment and sustainability (IES: Ispra, Italy), health and consumer protection (IHCP: Ispra, Italy), and prospective technological studies (IPTS: Seville, Spain).

33–07

---

[28] Art.8 (1) Euratom. See for instance Decision 2002/838 adopting a specific programme (Euratom) for research and training on nuclear energy (2002–2006) [2002] O.J. L294/74.

The JRC Work Programme[29] provides that the JRC should be competitive to maintain high-level research as well as being flexible to adjust to the evolving research priorities of the Commission.[30] Considerable research is devoted to support the European Chemicals Bureau, the European Integrated Pollution Prevention and Controls Bureau, and the European Laboratory for Air Pollution. With the implementation of the Framework Programmes, the JRC will focus on research in the areas of food, chemical products, and health; environment and sustainability; nuclear safety[31] and security; and dependability of information systems and services. Furthermore, the JRC provides horizontal support with the:

> "[P]roduction of reference materials and measurements, and the development of risk management tools for increased safety and public security, including fight against fraud. Technology foresight activities will be concentrated on networks of national institutes in this field, allowing for synergies and economies of scale."[32]

33–08   The JRC also plays an important role in research training through both courses and work experience as well as providing the ERA with access to its extensive facilities and networks.

Under the Union's Seventh Framework Programme and the Seventh Framework Programme of Euratom, the JRC's programme is organised into five themes:

1.   prosperity in a knowledge intensive society
2.   solidarity and the responsible management of resources;
3.   security and freedom;
4.   Europe as a world partner;
5.   the Euratom programme.

These five themes are subdivided into 17 policy agendas.[33] In 2009, the Commission concluded a Memorandum of Understanding with the European Organisation for Nuclear Research (CERN).[34]

The non-nuclear part of the Euratom research programme now represents about three-quarters of the Centre's activities; it has, for instance, adopted a medical intelligence system "MedSys" to identify public health threats by gathering and processing information published on the Internet. It also contributes to monitoring the forest fires which occur during the summer by providing satellite imaging and information generated by the European forest fire information service.

A supplementary research programme to be carried out by the JRC was adopted in 2009.[35]

---

[29] The multiannual work programme is based on a Council decision.
[30] For further information, see the Commission's Communication on "Fulfilling the JRC's Mission in the European Research Area", COM (2001) 215.
[31] The FRC provides national authorities with expertise on combating and tracing illicit nuclear materials: General Report 2007, 67.
[32] See *http://ec.europa.eu/dgs/jrc/index.cfm?id=1590* [accessed August 23, 2013].
[33] See *http://ec.europa.eu/dgs/jrc/index.cfm?id=1590* [accessed August 23, 2013].
[34] [2009] O.J. L161/13.
[35] [2009] O.J. L132/13.

Finally, the Commission must each year send a report to Parliament and the Council on its R&TD activities, the dissemination of results and the work programme for the current year.[36]

4. JOINT TECHNOLOGY INITIATIVES—JOINT UNDERTAKINGS

The programme provides for a long-term public-private partnership in the form of Joint Technology Initiatives, which can be implemented through Joint Undertakings, as provided for in the TFEU.[37] These enterprises are, generally, bodies of the Union, with legal personality and funded 50/50 by the Union and the private sector. The following joint undertakings were set up:

33–09

- ARTEMIS Joint Undertaking: embedded computer systems.
- Clear Sky Joint Undertaking: air transport[38] set up for the period up to December 31, 2017, to ensure the appropriate management of research activities, including exploitation of the results by the member of the joint enterprise.
- The ENIAC Joint Undertaking[39]: nano-electronics—it is a Community body that has legal personality and is located in Brussels. It will ensure and promote a safe, integrated and responsible approach to nano-electronics in keeping with the high safety standards already established in the industry and in accordance with public health, safety, environmental and consumer Union policies.
- IMI, the Joint Undertaking for the implementation of the Joint Technology Initiative on Innovative Medicine.[40]
- FCH Joint Undertaking[41]: fuel cells and hydrogen. The budget for 2008–2017 is €1 billion.
- SESAR Joint Undertaking: air traffic management.[42] The Commission has proposed a budget of €70 billion for the period 2007–2013. The detailed implementation of the programme was published in December[43] 2006.

In a communication "Competitive European regions through research and innovation: a contribution to more growth and more and better jobs",[44] the Commission describes the synergies of design of the European research, innovation and cohesion policies and calls on Member States and regions to make more effective use of European Union research, innovation and cohesion policies

---

[36] Art.190 TFEU.
[37] Art.187 TFEU: "The Union may set up joint undertakings or any other structure necessary for the efficient execution of the research, technological development and demonstration programmes."
[38] Regulation 71/07 [2007] O.J. L30/1, amended [2009] O.J. L175/14.
[39] Regulation 72/08 [2008] O.J. L30/21.
[40] Regulation 73/08 [2008] O.J. L30/38.
[41] General Report 2008, 261.
[42] General Report 2008, 261.
[43] [2006] O.J. L400/1; the whole issue (more than 400 pages) concerns the implementation of the Seventh Programme, for instance: rules for the participation of undertakings, research centres and universities.
[44] COM (2007) 474.

and instruments: greater effort could be made at the national and regional level to improve information about the instruments and their use.[45]

5.   THE EUROPEAN RESEARCH AREA[46]

33–10   The primary focus of the Sixth Framework Programme was the creation of the European Research Area (ERA),[47] an integrated science and technology complement to the internal market. While previous framework programmes have aimed to enhance co-operation among Member States, the Sixth Framework Programme went much further to create focused research at the Union level. Designed to improve competitiveness and innovation, the ERA will promote increased co-ordination among the relevant actors to produce integrated projects with clear objectives. To this end, the Sixth Framework Programme simplified procedures, reduced priorities, established new support mechanisms, and promoted collaboration and integration. These measures were intended to increase efficiency through more precise, focused and progressively integrated projects, and in turn create a broader, more lasting impact on scientific and technological development within the Union, that will enhance economic growth across the internal market. The ERA is the next step towards funding coherent Union-wide projects.

Framework funds are allocated based, not on national quotas, but on several criteria, among which, that: projects must involve partners from multiple Member States; projects follow the "calls for proposals" guidelines of the Commission meaning they are competitive and in line with the Commission's priorities; the scientific excellence, quality and relevance of the project is approved by five independent experts; and the funds allocated to a project must be applied to specific work, and may not be subsidies for broad research or companies. In order to ensure that the Commission's research priorities match those of the scientific community, the Commission published a "call for expression of interest" in March 2002 and successfully received 15,000 proposals from the scientific and industrial community. These proposals will influence the official "calls for proposals" that the Commission will publish when the new framework comes into effect. The "calls for proposals" not only invite teams to submit project ideas, but they provide transparent and equal access to funding for all applicants.

33–11   It is clear from the previous remarks that the multi-annual framework programmes play an important role in the implementation of the research and technological development activities of the Union. Those programmes are adopted by Parliament and the Council acting in accordance with the ordinary legislative procedure[48] after consulting the ESC.[49] They establish the scientific

---

[45] General Report 2007, 64.

[46] Decision 15/13/02 of Parliament and the Council concerning the Sixth Framework Programme of the EC for research, technical development and demonstration activities contributing to the creation of the European Research Area and to innovation (2002–2006) [2002] O.J. L232/1 and Decision of June 3, 2002 concerning the Euratom programme, same. at 34.

[47] Decision 2002/835 adopting a specific programme for RTD and demonstration: "Integrating and strengthening the European Research Area" (2002–2006) [2002] O.J. L294/1; see also Decision 2002/836 on "structuring the European Research Area" [2002] O.J. L294/44.

[48] Art.294 TFEU.

and technological objectives, fix the relevant priorities, indicate the broad lines of each activity and fix the maximum overall amount for Union financial participation. Those programmes are to be implemented through specific programmes developed for each activity. The rules for the participation of undertakings, research centres and universities in those programmes, and the dissemination of the results, are determined by Parliament and the Council in accordance with the ordinary legislative procedure[50] and after consulting the ESC.

The Treaty also provides that supplementary programmes may be financed by certain Member States only; this will, of course, influence the dissemination of the results of such programmes.[51] Also, the Union may participate in programmes carried out by several Member States,[52] while in its own programmes it may make provisions for co-operation with third countries or international organisations.[53]

It is also provided that the Union may set up joint undertakings or any other structure necessary for the execution of its research, technological development and demonstration programmes.[54] As indicated previously, R&TD programmes may be co-financed by the European Regional Development Fund and the European Social Fund in specific regions.[55]

See also a directive which lays down general rules for the establishment of the infrastructure for Special Information in the Union (INSPIRE)[56] and the implementing regulation.[57]

6. DISSEMINATION OF RESULTS

One of the most important aspects of an efficient R&TD program is that the results of the Union activities in this field must be disseminated and optimised. If results are not immediately and properly communicated to the undertakings which need them, such programmes will not fulfil the objectives set out in the Treaty. With the Sixth Framework Programme in mind, the Commission proposed new "rules for the participation of undertakings, research centres and universities and for the dissemination of research results for the implementation of the European Union Framework Programmes 2002–2006".[58] These rules adopted under the co-decision procedure are one mechanism towards the

33–12

---

[49] Art.183 TFEU.
[50] Art.294 TFEU.
[51] Art.184 TFEU.
[52] Art.185 TFEU.
[53] Art.186 TFEU.
[54] Art.187 TFEU. See, for instance, Regulation 71/2007 setting up the Clean Sky Joint Undertaking [2008] O.J. L30/1 and Decision 2000/1987 [2007] O.J. L90/58 setting up the Joint Undertaking for the international thermonuclear experimental reactor and the development of fusion energy; it will manage the contribution of Euratom to the International Fusion Energy Organisation of €1.717 billion.
[55] See above Ch.32: Regional Policy/Economic, Social and Territorial Cohesion—The Europe 2020 Strategy.
[56] [2007] O.J. L108/1.
[57] [2009] O.J. L274/9.
[58] [2006] O.J. L 400/1.

implementation of the new framework programme and are meant to simplify provisions for dissemination and make them more accessible. The decision lays down general rules on dissemination and protection of knowledge and provides for the implementation of centralised dissemination and exploitation measures.

One further task of the Union is to stimulate the training and mobility of researchers. This should be made easier by the Union activities with regard to education and training examined elsewhere in this book and, of course, the free movement of persons.[59]

7. CO-OPERATION WITH THIRD COUNTRIES

33–13   The implementation of the R&TD tasks is also carried out through the promotion of co-operation with third countries and international organisations. Supporting the objective of integration in the Sixth Framework Programme, the Commission established a separate international scientific co-operation policy. This policy aims at enhanced international co-operation in R&TD to allow for greater political and economic relations with non-EU countries. The European Research Advisory Board (EURAB) was established by the Commission in June 2001[60] to provide independent advice on the implementation of EU research policy. This board is entitled to present opinions and advice about policy as well as form working groups with other research groups or experts as it deems necessary. The 45 members nominated by academics and industrialists represent both Union and non-Union nationals providing a decisive point of influence for non-Union interests.

In this context mention must be made of certain special agreements concluded with third countries, namely Union participation in the following organisations: European Science Foundation (ESF), the European Space Agency (ESA), the European Molecular Biology Organisation (EMBO), the European Molecular Biology Laboratory (EMBL), the European Organisation for Nuclear Research (CERN), the European Southern Observatory (ESO), the European Synchrotron Radiation Facility (ESRF), the Institute Laue-Langevin (ILL), and the European Co-operation in the Field of Scientific and Technical Research. Furthermore, the Union participates in the International Science and Technology Centre with the USA, Japan, and the Russian Federation. This list is far from exhaustive and the Union has concluded agreements with countries around the world.

For instance, an agreement was concluded with Japan for the joint implementation of broader approach activities in the field of fusion energy research. A scientific and technology co-operation agreement was signed with South Korea, Switzerland, Israel and India. The Former Yugoslav Republic of Macedonia, Serbia and Turkey are eligible to participate in the Seventh Framework Programme on the same terms as the Member States.

---

[59] See Ch.16: The Free Movement of Persons.
[60] [2001] O.J. L192/21.

8. THE EUROPEAN SPACE POLICY[61]

The Treaty of Lisbon introduced "space" into the Union's activities. Based on the peaceful exploitation of outer space by all the Member States, the space policy is intended to promote scientific and technical progress, industrial competitiveness and the implementation of the Union's policies. To this end it may promote joint initiatives, support research and technological development and co-ordinate the efforts needed for the exploration and exploitation of space.
 33–14

Parliament and the Council, acting in accordance with the ordinary legislative procedure,[62] must establish the necessary measures, which may take the form of a European Space Programme. The Union is to establish any appropriate relations with the European Space Agency[63].

In 2008, the Council adopted a resolution "Taking forward the European Space policy"[64]. It refers to Galileo, which constitutes the first flagship space programme of the Union and GMES (Global Monitoring for Environment and Security), which is a user-driven initiative that should maximise the use of existing space and non-space Earth Observation centres, capacities and services in Europe. The resolution defines new priorities within the European Space policy: Space and climate change, contribution of Space to the Lisbon Strategy, Space and security and Space exploration. In 2007, the Commission adopted a Communication on European space policy.[65]

See also a directive which lays down general rules for the establishment of the infrastructure for Special Information in the Union (INSPIRE)[66] and the implementing regulation.[67]
 33–15

In April 2011, the Commission released the Communication "Towards a space strategy for the European Union that benefits its citizens", which reflects the crucial role of space for the economy and society. The Communication sets out the main priorities for the EU, which include insuring the success of the two flagship space programmes Galileo and GMES, the protection of space infrastructure, and space exploration. The communication also calls for the development of an industrial space policy in close co-operation with EU Member States and the European Space Agency.

The establishment of a space policy at European level demonstrates the ability of the EU to take a positive lead in areas of vital strategic importance that link a wide variety of policy areas—from telecommunications to humanitarian aid—and involve a complex interaction of players at regional, national and international levels.

As the policy is developed and implemented, it seeks to:

---

[61] Art.189 TFEU.
[62] Established in 1975, it is an intergovernmental organization dedicated to the exploitation of space. Its mission is to shape the development of Europe's space capability and ensure that investment in space continues to deliver benefits for the citizens of Europe and the World. Its headquarters are in Paris and it has centers in Germany, Spain, Italy and The Netherlands. It employs more than 2,000 people and had a budget, for 2009, of €9.3 billion. See the Agreement between the European Space Agency and the Union on the security and exchange of classified information.
[63] [2008] O.J. C 268/1.
[64] [2007] O.J. C181/17.
[65] [2007] O.J. L108/1.
[66] Text borrowed from *http://inspire.jrc.ec.europa.eu/* [accessed August 23, 2013].
[67] Text borrowed from *http://inspire.jrc.ec.europa.eu/* [accessed August 23, 2013].

- develop and exploit space applications that serve Europe's public policy objectives and the needs of Europe's citizens and enterprises;
- meet Europe's space-based security and defence needs;
- ensure Europe retains a strong and competitive space industry that is innovative and provides sustainable, high-quality and cost-effective services;
- develop a strong role in international space exploration.

CHAPTER 34

Environment

1. THE TREATY PROVISIONS[1]

The EU basis for environmental action is based on harmonisation of national laws and on an environmental policy, constantly updated. The first Union environmental legislation emerged in the 1970s, when environmental awareness first made an appearance on the global agenda. The Union and the Member States started to realise that—especially over the long term—the promotion of economic growth within the Union and the establishment of a single market economy required an underlying cross-border environmental protection regime. However, before the Single European Act of 1987, the Treaty did not explicitly provide for the adoption of environmental measures. Moreover, not all the Member States had any such measures in place. Consequently, the early legislation[2] was founded either on the internal market harmonisation provisions[3] or on the possibility for the Council to adopt the appropriate measures when action proved to be necessary, within the framework of the policies defined in the Treaties, to attain one of the objectives of the Treaties and the Treaties have not provided the necessary powers.[4] In both cases, a unanimous decision by the Council is required, on a proposal from the Commission and after obtaining the consent of Parliament. The Court, on the other hand, relied on the Preamble to the Treaty and on the tasks assigned to the Union to justify such measures. As mentioned, the SEA introduced environmental provisions into the Treaty: Title VII

34–01

---

[1] Arts 191–193 TFEU.

[2] For instance: Directive 67/548 [1967] O.J. L196/1 on classification, packaging and labelling of dangerous substances, modified for the 31st time [2009] O.J. L11/6, repealed by Regulation 1272/08 [2008] O.J. L353/1, amended [2009] O.J. L235/1; Directive 70/157 [1970] O.J. L42/16 on noise levels; Directive 70/220 [1970] O.J. L76/1 on automobile emissions.

[3] *Commission v Italy* (91/79) [1980] E.C.R. I-1099; [1981] 1 C.M.L.R. 331 and *Commission v Italy* (92/79) [1980] E.C.R. 1115; [1981] 1 C.M.L.R. 331.

[4] Art.352 TFEU. Since the Treaty did not refer to environmental protection as one of its objectives, the Court relied on an interpretation of Art.2 EC, which defines as a task of the Union "a harmonious development of economic activities, a continuous and balanced expansion, . . . (and) an accelerated raising of the standard of living", and of the Preamble stating that Union goals include "the constant improvement of living and working conditions". In 1985, the Court finally held that environmental protection is one of the Union's "essential objectives", reading it into the (then) EEC Treaty: *Procureur de la Rpublique v Association de dfense des bruleurs d'huiles usages* (240/83) [1985] E.C.R. I-531(549). Moreover, environmental protection also made its way into the mandatory requirements that justify possible derogations on the prohibition of quantitative restrictions, *Commission v Denmark* (302/86) [1988] ECR 4607.

"Environment" and into the harmonisation provisions.[5] The environment thus made its formal entry. Furthermore, according to the Treaty of Maastricht, one of the Union tasks was described as the promotion of a "sustainable and non-inflationary growth respecting the environment", an objective taken up and enhanced by the Treaty of Amsterdam of 1997, focusing on:

> "[A] harmonious, balanced and sustainable development of economic activities... sustainable and non-inflationary growth... a high level of protection and improvement of the quality of the environment, the raising of the standard in living and quality of life".

This objective was given even more weight by the inclusion, under the "activities" of the Union, of a "policy in the sphere of the environment".[6]

34–02   The Treaty of Amsterdam also enhanced the scope of environmental responsibility within the Union by "democratising" the decision-making process; this was achieved by conferring more power upon Parliament in this sector also.

The Charter of Fundamental Rights of the EU also reaffirms the principle of sustainable development and the high level of environmental protection and quality.[7]

The Union's objectives for environmental protection are now listed as follows[8]:

- preserving, protecting and improving the quality of the environment;
- protecting human health; see, for instance, the Air Quality Directive,[9] the Regulation on conditions for the export and import of certain dangerous chemicals,[10] and a Regulation on the banning and export of metallic mercury[11];
- prudent and rational utilisation of natural resources; see Framework Directive on waste,[12] a Directive on reducing the environmental impact of waste of electrical and electronic equipment,[13] and a Directive on the reduction of certain hazardous substances in those equipments[14];
- promotion of measures at international level to deal with regional or worldwide environmental problems and (added by Lisbon) in particular combating climate change.[15]

---

[5] Former Art.100a(3) EC granted the right to adopt measures progressively establishing the internal market and concerning health, safety, environmental protection and consumer protection.

[6] Currently, Arts 3–6 TFEU.

[7] Art.37.

[8] Art.191 TFEU.

[9] Directive 2008/50 [2008] O.J. L152/1, on ambient air quality and cleaner air for Europe: it sets standards and deadlines for the reduction of concentrations of fine particulate matter.

[10] Regulation 689/08 [2008] O.J. L204/1, Annexes I and V [2011] O.J. L59/8. Annex I modified [2012] O.J. L26/23

[11] Regulation 1102/08 [2008] O.J. L304/75.

[12] Directive 2008/98 [32008] O.J. L312/3, repealing certain Directives.

[13] Directive 2002/96 [2003] O.J. L37/24.

[14] Directive 2002/95 [2003] O.J. L37/19. See also Directive 85/337 on the assessment of the effects of certain public and private projects on the environment [1985] O.J. L175/40.

[15] Art.191,1 TFEU last indent.

The first of these objectives had also received some implementation with the establishment of a Union eco-label award system,[16] which is intended to promote the design, production, marketing and use of products which have a reduced environmental impact during their entire life cycle and provide consumers with better information on the environmental impact of products. Some of these products contain ozone-depleting substances and their destruction is regulated.[17] The system does not apply to food, drink and pharmaceuticals. The conditions for awarding the eco-label are defined by product groups. The decision to award is made by a "competent body" designated by each Member State. A revised eco-label award system was adopted by Parliament and the Council in 2002.[18]

2. GUIDING PRINCIPLES

While aiming at a "high level of protection", the Union policy must take into account the diversity of situations in various regions of the Union. It shall be based on the *precautionary principle*[19] and on the principles that *preventive* action should be taken, that environmental damage should, as a priority, be rectified at source: *proximity principle* and the *"polluter pays" principle.*[20]

34-03

The latter was enshrined in a 2004 Directive,[21] which became applicable on April 30, 2007. It applies to environmental damage caused by any of the occupational activities listed in annex III, such as: waste management operations, all discharges into the inland surface water and of substances into groundwater, etc. The Directive applies to any environmental damage and to any imminent threat of such damage, unless caused by an act of armed conflict or a natural phenomenon of exceptional character. Also excluded is damage arising from an incident in respect of which liability or compensation falls within the scope of any international convention listed in Annex IV. The Directive only applies to damage caused by pollution of a diffuse character, where it is possible to establish a causal link between the damage and the activities of individual operators. Preventive measures must be taken where there is an imminent threat of damage occurring. When damage has occurred, the operator must, without delay, inform the competent authority and take all practicable steps to control, contain, remove or otherwise manage the pollutants. The operator shall bear the costs of the preventive and remedial actions. The competent authority must recover from the

---

[16] Regulation 880/1992 [1992] O.J. L99/1.
[17] Regulation 2037/2000 [2000] O.J. L244/1.
[18] [2000] O.J. L237/1.
[19] Although not expressly defined in the Treaty, this principle entails that, despite scientific uncertainty concerning the likelihood of harm, certain measures should be taken before the environmental risk can be clearly evidenced. See Communication of the Commission of February 2, 2003 COM (2000) 1 and *National Farmers' Community* (C-157/96) [1998] E.C.R. I-2211(63), that, however, does not give a definitive answer.
[20] The principles were wrapped into a coherent whole in *Commission v France* (C-121/07) [2008] ECR I-9169. The polluter pays principle is regarded as the cornerstone of Union environmental policy. References to it are made, among others, in Directive 75/439 on the disposal of waste oils [1975] O.J. L194/23 and Directive 91/689 on dangerous waste [1991] O.J. L377/20, amended by Directive 94/31 [1994] O.J. L168/28.
[21] Directive 2004/35 on environmental liability with regard to the prevention and remedying of environmental damage [2004] O.J. L143/56.

operator who has caused the damage, the costs it has incurred in relation to the preventive or remedial actions taken under the Directive, inter alia, via security over property or other appropriate guarantees. Natural or legal persons affected or likely to be affected by environmental damage, or having sufficient interest in environmental decisions or, alternatively, alleging the impairment of a right when a member State requires this, shall be entitled to submit to the competent authorities any observations and to request them to take action under the directive.[22] Member States may, as in many other matters, adopt more stringent provisions.

34–04 In preparing its policy on the environment, the Union must take account of available scientific and technical data[23], environmental conditions in the various regions, the potential benefits and costs of action or lack of action, the economic and social development of the Union as a whole and the balanced development of its regions.

[The reader shall have noticed that in this single Treaty provision there are three references to the "regions"[24], which seems to indicate that regional policy, i.e. economic, social and territorial cohesion, must be taken into account when implementing environmental policy.]

By requiring that "environmental protection requirements shall be a component of the Union's other policies", this so-called *integration principle* led to a general obligation for Union institutions to seek to conciliate other Treaty objectives (e.g. single market economy) with environmental protection, determining the wide scope of environmental responsibility.[25]

34–05 A 1985 Directive provides that the public authorities must ensure that the public concerned is given the opportunity to express an opinion before a project is approved.[26] In 1992, a Directive on the freedom of public access to environmental information came into force; the aim is to trigger public participation in the decision-making and in the monitoring process by disseminating environmental information held by public authorities.[27] A

---

[22] See *Rafinerie Méditerranée* (C-378/08) E.C.R. I-1919 not necessary to establish fault, negligence or intend on the part of operators whose activities are held to be responsible for the damage. Also *RE ERG II Rafinerie Mediterranée* (Joined cases C-379 and 380/08) [2010] E.C.R. I-2007 is not precluded national legislation which permits authorities to make the exercise, by operators at whom recovery measures are directed, of the right to use their land to certain conditions.

[23] Thus, Directive 2010/75 on industrial emission for the manufacture of glass (integrated pollution prevention and control) and for iron and steel production establishes the BAT best available techniques principle.

[24] The use of the term "regions" in this context, related to the closer connection between regions and ecosystems, in a true subsidiarity spirit, and also to the fact that in decentralised systems of governance regions and the substate level are competent in environmental matters.

[25] The Treaty provides for the integration principle in Art.11 TFEU: "environmental protection requirements must be integrated into the definition and implementation of the Union policies and activities referred to in Arts 3, 4, 5 and 6, in particular with a view to promoting sustainable development."

[26] Directive 85/337 [1985] O.J. L175/40.See *Le Poumon Vert de la Hulpe and others* (C-177/09) order of November 17, 2011, not yet reported and also *Solvay and others* (C-182/10), judgment of February 16, 2012, not yet reported. Force and effect of the guidance in the Aarhus Convention—Habitat Directive—Imperative reasons to overriding public interest.

[27] Directive 2003/4 on public access to environmental information [2003] O.J. L41/26. See *Flachglass Torgau* (C-204/09) judgment of February 14, 2012, not yet reported: access to bodies or institutions acting in a legislative capacity—confidentiality of the proceedings of public authorities—condition the confidentiality must be provided by law.

regulation[28] applies the *Aarhus Convention* on Access to Information, Public Participation in Decision-making and Access to Justice in Environmental matters to Community institutions and bodies. The Union signed the United Nations Economic Commission for Europe (UNECE) Convention in 1998 but it was not ratified until 2005![29] Where public access to Parliament, the Council and Commission documents are concerned, the Aarhus Convention makes an exception for judicial and legislative acts; this would, however, be in contradiction to the rules applicable within the Union.[30] Access under Aarhus had therefore to be extended to legislative acts by the above-mentioned Regulation.[31]

Most significant, though, is the shift among Member States to accept the concept of "sustainable development",[32] as being fundamental to future economic Union policy leading to the prudent use of resources and to profound changes in current patterns of development, production, consumption and behaviour. In 2008, the Commission adopted a communication "Towards a Shared Environmental Information System" (SEIS), proposing to modify and modernise the existing Union system.[33] A Commission Communication of May 2000 set out long-term objectives for *sustainable development* concerning climate change, transport, health and natural resources.[34]

Finally, the *principle of subsidiarity*, first mentioned in the SEA in relation to the environment, was generalised by the EU Treaty: the Union is only to legislate if and in so far as the objectives stated above "cannot be sufficiently achieved by the Member States and can, therefore, by reason of the scale or effects of the proposed action, be better achieved by the Union".[35] But even where protective measures are adopted by the Union, the Treaty allows Member States to maintain or introduce stricter protective measures, as long as they are "compatible with the Treaty and notified to the Commission".[36] The latter will only approve them if it is satisfied that they are based on "grounds of major needs", or on new scientific evidence relating to the protection of the environment or the working environment. The Commission must also be convinced that those measures are neither means of arbitrary discrimination nor disguised restrictions on Union inter-State commerce nor other obstacles to the functioning of the internal market.[37]

As mentioned before, the EU Treaty substantially enhanced the decision-making power of Parliament in the area of environmental legislation. Where unanimous decisions of the Council, after prior consultation of Parliament, were required, the Treaty now provides for a decision of Parliament and Council, **34–06**

---

[28] Regulation 1367/2006 [2006] O.J. L264/13.

[29] [2005] O.J. L124/1.

[30] Regulation 1049/2001 [2001] O.J. L145/43.

[31] See *VLK* (C-240/09) [2011] E.C.R. I-1255 direct effect of convention.

[32] Following the Report of the World Commission on Environment and Development (Brundtland Commission), the term "sustainable development" can be defined as "development which meets the needs of the present, without compromising the ability of future generations to meet their own needs".

[33] COM (2008) 46 [2008] O.J. C118/10.

[34] COM (2001) 264 final.

[35] Protocol No.2 on the application of the principles of subsidiarity and proportionality annexed to the TFEU.

[36] Art.193 TFEU.

[37] Art.114(5) and (6) TFEU. See *Deponietzweckverband Eiterkpfe* (C-6/03) [2005] E.C.R. I-2753.

acting in accordance with the ordinary legislative provision[38] and after consulting the ESC and the Committee of the Regions.[39] See, for instance, the Directive on the assessment of the effects or impacts of certain plans and programmes on the environment (environmental impact assessment or EIA).[40]

Acting unanimously, the Council can, in accordance with a specific legislative procedure,[41] and after consulting Parliament, the ESC and the Committee of the Regions, adopt provisions primarily of a fiscal nature, measures affecting town and country planning, quantitative management of water resources or land use with the exception of waste management and measures significantly affecting Member States' choices between different energy sources and the general structure of its energy supply.[42] This is an area where the legal basis is often shared between internal market and environmental protection. Thus the 2009/28 Directive on renewables was adopted under both.[43]

3. ENVIRONMENTAL ACTS OF THE EU

34-07   Noticeably, almost all of the more than 300 Union legislative acts aiming at environmental protection are in the form of directives, leaving room for each Member State to implement them taking into account its own economic, social and cultural background. Thus, due to the diversity of situations within the various regions of the Union, Union environmental policy focuses rather on the harmonisation than on the unification of environmental standards.[44] In this context, the major sectors of environmental Union concern have been the protection of fresh and seawater,[45] the monitoring of atmospheric pollution,[46] the

---

[38] See Art.294 TFEU.

[39] Art.192,1 TFEU, which refers to Art.191 TFEU.

[40] Directive 2001/41 [2001] O.J. L.197/30. See *Inter-Environnement Wallonie and Terre wallone* (C41/11) judgment of February 28, 2012, not yet reported; application of Arts 2 and 3.

[41] See Art.289,2 TFEU.

[42] Art.192,2 TFEU.

[43] OJ 2009 L140/16

[44] In terms of national environmental legislation within the Member States, substantial differences exist due to diverse social, cultural and economic realities. Unification of standards would often neglect the respective socio-economic situation of a Member State. Therefore, the use of Directives leaves room for each Member State to adjust its laws accordingly. At present, for example, Member States such as Denmark, the Netherlands, Sweden, Austria and Germany are far more concerned about environmental protection than, for instance, Greece, Spain or Italy, but there are important internal divergences within these Member States as well, since environmental policy is a decentralised regional competence.

[45] Many Directives in this area are concerned with quality standards of water for specific uses, e.g. Directive 75/440 [1975] O.J. L194/26 to help ensure clean drinking water by protecting those rivers, lakes and reservoirs used as drinking water sources: See Directive 2008/105 on environmental quality standards in the field of water policy [2008] O.J. L348/84; Directive 76/160 [1976] O.J. L31/1 to safeguard the health of bathers and to maintain the quality of bathing water; Directive 78/659 [1978] O.J. L222/1 to protect freshwater bodies capable of supporting fish life; Directive 79/923 [1979] O.J. L281/47 to protect coastal and brackish waters to support shellfish populations; Directive 80/778 [1980] O.J. L229/11 to safeguard human health by imposing strict quality standards for water intended for direct or indirect human consumption. Various amendments and modifications have followed. Other legislation introduced emission standards for discharges to surface waters and groundwater, for instance, Framework Directive 76/464 [1976] O.J. L129/23 on the discharge of dangerous substances into the aquatic environment; Directive 80/68 on the protection of groundwater

prevention of noise,[47] the conservation of wild flora and fauna,[48] waste management,[49] the control of chemicals[50] and energy policies. With regard to atmospheric pollution, the Union set itself targets under the Kyoto Protocol; to this end it has approved a Programme on climate change and a Communication on its implementation.[51] In recent years, particular attention has been paid to a shift from "command and control" measures (e.g. fines, imprisonment, etc.) to

---

against pollution caused by certain dangerous substances [1980] O.J. L20/43), it established a system of information exchange on river water quality between the Member States.

[46] In the 1980s, especially under the impression of acid rain pollution, various Directives on air quality standards were enacted, for instance, Directive 80/779 [1980] O.J. L229/30 setting up quality standards for sulphur dioxide and suspended particulates; other Directives for lead and nitrogen dioxides followed. For new industrial plants prior authorisation schemes were developed verifying, among others, the use of "green" technologies and the compliance with certain air quality standards to prevent excessive air pollution: Framework Directive 84/360 [1984] O.J. L188/20; see *Commission v Greece* (C-364/03) [2005] E.C.R. I-6159, atmospheric pollution by electrical plant. Various "daughter" directives flowed from this, as well as legislation setting up emission standards for industrial plants and motor vehicles. See also Directive 2000/69 relating to limit values for benzene and carbon monoxide in ambient air [2000] O.J. L313/12 and Directive 2000/81 on national emission ceilings for certain atmospheric pollutants [2001] O.J. L309/22. An information exchange system was established by a Council decision concerning atmospheric pollution in each Member State.

[47] In order to give fresh impetus to the campaign against noise, a Directive was adopted in 2002 it defines a Union approach for the management and evaluation of ambient noise in order to protect public health, Directive 2002/49 [2002] O.J. L189/12 and Commission Recommendation [2003] O.J. L212/49.

[48] For instance, Directive 92/43 [1992] O.J. L206/7 on the conservation of European wildlife and natural habitats; Directive 79/409 [1979] O.J. L103/1 on the conservation of wild birds; other legislation banned the import of sea pup skins or the use of leg-hold traps within the Union and established common rules for the imports of whales and other cetacean products. See also Regulation 338/97 on the protection of species of wild fauna and flora by regulating trade therein [1997] O.J. L61/1, modified [2001] O.J. L209/14, amended by Regulation 407/09 and corrigendum [2009] O.J. L.139/35.

[49] For instance, Framework Directive 75/442 [1975] O.J. L194/39 on waste management, modified [1991] O.J. L78/32, see *Commune of Mesquer v Total* (C-188/07) [2008] E.C.R.I-4501, on the definition of waste and where the Court declared the International Convention on Civil Liability for Oil Pollution Damage non applicable. See also [1996] O.J. L135/32; Directive 75/439 [1975] O.J. L194/23, on the elimination of used oils, modified [1987] O.J. L42/43; Directive 91/689 [1991] O.J. L377/20 on waste management in hazardous waste; Regulation 259/93 [1993] O.J. L30/1, on the supervision and control of shipments of waste within, into and out of the EU (legislation implementing the obligations under the Basel Convention (1989) and the Lomé IV Convention (1991)); see *EU-Wood-Trading GmbH v Sonderabfall-Management* (C-277/02) [2004] E.C.R. I-11957; other Directives focused on landfill waste, Directive 1999/31 [1999] O.J. L182/1, packaging and packaging waste, waste disposal installations or the encouragement of the [2002] E.C.R. I-1961. A Directive of September 2000 on end-of-life vehicles provides for the introduction of a system for collecting such vehicles at the manufacturer's expense, Directive 00/53 [2000] O.J. L269/34. Similarly, Directive 2003/965 on waste electrical and electronic equipment (WEEE) [2002] O.J. L37/24 and restricting the use of certain dangerous substances in such equipment, Directive 2003/108 [2003] O.J. L345/106 and Directive 2008/34 [2008] O.J. L81/65.

[50] For instance, Framework Directive 67/548 [1967] O.J. L196/1 on the classification, packaging and labelling of dangerous chemical substances especially in the area of agriculture (use of pesticides and artificial fertiliser, etc.), amended for the 31st time [2009] O.J. L11/6, repealed by Regulation 1272/08 [2008] O.J. L353/1, amended [2009] O.J. L235/1; the so-called Seveso-Directive 82/501 [1982] O.J. L.230/1, on the prevention of major accident hazards of chemical industrial activities trying to set up a better control mechanism concerning actions entailing potential risk; Regulation 2455/92 [1992] O.J. L251/13, establishing a prior informed consent procedure for exports and imports of substances that are already severely restricted within the Union.

[51] Green Paper, COM (2000) 87 final and COM (2000) 88 final.

market-based incentives,[52] as well as to the above-mentioned improvement of public participation and information. An eco-audit regime allows for voluntary registration of private industrial companies in eco-management and audit schemes aiming at the improvement of the companies' environmental performance. They provide, for example, for the introduction of environmental reviews, programmes and management systems, audits and the publication of "environmental statements", while exposing them to public scrutiny.[53] See, for instance, the Directive on the assessment of the effects of certain public and private projects, on the environment,[54] and the Directive on industrial emissions[55] and the implementing Decision laying down rules concerning guidance on the collection of data and on the drawing up of BAT reference documents and on their quality assurance.[56]

As regards greenhouse gas emissions,[57] an allowance trading scheme was established[58]; aviation was brought within the remit of this scheme.[59] A Commission decision provided guidelines for the monitoring and reporting of greenhouse gas emissions.[60] Guidance to this end was given by the Intergovernmental Panel on Climate Change (IPCC), the International Standardisation organisation (ISO), the Greenhouse Gas Protocol Initiative of the World Business Council on Sustainable Development (WBCSD) and the World Resource Institute (WRI). The price of emission rights has plummeted in the years following the financial and economic crisis, putting the system at risk.

---

[52] In 1992, the proposal of a combined CO2/energy tax failed by not reaching the necessary unanimous consent [1992] O.J. C196/1. The negotiations appear to steer toward a voluntary system of national energy tax regimes.

[53] Regulation 1836/93 [1993] O.J. L168/1; by 1997 some 700 sites had been registered which are, in return, allowed to use a logo on their correspondence papers indicating their participation in the system.

[54] Directive 2011/92 [2012] O.J. L26/1.

[55] Directive 2010/75 [2010] O.J. L334/17.

[56] Decision 2012/119 [2012] O.J. L63/1.

[57] See Directive 2003/87 [2003] O.J. L275/32, amended to include aviation activities in the scheme for greenhouse gas emission allowance trading within the Union [2009] O.J. L8/3, Annex I of that directive specifies the administrating Member State for each aircraft operator also taking into consideration the expansion of the Union emission trading scheme to EEA-EFTA countries; Regulation 748/2009 on the list of aircraft operators that perform an aviation activity listed in the above-mentioned annex, amended [2012] O.J. L39/1. See also Regulation 1193/11 establishing a Union Registry for the trading period commencing on January 1, 2013, and subsequent trading periods, of the Union emission trading scheme pursuant to Directive 2003/87, and Regulation 920/2010 for a standardised and secured system of registries: [2010] O.J. L270/1 and Regulation 1031/10 [2010] O.J. L302/1 on the timing, administration and other aspects of auctioning gas emission allowances; see Decision determining Union-wide rules for harmonised free allocation of emission allowances pursuant to Art.10a of Directive 2003/87; see also Regulation 748/09 [2009] O.J. L219/1 list of aircraft operators. See *Germany v Commission* (C-374/04) [2006] E.C.R. I-11673. Since the scheme includes aviation, see Regulation 115/11 [2011] O.J. L39/1. The emission rights trading scheme extended to air traffic has given rise to tense relations with major air carriers outside Europe. See *Air Transport Association of America and others v Secretary of State for Energy and Climate Change* (C-366/10R) judgment of December 21, 2011, not yet reported.

[58] Directive 98/70, amended [2009] O.J. L140/88.

[59] Directive 2008/101 [2008] O.J. L8/3; the validity of that directive was confirmed by the Court in *Air Transport Association of America note 70 supra*.

[60] [2004] O.J. L59/1, replaced by [2007] O.J. L229/1.

In 2008, the Commission issued a series of regulations establishing minimum requirements and the conditions for mutual recognition of companies and personnel as regards items containing fluorinated greenhouse gases.[61]

The efforts of Member States to reduce their greenhouse gas emissions to meet the Union's greenhouse gas emission reduction commitments up to 2020, was the object of a decision of Parliament and the Council in 2009.[62] See also the Directive regarding the specifications of petrol, diesel and gas-oil and introducing a mechanism to monitor and reduce greenhouse gas emissions.[63]   **34–08**

The Seventh Annual Survey on the implementation of the Union's environmental law (some 633 acts),[64] shows serious shortcomings in the implementation. This deprives citizens of the high level of environmental protection that they expect. It shows also that Member States are late in transposing environmental directives: in 2005, the Commission issued 141 reasoned opinions[65] and brought 42 cases against Member States before the Court. The Commission also issued 21 letters of formal notice and 11 reasoned opinions for failure by a Member State to comply with a judgment of the Court.[66]

These lacks or defects of implementation also explain why the focus of the 7th EA Programme is more on implementation of existing legislative requirements in the directives than on the adoption of new instruments and new targets.

4.   ENVIRONMENT ACTION PROGRAMMES (EAP). THE SEVENTH PROGRAMME (2013–2020)

Since 1973, the Union environmental policy has been developed through the enactment by Parliament and the Council of a series of non-binding "EAP",[67] after consultation of the ESC and the Committee of the Regions.[68] Serving as an orientation for future Union action, the Fifth Programme was entitled "Towards Sustainability". It addressed the need for a greater use of market forces through market instruments and incentives (e.g. taxes, eco-labelling, liability schemes, eco-audits, voluntary agreements, deposit/refund systems, etc.). It also introduced the notion of shared responsibility between public authorities (see below), public and private undertakings and the general public, emphasising the need for their wider involvement in environmental affairs. The Sixth EAP (2001-2012) was entitled "Environment 2010: Our Future, Our Choice", and set out as major priorities: climate change; nature and biodiversity protection; enhancing environment and health and quality of life; and natural resources and waste. A   **34–09**

---

[61] [2008] O.J. L92/1–25.

[62] Decision 406/09 [2009] O.J. L140/136.

[63] Directive 2009/30 [2009] O.J. L140/88.

[64] *http://ec.europa.eu/environment/legal/law/implementation.htm* [accessed August 23, 2013].

[65] See Art.258,1 TFEU.

[66] See Art.260(2) TFEU.

[67] Passed either as resolutions or decisions: First Action Programme (1973–77) [1973] O.J. C112/1; Second Action Programme (1977–83) [1977] O.J. C139/1; Third Action Programme (1983–87) [1983] O.J. C46/1; Fourth Action Programme (1987–93) [1987] O.J. C328/1; Fifth Action Programme (1993–2000) [1993] O.J. C138/1; and Sixth Action Programme (2001–2012) [2002] O.J L242/1.

[68] Art.192(3) TFEU.

report on the main developments was adopted by the Commission in 2008.[69] One of its key innovations was the *integrated product policy*, aimed at developing a more ecological product market by making products more environmentally sustainable throughout their life cycle. The Sixth EAP contained important thematic strategies such as Clean Air For Europe (CAFE)[70]; soil protection; sustainable use of pesticides[71]; marine environment[72]; waste prevention and recycling[73]; sustainable use of natural resources and urban environment.[74]

The new 7th programme is entitled "Living well, within the limits of our planet" and was proposed by the Commission in 2012. On April 24, 2013 the European Parliament's Environmental Committee approved it and it is now (Spring 2013) pending Council approval. In preparing its proposal for a new EAP, the Commission built on the challenges highlighted in the European Environment Agency's State of the Environment Report 2010[75] and the conclusions of the Sixth EAP Final Assessment.[76] Accordingly, the new, more strategic EAP, sets out "priority objectives to be attained" in environment policy in the context of the Europe 2020 Strategy.

The Seventh EAP sets three priority objectives: (1) protecting and enhancing natural capital, especially soil and land use, including forestry, but also healthy oceans and seas; (2) encouraging more resource efficiency while accelerating the transition to the low-carbon economy; and (3) tackling the environmental causes of disease (health and quality of life, with an emphasis on updating air quality, noise and water legislation, and addressing concerns linked to chemicals and nano-materials). The strategic initiatives in the field of environment will be reinforced, in particular the Resource Efficiency Roadmap[77], the 2020 Biodiversity Strategy[78] and the Low Carbon Economy Roadmap (2050).[79]

34–10   The main tools to achieve these objectives are: better implementation of EU environment law, state of the art science, securing the necessary investments in support of environment and climate change policy, and improving mainstreaming of environmental considerations in other policies (e.g. the CAP). These tools are sometimes referred to as the four "I"s: implementation, information, investment and integration of environmental policy. Measures envisaged by the Programme include phasing out environmentally harmful subsidies, shifting taxation from labour to pollution, drawing up partnership agreements between Member States

---

[69] COM (2008) 409.

[70] [2008] O.J. L152/1.

[71] Directive 91/414 [1991] O.J. L230/1, amended [2011] O.J. L58/ 41,45 and 49, and [2011] O.J. L59/26,29,32 and 37. Also [2011] O.J. L102/24 and 28. See also the Biocidal Product Directive 98/8 [1998] O.J. L123/1, amended to include different coppers and bendiocarb, as active substances in Annex I [2012] O.J. L37/60 and 65.

[72] COM (2002) 539 final.

[73] See the Waste Management Directive 08/98 [2008] O.J. L312/3.

[74] See COM (2004) 60.

[75] See relevant documents at: *http://www.eea.europa.eu/soer* [accessed August 23, 2013].

[76] *http://eur-lex.europa.eu/LexUriServ/LexUriServ.do?uri=CELEX:52011DC0531:EN:NOT* [accessed August 23, 2013].

[77] *http://eur-lex.europa.eu/LexUriServ/LexUriServ.do?uri=CELEX:DKEY=615217:EN:NOT* [accessed August 23, 2013].

[78] *http://eur-lex.europa.eu/LexUriServ/LexUriServ.do?uri=CELEX:52011DC0244:EN:NOT* [accessed August 23, 2013].

[79] *http://eur-lex.europa.eu/LexUriServ/LexUriServ.do?uri=COM:2011:0112:FIN:EN:PDF* [accessed August 23, 2013].

and the Commission on the implementation of EU environmental law, introducing complementary inspection capacity at EU level to address areas of serious concern, tracking environment-related expenditure in the EU budget, integrating environment and climate-related considerations into the European semester process.

The spatial scope of action is to be focusing on the urban and the global dimensions. This also means working with local authorities.

5. CIVIL (ENVIRONMENTAL) LIABILITY

In 1989, the proposal of a civil liability scheme for damage caused by waste calling for a system of unlimited strict liability on the waste producer,[80] was heavily criticised and eventually not further approached.[81] In 1993, the Council of Europe initiated the Lugano Convention establishing a civil liability scheme for activities dangerous to the environment[82] and the same year, the Commission published a Green Paper[83] addressing the usefulness of a general liability system. This Green Paper was followed in February 2000 by a White Paper on environmental liability, and following its publication, the need for Union action on liability for damage caused to the environment and on making good such damage has been gaining ground.[84] The paper sets out objective principles. For the principle of liability to be effective, the polluters must be identifiable, the damage must be quantifiable and there must be a link between the polluter and the damage. In addition, the principle of liability cannot be applied for dealing with pollution of a widespread character (climate change).

34–11

In most of the Member States, there exist laws on liability for damage caused by activities that are hazardous to the environment, but these laws only apply with respect to damage to human health or property. What is needed is an environmental liability regime which covers damage to natural resources. The White Paper contains a proposal for the main features of a Union liability regime, such as a definition of the types of liability and the possible options for Union action. In conclusion, the Commission believes that the optimum solution would be to have a framework directive, which would invoke strict liability on the part of persons performing an activity and authorise certain defences as regards traditional environmental damage, and provide for fault-based liability in the case of damage caused to biodiversity by non-hazardous activities.

Certain Member States have introduced economic incentives (taxes) for undertakings to implement strict environmental rules. The environmental liability

34–12

---

[80] See amended proposal [1991] O.J. C192/6; this approach was based on the preventive action and polluter pays principles and entailed provisions for a compulsory insurance by producers and disposers of waste.

[81] Mainly the industrial and insurance lobby as well as France, Germany and the United Kingdom argued that the establishment of a civil liability regime should be left to each Member State and that the subsidiarity principle did not call for Union action in this area.

[82] This Convention set up an unlimited strict, joint, several and retroactive liability scheme in which access to justice was granted to individuals and non-governmental organisations. But at the end, only 8 of the 27 participants signed the document.

[83] Green Paper on remedying environmental damage, COM (93) 47 final.

[84] COM (95) 624 and COM (2000) 66 final.

Directive[85] is based on polluter pays and requires operators to prevent damage, or take the necessary steps to prevent it, to repair damage once produced and to report persisting risks. But the directive does not provide any right of action for environmental injury or damage caused. If civil environmental liability there be, it is rather limited.

The Council adopted, in 2003, a framework decision concerning the protection of the environment through criminal law.[86] It defines a number of infringements to the environment and invites the Member States to provide for penal sanctions.[87] However, this Framework Decision was annulled by the Court,[88] at the request of the Commission, which was of the opinion that the decision was based on the wrong provisions.[89]

6. PROTECTION OF THE ENVIRONMENT THROUGH CRIMINAL LAW

34–13 Criminal law is still the symbolic domain of Member State competence par excellence. It is therefore rather innovative for Art.192 TFEU to provide for the Union (Council) to require Member States to adopt criminal law measures in order to combat the particularly serious environmental crimes, which is something Council, i.e. Member State governments, need not always be eager to do in the field of environmental protection. Penalties should be based on the principles of effectiveness, proportionality and dissuasiveness of general prevention. Where criminal penalties are concerned, as a general rule, neither criminal law nor the rules of criminal procedure fall within the competence of the Union, but when the application of effective, proportional and dissuasive criminal penalties by the competent national authorities is an essential measure for combating serious environmental offences, the Union legislature might require the Member States to introduce such penalties for violation of Union environmental rules, as is the case, for instance, with the rules on ship-source pollution and transport.[90]

Concern grew at the rise in environmental offences and their effects, which are increasingly extending beyond the borders of the States in which the offences are committed. In 2008, a directive was adopted, which provides that, among other activities, the following acts can be considered criminal offences:

- illegal disposal of radioactive substances and illegal waste management, in particular waste transport when harmful;
- illegal operation of production plants pursuing hazardous activities likely to have harmful effects;

---

[85] Directive 2004/35 OJ 2004 L143/56.

[86] Framework Decision 2003/80/JAI on the protection of the environment through criminal law [2003] O.J. L29/55.

[87] This Decision was based on Arts 29, 31,e) and 34(2),b), EU Title VI, as they were drafted before Nice.

[88] *Commission v Council* (C-176/03) [2005] E.C.R. I-7879.

[89] According to the Commission the act should be based upon Art.175(1) EC.

[90] *Commission v Council* (C-176/03) [2005] E.C.R. I-7879; for an overview of the case law regarding penal sanctions, see Conclusions (34), and *Commission v Council* (C-440/05) [2007] E.C.R I-9097.

- illegal slaughter or destruction of protected animals or plants as well as any illegal action resulting in deterioration of habitat within a protected district;
- illegal production and use of substances that deplete the ozone layer.

Addressing both natural and legal persons, the Directive also provides that the criminal penalties must be effective proportionate and dissuasive.

7. EXTERNAL CO-OPERATION

The Treaty imposes a general obligation on the EU to contribute to the sustainable development of the Earth when establishing and engaging in external relations and co-operation[91]. Externally, the Union has become party to numerous international Conventions and related Protocols for the protection of the environment.[92] These international Treaties have without exception, the form of joint agreements between the Union and its Member States. This is due to the fact that their respective subject matters usually fall partly within the competence of the Union and partly within that of the Member States (shared competence).[93] In 2005, the European Union concluded the so-called Aarhus Convention on access to information, public participation in decision-making and access to justice in environmental matters, which aims at granting the public certain rights and imposes on parties and public authorities obligations regarding access, participation and justice. According to the Decision on the conclusion[94] of the Convention, its objective is consistent with the objectives of the Union's environmental policy listed in the Treaties.[95]

34–14

---

[91] See Regulation 1255/2011 for the sustainable use of seas and oceans in the context of the marine policy, O.J. 2011 L321, 1.

[92] For instance, Rio de Janeiro Convention on Biological Diversity [1993] O.J. L309/1; Vienna Convention on the Protection of the Ozone Layer and the Montreal Protocol on Substances that Deplete the Ozone Layer, both in [1988] O.J. L297/8; Basel Convention on the Control of Transport of Hazardous Waste [1993] O.J. L39/1; New York Convention on Climate Change [1994] O.J. L33/11; Bonn Convention on the Conservation of Migratory Species of Wild Animals [1982] O.J. L210/10; Paris Convention for the Prevention of Marine Pollution from Land-Based Sources: [1975] O.J. L194/5.

[93] Art.191(4) TFEU; this provision reserves, again, strong rights for the Member States to conclude international agreements individually and limits the power of the Union accordingly. However, the Treaty only refers in this respect to "their respective fields of competence" without further specification. Therefore, future disputes over the respective limits of each side's competence cannot be excluded until clear-cut criteria for such a distinction—similar to the "Protocol on the application of the principles of subsidiarity and proportionality" added by the Treaty of Amsterdam—will be established. See in this respect Opinion 2/00 of the Court, December 6, 2001 concerning the Cartagena Protocol 1997 on Living Modified Organisms [2001] E.C.R. I-9713; [1998] O.J. L127/11.

[94] [2005] O.J. L124/1.

[95] Art.191 TFEU.

8. THE EUROPEAN ENVIRONMENTAL AGENCY[96]

34–15 The establishment of the European Environmental Agency and the European Environment Information and Observation Network[97] in 1990, created an organisational basis for an independent, objective, comparative collection, screening and evaluation network of environmental data and information. Although it is a Union Agency, Norway, Iceland and Switzerland are members and so were the 12 candidate countries before accession.[98]

9. FINANCIAL INSTRUMENTS

34–16 In 1993, the Commission set up a European Environmental Forum with general consultative functions.[99] However, the fact that about 90 per cent of Union environmental legislation is in the form of directives means that the major problem with the environmental law of the Union resides in the too prudent and often insufficient implementation by the Member States.[100] Therefore, in 1992, a financial instrument for the environment (LIFE) was created, the main objective of which is the development and implementation of Union environmental policy by granting financial assistance.[101] Under the Financial perspectives 2007–2013, the budget for LIFE is €2.1 billion.[102] The new programme is divided in LIFE+ Nature and Biodiversity, LIFE+ Environment policy and governance and LIFE+ Information and communication.[103]

In 2007, Parliament and the Council adopted a Regulation on the LIFE+ financial instruments.[104] This new instrument merges a wide range of existing

---

[96] See also Ch.13: Decentralised Agencies and Bodies of the Union.
[97] Regulation 1210/90 [1990] O.J. L120/1, amended [1999] O.J. L117/1. The Agency is located in Copenhagen.
[98] [2001] O.J. L213/1. See Ch.13: Decentralised Agencies and Bodies of the Union.
[99] The Forum consists of 32 members elected from the sectors of economics and of environmental protection.
[100] From the start of the environmental legislation there has been a steady increase in the number of Court actions initiated by the Commission about lack of proper implementation by the Member States, particularly in the fields of drinking water quality, environmental impact assessments and the protection of wild birds. Finally, a new legal procedure was introduced to enable the Union to exert stronger influence on each Member State's implementation activities. Now, where a Member State does not comply with a judgment of the Court, although it has been previously found in breach of Union law by not appropriately implementing directives, the Commission can propose and specify to the Court the amount of a lump sum or penalty payment to be paid by the Member State concerned: Art.260 TFEU. The Court may then impose such penalty. In 1997, the first two environmental cases were submitted to the Court both against Germany asking for penalty payments of €26,400 and €158,000, per day respectively (both *Commission v Germany* (C-121/97) [1997] O.J. C166/7 [1990] E.C.R. I-272).
[101] Regulation 1973/92 [1992] O.J. L206/1; its annual budget is about €100 million. See also Regulation 1655/2000 concerning the Financial Instrument for the Environment [2000] O.J. L192/1. Concerning the implementation of the LIFE programme see *Commission v Parliament and Council* (C-378/00) [2003] E.C.R. I-937. See Regulation 1682/2004 amending Regulation 1655/2000 concerning the Financial Instrument for the Environment [2004] O.J. L308/1.
[102] In 2008, the Commission approved funding of €186 million for 143 new projects.
[103] IP/06/856. See Regulation 614/07 concerning LIFE+ [2007] O.J. L149/1.
[104] Regulation 614/07 [2007] O.J. L149/1.

environmental programmes and instruments into a single mechanism and has a budget of €1.9 billion for the period 2007–2013.

In 1993, the establishment of the Cohesion Fund which was designed to finance environmental and transport infrastructure projects in Member States whose gross domestic product is less than 90 per cent of the Union average, made even more financial support available.[105] Union pre-accession aid in the environment sector to the candidate countries has been stepped up considerably since 2000, using the pre-accession structural instrument (PASI), which concerns the environment and transport. Finally, the European Investment Bank funds environmental projects that pass a prior environmental assessment procedure.

10. COMPETITION

The Commission has, among others, adopted guidelines for State aid subsidies for environmental protection.[106] For more details see Ch.22: Competition Policy. **34–17**

FURTHER READING

L. Kramer *EC Environmental Law*, 5th edn (Sweet & Maxwell, London, 2003). **34–18**
Marco Onida "Europe and the Environment", *Legal Essays in honour of Ludwig Kramer*, (Europa Law Publishing, 2004).
Nerle Dhondt, *Integration of Environmental Protection into other EC policies*, (Europa Law Publishing, 2003).

---

[105] Regulation 1164/94 [1994] O.J. L130/1 and Regulation 16/2003 [2003], rules concerning eligibility; its budget for the period of 1993 to 1999 contains €15.15 billion. Currently, only Greece, Ireland, Portugal and Spain are eligible for financial assistance. Union pre-accession aid in the environment sector has been increased substantially since 2000, using pre-accession structural instruments such as PASI which relates to environment and transport [2000] O.J. L72/21.
[106] [2008] O.J. C82/1.

CHAPTER 35

Energy Policy

There was no Title on "Energy" in the EC Treaty, neither after nor before the **35–01** modifications introduced by the EU Treaty and the Treaties of Amsterdam and Nice.[1] However, a Chapter with a single article was introduced by the Treaty of Lisbon.[2] Energy is now a shared competence in the EU, in the sense of art.4(2)(i) TEU. This has important implications also for the external policy of the EU. The energy policy of the Union has the aim of ensuring the functioning of the energy market, ensuring the security of supply, promoting energy efficiency and saving and the development of new and renewable forms of energy, and promoting the interconnection of energy networks. But Member States keep the right to define the conditions for exploiting energy resources and to make their own political choices between different sources of energy or to determine the general structure of their grid and supply. Also there is a connection between energy supply structures and public security in the sense of Art.36 TFEU.

As is well known, coal—previously the main source of energy—has been the object of Union measures since 1952 under the now-extinct European Community for Coal and Steal Treaty, and the development of nuclear energy is the objective of Euratom since 1958; but a concerted effort in the energy field is required, especially now, from the Member States and the Union, as much as in the areas of agriculture, transport or commercial policy.

Notwithstanding the above-mentioned absence of Treaty provisions concerning an energy policy, the Union has developed over the years and is still expanding and implementing, in close co-operation with the Member States, a Union energy policy. This, however, raises the question of the competence of the Union to do so, since, as has been explained several times in the foregoing pages, the Union may only exercise those powers which have been explicitly conferred upon it. On the other hand, the connections between energy policy and other key objectives of the Union, like quality of the environment, combating climate change, reducing fossil energy dependence, reducing the macroeconomic impact of imported energy, securing passenger transport and trade in goods, and geostrategic security issues involved in nuclear, fuel and gas sources of energy, should not go unnoticed, and will be analysed infra. This places energy at a policy "hub" of the Union. As shall be seen, the institutions adopted directives, regulations and decisions in the energy field and it is interesting to examine at the onset what empowered the Union to do so.

---

[1] This might explain why, until the end of 2008, there was no Energy Directorate-General at the Commission.
[2] Art.194 TFEU.

35–02   A typical example is the Directive of Parliament and the Council concerning common rules for the internal market in electricity.[3] The institutions indicate, as legal bases for their acts, in the first place, the Treaty provisions concerning the right of establishment; among them the obligation of the Council to "issue directives for the co-ordination of provisions laid down by law, regulation or administrative action in the Member States concerning the taking-up and pursuit of activities as self-employed persons".[4] Secondly, they indicate the Treaty provisions concerning the freedom to provide services,[5] and, thirdly, the Treaty provisions concerning the harmonisation measures necessary for the establishment and functioning of the internal market.[6] Although an energy policy as such was not, as mentioned, provided for in the Treaties, the references to the above-mentioned provisions are ample justification for the Union to act in this domain.[7]

In December 1998, the Council adopted a multi-annual framework programme for actions in the energy sector (1998–2002) and connected measures. This programme was primarily to contribute to the balanced pursuit of security of supply, competitiveness and protection of the environment. The Council also adopted a multi-annual programme of studies, analyses, forecasts and other related work in the energy sector (1998–2002).[8] This multi-annual programme was followed by another one referred to as "Intelligent Energy-Europe" (2003–2006).[9] As a first step the Commission had to define, in consultation with the Programme Committee, the priority areas, the criteria for selection of projects, the funding arrangements, etc. The Commission then launched a call for proposals and a call for tenders. The "Intelligent Energy Europe II" programme (IEE II) was launched in 2007 together with the work programme for implementing it[10]; it now forms an integral part of the competitiveness and innovation framework programme.[11] In association with this programme, the Commission established the Executive Agency for Competitiveness and Innovation, with responsibility, in particular, for implementing IEE II.[12]

According to the Commission,[13] the overall objective of the Union's energy policy is to provide Europe with competitive and sustainable energy, the main

---

[3] Directive 96/92 [1997] O.J. L27/20, replaced by Directive 2003/54 [2003] O.J. L176/37, repealed by Directive 2009/72 [2009] O.J. L211/55, see *Citiworks A.G.* (C-439/06) [2008] E.C.R. I-3913 interpreting Art.20(1) Directive 2003/54.

[4] Art.53(1) TFEU.

[5] Art.62 TFEU which refers back to several provisions concerning the right of establishment, including the above-mentioned Art.53(2) TFEU.

[6] Art.114(1) TFEU.

[7] The absence of an explicit reference to Energy in the Treaty has nothing to do with the Commission's Communication to the Parliament and the Council concerning the repeal of several Union legislative texts in the field of energy policy [1996] O.J. C221/3.

[8] [1999] O.J. L7/16 and 20; the Decisions were based upon Art.352 TFEU and Art.203.

[9] [2003] O.J. L176/29; it entered into force on August 4, 2003.

[10] General Report 2007, 85.

[11] See Ch.31: Enterprise and Industrial Policy/Information Society.

[12] Decision 2007/372 [2007] O.J. L140/52 amending Decision 2004/20 in order to transform the Intelligent Energy Executive Agency into this new agency. See above, the chapter on Decentralised Bodies of the Union.

[13] See *http://www.europa.eu.int/comm/dgs/energy-transport/index-en.html* [accessed August 23, 2013], on which much of this chapter is based and from which some parts are reproduced here.

thrusts of which are the fight against climate change, boosting competitiveness with a regulatory framework conducive to it, and limiting the European Union's dependence on gas and oil imports.[14]

At the European Council of March 2007, the foundations for a European energy policy, including commitments, binding targets and procedures were adopted:

35–03

- with regard to climate change, an independent commitment by the Union to reduce greenhouse gas emissions by at least 20 per cent by 2020 compared with 1990, and a commitment to a 30 per cent reduction if other developed countries undertake to make comparable emissions reductions;
- as regards the single market for gas and electricity, effective separation of supply and production activities from network operations (unbundling);
- as regards, efficiency, an increase of 20 per cent in efficiency of energy production and consumption,
- as regards renewable energies, the binding target of 20 per cent by 2020 with a minimum share of bio-fuels of 10 per cent of overall petrol and diesel consumption in the Union.

Energy policy was one key theme in the February 2011 summit of the European Council, which set as an objective for the EU that of having in place a functioning internal energy market by 2014. In order to be able to implement its energy policy, the Union pursues different objectives—see below.

1. SECURITY OF ENERGY SUPPLY AND INTERNATIONAL CO-OPERATION

Besides the obligation imposed on the Member States to maintain minimum stocks of crude oil and/or petroleum products,[15] this includes the development of relations with the supplier countries through bilateral and multilateral agreements such as the Energy Charter. The Energy Charter Treaty[16] was adopted in 1997 and is designed to develop new relations between the main European countries and most of the independent states of the former Soviet Union and Central and Eastern Europe, Canada, the USA and Japan, covering trade, investment and energy co-operation. The main aim is to meet the challenge of developing the energy potential of the independent states of the former Soviet Union and Eastern Europe while helping to improve security of supply for the European Union.[17] Another aspect of those relations is the external interconnection of Trans-European Networks.[18] A series of guidelines for Trans-European Energy

35–04

---

[14] Communication "An energy policy for Europe" [2007] O.J. C138/14.

[15] Directive 2006/67 [2006] O.J. L217/8.

[16] See also the Decision with regard to the ECT, the Energy Charter Protocol on energy efficiency and related environmental aspects, and the amendments to the ECT [1998] O.J. L252/21, amended [2001] O.J. L209/32.

[17] [1997] Bull. 9, 26.

[18] Arts 170 and 171 TFEU. See above the chapter on Enterprise and Industrial Policy/Information Society, and the Communication from the Commission to Parliament and Council: "The external dimension of Trans-European Networks" COM(97) 125.

Networks were laid down by Parliament and the Council[19]; the latter also laid down general rules for the granting of Union financial aid,[20] and the Commission set out the specifications for projects of common interest identified in respect of those networks.[21] The actions also aim at the more efficient use of existing resources; a multi-annual programme was set up to promote energy efficiency in the Union (SAVE II),[22] the diversification of energy resources through the promotion of new energy sources,[23] the use of renewable sources[24] (hydroelectric, solar, wind, geothermal and bio-fuels), and the implementation of provisions concerning the supply of nuclear materials and safeguard measures.[25]

Other actions focus on energy demand, which include the promotion of energy saving and the development of a culture of energy-saving behaviour and rational energy consumption. A directive was adopted on end-use efficiency and energy services.[26]

(1) International Co-operation[27]

35–05   In December 1998, the Council adopted a multi-annual programme to promote international co-operation in the energy sector (1998–2002).[28] These include actions in the context of general technical assistance programmes: PHARE, TACIS[29] and MEDA.[30] These programmes finance international co-operation projects with third countries for developing, formulating and implementing their energy policy in fields of mutual interest. Those projects have to contribute to accomplishing the objectives defined in the Commission's White Paper on "An energy policy for the European Union". In 2004 the Council adopted a directive concerning measures to safeguard security of natural gas supply.[31] Also included are actions for the preparation of the accession of new States, co-operation with international organisations—IEA, IAEA, OECD, EBRD—and the World Bank, and the definition of crisis-management measures to be implemented for each type of energy source, if needed. In 2006 the Union concluded an Energy Community Treaty with the view of establishing an Integrated Energy Market Organisation in South-East Europe.[32]

---

[19] [1996] O.J. L161/147, amended [1999] O.J. L207/1.

[20] [1995] O.J. L228/1, amended several times.

[21] [2000] O.J. L305/1.

[22] Decision 647/2000 of Parliament and the Council adopting a multi-annual programme for the promotion of energy efficiency (SAVE) 1998–2002.

[23] See, for instance, Communication from the Commission on a Union strategy to promote combined heat and power (CHP) and to dismantle barriers to its development COM(97) 514 final.

[24] See the White Paper on energy for the future: renewable sources of energy COM(97) 599 final.

[25] See Communication from the Commission on the nuclear industries in the EU COM(97) 401 final.

[26] Directive 2006/32 [2006] O.J. L114/64.

[27] See General Report 2008, 90.

[28] [1999] O.J. L7/23.

[29] See Decision adopting a multi-annual programme (1998–2002) of actions in the nuclear sector, relating to the safe transport of radioactive materials and safeguards and industrial co-operation to promote certain aspects of the safety of nuclear installations in the countries currently participating in the TACIS programme [1999] O.J. L7/31.

[30] Regulation 701/97 amending a programme to promote international co-operation in the energy sector—Synergy programme [1997] O.J. L104/1.

[31] [2004] O.J. L127/92.

[32] [2006] O.J. L198/15.

2. INTEGRATING ENERGY MARKETS

The main objective of this action is the completion of the Internal Energy Market, **35–06** especially in the fields of electricity and gas. A directive was adopted by Parliament and the Council in 2003 concerning common rules for the internal market in electricity.[33] It concerns electrical energy, electricity supply, energy production, energy transport and the internal market. These institutions also adopted a regulation on conditions for access to the network for cross-border exchanges of electricity[34] and a decision laying down a series of guidelines for Trans-European Energy Networks.[35] During the same year, a directive was adopted regarding natural gas,[36] followed by a regulation on the conditions of access to the gas transport network.[37]

To clarify this legislation, the Commission published "interpretative notes" on various subjects such as "unbundling", "public service obligations", "distribution", "labelling", "gas storage", etc.[38] In order to consolidate the internal energy market, the Commission established the European Regulators Group for Electricity and Gas which later became the Agency for the Cooperation of Energy Regulators.[39] It shall facilitate consultation, co-ordination and co-operation of national regulatory authorities and take decisions when provided for in the legislation.[40] The Court reinforced the legislative framework by stipulating that existing long-term contracts could not deprive newcomers from access to existing facilities.[41] Other actions include the implementation of competition rules, including State aids,[42] the establishment of networks for the transport of energy throughout Europe,[43] taxation of energy products[44] and the promotion of standards for energy products. Those actions are closely linked with Union action in the field of regional policy.[45] The Commission sent a communication on energy and social and economic cohesion in the Union to the other institutions[46] and contributions for energy are provided for in the Structural Funds. Energy investments are also financed by the TENs, the EIB, the ECSC (until July 23, 2002) and Euratom aids and loans. The 2003 Directives had to be transposed by

---

[33] Directive 2003/54/EC O.J. L176/37 concerning common rules for the internal market in electricity, repealed by Directive 2009/72 [2009] O.J. L211/55.
[34] Regulation 1228/03 [2003] O.J. L176/1 repealed by Regulation 714/09 [2009] O.J. L211/15.
[35] Decision 1229/03 [2003] O.J. L176/11.
[36] Directive 2003/55 [2003] O.J. L176/57, repealed by Directive 2009/73 [2009] O.J. L211/94.
[37] Regulation 1775/05 [2005] O.J. L289/1, repealed [2009] O.J. L229/29. See Regulation 715/09 [2009] O.J. L211/36, corrigendum [2009] O.J. L229/29.
[38] These notes can be found *http://ec.europa.eu/energy/gas_electricity/doc/20121217_energy_market_2011_lr_en.pdf* (see gloassry at end of document) [accessed August 23, 2013].
[39] The Agency was established by Regulation 713/2009 [2009] O.J. L211/1.
[40] Arts 1 and 7 of Regulation 713/2009.
[41] *VEMV* (C-17/03) [2005] E.C.R. I-4983.
[42] See, for instance, Decision 3632/93 establishing Union rules for State aids to the coal industry [1993] O.J. L329/12.
[43] See, for instance, Directive 91/296 on the transit of natural gas through grids [1991] O.J. L147/37.
[44] In October 2003 the Council adopted a directive concerning taxation of energy and electricity; it extends to all the energy products, including coal and natural gas, the minimum tax rates, thereby reducing competition between various energy sources.
[45] See Ch.32: Regional Policy/Economic, Social and Territorial Cohesion—The Europe 2020 Strategy.
[46] COM (93) 645 final.

July 1, 2004 and since not all Member States had complied with this obligation, several court actions were introduced by the Commission. The Directives provide also for an annual report on the implementation of the Directives; according to the 2008 report, despite some encouraging improvements, especially with respect to the development of best practice solutions on a regional level, the overall analysis of progress shows that major barriers to the efficient functioning of the internal market still exist.[47] At the end of 2007, the Commission had to sound the alarm on the state of the internal gas and electricity market[48]: the final report on the sectoral inquiry on competition[49] demonstrated that numerous restrictions on free competition, and, in particular, obstacles to infrastructure access, lack of investment in interconnections[50] and excessive market concentration, have not yet allowed a truly competitive gas and electricity market to be created. In relation to state aids control, investment projects in the energy infrastructure within the European Union must be notified to the Commission.[51]

3. PROMOTING ENERGY TECHNOLOGY DEVELOPMENT

35–07   This is carried out in the context of the Research, Development and Demonstration programme, JOULE-THERMIE,[52] and Euratom programmes. In 2008 the Council set out fundamental principles, objectives and actions for a European policy on energy technology; it should improve synergies at Union level and take account of existing structures for co-operation on research, development, demonstration and development in the field of energy technology; the private sector must be fully involved.[53] See also the European strategic energy technology (SET).[54]

A programme to aid economic recovery by granting Union financial assistance to projects in the field of energy was adopted in 2009.[55]

Directives were issued in 2010 on the indication by labelling and standard product information of the consumption of energy and other resources by energy related products,[56] and on the energy performance of buildings.[57]

---

[47] General Report 2008, 89.

[48] [2007] O.J. C138/14.

[49] [2007] O.J. C138/14.

[50] As regards interconnections see Communication "Priority interconnection plan".

[51] Regulation 617/10, repealing Regulation 736/96 [2010] O.J. L180/7 and implementing Regulation 833/10 [2010] O.J. L248/36.

[52] A non-nuclear research, development and research programme designed to encourage the development of new, economically viable and environmental safe energy options.

[53] General Report 2008, 89.

[54] COM (2007) 723.

[55] [2009] O.J. L200/31.

[56] [2010] O.J. L153/1.

[57] [2010] O.J. L133/13.

4.   SECTORAL ASPECTS

Coal was within the ambit of the European Coal and Steel Community, which ceased to exist, as mentioned, on July 23, 2003, since it was concluded for a period of 50 years from its entry into force,[58] i.e. July 23, 1952. From 2003 on, coal is considered as a "good" in the sense of the EC Treaty, and subject to its rules; it now comes under the TFEU. The main problem with this solid fuel is the uneconomical extraction conditions prevailing in all the Member States.[59] Coal mines are still maintained in operation in Germany, France, Spain, Poland, Hungary, Romania and Slovakia. State aid to coal was governed by an ECSC Decision[60] until the expiry of that Treaty. On that day the Council adopted a regulation[61] providing for minimum coal production, which will help maintain an indigenous primary energy source. In December 1998, the Council adopted a multi-annual programme of technological actions promoting the clean and efficient use of solid fuels (1998–2002).[62] After the expiry of the ECSC Treaty, the Union activities in this field were, as indicated, taken over by the EC Treaty.[63]

35–08

In a 2007 communication, the Commission stressed that the future use of coal must be made compatible with sustainable objectives and climate-change policy.[64] A proposal was made in 2010 to close all loss-making coal mines by the end of 2014, since the Regulation about state aid expires at the end of 2010. See in this regard above the chapter on Competition.

Oil and petroleum products are, as mentioned, mainly imported from third countries; consequently, the Union attaches great importance to prospecting, exploration and production within the Union itself.[65]

As for *natural gas*, which is also produced in limited quantities within the Union, the Union has established conditions for access to the natural gas transmission networks[66] and common rules for the internal market in gas,[67] which are similar to those for electricity.

35–09

The common rules for *electricity* entered into force in February 1997.[68] They are based on a balanced approach to public service obligations and competition rules and on the broad application of the subsidiarity principle, in order to take

---

[58]   Art.97 ECSC.

[59]   Coal imported from Australia is cheaper on arrival in Rotterdam than European coal.

[60]   Decision 3632/93/ECSC [1993] O.J. L205/1 and Regulation 1047/02 [2002] O.J. L329/12.

[61]   Report on Competition 2002/474.

[62]   [1999] O.J. L7/28.

[63]   See, for instance, Regulation 1047/02 on aid to the coal industry [2002] O.J. L329/12.

[64]   [2007] O.J. C138/14.

[65]   See Directive 94/22 on the conditions for granting and using authorizations for the prospection, exploration and production of hydrocarbons [1994] O.J. L164/3. On 7 September 2012 the European Commission published three new studies on unconventional fossil fuels, in particular shale gas, see the reports "Unconventional Gas: Potential Energy Market Impacts in the European Union", "Climate impact of potential shale gas production in the EU" and "Support to the identification of potential risks for the environment and human health arising from hydrocarbons operations involving hydraulic fracturing in Europe". See the 2012 Report on unconventional gas in Europe by the Commission. All these documents are available at *http://ec.europa.eu/energy/studies/energy_en.htm* [accessed August 23, 2013].

[66]   Regulation 1775/2005: [2005] O.J. L289/1, replaced [2009] O.J. L211/36.

[67]   Directive 2003/55 [2003] O.J. L76/57, repealed [2009] O.J. L211/94.

[68]   [1997] O.J. L27/20.

account of the different gas and electricity systems existing in the Member States. They provide for the opening-up of the market over a period of 10 years.[69]

Nuclear energy is submitted to the rules of the Euratom Treaty, which shows great similarities with the EC Treaty and now the TFEU. One of the main particularities consists of the fact that nuclear fissile materials are the property of the Union. This property right is exercised, among others, by the right of option of Euratom's Supply Agency on all fissile material.[70] Furthermore, all operations concerning nuclear material must be handled by the said Agency. The latter will be examined hereafter. Another important aspect is the necessity to safeguard the use of the fissile material for non-military purposes, when they have been declared to be destined for peaceful purposes.[71] Bilateral agreements exist with Australia, Canada and the United States; supply agreements were also signed with Uzbekistan (2004), Kazakhstan, Ukraine, Japan (2006) and Russia (2007).

Renewable Energy

35–10   Renewable sources of energy—wind power, solar power (thermal and photovoltaic), hydroelectric power, tidal power, geothermal energy and biomass—are an essential alternative to fossil fuels. See Commission Communication "Renewable energy in the 21st century: building a more sustainable future".[72] In it, the Commission proposed establishing a legal binding target of 20 per cent for renewable energy's share of energy consumption in the Union by 2020, and a new legislative framework for the promotion and use of renewable energy in the Union. A Directive establishing National Renewable Energy Action Plans was adopted in 2009.[73]

A specific programme was put in place: ALTENER. The development concerns energy from wind, water, solar power and biomass. Renewable energy has indeed an important role to play in reducing carbon dioxide; it enhances sustainability and helps to improve the security of energy supply by reducing the Union's growing dependence on imported energy sources. It is expected to become competitive with conventional energy in the medium- to long-term. It is, by definition local, and therefore can create new business, bring employment and encourage economic and social cohesion in regions that otherwise lack industrial development. ALTENER II applied until December 2002. It was replaced by the ALTENER programme for which a budget of €77 million is provided.

---

[69] See, for instance, Directive 2003/54 concerning common rules for the internal market in electricity [2003] O.J. L176/37, replaced [2009] O.J. L211/55. For third-party access to the transmission and distribution systems see *Sabatauskas A.O.* (C-239/07) [2008] E.C.R. I-7523.

[70] See *ENU v Commission* (Joined Cases T-458/93 and T-523/93 [1995] E.C.R. II-2459).

[71] See the Agreement for co-operation in the peaceful use of nuclear energy between Euratom and the US [1996] O.J. L120/1.

[72] [2007] O.J. C138/14.

[73] [2009] O.J. L140/16 and Commission Decision establishing a template for it [2009] O.J. L182/33.

5. NUCLEAR ENERGY—EURATOM'S SUPPLY AGENCY AND SAFEGUARDS

Nuclear power stations currently produce around a third of the electricity and 15 per cent of the energy consumed in the Union. The sector represents a source of energy with low carbon levels and relatively stable costs, which makes it attractive from the point of view of security of supply and fighting climate change. It is up to each Member State, however, to decide whether or not to -pursue the option of nuclear power.[74] After the Fukushima plant accident, following a tsunami in the Pacific in 2011, the debate on the "nuclear energy" question is back on the agenda. Also, the thorny problem of spent fuel and radioactive waste and its disposal in repositories, management and trade raises legal and political issues. On July 19, 2011, the Council adopted the "Radioactive waste and spent fuel management Directive", proposed by the Commission on November 3, 2010. The Directive asks Member States to present national programmes, indicating when, where and how they will construct and manage final repositories guaranteeing the highest safety standards. The safety standards become legally binding and enforceable in the European Union. Member States have to submit the first report on the implementation of their national programmes in 2015.[75]

35–11

The main function of Euratom consists in furthering co-operation in the field of research, protecting the public by establishing common safety standards, ensuring an adequate and equitable supply of ores and nuclear fuel, monitoring the peaceful use of nuclear material, and co-operating with other countries and international organisations.[76]

The property of all special fissionable material within the territory of the Member States is, as indicated, vested in the Union,[77] in so far as this material is subject to Euratom's safeguard control. The latter does not extend to materials "intended to meet defence requirements".[78] The Treaty provides for the creation of a Supply Agency[79] having a right of option on all ores, source materials and special fissile materials produced in the territories of the Member States. It also has the exclusive right to conclude contracts relating to the supply of ores, source material and special fissile materials coming from inside or outside the Union.[80] New Statutes of the Agency were laid down by the Council in 2008[81] and various regulations have specified the conditions under which nuclear materials can be

---

[74] Taken from *http://ec.europa.eu/energy/nuclear/index_en.htm* [accessed August 23, 2013].
[75] [2011] O.J. L199/48.
[76] Taken from *http://ec.europa.eu/energy/nuclear/euratom/euratom_en.htm* [accessed August 23, 2013]. See there for further information on Euratom.
[77] Art.86 Euratom.
[78] Art.85 Euratom.
[79] Art.52(2)(b) Euratom.
[80] Art.52(2)(b) Euratom. In 2007, e.g. the Agency concluded or was notified of, 58 contracts for natural uranium and 18 for special fissile material (Euratom Supply Agency, 2007 Report). See *Commission v France* (7/71) [1971] E.C.R. 1003; [1972] C.M.L.R. 453. See also *Kernkraftwerke Lippe-Ems v Commission* (C-161/97 P) [1999] E.C.R. I-2057, concerning, among other things, the conclusion of contracts and the powers of the Agency to refuse to do so.
[81] [2008] O.J. L41/15.

acquired, sold or transferred.[82] Currently, the supply of natural uranium, special fissile material and enrichment services to Union users and the provisions of services for the whole fuel cycle do not present any problems.[83] The Union depends on imports for some 94 per cent of its supplies of natural uranium.[84] Canada (18.15 per cent), Russia (24.65 per cent), Niger (16.92 per cent) and Australia (15.38 per cent) are the main suppliers of nuclear materials to the Union.[85]

35–12   The Council decided to support the creation of a nuclear fuel bank under the control of the International Atomic Energy Agency (IAEA). The Union contributes €25 million to this project. It is part of a wider effort aimed at establishing multilateral fuel supply mechanisms.[86]

In this context must also be mentioned the Euratom safeguards. In pursuance of the Euratom Treaty:

> "[T]he Commission must satisfy itself that, in the territories of the Member States, ores, source materials and special fissile materials are not diverted from their intended uses as declared by the users, and that the provisions relating to supply and any particular safeguarding obligation assumed by the Union, under an agreement concluded with a third State or an international organisation, are complied with".[87]

To fulfil those obligations, the Commission must carry out inspections and its inspectors have access to all places and data and all persons who, by reason of their occupation, deal with materials, equipment or installations which are subject to the Euratom safeguards. If serious irregularities are discovered, the Commission imposes sanctions.[88]

As far as the International Atomic Energy Agency (IAEA) is concerned, joint IAEA–Euratom safeguards are applied in certain Union installations in compliance with the Verification Agreement in force since 1973.[89] Safeguard provisions are an essential element in all the agreements which the Union has concluded with third-world countries.[90]

---

[82] See J.O. 777/60 [1959–1962] (manner in which demand is to be balanced against supply); J.O. 4057/66 (implementation of supply provisions) and J.O. 1460/60 and 240/64 (communications of the Agency). For the Rules of the Agency see [160] O.J. No. 60 and [1975] O.J. L 123/37.

[83] Directive 2003/55 concerning common rules for the internal market in natural gas [2003] O.J. L76/57, corrigendum [2004] O.J. L16/74.

[84] Directive 2003/55, above.

[85] Euratom Supply Agency 2007 Annual Report.

[86] General Report 2008, 89.

[87] Art.77 Euratom.

[88] See General Report 1992, 236. See also Decision 99/25, Euratom adopting a multi-annual programme (1998–2002) of actions in the nuclear sector, relating to the safe transport of radioactive materials and to safeguards and industry co-operation to promote certain aspects of safety of nuclear installations in the countries currently participating in the TACIS programme [1999] O.J. L7/31. See Bull. 12, 2003, 1.4.73: report on safeguards.

[89] See amendment to Council Declaration attached to the Decision approving the accession to the Vienna Convention, following a Court's ruling: *Commission v Council* (C-29/99) [2002] E.C.R. I–11221.

[90] Decision approving the accession to the Vienna Convention following *Commission v Council* (C-29/99) above, fn. 89. See also General Report 2003, 659.

6. NUCLEAR SAFETY

Various international conventions concern nuclear safety. The Council authorised **35–13**
the Member States, which are contracting parties to the 1960 Paris Convention on
Third Party Liability in the field of Nuclear Energy, to ratify, in the interest of the
Union, a Protocol amending that Convention, or to accede to it.[91] The Council
also called on the Member States to accede to the 1994 Vienna Convention on
Nuclear Safety and the Joint Convention on the Safety of Spent Fuel
Management and on the Safety of Radioactive Waste Management. The Council
has also approved the 1986 Convention on Early Notification of a Nuclear
Accident and on Assistance in the Case of Nuclear Accident or Radiological
Emergency.[92]

FURTHER READING

Christiane Trüe, "Legislative competences of the European Community in the **35–14**
energy sector: the 'Nuclear Package' of the Commission" (2003) E.L.Rev. 664.

Christopher W, "EU Energy Law in Europe", in Vol.2, *EU Competition law
and Energy markets* (Jones-Claeys & Casteels, 2005).

Martha M. Roggenkamp, Catherine Redgwell, Inigo del Guayo and Anita
Ronne, *Energy Law in Europe* (Oxford University Press, 2007).

---

[91] [2004] O.J. L97/53.
[92] General Report 2004, 176.

PART 6

External Action by the Union, the Common Foreign and Security Policy and Enlargement

INTRODUCTION

Contrary to the old EU and EC Treaties, both the actual Treaty on European Union and the TFEU contain extensive and co-ordinated provisions concerning the external activities of the Union. While the EU Treaty provides for general provisions concerning this action[1] and specific provisions on the Common Foreign and Security Policy (CFSP),[2] the TFEU[3] contains a new Part V "External action by the Union" consisting of:

VI–01

- "General provisions",
- "Common Commercial Policy",[4] and
- "Co-operation with third Countries and Humanitarian Aid", which, encompasses:
  - "Development Co-operation",[5]
  - "Economic, Financial and Technical Co-operation with Third Countries",[6]
  - "Humanitarian Aid",[7]
  - "Restrictive Measures",[8]
  - "International Agreements",[9]
  - "The Union's Relations with International Organisations and Third Countries and Union's Delegations"[10],
  - "Solidarity Clause"[11] and
  - the European Neighbourhood Policy

---

[1]   Arts 21 and 22 EU.
[2]   Arts 23 to 46 EU.
[3]   Arts 205 to 222 TFEU.
[4]   Arts 206 and 207 TFEU. See Ch.38: Common Commercial Policy and Relations with Third Countries.
[5]   Arts 208 to 211 TFEU. See Ch.39: Development Co-operation.
[6]   Arts 212 and 213 TFEU.
[7]   Art.214 TFEU.
[8]   Art.215 TFEU.
[9]   Arts 216 to 219 TFEU.
[10]   Arts 220 and 221 TFEU.
[11]   Art.222 TFEU.

The Treaties (TEU and TFEU) distinguish between the Union's "common foreign policy", which covers "all areas of foreign policy",[12] and the Union's "external action", which refers to a series of specific activities. Both must "be guided by the principles, pursue the objectives and be conducted in accordance with the general provisions laid down"[13] in the Treaty on European Union.[14]

All these provisions will be briefly examined hereafter, together with the Union's "Neighbouring Policy", however, not necessarily in the order they are mentioned above: the Common Foreign and Security Policy, the Common Commercial Policy and Development Co-operation are each examined in separate chapters below, after the chapter on the General Provisions concerning the Union's External Action. Enlargement will be examined in the last chapter of this book.

---

[12] Art.24(1) EU.
[13] Both Art.23 EU and Art.205 TFEU contain exactly the same text.
[14] EU Ch.I, Title V, Arts 21 and 22.

CHAPTER 36

General Provisions concerning the Union's External Action[1]

The EU Treaty provides, under the Title "General provisions on the Union's external action", that:

> "[T]he Union's action on the international scene, shall be guided by the principles which have inspired its own creation, development and enlargement, and which it seeks to advance in the wider world: democracy, the rule of law, the universality and indivisibility of human rights and fundamental freedoms, respect for human dignity, the principle of equality and solidarity, and respect for the principles of the United Nations Charter and international law."[2]

36–01

The Union must seek to develop relations and build partnerships with third countries and international, regional and global organisations which share the above principles.[3]

As will appear, the means provided to achieve those lofty objectives do not seem to be sufficient; this is probably due to the opposition from those Member States which resent any encroachment on their so-called national sovereignty, of which foreign affairs and defence are symbols. Nonetheless, over the years, the external competences of the Union were enlarged in several ways; first, by the simple fact that its internal competences were increased and these constitute the basis for external action,[4] and secondly, by the inclusion in the former EC Treaty of a new external policy: "Development Co-operation"[5] and finally, by the addition to the EU Treaty of "Provisions on a Common Foreign and Security Policy".[6] With regard to the competences of the Union that existed previously under the EC Treaty, except for the provisions concerning the conclusion of international agreements,[7] not much was changed however, and the CFSP remained under different institutional arrangements.

The Union must define and pursue common policies and actions and work to a high degree of co-operation in all fields of international relations, in order to:

36–02

---

[1] Arts 21 and 22 EU.
[2] Art.21(1)1 EU.
[3] Art.21(1)2 EU.
[4] As pointed out at the beginning of this book, the Union's competences were enlarged with Education, Culture, Public Health, Consumer Protection, Trans-European Networks, etc. Another example is the possibility for the Union to conclude agreements concerning monetary and foreign exchange regime matters, Art.219(3) TFEU.
[5] Arts 208–211 TFEU.
[6] Art.24 EU.
[7] Art.218 TFEU.

1. safeguard its values, fundamental interests, security, independence and integrity;
2. consolidate and support democracy, the rule of law, human rights and the principles of international law;
3. preserve peace, prevent conflicts and strengthen international security, in accordance with the purposes and principles of the United Nations Charter, with the principles of the Helsinki Final Act and with the aims of the Charter of Paris, including those relating to external borders;
4. foster the sustainable economic, social and environmental development of developing countries with the primary aim of eradicating poverty[8];
5. encourage the integration of all countries into the world economy, including the progressive abolition of restrictions on international trade;
6. help develop international measures to preserve and improve the quality of the environment and the management of natural resources;
7. assist populations, countries and regions confronting natural or man-made disasters[9];
8. promote an international system based on stronger multilateral co-operation and global governance.[10]

The Council and the Commission, assisted by the High Representative of the Union for Foreign Affairs and Security Policy ("High Representative"), must ensure consistency between the different areas of the Union's external action and between these and its other policies.

It is the task of the European Council to identify the strategic interests and objectives of the Union; its decisions may concern relations with a specific country or region or may be thematic in approach. They must define their duration, and the means to be made available by the Union and the Member States. The European Council must act unanimously on a recommendation from the Council or joint proposals from the High Representative and the Commission.[11]

36–03 One should realise that the absence, in the former EC Treaty, of provisions conferring upon the "Community", as it was then called, a general competence with regard to foreign policy, has not prevented it from developing a particularly active one. This was made possible, as will be seen, with the help of the Court. According to the latter the Union is a body created by an international treaty concluded between sovereign States with the task, among others, of exercising activities in the international field. This body enjoys international legal personality and participates in activities which come within the ambit of international law.[12]

However, it is only to the extent that other subjects of international law recognise the Union as a member of the international community, that it can take initiatives and play an active role in the international sphere. This recognition was never a problem. It was rather among the Member States that some disagreement existed as to the extent of the Union's jurisdiction in international affairs. The

---

[8] See Ch.39: Development Co-operation.
[9] See below, the chapter on Development Co-operation (4. Humanitarian Aid).
[10] Art.21(2) EU.
[11] Art.22 EU.
[12] *Commission v Council* (22/70), [1971] E.C.R. 263.

question was raised mainly with regard to the Union's treaty-making power; in other words, how much of the Member States' treaty-making power was transferred to the Union? That some powers were transferred was not questioned, but it was not clear whether those powers were to be exercised exclusively by the Union or in conjunction with the Member States. The views of the Court were formulated in 1971[13] and repeated in later judgments. They were based on the former EC Treaty that provides that, "the Community shall have legal personality".[14] According to the Court, this provision, placed at the head of Part Six of the Treaty devoted to "General and Final Provisions", means that in its external relations, the Union enjoys the capacity to enter into international commitments over the whole field of objectives defined in Part One of the Treaty, which Part Six supplements. The following statement is also important:

> "[T]o establish in a particular case whether the [Union] has authority to enter into international commitments, regard must be had to the whole scheme of [Union] law no less than to its substantive provisions. Such authority arises not only from express conferment by the Treaty but may equally flow implicitly from other provisions of the Treaty, from the Act of accession and from measures adopted within the framework of those provisions, by the [Union] institutions."[15]

In other words, whenever Union law has created powers for the institutions, **36–04** within the internal system, for the purpose of attaining a specific objective, the Union has authority to enter into the international commitments necessary for the attainment of that objective, even in the absence of an express provision in that connection.[16] This is particularly so in all cases where internal power has already been used by the Union institutions in order to adopt measures which come within the attainment of common policies.[17]

With regard to the second question (exclusive or shared jurisdiction), the Court admits a "mixed procedure", i.e. both the Union and the Member States are the contracting parties when an agreement covers matters for which the Union is competent and others coming within the ambit of the Member States.[18] Mixed

---

[13] *Commission v Council* (better known as the *AETR* case: Accord Européen sur les Transports Routiers (European Road Transport Agreement)) (22/70) [1971] E.C.R. 263, para.14; [1971] C.M.L.R. 335. See also the Opinions of the Court given under former Art.300(6) EC (now 218(11)): Opinion 1/75 [1975] E.C.R. 1355, compatibility with the EEC Treaty of a draft "Understanding on a Local Cost Standard" drawn up under the auspices of the OECD; Opinion 1/76 [1977] E.C.R. 741, compatibility of a draft agreement establishing a European lying-up Fund for inland waterway vessels; Opinion 1/78 [1979] E.C.R. 2871 compatibility of the draft International Agreement on Natural Rubber negotiated in the UNCTAD; *Commission v Council* (C-25/94) [1996] E.C.R. I-1469; *Kramer* (Joined Cases 3/76, 4/76 and 6/76) [1976] E.C.R. 1279; [1976] 2 C.M.L.R. 440; Opinion 2/91, [1993] E.C.R. I-1061; [1993] 3 C.M.L.R. 800 concerning the compatibility of the ILO Convention 170 on safety in the use of chemicals at work; and Opinion 1/94 [1994] E.C.R. I-5267.
[14] Former Art.281 EC.
[15] *Commission v Council* (22/70) (quoted above) at para.17–18. In its Opinion 2/91, the Court expressed it as follows: "Whenever [Union] law created for the institutions of the [Union] powers within its internal system for the purpose of attaining a specific objective, the [Union] has authority to enter into the international commitments necessary for the attainment of that objective even in the absence of an express provision in that connection."
[16] Opinion 1/76: Lying-up Fund (quoted above), at 755.
[17] Opinion 1/76: Lying-up Fund, above.
[18] Opinion 1/76: Lying-up Fund, above at para.7. In Opinion 2/91 (quoted above) the Court came to the conclusion that the ILO Convention 170 is a matter which falls within the joint competence of the

agreements require concurrent ratifications and collaboration—sincere co-operation in the spirit of art.4(3) TEU between Member State authorities and the EU institutions to adopt a concerted strategy and to ensure consistency of results and avoiding the frustration of EU objectives and the scope of application of EU law.[19] However:

> "[E]ach time the [Union], with a view to implementing a common policy envisaged by the Treaty, adopts provisions laying down common rules, whatever form these may take, the Member States no longer have the right, acting individually or even collectively, to undertake obligations with third countries which affect those rules".[20]

However, as long as the Union has not exercised its right to conclude agreements, the Member States retain the power to do so.[21] Nonetheless, this authority is only of a transitional nature and Member States are bound by Union obligations in their negotiations with third countries: they may not enter into or renew any commitment which could hinder the Union in the carrying out of the tasks entrusted to it by the Treaties.[22]

36–05 The emergence of a Union competence should not, however, be seen as a -sudden break; Union law being "evolutive", the transfer of power from the Member States to the Union is necessarily gradual.[23] In some cases international conventions, especially in the field of private international family law or in the law of obligations (Rome I and II, and Brussels II bis[24]), might be restricted to States and even if there is recognised Union (shared) competence, the EU cannot sign it, only the Member States can, assuming they are authorised by the EU. There is also the question of the consequences for the Union and Union law of collective international commitments undertaken by the Member States before the establishment of the Union. Here the Court has, through various judgments, formulated the basic principles. For instance, with regard to tariffs and trade policy the Member States have progressively transferred to the Union their

---

Member States and the Union. As the Court mentioned in its Opinion 3/94 [1995] E.C.R. I-4577, with regard to the Uruguay Round multilateral negotiations, the Council adopted Decision 94/800 concerning the conclusion, on behalf of the European Union, "as regards matters within its competence". The other matters were adopted by the Member States.

[19] *Commission v Sweden* (C-246/07) [2010] ECR I-3317.

[20] *AETR* (22/70) (quoted above) at para.17.

[21] See answer to Parliamentary question no.173/77 [1978] O.J. C72/1.

[22] *Kramer* (Joined Cases 3/76, 4/76 and 6/76) (quoted above) at para.40. See also Art.351 TFEU: agreements concluded, before January 1, 1958 or before accession, between one or more Member States and one or more third countries are not affected by the entry into force of the Treaty. Art.267 TFEU (preliminary ruling) takes effect only if the agreement imposes on a Member State an obligation that is incompatible with the Treaty: *Evans Medical and MacFarlan Smith* (C-324/93) [1995] E.C.R. I-563.

[23] *AETR* (22/70) (quoted above) at para.81–92.

[24] Two Regulations adopted in 2009 are examples to the point: Regulation 662/2009 [2009] O.J. L200 establishing a procedure for the negotiation and conclusion of agreements between Member States and third countries on particular matters concerning the law applicable to contractual and non-contractual obligations; and Council Regulation No.664/2009 [2009] O.J. L200 establishing a procedure for the negotiation and conclusion of agreements between Member States and third countries concerning jurisdiction, recognition and enforcement of judgments and decisions in matrimonial matters, matters of parental responsibility and matters relating to maintenance obligations, and the law applicable to matters relating to maintenance obligations.

jurisdiction. By doing so they have also conferred upon the Union the international rights and obligations connected with the exercise of this jurisdiction, particularly with regard to the General Agreement on Tariffs and Trade (GATT), now World Trade Organisation (WTO). It follows that the Union itself is bound by that agreement.[25] This constitutes a clear case of substitution of the Union for the Member States in the implementation of multilateral treaties bearing on the subject matter of the Treaty.

As for the rights which derive for the Union from those agreements, their exercise depends on recognition of the Union by the other contracting parties; as -mentioned, this was never a problem. The internal problems of the Union in this field may not, of course, obliterate the interests of third countries. In the various Court statements referred to above, this principle was underlined several times.[26] However, third States may not intervene in internal matters of the Union and, more particularly, in the determination of the very complex and delicate relationship between the Union and its own Member States.[27]

1. ECONOMIC, FINANCIAL AND TECHNICAL CO-OPERATION WITH THIRD COUNTRIES[28]

This action of the Union concerns third countries other than developing countries. It must carry out economic, financial and technical co-operation measures, including assistance and financial assistance. Those measures must be consistent with the Union's "development policy" examined below and with the principles and objectives of its external action, described above.

36–06

Since this Union activity concerns a, "shared competence between the Union and the Member States", it has competence to carry out activities and conduct a common policy, which may not, however, result in Member States being prevented from exercising theirs.[29] The Union's operations and those of the Member States must complement and reinforce each other.[30] Parliament and the Council, acting in accordance with the ordinary legislative procedure,[31] must adopt the necessary measures.

Within their respective spheres of competence, the Union and the Member States co-operate with third countries and the competent international organisations (see point 5 below). The arrangements for such co-operation may be the

---

[25] *International Fruit Company v Produktschap voor Groenten en Fruit* (Joined Cases 21/72, 22/72, 23/72 and 24/72) [1972] E.C.R. 1219 at para. 18; [1975] 2 C.M.L.R. 1. The Union has assumed those powers in pursuance of Arts 206 and 207 TFEU. See also *Nederlandse Spoorwegen v Inspecteur der invoerrechten en accijnzen* (38/75) [1975] E.C.R. 1439 at 1450(21); [1976] 1 C.M.L.R. 1; *Amministrazione delle Finanze dello Stato v SPI and SAMI* (Joined Cases 267/81, 268/81 and 269/81) [1983] E.C.R. 801; [1984] 1 C.M.L.R. 334; and *Singer and Geigy v Amministrazione delle Finanze dello Stato* (Joined Cases 290/81 and 291/81) [1983] E.C.R. 847.

[26] See, for example, Opinion 1/75: Local Cost Standards and Opinion 1/76, Laying-up Fund, both quoted above.

[27] Ruling 1/78 [1978] E.C.R. 2151, compatibility with the Euratom Treaty of a draft Convention of the IAEA on the Physical Protection of Nuclear Materials, Facilities and Transport.

[28] Arts 212 and 213 TFEU.

[29] Art.4(4) TFEU.

[30] Art.212(1) TFEU.

[31] See Art.294 TFEU.

subject of agreements between the Union and the third parties concerned (see point 4 below) but, the Member States retain the right to negotiate in international bodies and to conclude international agreements on their own, except, of course, in matters that have been dealt with already by the Union, since it is not possible for Member States to assume obligations which might affect Union rules or alter their scope.[32]

36–07   As already indicated, Member States consider these relations with third countries and international organisations as important symbols of what is left, according to them, of their "sovereignty",[33] and refuse to include these relations within common Union actions. This dichotomy enfeebles the Union's external influence, since it is not only unable to speak with one voice in the world bodies, but presents to the rest of the world a very divided image,[34] which does not correspond to its economic weight as the largest economic unit in the world.

The TFEU also provides that when the situation in a third country requires urgent financial assistance from the Union, the Council shall adopt the necessary decisions on a proposal from the Commission.[35] It is interesting to note that no legislative procedure is prescribed in this case. In this sense, a Guarantee Fund for external action was established.[36]

2. HUMANITARIAN AID[37]

36–08   Under the former EC Treaty, Humanitarian Aid was part of "Development Co-operation", but now constitutes an independent Union activity. It is intended to provide ad hoc assistance and relief and protection for people in third countries who are victims of natural or man-made disasters,[38] in order to meet the humanitarian needs resulting from these different situations. Here again the TFEU provides that the, "Union's measures and those of the Member States shall complement and reinforce each other"[39]; the Commission may take any useful initiative to promote co-ordination between actions of the Union and those of the Member States in order to enhance the efficiency and complementary nature of each other's measures. The TFEU also provides that, "humanitarian aid operations shall be conducted in compliance with the principles of international law and with the principle of impartiality, neutrality and non-discrimination".[40] The TFEU also provides that:

---

[32] See *Commission v Greece* (C-45/07) [2009] E.C.R. I-701.

[33] Needless to say that in the present world the freedom of countries to operate in total independence (sovereignty) is extremely limited: their inter-dependence with other countries and international institutions, in every field, indeed dictates most of their actions.

[34] Remember what Henry Kissinger, US Foreign Secretary, said: "the EU lacks a single telephone number for foreign leaders to call when they want to speak to 'Europe'".

[35] Art.213 TFEU.

[36] Regulation 480/09 [2009] O.J. L145/10.

[37] Art.214 TFEU.

[38] This distinction is relative, since many natural disasters are linked to climate change, and the human causes of climate change are obvious.

[39] Art.214(1) TFEU.

[40] Art.214(2) TFEU.

"[I]n the areas of development cooperation and humanitarian aid, the Union shall have competence to carry out activities and conduct a common policy; however the exercise of the competence shall not result in Member States being prevented from exercising theirs."[41]

Parliament and the Council are to establish the measures defining the framework within which the Union's humanitarian aid operations are to be implemented.

The principal objectives of the humanitarian aid operations are, according to existing provisions, the following:

36–09

- save and preserve life during emergencies and their immediate aftermath and natural disasters;
- provide assistance and relief to people affected by longer-lasting crises;
- help finance the transport of aid;
- carry out short-term rehabilitation and reconstruction work;
- cope with the consequences of population movements;
- assure preparedness for risks of natural disasters;
- support civil operations to protect the victims of fighting and comparable emergencies.

To carry out those tasks, the European Office for Emergency Humanitarian Aid (ECHO) was set up in 1996. In recent years, assistance has been granted, among others, to victims of the war in the former Yugoslavia and victims of conflicts in Afghanistan, Armenia, Azerbaijan and Tajikistan, and more recently Africa, especially the Horn of Africa.

In order to underpin existing Union policies and programmes (such as -development aid, macro-financial aid, aid for economic, regional and technical co-operation, aid for reconstruction, for refugees and displaced persons, etc.) and to enable the Union to take urgent action to help re-establish or safeguard normal conditions, a Rapid Reaction Fund was set up. It is referred to as "the Rapid Reaction Mechanism".[42]

A very interesting novelty introduced by the Lisbon Treaty is the setting up of a European Voluntary Humanitarian Aid Corps: a framework for joint contributions from young Europeans to the humanitarian aid operations of the Union.[43] Parliament and the Council, acting by means of regulations in accordance with the ordinary legislative procedure,[44] will determine the rules and procedures for the operation of the Corps.

36–10

The Union may conclude with third countries and competent international organisations any agreement helping to achieve the objectives of humanitarian aid. It must ensure that its humanitarian aid operations are co-ordinated and consistent with those of international organisations and bodies, in particular those forming part of the United Nations system.

---

[41] Art.4(4) TFEU.
[42] Regulation 381/2001 [2001] O.J. L57/5.
[43] Art.214(5) TFEU.
[44] Art.294 TFEU.

3.   RESTRICTIVE MEASURES[45]

36–11   When a decision adopted under the Special Provisions on the Common Foreign and Security Policy[46] provides for the interruption or reduction, in part or completely, of economic and financial relations with one or more third countries, the Council, acting by a qualified majority on a joint proposal from the High Representative and the Commission, shall adopt the necessary measures. The Council must inform Parliament. Such measures were already provided for under the previous EU Treaty.[47]

Under the same conditions, the Council may adopt restrictive measures against natural or legal persons and groups and non-State entities.

The TFEU adds that those acts shall, "include necessary provisions on legal safeguards."[48]

4.   INTERNATIONAL AGREEMENTS[49]

36–12   The TFEU provides for four cases in which the Union may conclude an agreement with one or more third countries or international organisations:

- where the Treaties so provide,[50]
- where the conclusion of an agreement is necessary in order to achieve, within the framework of the Union policies, one of the objectives referred to in the Treaties,
- where it is provided for in a legally binding Union act, and
- where it is likely to affect common rules or alter their scope.

It should be noted that such agreements constitute, "acts of the institutions of the Union" and as such can be challenged in the courts as to their compatibility with the Treaties.[51] In the second place, provisions of international agreements concluded by the Union in conformity with the procedures provided for in the Treaties (see below), "are binding upon the institutions of the Union and on its Member States".[52] Such provisions are directly applicable in the Union. They can

---

[45] Art.215 TFEU.

[46] Arts 23 to 46 EU.

[47] Title IV of the former EU Treaty. See, for instance, restrictive measures against the Democratic Republic of the Congo [2009] O.J. L106/60.

[48] Art.215(3) TFEU.

[49] Arts 216 to 219 TFEU.

[50] See, for instance, point 2 above.

[51] Arts 263 and 267 TFEU.

[52] Art.216(2) TFEU. See also Opinion 1/76, Laying-up Fund (quoted above), para. 6 and 7. See especially *Kupferberg* (104/81) [1982] E.C.R. 3641: according to Art. 216(2) TFEU, Member States are bound in the same manner as the institutions of the Union, by the international agreement which the latter are empowered to conclude. When they ensure respect for commitments arising from an agreement concluded by the Union institutions, they fulfill an obligation, not only in relation to the non-member country concerned, but also and above all in relation to the Union, which has assumed responsibility for the due performance of the agreement. That is why the provisions of such an agreement form an integral part of the Union legal system. It follows from the Union nature of such provisions that their effect in the Union may not be allowed to vary according to whether this

also have direct effect. Indeed, an agreement concluded by the Union with third countries must be considered as having direct effect when, taking into account its provisions and the object and nature of the agreement, it contains a clear and precise obligation, which is not submitted, in its implementation or effects, to a subsequent act. International agreements also override conflicting provisions of Member States' domestic law.[53]

The Union may conclude with one or more third countries or international organisations agreements establishing an association involving reciprocal rights and obligations, common action and special procedure.[54]

Procedures for the Adoption of International Agreements by the Union

Taking into account that special procedures are provided for the conclusion of **36–13** international agreements within the framework of the common commercial -policy,[55] agreements between the Union and third countries or international organisations shall be negotiated and concluded in accordance with the following procedure,[56] under which it is the Council, acting by a qualified majority,[57] that authorises the opening of negotiations, adopts negotiating directives, authorises the signing of agreements and concludes them. Parliament must be fully and immediately informed at all the stages of the procedure.

- The Commission (or the High Representative when the agreement relates exclusively or principally to the Common Foreign and Security Policy) submits recommendations to the Council;
- the Council adopts a decision authorising the opening of negotiations and,
- depending on the subject of the agreement, nominating the Union negotiator or the head of the Union's negotiating team;
- the Council may address directives to the negotiator and designate a special committee in consultation with which the negotiations must be conducted;
- the Council, on a proposal by the negotiator, adopts a decision authorising the signing of the agreement and, if necessary, its provisional application before entry into force;
- except where the agreement relates exclusively to the Foreign and Security Policy,[58] the Council, on a proposal by the negotiator, adopts a decision concluding the agreement, either, after obtaining the consent of Parliament in the following cases:
  - association agreement;

---

application is in practice the responsibility of the Union institutions or of the Member States. Violation by a Member State of obligations resulting from such an international agreement engages the responsibility of said Member State.

[53] *Bresciani v Amministrazione Italiana delle Finanze* (87/75) [1976] E.C.R. 129 at 141(23); [1976] 2 C.M.L.R. 62. See also *Razanatsimba* (65/77) [1977] E.C.R. 2229; [1978] 1 C.M.L.R. 246; *Demuel* (12/86) [1987] E.C.R. 3719(14).

[54] Art.217 TFEU.

[55] See Art.207 TFEU.

[56] Art.218 TFEU.

[57] Unanimity is required where it is required for the adoption of a Union act, for instance: association agreements.

[58] In which case the recommendation to negotiate can come from the High Representative.

- agreement on the Union accession to the European Convention for the Protection of Human Rights and Fundamental Freedoms[59];
- agreement establishing a specific institutional framework by organising co-operation procedures;
- agreements with important budgetary implications for the Union;
- agreements covering fields to which either the ordinary legislative pro-cedure[60] applies, or the special legislative procedure,[61] where consent by Parliament is required, in the latter case the Council and Parliament may agree upon a time limit for consent, or, after consulting Parliament in other cases; Parliament must deliver its opinion within a time limit set by the Council depending on the urgency of the matter; in the absence of an opinion the Council may act.

36–14 When concluding an agreement, the Council may authorise the negotiator to approve, on behalf of the Union, modifications to the agreement where it provides for them to be adopted by a simplified procedure or by a body set up by the agreement. The Council may attach specific conditions to such authorisation.[62] However, when a body set up by an agreement is called upon to adopt acts having legal effects, the Council, on a proposal from the Commission or the High Representative, shall adopt a decision suspending the application of an agreement and establishing the position to be adopted on the Union's behalf in the said body.[63]

Member States, Parliament, the Council and the Commission may obtain an opinion of the Court as to whether the envisaged agreement is compatible with the Treaties. Where the opinion is adverse, the agreement may not enter into force unless it is amended or the Treaties revised.[64]

Special rules are provided for agreements on an exchange-rate system or concerning monetary or foreign exchange regime matters.[65]

The TFEU also provides that Member States may negotiate in international bodies and conclude international agreements without prejudice to Union competence and Union agreements, as regards economic and monetary union.[66]

---

[59] In this case the Council must act unanimously and the decision must be approved by the Member States: Art.118(8) TFEU.

[60] Art.294 TFEU.

[61] Art.189 TFEU.

[62] Art.118(7) TFEU.

[63] Art.118(9) TFEU.

[64] Art.218(11) TFEU.

[65] Art.219(1),(2),(3) TFEU.

[66] Art.219(4) TFEU.

5. THE UNION'S RELATIONS WITH INTERNATIONAL ORGANISATIONS AND THIRD COUNTRIES AND THE UNION'S DELEGATIONS[67]

Under the EC Treaty it was for the Commission to, "ensure the maintenance of all appropriate relations with the organs of the United Nations",[68] it is now the Union, acting via the High Representative and the Commission,[69] which establishes:

36–15

> "[A]ll appropriate forms of cooperation with the organs of the United Nations and its Specialised Agencies, the Council of Europe, the Organisation for Security and Cooperation in Europe and the Organisation for Economic Cooperation and Development."

The Union is to maintain also such relations as are appropriate with other international organisations.

(1) The Union's Right of Passive and Active Legation

With regard to diplomatic representation with the Union, the only relevant Treaty provisions are to be found in the Protocol on the Privileges and Immunities.[70] The Member States in whose territory the Union has its seats, shall accord the customary diplomatic immunities and privileges to missions of third countries accredited to the Union.[71] Reference can also be made to the Statement issued after the extraordinary meeting of the Council in January 1966, held in Luxembourg. It provides that the credentials of the Heads of Missions of non-Member States accredited to the Union will be submitted jointly to the President of the Council and the President of the Commission, meeting together for this purpose.

36–16

(2) The Union Delegations/The European External Action Service[72]

The representatives of the Union in third countries enjoy the same diplomatic immunities and privileges. This is the case also for the Commission delegations to various third countries and International Organisations such as the WTO, the OECD, the United Nations and its Specialised Agencies.

36–17

The TFEU now provides that the Union is represented in third countries and at international organisations by "Union delegations",[73] which are placed under the

---

[67] Arts 220 and 221 TFEU.

[68] Former Art.302 EC.

[69] Art.220(2) TFEU.

[70] Annexed to the Merger Treaty. Another mention is to be found, but in a different context, in Part Two of the TFEU concerning "Citizenship": every citizen of the Union shall, in the territory of a third country in which the Member State of which he is a national is not represented, be entitled to protection by the diplomatic or consular authorities of any Member State, Art.23 TFEU

[71] TFEU Protocol No.7, Art.10. For a list of the accredited missions, see "Corps diplomatique accredité auprés des Communautés Européennes", Directorate-General External Relations.

[72] Art.27(3) EU.

[73] Art.221(1) TFEU.

authority of the High Representative and that they shall act in close co-operation with Member States' diplomatic and consular missions.

The European External Action Service[74] is a functionally autonomous body of the Union assisting and supporting and under the authority of the High Representative. This service somehow constitutes in all aspects but name, the "diplomatic corps" of the Union. The Service works in co-operation with the diplomatic services of the Member States and comprises geographically representative officials from relevant departments of the General Secretariat of the Council and of the Commission as well as staff seconded from national diplomatic (and consular) services of the Member States,.

36–18 The organisation and functioning of the Service is established by a decision of the Council which acts on a proposal from the High Representative after consulting Parliament and after obtaining the consent[75] of the Commission. It comprises a central administration with directorates-general and under the direction of an executive Secretary-General and the external delegations of the Union, each guided by a head of delegation It was established in 2010.[76] See also Draft Declaration by the High Representative on political accountability.[77]

Without it being more explicitly provided for in the Treaty, the Union thus exercises the right of active and passive legation.

6. SOLIDARITY CLAUSE[78]

36–19 Under this title the TFEU provides for joint action by the Union and the Member States in case a Member State is the object of a terrorist attack or the victim of a natural or man-made disaster. If this happens, the Union must mobilise all the instruments at its disposal, including the military resources made available by the Member States, in order to:

- prevent the terrorist threat,
- protect democratic institutions and the civilian population, and
- assist a Member State in its territory, at the request of its political authorities.

Similarly, the other Member States must assist it and co-ordinate their action within the Council.

The arrangements for the implementation of the Solidarity Clause shall be defined by a Council decision acting on a joint proposal from the Commission and the High Representative. Where this decision has defence implications the Council must act unanimously and legislative acts are excluded.[79] The Council

---

[74] Art.27(3) EU. See *http://www.eeas.europa.eu/background/organisation/index_en.htm* [accessed August 23, 2013].

[75] This term is normally used in relation to the involvement of Parliament in the legislative procedure: it confers what amounts to a veto right.

[76] [2010] O.J. L201/30.For the conditions of employment see Regulation 1080/10 [2010] O.J. L311/1 and for the budgetary aspects, see Regulation 1081/10 [2010] O.J. L311/9.

[77] [2010] O.J. C210/1.

[78] Art.222 TFEU.

[79] Art.31(1) EU.

shall be assisted, as always, by COREPER, but also by the Political and Security Committee (PSC)[80] and by the standing committee set up within the Council to ensure that operational co-operation on internal security is promoted and strengthened within the Union.[81]

The European Council must regularly assess the threats facing the Union in order to enable the Union and the Member States to take effective action.[82]

7. THE EUROPEAN NEIGHBOURHOOD POLICY (ENP)[83]

This policy was developed in 2004 with the object of avoiding the emergence of new dividing lines between the enlarged EU and its neighbours, and instead, strengthening the prosperity, stability and security of all concerned, in line with the EU Security Strategy of December 12, 2003. The EU offers its neighbours a "privileged relationship" based upon a mutual commitment to common values: democracy and human rights, the rule of law, good governance, market economy principles and sustainable development. It goes beyond existing relationships; it remains distinct from the process of enlargement. It applies to the Union's immediate neighbours by land and sea: Algeria, Armenia,[84] Azerbaijan,[85] Belarus, Egypt,[86] Georgia,[87] Israel (associated), Jordan,[88] Lebanon,[89] Libya, Moldavia,[90] Morocco,[91] Occupied Palestinian Territory,[92] Syria, Tunisia[93] and Ukraine.[94]

36–20

The central element of the ENP is the bilateral ENP Action Plans agreed between the Union and each partner. The Action Plans are built upon existing agreements such as *Partnership and Co-operation Agreements (see hereunder)* or Association Agreements in the framework of the Euro-Mediterranean Partnership Those action plans or individual country programmes support cross-border contacts and co-operation between regional actors and civil society.[95]

---

[80] The PSC is the permanent body in the field of foreign and security policy; see Ch.37: Common Foreign and Security Policy.

[81] Art.71 TFEU.

[82] Art.222(4) TFEU.

[83] Regulation 1638/06 [2006] O.J. L310/1, laying down general provisions establishing a European Neighbourhood and Partnership Instrument. See General Report 2009, 59 and implementing Regulation 435/11 [2011] O.J. L118/1.

[84] The overall allocation for 2007–2010 for Armenia: €964 million.

[85] Allocation for Azerbaijan: €92 million.

[86] Allocation for Egypt: €558 million.

[87] Allocation for Georgia: €170 million.

[88] Allocation for Jordan: €265 million.

[89] Alloation for Lebanon: €187 million.

[90] Allocation for Moldavia: €250 million. See Decision providing macro-financial assistance: [2010] O.J. L277/1.

[91] Allocation for Morocco: €654 million.

[92] Allocation for Palestine: €664 million.

[93] Allocation for Tunisia: €300 million.

[94] Allocation for Ukraine: €500 million.

[95] See ENPI Cross-Border Co-operation Strategic Paper.

The European Neighbourhood and Partnership Instrument (ENPI),[96] which from January 1, 2007 replaced the MEDA, TACIS and various other instruments, was established in 2006 and a Regulation laying down implementing rules, for cross--border co-operation programmes financed under the ENP, was issued in 2007.[97]

(1) Eastern Partnership[98]

36–21 The countries concerned are: Armenia, Azerbaijan, Georgia, Moldova and the Ukraine, and not completely, Belarus. The Commission put forward concrete ideas for enhancing the relationship between the Union and those countries. This will imply new association agreements including deep and comprehensive free trade agreements with those countries willing and able to enter into a deeper engagement and gradual integration into the Union's economy. The partnership will promote democracy and good governance, strengthen energy security, promote sector reform and environment protection, encourage people to people contacts, support economic and social development and offer additional funding for projects to reduce socio-economic imbalances and increase stability.

Between 2007 and 2010, Armenia received €98.4 million, Azerbaijan: 92, Georgia: 120.4, Moldova: 209.7 and Ukraine: 494.[99]

In 2011 Parliament announced the constitution of the *Euronest Parliamentary Assembly* as the parliamentary institution of the Eastern Partnership.[100]

(2) Partnership and Co-operation Agreements (PCAs)[101]

36–22 These apply to Russia, Eastern Europe, the Southern Caucasus and central Asia. The aim of these agreements is to strengthen their democracies and develop their economies through co-operation in a wide range of areas and through political dialogue. A Co-operation Council has been set up to ensure implementation of the agreements.

PCAs were concluded[102] with Armenia, Azerbaijan, Georgia, Kazakhstan, the Kyrgyz Republic, Moldova,[103] the Russian Federation, Ukraine,[104] Uzbekistan and Tajikistan.

---

[96] Regulation 1638/06 [2006] O.J. L310/1. For the period 2007–2013 approximately €12 billion in Union funding is available, of which each cross-border co-operation programme receives €1 billion.

[97] Regulation 951/07 [2007] O.J. L210/10, corrigendum [2009] O.J. L221/7.

[98] From *http://www.eeas.europa.eu/eastern/index_en.htm* [accessed August 23, 2013].

[99] EUROPA—Press releases Eastern partnership.

[100] [2011] O.J. C198/4.

[101] For more information, see *http://europa.eu/legislation_summaries/external_relations/relations_ with_third_countries/eastern_europe_and_central_asia/r17002_en.htm* [accessed August 23, 2013].

[102] Council and Commission Decisions 99/602/EC, 99/614/EC, 99/515/EC, 99/490/EC, 99/491/EC, 98/401/EC, 97/800/EC, 98/149/EC, 99/593/EC, 2009/989/EC on the conclusion of the Partnership and Cooperation Agreement between the European Communities and their Member States, of the one part, and the Republic of Armenia, the Republic of Azerbaijan, Georgia, the Republic of Kazakhstan, the Kyrgyz Republic, the Republic of Moldova, the Russian Federation, Ukraine, and the Republic of Uzbekistan, Tajikistan of the other part, respectively.

[103] A Protocol to the PCA on the general principles for the participation of Moldova in Union programmes was added: [2011] O.J. L14/2.

[104] Conclusion of a Protocol to the PCA on the general principles for the participation of Ukraine in Union programmes [2011] O.J. L18/1.

FURTHER READING

Panos Koutrakos, "Primary law and policy in EU external relations—moving   **36–23**
away from the big picture" (2008) 33 E.L.Review 666.

Marise Cremona and Bruno De Witte, *EU Foreign Relations Law: Constitutional Fundamentals* (Oxford, Hart Publishing, 2008).

Rass Holdgaard, *External Relations Law of the European Community* (Kluwer Law International, 2009).

CHAPTER 37

The Common Foreign and Security Policy[1] (CFSP)

37–01

The Preamble to the EU Treaty refers, among others, to the implementation of:

"a common foreign and security policy including the progressive framing of a common defence policy, which might lead to a common defence in accordance with the provisions of Article 4 [concerning the common security and defence policy],[2] thereby reinforcing the European identity and its independence in order to promote peace, security and progress in Europe and in the world.[3] It follows that the 'Common Foreign and Security Policy' includes a 'Common Security and Defence Policy'.

The Union's competences in the field of the Common Foreign and Security Policy (CFSP) cover all areas of foreign policy and all questions relating to the Union's security, including the progressive framing of a defence policy that might lead to a common defence.[4]

The CFSP is subject to specific rules and procedures: it is defined and implemented by the European Council and the Council acting unanimously, unless otherwise provided in the Treaties. The adoption of legislative acts is excluded; it shall be put into effect by the High Representative of the Union for Foreign Affairs and Security policy, and by Member States; there is a specific role for Parliament and for the Commission. The Court has no jurisdiction with respect to the provisions relating to the CFSP and the acts adopted under it.[5] However, the Court has jurisdiction to monitor compliance with the strict separation of the procedures and the extent of the powers of the institutions, laid down by the Treaties, for the exercise of the competences referred to in Articles 3 to 6 of the TFEU and the implementation of the CFSP,[6] and to review the legality of certain 'decisions providing for restrictive measures against natural or legal persons'.[7]"

The CFSP must be conducted, defined and implemented based on the development of mutual political solidarity among Member States, the identification of questions of general interest and the achievement of an ever increasing degree of convergence of the Member States' actions.[8]

---

[1] Arts 23–41 EU.
[2] Provisions on the common security and defence policy.
[3] EU Preamble, para.11.
[4] Art.24(1) EU.
[5] Art.24(1)2 EU.
[6] Art.40 EU.
[7] Art.275 TFEU.
[8] Art.24(2) EU.

The Council and the High Representative shall ensure compliance with the above principles.[9]

The CFSP is conducted by:

1. defining the general guidelines;
2. adopting decisions defining:
   (a) actions to be undertaken by the Union[10];
   (b) positions to be taken by the Union; and
   (c) arrangements for the implementation of these decisions;
3. strengthening systematic co-operation between Member States in the conduct of policy.[11]

37–02   The European Council identifies the Union's strategic interests, determines the objectives and defines general guidelines, while the Council takes the necessary decisions for defining and implementing the CFSP; the latter and the High Representative ensure the unity, consistency and effectiveness of actions by the Union.[12]

Where the international situation requires operational action, the Council adopts the necessary decisions that lay down the objectives, scope, the means to be made available to the Union, if necessary their duration and the conditions of their implementation. Those decisions shall commit the Member States in the positions they adopt and in the conduct of their activity.[13] These operational actions correspond to the "joint actions"[14] previously provided for in the EU Treaty.

The Council also adopts decisions that define the approach of the Union to a particular matter of a geographical or thematic nature.[15] They correspond to the former "common positions".

37–03   As indicated, decisions with regard to the CFSP are taken by the European Council and the Council acting unanimously; however, there are exceptions.[16]

Member States must consult one another within the European Council and the Council on any matter of foreign and security policy of general interest in order to determine a common approach.[17] The latter may be defined by the European Council or the Council. Member States must co-ordinate their action in international organisations and conferences. Member States that are also members of the United Nations Security Council must concert and keep the other Member States and the High Representative fully informed.[18]

---

[9] Art.24(3),3 EU. The Treaty does not indicate how they are supposed to do this.

[10] See, for instance, Joint Action 2008/124/CFSP on the European Union rule of law mission in Kosovo [2008] O.J. L42/22 and the agreement with the Swiss Confederation on its participation in it [2008] O.J. L217/23.

[11] Art.25 EU.

[12] Art.26 EU.

[13] Art.28 EU.

[14] In 2008, more than 30 Joint Actions and more than 20 Common Positions concerned the Balkans, South Caucasus, Asia, Africa, Indian Ocean, the Middle East and Eastern Europe, the European Security Strategy and the European Security and Defence Policy; see General Report 2008, 201.

[15] Art.29 EU.

[16] See Art.31(2) EU.

[17] Art.32 EU.

[18] Art.34(2)2 EU.

A Special Representative may be appointed by the Council with a mandate in relation to particular policy issues.[19]

Diplomatic and consular missions of the Member States and the Commission Delegations in third countries and international conferences, and their representations to international organisations, shall co-operate in ensuring that decisions defining Union positions and actions adopted pursuant to the EU Chapter on CFSP are complied with and implemented.[20]   **37–04**

The Treaty provides that the Union may conclude international agreements in implementation of the CFSP.[21]

A Political and Security Committee[22] was set up to monitor the international situation in the areas covered by the CFSP and to contribute to the definition of policies by delivering opinions to the Council, at the request of the Council or of the High Representative, or on its own initiative. The Committee exercises, under the responsibility of the Council and of the High Representative the political control and strategic direction of crisis management operations provided for under the Common Security and Defence Policy.[23] The Committee may be authorised by the Council to take the relevant decisions[24] concerning political control and strategic direction of the operations.

It should be noted that the implementation of the CFSP does not affect the application of the procedures and the extent of the powers of the institutions laid down by the Treaties for the exercise of the Union competences referred to in the TFEU.[25]   **37–05**

All expenditures following from the implementation of the CFSP are charged to the Union's budget, unless they are financed by a "start-up" fund made up of Member States' contributions.[26]

An Instrument for Stability[27] with a total budget for 2007–2013 of €2 billion was set up to respond urgently to the needs of countries threatened with or undergoing severe political instability or suffering from the effects of a technological or natural disaster. (It replaces the Rapid Reaction Mechanism.) In short, it is a mechanism for preventing crises and conflicts, managing crises and emerging conflicts, and restoring peace. It may also be deployed to address trans-border challenges including nuclear safety and non-proliferation, the fight against trafficking, organised crime and terrorism. It can only finance operations where other financial instruments cannot respond within the timeframe necessary; it cannot, for instance, finance humanitarian assistance. A simplified decision process is used: the Commission may adopt measures which apply immediately, it is assisted by a committee and if the Commission's action is not

---

[19] Art.33 EU.

[20] Art.35 EU.

[21] Art.37 EU.

[22] Art.38 EU.

[23] Art.42 EU.

[24] See, for instance, Decision Atalanta/3/2009 on the setting up of the Committee of Contributors for the European Union military operation to contribute to the deterrence, prevention and repression of acts of piracy and armed robbery of the Somali coast [2009] O.J. L119/40.

[25] Art.40 EU with reference to Arts 3–6 of the TFEU.

[26] Art.41 EU.

[27] Regulation 1717/06 [2006] O.J. L327/1. It became fully operational in 2008. See General Report 2008, 200.

in accordance with the opinion of the committee, the Council will immediately be informed and may overrule the Commission within 30 days. Parliament is kept informed.

1. THE COMMON SECURITY AND DEFENCE POLICY (CSDP)[28]

37–06   The CSDP is an integral part of the Common Foreign and Security policy (CFSP). It provides the Union with an operational capacity drawing on civilian and military assets. The Union may use them on missions outside the Union for joint disarmament operations, humanitarian and rescue tasks, military advice and assistance, conflict prevention and peace keeping and tasks of combat forces in crisis management, including peace-making and post-conflict stabilisation, in accordance with the principles of the United Nations Charter.[29] The performance of those tasks is undertaken using capabilities provided by the Member States.[30] The latter must make civilian and military capabilities available to the Union for the implementation of the CSDP and to contribute to the objectives defined by the Council. Multinational forces may also be made available.[31] All these tasks may contribute to the fight against terrorism, sometimes by supporting non-EU countries in combating terrorism on their soil.

In the last decade, the EU has launched 23 civilian missions and military operations on three continents. They were responses to crises, such as post-tsunami peace-building in Aceh (Indonesia), protecting refugees in Tchad, and fighting piracy of Somalia and the Horn of Africa.

Since January 2007, the EU has been able to undertake rapid-response operations with two concurrent 1,500-strong single-battle groups and, if required, to launch both operations aimed almost simultaneously. Deployment decisions are taken by ministers from the Member States meeting in the Council.[32]

37–07   The CSDP includes the progressive framing of a Common Defence Policy, which will lead to a common defence, when the European Council, acting unanimously, so decides. The Council shall then recommend the Member States adopt such a decision in accordance with their respective constitutional requirements. Decisions relating to the CSDP are adopted by the Council acting unanimously on a proposal from the High Representative or an initiative from a Member State. The High Representative may propose the use of both national resources and Union instruments, together with the Commission where appropriate.[33]

---

[28] Arts 42–46 EU.

[29] *http://europa.eu/pol/cfsp/index_eu.htm* [accessed August 23, 2013], from which certain passages are borrowed.

[30] Art.42(1) EU.

[31] Art.42(3)1 EU.

[32] Same.

[33] Art.42(4) EU.

The Member States undertake progressively to improve their military capabilities. A European Defence Agency is provided for in the Treaty.[34] A European Security and Defence College (ESDC) was established in 2005.[35]

At the Helsinki European Council, the Member States decided to establish, within the Council, new permanent political and military bodies enabling the EU to assume its responsibilities for the full range of conflict prevention and crisis management, tasks defined in the EU Treaty, the "Petersberg tasks".[36] As mentioned, these tasks concern humanitarian and rescue tasks, peacekeeping tasks and tasks of combat forces in crisis management, including peacemaking.[37] The implementation of those tasks may be entrusted, by the Council, to a group of Member States which are willing and have the necessary capabilities.[38] The defence policy of the Union may not prejudice the defence policy of certain Member States, and respects the obligations of certain Member States, which see their common defence realised in the North Atlantic Treaty Organisation (NATO), under the North Atlantic Treaty.[39]

In 2001, the Council set up a Military Committee and established a Military Staff of the European Union (EUMS).[40] This was decided within the framework of the strengthening of the CFSP, and in particular of the Common Security and Defence Policy (CSDP).[41] In accordance with this decision, a military personnel is seconded from Member States to the General Secretariat of the Council, of which the EUMS is part. The Mission and functions of the Military Staff are reproduced in the Annex to the decision: "within the Council structures [to] provide[s] military expertise and support to the CSDP, including the conduct of EU-led military crisis operations." A mechanism was established in 2004 to administer the financing of the common costs of European Union operations having military or defence implication (Athena).[42]

37–08

The military staff is to perform "early warning, situation assessment and strategic planning for 'Petersberg tasks', including identification of European national and multinational forces" and implement policies and decisions as directed by the European Union Military Committee (EUMC).

A permanent structure of co-operation within the Union framework can be established by those Member States whose military capabilities fulfil higher criteria, and which have made more binding commitments to one another with a view to the most demanding missions.[43] Member States that wish to participate,

---

[34] Art.42(3)2 EU. See Ch.13: Decentralised Agencies and Bodies of the Union.
[35] Joint Action 2005/575 [2005] O.J. L194/15, replaced by [2008] O.J. L176/20.
[36] These tasks were set out in the Petersberg Declaration adopted at the Ministerial Council of the Western European Union (WEU) in June 1992. They are an integral part of the ESDP and were explicitly included in art.17 of the EU Treaty, now Art.42.
[37] Art.43 EU. Decisions relating to those tasks shall be adopted by the Council and will define their objectives, scope and the general conditions for their implementation (Art.43(2) EU).
[38] Art.44 EU.
[39] Art.42(2)2 EU.
[40] Regulation 79/2001 [2001] O.J. L27/4 and 7, amended [2008] O.J. L102/25.
[41] Art.42 EU.
[42] Decision 2007/384 [2007] O.J. L152/14.
[43] Art.42(6) EU.

fulfil the criteria and have made the commitments on military capabilities, shall notify their intention to the Council and the High Representative. The Council shall adopt the necessary decisions.[44]

37–09   If a Member State is the victim of armed aggression on its territory, the other Member States shall have towards it an obligation of aid and assistance by all the means in their power, in accordance with the United Nations Charter.[45]

None of the actions taken under the CSDP may prejudice the specific character of the security and defence policy of certain Member States. Commitments and co-operation in this area shall be consistent with commitments under the North Atlantic Treaty Organisation, which for its members remains the foundation of their collective defence and the forum for its implementation.[46]

The EU is moving to strengthen ties with Georgia, Armenia, Azerbaijan, Moldova, Ukraine and Belarus. The 2008 Russia–Georgia war, which ended in a EU-brokered ceasefire, and the deployment of an EU monitoring mission in Georgia, raised concerns over the region's stability. The EU offers considerable funding to those countries, as well as the project of free-trade agreements if they undertake political and economic reforms to strengthen democracy.

37–10   In the wake of the "Arab Spring" in 2011, the EU re-launched its European Neighbourhood Policy to express its solidarity with those calling for democracy. Designed to strengthen the EU's relations with its neighbours to the east and south, the policy offers political association, economic integration and increased mobility. The re-launch promised more EU support for those neighbours committed to political and economic reform, and more interaction with the people living in these neighbouring countries.[47] See for instance, to mention only a very few, the Agreement between the EU and the Federal Republic of Yugoslavia on the activities of the EU Monitoring Mission;[48] the Agreement between the EU and the Republic of Poland on the participation of the latter in the EU Police Mission in Bosnia and Herzegovina;[49] and the Agreement between the EU and New Zealand on the participation of New Zealand in the EU Police Mission in Afghanistan [2007] O.J. L274/18. The Agreement between the EU and Montenegro on the participation of Montenegro in the EU military operation to contribute to the deterrence, prevention and repression of acts of piracy and armed robbery off the Somalia coast [2010] O.J.L88/3; Framework Agreement between the EU and the USA on the participation of the US in EU crisis management operations [2011] O.J. L143/2. Idem with Macedonia [2012] O.J. L338/3, and the Agreement with Moldova establishing a framework for the participation of Moldova in EU crisis management operations [2013] O.J. L8/2.

---

[44] Art.46 EU.
[45] Art.42(7) EU. Similar provisions are to be found in the "Solidarity Clause" in the Art.222 TFEU.
[46] Art.42(7)2 EU.
[47] Same.
[48] [2001] O.J. L125/2.
[49] [2003] O.J. L64/38.

2.   THE HIGH REPRESENTATIVE[50]

The High Representative chairs the Foreign Affairs Council, contributes towards **37–11** the preparation of the CFSP through his or her proposals, and ensures the implementation of the decisions adopted by the European Council and the Council. The Representative "represents" the Union in matters relating to the CFSP. He or she conducts political dialogue with third parties on the Union's behalf and expresses the Union's position in international organisations and at international conferences. He or she is assisted by the *European External Action Service* (see below).

The High Representative must regularly consult Parliament on the main aspects and the basic choices of the CFSP and inform it of how these policies evolve. He or she must ensure that the views of Parliament are duly taken into consideration. Parliament may ask questions of the Council or make recommendations to it and to the High Representative.[51]

3.   THE EUROPEAN SECURITY AND DEFENCE COLLEGE (ESCD)

Set up by a Council decision in 2013.[52]   **37–12**

The ESCD provides training in the field of the Union Common security and defence policy, in the context of the Common Foreign and Security Policy at the strategic level in order to develop and promote a common understanding of CSDP among civilian and military personnel, and to identify and disseminate, through its training activities ("ESDC training activities") best practice in relation to various CSDP issues.

(For more details, see the Council Decision.)

---

[50] Art.27 EU.
[51] Art.36 EU.
[52] Decision 2008/550/CFSP [2013] O.J. L112/22.

CHAPTER 38

Common Commercial Policy[1] and Relations with Third Countries

GENERAL PRINCIPLES

The European Union is now the largest trading group in the world, accounting for just over 20 per cent of total global trade in goods. This gives the Union the capacity, for instance, to play a leadership role in global negotiations to liberalise world trade; indeed it is one of the tasks imposed upon the Union by the TFEU:

> "[B]y establishing a customs union in accordance with Arts 28 to 32 the Union shall contribute, in the common interest, to the harmonious development of world trade, the progressive abolition of restrictions on international trade and on foreign direct investment, and the lowering of customs and other barriers."[2]

38–01

The TFEU also provides that, when establishing the Customs Union, the Commission shall be guided, among others things, by, "the need to promote trade between Member States and third countries".[3] Furthermore, free trade has traditionally been one of the main aims of the Union, because it is heavily dependent on international commerce, more so than, for example, the US. This broad objective has been pursued multilaterally first in the GATT, now in the World Trade Organisation (WTO), through regional agreements, and in bilateral relations with other countries.

As previously indicated, the Union has sole responsibility for commercial trade policy. Indeed, one of the first TFEU articles[4] provides that, the Union shall have exclusive competence in the area of "common commercial policy".[5] Further on, it is stated that the Union is based upon a Customs Union which involves "the adoption of a common customs tariff in their relations with third countries".[6] As was pointed out in the chapter on Free Movement of Goods, the elimination of internal customs tariffs does indeed require the adoption of a common customs tariff with regard to third countries since, without it, trade from third countries would be deflected towards the Member State with the lowest external tariffs. Customs tariffs, furthermore, are one of the main instruments of commercial -policy, i.e. in the relations with third countries.

---

[1] Arts 206–207 TFEU.
[2] Art.206 TFEU.
[3] Art.32 TFEU.
[4] Art.3(1).
[5] Art.3(1)(e) TFEU.
[6] Art.28(1) TFEU.

38–02   Since the external customs tariffs had to be "common", the commercial policy itself must be a policy common to the 28 Member States. The TFEU, consequently, provides that:

> "[T]he common commercial policy must be based on uniform principles, particularly with regard to changes in tariff rates, the conclusion of tariff and trade agreements relating to trade in goods and services, and the commercial aspects of intellectual property, foreign direct investment, the achievement of uniformity in measures of liberalisation, export policy and measures to protect trade such as those to be taken in the event of dumping or subsidies".[7]

As the Court indicated, commercial policy was thus transferred by the Treaty from the national ambit to the Union's jurisdiction.[8] Unfortunately, this evidence is not always fully accepted by all the national governments; this can maybe be explained by the fact that commercial policy formed part of external relations in general, and the latter, until recently were strictly reserved to the Member States themselves. Theoretically, national measures of commercial policy are no longer possible, but can still be taken with the Union's authorisation.[9] This situation is necessarily detrimental to the conduct of a coherent commercial policy towards third countries. It is to be hoped therefore, that the Treaties' provisions concerning the external action of the Union, introduced by the Treaty of Lisbon, will "communitarise" the whole spectrum of relations with third countries. Indeed, the TFEU provides for the achievement of, "an ever-increasing degree of convergence of Member States' action."[10]

However, where customs tariffs are concerned, it was accepted from the beginning by all the Member States that they can only be modified by the Council, as provided for in the Treaty.[11] Changes in tariff rates and the conclusion of tariff agreements must, as was just pointed out, be based on uniform principles. The Treaty provides for two procedures in this field: first, the so-called "autonomous" modification of tariffs, where the Union acts on its own,[12] but that is now very limited, since most duties have been "consolidated" under the WTO; and, secondly, those that take place pursuant to agreements with third countries.

38–03   Those agreements are negotiated in the same way as those described above in the chapter on General Provisions concerning the Union's External Action, i.e. by the Commission, in consultation with a Special Committee on the basis of a

---

[7] Art.207 TFEU.

[8] Court Opinion 1/75 [1975] E.C.R. 1355.

[9] *Donckerwolcke v Procureur de la République* (41/76) [1976] E.C.R. 1921 at para.32; [1977] 2 C.M.L.R. 535. See Council Decision of 91/169, 1991 authorising prorogation or tacit renewal of certain commercial agreements concluded by the Member States [1991] O.J. L83/13. Art.207 TFEU and Council Decision 69/494 concerning progressive uniformisation of existing trade agreements [1969] O.J. L326/39. See also Council decision 91/167 [1991] O.J. L82/52 authorising the automatic renewal or maintenance in force of provisions governing matters covered by the common commercial policy contained in the friendship, trade and navigation treaties and similar agreements concluded between Member States and third countries.

[10] Art.24(2) EU. Progress was recently made with regard to the so-called open sky agreements with the US, following a judgment of the Court. See, for instance, *Commission v Sweden* (C-468/98) [2002] E.C.R. I-9575, affirming the exclusive competence of the Union.

[11] Arts 31 and 207 TFEU.

[12] Art.31 TFEU.

mandate that it proposes to, and receives from, the Council, and within the framework of such directives as the Council may issue to it. These agreements are concluded by the Council.[13]

For the negotiation and conclusion of international agreements in the area of the Common Commercial Policy, the Council acts by qualified majority.[14] However, when it concerns trade in services and the commercial aspects of intellectual property, as well as foreign direct investment, the Council must act unanimously, where such agreements include provisions for which unanimity is required for the adoption of internal rules.[15]

Furthermore, the TFEU specifies that the Council must also act unanimously for agreements in the field of trade in cultural and audio-visual services, where those agreements risk prejudicing the Union's cultural and linguistic diversity. Unanimity is also provided for trade in the field of social, education and health services, where these agreements risk seriously disturbing the national organisation of such services and prejudicing the responsibility of Member States to deliver them.

Finally, the TFEU provides that the competences conferred in the area of the common commercial policy may not affect the delimitation of competences between the Union and the Member States and shall not lead to harmonisation unless this is provided for by the Treaties.[16]

1. COMMERCIAL POLICY INSTRUMENTS AND IMPORT AND EXPORT ARRANGEMENTS

It will be noted that the specific Treaty provisions concerning commercial policy refer to, "the achievement of uniformity in measures of liberalisation, export policy and measures to protect trade such as those to be taken in the event of dumping or subsidies."[17]   **38–04**

(1) Liberalisation and Export Policy

Member States must harmonise the systems whereby they grant aid for export to third countries, to the extent necessary to ensure that competition between enterprises is not distorted. In this context reference must be made to the OECD Arrangement on Guidelines for Officially Supported Export Credits "Consensus". The application of the agreement was made compulsory for the Member States.[18] Generally speaking, exports from the Union are free, although the Council is empowered to impose restrictions in certain cases. For instance, in 1992, the Council adopted a regulation requiring prior authorisation for the export of eight chemical products. This authorisation may not be given if there is reason to believe that the products in question will be used for the development or   **38–05**

---

[13] Art.207 TFEU. This Committee is composed of national officials appointed by the Council.
[14] Art.207(4) TFEU.
[15] Art.207(4)2 TFEU.
[16] Art.207(6) TFEU.
[17] Art.207(1) TFEU.
[18] [1997] O.J. L216/77, repealed by Council Decision 2001/76 [2001] O.J. L32/1.

the production of chemical weapons or that there is a risk of their being delivered directly or indirectly to belligerent countries or to areas of serious international tension.[19]

On the other hand, the Commission supplements Member States' export promotion efforts with a programme based on fairs, trade forums and co-ordinated Union initiatives; it gave, for instance, priority to promoting exports to the Gulf and Asian countries. See Council Decision on the implementation by the Commission of activities relating to the Union market access strategy.[20] See the 2009 regulation establishing common rules for exports, accepting as a Union principle that exports to third countries are not subject to any quantitative restrictions, subject to certain exceptions and measures as Member States may take in conformity with the TFEU.[21]

(2)   Measures to Protect Trade[22]

38–06   The instruments concerning imports consist mainly of anti-dumping and anti-subsidy measures.[23] The purpose of anti-dumping measures is to eliminate the prejudice suffered by Union producers of a given product because of imports of a similar product being "dumped". Dumping exists when an exporter applies to exported products a price that is lower than the so-called normal value. The latter is the price asked for that product on the exporter's home market. In case the products were sold domestically for a loss, then the normal value would be construed by adding a profit margin to the production costs, the so called constructed value.

Union action, generally speaking, takes the form of provisional anti-dumping duties imposed on the imported product causing injury. This is followed either by an undertaking from the exporter concerning his export price to the Union or by definitive duties. Such action is taken at the end of a procedure which starts with a complaint containing sufficient proof, submitted to the Commission, by a majority of the European producers of a given branch or by a Member State. The Commission can then initiate proceedings and an investigation, after consultation of a consultative committee. The initiation of proceedings is announced in the *Official Journal*. The Commission could also open proceedings on its own initiative, but never does so, deeming the industry better placed to gather the

---

[19] General Report 1992, 311. See, for instance, the suspension of trade concession to former Yugoslavia: *Racke* (C-162/96) [1998] E.C.R. I-3655 concerning the EEC/Yugoslavia Co-operation Agreement and the Vienna Convention on the Law of Treaties: application of the rule *rebus sic stantibus*.

[20] [1998] O.J. L265/31. See General Report 2003, 799.

[21] [2009] O.J. L291/1.

[22] Also commonly referred to as "trade defence instruments" (TDI).

[23] Regulation 384/96 on protection against dumped imports from countries not members of the Union [1996] O.J. L56/1, replaced by Regulation 1225/2009 [2009] O.J. L343/51, and Regulation 597/2009 [2009] O.J. L188, on protection against subsidised imports from countries not members of the European Union. See also Guidelines for the calculation of the amount of subsidy in countervailing duty investigations [1998] O.J. C394/6. Also of interest is Regulation 519/94 on common rules for imports from certain third-world countries [1994] O.J. L67/89, amended [2009] O.J. L37/4, codified [2009] O.J. L185/1. See also *BEUC v Commission* (T-256/97) [2000] E.C.R. II-101, where it was decided that consumer organi-sations could not be "interested parties" in proceedings involving products not commonly sold at retail level.

necessary proofs. The complaint should be submitted by producers of a similar product that, furthermore, must be "communautaire".

Next, the existence of dumping and of a prejudice must be ascertained by the Commission. The Commission's investigation covers a period of six months following the submission of the complaint. To conduct the investigation the Commission needs the full co-operation of all interested parties. The Commission cannot however impose coercive measures, but in case of a refusal to furnish the requested information, the Commission may, in pursuance of the WTO Anti-Dumping Code, decide on the basis of the existing evidence. Indeed, mention should be made of the fact that the Union rules in this field are based upon the General Agreement for Tariffs and Trade (GATT), now WTO.[24]

The proceedings are closed either by a decision that there is no need for protective measures, by the expiration or abrogation of the anti-dumping measures or by the nullity of the price undertaking. This means that, as long as one of these three events has not occurred, the Council can take a new measure without opening proceedings again.

38–07

Measures can only be imposed by the Union after it has ascertained that there is dumping and that it causes injury to Union producers. This may be a lengthy procedure and reactions to a complaint cannot therefore be immediate. There is however, a further requirement namely that the interest of the Union does require such measures. In practice, injury to a Union industry is considered as constituting an Union interest. As for the undertaking made by an exporter, it consists in applying a price which will eliminate the dumping effect and the injury to the Union producers. The implementation of the undertaking is verified by periodical reports from the exporter to the Commission.

The anti-dumping duties are established for five years and are levied when the product is put in free circulation. The proceedings and measures described above are similar for anti-subsidy measures; in order to offset any subsidy bestowed, directly or indirectly, in the country of origin or export, upon their manufacture, production, export or transport of any product whose release in the free circulation in the Union causes injury, a countervailing duty may be imposed.[25]

Anti-dumping or countervailing duties imposed by the Union are subject to the judicial control of the Court; this control has given rise to an abundant case law.[26]

38–08

"Many trading partners, many commercial agreements." Those are the words of the Commission[27] to indicate that, in addition to full participation in the

38–09

---

[24] The Union rules must be interpreted in accordance with the WTO rules that they intend to implement ; however the WTO rules do not have direct applicability in the Union legal order, and the Union's failure to comply with WTO law cannot generally trigger off the Union's liability, see for instance, *Montecchio SpA and Montecchio Technologies LLC v Council of the European Union and Commission* (joined cases C-120/06 and C-121/06 P) [2008] E.C.R. I-6513; *Etablissements Biret et Cie SA v Council* (C-94/02 P) [2003] E.C.R. I-10565; and *Germany v Council (Bananas)* (C-280/93) [1994] E.C.R. I-4973.

[25] See General Report 2003, 792.

[26] See for instance *Council and Commission v Interpipe Niko Tube and Interpipe NTRP* (joined cases C-191/09 and C-200/09 P) judgement of February 16, 2012, not yet reported, and *Brosmann Footwear (HK) and others* (C-249/10 P) judgement of February 2, 2012, not yet reported, where the Court annulled a Council Regulation imposing a definitive anti-dumping duty.

[27] Parts of this chapter are based on, or borrowed from, *http://ec.europa.eu/trade/index_en.htm* [accessed August 23, 2013].

multilateral negotiation and management activities of the WTO, the Union also has a broad range of commercial agreements of differing types with its many partners; these are, for instance:

- agreements creating Customs Union with Turkey;
- free trade agreements with the EFTA States;
- "Europe" agreements (also known as association agreements), which were concluded before accession, with Central and Eastern European countries. Those aimed to integrate their economies with the Union in view of their accession;
- preferential agreements with Mediterranean countries and, through the Cotonou Convention, with more than 70 African, Caribbean and Pacific countries. These arrangements give their exports privileged access to the EU as well as financial and technical assistance;
- non-preferential commercial and economic co-operation agreements with many countries of Latin America and Asia, such as the recently concluded New Generation Free Trade Agreement of 2010 with South Korea and the Partnership and Co-operation Agreement of 2012 with Iraq;
- sectoral agreements, such as in textiles and clothing, guaranteeing third-world producers access to the Union market;
- international commodity agreements, such as the Cocoa Agreement 1993; and[28]
- generalised system of preferences[29] (see below, see the chapter on Development Co-operation).

A regulation lays down Union procedures in the field of the common commercial policy, in order to ensure the exercise of the Union's rights under international trade rules, in particular those established under the auspices of the World Trade Organisation.[30]

2. RELATIONS WITH OTHER EUROPEAN COUNTRIES

(1) The European Economic Area (EEA)

38–10 The European Economic Area was born on January 1, 1994; it joins together the three EFTA States—**Iceland, Liechtenstein** and **Norway**—with the Union in one single market.[31] Among other things, it grants those countries the basic freedoms of goods, services, capital and persons, and requires them to adopt most EU

---

[28] Decision 98/489 concerning the conclusion of the International Cocoa Agreement 1993, on behalf of the Union [1998] O.J. L220/1.

[29] See Scheme for the period January 1, 2009 to December 31, 2011 [2008] O.J. L211/1. General Report 2008, 171.

[30] Regulation 3286/94 [1994] O.J. L349/71, modified [2008] O.J. L40/1; see *FICF v Commission* (T-317/02) [2004] E.C.R. II-4325.

[31] The Union also has free-trade agreements with Iceland and Norway, dating back to the beginning of the 1970s, and which may still have relevance in the limited areas not governed by the EEA Agreement.

policies on mergers, State aids, consumer protection, labour markets and the environment. The agreement gives the three States the right to be consulted by the Commission during the formulation of Union legislation, although they have no say in the decision-making.[32] All new Union legislation, in the areas covered by the EEA, is integrated into the agreement through a Joint Committee decision and subsequently made part of the national legislation of the EEA States. From an institutional point of view, it might be interesting to note that the EEA has a Council, a Joint Committee and a Consultative Committee, which meet either in Brussels or in the capital of one of the member countries. The three EFTA States have set up an independent EFTA Surveillance Authority (ESA) which powers that mirror those the Commission has in monitoring compliance with Union law, and an EFTA Court whose jurisdiction is similar to that of the Court of Justice and the General Court before the Maastricht Treaty. An overriding principle of the EEA is that of homogeneity, by which is meant that the EEA rules shall, all things being equal, be interpreted as the Union rules which they mirror. Members of the EEA participate in several Union activities: Norway and Iceland, for instance, participate in the European Medicines Agency, in the European Environment Agency and in other schemes. It should be noted that those three countries and Switzerland do apply, for instance, the Union Directive on the right of establishment of lawyers.[33]

(2) Switzerland

Relations with **Switzerland**, that in a referendum rejected membership of the EEA, will continue to be governed by the existing co-operation agreements.[34] An agreement on scientific and technological co-operation was signed in 2007[35] and one on trade in agricultural products in 2009.[36] In 2010 an agreement was signed establishing the terms and conditions for the participation of the Swiss Confederation in the "Youth in action" programme and the action programme in the field of lifelong learning,[37] a similar agreement concerns the participation of the Swiss Confederation in the MEDIAZ 2007 programme.[38] An agreement with the Union on supplementary rules in relation to the External Borders Fund for the period 2007 to 2013 was concluded by Switzerland and the EEA States in 2011 ([2011] O.J. L137/1).

38–11

---

[32] General Report 1997, 305.

[33] The EEA agreement involves a "high degree of integration, with objectives which exceed those of a mere free trade agreement", see *Opel Austria* (T-115/94) [1997] E.C.R. II-39, para.107. The EFTA Court which has for instance held that the three EFTA States may incur liability for their failure to comply with EEA law, has held that the agreement is "an international treaty *sui generis* which contains a distinct legal order of its own", see *Sveinbjörnsdóttir* (E-9/97) [1998] EFTA Court Report 120, para.59.

[34] See [2002] O.J. L11k/1 and [2004] O.J. L368/26 (Schengen). See agreement on scientific and technological co-operation ([2007] O.J. L189/24) and agreement on the carriage of goods and passengers by rail and road ([2011] O.J. L19/34).

[35] [2008] O.J. L86/25.

[36] [2009] O.J. L136/1.

[37] [2010] O.J. L322/1.

[38] [2011] O.J. L53/1.

(3)   Other European Countries

38–12   A co-operation and Customs Union Agreement was concluded and entered into force with San Marino.[39] A co-operation agreement exists with Andorra, in respect of the environment, communications, education, transport, and regional and trans-frontier co-operation and veterinary matters. A monetary agreement with Monaco was signed by France on behalf of the Union.[40] For more information on those various subjects the reader is referred to the Commission's annual General Reports.[41]

(3)   The New Independent States (NIS)

38–13   Relations with these republics of the former Soviet Union are regulated by partnership and co-operation agreements whose scope is political, economic, commercial and cultural. They aim to pave the way for the integration of these countries into the wider European economy. Such agreements and others have been signed with Ukraine,[42] Moldova,[43] Kyrgyz Republic,[44] Belarus,[45] Kazakhstan,[46] Georgia,[47] Armenia,[48] Azerbaijan,[49] Turkmenistan,[50] Tajikistan[51] and Uzbekistan[52].

Substantial allocations—€132.5 million, including Russia—were committed over the period 1996–2000, which represents approximately 5 per cent of the total the TACIS budget. The purpose of the programme is to aid the NIS in their transition to a market economy and to entrench democracy. In 2011, €93 million was allocated for assistance to central Asia.[53] It covered six fields of co-operation: institutional, judicial and administrative reform; support for the private sector; social consequences from transition to market economy;

---

[39] [1991] O.J. C302/10.

[40] [2002] O.J. L142/59. Renegotiated [2011] O.J. L81/3.

[41] [1989] O.J. L54/1.

[42] [2000] O.J. L283/27. See also the agreement on trade in certain steel products [2004] O.J. L384/23 and General Report 2004, 253. See Decision providing macrofinancial assistance to Ukraine: [2010] O.J. L179/1 and the agreement for scientific and technical co-operation [2011] O.J. L79/3 and [2012] O.J.L40/1: entry into force.

[43] [2000] O.J. L283/27 at 36 and General Report 2004, 251. See Framework Agreement on the general principles for the participation of Moldova in Union programmes [2011] O.J. L131/1.

[44] [1999] O.J. L196/46.

[45] See http://ec.europa.eu/trade/policy/countries-and-regions/countries/belarus [accessed August 23, 2013]. Relations of the EU with Belarus, General Report 2004, 250.

[46] [1999] O.J. L196/1. See also Regulation 2265/04 on trade in certain steel products between the Union and the Republic of Kazakhstan [2004] O.J. L395/1. See Partnership and Co-operation Agreement [1999] O.J. L299/3 and Protocol on trade in textiles [2011] O.J. L106/1 and Protocol on a Framework Agreement for the participation of Ukraine in Union programmes [2011] O.J. L133/1.

[47] See, for instance, [1999] O.J. L343/1 and General Report 2004, 251. A common aviation agreement was signed and provisionally applied [2011] O.J. L25/1.

[48] [1999] O.J. L343/1.

[49] [1999] O.J. L343/1 and General Report 2004, 250.

[50] [1999] O.J. L343/1. The Partnership and Cooperation Agreement with Turkmenistan is still pending notification.

[51] [2009] O.J. L350/1.

[52] [1999] O.J. L343/1. For interim agreement on trade and trade-related matters, [2011] O.J. L1 and 19.

[53] See Annual Report on Union's Development and External Assistance 2012, s.5.2.4.

infrastructure networks; protection of the environment and management of natural resources; development of rural economy.

3. RELATIONS WITH MAJOR INDUSTRIALISED COUNTRIES[54]

(1) The United States

The relations between the United States and the Union are rather ambiguous. On the one hand, both sides claim to attach great importance to closer co-operation and to a strengthening of their relations, and on the other hand they are involved in several disputes[55] (threats, retaliation measures, counter-retaliations, WTO panels, Boeing/Airbus, etc.). These two economic powers are, however, bound to co-operate very closely in the economic and political fields. This they successfully do, for example, within the Western Economic Summits held every year and recently with joint proposals for the new WTO multilateral round, which unfortunately, did not get very far, and also in the G8 and G20. The EU and the US form a global partnership, covering not only trade and economics but also co-operation on a whole range of foreign issues and global challenges. **38–14**

The economic relationship between the two is characterised by close economic interdependence. Together the EU and the US produce 57 per cent of the world GDP and are responsible for about two-fifths of world trade. The EU and the US are each other's most important partners in trade and in investment. The total amount of two-way investments amounts to over €1.5 trillion, with each partner employing about six million people in the other. In 2005, the EU exported goods to the US for €260 billion and imported from the US for €180 billion.

Where services are concerned, in 2004 the Union exported to the US for €139 billion and imported from the US €127.9 billion.

Agreements were signed between the parties concerning mutual recognition of technical norms and certificates,[56] establishing a co-operation programme in higher education and vocational education and training,[57] on sanitary measures to protect public and animal health in trade in live animals and animal products,[58] **38–15**

---

[54] Information in this section is based on *http://ec.europa.eu/trade/policy/countries-and-regions/* [accessed August 23, 2013]. See same for more details.

[55] For details about those disputes, consult the General Reports published by the Commission each February; see, for instance, General Report 2004, 210. General Report 1997, 333, where mention is made, among other things, of the US legislation with an extraterritorial effect like the Cuban liberty and democratic solidarity (Helms–Burton) Act and the Iran and Libya Sanctions Act (d'Amato), about which the EU and the US reached an understanding in April 1997; see also General Report 1996, point 878, and lately the banana dispute.

[56] Under this agreement, a Joint Committee was established and empowered to take decisions; see, for instance, [2001] O.J. L306/34, listing of Conformity Assessment Bodies under the Sectoral Annex on Telecommunication Equipment and on Electromagnetic Compatibility, and concerning medical devices: [2002] O.J. L302/30.

[57] [1995] O.J. L279/13, renewed [2001] O.J. L71/7.

[58] [1998] O.J. L118/3.

for scientific and technological co-operation,[59] on trade in wine,[60] on air transport,[61] and on the participation of the United States in European Union crisis management operations.[62]

Notwithstanding the above-mentioned disputes, the bilateral dialogue and consultations are increasing both in the economic and political fields.[63] Examples are the already mentioned Transatlantic Business Dialogue, the Transatlantic Environment Dialogue, the Transatlantic Consumers Dialogue, the Transatlantic Labour—Legislators'—and Development Dialogue. In 2003 an EU–US Agreement was signed on extradition and mutual assistance in criminal matters.[64] An agreement was signed on extradition between the Union and the United States and one on mutual legal assistance,[65] and another on the processing and transfer of Financial Messaging Data.[66] Mention should also be made of the Bilateral Positive Economic Agenda concerning financial markets dialogue, the launch of regulatory co-operation in four priority sectors (cosmetics, automobile, nutritional labelling and metrology) and the conclusion of an agreement on marine safety equipment.

An Air Transport Agreement was signed and provisionally applied in 2007,[67] a memorandum of co-operation in civil aviation research and development was signed,[68] and an agreement was concluded on the security of classified -information.[69] See also an implementing arrangement for co-operation activities in the field of homeland/civil security research.[70] An Air Transport Agreement was signed between the US and the Union and its Member States in 2011.[71] See also the agreement on co-operation in the regulation of civil aviation safety.[72]

38–16   See the Agreement on Mutual Recognition of 2011 related to the listing of Conformity Assessment Bodies[73] and the agreement on the promotion, provision and use of Galileo and GPS satellite-based navigation systems and related applications.[74] See also the arrangement for imports of organic products.[75] In February 2013, the EU and the United States agreed to start internal procedures to launch negotiations on a Transatlantic Trade and Investment Partnership. The venture is ambitious and is likely to be a time-consuming process before the parties manage to agree on all aspects of such a comprehensive agreement.

---

[59] [1998] O.J. L284/37, renewed [2004] O.J. L335/5 and amended [2009] O.J. L90/20.
[60] [2006] O.J. L87/1.
[61] See [2010] O.J. L223/1.
[62] [2011] O.J. L143/1.
[63] [1996] Bull.12, 171.
[64] [2003] O.J. Ll81/25.
[65] [2009] O.J. L291/40.
[66] [2010] O.J. L8/9.
[67] [2007] O.J. L134/4.
[68] [2011] O.J. L89/1
[69] [2007] O.J. L115/29.
[70] [2010] O.J. L125/53.
[71] [2011] O.J. L283/1.
[72] [2011] O.J. L291/3.
[73] [2011] O.J. L328/56.
[74] [2011] O.J. L348/1.
[75] [2011] O.J. L153/1.

(2) Canada

Links between Europe and Canada have traditionally been close.   38–17

> "What started out in 1950 as a purely economic relationship has evolved over the years to become a close strategic alliance. The EU and Canada now work together on a great range of diverse issues ranging from research into alternative energy sources to providing police training in Afghanistan."[76]

The Union is Canada's second trade partner, while Canada ranks 11th in terms of Union trade. The first co-operation agreement ever signed by the Union with an industrialised country was with Canada in 1976, the Framework Agreement for Commercial and Economic Co-operation. This provided for closer business and commercial links, economic co-operation and joint undertakings between industries and companies.

The Union and its Member States and Canada adopted a Joint Declaration in 1996 and an Action Plan on relations between the Union and Canada. While less tense than those with the United States, economic and trade relations between Canada and the Union were clouded by numerous disagreements. The worst of these concerned fish and lasted many years.

At the summit held in Ottawa in March 2004, the Union and Canada adopted   38–18
the Framework for the Canada–EU Trade and Investment Enhancement Agreement (TIEA), the key element of which is co-operation between Union and Canadian regulators. In addition the agreement addresses issues such as: mutual recognition of professional qualifications; e-commerce; financial services; government pro-curement; trade and investment facilitation; intellectual property rights; science and technology, etc. In addition, the Union and Canada adopted the EU–Canada Partnership Agenda.

Trade in goods to Canada in 2008 amounted to €26.1 billion and imports from Canada to €23.8 billion. The equivalent figures for trade in services are respectively €11.3 and €9.5 billion.

In order to facilitate trade between the two partners, they signed an agreement on mutual recognition,[77] and an agreement establishing a Co-operation programme in higher education and vocational education and training,[78] an agreement for Scientific and Technological Co-operation,[79] a 1997 Agreement on Customs Co-operation and Mutual Assistance, another in 1998 on Mutual Recognition of Conformity Assessments, a 1999 Veterinary Agreement and a Competition Agreement in view of the increasing number of cases reviewed both by the Commission Directorate-General for Competition and the Canadian Bureau of Competition Policy. (See above, Ch.22: Competition Policy.)

In 2004 the EU and Canada adopted a Partnership Agenda for joint action in   38–19
foreign and security policy, in the field of justice and home affairs, multilateral trade talks and tackling global challenges such as climate change and poverty in developing countries.

---

[76] *http://www.eeas.europa.eu/canada/index_en.htm* [accessed August 23, 2013].
[77] [1998] O.J. L280/3.
[78] [1995] O.J. L300/19, renewed [2001] O.J. L71/15.
[79] [1996] O.J. L74/25, amended [1999] O.J. L156/23.

Summit meetings are held yearly. The conclusion of a Comprehensive Economic and Trade Agreement is envisaged in the second half of 2013.[80]An agreement on civil aviation safety was concluded in 2011.[81]

(3) Japan

38–20 Japan and the EU together represent nearly 40 per cent of world GDP (2001) and Japan is the EU's third largest export market (after the US and Switzerland) and the third largest source of imports. Relations with Japan were strained for a long time due to the Japanese trade surplus and the difficulties encountered by exporters in Japan. The latter has, however, especially since its "financial bubble" collapsed, began to accept that it has to make special efforts to open its economy to international competition and embark on structural reforms for its own good and for the benefit of the international economy. Relations improved after the EC–Japan Political Declaration of 1991[82] on relations between the EC and its Member States and Japan. It established common principles and shared objectives in the political, economic, co-operation and cultural areas and established a consultation framework including annual summit meetings.[83]

The co-operation covers various fields such as trade, the environment, industry, scientific research, social affairs, competition policy and energy. However, the commercial relations with Japan were a constant worry for the Union, as shown in the Commission Communication entitled "A consistent and global approach: a review of the Union's relations with Japan".[84] The Council therefore asked the Commission to analyse, on a regular basis, statistically, the development of trade with Japan in goods and services.[85] The Union's trade balance with Japan started to improve in April 1993 and this trend continued, albeit rather slowly. In 2007, Union exports to Japan were €12.38 billion and imports from Japan were €14.24 billion. Japan is also a major investor in the Union.

Co-operation between the Union and Japan now takes place across a wide range of areas, including, besides those already mentioned, development assistance, macroeconomic and financial affairs and transport. An agreement on mutual recognition was concluded in 2001.[86] The Commission operates an executive training programme that takes young European business people to Japan for 12 months of in-house training in a Japanese company. Important agreements were signed. The EU–Japan Mutual Recognition Agreement (MRA), which entered into force on January 1, 2002, permits acceptance of conformity assessments conducted in one party according to the regulations of the other for telecommunication terminal equipment and radio equipment, electrical products, Good Laboratory Practice for chemicals and Good Manufacturing Practice for pharmaceuticals. Agreements on Co-operation on Anti-competitive Activities,[87]

---

[80] General Report 2008, 175.
[81] [2011] O.J. L195/5.
[82] General Report 1991, 272.
[83] The 14th Summit meeting took place in Luxembourg in June 2004.
[84] COM (92) 219; [1992] Bull.5-1992.
[85] [1992] Bull.6, 95. General Report 1993, 257.
[86] [2001] O.J. L284/1.
[87] [2003] O.J. L183/111

on customs co-operation (2008) and an assistance in criminal matters (2010) were signed. An agreement was signed in 2010 on mutual legal assistance in criminal matters[88] and another, in 2011, on co-operation in science and technology.[89]

On March 25, 2013, the Union and Japan officially launched negotiations for a Free Trade Agreement. The negotiation will centre around long-standing EU concerns, including non-tariff barriers and the further opening of the public procurement market.

38–21

(4) Russia

The EU is Russia's largest trading partner by far, accounting for close to 52 per cent of the latter's foreign trade. Political and economic relations are governed by a Partnership and Co-operation Agreement (PCA)[90] that entered into force on December 1, 1997. The agreement establishes a political dialogue at all levels, regulates the trade in nuclear fuels, allows free EU investment in Russia with full repatriation of profits, liberalises the activities of foreign banks in Russia, removes all EU quotas on Russian exports apart from certain textile and steel products[91] and allows temporary Russian quotas on some EU imports. After enlargement, Russia and the EU became direct neighbours; hence the interest of both parties in maintaining and strengthening solid, predictable, transparent and open trade relations.

38–22

In 2012, bilateral trade in goods amounted to €336.5 billion, with Union exports of €123.2 billion, and imports of €213.3 billion. In 2011, services were €39 billion as against €11.7 in favour of the Union. Foreign direct investments in 2010 were of €120 billion to Russia and €42 billion from Russia.

The relationship is based on a Partnership and Co-operation Agreement (PCA); the negotiation of a new agreement is currently stalled.

An agreement on co-operation in science and technology was renewed in March 2009.[92] Four Council Decisions were taken in 2011 on the signing of Agreements on tariff-rate quotas on export of wood, on trade in parts and components of motor vehicles, relating to the preservation of commitments contained in services and to export duties on raw materials.[93]

38–23

(5) China

In 1995, China became the Union's fourth largest export market and its fourth largest supplier, with the EU's imports exceeding its exports. In 2004 China had become the second largest trade partner of the EU (after the US) with a total trade of €175 billion and an EU deficit of €78.5 billion (the greatest trade deficit). In 2012 the trade total reached €472.1 billion, with an EU deficit of €139.8 billion.

38–24

---

88 [2010[O.J. L271/3.

89 [2011] O.J. L90/1.

90 *Simuntenkov* (C-265/03) [2005] E.C.R. I-2581 gave the Court an opportunity to rule, for the first time, on the effects of a partnership agreement between the EC and a non-Member State.

91 See Regulation 2267/04 on trade in certain steel products between the EC and the Russian Federation [2004] O.J. L395/38.

92 [2009] O.J. L92/3.

93 [2012] O.J. L57/1 to 53.

China is the EU's largest supplier of textiles and clothing (see General Report 2005, 145). The legal framework for commercial relations and a programme of co-operation and development are provided by the EC–China Trade and Co--operation Agreement, signed in 1985. At the end of 1995, the Council issued guidelines for an EU strategy towards China, whose objectives emphasised the "smooth and gradual integration of China into the world economy, together with the promotion of democracy, structures based on the rule of law and respect for human rights". As the Commission writes, "two of the biggest markets in the world have everything to gain from deepening their commercial ties."

Trade in goods represented, in 2010, for the Union €282.5 billion in imports and only €113.3 billion in exports; trade in services was better with exports of €22.3 billion and imports of €16.3 billion, seeing a balance of €6 billion in favour of the Union. Union investments in China reached €75.1 billion, while Chinese investments in the Union were €6.7 billion.

38–25 A High Level Economic and Trade Dialogue was launched in Beijing in 2008, a High Level Strategic Dialogue was established in 2010 and finally a High Level People-to-People Dialogue was initiated at the latest summit between the parties in February 2012.

EU–China Co-operation

38–26 The current strategy for EC co-operation with China is defined in the EU–China Strategy Paper 2007–2013 (CSP), which proposes a concentration of activities in three areas:

1. support for areas covered by EU-China policy dialogues, including bilateral relationship in trade, business exchanges, socio-economic development and support for the internal reform process;
2. global concerns over climate change, the environment and energy;
3. human resources development.

Financing for the first four years of the 2007–2013 CSP amounted to €128 million.

Other agreements are a Science and Technology agreement, an agreement on co-operation in EU's Galileo satellite navigation programme, joint research in the peaceful use of atomic energy, maritime transport,[94] and customs co-operation.

Political dialogue and human rights dialogue: a political dialogue was formally established in 1994; it has grown into regular, structured series of meetings at -several levels. In 2010 a new high level dialogue on strategic and foreign policy issues was established to further expand the political dialogue. The latest summit meeting took place in September 2012. A Human Rights Dialogue was formally established in 1995 and May 2012 saw the Dialogue's 31st round being held in Brussels with a focus on criminal punishment and deprivation of liberty, treatment of minorities and racism and xenophobia.

---

[94] See agreement on maritime transport [2008] O.J. L46/23, modified [2009] O.J. L294/10.

(6) Australia

The Union is Australia's main trading partner; trade between the two continues to grow: Australia's exports to the EU in 2012 rose to €14.4 billion, while Union exports to Australia amounted to €33.8 billion. Trade in services was, in 2010, from Australia, €6.7 billion and to Australia, €14.3 billion.   **38–27**

In 2008, Union and Australia signed an agreement on certain aspects of air service.[95] In March 2011, Australia and Euratom concluded an agreement for co-operation in the peaceful uses of nuclear energy.[96]

The Union is still Australia's second largest supplier and its fourth largest export market. It is its leading partner for services while the Union is also the chief source of cumulative investment and the second home for Australian overseas investments.[97]

Since early 2012, Australia and the Union have been negotiating a formal Framework Agreement that contains several mutually beneficial economic and trade cooperation provisions.

(7) New Zealand

Co-operation between the EU and New Zealand is based on preferential agreements largely focused on agricultural products. Thus, butter and lamb imports into the EU from New Zealand have enjoyed preferential access for many years. Total trade in goods between the two is about €7 billion with a small balance in favour of the Union. In 1991, the two sides signed a scientific and technical co-operation agreement covering agriculture, biomass, biotechnology, environment, forests, renewable sources of energy and information technology. Other agreements cover, for instance, sanitary measures applicable to trade in live animals and animal products,[98] mutual recognition in relation to conformity assessments,[99] establishment of a framework for the participation of New Zealand in European Union crisis management operations.[100]   **38–28**

4. RELATIONS WITH MEDITERRANEAN COUNTRIES

Implementation of a new Mediterranean policy started in 1992 with three regulations. The first of these concerns financial co-operation in respect of all the non-member countries of the area,[101] the second concerns the detailed implementation of financial co-operation under the existing protocols with all those countries,[102] and the third concerns improving the arrangements for the import into the Union of certain agricultural products originating in Algeria,[103]   **38–29**

---

[95] [2008] O.J. L14965.

[96] [2012] O.J. L29/3.

[97] General Report 1992, 278.

[98] [2003] O.J. L214/36.

[99] [1998] O.J. L229/61.

[100] [2012] 0.J. L160/1.

[101] Regulation 1763/92 [1992] O.J. L181/5.

[102] Regulation 1762/92 [1992] O.J. L181/1.

[103] An agreement was signed in 2012 on scientific and technological co-operation: [2012] O.J. L99/1.

Egypt,[104] Israel, Jordan,[105] Lebanon, Morocco,[106] the Palestinian Authority, Syria, Tunisia and Turkey.[107] A Customs Union Association Agreement exists with Turkey. Regular Association Agreements exist also with the Maghreb Countries, Algeria,[108] Morocco and Tunisia,[109] the Mashreq countries, Egypt, Jordan,[110] Lebanon[111] and with Israel, the West Bank and the Gaza Strip ("occupied territories"). Steps towards the signature of an Association Agreement with Syria were initialled in 2008, but are currently suspended. Those agreements cover agriculture, energy, industry, distribution trades, infrastructure, education and training, health and environment and scientific co-operation. Those activities are financed by the resources provided for in the financial protocols. In 1992, the Council adopted the 4th Financial Protocols with Algeria, Israel, Jordan and Lebanon in the context of the new Mediterranean policy. Similar protocols with the other countries were already concluded or on the point of being concluded. In December 1994, the Essen European Council endorsed a strategy set out by the Commission in the framework of a Euro-Mediterranean partnership with a view of strengthening the Union's policy for peace, security and welfare of the Mediterranean. The long-term goal was the creation of an extensive trade area, backed up by substantial financial aid.[112]

A Euro-Mediterranean ministerial conference took place in Barcelona in November 1995.[113] The EU and its 12 Mediterranean partners[114] adopted a Declaration[115] in which they decided to put their relations on a multilateral and durable footing based on a spirit of partnership and on a work programme. The partnership's three components are reinforced and regular political dialogue, enhanced economic and financial co-operation in support of the creation of a free-trade area, and a further strengthening of the social, cultural and human dimension. Those three facets are being implemented, and the process was

---

[104] An agreement was signed in 2011 establishing a dispute settlement mechanism applicable to disputes under the trade provisions of the Euro-Mediterranean Agreement: [2011] O.J.L27/2.

[105] In 2011, agreements were concluded on scientific and technological co-operation ([2011] O.J. L159/1) and on establishing a dispute settlement mechanism ([2011] O.J. L177/1).

[106] An agreement establishing a dispute settlement mechanism was signed in 2011: [2011] O.J. L27/1 and L176/1. In 2012, a Protocol to the Euro-Mediterranean Agreement established a framework agreement on the general principles for the participation of Morocco in Union programmes: [2012] O.J. L90/1.

[107] Regulation 1764/92 [1992] O.J. L181/9.

[108] A Euro-Mediterranean Agreement establishing an Association between the Union and its Member States, of the one part, and the People's Democratic republic of Algeria, of the other part, was concluded in July 2005: [2005] O.J. L265/1. In 2005, a Euro-Mediterranean Agreement established an association with Algeria: [2005] O.J. L292/10.

[109] See the Decision of September 20, 2005 establishing an association between the European Communities and their Member States and the Republic of Tunisia: [2005] O.J. L278/1.

[110] Agreement establishing an Association [2002] O.J. L129/1, modified [2006] O.J. L41/1. See also signing of a protocol [2005] O.J. L283/2, Association Agreement amended [2008] O.J. L207/16. An agreement establishing a dispute settlement mechanism, applicable to disputes under the trade provisions of the Euro-Mediterranean Agreement was signed in 2011: [2011] O.J. L34/1. See also the Euro Mediterranean Aviation Agreement [2011] O.J. L79/1 between the Union and Jordan.

[111] Decision concerning the conclusion of the Euro-Mediterranean Agreement [2006] O.J. L143/1.

[112] General Report 1995, 327.

[113] [1995] Bull.11, point 1.4.56 and Suppl.2/95.

[114] Algeria, Cyprus, Egypt, Israel, Jordan, Lebanon, Malta, Morocco, Syria, Tunisia, Turkey and the Palestinian Authority.

[115] The full text of the Declaration and the work programme can be found in [1995] Bull.11.

spurred on by a second Euro-Mediterranean ministerial[116] conference in 1997, in Malta.[117] The concrete implementation is carried out through Euro-Mediterranean Association Agreements. The existing association or co-operation agreements were "re-launched" on the basis of the Barcelona Declaration. The latter also set the ambitious target of a free-trade zone by 2010 between the Union and the 12 countries from the Southern and Eastern Mediterranean. This goal has not yet been attained, but the Union is constantly working to increase the scope of the bilateral agreements and has supported several states in their accession process to the WTO (Algeria is currently in the process of joining with strong support from the EU).[118] A Euro-Mediterranean Conference of Foreign Ministers took place in Valencia in April 2002, followed by a series of Euro-Mediterranean sectoral ministerial conferences.[119] Financial and technical measures were provided to accompany the reform of economic and social structures. Euro-Mediterranean co-operation in higher education was considered an indispensable instrument to achieve the key objectives set out in the Barcelona declaration (MEDA).[120] On the other hand, it will be remembered that the Union set up a Trans-European Co-operation Scheme for Higher Education (TEMPUS). The geographical scope of the TEMPUS III programme was enlarged to the Mediterranean non-member countries and territories.[121] The financial envelope for MEDA for the period 2000–2006 was set at €5.35 billion.

Following the Laeken European Council the Euro-Mediterranean Investment Facility was set up within the EIB. The latter also manages technical assistance and venture capital projects financed from the Union budget. Current agreements give duty-free access into the EU to all, or most, of the Mediterranean industrial products, with some concessions for agricultural produce and financial aid in the form of grants and loans. Mention must also be made of the Co-operation Agreement between the EEC, on the one part, and the countries party to the Charter of the Co-operation Council for the Arab States of the Gulf (the State of the United Arab Emirates, the State of Bahrain, the Kingdom of Saudi Arabia, the Sultanate of Oman, the State of Qatar and the State of Kuwait), on the other part, signed in 1988.[122]

In 2008, a framework agreement was concluded between the Union and Israel **38–30** on the general principles governing the State of Israel's participation in Union programmes.[123]In 2010 a framework protocol to the Euro-Mediterranean Agreement was signed.[124] The Euro-Mediterranean relations are currently governed by the Euro-Mediterranean Regional Strategy and Indicative Pro-gramme 2007–2013 (EUROMED) and forms part of the broader European

---

[116] 27 foreign ministers met in April 1997.

[117] General Report 1997, 315.

[118] *http://ec.europa.eu/trade/policy/countries-and-regions/countries/algeria/* [accessed August 23, 2013].

[119] General Report 2002, 880 and *http://eeas.europa.eu/euromed/conf/index_en.htm* [accessed August 23, 2013].

[120] Regulation 1488/96 [1996] O.J. L189/1, amended [2000] O.J. L311/1, repealed [2006] O.J. L310/1.

[121] Decision amending Decision 1999/311 adopting the third phase of TEMPUS (2000 to 2006) [2002] O.J. L195/34.

[122] See Ch.40: Enlargement, [1989] O. J. L54/1.

[123] Decision 2008/372 [2008] O.J. L129/39.

[124] [2010] O.J. L273/1.

Neighbourhood Policy. This programme seeks to add a further dimension to the Barcelona Declaration by strengthening its impact beyond bilateral relations.

5. RELATIONS WITH ASIA

38–31 In 2004, €272 million was committed under financial and technical co-operation with the countries of Asia.[125] Afghanistan received €18 million to cover rehabilitation and reconstruction schemes.[126] Operations to support uprooted people amounted to €25 million, while €3.4 million was allocated under the heading of political, economic and cultural co-operation. Along the same lines, €5 billion have been allocated to Asia for development cooperation for the period 2007–2013.[127]

Mention must be made of the Asia-Europe Meetings (ASEM) comprising the seven members of the ASEAN (Association of South-East Asian Nations) plus China, Japan and South Korea.[128]

(1) South Korea

38–32 A Framework Agreement for Trade and Co-operation and its attached political declaration was signed in October 1996 in South Korea. It aims at promoting closer economic relations and exchanges of information and mutually beneficial investment.[129] In 2012, The Union exported €37.7 billion in goods and services, and the EU imported €37.8 billion from South Korea, becoming the fourth most important export area for South Korea after China, Japan and the US. With registered investment stock of €39 billion (2010) the EU remains the largest investor in South Korea. In 2010, the Union and the Republic of South Korea signed a Free Trade Agreement (FTA).[130] It constitutes a new generation of FTA's and is the most comprehensive one entered into to date; it will come into force in 2011. Many of the import duties will be removed at that date and the rest will disappear over a period of five years. More important are the Korean Non-Tariff Barriers (NTBs): most of them will be eliminated. Investments in various industries will be liberalised. The FTA also contains detailed provisions on copyright, designs and geographical indications. There are also chapters on competition, transparency, government procurement, trade and sustainable development and cultural cooperation. A Free Trade Agreement was signed in 2011.

In addition, the EU is contributing to the Korean Peninsula Energy Development Organisation in support of the search for peace and stability in the

---

[125] General Report 2004, 264.
[126] General Report 2004, 260.
[127] EU External Action Service—Asia (*http://eeas.europa.eu/asia/index_en.htm* [accessed August 23, 2013]).
[128] General Report 2004, 259.
[129] See [2005] O.J. L332/1
[130] [2011] O.J. L127/1. See Regulation implementing its bilateral safeguard clause [2011] O.J. L145/10. An agreement for co-operation in the field of fusion energy research was concluded in 2006, published [2011] O.J. L154/2.

region. The EU supports the inter-Korean reconciliation process. From a commercial point of view there are a certain number of regulatory and access issues that remain unresolved.[131]

(2)   India

The current 1994 co-operation agreement goes well beyond trade and economic co-operation. The EU is India's largest trading partner. Total trade in 2011 was €79.9 billion (imports €39.3 billion, exports €40.4 billion). India benefits from the Generalised Preferential System. Overall high tariff levels and non-tariff trade barriers remain an obstacle for European industry. Various agreements have been concluded: on sugar cane, on trade in textiles, on science and technology[132] and -customs co-operation.

38–33

A Framework Agreement on Trade and Co-operation is in force since 2001. Back in 1997, two agreements were concluded on Co-operation and Mutual Administrative Assistance in Customs matters and on Telecommunications Procurement. EU–India relations were upgraded to a "strategic partnership" in 2004[133] and in 2005 India decided to participate in the European satellite radio navigation programme "Galileo"; it ensures the availability of the highest quality Galileo services in India as well as co-operation to establish regional augmentation systems based on EGNOS and Galileo. The parties entered into Free Trade Agreement negotiations in 2007 which are still on-going in 2013. Important issues include market access for goods, service provision and public procurement.

(3)   Other Asian Countries

Where other Asian Countries are concerned, the 25-nation summit in Bangkok between European and Asian leaders in March 1996, was a major step towards widening and deepening the dialogue between the two regions. The meeting brought together the 15 EU members with the seven members of ASEAN as well as China, Japan and Vietnam.

38–34

Co-operation agreements were signed with Cambodia and Laos, while Myanmar (Burma) was withdrawn from the Generalized System of Preferences (GSP). After the recent political developments in Myanmar, its relationship with the EU is now governed by the Council Conclusions of 23 April 2012, which marked a new chapter in bilateral relations between the two parties.[134] All restrictive measures have been suspended with the exception of the arms embargo. The Union supports reinstating the GSP for Myanmar as soon as possible, following the assessment of the ILO.[135]

---

[131] See, for instance, Commission Decision of October 8, 2002 concerning trade practices maintained by Korea affecting trade in commercial vessels [2002] O.J. L281/15.

[132] The 2007 agreement for scientific and technological co-operation was renewed in 2010: [2010] O.J. L304/1.

[133] General Report 2004, 262.

[134] Council Conclusions on Burma/Myanmar, 3159th Foreign Affairs Council Meeting, April 23, 2013: *http://eeas.europa.eu/myanmar/docs/council_conclusions_april_2012_en.pdf* [accessed August 23, 2013].

[135] Council Conclusions on Burma/Myanmar (above fn.20)

Co-operation agreements exist with Bangladesh, Pakistan and Sri Lanka in the fields of rural development, food aid, scientific and technical co-operation and industrial and trade promotion. Under a system of compensation for loss of export earnings for least-developed countries not signatories to the Lomé Convention,[136] Nepal, Bangladesh and have received Union financial aid. Diplomatic relations with Vietnam were established in 1990.[137] Relations were established with Singapore, Indonesia,[138] Bhutan, Cambodia and Pakistan.[139] The main activities covered a programme to protect EC–Asian patents and registered trademarks, education, environmental technology, energy co-operation, medical co-operation, refugee aid, etc.[140]

6. LATIN AMERICA

38–35   Agreements exist with Mexico[141] (Global Agreement 2000 establishing a Free Trade Area between the parties), Brazil (2007 Strategic Partnership),[142] Paraguay (Framework Co-operation Agreement 1992), Uruguay (Framework Cooperation Agreement 1992), Chile (2002 Association Agreement) and Argentina (1990 Framework Co-operation Agreement). An agreement with Ecuador was signed in 2003, but has not yet entered into force as it is awaiting ratification by all 27 EU states. The EU is the main trading partner, after the US, of most of these countries. Details can be found on the Commission website. The Union has established relations with the Rio Group Countries (Argentina,[143] Bolivia, Brazil,[144] Chile,[145] Columbia, Ecuador, Panama, Paraguay, Peru, Uruguay and

---

[136] [1987] O.J. L43/1.

[137] An agreement on certain aspects of air service was concluded in 2011: [2011] O.J. L132/5.

[138] An agreement on certain aspects of air service was signed in 2011: [2011] O.J. L264/2 and [2012] O.J. L52/1.

[139] For information concerning the relations of Europe with these countries, see the Bulletin and the General Reports.

[140] General Report 1992, 299. See Decision of December 2, 1993; agreement on trade in textiles with Hong Kong, Singapore, Macao, Indonesia, the Philippines, China, Bangladesh, South Korea, India, Malaysia, Pakistan, Sri Lanka and Thailand [1994] O.J. L110/1.

[141] An Economic Partnership, Political Co-ordination and Co-operation Agreement was signed in 1997 with the Community and its Member States [2000] O.J. L276/45 and a Joint Council was set up; see [2008] O.J. L198/55.

[142] See also agreement on civil aviation safety [2011] O.J. L273/1.

[143] See Regulation 1150/02 opening an additional autonomous quota for imports of high-quality beef [2002] O.J. L170/14.

[144] In 2002, the EC and Brazil signed a Memorandum of Understanding on Co-operation. It reflected the priorities for bilateral EC–Brazilian co-operation until the end of 2006. It foresees an indicative budget of close to €64 million and includes the possibility of adjustments when the parties -considered this necessary, IP/02/1707. In 2005, an agreement was concluded for scientific and technological co-operation: [2005] O.J. L295/37, and in 2012 agreements in the form of Exchange of Letters were published: [2012] O.J.L117/1.

[145] An agreement establishing an association between the European Union and its Member States, of the one part, and the Republic of Chile, of the other part, was concluded at the end of 2002 [2002] O.J. L352/1 and 3; it entered into force on March 1, 2005. In 2005, the EU concluded an aviation agreement with Chile; it is the first of its kind, it allows EU airlines to fly between Chile and the EU Member States. An Understanding was signed and provisionally applied concerning the conservation of swordfish stocks in the South Eastern Pacific Ocean [2010] O. J. L155/1.

Venezuela), the countries of Central America and Mercosur[146] and the Andean Group. There is also the San José Group composed of Costa Rica, El Salvador, Guatemala, Honduras, Nicaragua and Panama; with all those groups the Union holds regular meetings at ministerial level. In June 2012 the Union signed a comprehensive Trade Agreement with Central America, which will open up markets on both sides once fully implemented.

Besides those multilateral relations the Union has bilateral relations with a number of Latin American countries.

Following the establishment of the common organisation of the banana market a five-year diversification and development programme was established for the Latin American banana-producing countries: Panama, Costa Rica, Nicaragua, Honduras, El Salvador, Guatemala, Columbia, Venezuela, Ecuador, Peru and Bolivia.

The main economic co-operation activities were geared to trade promotion, training, regional integration, energy co-operation, investment promotion, development of democracy in the region, refugee aid, etc.[147]   **38–36**

7. AFRICA

South Africa is an important trade partner: an agreement on trade, development   **38–37**
and co-operation between the Union and its Member States and South Africa has been in existence for some time.[148]Many agreements were concluded with various African countries and their regional organisations; see, for instance, the agreement between the Union and the West African Economic and Monetary Union on certain aspects of air services[149]; the agreement establishing a framework for an Economic Partnership Agreement between the Eastern and Southern African States and the European Union and its Member States.[150]

8. EURATOM'S EXTERNAL RELATIONS

Contrary to the EC Treaty, the Euratom Treaty contains a Chapter concerning the   **38–38**
"External Relations" of that Union. It explicitly provides for the necessary powers and jurisdiction to "enter into obligations by concluding agreements or contracts with a third State, an international organisation or a national of a third State".[151] Such agreements are negotiated by the Commission in accordance with the directives of the Council, and are concluded by the Commission with

---

[146] General Report 1993, 271. The Association Agreement contained an Agreement on trade in Wines (Annex V [2002] O.J. L352/1083), the latter was amended [2006] O.J. L 54/23.
[147] EEC–Central America Co-operation Agreement [1986] O.J. L172/1.
[148] See Decision of the South African Co-operation Council of 2009 [2009] O.J. L265/34.
[149] [2011] O.J. L51/1.
[150] [2012] O.J. L111/1.
[151] Art.101, Euratom.

approval of the Council.[152] However, agreements and contracts whose implementation does not require action by the Council and can be effected within the limits of the relevant budget, are negotiated and concluded solely by the Commission, which must keep the Council informed.

Furthermore, Member States must communicate to the Commission the draft agreements or contracts with a third State, an international organisation or a national from a third State when such agreements or contracts concern matters within the ambit of the Euratom Treaty.[153] The Commission can oppose the conclusion of such acts and the Court of Justice must decide on disputes when called upon by the Member States in question.

9. MULTILATERAL RELATIONS

(1) GATT[154]

38–39   The negotiations for the Uruguay Round started on September 20, 1986 at Punte del Este and ended in Geneva on December 15, 1993. The final text was signed on April 15, 1994.

(2) The World Trade Organisation (WTO)

38–40   The Uruguay Round agreement established the World Trade Organisation (WTO), and thanks to the institutional framework of the WTO it makes possible the establishment the rules of world trade on a stable basis and on a commitment of the participants to· all the results of the negotiation, without exception. It encompasses an effective system for the settlement of disputes and, finally, it allows for a better co-ordination with the International Monetary Fund (IMF) and the Bank for Industrial Reconstruction and Development (BIRD). The institutions of the WTO consist of the Ministerial Conference which meets at least once every two years and takes the basic decisions and a General Council, which oversees the functioning of the WTO and the implementation of the ministerial decisions. It is, at the same time, the Organ for the Settlement of Disputes and the Organ for the Examination of the Commercial Policies. Councils for goods, services (GATS: General Agreement for Trade in Services)[155] and TRIPs (Trade Related Intellectual Property Rights) were set up. The functioning of the WTO, like that of the GATT, is based on consensus, and when a vote is necessary, decisions are, save exceptions, taken by a majority of the votes cast. However, decisions concerning the interpretation of the agreement and the granting of exemptions must be taken by a two-third majority of the members. Specific rules are provided for amendments to the agreement.

---

[152] Several such agreements were concluded right from the beginning for the purchase of nuclear material, among others with the US and the UK. See also the agreement between the EEC and Euratom and the USSR of 1990: [1990] O.J. L68/2 and a similar agreement with the republic of Tajikistan: [2004] O.J. L340/21.

[153] Art.103, Euratom.

[154] This summary is based on the Commission's weekly reports.

[155] See Court's Opnion 1/08 (2011/C 211/02): the conclusion of the agreement falls within the sphere of shared competences of the Union and the Member States [2011] O.J. C211/2.

The agreement contains one binding provision concerning the conformity of the national legislations with the rules of the WTO. Special attention is also given to the tandems "trade and environment" and "trade and competition". The WTO permits a reduction of the trade obstacles resulting in an improvement of the free "market access". It should also put an end to the bilateral and unilateral trade measures, which, particularly, the United States has a tendency to prefer above the agreed-upon multilateral arrangements. The final results of the Uruguay Round were put in the form of various agreements: on trade in goods, in services, trade related to intel-lectual property rights (TRIPS), dispute settlement regarding anti-dumping and anti-subsidy, trade policy review mechanisms and plurilateral trade agreements.

The Uruguay Round Agreement ended with a Declaration on the Functioning of the GATT which, among other things, aims at establishing a link between trade, monetary and financial policies.

(3)   The Doha Negotiations for a New Round

On November 14, 2001, the WTO members agreed on a Declaration providing **38–41** for a new round of global trade negotiations. Special attention was to be given to the "Least Developed Countries", social development, services, market access for non-agricultural products, competition, investment, simplifying customs and related procedures, government procurement, trade-related aspects of intellectual property (TRIPS), environment, public health, etc.[156] This list is very long indeed, and was so at the insistence of the EU; one might wonder whether the EU did not thereby overplay its hand. The Doha round has not yet come to a conclusion.

FURTHER READING

Dr Robert Maclean, *EU Trade Barrier Regulation: Tackling Unfair Foreign* **38–42** *Trade Practices* (Sweet & Maxwell, 2005).

Mistuo Matsushita, Thomas J. Schoenbaum, Petros C. Mavroidis, *The World Trade Organisation* (Oxford University Press, 2003).

Van Bael & Bellis, *Anti-dumping and other trade protection laws of the E.C.* (Kluwer Law International, 2004).

---

[156] *http://www.wto.org/english/tratop_e/dda_e/dohasubjects_e.htm* [accessed August 23, 2013].

CHAPTER 39

Development Co-operation

1. GENERAL REMARKS

According to the TFEU, Union policy in the field of development co-operation **39–01** must be conducted within the framework of the principles and objectives of the Union's external action (see above, the chapter on General Provisions concerning the Union's external action). Moreover, the Union's development co-operation and that of the Member States must complement and reinforce each other.[1] The TFEU provides that:

> "In the areas of development cooperation and humanitarian aid, the Union shall have competence to carry out activities and conduct a common policy; however, the exercise of that competence shall not result in Member States being prevented from exercising theirs."[2]

The primary objective of the Union's development co-operation is the reduction and, in the long-term, the eradication of poverty.

This policy must comply with the Union's international commitments.[3] More specifically, the TFEU provides that the Union and the Member States must comply with the commitments and take account of the objectives they have approved in the context of the United Nations and other competent international organisations.[4] In this regard, account must be taken of the Millennium Development Goals (MDGs), which the Member States of the United Nations adopted in 2000. The MDGs are intended to focus the efforts of the world community on achieving significant, measurable improvements in people's lives by the year 2015. The eight MDGs are:

- eradicate extreme poverty and hunger;
- achieve universal primary education;
- promote gender equality and empower women;
- reduce child mortality;
- improve maternal health;
- combat HIV/AIDS, malaria and other diseases;
- ensure environmental sustainability; and

---

[1] Art.208(1) TFEU.
[2] Art.4(4) TFEU.
[3] Art.208(2) TFEU.
[4] Art.208(2) TFEU.

- develop a global partnership for development.[5]

39–02   Related to these targets is the pledge of the participating developed countries to contribute 0.7 per cent of their GNI towards poverty reduction. The European Union has reaffirmed its commitment to the 0.7 per cent target and has worked sustainably to realise the eight MDGs.

More than half of global official development assistance comes from the Union and its Member States, making it the world's biggest aid donor.[6]

Furthermore, the Union's development policy must pursue so-called policy coherence for development (normally referred to as PCD) which means that the development objective must be taken into account when implementing other Union policies that are likely to affect developing countries.[7] This aspect has been given much increased attention since the turn of the millennium.

39–03   By definition, the Union's development co-operation is aimed at developing countries. However, the size and type of assistance provided by the Union differs considerably between the different recipients. Traditionally the Union has focussed its development co-operation upon Sub-Saharan African States as well as Caribbean and Pacific States. At the time of writing, this group of African, Caribbean and Pacific (ACP) States numbers 79. The Union has entered into a special agreement with this group of countries (see below). Moreover, a number of so-called overseas countries and territories belonging to some of the Union's Member States are offered preferential treatment. Finally, the Union also provides development co-operation assistance to other developing countries in Latin America, Northern Africa, Europe and Asia.

Despite growing pressure on public budgets, the Union and its Member States remain at the centre of global efforts to promote aid and development in the developing countries. In 2010, EU development co-operation aid totalled €53.8 billion (of which €9.57 billion was from the EU institutions). The objective is to increase the Member States' collective development aid to 0.7 per cent of GNI by 2015. However, in 2011 the figure had only reached 0.42 per cent, meaning that it appears increasingly unlikely that the 0.7 per cent target will be achieved. The European figure may, however, be compared with that of the US of 0.21 per cent of GNI in 2010 (this figure does not include the very substantial private donations from the US) and 0.2 per cent of GNI coming from Japan. The Union Institutions are responsible for around 17 per cent of the total aid given by the Union (including both institutions and Member States).

The Union is a vital market for developing countries and this is particularly true with regard to several African countries. Previously the Union offered ACP countries as a group preferential access without offsetting concessions. This, however, discriminated between different developing countries (ACP countries versus non-ACP countries) and was found to contravene WTO-rules. The Union's trade preferences have therefore been amended very considerably.

---

[5] For more information of the Union's activities in some of these areas, see Communication from the Commission to the European Parliament, the Council, the European Economic and Social Committee, and the Committee of the Regions – A twelve-point EU action plan in support of the Millennium Development Goals, COM(2010)159 final.

[6] For updated data, see further *http://www.oecd.org/dac/stats* [accessed August 23, 2013].

[7] Art.208(1) TFEU.

The Union has adopted a so-called Generalised System of Preferences (or GSP **39–04** as it is normally called) which gives developing countries duty-free or reduced-duty access to the Union market for their finished and semi-finished products.[8] This GSP scheme is divided into three different arrangements. The principal one is the general arrangement which is available to all developing countries. This arrangement provides preferential access with respect to a number of products. Even better access is provided under the so-called GSP+ incentive arrangement which applies to countries that are considered to be "vulnerable" in terms of their size or the limited diversification of their exports and which have ratified and effectively implemented 27 specific international conventions in the fields of human rights, core labour standards, sustainable development and good governance.[9] Finally, the Union's GSP scheme operates a third arrangement which is only available to the world's poorest countries; i.e. the least-developed countries or LDCs.[10] This arrangement provides these countries with duty free access to the Union market on all products with the sole exception of arms and it is therefore known as the everything-but-arms (EBA) arrangement.

In order to simplify the financing of the Union's development co-operation as from 2007 the previous system with many different financial instruments was replaced with a system based upon five financial instruments of which the so-called Development Cooperation Instrument or DCI is the most important when it comes to traditional development cooperation aid.[11] Moreover, the Union is distributing its development cooperation assistance through multi-annual strategies and programmes. One of the consequences of this "programming" approach is that the Union may withhold funding to on-going development co-operation projects if it finds that a developing country does not comply with the conditions for the assistance, thereby essentially giving the Union a stronger negotiation position vis-à-vis the developing countries.

The Union may also conclude agreements with third countries and international organisations[12] helping to achieve the objectives of development co-operation and those referred to in the general provisions on the Union's external action.[13]

The Union and the Member States have parallel competences within the field **39–05** of development co-operation policy.[14] This means that the Member States retain the necessary powers to continue to carry out their own development policy. Consequently, the Treaty provides for co-ordination of those policies and instructs the Union and the Member States to consult each other on their aid programmes, including in international organisations and during international

---

[8] Regulation 978/2012 of the European Parliament and of the Council of 25 October 2012 applying a scheme of generalised tariff preferences and repealing Council Regulation732/2008 [2012] O.J. L303/1.

[9] See further Annex VIII to Regulation 978/2012 of the European Parliament and of the Council of October 25, 2012 applying a scheme of generalised tariff preferences and repealing Council Regulation 732/2008 [2012] O.J. L303/1.

[10] At the time of writing, 49 States qualified as LDCs for the purposes of the Union's GSP scheme.

[11] Regulation 1905/2006 [2006] O.J. L378/41 of the European Parliament and of the Council of 18 December 2006 establishing a financing instrument for development cooperation.

[12] Arts 209(2) and 211 TFEU.

[13] Arts 21 TEU and 208 TFEU.

[14] Art.4(4) TFEU.

conferences.[15] They may also undertake joint action and Member States shall contribute, if necessary, to the implementation of the Union aid programmes.[16] Moreover, the Union development cooperation policy and those of the Member States shall be mutually complementary.[17]

The Union's co-operation with third countries and international organisations may be the subject, as indicated, of agreements which are concluded in accordance with the Treaty provisions on the conclusion of international agreements.[18]

Administration of EU development cooperation assistance

39–06 EU development cooperation assistance is primarily managed by the European Commission's "Directorate-General Development and Co-operation – Europe Aid". This directorate general must co-operate, however, with the European External Action Service (EEAS) and must work through the Union's delegations which are under the authority of the Union's High Representative (in practice under the authority of the EEAS).

2. RELATIONS WITH THE AFRICAN, CARIBBEAN AND PACIFIC COUNTRIES (ACP)

39–07 The main feature of the Union policy towards developing countries is the ACP–EU Agreement, initially known as the Yaoundé Convention (Yaoundé I and II), subsequently replaced by the Lomé Convention (Lomé I, II, III and IV), and presently known as the Cotonou Agreement, signed on June 23, 2000.[19] The designation of the Cotonou Agreement as a 'partnership agreement' is intended to signal that the two sides are equal partners. The Cotonou Agreement entered into force on April 1, 2003. The objective is to:

> "promote and expedite the economic, cultural and social development of the ACP States, with a view of contributing to peace and security and to promote a stable and democratic political environment."[20]

It establishes commercial, industrial and financial relations between the Union on the one hand, and now 78 African, Caribbean and Pacific countries,[21] on the other.

---

[15] Art.210(1) TFEU.

[16] Art.210(1) TFEU.

[17] Art.208(1) TFEU.

[18] Arts 209(2) and 218 TFEU.

[19] Partnership agreement between the members of the African, Caribbean and Pacific Group of States of the one part, and the European Community and its Member States, of the other part, signed in Cotonou on June 23, 2000, [2000] O.J. L317/3, as amended most recently by Decision 1/2012 [2012] O.J. L174/27 of the ACP-EU Council of Ministers of June 15, 2012 regarding the revision of terms and conditions of investment financing.

[20] Art.1 of the Cotonou Agreement.

[21] Angola, Antigua and Barbuda, the Commonwealth of the Bahamas, Barbados, Belize, Benin, Botswana, Burkina Faso, Burundi, Cameroon, Cape Verde, Central African Republic, Chad, Cape Verde, Comoros, Congo (Democratic Republic of the), Congo (Republic of the), Cook Islands, Cote

This relationship grew out of a quite different set of links which existed when the Community was first established. Most of the countries that today are "associated" with the Union were colonies at the time of the Union's inception and the Member States, that were colonial powers, had special responsibilities towards their colonies. The EEC Treaty provided for the association of "overseas countries and territories", in order to increase trade and to promote jointly economic and social development.[22] Consequently, countries which at the time when the Union was established had special relations with (i.e. were colonies of) Belgium, France, Italy and the Netherlands and, after accession, Denmark as well as the United Kingdom (and to a lesser extent Portugal and Spain) were associated with the Union. The Treaty provisions were drafted at a time when most of these overseas countries were still dependent, but in particular France insisted that the principle of a special relationship was maintained also after its (former) colonies gained independence.

For a first period of five years, the details and the procedures of the association were determined by an implementing convention[23] annexed to the Treaty.[24] This convention was replaced by an agreement negotiated between the Union and the emerging African and Malagasy States, known as the Yaoundé I Convention.[25] A second Yaoundé Convention, fairly similar to the first, came into force on January 1, 1971.[26] It did not apply to the United Kingdom, Ireland and Denmark until January 1, 1975.[27] An entirely new convention was signed at Lomé (Togo) on February 28, 1975, between the Union of nine and 46 countries situated in Africa, the Caribbean and the Pacific.[28] It came into force on April 1, 1976,[29] and expired on March 1, 1980. The Lomé II Convention expired in 1985 and the Lomé III Convention in 1990.

39–08

The Lomé Conventions differed from the Yaoundé Conventions in that they aimed to establish a kind of partnership between the developing countries and the Union and its Member States. This partnership aspect was emphasised in the Cotonou Agreement that, as indicated, is officially designated a "Partnership Agreement". The main features of the latter agreement concern "co-operation

---

d'Ivoire, Djibouti, the Commonwealth of Dominica, Dominican Republic, East Timor, Equatorial Guinea, Eritrea, Ethiopia, Fiji, Gabon, the Gambia, Ghana, Grenada, Guinea, Guinea-Bissau, the Republic of Guyana, the Republic of Haiti, Jamaica, Kenya, Kiribati, Lesotho, Liberia, Madagascar, Malawi, Mali, Marshall Islands, Mauritania, Mauritius, Micronesia (Federated States of), Mozambique, Namibia, Nauru, Niger, Nigeria, Niue, Palau, Papua New Guinea, Rwanda, Saint Christopher and Nevis, Saint Lucia, Saint Vincent and the Grenadines, Samoa, Sao Tomé & Principe, Senegal, Seychelles, Sierra Leone, Solomon Islands, Somalia, South Africa, Sudan, the Republic of Surinam, Swaziland, Tanzania, Cape Verde Togo, Tonga, the Republic of Trinidad and Tobago, Tuvalu, Uganda, Vanuatu, Zambia, Zimbabwe. In addition, Cuba is an ACP country, but is not a signatory to the Cotonou Agreement.

[22] Art.131 of the EEC Treaty.

[23] This was a convention concluded between the Member States themselves, not with the overseas countries.

[24] Art.136 of the EEC Treaty.

[25] [1964] O.J. 93/1431 and 93/1490.

[26] [1970] O.J. L282/1; O.J. Spec. Ser. I (2) 7.

[27] Arts 109 and 115(1) Act of Accession.

[28] [1976] O.J. L25/1.

[29] [1976] O.J. L25/1. Since it expired before the Lomé II Convention became effective, transitional measures were adopted [1980] O.J. L55/1. The Lomé III Convention, see [1984] Bull. 11, 7 and General Report 1984, 275.

strategies" and "development finance co-operation". The strategies put the emphasis on private investment and the development of a dynamic, viable and competitive private sector, the improvement of the quality, availability and accessibility of financial and non-financial services to private enterprises and the promotion of business development through the provision of finance, guarantee facilities and technical support for the creation, establishment, expansion, diversification, rehabilitation, restructuring, modernisation or privatisation of dynamic, viable and competitive enterprises in all economic sectors.[30] The emphasis is on private business and thereby downplays the role of the "State", which, until recently, was the principal actor in this so-called partnership between the ACP States and the Union. The agreement also provides for economic sector development, tourism, social sector development, youth issues and cultural development.[31] Assistance is also provided for "regional co-operation and integration". In the Agreement the parties recognise the need to ensure a better operation of the international commodity market and to increase market transparency. The same applies to services, information and communication technology, the information society and trade-related areas.[32] Also need to be considered competition policy, the protection of intellectual property rights, standardisation and certification, sanitary and phytosanitary measures, environment, labour standards and consumer protection and health.[33]

Of particular importance for the ACP countries is the development of finance co-operation.[34] Operations finance is implemented by the Parties in close co-operation. The ACP States are responsible for defining the objectives and priorities, choosing projects and programmes, preparing and presenting dossiers, preparing, negotiating and concluding contracts, implementation and management and maintaining the projects and the programmes. The Union is responsible for taking the financing decisions.[35] Eligible for financial support are: ACP States, regional and inter-State bodies and joint bodies set up by the ACP States and the Union. Private companies, firms and other private organisations and private operators are also eligible, subject to the agreement of the ACP State or States. This constitutes a novelty and is the logical consequence of the emphasis put on private investment.[36] The latter can also profit from the Centre for Development of Enterprise (CDE).[37]

39–09   The scope of financing may include measures to attenuate the debt burden of an ACP State, macroeconomic reforms, mitigation of instability of export earnings, sectoral policies, institutional development, technical co-operation and

---

[30] Art.21 Agreement.
[31] Arts 23–27 Agreement.
[32] Arts 40–44 Agreement.
[33] Arts 45–51 Agreement.
[34] Arts 55–83 Agreement.
[35] See Internal Agreement of July 17, 2006 between the Representatives of the Member States on the financing of Community aid under the multi-annual financial framework for the period 2008–2013 in accordance with the ACP-EC Partnership Agreement and the allocation of financial assistance to the Overseas Countries and territories [2007] O.J. L202/35 and the Financial Regulation applicable to the 9th European Development Fund [2003] O.J. L83/1, amended [2007] O.J. L82/1.
[36] Art.74 and following Agreement.
[37] This centre is a joint institution of the European Union and the ACP; it is endowed with €110 million from the European Development Fund; it operates to complement the Commission, the ACP Secretariat and the European Investment Bank.

humanitarian and emergency assistance. The overall amount and the method of financing are decided jointly by the ACP State and the Union.[38] The Cotonou Agreement also contains special provisions for the least-developed, landlocked and island ACP States.[39]

Arguably the most important novelty of the Cotonou Agreement is that it replaces the Union's previous unilateral trade preferences to the ACP States that applied under the Lomé IV Convention, by new reciprocal trade arrangements that are in conformity with the WTO rules. These new trade arrangements are called Economic Partnership Agreements (EPAs)[40] and were to be completed before the end of 2007 so that they could enter into force on January 1, 2008 at the latest. The intention was that the Union, on the one hand, and different groups of ACP countries, on the other hand, should enter into EPAs whereby the ACP countries would gain preferential access to the Union market—but at the same time the Union would be given preferential access to the ACP markets (reciprocity). The ACP States have shown considerable reluctance vis-à-vis the EPAs so that at the beginning of 2013 only one EPA had entered into force; namely the one between the Caribbean ACP countries (the CARIFORUM States) and the European Union and its Member States.[41] The main parts of this Agreement concern trade partnerships and sustainable development, trade-related matters, competition, environment, investment and trade-related services, e-commerce, etc.

The Cotonou Agreement is concluded for 20 years, having commenced on March 1, 2000; financial Protocols are defined for five years. For the period 2008–2013 the financial resources are the 10th European Development Fund (EDF)[42] which provides €21.97 billion for the ACP countries.[43] For the period 2014-2020 an 11th European Development Fund is expected to be adopted sometime before the end of 2013. Finally, the Cotonou Agreement lays down provisions on consultation procedures and appropriate measures as regards infringements of human rights, democratic principles and the rule of law. In case of presumed violation of these principles, consultations may be requested, which may not last more than 60 days. If no solution acceptable to both Parties is found or if consultation is refused, "appropriate measures" may be taken in accordance with international law and proportional to the violation. It is understood that suspension shall be a measure of last resort.[44] Nevertheless, suspension has been applied against ACP countries on several occasions since the Cotonou Agreement

---

[38] Arts 62 and 63 Agreement.

[39] Arts 84–90 Agreement.

[40] Art.37 Agreement.

[41] [2008] O.J. L289/1. These ACP countries are: Antigua and Barbuda, the Commonwealth of the Bahamas, Barbados, Belize, the Commonwealth of Dominica, the Dominican Republic, Grenada, the Republic of Guyana, the Republic of Haiti, Jamaica, Saint Christopher and Nevis, Saint Lucia, Saint Vincent and the Grenadines, the Republic of Suriname and the Republic of Trinidad and Tobago. The Agreement provides for a CARIFORUM-EU Council and a Trade and Development Committee.

[42] [2007] O.J. L314/1; see also Regulation 215/2008 on the Financial Regulation applicable to the 10th EDF [2008] O.J. L78/1 and Decision adopting the rules of procedure of the EDF Committee [2008] O.J. L78/35.

[43] See Regulation 215/2008 on the Financial Regulation applicable to the 10th EDF [2008] O.J. L78/1, amended [2011] O.J. L102/1.

[44] Art.96 Agreement.

entered into force.[45] The Cotonou Agreement was modified for the first time in 2008,[46] inter alia to allow the Union to take appropriate measures, including partial suspension, where an ACP State fails to fulfil an obligation under the Agreement on non-proliferation of weapons of mass destruction.[47] In March 2010, the Union and the ACP States concluded the second revision of the Cotonou Partnership Agreement and provisionally applied this revised agreement as from October 31, 2010.[48]

Institutional Aspects of the EU–ACP Agreement

39–10   The Cotonou Agreement provides for three joint institutions: the Council of Ministers (Council),[49] the Committee of Ambassadors (Committee)[50] and the Joint Parliamentary Assembly (Assembly). The Council is composed of, on the one hand, the members of the Council of the Union and members of the European Commission and, on the other hand, of a member of the government of each ACP State. Its function is to conduct the political dialogue, adopt the policy guidelines and take the decisions necessary for the implementation of the Cotonou Agreement, settle disputes,[51] and ensure the smooth functioning of the political dialogue. Decisions are taken by common agreement. Proceedings are valid when half of the members of the Council and one member of the Commission and two-thirds of the members representing the ACP States are present; members may be represented. The Committee is composed of, on the one hand, the Permanent Representatives of the EU Member States, a member of the European Commission and, on the other hand, of the Heads of Mission of the ACP States to the Union. It assists the Council in the implementation of its tasks and follows the application of the Agreement. The Assembly is composed in equal numbers of members of the European Parliament and members of the ACP parliaments; failing this, the persons designated must first be approved by the Assembly. It is a purely consultative body.

3.   ASSOCIATION OF THE OVERSEAS COUNTRIES AND TERRITORIES (OCT)

39–11   According to Art.198 TFEU, a number of non-European countries and territories, which have special relations with Denmark, France, the Netherlands and the United Kingdom, are awarded a special status. These countries and territories are listed in Annex II to the TFEU. In practice this "association" to the Union means that the overseas countries and territories are offered particularly preferential treatment vis-à-vis the Union, both with regards to financial assistance and with

---

[45] See for example General Report 2002, 1004.
[46] [2005] O.J. L287/3.
[47] [2008] O.J. L129/44.
[48] [2011] O.J. L13/1.
[49] Decision 1/2005 of the ACP-EC Council of Ministers of March 8, 2005 concerning the adoption of the Rules of Procedure of the ACP-EC Council of Ministers [2005] O.J. L95/44.
[50] Decision 3/2005 of the ACP-EC Council of Ministers of March 8, 2005 concerning the adoption of the Rules of Procedure of the ACP-EC Committee of Ambassadors [2005] O.J. L95/51.
[51] Art.98 Agreement.

regards to access to the Union market. Major fields of co-operation are environment, agriculture, fisheries, industrial development, services, tourism and trade. The declared aim of the decision is to promote the economic and social development of the countries and territories and to establish close economic relations between them and the Union as a whole.[52]

4. HUMANITARIAN AID

Jointly the Member States and the Union institutions are the world's biggest donor of humanitarian aid, providing more than 50 per cent of humanitarian aid worldwide. The Union's humanitarian aid is administered by the Commission's Directorate-General for Humanitarian Aid & Civil Protection. In practice this directorate general provides financing whilst the actual humanitarian aid work on the ground primarily is carried out by a number of non-governmental organisations as well as by international organisations like the United Nations. The Union's humanitarian aid is primarily directed towards developing countries, but differs from development co-operation assistance: whereas the latter is aimed at poverty cradication and sustainable development, humanitarian aid is aimed at emergency situations. Moreover, the Union's humanitarian aid operations shall not only be conducted in compliance with the principles of international law, but also in compliance with the principles of impartiality, neutrality and non-discrimination.[53] These last-mentioned principles do not apply to the provision of development cooperation assistance. Specific procedures for the provision of humanitarian aid have been laid down in the humanitarian aid regulation.[54]

39–12

FURTHER READING

D. Sicurelli, *The European Union's Africa Policies: Norms, Interests and Impact* (Ashgate Publishing, 2010).

39–13

European Commission, *Economic Partnership Agreements (EPAs): African, Caribbean and Pacific voices speak up for trade and development* (Publications Office, 2012).

European Investment Bank, *The European Investment Bank in Africa, the Caribbean, the Pacific and the Overseas Territories* (EIB, 2013).

Online Publications Catalogue of the Directorate General for Development: *http://ec.europa.eu/europeaid/multimedia/publications/index_en.htm*.

O. Barbarinde & G. Faber, *The European Union and the Developing Countries, The Cotonou Agreement* (Martinus Nijhoff, 2006).

P. Hoebink, *European Development Cooperation: In Between the Local and the Global* (Amsterdam University Press, 2010).

S. Bartelt, *ACP-EU Development Cooperation at a crossroads?: One year after the second revision of the Cotonou Agreement* (European Foreign Affairs Review 2012, v.17, n. 2).

---

[52] Art.198 TFEU. See generally Arts 198–204 TFEU.

[53] Art.214(2) TFEU.

[54] Council Regulation1257/96 [1996] O.J. L163/1 of June 20, 1996 concerning humanitarian aid.

DEVELOPMENT CO-OPERATION

S. Gänzle, S. Grimm & D. Makhan, *The European Union and Global Development: An 'Enlightened Superpower' in the Making?* (Palgrave Macmillan, 2012).

CHAPTER 40

Enlargement

It might be useful to recall what has happened before 2013. The Union was **40–01** founded in 1957, in Rome, by six States: Belgium, Germany, France, Italy, Luxembourg, and the Netherlands. In 1973 it was enlarged a first time to Denmark, Ireland and the United Kingdom. In 1981 Greece joined, followed in 1986 by Portugal and Spain and, in 1995, the Union was enlarged to Austria, Finland and Sweden, bringing the number of Member States to 15. In 2004, 10 countries joined the Union: Cyprus, Czech Republic, Estonia, Hungary, Latvia, Lithuania, Malta, Poland, Slovakia and Slovenia. In 2007, Bulgaria and Romania joined and, in 2013, Croatia. The possibility of such enlargements was provided for by the various European Treaties, right from the beginning, since the objective has always been to unite Europe. See above, the chapter on History, where it is mentioned that already in 1946, barely a year after the end of the Second World War, Churchill proposed to "recreate the European family" by "building a kind of United States of Europe". The reader will therefore also understand that there may still be more enlargements to come.

Any European State which respects the principles of liberty, democracy, respect for human rights and fundamental freedoms, and the rule of law,[1] may apply to become a member of the Union. It must address its application to the Council, which shall act unanimously, after consulting the Commission and receiving the assent of Parliament.[2]

The Commission periodically adopts strategy papers for the EU enlargement policy. It gives an updated overview of the enlargement policy and a summary of progress made by each of the candidate and potential candidate countries, the latest dating from the autumn 2011.[3]

Once negotiations with a candidate country have started, the Commission **40–02** issues regular reports on the process towards accession. The Commission uses objective economic and political criteria to assess each applicant's ability to fulfil, in the medium term, the obligations arising out of accession. These criteria were defined by the European Council in Copenhagen in 1993 (often referred to as the "Copenhagen criteria")[4]; they ensure equal treatment of all applicants. An applicant country must have:

- stable institutions guaranteeing democracy, the rule of law, human rights and respect for and protection of minorities;

---

[1] Arts 49(1) and 2 TEU.
[2] Art.49 TFEU.
[3] COM(2011) 666 final.
[4] EC Bull. 1993–6, 1013.

- a functioning market economy and the capacity to cope with competitive pressure and market forces within the Union;
- the ability to take on the obligations of membership, including adherence to the aims of political, economic and monetary union.

The Commission seeks to evaluate the progress each applicant might reasonably be expected to make in the years ahead, bearing in mind that the *acquis communautaire* (existing Union law and practice acquired over the years) would continue to evolve. Without prejudice to the actual date of accession, the Commission's opinion is, therefore, based on the foreseeable economic situation in the relevant country and its probable capacity to apply existing Union rules in the medium term.

1. THE ACCESSION PROCESS

40-03   The accession process consists of several stages, which can be summarised as follows. The first step is that the country becomes an official candidate for membership; however, this does not in itself entail that the accession negotiations are opened. The next step is referred to as the "screening"; it is normally not initialised until there is a high degree of certainty that the results of the "screening" will be that formal negotiations can be opened. The "screening" entails that the Commission, assisted by the candidate country, examines how well prepared the country is for taking over Union Law. The examination is conducted by "chapters" of which there are 35, each one being a major policy field or separate issue; for instance, agriculture or financial questioning. The Union law that the country has to take over is normally referred to as the "*acquis communautaire*". If the result of the screening is positive, formal negotiations are opened. They are also conducted by chapter. The main principles governing the negotiations are that the negotiation on one individual chapter is only provisionally closed until the whole negotiation process is conducted definitely. The results of the negotiation process are laid down in the accession treaty. It must be signed and ratified by the candidate country as well as all existing Member States. In the time from the signature to the accession date, i.e. during the time the national ratification processes take place, the candidate country has the status of "acceding country". This means in essence that it has "observer status" in the decision-making processes of the Union; it can thus comment on draft legislation but it has no vote.

2. FINANCIAL AND ECONOMIC ASSISTANCE

40-04   In order to help the countries that apply to become members of the Union to carry out the required reforms, the Union provides financial assistance in various areas under the Instrument for Pre-accession Assistance (IPA).[5] The assistance given

---

[5] Council Regulation 1085/2006 [2006] O.J. L210/82, with later amendments, implemented through Commission Regulation 718/2007 [2007] O.J. L170/1, with later amendments. The IPA replaces a number of separate instruments, applied previously.

depends on the different needs of the countries. The assistance falls in these five major groups: (a) transition assistance and institution building; (b) cross-border co-operation; (c) regional development; (d) human resources development; and (e) rural development. In 2008, the Commission adopted the multi-annual financing framework document for all candidate and potential candidate countries, establishing the 2010–2012 financial framework with indicative allocation for each beneficiary.[6] Over that period the amount of assistance is €5.334 billion.

A donor conference was organised aimed at raising pledges of funding for Kosovo's socioeconomic development; participants pledged €1.2 billion including 70 per cent from the Union and the Member States.

3.   CANDIDATE COUNTRIES

(1)   Turkey

The history of the accession of Turkey to the Union is a long one and has known many ups and downs. For instance, an Association Agreement was conducted in 1963 for the progression establishment of a Customs Union between Turkey and the Union was achieved in 1995, and in 2006 Turkey became the 7th largest trading partner of the Union. In 1999, at the Helsinki European Council, Turkey was officially recognised as a candidate State, on an equal footing with other States; negotiations for accession finally started on October 3, 2005. They are still on-going.   **40–05**

The attitude of certain Member States to Turkey joining the Union is, to say the least, ambiguous. Nevertheless, the European Council always formally acted as if there were no doubts about starting negotiations. The conclusions of one of the European Councils read as follows.

> "The European Council welcomes the commitments of the Turkish government to carry forward the reform process, in particular the remaining legislative work by the end of 2003, and supports its on-going effort to fulfil the Copenhagen political criteria for opening access negotiations with the Union. Taking into account progress achieved, significant further efforts to this end are required."

With a view to helping Turkey achieve this objective, the Council adopted recently a revised accession partnership,[7] which sets out the priorities which Turkey should pursue, supported by substantially increased pre-accession financial assistance. In accordance with the Helsinki conclusions, fulfilment of these priorities will assist Turkey towards EU membership. The Accession Partnership[8] constitutes the cornerstone of EU/Turkey relations. In January 2006, the Council decided on the principles, priorities and conditions contained in the Accession partnership.[9] Between 1996 and 2004, Turkey received around €1.5

---

[6] COM (2008) 705.
[7] [2003] O.J. L 145/40.
[8] See Regulation 390/2001 on assistance to Turkey in the framework of the pre-accession strategy, and in particular on the establishment of an Accession Partnership [2001] O.J. L58/1.
[9] [2006] O.J. L22/34.

billion in Union assistance for different projects; €300 million in 2005 and €500 million in 2006. From 2007 on Turkey, with other candidates will be a beneficiary of the Instrument for Structural Policy for pre-Accession (IPA)[10]; the annual allocation for Turkey in the 2007–2013 period will be €1 billion.

40–06   During 2008, the accession negotiations continued and by the end of that year negotiations had been opened on 10 of the 35 Chapters[11] and provisionally closed on one! According to the monitoring report,[12] Turkey continued to fulfil the Copenhagen political criteria sufficiently, although progress on reform was limited in 2008, but it had made progress on alignment with the Union's legal order and, as regard the economic criteria, was a functioning market economy.

(2)   Macedonia (former Yugoslav Republic of)

40–07   A Stabilisation and Association Agreement (SAA)[13] was signed in April 2001; it entered into force in April 2004. Macedonia applied for membership in March 2004. In June 2004, the Council decided on the European partnership[14] and on the principles, priorities and conditions contained in the European Partnership.[15] Macedonia benefited from a total EU assistance of about €728 million between 2002 and 2004. In addition, Macedonia benefited from the Community Assistance for the Reconstruction, Development and Stability (CARDS)[16] regional programme, macroeconomic assistance and humanitarian assistance. Several agreements were concluded with the Union on wine, trade in agricultural and fisheries products, on the participation in Union programmes, on transport, on the presence of the European Union Monitoring Mission and on the EU Police Mission and the Status of Force (SOFA).[17]

In 2005, the Council granted the country candidate status. In 2009, the Commission recommended that accession negotiations be opened with Macedonia. For the Council to act upon this, unanimity is requested and Greece has an outstanding issue with Macedonia concerning the very name of Macedonia.

---

[10] Regulation 1267/1999 [1999] O.J. L161/73. IPA replaces PHARE, ISPA, SAPARD and CARDS.
[11] The negotiations concern in particular the following 31 chapters: 1. free movement of goods; 2. free movement of persons; 3. freedom to provide services; 4. free movement of capital; 5. company law [which includes the basic freedom of establishment]; 6. competition policy; 7. agriculture; 8. fisheries; 9. transport; 10. taxation; 11. economic and monetary union; 12. statistics; 13. social policy and employment; 14. energy; 15. industrial policy; 16. small- and medium-sized enterprises; 17. science and research; 18. education and training; 19. telecommunications and information technology; 20. culture and audio-visual policy; 21. regional policy and co-ordination of structural instruments; 22. environment; 23. consumer and health protection; 24. co-operation in the field of justice and home affairs; 25. customs union; 26. external relations; 27. common foreign and security policy; 28. financial control; 29. financial and budgetary provisions; 30 institutions; and 31. others.
[12] COM (2008) 674.
[13] [2004] O.J. L86/1.
[14] Regulation 533/2004 [2004] O.J. L86/1.
[15] [2004] O.J. L222/20, replaced [2006] O.J. L35/57.
[16] Regulation 2666/2000 [2000] O.J. L306/1.
[17] For further information consult, *http://ec.europa.eu/enlargement/candidate-countries/the_former_ yugoslav_republic_of_macedonia/eu_the_former_yugoslav_republic_of_macedonia_relations_ en.htm* [accessed August 23, 2013].

(3) Iceland

The Icelandic Parliament voted on July 16, 2009 to seek membership of the European Union and a formal request for membership was filed with the Union on July 23, 2009. The country is very aligned with the *acquis communautaire* given its membership of the EEA. The negotiations are still on-going in the summer of 2013. Parliamentary elections in Iceland brought a new government in May 2013. The new government announced that the accession negotiations will not be continued without a prior referendum.

40–08

(4) Montenegro

Montenegro declared independence from Serbia in 2006. An agreement on trade and trade-related matters entered into force on January 1, 2008 and its implementation is proceeding satisfactorily. Montenegro has made significant progress in addressing the political criteria for Union membership by improving its legal framework and strengthening its institutional infrastructure. A Stabilisation and Association Agreement entered into force in 2010.[18] In 2012 the accession negotiations were opened.

40–09

4. POTENTIAL CANDIDATE COUNTRIES

The Union grants autonomous trade preferences to the Western Balkans (Albania, Bosnia and Herzegovina, the former Yugoslav Republic of Macedonia, and Serbia). They have been key instruments in the revitalisation of that area's economies by providing privileged access to the Union market. In 2000, the Union granted exceptional unlimited duty-free access for nearly all products originating in the countries and territories benefiting from the Stabilisation and Association Process: Albania, Bosnia and Herzegovina, Croatia, the former Yugoslav Republic of Macedonia, Serbia and Montenegro, including Kosovo. The preferences were originally adopted for a period until the end of 2005. The country has moved closer towards becoming a functioning market economy.

40–10

The EU's policy framework for the countries of the Western Balkans is the Stabilisation and Association Process (SAP). It supports the countries' development and preparations for future Union membership by combining three main instruments:

- the Stabilisation and Association Agreements,
- autonomous trade measures, and
- substantial financial assistance.

Regional co-operation constitutes a cornerstone of the SAP. The European perspectives of the countries in question were confirmed by the European Council of Thessaloniki in June 2003.

---

[18] [2010] O.J. L108/3.

(1) Albania

40–11   In March 2004 the Council adopted a Regulation on the establishment of European Partnerships in the framework of the Stabilisation and Association Process,[19] while in 2003, the Thessaloniki European Council endorsed the "Thessaloniki Agenda for the Western Balkans: moving towards European integration", which mentioned European Partnerships as one of the means to intensify the Stabilisation and Association Process (SAP).

The June 2000 European Council stated that all the SAP countries are "potential candidates" for Union membership. The principles, priorities and conditions contained in the European Partnership with Albania were laid down by the Council in June 2004[20] and revised in February 2006.[21]

Albania profited from autonomous trade preferences, national and regional financial assistance under Community Assistance for Reconstruction, Development and Stabilisation (CARDS).[22] A Stabilisation and Association Agreement (SAA) like the one signed with Croatia (see above) was signed on June 12, 2006 and entered into force on April 1, 2009.[23] The EC/Albania readmission Agreement was signed on April 14, 2005. In 2009 Albania submitted its formal application for membership. In its opinion on the application the Commission considered that Albania still needed to make progress in complying with the membership criteria, in particular as concerns judicial and electoral reforms, the rule of law and guarantees as to the proper functioning of state institutions. Late 2012 the Commission recommended that Albania be granted candidate status.

(2) Bosnia and Herzegovina

40–12   In 1999, the Union proposed the Stabilisation and Association Process (SAP) for five countries of South-East Europe, including Bosnia and Herzegovina. Since all the SAP countries are "potential candidates" for Union membership, negotiations for the conclusion of a Stabilisation and Association Agreement (SAA) were opened in November 2005 and concluded in 2008, as well as an Interim Agreement on trade and trade-related matters were signed with the Union.[24] The former is aimed at supporting efforts to strengthen democracy and the rule of law and to complete the transition to a market economy.

Although there are no contractual links between Bosnia and Herzegovina and the Union, the latter is their main trade partner, thanks to an autonomous preferential regime adopted by the Union in 2000. Bosnia and Herzegovina need to achieve the necessary political consensus and to proceed with reforms; in particular to ensure functional institutions and respect of fundamental rights.[25]

---

[19] Regulation 533/2004 [2004] O.J. L86/1.
[20] [2004] O.J. L223/20.
[21] [2006] O.J. L35/1.
[22] Regulation 2666/2000 [2000] O.J. L306/1. It was replaced by the Instrument for Pre-Accession Assistance (IPA).
[23] [2009] O.J. L104/57.
[24] [2008] O.J. L233/6.
[25] Commission communication COM (2011) 666 final on Enlargement Strategy and Main Challenges.

(3) Serbia

Serbia's way to the Union has been hindered by issues such as lack of co-operation with the International Criminal Tribunal for the former Yugoslavia, and its relations with Kosovo. In 2008 a Stabilisation and Association Agreement and an Interim Agreement on trade and trade related issues were signed. In 2009, Serbia applied for membership, and in 2011 the Commission delivered its opinion, identifying a number of issues on which Serbia would have to make progress before accession negotiations can be opened.[26] In 2012, the European Council confirmed Serbia as a candidate country. In late spring 2013, Serbia reached an agreement with Kosovo to normalise relations; the agreement will make possible advancing the membership negotiations.

40–13

(4) Kosovo

Kosovo is a potential candidate country. In 2012, the Commission issued its Study for a Stabilisation and Association Agreement between the Union and Kosovo.

40–14

FURTHER READING

"Enlargement of the Union", *http://ec.europa.eu/enlargement/index_en.htm* [accessed August 23, 2013].

40–15

Marise Cremona, *The Enlargement of the European Union* (Oxford University Press, 2003).

Giandomenico Majone, "Unity in diversity: European integration and the enlargement process", (2008) E.L.Review 457.

Hurbert Isak, *A European perspective for the Western Balcans* (Neuer Wissenschaftilicher Verlag, Vienna, 2008).

---

[26] Commission communication COM(2011) 668 final.

INDEX

This index has been prepared using Sweet and Maxwell's Legal Taxonomy. Main index entries conform to keywords provided by the Legal Taxonomy except where references to specific documents or non-standard terms (denoted by quotation marks) have been included. These keywords provide a means of identifying similar concepts in other Sweet and Maxwell publications and online services to which keywords from the Legal Taxonomy have been applied. Readers may find some minor differences between terms used in the text and those which appear in the index. Suggestions to *sweetandmaxwell.taxonomy@thomson.com*.

All references are to paragraph number

Common transport policy
see also **Transport**
acquis communautaire, 27–01
conclusion, 27–28
generally, 27–01
new approach, 27–02
"Communiqués"
legal Acts of the EU, and, 3–03
Community Acts *see* **EU Acts**
Community agencies *see* **EU agencies**
Community bodies *see* **EU agencies**
Community designs
intellectual property, and, 20–09–20–10
Community Fisheries Control Agency
generally, 13–24
Community Plant Variety Office
generally, 13–14
Community trade marks
intellectual property, and, 20–07–20–08
Companies
freedom of establishment, and, 17–13–17–17
tax, and, 25–15
Company law
freedom of establishment, and, 17–13–17–17
Compensation
jurisdiction of European Court of Justice, and,
9–25–9–27
Competence
introduction, 1–04
jurisdiction of European Court of Justice
attribution, 9–39
grounds for annulment, 9–18
introduction, 9–03
Competition policy
abuse of dominant position
'abuse', 22–42–22–43
'dominant position', 22–40–22–41
generally, 22–39
implementation of rules, 22–59–22–65
market definition, 22–03–22–04
'may affect trade between member states',
22–39
specific economic sectors, 22–44–22–58
access to the files, 22–75
agency agreements, 22–73
agriculture, 22–56
air transport, 22–49–22–50
anti-competitive practices
exemptions from prohibition, 22–17–22–38
general prohibition, 22–06–22–15
generally, 22–05
implementation of rules, 22–59–22–65
market definition, 22–03–22–04
nullity, 22–16
specific economic sectors, 22–44–22–58
application of rules to member states
public undertakings, 22–83
services of general economic interest, 22–84

state aid, 22–85–22–107
application of rules to undertakings
abuse of dominant position, 22–39–22–43
anti-competitive practices, 22–05–22–38
cartels, 22–05–22–38
concentrations, 22–02
introduction, 22–02
market definition, 22–03–22–04
relevant geographic market, 22–03–22–04
relevant product market, 22–03–22–04
best practices for conduct of proceedings, 22–77
block exemptions
categories of agreements, for, 22–21
horizontal co-operation agreements, 22–22
introduction, 22–17
motor vehicles, 22–28–22–29
research and development agreements,
22–32–22–34
specialisation agreements, 22–30–22–31
technology transfer agreements, 22–35–22–38
vertical agreements, 22–23–22–27
cartels
exemptions from prohibition, 22–17–22–38
general prohibition, 22–06–22–15
generally, 22–05
implementation of rules, 22–59–22–65
market definition, 22–03–22–04
nullity, 22–16
specific economic sectors, 22–44–22–58
coal and steel, 22–58
comity, 22–80
Commission Notices
abuse of dominant position, 22–76
access to the files, 22–75
agency agreements, 22–73
best practices for conduct of proceedings,
22–77
co-operation between national competition
authorities, 22–78
enforcement priorities, 22–76
exclusive dealing contracts made with
commercial agents, 22–73
implementing provisions, 22–79
international co-operation, 22–80–22–82
introduction, 22–72
subcontracting agreements, 22–74
concentrations
ancillary restraints, 22–69
generally, 22–66–22–68
joint or collective dominance, 22–69–22–71
main features, 22–69–22–71
market definition, 22–03–22–04
scope, 22–67
concerted practices, 22–05–22–38
co-operation between national competition
authorities, 22–78
decisions by associations of undertakings,
22–05–22–38
energy, 22–57